■ THE RESOURCE FOR THE INDEPENDENT TRAVELER

"The guides are aimed not only at young budget travelers but at the indepedent traveler; a sort of streetwise cookbook for traveling alone."

—The New York Times

"Unbeatable; good sight-seeing advice; up-to-date info on restaurants, hotels, and inns; a commitment to money-saving travel; and a wry style that brightens nearly every page."

—The Washington Post

"Lighthearted and sophisticated, informative and fun to read. [Let's Go] helps the novice traveler navigate like a knowledgeable old hand."

—Atlanta Journal-Constitution

"A world-wise traveling companion—always ready with friendly advice and helpful hints, all sprinkled with a bit of wit."

—The Philadelphia Inquirer

■ THE BEST TRAVEL BARGAINS IN YOUR PRICE RANGE

"All the dirt, dirt cheap."

—People

"Anything you need to know about budget traveling is detailed in this book."

—The Chicago Sun-Times

"Let's Go follows the creed that you don't have to toss your life's savings to the wind to travel—unless you want to."

—The Salt Lake Tribune

■ REAL ADVICE FOR REAL EXPERIENCES

"The writers seem to have experienced every rooster-packed bus and lunar-surfaced mattress about which they write."

—The New York Times

"A guide should tell you what to expect from a destination. Here Let's Go shines."

—The Chicago Tribune

LET'S GO PUBLICATIONS

TRAVEL GUIDES

Alaska & the Pacific Northwest 2003
Australia 2003
Austria & Switzerland 2003
Britain & Ireland 2003
California 2003
Central America 8th edition
Chile 1st edition **NEW TITLE**
China 4th edition
Costa Rica 1st edition **NEW TITLE**
Eastern Europe 2003
Egypt 2nd edition
Europe 2003
France 2003
Germany 2003
Greece 2003
Hawaii 2003 **NEW TITLE**
India & Nepal 7th edition
Ireland 2003
Israel 4th edition
Italy 2003
Mexico 19th edition
Middle East 4th edition
New Zealand 6th edition
Peru, Ecuador & Bolivia 3rd edition
South Africa 5th edition
Southeast Asia 8th edition
Southwest USA 2003
Spain & Portugal 2003
Thailand 1st edition **NEW TITLE**
Turkey 5th edition
USA 2003
Western Europe 2003

CITY GUIDES

Amsterdam 2003
Barcelona 2003
Boston 2003
London 2003
New York City 2003
Paris 2003
Rome 2003
San Francisco 2003
Washington, D.C. 2003

MAP GUIDES

Amsterdam
Berlin
Boston
Chicago
Dublin
Florence
Hong Kong
London
Los Angeles
Madrid
New Orleans
New York City
Paris
Prague
Rome
San Francisco
Seattle
Sydney
Venice
Washington, D.C.

IRELAND 2003

David James Bright Editor
Kathleen Marie Rey Associate Editor

Researcher-Writers
Chris Gregg
Sarah Jessop
Jack Pettibone Riccobono
Abigail E. Shafroth
Kira Whelan

Angela Mi Young Hur Managing Editor
Damian Williams Map Editor
Chris Clayton Typesetter

St. Martin's Press New York

HELPING LET'S GO

If you want to share your discoveries, suggestions, or corrections, please drop us a line. We read every piece of correspondence, whether a postcard, a 10-page email, or a coconut. Please note that mail received after May 2003 may be too late for the 2004 book, but will be kept for future editions. **Address mail to:**

Let's Go: Ireland
67 Mount Auburn Street
Cambridge, MA 02138
USA

Visit Let's Go at **http://www.letsgo.com,** or send email to:

feedback@letsgo.com
Subject: "Let's Go: Ireland"

In addition to the invaluable travel advice our readers share with us, many are kind enough to offer their services as researchers or editors. Unfortunately, our charter enables us to employ only currently enrolled Harvard students.

Distributed outside the USA and Canada by Macmillan.

ISBN: 0-312-30579-6

First edition
10 9 8 7 6 5 4 3 2 1

Let's Go: Ireland is written by Let's Go Publications, 67 Mount Auburn Street, Cambridge, MA 02138, USA.

Printed in the USA on recycled paper with soy ink.

WHO WE ARE

A NEW LET'S GO FOR 2003

With a sleeker look and innovative new content, we have revamped the entire series to reflect more than ever the needs and interests of the independent traveler. Here are just some of the improvements you will notice when traveling with the new *Let's Go*.

MORE PRICE OPTIONS

Still the best resource for budget travelers, *Let's Go* recognizes that everyone needs the occassional indulgence. Our "Big Splurges" indicate establishments that are actually worth those extra pennies (pulas, pesos, or pounds), and price-level symbols (❶ ❷ ❸ ❹ ❺) allow you to quickly determine whether an accommodation or restaurant will break the bank. We may have diversified, but we'll never lose our budget focus—"Hidden Deals" reveal the best-kept travel secrets.

BEYOND THE TOURIST EXPERIENCE

Our Alternatives to Touism chapter offers ideas on immersing yourself in a new community through study, work, or volunteering.

AN INSIDER'S PERSPECTIVE

As always, every item is written and researched by our on-site writers. This year we have highlighted more viewpoints to help you gain an even more thorough understanding of the places you are visiting.

IN RECENT NEWS. *Let's Go* correspondents around the globe report back on current regional issues that may affect you as a traveler.

CONTRIBUTING WRITERS. Respected scholars and former *Let's Go* writers discuss topics on society and culture, going into greater depth than the usual guidebook summary.

THE LOCAL STORY. From the Parisian monk toting a cell phone to the Russian *babushka* confronting capitalism, *Let's Go* shares its revealing conversations with local personalities—a unique glimpse of what matters to real people.

FROM THE ROAD. Always helpful and sometimes downright hilarious, our researchers share useful insights on the typical (and atypical) travel experience.

SLIMMER SIZE

Don't be fooled by our new, smaller size. *Let's Go* is still packed with invaluable travel advice, but now it's easier to carry with a more compact design.

FORTY-THREE YEARS OF WISDOM

For over four decades *Let's Go* has provided the most up-to-date information on the hippest cafes, the most pristine beaches, and the best routes from border to border. It all started in 1960 when a few well-traveled students at Harvard University handed out a 20-page mimeographed pamphlet of their tips on budget travel to passengers on student charter flights to Europe. From humble beginnings, *Let's Go* has grown to cover six continents and *Let's Go: Europe* still reigns as the world's best-selling travel guide. This year we've beefed up our coverage of Latin America with *Let's Go: Costa Rica* and *Let's Go: Chile;* on the other side of the globe, we've added *Let's Go: Thailand* and *Let's Go: Hawaii*. Our new guides bring the total number of titles to 61, each infused with the spirit of adventure that travelers around the world have come to count on.

CONTENTS

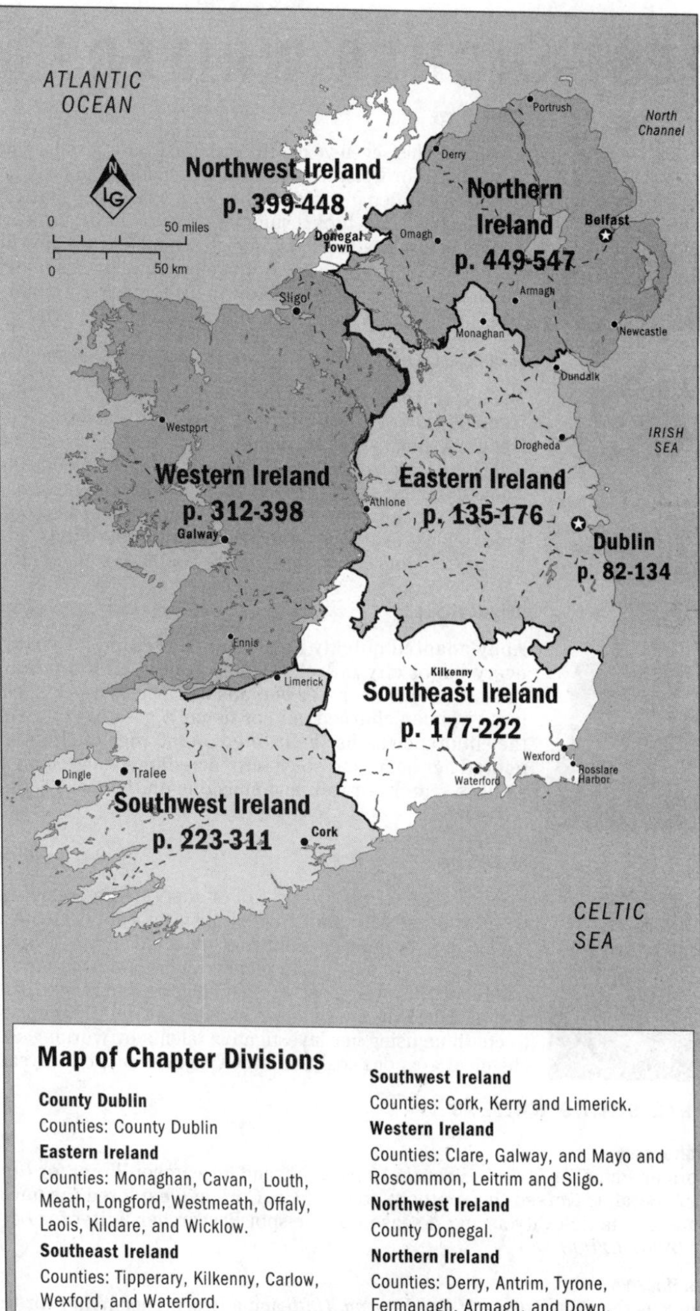
ATLANTIC OCEAN
0
50 miles
0
50 km
Northwest Ireland
p. 399-448
Northern Ireland
p. 449-547
Western Ireland
p. 312-398
Eastern Ireland
p. 135-176
Dublin
p. 82-134
Southeast Ireland
p. 177-222
Southwest Ireland
p. 223-311
Portrush
North Channel
Derry
Belfast
Omagh
Donegal Town
Armagh
Sligo
Monaghan
Newcastle
Dundalk
Westport
IRISH SEA
Drogheda
Athlone
Galway
Ennis
Limerick
Kilkenny
Wexford
Rosslare Harbor
Waterford
Dingle
Tralee
Cork
CELTIC SEA
Map of Chapter Divisions
County Dublin
Counties: County Dublin
Eastern Ireland
Counties: Monaghan, Cavan, Louth, Meath, Longford, Westmeath, Offaly, Laois, Kildare, and Wicklow.
Southeast Ireland
Counties: Tipperary, Kilkenny, Carlow, Wexford, and Waterford.
Southwest Ireland
Counties: Cork, Kerry and Limerick.
Western Ireland
Counties: Clare, Galway, and Mayo and Roscommon, Leitrim and Sligo.
Northwest Ireland
County Donegal.
Northern Ireland
Counties: Derry, Antrim, Tyrone, Fermanagh, Armagh, and Down.

RESEARCHER-WRITERS

Chris Gregg *Dublin, Midlands, Southeast*

Chris used his seven-year stint with the US Navy to help him in his hunt for Ireland's best water activities and local surf spots. A qualified physics teacher with a degree in electrical engineering, Chris took a summer off to cover the streets of Dublin before heading back to high school. His detailed hiking maps will make it easy for travelers to follow his route—though no one could ever follow in his footsteps; a charmer and smooth talker, you'll never find another like Chris.

Jack Riccobono *The Southwest*

Jack, a researcher for *Let's Go: Eastern Europe 2002*, took his experience all the way to the far reaches of rural Ireland. Using his background in visual and environmental sciences, Jack had no problems describing the Southwest. Though transportation proved daunting, nothing could have stopped this intrepid researcher from finishing his route; tired of looking at the country through a window, he traded his car for boots and tramped in the southern mountains.

Abigail Shafroth *Belfast, Derry, Sligo, Galway*

Abby adapted quickly to the mixed blessing of visiting every major city in Ireland. Despite the all-too-reliable "unsettled" weather—or perhaps because of it—this fearless Virginian churned out consistently great work. Using the endurance skills she learned on the rugby field, Abby poured her heart and soles into incredible research on an endless search for tofu and sunshine on the meat-eating, misty Isle.

Kira Whelan *The Northwest*

Confident, determined, and full of energy, Kira conquered the northwest with unrivaled enthusiasm—not even a car-eating ditch or bumper-trailing *garda* could slow her down. The surfing skills that Kira picked up in California proved helpful on the west coast. From hiking to swimming to driving—if there was a way to see Ireland, she did it. Kira plans to continue using her investigative talents by working as a chemical weapons analyst for the US government next year.

CONTRIBUTING WRITERS

Sarah Jessop
A former editor for *Let's Go: South Africa 2002* and Researcher-Writer for *Italy 2001*, Sarah traversed the southern coast of Co. Cork and explored the music scene of Limerick City as an off-season on-the-spot Researcher-Writer for *Let's Go: Ireland 2003*.

Ryan Hackney
Ryan was the Editor of *Let's Go: Ireland 1996* and a Researcher-Writer for Ireland 1995 and Ecuador 1997. He is now pursuing a career as a novelist.

ACKNOWLEDGMENTS

SPECIAL THANKS TO our stellar R-Ws, who went above and beyond; Angela, whose shoulder rubs gave us strength; Damian, for his divine cartography; Hannah, who was always there; Anne, Caleb, Chris, and David, who were there when we needed them most; Rebecca and Mark, for being our 'pod' buddies; and Sarah, thank you, sweetheart.

DAVID THANKS his mother Marian and brother Robert (bobo). Mom—thanks for birthing me. Rob—thanks for not beating me up. And, with more relevance, Kathleen, thank you. Your faith in me gave me faith in myself. I couldn't have asked for a better partner. Rebecca, you make me want to shower, daily. Mark, thanks for not kicking me while I slept under the desk. Angela, honestly love, thank you. I want to thank people in the office, but don't want to single anyone out. You know who you are—you rock. Other people: you know who *you* are—tsk tsk tsk.

KATHLEEN THANKS David, thank you for trusting me with your labor of love. Your heart is bigger than the Isle itself. Angela, I owe you a million (smoothies or kidburgers?). Thanks to all my friends, especially SJ for the cheesecake and apartment-hunting escapes; Rebecca and Amber for keeping me sane; and Lucy—the 'Beer Brat'—for being the best roommate. So much loves and thanks to my "favorite." Now I'm famous too! To my wonderful family, thank you for your constant love and support. Finally, I dedicate my work on this book to my grandmother, Eileen Hennessy.

DAMIAN THANKS David and Kathleen, you guys are the best. To my Mapland mates, this one is for you.

Editor
David James Bright
Associate Editor
Kathleen Marie Rey
Managing Editor
Angela Mi Young Hur
Map Editor
Damian Williams

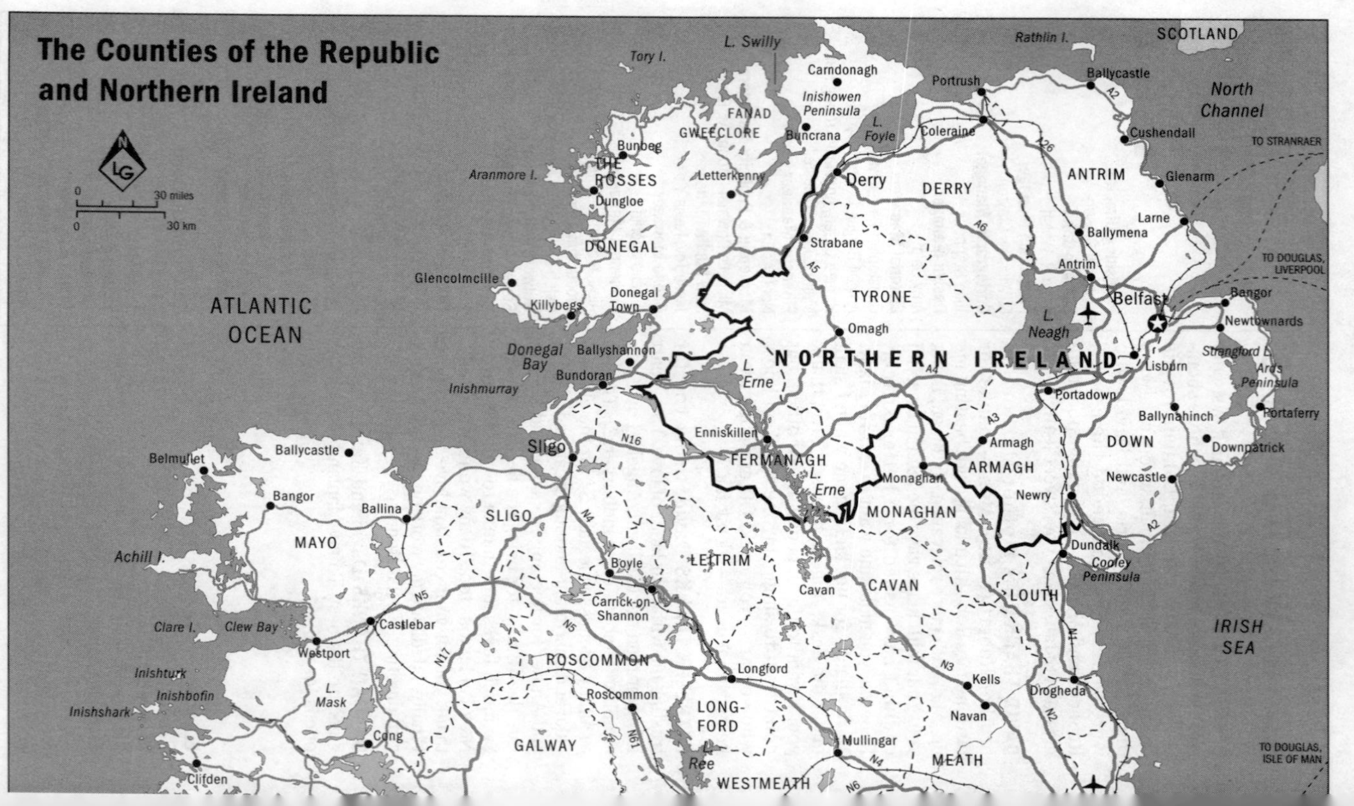
The Counties of the Republic and Northern Ireland
0 30 miles
0 30 km
ATLANTIC OCEAN
NORTHERN IRELAND
SCOTLAND
North Channel
IRISH SEA
TO STRANRAER
TO DOUGLAS, LIVERPOOL
TO DOUGLAS, ISLE OF MAN
Tory I.
L. Swilly
Rathlin I.
Carndonagh
Inishowen Peninsula
FANAD
GWEECLORE
Buncrana
L. Foyle
Portrush
Coleraine
Ballycastle
Cushendall
Glenarm
Larne
Bunbeg
THE ROSSES
Aranmore I.
Dungloe
Letterkenny
Derry
DERRY
ANTRIM
Ballymena
Antrim
DONEGAL
Strabane
A5
A6
A26
A2
Glencolmcille
Killybegs
Donegal Town
TYRONE
Omagh
L. Neagh
Belfast
Bangor
Newtownards
Strangford L.
Ards Peninsula
Portaferry
Lisburn
Donegal Bay
Ballyshannon
Bundoran
Inishmurray
L. Erne
A4
Portadown
A3
Ballynahinch
Downpatrick
DOWN
Armagh
ARMAGH
Enniskillen
FERMANAGH
Monaghan
MONAGHAN
Newry
Newcastle
Dundalk
Cooley Peninsula
Belmullet
Ballycastle
Bangor
Ballina
SLIGO
Sligo
N16
N4
MAYO
Achill I.
Boyle
LEITRIM
Cavan
CAVAN
LOUTH
Carrick-on-Shannon
N5
Castlebar
Clare I.
Clew Bay
Westport
N17
ROSCOMMON
Longford
N3
Kells
Navan
Drogheda
N1
N2
Inishturk
Inishbofin
Inishshark
L. Mask
Cong
Roscommon
N61
LONG-FORD
L. Ree
GALWAY
Mullingar
MEATH
WESTMEATH
N6
Clifden

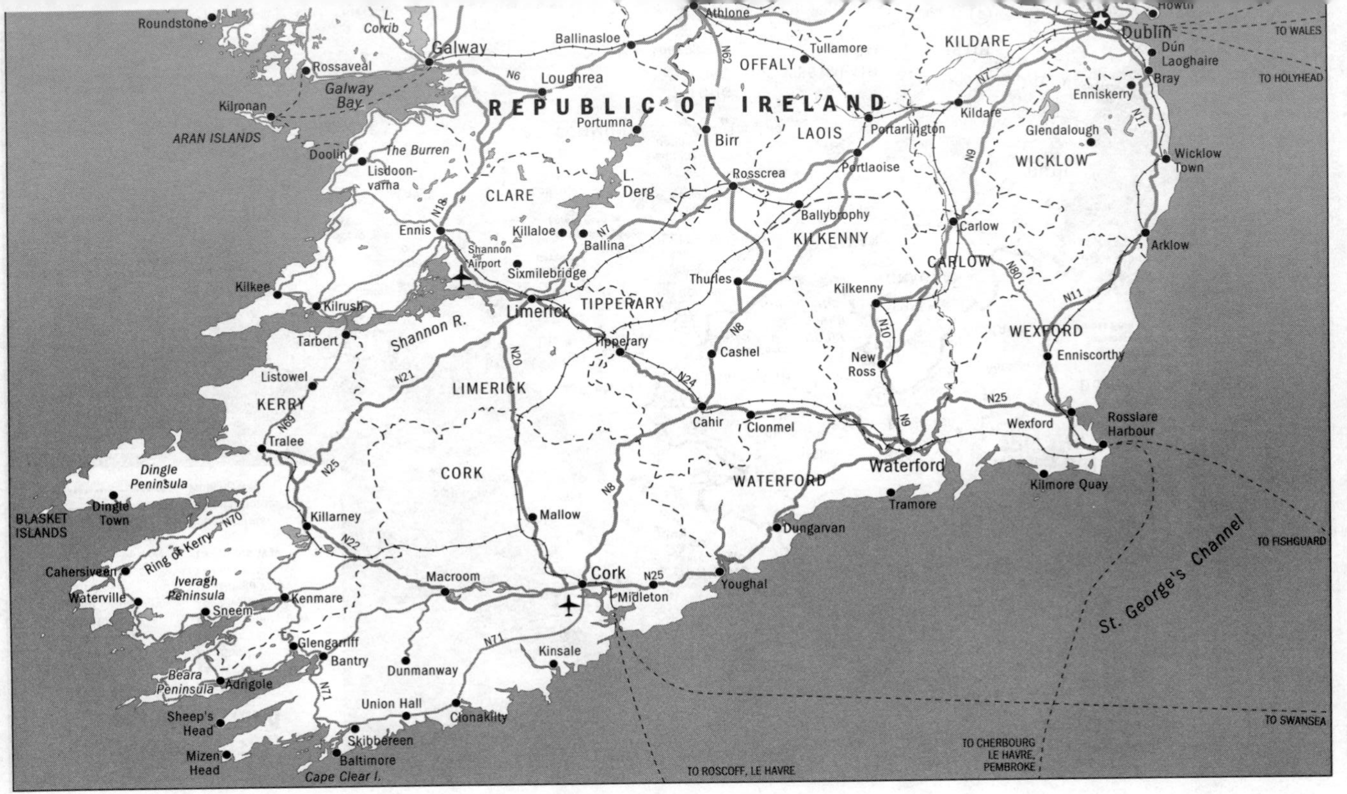
REPUBLIC OF IRELAND
KILDARE
OFFALY
LAOIS
WICKLOW
CLARE
KILKENNY
CARLOW
TIPPERARY
WEXFORD
LIMERICK
KERRY
CORK
WATERFORD
Roundstone
L. Corrib
Galway
Ballinasloe
Athlone
Tullamore
Dublin
Howth
Dún Laoghaire
Bray
Enniskerry
Glendalough
Wicklow Town
Arklow
Rossaveal
Galway Bay
Kilronan
ARAN ISLANDS
Loughrea
Portumna
Birr
Portarlington
Kildare
Portlaoise
Rosscrea
Ballybrophy
Carlow
Doolin
The Burren
Lisdoon-varna
L. Derg
Ennis
Killaloe
Ballina
Shannon Airport
Sixmilebridge
Thurles
Kilkenny
Kilkee
Kilrush
Limerick
Shannon R.
Tarbert
Tipperary
Cashel
New Ross
Enniscorthy
Listowel
Cahir
Clonmel
Wexford
Rosslare Harbour
Tralee
Waterford
Kilmore Quay
Dingle Peninsula
Dingle Town
BLASKET ISLANDS
Killarney
Mallow
Tramore
Dungarvan
Ring of Kerry
Cahersiveen
Iveragh Peninsula
Waterville
Kenmare
Sneem
Macroom
Cork
Midleton
Youghal
St. George's Channel
Glengarriff
Bantry
Dunmanway
Kinsale
Beara Peninsula
Adrigole
Union Hall
Clonakilty
Sheep's Head
Skibbereen
Mizen Head
Baltimore
Cape Clear I.
N6
N62
N7
N9
N11
N18
N20
N21
N69
N25
N8
N10
N24
N80
N70
N22
N71
TO WALES
TO HOLYHEAD
TO FISHGUARD
TO SWANSEA
TO CHERBOURG LE HAVRE, PEMBROKE
TO ROSCOFF, LE HAVRE

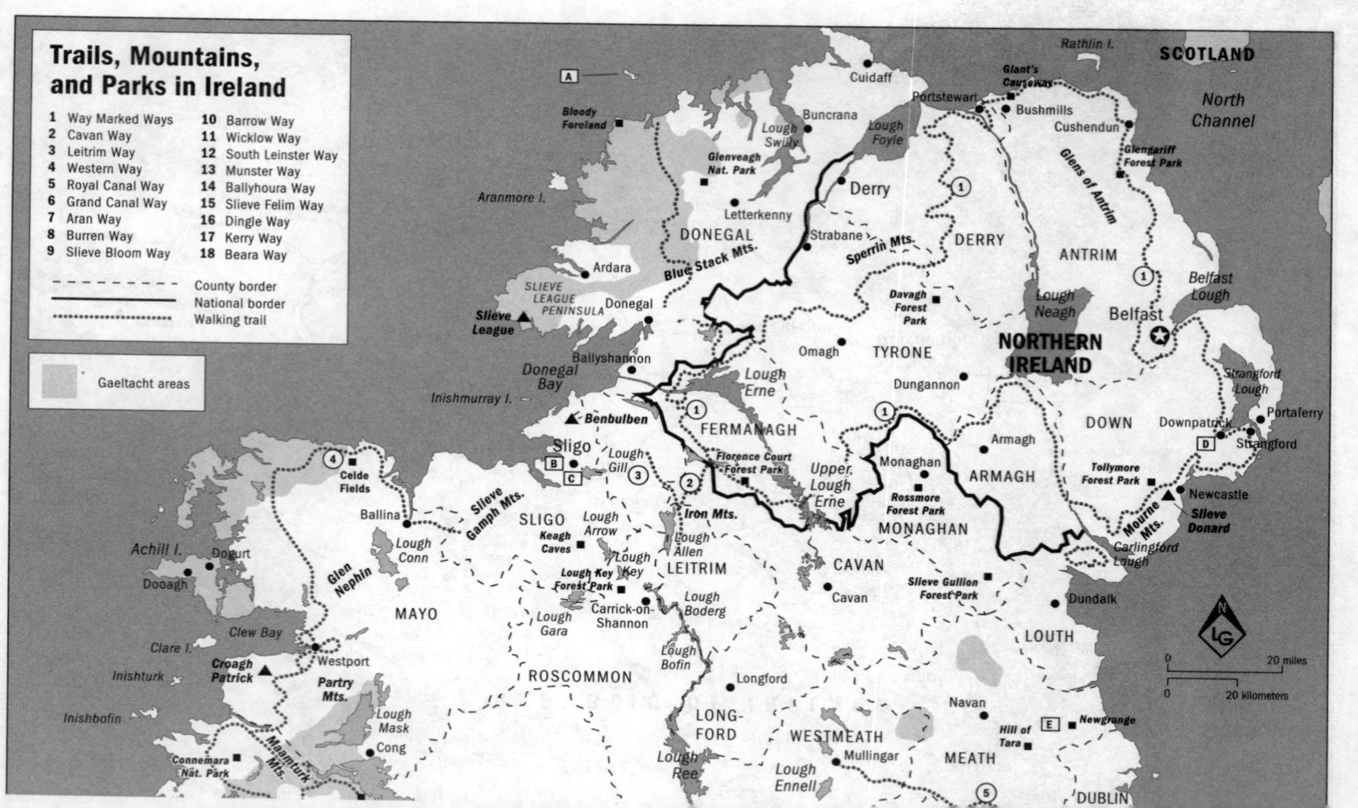
Trails, Mountains, and Parks in Ireland
1 Way Marked Ways
2 Cavan Way
3 Leitrim Way
4 Western Way
5 Royal Canal Way
6 Grand Canal Way
7 Aran Way
8 Burren Way
9 Slieve Bloom Way
10 Barrow Way
11 Wicklow Way
12 South Leinster Way
13 Munster Way
14 Ballyhoura Way
15 Slieve Felim Way
16 Dingle Way
17 Kerry Way
18 Beara Way
County border
National border
Walking trail
Gaeltacht areas
SCOTLAND
North Channel
Rathlin I.
Giant's Causeway
Portstewart
Bushmills
Cushendun
Glengariff Forest Park
Glens of Antrim
ANTRIM
Belfast Lough
Belfast
Lough Neagh
NORTHERN IRELAND
DERRY
Cuidaff
Buncrana
Lough Swilly
Lough Foyle
Derry
Strabane
Sperrin Mts.
Bloody Foreland
Glenveagh Nat. Park
Letterkenny
DONEGAL
Blue Stack Mts.
Aranmore I.
Ardara
SLIEVE LEAGUE PENINSULA
Slieve League
Donegal
Ballyshannon
Donegal Bay
Inishmurray I.
Davagh Forest Park
Omagh
TYRONE
Dungannon
Lough Erne
FERMANAGH
Florence Court Forest Park
Upper Lough Erne
Monaghan
Rossmore Forest Park
MONAGHAN
Armagh
ARMAGH
DOWN
Downpatrick
Strangford Lough
Portaferry
Strangford
Tollymore Forest Park
Newcastle
Slieve Donard
Mourne Mts.
Carlingford Lough
Slieve Gullion Forest Park
Dundalk
LOUTH
Benbulben
Sligo
Lough Gill
Iron Mts.
Lough Allen
LEITRIM
Celde Fields
Ballina
Slieve Gamph Mts.
SLIGO
Lough Arrow
Keagh Caves
Lough Key
Lough Key Forest Park
Carrick-on-Shannon
Lough Boderg
CAVAN
Cavan
Achill I.
Dogurt
Dooagh
Glen Nephin
Lough Conn
MAYO
Lough Gara
Clew Bay
Clare I.
Westport
Croagh Patrick
Inishturk
Partry Mts.
Inishbofin
Lough Mask
Cong
Connemara Nat. Park
Maamturk Mts.
ROSCOMMON
Lough Bofin
Longford
LONG-FORD
Lough Ree
WESTMEATH
Mullingar
Lough Ennell
Navan
Hill of Tara
Newgrange
MEATH
DUBLIN
0 20 miles
0 20 kilometers

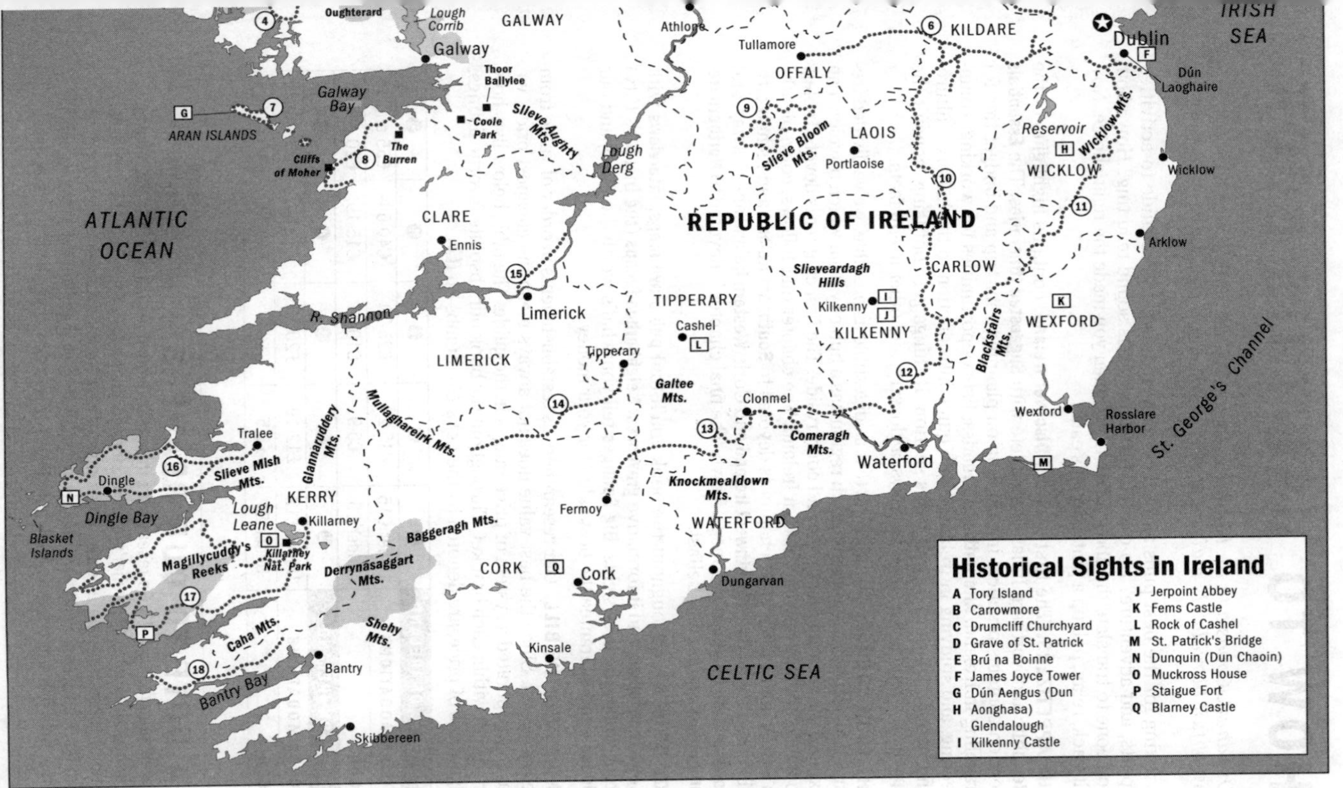
Historical Sights in Ireland
A Tory Island
B Carrowmore
C Drumcliff Churchyard
D Grave of St. Patrick
E Brú na Boinne
F James Joyce Tower
G Dún Aengus (Dun Aonghasa)
H Glendalough
I Kilkenny Castle
J Jerpoint Abbey
K Fems Castle
L Rock of Cashel
M St. Patrick's Bridge
N Dunquin (Dun Chaoin)
O Muckross House
P Staigue Fort
Q Blarney Castle
ATLANTIC OCEAN
IRISH SEA
CELTIC SEA
St. George's Channel
REPUBLIC OF IRELAND
GALWAY
KILDARE
OFFALY
LAOIS
WICKLOW
CARLOW
WEXFORD
KILKENNY
TIPPERARY
CLARE
LIMERICK
KERRY
CORK
WATERFORD
Dublin
Dún Laoghaire
Wicklow
Arklow
Rosslare Harbor
Wexford
Waterford
Dungarvan
Kinsale
Cork
Fermoy
Clonmel
Kilkenny
Portlaoise
Tullamore
Athlone
Galway
Oughterard
Lough Corrib
Galway Bay
ARAN ISLANDS
Cliffs of Moher
The Burren
Coole Park
Thoor Ballylee
Slieve Aughty Mts.
Lough Derg
Ennis
Limerick
R. Shannon
Cashel
Tipperary
Galtee Mts.
Slieveardagh Hills
Slieve Bloom Mts.
Reservoir
Wicklow Mts.
Blackstairs Mts.
Comeragh Mts.
Knockmealdown Mts.
Mullaghareirk Mts.
Glannaruddery Mts.
Tralee
Slieve Mish Mts.
Dingle
Dingle Bay
Blasket Islands
Lough Leane
Killarney
Killarney Nat. Park
Magillycuddy's Reeks
Baggeragh Mts.
Derrynasaggart Mts.
Shehy Mts.
Caha Mts.
Bantry
Bantry Bay
Skibbereen

HOW TO USE THIS BOOK

Dia dhuit. Conas a tá tú. Is mise Let's Go Ireland 2003.
An bhfuil tú réidh? Is maith: Let's Go.

Looking for the best pubs and music scenes in Ireland? A guide to activities, sports, and adventure? Do castles, forts, and cliffs sound tempting? How about someone to translate the above text? Good, then you made the right choice. Now sit back, relax, pull up a pint, and let's eat.

THE APPETIZERS. The first section, **Discover Ireland,** contains highlights of the Republic and Northern Ireland, complete with **Suggested Itineraries.** The **Essentials** section contains practical information on planning your trip and budget tips for traveling in Ireland. **Alternatives to Tourism** lists opportunities for working, volunteering, and studying in Ireland. For a quick introduction to the history, culture, and people, try our **Life and Times** section. If things get confusing, consult the **Appendix,** which has a list of holidays, a glossary, and other useful facts.

THE MAIN COURSE. To make the text as digestible as possible, we've divided Ireland into six separate regions. Each region has a hub city from which travelers can explore the surrounding towns and countryside. The first chapter is devoted solely to **Dublin,** the hub city for Eastern Ireland. The chapter that follows, conveniently, is **Eastern Ireland.** The next chapter is devoted to **Southeast Ireland** and its hub city, Kilkenny. Then comes **Southwest Ireland** and Cork, **Western Ireland** and Galway, and **Northwestern Ireland** and Donegal Town. The final chapter is devoted to **Northern Ireland** and cosmopolitan Belfast.

FOR DESSERT. Throughout the book you'll find **pub crawl maps, interviews** with locals, **hot topics,** and informative **grayboxes. Neighborhood maps** (the Insider's City) point you to the best sights, **Big Splurges** tell you what's worth the price, and our **Hidden Deals** guarantee the best value for your money.

AND ABOUT THE BILL. Our researchers list establishments in order of value from best to worst. Since the best value does not always mean the cheapest price, we have incorporated a system of price ranges in the guide. The table below lists how prices fall within each bracket. Throughout the book our absolute favorite listings, regardless of price, are denoted by the *Let's Go* thumbs-up (☒).

REPUBLIC OF IRELAND	❶	❷	❸	❹	❺
ACCOMMODATIONS	Under €15	€15-24	€25-39	€40-54	€55 and up
FOOD	Under €5	€5-9	€10-14	€15-19	€20 and up
NORTHERN IRELAND	❶	❷	❸	❹	❺
ACCOMMODATIONS	Under £12	£12-19	£20-29	£30-44	£45 and up
FOOD	Under £3	£3-5	£6-9	£10-14	£15 and up

A NOTE TO OUR READERS The information for this book was gathered by *Let's Go* researchers from May through August of 2002. Each listing is based on one researcher's opinion, formed during his or her visit at a particular time. Those traveling at other times may have different experiences since prices, dates, hours, and conditions are always subject to change. You are urged to check the facts presented in this book beforehand to avoid inconvenience and surprises.

DISCOVER IRELAND

To Ireland, I.
—Shakespeare, *Macbeth*.

Literary imaginations have immortalized Ireland's natural scenery since ancient times, and travelers who come with their heads filled with poetic imagery will not be disappointed: this largely agricultural and sparsely populated island still looks very much the same as it did when Celtic bards roamed the land. Windswept scenery wraps around the coast, and mountain chains ripple the interior expanses of bogland. The landscape is punctuated with pockets of civilization, ranging in size from one-street villages to small market towns to urbane cities. Dublin and Belfast are cosmopolitan city centers, radiating sophistication into their immediate surroundings. While some fear that international influence threatens their native culture, the survival of traditional music, dance, and storytelling in rural and urban areas proves otherwise. The Irish language lives on in small, secluded areas known as *gaeltachts*, as well as on road signs, in national publications, and in a growing body of modern literary works. Today's Ireland promises her visitors an old-world welcome with just the right amount of urban edge counterculture.

FACTS AND FIGURES

Capitals: Dublin and Belfast.

Number of female presidents: 2

Highest Point: 3415 ft.

Natural Resources: Zinc, lead, natural gas, *craic*, copper, gypsum, limestone, poets, peat, silver, stout.

Populations: 3,797,257 people live in the Republic. 1,663,200 people live in Northern Ireland.

Population Distribution: More than 35% lives within 60 mi. of Dublin.

Land Area: 32,589 sq. mi.

Population Under 25: 40.1%.

Most Popular Names: Jack & Aoife.

Daily Caloric Intake: 3638 calories.

Annual Beer Consumption: 32.5 gallons per person.

Number of Sheep per person: 2:1

WHEN TO GO

Traveling during the off-season (mid-Sept. to May) brings cheaper airfares and accommodation and frees you from the tourist hordes. The flip side is that many attractions, hostels, B&Bs, and tourist offices close in winter, and in some rural areas, local transportation dwindles to a trickle or shuts down altogether. Most of Ireland's best festivals also take place during the summer months.

The 'unsettled' Irish weather is subject to frequent changes but relatively constant temperatures. The southeastern coast is the driest and sunniest, while western Ireland is considerably wetter and cloudier. May and June are the sunniest months, and July and August are the warmest. December and January have the worst weather of the year. Take heart when you wake to clouded, foggy mornings—the weather usually clears by noon.

THINGS TO DO

WONDERS AND WANDERS

The west coast is strewn with a gorgeous and dense concentration of geologic curiosities, including the limestone moonscape of **The Burren** (p. 329) and the towering **Cliffs of Moher** (p. 328), which soar 700 ft. above the sea. The tranquil, gorgeous **Beara Peninsula** (p. 257) and its 125 mi. of **Beara Way** don't know the meaning of tour buses. **Killarney National Park** (p. 272) is a hiking-biking-climbing paradise, and makes a good gateway to the understandably heavily touristed **Ring of Kerry** (p. 276). For a less-populated, more beautiful version of the Ring, you can trek the **Kerry Way** (p. 276). In remote Co. Donegal, the **Slieve League** (p. 414) mountains are fronted by the highest sea cliffs in Europe. Donegal's **Glenveagh National Park** (p. 427) contains salt-and-peppered **Mount Errigal,** close to the bewitching **Poison Glen** (p. 426). The bizarre honeycomb columns of **Giant's Causeway** (p. 527) spill out from the **Antrim Coast,** a long strip of rocky crags and white beaches. Several developed paths allow hikers to spend any number of days exploring Ireland's mountain chains—the **Wicklow Way** passes through the **Wicklow Mountains** (p. 141) in Dublin's backyard, while the currently-being-revamped and soon-to-be-renamed **Ulster Way** treks through the **Sperrin Mountains.**

THE ISLAND'S ISLANDS

The people of the **Aran Islands** (p. 351) still live much like the rest of the country did at the turn of the century—speaking Irish, eking out their living fishing in *curraghs,* and enjoying numerous quirky superstitions, including one that prevents fishermen from learning to swim. Off the Dingle Peninsula, the now depopulated **Blasket Islands** (p. 295) were once home to several impoverished memoirists, and today provide little talk but great walks in exquisite scenery and haunting village ruins. **Tory Island's** (p. 430) counterculture is undoubtedly Ireland's most eclectic: this island of 160 individuals elects its own king, sponsors its own school of painters, and refers to the mainland as "the country." Down south in the Republic, **Sherkin Island** (p. 251) beckons visitors with its sandy, cliff-enclosed beaches, overabundance of cows, and under-abundance of visitors and residents. Nearby **Cape Clear Island** (p. 249) trades goats for cows, offering some of the best homemade goat's milk ice cream in all of Ireland.

STONES AND THRONES

In Co. Meath, the 5000-year-old passage tombs of the **Boyne Valley** (p. 150) are architectural feats that stump even today's engineers. The nearby **Hill of Tara** (p. 152) has been the symbolic throne for Irish bigwigs from pre-Christian rulers to St. Patrick to 19th-century Nationalists. On the west coast, the **Poulnebrane Dolmen** (p. 333) marks a group grave site with a 25-ton capstone that rests atop two standing rocks. On the magnificent limestone **Rock of Cashel** (p. 189), a mish-mash of early Christian structures pop up across the skyline, including a medieval cathedral and a Celtic cross. **Glendalough** (p. 141) is the picturesque home of St. Kevin's 6th-century monastery, a 100 ft. round tower, and the small stone kitchen of the saint himself. In Donegal, just outside of Derry, **Grianan Ailigh** (see p. 442) was first a Druidic temple, then the burial place for Aedh (divine king of the Túatha De Dannan), and finally, a seat of power for the northern branch of the Uí Néill (O'Neill) Clan. Today, only the hilly remnants of the fort remain. The monastic ruins of **Clonmacnois** (see p. 171), just south of Athlone, keep watch over the River Shannon's boglands. St. Ciaran founded his monastery here in AD 548, and all that remains—nun's church, the whispering arch, and O'Conner's cathedral—lure many a traveler to the country's otherwise untouristed midlands.

LITERARY LANDMARKS

Natural beauty and urban grime have inspired many centuries of superb Irish literary output. Dublin (p. 84) has promoted (and suffered) the caustic wit of **Jonathan Swift, Oscar Wilde, George Bernard Shaw, James Joyce, Sean O'Casey, Samuel Beckett, Brendan Behan, Flann O'Brien,** and **Roddy Doyle,** to name but a few. **W.B. Yeats** scattered his poetic settings throughout the island, but he chose Co. Sligo for his grave site (p. 394). **John Millington Synge** found literary greatness by depicting the domestic squabbles of Aran Islanders (p. 351). **Seamus Heaney** has compared the bogland's fossilized remains of pre-Christian sacrifices to The Troubles of present-day Northern Ireland. In Belfast (p. 462), **Brian Moore** and **Paul Muldoon** illustrate the ordinary life of individuals in a city that receives world recognition only for its extraordinary events. **Brian Friel's** plays bring to life the wilds and folkways of Co. Donegal (p. 399). Limerick (p. 304) has had a successful face-lift since the poverty-stricken days described by **Frank McCourt** in his childhood memoirs. Ireland's ancient **mythology** is the most pervasive of all its literary forms—virtually every bump and bauble on the island is accountable to fairies, giants, gods, and heroes.

BREWERIES AND DISTILLERIES

The Irish claim that stout is blessed and that whiskey is the "water of life": it follows that the island's breweries and distilleries are its holy wells. The **Guinness Storehouse** (p. 116) provides only a handful of clues about how to concoct the black magic. Free samples abound at the tour's end, and you're sure to get even more if you mention the infamous "Hennessy Tap" to the guide. Smaller, though just as intoxicating, the **Dublin Brewing Company** (see p. 119) is the city's new kid on the block, offering personal tours with plenty of hops to smell and beer to 'taste.' **Smithwicks** (p. 177) stores a blonder brew in a former monastery in Kilkenny. Monks first brewed the stuff in the early 14th century, and though commercial use didn't start until 1710, it's still the oldest brewery in Ireland—50 years older than its black cousin on the Liffey. Back in Dublin, the **Old Jameson Distillery** (p. 119) makes a slightly sweeter version of whiskey than the hard stuff stored in barrels at **Bushmills Distillery** (p. 528) in Co. Antrim, though the folks at Bushmills provide more 'fullfilling' tours, if you know what we mean.

FESTIVALS AND FESTIVITIES

Most seaside towns manage to scrape together a **regatta** or two; **Wicklow's Regatta Festival** is the oldest on the Isle (p. 139). In mid-July, the **Galway Arts Festival** (p. 351) hosts theater, trad, rock, and film during two weeks of vigorous revelry, second in fun only to the island-wide frenzy of **St. Patrick's Day** (March 17th). Mid-May brings **Armagh's Apple Blossom Festival** (p. 507). James Joyce enthusiasts take part in an 18hr. ramble through Dublin's streets every year on June 16, **Bloomsday** (p. 123). Early August brings all types of musicians, artists, and merrymakers to Waterford's **Spraoi festival** (p. 222). He-goats compete for the title of alpha male in **Killorglin's Puck Fair** (p. 276) in mid-August. The **Connemara Pony Show** (p. 362) brings its colts to Clifden in late August. Around the same time, every set in Ireland tunes in to the nationally televised **Rose of Tralee Festival and Pageant** (p. 299). Cape Clear Island spins yarns at the **International Storytelling Festival** (p. 249), also in late August. Many return home happy from the **Lisdoonvarna Matchmaking Festival** (p. 331) in early September. Fat ladies sing at the **Wexford Festival Opera** (p. 206) in late October. Ireland's largest arts festival, the **Belfast Festival** (p. 485) at Queen's College, is a citywide three-week winter potluck of cultural events.

LET'S GO PICKS

BEST PUBS: Most Dubliners consider **The Palace** to be the only *real* pub in the city (p. 104). Raise your spirits at **Johnnie Fox's** on the Wicklow Way (p. 146), the highest pub in all of Ireland. **An Droichead Beag** keeps Dingle tipsy and toe-tapping with constant trad sessions (p. 293). The folks at **McCarthy's Hotel** in Fethard promise to "wine you, dine you, and bury you" (p. 190). And anyone who's anyone goes to **Matt Molloy's** in Westport, owned by the flautist of the Chieftans (p. 374).

BEST VIEWS: Yeats admired the mile-high cliff views from **Drumcliffe** towards **Ben Bulben** (p. 394)—so will you. The finest views in two counties await you from high on **The Healy Pass** (p. 260). The sheer **Bunglass** (p. 414) cliffs near the Slieve League are Europe's highest coastal ledges. The views from **Slea Head** (p. 295) have brought many a filmmaker to the Isle. The towering heights of the cliffs around the **Giant's Causeway** (p. 527) both terrify and tantalize.

BEST ODDBALL COLLECTIONS: The Irish National Stud, Kildare, is an unforgettable Zen/equine experience (p. 148). **Fox's Lane Folk Museum** in Youghal has razor-sharp exhibits (p. 240). The **Ceim Hill Museum** in Union Hall has dinosaur dung, revolutionary rifles, and a remarkably remarkable curator (p. 246). The doll house exhibit at **Malahide Castle's Museum** (p. 128) amazes both young'uns and old'uns alike.

BEST AQUATIC FUN: Ride some of Europe's best waves at the sandy strands near **Tramore Bay Surf Centre** (p. 215), or hang ten up north in **Bundoran** (p. 407), where the North's best surfers strut their stuff. Snorkelers often see U-boat and galleon wrecks in the waters off **Baltimore** (p. 248). For windsurfing, canoeing, sailboating, motorboating, and anything else that can get you wet, head south to Co. Clare's **Killaloe** (p. 320). The folks at **Leeane's** Killary Adventure Company (p. 369) can also outfit you for anything adventure-aquatic related.

BEST PLACES TO STAY: Try a night in one of the three colorful gypsy trailers of Dunmanway's **Shiplake Mountain Hostel** (p. 241). **Maria's Schoolhouse,** Union Hall, has the best and the brightest of everything (p. 246). Relax in the gentle embrace of the cushy, beachfront **Downhill Hostel** (p. 529). Abandon technology and get back to nature inside the gas-lamp-lit **Flax Mill Hostel** in the Sperrins (p. 539). Stay in **the Bastion** (p. 169) of cool in Athlone.

BEST LEGENDARY LANDSCAPES: The spurge is poisonous, so gaze but don't graze at the **Poison Glen,** Donegal (p. 399). Take in the lake views at **Glendalough,** which St. Kevin preferred to women (p. 141). **Navan Fort,** near Armagh, is not only home to men with childbirth pangs, but is a fascinating archaeological site as well (p. 511).

BEST CASTLES AND FORTS: Eastern Ireland is filled with ancient castles and forts—**Trim Castle** (p. 152) is the granddaddy of them all. While the ruins at Trim stand untouched, the folks at **Kilkenny Castle** (p. 184) have refurbished their castle to make it look as it would have in the 17th century—you walk in, and wouldn't know what year it is. On the Aran Islands, 7000-year-old **Dún Aengus** (p. 354) makes the 17th century seem not so cool anymore.

BEST CRITTERS: Eleven pound **Lobzilla** was last spotted at the Seaworld and Leisure Centre in Lahinch (p. 325). Discover the **mummified cat and mouse** at Dublin's Christ Church (p. 115). Knocknarea's **bilingual sheep** beckon you in two different languages (p. 391). Check out Fota Island's very confused **Chilean flamingos** (p. 238). **Fungi** and his Ego await you in Dingle Bay (p. 293). And who could forget the **goats** of Cape Clear Island (p. 249)...or their ice cream?

SUGGESTED ITINERARIES

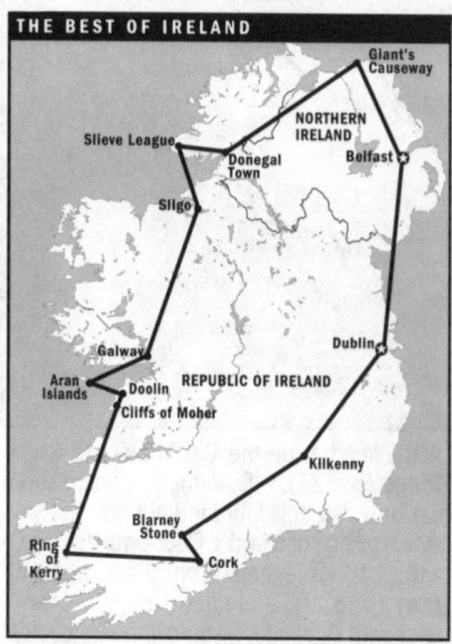

THE BEST OF IRELAND (3½ WEEKS)
Spend a few days in **Dublin** (p. 84) exploring its many pubs. Drink a pint of the dark stuff at the Guinness Brewery and catch a football match at Croke Park before moving on to **Belfast** (p. 467). The complex history of this capital is spectacularly illustrated in the murals decorating its sectarian neighborhoods. Catch the bus to the **Giant's Causeway** (p. 527), a strange formation of octagonal rocks referred to as the earth's eighth natural wonder. Ride the bus back to the Republic and on to **Donegal Town** (p. 402). Get a good night's rest at one of Ireland's best hostels–tomorrow it's on to **Slieve League** (p. 410) to hike and view Europe's tallest sea cliffs. For nighttime entertainment, dip down to **Sligo** (p. 385), once the beloved home of W.B. Yeats. From there, head to **Galway** (p. 336), a raging student center that draws the best musicians on the island. Jump on a ferry to the desolate **Aran Islands** (p. 351) and relax for a few days. Return via **Doolin,** which rests right near the **Cliffs of Moher** (p. 328). Travel south and take a bus or bike ride around the **Ring of Kerry** (p. 276), a peninsula captured on Irish postcards worldwide. Return to civilization in **Cork** (p. 223), where you can daytrip out to see the **Blarney Stone** (p. 223). On your way back to Dublin, take a detour to medieval **Kilkenny** (p. 177), where a former monastery is now Ireland's oldest brewery.

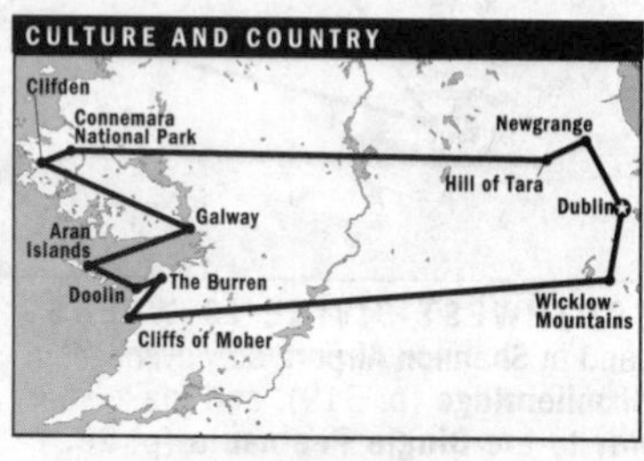

CULTURE AND COUNTRY (3 WEEKS)
For a taste of both urban and rural Ireland, begin in **Dublin** (p. 84). Hit the National Museums by day, spend the evening on a literary pub crawl, and finish off the night in Temple Bar, one of the trendiest nightspots in Europe. From Dublin, take a daytrip to **Newgrange** (p. 150), a neolithic burial site that's older than the pyramids; nearby **Hill of Tara** (p. 152) was the seat of Irish Kings from pre-Christian times up until just 400 years ago. Race across the country to **Connemara National Park** (p. 368). Connemara is an Irish-speaking region with **Clifden** (p. 362) as its accommodating capital. Wind along the breathtaking coastal road to **Galway** (p. 336), a friendly city that entertains thousands of international visitors in its small, pedestrianized streets. Take a plane out from Galway to the **Aran Islands** (p. 351) and check out ancient ring forts and newly knit Aran sweaters. Ferry back from the islands to **Doolin** (p. 326), a superbly musical village snuggled into the unique and rocky **Burren** (p. 329). South of Doolin, waves smash against the looming **Cliffs of Moher** (p. 328). Return to Dublin via the **Wicklow Mountains** (p. 141), and spend two days hiking through "The Garden of Ireland" on the Wicklow Way.

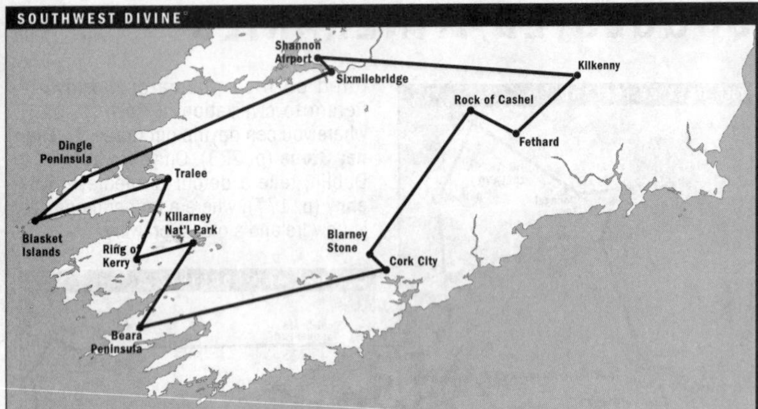

SOUTHWEST DIVINE (3 WEEKS)

Land at **Shannon Airport,** stay overnight in **Sixmilebridge** (p. 319), and make your way to the **Dingle Peninsula** (p. 289), where mountains, beaches, and Irish speakers abound. Don't leave before hitting the isolated *gaeltacht* in the **Blasket Islands** (p. 295). Move east through **Tralee** (p. 299), home of Ireland's most famous festival. Next, circle the **Ring of Kerry** (p. 276). Home to magnificent **Killarney National Park** (p. 272), this highly touristed peninsula provides access to **Valentia Island** (p. 279) and the **Skellig Rocks** (p. 279). Don't miss a third finger of land: the **Beara Peninsula** (p. 257), most remote and splendid of the three. Try **Cork City** (p. 223) for a taste of urbanania as you move inland. After a daytrip to the **Blarney Stone,** travel onward to **Cashel** (p. 189), whose monolithic **Rock** attracts thousands of visitors each year. Stop in at the small town of **Fethard** (p. 191) for some medieval porn before moving onward to **Kilkenny** (p. 177), where you can reacclimatize yourself to a busier way of life and raise a parting glass.

TREKKING THE NORTH (3 WEEKS)

Step off the plane in **Belfast** (p. 462) and leap into a Black Cab for a tour of the Golden Mile, the murals, and the peace line of this infamous and misunderstood city. Take the Antrim Coaster bus north along the waterfront past the glorious **Glens of Antrim** (p. 514). Farther along the coast, Ballintoy village lies beside the **Carrick-a-rede Rope Bridge** (p. 523), a fishermen's construction that provides thrills for landlubbers. The volcanic spillage of **Giant's Causeway** (p. 527) is the stuff of legend. From there, head to **Derry** (p. 530), a medieval city that competes with Dublin for historic importance. It's just a hop across the border to Co. Donegal, the most remote and untouched area on the island. Head up the Inishowen Peninsula to reach **Malin Head** (p. 445), Ireland's northernmost point. Back inland, **Letterkenny** (p. 436) serves as a transport hub to the rest of the county. To the west lies the mountainous **Glenveagh National Park** (p. 427) and the Irish-speaking, trad-loving region of **Gweedore** (p. 426). Continue on to the **Slieve League Peninsula** (p. 414), where soaring cliffs are a bus ride away from the conveniences of **Donegal Town** (p. 402). Before heading back to Belfast, tour Yeats Country around **Sligo** (p. 385).

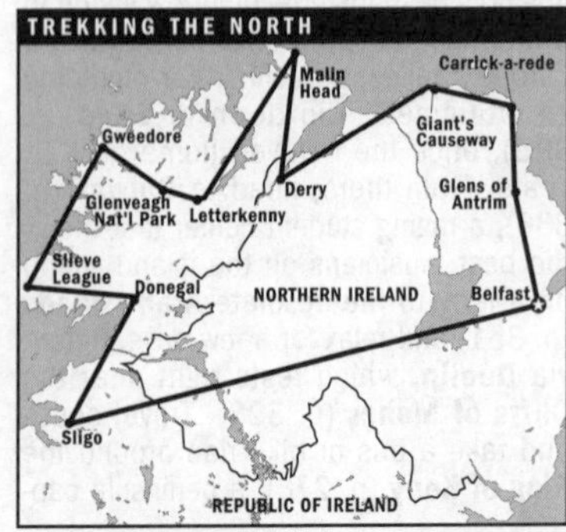

ESSENTIALS

FACTS FOR THE TRAVELER

ENTRANCE REQUIREMENTS.

Driving Permit (p. 32). A valid foreign driver's licence is required for all drivers; a driving permit is required only if you plan to drive for longer than 3 months.

Passport (see below). Required of all foreign nationals, though they may not be checked for EU citizens.

Visa (p. 9). Not required for short-term travel from EU, Commonwealth, and North American countries.

Work Permit (p. 9). Required for non-EU citizens planning to work in Ireland.

EMBASSIES & CONSULATES

IRISH EMBASSIES AND CONSULATES IN...

For other Irish embassies, check the Worldwide Embassies and Consulates Search Engines at www.embassyworld.com and www.irelandemb.org.

Australia: Irish Embassy, 20 Arkana St., Yarralumla, Canberra ACT 2600 (☎062 73 3022).

Canada: Irish Embassy, Suite 1105, 130 Albert St., Ottawa, K1P 5G4, Ontario (☎613-233-6281; emb.ireland@sympatico.ca).

New Zealand: Honorary Consul General, 6th fl., 18 Shortland St. 1001, Auckland 1 (☎09 997 2252, www.ireland.co.nz).

South Africa: Irish Embassy, 1st fl., Southern Life Plaza, 1059 Shoeman St., Arcadia 0083, Pret. (☎012 342 5062).

UK: Irish Embassy, 17 Grosvenor Pl., London SW1X 7HR (☎020 7235 2171). Consulates: 16 Randolph Crescent., Edinburgh EH3 7TT Scotland (☎0131 226 7711); Brunel House, 2 Fitzalan Rd., Cardiff CF24 0EB (☎0207 225 7700).

US: Irish Embassy, 2234 Massachusetts Ave. NW, Washington, D.C. 20008 (☎202-462-3939). Consulates: 345 Park Ave., 17th fl., New York, NY 10154-0037 (☎212-319-3552); 400 N. Michigan Ave., Chicago, IL 60611 (☎312-337-1868); 44 Montgomery St., #3830, San Francisco, CA 94104 (☎415-392-4214); 535 Boylston St., Boston, MA 02116 (☎617-267-9330).

UK EMBASSIES AND CONSULATES IN...

For embassies in countries not listed here, check the Foreign and Commonwealth Office website at www.fco.gov.uk/directory/posts.asp (☎020 7270 1500).

Australia: British High Commission, Commonwealth Ave., Yarralumla, ACT 2606 (☎02 6270 6666; www.uk.emb.gov.au). Consulate-General also in Brisbane, Melbourne, Perth, and Sydney; Consulate in Adelaide.

Canada: British High Commission, 80 Elgin St., Ottawa, ON, K1P 5K7 (☎613-237-1530; www.britain-in-canada.org). British Consulate-General, College Park, 777 Bay St., Suite 2800, Toronto, ON, M5G 2G2 (☎416-593-1290). Consulate-General also in Montreal and Vancouver.

France: British Embassy, 35 Rue du Faubourg St. Honoré, 75383 Paris CEDEX 08 (☎331 44 51 31 00; www.amb-grandebretagne.fr). British Consulate-General, 18 bis Rue d'Anjou, 75008 Paris (☎331 44 51 31 00). Consulates-general also in Bordeaux, Lille, Lyon, and Marseille.

Ireland: British Embassy, 29 Merrion Rd., Ballsbridge, Dublin 4 (☎01 205 3700/3822; www.britishembassy.ie).

New Zealand: British High Commission, 44 Hill St., Thorndon, Wellington 1 (☎04 924 2888; www.britain.org.nz). Consulate-General, 17th fl., NZI House, 151 Queen St., Auckland 1 (☎09 303 2973).

South Africa: British High Commission, 91 Parliament St., Cape Town 8001 (☎021 405 2400); also at 255 Hill St., Arcadia 0002, Pretoria (☎012 483 1400). Consulates-General in Johannesburg and Cape Town; consulates in Port Elizabeth and Durban.

US: British Embassy, 3100 Massachusetts Ave. NW, Washington, D.C. 20008 (☎202-588-6500; www.britainusa.com). Consulate-General, 845 3rd Ave., New York, NY 10022 (☎212-745-0200). Other Consulates-General in Atlanta, Boston, Chicago, Houston, Los Angeles, and San Francisco. Consulates in Anchorage, Dallas, Kansas City, Miami, New Orleans, Salt Lake City, San Diego, Seattle, and Puerto Rico.

EMBASSIES AND CONSULATES IN IRELAND

Below is a list of the foreign embassies and consulates in Ireland. Should you run into any troubles along the way, contact your national branch immediately.

Australia: The Republic, 2nd fl., Fitzwilton House, Wilton Terr., Dublin 2 (☎01 676 1517). **UK,** Australia House, the Strand, London WC2B 4LA (☎020 7379 4334).

Canada: The Republic, Canadian Embassy, 65/68 St. Stephen's Green, 4th fl., Dublin 2 (☎01 478 1988). **Northern Ireland,** Consulate of Canada, 378 Stranmills Rd., Belfast, N.I., BT9 5 ED (☎028 660 212).

New Zealand: UK, New Zealand Embassy, New Zealand House, the Haymarket, London SW1Y 4TQ (☎0171 930 8422).

South Africa: The Republic, South Africa Embassy, Alexandra House, Earlsfort Terr., 2nd fl., Dublin 2 (☎01 661 5553). **UK,** South African High Commission, South Africa House, Trafalgar Sq., London WC2N 5DP (☎020 7925 8900).

United Kingdom: See **UK Embassies and Consulates,** above.

United States: The Republic, Embassy of the United States of America, 42 Elgin Rd., Dublin 4 (☎01 668 8777/7122). **Northern Ireland,** Consulate General, Queen's House, 14 Queen St., Belfast BT1 6EQ (☎028 9032 8239).

TOURIST OFFICES

Almost every town in Ireland has a tourist office. Their offerings, however, range from the useful (free local maps and pamphlets, transportation schedules, and accommodation booking services) to the partial (many tourist boards, especially in the Republic, will only list accommodations that have paid them a fee). All national tourist boards offer information on national hikes, parks, and trails.

Below are the main offices of the national tourist boards; for countries not listed here, check www.ireland.travel.ie and www.discovernorthernireland.com.

Irish Tourist Board (Bord Fáilte): Main office: Baggot St. Bridge, Dublin 2. (☎01 850 230 330 or 602 4000; www.ireland.travel.ie). **Australia:** Level 5, 36 Carrington St., Sydney NSW 2000 (☎02 299 6177). **Canada:** 120 Eglington Ave. E., Ste. 500, Toronto, ON, M4P 1E2 (☎800-223-6470). **New Zealand:** Dingwall Building, 2nd fl., 87 Queen St., Auckland (☎09 379 8720). **South Africa:** Everite House, 7th fl., 20 De

Korte St., Braamfontein, 2001, Johannesburg (☎011 339 4865). **UK:** 150 New Bond St., London W1Y 0AQ (☎7493 3201). **US:** 345 Park Ave., New York, NY 10154 (☎800-223-6470 or 212-418-0800; www.irelandvacations.com).

Northern Ireland Tourist Board: Main Office: 59 North St., Belfast, BT1 1NB, Northern Ireland (☎028 9023 1221; fax 9024 0960; www.discovernorthernireland.com). **Australia:** 36 Carrington St., 5th fl., Sydney NSW 2000 (☎02 299 6177; fax 299 6323; info@tourismireland.com.au). **Canada:** 2 Bloor St., Ste. 1501, Toronto, ON, M4W 3E2 (☎800-223-6470). **New Zealand:** 18 Shortland St., Private Bag 92136, Auckland 1 (☎09 379 3708; fax 309 0725). **The Republic:** 16 Nassau St., Dublin 2 (☎01 679 1977; fax 01 679 1863; infodublin@nitb.com). **UK:** 24 Haymarket, London SW1 4DG (☎020 7766 9920; fax 020 7766 9929). **US:** 551 5th Ave., #701, New York, NY 10176 (☎800-326-0036 or 212-922-0101; fax 922-0099). From elsewhere overseas, contact any British Tourist Office. Tourist boards should have free brochures as well as *Where to Stay in Northern Ireland 2000*, a list of all B&Bs and campgrounds (UK£4).

ESSENTIALS

DOCUMENTS & FORMALITIES

PASSPORTS

REQUIREMENTS. Citizens of Australia, Canada, New Zealand, South Africa, the UK, and the US need valid passports to enter Ireland and to re-enter their home countries. You cannot enter Ireland if your passport expires in under six months; returning home with an expired passport is illegal and may result in a fine.

NEW PASSPORTS. Citizens of Australia, Canada, New Zealand, the UK, and the US can apply for a passport in their home countries at any post office, passport office, or court of law. Citizens of South Africa can apply for a passport at the nearest Home Affairs office. Any new passport or renewal applications must be filed well in advance of the departure date, although most passport offices offer rush services for a steep fee.

PASSPORT MAINTENANCE. Be sure to photocopy the page of your passport with your photo, as well as your visas and traveler's check serial numbers. Carry one set of copies in a safe place, apart from the originals, and leave another set at home. If you lose your passport, immediately notify the local police and the nearest embassy or consulate of your home government. To expedite its replacement you will need to know all information previously recorded and show ID and proof of citizenship. In some cases, a replacement may take weeks to process, and it may be valid only for a limited time. Any visas stamped in your old passport will be irretrievably lost. In an emergency, ask for immediate temporary traveling papers that will permit you to re-enter your home country.

VISAS AND WORK PERMITS

VISAS. Citizens of most countries, including Australia, Canada, EU countries, New Zealand, South Africa, the UK, and the US, do not need visas for visits of less than 90 days in duration. For longer stays, contact the Irish Department of Justice (☎ 01 6028 202) to obtain official permission. If in doubt, or if your home country is not one of these, check with your embassy.

WORK & STUDY PERMITS. Admission as a visitor does not include the right to work, which is authorized only by a work permit. Students wishing to study in Ireland may enter the country without a visa, but must apply to the Aliens Office within seven days (Harcourt Sq., Dublin 2. ☎01 475 5555). Contact your own embassy for information. Also see **Alternatives to Tourism,** p. 47.

ONE EUROPE. The idea of European unity has come a long way since 1958, when the European Economic Community (EEC) was created to promote solidarity and cooperation. Since then, the EEC has become the European Union (EU), with political, legal, and economic institutions spanning 15 states: Austria, Belgium, Denmark, Finland, France, Germany, Greece, Ireland, Italy, Luxembourg, the Netherlands, Portugal, Spain, Sweden, and the UK.

What does this have to do with the average non-EU tourist? In 1999, the EU established **freedom of movement** across 14 European countries—the entire EU minus Ireland and the UK, but plus Iceland and Norway. This means that border controls between participating countries have been abolished, and visa policies harmonized. While you're still required to carry a passport (or government-issued ID card for EU citizens) when crossing an internal border, once you've been admitted into one country, you're free to travel to all participating states. Britain and Ireland have also formed a **common travel area,** abolishing passport controls between the UK and Ireland. This means that the only times you'll see a border guard within the EU are traveling between the British Isles and the Continent.

For more important consequences of the EU for travelers, see **The Euro** (p. 11) and **European Customs** and **EU customs regulations** (p. 11).

IDENTIFICATION

When you travel, always carry two or more forms of identification on your person, including at least one photo ID; a passport combined with a driver's license or birth certificate is usually adequate. Many establishments, especially banks, may require several IDs in order to cash traveler's checks. Never carry all your forms of ID together; split them up in case of theft or loss.

STUDENT, TEACHER & YOUTH IDENTIFICATION. The **International Student Identity Card (ISIC),** the most widely accepted form of student ID, provides discounts on sights, accommodations, food, and transport; access to 24hr. emergency helpline (in North America call ☎877-370-ISIC; elsewhere call US collect ☎+1 715-345-0505); and insurance benefits for US cardholders (see **Insurance,** p. 19). The ISIC is preferable to an institution-specific card (such as a university ID) because it is more likely to be recognized and honored abroad. Applicants must be degree-seeking students of a secondary or post-secondary school and must be at least 12 years of age. Because of the proliferation of fake ISICs, some services (particularly airlines) require additional proof of student identity, such as a school ID or a letter attesting to your student status, signed by your registrar.

The **International Teacher Identity Card (ITIC)** offers teachers the same insurance coverage as well as similar but limited discounts. For travelers who are 25 years old or under but are not students, the **International Youth Travel Card (IYTC;** formerly the **GO 25** Card) also offers many of the same benefits as the ISIC.

Each of these identity cards costs US$22/€23. ISIC and ITIC cards are valid for one and a half academic years; IYTC cards are valid for one year from the date of issue. Many student travel agencies (see p. 22) issue the cards, including STA Travel in Australia and New Zealand; Travel CUTS in Canada; usit in the Republic of Ireland and Northern Ireland; SASTS in South Africa; Campus Travel and STA Travel in the UK; and Council Travel and STA Travel in the US. For a listing of issuing agencies and more information contact the **International Student Travel Confederation (ISTC),** Herengracht 479, 1017 BS Amsterdam, Netherlands (☎+31 20 421 28 00; www.istc.org).

CUSTOMS IN THE EU. As well as freedom of movement of people within the EU (see p. 10), travelers in the countries that are members of the EU can also take advantage of the freedom of movement of goods. This means that there are no customs controls at internal EU borders (i.e., you can take the blue customs channel at the airport), and travelers are free to transport whatever legal substances they like, as long as it is for their own personal (non-commercial) use—up to 800 cigarettes, 10L of spirits, 90L of wine (60L of sparkling wine), and 110L of beer. You should also be aware that duty-free was abolished on June 30, 1999, for travel between EU states; however, travelers between the EU and the rest of the world still get a duty-free allowance when passing through customs.

ESSENTIALS

CUSTOMS

ENTERING IRELAND. Upon entering Ireland, you must declare certain items from abroad and pay a duty on the value of those articles if they exceed the allowance established by Ireland's customs service. Note that goods purchased at **duty-free** shops abroad are not exempt from duty or sales tax; "duty-free" merely means you do not pay a tax in the country of purchase. (Also see **Customs in the EU,** below.)

LEAVING IRELAND. If you're leaving for a non-EU country, you can reclaim any **Value Added Tax (VAT).** Keeping receipts for purchases made abroad will help establish values when you return. Upon returning home, you must similarly declare all articles acquired abroad and pay a duty on the value of articles in excess of your home country's allowance. To expedite your return, make a list of any valuables brought from home, and be sure to keep receipts for all goods acquired abroad.

MONEY

CURRENCY AND EXCHANGE

On February 9th, 2002, the Republic of Ireland's legal tender became the **euro,** denoted €. Euro coins come in denominations of 1, 2, 5, 10, 20, and 50 cents, and €1 and €2. Euro notes begin at €5. Legal tender in Northern Ireland is the **British pound.** Northern Ireland has its own bank notes, identical in value to English, Scottish, and Manx notes of the same denominations. Although all of these notes are accepted in Northern Ireland, Northern Ireland notes are not accepted across the water. UK coins come in denominations of 1p, 2p, 5p, 10p, 20p, 50p, and £1. Residents of both nations refer to pounds and euros as "**quid,**" as in "ten quid" (never "quids"). Also expect to hear the terms "**fiver**" (€5 or £5), and "**tener**" (€10 or £10).

THE EURO. The official currency of 12 members of the European Union is now the euro. The currency has some important—and positive—consequences for travelers hitting more than one euro-zone country. For one thing, money-changers across the euro-zone are obliged to exchange money at the official, fixed rate (see below), and at no commission (though they may still charge a small service fee). Second, euro-denominated travelers' checks allow you to pay for goods and services across the euro-zone, again at the official rate and commission-free.

When changing money abroad, try to go only to banks or bureaux de change offices that have at most a 5% margin between their buy and sell prices. Since you lose money with every transaction, **convert large sums** (unless the currency is depreciating rapidly), **but no more than you'll need.**

If you use traveler's checks or bills, carry some in small denominations (the equivalent of US$50 or less) for times when you are forced to exchange money at disadvantageous rates, but bring a range of denominations since charges may be levied per check cashed. Store your money in a variety of forms; ideally, at any given time you will be carrying some cash, some traveler's checks, and an ATM and/or credit card. All travelers should also consider carrying some US dollars (about US$50), which may sometimes be accepted by local teller.

The currency chart below is based on August 2002 exchange rates between Euro currency and Australian dollars (AUS$), Canadian dollars (CDN$), New Zealand dollars (NZ$), South African Rand (ZAR), British pounds (UK£), US dollars (US$). Check the currency converter on financial websites such as www.bloomberg.com and www.xe.com for the latest exchange rates.

THE EURO

AUS$1 = €0.55	€1 = AUS$1.81
CAD$1 = €0.65	€1 = CAD$1.53
NZ$1 = €0.48	€1 = NZ$2.10
ZAR1 = €0.10	€1 = ZAR10.14
US$1 = €1.03	€1 = US$0.97
UK£1 = €1.57	€1 = UK£0.64

As a general rule, it's cheaper to convert money in Ireland than at home. While currency exchange will probably be available in your arrival airport, it's wise to bring enough foreign currency to last for the first 24 to 72 hours of a trip.

TRAVELER'S CHECKS

Traveler's checks are one of the safest and least troublesome means of carrying funds. American Express, Travelex/Thomas Cook, and Visa are the most widely recognized brands in the UK. Many banks and agencies sell them for a small commission. Check issuers provide refunds if the checks are lost or stolen, and many provide additional services, such as toll-free refund hotlines abroad, emergency message services, and stolen credit card assistance.

While traveling, keep traveler's check receipts and a record of which ones you've cashed separate from the checks themselves. Also leave a list of check numbers with someone at home. Never countersign traveler's checks until you're ready to cash them, and always bring your passport with you to cash them. If your checks are lost or stolen, immediately contact a refund center (of the company that issued them) to be reimbursed; they may require a police report verifying the loss or theft. Ask about toll-free refund hotlines and the location of refund centers when purchasing checks, and always carry emergency cash.

CREDIT & DEBIT CARDS

Credit cards are generally accepted in urban and larger Irish establishments, but small businesses, B&Bs, and hostels often do not take them. Where they are accepted, credit cards often offer superior exchange rates—up to 5% better than the retail rate used by banks and bureaux de change. Credit cards may also offer services such as insurance or emergency help, and are sometimes required to reserve hotel rooms or rental cars. **MasterCard** and **Visa** are the most welcomed; **American Express** cards work at some ATMs and at AmEx offices and major airports. The **Discover Card** may not be readily accepted in Ireland.

Credit cards are also useful for **cash advances,** which allow you to withdraw Irish pounds from associated banks and ATMs throughout Ireland instantly. However, transaction fees for all credit card advances (up to US$10 per advance, plus 2-3% extra on foreign transactions after conversion) tend to make credit cards a more costly way of withdrawing cash than ATMs or traveler's checks. In an emergency, however, the transaction fee may prove worth the cost.

Debit cards are a relatively new form of purchasing power. A debit card can be used wherever its associated credit card company (usually Mastercard or Visa) is accepted. The difference between a debit card and a credit card is that with a debit card purchase, money is withdrawn directly from the holder's checking account. Debit cards also function as ATM cards and can be used to withdraw cash from banks and ATMs throughout Ireland. Ask your local bank about obtaining one.

CASH CARDS (ATM CARDS)

Cash cards—popularly called ATM cards—are widespread in Ireland, though a few of the islands and smallest towns still do without. ATMs get the same wholesale exchange rate as credit cards, but there may be a limit on the amount of money you can withdraw per day (around US$500), and unfortunately computer networks sometimes fail. There is typically also a surcharge of US$1-5 per withdrawal.

The two major international money networks are **Cirrus** (US ☎800-424-7787) and **PLUS** (US ☎800-843-7587). **Ulster Bank Limited, AIB,** and **Bank of Ireland** typically accept Cirrus transactions. To locate ATMs around the world, call the above numbers, or consult www.visa.com/pd/atm or www.mastercard.com/atm.

Visa TravelMoney is a system allowing you to access money from any ATM that accepts Visa cards. (For local customer assistance in Ireland, call ☎800 559 345.) You deposit an amount before you travel (plus a small administration fee), and you can withdraw up to that sum. Obtain a card by either visiting a **Thomas Cook** or **Citicorp** office, by calling toll-free in the US ☎877-394-2247, or check with your local bank or to see if it issues TravelMoney cards.

PIN NUMBERS & ATMS. To use a cash or credit card to withdraw money from a cash machine (ATM) in Europe, you must have a four-digit **Personal Identification Number (PIN).** If your PIN is longer than four digits, ask your bank whether you can just use the first four, or whether you'll need a new one. **Credit cards** don't usually come with PINs, so if you intend to hit up ATMs in Europe with a credit card to get cash advances, call your credit card company before leaving to request one.

People with alphabetic, rather than numerical, PINs may also be thrown off by the lack of letters on European cash machines. The following handy chart gives the corresponding numbers to use: 1=QZ; 2=ABC; 3=DEF; 4=GHI; 5=JKL; 6=MNO; 7=PRS; 8=TUV; and 9=WXY. Note that if you mistakenly punch the wrong code into the machine three times, it will swallow your card for good.

GETTING MONEY FROM HOME

If you run out of money while traveling, the easiest and cheapest solution is to have someone back home make a deposit to your credit card or cash (ATM) card. Failing that, consider one of the following options.

WESTERN UNION. Travelers from Australia, Canada, the UK, and the US can wire funds through Western Union's international money transfer services. In Australia, call ☎800 501 500; Canada ☎800 235 000; Ireland ☎800 395 395; UK ☎0900 83 38 33; US ☎800-325-6000. Rates for sending cash are US$10 cheaper than with a credit card, and the money is often available at the place you're sending it within an hour. For the nearest Western Union location, consult www.westernunion.com.

US STATE DEPARTMENT (US CITIZENS ONLY). In dire emergencies only, the US State Department will forward money within hours to the nearest consular office, which will then disburse it according to instructions for a US$15 fee. If you wish to use this service, you must contact the Overseas Citizens Service division of the US State Department (☎202-647-5225; nights, Sundays, and holidays ☎202-647-4000).

COSTS

The cost of your trip will vary considerably, depending on when you go, how you travel, and where you stay. The single biggest cost of your trip will probably be your round-trip (return) **airfare** (see **Getting There: By Plane,** p. 20). Before you go, spend some time calculating a reasonable per-day **budget** that will meet your needs. To give you a general idea, a day in Ireland would cost about €30 (US$32) if you were to camp or stay in hostels and cook your own food. Also, don't forget to factor in emergency reserve funds (at least €200 euro) when planning how much money you'll need.

Considering that saving just a few dollars a day over the course of your trip might pay for days or weeks of additional travel, the art of penny-pinching is well worth learning. Bring a **sleepsack** (see p. 20) to save on sheet charges in some hostels, and do your **laundry** in the sink (unless you're prohibited from doing so). You can split **accommodations** costs (in hotels and some hostels) with trustworthy fellow travelers; multi-bed rooms almost always work out cheaper per person than singles. With that said, don't go overboard with your budget obsession. Though staying within your budget is important, don't do so at the expense of your sanity or health.

TIPPING

Some restaurants in Ireland figure a service charge into the bill; some even calculate it into the cost of the dishes themselves. The menu often indicates whether or not service is included. Most people working in restaurants, however, do not expect a tip, unless the restaurant is targeted exclusively toward tourists. In those incidences, consider leaving 10-15%, depending upon the quality of the service. Tipping is very uncommon for other services, such as taxis and hairdressers, especially in rural areas. In most cases, people are usually happy if you simply round off the bill to the nearest euro. Barmen at older or rural pubs may be surprised if you leave them a gratuity, while in cities or at bars with a younger clientele a tip may be expected—the trick is to watch and learn from other customers.

VALUE ADDED TAX

Both the Republic and Northern Ireland charge a **Value Added Tax (VAT),** a national sales tax on most goods and some services. In Ireland, the VAT does not apply to food and children's clothing but goes as high as 17% in restaurants and 21% on large consumer items. The VAT is almost always included in listed prices. The British rate, applicable to Northern Ireland, is 17.5% on many services (such as hairdressers, hotels, restaurants, and car rental agencies) and on all goods (except books, medicine, and food). Refunds are available only to non-EU citizens and only for goods taken out of the country, not services. In Ireland, **VAT refunds** are available on goods purchased in stores displaying a "Cashback" sticker (ask if you don't see one). Ask for a voucher with your purchase, which you must fill out and present at the Cashback service desk in Dublin or Shannon airports. Purchases greater than €250 must be approved at the customs desk first. Your money can also be refunded by mail, which takes six to eight weeks.

Visitors to Northern Ireland can get a **VAT refund** on goods taken out of the country through the **Retail Export Scheme.** Look for signs like "Tax Free Shopping" or "Tax Free for Tourists" and ask the shopkeeper about minimum purchases (usually €65-130) as well as for the appropriate form. Keep purchases in carry-on luggage so a customs officer can inspect the goods and validate refund forms. To receive a refund, mail the stamped forms back to the store in the envelope provided. Refunds can take up to three months to be processed. To use this scheme, you must export the goods within three months of purchase.

SAFETY AND SECURITY

The **national emergency number** in Ireland for police, ambulance, fire, and (in appropriate areas) mountain rescue services is ☎**999.**

Ireland's friendliness makes for a relatively safe country with a low rate of violent civilian crime, but there are incidents of petty crime by **muggers** and **pickpockets** (see **Financial Security,** below). Certain areas of larger cities are particularly dangerous at night—don't walk alone, don't wear revealing clothing, and don't carry valuables. Check with the reception at hostels for more information on dangerous areas. When walking at night, stick to busy streets and avoid dark alleyways. If you feel uncomfortable, leave as quickly and directly as you can, but don't allow fear of the unknown to spoil your travels. If you're by yourself, be sure that someone at home knows your itinerary, and never admit that you're traveling alone.

SELF DEFENSE. There is no sure-fire way to avoid all the threatening situations you might encounter when you travel, but a good self-defense course will give you concrete ways to react to unwanted advances. **Impact, Prepare,** and **Model Mugging** can refer you to local self-defense courses in the US (☎800-345-5425). Visit the website at www.impactsafety.org/chapters for a list of nearby chapters. Workshops (2-3hr.) start at US$50; full courses run US$350-500.

TRANSPORTATION. The main concern for most drivers visiting the Republic or Northern Ireland is adjusting to driving on the left-hand side of the road (especially dealing with right turns). If you are using a **car,** learn local driving signals and wear a seatbelt. Study route maps before you hit the road, and if you plan on spending a lot of time on the road, you may want to bring spare parts. For long drives in desolate areas, consider a cellular phone and a roadside assistance program (see p. 32). Be sure to park your vehicle in a garage or well traveled area, and use a steering wheel locking device in larger cities. **Sleeping in your car** is one of the most dangerous (and often illegal) ways to get your rest.

If you're **cycling,** wear reflective clothing, drink plenty of water, and ride on the same side as the traffic. Learn the international signals for turns, and use them. Know how to fix a modern derailleur-equipped chain mount and change a tire, and practice on your own bike; a few simple tools and a good bike manual will be invaluable. Exercise caution when biking at night and on heavy-traffic roads.

Let's Go doesn't recommend **hitchhiking,** particularly not for women. For more information on the perils of traveling by thumb, see p. 33.

TERRORISM. Terrorism has become a serious international concern, but it is enormously difficult to predict where or when attacks will occur. Over the past several decades, Northern Ireland has combatted its own domestic terrorist organizations. Most of these terrorist organizations set out to cause maximum monetary damage but minimum casualties. Travelers are almost never targeted, and since the a Good Friday Agreement in 1998, terrorism has ceased to be a concern for most Irish, even in the North.

The most important thing for travelers is to gather as much information as possible before leaving and to **keep in contact** while overseas. The US Department of State website (travel.state.gov) is a good place to research the current situation anywhere you may be planning to travel. Depending on the circumstances, you may want to register with your home embassy or consulate when you arrive. The **Travel Advisories** box (below) lists offices to contact and webpages to visit for the most updated list of your home country's government traveling advisories.

TRAVEL ADVISORIES. The following government offices provide travel information and advisories by telephone, by fax, or via the web:

Australian Department of Foreign Affairs and Trade: ☎1300 555135; fax-back service 02 6261 1299; www.dfat.gov.au.

Canadian Department of Foreign Affairs and International Trade (DFAIT): In Canada and the US call ☎800-267-6788, elsewhere call ☎613-944-6788; www.dfait-maeci.gc.ca. Call for their free booklet, *Bon Voyage...But.*

New Zealand Ministry of Foreign Affairs: ☎04 494 8500; fax 494 8506; www.mft.govt.nz/trav.html.

United Kingdom Foreign and Commonwealth Office: ☎020 7008 0232; fax 7008 0155; www.fco.gov.uk.

US Department of State: ☎202-647-5225, toll-free 888-407-4747; http://travel.state.gov. For *A Safe Trip Abroad,* call 202-512-1800.

FINANCIAL SECURITY

PROTECTING YOUR VALUABLES. There are a few steps you can take to minimize the financial risk associated with traveling. First, **bring as little with you as possible.** Second, buy a few combination **padlocks** to secure your belongings either in your pack—which you should **never leave unattended**—or in a hostel or train station locker. Third, **carry as little cash as possible;** instead carry traveler's checks and ATM/credit cards, keeping them in a **money belt**—not a "fanny pack"—along with your passport and ID cards. Fourth, **keep a small cash reserve separate from your primary stash,** along with your traveler's check numbers and important photocopies.

ACCOMMODATION & TRANSPORTATION. Never leave belongings unattended; crime occurs in even the most demure-looking hostel or hotel. Bring your own **padlock** for hostel lockers, and don't ever store valuables in any locker. Be particularly careful on **buses** and **trains,** carry your backpack in front of you where you can see it, and try not to sleep on any public transportation. If traveling by **car,** don't leave valuables in it while you are away, and hide removable CD players in the trunk.

CON ARTISTS & PICKPOCKETS. Con artists often work in groups, and children are among the most effective. **Don't ever let your passport or your bag out of your sight.** Beware of **pickpockets** in city crowds, especially on public transportation. Also, be alert in public telephone booths. If you must say your calling card number, do so quietly; if you punch it in, make sure no one looks over your shoulder.

DRUGS & ALCOHOL

A meek "I didn't know it was illegal" will not suffice. Remember that you are subject to the laws of the country in which you travel, not to those of your home country. The Republic of Ireland and the UK both regulate the possession of recreational drugs, with penalties ranging from a warning to lengthy prison sentences. Minor marijuana use generally results in a fine or warning, but harder substances are treated with severity. If you carry **prescription drugs** while you travel, it is vital to have a copy of the prescription and a note from a doctor, readily accessible at country borders. The drinking age is 18 throughout Ireland.

HEALTH

Traveling in Ireland is not without its share of health risks—most of which can be prevented with little more than common sense and a little bit of foresight. For instance: drink lots of fluids, wear sturdy, broken-in shoes and clean socks, and use talcum powder to keep your feet dry.

BEFORE YOU GO

In your **passport,** write the names of any people you wish to be contacted in case of a medical emergency, and also list any allergies or medical conditions of which you want doctors to be aware. Allergy sufferers might want to obtain a full supply of any necessary medication before the trip. Matching a prescription to a foreign equivalent is not always easy, safe, or possible. Carry up-to-date, legible prescriptions or a statement from your doctor stating the medication's trade name, manufacturer, chemical name, and dosage. While traveling, be sure to keep all medication with you in your carry-on luggage. For tips on packing a basic first aid kit or other health essentials, see p. 17.

USEFUL ORGANIZATIONS & PUBLICATIONS

The US **Centers for Disease Control and Prevention** (**CDC;** ☎877-FYI-TRIP; toll-free www.cdc.gov/travel) maintains an international travelers' hotline and an informative website. The CDC's comprehensive booklet *Health Information for International Travel*, an annual rundown of disease, immunization, and general health advice, is free online or for US$25 via the Public Health Foundation (☎877-252-1200). Consult the appropriate government agency of your home country for consular information sheets on entry requirements and other issues for various countries (see the listings in **Travel Advisories,** p. 16). For quick information on health and travel warnings, call the **Overseas Citizens Services** (☎202-647-5225; after-hours 202-647-4000), or contact a passport agency, embassy, or consulate abroad. For information on medical evacuation services and travel insurance firms, see the US government's website at http://travel.state.gov/medical.html or the **British Foreign and Commonwealth Office** (www.fco.gov.uk). For detailed information on travel health, including a country-by-country overview of diseases try the **International Travel Health Guide,** by Stuart Rose, MD (www.travmed.com). For general health information, contact the **American Red Cross** (☎800-564-1234; www.redcross.org).

MEDICAL ASSISTANCE ON THE ROAD

In the event of sudden illness or an accident, dial ☎**999,** the general **emergency** number for the Republic and Northern Ireland. It's a free call from any pay phone to an operator who will connect you to the local police, hospital, or fire brigade. EU citizens receive health care; others must have medical insurance or be prepared to pay, though emergency care is provided free of charge. Hospitals are plentiful and listed in the **Practical Information** sections.

If you are concerned about being able to access medical support while traveling, there are special support services you might employ. The *MedPass* from **GlobalCare, Inc.,** 6875 Shiloh Rd. East, alpharetta, GA 30005-8372, USA (☎800-860-1111; www.globalems.com), provides 24hr. international medical assistance, support, and medical evacuation resources.

Those with medical conditions (diabetes, allergies to antibiotics, epilepsy, heart conditions) may want to obtain a stainless-steel **Medic Alert** ID tag (first year US$35, annually thereafter US$20), which identifies the condition and gives a 24hr. collect-call number. Contact the Medic Alert Foundation, 2323 Colorado Ave, Turlock, CA 95382, USA (☎888-633-4298; www.medicalert.org).

PREVENTING DISEASE

INSECT-BORNE DISEASES. Beware of insects—particularly mosquitoes, fleas, and lice—in wet or forested areas in Ireland (particularly in the northwest and near boglands). **Ticks**—responsible for Lyme and other diseases—can be particularly dangerous in rural and forested regions. Pause periodically while walking to brush off ticks using a fine-toothed comb on your neck and scalp. Do not try to remove ticks by burning them or coating them with nail polish remover or petroleum jelly. If you find a tick attached to your skin, grasp the head with tweezers as close to your skin as possible and apply slow, steady traction. Removing a tick within 24 hours greatly reduces the risk of infection.

FOOT AND MOUTH DISEASE. Although easily transmitted between cloven-hoofed animals (cows, pigs, sheep, goats and deer), Foot and Mouth Disease (FMD) does not pose a known health threat to humans. It is, however, devastating to livestock—causing severe depletions of milk and meat production—and can be transmitted by human traffic as well as animal contact. FMD is believed to be killed by heat, making cooked meats apparently safe for consumption. Fish, poultry, fruits and vegetables pose no FMD risk. In 2001, several European countries experienced a severe outbreak of FMD. Incidents in the Republic and Northern Ireland were relatively minor and contained. As of publication of this guide, general travel is not restricted in Ireland. For more information, contact the Republic's Department of Agriculture, Food, and Rural Development (☎01 607 2000; www.irlgov.ie/daff) or the North's Department of Agriculture and Rural Development (☎028 90 524 279 or 90 524 590; www.dani.gov.uk).

MAD COW DISEASE. Bovine spongiform encephalopathy (BSE), better known as Mad Cow Disease, is a disease affecting the central nervous system of cattle. The human variant is called Creutzfeldt-Jakob disease (nvCJD), and both forms of the disease involve fatal brain diseases. Information on nvCJD is not conclusive, but the disease is supposedly caused by consuming infected beef; however, the risk is very small (around 1 case per 10 billion servings of meat). The US Centers for Disease Control has further information (www.cdc.gov/travel), as does the EU Commission on Food Safety (http://europa.eu.int/comm/food).

FOOD- AND WATER-BORNE DISEASES. Prevention is the best cure: be sure that everything you eat is cooked properly and that the water you drink is clean. **Parasites** hide in unsafe water and food. Symptoms of parasitic infection include swollen glands or lymph nodes, fever, digestive problems, and anemia. Tap water in Ireland is generally safe, but river, streams, and lakes may carry bacteria, and water from them should always be purified. To purify your own water, bring it to a rolling boil or treat it with **iodine tablets,** available at any camping goods store.

HEPATITIS. **Hepatitis B** is a viral infection of the liver transmitted via bodily fluids or needle-sharing. Symptoms may not surface until years after infection. Vaccinations are recommended for health-care workers, sexually-active travelers, and anyone planning to seek medical treatment abroad. The 3-shot vaccination series must begin 6 months before traveling. **Hepatitis C** is like Hep B, but the mode of transmission differs. IV drug users, those with occupational exposure to blood, hemodialysis patients, and recipients of blood transfusions are at the highest risk, but the disease can also be spread through sexual contact or sharing items like razors and toothbrushes that may have traces of blood on them.

AIDS & HIV. For detailed information on **Acquired Immune Deficiency Syndrome (AIDS)** in Ireland, call the National AIDS Helpline Éire (☎01 872 4277), AIDS Ireland (☎800 232 320), or the Northern Ireland National AIDS Helpline (☎0800 137

437). You can also contact the US Centers for Disease Control's 24hr. hotline at ☎800-342-2437, or the Joint United Nations Programme on HIV/AIDS (UNAIDS), 20, av. Appia, CH-1211 Geneva 27, Switzerland (☎41 22 791 36 66; fax 22 791 41 87). The Council on International Educational Exchange's pamphlet, *Travel Safe: AIDS and International Travel*, is posted on their website (www.ciee.org/Isp/safety/travelsafe.htm), along with links to other online and phone resources.

WOMEN'S HEALTH

Reliable **contraceptive devices** may be difficult to find, especially in rural areas. Women on birth-control should bring enough to allow for extended stays. Bring a prescription, since forms of the Pill vary. **Abortion** is illegal in Ireland, except when the life of the mother is in danger. Women who need an abortion while abroad should contact the **International Planned Parenthood Federation,** European Regional Office, Regent's Park, London NW1 4NS (☎020 7487 7900; www.ippf.org).

MEDICAL AND TRAVEL INSURANCE

Travel insurance covers four basic areas: medical/health problems, property loss, trip cancellation/interruption, and emergency evacuation. Prices for travel insurance purchased separately run about US$50 per week for full coverage, while trip cancellation/interruption may be purchased separately at a rate of about US$5.50 per US$100 of coverage.

Medical insurance often covers costs incurred abroad; check with your provider. **US Medicare** does not cover foreign travel. **Canadians** are protected by their home province's health insurance plan for up to 90 days after leaving the country; check with the Ministry of Health or Health Plan Headquarters. **Australians** traveling in the UK are entitled to many of the services that they would receive at home as part of the Reciprocal Health Care Agreement. **Homeowners' insurance** (or your family's coverage) often covers theft during travel and loss of travel documents (passport, plane ticket, railpass, etc.) up to US$500.

ISIC and **ITIC** (see p. 10) provide basic insurance benefits, including US$100 per day of in-hospital sickness for up to 60 days, US$3000 of accident-related medical reimbursement, and US$25,000 for emergency transport. Cardholders have access to a toll-free 24hr. helpline (run by **TravelGuard**) for medical, legal, and financial emergencies overseas (US and Canada ☎877-370-4742, elsewhere call US collect ☎+1 715-345-0505). **American Express** (US ☎800-528-4800) grants most cardholders automatic car rental insurance (collision and theft, not liability) and ground travel accident coverage of US$100,000 on flight purchases made with the card.

INSURANCE PROVIDERS. **Council** and **STA** (see p. 22) offer plans that can supplement your basic coverage. Other private insurance providers in the US and Canada include: **Access America** (☎800-284-8300; www.accessamerica.com); **Berkely Group/Carefree Travel Insurance** (☎800-323-3149; www.berkely.com); and **Travel Assistance International** (☎800-821-2828; www.travelassistance.com). Providers in the **UK** include **Columbus Direct** (☎020 7375 0011; www.columbusdirect.net).

PACKING

Pack lightly. Lay out only what you absolutely need, then take half the clothes and twice the money. The less you have, the less you have to lose (or store, or carry on your back). Any extra space will be useful for souvenirs or items you might pick up along the way. If you plan to do a lot of hiking, see **Camping & the Outdoors** (p. 36).

CLOTHING. No matter when you're traveling, it's a good idea to bring a **warm jacket** or wool sweater, a **rain jacket,** sturdy shoes or **hiking boots,** and **thick socks.**

Flip-flops or waterproof sandals are key for surviving grubby hostel showers. You may also want to a nicer change of clothes for hitting the town at night. Remember to dress respectfully when visiting churches and cathedrals.

CONVERTERS & ADAPTERS. In Ireland, electricity is 220 volts AC, enough to fry any 110V North American appliance. 220/240V electrical appliances don't like 110V current, either. **Americans** and **Canadians** should buy an **adapter** (which changes the shape of the plug) and a **converter** (which changes the voltage). Don't make the mistake of using only an adapter (unless appliance instructions explicitly state otherwise). **New Zealanders** and **South Africans** (who both use 220V) as well as **Australians** (240/250V) won't need a converter but will need a set of adapters.

FILM. Film and developing in Ireland is expensive, so bring enough film for your entire trip and developing it at home. Less serious photographers should bring a **disposable camera** rather than an expensive permanent one.

FIRST-AID KIT. For a basic first-aid kit, pack: bandages, pain reliever, antibiotic cream, a thermometer, a Swiss Army knife, tweezers, moleskin, decongestant, motion-sickness remedy, diarrhea or upset-stomach medication (Pepto Bismol or Immodium), an antihistamine, sunscreen, insect repellent, burn ointment, and a syringe for emergencies (get an explanatory letter from your doctor).

IMPORTANT DOCUMENTS. Don't forget your passport, traveler's checks, ATM and/or credit cards, and adequate ID (see p. 10). Also check that you have any of the following that might apply to you: a hosteling membership card (see p. 35); driver's license (see p. 10); travel insurance forms; and rail/bus passes (see p. 29).

LUGGAGE. If you plan to cover most of your itinerary by foot, a sturdy **frame backpack** is unbeatable. (For the basics on buying a pack, see p. 37.) Toting a **suitcase** or **trunk** is fine if you plan to live in one or two cities and explore from there, but a very bad idea if you're going to be moving around a lot. In addition to your main piece of luggage, a **daypack** (a small backpack or courier bag) is a must.

SLEEPSACK. Some hostels require that you provide your own linen or rent sheets from them. Save cash by making your own sleepsack: fold a full-size sheet in half the long way, then sew it closed along the long side and one of the short sides.

OTHER USEFUL ITEMS. For safety purposes, you should bring a **money belt** and small **padlock.** Basic **outdoors equipment** (plastic water bottle, compass, waterproof matches, pocketknife, sunglasses, sunscreen, hat) may also prove useful. Quick repairs of torn garments can be done on the road with a **needle and thread;** also consider bringing electrical tape for patching tears. Doing your **laundry** by hand (where it is allowed) is both cheaper and more convenient than doing it at a laundromat. **Other things** you're liable to forget: an umbrella; sealable **plastic bags** (for damp clothes, soap, food, shampoo, and other spillables); an **alarm clock;** safety pins; rubber bands; a flashlight; earplugs; garbage bags; and a small **calculator.**

GETTING THERE

Ireland is best visited in July and August, when the climate becomes something near summery. There are a wealth of travel options available—if you want to get to Ireland cheaply, fly into London, and take a ferry from Wales.

BY PLANE

A little effort can save you a bundle. If your plans are flexible enough, courier fares are cheapest. Tickets bought from consolidators and standby seating are also

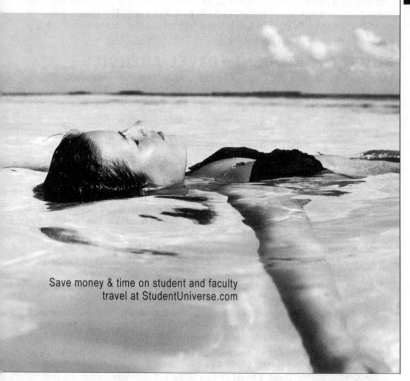

good deals, but last-minute specials, airfare wars, and charter flights often beat these fares. The key is to hunt around, to be flexible, and to ask persistently about discounts. Students, seniors, and those under 26 should never pay full price.

AIRFARES

Airfares to Ireland peak between early June and late August; holidays are also expensive. The cheapest times to travel are in October and February. Midweek (M-Th morning) round-trip flights run US$40-50 cheaper than weekend flights, but they are more crowded and less likely to permit frequent-flier upgrades. Traveling with an "open return" ticket can be pricier than fixing a return date when buying the ticket. Round-trip flights are by far the cheapest; "open-jaw" (arriving in and departing from different cities) tickets tend to dent the wallet. Patching one-way flights together is the most expensive way to travel. Flights between capitals or regional hubs will usually be cheaper.

Fares for roundtrip flights to Dublin from the US or the Canadian east coast cost roughly US$700/$450 (summer/off-season); from the US or Canadian west coast US$850/$600; from London UK£70/£35; from Australia AUS$2700/$2000. Flying into Shannon can be cheaper, while flights into Belfast cost about the same but arrive only from major cities such as New York and Paris. The cheapest way to enter Ireland is by flying into London and buying a return ticket that takes you from London to Dublin (or by taking the bus from London to Dublin).

BUDGET & STUDENT TRAVEL AGENCIES

Travelers with **ISIC and IYTC cards** (see p. 10) qualify for big discounts from student travel agencies.

Council Travel (www.counciltravel.com). Countless US offices, including branches in Atlanta, Boston, Chicago, L.A., New York, San Francisco, Seattle, and Washington, D.C. Check the website or call ☎800-2-COUNCIL (226-8624) for the office nearest you. Also an office at 28A Poland St. (Oxford Circus), **London,** W1V 3DB (☎0207 437 77 67).

STA Travel, 7890 S. Hardy Dr., Ste. 110, Tempe AZ 85284, USA (24hr. reservations and info ☎800-781-4040; www.sta-travel.com). A student and youth travel organization with over 150 offices worldwide (check their website for a listing of offices), including US offices in Boston, Chicago, L.A., New York, San Francisco, Seattle, and Washington, D.C. Ticket booking, travel insurance, railpasses, and more. In the **UK**, walk-in office 11 Goodge St., London W1T 2PF or call 0207-436-7779. In **Australia,** 366 Lygon St., Carlton Vic 3053 (☎03 9349 4344).

StudentUniverse, 545 Fifth Ave., Suite 640, New York, NY 10017 (toll-free customer service ☎800-272-9676, outside the US 212-986-8420; help@studentuniverse.com; www.studentuniverse.com), is an online student travel service offering discount ticket booking, travel insurance, railpasses, destination guides, and much more. Customer service line open M-F 9am-8pm and Sa noon-5pm EST.

Travel CUTS (Canadian Universities Travel Services Limited), 187 College St., **Toronto,** ON M5T 1P7 (☎416-979-2406; fax 979-8167; www.travelcuts.com). 60 offices across Canada. Also in the UK, 295-A Regent St., **London** W1R 7YA (☎020 7255 1944).

usit world (www.usitworld.com). Nearly 20 **usit NOW** offices in Ireland, including 19-21 Aston Quay, O'Connell Bridge, **Dublin** 2 (☎01 602 1600; www.usitnow.ie), and Fountain Centre, College Street, **Belfast** (☎028 9032 7111; www.usitnow.com). Over 50 **usit campus** branches in the UK (www.usitcampus.co.uk), including 52 Grosvenor Gardens, **London** SW1W 0AG (☎0870 240 1010); **Manchester** (☎0161 273 1880); and **Edinburgh** (☎0131 668 3303). Offices also in Athens, Auckland, Brussels, Frankfurt, Johannesburg, Lisbon, Luxembourg, Madrid, Paris, Sofia, and Warsaw.

Wasteels, Skoubogade 6, 1158 Copenhagen K. (☎3314 4633; fax 7630 0865, www.wasteels.dk/uk). A huge chain with 165 locations across Europe. Sells Wasteels BIJ tickets discounted 30-45% off regular fare, 2nd-class international point-to-point train tickets with unlimited stopovers for those under 26 (sold only in Europe).

COMMERCIAL AIRLINES

The commercial airlines' lowest regular offer is the **APEX** (Advance Purchase Excursion) fare, which provides confirmed reservations and allows "open-jaw" tickets. Generally, reservations must be made seven to 21 days ahead of departure, with seven- to 14-day minimum-stay and up to 90-day maximum-stay restrictions. Book peak-season APEX fares early; by May you will have a hard time getting your desired departure date. Use **Microsoft Expedia** (http://msn.expedia.com) or **Travelocity** (www.travelocity.com) to get an idea of the lowest published fares, then use the resources outlined here to try and beat those fares. Low-season fares should be appreciably cheaper than the high-season (mid-June to Aug.) ones listed here.

Specials advertised in newspapers may be cheaper but have more restrictions. A popular carrier to Ireland is its national airline, **Aer Lingus** (☎01 886 8888; US ☎800-IRISHAIR; www.aerlingus.ie), which has direct flights to the US, London, and Paris. **Ryanair** (☎01 609 7900; www.ryanair.ie) is a smaller airline that offers a "lowest-fare guarantee"; check the website for details. The web-based phenom **easyJet** (UK☎08706 000 000; www.easyjet.com) has recently begun flying from England and Scotland to Belfast. If another airline doesn't fly directly to one of Ireland's airports, it can almost certainly get you to London.

FLIGHTS FROM NORTH AMERICA

Round-trip fares range from US$450-700. Standard commercial carriers like **American** (☎800-433-7300; www.aa.com) and **United** (☎800-241-6522; www.ual.com) offer the most convenient flights, but they may not be the cheapest. Foreign carriers often offer better deals. **Icelandair** (☎800-223-5500; www.icelandair.com) offers free stopovers in Iceland and flies from the east coast of the US to London, after which you can buy a ticket taking you from London to Dublin and back again.

FLIGHTS FROM BRITAIN

Flying to London and connecting to Ireland is often easiest and cheapest. Aer Lingus (see p. 25) and several other carriers offer service on these routes. **British Midland Airways** (UK ☎0870 607 0555; from abroad 1332 854 854; Republic ☎01 814 4259; www.flybmi.com) flies about seven times per day to London Heathrow. **British Airways** (UK ☎0845 773 3377; Republic ☎800 626 747; in the US ☎800 AIRWAYS; www.british-airways.com) flies into most Irish airports daily and into some Irish airports many, many times a day. Prices range from UK£60-225 round-trip but can drop from time to time. Check their website for specials. **Ryanair** (UK ☎0870 1 569 569, Republic ☎0818 30 30 30; www.ryanair.com) connects Kerry, Cork, and Knock to London and more than nine other destinations in England and Scotland.

FLIGHTS FROM AUSTRALIA & NEW ZEALAND

Expect to pay somewhere between AUS$2000 (off-season) and AUS$2700 (peak-season) for a basic round-trip fare to Ireland. Commercial carriers like Quantas (Australia ☎13 13 13, New Zealand ☎0800 808 767; www.qantas.com.au) will take you from major cities in Australia and New Zealand to London, where you will have to purchase a return-ticket taking you from London to Ireland. Others, such as Thai Airways (Australia ☎1300 65 19 60, New Zealand ☎09 377 02 68; www.thaiair.com), will take you directly to Dublin. Other commercial carriers include Air New Zealand (☎0800 73 70 00; www.airnz.co.nz.) and Singapore Air (Australia ☎13 10 11, New Zealand ☎0800 808 909; www.singaporeair.com.)

SHE'S GOT AN E-TICKET TO RIDE. Most airline sites offer special last-minute deals on the Web. Other sites do the legwork and compile the deals for you—try www.bestfares.com,www.onetravel.com, and www.travelzoo.com. Student Universe (www.studentuniverse.com), STA (www.sta-travel.com), and Orbitz.com provide quotes on student tickets, while Expedia (www.expedia.com) and Travelocity (www.travelocity.com) offer full travel services. Priceline (www.priceline.com) allows you to specify a price, and obligates you to buy any ticket that meets it; be prepared for antisocial hours and odd routes. Skyauction (www.skyauction.com) allows you to bid on last-minute and advance-purchase tickets. An indispensable resource on the Internet is the *Air Traveler's Handbook* (www.cs.cmu.edu/afs/cs/user/mkant/Public/Travel/airfare.html), a comprehensive listing of links to everything you need to know before you board a plane.

ESSENTIALS

AIR COURIER FLIGHTS

Those who travel light should consider courier flights. Couriers help transport cargo on international flights by using their checked luggage space for freight. Couriers require carry-ons only and often have complex flight restrictions. Most flights are round-trip, with short fixed-length stays (usually one week) and a limit of one ticket per issue. These flights usually operate out of major gateway cities, primarily from North America. Generally, you must be over 21 (in some cases 18) and purchase a one-year membership (usually US$50) before you can take advantage of discounted rates. In summer, popular destinations require an advance reservation of about two weeks (you can often book up to two months ahead). Super-discounted fares are common for "last-minute" flights (three to 14 days early).

Round-trip courier fares from the US to Ireland run around US$250-650. For direct flights from North America to Dublin, contact **NOW Voyager** (☎212-459-1616; fwww.nowvoyagertravel.com). For direct flights from North America, Canada, Australia and New Zealand, contact **Global Courier Travel** (US ☎866-470-3061; www.globalcouriertravel.com). For flights from North America to London, contact **Air Courier Association** (☎800-282-1202; www.aircourier.org), and for flights between London and Dublin, contact the **British Airways Travel Shop** (☎0870 240 0747; www.batravelshops.com), which can arrange flights from London to destinations throughout Europe (specials as low as UK£60; no registration fee).

STANDBY FLIGHTS

Traveling standby requires considerable flexibility in arrival and departure dates and cities. Companies dealing in standby flights sell vouchers rather than tickets, along with the promise to get to your destination within a certain window of time (typically 1-5 days). You call in before your specific window of time to hear your flight options and the probability that you will be able to board each flight. You can then decide which flights you want to try to make, show up at the appropriate airport at the appropriate time, present your voucher, and board if space is available.

Carefully read agreements with any company offering standby flights as tricky fine print can leave you in a lurch. To check on a company's service record in the US, call the **Better Business Bureau** (☎212-533-6200). It is difficult to receive refunds, and clients' vouchers will not be honored when an airline fails to receive payment in time. One established standby company in the US is **Whole Earth Travel,** 325 W. 38th St., New York, NY 10018 (☎800-326-2009; www.4standby.com) and Los Angeles, CA (☎888-247-4482), which offers one-way flights to Europe from the Northeast (US$169), West Coast (US$249), Midwest (US$219), and Southeast (US$199). Intra-continental connecting flights within Europe cost US$79-139.

TICKET CONSOLIDATORS

Ticket consolidators, or **"bucket shops,"** buy unsold tickets in bulk from commercial airlines and sell them at discounted rates. The best place to look for their ads is in the Sunday travel section of any major newspaper. Call quickly, as availability is typically limited. Not all bucket shops are reliable, so insist on a detailed receipt and pay by credit card (in spite of the 2-5% fee) so you can stop payment if you never receive your tickets. For more information, see www.travel-library.com/air-travel/consolidators.html. In London, the **Air Travel Advisory Bureau** (☎020 7636 5000; www.atab.co.uk) can provide names of reliable consolidators.

Numerous ticket consolidators are based in North America. **Travel Avenue** (☎800-333-3335; www.travelavenue.com) searches for best available fares and then uses several consolidators to attempt to beat that fare. Other consolidators worth trying are **Cheap Tickets** (☎800-377-1000; www.cheaptickets.com); **Interworld** (☎305-443-4929); **Pennsylvania Travel** (☎800-331-0947); **Rebel** (☎800-227-3235; www.rebeltours.com); and **Travac** (☎800-872-8800). Yet more consolidators on the web include the **Internet Travel Network** (www.itn.com); **Travel Information Services** (www.tiss.com); **TravelHUB** (www.travelhub.com); and **The Travel Site** (www.thetravelsite.com). Keep in mind that these are just suggestions to get you started in your research; *Let's Go* does not endorse any of these agencies. As always, be cautious, and research companies before giving over your credit card number.

CHARTER FLIGHTS

Charters are flights a tour operator contracts with an airline to fly extra loads of passengers during peak season. Flights are often fully booked, and schedules and itineraries may change or be cancelled at the last moment (as late as 48 hours before the trip, and without a full refund), and check-in, boarding, and baggage claim are often much slower. However, they can also be cheaper.

Discount clubs and **fare brokers** offer members savings on last-minute charter and tour deals. Study contracts closely; you don't want to end up with an unwanted overnight layover. Discount travel to Ireland is the specialty of **O'Connors Fairways Travel,** located in the USA at 342 Madison Ave., Suite 437, New York, NY, 10173 (☎212-661-0550; reservations ☎800-662-0550; www.oconnors.com). **Travelers Advantage,** Trumbull, CT, USA (☎203-365-2000; www.travelersadvantage.com) specializes in European travel and tour packages.

BY FERRY

Ferries are popular and usually a more economical, albeit considerably more time-consuming, form of transportation than airplanes. Almost all sailings in June, July, and August are "controlled sailings," which means that you must book the crossing ahead of time (a few days in advance is usually sufficient).

Fares vary tremendously depending on time of year, time of day, and type of boat. Traveling mid-week, during the night, in spring, fall, or winter, promises the cheapest fares. Adult single tickets usually range from UK£18 to £35 (€28-55), and there are many discount rates available. Some people tag along with car drivers who are allowed four free passengers. *Let's Go* does not recommend this or any form of hitchhiking. Bikes can usually be brought on for no extra charge. Students, seniors, families, and youth traveling alone typically receive discounts; **An Óige (HI) members** receive up to a 20% discount on fares from Irish Ferries and Stena Sealink, while **ISIC cardholders** with the **TravelSave Stamp** (€10; available at **usit NOW,** see p. 22) receive a 15% discount from Irish Ferries and an average 17% discount (variable among four routes) on Stena Line ferries. Ferry passengers from the Republic are taxed an additional €6.50 when traveling home from England.

ESSENTIALS

BRITAIN AND FRANCE TO IRELAND

Assorted bus and train tickets that include ferry connections between Britain and Ireland are also available as package deals through ferry companies, travel agents, and usit offices. Contact Bus Éireann for information (see **By Bus,** p. 29).

Brittany Ferries: UK ☎08703 665 333; France 08 25 82 88 28; www.brittany-ferries.com. Cork to Roscoff (13½hr., Apr.-Sept. 1 per week, €52-99).

Cork-Swansea Ferries: Between Swansea, South Wales, and Ringaskiddy in Co. Cork (10hr., UK£24-34/€38-53). Contact them at ☎021 271 166 or www.swansea-cork.ie.

Irish Ferries: Republic ☎1890 31 31 31, after-hours info line ☎01 661 0715; **Northern Ireland** ☎0800 018 2211; **UK** ☎08705 17 17 17; **France** ☎01 44 88 54 50; www.irishferries.ie. From Holyhead, North Wales, to Dublin (3hr.), and Pembroke, Wales, to Rosslare Harbour (4hr.), return tickets range from UK£22-24/€34-38, and for students, UK£18/€28. Also from Cherbourg and Roscoff, France to Cork and Rosslare Harbour (about 18hr.); **Eurail passes** grant passage on ferries from France. For specific schedules and fares contact them at: **Dublin,** 2-4 Merrion Row (☎01 638 3333); **Cork,** St. Patrick's Bridge (☎021 455 1995); **Rosslare Harbour** (☎053 33158); **Holyhead, Wales** (☎08705 329 129); and **Pembroke, Wales** (☎08705 329 543).

Steam Packet Company: Sends SeaCats between Belfast and Heysham (4hr.; UK£34/€38, under 16 UK£20/€32) and Troon (2½hr.; UK£17-31/€27-49, under 16 UK£9-17/€14-27), also between Liverpool and Dublin (4hr.; UK£29-39/€49-61, under 16 UK£15-20/€24-32). SeaCat trips are faster than ferries but considerably pricier. For info and bookings, call UK ☎08705 523 523, or visit their website at www.steam-packet.com.

Stena Line: Cork (☎021 272 965); **Dún Laoghaire** (☎01 204 7777); **Ferrycheck** (☎08705 755 755) has 24hr. recorded info; Tourist Office, Arthurs Quay, **Limerick** (☎061 316 259). **Rosslare Harbour** (☎053 33115); **UK,** ☎1233 64 68 26; www.stenaline.co.uk. Ferries from Holyhead, North Wales, to Dún Laoghaire (3½hr. on the Superferry, UK£23-29/€35-45); from Fishguard, South Wales, and Pembroke, Wales to Rosslare Harbour (3½-3¾hr. UK£18-23/€28-35); and from Stanraer, Scotland, to Belfast (90min. on the Stena Line, 3hr. on the SeaCat, UK£14-36/€22-56). Package deals include train service from London. Contact them at: Charter House, Park St., Ashford, Kent TN24 8EX, England (☎08705 707 070).

BY BUS

Bus Éireann (the Irish national bus company) reaches Britain and even the continent by working in conjunction with ferry services and the bus company **Eurolines** (Republic ☎08705 143 219, UK ☎08705 143 219; www.eurolines.com). Most buses leave from Victoria Station in London (to Belfast: 15hr., €49/UK£74, return €79/UK£51; Dublin: 12hr., €42/UK£27, return €69/UK£45), but other major city stops include Birmingham, Bristol, Cardiff, Glasgow, and Liverpool. Services run to Cork, Derry, Galway, Limerick, Waterford, and Tralee, among others. The immense Eurolines network connects with many European destinations (Dublin-Paris 9hr.; €90/UK£58, return €143/UK£92). Prices given are for adult fares during the summer—cheaper fares are available in the off-season, as well as for children (under 13), young people (under 26), and seniors (60+). Tickets can be booked through usit, any Bus Éireann office, Irish Ferries, Stena Line, any Eurolines office or **National Express** office in Britain (☎08705 808 080). You might also contact the Bus Éireann General Inquiries desk in Dublin (☎01 836 6111) or a travel agent for further information.

ONCE THERE

Public transportation is, for the most part, regular and extensive. Most travel is done via buses, as the train system can only effectively be used to travel between urban centers. Travel in Co. Clare, Kerry, and Donegal, can be particularly spotty.

GETTING AROUND

Fares on all modes of transportation are either **single** (one-way) or **return** (round-trip). "Period returns" require you to return within a specific number of days; "day return" means you must return on the same day. Unless stated otherwise, *Let's Go* always lists single fares. Roundtrip fares are generally 30% above the one-way fare.

Roads between Irish cities and towns have official letters and numbers ("N" and "R" in the Republic; "M," "A," and "B" in the North), but most locals refer to them by destination ("the Kerry road"). Signs and printed directions sometimes give only the numbered and lettered designations, sometimes only the destination. Most signs are in English and Irish; destination signs in outlying *gaeltacht* are most often only in Irish. Old black-and-white road signs give distances in miles; new green and white signs are in kilometers. Speed limit signs are in miles.

BY BUS

Buses in the Republic of Ireland reach many more destinations and are less expensive than trains. Bus drivers are often very accommodating in where they will pick you up and drop you off. The national bus company, **Bus Éireann** (Dublin general helpline ☎01 836 6111; www.buseireann.ie), operates both long-distance Expressway buses, which link larger cities, and local buses, which serve the countryside and smaller towns. The invaluable bus timetable book is hugely difficult to obtain for personal ownership, though you may find one at Busáras Central Bus Station in Dublin. In Donegal, **private bus providers** take the place of Bus Éireann's nearly-nonexistent local service. *Let's Go* lists these providers when appropriate.

Bus Éireann's **Rambler** ticket offers unlimited bus travel within Ireland for 3 of 8 consecutive days (€45; under 16 €25), 8 of 15 consecutive days (€100; under 16 €55), or 15 of 30 consecutive days €145; under 16 €80), but is generally less cost-effective than buying individual tickets. A combined **Irish Explorer Rail/Bus** ticket allows unlimited travel on trains and buses for 8 of 15 consecutive days (€145; under 16 €72). Tickets can be purchased at any Bus Éireann big-city terminal.

Ulsterbus, (☎028 9033 3000, Belfast office 028 9032 0011; www.ulsterbus.co.uk), the North's version of Bus Éireann, runs extensive and reliable routes throughout Northern Ireland, where there are no private bus services. Coverage expands in summer, when several buses run a purely coastal route and full- and half-day tours leave from Belfast for key tourist spots. Pick up a free regional timetable at any station. There are excellent discounts for students (with ISIC cards) and families.

The **Irish Rover** pass covers both Bus Éireann and Ulsterbus services. It sounds ideal for visitors intending to travel in both the Republic and Northern Ireland, but unless you plan to travel extensively on the bus, its true value is debatable (unlimited travel for 3 of 8 days €60/UK£90, child €33/UK£50; for 8 of 15 days €135/UK£200, child €75/UK£113; for 15 of 30 €195/UK£293, child €110/UK£165). The **Emerald Card** offers unlimited travel on: Ulsterbus; Northern Ireland Railways; Bus Éireann Expressway, Local, and City services in Cork, Dublin, Galway, Limerick, and Waterford; and intercity, DART, and suburban rail Iarnród Éireann services. The card works for 8 out of 15 consecutive days (€168/UK£108, under 16 €84/UK£54) or 15 out of 30 consecutive days (€290/UK£187, under 16 €145/UK£94).

BUS TOURS. Though some find that they limit a traveler's independence, bus tours often free a traveler from agonizing over the minutiae of your trip while exposing you to a knowledgeable tour leader. Tours cost around €45 per day, with longer tours costing less per day. **Tír na nÓg Tours** (☎01 836 4684; www.tirnanogtours.com) offers 3- to 6-day tours which include breakfast, hostels, and entrance to sights. **Paddywagon Tours** (☎01 672 6007; 0800 783 4191 from the UK; www.paddywagontours.com) have 1-, 3-, and 6-day packages, including breakfast, hostels, and sights. The **Stray Travel Network** in London (☎0171 373 7737; www.straytravel.com) provides flexible tours of Ireland, minus accommodation or food provisions so you can choose where to spend your money. **Contiki Travel** (☎1-888-CONTIKI; www.contiki.com) runs comprehensive nine-day bus tours starting at $739/€759. Tours include accommodation, transportation and some meals.

BY TRAIN

Iarnród Éireann (Irish Rail), is useful only for travel to urban areas, from which you'll need to find another form of transportation to reach Ireland's picturesque villages and wilds. Trains from Dublin's Heuston Station chug toward Cork, Ennis, Galway, Limerick, Tralee, Waterford, and Westport; others leave from Dublin's Connolly Station to head for Belfast (express), Rosslare (express), Sligo, and Wexford. For schedule information, pick up an InterCity Rail Travelers Guide (€0.60), available at most train stations. The **TravelSave** stamp, available for €10 at any **usit** agency if you have an ISIC card, cuts fares by 30-50% on national rail. (It also provides up to 30% discounts on bus fares above €1.30.) A **Faircard** (€10.10) can get anyone age 16 to 26 up to 50% off the price of any InterCity trip. Those over 26 can get the less potent **Weekender card** (€6.35; up to a third off, valid F-Tu only). Both are valid through the end of the year. The **Rambler** rail ticket allows unlimited train travel on five days within a 15-day travel period (€122). For combined bus-and-train travel passes, see **By Bus,** p. 29. Information is available from Irish Rail information office, 35 Lower Abbey St., Dublin (☎01 836 3333; www.irishrail.ie). Unlike bus tickets, train tickets sometimes allow travelers to break a journey into stages yet still pay the price of a single-phase trip. Bikes may be carried on trains for a fee of €3-7; check at the station for specific restrictions.

While the **Eurailpass** is not accepted in Northern Ireland, it *is* accepted on trains in the Republic. Youth and family passes are also available but are cost-effective only if you plan to travel to the Continent as well. The BritRail pass does not cover travel in Northern Ireland, but the month-long **BritRail+Ireland** works in both the North and the Republic with rail options and round-trip ferry service between Britain and Ireland (5 days US$399; 10 days US$569). A traveler under 26 should look into a youth pass. You'll find it easiest to buy a Eurailpass before you arrive in Europe; contact Council Travel, Travel CUTS (see p. 22), or another travel agent. **Rail Europe Group** (US ☎877-456-RAIL (7245), UK 08705 848 848; www.raileurope.com), also sells point-to-point tickets.

Northern Ireland Railways (☎028 9066 6630; www.nirailways.co.uk) is not extensive but covers the northeastern coastal region well. The major line connects Dublin to Belfast. When it reaches Belfast, this line splits, with one branch ending at Bangor and one at Larne. There is also rail service from Belfast and Lisburn west to Derry and Portrush, stopping at three towns between Antrim and the coast. British Rail passes are not valid here, but Northern Ireland Railways offers its own discounts. A valid **Northern Ireland Travelsave** stamp (UK£6, affixed to back of ISIC) will get you up to 33% off all trains and 15% discounts on bus fares over UK£1.45 within Northern Ireland. The **Freedom of Northern Ireland** ticket allows unlimited travel by train and Ulsterbus and can be purchased for seven consecutive days (UK£40), three out of eight days (UK£27.50), or a single day (UK£11).

ESSENTIALS

BY CAR

Traveling by car has obvious advantages: speed, freedom, and direct access to the countryside. Unfortunately, disadvantages include gas (petrol) prices, unfamiliar automobile laws, and, for many travelers, the switch to **driving on the left side of the road.** Be particularly cautious at roundabouts (rotary interchanges): remember to **give way to traffic from the right.** For an informal primer on European road signs and conventions, check www.travlang.com/signs. Additionally, the Association for Safe International Road Travel (ASIRT), 11769 Gainsborough Rd., Potomac, MD 20854 (US ☎301-983-5252; www.asirt.org), can provide specific information on road conditions.

INTERNATIONAL DRIVING PERMIT (IDP). If you plan to drive a car while in Ireland for longer than a three-month period, you must have an International Driving Permit (IDP). If you intend to drive for longer than one year, you'll need to get an Irish driver's license. Your IDP, valid for one year, must be issued in your own country before you depart. An application for an IDP usually needs to include one or two photos, a current local license, an additional form of identification, and a fee. To apply, contact your home country's Automobile Association.

CAR INSURANCE. Most credit cards cover standard insurance. If you rent, lease, or borrow a car, you will need a **green card,** or **International Insurance Certificate,** to certify that you have liability insurance and that it applies abroad. Green cards can be obtained at car rental agencies, car dealers (for those leasing cars), some travel agents, and some border crossings. Rental agencies may require you to purchase theft insurance in countries that they consider to have a high risk of auto theft.

RENTING A CAR. Renting (hiring) an automobile is the cheapest option if you plan to drive for a month or less, but the initial cost of renting a car and the price of gas will astound you in Ireland. Prices range €150-370 (plus VAT) per week with insurance and unlimited mileage. Automatics are 40% more expensive to rent than manuals (stick-shifts). For insurance reasons, most companies require renters to be over 23 and under 70. **Dan Dooley** (☎062 53103, UK 0181 995 4551; US 800-331-9301; dandooley.com) is the only company in Ireland that will rent to drivers between 21 and 24, though such drivers incur an added daily surcharge. Major rental agencies convenient to major airports are **Budget Rent-A-Car** (Central Office ☎903 27711; Shannon Airport 061 471 361; Dublin Airport (01 844 5150; www.budgetcarrental.ie), and **Thrifty** (Freephone in Ireland ☎800 515 800, Dublin Airport 01 840 0800, Shannon Airport 061 472 649; www.thrifty.ie). It is always significantly less expensive to reserve a car from the US than from Europe.

BY BICYCLE

Many insist that cycling is *the* way to see Ireland and Northern Ireland. Much of the Island's countryside is well suited for pedaling by daylight, as many roads are not heavily traveled. Single-digit N roads in the Republic, and M roads in the North, are more busily trafficked; try to avoid these. Begin your trip in the south or west to take advantage of prevailing winds.

Many **airlines** will count your bike as your second free piece of luggage, and some charge extra. Check with the individual company for any special packaging procedures. Most ferries let you take your bike for free or for a nominal fee. You can ship your bike on some **trains,** but the cost varies; inquire at the information desk. You'll have better luck getting your bike on a **bus** if you depart from a terminal, not a wayside stop. Bikes are allowed on Bus Éireann at the driver's discretion for a fee of €3.80-6.35 (not always enforced).

Riding a bike with a frame pack strapped on it or your back is about as safe as pedaling blindfolded over a sheet of ice; **panniers** are essential. The first thing to buy, however, is a suitable **bike helmet** (US$25-50). U-shaped **locks** are expensive (starting at US$30), but most companies insure their locks against theft.

Raleigh Rent-A-Bike (☎01 626 1333; www.iol.ie/raleigh) has rental shops across Ireland. You can hire a bike for €15-20 per day, €65-80 per week, plus deposit (usually €80). The shops will equip you with locks, patch kits, pumps, and, for longer journeys, pannier bags (€10 per week). The **One-Way Rental** plan allows you to rent a bike at one shop and drop it off at another for a fee of €19. **Celtic Cycling** (☎0503 75282; www.celticcycling.com) serves the Southeast, including Carlow, Kilkenny, Waterford and Wexford. Bikes are €10 per day, €60 per week, and require a credit card deposit. They also offer cycling tour packages of varing length, that include accommodations and pickup at the airport (€527 for 7 days).

Many small local dealers and hostels also rent bikes. Rates are about €8-16 per day and €40-70 per week. Tourist offices can direct you to bike rental establishments and distribute leaflets on local biking routes, as well as providing the extensive *Cycle Touring Ireland* (€9). Adequate **maps** are a necessity; *Ordnance Survey* maps (€7) or Bartholomew maps are available in most bookstores.

ESSENTIALS

BY FOOT

Ireland's mountains, fields, and heather-covered hills make walking and hiking an arduous joy. The **Wicklow Way,** a popular trail through mountainous Co. Wicklow, has hostels designed for hikers within a day's walk of each other. The best hill-walking maps are the *Ordnance Survey Discovery Series* (€6.60 each). Other remarkable trails include the **Kerry Way** (see p. 276), the **Burren Way** (p. 329), the **Western Way** (p. 358), and the **Fore Trail.** There are a multitude of other trails all over the island; consult Bord Fáilte (see p. 8) for more information and free pamphlets. *Let's Go* lists many of these longer hikes in the **Sights** sections, as well as a plethora of shorter strolls in virtually every Irish town.

The 560 mi. Ulster Way no longer exists, but is in the process of being split into new regional **Waymarked ways.** Contact any local tourist information office in Northern Ireland for more information.

WALKING TOURS. For those looking to avoid some of the pitfalls of hiking, **guided tours** may be the solution. Though expensive (upwards of €80 per day), an area expert will guide hiking greenhorns over the green hills as a bus transports their luggage, meals are served, and accommodations await. Less expensive and more independent, **self-guided tours** include the luggage transport and accommodations but usually do away with meals (and, of course, the guide). For a list of tours, see www.kerna.ie/wci/walking or www.walking.travel.ie. **Tír na nÓg Tours** (57 Lower Gardiner St., Dublin 1; ☎01 836 684), is a reputable and acclaimed choice.

BY THUMB

No one should hitch without careful consideration of the risks involved. Hitching means entrusting your life to a random person, risking theft, assault, sexual harassment, and unsafe driving. Although hitching in Ireland is probably safer than any where else in the world, the risks of such travel have increased over recent years. Locals do not recommend hitchhiking in Northern Ireland; some caution against it in Co. Dublin, as well as the Midlands.

For women traveling alone, hitching is just too dangerous. A man and a woman are a safer combination, two men will have a harder time, and three will go nowhere. In all cases, **safety** should be the first concern. Safety-minded hitchers avoid getting in the back of a two-door car (or any car they wouldn't be able to get out of in a hurry) and never let go of their backpacks. If they ever feel threatened, they insist on being let off immediately. Acting as if they are going to open the car door or vomit will usually get a driver to stop.

In the **Practical Information** section of many cities, *Let's Go* lists the tram or bus lines that take travelers to strategic hitching points. Success will depend on appearance. Placement is crucial—experienced hitchers stand where drivers can stop, have time to look over potential passengers, and return to the road without causing an accident. Hitching on hills or curves is hazardous and usually fruitless; roundabouts and access roads to highways are better. You can get a sense of the amount of traffic a road sees by its letter and number: in the Republic, single-digit N-roads (A-roads in the North) are as close as Ireland gets to highways, double-digit N-roads see some intercity traffic, R-roads (B-roads in the North) generally only carry local traffic but are easy hitches, and non-lettered roads are a **hitcher's purgatory.** In Northern Ireland, hitching (or even standing) on motorways (M-roads) is illegal: you may only thumb at the entrance ramps—*in front* of the blue-and-white superhighway pictograph (a bridge over a road).

Let's Go strongly urges you to consider the risks before you choose to hitch. We do not recommend hitching as a safe means of transportation, and none of the information presented here is intended to do so.

ACCOMMODATIONS

Bord Fáilte (bored FAHL-tshah; "welcome board") is the Republic of Ireland's tourism authority. Its system for approving accommodations involves a more-or-less frequent inspection and a fee. Approved accommodations get to use Bord Fáilte's national booking system and display its icon, a green shamrock on a white field. Approved campgrounds and bed and breakfasts are listed with prices in the *Caravan and Camping Ireland* and *Bed and Breakfast Ireland* guides, respectively, available from any Bord Fáilte office. Bord Fáilte's standards are very specific and, in some cases, far higher than what hostelers and other budget travelers expect or require. Unapproved accommodations can be a better value than their approved neighbors, though some unapproved places are, of course, real dumps. Most official tourist offices in Ireland will refer *only* to approved accommodations, and will book rooms for a €1-4 fee. **Credit card reservations** can be made through Dublin Tourism (☎800 6686 6866). Approval by the **Northern Ireland Tourist Board** is legally required of all accommodations in the North. Their tourist offices can provide you with all the contact information you'll need to find lodging.

HOSTELS

Hostels are generally laid out dorm-style, often with large single-sex rooms and bunk beds, although some offer private rooms for families and couples. They sometimes have kitchens and utensils for your use, bike or moped rentals, storage areas, and laundry facilities. The Internet is becoming an increasingly common hostel amenity, though web access is often via mind-numbingly slow connections. There can be drawbacks to hostels: some close during daytime "lockout" hours, have a curfew, don't accept reservations, impose a maximum stay, or, less frequently, require that you do chores. In Ireland, a hostel bed will average €12-18.

In Ireland more than anywhere else, senior travelers and families are invariably welcome. Some hostels are strikingly beautiful (a few are even housed in castles), but others are little more than run-down barracks. You can expect every Irish hostel to provide blankets, although you may have to pay extra for sheets (see **Pack-**

ing, p. 19). Hostels listed are chosen based on location, price, quality, and facilities. In recent years, a number of Irish hostels have been turned into refugee houses and have closed their doors to the budget traveling scene—it is always a good idea to call ahead to hostels to ensure that they are open for business.

A HOSTELER'S BILL OF RIGHTS. There are certain standard features that we do not include in our hostel listings. Unless we state otherwise, you can expect that every hostel has no lockout, no curfew, a kitchen, free hot showers, some system of secure luggage storage, and no key deposit.

HOSTELLING INTERNATIONAL

Joining the youth hostel association in your own country automatically grants you membership privileges in **Hostelling International (HI),** a federation of national hosteling organizations. This is rarely necessary in Ireland, although there are sometimes member discounts. Most HI hostels also honor **guest memberships:** You'll get a blank card with space for six validation stamps, then each night you'll pay a nonmember supplement (one-sixth the membership fee) and earn one guest stamp; get six stamps, and you're a member. Many HI hostels accept reservations via the **International Booking Network** (The Republic ☎01 830 1766; Northern Ireland ☎1232 32 47 33; Australia ☎02 9261 1111; Canada ☎800-663-5777; England and Wales ☎1629 581 418; NZ ☎03 379 9808; Scotland ☎8701 55 32 55; US ☎800-909-4776; www.hostelbooking.com). HI's umbrella organization's web page (www.iyhf.org) lists the web addresses and phone numbers of all national associations.

Travelers can apply for a HI card at most student travel agencies (see p. 22), or at the national hosteling organization of the country they are visiting. Listed below is **An Óige,** the national hosteling organization of Ireland, and **HINI,** the national hosteling organization of Northern Ireland. **Independent Holiday Hostels** offers similar and more extensive service in both the Republic and the North.

AN ÓIGE. In Ireland, **An Óige** (an OYJ), the **HI** affiliate, operates 32 hostels countrywide (☎01 830 4555; www.irelandyha.org; 61 Mountjoy St., Dublin 7; one-year membership €15 under 18 €7.50). Many An Óige hostels are in remote areas or small villages and were designed primarily to serve hikers, long-distance bicyclists, anglers, and others seeking nature, not noise. The North's HI affiliate is **HINI** (Hostelling International Northern Ireland; formerly known as **YHANI**). It operates only 8 hostels, all comfortable (22-32 Donegal Rd., Belfast BT12 5JN. ☎028 9031 5435; www.hini.org.uk; one-year membership UK£10, under 18 UK£6).

INDEPENDENT HOLIDAY HOSTELS. A number of hostels in Ireland belong to the **Independent Holiday Hostels (IHH).** Most of the 140 IHH hostels have no lockout or curfew, accept all ages, require no membership card, and have a comfortable atmosphere that generally feels less institutional than that at An Óige hostels; all are Bord Fáilte-approved. Pick up a free booklet with complete descriptions of each at any IHH hostel. Contact the IHH office at 57 Lower Gardiner St., Dublin 1 (☎01 836 4700; www.hostels-ireland.com).

BED & BREAKFASTS

For a cozy alternative to impersonal hostel dorms, B&Bs (private homes with rooms available to travelers) range from the tolerable to the sublime. Hosts will sometimes go out of their way to be accommodating, often accepting travelers with pets and giving personalized tours. "Full Irish breakfasts"—eggs, bacon, bread, sometimes black or white pudding, fried vegetables, cereal, orange juice, and coffee or tea—fill tummies until dinner. Singles run about €20-30, doubles €35-50. Many B&Bs do not provide phones, TVs, or private bathrooms, but by and large, Irish B&Bs are excellent ways to meet locals who are laden with insights on their island. B&Bs displaying a shamrock are officially approved by Bord Fáilte. For accommodations in the North, check the Northern Ireland Tourist Board's *Where to Stay in Northern Ireland* (UK£4), available at most tourist offices.

UNIVERSITY DORMS

Many **colleges and universities** open their residence halls to travelers when school is not in session; some do so even during term-time. These dorms are often close to student areas—typically areas of town chock-full of things to do and people to meet—and are usually very clean. Getting a room may take a couple of phone calls and require advanced planning, but rates tend to be low, and many offer free local calls. For appropriate cities, including **Dublin, Galway,** and **Belfast,** *Let's Go* lists colleges which rent dorm rooms in the Accommodations sections. **Cork** and **Limerick** are also big university towns with student housing available in summer.

GOING GREEN

ECEAT International (the European Centre for Eco Agro Tourism) publishes a *Green Holiday Guide to Ireland*, in which it lists hostels, B&Bs, campgrounds, and guest houses that are either organic farms or otherwise environmentally friendly. All ECEAT-listed accommodations are in beautiful, wild areas, and frequently beside protected parkland. Contact ECEAT-International at P.O. Box 10899, 1001 EW, Amsterdam (☎31 206 681 030; www.pz.nl/eceat). For more about work exchanges on Irish organic farms see **Alternatives to Tourism,** p. 46.

CAMPING AND THE OUTDOORS

Camping brings you closest to the land, the water, the insects, and continued financial solvency. Youth hostels often have camping facilities, which is fortunate for backpackers as many campsites are designed for people with caravans (RVs), not tents. Sites cost €5-13, depending on the level of luxury. It is legal to cross private land by **public rights of way;** any other use of private land without permission is considered trespassing. Remember, **bogs catch fire** extremely easily.

Camping in State Forests and National Parks is not allowed, nor is camping on public land if an official campsite is in the area. It is also illegal start campfires within 2 mi. of these forests and parks. Caravan and camping parks provide all the accoutrements of bourgeois civilization: toilets, showers, and sometimes kitchens, laundry facilities, and game rooms. At many sites, caravans are available for hire. **Northern Ireland** treats its campers royally; there are well-equipped campsites throughout, and spectacular parks often house equally mouth-watering sites.

USEFUL PUBLICATIONS AND WEB RESOURCES. An excellent general resource for travelers planning on camping or spending time in the outdoors is the **Great Outdoor Recreation Pages** (www.gorp.com). For information about camping, hiking, and biking, call the publishers listed below for a free catalogue.

Automobile Association, Contact Centre, Car Ellison House, William Armstrong Dr., Newcastle-upon-Tyne NE4 7YA, UK. (☎0870 600 0371; www.theaa.co.uk). Publishes Caravan and Camping: Europe (UK£9) and Britain & Ireland (UK£8).

The Caravan Club, East Grinstead House, East Grinstead, West Sussex, RH19 1UA, UK (☎01342 32 69 44; www.caravanclub.co.uk). For UK£27.50, members receive equipment discounts, a 700pp directory and handbook, and a monthly magazine.

The Mountaineers Books, 1001 SW Klickitat Way, #201, Seattle, WA 98134, USA (☎800-553-4453 or 206-223-6303; www.mountaineersbooks.org). Over 400 titles on hiking, biking, mountaineering, natural history, and conservation.

ESSENTIALS

WILDERNESS SAFETY

THE GREAT OUTDOORS. Stay warm, stay dry, and stay hydrated. The vast majority of life-threatening wilderness situations can be avoided by following this simple advice. Prepare yourself for an emergency, however, by always packing raingear, a hat and mittens, a first-aid kit, a reflector, a whistle, high energy food, and extra water for any hike. Dress in wool or warm layers of synthetic materials designed for the outdoors; never rely on cotton for warmth, as it is useless when wet. Check **weather forecasts** and pay attention to the skies when hiking as weather patterns can change suddenly. Whenever possible, let someone know when and where you are going hiking, and do not attempt a hike beyond your ability. See **Health,** p. 17, for information about outdoor ailments and basic medical concerns.

ENVIRONMENTALLY RESPONSIBLE TOURISM. The idea behind responsible tourism is to leave no human trace. A campstove is a safer (and more efficient) way to cook than using vegetation, but if you must make a fire, keep it small and use only dead branches or brush rather than cutting vegetation. Make sure your campsite is at least 150 ft. (50m) from water supplies or bodies of water. If there are no toilet facilities, bury human waste (but not paper) at least 4 in. (10cm) deep and above the high-water line, and 150 ft. or more from any water supplies and campsites. Always pack your trash in a plastic bag and carry it with you until you reach the next trash can.

CAMPING AND HIKING EQUIPMENT

Backpack: Internal-frame packs mold better to your back, keep a lower center of gravity, and flex adequately to allow you to hike difficult trails. **External-frame packs** are more comfortable for long hikes over even terrain, as they keep weight higher and distribute it more evenly. Make sure your pack has a strong, padded hip-belt to transfer weight to your legs. Any serious backpacking requires a pack of at least 4000 in^3 (16,000cc), plus 500 in^3 for sleeping bags in internal-frame packs. Sturdy backpacks cost anywhere from US$125-420—this is one area in which it doesn't pay to economize. Either buy a **waterproof backpack cover,** or store all of your belongings in plastic bags inside your pack. Also see **Packing,** p. 19.

Boots: Be sure to wear hiking boots with good **ankle support.** They should fit snugly and comfortably over 1-2 pairs of wool socks and thin liner socks. Break in boots over several weeks first in order to spare yourself painful and debilitating blisters.

Sleeping Bag: Most sleeping bags are rated by season ("summer" means 30-40°F at night; "four-season" or "winter" often means below 0°F). They are made either of **down** (warmer and lighter, but more expensive, and miserable when wet) or of **synthetic** material (heavier, more durable, and tolerable when wet). Prices range US$80-210 for a summer synthetic to US$250-300 for a good down winter bag. **Sleeping bag pads** include foam pads (US$10-20), air mattresses (US$15-50), and Therm-A-Rest self-inflating pads (US$45-80). Bring a **stuff sack** to store your bag and keep it dry.

Tent: The best tents are free-standing (with their own frames and suspension systems), set up quickly, and only require staking in high winds. Low-profile dome tents are the best all-around. Good 2-person tents start at US$90, 4-person at US$300. Seal the seams of your tent with waterproofer, and make sure it has a rain fly. Other tent accessories include a **battery-operated lantern,** a **plastic groundcloth,** and a **nylon tarp.**

Other Necessities: Synthetic layer and a **pile jacket** will keep you warm even when wet. A **"space blanket"** will help you to retain your body heat and doubles as a groundcloth (US$5-15). Plastic **water bottles** are virtually shatter- and leak-proof. Bring **water-puri-**

fication tablets for when you can't boil water. For those places that forbid fires or the gathering of firewood, you'll need a **camp stove** (the classic Coleman starts at US$40) and a propane-filled **fuel bottle** to operate it. Also don't forget a **first-aid kit, pocket-knife, insect repellent, calamine lotion,** and **waterproof matches** or a **lighter.**

...AND WHERE TO BUY IT

Discount Camping, 880 Main North Rd., Pooraka, South Australia 5095, Australia (☎08 8262 3399; www.discountcamping.com.au).

Eastern Mountain Sports (EMS), 327 Jaffrey Rd., Peterborough, NH 03458, USA (☎888-463-6367 or 603-924-7231; www.shopems.com).

L.L. Bean, Freeport, ME 04033 (US and Canada ☎800-441-5713, UK ☎0800 891 297, elsewhere US ☎207-552-3028; www.llbean.com).

YHA Adventure Shop, 14 Southampton St., London, WC2E 7HA, UK (☎020 7836 8541). The main branch of one of Britain's largest outdoor equipment suppliers.

CAMPERS, CARAVANS, AND RVS

Renting an RV (called a "camper" or "caravan" in Ireland), will always be more expensive than tenting or hosteling, but the costs compare favorably with staying in hotels and renting a car. The convenience of bringing along your own bedroom, bathroom, and kitchen makes it an attractive option, especially for older travelers and families. Rates vary by region, season, and type of caravan. Rental prices for a standard caravan range from €500-950 per week. It always pays to contact several different companies to compare vehicles and prices. **Motorhome Ireland** (028 97 519 519; www.motorhome-irl.co.uk), based in Co. Down, Northern Ireland, has offices in the North, in Co. Down, and the Republic, in Co. Meath.

ORGANIZED ADVENTURE TRIPS

Organized adventure tours offer another way of exploring the wild. Activities include hiking, biking, skiing, canoeing, kayaking, rafting, climbing, photo safaris, and archaeological digs. **Specialty Travel Index** (☎800-442-4922 or 415-459-4900; info@specialtytravel.com; www.specialtytravel.com) lists more than 500 adventure and specialty tour operators worldwide; tourist bureaus and outdoors organizations are also good sources of information.

KEEPING IN TOUCH

The Irish postal service is both reliable and speedy. Though Internet is readily available in the cities, it can often be hard to find in rural Donegal and Kerry.

BY MAIL

SENDING MAIL FROM IRELAND. Airmail from Ireland to the US averages five to six days; to Europe it averages three to four days. To Australia, NZ, or South Africa, it will take one to two weeks. Times are less predictable from small towns. To send a postcard or letter (up to 25g) to Britain costs €0.41; to Europe, €0.44; to other international destinations, €0.57. Add €3.40 for Swiftpost International. Domestic letter rate within Ireland is €0.41.

RECEIVING MAIL IN IRELAND. An Post is Ireland's national postal service (☎1850 57 58 59; www.anpost.ie). Dublin is the only place in the Republic with postal codes. Even-numbered codes are for areas south of the Liffey, odd-numbered are for the north. The North has number-and-letter postal codes like the rest of the

UK. **Airmail** letters under 1oz. between the US and Ireland take 6-8 days and cost US$0.80. Letters under 20g from Canada are CDN$1.05. Allow at least 5-7 days from Australia (postage AUS$1 for up to 20g) and 3 days from Britain (postage 36p for up to 20g). Make sure to write "air mail" or "par avion" on your envelope. There are several ways to arrange pickup of letters sent to you while you're abroad:

General Delivery: Mail can be sent to Ireland through **Poste Restante** (the international phrase for General Delivery) to almost any city or town with a post office. Address *Poste Restante* letters to (for example): "Robert BRIGHT, Poste Restante, Dunboyne, Co. Meath, Ireland." The mail will go to a special desk in the central post office, unless you specify a post office by street address or postal code. When picking up mail, bring a form of photo ID. There is generally no surcharge.

American Express: AmEx offices throughout the world offer a free **Client Letter Service** (mail held up to 30 days and forwarded upon request) for cardholders who contact them in advance. Address the letter in the same way shown above. Some offices will offer these services to non-cardholders (especially AmEx Travelers Cheque holders), but call ahead to make sure. *Let's Go* lists AmEx office locations for most large cities in **Practical Information** sections; for a complete, free list, call 800-528-4800.

If regular airmail is too slow, **Federal Express** can get a letter from New York to Dublin in 2 days for US$29; rates among non-US locations are prohibitively expensive (London to Dublin, for example, costs upwards of US$50). By **US Global Priority Mail,** a letter from New York would arrive in Dublin within 3-5 days and would cost US$5. From Australia, **EMS** can get a letter to Ireland in 3-4 working days for AUS$67. **Surface mail** is by far the cheapest and slowest way to send mail. It takes 1-3 months to cross the Atlantic and 2-4 to cross the Pacific.

BY TELEPHONE

CALLING IRELAND FROM HOME

To call Ireland from home, you must first dial the **international access code** of your home country. International access codes include: Australia 0011; NZ 00; South Africa 09; UK 00; US 011. After dialing the international code, dial the **country code** of the region you are calling. Country codes include: 353 to reach the **Republic of Ireland;** 44 to reach **Northern Ireland** and **Britain**; 048 to reach **Northern Ireland** from the Republic. Then dial the **city code.** City codes start with a 0 (e.g., Dublin is 01). This zero is dropped when dialing from overseas. *Let's Go* lists telephone codes opposite each city header (marked by a ☎ icon), except when covering rural areas where more than one telephone code may apply—here we list the area code before the number. **The city code is 028 throughout the north.** After dialing the area code, you must finally dial the **local number.** Regional telephone codes range from 2-5 digits, and local telephone numbers range from five to seven digits. For example, to call the US embassy in Dublin from New York, dial 011 353 1 668 8777. To call the Irish embassy in New York from Dublin, dial 00 1 212 745 0200.

LET'S GO PHONE HOME Let's Go has recently partnered with ekit.com to provide a calling card that offers a number of services, including email and voice messaging. Before purchasing any calling card, always compare rates with other cards, and make sure it serves your needs (a local phonecard is generally better for local calls). For more info, visit www.letsgo.ekit.com

CALLING HOME FROM IRELAND

A **calling card** is your cheapest option. Calls are billed collect or to your account. You can often call collect without possessing a company's calling card just by calling their access number and following the instructions. **To obtain a calling card** from your national telecommunications service before leaving home, contact the appropriate company listed below (using the numbers in the first column). To **call home with a calling card,** contact the operator for your service provider in Ireland by dialing the appropriate toll-free access number (listed below in the second column).

COMPANY	TO OBTAIN A CARD, DIAL:	TO CALL ABROAD, DIAL:
AT&T (US)	800-361-4470	800 550 000 (Republic) 0800 013 0011 (Northern Ireland)
British Telecom Direct	800 34 51 44	800 55 01 44 (Republic)
Canada Direct	800-668-6878	800 555 001 (Republic) 0800 89 00 16 (Northern Ireland)
MCI (US)	800-444-3333	800 55 1001 (Republic and Northern Ireland)
New Zealand Direct	0800 00 00 00	800 55 00 64 (Republic) 0800 89 00 64 (Northern Ireland)
Sprint (US)	888-523-2102	800552 011 (Republic) 0800 890 877 (Northern Ireland)
Telkom South Africa	10 219	800 550 027 (Republic) 0800 890 027 (Northern Ireland)
Telstra Australia	13 22 00	800 55 00 61 (Republic) 0800 856 6161 (Northern Ireland)

Where available, prepaid Irish phone cards and occasionally major credit cards can be used for direct international calls. **Swiftcall** phone cards or other prepaid Irish phone cards (available at post offices and newsagents) can score you great rates after 9pm, Irish time—often as low as €0.20-€0.30 per minute.

If you do dial direct, dial 00 (the international access code in both the Republic and Northern Ireland), and then dial the country code and number of your home. **Country codes** include: Australia 61; New Zealand 64; South Africa 27; UK 44; US and Canada 1. Alternatively, you can access an Irish international operator at 114. Note that to call the North from the Republic, you dial 048 plus the number. Phone rates tend to be highest in the morning, lower in the evening, and lowest on Sunday and late at night. International calls from the Republic are cheapest during **economy periods.** The low-rate period to North America is Monday through Friday 10pm to 8am and Saturday and Sunday all day; to EU countries it's Monday through Friday 6pm to 8am and Saturday and Sunday all day; to Australia and New Zealand call Monday through Friday 2 to 8pm and midnight to 8am, and Saturday and Sunday all day. There are no economy rates to the rest of the world.

Placing a **collect call** through an international operator is even more expensive, but may be necessary in case of emergency. You can place collect calls through the service providers listed above even if you don't have one of their phone cards.

CALLING WITHIN IRELAND

The simplest way to call within the country is to use a coin-operated phone. Using Irish pay phones can be tricky. Public phones come in two varieties: **coin phones** and **card phones.** Public coin phones will give you back unused coins (but not fractions of coins; don't insert a €1 coin for a 20 cent call) but private pay phones (called "one-armed bandits") in hostels and restaurants do not—once you plunk in your change, kiss it good-bye. In any pay phone, do not insert money until asked to, or until the call goes through. The pip-pip noise that the phone makes as you wait for it to start ringing is normal and can last up to 10 seconds. Local calls cost 20 cents on public phones; "one-armed bandits" can charge 30 cents, or whatever they please. Local calls are not unlimited—one unit pays for 4min.

The smart option for non-local calls is buying a **prepaid phone card,** which carries a certain amount of phone time depending on the card's denomination. The time is measured in minutes or talk units (e.g. one unit/one minute), and the card usually has a toll-free access telephone number and a personal identification number (PIN). News agents sell phone cards in denominations of €2, €5, €10, or €20. Card phones have a digital display that ticks off the perilous plunge your units are taking. When the unit number starts flashing, you may push the eject button on the card phone; you can then pull out your expired calling card and replace it with a fresh one. If you try to wait until your card's units fall to zero, you'll be disconnected. Eject your card early and use the remaining unit or two for a local call.

CALLING FROM THE REPUBLIC OF IRELAND.
Operator: 10 (not available from card phones).
Directory inquiries: 11850 or 11811 (for the Republic and the North).
International access code: 00.
International operator: 114.
International directory inquiries: 11818.

Pay phones in Northern Ireland initially charge 10p for local calls; most calls cost 20p. A series of harsh beeps warns you to insert more money when your time is up. The digital display ticks off your credit in 1p increments so you can watch your pence in suspense. Only unused coins are returned. You may use all remaining credit on a second call by pressing the "follow on call" button (often marked "FC"). Phones don't accept 1p, 2p, or 5p coins. The dial tone is a continuous purring sound; a repeated double-purr means the line is ringing. Northern **British Telecom Phonecards,** in denominations of UK£2, £5, £10, and £20, are sold at post offices and newsstands, and are accepted at most public phones.

CALLING FROM NORTHERN IRELAND AND LONDON.
Operator: 100.
Directory inquiries: 192.
International access code: 00.
International operator: 155.
International directory assistance: 153.

BY INTERNET

The **Internet,** delightful plague that it is, has infected even the Emerald Isle. **Electronic mail (email)** is a wonderful way to stay in touch, though slow connections in Ireland may make the experience more trying than you're accustomed to. Free, web-based email providers include Hotmail (www.hotmail.com), Yahoo! Mail (www.yahoo.com) and, in Ireland, Ireland.com. Internet access is available in Irish cities in cafes, hostels, and usually in libraries. One hour of webtime costs about €4-6(an ISIC card may win you a discount). Look into a county library membership in the Republic (€2.50-3), which will give you unlimited access to participating libraries, and their Internet. Such membership is particularly useful in counties where Internet cafes are sparse, like Donegal, Mayo, and Kerry.

TIME DIFFERENCES

Britain and Ireland are on **Greenwich Mean Time (GMT).** GMT is 5hr. ahead of New York, 8hr. ahead of Vancouver and San Francisco, 2hr. behind Johannesburg, 10hr. behind Sydney, and 12hr. behind Auckland, although the actual time differences depend on daylight savings time. Both Britain and Ireland observe **daylight savings time** between the last Sunday of March and the last Sunday of October.

SPECIFIC CONCERNS

Traveling is never easy, and for some of us, it can be especially hard. *Let's Go* has compiled some information below that should help answer many of the questions that those with special needs or specific concerns might generally have.

DIETARY CONCERNS

Let's Go lists restaurants with vegetarian options when we find them. You're not likely to find much pub grub without meat, but in almost every town at least one restaurant will have something for vegetarians. Eating in larger cities, particularly Dublin and Belfast, should pose no problems. Vegans will have more of a challenge and may need to cook for themselves.

For more information, contact the **North American Vegetarian Society,** P.O. Box 72, Dolgeville, NY 13329 (☎518-568-7970; www.navs-online.org), which publishes information on veggie-happy travel, including *Transformative Adventures: A Guide to Vacations and Retreats* (US$15). Another good book to consult us *The Vegetarian Traveler*, by Jed and Susan Civic (Larson Publications; US$16).

Travelers who keep kosher should contact synagogues in larger cities for information on kosher restaurants. Your own synagogue or college Hillel should have access to lists of Jewish institutions across the nation. Kosher is not a common term or practice in Ireland; if you are strict in your observance, you may have to prepare your own food. A good resource is the *Jewish Travel Guide*, by Michael Zaidner (Vallentine Mitchell; US$17).

TRAVELING ALONE

There are many benefits to traveling alone, including independence and greater interaction with locals. On the other hand, any solo traveler is a more vulnerable target of harassment and street theft. Lone travelers need to be friendly, well-organized, and confident at all times. If questioned, never admit that you are traveling alone. Maintain regular contact with someone at home who knows your itinerary. For more tips, pick up *Traveling Solo* by Eleanor Berman (Globe Pequot Press) or subscribe to **Connecting: Solo Travel Network,** 689 Park Road, Unit 6, Gibsons, BC V0N 1V7 (☎604-886-9099; www.cstn.org; membership US$35).

Several services link solo travelers with companions who have similar travel habits and interests; for a bi-monthly newsletter for single travelers seeking a travel partner (subscription US$48), contact the **Travel Companion Exchange,** P.O. Box 833, Amityville, NY 11701 (☎631-454-0880; www.whytravelalone.com).

WOMEN TRAVELERS

Though Ireland is n extremely safe place in which to travel, women exploring on their own will inevitably face additional safety issues. If you are concerned, consider staying in **centrally located accommodations.** Stay in places that offer single rooms that lock from the inside, avoid solitary late-night treks, and always choose train compartments occupied by other women or couples. **Hitchhiking** is never safe for lone women, or even for two women traveling together.

Carry a **whistle** on your key chain or a **rape alarm** (about €10), and don't hesitate to use them in an emergency. Mace and pepper sprays are illegal in Ireland. The national **emergency** number is ☎999, and the EU number is ☎112. The **Dublin Rape Crisis Centre** helpline is ☎1800 778 888. *Let's Go* lists other hotlines in the **Practical Information** section of our city write-ups. An **IMPACT Model Mugging** self-defense course can prepare you for a potential attack, as well as raise your level of awareness of your surroundings and your confidence (see **Self Defense,** p. 15).

HEY, LADIES... The world isn't half as big and bad as the women who wrote the books listed below—let them show you around.

A Journey of One's Own: Uncommon Advice for the Independent Woman Traveler, by Thalia Zepatos. Eighth Mountain Press (US$17).

A Foxy Old Woman's Guide to Traveling Alone, by Jay Ben-Lesser. The Crossing Press (US$11).

Travel Alone & Love It: A Flight Attendant's Guide to Solo Travel, by Sharon B. Wingler. Chicago Spectrum Press, (US$15).

WOMEN'S HEALTH. Women who need an **abortion** or **emergency contraception** while in Northern Ireland should call the **fpa** (formerly the Family Planning Association) helpline (UK ☎0845 310 1334, M-F, 9am-7pm), visit their website (www.fpa.org.uk/), or contact the London office, 2-12 Pentonville Rd., N1 9PF (☎020 7837 5432), for more information. Abortions are illegal in the Republic of Ireland; call the London office if you need help.

OLDER TRAVELERS

Senior citizens are eligible for a wide range of discounts on transportation, museums, movies, theaters, concerts, restaurants, and accommodations. If you don't see a senior citizen price listed, ask, and you may be delightfully surprised. **Age and Opportunity** (☎01 837 0570; indigo.ie/~ageandop/) promotes the participation of the elderly in all aspects of Irish society. The books *No Problem! Worldwise Tips for Mature Adventurers*, by Janice Kenyon (Orca Book Publishers; US$16) and *Unbelievably Good Deals and Great Adventures That You Absolutely Can't Get Unless You're Over 50*, by Joan Rattner Heilman (NTC/Contemporary Publishing; US$13) are both excellent resources. For more information, contact:

ElderTreks, 597 Markham St., Toronto, ON M6G 2L7 (☎800-741-7956; www.eldertreks.com). Adventure travel programs for the 50+ traveler in Ireland.

Elderhostel, 11 Ave. de Lafayette, Boston, MA 02111 (☎877-426-8056; www.elderhostel.org). Organizes 1- to 4-week "educational adventures" in Ireland for those over 55.

The Mature Traveler, P.O. Box 15791, Sacramento, CA 95852 (☎800-460-6676). Deals, discounts, and travel packages for the 50+ traveler. Subscription US$30.

GAY AND LESBIAN TRAVELERS

Ireland is more tolerant of homosexuality than one might expect, but less tolerant than one might hope. People in rural areas may not have progressed as far as those in cities have since homosexuality was decriminalized in the Republic in 1993. Dublin now supports a small gay community, with growing student societies at Trinity and UCD and a growing array of pubs and clubs. Belfast and, to a lesser degree, Cork and Galway, also have growing gay communities. *Gay Community News* covers Irish gay-related news, and its listings page covers gay locales in all of Ireland. *Let's Go: Ireland* has gay pub and nightlife listings as well as phone numbers for gay information in Dublin, Belfast, Cork, and elsewhere (see the **Practical Information** sections). Listed below are contact organizations, mail-order bookstores, and publishers that offer materials addressing some specific concerns. **Out and About** (www.outandabout.com) offers a bi-weekly newsletter and a comprehensive site addressing gay travel concerns. **Gay Ireland** (www.gay-ireland.com) provides information on gay locales and events in Ireland and offers a personals/chat services. Other useful websites include www.gcn.ie, www.time-out.com/dublin/, and www.esatclear.ie/~gay-hiking/.

Gay and Lesbian Youth in Northern Ireland (GYLNI), Cathedral Buildings, 64 Donegall Street, Belfast, BT1 1SH, (☎028 9027 8636; www.glyni.org.uk). Offers a forum for meeting gay men and lesbians (ages 18-26), and info on gay locales in the North.

Ireland's Pink Pages (www.pink-pages.org). Ireland's web-based bisexual, gay, and lesbian directory. Extensive urban and regional info for both the Republic and the North.

International Lesbian and Gay Association (ILGA), 81 rue Marché-au-Charbon, B-1000 Brussels, Belgium (☎+32 2 502 2471; www.ilga.org). Provides political information, such as homosexuality laws of individual countries.

FURTHER READING: BISEXUAL, GAY, & LESBIAN.

Spartacus International Gay Guide 2001-2002. Bruno Gmunder Verlag (US$33).

Damron's Accommodations, and *The Women's Traveller.* Damron Travel Guides (US$14-19). For more info, call 800-462-6654 or visit www.damron.com.

Ferrari Guides' Gay Travel A to Z, Ferrari Guides' Men's Travel in Your Pocket, and *Ferrari Guides' Inn Places.* Ferrari Publications (US$16-20).

TRAVELERS WITH DISABILITIES

Ireland is not particularly wheelchair-friendly. Ramps, wide doors, and accessible bathrooms are less common than in the US, even in cities like Dublin. *Let's Go* lists and indexes **wheelchair-accessible facilities. Guide dogs** are always conveyed free, but until recently both the UK and Ireland imposed a six-month quarantine on all animals entering the country and require that the owner obtain an import license. For more information, call the PETS Helpline in the UK at ☎870 241 1710 (pets@ahvg.maff.gsi.gov.uk). For general information and free guides on disability access, write to the British Tourist Authority or Bord Fáilte.

Those with disabilities should inform airlines and hostels of their disabilities when making reservations; some time may be needed to prepare special accommodations. Call ahead to restaurants, museums, and other facilities to find out about ramps, door widths, elevator dimensions, etc. **Rail** is probably the most convenient form of travel for disabled travelers in Ireland. Not all train stations are wheelchair-accessible. On the web, *Global Access* (www.geocities.com/Paris/1502/disabilitylinks.html) has links for disabled travelers in Ireland. The **Green Book** (http://members.nbci.com/thegreenbook/home.html) has a partial listing of disabled-access accommodations and sights in Ireland.

USEFUL ORGANIZATIONS

Mobility International USA, P.O. Box 10767, Eugene, OR 97440 (☎541 343 1284, voice and TDD; www.miusa.org). Sells *A World of Options: A Guide to International Educational Exchange, Community Service, & Travel for Persons with Disabilities* (US$35).

Society for Accessible Travel and Hospitality (SATH), 347 Fifth Ave., #610, New York, NY 10016 (☎212-447-7284; www.sath.org). An advocacy group that publishes free online travel info and the travel magazine *OPEN WORLD* (US$18, free for members). Annual membership US$45, students and seniors US$30.

Directions Unlimited, 123 Green Ln., Bedford Hills, NY 10507 (☎800-533-5343). Books individual and group vacations for the physically disabled; not an info service.

The Guided Tour Inc., 7900 Old York Rd., #114B, Elkins Park, PA 19027, USA (☎800-783-5841; www.guidedtour.com). Organizes travel programs for persons with developmental and physical challenges in countries including Ireland.

MINORITY TRAVELERS

Most of Ireland's five million people are white and Christian (largely Catholic in the Republic, mixed Catholic and Protestant in the North). Until recently, the Irish have never had to address racial diversity on a large scale. Recent influxes of non-European immigrants (drawn by Ireland's present economic boom) and a growing Malaysian, Indian, and Pakistani population in Dublin has changed this, however.

Darker-skinned travelers are common subjects of attention, especially in rural areas. Minority travelers may be subject to racial comments and refused service in more certain establishments. In a 2002 survey of minority travelers in Ireland, Sinead O'Casey and Michael O'Connelly found that over 64% of the people had experienced racial insults and 16% suffered physical attacks of some sort. Most comments happen in public places, like pubs, B&Bs, and shops. For more statistical information, check www.amnesty.ie/act/racism/a-experience.shtml, and for community resources, consult www.nicem.org.uk.

That said, most of the time comments and stares are motivated by curiosity, rather than ill will. The Irish are a very welcoming and friendly people, but as in any place else, what is different, stands out.

TRAVELING WITH CHILDREN

Family vacations often require that you slow your pace, and always that you plan ahead. When deciding where to stay, remember the special needs of young children; call ahead to hostels and B&Bs to make sure they are child-friendly. If you rent a car, make sure the rental company provides a car seat for younger children. Consider using a papoose-style device to carry a baby on walking trips. **Be sure that your child carries some sort of ID** in case of an emergency or he or she gets lost, and arrange a reunion spot in case of separation when sight-seeing.

Virtually all museums and tourist attractions also have a children's rate. Children under two generally fly for 10% of the adult airfare on international flights (this does not necessarily include a seat). International fares are usually discounted 25% for children from two to 11.

TEACH YOUR CHILDREN WELL. Travel is an invaluable learning experience, for kids from one to ninety-two; the books listed below will help you research for the perfect family vacation.

Backpacking with Babies and Small Children, by Goldie Silverman. Wilderness Press (US$10).

Take Your Kids to Europe, by Cynthia W. Harriman. Cardogan Books (US$18).

How to take Great Trips with Your Kids, by Sanford and Jane Portnoy. Harvard Common Press (US $10).

Have Kid, Will Travel, by Claire and Lucille Tristram. Andrews McMeel (US$9).

Adventuring with Children: An Inspirational Guide to World Travel and the Outdoors, by Nan Jeffrey. Avalon House Publishing (US$15).

Trouble Free Travel with Children, by Vicki Lansky. Book Peddlers (US$9).

OTHER RESOURCES

Listed below are books and websites useful for independent research.

TRAVEL PUBLISHERS & BOOKSTORES

Hunter Publishing, 130 Campus Dr., Edison, NJ 08818, USA (☎800-255-0343; www.hunterpublishing.com). Extensive catalog of travel and adventure travel books.

Rand McNally, 150 S. Wacker Dr., Chicago, IL 60606, USA (☎800-234-0679 or 312-332-2009; www.randmcnally.com), publishes road atlases (each US$10).

Adventurous Traveler Bookstore, 245 S. Champlain St., Burlington, VT 05401, USA (☎800-282-3963 or 802-860-6776; www.adventuroustraveler.com).

Travel Books & Language Center, Inc., 4437 Wisconsin Ave. NW, Washington, D.C. 20016 (☎800-220-2665; www.travelbks.com). 60,000 titles from around the world.

USEFUL PUBLICATIONS

Ireland: An Encyclopedia for the Bewildered, K.S. Daly. Ten Speed Press (US$8).

Dublin Pub Life and Lore: An Oral History, Kevin C. Kearns. Roberts Rinehart (US$16).

A Pocket History of Irish Traditional Music, Gearóid Ó hAllmhuráin. O'Brien Press (US$8).

Teach Yourself Irish, Diarmuid Ó Sé & Joseph Sheils. Hodder & Stoughton (US$10).

WORLD WIDE WEB

As website turnover is so high, also use search engines to strike out on your own.

THE ART OF BUDGET TRAVEL

Backpacker's Ultimate Guide: www.bugeurope.com. Tips on packing, transportation, and where to go. Also tons of country-specific travel info.

Backpack Europe: www.backpackeurope.com. Helpful tips, a bulletin board, and links.

How to See the World: www.artoftravel.com. A compendium of great travel tips, from cheap flights to self defense to interacting with local culture.

Lycos: http://travel.lycos.com/. General introductions to cities and regions throughout Ireland, accompanied by links to applicable histories, news, and local tourism sites.

Rec. Travel Library: www.travel-library.com. Fantastic links for personal travelogues.

INFORMATION ON IRELAND

CIA World Factbook: www.odci.gov/cia/publications/factbook/index.html.

The Irish Times: www.ireland.com. The Republic's major daily newspaper online.

MyTravelGuide: www.mytravelguide.com. Country overviews, with everything from history to transportation to live web cam coverage of Ireland.

World Travel Guide: www.travel-guides.com/navigate/world.asp. Helpful practical info.

WWW.LETSGO.COM Our newly designed website now features the full online content of all of our guides. In addition, trial versions of all nine City Guides are available for download on Palm OS™ PDAs. Our website also contains our newsletter, links for photos and streaming video, online ordering of our titles, information about our books, and a travel forum buzzing with stories and tips.

ALTERNATIVES TO TOURISM

Travel can be a worthwhile and memorable experience, but for more comprehensive insights into a country, you may want to consider alternatives to tourism. Working, volunteering, or studying for an extended period of time is often the best way to attain an understanding of local life. With a diverse landscape and growing economy, Ireland allows visitors the opportunity to engage in a broad range of activities. Students may take courses at campuses around the country, from urban universities to rural colleges. For the ambitious admirer of Gaelic, Irish language courses are taught in several schools and cultural centers in the North and South. Amidst the economic boom of the Celtic Tiger, more and more employment opportunities—and job placement agencies—are springing up in the cities. And with hundreds of urban and rural sites of activism, volunteering in Ireland offers one of the best ways to immerse oneself in both the history and future of Ireland. Whether studying at Trinity or volunteering at an archelogical dig in the South, taking advantage of the alternatives to tourism available in Ireland will earn you a meaningful and educational experience.

For an extensive listing of specialty travel opportunities and other alternatives to tourism, try the **Specialty Travel Index,** 305 San Anselmo Ave., Ste. 313, San Anselmo, CA 94960, USA (☎800-442-4922 or 415-459-4900; www.specialtytravel.com; US$10). **Transitions Abroad** (www.transitionsabroad.com) also publishes a bimonthly on-line newsletter for work, study, and specialized travel abroad (US$6.45 per issue).

VISA AND PERMIT INFORMATION

Citizens of the EU and most Western countries need only a passport to enter Ireland. To remain for longer than 90 days, visitors must obtain permission from the Alien's Registration Office in Dublin, or the local Garda (police) station.

Though EU nationals may work in Ireland without a permit, non-EU visitors must obtain proper documentation. For **work permits,** non-EU visitors must have potential employers submit an application to the Department of Enterprise, Trade and Employment. Employers will usually be willing to pay the large fees attached to the application only if the worker has technical skills to offer.

To **study in Ireland,** students need to submit a copy of their acceptance letter from an education institution in Ireland, verifying the duration and nature of the course and that the requisite fees have been paid, to the Department of Foreign Affairs Visa Office in St. Stephen's Green.

STUDYING IN IRELAND

It's easy to spend a summer, a term, or even a year studying in Ireland or Northern Ireland. Each of the major cities in Ireland is home to several universities, and smaller *gaeltacht* communities support many Irish language and cultural programs. To choose a program that best fits your needs, you will want to research all you can before making your decision—determining costs and duration, as well as what kind of students participate in the program and what sort of accommodations are provided. To fully immerse yourself in the culture, try to arrange housing with an Irish family through the university.

EU students will find it easier to gain acceptance to an Irish unviersity than most other students. The standards for admission are much lower for those who have attended an EU secondary school, and while other students will have to pay between €15,000-30,000 a year, educational programs are free of charge for EU students. American students seeking to enroll in an Irish university will find it cheaper to enroll directly to the university from abroad, though gaining admission and college credit may prove more difficult. For all students, spots in Irish schools are scarce, especially in history and English departments.

A good resource for finding programs that cater to your particular interests is **www.studyabroad.com,** which has links to various semester abroad programs based on a variety of criteria, including desired location and focus of study. Also try **www.goabroad.com.** The following is a list of other organizations that can help place students in university programs in Ireland.

AMERICAN PROGRAMS

The following is a list of American organizations that can help arrange study abroad opportunities.

Academic Programs International, 129 E. Hopkins, Ste. 101, San Marcos, TX 78666, USA (☎800-844-4124; www.academicintl.com). Arranges placement in Galway and Limerick. Fees range from US$4000 (summer) to US$17,400 (full-year).

American Institute for Foreign Study, College Division, River Plaza, 9 West Broad St., Stamford, CT 06902, USA (☎800-727-2437, ext. 5163; www.aifsabroad.com). Organizes programs for study at the University of Limerick. Costs range from US$10,495 (semester) to US$20,145 (full-year); scholarships available.

Arcadia University, Center for Education Abroad, 450 S. Easton Rd., Glenside, PA 19038, USA (☎866-927-2234; www.arcadia.edu/cea). Operates programs throughout Ireland. Costs range from $2200 (summer) to $29,000 (full-year).

College Consortium for International Studies, Truman State University, 120 Kirk Building, Kirksville, MO 63501, USA (☎660-785-4076; www.ccisabroad.org). Term-time programs in the North from US$4500, summer courses in the Republic US$1500-2224.

School for International Training, College Semester Abroad, Kipling Rd., P.O. Box 676, Brattleboro, VT 05302, USA (☎800-336-1616 or 802-257-7751; www.sit.edu). Semester- and year-long programs in Ireland run US$10,600-13,700. Also sponsors the **Experiment in International Living** (☎800-345-2929; www.usexperiment.org), 3- to 5-week summer programs that offer high-school students cross-cultural homestays, community service, language training and more from US$1900-5000.

North American Institute for Study Abroad, Mill St., Danville, PA 17821, USA (☎570-275-5099; www.naisa.com). Arranges placement in universities throughout the Republic and Northern Ireland (fees vary by school; check website for details).

UNIVERSITY PROGRAMS IN IRELAND

Most American undergraduates enroll in programs sponsored by US universities. Local universities can be much cheaper, though it may be more difficult to receive academic credit. Some schools that offer study abroad programs to international students are listed below.

GET CARD.
TRAVEL HARD.
International Student Identity Card
STUDENT
Beijing University
LEE, M.
05/07/1978
ISIC
S 000 123 456 789
SCENIC DRIVE
FOOD + GAS
LOOKOUT

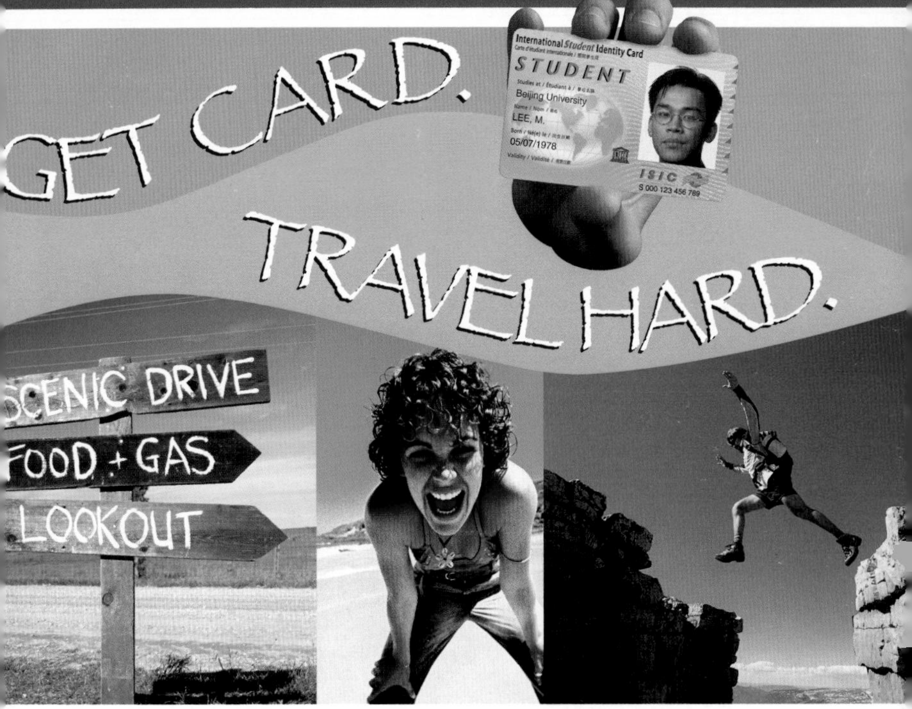

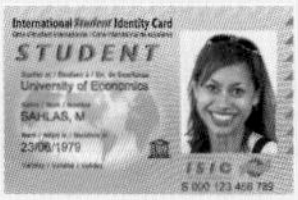

Irish Studies Summer School, usit NOW, 19-21 Aston Quay, O'Connell Bridge, Dublin 2, Ireland (☎01 602 1600; www.usitnow.ie). A 7-week-long program (US$5200) offering courses in Irish history and contemporary culture. usit also administrates the summer program **Ireland in Europe,** a 2 week course focused on Irish civilization.

National University of Ireland, University Rd., Galway, Ireland (☎091 524 411; www.nuigalway.ie). Offers half- or full-year opportunities for junior-year students who meet the college's entry requirements. **Summer school** courses include Irish Studies, Education, and Creative Writing (€800-1000, without accommodation).

Queen's University Belfast, University Rd., Belfast BT7 1NN (International Office ☎028 9033 5415; www.qub.ac.uk). Study in Belfast from a semester (UK£2,800) to a full year (UK£5700). The 3-week **Introduction to Northern Ireland** program in January addresses political, social, and economic questions unique to the North (UK£650).

Trinity College Dublin, Office of International Student Affairs, Trinity College, Dublin 2, Ireland (☎01 608 2011; www.tcd.ie/isa). Offers a 1-year program of undergraduate courses for visiting students. Fees €9450-14,700.

University College Cork, The Information Office, University College, Cork (☎021-490-3000; www.ucc.ie). Students who enroll directly in the college are presented with a wide selection of subjects and classes from which to choose. Those seeking help with applying may enroll through **Cultural Experiences Abroad** (☎800-266-4441; www.gowithcea.com), which offers semester- or year-long programs in various disciplines. Fees range from US$8995 (semester) to US$18,495 (full-year).

University College Dublin, International Summer School, Newman House, 86 St. Stephen's Green, Dublin 2 (☎01 475 2004; www.ucd.ie/summerschool). Offers a 2-week international summer course examining Irish culture and tradition (€650).

University of Ulster, Shore Rd., Newtownabbey, Antrim, BT37 0QB, Northern Ireland (☎028 9036 6151; www.ulst.ac.uk). Offers semester- or year-long programs for visiting international students. Fees UK£2500-10,000.

LANGUAGE SCHOOLS

Although most university courses in Ireland are conducted in English, there are Irish (or *Gaeilge*) language classes and schools offering intensive training for beginners through to the advanced Gaelic-speaker. These language schools, often independently-run international or local organizations, or divisions of foreign universities, rarely offer college credit. Language schools are a good alternative to university study if you desire a deeper focus in Gaelic or a slightly less-rigorous courseload. Some good programs include:

Daltaí na Gaeilge, (www.daltai.com). Gaelic for "Students of the Irish Language," this non-profit corporation runs language programs throughout the US, Europe, and Australia. Website includes an extensive list of course offerings (check for individual contacts and fees), as well as online grammar and language games and exercises.

Donegal Gaeltacht Cultural Centre, Loughanure, Annagry, Co. Donegal, Ireland (☎075 48081; www.lochgael.com). In addition to offering accommodations and weekends of dance, song, and literature, the center offers week-long Irish language courses (summer US$425, winter US$280), and cultural weekends (US$40).

Oideas Gael, Glencolmcille, Co. Donegal, Ireland (☎073 30248; www.oideas-gael.com). Offers week-long Irish language and cultural courses in dance, music, and local arts, from April to late August (US$150). Teachers from Oidas Gael also offer an **intensive weekend course** once a year in San Francisco (US$215 for tuition and food; ☎510-881-5958; gaeilge@onesourcegraphics.com).

WORKING IN IRELAND

In spite of the country's recent economic boom, unemployment in Ireland is high for an EU country. Travelers are most likely to find work in touristed urban centers such as Dublin, Galway, Belfast, or Cork. European Union citizens can work in any EU country, and if your parents were born in an EU country, you may be able to claim dual citizenship with Ireland, or at least the right to a **work permit.** Commonwealth residents with a parent or grandparent born in the UK do not need a work permit to work in Northern Ireland. Contact your British Consulate or High Commission (see p. 7) for details before you go and the **Department of Employment** (☎01 631 2121; www.entemp.ie) when you arrive. If you do not fit into any of these categories, you must apply for a **work permit** to be considered for paid employment in the Republic or Northern Ireland. The permit takes approximately four weeks to process, is valid for between one month and one year, and can be renewed upon expiration. Your prospective employer must obtain this document for you.

There are two main schools of thought when it comes to working abroad. Some travelers want long-term jobs that allow them to get to know another part of the world in depth (e.g. teaching or working in the tourist industry). Other sojourners seek out short-term jobs to finance their future travel. They often seek employment in the service sector or in agriculture, working for a few weeks at a time to finance the next leg of their journey. This section discusses both short-term and long-term opportunities for working in Ireland.

LONG-TERM WORK

If you're planning on spending a substantial amount of time (i.e., more than three months) working in Ireland, it is best to search for a job well in advance. International placement agencies are often the easiest way to find employment abroad, especially if you wish to teach, but be wary of advertisements or companies that claim the ability to get you a job abroad for a fee—often times the same jobs are freely listed online or in newspapers. For US college students, recent graduates, and young adults, the simplest way to get legal permission to work abroad is through **Council on International Educational Exchange's Work Abroad Programs** (☎888 COUNCIL; www.ciee.org). Council Exchanges can help you obtain a three to six month work permit/visa and also provides assistance finding jobs and housing. Fees average around US$350. Internships, for college students, are a good way to segue into working abroad. Though they are often unpaid, or poorly paid, many say the overall experience is well worth the financial inconvenience. **Search Associates** (www.search-associates.com) recruits for internships abroad. If you wish to obtain work through an organization, **Working Ireland,** 26 Eustace St., Dublin 2, Ireland (☎01 677 0300; www.workingireland.ie) is the place to go. This multi-tasking agency arranges short- and long-term job placement throughout the country and assits visitors in finding accommodation. When it's time to leave Ireland, they will also help you collect your tax refund and arrange travel home. In the South, you may also want to pay a visit to the **Job Options Bureau,** Tourist House, 40-41 Grand Parade, Cork, Ireland (☎21 427 5369; info@joboptionsbureau.ie).

TEACHING

Teaching jobs abroad are rarely well-paid, though some private American schools in Ireland pay relatively competitive salaries. In most cases, you must have a bachelor's degree to work as a full-time teacher. College undergraduates lacking these degrees can often get summer positions teaching or tutoring. If you wish to teach in an American school overseas you must have an American teaching certification.

A popular option for many is to volunteer as a teacher. While most fund their own way, some volunteers get free accommodations, while others manage to obtain a daily stipend from their college. Those interested are encouraged to inquire at colleges and secondary schools for information specific to the school in question.

The International Educator (☎508-362-1414; www.tieonline.com) lists overseas teaching vacancies and offers job search and resume posting online. A good teacher-job website specific to Ireland, complete with a tutorial on the Irish education system and firsthand accounts from student teachers, is **Americans in Ireland** (www.geocities.com/teachingirish). Also see **www.teachabroad.com** for a comprehensive list of paid and volunteer teaching opportunities in Ireland. Other programs that may arrange placement for teaching jobs in Ireland include:

European Council of International Schools, 105 Tuxford Terr., Basking Ridge, NJ 07920, USA (☎908-903-0552; www.ecis.org).

Institute of International Education, 809 United Nations Plaza, New York, NY 10017, USA (☎212-883-8200).

North American Institute of Study Abroad, Mill St., Danville, PA 17821, USA (☎570-275-5099; www.naisa.com).

AU PAIR WORK

Au pairs are typically females (aged 18-30) who work as live-in nannies, caring for children and doing light housework in exchange for room, board, and a small stipend. The average weekly pocket money allowance is between €60-70. All agencies stress that an au pair must have a strong love of children.

Though most au-pairs speak favorably of their experience, drawbacks often include long hours of on-duty call, and severely decrepit pay. Much of the experience depends on the family with which you're placed. The agencies below are a good starting point for looking for employment as an au pair.

Accord Cultural Exchange, 750 La Playa, San Francisco, CA 94121, USA (☎415-386-6203; www.cognitext.com/accord).

Au Pair in Europe, P.O. Box 68056, Blakely Postal Outlet, Hamilton, Ontario, Canada L8M 3M7 (☎905-545-6305; www.princeent.com).

Douglas Au Pair Agency Ltd., 28 Frankfield, Douglas, Cork, Ireland (☎21 489 1489; www.aupairhere.com).

Dublin Childcare Recruitment Agency, Newcourt House, Strandville Ave., Clontarf, Dublin 3, Ireland (☎01 833 2281; www.childcare-recruitment.com).

Shamrock Au Pair Agency, Magheree, Kilmorony, Athy, Co. Kildare, Ireland (☎507 25 533; www.aupairireland.com).

SHORT-TERM WORK

Roaming for long periods of time can get expensive; many travelers try their hand at odd jobs for a few weeks at a time to make some extra cash. Some of the most common forms of short-term work in Ireland include hostessing, waitressing, bartending, temping, childcare, farm work, and volunteering. Another popular option is to work several hours a day at a hostel in exchange for free or discounted room and/or board. Most often, these short-term jobs are found by word of mouth, or by talking to the owners of hostels and restaurants. Due to the high turnover in the tourism industry, many establishments are eager for help, even if only temporary. Ireland does not issue work permits for short-term manual or domestic labor, but depending on your employer, you may not need one. *Let's Go* tries to list temporary jobs like these whenever possible; check under the **practical information** sections of all towns and cities for **work opportunities** listings.

FARMING IN IRELAND

Agricultural work may be one of the most interesting and rewarding experiences you can have in Ireland—working on a farm offers you a chance to get away from the urban sprawl of Dublin and the big cities and to wander among flocks of sheep rather than hordes of tourists. **World Wide Opportunities on Organic Farms (WWOOF),** (www.wwoof.org) can help you arrange volunteer work with independent host farms across Northern Ireland.

VOLUNTEERING IN IRELAND

Unlike some countries in Western Europe, the opportunities for volunteerism in Ireland and Northern Ireland are endless. Most people choose to go through a parent organization that handles logistical details and provides a group environment and support system. There are two main types of organizations—religous (often Catholic), and non-sectarian—although there are rarely restrictions on participation for either. Some volunteer services charge a surprisingly hefty fee to participate (although they frequently cover airfare and most, if not all, living expenses). Do research on a program before committing—talk to people who have previously participated and find out exactly what you're getting into, as living and working conditions can vary greatly. Different programs are geared toward different ages and levels of experience, so make sure that you're not taking on too much or too little. The more informed you are and the more realistic expectations you have, the more enjoyable the program will be.

Volunteer jobs are readily available in Ireland and Northern Ireland. You can sometimes avoid high application fees by contacting individual sites and workcamps directly. Northern Ireland's **FREEPHONE** connects callers to local volunteer bureaus (☎0800 052 2212). Opportunities in the Republic range from building houses with **Habitat for Humanity,** to advocating for the homeless with **Focus Ireland,** to counseling the mentally ill with **Mental Health Ireland.** For those who would rather tend to crops, membership in **Willing Workers on Organic Farms (WWOOF)** (www.phdcc.com/sites/wwoof; US$20; UK£10) allows you the opportunity to receive room and board at a variety of organic farms in Ireland in exchange for help on the farm. The **Donegal Organic Farm,** in northwestern Ireland, offers camps and programs for organic-oriented individuals.

Archaeological Institute of America, Boston University, 656 Beacon St., Boston, MA 02215, USA (☎617-353-9361; www.archaeological.org). The *Archaeological Fieldwork Opportunities Bulletin*, available on the organization's website, lists field sites throughout Europe, including parts of Ireland.

Christian Aid, The Republic: 17 Clanwilliam Terr., Grand Canal Dock, Dublin 2 (☎01 611 0801). **Northern Ireland:** 30 Wellington Park, Belfast, BT9 6DL (☎028 9038 1204; www.christian-aid.org.uk). Individuals or groups of volunteers work in various fundraising and administrative roles, occasionally for a small stipend.

Earthwatch, 3 Clocktower Pl., Ste. 100, Box 75, Maynard, MA 01754, USA (☎800-776-0188 or 978-461-0081; www.earthwatch.org). Arranges 1- to 3-week programs in Ireland to promote conservation of natural resources. Programs average US$1700.

Elderhostel, Inc., 11 Avenue de Lafayette, Boston, MA 02111, USA (☎877-426-8056; www.elderhostel.org). Sends volunteers ages 55+ to work in construction, research, teaching, and many other projects. Costs average US$100 per day plus airfare.

Focus Ireland, 1 Lord Edward Court, Bride St., Dublin 8, Ireland (☎01 475 1955; www.focusireland.ie). Offers volunteers the opportunity to become involved in advocacy, fundraising, and assistance efforts for the homeless of Ireland.

Habitat for Humanity International, 121 Habitat St., Americus, GA 31709, USA (☎229-924-6935; www.habitat.org). Volunteers build houses in over 83 countries, including Northern Ireland, for anywhere from 2 weeks to 3 years. Costs start at US$1200.

Mental Health Ireland, Mensana House, 6 Adelaide House, Dun Laoghaire, Co. Dublin, Ireland (☎01 284 1186; www.mentalhealthireland.ie). Volunteer activities include fundraising, housing, "befriending," and promoting mental health in various regions of Ireland. Opportunities listed in their newsletter, *Mensana News*, available online.

Northern Ireland Volunteer Development Agency, Annsgate House, 70-74 Anne St., Belfast, BT1 4EH (☎0232 236 100; info.nivda@cinni.org). A representative of the **International Association for Volunteer Effort (IAVE),** the center helps arrange individual and group volunteer efforts in Northern Ireland. IAVE membership fees for individuals US$30/yr; for groups US$100/yr.

Service Civil International Voluntary Service (SCI-IVS), 3213 W. Wheeler St., Seattle, WA 98199, USA (☎/fax 206-350-6585; www.sci-ivs.org). Arranges placement in several types of camps in Dublin and Northern Ireland for those 18+. Registration US$125.

Volunteering Ireland, Carmichael Centre for Voluntary Groups, Coleraine House, Coleraine St., Dublin 7, Ireland (☎01 872 2622; www.volunteeringireland.com). Offers opportunities for individuals or groups in various volunteering and advocacy settings. Options listed online and placement service is free.

Volunteers for Peace, 1034 Tiffany Rd., Belmont., VT 05730, USA (☎802-259-2759; www.vfp.org). Places volunteers in work camps in Ireland, although camps are small so spaces are limited. Membership required for registration. Annual *International Workcamp Directory* US$20. Programs average US$200 for 2-3 weeks.

FOR FURTHER READING ON ALTERNATIVES TO TOURISM

Alternative Travel Directory: The Complete Guide to Traveling, Studying, and Living Overseas, by Clayton A. Hubbs. Transitions Abroad Publishing, 2002.

How to Get a Job in Europe, by Sanborn and Matherly. Surrey Books, 1999.

How to Live Your Dream of Volunteering Oversees, by Collins, DeZerega, and Heckscher. Penguin Books, 2002.

International Directory of Voluntary Work, by Whetter and Pybus. Peterson's Guides and Vacation Work, 2000.

Jobs for People Who Love to Travel, by Krannich, Krannich, and Krannich. Impact Publications, 1999.

Live and Work Abroad, by Francis and Callan. Vacation-Work, 2001.

Living and Working Abroad, by David Hampshire. Survival Books, 2001.

The Back Door Guide to Short-Term Job Adventures, by Michael Landes. Ten Speed Press, 2001.

The Insider's Guide to Study Abroad, by Ann M. Moore. Peterson's, 2001.

Work Abroad: The Complete Guide to Finding a Job Overseas, by Hubbs, Griffith, and Nolting. Transitions Abroad Publishing, 2000.

Work Your Way Around the World, by Susan Griffith. Worldview Publishing Services, 2001.

LIFE AND TIMES

I know tolerably well what Ireland was, but have a very imperfect idea of how Ireland *is*.

—John Stuart Mill.

Jagged coastal cliffs, thatch-roofed fishing cottages, clouded, misty days, and, of course, the green rolling hills—poetic images of Ireland dominate the tourist's mind. What most travelers don't realize, however, is that Ireland is now a country on the rise. Poverty and unemployment have historically been widespread, but the EU has brought new life; impressed by the island's recent economic boom, the international media has christened Ireland the "Celtic Tiger." In the face of an influx of new faces—refugees and emigrants have recently brought Ireland its first population increase—the country's conservatism is slowly cracking. The short-term result is a growing generation gap and disparity between rural and urban areas. Amid the necessary grime of modernization, however, the lifestyle of the Irish lives on unsullied, continuing to center itself around music, sports, a laid-back attitude, and The Pub.

Six of Ulster's nine counties make up Northern Ireland, officially a territory of the United Kingdom. Under the 1998 Northern Ireland Peace Agreement, residents of Northern Ireland may choose whether to individually identify themselves as Irish or British, but word choice can still be tricky. "Ulster" is a term used exclusively by Protestants in the North. It's best to refer to "Northern Ireland" or "the North" and "the Republic" or "the South." "Southern Ireland" is not a viable term.

HISTORY

History may seem, as it did to Joyce's Stephen Daedalus, a nightmare from which we're trying to awake, but visitors to Ireland unfamiliar with historical conflicts will pass by some of the island's most worthwhile attractions—namely, the character of its people and their cultural productions—with little sense of what lies beyond their surface charm. The following should provide you with a taste of the complexities underlying modern Ireland.

ANCIENT IRELAND (TO AD 350)

IMPORTANT EVENTS

circa 7000 BC Ireland's first settlers arrive from Britain. Ireland is one of the last areas in Europe to be colonized by human populations.

Our fragmented knowledge of ancient Irish culture comes from the scant remains of its stone structures and metalwork. From these we have learned that Ireland's first settlers quickly founded an agrarian civilization upon arriving from Britain in about 7000 BC. This civilization created and left behind many structures still prominent in the Irish landscape. Among them were **dolmens,** arrangements of huge stones in table-like forms, which were created as tombs and shrines for the recently dead (see **Poulnabrane Dolmen,** p. 333). **Passage tombs** were less common; these underground stone hallways and chambers often contained corpses and cinerary urns (see **Newgrange,** p. 150). **Stone circles** were rings of pint-sized gravestones that likely marked spots of religious significance.

Bronze poured into Ireland circa 2000 BC, and the agrarian society was slowly retooled into a warrior aristocracy. By 900 BC, it was bronze, schmonze—the **Irish Golden Age** brought about an evolution from the simpler stone structures of the past to more impressive projects: **ring forts** (see **Dún Aengus,** p. 354), which were protective walls that circled encampments and villages; **souterrains,** underground hideouts for storing loot and escaping from various marauders; and **clochans,** mortarless beehive-shaped stone huts.

Although a few groups of **Celts** may have arrived as early as 2000 BC, their real migration didn't start until 600 BC. First refered to by the Greeks as the *Keltoi* (hidden people), named in reference to their vast but unwritten stores of scholarship and knowledge, the Celts quickly settled down to their new western outpost. (Their pan-European movement had already brought them as far east as Asia Minor.) At the time, the Romans were too busy conquering Germanic tribes to set their greedy sights on Ireland.

The Celts prospered on their peaceful isle, speaking a hybrid of Celtic and indigenous languages (called Old Irish) and living in small farming communities. Under their system, regional chieftains ruled territories called *tuath*, while provincial kings controlled several *tuatha*. The **Uliad of Ulster,** a northern kingdom of chariot warriors, dominated the La Tène culture from their capital near Armagh (see **Navan Fort,** p. 511). These kings organized raids on Britain, established settlements in Scotland and Wales, and generally set themselves up for a long and brutal comeuppance. Their valor and relative success inspired the tales of mythic heroism prominent in the *Táin* and other Irish epics (see **Legends and Folktales,** p. 71).

CHRISTIANS & VIKINGS & PIRATES, OH MY! (350-1200)

The wind is fierce to-night
It tosses the sea's white hair
I fear no wild Vikings
sailing the quiet main.
—unnamed 9th-century scribe, doodling on his manuscript

Starting in the 5th century with **St. Patrick,** Ireland was shown the light, Christian-style, by a series of hopeful missionaries. According to legend, Paddy was born in Scotland and kidnapped by Irish pirates (*arr*). Enslaved and forced to tend Irish pirate sheep (*baa…arr*), he quickly found Jesus. He escaped back home, but at the command of a prophetic vision, he performed an about-face and returned to proselytize in Ireland.

The missionaries and monks that followed St. Paddy recorded observations of the unfamiliar Celtic culture, describing, among other things, the system of writing found on **ogham stones.** These large obelisks, which recorded lineages in a script of dots and slashes, are still present in the **Burren** (see p. 329), at the **Hill of Tara** (see p. 152), and at **Brú na Boínne** in Co. Meath (see p. 150). Missionaries also introduced the Viking-inspired **round tower** to the architectural lexicon. These towers were built as fortifications against invaders; their sturdy forms still rise from dozens of fields across the island, causing modern Vikings on modern tour buses to sigh wistfully and pine for the

circa 3000 BC
Mound-builders build their mounds. The Hill of Tara is established.

2000 BC
Bronze becomes the latest craze.

900 BC-700 BC
The Irish Golden Age (bronze is SO last millennium).

600 BC-AD 0
The Celts migrate from central Europe.

circa AD 379
More southern (Co. Meath) Uí Néill clan gains prominence.

AD 350
The first Christians arrive in Ireland and begin their missionary work.

AD 432
St. Patrick's estimated time of arrival in Ireland.

circa AD 600
Monks illuminate the Book of Durrow.

fjords. **High crosses,** or Celtic crosses, combine the Christian cross with the Celtic circle. These stone crucifixes can be large enough to dwarf bystanders and sometimes feature elaborate carvings illustrating Bible stories or saintly legends.

AD 500-700
Huge monastic cities flourish.

AD 795
Full-scale Viking invasions begin.

early AD 800s
Monks ignore Vikings and instead spend time illuminating the Book of Kells.

1000-1100
Irish chieftains fight amongst themselves.

1002
Dal Cais clan of Co. Clare captures Armagh.

1014
Battle of Clontarf: Vikings get trounced once and for all.

1171
Strongbow grovels before English crown.

1172
Pope decrees that Henry II of England is feudal lord of Ireland.

In the 5th century, Barbarians took their pillaging on the continent a bit too far, and asylum-seeking monks began arriving in Ireland. These events predated the policy of converting hostels into asylums (see **Wexford,** p. 204); instead, monks erected enormous **monastic cities,** which during the 6th through 8th centuries earned Ireland its reputation as the "land of saints and scholars." At their bases in **Glendalough** (see p. 141), **Clonmacnois** (see p. 171), and elsewhere, the monastics of the Early Irish Church recorded the old epics and composed long religious poems in both Latin and Old Irish. The monks also shed some of their Divine Light on the classics by illuminating manuscripts. The 7th-century **Book of Durrow** is the earliest surviving such manuscript; it is now exhibited at Trinity College (see p. 111) with the early 9th-century **Book of Kells.** Rather than bowing to Rome, monastic cities allied themselves with up-and-coming Irish chieftains. Armagh, an important religious center, owed its prominence in part to the **Uí Néill** (O'Neill) clan, whose jurisdiction gradually spread from Meath to central Ulster.

Before we get too much further along, we should explain that Ireland of yore was divided into four counties: **Leinster** (east and southeast), **Munster** (southwest), **Connacht** (west), and **Ulster** (north). Very well, then—proceed.

The Golden Age of Irish Scholasticism (not to be confused with the Irish Golden Age) was interrupted by **Viking** invasions in the 9th and 10th centuries. Their raids were most frequent along the southern coast, where they founded permanent settlements at Limerick, Waterford, and Dublin. The horned ones built Ireland's first castles, allied themselves with equally fierce chieftains, and littered the southeast with Norse-derived place names (Smerwick and Fota being choice examples).

In 1002, High King **Brian Ború** and his militant **Dal Cais** clan set off a period of bitter inter-*tuath* strife by capturing Armagh and challenging the Uí Néills for control of Ireland. The Dal Cais won a heroic victory but lost Brian Ború in the epic **Battle of Clontarf,** fought against the Vikings near Dublin in 1014. The island was then divided between chieftains **Rory O'Connor** and **Dermot MacMurrough,** who continued to duke it out for the crown. Dermot ill-advisedly sought the assistance of English Norman nobles—Richard de Clare (a.k.a. **Strongbow**) was all too willing to help. Strongbow and his Anglo-Normans arrived in 1169 and cut a bloody, Anglo-Norman swath through south Leinster. Strongbow married Dermot's daughter **Aoife** after Dermot's death in 1171 and for a time seemed ready to proclaim an independent Norman kingdom in Ireland. Instead, he affirmed his loyalty to King Henry II and with characteristic generosity offered to govern Leinster on England's behalf.

FEUDALISM AND ITS DISCONTENTS (1200-1607)

Thus the English came to Ireland and settled down for a nice, long occupation. The subsequent feudal period saw constant bickering between Gaelic and Norman-descended English lords. While the Norman strongholds in Leinster had more towns—including the **Pale,** a fortified domain around Dublin—and more trade, Gaelic Connacht and Ulster remained intimidatingly agrarian. The two sides were of surprisingly unified culture: English and Irish fiefdoms built similar castles, ate similar foods, enjoyed the same poets, and hired the same mercenaries. The Crown fretted up a storm over this cultural cross-pollination and sponsored the notorious **Statutes of Kilkenny** in 1366. These fretful decrees banned English colonists from speaking, dressing, or marrying Irish and forbade the Irish from entering walled cities like Derry. But the Gaelic lords went on reclaiming their territorial inheritance, and the new laws did little to alleviate English trepidation.

1366
Statutes of Kilkenny passed.

1470-1534
Anglo-Irish Earls of Kildare bring relative stability to Irish politics.

Feudal skirmishes and economic decline plagued the English lords until the rise of the "Geraldine Earls," two branches of the FitzGerald family who initially fought for control of south Leinster. The victors, the **Earls of Kildare,** ruled Ireland with panache, elan, and occasionally a bit of gusto, from 1470 to 1534; their reign was marked with such brio, such ardor, that the English crown quickly grew wary. In 1494, **Poynings' Law** limited Earl-ly authority, declaring that the Irish Parliament could convene only with English consent and could not pass laws that did not meet the approval of the Crown. The Irish people were divided: half were not surprised while the other half were just slow on the uptake.

1494
The Fretful Crown attempts to limit the Earls' power through Poynings' Law.

1537
Henry VIII claims Ireland for his own. Yoink.

The English Crown increased its control over Ireland throughout the next century, and the latter group finally began to catch on. When Henry VIII created the Church of England, the Dublin Parliament passed the 1537 **Irish Supremacy Act,** declaring Henry head of the Protestant **Church of Ireland** and effectively making the island property of the Crown. The Church of Ireland held a privileged position over Irish Catholicism, even though the English neither articulated any difference between the two religious outlooks nor attempted to convert the Irish masses. The lords of Ireland wished to remain loyal both to Catholicism and to the Crown—a daunting proposition even by 16th-century standards. Bold **Thomas FitzGerald** sent a missive to Henry VIII stating this position. In response, Henry denied his aristocratic title. FitzGerald, who was clearly not getting it, sponsored an uprising in Munster in 1579, thus planting in the English imagination the idea that a loyal Ireland could only be achieved under direct Protestant control.

1579
Catholic-minded FitzGerald uprising against the English.

1595-1601
Another uprising: Hugh O'Neill vs. English Crown.

Not to be outdone by Leinster, the equally defiant Ulster Earl **Hugh O'Neill** led a rebellion in the late 1590s. The King of Spain promised naval assistance; his Armada arrived in Kinsale Harbour in 1601 but sat around polishing their blunderbusses while armies from England demolished Irish forces. Relieved of their power, O'Neill and the rest of the major Gaelic lords soared out of Ireland in 1607 in what came to be known as the **Flight of the Earls.** Though they aimed to return with assistance from the forces of Catholic rulers on the mainland continent, few ever returned to Ireland. While the world looked on in feigned astonishment, the English took control of the land and parceled it out to Protestants.

1601
The Armada sits passive in Kinsale Harbour.

1607
The Flying Earls. Irish land is systematically parceled out to Protestants.

1607-41 Under James I, Protestants from the Scotland lowlands are settled in the northern counties of Ireland

1641 Landless Irish revolt in Ulster.

1642 Confederation of Kilkenny is formed between the Church, Irish Lords, and English Earls.

1649 Cromwell arrives in Ireland.

1654-1655 Cromwell's policy of Plantation implemented.

1665 Act of Explanation passed under English Restorers: Catholics receive some meagre compensation for losses.

1688 Deposed King James II flees to Ireland.

1689 The Siege of Derry: Apprentice Boys do their trick with the gates.

1690 Battle of the Boyne: James is defeated.

CROMWELL (1607-1688)

The English project of dispossessing Catholics of their land and replacing them with Protestants (let's see if they notice the difference!) was most successful in Ulster. Scottish tenants and laborers, themselves displaced by the English but too polite to mention it, joined the rag-tag mix of adventurers, ne'er-do-wells, and ex-soldiers. The northern part of the settlement project was known as the **Ulster Plantation.** In 1641, a loose-knit group of Gaelic-Irish chiefs led the now landless Irish in a revolt in Ulster.

Owen Roe O'Neill returned from the Continent to lead the insurrection, Rome's blessing in hand. The rebels advanced south and in 1642 formed the **Confederation of Kilkenny,** an uneasy alliance between the Church and Irish and Old English lords. Some English lords believed they were rebelling against a treasonous viceroy but remaining loyal to the King, and the concurrent English Civil War just made a *really* big mess of things. **Oliver Cromwell's** victory in England made the negotiations between King and Confederation something of a moot point. After a celebratory glass of sparkling white wine, Ollie and his Puritan army turned to Ireland.

Following standard Cromwellian procedure, the Lord Protectorate destroyed anything he did not occupy, and then some. Catholics were massacred and whole towns razed. Entire tracts of land were confiscated, gift-wrapped, and handed out to soldiers and Protestant vagabonds. Native Irish landowners were presented with the option of going **"to Hell or to Connacht,"** both desolate and infertile, one with a slightly more tropical climate. By 1660, the vast majority of Irish land was owned, maintained, and policed by Protestant immigrants. After sending naughty Oliver to his room, Restored King Charles II passed the 1665 **Act of Explanation.** The Act required Protestants to relinquish one-third of their land to the "innocent papists." The Catholics did not hold their breath for this to happen.

THE ASCENDANCY (1688-1801)

Thirty years after the Civil War, English political disruption again resulted in Irish bloodshed. In 1688, Catholic **James II,** driven from England by Protestant William of Orange and his Glorious Revolution, came to Ireland to gather military support and reclaim his throne. Irish Jacobites began bashing Williamites whenever the opportunity presented itself. This was fine with the Williamites, who had made their own decision to beat up Jacobites any chance they got. James tried to take Derry in 1689, but a rascally band of **Apprentice Boys** closed the gates on him and started the 105-day **Siege of Derry** (see p. 530). William ended the war and sent his rival into exile on July 12, 1690, at the **Battle of the Boyne.** Northern Protestants still celebrate the victory on July 12 (called **Orange Day** in honor of King Billy; for more on **"the silly season,"** see **Northern Ireland,** p. 452). The war was concluded with the **Treaty of Limerick,** which ambiguously guaranteed the defeated their civil rights. "Ambiguously" meaning that, at the turn of the 18th century, a set of **Penal Laws** were enacted for the purposes of further oppression, banning (among other things) the practice of Catholicism.

In Dublin and the Pale, Anglo-Irish muckedy-mucks garden-partied, gossiped, and architectured their way into creating a second London. The term **"Ascendancy"** was coined just for them; it described a social elite whose elitehood depended upon Anglicanism. **Trinity College** was the quintessential institution of these Ascended Protestants. Cultural ties notwithstanding, many aristocrats felt little political allegiance to England. **Jonathan Swift** pamphleteered on behalf of both the Protestant Church and the Irish masses. Meanwhile, displaced peasants filled Dublin's poor quarters, creating the horrific slums that led to his "Modest Proposal" (see **Wit & Resistance,** p. 71).

Away from the Protestants and their Ascended nonsense, the Catholic merchant class grew in cites like Galway and Tralee. Early 18th-century Catholics practiced their religion furtively, using large, flat rocks (dubbed **Mass rocks**) when they couldn't get their hands on an altar. Denied official education, Gaelic teens learned literature and religion in secret **hedge schools,** whose teachers who were often fugitive priests. Meanwhile, secret agrarian societies, like the **Defenders,** formed to protect peasants against Protestant landlords and their brutal rents.

1695
Penal Laws make life miserable for Catholics.

1713
Jonathan Swift becomes Dean of St. Patrick's Cathedral in Dublin.

1744
Edmund Burke, the son of a Protestant Dublin solicitor and a Roman Catholic mother, enters Trinity College.

Early 1700s
Catholics practice their religion in hiding on Mass rocks. Catholic youngsters educated in underground "hedge schools."

REBELLION & UNION (1775-1848)

The Irish were not immune to the highfalutin' notions of independence that emerged from the American and French Revolutions. The *liberté*-fever was particularly strong among the **United Irishmen,** which had begun as a radical Protestant Ulster debating society. (That's no typo; the major rebels against the English at this time were in fact Protestant.) Although outlawed, the United Irishmen reorganized themselves as a secret society. Their leader, **Theobald Wolfe Tone,** hoped that a general rebellion would create an independent, non-sectarian Ireland. To this end, he admitted Catholics among the ranks of the United Irishmen. The bloody **Rebellion of 1798** erupted with a furious band of peasants and priests, and ended with their last stand at **Vinegar Hill,** near Enniscorthy in Co. Wexford (see p. 199). Always looking for an excuse to tussle with the Brits, French troops arrived and managed to hold their ground for about a month before being utterly destroyed. The Irish rebels, as they were led to the gallows, thanked them for trying anyway.

Any hopes England had held of making Irish society less volatile by relaxing anti-Catholic laws were canceled by such rebellious misbehavior. With the 1801 **Act of Union,** the Crown abolished Irish "self-government" altogether. The Dublin Parliament died and "The United Kingdom of Great Britain and Ireland" was born. The Church of Ireland entered into an unequal arranged marriage, changing her name to the "United Church of England and Ireland." Noble Wolfe Tone committed suicide in captivity, and other United Irishmen escaped to France.

The carnage continued. Dublin's mad gaiety vanished, the Anglo-Irish gentry collapsed, and agrarian violence and poverty escalated. Meanwhile, the Napoleonic Wars raged in Europe, and many feared that Monsieur Bonaparte would notice the little green island in the Atlantic. Paranoid generals constructed squatty structures along the coast called **Martello towers.**

1775-1789
The American and French Revolutions foment Irish unrest.

1798
The bloody, unsuccessful, but very heroic Rebellion of 1798.

1801
The Act of Union: British dissolve the Irish Parliament and create "the United Kingdom of Great Britain and Ireland."

LIFE AND TIMES

1803
Robert Emmett is hanged for organizing a rising against the British.

1829
Daniel "The Liberator" O'Connell is elected and Catholics finally allowed to sit in Parliament.

1841
Population of Ireland over 8 million.

1845-1847
Potato and other crops fall prey to a fungal disease.

1847-1851
The Great Famine: 2 to 3 million people die, another million emigrate. Social structure of Ireland completely revamped.

1849-1899
The British began to remove the Irish landlords from their properties.

1858
Irish Republican Brotherhood (IRB), a.k.a the Fenians, founded.

1868
William Gladstone elected as British Prime Minister; continues land reform

Union meant Irish representatives now held seats in the British Parliament. Thanks to a delightful set of electoral reforms, Catholic farmers found that they too could go to the polls. With their newfound suffrage they elected Catholic **Daniel O'Connell** in 1829, forcing Westminster to repeal the remaining anti-Catholic laws that would have barred him from taking his seat. "The Liberator" promptly forced Parliament to allot money for improving Irish living conditions, health care, and trade. When unsympathetic Tories took power, O'Connell convened huge rallies in Ireland, showing popular support for repealing the Act of Union. From this political enthusiasm arose unprecedented social reform.

THE FAMINE (1845-1870)

In the first half of the 19th century, the potato was the wondercrop of the rapidly growing Irish population. This reliance had devastating effects when the heroic spud fell victim to an evil fungal disease. During the years of the **Great Famine** (1847-51), an estimated two to three million people died and another million emigrated to Liverpool, London, Australia, and America on overcrowded boats known as **coffin ships** (see **New Ross,** p. 210). British authorities often forcibly traded inedible grain for what few potatoes peasants could find. The Irish, whose diet was supplemented by delicacies like grass, had little choice but to accept. Hungry Catholics converted to Protestantism in exchange for British soup, earning for themselves and their descendants the disdainful title "Soupers."

After the Famine, the societal structure of surviving Irish peasants completely reorganized itself. The bottom layer of truly penniless farmers had been eliminated altogether. Eldest sons inherited the family farm, while unskilled younger sons often had little choice but to leave the Emerald Isle for greener pastures. Depopulation continued, and **emigration** became an Irish way of life. Fifty years of land legislation converted Ireland, with the exception of Dublin and northeast Ulster, into a nation of conservative, culturally uniform smallholders.

English injustice, functioning like a splash of British Petrol, fueled the formation of more angry young Nationalist groups. In 1858, crusaders for a violent removal of their oppressors founded the Irish Republican Brotherhood (IRB), a secret society known as the **Fenians.** With signs of encouragement from a purportedly sympathetic Parliament, agrarian thinkers and republican Fenians created the **Land League** of the 1870s and pushed for further reforms.

PARNELL AND IRISH NATIONALISM (1870-1914)

In 1870, Member of Parliament **Isaac Butt** founded the **Irish Home Rule Party.** Its several dozen members adopted obstructionist tactics—they made long speeches, introduced amendments, and generally kept the opposing MPs so angry, bored, and ineffective that they would have little choice but to grant Ireland its autonomy. Home Ruler **Charles Stewart Parnell** was a charismatic Protestant aristocrat with a hatred for everything English. Backed by Parnell's invigorated Irish party, British Prime Minister **William Gladstone** introduced an ill-fated **Home Rule Bill.** Despite surviving implication in the **Phoenix Park murders** (see p. 119; we *told* you we didn't recommend camping there), Parnell couldn't beat an adultery rap. In 1890, allegations that he was having an extra-marital affair were confirmed. The scandal split Ireland into Parnellites and anti-Parnellites.

While politicians, bickering over whether he did or did not have sexual relations with "that woman," let their ideals fall by the wayside, civil society waxed ambitious. Following the lead of their British and American sisters, the fairer sex established the **Irish Women's Suffrage Federation** in 1911. Marxist **James Connolly** led strikes in Belfast, and Dubliner **James Larkin** spearheaded an enormous general strike in 1913. Conservatives, attempting to "kill Home Rule by kindness," also pushed for (that is, vaguely in the general direction of) social reform.

Meanwhile, various groups tried to revive an essential "Gaelic" culture, unpolluted by foreign influence. The **Gaelic Athletic Association** (see **Sports,** p. 77) attempted to replace English sports with hurling, camogie, and Gaelic football. The **Gaelic League** spread the use of the Irish language (see **The Revival,** p. 70). Culture was not only trendy, but a politically viable weapon—the Fenians seized the opportunity to disseminate their ideas and became the movers and shakers in Gaelic organizations. Arthur Griffith began a tiny movement and a little-read newspaper advocating Irish abstention from British politics, both of which went by the name **Sinn Féin** (SHIN FAYN, "Ourselves Alone"). Equal and opposite reactions led thousands of Northern Protestants who opposed Home Rule to join mass rallies, sign a covenant, and organize a quasi-militia called the **Ulster Volunteer Force (UVF).** Nationalists led by **Eoin MacNeill** in Dublin responded by creating the **Irish Volunteers,** which the Fenians correctly saw as a potentially revolutionary force.

THE EASTER RISING (1914-1918)

Summer 1914: Irish Home Rule seemed imminent, and Ulster was ready to go up in flames. As it turned out, someone shot an archduke, and the world went up in flames. British PM Henry Asquith passed a **Home Rule Bill** in return for some Irish bodies to fill trenches for the British army. A **Suspensory Act** followed, delaying home rule until peace returned to Ulster; meanwhile, 670,000 Irishmen signed up to fight the Kaiser.

An 11,000-member armed guard, the remnants of the Volunteers, remained at home. They were officially led by Eoin MacNeill, who knew nothing of the revolt that the Fenians were brewing. If an architect could be ascribed to the ensuing mayhem, it would be poet and schoolteacher **Padraig Pearse,** who won his co-conspirators over to an ideology of "blood sacrifice"—the notion that if a small cache of committed men died public martyrs' deaths, then the island's entire population would join in the struggle for independence.

1870
Isaac Butt founds the Irish Home Rule Party and seeks to disrupt parliamentary procedure.

1880
Gladstone and Parnell's Home Rule Bill is defeated.

1884
The Gaelic Athletic Association founded.

1890
Parnell scandal divides the Home Rule contingent.

1893
Gaelic League founded to reinvigorate the Irish language.

1905
Arthur Griffith forms Sinn Féin.

1911
Women's Suffrage movement established.

1910-1913
Northern Protestants commence mass rallies to protest Home Rule.

1913
Dublin general strike

1913
Nationalist Irish Volunteers founded. Unionist Ulster Volunteers founded.

1914
Home Rule Bill passed with an amendment excluding Ulster. 770,000 Irishmen enlist to fight with the Allies in WWI.

1915-1916
The Irish Volunteers and the Fenians prepare for the Easter Rising.

1916
Easter Rising begins a day late in Dublin. The insurrection fails and its leaders are executed right into martyrdom.

1917
Sinn Féin is reorganized under Éamon de Valera as a national movement fighting for Irish independence

1917
The Irish Volunteers reorganize under Fenian Michael Collins.

1918
The Irish public turns to Sinn Féin to resist British plans for Irish conscription.

1919
Ireland fights for its Independence.

1920
The first Black and Tans recruited. Government of Ireland Act is passed, dividing Northern Ireland from the rest of the island.

The Volunteers conducted a series of unarmed maneuvers and parades in an effort to convince the Dublin government of their harmlessness. Meanwhile, Fenian leaders were plotting to receive a shipment of German arms for use in a nationwide revolt on **Easter Sunday 1916.** However, the arms arrived early (chalk it up to German efficiency) and were never picked up. Unsuspecting Fenian leaders continued planning their rebellion; they attempted to coerce MacNeill, who gave orders for Volunteer mobilization on Easter Sunday. On that Saturday he learned that he had been manipulated by a weaponless bunch of brigands. Putting his trust in mass media, he inserted a plea into the Sunday papers asking all Volunteers to forego the rebellion and stay home.

Although MacNeill and most Fenian leaders had been thinking in terms of military success, Pearse's followers wanted martyrdom. On Sunday, the group met and rescheduled their uprising shindig for the following Monday, April 24. Pearse, James Connolly, and about a thousand of their closest friends seized the **General Post Office** on O'Connell St. (see p. 117), read aloud a "Proclamation of the Republic of Ireland," and hunkered down for five days of brawling in the streets of Dublin. As their only tangible accomplishment was massive property damage, the rebels were initially seen as criminals in the eyes of most Dubliners.

The Crown retaliated with swift, vindictive punishments—in May, 15 "ringleaders" received the death sentence. Among the executed were Pearse, Pearse's brother (whose primary crime was being Pearse's brother), and James Connolly, who was shot while tied to a chair because his wounds prevented him from standing. **Éamon de Valera** was spared when the Crown discovered he was American.

The British, with their hasty martial law, proved Pearse a true prophet—the public grew increasingly anti-British and sympathetic to the rebels. Wicklow's **Kilmainham Gaol** (see p. 116), the site of the executions, became a shrine of martyrdom. Everything was falling together: the Volunteers reorganized under master spy and Fenian bigwig **Michael Collins,** and the Sinn Féin party became the political voice of military Nationalism. Collins brought the Volunteers to Sinn Féin, and Éamon "Don't Call Me Yankee" de Valera became the party president. In 1918, misjudging popular sentiment yet again, the British tried to introduce a military draft in Ireland and the Irish lost what little complacency they had left.

INDEPENDENCE AND CIVIL WAR (1919-1922)

Extremist Irish Volunteers became Sinn Féin's military might and started calling themselves the **Irish Republican Army (IRA).** Thus the British saw another, though not their last, **War for Independence** (all in an Imperialist power's day's work). The Crown reinforced its police with brutal **Black and Tans**—demobilized soldiers nicknamed for their patched-together uniforms. In 1920, British Prime Minister **David Lloyd George** passed the **Government of Ireland Act,** which divided the island into Northern

Ireland and Southern Ireland, two partially self-governing areas within the United Kingdom. Pressed by a newly elected Parliament, George conducted hurried negotiations with de Valera and produced the **Anglo-Irish Treaty,** creating a 26-county Irish Free State but recognizing British rule over the northern counties. The treaty imposed on Irish officials an oath of allegiance to the Crown, but not to the British government. Resourceful Lloyd George pushed the treaty through with the threat of war.

Sinn Féin, the IRA, and the population all split on whether to accept the treaty. Collins said yes; de Valera said no. Parliament said yes, and de Valera said "Fine, then I don't wanna be President anymore." Arthur Griffith said he'd assume the position. Amid this and other sayings, the capable Collins government began the business of setting up a nation. A portion of the IRA, led by **General Rory O'Connor,** opposed the treaty; these nay-sayers occupied the Four Courts in Dublin, took a pro-treaty army general hostage, and were attacked by the forces of Collins's government. Two years of **civil war** followed. Skipping all the ugly details: the pro-treaty government won, Griffith died from the strain of the struggle, Collins was assassinated (see **Clonakilty,** p. 244), and the dwindling minority of anti-treaty IRA officers went into hiding. Sinn Féin denied the legitimacy of the Free State government and expressed their disapproval by referring to the Republic as "the 26-county state" or "the Dublin Government," rather than the official "Éire."

THE ERA DE VALERA (1922-1960)

Éire emerged from its civil war looking quite a bit worse for the wear—it had lost its most prominent leaders and frankly felt a little underdressed without them. The Anglo-Irish Treaty required a constitution by December 6, 1922. With time running out, **W.T. Cosgrave** was elected prime minister and passed a hasty preliminary constitution. Under the guidance of **Éamon de Valera,** the government ended armed resistance by Republican insurgents, executed 77 of them, and imprisoned several more. Cosgrave and his party **Cumann na nGaedheal** (which evolved into today's **Fine Gael**) headed the first stable Free State administration. His government restored civil order, granted suffrage to women in 1923, and brought **electrical power** (yee-haw) to much of western Ireland. In the Republic's first elections, the anti-treaty voters supported abstentionist Sinn Féin. Then, in 1927, de Valera broke with Sinn Féin and the IRA and founded his own political party, **Fianna Fáil,** in order to both participate in government and oppose the treaty non-violently. Fianna Fáil won the 1932 election, and de Valera held power for much of the next 20 years. In line with the vision of Ireland as a small nation of small farmers, Fianna Fáil broke up the remaining large landholdings and imposed high tariffs, instigating a trade war with Britain that battered the Irish economy until 1938. Meanwhile, IRA hard-liners trickled out of jails, resumed violence, and saw their party outlawed in 1936.

1921
The Anglo-Irish Treaty produces the 26-county Free State of Ireland. The British retain control of the six Northern counties.

1922
Arthur Griffith is elected President and begins makin' a nation.

1922-1923
The Irish Civil War.

1922
A first constitution is framed for the Irish Free State.

1923
de Valera's government squelches Republican insurgents and ends armed resistance to the Irish State.

1923-1932
Cosgrave rules, granting women's suffrage and bringing electricity to the West.

1927
de Valera splits with Sinn Féin and establishes Fianna Fáil.

1936
The IRA is outlawed.

1937
The Irish Constitution is ratified. The official name of the country is changed to Éire.

1939
The IRA begin its bombing campaign in England.

1939
Britain enters WWII; Ireland maintains "neutrality" throughout "The Emergency."

1948
An intermittently Fine Gael government declares the Republic of Ireland and ends Irish membership in the British Commonwealth. Hoo-ah!

1949
Britain recognizes the Republic but decides to maintain control over Northern Ireland.

1955
The Republic is admitted to the United Nations.

1969
"Troubles" and clashes intensify in Northern Ireland. Protestants launch siege of Catholic Bogside neighborhood in Derry. For more information on Northern Ireland, see p. 452

1973
Ireland enters the European Economic Community. Secularization of Irish society marches forward.

1983
Abortion is reaffirmed as national policy by way of public referendum

In 1937 and "in the name of the most Holy Trinity," de Valera and the voters approved the permanent Irish Constitution. It declares the state's name to be Éire and establishes the country's legislative structure, consisting of two chambers. The **Dáil** (DAHL), or big, bad, lower house, is composed of 166 seats directly elected in proportional representation. The second-banana upper house, or **Seanad** (SHA-nud), has 60 members chosen by electoral colleges. The Prime Minister is the **Taoiseach** (TEE-shuch), and he calls his deputy **Tánaiste** (tah-NESH-tuh). They lead a Cabinet (CAB-in-et). The **President** is the ceremonial head of state, elected to a seven-year term.

Ireland stayed neutral during WWII (known as **The Emergency**), though many Irish citizens identified with the Allies and around 50,000 served in the British army. This may have had something to do with the fact that Hitler was bombing Dublin, though we don't want to jump to any conclusions. While the young government lacked the monetary and military strength to make much difference on the Front, Éire's brand of neutrality didn't exactly hinder the Allies. For example, downed American or British airmen were shipped north to non-neutral Belfast; German pilots were detained in P.O.W. camps.

In 1948, a Fine Gael government under **John Costello** had the honor of officially proclaiming "the Republic of Ireland" free, thus ending British Commonwealth membership altogether. Britain, who didn't quite catch all that, recognized the Republic a year later. They declared (harumph) that the UK would maintain control over Ulster until the Parliament of Northern Ireland consented to join the Republic.

The last de Valera government (1951-59), and its successor, under **Sean Lemass,** boosted the Irish economy by ditching protectionism in favor of attracting foreign investment. Instead of the verbal and military skirmishes over constitutional issues that dominated the 20s, Irish politics became a contest between the ideologically similar Fianna Fáil and Fine Gael parties.

IRELAND TODAY

Ireland's post-war boom, ushered in with the efforts of Lemass, didn't arrive until the early 1960s. Economic mismanagement and poor governmental policies kept the boom short. By the early 1970s, Ireland was on its way back down again. In an effort to revitalize the nation, Ireland entered the European Economic Community, now the **European Union** (**EU**), in 1973. EU membership and an increased number of international visitors spurred by the creation of **Bord Fáilte** helped introduce the slow, painful process of secularization. **Garret FitzGerald** revamped Fine Gael under a secular banner and alternated Prime Ministership with Fianna Fáil's **Charlie Haughey** throughout the late 70s and early 80s. EU funds proved crucial to helping Ireland out of a severe mid-80s recession and reducing its dependence on the UK. In 1985, FitzGerald signed the **Anglo-Irish agreement,** which let Éire stick an official nose into Northern negotiations.

The Irish broke progressive social and political ground in 1990 by choosing **Mary Robinson,** of the female persuasion, as their President. Formerly a progressive barrister who had championed the rights of single mothers and gays, Robinson fought vigorously to overcome international (and local) evaluations of the Irish as conservative cronies. In 1993, the age of consent between gay men was lowered to 17, and in 1995, a national referendum finally made divorce legal in the Republic. When fair Mary was appointed the United Nation's High Commissioner for Human Rights in 1997, she was replaced by **Mary McAleese.** Irish men across the country stood up and cried out in unison - "huh?" Irish women replied—"ha!"

Robinson's small, leftist **Labour Party** enjoyed enormous, unexpected success, paving the way for further, even more harebrained, social reform. In 1993, Taoiseach **Albert Reynolds** declared his top priority was to stop violence in Northern Ireland. A year later he announced a cease-fire agreement between Sinn Féin and the IRA. In spite of his miracle-working in the North, Reynolds was forced to resign following a scandal involving his appointee for President of the High Court. His choice, Attorney General **Harry Whelehan,** had been heavily criticized for his lack of action in a case involving a pedophilic priest, **Father Brendan Smyth.** During the week following Whelehan's appointment, Fine Gael, led by **John Bruton,** introduced a no-confidence motion against the government. After Reynold's resignation, the Labour Party formed a coalition with Fine Gael, with Bruton as Taoiseach.

In June 1997, Fianna Fáil won the general election, making **Bertie Ahern,** at a spring-chickenish 45, the youngest Taoiseach in Irish history. Ahern joined the peace talks that produced the **Good Friday Peace Agreement** in April of 1998 (see p. 458). On May 22, 1998, in the first island-wide election since 1918, an overwhelming 94% of voters in the Republic voted for the enactment of the Agreement. (For the recent status of the Good Friday Agreement, see p. 458.)

In the summer of 2001, the Irish populace trickled out to the polls and defeated the **Nice Treaty.** The Treaty was the first step in the addition of 12 eastern European nations to the European Union. The result of the referendum shocked Ireland's pro-Treaty government and caused quite a stir on the continent. In other European Union related news, the **euro** was formally introduced into Ireland on January 1, 2002 (see **The Euro,** p. 11). The Irish pound, the punt, has since gotten the boot.

With the money Ireland has garnered from the European Union over the years (in 1992 alone they received **6 million dollars** for agreeing to sign onto the Maastrict Treaty); with increased foreign investment and the establishing of Ireland as a center for computer software development; and with a thriving tourism industry bringing millions of dollars into Ireland yearly, the Irish economy is thriving like never before. According to a 1999 report, the unemployment rate should be reduced to three percent by the year 2005. With each boom comes a bust, however, and with the introduction of the euro, and waning foreign investment, many fear the roar of the **Celtic Tiger** will soon be reduced to a Celtic Kitty purr.

1985
The Republic gains an official place in Northern Ireland negotiations.

1990
Mary Robinson is elected President. And she's a *girl.*

1993
Conservative Ireland goes liberal and lowers the age of consent for gay men to just 17.

1994
Peace-minded President Reynolds is forced to step down over Church scandals.

1995
Divorce is legalized in Ireland.

1997
Bertie Ahern is Prime Minister–the youngest ever.

1998
The Good Friday Peace begins in the North.

2002
The Euro is introduced to Ireland and the punt is phased out.

THE IRISH

> The Irish...have one of the most vivid public images in the world, though a remarkably self-contradictory one. They are seen as...genial and aggressive, witty and thick-headed, quick and slow, eloquent and blundering, laid back and hot tempered...lying and loyal. So either they're schizoid, or they defy the laws of logic.
>
> —Terry Eagleton, *The Truth About the Irish*

DEMOGRAPHICS

Recent estimates put the Republic of Ireland's population at around 3.8 million—with over 35% living within 60mi. of Dublin—and Northern Ireland's at approximately 1.7 million. Over 50% of Ireland's population is under 25 while 73% of them own mobile phones. The birthrate in Ireland is one of the highest in Europe, with 14.6 births per thousand in 2000. However, rates are expected to drop slightly as Irish couples have recently begun to wait longer before having children.

The demographic composition of Ireland is often described as generally monoracial, but the recent economic growth and prosperity of the "Celtic Tiger" has inspired unprecedented immigration to Ireland. This influx, a happy reverse of the historic emigration of the Irish people, includes, among others, the return of Irish citizens, foreigners in search of jobs, and refugees seeking asylum. Because of the limited diversity at present, racial strife remains negligible, especially when compared to the more diverse urban areas of the United Kingdom.

Though Britain itself may boast a multi-racial population, the demographic make-up of Northern Ireland more closely resembles that of the Republic. Historically and presently, the most pervading cultural distinctions and disagreements in the Republic, and especially in Northern Ireland, have been between people of different creeds (Protestants and Catholics, Republicans and Loyalists), not color.

RELIGION

The Republic of Ireland is blessed with a population over 92% Catholic, making it one of the most Christian countries in the world. But the emergence of Catholicism didn't begin until St. Patrick's arrival some 1500 years ago. Before the coming of St. Paddy, the island was overwhelmed with heathen hordes, or Celts. The Celts were a very religious, though pagan, people, who worshipped a number of natural gods. When Christianity arrived in the 5th century, the Celts readily adopted the new faith; by incorporating Celtic pagan beliefs into the Chrisitan religion (Halloween is an old pagan Irish holiday), St. Paddy and his followers were able to capture the country for Jesus.

Fully converted, Catholicism has since become a cult in Ireland, nay, a religion. Until recently, church and state were one in the same. Though divorce has since been legalized, abortion is still outlawed in the Republic. Public schools have mandatory religion classes and Sunday mass is a family event (often followed up by a pint in the pub), enjoyed, not mourned, by parishioners. The importance of Catholicism to the lives of the Irish is further demonstrated by the respect garnered by the local parish priests (who often spring for parishioners in the pub after services). Though Catholicism is certainly the religion of choice on the isle, small Jewish and Buddhist populations can be found in the cities.

The ties between religion, politics, and culture, are more intertwined in the north. Northern Ireland's primary religions are Catholicism and Protestantism. Though Protestants have a slightly larger population, it is predicted that due to the higher birth rates of Catholics in the country, Catholics will outnumber Protestants within a couple of decades.

Though the troubles in the North are often attributed to religious disagreement, the contemporary problem is more an issue of nationalism, not religion. Fighting in the North often erupts between Catholics and Protestants, especially during the summer months, but religion is not the cause. Rather, Protestants, descended from the English imported to Ireland over the years, more often than not claim loyalty to England (Loyalists), while Catholics, more likely to be descended from the Irish masses abused by the English over the years, claim loyalty to the Republic (Republicans). Fighting usually erupts over one's loyalty to country, not savior.

LANGUAGE

The English language came to Ireland with the Normans in the 12th Century. Since this time it has become the primary language spoken in Ireland, but like many things British, the Irish have molded the language to make it their own. The Irish accent, or "lilt", differs from county to county. In the southern and western counties, bring a notebook for communication, as the accent is often so thick and guttural that visitors sometimes find it hard to understand conversations. In Dublin, and in the North expect clearer pronunciation and a sing-song style of conversing.

Because English is so commonly spoken in Ireland, the strong linguistic history of the Irish language is often unknown or unseen by the average traveler. Though the constitution declares Irish the national language of the Republic, there are only 86,000 individuals in the exclusively Irish-speaking community, or **gaeltacht** (GAYL-tacht). The larger *gaeltacht* is composed of small settlements scattered about the most remote regions of the island. The most prominent of these are located in Connemara (see p. 361), in patches of Co. Donegal (p. 426), on the Dingle Peninsula (p. 257), Cape Clear Island (p. 249), and in the Aran Islands (p. 351). These geographically disparate communities are further divided by three different dialects: Ulster, Connacht, and Munster Irish.

The Irish government continues efforts to preserve and promote modern Irish; Irish citizens are required to take *Gaelige* throughout their educational experience. A Connemara-based Irish radio station and a new Irish language television station, *Telifís na Gaelige* (T na G [TEE NUH JEE] to locals), expand Irish-hearing opportunities. Peruse the **Glossary** (p. 559) for useful Irish words and phrases.

IRISH CULTURE

I was blue mouldy for the want of that pint. Declare to God
I could hear it hit the pit of my stomach with a click.
—James Joyce, *Ulysses* (1922)

MEAT AND POTATOES

Irish food can be fairly expensive, especially in cities and in restaurants. The basics—and that's what you'll get—are simple and filling. The restaurant business is a fairly recent phenomenon in Ireland; up until the economy took off about 20 years ago, only a few restaurants graced even the streets of Dublin. Today, eateries clutter Ireland's mini-metropoli, many of which specialize in international fare. The rural byways of the island remain limited in their culinary offerings. Quick and greasy staples are **chippers** (fish n' chip shops) and **takeaways** (takeout joints). At chippers, "fish" is a whitefish, usually cod, and chips are served with salt and vinegar; ketchup sometimes costs extra. Fried food delicacies include chips with gravy, potato cakes (pancakes made of potato flakes), or the infamous spiceburger (fried patty of spiced breadcrumbs). Most pubs serve food, and **pub grub** is a good option for a cheap but substantial meal. Typical pub grub includes Irish stew (meat, potatoes, carrots, and onions), burgers, soup, and sandwiches.

Most Irish meals are based on a simple formula: meat, potatoes, greens, and more meat. *Colcannon* (a potato, onion, and cabbage dish), "ploughman's lunch," and Irish stew are Irish specialties. Loud and long will Irish bards sing the praises of the Clonakilty man who first concocted **black pudding.** This delicacy was invented during a shortage and makes the most of the bits of the pig not usually eaten. Black pudding is, as one local butcher put it, "some pork, a good deal of blood, and grains and things—all wrapped up in a tube." White pudding is a similar dish that uses milk instead of blood. **Irish breakfasts,** often served all day and a given at any B&B, include eggs, sausage, white or black pudding, **rashers** (similar to thick American bacon), a fried tomato, brown bread, and toast.

The true culinary strength of the Irish is their bread. Most famous is **soda bread:** heavy, white, sweetened by raisins, and especially yummy when fried. Most common are **brown bread** and **batch loaves.** The brown stuff is thick and grainy, while batch loaves are square-shaped, white, and ideal for sandwiches. Another indigenous bread is **barm brack;** perfect for holidays, it is a spicy mixture of dried fruits and molasses mixed to a lead-like density. Sandwiches are often served on a **bap,** a round, white bun. All of these breads are excellent in combination with locally produced cheeses.

TURLOUGH'S IRISH SODA BREAD

Dry Ingredients

2½ cups coarse brown flour
1 cup white flour
¼ cup rolled oats
¼ cup bran
2 tsp. baking soda (NO clumps!)

Wet Ingredients

¼ cup vinegar
2 cups milk
1 Guinness beer

Directions:

Preheat oven to 400°F. Mix dry ingredients well (the baking soda needs to be well-distributed). Add wet ingredients, except Guinness, and mix through to the bottom. Pour mixture into a greased, regular-sized bread-pan. Open Guinness and enjoy your reward as you wait 40 minutes for your bread to bake!

Seafood can be a real bargain in smaller towns; mussels and oysters are delectable, as is anything marinated in Guinness. In addition to the widespread fried fish, smoked mackerel is splendid year-round, and Atlantic salmon is freshest in July. Regional specialties include **crubeen** (pigs' feet) in Cork, **coddle** (sausages and bacon with potatoes) in Dublin, and **blaa** (sausage rolls) in Waterford. **Coffee** is gaining ground in its rivalry with **tea** for the standard washer-down of unwanted cabbage.

In the North, an Irish Breakfast is called an **Ulster Fry.** Aside from terminology, Northern food is much the same as in the Republic.

GUINNESS AND CRAIC

A 1998 study found that Irish students spend roughly €100 a month on drinks, which is no wonder considering the centrality of pubs in Irish culture. More so in the Republic than in the North, the pub is, in a sense, the living room of the Irish household. Locals of all ages from every social milieu head to the public house for conversation, food, singing, and ***craic*** (crack), an Irish word meaning "a good time." In the evening, some pubs host traditional music. Local and traveling musicians toting fiddles, guitars, and *bodhráns* drop in about 9:30pm to start impromptu sessions (see **Music,** p. 74). In rural pubs, there's also a chance that a *seanachaí (*SHAN-ukh-ee, a storyteller), might make an appearance. Before hitting the street, you should learn the ground rules (see **Pub Ground Rules,** p. 69).

Cocktails are an oddity found mainly in American-style bars and discos. In Ireland, expect **beer,** and not much else. Beer comes in two basic varieties, **lagers** (blond,

PUB GROUND RULES **Pubs in the Republic** are generally open Monday through Saturday from 10:30am to 11:30pm (11pm in winter) and Sunday from 12:30 to 2pm and 4 to 11pm (closed 2-4pm for the Holy hour). Late-hours licenses, becoming increasingly common in Dublin, allow some pubs to stay open until somewhere between midnight and 2am. Some pubs, especially ones catering to a clientele of fishermen, have been granted special "early" licenses, requiring an act of Parliament to revoke, which allow them to open at 7:30am. Pubs almost never charge a cover or require a drink minimum. **Pubs in the North** tend to be open Monday through Saturday from 11:30am to 11pm (or recently until 1 or 2am on the weekends since the Troubles have calmed) and Sunday from 12:30 to 2:30pm and 7 to 10pm. Some rural pubs close for a few hours on weekday afternoons as well. Pub lunches are usually served Monday to Saturday from 12:30 to 2:30pm, while soup, soda bread, and sandwiches are served all day. Children are often not allowed in pubs after 7pm. The legal drinking age in Ireland and Northern Ireland is 18.

fizzy brews served cold, a bit weaker than ales or stouts) and **ales** (slightly darker, more bitter, and sometimes served warmer than lagers). **Stout,** a type of ale, is thick, dark-ruby colored, and made from roasted barley to impart an almost meaty flavor. **Guinness** stout inspires a reverence otherwise reserved for the Holy Trinity. Known variously as "the dark stuff," "the blonde in the black skirt," or simply "I'll have a pint, please," it's a rich, dark brew with a head thick enough to stand a match in. For a sweeter taste, try it with blackcurrant or cider. **Murphy's,** brewed in Cork, is a similar, slightly creamier stout. Cork also produces **Beamish,** a tasty "economy" stout (read: cheap date drink). Stout takes a while to pour properly (usually 3-4min.); it should be drunk in slow measure as well, and never before it settles. **Smithwicks** is a hoppy, English-style bitter commonly perceived as an old man's drink. Two more popular domestic lagers are **Kilkenny** and **Harp.** You may be surprised by the many pubs serving Budweiser or Heineken and by the number of young people quaffing such imported lagers. In general, the indigenous brews are far worthier. Beer is served in **pint glasses** (20 oz.) or half-pints (called a "glass"). Ordering a beer by name will bring you a full pint, so be loud and clear if you can only stay for a half (or just take the pint and drink faster). A pint of Guinness usually costs about €4 in the Republic and about UK£3 in the North, with prices rising in urban settings.

Life in Ireland is tough. When beer doesn't cut it, the Irish quickly turn to the hard stuff for support. **Irish whiskey,** which Queen Elizabeth once claimed was her only true Irish friend, is sweeter than its Scotch counterpart, spelled "whisky" (see p. 237). In Ireland, whiskey is served in larger measures than you might be used to. **Jameson** is popular everywhere. Dubliners are partial to **Powers and Sons. Bushmills,** distilled near Portstewart, is the favorite in the North. Drinkers in Cork enjoy **Paddy's. Irish coffee** is sweetened with brown sugar and whipped cream and laced with whiskey. It's been more popular with the tourists than the natives ever since its alleged invention at Shannon Airport by a desperate bartender looking to appease cranky travelers on a layover. **Hot whiskey** (spiced up with lemon, cloves, and brown sugar) can provide a cozy buzz. In the west, you may hear some locals praise "mountain dew," a euphemism for ***poitín*** (put-CHEEN), an illegal distillation sometimes given to cows in labor that ranges in strength from 115 to 140 proof (see **Love Poitín #9,** p. 416). *Poitín* makes after-hour appearances in pubs throughout the island, but be warned that *poitín* is a highly toxic substance. While most alcoholic drinks are based on ethanol, *poitín* uses lethal methanol. *Let's Go* generally does not recommend drinking methanol.

CUSTOMS AND ETIQUETTE

Like in any other country, a set of culturally specific customs dictate how the Irish interact with one another. Those unfamiliar with these customs run the risk of accidently insulting locals. Some important customs include the following:

JUMPING THE QUEUE. In Ireland, when the occasion calls, people usually form orderly lines, or 'queues.' When people line up to get on a bus, enter a theater, or what have you, the 'queue' that forms is usually considered quite sacred. To 'jump the queue'—to ignore the order of the line and push your way to the front—will earn you disapproving stares, and often, verbal confrontations.

FLIPPING THE BIRD(S). Another easy way to anger the locals is to flip someone the fingers. Yes, fingers. While people in other countries usually flip only their middle finger when letting friends know what they really think, the Irish flip both their middle finger and their index finger, forming a V shape. Flipping the birds is only insulting when you position your hand so that the palm is facing inward; if the palm is facing outward, you've just said 'peace'—you damned hippy.

BUYING THE ROUND. Ordering at an Irish pub can become a complex affair. Rather than buying individual drinks, when in a small group, one individual will usually approach the bar and buy a round of drinks for everyone. Once those drinks are downed, another individual will buy the next round. This continues until everyone has bought a round. Don't order a whiskey when someone else is buying a round and order a half-pint of something cheap when you're buying. And don't think no one will notice if you forget to buy a round. Though they might not comment on it, everybody notices everything and nobody forgets anything. It's also considered extremely poor form to refuse someone's offer to buy you a drink.

CHASING THE RAINBOW. What may be funny in one culture can be terribly annoying in another. Try to avoid jokes or references to leprechauns, Lucky Charms, pots of gold, and the 'wee' people. Such comments will not earn you any friends at the local pub. Abortion, divorce, gay marriages, and the Troubles up North, likewise, do not make for casual conversation; these topics are largely avoided in pubs and public places. Discussing these subjects is likely to bring you serious troubles of your own—restrict questions and curiosity for another time.

IRISH LITERARY TRADITIONS

> The old literature of Ireland...has been the chief illumination of my imagination all my life.
> —W.B. Yeats (from a speech to the Irish Senate, 1923)

THE IRISH LANGUAGE

The oldest vernacular literature, and the largest collection of folklore in all of Europe, lies within the Irish language. Irish is a Celtic language that shares its Indo-European origin with Scottish Gaelic and Manx, and more distantly with Breton, Welsh, and Cornish. The Irish language is called *Gaeilge* (GALE-ga) by its speakers; the English word "Gaelic" (GAL-lik) refers to the Scottish language. In 1600, there were as many speakers of Irish worldwide as of English. The Anglophones, however, had more money and better armies; over the next 250 years, Irish became the language of the disenfranchised.

Irish re-entered the lives of the privileged classes with the advent of the Gaelic Revival. In 1893, **Douglas Hyde** (Éire's first President) founded the **Gaelic League** to inspire enthusiasm for Irish among those who didn't speak it. The League aimed to spread the everyday use of Irish as part of a larger project of de-Anglicization. W.B. Yeats and Lady Gregory count among Hyde's admirers; to help the cause, they founded the Abbey Theatre in Dublin for the promotion of Irish playwrights.

LEGENDS AND FOLKTALES

In early Irish society, what the bard (from the Irish *baird*) sang about battles, valor, and lineage was the only record a chieftain had by which to make decisions. Poetry and politics of the Druidic tradition were so intertwined that the *fili*, trained poets, and *breitheamh* (BREH-huv), judges of the Brehon Laws, were often the same people. The poet-patron relationship was as symbiotic in Ireland as anywhere else—the poet bought his lord's favor (and food and shelter) by selling his poetic soul in long praise poems.

In later years, legendary tales were written down for prosperity. The famous **Book of Invasions** (*Leabhar Gabhála*; LOWR GA-vah-lah) is a long-winded record of the pre-Christian cultures and armies that have invaded Ireland. The **Ulster Cycle,** a collection of old Irish folktales, includes the adventures of King Conchobar (Conor) of Ulster and his clan, the **Ulaid.** Conor's archenemy is his ex-wife Queen Medbh (MAVE) of Connacht. Ulster's champion is **Cúchulainn** (coo HOO-lin), the king's nephew and an athlete extraordinare known as the "Hound of Ulster." The central tale of the Ulster Cycle is the **Táin bo Cuailnge** (Cattle Raid of Cooley), in which Queen Medbh decides first to borrow, and then to steal, the most famous bull in the country, the Donn of Cooley.

WIT AND RESISTANCE

After the English dispossessed the Irish chieftains at the Battle of Kinsale (see p. 56), most Irish writers predicted the imminent collapse of Irish language and culture. As the bards of the Irish courts lost their high status, they carried on their work among the peasant classes, so that Ireland developed a vernacular literary culture. Most of the authors writing in Irish at this time lamented their home as a land under cultural attack; a common theme in their poetry is the metaphor of Ireland as a captive woman, like the dark and beautiful "Roisin Dubh" (black rose).

By the 17th century, wit and satire began to characterize the emerging modern Irish literature. In Dublin, **Jonathan Swift** (1667-1745), Dean of St. Patrick's Cathedral, wrote some of the most sophisticated, misanthropic, and marvelous satire in the English language. Like writers throughout the island, Swift felt compelled to address the sad condition of starving Irish peasants. Besides his masterpiece *Gulliver's Travels*, Swift's razor-sharp pamphlets and essays took pot-shots at cruel English lords but still managed to defend the Protestant Church of Ireland.

In the mid-19th century, the Famine hit, and folk culture fell by the wayside in the face of destitution; while the peasants starved, the Industrial Revolution passed Ireland by. Cosmopolitan Dublin managed to breed talent, but gifted young writers traded the Liffey for the Thames in order to make their names. **Oscar Wilde** (1856-1900) moved to, or perhaps created, the high aesthetic culture of London. He wrote many vicious and delightful works, including his best-known play, *The Importance of Being Earnest* (1895). His work critiqued society and propriety while fetishizing it; he challenged Irish clichés and Victorian determinism by perfecting a pithy style whose absurd truths still stand today. Prolific playwright **George Bernard Shaw** (1856-1950) was also born in Dublin but moved to London in 1876, where he became an active socialist. *John Bull's Other Island* (1904) depicts the increasing hardships of the Irish peasant laborer.

THE REVIVAL

Toward the end of the 19th century, a portion of Ireland's crop of young writers no longer turned to London to cultivate their talent. Rather, a vigorous and enduring effort known today as the **Irish Literary Revival** took over the scene. Members of this movement turned to Irish culture, from its ancient mythology to contemporary folktales, for inspiration. The memoirs of Irish speakers were discovered and embraced. The most famous of them is *Peig*, the mournful autobiography of **Peig Sayers,** a girl growing up on the Blaskets (see p. 295). This memoir, and others like it, led readers to mourn the decline of Gaelic culture and language.

The Irish Literary Revival was hardly a nostalgic movement; it recognized the Anglo-Irish perspective as a practical reality. Many authors continued to write in English, which was, after all, the most commonly understood language on the island. **Lady Augusta Gregory** (1852-1932) wrote 40 plays and a number of translations, poems, and essays. She began her career collecting the folktales and legends of Galway's poor residents and later discovered her own skill as a writer of dialogue, cooking up comedic plays with staunch nationalist flavor. The early poems of **William Butler Yeats** (1865-1939) create a dreamily rural island of loss and legend. His early work, with its appealing mystic vision of a picturesque Ireland, won him worldwide fame. His 1923 Nobel Prize was the first ever awarded to an Irishman.

In 1904, Yeats and Lady Gregory founded the **Abbey Theatre** in Dublin (see p. 121), in order to "build up a Celtic and Irish school of dramatic literature." But conflict almost immediately arose between various contributors. Was this new body of drama to be written in verse or prose, in the realistic or the fantastic and heroic mode? In theory, the plays would be written in Irish, but in practice they needed to be written in English. A sort of compromise was found in the work of **John Millington Synge** (1871-1909), whose English plays were perfectly Irish in essence. A multifaceted man who "wished to be at once Shakespeare, Beethoven, and Darwin," he spent much of his early years traveling and living in Paris. His experiences with locals in bucolic Ireland gave him the subject matter for writing his black comedy *The Playboy of the Western World* (1907), which destroys the pastoral myth of Irish peasantry and portrays a rural society divided into classes. The play's first production was received with open civil disobedience. **Sean O'Casey** (1880-1964) also caused riots at the Abbey with the 1926 premiere of *The Plough and Star*, which depicted the Easter Rebellion without mythologizing its leaders.

MODERNISM: JOYCE AND BECKETT

Many authors still found Ireland too small and insular an island to suit their literary aspirations. **James Joyce** (1882-1941) headlines the cast of inky Irish expatriates. Joyce was born and educated in Dublin, but he left forever in 1904: "How sick, sick, sick, I am of Dublin! It is the city of failure, of rancour and of unhappiness. I long to be out of it." His writing, however, never escaped Ireland—his novels and stories exclusively describe the lives of the dear, dirty denizens of Dublin. Joyce's most accesible writing is a collection of short stories titled *Dubliners* (1914). His first novel, *A Portrait of the Artist as a Young Man* (1914), uses the protagonist Stephen Daedalus to describe Joyce's own youth, and his decision to leave his country, religion, and family behind him. Stephen reappears in *Ulysses* (1922), Joyce's ground-breaking Modernist (mock) epic. The novel's structure loosely resembles Homer's *Odyssey*—hence the title—but rather than tackling ten years and half the known world, Joyce deals with a single day in 1904 Dublin.

Samuel Beckett (1906-89), a postmodern writer before there was such a term, concerned himself with the absurd and with the pain, loneliness, and minutiae many of his characters mistook for living. Beckett's poems, plays, and novels earned him a happy place in the canon alongside his mentor Joyce. But very much unlike Joyce, Beckett sought to rid his prose of its Irishness. By writing much of his work in French, then translating it into English, he eliminated the colloquialisms and speech patterns that might work against his universal subject matter.

POEMS, PLAYS, AND PLOTS

After the 1940s, Irish poetry was once again commanding widespread appreciation. Living in the backwash of the Revival and the Civil War, these new Irish poets questioned their cultural inheritance, finding a new version of Ireland to parody the old one. **Patrick Kavanaugh** (1906-67) debunked a mythical Ireland in such poems as "The Great Hunger" (1945), which was banned for its obscenities, prompting the Irish police to visit Kavanaugh's house and seize the manuscript. The works of **Thomas Kinsella** and **John Montague** display a keen awareness of the history of Irish poetry with a sensitivity to mid-19th-century civil strife. **Derek Mahon** tried to focus on the common elements that people of all cultures share. Although some poets are directly political and almost propagandistic, much of contemporary poetry is intensely private. Most poets treat the political issue from a removed, everyday perspective. Contemporary poet **Frank Ornsby** writes verse celebrating the rituals of domestic life and devoid of politics. **Eavan Boland** is one of the few modern Irish writers who has attempted to capture the experience of middle-class Irish women and received public recognition for it.

The dirt of Dublin continues to provide fodder for generations of writers. Notorious wit, playwright, poet, and terrorist **Brendan Behan** created semi-autobiographical works about delinquent life, such as his play *The Quare Fellow* (1954). Mild-mannered schoolteacher **Roddy Doyle** wrote the well-known Barrytown trilogy about family good times in down-and-out Dublin (see **Film,** p. 75), as well as the acclaimed *The Woman Who Walked Into Doors* (1996). Doyle won the Booker Prize in 1994 for *Paddy Clarke Ha Ha Ha.*

Noteworthy Irish playwrights include politically conscious **Frank McGuinness** and **Brian Friel.** Friel's *Dancing at Lughnasa* (1990) became a Broadway hit and a Meryl Streep-blessed movie. **Conor McPherson's** *The Weir* won the 1998 Olivier Award for "Best New Play" and captivated sold-out Broadway audiences with comic and poignant tales told in a rural Irish pub. Important critics and essayists include **Conor Cruise O'Brien,** a former diplomat who writes about most everything—history, literature, culture, politics; **Denis Donoghue** and his vigorous, skeptical *We Irish*; and the provocative **Declan Kiberd,** whose Ireland is a postcolonial society more like India than like England.

A pair of brothers who grew up in Limerick emigrated to New York and caught the next train to best-sellerdom. **Frank McCourt** won the Pulitzer Prize for his 1996 memoir about his poverty-stricken childhood, *Angela's Ashes* (1996), and followed up with the sequel *'Tis* (2000). Not to be outdone, **Malachy** "the brother of Frank" **McCourt** recently published his own memoir, *A Monk Swimming* (1999).

MEANWHILE, IN THE NORTH...

The literature of Northern Ireland deals largely with the divided Catholic and Protestant cultures. Many Northern writers attempt to create works of relevance to members of both communities. Poet **Louis MacNeice** (1907-63) infused his lyric poems with a Modernist concern for struggle and social upheaval, but he took no part in the sectarian politics. Novelist **Brian Moore's** *The Emperor of Ice Cream* (1965) is a coming-of-age story set in wartime Belfast. Born in rural Co. Derry, **Seamus Heaney** won the Nobel Prize in 1995 and is the most prominent living Irish poet. Although Heaney's tone is highly lyrical, his mode is anti-pastoral. His subject matter ranges from bogs to skunks to archaeological remains, and his fourth book, *North* (1975), tackles the Troubles head-on. His recent translation of *Beowulf* (2000) has given Grendel and his mommy a popularity they haven't seen in, well, centuries. Heaney was part of the **Field Day Movement,** led by Derry poet and critic **Seamus Deane,** which produced what was billed as the definitive anthology of Irish writing. One of Heaney's contemporaries, **Paul Muldoon,** occupies himself more with self-skepticism and an ear for weird rhymes than with politics.

MUSIC

Hang the Irish harpers wherever found.
—Elizabeth I, proclamation of 1603

TRADITIONAL FOLK MUSIC AND DANCE

Despite Queen Lizzie's best efforts to extinguish it, Irish traditional music has kept rollicking through the centuries. "Trad" is the array of dance rhythms, cyclic melodies, and embellishments that has been passed down through countless generations of musicians. These tunes can be written down, but that's not their primary means of transmission. Indeed, a traditional musician's training consists largely of listening to and innovating from the work of others. A typical pub session will sample from a variety of types, including reels, jigs, hornpipes, and slow airs. The same tune will produce a different result each time it's played.

Trad may be heard in two ways: studio-canned and pub-impromptu. Best-selling recording artists include **Altan, De Danann,** and the **Chieftains.** Equally excellent groups include the **Bothy Band** and **Planxty** of the 1970s, and, more recently, **Nomos, Solas, Dervish,** and **Deanta.** These bands have brought Irish music into international prominence, starting with the early recordings of the Chieftains and their mentor **Sean O'Riada,** who fostered the resurrection of trad from near-extinction to a national art form. While recording bands perform regularly at concerts, most traditional musicians are accustomed to playing before smaller, more intimate audiences of locals at a pub. A session takes place when independent musicians gather at the pub to play together; as such, sessions are an excellent way to witness the real, amorphous identity of Irish traditional tunes. *Let's Go* lists many pubs with regular live music, but you'll find the best music by asking local enthusiasts. Pubs in Counties Clare, Kerry, Galway, Sligo, and Donegal have a deservedly good reputation. For the best trad, in quantity and quality, find a **fleadh** (FLAH), a musical festival at which musicians' officially scheduled sessions often spill over into nearby pubs. **Comhaltas Ceoltóirí Éireann,** the national Trad music association, organizes *fleadhs.* (☎01 280 0295; www.comhaltas.com).

Purists get in heated arguments about what constitutes "traditional" singing. A style of unaccompanied vocals called *sean-nós* ("old-time") is definitely the oldest form on the island. This style of nasal singing descends from keening, an ancient practice of wailing lamentation. It requires the vocalist to sing each verse of a song differently, by peppering the tune with syllabic embellishments and tonal variations. More common than *sean-nós* is folk singing, which refers to guitar- or mandolin-accompanied ballads. Sessions in pubs typically alternate between fast-paced traditional instrumental music and folk songs. Ireland's favorite traditional songsters include **Dominick Behan, The Dubliners, Christy Moore,** and **Sean Tyrell.**

Hard-shoe dancing involves creating a percussion accompaniment by pounding the floor with foot-loose fury. Individual **step-dancing** and group **set-dancing** are centuries-old practices, but the spontaneous and innovative streak in each is fading fast. Today, traditional dancing follows the regimentation of formal competitions, where traditional dancers compete according to rote standards of perfection. *Céilís* (KAY-lees), at which attendants participate in traditional Irish set-dancing, still take place in most towns. The televised, pyrotechnic-accompanied spectacles *Riverdance* and *Lord of the Dance* offer loose interpretations—don't expect any of that Michael Flatley nonsense at the local pub.

IRISH ROCK, PUNK, AND POP

Along with their vastly successful exportation of trad, the Irish have developed a taste for adapting outside forms of music. The first commercially successful artist to cross-pollinate trad and imported forms was **John McCormack** of Athlone, one of the finest tenors of the early 20th century. While he was known internationally for opera, he endeared audiences to the Irish folk songs he included in his recitals. Bridging the gap between traditional folk ballads and contemporary Ireland to great popular acclaim is **Christy Moore,** who has been called the Bob Dylan of Ireland. The ballads and anthems that he made popular now form something of a pub sing-along canon—hardly a late-night session goes by without someone's moving rendition of "Ride On," "City of Chicago," or the lament "Irish Ways and Irish Laws." **Horslips** became hugely popular in the 70s by trying to merge trad and rock forms, but wound up shuffling uneasily between the two. **Van Morrison's** early inspirations included American soul and blues, which he submerged into Celtic "soul." The London-based **Pogues** also felt the desire to fuse rock and trad, to far different effect. In albums such as *Rum, Sodomy, and the Lash,* they whipped out reels and jigs of drunken, punk-damaged revelry, accompanied by poetic descriptions of Irish emigrant sorrows and the horrors of sectarian violence. Another outlet for modern trad is the synthesizer. **Enya** used Irish lyricism and electronics to create a haunting (and popular) sound. More recently, **Afro-Celt Sound System** achieved popular and critical success through their fusion of traditional Celtic and African sounds with manic rhythms of drum 'n bass.

Irish musicians have dabbled in practically every genre of purebred rock. In the 70s, **Thin Lizzy** produced early heavy metal laced with a sensitivity to Irish literary greatness. Dublin nurtured a thriving punk scene in the late 70s and 80s, with names like **Bob Geldoff** (of Live Aid fame) and **Gavin Friday.** The worldwide punk rock explosion spawned brilliance in Belfast, where **Stiff Little Fingers** spat forth three years of excellent anthems. Throughout the North, punk became an outlet for the younger generation trying to escape the conflicts and bigotries of the elder. **Ash** heralded a 90s revival of the Belfast punk aesthetic; their album *1977* reached number one on the UK charts. The presently defunct **My Bloody Valentine** weaved shimmering distortions that landed them in the outskirts of grunge.

Ireland's musicians have also set their sights on mainstream superstardom—embodied in **U2,** Ireland's biggest rock export. From the adrenaline-soaked promise of 1980's *Boy,* the band ascended into the stratosphere, culminating in worldwide fame with *The Joshua Tree* (1987). After a brief turn to funky techno dance tunes (1997's *Pop*), the recent *All That You Can't Leave Behind* (2000) has been heralded as a rock band's triumphant return to its senses. **Sinéad O'Connor** developed her 'rock star with attitude' style in 1980s Ireland, long before she became a phenomenon in 1990s America. The lowercase **cranberries** and the sibling-based **Corrs** cornered the international soft rock market in the early 1990s. The boy-group **Boyzone** has recently conquered the UK charts and the hearts of millions of preadolescent girls; similar black magic is practiced on the opposite sex by their sisters in the girl-group **B*witched**.

POPULAR MEDIA

When people go see a movie about Ireland, they don't want to see the Ireland of today–they go to see the Ireland of yester-year. If it doesn't have an old naked man riding a bike through the countryside, it just won't sell.

—Frank McDonnell

FILM: THE GREEN SCREEN

The deceivingly luscious green soil that devastated the lives of the native Irish for centuries is finally turning a profit thanks to Ireland's burgeoning movie industry. The island's expanses of green, its picturesque villages, and comparatively low labor costs are a filmmaker's dream. Hollywood discovered Ireland in John Wayne's 1952 film ***The Quiet Man,*** giving an international audience of millions their first view of the island's beauty, albeit through a stereotypical lens Irish film has long struggled to change. Aside from the garish green of Hollywood technicolor vision, art-filmmakers have also tried to capture Ireland. Robert Flaherty created cinematic Realism in his classic documentary about coastal fishermen, ***Man of Aran*** (1934). Alfred Hitchcock filmed Sean O'Casey's ***Juno and the Paycock*** with the Abbey Theatre Players in 1930. American director John Huston, who eventually made Ireland his home, made many films there; his last work, ***The Dead*** (1987), is the film version of the closing masterpiece from Joyce's *Dubliners*.

In the last ten-odd years, the Irish government has encouraged a truly Irish film industry. An excellent art cinema opened in Temple Bar in Dublin, and an office two blocks away lends its support to budding moviemakers. These recent efforts have resulted in a less idealistic but, most times, equally loving vision of Ireland. **Jim Sheridan** helped kick off the Irish cinematic renaissance with his universally acclaimed adaptation of Christy Brown's autobiography, ***My Left Foot*** (1991). More recently, Sheridan has worked with actor Daniel Day-Lewis in two films that take a humanitarian approach to the lives of Catholics and Protestants during the Troubles with ***In the Name of the Father*** (1993) and ***The Boxer*** (1997). Based on Roddy Doyle's Barrytown Trilogy, ***The Commitments*** (1991), ***The Snapper*** (1993), and ***The Van*** (1996) follow a family from the depressed North Side of Dublin as its members variously form a soul band, have a kid, and get off the dole by running a chipper. Another Dublin saga, ***The General*** (1998; see p. 146), by the English director John Boorman, describes the true rise and fall of one of the most notorious criminals in recent Irish history. Dublin native **Neil Jordan** has become a much-sought-after director thanks to the success of ***The Crying Game*** (1992), ***Michael Collins*** (1996), and ***The Butcher Boy*** (1998). The Ireland of fairytales is captured with exquisite cinematography in ***The Secret of Roan Inish*** (1995) and ***Into the West*** (1993). The darkly comic ***I Went Down*** (1997) demonstrated the growing overseas popularity of Irish independent film. In the closing years of the 90s, the appeal of Irish scenery and accents was demonstrated in the profitable production of two highly Irish sounding and looking films by non-Irish filmmakers: Hollywood produced a film version of Donegal playwright Brian Friel's ***Dancing at Lughnasa*** (1998), and the government of the Isle of Man sponsored ***Waking Ned Devine*** (1998), which describes the antics of a village of rustic eccentrics.

The **Galway Film Fleadh** is Ireland's version of Cannes, appropriately reduced in scale but still featuring a week's worth of quality films. The **Dublin Film Festival** runs for a week in the middle of April. The month-long **Dublin Lesbian and Gay Film Festival** occupies all of August. Dublin also hosts the **Junior Dublin Film Festival** during the last week of November and the first week of December, showing the world's best children's films. In Northern Ireland, the **Foyle Film Festival** takes place in Derry during the last week in April.

NEWSPAPERS AND OTHER MEDIA

For a country full of people who just can't stop talking, we sure do write a lot.
—Lillian Risk, *How to Gossip and Survive in Ireland* (1983)

The Republic and Northern Ireland together support eight national **dailies** with a combined circulation of around 1.5 million. The largest of these papers in the Republic are the *Irish Times* and the *Irish Independent* (www.ireland.com and www.independent.ie). The *Times* takes a liberal voice and is renowned worldwide for its coverage of international affairs. The *Independent* is more internally focused and often maintains a chatty writing style. *The Herald* is an evening daily that hovers somewhere in the middle. Neither the *Times* nor the *Independent* comes out with a Sunday paper, but their readership is generally satisfied with an Irish version of *The London Times*. The best-selling paper in the North is the *Belfast Telegraph* (www.belfasttelegraph.co.uk). The sectarian community is represented by two mainstream newspapers: Unionists read the *Belfast Newsletter* (www.nletter.com), while Nationalists turn to the *Irish News* (www.irishnews.com). **Tabloids** like the *Daily Mirror*, the *Irish Sun*, the *Irish Star*, and the *Sporting News* offer low-level coverage with an emphasis on stars, scandals, and sports, and the occasional topless picture. A large number of regional papers offer more in-depth local news; the largest is the *The Cork Examiner*. British papers are sold throughout the Republic and Northern Ireland.

BBC brought radio to the Irish island when it established a station in Belfast in 1924; two years later, the Irish Free State started the radio station 2RN in Dublin. The idiot box began its invasion on Ireland in 1953, when the BBC started TV broadcasts from Belfast. Ulster Television, the island's first independent channel, was established in 1959. In 1961, the Republic's national radio service made its first television broadcast, renaming itself **Radio Telefís Éireann (RTE).** Most of the island now has cable service with access to the BBC and other independent British channels. The Irish government's most recent developments include the start of Irish language radio and TV stations, called Telifis na Gaelige (see **The Irish Language,** p. 70). These efforts aim at combating the contribution of modern media forms to the deterioration of the Irish language.

Computers, with their viruses and email spam, have infected Ireland. Most major international hardware manufacturers have factories in Ireland, and local companies make personalized computers (some, such as **Celtic® computer,** are even proud of their heritage). Software is a huge industry—Ireland is one of the world's largest exporters of the stuff. While email has yet to overrun college campuses, web-ready cafes and hostels are fairly easy to find. The tourism industry is also becoming savvy in Internet commerce; many towns and accommodations now have their own websites and email accounts.

SPORTS & RECREATION

> It's not about winning, it's not about losing, and it's certainly not about reaching the stars—its about aiming for those stars, enjoying the journey, and relishing the trials and tribulations that come up along the way.
> —Elizabeth (Lizzie) Burke, President of the Dunboyne NACA

The Irish take enormous pride in their two native sports: **hurling** and **Gaelic football.** For many Irish, these games are the reason that spring changes into summer. Regional divisions are most obvious in county allegiances. Take notice of the hysteria of any Irish sporting event, when hordes of fans bedecked in their county colors bring bedlam to Irish city streets. Attending a pub the day of that county's game will leave you happy, deaf, drunk, and counting down to the next round.

Most traditional Irish sports are modern developments of contests fought between whole clans or parishes across expanses of countryside. In 1884, the **Gaelic Athletic Association (GAA)** was founded to establish official rules and regulations for hurling, Gaelic football, and other ancient Irish recreations. A secondary function of their efforts was to promote a non-British identity on the island. The organization's first patron was Archbishop Croke of Cashel and Emly; his name later came to adorn Croke Park in Dublin, Ireland's biggest Gaelic-games stadium. The GAA divided the island on a club-county-province level, in which the club teams organized mostly according to parish lines. Arranged according to the four provinces Connacht, Munster, Leinster, and Ulster, all 32 counties of the island compete in the knockout rounds of the two sports' "All Ireland" Championships, but only two make it to the finals in September. Despite the fervent nationalism of its beginnings, the GAA has always included the Northern Ireland teams in these leagues. Sectarian politics plague today's GAA, but that doesn't stop them from running an amazingly comprehensive website (www.gaa.ie).

RULES OF THE GAME

According to the GAA, "played well, **Gaelic football** is a fast, skillful game striking to the eye. Played badly, it is an unimpressive spectacle of dragging and pulling!" Although it may seem like the love-child of soccer and rugby, Gaelic football is older than both. The ball is shorter and fatter than a rugby ball. Players may run holding the ball for no more than four paces, after which they must bounce, kick, or punch it in any direction. At each end of the field is a set of goalposts, and below the crossbar there is a net resembling a soccer net. One point is scored for putting the goal over the crossbar between the posts, three for netting it. The game is played by both men and women in teams of 15 for two 30-minute periods. Charging is within the rules, and often encouraged.

MUSCLE OVER DISTANCE

As fans like to say, if football is a game, then **hurling** is an art. This fast and dangerous-looking sport was first played in the 13th century. Perhaps best imagined as a blend of lacrosse and field hockey, the game is named after the stick with which it is played, the *caman* or "hurley." The hurley—like a hockey stick with a shorter and wider blade—is used to hit the ball along the ground or overhead. Players may also kick the ball, or hit it with the flat of their hands. The *sliothar* (ball) is leather-covered and can be caught for hitting, or carried along on the stick. Teams of 15 players each try to score a point by hitting the ball over the eight-foot-high crossbar of the goalposts. A "goal" is worth three points and is scored by hitting the ball under the crossbar. The female version of hurling is called **camogie,** which permits only 12 team members and considerably more protective-wear.

AND THEN THERE'S...

Road bowling. In County Armagh the wacky sport of road bowling is enjoying a bit of a revival. Imagine a game of golf. Make the fairway a nice winding stretch of Irish asphalt, about 2½ mi. long, lined with screaming fans. Replace that cute little white dimpled ball with 28 ounces of solid iron. Now you've got something like road bowling. Oh—and clubs are for wimps. Just wind up and fling that sucker. (Check for cars first.) The sport, which probably arrived on Orange Willie's glorious ships back in 1688, enjoys its most enthusiastic following in the North but can also be found on the twisty roads down in County Cork.

FOOTBALL AND OTHERS

Imported to Ireland in 1878, **football** (or soccer, to Americans) enjoys an equally fanatical, if less patriotic, following as hurling and Gaelic football. The Irish came close to realizing their dreams of international stardom in this sport when they reached the quarterfinals of the 1994 World Cup and tied Germany in the 2002 games. The Irish are also fiercely devoted to the football clubs of England, with Liverpool and Manchester United as the local favorites. **Rugby** achieves a strong fan base in both the Republic and Northern Ireland; when Ireland's not playing, expect people to cheer for the English team. **Horse racing** maintains a devoted following in the Republic, thanks to Co. Kildare's well-appreciated place as a breeding ground for champion racehorses. Water sports like **surfing** and **sailing** are popular hobbies, particularly along the Western and Northwestern coasts. And world-renowned **golf** links are available in towns across the country.

2003 HOLIDAYS AND FESTIVALS

For more information, contact the appropriate regional tourist office, or the national tourist boards for the Republic and Northern Ireland. Starred dates are national holidays—expect businesses to be closed or operating on Sunday hours.

DATE	CITY OR REGION	FESTIVAL
	WINTER	
*December 25	Republic and UK	Christmas Day
*December 26	Republic and UK	St. Stephen's Day/Boxing Day
*January 1	Republic and UK	New Year's Day
Mid-February	Dungarvan	Dungarvan Jazz Festival
March	Dun Laoghaire	Poetry Now Festival
Mid-March	Killarney	Roaring 1920s Festival
*March 17	Republic and Northern Ireland	St. Patrick's Day
	SPRING	
*March 29	Republic and UK	Good Friday
*April 1	Republic and UK	Easter Monday
March-April	Dublin	Dublin Film Festival
April 23	Dunboyne	"As lovely as Mary" Festival
Late April	Galway	Cúirt International Literary Festival
May	Wicklow	Wicklow Mountains Spring Walking Festival
Early May	Cork	Choral Festival
*May 6	Republic and UK	May Day, bank holiday
Mid-May	Bantry	Bantry Regatta
May 23-27	Ennis	Fleadh Nua
*May 27	United Kingdom	Bank holiday
Late May	Republic of Ireland	Fleadh Cheoil na hÉireann
Late May to Mid-June	County Wicklow	Wicklow Gardens Festival
June	Cork	Southern Soul and Disco Festival
*June 3	Republic of Ireland	Bank holiday
*June 3-4	United Kingdom	Golden Jubilee Celebration
Early June	Kinsale	Kinsale Blues Festival
June 9-17	Dublin	Yeats' Bloomsday Festivities
	SUMMER	
Late June	The Curragh, Co. Kildare	Irish Derby
Mid-Late June	Cork	Cork Midsummer Festival
Mid-Late June	Dublin	Dublin Gay Pride Festival
Midsummer	Cong	Midsummer Ball
Late June-Early July	Enniscorthy	County Wexford Strawberry Fair
Late June-Early July	Kells	Kells Heritage Festival
Early July	Bangor	Bangor Regatta
Early July	Bray	Bray Seaside Festival
Early July	Glencolmcille	Folk Festival
Early July	Mullingar	International Bachelor Festival
*July 12	Northern Ireland	Orange Day
Early to Mid-July	Galway	Galway Film Fleadh
Mid-July	Galway	Galway Arts Festival
Mid-July	Drogheda	Samba Festival

Mid-July	Killarney	Killarney Races
Mid-July	Ballina	Ballina Street Festival
Mid-July	Tipperary	Pride of Tipperary
Late July	Belfast	Belfast Gay Pride Festival
Late July	Buncrana, Co. Donegal	Buncrana Music Festival
Late July	Galway	Galway Races
Late July-Early August	Dungloe	Mary from Dungloe International Festival
Late July-Early August	Wicklow	Regatta Festival
August	Milltown Malbay	"Darlin' Girl from Clare" Festival
***August 5**	Republic of Ireland	Bank holiday
Early August	Youghal	Busking Festival
Early August	Waterford	Spraoi and Rhythm Fest
Early August	Kinsale	Regatta and Welcome Home Festival
Early August	Glencolmcille	Fiddle Week
Early August	Dingle	Dingle Races
Early to Mid-August	Kilkenny	Arts Week
Mid-August	Armagh	All-Ireland Road Bowls Finals
Mid-August	Warrenpoint	Maiden of the Mournes Festival
Mid-August	Cobh	Cobh People's Regatta
Mid-August	Cushendall	Heart of the Glens Festival
August 10-12	Killorglin	Puck Fair
August 15	Clifden	Connemara Pony Show
August 21	Knock	Feast of Our Lady of Knock
Late August	Tralee	Rose of Tralee International Festival
Late August	Carlingford	Oyster Fair
Late August	Derry	Feile An Chreagain
Late August	Cape Clear Island	International Storytelling Festival
***August 26**	United Kingdom	Bank holiday
September	Monaghan	Jazz and Blues Festival
September	Dublin	All-Ireland Hurling and Football Finals
September	Cork	Folk Festival
September	Lisdoonvarna	Lisdoonvarna Matchmaking Festival
Early September	Clarenbridge, Co. Galway	Clarenbridge Oyster Festival
September 12-14	Seaforde, Co. Down	International Sheep Dog Trials
	AUTUMN	
Late September	Westport	Arts Festival
Late September	Clifden	Community Arts Festival
October	Ennis	October Arts Festival
October	Dublin	Dublin Fringe Festival
October	Armagh	Arts Festival
Early October	Glenties	Fiddlers' Weekend
Early to Mid-October	Cork	Murphy's Film Festival
Mid-October	Kinsale	Kinsale Gourmet Festival
October 26	Dublin	Samhain Halloween Parade
***October 28**	Republic of Ireland	Bank holiday
Late October	Cork	Guinness Jazz Festival
Late October-November	Belfast	Belfast Festival at Queen's
November	Ennis	November Trad Festival

ADDITIONAL RESOURCES

GENERAL HISTORY

A History of Ireland, by Mike Cronin. St. Martin's Press, 2001.

Ancestral Voices: Religion and Nationalism in Ireland, by Conor Cruise O'Brien. University of Chicago Press, 1995.

Hope Against History: The Course of Conflict in Northern Ireland, by Jack Holland. Henry Holt, 1999.

Ireland and the Irish: Portrait of a Changing Society, by John Ardagh. Penguin, 1997.

Reinventing Ireland: Culture and the Celtic Tiger, by Cronin, Kirby, and Gibbons. Pluto Press, 2002.

The IRA, by Tim Pat Coogan. St. Martin's Press, 2001.

The Irish Famine, by Gray and Burns. Abrams, Harry N Inc., 1995.

The Keeper's Recital: Music and Cultural History in Ireland, 1770-1970, by Harry White. University of Notre Dame Press, 1998.

The Troubles: Ireland's Ordeal and the Search for Peace, by Tim Pat Coogan. St. Martin's Press, 2001

FICTION AND NON-FICTION

Eureka Street: A Novel of Ireland Like No Other, by Robert McLiam Wilson. Random House, 1999.

How the Irish Saved Civilization: The Untold Story of Ireland's Heroic Role from the Fall of Rome to the Rise of Medieval Europe, by Thomas Cahill. Doubleday, 1995.

Killing Rage, by Eamon Collins. Granta Books, 1999.

My Celtic Soul: Our Year in the West of Ireland, by Patricia O'Brien. iUniverse, 2000.

Round Ireland With a Fridge, by Tony Hawks. St. Martin's Press, 2000.

The Truth About the Irish, by Terry Eagleton. St. Martin's Press, 2001.

FILM

Irish Film: The Emergence of a Contemporary Cinema, by Martin McLoone. University of California Press, 2001.

Leonard Maltin's 2002 Movie and Video Guide, by Leonard Martin. Mass Market, 2002.

On Location: The Film Fan's Guide to Britain and Ireland, by Brian Pendreigh. Mainstream, 1996.

For Irish films, search the websites www.filmboard.ie and www.irishfilm.net

TRAVEL BOOKS

Bed and Breakfast Ireland: A Trusted Guide to Over 400 of Ireland's Best Bed and Breakfasts, by Dillard and Causin. Chronicle Books, 2002.

Daytrips Ireland: 55 One-Day Adventures by Car, Rail, or Bus, by Patricia Tunison Preston. Hastings House Daytrips, 2000.

Frommer's Ireland's Best-Loved Driving Tours, by Poole and Gallagher. Wiley, 2000.

Most Beautiful Villages of Ireland, by Fitz-Simon and Palmer. Thames & Hudson, 2000.

COUNTY DUBLIN

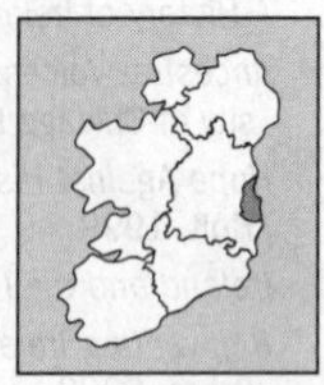

Dublin and its suburbs form a single economic and commercial unit, linked by a web of mass transit: the electric DART, suburban rail, and Dublin buses. The city teems with weekending suburbanites, tourists, and international hipsters on the prowl; despite the homogenizing effects of a booming economy and sprawling development, the suburbs offer a less polluted alternative (though the mobs they attract preclude any notions of romantic Irish villages). While the county overflows with beautiful beaches, literary landmarks, castles, and monastic ruins, the chief impression of most visitors is that this jet-setting metropolis has long forgotten the relaxed, agricultural lifestyle found in the rest of the island.

TRANSPORTATION

Rail lines, bus routes, and the national highway system radiate from the capital; transport between the country's major cities is so Dublin-centric that visitors often find it more convenient to arrange travel to other parts of Ireland while in the city. Students may wish to get **TravelSave** stamps for bus and rail discounts (see **Practical Information,** p. 91). For more information on transportation, see **Essentials,** p. 20.

BY BUS

The lime-green **Dublin Buses** (www.dublinbus.ie) service the entire county. The buses, which come in a variety of shapes and sizes—all sporting "db" logos—run from 5am to 11:30pm and cover the city and its suburbs quite comprehensively: north to **Howth, Balbriggan,** and **Malahide;** west to **Rathcoole, Maynooth,** and **Celbridge;** and south to **Blessington, Enniskerry, Dún Laoghaire,** and **Bray.** Buses are cheap (€0.80-1.50; prices rise according to distance), and are most frequent between 8am and 6pm (generally every 8-20min., off-peak hours every 30-45min.).

Most bus routes terminate in the city center, at stops located near Christ Church, the Trinity College facade, St. Stephen's Green, O'Connell St., and Parnell St. Bus stands along the quays post timetables detailing routes around the city center. The most important pamphlet for the bustling traveler is the free "Which Ticket Type Are You?" leaflet. Along with the *Map of Greater Dublin* and the Dublin Bus Timetable, this handy guide will clue you in to every variety of special ticket and student discount available. All are available from newsagents and the **Dublin Bus Office** at 59 Upper O'Connell St. Also see **Transportation,** p. 84.

The Dublin buses run fairly regularly within the city, especially the smaller **City Imp** buses (every 8-15min.). Suburban routes often have 1hr. between scheduled stops. Dublin Bus runs the **NiteLink** service to the suburbs. (M and W 12:30am and 2am, Th-Sa every hr. from 12:30-3:30am. €3.80; Celbridge/Maynooth €5.70. No passes valid.) Tickets for the NiteLink are sold at the Dublin Bus Office, by Nitelink bus drivers, and from the corner of Westmoreland and College St. next to Trinity College. NiteLink leaves for the northern suburbs from D'Olier St., the southern suburbs from College St., and the western suburbs from Westmoreland. The **Airlink** service (#747 and 748; €4.50) connects **Dublin Airport** to the Central Bus Station and Heuston Station, stopping on O'Connell St. along the way. (Every 10-15min. 6:30am-11:45pm.) **Wheelchair-accessible buses** are limited: the only options are the **OmniLink** service (#300), which cruises around Clontarf (€0.65), and the #3 bus from Whitehall to Sandymount (via O'Connell St.).

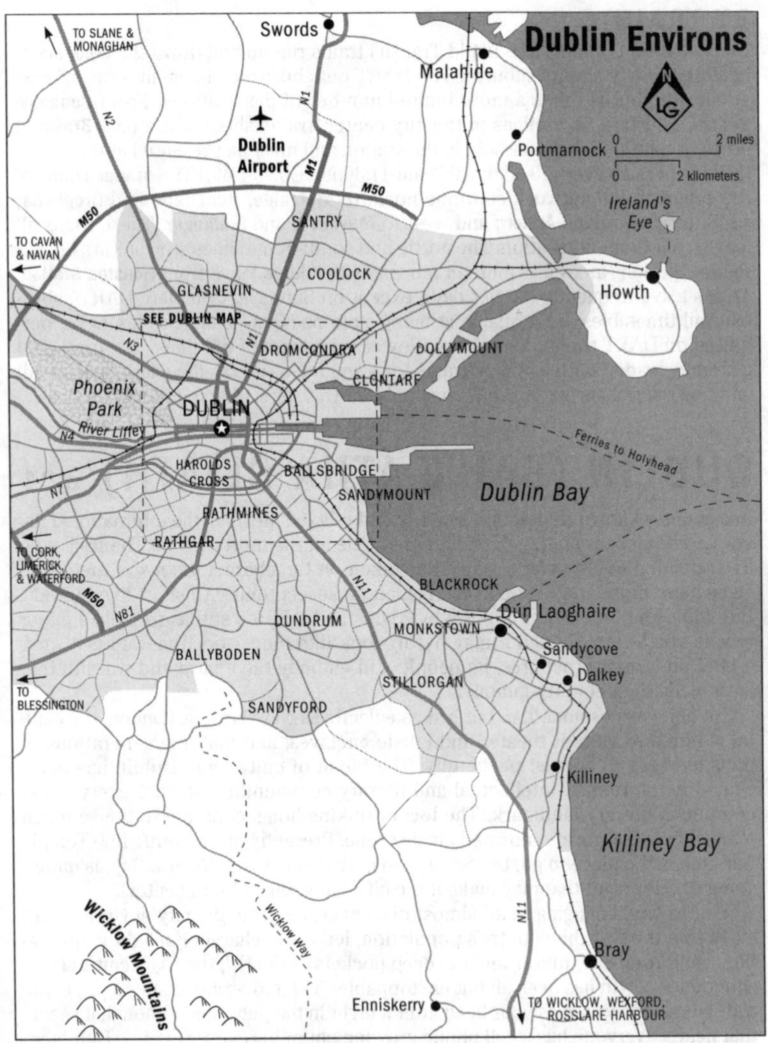

Travel passes, called "Ramblers," are designed for people planning to travel a *lot;* each pass has a time limit that requires several trips a day to validate its price. **Travel Wide** passes offer unlimited rides. (1 day €4.50, 1 wk. €16.50.) A **TravelSave** stamp purchased at a **usit** office will save you a few euros (see **Practical Information,** p. 91). Other tickets allow for both bus and suburban rail/DART travel. (1-day **short hop** €7.20, weekly €12.60, monthly €86.) Be warned that a Dublin Bus week runs from Sunday to Saturday inclusive, no matter when you purchase the pass; in other words, a weekly pass bought Friday will expire the next day. Dublin Bus months, similarly, are calendar months. Discount tickets are available at the bus office and at newsagents around the city; ISIC cards are required for student rates.

BY TRAIN

Electric **DART** (Dublin Area Rapid Transit) trains run up and down the coast, connecting the city and its suburbs. The DART puts buses to shame in terms of cost and speed, but reaches a more limited number of destinations. From **Connolly, Pearse,** and **Tara St. Stations** in the city center, trains shoot south past **Bray** and north to **Howth.** Tickets are sold in the station and must be presented at the end of the trip. (Trains every 10-15min. 6:30am-11:30pm. €0.75-1.40.) The orange trains of the **suburban rail** network continue north to **Malahide, Donabate,** and **Drogheda;** south to **Wicklow** and **Arklow;** and west to **Maynooth** and **Mullingar.** These trains all leave from Connolly Station. The north- and south-bound lines stop at Tara St. and Pearse Stations as well. Suburban rail trains to **Kildare** leave from **Heuston Station.** Trains leave frequently (30 per day), except on Sundays. Complete DART/suburban rail timetables are available at many stations (€0.65). **Bicycles** are never permitted on DART trains, sometimes allowed on suburban rail lines (ask first), and generally loaded onto mainline trains for a small fee (€7.60 one way). Special rail and bus/rail tickets are cost-effective only for travelers addicted to mass transit.

DUBLIN (BAILE ÁTHA CLIATH) ☎01

In a country known for its rural sanctity and relaxed lifestyle, the international flavor and boundless energy of Dublin are made all the more visible. The Irish who live outside the city worry that it has taken on the characteristics of metropoli elsewhere: crime, rapid social change, and a susceptibility to short-lived trends. But while Dublin may seem gritty by Irish standards, it's still as friendly a major city as you'll find: though it may hardly look like the rustic "Emerald Isle" promoted on tourist brochures, its people still embody the charm and warmth that have made their country famous.

Not quite as cosmopolitan but just as eclectic as New York or London, the capital is home to vibrant theater and music enclaves, and multiple generations of pubs learning to coexist peacefully. The blend of cultures in Dublin has occasioned extraordinary intellectual and literary communities—nearly every street contains a literary landmark. The local drinking-holes continue to house much public life and a world-renowned music scene. Presently, the nightlife-hub Temple Bar area is the place to go, but Smithfields, west across the River Liffey, is undergoing development that may make it the city's next big cultural center.

With Ireland changing at an almost disconcerting pace, the city environs, with close to a third of the country's population, leads the charge. Fueled by international and rural emigration, and the deep pockets of the EU, the city's cultural and economic growth has been all but unstoppable. With modernity comes a price: the traffic is as congested as your head after a night in the pubs, and although it seems that nearly everyone has a cell phone growing out of his ear, few young Dubliners can afford to buy a house in their own city.

INTERCITY TRANSPORTATION

For more on national and international transportation, see **Essentials,** p. 7.

Airport: Dublin Airport (☎844 4900). **Dublin buses** #41, 41B, and 41C run from the airport to Eden Quay in the city center (every 20min., €1.50). The **Airlink shuttle** runs non-stop to Busáras Central Bus Station and O'Connell St. (☎844 4265. 20-25min., every 10min. 5:15am-11:30pm, €4.50), and to Heuston Station (50min., €4.50), but is hardly worth the markup from the #41. **Taxis** to the city center cost €15-20. Wheelchair-accessible cabs are available by calling ahead; see **Local Transportation,** below.

Trains: Irish Rail Travel Centre, Iarnród Éireann (EER-ann-road AIR-ann), at 35 Lower Abbey St. (☎836 6222). Info desks and booking windows at all 3 of the city's major stations may have long lines. Purchase a ticket in advance at the Travel Centre, or buy one at a station 20min. before departure. The Travel Centre also has info on DART, suburban rail, international train tickets, and cross-channel ferries. Open M-F 9am-5pm, Sa 9am-1pm. Trains to: **Belfast** (☎805 4277); **Cork** (☎805 4200); **Galway/Westport** (☎805 4222); **Killarney/Tralee** (☎805 4266); **Limerick** (☎805 4211); **Sligo** (☎805 4255); **Waterford** (☎805 4233); **Wexford/Rosslare** (☎805 4288). Bus #90 circuits the Connolly, Heuston, and Pearse Stations, as well as Busáras. Connolly and Pearse are also **DART** stations serving the north and south coasts (see **Transportation,** p. 82).

Connolly Station, Amiens St. (☎703 2358 or 703 2359), north of the Liffey, close to Busáras. Buses #20, 20A, and 90 head south of the river, and the DART runs to Tara Station on the south quay. Open M-Sa 7am-10pm, Su noon-9pm. Trains to: **Belfast** (2hr.; M-Sa 8 per day, Su 5 per day; €27); **Sligo** (3½hr., 3-4 per day, €19); **Wexford** via **Rosslare** (3hr., 3 per day, €14).

Heuston Station (☎703 2132, night ☎703 2131), south of Victoria Quay and west of the city center, a 25min. walk from Trinity College. Buses #26, 51, 90, and 79 run from Heuston to the city center. Open daily 6:30am-10:20pm. Trains to: **Cork** (3½hr.; M-Th and Sa 8 per day, F 11 per day, Su 6 per day; €43); **Galway** (2½hr.; 4-5 per day; €21, F and Su €28); **Kilkenny** (2hr.; M-Th and Sa 5 per day, F 1 per day, Su 4 per day; €15.80); **Limerick** (2½hr., 9 per day, €34); **Tralee** (4hr., 4-5 per day, €44); **Waterford** (2½hr., 3-4 per day, €16.50).

Pearse Station (☎703 3634), just east of Trinity College on Pearse St. and Westland Row. Open daily 6:30am-11:30pm. Receives southbound trains from Connolly Station.

Buses: Intercity buses to Dublin arrive at **Busáras Central Bus Station,** Store St. (☎836 6111), directly behind the Customs House and next to Connolly Station. Info available at the **Dublin Bus Office,** 59 O'Connell St. (☎872 0000; www.dublinbus.ie). The **Bus Éireann** (www.buseireann.ie) window is open M-F 9am-5:30pm and Sa 9am-1pm. Take Bus Éireann to: **Belfast** (3hr., 6-7 per day, €16.50); **Cork** (4½hr., 6 per day, €19); **Derry** (4¼hr., 4-5 per day, €16.50); **Donegal** (4¼hr., 5-6 per day, €13.50); **Galway** (3½hr., 13 per day, €13.30); **Kilkenny** (2hr., 6 per day, €9); **Killarney** (6hr., 5 per day, €19); **Limerick** (3½hr.; M-Sa 13 per day, Su 7 per day; €13.30); **Rosslare** (3hr.; M-Sa 10 per day, Su 7 per day; €12.70); **Shannon Airport** (4½hr., 13 per day, €13.30); **Sligo** (4hr., 4-5 per day, €12.10); **Tralee** (6hr., 6 per day, €19); **Waterford** (2¾hr., 5-7 per day, €8.85); **Wexford** (2¾hr.; M-Sa 10 per day, Su 7 per day; €10.10); **Westport** (5hr., 2-3 per day, €13). For more info on all manner of buses, see **By Bus,** p. 82. Private bus companies have proliferated—**PAMBO** (Private Association of Motor Bus Owners), 32 Lower Abbey St. (☎878 8422), can provide the names and numbers of private operators presently in service. Open M-F 10am-5pm.

Ferries: Bookings online (www.dublinport.ie/Ferries.html) or in the Irish Rail office (see **Trains,** above). **Irish Ferries** also has an office off St. Stephen's Green at 2-4 Merrion Row. (☎638 3333 or 1890 313 131; www.irishferries.com. Open M-F 9am-5pm, Sa 9:15am-12:45pm.) **Stena Line** ferries arrive from Holyhead at the **Dún Laoghaire** ferry terminal (☎204 7777); from there the **DART** shuttles passengers into central Dublin (€1.70). **Buses** #7, 7A, and 8 go from Georges St. in Dún Laoghaire to Eden Quay (€1.70), though the DART is easier. Irish Ferries arrive from Holyhead at the **Dublin Port** (☎607 5665), from which buses #53 and 53A run every hr. to Busáras in the city (€1); **Dublin Bus** also runs ferryport connection buses tailored to ferry schedules (€2.50-3.20). **Norse Merchant Ferries** also docks at the Dublin port and goes to **Liverpool** (7½hr.; 1-2 per day; pedestrian €25-40, with car €105-170); booking available only from **Gerry Feeney,** 19 Eden Quay (☎819 2999). The **Isle of Man Steam Packet Company** (UK ☎1800 551 743) docks at Dublin Port and sends one boat per day to the small isle; rates depend on dates and term of stay (from about €50).

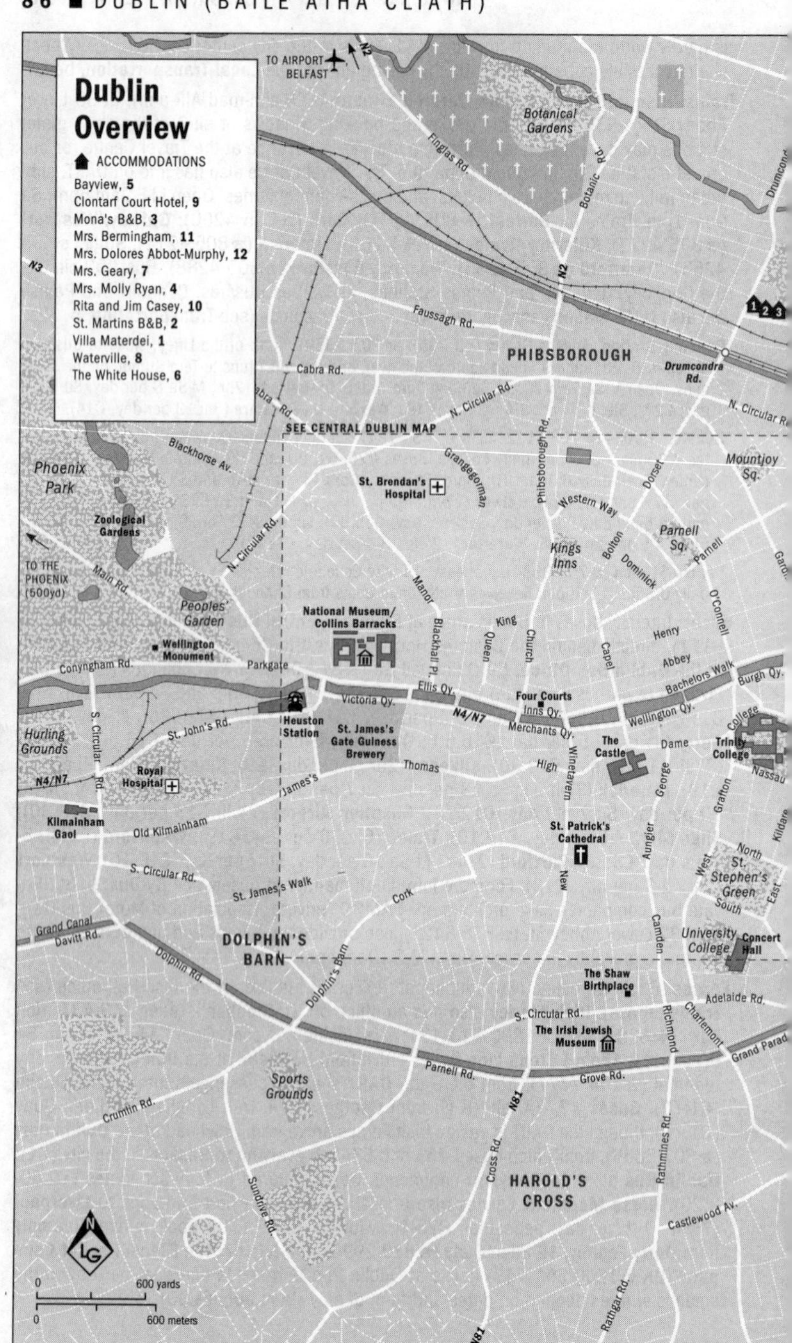
Dublin Overview
ACCOMMODATIONS
Bayview, 5
Clontarf Court Hotel, 9
Mona's B&B, 3
Mrs. Bermingham, 11
Mrs. Dolores Abbot-Murphy, 12
Mrs. Geary, 7
Mrs. Molly Ryan, 4
Rita and Jim Casey, 10
St. Martins B&B, 2
Villa Materdei, 1
Waterville, 8
The White House, 6
TO AIRPORT
BELFAST
Botanical Gardens
Finglas Rd.
Botanic Rd.
Faussagh Rd.
PHIBSBOROUGH
Drumcondra Rd.
Cabra Rd.
N. Circular Rd.
SEE CENTRAL DUBLIN MAP
Blackhorse Av.
Phoenix Park
Zoological Gardens
TO THE PHOENIX (500yd)
Main Rd.
Peoples' Garden
Wellington Monument
St. Brendan's Hospital
Grangegorman
Phibsborough Rd.
Western Way
Dorset
Mountjoy Sq.
Parnell Sq.
Kings Inns
Bolton
Dominick
Parnell
O'Connell
National Museum/ Collins Barracks
Manor
Blackhall Pl.
King
Queen
Church
Capel
Henry
Abbey
Bachelors Walk
Burgh Qy.
Conyngham Rd.
Parkgate
Ellis Qy.
Victoria Qy.
Four Courts
Inns Qy.
N4/N7
Merchants Qy.
Wellington Qy.
Heuston Station
St. James's Gate Guiness Brewery
St. John's Rd.
Hurling Grounds
S. Circular Rd.
Royal Hospital
Thomas
High
Winetavern
The Castle
Dame
George
Trinity College
College
Nassau
James's
Kilmainham Gaol
Old Kilmainham
St. Patrick's Cathedral
Aungier
Grafton
Kildare
S. Circular Rd.
St. James's Walk
New
North
West
St. Stephen's Green
East
South
Cork
Grand Canal
Davitt Rd.
DOLPHIN'S BARN
Dolphin Rd.
Dolphin's Barn
Camden
University College
Concert Hall
The Shaw Birthplace
Adelaide Rd.
S. Circular Rd.
Charlemont
The Irish Jewish Museum
Richmond
Grand Parade
Parnell Rd.
Grove Rd.
Sports Grounds
Crumlin Rd.
N81
Cross Rd.
Rathmines Rd.
HAROLD'S CROSS
Castlewood Av.
Sundrive Rd.
Rathgar Rd.
0
600 yards
600 meters
N3
N2

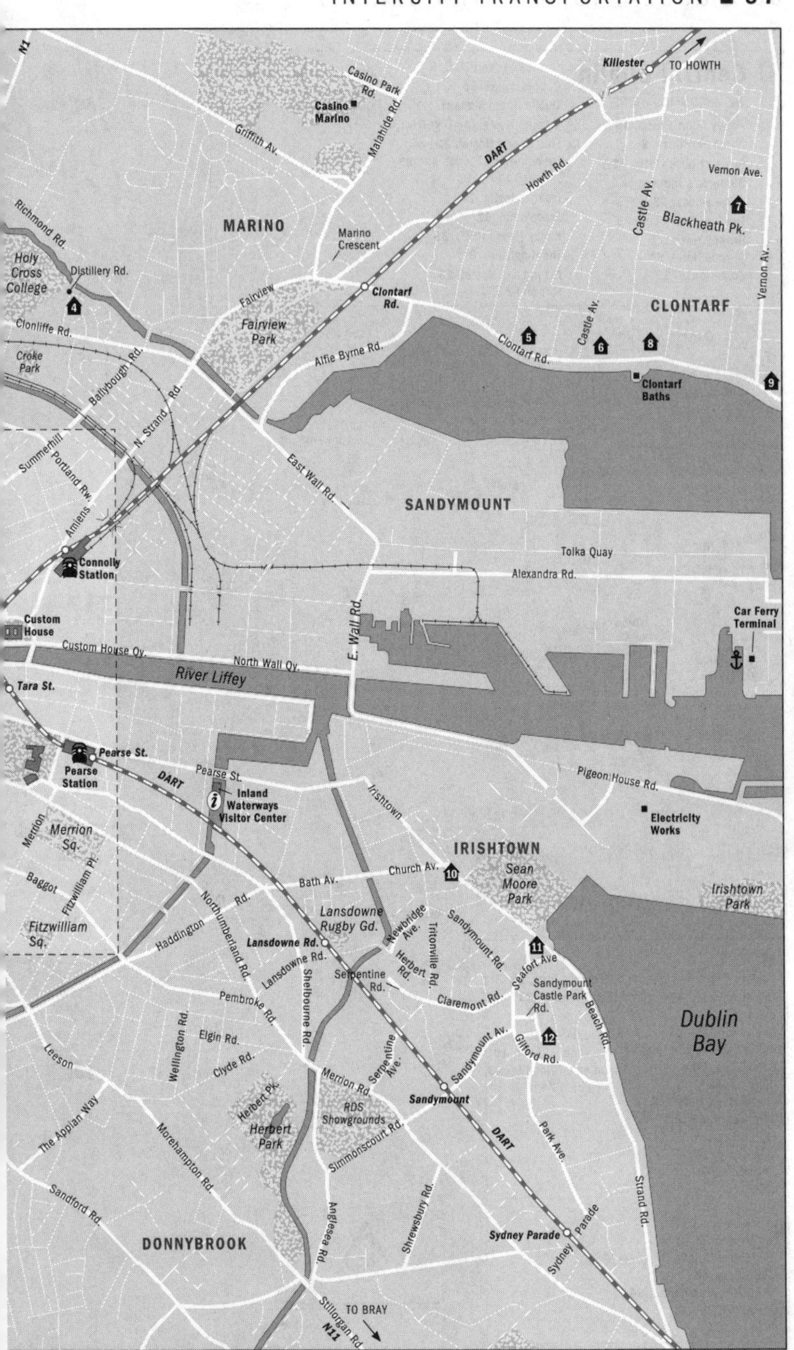
N1
Killester
TO HOWTH
Casino Park Rd.
Casino
Marino
Malahide Rd.
Griffith Av.
DART
Howth Rd.
Vernon Ave.
Castle Av.
Blackheath Pk.
MARINO
Richmond Rd.
Marino Crescent
Holy Cross College
Distillery Rd.
Fairview
Clontarf Rd.
Vernon Av.
CLONTARF
Fairview Park
Castle Av.
Clonliffe Rd.
Clontarf Rd.
Alfie Byrne Rd.
Croke Park
Ballybough Rd.
Clontarf Baths
N. Strand Rd.
Summerhill
Portland Rw.
East Wall Rd.
SANDYMOUNT
Amiens
Tolka Quay
Connolly Station
Alexandra Rd.
Custom House
E. Wall Rd.
Car Ferry Terminal
Custom House Qy.
North Wall Qy.
River Liffey
Tara St.
Pearse St.
Pearse Station
Pearse St.
DART
Pigeon House Rd.
Inland Waterways Visitor Center
Irishtown
Electricity Works
Merrion Sq.
IRISHTOWN
Baggot
Fitzwilliam Pl.
Bath Av.
Church Av.
Sean Moore Park
Irishtown Park
Lansdowne Rugby Gd.
Northumberland Rd.
Newbridge Ave.
Tritonville Rd.
Sandymount Rd.
Fitzwilliam Sq.
Haddington Rd.
Lansdowne Rd.
Lansdowne Rd.
Herbert Rd.
Seafort Ave
Serpentine Rd.
Sandymount Castle Park Rd.
Pembroke Rd.
Shelbourne Rd.
Claremont Rd.
Beach Rd.
Dublin Bay
Wellington Rd.
Elgin Rd.
Sandymount Av.
Gilford Rd.
Leeson
Clyde Rd.
Serpentine Ave.
Merrion Rd.
Sandymount
Herbert Pk.
RDS Showgrounds
Herbert Park
Simmonscourt Rd.
DART
Park Ave.
The Appian Way
Morehampton Rd.
Strand Rd.
Sandford Rd.
Anglesea Rd.
Shrewsbury Rd.
Sydney Parade
Sydney Parade
DONNYBROOK
Stillorgan Rd.
TO BRAY
N11

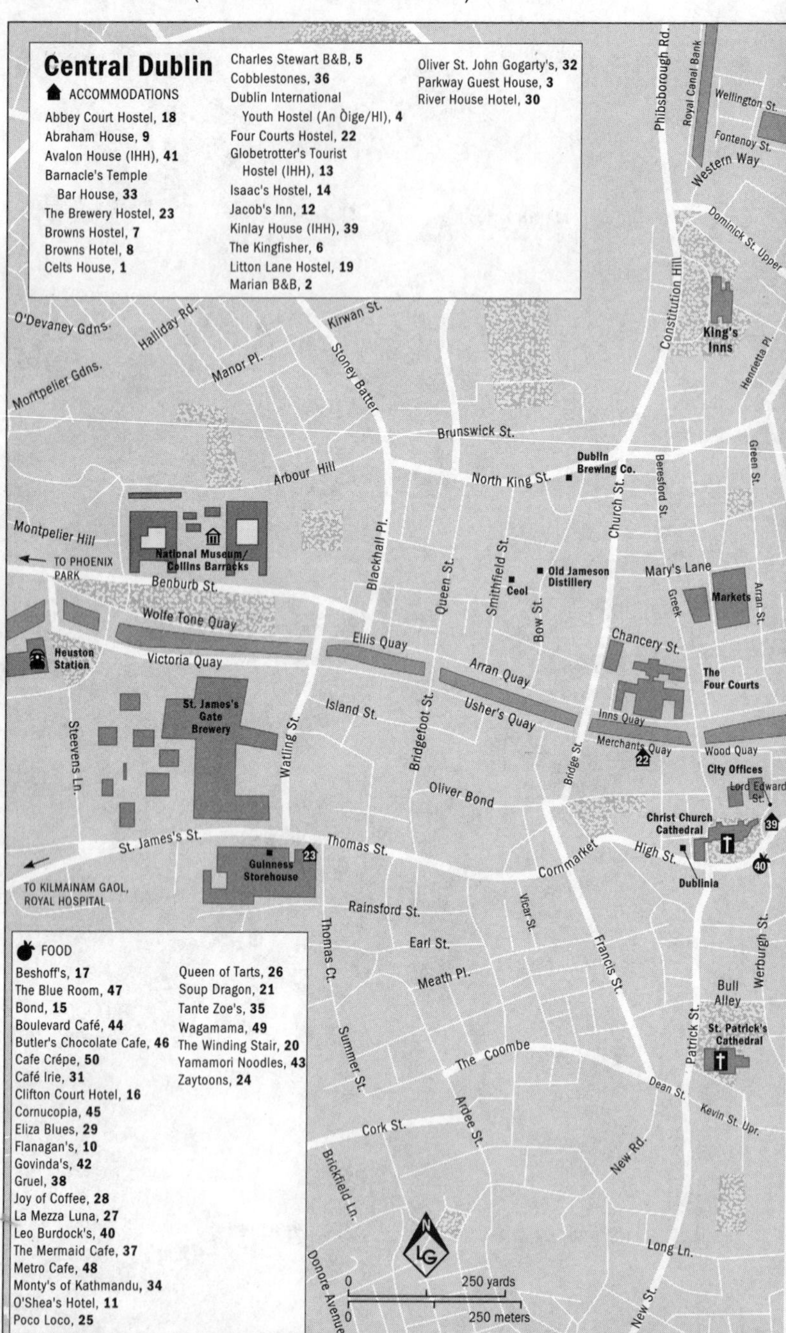

COUNTY DUBLIN

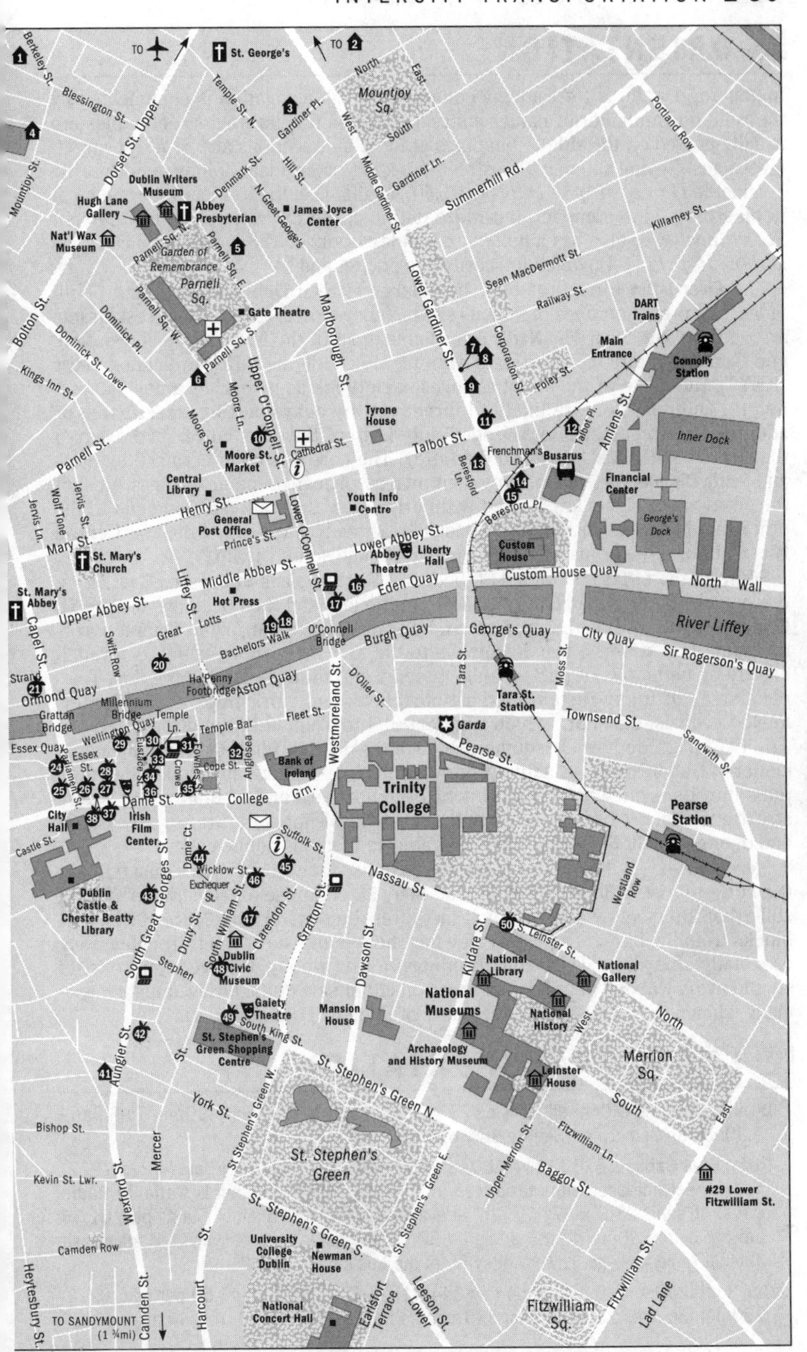

COUNTY DUBLIN

ORIENTATION

In general, Dublin is refreshingly compact, though navigation is complicated by the ridiculous number of names a street adopts along its way; street names are usually posted on the side of buildings at most intersections and never on street-level signs. Buying a map with a street index is a smart idea. Collins publishes the invaluable *Handy Map of Dublin* (€6.50), available at the tourist office and most book stores. Less compact, but more detailed, the *Ordnance Survey Dublin Street Map* (€6) also has a hefty street index booklet. The most compact is *The Dublin Popout* (€4), which fits easily in a pocket and has excellent detail.

The **River Liffey** forms a natural boundary between Dublin's North and South Sides. The preponderance of famous sights, fancy stores, and fabulous restaurants are on the **South Side.** The **North Side** claims most of the hostels, the bus station, and Connolly Station. The streets running alongside the Liffey are called **quays** (KEYS); the name of the street changes each block as it reaches a new quay. A helpful Dubliner is more likely to direct you by quays, not by street name or address. If a street is split into "Upper" and "Lower," then the "Lower" is the part of the street farther east, closer to the Liffey. The core of Dublin is ringed by **North** and **South Circular Rd.,** which enjoy their own assortment of name changes. Most of the city's major sights are located within this area; the walk from one end to the other should take about 40min. **O'Connell St.,** three blocks west of Busáras Central Bus Station, is the primary link between north and south Dublin.

South of the Liffey, O'Connell St. becomes **Westmoreland St.,** passes **Fleet St.** on the right, curves around Trinity College on the left, and then becomes **Grafton St.** One block south of the Liffey, **Fleet St.** becomes **Temple Bar.** While Temple Bar is the name of a street, it usually applies to the area as a whole, which is invaded nightly by battalions of pub-seeking students and tourists. During the day, Temple's array of funky restaurants, art museums, and workshops attract better-heeled crowds. **Dame St.,** which runs parallel to Temple Bar and terminates at Trinity College, defines the southern edge of the district. **Trinity College** is the nerve center of Dublin's cultural activity, drawing many bookshops and student-oriented pubs into its orbit. The college touches the northern end of **Grafton St.,** where street entertainers brush elbows with world-class shoppers. Grafton's southern end opens onto **St. Stephen's Green,** a sizable and famous public park.

Merchants on the North Side hawk merchandise for cheaper prices than those in the more touristed South. **Henry St.** and **Mary St.** comprise a pedestrian shopping zone that intersects with O'Connell just after the **General Post Office (GPO),** two blocks from the Liffey. The North Side has the reputation of being a rougher area, especially after dark. This reputation may not be wholly deserved, but tourists should avoid walking in unfamiliar areas on either side of the Liffey at night, especially when alone. It is wise to steer clear of Phoenix Park after dark.

LOCAL TRANSPORTATION

Dublin Bus, 59 O'Connell St. (☎873 4222). Open M 8:30am-5:30pm, Tu-F 9am-5:30pm, Sa 9am-1pm. (See **By Bus,** p. 82.)

Taxis: Blue Cabs (☎676 1111), **ABC** (☎285 5444), and **City Group Taxi** (☎872 7272) have wheelchair-accessible taxis (call in advance). Another option is **National Radio Cabs,** 40 James St. (☎677 2222). All available 24hr. €2.75 initial charge plus €1.35 per mi. before 10pm, €1.80 after; €1.50 call-in charge. Alternatively, taxi stands sit outside Trinity College, Lower Abbey St. at the bus station, and Parnell St.

Car Rental: Alamo, Dublin Airport (☎844 4162). Economy €38-44.50 per day, €220-250 per wk. Ages 25-74. **Argus,** 59 Terenure Rd. East (☎490 4444; www.argus-rental-car.com), also in the tourist office on Suffolk St., and the airport. Economy €50 per day, €111-250 per wk. Ages 25-70. **Budget,** 151 Lower Drumcondra Rd. (☎837 9611; www.budget.ie), and at the airport. Economy €38-40 per day, €138-158 per wk. Ages 23-75. Be warned that Dublin traffic is heavy, and parking spaces are scarce.

Bike Rental: Raleigh Rent-A-Bike, Kylemore Rd. (☎626 1333). Helps with arranging 1-way bike rentals: pickup in Dublin and drop-off in another city. €19 surcharge. **Cycle Ways,** 185-6 Parnell St. (☎873 4748). Rents quality bikes, but be sure to bring your own helmet. €20 per day, €80 per wk. Deposit €80. Open M-W and F-Sa 10am-6pm, Th 10am-8pm. (See **By Bicycle,** p. 32.)

Bike Repair and Storage: Square Wheel Cycleworks, Temple Ln. South (☎679 0838), off Dame St. Expert repair and excellent advice on bike touring. Storage available. Open M-F 8:30am-6:30pm. **Cycle Ways** does same-day repairs. (See **Bike Rental,** above.)

Hitchhiking: Since Dublin is well served by bus and rail, there is no good reason to thumb it, and *Let's Go* does not recommend trying. Still, those who choose to hitch from Dublin usually take buses to the outskirts where the motorways begin. Buses #25, 25A, 66, 66A, 67, and 67A from Wellington Quay go to Lucan Rd., which turns into N4 (to Galway and the West). For a ride to Cork, Limerick, and Waterford (N7), hitchers usually take bus #51, 51B, 68, or 69 from Fleet St. to Aston Quay to Naas ("nace") Rd. N11 (to Wicklow, Wexford, and Rosslare) can be reached by bus #84 from Eden Quay, or #46A from Fleet St. toward Stillorgan Rd. Bus #38 from George Quay or #39 from Burgh Quay to Navan Rd. goes to N3 (to Donegal and Sligo). Buses #33, 41, and 41A from Eden Quay toward Swords send hitchers on their way to N1 (Belfast and Dundalk). Again, *Let's Go* does not recommend hitchhiking.

PRACTICAL INFORMATION

TOURIST AND FINANCIAL SERVICES

Tourist Information: Main Office, Suffolk St. (☎1850 230 330 or 605 7700; UK ☎0171 493 3201; international ☎669 792 083; www.visitdublin.com). From Connolly Station, walk left down Amiens St., take a right onto Lower Abbey St., pass Busáras, and continue until you come to O'Connell St. Turn left, cross the bridge, and walk past Trinity College; the office will be on your right, down Suffolk St., in a converted church. Accommodation service with €4 booking fee. The tourist information office contracts to **Gulliver Ireland** travel agency for credit card bookings by phone (☎0800 6686 6866). **American Express** maintains a branch office with **currency exchange** here (☎605 7709; open M-Sa 9am-5pm); there is another at 41 Nassau St. **Bus Éireann** has representatives to provide info and tickets. **Argus Rent a Car** has a desk here (☎605 7701 or 490 4444; open M-F 9am-5pm, Sa 9am-1pm). A list of car rental agencies and other goodies are available at **Bord Fáilte.** You can also book tours, concerts, plays, and most anything else in Dublin that requires a ticket (through **TicketMaster**); booking fee €2. Main Office open July-Aug. M-Sa 9am-8:30pm, Su 11am-5:30pm; Sept.-June M-Sa 9am-5:30pm. Reservation desks close 30min. early.

Branch Offices: Dublin Airport. Open daily 8am-10pm. **Dún Laoghaire Harbour,** Ferry Terminal Building. Open M-Sa 10am-1pm and 2-6pm. **Tallaght,** the Square. Open M-Sa 9:30am-noon and 12:30-5pm. **Baggot St.** Open M-F 9:30am-5pm. **13 Upper O'Connell St.** Open Apr.-Aug. M-Sa 9am-5pm. The latter 4 branches are well stocked and less crowded than the airport and main branches. All telephone inquiries handled by the central office (☎1850 230 330).

Northern Ireland Tourist Board: 16 Nassau St. (☎679 1977 or 1850 230 230). Books accommodations up North. Open M-F 9:15am-5:30pm, Sa 10am-5pm.

Community and Youth Information Centre: Sackville Pl. (☎878 6844), at Marlborough St., east of O'Connell St. Library of resources on youth and special-needs groups, careers, outings, travel, hostels (no bookings), sports, counseling, and referrals. Comprehensive **work opportunities** listing board and free **Internet access** (call ahead). Open M-W 9:30am-1pm and 2-6pm, Th-Sa 9:30am-1pm and 2-5pm.

Budget Travel: usit NOW, 19-21 Aston Quay (☎602 1777), near O'Connell Bridge. The place for Irish travel discounts. ISIC, HI, and EYC cards; **TravelSave** stamps €10 (see **Student Travel Agencies,** p. 22). Photo booths €6. Big discounts, especially for ISIC cardholders and people under 26. **Internet access** with ISIC card €1 per 15min., €2.50 per 45min. Open M-W and F 8:30am-6:30pm, Th 8:30am-8:30pm, Sa 9:30am-5pm. **Dust Travel** (☎677 5076), located on the Trinity College campus, also specializes in student travel. Turn left inside the main gate. Open M-F 9am-5pm.

Hosteling Organization: An Óige Head Office (Irish Youth Hostel Association/HI), 61 Mountjoy St. (☎830 5808; www.irelandyha.org), at Wellington St. Follow O'Connell St. north, ignoring its name changes. Mountjoy St. is on the left, 20min. from O'Connell Bridge. Book/pay for HI hostels here. Also sells bike and rail package tours. The *An Óige Handbook* lists all HI hostels in Ireland and Northern Ireland. Hugely beneficial membership card €15, under 18 €7.50. Open M-F 9:30am-5:30pm. (Also see **Hostels,** p. 35.)

Embassies: For an extensive list of embassies and consulates, see **Essentials,** p. 7.

Banks: Bank of Ireland, AIB, and **TSB** branches with **bureaux de change** and **24hr. ATMs** cluster on Lower O'Connell St., Grafton St., and in the Suffolk and Dame St. areas. Most banks are open M-F 10am-4pm. Bureaux de change also found in the General Post Office and in the tourist office main branch.

American Express: 41 Nassau St. (☎679 9000). Traveler's check refunds. Currency exchange. Client mail held. Open M-F 9am-5pm. Smaller branch inside the Suffolk St. tourist center is also open Su.

LOCAL SERVICES

Luggage Storage: Connolly Station. €2.50 per item per day. Open M-Sa 7:40am-9:20pm, Su 9:10am-9:45pm. **Heuston Station.** €2-5 per item, depending on size. Open daily 6:30am-10:30pm. **Busáras.** €3 per item, lockers €4-9. Open M-Sa 8am-7:45pm, Su 10am-5:45pm.

Lost Property: Connolly Station (☎703 2363), **Heuston Station** (☎703 2102), **Busáras** (☎703 2489), and **Dublin Bus** (☎703 3055).

Library: Dublin Corporation Central Library, Henry and Moore St. (☎873 4333), in the ILAC Centre. Video facilities, a kids library, EU telephone directories, and free **Internet access** (call ahead) are all available. To check out books you must provide proof of residence in Dublin. Tourists may apply for a reference ticket, which allows use of library facilities, minus check-out privileges. Open M-Th 10am-8pm, F-Sa 10am-5pm.

Women's Resources: Women's Aid Helpline (☎1800 341 900) offers info on legal matters and support groups (10am-10pm). **Dublin Rape Crisis Centre** (24hr. hotline ☎1800 778 888). **Dublin Well Woman Centre,** 35 Lower Liffey St. (☎872 8051), is a private health center for women. It also runs a clinic (☎668 3714) at 67 Pembroke Rd.

Ticket Agencies: HMV (☎679 5334) record stores and **TicketMaster** (www.ticketmaster.ie) are linked at the hip; try HMV on Grafton St. or the TicketMaster ticket desk at the Suffolk St. tourist office. Additional TicketMaster desk at Celtic Note, 14-15 Suffolk St.

Laundry: Laundry Shop, 191 Parnell St. (☎872 3541), near Busáras. Wash and dry €8-12. Open M-F 8am-7pm, Sa 9am-6pm, Su 11am-5pm. **All-American Launderette,** 40 South Great Georges St. (☎677 2779). Wash and dry €7; full service €8. Open M-Sa 8:30am-7pm, Su 10am-6pm.

Work Opportunities: Check out the helpful job listing board at the **Community and Youth Information Center** (see **Tourist and Financial Services,** above). If you wish to obtain work through an organization, **Working Ireland,** 26 Eustace St. (☎01 677 0300;

www.workingireland.ie), is a multi-tasking agency that arranges short- and long-term job placement throughout Ireland. **The Job Shop,** 50 Grafton St. (☎672 7755) can also help.

EMERGENCY AND COMMUNICATIONS

Emergency: ☎999 or 112; no coins required.

Police *(Garda)*: Dublin Metro Headquarters, Harcourt Terr. (☎666 9500); Store St. Station (☎666 8000); Fitzgibbon St. Station (☎666 8400); Pearse St. (☎666 9000). **Police Confidential Report Line:** ☎1800 666 111.

Counseling and Support: Tourist Victim Support, Harcourt Sq. (☎478 5295; 10am-5pm helpline ☎1800 661 771; www.victimsupport.ie). Helps robbery victims find accommodations and contact embassies or families; a loss or crime report must first be filed with the police. Also offers telephone, email, assistance with language difficulties, emergency meals and shelter, and can help with re-issuing travel tickets and canceling credit cards. Open M-Sa 10am-6pm, Su noon-6pm. **Samaritans,** 112 Marlborough St. (☎1850 609 090 or 872 7700), for anything and everything. **Rape Crisis Centre,** 70 Lower Leeson St. (☎661 4911; 24hr. hotline ☎1800 778 888). Office open M-F 8:30am-7pm and Sa 9am-4pm. **Cura,** 30 South Anne St. (☎505 3040; Dublin office ☎671 0598), is a Catholic-funded support organization for women with unplanned pregnancies. Open M and W 10:30am-6:30pm, Tu and Th 10:30am-8:30pm, F-Sa 10:30am-2:30pm. **AIDS Helpline** (☎1800 459 459). Open daily 10am-5pm.

Pharmacy: O'Connell's, 56 Lower O'Connell St. (☎873 0427). Convenient to city bus routes. Open M-Sa 7:30am-10pm and Su 10am-10pm. Other branches are scattered about the city, including 2 on Grafton St. **Dowling's,** 6 Baggot St. (☎678 5612), near the Shelbourne Hotel and St. Stephen's Green. Also on Church St. (☎674 0204), by the Four Courts. Both open M-W and F 8am-7pm, Th 8am-8pm, Sa 9am-7pm.

Hospital: St. James's Hospital, James St. (☎453 7941). Take bus #123. **Mater Misericordiae Hospital,** Eccles St. (☎830 1122), off Lower Dorset St. Buses #10, 11, 13, 16, 121, and 122. **Beaumont Hospital,** Beaumont Rd. (☎837 7755 or 809 3000). Buses #27B, 51A, 101, 103, and 300. **Tallaght Hospital** (☎414 2000), farther south, is served by buses #49, 49A, 50, 54A, 65, 65B, 75, 76, 77, 77A, 201, and 202.

Phones: Telecom Éireann (inquiries ☎1901; phonecard refunds ☎1850 337 337). Public pay phones are on almost every corner. Recent privatization of Ireland's phone industry means other companies are putting up their own pay phones; pay careful attention to varying rates for local calls. (Also see **Telephones,** p. 39.)

Directory Inquiries: ☎11850 (€0.59 per min.) or ☎11811 (3 inquiries €0.50); international ☎11818 (€0.58 for the 1st 30sec., €0.02 per sec. after).

Internet Access: Free Internet is available at the **central library** (see **Local Services,** above) and at the **Community and Youth Information Centre** (book ahead by phone in both cases). Several chains abound, the best being **The Internet Exchange,** with branches at 146 Parnell St. (☎670 3000) and Fownes St. in Temple Bar (☎635 1680). €4 per hr., members €2.50 per hr. Membership card €5. Open daily 9am-10:30pm. **Global Internet Cafe,** 8 Lower O'Connell St. (☎878 0295), a block north of the Liffey and on the right. Wide array of services, excellent coffee and smoothies. €6 per hr., students €5, members €3. Membership card €5. Open M-F 8am-11pm, Sa 9am-11pm, Su 10am-11pm. **The Planet Cyber Cafe,** 13 St. Andrews St. (☎670 5182). Science-fiction theme, with tasty nibblies. €6 per hr., students €5. Open M-W and Su 10am-10pm, Th-Sa 10am-11pm.

Post Office: General Post Office (GPO), O'Connell St. (☎705 7000). *Poste Restante* pickup at the **bureau de change** window (see **Mail,** p. 38). Open M-Sa 8am-8pm, Su 10am-6:30pm. Smaller post offices around the city open M-F 8:45am-6pm. **Postal code:** Dublin 1. Dublin is the only place in the Republic with postal codes. Even-numbered codes are for areas south of the Liffey, odd-numbered are for the north.

ACCOMMODATIONS

Reserve at least a week in advance, particularly around Easter weekend, bank holiday weekends, sporting weekends, St. Patrick's Day, New Year's, and the peak summer season (June-Aug.). The tourist office books local accommodations for a fee of €4, but they only deal in Bord Fáilte-approved B&Bs and hostels, which aren't necessarily better than unapproved ones (though they do tend to be cleaner). Phoenix Park may tempt the desperate, but camping there is a terrible idea, not to mention big-time illegal—if the *Garda* or park rangers don't deter you, the threat of thieves and other unsavories should. If the accommodations below are full, consult Dublin Tourism's annually updated and incredibly helpful *Dublin Accommodation Guide* (€3.80), or ask hostel and B&B staff for referrals.

Hostels in **Dún Laoghaire** (see p. 129), only a DART ride away, offer an alternative to city life. In addition to hostels, a blanket of high-quality B&Bs warms Dublin and its suburbs. Those with a green shamrock sign out front are registered, occasionally checked, and approved by Bord Fáilte. B&Bs without the shamrock haven't been inspected but may be cheaper and better located— popular establishments often find that Bord Fáilte's advertising is unnecessary. Rooms range from €15 at the very lowest to upwards of €38 per person sharing. On the North Side, B&Bs cluster along **Upper** and **Lower Gardiner St.**, on **Sheriff St.**, and near **Parnell Sq.** Exercise caution when walking home through the inner-city area at night. **Clonliffe Rd.**, **Sandymount**, and **Clontarf** are no more than a 15min. bus ride from Eden Quay. Chances for decent B&Bs are greater farther out, especially if you aren't the reservation type. Dublin Tourism's annually updated *Dublin Accommodation Guide* (€3.80) lists the locations of all approved B&Bs.

INSIDE THE CITY CENTER

TEMPLE BAR AND THE QUAYS

With chic cafes and trendy pubs, Temple Bar is *the* destination for fashionable and stylish wannabes trying to keep up with the latest fads. Dublin's student population converges on the pubs here nightly; during the day you'll find them winding in and out of the area's coffee shops and small museums. Ignoring the pretense, or because of it, this is where you want to be.

Abbey Court Hostel, 29 Bachelor's Walk, O'Connell Bridge (☎878 0700). From O'Connell Bridge, turn left and it's just up the street. Great location. Clean, smoke-free, and with bathrooms/showers in most rooms. Knowledgeable staff will spend hours helping you plot your way around the city. Continental breakfast included. **Internet access** €1 per 15min. Free luggage storage; security box €1. Full service laundry €8 per load. 12-bed dorms €17-20; 6-bed €22-25; 4-bed €25-28. Doubles €76-88. ❷

Oliver St. John Gogarty's Temple Bar Hostel, 18-21 Anglesea St. (☎671 1822). Joyce once roomed here with Gogarty. Drink and boogie with the ghosts of both at the pub and disco next door. The location is unbeatable if you're frolicking in Temple Bar. **Internet access** available. Laundry €4. Dorms €13-23; doubles €46-56; triples €63-75. Oct.-May prices €2-4 less. ❷

Cobblestones, 29 Eustace St. (☎677 5614). A breath of fresh air from the more industrial hostels, right in the middle of Temple Bar. Friendly staff, bright rooms, and a kitchen with fridge and microwave. Book before Feb. and watch the St. Paddy's Day parade from the patio roof. Breakfast included. Cheap **Internet access.** Dorms €18-21; doubles €48. Long-term stays welcome. Student and group discounts available. ❷

Litton Lane Hostel, 2-4 Litton Ln. (☎872 8389), off Bachelors Walk. A former studio for the likes of U2, Van Morrison, and Sinead O'Connor. In addition to standard dorm accommodations, the hostel also offers shining new apartments, complete with their own separate lounge area, kitchen, bathroom, TV, and laundry facilities. **Internet access** €1 per 20min. Laundry €5. Key deposit €1. Check-in 3pm, check-out 10:30am. Dorms €16-25; doubles €70-80. 1-bedroom apartments €80-110; 2-bedroom €120-150. ❷

Barnacle's Temple Bar House, 19 Temple Ln. (☎671 6277). "The burning hot center of everything." So close to the hopping (and noisy) heart of Dublin that you can crawl home to your bed from the Temple Bar pubs. Lounge with open fire and TV. Skylights in some rooms. All rooms with bath and water pressure that will make you sing. Continental breakfast included. Laundry and luggage storage available. 12-bed dorms €13-16.50; 10-bed €15.50-19; 6-bed €18-21.50; 4-bed €20.50-23. Doubles €62-74. ❶

River House Hotel, 23-24 Eustace St. (☎670 7655; www.visunet.ie/riverhouse). A quiet establishment right in the middle of thumping Temple Bar. Modern rooms and a space-age pub. Delicious and filling full Irish breakfast included. Mar.-Oct. singles €90; doubles €135; triples €180. Nov.-Feb. singles €70; doubles €95; triples €115. ❺

GARDINER ST. AND CUSTOMS HOUSE

Unsuspecting visitors arrive here late at night by bus or train, wander around aimlessly looking for a place to stay, and usually get plundered. Plan ahead, or face the consequences. **Gardiner St.** runs parallel to **O'Connell St.** and leads to the **Custom House; Parnell Sq.** sits at the top of **Upper Gardiner St.** Both Lower and Upper Gardiner St. are within walking distance of **Busáras** and **Connolly station;** buses #41, 41B, and 41C from Eden Quay travel to the end of the road.

Globetrotter's Tourist Hostel (IHH), 46-7 Lower Gardiner St. (☎873 5893; www.iol.ie/globetrotters). A dose of luxury for the weary. Beds are snug, but there's plenty of room to stow your stuff. Full Irish breakfast included. **Internet access** available. Free luggage storage. Towels €1. Dorms €19-21.50; singles €60-66.50; doubles €102-110. ❷

Browns Hostel, 89-90 Lower Gardiner St. (☎855 0034; www.brownshostelireland.com). Brand-new hostel attached to the Georgian decorated **Browns Hotel** (see below). Glistening yellow decor with TVs, closets, and A/C in every room. Dorms are named after Irish rivers; be sure to ask for the Shannon room. Breakfast included. **Internet access** available. Lockers €1. Towels €1. 20-bed dorm €12.50-15; 10- to 14-bed €15-20; 4- to 6-bed €20-25. Long-term bargains available. ❶

Browns Hotel, 90 Lower Gardiner St. (☎855 0034; www.brownshotelireland.com). Elegant Georgian building with newly refurbished rooms and a professional, hospitable staff that aims to take care of all your needs. Full hot breakfast included. Connected to **Browns Hostel** (see above). Singles €65-75; doubles €70-100. ❺

Abraham House, 82-3 Lower Gardiner St. (☎855 0600). An accommodating receptionist and respectable, tidy rooms with peaceful green and yellow color schemes calm the harried traveler. New expansion includes a wing of hotel-esque rooms for those desiring a private TV and kettle. Light breakfast included. **Bureau de change. Internet access** €1.20 per 15min. Free luggage and bike storage. Laundry €5. 12-bed dorms €13-17; 8-bed €17-22; 6-bed €18-25; 4-bed €20-29. Triples €60-72, with bath €80-105; quads €80-104/€96-126. ❷

Jacob's Inn, 21-28 Talbot Pl. (☎855 5660). 2 blocks north of the Custom House, Talbot Pl. stretches from the back of the bus station up to Talbot St. Rooms, all with bath, are spacious, clean, and cheery. Gigantic luggage room with individual cages. Wheelchair-accessible. Breakfast €3.50-6. **Internet access** €1 per 20min. Bike storage. Lockers €1.30 per night, deposit €6.35. Towels €1.30. Laundry €7. Lockout 11am-3pm. Dorms €13-19; doubles €60-64; triples €78-84. Weekend prices €2 higher. ❷

Isaac's Hostel, 2-5 Frenchman's Ln. (☎855 6215), off the lower end of Gardiner St., behind the Custom House. Especially attractive to the young and energetic. Bustling cafe attached to the lobby. **Internet access** €1 per 15min. Bike storage. Towels €2. Laundry

IN RECENT NEWS

"DAMN THE EURO TO BLOODY HELL"

Many an Irish citizen has been heard declaring these words recently, as well as a fair number of tourists, too. Since the switch over from the old Irish punt to the currency of the continent, it seems that prices in Ireland have risen across the board. Dublin was rated the third most expensive city in Europe in 2002, and restaurant and accommodation rates have rounded up higher than the normal annual rate of inflation.

The real costs of the euro may be cultural, however. A country's currency is not as dispensable as an ATM would have you believe. The currency of a country marks a people, and they mark it. In sacrificing their currency for the blue and neon pink of the euro, the Irish may also have lost part of their heritage, for with the loss of the Irish currency comes the loss of some of Ireland's most flavorful colloquialisms. Soon, you'll no longer be able to walk down Moore St. and listen to the cries of old women hawking their fruit and veggies by the roadside, shouting "fiv' fer a pound" or "three for a fiver." No longer will you be able to spare your friend a "few quid," or pay him back the "tener" you borrowed from him last week. And forget about buying your girlfriend a cheap gift from the 'pound store.' It seems that the "punt" has been booted, and we can't even console ourselves by dipping into the shop and buying some "penny sweets."

€8. Bed lockout 11am-2:30pm. Mar.-Oct. 8- to 10-bed dorms €11.75-14; 4-bed €20. Singles €32; doubles €58. Nov.-Feb. €2 less. Weekend prices €2 higher. ❶

WEST OF TEMPLE BAR

Farther from the action, but closer to the city's main sights, the area west of Temple Bar is more industrial than the city center. Among the many duds in the area, several star accommodations stand out. While you might find yourself a 30min. walk from the action of Temple Bar, in the morning you'll awake and find yourself on the doorstep of the Guinness Brewery or Christ Church.

Four Courts Hostel, 15-17 Merchants Quay (☎672 5839). South side of the river, near O'Donovan Rossa Bridge. The #748 bus from the airport drops you next door. If you come into town late without a place to stay, try here first. The non-central location of this 250-bed, first-rate mega-hostel is made up for by its extremely friendly staff and relaxing atmosphere. Clean rooms (most with showers), kitchen facilities, laundry (€5 per load), carpark facilities, and long-term stays available. Continental breakfast included. **Internet access** €1 per 10min. 16-bed dorms €15-16.50; 8-bed €17-19; 4- to 6-bed €20-21.50. Doubles €54-65; family room €25-26.50 per person. ❷

Avalon House (IHH), 55 Aungier St. (☎475 0001; www.avalon-house.ie). Turn off Dame St. onto Great Georges St.; the hostel is a 10min. walk down on your right and just a stumble away from Temple Bar. Large but not overwhelming, Avalon hums with the energy of transcontinental travelers. Dorms provide privacy with a split-level setup connected by cool spiral staircases. Wheelchair-accessible. Very secure. Continental breakfast included. **Internet access** available. Storage cages €1 per day. Towels €2, deposit €8. Large dorms €15-20; 6-bed €20-30. Singles €30-37; doubles €56-70. ❷

Kinlay House (IHH), 2-12 Lord Edward St. (☎679 6644). Slide down the oak banisters in the lofty entrance hall, snuggle into the soft couches in the TV room, or gaze at Christ Church Cathedral from your room window. Get a crash course in Irish culture from the Irish icon posters lining the walls. Breakfast included. **Internet access** €1 per 15min. Free luggage storage. Lockers €2, deposit €5. Laundry €7. 15- to 24-bed dorms €15-17; 20-bed partitioned into 4-bed nooks €16-18; 4- to 6-bed €20-24, with bath €22-26. Singles €40-46; doubles €50-56, with bath €54-60. Nov.-May prices €2 less. ❷

The Brewery Hostel, 22-23 Thomas St. (☎453 8600). Follow Dame St. past Christ Church through its name changes, or take bus #123. So close to the Guinness

Brewery you can smell the hops, and only a 15min. walk from Temple Bar. Rooms are a bit snug but the beds are good. Continental breakfast included. All rooms with bath. Free carpark. Free luggage storage. Awkward 1 key per room system. 10-bed dorms €16-22; 8-bed €18-24; 4-bed €19-28. Doubles €65-78. One-bedroom apartment €75-100. ❷

NORTH OF O'CONNELL ST.

While Temple Bar has Dublin's small and eclectic museums and theaters, the big boys reside just north of O'Connell St., around Parnell Sq.: Gate Theatre, the Dublin Writers Museum, and the National Wax Museum are all found in the area.

Parkway Guest House, 5 Gardiner Pl. (☎874 0469). Rooms are high-ceilinged and tidy, and the location (off Gardiner St. near Croke Park) is perfectly central. Run by a mother-and-son team. The son, a hurling veteran, offers discerning advice on the city's restaurants and pubs and can talk for hours about sports. Full Irish breakfast. Singles €32; doubles €52-60, with bath €60-70. ❸

Dublin International Youth Hostel (An Óige/HI), 61 Mountjoy St. (☎830 4555; www.irelandyha.org), in a converted convent. O'Connell St. changes names 3 times before the left turn onto Mountjoy St. Calling home from the confessional-turned-phone-booths may make you say things you'll later regret. Don't forget to say grace during the free breakfast, served in the chapel. Carpark and buses to Temple Bar. Wheelchair-accessible. Towels €1. Laundry €5. Dorms €20; doubles €52-56; triples €75-81. ❷

Celts House, 32 Blessington St. (☎830 0657), 15min. from the city center. 38 comfy wooden bunks in a brightly painted setting. Plenty of parking. Key deposit €5. Reception 9am-11pm. 8-bed dorms €13-15; 6-bed €20; 4-bed €18.50. Doubles €51. ❷

Marian B&B, 21 Upper Gardiner St. (☎874 4129). Brendan and Catherine McElroy provide lovely rooms at a better price than comparable neighborhood accommodations. Singles €30; doubles €54. ❸

Charles Stewart B&B, 5-6 Parnell Sq. E. (☎878 0350). Continue up O'Connell St. past Parnell St. and look to your right. More a hotel than a B&B. Renovations expected to be complete by 2003. Full Irish breakfast. Singles €50-63.50; doubles €76-89; triples €120; quads €140. Very small private room with shared bath facilities €31.75. ❺

The Kingfisher, 166 Parnell St. (☎872 8732). A combined B&B, restaurant, and Internet cafe. Offers clean, modern rooms, uncomplicated food (fish and chips €8), and a full Irish breakfast. Cheap **Internet access.** TV/VCR in each room, kitchenettes in some. Singles €60; doubles €110; triples €165. Prices drop in winter. ❺

OUTSIDE THE CITY CENTER

CLONLIFFE ROAD

This is an ideal place to stay if you're planning to attend (or eavesdrop on) events at **Croke Park.** To make the 20min. walk from the city center, go up O'Connell St., take a right on Dorset St., head across the Royal Canal, then turn right onto Clonliffe Rd. Buses #41A, 41B, and 41C serve the area from the airport.

Mona's B&B, 148 Clonliffe Rd. (☎837 6723). Gorgeous house run for 37 years (and probably 37 more) by Ireland's most lovely proprietress. Homemade brown bread accompanies the full Irish breakfast. Open May-Oct. Singles €35; doubles €66. ❸

Mrs. Molly Ryan, 10 Distillery Rd. (☎837 4147), off Clonliffe Rd. On your left if you're coming from the city center, in a yellow house attached to #11. The unsinkable Molly Ryan, in her countless years, has never marked the B&B with a sign. Small rooms, small prices, no breakfast. As honest as they come. Singles €15; doubles €30. ❷

Villa Materdei, 208 Clonliffe Rd., and **St. Martins B&B,** 186 Clonliffe Rd. (☎857 0920). Sri Lankan owner Bala has renovated these two beautiful Victorian houses with modern amenities. TVs and VCRs keep you company at night. Blurs the line between B&B and more commercial hotel experiences. All rooms with bath. €35 per person. ❸

SANDYMOUNT

Sandymount is a peaceful neighborhood near **Dublin Port,** 2 mi. south of the city and famous for its Joycean associations. Take bus #3 from Clery's Department Store on O'Connell St. or the DART to Lansdowne Rd. or Sandymount (10min.).

Mrs. Bermingham, 8 Dromard Terr. (☎668 3861), on Dromard Ave. Take the #2 or 3 bus. Disembark at the Tesco and make the next left. Down the street, the road forks—the left fork is Dromard Terr. The colorful Mrs. Bermingham resides in the red brick house covered with ivy. One room has a lovely bay window over the garden. Soft beds with fluffy comforters. Open Feb.-Nov. Singles €28; doubles with bath €52. ❸

Rita and Jim Casey, Villa Jude, 2 Church Ave. (☎668 4982), off Beach Rd. Bus #3 to the first stop on Tritonville Rd.; Church Ave. is back a few yards. Call for directions from the Lansdowne Rd. DART stop. Mr. Casey is the former mayor of Sandymount, and he and lovely Rita specialize in the royal treatment. Clean rooms, big breakfasts, and good company. Doubles €45. ❷

Mrs. Dolores Abbot-Murphy, 14 Castle Park (☎269 8413). Ask the #3 bus driver to drop you off at Sandymount Green. Continue past Browne's Deli and take the 1st left; at the end of the road look right. A 5min. walk from Sandymount DART stop. Cheerful rooms in a charming cul-de-sac. Open May-Oct. €28 per person, with bath €32. ❸

CLONTARF

Clontarf Rd. runs north along Dublin Bay to the neighborhood that bears its name. Sea breezes are more pleasant than the harbor traffic; B&Bs are inland a few blocks and avoid both. Many B&Bs in Clontarf are unmarked; call ahead. Bus #130 goes from Lower Abbey St. to Clontarf Rd. (15min.).

COUNTY DUBLIN

The White House, 125 Clontarf Rd. (☎833 3196). Sink into your bed and gaze out at pristine rose gardens. Large garden and yard out back. Full Irish breakfast. Singles €36; doubles €68. ❸

Bayview, 98 Clontarf Rd. (☎833 3950). The Barry family provides fresh, airy rooms and a friendly spot of tea on arrival. Lucky travelers get Irish piano tunes in the evening. Singles €35; doubles with bath €70-74. ❸

Mrs. Geary, 69 Hampton Ct. (☎833 1199). Take bus #130 from Lower Abbey St., and up Vernon Ave. in Clontarf. Ask the bus driver to drop you at Hampton Court, a walled cul-de-sac. Spacious and relaxing, with an enclosed sun deck overlooking a tidy garden. Open Apr.-Sept. Singles €36; doubles €54, with bath €60. ❸

Waterville, 154 Clontarf Rd. (☎833 0238). Wood floors and modern decor with a dining room overlooking the bay. All rooms with bath, TV, and phone. **Internet** hookup available. €40-45 per person. ❹

Clontarf Court Hotel, 225 Clontarf Rd. (☎833 2680). Family owned hotel/restaurant/pub overlooking a sailboat harbor. Room 104 has the best views. Golf courses close by. W you'll find trad in the pub, Su features two locals banging out Irish tunes on the piano. Full Irish breakfast included. Singles €60; doubles €90; family room €120. ❺

CAMPING

Most campsites are far from the city center, but camping equipment is available in the heart of the city. **The Great Outdoors,** on Chatham St. off the top of Grafton St., has an excellent selection of tents, backpacks, and cookware. (☎679 4293. 10% discount for An Óige/HI members. Open M-W and F-Sa 9:30am-5:30pm, Th 9:30am-8pm.) **O'Meara's Camping,** 4-6 Bridgefoot St., off Thomas St. near the Guinness Brewery, sells camping equipment and rents tents. (☎670 8639. 3-person tents €40 to buy; 3-room tents €150 to rent per wk. Open year-round M-Sa 10am-6pm, Su 2:30-5:30pm.) It is illegal and unsafe to camp in Phoenix Park.

Camac Valley Tourist Caravan & Camping Park, Naas Rd., Clondalkin (☎464 0644), near Corkagh Park. Accessible by bus #69 (35min. from city center, €1.50). Food shop and kitchen facilities. Wheelchair-accessible. Dogs welcome. €7 per person; €14 per 2 people with car; €17 per 2 people with caravan; €15 per 2 people with camper. Showers €1. Laundry €4.50. ❶

Shankill Caravan and Camping Park (☎282 0011). The DART and buses #45 and 84 from Eden Quay run to Shankill, as does bus #45A from the Dún Laoghaire ferryport. Welcomes all ages. €9 per tent plus €2 per adult, €1 per child. Showers €1. ❶

North Beach Caravan and Camping Park, in Rush (☎843 7131; www.northbeach.ie). Bus #33 from Eden Quay (1hr., 25 per day) and the suburban rail come here. Peaceful, beach-side location in a quiet town just outside Dublin's urban jumble. Kitchen available. Open Mar.-Oct. €6 per person, children €3. Electricity €1.50. Showers €0.50. ❶

LONG-TERM STAYS

Visitors expecting to spend several weeks in Dublin may want to consider a bedsit or a sublet. Longer stays are often most economical when sharing the cost of rent with others. Many hostels give special rates for long-termers, especially in the winter; ask at individual hostels for details. Rooms in locations outside the city center, like Marino and Rathmines, go for about €70-110 per week (ask whether electricity, phone, and water are included). B&Bs sometimes offer reduced rates for long-term stays but are reluctant to do so in the high season.

There are a number of sources for finding roommates and possible sublets; Dublin's countless university students are often looking for them, usually for the summer but also on a weekly basis. The most up-to-date and comprehensive postings of vacancies are at **usit NOW,** 19-21 Aston Quay (see **Practical Information,** p. 91). Supermarket notice boards are another source. **Trinity College** has two spots worth checking out: one notice board is near the guard's desk in the Student Union and the other is on the main gate. Also check out the tourist office's *Dublin Accommodation Guide* (€3.80), or classified ads in the *Irish Independent*, the *Irish Times*, and particularly the *Evening Herald*. If you'd rather someone else did the legwork, **Dublin Central Reservations,** 3 Sandholes, Castleknock, arranges short or long stays in locations both humble and snazzy. (☎820 0394; bookings@dublinreservations.com. From €190.50 per wk. No finder's fee. Open M-F 9am-7pm, Sa noon-5:30pm.) **Working Ireland,** 26 Eustace St. (☎01 677 0300; www.workingireland.ie), also assists travelers in finding long-term accommodation.

Another reasonable option is **university housing,** available during the summer holiday—roughly mid-June to mid-September. You shouldn't expect anything fancy, but prices are only a fraction more expensive than those of hostels. **Dublin City University,** Glasnevin, can be reached on bus #11, 11A, 11B, 13, or 19A from the city center. (☎700 5736. Free morning breakfast. Singles with bath €42 per night; doubles with bath €70.) Other options are available through **usit** (see **Practical Information,** p. 91), which operates **University College Dublin** dorms in Belfield. (☎269 7111. Take bus #3. Single private room in an apartment of 4 €33 per night.)

FOOD

Dublin's many **open-air markets** sell fixin's fresh and cheap. Vendors hawk fruit, fresh strawberries, flowers, and fish from their pushcarts. The later in the week, the more lively the market. Actors might head to **Moore St. Market** to perfect their Dublin accent, and get fresh veggies at the same time. (Between Henry and Parnell St. Open M-Sa 7am-5pm.) The **Thomas St. Market,** along the continuation of Dame St., is a calmer alternative for fruit and veg shopping. (Open M-Sa 9am-5pm.) On Saturdays, **Temple Bar's** gourmet open-air market takes place in Meeting House Sq.

The cheapest **supermarkets** around Dublin are in the **Dunnes Stores** chain, with full branches at St. Stephen's Green (☎478 0188; open M-W and F-Sa 8:30am-7pm, Th 8:30am-9pm, Su noon-6pm), the ILAC Centre off Henry St., on N. Earl St. off O'Connell, and a small convenience version on Georges St. The **Runner Bean,** 4 Nassau St., vends whole foods, homemade breads, veggies, fruits, and nuts. (☎679 4833. Open M-F 7:30am-6pm, Sa 7:30am-3pm.) **Down to Earth,** 73 South Great Georges St., stocks health foods, herbal medicines, and a dozen granolas. (☎671 9702. Open M-Sa 8:30am-6:30pm.) Health food is also available around the city at various branches of **Nature's Way;** the biggest is at the St. Stephen's Green shopping center. (☎478 0165. Open M-W and F-Sa 9am-6pm, Th 9am-8pm.)

TEMPLE BAR

This neighborhood is bursting with creative eateries catering to every budget. Temple Bar has more ethnic diversity in its restaurants than counties Louth, Meath, Wicklow, and Longford combined. (And probably Offaly, too.)

La Mezza Luna, 1 Temple Ln. (☎671 2840), on the corner of Dame St. Refined and classy, minus the pretension. Celestial food with a giant a la carte dinner menu ranging from pasta and seafood to Asian noodles and tortilla wraps. Try the wok-fried chicken (€8.25). Open M-Th 8am-11pm, F-Sa 9:30am-11:30pm, Su 9:30am-10:30pm. ❷

Cafe Irie, 11 Fownes St. (☎672 5090). Travel up Fownes St. from Temple; it's on the left above the clothing store Sé Sí Progressive. A small, hidden eatery with an impressive selection of lip-smackingly good sandwiches (€2-4). A little crunchy, a little jazzy, and a whole lotta good. Vegan-friendly. Open M-Sa 9am-8pm, Su noon-6pm. ❶

Monty's of Kathmandu, (☎670 4911), just off of Dame St. on the right. Nepalese food with decor to match. Mains €13-18; try the Sekuwa Chatpate Chicken or the spicy Begum Bahar with the unorthodox mix of chicken and lamb (both €14). Open M-Sa noon-2:30pm and 6-11:30pm, Su 6-11:30pm. ❹

Tante Zoe's, 1 Crowe St. (☎679 4407), across from the back entrance of the Foggy Dew pub. New Orleans Creole food in an elegantly casual setting. Staff will help you get just the right spiciness. Mains €16.50-19. Open daily noon-4pm and 6pm-midnight. ❹

Eliza Blues (☎671 9114), on Wellington Quay, across from Millennium bridge. A circular glass door ushers patrons into this modern restaurant overlooking the Liffey. Crowded for brunch on Su when live jazz fills the room. Large a la carte menu (5:30-11pm, mains €10-24); try the juicy organic lamb burger (€10) or the pre-theater 3-course menu (€19). Open M-Sa 7:30am-11pm, Su 7:30am-12:30pm and 6-11pm. ❸

The Mermaid Cafe, 72 Dame St. (☎670 8236), near South Great Georges St. Modern art lines the walls at this flashy cafe. 2- and 3-course meals for €17.95 and €21.95 respectively. Excellent Su brunch. Try the Confit Duck with smoky tomato (€13.95). Open M-Sa 12:30-2:30pm and 6-11pm, Su noon-3:30pm and 6-9pm. ❺

Gruel, 68 Dame St. (☎670 7119). Keep your eye out for the lowercase "g" sign. Come in for a sit-down or takeaway meal like mom used to make. That is, if your mom was a world-class chef. Their motto: "We gruel, you drool." Lunch changes daily; go F for roast lamb with apricot chutney (€6). Huge dinners €6-12. Eye-opening cheap coffee €1. Open for breakfast 8:30-11:30am, lunch 11:30am-6:30pm, dinner 6:30-9:30pm. ❷

Queen of Tarts, 3 Cork Hill (☎670 7499). This little red gem offers homemade pastries, scones, cakes, and coffee. Limited seating in the courtyard. Continental breakfast €4-6. Open M-F 7:30am-6pm, Sa 9am-6pm, Su 10am-6pm. ❷

Poco Loco, 32 Parliament St. (☎679 1950), between Grattan Bridge and City Hall. A wide variety of good Mexican food to choose from. Dinner mains €8.75-12. Open M-Th 5-11pm, F-Sa 5pm-midnight, Su 4-10pm. ❸

Joy of Coffee, 25 Essex St. (☎679 3393). Joy is right—communal feeling and happy folksy-jazzy tunes. Limited seating encourages conversation mergers. Coffee from €2. Open M-Th 9am-10pm, F-Sa 9am-11pm, Su 10am-10pm. ❶

Zaytoons, 14-15 Parliament St. (☎677 3595). Persian food served on big platters of warm bread. A good lunch or a healthy way to satisfy the munchies. Excellent chicken kebab €6.50. Open M-Sa noon-4am. ❷

GRAFTON AND SOUTH GREAT GEORGES STREETS

The power-shoppers of streets Grafton and South Great Georges are kept on their feet by the trendy eateries that proliferate in the area.

The Blue Room, Copperinger Row (☎670 6982). Wonderful, family-friendly pastel cafe. Sandwiches to die for (€6.35), sweets, and coffee. Known for their pesto and home-made cranberry sauce. Open M-F 10am-6:30pm. ❷

Cornucopia, 19 Wicklow St. (☎677 7583). If you can find the space, sit down for a rich meal (about €8.50) or snack (€2). This vegetarian horn o' plenty spills huge portions onto your plate. Open M-W and F-Sa 8:30am-8pm, Th 9am-9pm. ❷

Boulevard Café, 27 Exchequer St. Walk inside to the outside of an Italian street. This funky little place has recreated an Italian boulevard within its walls. Flower pots even line the faux balconies. Good tapas (€5.70) and pasta (€8.25); dinner mains €14-22. Cafe open daily 10am-6pm; restaurant open daily 6pm-midnight. ❸

Yamamori Noodles, 71-72 South Great Georges St. (☎475 5001 or 475 5002). Exceptional and reasonably priced Japanese cuisine. Cleaner than a hospital. Traditional black, red, and white decor. Tofu steak €12; mains €12-14. Open M-W and Su 12:30-11pm, Th-Sa 12:30-11:30pm. ❸

Cafe Crepe, 15 South Leinster St. (☎661 0085). Across from Trinity College near the National Museums. Scrumptious crepes make for a more interesting meal than the generic cafe fare you'll find at the pricey museums. Fine Italian coffee. Sandwiches €3; Bailey's, mocha, and banana crepe €6.50. Open M-F 7:30am-6pm, Sa 9am-5pm. ❷

Butler's Chocolate Cafe, 24 Wicklow St. (☎671 0591). Sinning never felt so good. In this luxury sweet shop lattes start at €2.20 and a Bailey's milkshake is just €2.90. Open M-W and F-Su 8am-6pm, Th 8am till late. ❶

Metro Cafe, 43 South William St. (☎679 4515). New-wave cafe with a fine, freshly ground coffee selection and homemade breads. Simple but scrumptious. If the sun's out, bring your meal to the outside seating area. Sandwiches €4-5. Open M-Tu and F 8am-8pm, W 8am-9pm, Th 8am-10pm, Sa 9am-7pm, Su 10:30am-6pm. ❶

Govinda's, 4 Aungier St. (☎475 0309). Fabulous veggie fare in a bright, airy oasis with a soothing Hare Krishna sensibility. Dinner special €7.50. Open M-Sa 11am-9pm. ❷

Wagamama, South King St. (☎478 2152). Sate your noodle lust at this London-based chain. Service is efficient to the point of being industrial. Ramen €9-12. Open M-Sa noon-11pm, Su 11am-10pm; last orders 15min. before closing. ❸

Leo Burdock's, 2 Werburgh St. (☎454 0306), up from Christ Church Cathedral. The real deal fish and chips. A holy ritual for many Dubliners. Takeaway only. Fish €4; chips €1.50. Open M-Sa noon-midnight, Su 4pm-midnight. ❶

Harrison's, Westmoreland St. (☎679 9373). Good cheap eats in a modern setting. Lunch specials for just €7.55; 4-course dinner €17-20. Open M-Sa noon-10pm. ❹

Bendini & Shaw. Retro gourmet sandwich shop with locations around Dublin. Grab off the shelf for a quick bite on the run. Irish smoked salmon, avocado, and ham salad on a baguette just €3.80. Try the hot dog with mustard in a fancy braided pastry bun. Delivery available for orders over €15. Five branches: 4 St. Stephen's Green (☎671 8651); 20 Upper Baggot St. (☎660 0131); 1A Lower Pembroke St. (☎678 0800); 2A

Upper Fownes St. (☎671 0800); 4 Lower Mayor St. (☎829 0275). All open M-F 7am-5pm, Sa 8am-6pm, Su 9am-5pm. ❷

NORTH OF THE LIFFEY

Eateries here are less interesting than their counterparts on the South Side. **O'Connell St.** sports blocks of neon fast-food chains, while side streets overflow with chippers between newsagents hawking overpriced groceries.

The Winding Stair Bookshop and Cafe, 40 Lower Ormond Quay (☎873 3292), near the Ha'penny Bridge. A relaxed cafe overlooking the river shares its lower level with a bookshop (see p. 124). Contemporary Irish writing, periodicals, and soothing music wind you down. Salads around €8; sandwiches €4. Open M-Sa 9:30am-6pm, Su 1-6pm. ❷

Flanagan's, 61 Upper O'Connell St. (☎873 1388). "A well-regarded establishment whose tourist trade occasionally suffers from being too close to a McDonald's," writes Tom Clancy in *Patriot Games.* (Sorry, Tom—now there's a Burger King across the way too.) Mains €8.50-13.50. There are cheaper eats (€8-10) and leopard-print seats at the pizza-pasta joint upstairs. Open daily noon-11pm. ❸

Soup Dragon, 168 Capel St. (☎872 3277). A dozen different soups (€4.10-11.35) by kitchen wizards, as well as healthy juices, fruits, and breads. Open M-F 8am-5:30pm and Sa 11am-5pm. ❷

Clifton Court Hotel, Eden Quay (☎874 3535). Excellent grub served with cigars in a convivial atmosphere. Chef's, vegetarian, or seafood special €8. Food served daily noon-9pm. Trad nightly 9pm. Open M-W and Su until 11:30pm, Th-Sa until 12:30am. ❷

Bond, Beresford Pl. (☎855 9249). Minimalist design accented by bright blue chairs. Young professionals power-lunch on a range of exquisitely prepared French cuisine. Choose a wine from downstairs and enjoy it with your meal. 8oz. fillet of beef served with Cajun-herbed and mozzarella potatoes (€22). Dress casual plus. Open for lunch daily noon-3pm; coffee 3-6pm; dinner M-W 6-9pm, Th-Sa 6-10pm. ❺

O'Shea's Hotel, 19 Talbot St. (☎836 5670), at Lower Gardiner St. Good bar vittles and a high window for peeking on pedestrians. Very convenient to the North Side accommodations. Specials from €7, sandwiches €5.25. Open daily 7:30am-10pm. ❷

Beshoff's, 6 Lower O'Connell St. (☎872 4400). Named for the cook in the 1925 Russian film *Battleship Potemkin.* Takeaway counter with a touch of class. Lots of seats, various levels, and loads of fish specials. Open daily 10am-10pm. Another branch at 14 Westmoreland St. (open daily 11am-11pm). ❷

Bewley's Cafes. A Dublin institution, though some locals claim it ain't what it used to be. Dark wood paneling and marble table tops. Meals are plain but affordable. Decadent pastries €1.60. Many branches: 78 Grafton St., with a room honoring its most famous patron, James Joyce (☎635 5470; open daily 7:30am-11pm, later on weekends); 12 Westmoreland St. (☎677 6761; open M-Sa 7:30am-7:30pm, Su 9:30am-8pm); 13 South Great Georges St. (open M-Sa 7:45am-6pm); Mary St. past Henry St. (open M-W 7am-9pm, Th-Sa 7am-2am, Su 10am-10pm). ❷

PUBLIN

James Joyce proposed that a "good puzzle would be to cross Dublin without passing a pub." When a local radio station once offered £100 to the first person to solve the puzzle, the winner explained that you could take any route—you'd just have to stop in each one along the way. Dublin's pubs come in all shapes, sizes, specialties, and subcultures. This is the place to hear country-and-western, Irish rock, and, on occasion, trad. Ask around or check *In Dublin*, *Hot Press*, or *Event Guide* for music listings. Normal pub hours in Ireland end at 11:30pm Sunday through

Wednesday and 12:30am Thursday through Saturday, but the laws that dictate these hours are changing—often you'll get about a half-hour after "closing" to kill your drink. An increasing number of pubs have permits for late hours, at least on some nights; drink prices tend to rise around 11pm in order to cover the permit's cost (or so they claim). Bars will post their closing time as "late," meaning after midnight and, sometimes, after their legal limit. ID-checking almost always takes place at the door rather than at the bar, and is more enforced in Dublin than in most of Ireland. Note that a growing number of places are blurring the distinction between pubs and clubs, with rooms or dance floors opening after certain hours. So pay attention, and hit two birds with one pint.

The *Let's Go* **Dublin Pub Crawl** will help you in discovering the city while researching the perfect pint. We recommend you begin your expedition at Trinity gates, stroll up Grafton St., teeter to Camden St., stumble to South Great Georges St., then triumphantly drag your soused and sorry self to Temple Bar. Start early—say, noon. In your search for the best Guinness along the way, try the new **Guinness Storehouse,** which has replaced the Guiness Hop Store (see p. 116). Next in the line for the coveted title of "Ireland's Best Pub for Guinness" is **Mulligan's** (p. 105). Honorable mentions go to **The Stag's Head** (p. 104) and **Brogan's Bar** (p. 105).

GRAFTON STREET AND TRINITY COLLEGE AREA

The Long Stone, 10-11 Townsend St. (☎671 8102). Old books and handcarved banisters lend a rustic medieval feel. Lots of interesting rooms; the largest has a huge carving of a bearded man whose mouth serves as a fireplace. Carvery lunches 12:30-2:30pm. Open M-W noon-11:30pm, Th-F 10am-12:30am, Sa 3pm-12:30am, Su 4-11pm.

Sinnott's, South King St. (☎478 4698). A classy crowd of 20-somethings gathers in this spacious, wooden-raftered basement pub. Fancies itself a spot for writers, but let's be honest: it's for drinkers. Dance floor packed 'til 2am. Big screen TV is great for watching the big match. Open M-F 10:30am-2:30am, Sa noon-2:30am, Su 4pm-1am.

McDaid's, 3 Harry St. (☎679 4395), off Grafton St. across from Anne St. The center of Ireland's literary scene in the 50s. Book-covered walls and a gregarious crowd downstairs; during peak hours it's hotter than the devil's behind. Open M-W 10:30am-11:30pm, Th-Sa 11am-12:30am, Su 11am-11pm.

M.J. O'Neill's, Suffolk St. (☎679 3614), across from the tourist office. The enormous yet intimate maze of rooms is fairly quiet by day, but by night a fun, young crowd has it pulsing. Big screen TVs. Late closing Th-F 12:30am, Sa midnight.

Bruxelles (☎677 5362), across from McDaid's. Dark, comfortable pub, with international flags hanging from ceiling. Blues funk (Su-W) will draw you in off the street to shake your soul. Open M-W and Su until 1:30am, Th-Sa 2:30am.

Davy Byrne's, 21 Duke St. (☎677 5217), off Grafton St. A lively, middle-aged crowd fills the pub in which Joyce set the "Cyclops" chapter of *Ulysses*. The images of the writer himself on the walls hint at more recent redecorating. Open M-W 11am-11:30pm, Th-Sa 11am-12:30am, Su 11am-11pm.

The International Bar, 23 Wicklow St. (☎677 9250), on the corner of South William St. A great place to meet kindred wandering spirits. Excellent improv comedy M, stand-up W and Th, jazz Tu and F, trad Su. W-F cover €8. Go early for a seat during the comedy shows. Open M-W 10:30am-11:30pm, Th-Sa 10:30am-12:30am, Su 12:30-11pm.

The Pavilion, Trinity College (☎608 1000). Head to the far right corner of campus from the main gate. Enjoy a summer cricket match over Guinness with Trinity heads. Open M-F noon-11pm. During term, join the students under the vaults of **The Buttery,** in a basement to the left as you enter campus. Open M-F 2-11pm.

HARCOURT AND CAMDEN STREETS

The Bleeding Horse, 24 Upper Camden St. (☎475 2705). You can't beat it, 'cause it ain't dead yet. All sorts of little nooks for private affairs. Late bar with DJ Th-Sa. Open M-W until 11:30pm, Th 2:30am, F-Sa 2am, Su 11pm.

The Odeon, Old Harcourt Train Station (☎478 2088). The Odeon has a columned facade and the 2nd-longest bar in Ireland (after the one at the Galway races). Everything here is gargantuan, though the upstairs is cozier. Come to be seen. Sa DJ. Other nights casino, lounge, and dance. Cover €9. Open Su-W 'til 12:30am, Th-F 2:30am, Sa 3am.

The Chocolate Bar, Harcourt St. (☎478 0225), in the Old Harcourt Train Station. Young clubbers drink here every night. Dress sharp. Arrive early on Th-Sa and you've got the golden ticket to escape the €10-20 cover at **The PoD** (see **Clublin,** below).

WEXFORD AND SOUTH GREAT GEORGES STREETS

Whelan's, 25 Wexford St. (☎478 0766), continue down South Great Georges St. People in the know know Whelan's. The stage venue in back hosts big-name trad and rock, with live music every night starting at 9:30pm (doors open at 8pm). Cover €7-12. Open 12:30-2:30pm for lunch (€8-12). Open late W-Sa.

The Stag's Head, 1 Dame Ct. (☎679 3701). The beautiful Victorian pub has stained glass, mirrors, and yes, you guessed it, evidence of deer decapitation. The student crowd dons everything from t-shirts to tuxes and spills out into the alleys. Excellent grub; mains €10. Food served M-F noon-3:30pm and 5-7pm, Sa 12:30-2:30pm. Bar open M-W 11:30am-11:30pm, Th-Sa 11:30am-12:30am.

The Globe, 11 South Great Georges St. (☎671 1220). Frequented by artsy-fartsy wannabe artists (according to one barkeep)—attracts those who like to get a little freaky, but nothing to get nervous and dye your hair over. A fine spot to relax with a Guinness or a frothy cappuccino. Open M-W noon-11:30pm, Th-Sa noon-midnight, Su 2-11pm. **Rí Rá** nightclub attached (see **Clublin,** below).

Hogan's, 35 South Great Georges St. (☎677 5904). Attracts an attractive, trendy crowd, despite its no-frills name and minimalist decor. Self-proclaimed "surly bar staff" (not really). Su DJ from 4pm. Late bar Th-Sa.

TEMPLE BAR

The Porter House, 16-18 Parliament St. (☎679 8847). Way, way, way more than 99 bottles of beer on the wall. The largest selection of world beers in the country plus 8 self-brewed porters, stouts, and ales. Excellent sampler tray includes a sip of stout made with oysters (€9). Occasional trad, blues, and rock. Open M-W 10:30am-11:30pm, Th-F 10:30am-1:30am, Sa 10:30am-2am, Su 12:30-11pm.

The Palace, 21 Fleet St. (☎677 9290), behind Aston Quay. This classic, neighborly pub has old-fashioned wood paneling and close quarters; head for the comfy seats in the sky-lit back room. The favorite of many a Dubliner and the only true Irish Pub in Temple Bar. Open M-W 10:30am-11:30pm, Th-Sa 10:30am-12:30am, Su 12:30-11pm.

The Foggy Dew, Fownes St. (☎677 9328). Like a friendly, mellow village pub but twice as big. The Foggy Dew makes a great spot for a pint or two without the flash of other Temple Bar pubs. Live rock Su nights. Late bar Th-Sa until 2am.

Oliver St. John Gogarty (☎671 1822), at Fleet and Anglesea St. Lively and convivial atmosphere in a traditional but touristed pub. Named for Joyce's nemesis and onetime roommate, who appears in *Ulysses* as Buck Mulligan (see p. 131). Start or finish your pub crawl here. Trad daily from 2:30pm. Open daily 10:30am-2am.

Messrs. Maguire, Burgh Quay (☎670 5777). Hours of enjoyment for those who explore this classy watering hole under the spell of homemade microbrews. The Weiss stout is a spicy delight (€4.20). Late bar W-Sa. Trad Su-Tu 9:30-11:30pm. Open Su-Tu 10:30am-12:30am, W-Th 10:30am-1:30am, F 10:30am-2am, Sa 12:30pm-2am.

Q-Bar, Burgh Quay (☎677 7435), at the O'Connell bridge. Modernistic and funky, with chrome pillars and bright red, cushy airline chairs. Draws a young, hip crowd. The dance floor opens with pop and chart at about 10pm. Open 10:30am-late.

Brogan's Bar, 75 Dame St. (☎679 9570). Unassuming little ditty ignored by tourists in spite of its location. Spend a night on an internal pub crawl marveling their impressive collection of Guinness paraphernalia. Open Su-W 4-11:30pm, Th-Sa 4pm-12:30am.

Buskers, Fleet St. (☎677 3333, ext. 2145). Large, industrial bar with bright colors and a small dance floor in the back. Open M-W 11am-11:30pm, Th-Sa 11am-12:30am (club downstairs until 3am), Su 11am-11pm.

Temple Bar Pub, Temple Ln. South (☎672 5286). This sprawling bar is a worthwhile stop, and one of the very few wheelchair-accessible pubs. Outdoor beer garden is great on nice summer nights. Music M-Sa 4-6pm and 8pm-closing, Su all day.

THE BEST OF THE REST

The Brazen Head, 20 North Bridge St. (☎679 5186), off Merchant's Quay. Dublin's oldest and one of its liveliest pubs, established in 1198 as the first stop after the bridge on the way into the city. The courtyard, with its beer barrel tables, is quite the pickup scene on summer nights. The United Irishmen once met here to plan their attacks on the British (see **Rebellion,** p. 59). Nightly Irish music. Late bar F-Sa until 1am.

The Celt, 81-82 Talbot St. (☎878 8655). Step out of the city and into Olde Ireland. Small, but not cramped, comfortably worn, and genuinely welcoming. Nightly trad. Open Su-W 10:30am-11:30pm, Th-Sa 10:30am-12:30am.

Zanzibar (☎878 7212), at the Ha'penny Bridge. Mix of Oriental/Arab decor and pop culture. Quite the hot spot. Get your heart in rhythm as you make your way through the fabulous high-ceilinged bar to the dance floor in back. DJ M-Th from 10pm, F-Sa from 9pm. Open M-Th 5pm-2:30am, F-Sa 4pm-2:30am, Su 4pm-1am.

Mulligan's, 8 Poolbeg St. (☎677 5582), behind Burgh Quay off Tara St. Upholds its reputation as one of the best pint-pourers in Dublin. Try to collect all 6 Guinness coasters to learn how. A taste of the typical Irish pub: low-key and nothing fancy.

Lanigans, Clifton Court Hotel, Eden Quay (☎874 3535). Imagine a pub with Irish singers that actually attracts more Dubliners than tourists. Stop imagining

THE PERFECT PINT

Bartender Glenn, of a local Dublin Pub, helps *Let's Go* resolve the most elusive question of all...

LG: *Tell us, what's the most important thing about pouring a pint*

BG: The most important thing is to have the keg as close to the tap as possible. The closer, the better.

LG: *And why's that?*

BG: Well, you don't want the Guinness sitting in a long tube while you wait to pour the next pint. You want to pull it straight out of the keg, without any muck getting in between.

LG: *Does stopping to let the Guinness settle make a big difference?*

BG: Well, you can top it straight off if you want, but you might get too big a head with that. You don't want too small or big a head, so if you stop ¾ of the way, you can adjust the pint until the head is perfect. A true Guinness lover will taste the difference.

LG: *Because of the head?*

BG: No, because of the gas. If you pull the Guinness straight from the tap and get a big head, it means you've gotten too much gas. It kills the taste. Thats why you have to tilt the glass.

LG: *Anything else to look for?*

BG: Well what you don't want is a window-clean glass; you don't want a glass that you can see through when you're done. Good Guinness leaves a healthy film on the glass. If it doesn't, you didn't get a good Guinness.

LG: *Well, Glenn, you sure make pouring pints sound like an art form.*

BG: Oh aye, but only with Guinness—everything else you just chuck into a glass and hand out.

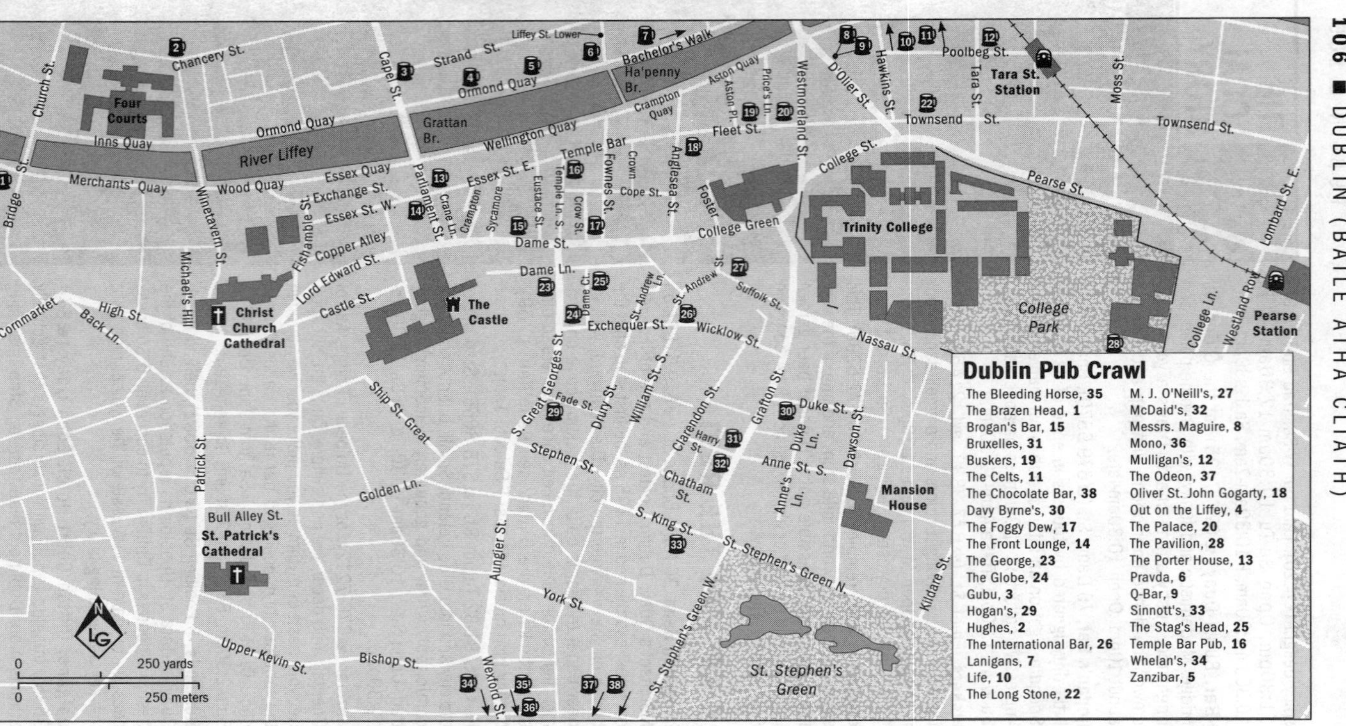
Dublin Pub Crawl
The Bleeding Horse, 35
The Brazen Head, 1
Brogan's Bar, 15
Bruxelles, 31
Buskers, 19
The Celts, 11
The Chocolate Bar, 38
Davy Byrne's, 30
The Foggy Dew, 17
The Front Lounge, 14
The George, 23
The Globe, 24
Gubu, 3
Hogan's, 29
Hughes, 2
The International Bar, 26
Lanigans, 7
Life, 10
The Long Stone, 22
M. J. O'Neill's, 27
McDaid's, 32
Messrs. Maguire, 8
Mono, 36
Mulligan's, 12
The Odeon, 37
Oliver St. John Gogarty, 18
Out on the Liffey, 4
The Palace, 20
The Pavilion, 28
The Porter House, 13
Pravda, 6
Q-Bar, 9
Sinnott's, 33
The Stag's Head, 25
Temple Bar Pub, 16
Whelan's, 34
Zanzibar, 5
Trinity College
College Park
Pearse Station
Tara St. Station
Mansion House
St. Stephen's Green
The Castle
Christ Church Cathedral
St. Patrick's Cathedral
Four Courts
River Liffey
250 yards
250 meters

and head to Lanigans. Half of it is quiet and dark throughout the day, lit by solitary candles in Bailey's bottles. The other half has live music nightly at 9pm. Patches the generation gap with Irish dancing M-Th. Open M-W 10:30am-11:30pm, Th-Sa until 1am, Su until 11:30pm.

Pravda (☎874 0090), on the north side of the Ha'penny Bridge. The Russian late bar and Russian DJ action goes Russian Th-Sa. Actually, there's nothing Russian about the place, other than Cyrillic on the wall murals. Trendy, popular, gay-friendly, and crowded. Late bar F-Sa until 2:30am.

Life, Lower Abbey St. (☎878 1032), next to the Irish Life Centre–go to the left of the large "Chariot of Life" fountain and sculpture. The young and the beautiful head here after work to talk about important things like image. Cool aquarium in the middle of the bar. Pink-tinted skylights on upper level. Mediterranean-ish lunch €8-12.

Hughes, 19 Chancery St. (☎872 6540), behind the Four Courts. Attracts the prosecution and the defense, and is loaded with the *Garda* at lunch. A delightful neighborhood venue for authentic nightly trad and set dancing M and W-Th around 9:30pm. Join the Monday Morning Club and be the first in Dublin to down a Guinness; pub opens at 7am (woo hoo!), closes Su-W at 11:30pm, Th-Sa at 12:30am.

CLUBLIN

In Dublin's nightlife war, clubs currently have a slight edge over pub rock venues, though the pubs are fighting back with later hours. As a rule, clubs open at 10:30 or 11pm, but the action really heats up after the 11:30pm pub closings. Clubbing is an expensive way to end the night, since covers run €7-20 and pints are a steep €5. Find a club with an expensive cover but cheap drink prices and you'll be set for the night. **Concessions** provide discounts with varying restrictions. Stag's Head (see **Publin,** p. 104) offers them around 11pm, but any nightclub attached to a pub distributes them in its home bar. There are a handful of smaller clubs on **Harcourt** and **Leeson St.** that can be fun, if a bit austere. Most clubs close between 1:30 and 3am, but a few have been known to last until daybreak. To get home after 11:30pm, when Dublin Bus stops running, dancing queens take the **NiteLink bus** (1 per hr., Th-Sa 12:30-3:30am, €3.30), which runs designated routes from the corner of Westmoreland and College St. to Dublin's suburbs. **Taxi** stands are located in front of Trinity, at the top of Grafton St. by St. Stephen's Green, and on Lower Abbey St. Be prepared to wait 30-45min. on weekend nights.

Rí-Rá, 1 Exchequer St. (☎677 4835), in the back of the Globe (see **Publin,** p. 104). Generally good music that steers clear of pop and house extremes. 2 floors, several bars, more nooks and crannies than a crumpet, and really quite womb-like downstairs. Open daily 11pm-2am. Cover €7-10.

The PoD, 35 Harcourt St. (☎478 0225). Corner of Hatch St., in an old train station. Spanish-style decor meets hard-core dance music. The truly brave venture upstairs to **The Red Box** (☎478 0225), a separate, more intense club with a warehouse atmosphere, brain-crushing music, and an 8-deep crowd at the bar designed to winnow out the weak. Often hosts big-name DJs–cover charges skyrocket. Cover €10-20; Th ladies free before midnight; Th and Sa €7 with ISIC card. Open until 3am. Start the evening at the **Chocolate Bar** or **The Odeon,** which share the building (see **Publin,** p. 104).

The Shelter, Thomas St. (☎454 6656), at the Vicar St. theater where Cornmarket changes names. Near the Guinness Brewery. Funk, soul, and a little bit of Austin Powers sound mixed with people wearing multiple shades of gray, black, and brown. Live bands and DJs. Cover €9. Open Th-Sa.

Gaiety, South King St. (☎677 1717), just off Grafton St. This elegant theater shows its late-night wild side midnight-4am every F and Sa. 4 bar areas. Enjoy the best of all worlds with DJs and live music, salsa, jazz, swing, latin, and soul. Cover around €10.

Club M, Blooms Hotel, Anglesea St. (☎671 5622), in Temple Bar. Look for the big orange building. One of Dublin's largest clubs, attracting a crowd of all ages and styles, with multiple stairways and a few bars in the back. If at first you don't succeed, grind, grind again. Cover Su-Th €7, ladies free before midnight; F-Sa €12-15.

Tomato, 60 Harcourt St. (☎476 4900). A smaller venue, usually blasting house and glam-girly sounds. College-age crowd during the school year. Open nightly. Serves very cheap drinks. Cover W-Th student night €4 or free; F-Sa €10.

Club Aquarium (Fibber's), 80-82 Parnell St. (☎872 2575). No charts here; mostly indie. Houses Ireland's only metal club. Occasional goth nights. If the darkness, heat, or doom gets to be too much, head outside to the deck to finish things up (your drink, that is). Weekend cover €7. Open daily until 2am, later Th-Sa.

Switch, 21-25 Eustace St. (☎670 7655). The only 18+ club in Temple Bar, so a younger crowd flocks. M gay night, F drum and bass, Sa techno, Su funky groove, otherwise a lot of deep house. Cover Su-Th €7, F €10, Sa €13.

The Palace Niteclub, Camden St. (☎478 0808), in Camden de Luxe Hotel. A meat market for a mostly young-20s crowd. Pop faves blast under a barrel-vaulted ceiling. Upstairs for charts, downstairs for 70s-80s. Cover M-Th €5.50 with €2 drinks, Sa free until 10pm. Open M-Sa until 2:30am.

Mono, 26 Wexford St. (☎475 8555). Newly renovated 2-floor glittering pub/club. Bands play Th-Sa from 7-10:30pm (cover €5-15), then DJs come in for chill-out, jungle, and house downstairs. Cover €10 after 11pm. Open Th-Sa until 3am.

The Turk's Head, Parliament St. (☎679 2606), beneath the pub. Think Istanbul in a jar. A selection of 70s and 80s classics. F-Sa cover €5, free if you come early in the night.

COUNTY DUBLIN

GAY AND LESBIAN NIGHTLIFE

The gay nightclub scene is alive and well, with gay venues (usually rented-out clubs) just about every night. Keep up-to-date by checking out the various entertainment publications around town (see **Gay and Lesbian Dublin,** p. 108.)

The George, 89 South Great Georges St. (☎478 2983). This throbbing, purple man o' war is Dublin's first and most prominent gay bar. A mixed-age crowd gathers throughout the day to chat and sip. The attached nightclub opens W-Su until 2am. Frequent theme nights. Su night drag Bingo is accompanied by so much entertainment that sometimes the Bingo never happens. Look spiffy—no effort, no entry. Cover €8-10 after 10pm.

The Front Lounge, Parliament St. (☎670-4112). The velvet seats of this gay-friendly bar are popular with a very mixed, very trendy crowd. Open M and W noon-11:30pm, Tu and Sa noon-12:30am, F noon-1:30am, Su 4-11:30pm.

Out on the Liffey, 27 Upper Ormond Quay (☎872 2480). Ireland's 2nd gay bar; its name plays on the more traditional Inn on the Liffey a few doors down. Lots of dark nooks in which to chat and drink. The short hike from the city center ensures a local crowd most nights. Tu drag, W karaoke, F-Sa DJ. No cover. Late bar W-Th until 12:30am, F-Sa until 2am.

Gubu, 7-8 Capel St. (☎874 0710). Modern with a small dance floor, it is a pleasant oasis in Dublin's working class neighborhood. Everything from disco to jazz to comedy during the week. Ask about the inside joke responsible for the bar's name. Open Su-W 5-11:30pm, Th-Sa 5pm-12:30am.

TOURS

SELF-GUIDED WALKING TOURS

Dublin is definitely a walking city, as most major sights lie within 1 mi. of O'Connell Bridge. The tourist office sells *Dublin's Top Visitor Attractions*, which lists the main attractions, essential information, and directions. The first three walking tours listed below are in *Heritage Trails: Signpost Walking Tours of Dublin*. Individual trail pamphlets can be purchased for the Ulysses Trail and the Rock 'N' Stroll Trail. All guides are available at the tourist office (€1.50-3.50).

THE CULTURAL TRAIL. Starring James Joyce and Sean O'Casey, this route zips past the North Side's important sights: the Four Courts, the Custom House and King's Inns, the Municipal Gallery, and the Dublin Writers Museum.

THE OLD CITY TRAIL. This walk begins on College Green and weaves its way through the Liberties and the markets, ending in Temple Bar. Ironically, the Old City trail hits some of the city's newest, most garish exhibits, including Dublinia.

GEORGIAN HERITAGE TRAIL. No visitors to Dublin should deny themselves the pleasure of viewing the best-preserved Georgian streets, terraces, and public buildings south of the Liffey.

ULYSSES MAP OF DUBLIN. Charts Poldy's haunts and retraces his heroic actions, beginning with kidneys for breakfast. The walk takes a full 18hr. (including drinking and debauching), but it's faster than reading *Ulysses*. Take your pick.

ROCK 'N' STROLL TRAIL. Circuits the significant sights in Dublin's recent musical history. It covers U2's Windmill Lane Studios and provides the grim details of Sinead O'Connor's waitressing job at the Bad Ass Cafe.

GUIDED WALKING TOURS

If you're more the social type, enjoy big groups, and don't mind the idea of a tour guide saying "Come on, move on, we can't let the rest of the group down," there are several tours which you can take advantage of. Most tours are about 2hr. long, but entertaining anecdotes and continuous movement keep boredom at bay.

HISTORICAL WALKING TOUR. Provides a crash course in Dublin and Irish history, stopping at a variety of Dublin sights. Guides seamlessly transition from one era to another and one street to another, protecting you both from ignorance and Dublin's maniac drivers. *(Meet at Trinity's front gate. ☎878 0227. May-Sept. M-F 11am and 3pm; Sa-Su 11am, noon, and 3pm. Oct.-Apr. F-Su noon. €10, students €8.)*

TRINITY COLLEGE WALKING TOUR. Moderately irreverent and enormously pretentious, this tour is run by students and concentrates on University lore, with glimpses of Dublin history. All that pretension *does* get you to the front of the line at the Book of Kells. *(☎608 1000. Wheelchair-accessible. 30min. tours June-Sept. 10:15am-3:40pm leave every 45min. from the info booth inside the front gate. Mar.-May weekends only. €7, students €6; includes admission to the Old Library and the Book of Kells.)*

DUBLIN FOOTSTEPS. This tour treads the beaten and offbeat paths of Irish literary greats past the Georgian architecture that housed them. *(Meet upstairs at the Grafton St. Bewley's. ☎496 0641 or 490 9341. Tour lasts 2hr. M, W, and F-Sa 10:30am. €7.)*

1916 REBELLION WALKING TOUR. The creation of the Republic arguably began with the 1916 Rebellion (see p. 61), which took place solely in Dublin. See the scars it left and the state it created. *(Meet at the International Bar, 23 Wicklow St. ☎676 2493. Tour lasts 2hr. Mid-Apr. to mid-Oct. Tu-Sa 11:30am and 2pm. €10.)*

AUDIO WALKING TOUR OF DUBLIN. A comprehensive if somewhat mechanical guide for those who aren't into asking questions. Available in several languages. *(Aston Quay. ☎670 5266. Open daily 10am-5pm. Half-day €8, students €6; full-day €11.)*

GUIDED PUB CRAWLS

THE DUBLIN LITERARY PUB CRAWL. The tour traces Dublin's liquid history in reference to its literary history, spewing informative factoids between entrancing monologues. *(Meet at The Duke, 2 Duke St. ☎670 5602; www.dublinpubcrawl.com. Apr.-Oct. M-Sa 7:30pm, Su noon and 7:30pm; Nov.-Mar. Th-Sa 7:30pm, Su noon and 7:30pm. €10, students €8. Suffolk St. tourist office takes bookings.)*

MUSICAL PUB CRAWL. An enjoyable jaunt led by two musicians (and their instruments), who'll teach you how to differentiate between one session and another. *(Show up a little early upstairs at Oliver St. John Gogarty's, on the corner of Fleet and Anglesea St. ☎478 0193; www.musicalpubcrawl.com. Apr.-Oct. daily 7:30pm; Nov. and Feb.-Apr. F-Sa 7:30pm. €10, students and seniors €8.)*

BUS TOURS

Dublin Bus runs a number of tours through and around the city, including the first three listings below. All three depart from the Dublin Bus office, at 59 O'Connell St. *(☎873 4222. Open M-Sa 9am-7pm.)*

THE GRAND DUBLIN TOUR. Plows non-stop through all the major sights and every corner of the city. Take photographs from an open-top bus or a normal double-decker in the "unlikely" event of rain. *(3hr. Daily 10:15am and 2:15pm. €13.)*

THE DUBLIN CITY HOP-ON HOP-OFF. This tour lets you explore Dublin's major sights in depth, including the Writers Museum, Trinity, and the Guinness Brewery. Exit and board the bus at your leisure. *(Roughly 1¼hr. Departs Apr.-Sept. daily every 10min. 9:30am-5pm, then every 30min. until 7pm. €10. Ticket brings discounts at many sights.)*

THE GHOSTBUS TOUR. The "world's only Ghostbus" lets you see the dead and undead aspects of the city. *(2¼hr. Tu-F 8pm and Sa 7, 7:30, and 9:30pm. €20.)*

GUIDE FRIDAY. Get the perspective of a private bus line with open-top buses and full hop-on/hop-off privileges, not to mention discounts at a number of sights. *(Tours depart from O'Connell St. ☎676 5377. Buses run frequently Apr.-Sept. 9:30am-5:30pm, Oct.-Mar. 9:30am-3:30pm. €12, students and seniors €10, children €4.)*

VIKING SPLASH TOURS. Cruise on land and water in converted World War II amphibious vehicles. Razz other tours with the Viking Roar, and hear diverse tales of Dublin history from the surprisingly amiable Norsemen at the helm. *(1¼hr. Tours depart on the hour from Bull Alley St. behind St. Patrick's Cathedral. ☎296 6047; www.vikingsplashtours.com. M-Sa 9am-6:30pm, Su 11am-6:30pm. €13.50, children €7.)*

SIGHTS

SOUTH OF THE LIFFEY

WITHIN TRINITY COLLEGE AND NEARBY

With 12,000 students and 1200 staff to cater to the area around, Trinity College is like a self-contained city within a city. To get there from North of the Liffey, follow O'Connell St. across the river and bear right onto Westmoreland St.

TRINITY COLLEGE. Behind ancient walls sprawls Trinity's expanse of stone buildings, cobblestone walks, and grassy-green grounds. The British built Trinity in 1592 as a Protestant seminary that would "civilize the Irish and cure them of Popery." The college became part of the path members of the Anglo-Irish elite trod on their way to high positions. The Catholic Jacobites who briefly held Dublin in 1689 used the campus as a barracks and a prison (see **The Ascendancy,** p. 58). Jonathan Swift, Robert Emmett, Thomas Moore, Edmund Burke, Oscar Wilde, and Samuel Beckett are just a few of the famous Irishmen who studied here. Bullet holes from Easter 1916 mar the stone entrance. Until the 1960s, the Catholic church deemed it a cardinal sin to attend Trinity; once the church lifted the ban, the size of the student body more than tripled. *(Hard to miss–between Westmoreland and Grafton St., in the very center of South Dublin. The main entrance fronts the block-long traffic circle now called College Green. Pearse St. runs along the north edge of the college, Nassau St. to the south. ☎608 1000. Grounds always open. Free.)*

THE OLD LIBRARY. This 1712 chamber holds an invaluable collection of ancient manuscripts, including the duly renowned **Book of Kells.** Around AD 800, four Irish monks squeezed multicolored ink from bugs and plants to illustrate this four-volume edition of the Gospels. Each page holds an intricate latticework of Celtic designs, interwoven with images of animals and Latin text. In 1007 the books were unearthed at Kells (see p. 155), where thieves had apparently buried them. For preservation purposes, the display is limited to two volumes, of which one page is turned each month. A new exhibit elegantly details the history of the book's illustration, and also describes the library's other prize holdings. The **Book of Durrow,** Ireland's oldest manuscript (see **Christians and Vikings,** p. 55), is also on display periodically. Upstairs, the library's **Long Room** contains Ireland's oldest harp—the **Brian Ború Harp,** used as the design model for Irish coins—and one of the few remaining **1916 proclamations** of the Republic of Ireland. The room seethes with scholarship, although the catalogue system (smallest books on the top shelf, largest on the bottom) seems to be more for practical reasons than for academic. *(From the main gate, the library is on the south side of Library Sq. Open June-Sept. M-Sa 9:30am-5pm, Su noon-4:30pm; Oct.-May M-Sa 9:30am-5pm, Su noon-4:30pm. €6, students and seniors €5.)*

BANK OF IRELAND. Staring down Trinity from across College Green is the monolithic Bank of Ireland. Built in 1729, the building originally housed the **Irish Parliament,** a body that represented only the Anglo-Irish landowner class. After the Act of Union (see **Rebellion,** p. 59), the Brits sold the building to the bank on the condition that it destroy all material evidence of the parliament's previous existence. In spite of the bank's effort, tourists can still visit the former chamber of the **House of Lords,** which contains a huge 1780s chandelier and Maundy Money—special coins once given to the poor on the Thursday before Easter and legal tender only for that day. *(☎677 6801. Open M-F 10am-4pm, Th until 5pm. 45min. guided talks Tu 10:30, 11:30am, and 1:45pm. Free.)*

GRAFTON STREET. The few blocks south of College Green are off-limits to cars and ground zero for shopping tourists and residents alike. Grafton's **street performers** range from string octets to jive limboists. Upstairs at the Grafton St. branch of Bewley's and inside the chain's former chocolate factory is the **Bewley's Museum.** Tea-tasting machines, corporate history, and a Bewley's Quaker heritage display number among the marvels. *(Open daily 7:30am-11pm. Free.)*

THE DUBLIN CIVIC MUSEUM. This pint-sized, two-story townhouse holds photos, antiquities, and knick-knacks relating to the whole range of Dublin life, from the accessories of the Vikings to the shoes of Patrick Cotter, the 8½ ft. "Giant of Ireland." *(58 South William St. ☎679 4260. Open Tu-Sa 10am-6pm, Su 11am-2pm. Free.)*

THE EMERALD ISLE'S GOLDEN EGG

Many of Ireland's most touristed sights—its national parks, museums, monuments and gardens—are owned and operated by the Irish Department of Arts and Heritage. While this government-run department keeps the price of admission to these sights quite low, the accumulated cost of visiting each can grow too high for the ordinary budget traveler to afford.

Recently, the Department of Heritage has started to offer discount cards to those wishing to visit multiple sights. Their **Dúchas Heritage Discount Card** may just be Ireland's greatest hidden deal. Not only does the ticket give you access to all of the sights owned and operated by the Department of Heritage, it also grants you one full year of access so that you can return again and again to refresh your memory on why it is you bought the card in the first place.

There are ten sights in Dublin alone, including the Casino, Kilmainham Gaol, St. Audeon's Church, and the Royal Hospital Kilmainham. Other sights around Ireland include a slew of castles and ruins. The average price to visit one sight is between €2.50-5, so this card—at €19—is Ireland's best steal.

The Irish Heritage Discount Card. €19, students and children €7.62, seniors €12.70, families €45.72. For more info call ☎01 647 2461; or within Ireland ☎1850 600 601; www.heritageireland.ie/en/HeritageCard.

KILDARE STREET

The block bordered by Kildare St., Merrion St. (the continuation of Nassau St.), and St. Stephen's Green is loaded with important-type buildings.

THE NATIONAL GALLERY. This collection of over 2400 canvases includes paintings by Brueghel, Goya, Carravaggio, Vermeer, Rembrandt, and El Greco. Works by 19th-century Irish artists comprise a major part of the collection. The works of **Jack Yeats,** brother of W.B., are of particular interest. Portraits of Lady Gregory, James Joyce, and George Bernard Shaw complete the display. The new **Millennium Wing** houses a 20th-Century Irish Art exhibit, a Yeats archive, and a multimedia system that allows you to explore many of the museum's rooms in virtual reality. Concerts and art classes legitimize a lazy summer. *(Merrion Sq. West. ☎661 5133. Open M-Sa 9:30am-5:30pm, Th 10am-8:30pm, Su noon-5pm. Free guided tours Sept.-June Sa 3pm; Su 2, 3, and 4pm. July-Aug. daily 3pm. Admission free. Concerts and art classes range from €6-20.)*

LEINSTER HOUSE. The Duke of Leinster made his home on Kildare St. back in 1745, when most of the urban upper-crust lived north of the Liffey. By building his house so far south, where land was cheaper, he was able to afford an enormous front lawn. Today, Leinster House provides chambers for the **Irish Parliament,** or **An tOireachtas** (on tir-OCH-tas). It holds both the **Dáil** (DOIL), which does most of the government work, and the **Seanad** (SHAN-ad), the less powerful upper house (see p. 63). The Dáil meets, very roughly and with lots of breaks, from October to Easter, Tuesday and Wednesday 3-9pm, and Thursday 10am-3pm. When the Dáil is in session, visitors can view the proceedings by contacting the Captain of the Guard, who conducts **tours** of the galleries. *(☎678 9911. Passport necessary. Tours leave from the adjacent National Gallery Sa on the hour.)*

THE NATURAL HISTORY MUSEUM. When taxidermists and entomologists die, St. Peter meets them here. Three creepy skeletons of giant (yes, huge) Irish deer greet visitors at the front, and the museum is stocked with tons more beautiful and fascinating examples of classic taxidermy, all displayed in old Victorian cabinets. The dodo skeleton draws crowds away from the Irish parasitic worms exhibit, and red tarps cover scary insect exhibits—lift them only if brave. *(Upper Merrion St. ☎677 7444. Open Tu-Sa 10am-5pm and Su 2-5pm. Free.)*

THE NATIONAL MUSEUM OF ARCHAEOLOGY AND HISTORY. The largest of Dublin's museums has extraordinary artifacts spanning the last two millennia. One room gleams with the **Tara Brooch,** the **Ardagh Hoard,** and other Celtic goldwork. Another section is devoted to the Republic's founding years and shows off the bloody vest of nationalist hero **James Connolly.** *(Kildare St., next to Leinster House. ☎677 7444. Open Tu-Sa 10am-5pm and Su 2-5pm. Free. Guided tours €1.50; call for times.)*

THE NATIONAL LIBRARY. Chronicles Irish history and exhibits literary goodies in its entrance room. A genealogical research room can help visitors trace even the thinnest twiglets of their Irish family trees. The reading room is quite elegant, with an airy, domed-bridged ceiling. *(Kildare St., adjacent to Leinster House. ☎661 2523. Open M-W 10am-9pm, Th-F 10am-5pm, Sa 10am-1pm. Free. Academic reason required to obtain a library card and entrance to the reading room; just "being a student" is usually enough.)*

ST. STEPHEN'S GREEN AND MERRION SQUARE

Home to Ireland's trendiest shops and most expensive city homes, travelers and locals alike come to shop, gawk, and relax on the grass of Dublin's finest park.

ST. STEPHEN'S GREEN. This 22-acre park was a private estate until the Guinness clan bequeathed it to the city. Today, the grounds are teeming with public life: punks, couples, gardens, fountains, gazebos, strollers, swans, an artificial lake, a waterfall, a statue of Henry Moore, and a partridge in a pear tree. During the summer, musical and theatrical productions are given near the old bandstand. *(Kildare, Dawson, and Grafton St. all lead to it. Open M-Sa 8am-dusk, Su 10am-dusk.)*

MERRION SQUARE. The Georgian buildings and elaborate doorways of Merrion Sq. and adjacent **Fitzwilliam St.** feed your architectural longings. After leaving 18 Fitzwilliam St., Yeats took up residence at 82 Merrion Sq. Farther south on **Harcourt St.,** playwright George Bernard Shaw and Dracula's creator, Bram Stoker, were neighbors at #61 and #16, respectively. At one point the Electricity Supply Board tore down a row of the townhouses to build a monstrous new office. Irate Dubliners had a row of a different sort, and to compensate, the ESB now funds **#29 Lower Fitzwilliam St.,** a completely restored townhouse-turned-museum demonstrating the lifestyle of the 18th-century Anglo-Irish elite. *(☎702 6165. Open Tu-Sa 10am-5pm, Su 2-5pm. A short audio-visual show leads to a 25min. tour of the house. €3.15, students and seniors €1.25.)* The prim Georgians continue up **Dawson St.,** which connects St. Stephen's Green to Trinity College one block west of Leinster House. Dawson St. has the honor of providing an address for the **Mansion House,** home to the Lord Mayors of Dublin since 1715. The house's eclectic facade exhibits evidence of several aesthetic eras. The Irish state declared its independence here in 1919, and the Anglo-Irish truce was signed in the mansion two years later.

NEWMAN HOUSE. This fully restored building was once the seat of **University College Dublin,** the Catholic answer to Trinity. *A Portrait of the Artist as a Young Man* chronicles Joyce's time here. The poet Gerard Manley Hopkins spent the last years of his life teaching classics at the college. The cursory tour is geared to the architectural and the literary. *(85-86 St. Stephen's Green South. ☎706 7422. Admission by guided tour. Open to individuals only in June-Aug. Tu-F noon-5pm and Sa 2-5pm. Groups admitted throughout the year with advance booking. €4.)*

THE SHAW BIRTHPLACE. Suitable as either a period piece or a glimpse into the childhood of G.B. Shaw. Mrs. Shaw held recitals here, sparking little George's interest in music; her lovely Victorian garden inspired his fascination with landscape painting. *(33 Synge St. Stroll down Camden, make a right on Harrington, and turn left onto Synge St. Convenient to buses #16, 19, or 122 from O'Connell St. ☎475 0854 or 872 2077. Open May-Sept. M-Sa 10am-5pm, Su 11am-5pm; no tours 1-2pm. Open for groups outside hours by request. €5.50, concessions €5, children €3; joint ticket with Dublin Writers Museum €7, with James Joyce and Writers Museums €9.)* Nearby is the **Grand Canal,** where a stony version of the poet **Patrick Kavanagh** sits on his favorite bench by the water.

THE IRISH JEWISH MUSEUM. This museum resides in a restored former synagogue and houses a large collection of artifacts, documents, and photographs chronicling the history of the Jewish community in Ireland from 1079 (five arrived and were soon sent packing) through later waves of European migration (things didn't get much better). The most famous Dublin Jew covered is, predictably, Leopold Bloom of *Ulysses* fame. *(3-4 Walworth Rd., off Victoria St. South Circular Rd. runs to Victoria St.; from there the museum is signposted. Any bus to South Circular Rd., including #16 and 20, will get you there. ☎490 1857. Open May-Sept. Tu, Th, and Su 11am-3:30pm; Oct.-Apr. Su 10:30am-2:30pm. Groups may call to arrange an alternate visiting time.)*

TEMPLE BAR

West of Trinity, between Dame St. and the Liffey, the Temple Bar neighborhood writhes with activity. Narrow neo-cobblestone streets link cheap cafes, hole-in-the-wall theaters, rock venues, and used clothing and record stores. In the early 1980s, the Irish transport authority intended to replace the neighborhood with a seven-acre transportation center. The artists and nomads who lived there started a typical artist-and-nomad brouhaha about being forced into homelessness. In 1985, they circulated petitions and saved their homes and businesses from the heartless corporate interests of the transit project. It was like a movie or something. Temple Bar immediately grew into one of Europe's hottest spots for nightlife, forcing the artists and nomads into homelessness. (Ah, the sweet irony of life.) To steer the growth to ends more cultural than alcoholic, the government-sponsored Temple Bar Properties has spent over €40 million to build a whole flock of arts-related tourist attractions, with independent coattail-riders springing up as well.

TEMPLE BAR MUSIC CENTRE. The Centre holds terrific musical events virtually every night of the week. It also has a rehearsing and recording facility for those looking to break out on their own. *(Curved St. Walk from the city center or take the DART train to Pearse St. ☎670 9202; www.tbmc.ie. Box office daily 10am-6pm.)*

THE IRISH FILM CENTRE. In addition to a continuous program of new releases, festivals, and special retrospectives, the IFC also plays home to a film-centered bookshop, a memorabilia-filled restaurant, and a lively bar. One theater usually shows art-house films, while the other offers seminars and screenings of silent films, sometimes accompanied with live music. The **Irish Film Archive** and a library can be seen upon request. *(6 Eustace St. ☎679 3477; www.fii.ie. Open M-Th 11am-9pm, F-Sa 11am-7pm, Su 2-7pm. See* ***Cinema,*** *below.)*

GALLERY OF PHOTOGRAPHY. Ireland's only photo studio, the walls of this four-story gallery are lined with contemporary photographs from Irish and some international photographers. The gallery also runs workshops and an advanced photography course, and has B&W/color darkrooms available for hire. Patient and friendly staff will wait (and nurture) your progress. *(Meeting House Sq. ☎671 4654. 6-session B&W photography course €150-170. 3hr. darkroom rental €15. Open M-Sa 11am-6pm.)*

TEMPLE BAR GALLERY & STUDIOS. One of Europe's largest studio complexes, artists from all around Ireland, from all different fields, come to take advantage of the gallery's resources. Though the studio has a couple dozen live-in artists at any one time, each working on a variety of visual arts, the gallery is open, and free, to the public. *(5-9 Temple Bar. ☎671 0073; www.paddynet.ie/tbgs.)*

DAME STREET AND THE CATHEDRALS

If you came to Dublin in search of medieval castles, religious ruins, and tales of Vikings and past Irish warriors, look no further.

COUNTY DUBLIN

DUBLIN CASTLE. Norman King John built the castle in 1204 on top of the Viking settlement *Dubh Linn;* more recently, a series of structures from various eras (mostly the 18th and 19th centuries) has covered the site, culminating in an uninspired 20th-century office complex. For the 700 years after its construction, Dublin Castle was the seat of British rule in Ireland. Fifty insurgents died at the castle's walls on Easter Monday, 1916 (see **The Easter Rising,** p. 61). Since 1938, every Irish president has been inaugurated here. Next door, the intricate inner dome of **Dublin City Hall** (designed as the Royal Exchange in 1779) shelters statues of national heroes like Daniel O'Connell. *(Dame St., at the intersection of Parliament and Castle St. ☎677 7129. State Apartments open M-F 10am-5pm, Sa-Su and holidays 2-5pm; closed during official functions. €4.50, students and seniors €3.50. Grounds free.)*

CHESTER BEATTY LIBRARY. Honorary Irish citizen Alfred Chester Beatty was an American rags-to-riches mining engineer who amassed an incredibly beautiful collection of Asian art, sacred scriptures, and illustrated texts. He donated this collection to Ireland upon his death, and a new library behind Dublin Castle houses and exhibits his cultural wonderland. An illustrated book by Matisse and a collection of Chinese snuff bottles are just two highlights of the eclectic displays. Special exhibits and public lectures complete the academic environment. *(Behind Dublin Castle. ☎407 0750. Open Tu-F 10am-5pm, Sa 11am-5pm, Su 1-5pm. Free.)*

CHRIST CHURCH CATHEDRAL. Originally built in the name of Catholicism, Irish cathedrals were forced to convert to the Church of Ireland in the 16th century. Sitric Silkenbeard, King of the Dublin Norsemen, built a wooden church on this site around 1038; Strongbow rebuilt it in stone in 1169. Further additions were made in the following century and again in the 1870s. Stained glass sparkles above the raised crypts, one of which supposedly belongs to Mr. Strongbow and his favorite lutefisk. In merrier times the cavernous crypt held shops and drinking houses, but nowadays cobwebs hang down from the ceiling, fragments of ancient pillars lie about like bleached bones, and a mummified cat chases a mummified mouse. *(At the end of Dame St., uphill and across from the Castle. Take bus #50 from Eden Quay or 78A from Aston Quay. ☎677 8099. Open daily 9:45am-5:30pm except during services. Donation of €3 strongly encouraged.)*

DUBLINIA. Across the street and attached via bridge to Christ Church Cathedral, Dublinia recreates the medieval city of Dublin with a little help from a cadre of life-sized replicas. It's informative, if a little underwhelming, though you do get to throw a ball at a mannequin in stockades, just for the hell of it. *(Next to the cathedral. ☎679 4611. Open Apr.-Sept. daily 10am-5pm, Oct.-Mar. 11am-4pm. €7, concessions €5.15; with admission to cathedral €8/€6.15.)*

ST. PATRICK'S CATHEDRAL. The body of this church dates to the 12th century, although Sir Benjamin Guinness remodeled much of the building in 1864. Measuring 300 ft. from bow to stern, it's Ireland's largest cathedral. Jonathan Swift spent his last years as Dean of St. Patrick's, and his crypt is above the south nave. *(From Christ Church, Nicholas St. runs south and downhill, eventually becoming Patrick St. Take bus #49, 49A, 50, 54A, 56A, 65, 65B, 77, or 77A from Eden Quay. ☎475 4817. Open Mar.-Oct. daily 9am-6pm, Nov.-Feb. Sa 9am-5pm and Su 9am-3pm. €4; students, seniors, and children free.)* **Marsh's Library,** beside the cathedral, is Ireland's oldest public library. A peek inside reveals elegant wire alcoves and an extensive collection of early maps. Occasional exhibits. *(☎454 3511. Open M and W-F 10am-12:45pm and 2-5pm, Sa 10:30am-12:45pm. €3, students and seniors €1.50.)*

ST. AUDOEN'S CHURCH. The Normans founded this, Dublin's oldest parish church. Please do not confuse it with the more modern (more Catholic) St.

Audoen's. *(High St. Open Sa-Su 2:30-5pm.)* **St. Audoen's Arch,** built in 1215 and now obscured by a narrow alley, is the only surviving gate from Dublin's medieval **city walls.** During the 16th century, the walls ran from Parliament St. to the castle, then to Little Ship St., along Francis St. to Bridge St., and then along the Liffey.

GUINNESS BREWERY AND KILMAINHAM

Within walking distance of Dublin central, you'd be better advised to take a bus west along the quays, or to hop on a train to nearby Heuston Station; the long, anti-scenic walk from O'Connell St. passes industrial buildings and vacant factories.

GUINNESS STOREHOUSE. Discover how the storehouse brews its black magic and creates the world's best stout. The admirably farsighted Arthur Guinness signed a 9000-year lease on the original 1759 brewery. You can see the lease displayed on the floor of the atrium, an architectural triumph that rises seven floors and has a center shaped like a pint glass. The Storehouse offers a self-guided tour with multimedia eye-candy and hyper-technical fun. Learn about ingredients, brewing, the histories of advertising and transportation, and cooperage (the science of making beer barrels). As your great reward, ye shall conclude your pilgrimage on the top floor, overlooking 64 acres of Guinness and imbibing a free pint of dark and creamy goodness. *Sláinte. (St. James's Gate. From Christ Church Cathedral, follow High St. west through its name changes—Cornmarket, Thomas, and James. Take bus #51B or 78A from Aston Quay or #123 from O'Connell St. ☎408 4800. Open Oct.-Mar. 9:30am-5pm, Apr.-Sept. 9:30am-7pm. €12, students €8, seniors and children €5.30.)*

KILMAINHAM GAOL. A place of bondage and a symbol of freedom—almost all the rebels who fought in Ireland's struggle for independence between 1792 and 1921 spent time here. "The cause for which I die has been rebaptized during this past week by the blood of as good men as ever trod God's earth," wrote Sean MacDiarmada in a letter to his family while he awaited execution for participation in the 1916 Easter Rising (see p. 61). The jail's last occupant was **Éamon de Valera,** the future leader of Éire. Today, Kilmainham is a museum that traces the history of penal practices over the last two centuries. Lengthy tours wander through the chilly limestone corridors of the prison and end in the haunting wasteland of the execution yard. *(Inchicore Rd. Take bus #51 from Aston Quay, #51A from Lower Abbey St., or #79 from Aston Quay. ☎453 5984. Open Apr.-Sept. daily 9:30am-4:45pm, Oct.-Mar. M-F 9:30am-4pm and Su 10am-4:45pm. Tours every 35min. €4.40, students €1.90, seniors €3.10.)*

THE ROYAL HOSPITAL KILMAINHAM. Built in 1679 as a hospice for retired and disabled soldiers, today the compound houses the **Irish Museum of Modern Art.** The hospital's facade and courtyard mimic Les Invalides in Paris; the Baroque chapel is also stunning. Museum curators have taken some heat over the avant-garde use of this historic space. Modern Irish artists are mixed with others as the gallery builds up its permanent collection. *(Military Rd. Bus #90 or 91 from Heuston Station, #78A or 79 from the city center. ☎612 9900. Open Tu-Sa 10am-5:30pm, Su noon-5:30pm. Guided tours W and F 2:30pm, Su 12:15pm. Free. Call for events.)*

THE COLLINS BARRACKS. The barracks are home to the **National Museum of Decorative Arts and History.** The most sophisticated of Dublin's three national museums, the barracks gleam with exhibits that range from the deeply traditional to the subversively multi-disciplinary. The Curator's Choice room displays a range of objects in light of their artistic importance, cultural context, and historical significance. *(Benburb St., off Wolfe Tone Quay. Take the Museum Link bus which leaves from the adjacent Natural History and Archaeology museums once per hr. All-day pass €2.50; one-way €1. Or hop on bus #10 from O'Connell St., or the #90, which goes to Heuston Station and stops across the street from the museum. ☎677 7444. Open Tu-Sa 10am-5pm and Su 2-5pm. Museum free. Guided tours €1.30; call for times.)*

DUBLINESE Mastering the Dublin dialect has been a persistent challenge to writers and thespians of the 20th century. James Joyce, Brendan Behan, and Roddy Doyle are just a few ambitious scribes who have tried to capture the nuances of this gritty, witty city. The following is a short introduction to Dubliners' favorite phrases.

Names for Outsiders: The rivalry between Dubliners and their country cousins is fierce. For Dubliners, all counties outside their own blur into one indiscriminate wasteland populated with "culchies," "plonkers," "turf-gobblers," and "muck-savages."

In Times of Difficulty: Dublinese is expeditious in keeping others in line. Idiots are rebuked as "eejits" or "gobshites." Total exasperation calls for "shite and onions." When all is restored to order, "the job's oxo and the ship's name is Murphy."

Affectionate Nicknames for Civic Landmarks: Over the past couple of decades, the government has graced the city with several public artworks that personify the Irish spirit in the female form. Dubliners have responded with poetic rhetoric. Off Grafton St., the statue of the fetching fishmongress Molly Malone is commonly referred to as "the dish with the fish" and "the tart with the cart."

NORTH OF THE LIFFEY

O'CONNELL ST. AND PARNELL SQUARE

While tourists flock to the south, locals congregate and converse in the North. Less trendy than its southern partner, the area is flooded with street vendors and performers. If you're looking for the Real Dublin, dart off to one of the area's many side streets, where fresh fruit and fish markets reside.

O'CONNELL STREET. Dublin's biggest shopping thoroughfare starts at the Liffey and leads to **Parnell Square.** At 150 ft., it was once the widest street in Europe. In its pre-Joycean heyday, it was known as Sackville St.; later the name was changed in honor of "The Liberator" (see **Rebellion,** p. 59). The central traffic islands contain monuments to Irish leaders O'Connell, Parnell, and James Larkin, who organized the heroic Dublin general strike of 1913 (see **Parnell,** p. 60). **O'Connell's statue** faces the Liffey and O'Connell Bridge; the winged women aren't angels but Winged Victories, although one has a bullet hole from 1916 in a rather inglorious place. At the other end of the street, **Parnell's statue** points toward nearby Mooney's pub, while the engraved words at his feet proclaim "Thus far and no further." On Grafton St., a newer statue of **Molly Malone,** of ballad fame, has her own aliases (see **Dublinese,** above). One monument you won't see is **Nelson's Pillar,** a freestanding column that remembered Trafalgar and stood outside the General Post Office for 150 years. In 1966 the IRA commemorated the 50th anniversary of the Easter Rising by blowing the Admiral out of the water.

THE GENERAL POST OFFICE. Not just a fine place to send a letter, the Post Office was the nerve center of the 1916 Easter Rising (see **The Easter Rising,** p. 61); Patrick Pearse read the Proclamation of Irish Independence from its steps. When British troops closed in, mailbags became barricades. Outside, a number of bullet nicks are still visible. *(O'Connell St. ☎ 705 7000. Open M-Sa 8am-8pm, Su 10am-6:30pm.)*

HUGH LANE MUNICIPAL GALLERY OF MODERN ART. A small but impressive collection hangs in Georgian **Charlemont House.** When American painter Lane offered to donate his collection of French Impressionist paintings to the city, he did so on the condition that the people of Dublin contribute to this gallery's construction. Because his collection and the architect chosen were foreign, Dubliners refused to lend their support; Yeats then lamented their provincial attitudes in a string of poems. Lane's death aboard the *Lusitania* in 1915 raised decades of disputes over his will, resolved by a plan to share the collection between Dublin and the Tate Gallery in London. *(Parnell Sq. North. Buses #3, 10, 11, 13, 16, and 19 all stop near Parnell Sq. ☎874 1903. Open Tu-Th 9:30am-6pm, F-Sa 9:30am-5pm, Su 11am-5pm. Free.)*

THE DUBLIN WRITERS MUSEUM. Read your way through placard after placard describing the city's rich literary heritage, or listen to it all on an audio headset tour. Manuscripts, rare editions, and memorabilia of Swift, Shaw, Wilde, Yeats, Beckett, Brendan Behan, Patrick Kavanagh, and Sean O'Casey blend with caricatures, paintings, a great bookstore, and an incongruous Zen Garden. *(18 Parnell Sq. North. ☎872 2077. Open June-Aug. M-F 10am-6pm, Sa 10am-5pm, Su 11am-5pm; Sept.-May M-Sa 10am-5pm. €5.50, students and seniors €5. Combined ticket with either Shaw birthplace or James Joyce Centre €8.)* Adjacent to the museum, the **Irish Writers Centre** is the center of Ireland's living community of writers, providing for today's aspiring penwrights and sponsoring frequent fiction and poetry readings. The Centre is not a museum, but if you ring the doorbell you can get information about Dublin's literary happenings. *(19 Parnell Sq. North. ☎872 1302; www.writerscentre.ie. Open M-F 9:30am-6pm.)*

JAMES JOYCE CULTURAL CENTRE. The museum features Joyceana ranging from portraits of individuals who inspired his characters to the more arcane fancies of the writer's nephew, who runs the place. Feel free to mull over Joyce's works in the library or the tearoom. Call for information on lectures and Bloomsday events. *(35 N. Great Georges St. Up Marlborough St. and past Parnell St. ☎878 8547. Open M-Sa 9:30am-5pm, Su 12:30-5pm; July-Aug. extra Su hours 11am-5pm. €4, students and seniors €3.)*

HOT PRESS IRISH MUSIC HALL OF FAME. Dublin's anthem to its musical wonders has found itself a great location. A headset tour takes you through memorabilia-laden displays on the history of Irish music from bards to the studio, heaping lavish praise on such stars as Van Morrison, U2, and, uh, Boyzone. The concert venue **HQ** (see **Music,** p. 120) is attached. *(57 Middle Abbey St. ☎878 3345; www.irishmusichof.com. Open daily 10am-6pm. €7.60; students, seniors, and children €5.)*

OTHER SIGHTS. Just past Parnell Sq., the **Garden of Remembrance** eulogizes the martyrs who took and lost the General Post Office (see **The Easter Rising,** p. 61). A cross-shaped pool is anchored at one end by a statue representing the mythical Children of Lir, who turned from humans into swans. They proclaim their faith in freedom (in Irish): "In the winter of bondage we saw a vision. We melted the snows of lethargy and the river of resurrection flowed from it." *(Open until dusk.)* Turn right on Cathedral St. to find the inconspicuous **Dublin Pro-Cathedral,** the city's center of Catholic worship where tens of thousands gathered for Daniel O'Connell's memorial service. "Pro" means "provisional"—many Dublin Catholics still want Christ Church Cathedral returned (see p. 115). On Granby Row, the **National Wax Museum** features life-size replicas of everyone from Hitler to the Teletubbies, including the Pope (complete with Popemobile).

ALONG THE QUAYS

Not quite the Seine, a walk along the River Liffey can be pleasant enough, especially when broken up with quick visits to the following sights.

THE CUSTOM HOUSE. Dublin's greatest architectural triumph, the Custom House was designed and built in the 1780s by James Gandon, who gave up the chance to be Russia's St. Petersburg's state architect and settled in Dublin. The building's Roman and Venetian columns and domes hint at what the city's 18th-century Anglo-Irish highbrows wanted Dublin to become. Carved heads along the frieze represent the rivers of Ireland; Liffey is the only lady. *(East of O'Connell St. at Custom House Quay, where Gardiner St. meets the river. ☎878 7660. Visitors center open mid-Mar. to Nov. M-F 10am-5pm, Sa-Su 12:30-2pm; Nov. to mid-Mar. W-F 10am-5pm and Su 2-5pm. €1.50.)*

FOUR COURTS. Another of Gandon's works, this building appears monumentally impressive from the front, but the back and sides reveal 20th-century ballast. On April 14, 1922, General Rory O'Connor seized the Four Courts on behalf of the anti-Treaty IRA; two months later, the Free State government of Griffith and Collins attacked the Four Courts garrison, starting the Irish Civil War (see **Independence,** p. 62). The building now houses Ireland's highest court. *(Inn's Quay, several quays to the west of the Custom House. ☎872 5555. Open M-F 9am-4:30pm. No scheduled tours. Free.)*

ST. MICHAN'S CHURCH. The dry atmosphere in the church has preserved the corpses in the vaults, which inspired Bram Stoker's *Dracula.* Of particular interest is a 6½ ft. tall crusader (dead) and the hanged, drawn, and quartered bodies of two (very dead) 1798 rebels. *(Church St. Open Mar.-Oct. M-F 10am-12:45pm and 2-4:45pm, Sa 10am-12:45pm; Nov.-Feb. M-F 12:30-3:30pm, Sa 10am-12:45pm. Church of Ireland services Su 10am. €2.50, students and seniors €2, under 16 €1.)*

SMITHFIELD

With the government pouring thousands of euros into local development, this area is on its way to becoming the next Temple Bar. Don't rush here yet though, as true progress won't be seen for another few years. In the meantime, drink up.

OLD JAMESON DISTILLERY. Learn how science, grain, and tradition come together to form liquid gold—whiskey, that is. A film recounts Ireland's spirit-ual rise, fall, and renaissance; the subsequent tour walks you through the actual creation of the drink. The experience ends with a glass of the Irish firewater of your choice; be quick to volunteer in the beginning and you'll get to sample a whole tray of different whiskeys. *(Bow St. From O'Connell St., turn onto Henry St. and continue straight as the street dwindles to Mary St., then Mary Ln., then May Ln.; the warehouse is on a cobblestone street on the left. ☎807 2355. Tours daily 9:30am-5:30pm. €7, students and seniors €4.)*

DUBLIN BREWING COMPANY. New kid on the block trying to best the heavyweights, this mall brewery runs fun, personal tours with plenty of hops to smell and beer to taste. The tour takes visitors step by step through the brewing process. You also get more beer for your money than at the *other* brewery, and more often than not, the tour guide partakes as well. *(144-146 N. King St. From Old Jameson, go up to N. King St., turn left, and it's on the left. ☎872 8622. Tours every hr. noon-6pm, and by appointment. €9.)*

DISTANT SIGHTS

Far removed from the hustle and bustle of Dublin's main center, several attractions tempt on the outskirts.

PHOENIX PARK AND DUBLIN ZOO. Europe's largest enclosed public park is most famous for the "Phoenix Park murders" of 1882. The Invincibles, a Republican splinter group, stabbed Lord Cavendish, Chief Secretary of Ireland, and his trusty Under-Secretary 200 yd. from the **Phoenix Column.** A Unionist journalist forged a series of letters linking Parnell to the murderers (see **Parnell,** p. 60). The Phoenix Column, of the Corinthian kind and capped with a phoenix rising from flames, is something of a pun—the park's name actually comes from the Irish *Fionn Uísce,* "clean water." The 1760 acres incorporate the **President's residence** *(Áras an Uachtaraín),* the US Ambassador's residence, cricket pitches, polo grounds, and red deer. The deer are quite tame and not to be missed; they often graze in the thickets near Castleknock Gate. The park is peaceful during daylight hours but unsafe at night. *(Take bus #10 from O'Connell St. or #25 or 26 from Middle Abbey St. west along the river.)* **Dublin Zoo,** one of the world's oldest and Europe's largest, is in the park. It contains 700 critters and the **world's biggest egg.** For an urban zoo, the habitats are large and the animals tend to move around a bit, except for the lions, who feel it is their royal prerogative to sleep over 20 hours a day. *(Bus #10* *from O'Connell St. ☎677 1425. Open M-Sa 9:30am-6:30pm, Su 10:30am-6:30pm. Last admission at 5pm. Zoo closes earlier in winter. €10, students €7.70, children and seniors €6.30.)*

CASINO MARINO. This is an architectural gem and house of tricks. You can certainly gambol here, but forget the slot machines—this is a casino only in the sense of "small house," built for the Earl of Charlemont in 1758 as a seaside villa. Funeral urns on the roof are actually chimneys, and hollow columns serve as drains. The casino has secret tunnels, trick doors, and stone lions standing guard. *(Off Malahide Rd. Take bus #123 from O'Connell St.; #27 or 42 from the quays by Busáras. ☎833 1618. Open June-Sept. daily 10am-6pm, Feb.-Mar. Th and Su 10am-4pm, Apr. Th and Su noon-5pm, May and Oct. daily 10am-5pm. Admission by tour only. €2.50, seniors €2, students and children €1.50.)*

GAELIC ATHLETIC ASSOCIATION MUSEUM AND CROKE PARK. Those intrigued and/or mystified by the world of Irish athletics—hurling, camogie, Gaelic football, and handball—will appreciate the museum located at **Croke Park Stadium.** The GAA museum spells out the rules and history of every Gaelic sport, with the help of touchscreens and audio-visual displays, while a 1hr. tour of the stadium brings you up close to the fields on which they are played. *(☎855 8176. Museum open May-Sept. daily 9:30am-5pm; Oct.-Apr. Tu-Sa 10am-5pm, Su noon-5pm. Last admission 4:30pm. €5, students and seniors €3.50, children €3. Stadium tour plus museum €2-4 more.)*

INLAND WATERWAYS VISITOR CENTRE. Known as the "box on the docks" in Dublinese, this floating museum educates those ignorant of the significance of the inland waterway. The canals don't get no respect, it seems—this takes you back to school. *(Take bus #3 to the Grand Canal. Open June-Sept. 9:30am-5:30pm, Oct.-May W-Su 12:30-5pm. €2.50, student €1.50.)*

COUNTY DUBLIN

ARTS AND ENTERTAINMENT

Whether you fancy poetry or punk, Dublin is well equipped to entertain you. The *Event Guide* (free) is available at the tourist office, Temple Bar restaurants, and the Temple Bar Info Center. It comes out every other Friday, and has ads in the back, fawning reviews in the front, and reasonably complete listings of museums and literary, musical, and theatrical events in between. The glossier *In Dublin* (€2.50) comes out every two weeks with feature articles and listings for music, theater, art exhibitions, comedy shows, clubs, museums, gay venues, and movie theaters. *Events of the Week*—a much smaller, free booklet—is jammed with ads, but also has good info buried in it. Hostel staffers are often reliable, if opinionated, sources of information. Click to www.visitdublin.com for hot spots updated daily.

MUSIC

Dublin's music scene attracts performers from all over the world. Pubs see a lot of musical action, as they provide musicians with free beer and a venue. There is often a cover charge (€4-7) for better-known acts. *Hot Press* (€1.90) has the most up-to-date listings, particularly for rock. Its commentaries on the musical scene are insightful, and its left-leaning editorials give a clear impression of what the Dublin artistic community is thinking. **Tower Records** on Wicklow St. has reams of leaflets, and bills posted across the city broadcast coming attractions. Scheduled concerts tend to start at 9pm; impromptu ones start later.

Traditional music (trad) is not only a tourist gimmick, but a vibrant and important element of Dublin's music world. Some pubs in the city center have trad sessions nightly, others nearly so: **Hughes, Slattery's, Oliver St. John Gogarty,** and **McDaid's** are all good choices (see **Publin,** p. 102). The best pub for trad in the entire city is **Cobblestones,** King St. North (☎872 1799), in Smithfield. No rock here, but live shows every night, a trad session in the basement, and real live spontaneity. Another great small venue for live music is **Whelan's,** at 25 Wexford St., the continuation of South Great Georges St. (☎478 0766. Live music nightly. Cover €7-12.) Big-deal bands frequent the **Baggot Inn,** 143 Baggot St. (☎676 1430). U2 played here in the early 80s; some people are still talking about it.

The Temple Bar Music Centre, Curved St. (☎670 9202), has events and concerts every night. The **National Concert Hall,** Earlsfort Terrace, provides a venue for classical concerts and performances. They have nightly shows in July and August, and their summer lunchtime series makes a nice break on occasional Tuesdays and Fridays. (☎671 1533. Tickets €8-16, students half-price; summer lunchtime tickets €4-8.) Programs for the **National Symphony** and smaller local groups are available at classical music stores and the tourist office. **Isaac Butt** on Store St. and the **Life** bar (see **Publin,** p. 102) have periodic jazz. The new **HQ** (☎878 3345), in the Irish Music Hall of Fame on Middle Abbey St., considers itself one of the nicest venues in Europe. Big acts play **Olympia,** 72 Dame St. (☎677 7744), and at **Vicar St.,** 99 Vicar St., off Thomas St. (☎454 6656). The stars also perform for huge crowds at the **Tivoli Theatre,** 135-138 Francis St. (☎454 4472), and the musical monsters come to **Croke Park,** Clonliffe Rd. (☎836 3152), and the **R.D.S.** (☎668 0866), in Ballsbridge.

THEATER

Dublin's curtains rise on a range of mainstream and experimental theater. There is no true "Theatre District," but smaller theater companies thrive off Dame St. and Temple Bar. Box office hours are usually for phone reservations; box offices stay open until curtain on performance nights. Showtime is generally 8pm.

Abbey Theatre, 26 Lower Abbey St. (☎878 7222). Founded by Yeats and his collaborator Lady Gregory in 1904 to promote the Irish cultural revival and modernist theater, which turned out to be a bit like promoting corned beef and soy burgers. Synge's *Playboy of the Western World* was first performed here in 1907. The production occasioned storms of protest and yet another of Yeats's hard-hitting political poems (see **The Revival,** p. 71). Today, the Abbey (like Synge) has gained respectability; it is now Ireland's National Theatre. Tickets €12-25; Sa matinees 2:30pm, €10; M-Th student rate €10. Box office open M-Sa 10:30am-7pm.

Peacock Theatre, 26 Lower Abbey St. (☎878 7222). The Abbey's experimental downstairs studio theater. Evening shows (8:15pm curtain) plus occasional lunchtime plays, concerts, and poetry. Theater tickets €17, Sa 2:45pm matinees €12.50. Box office open M-Sa at 7:30pm.

Gate Theatre, 1 Cavendish Row (☎874 4045), specializes in international period drama. Tickets €16-24; M-Th student discount with ID at curtain €10, subject to availability. Box office open M-Sa 10am-8pm.

Project Arts Centre, 39 E. Essex St. (☎1850 260 027). Sets its sights on the avant-garde and presents every imaginable sort of artistic production. Tickets under €15; student concessions available. Box office open daily 11am-7pm. The **gallery** hosts rotating visual arts exhibits. Open same time as box office. Free.

Gaiety, South King St. (☎677 1717; www.gaietytheatre.com), just off Grafton St. Provides space for modern drama, ballet, music, and the Opera Ireland Society. Tickets €15-25. Box office open M-Sa 10am-7pm. Also see **Clublin,** p. 107.

Andrews Lane Theatre, Andrews Ln. (☎679 5720), off Dame St. Dramas of every sort presented on 2 different stages; the studio stage is usually more experimental. Mainstage tickets €15-20, studio €15. Box office open daily 10:30am-7pm.

City Arts Centre, 23-25 Moss St. (☎677 0643), parallel to Tara St. off Georges Quay. Avant-garde exploration of significant contemporary issues. Tickets €8, students €5. Box office open daily 9:15am-5pm.

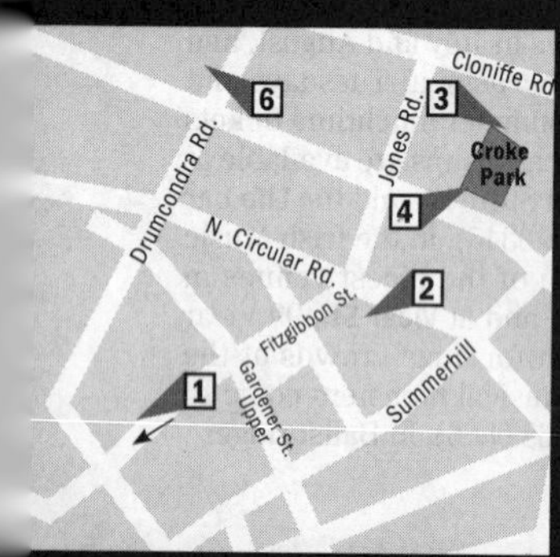

A DAY AT CROKE PARK

Before you can brag about having "done" Dublin, you have to first experience what it's like to participate as a spectator at one of the city's raucous Gaelic Football Matches.

1. Spend Saturday night at **Parkway B&B** (see p. 97) so you can get to the park early the next morning. Follow North St. to Gardner Place.
2. Push and shove and bite and pinch—whatever it takes to get to the **ticket booth,** on Fitzgibbon St.
3. Run into the **GAA museum** inside the stadium to learn all you will need to know about the game.
4. Watch the game from the stadium's best seats at **Hill 16** or **Hogan's Stand,** where you'll find local Dubliners sitting and drinking.
5. Celebrate the victory or mourn the loss with the rest of the locals at **Quinn's Pub** (42 Lower Drumcondra Rd; ☎830 4973).
6. Pass out on the **left side of the street** if your team lost, and on the **right side of the street** if they won: left-side street cleaning takes place Monday morning.

Samuel Beckett Theatre, Trinity College (☎608 2461). Inside the campus. Hosts anything it happens upon, including scores of student shows. Tickets €18, students €14.

Olympia Theatre, 72 Dame St. (☎677 7744). Hosts commercial musical theater, plus midnight revues and tributes to the likes of ABBA and pivotal Northern European pop bands. Tickets €11-45. Box office open daily 10:30am-6:30pm.

The New Theatre, 43 E. Essex St. (☎670 3361), in the Temple Bar district. Opposite the Clarence Hotel, inside Connolly Books. Mission statement is to provide plays by established playwrights dealing with contemporary issues. Small and intimate. Shows at 8pm M-Sa. Tickets €12.50, students €10.

CINEMA

Ireland's well-subsidized film industry reeled with the arrival of the **Irish Film Centre,** 6 Eustace St., in Temple Bar. The IFC mounts tributes and festivals, including a French film festival in October and a **gay and lesbian film festival** in early August. A variety of classic and European art house films appear throughout the year. You have to be a "member" to buy most tickets. (☎679 3477; www.fii.ie. Weekly membership €1.30; yearly membership €14, students €10. Membership must be purchased at least 15min. before start of show. Matinees €5; after 5pm €6.30. 18+.) **The Screen,** D'Olier St. (☎672 5500), also rolls artsy reels. First-run movie houses cluster on O'Connell St., the quays, and Middle Abbey St. The **Savoy,** O'Connell St. (☎874 6000), and **Virgin,** Parnell St. (☎872 8400), offer a wide selection of major releases. General movie tickets cost about €7.50 per person.

SPORTS AND RECREATION

Dubliners aren't as sports-crazed as their country cousins, but that's not saying much. Games are still a serious business, especially since most tournament finals take place here. The season for **Gaelic football** and **hurling** (see **Sports,** p. 77) runs from mid-February to November. Action-packed and often brutal, these contests are entertaining for any sports-lover. Provincial finals take place in July, national semifinals on Sundays in August (hurling the first week, football the second and third), and **All-Ireland Finals** in either late August or early September. Games are played in **Croke Park** (☎836 3222; www.gaa.ie; Clonliffe Rd., a 15min. walk from Connolly station; bus routes 3, 11, 11A, 16, 16A, 51A, and 123; tickets run €15-40) and on **Phibsborough Rd.** Tickets are theoretically available at the turnstiles, but they tend to sell out quickly; All-Ireland Finals sell out immediately. Your best bet is to hit the Dublin pubs on game day and see who's selling. Home games of the Irish **rugby** team are played in **Lansdowne Road Stadium;** the peak season runs from February to early April. **Camogie** (women's hurling) finals also occur in September. For more sports information, check the Friday papers or contact the **Gaelic Athletic Association** (☎836 3232; www.gaa.ie). **Greyhounds** race all year. (W-Th and Sa at 8pm at Shelbourne Park; ☎668 3502. M-Tu and F at 8pm at Harold's Cross; ☎497 1081.) **Horse racing** and its attendant gambling are at Leopardstown Racetrack in Foxrock (☎289 2888). At the beginning of August, the **Royal Dublin Horse Show** comes to the RDS in Ballsbridge (see **Music,** above).

FESTIVALS

The tourist office's annual *Calendar of Events* (€1.30) offers info on events throughout Ireland, including Dublin's many festivals, antique and craft fairs, flower marts, horse shows, and the like. The biweekly *Events Guide* or *In Dublin* (€2.50) are also good sources.

BLOOMSDAY. Dublin returns to 1904 each year on June 16, the day of Leopold Bloom's 18hr. journey, which frames the narrative (or lack thereof) of Joyce's *Ulysses.* Festivities are held all week long, starting before the big day and (to a lesser extent) continuing after it. The James Joyce Cultural Centre (see p. 118) sponsors a reenactment of the funeral and wake, a lunch at Davy Byrne's, and a Guinness breakfast. *(☎873 1984.)*

MUSIC FESTIVALS. The **Festival of Music in Great Irish Houses,** held during mid-June, organizes concerts of period music in 18th-century homes across the country, including some in the city. *(☎278 1528.)* The **Feis Ceoil** music festival goes trad in mid-March. *(☎676 7365.)* The **Dublin International Organ and Choral Festival** lifts every voice in Christ Church Cathedral. *(☎677 3066.)* The **Guinness Blues Festival,** a three-day extravaganza in mid-July, gets bigger and broader each year. *(☎497 0381; www.guinnessbluesfest.com.)* Ask at the tourist office about *fleadhs* (FLAHS), day-long trad festivals that pop up periodically.

ST. PATRICK'S DAY. The half-week leading up to March 17 occasions a city-wide carnival of concerts, fireworks, street theater, and intoxicated madness, celebrating one of Ireland's lesser-known saints. Many pubs offer special promotions, contests, and extended hours. *(☎676 3205; www.paddyfest.ie.)*

THE DUBLIN THEATRE FESTIVAL. This premier cultural event, held the first two weeks of October, screens about 20 works from Ireland and around the world. Tickets may be purchased all year at participating theaters, and, as the festival draws near, at the Festival Booking Office. *(47 Nassau St. ☎677 8439. Tickets €13-20, student discounts vary by venue.)*

THE DUBLIN FILM FESTIVAL. Nearly two weeks of Irish and international movies with a panoply of seminars in tow. *(Early to mid-Mar. ☎679 2937; www.iol.ie/dff.)*

ACTIVITIES

Drinking stout and/or watching sporting events takes precedence in Dublin, so finding activities to participate in can be tricky. Most outdoor activities take place outside the city limits, but you can fish on certain sections of the Liffey, rent bicycles for a ride around town, and various parks have public tennis courts. Dublin is not a big adventure activity city, but hang gliding is available for those who dare.

BICYCLING. Cycle Ways rents bikes cheap. But remember to bring your own helmet, as the shop doesn't provide any for their customers. *(185-6 Parnell St. ☎873 4748. €20 per day, €80 per wk.; deposit €80. Open M-W and F-Sa 10am-6pm, Th 10am-8pm.)*

FISHING. You can fish the Liffey for perch, salmon and trout, among many other types of fish. Tackle shops can direct you to the best spots to fish. Few places in town hire out fishing equipment, so you'll have to buy your own gear or hire from out of town. For more information, contact **Cleere Patk & Son** *(5 Bedford Row, ☎677 7406, off Aston Quay)* or **Rory's Fishing Tackle** *(17A Temple Bar, ☎677 2351).*

GO-CARTS. There are two places around Dublin to get behind the small wheel, and both have indoor tracks. Be sure to book ahead. **Kart City** *(Old Airport Rd, ☎842 6322; €20 per 15min., €26 per 20min, €38 per 30min.; open daily noon-10pm)* and **Kylemore Karting Centre** *(Killeen Road, ☎626 1444; €16 per 15min., €26 per 25min.; open M-F 11am-10pm and Sa-Su 10am-10pm).*

GOLF. Most of the golf clubs around Dublin are private, but some allow visitors, usually on weekdays. There are also municipal courses, par-3, and pitch and putt courses around the city. For more info, contact the **Clontarf Golf Club** *(Malahide Rd., ☎833 1892, in Clontarf)*, **Royal Dublin Golf Course** *(☎833 6346)*, **Glencullen Golf** *(☎294 0898)*, and **Open Golf Centre** *(☎864 0324).*

HANG GLIDING. If you're looking for greater thrills, **Adventure Ireland** can help provide activity planning for singles or groups that include hang gliding lessons *(☎490 0246).* **Amazing Days** offers paragliding lessons *(☎045 630 3046, in Kildare).*

TENNIS. Public courts are available in **Bushy Park** in Terenure *(☎490 0320)*, **Herbert Park** in Ballsbridge *(☎668 4364)*, and **St. Anne's Park** in Raheny *(☎833 1859).*

COUNTY DUBLIN

SHOPPING

Dublin is hardly a center for international trade, and consumer goods here are generally expensive—your time may be better spent in pubs and castles. That said, if an item is made anywhere in Ireland, you can probably find it in Dublin. Stores are usually open Monday through Saturday from 9am to 6pm, with later hours on Thursdays (until 7-8pm). Tiny shops pop up everywhere along the streets both north and south of the Liffey, but Dublin's serious shopping is on **Grafton** and **Henry St.** On pedestrianized Grafton St., well-dressed consumers crowd into boutiques and restaurants while sidewalk buskers lay down their caps for money. Teens and barely-twenties buy used clothes and punk discs in **Temple Bar.** Across the river, **Henry St.** and **Talbot St.** have the goods for those on a tighter budget. On **Moore St.,** vendors sell fresh produce at very low prices. (Open M-Sa 7am-5pm.) **Clery's,** Upper O'Connell St., is Dublin's principal department store. (☎878 6000. Open M-W and Sa 9am-6:30pm, Th 9am-9pm, F 9am-8pm.)

At the top of Grafton St., **St. Stephen's Green Shopping Centre** mauls shoppers. Lord Powerscourt's 200-year-old townhouse on Clarendon St. has been converted into the **Powerscourt Townhouse Centre**—a string of chic boutiques carrying Irish crafts. Gen-Xers and hippie-holdouts head to **Georges St. Market Arcade,** on South Great Georges St. near Dame St., which includes a fortune teller and many vintage clothing and used-record stalls. (Open M-W and F-Sa 10am-6pm, Th 8am-7pm.)

DUBLIN'S LITERARY SHOPPING

Eason, 80 Middle Abbey St. (☎873 3811), off O'Connell St. A floor-space behemoth. Lots of serious tomes and an extensive "Irish interest" section. Wide selection of local and foreign magazines and newspapers. Their bargain shelves are in the cleverly named

Bargain Books, residing diagonally across Abbey St. Open M-W and Sa 8:30am-6:45pm, Th 8:30am-8:45pm, F 8:30am-7:45pm.

Winding Stair Bookstore, 40 Ormond Quay (☎873 3292), on the North Side. 3 floors of good tunes, great views, and cheap food. New and used books, contemporary Irish lit, and literary periodicals. Open M-W 9:30am-6pm, Th-Sa 9:30am-10pm, Su 1-6pm.

Eason Hanna's, 27-29 Nassau St. (☎677 1255), across from Trinity College at Dawson St. Knowledgeable staff answers all questions about contemporary Irish writing. Open M-W and F-Sa 8:30am-6:30pm, Th 8:30am-8pm, Su 1:45-5:45pm.

Books Upstairs, 36 College Green (☎679 6687), across from Trinity Gate. Extensive sections on **gay literature** and women's studies. The principal distributor for *Gay Community News*. Open M-F 10am-7pm, Sa 10am-6pm, Su 1-6pm.

RECORDS, TAPES, AND CDS

Claddagh Records, 2 Cecilia St. (☎677 0262), in Temple Bar between Temple Ln. and Crow St. Has a good selection of trad and a variety of international music. Open M-F 10:30am-5:30pm, Sa noon-5:30pm.

Celtic Note, 14-15 Nassau St. (☎670 4157). Specializes in traditional Irish music. Open M-W and F-Sa 9am-6:30pm, Th 9am-8pm, Su 11am-6:30pm.

Freebird Records, 1 Eden Quay (☎873 1250), the North Side facing the river. Crowded basement has perhaps Dublin's best selection of indie rock. Proprietors can recommend local bands. Open M-F 10:30am-7:30pm, Sa 10:30am-6pm, and Su 1:30-6pm.

GAY AND LESBIAN DUBLIN

Dublin's less-retrograde-than-you-might-fear (but more than you might hope) thinking allows the celebration of **PRIDE,** an annual, week-long festival in July celebrating gay identity. **Gay Community News (GCN),** 6 South William St. (☎872 9417 or 872 9418), is free and comes out monthly, offering the most comprehensive and up-to-date information possible on gay life and nightlife in Dublin and beyond. *GCN* is available at Books Upstairs (see **Literary Shopping,** above), Cornucopia, the George, and venues around Temple Bar. It has extensive listings of support groups and other organizations. *Sceneout* magazine is a periodic supplement to *GCN* that focuses on nightlife and prints classifieds. The queer pages of *In Dublin* list gay-friendly pubs, dance clubs, restaurants, bookshops, hotlines, and organizations. Since gay Dublin seems to be consistent in its rapid rate of change, the listings are comprehensive but often outdated. **The George, Gubu, Out on the Liffey,** and **The Front Lounge** (see **Gay and Lesbian Nightlife,** p. 104) are always safe bets. If nothing is happening at night, **Books Upstairs** was Dublin's first bookstore to have a gay literature shelf, and it's still got the best selection of reading material around.

Gay Switchboard Dublin is a good resource for events and updates and sponsors a hotline (☎872 1055; Su-F 8-10pm, Sa 3:30-6pm). **The National Gay and Lesbian Federation,** Hirschfield Centre, 10 Fownes St. (☎671 0939), in Temple Bar, offers counseling on legal concerns. The lesbian community meets at **Lesbians Organizing Together (LOT),** 5 Capel St. (☎872 7770. Drop-in resource center and library open Tu-Th 10am-5pm.) **Outhouse,** 65 William St. (☎670 6377), is a queer community resource center, offering a library, a cafe, information, and advice. Outhouse organizes all sorts of social groups, support groups, seminars, and information sessions for gays, lesbians, teenagers, alcoholics, various permutations of the above, and everyone else. **Gay Information Ireland** has a website at www.geocities.com/WestHollywood/9105. Tune into local radio for gay community talk shows: **Innuendo** is broadcast on 104.9FM (Tu 2-3pm); 103.8FM has **Out in the Open** (Tu 9-10pm); and **Equality** airs on 101.6FM (Th 4:30pm).

DUBLIN'S SUBURBS

Strung along the Irish Sea from Donabate in the north to Bray in the south, Dublin's suburbs are a calm alternative to the voracious human tide swarming about the Liffey. Two regions stand out from the sprawl: the tranquil Howth Peninsula to the north and the cluster of suburbs around Dún Laoghaire to the south. Castles and factories are surrounded by housing developments, all clamoring for a view of the rocky shore. Howth, in particular, is quiet and offers splendid views of the water and of Dublin itself. Bragging rights for Dublin's best beach go to the Velvet Strand, a plush stretch of rock and water between Malahide and Portmarnock (see p. 128). Dublin's southern suburbs tend to be tidy and fairly well-off—the coastal yuppie towns form a chain of snazzy houses and bright surf. The DART, suburban rail, and local buses make the area accessible for afternoon jaunts.

HOWTH (BINN EADAIR) ☎01

Maud Gonne, winner of Yeats's unyielding devotion, described her childhood in Howth in *A Servant of the Queen:* "After I was grown up I have often slept all night in that friendly heather… From deep down in it one looks up at the stars in a wonderful security and falls asleep to wake up only with the call of the sea birds looking for their breakfasts." The secret is out. Howth (rhymes with "both"), an affluent Eden dangling from the mainland, is becoming an increasingly popular destination. If the sun is shining on a weekend, expect the place to be full of maddening crowds. And who could blame them? Less than 10 mi. from the center of Dublin, Howth plays like a highlight reel of Ireland: rolling hills, pubs, a literary landscape, fantastic sailing, and a castle. The town's buildings are densest near the harbor, where the fishing industry sometimes renders the air less than pristine. Man-made structures from various millennia pepper the area, connected by quiet paths around hills of heather and stunning cliffs.

COUNTY DUBLIN

TRANSPORTATION AND PRACTICAL INFORMATION

The easiest way to reach Howth is by **DART.** Just take a northbound train to the end of the line. (30min., 6 per hr., €1.45.) Pay attention at the Howth Junction, as the line splits to serve Malahide as well. **Buses** leave from Dublin's Lower Abbey St.: #31 runs every hour to the center of Howth, near the DART station, and #31B adds a loop that climbs Howth Summit. Turn left out of the DART station and walk toward the harbor on the aptly-named Harbour Rd. The **tourist office** is on the right in the Old Courthouse. (☎844 5976. Open May-Aug. M 11am-1pm, Tu-F 11am-1pm and 1:30-5pm.) If the tourist office is closed, head to the other side of the street, where there is a hand-drawn map of the peninsula posted at the harbor entrance. There is an **ATM** at the **Bank of Ireland** on Main St. To fill the tank or get some groceries, head to **Sutton** (2 mi. or one DART stop away). Down the street is **McDermott's Pharmacy,** 6 Main St. (☎832 2069. Open M-Sa 9am-6pm, Su 10:30am-1pm.) The **post office** (☎831 8210; open M-F 9am-1pm and 2:15-5:30pm; Sa 9am-1pm) leads a tenuous existence at 27 Abbey St. The library has free **Internet access,** but you must call ahead for a time slot. Across the street, **Global Net Cafe** also has access. (Open M-F 9am-6pm, Sa 10am-1pm and 2-6pm. €5 per hr.)

ACCOMMODATIONS

Most B&B proprietors will pick up at the DART stop; otherwise it is quite a climb or a short bus ride to their hilly locations. **Gleann na Smól** ❸ ("The Valley of the Thrush"), on the left at the end of Nashville Rd. off Thormanby Rd., is the affordable option closest to the harbor. They have firm beds for the weary, in-room TVs, and a generous supply of reading matter to suit bookwormier guests. The gregarious owners, with star tour-guide skills, will fill you in on everything the town offers. (☎832 2936. Singles €38; doubles €60.) The top-notch beds of **Hazelwood ❸** are 1 mi. up Thormanby Rd., at the end of the cul-de-sac in the Thormanby Woods estate. Bus #31B runs up Thormanby Rd. (☎839 1391. All rooms with bath. Doubles €64.) **Highfield ❸,** also on Thormanby Rd., is on the left a ½ mi. past the Church of Assumption. When the weather cooperates, a lovely view of the harbor complements tidy floral-themed bedrooms and a traditional dining room brimming with antiques. (☎832 3936. All rooms with shower and TV. Singles €38; doubles €64.) On the side of a hill on Balkill Road lies **Inisradharc ❸,** with its brilliant views of **Ireland's Eye** from its sunny conservatory. Go up Thormanby Rd. and take a right at **The Summit;** it's down the windy road on the left. (☎832 2306. Two night minimum stay. Doubles with bath €66.)

FOOD AND PUBS

Hungry shoppers head to **Mace,** on Harbour Rd. (Open M-F 7am-11pm, Sa-Su 8am-11pm.) **Maud's ❶,** Harbour Rd., is a spunky cafe with sandwiches and ice cream. (☎839 5450. Ice cream €1-4.50; try their signature "Pooh Bear Delight," €4.50. Open 10am-8pm.) **Caffe Caira ❷,** on the corner of Harbour Rd. and Abbey St., is an above-average chipper. The takeaway window serves the same food for a fraction of the price. (☎832 3699. Open daily noon-9:30pm; takeaway noon-1am.) The newest entrant in the best of Harbour St. is **Citrus ❹,** a Thai restaurant offering unique selections (chicken stir-fry with oyster sauce €15.95). Try to grab a table outside for people-watching. (☎832 0200. Open Tu-Su 5pm-late, also Sa-Su noon-4pm.) On Main St., **Kruger's ❸** offers tasty and inexpensive specials (Cajun chicken €9.55). Lucky diners will get the "Beef and Guinness Hot Pot" special. Climb Thormanby Rd. for drinks and an incredible view of North Howth at **The Summit** and its adjoining nightclub **K2.** (☎832 4615. Club open F-Su. Cover €3 before 11pm, €9 after.) Join the fishermen at the **Lighthouse,** Church St., and relax with a pint and some trad. Take Harbour St. from the train station, then right at El Paso and up the hill to Church. (☎832 2827. Sessions M and F from 9pm, Su afternoons.)

SIGHTS AND ACTIVITIES

A great way to experience Maude Gonne's heather and seabird nests is on the 3hr. **cliff walk,** well-trod but narrow, which rings the Howth peninsula. The best section is a 1hr. hike that runs between the harbor and the lighthouse at the southeast tip of the peninsula. At the harbor's end, **Puck's Rock** marks the spot where the devil fell when St. Nessan shook a Bible at him (it was just that easy). The nearby **lighthouse,** surrounded by tremendous cliffs, housed Salman Rushdie for a night during the height of the *fatwa* against him. To get to the trailhead from town, turn left at the DART and bus station and follow Harbour Rd. around the coast for about 20min. From the lighthouse, if you don't want to trek it back around the way you came, climb the path to the Summit Carpark and either hop the #31B back down to the heart of town or pound the pavement down Thormanby Rd. Take a moment in the parking lot to admire the magnificent view: on a clear day you can see the Mourne Mountains in Northern Ireland.

Several sights are clustered in the middle of the peninsula; go right as you exit the DART station and then left after ¼ mi. at the entrance to the Deer Park Hostel. Up that road lies the private **Howth Castle,** a charmingly awkward patchwork of materials, styles, and degrees of upkeep. Unfortunately, the castle's denizens prefer to keep all their toys to themselves and don't open their house to the public

COUNTY DUBLIN

AMAZING GRACE Howth Castle is a private residence, belonging to the St. Lawrence family, which has occupied it for four centuries, but you might try knocking if your surname is O'Malley. In 1575, the pirate queen Grace O'Malley (see **Clare Island,** p. 376) paid a social call but was refused entrance on the grounds that the family was eating. Not one to take an insult lightly, Grace abducted the St. Lawrence heir and refused to hand him back until she had word that the gate would always be open to all O'Malleys at mealtimes.

rabble. Such rabble can instead ramble in the bloomin' **Rhododendron Gardens,** in which Molly remembers romance (and such) at the end of *Ulysses*. (Always open. Free.) Turn right as you enter the gardens for views of a collapsed **portal dolmen** with a 90-ton capstone, marking the grave of someone who was more important in 2500 BC than he is now. Just offshore, **Ireland's Eye** once provided both religious sanctuary and strategic advantage for monks, whose former presence is visible in the ruins of **St. Nessan's Church,** and one of the coast's many **Martello towers** (see **Rebellion,** p. 59), which opened for visitors in the summer of 2001. The monks abandoned their island refuge when they got sick of marauding pirates, and the island's long beach is now primarily a bird haven. **Ireland's Eye Boat Trips** jets passengers across the water. (☎831 4200 or 087 267 8211. 15min.; every 30min. 11am-6pm, weather permitting; €8 return, students and children €4.) Find them on the East Pier, toward the lighthouse. For a picturesque day of golf, play at the **Deer Park Golf Club,** right from the DART terminal and up Howth Hill, about a 10min. walk. (☎832 3487. €15.50 per 18-hole round. Open 8am to dusk.)

MALAHIDE (MULLACH ÍDE) ☎01

Eight miles north of Dublin, Malahide presides over its little bay with quiet suburban hauteur. Rows of shops line the main street, smiling at you with smug satisfaction. The town's pride may be due to something in the drinking water, but a more likely culprit would be **Malahide Castle** and its gorgeous parklands. To complement the lovely grounds, the National Gallery has stocked the interior with furnishings and portraits from various periods between the 14th- and 19th-centuries. The dark-paneled oak room and the great hall are magnificent. (☎846 2184. Park open dawn to dusk. Castle open Apr.-Oct. Sa 10am-5pm, Su 11am-6pm; Nov.-Mar. M-Sa 10am-5pm, Su 11am-5pm. Admission by tour only. Tours last 35min. €5.50, students and seniors €5.) Next to the castle, track on over to the **Fry Model Railway,** a 2500 sq. ft. working model with detailed miniatures of all your favorite Dublin landmarks. The 20min. tour gives the surprisingly interesting history of railroads and other transport throughout Ireland. (☎846 3779. Open Apr.-Oct. M-Sa 10am-1pm and 2-5pm, Su 2-6pm; Nov.-Mar. Sa-Su 2-5pm. €5. Admission by tour only; tours every 30min.) The best secret in the castle complex is the incongruous **Museum of Childhood,** which holds a veritable antiques roadshow of 18th-century dollhouses and toys. This charity trust can't afford to advertise, so few know of the world's oldest known dollhouse (circa 1700) that lies in its midst. Upstairs is the spectacular Tara's Palace, a huge model mansion that fills an entire room. (€2 donation for charity requested.) In town, make sure to hit Malahide's gorgeous **beach.** Closer to neighboring Portmarnock is the even softer, more luxurious **Velvet Strand.**

Getting here from Dublin has become easier now that the **DART** and **suburban rail** serve Malahide station (☎845 0422). Alternatively, take **bus** #42, 32A, or 230. All forms of transport to Dublin (except #32A) run at least once per hour and cost around €1.45. From the DART/train station on Main St., turn right for the nearby castle, or left to reach The Diamond, the central intersection of town. The folks at the **Citizens Information Centre,** Main St., in the parking lot behind the library, provide free maps and info. (Open M-F 10am-noon and 2:30-4pm.) The **library** has limited **Internet access** by appointment. (☎845 2026. Open M, W, and F-Sa 10am-1pm and 2-5:15pm; Tu and Th 2-8:30pm.) You can rent wheels at **Malahide Cycles,** across from the library, downstairs in the Malahide Shopping Centre. (☎845 0945. Open M-Sa 10am-1pm and 2-6pm. €15 per day.) The **post office** is just a few doors down in the Shopping Centre. (Open M-F 9am-1pm and 2:15-5:30pm, Sa 9am-1pm.)

Continue on Main St. for 10min., as it becomes Coast Rd., to reach **Pegasus ❸,** 56 Biscayne, home to Betty O'Brien and her lovely, veggie-friendly breakfasts. (☎845 1506. Open Mar.-Oct. Doubles €60.) On Main St., across from the Grand Hotel on Grove Rd., is **Maud Plunkett's ❺,** a pub/hotel decorated like a 19th-century apothecary. Named after an unfortunate local resident who was a maiden, bride, and widow on the same day; she married a soldier during WWI who was killed in battle the evening of their wedding day. Cozy but comfortable rooms with full hotel accommodations are available. (Breakfast included. Singles €57; doubles €100.) Malahidean restaurants tend to cater to heavy purses; try the **L&N SuperValu** at the shopping center (☎845 0233; open M-W 8am-8pm, Th-Sa 8am-9pm, Su 9:30am-6pm) or **Kupz ❷,** on Main St., across from the DART, which has a varied menu of Spanish tapas, freshly-squeezed juices, coffees, and gargantuan bowls of soup, all for under €6.35. (☎845 6262. Open M-Th 10am-8pm, F-Sa 10am-10pm.)

DÚN LAOGHAIRE ☎01

As one of Co. Dublin's major ferryports, Dún Laoghaire (dun-LEER-ee) is many tourists' first peek at Ireland. Fortunately, this is as good a place as any to begin your rambles along the coast. The surrounding towns, from north to south, are Blackrock, Monkstown, Dalkey, and Killiney; getting from one town to the next is quick and simple if you stay within a few blocks of the sea. An entertaining jaunt would begin with a ride on bus #59 from the Dún Laoghaire DART station to the top of Killiney Hill and continue along the path through the park and down into Dalkey. Or you can disembark at the Dalkey DART and ramble over the hills to Killiney's wonderful beach. On summer evenings, couples stroll down the Dún Laoghaire waterfront, and the whole town turns out for weekly sailboat races.

ORIENTATION AND PRACTICAL INFORMATION

You can reach Dún Laoghaire in a snap with the **DART** from Dublin (€1.40), or on southbound **buses** #7, 7A, 8, or (a longer, inland route) #46A from Eden Quay. If you're staying here but want to party like a rock star downtown, the 7N **nightbus** departs for Dún Laoghaire from College St. in Dublin. (M-W 12:30 and 2am, Th-Sa every 20min. 12:30-4:30am.) From the ferryport, **Marine Rd.** climbs up to the center of town. **George's St.,** at the top of Marine Rd., holds most of Dún Laoghaire's shops; many are right at the intersection in the **Dún Laoghaire Shopping Centre.** You can reach the **Bloomfield Shopping Centre** by heading up Marine Rd. from the harbor, taking a right on George's St., and then taking your third left. **Patrick St.,** the continuation of Marine Rd., is the place for cheap eateries.

Danae and her comrades keep the **tourist office** humming at the ferry terminal and will outfit you with maps and pamphlets. (Open M-Sa 10am-6pm.) Exchange money at the ferry terminal's **bureau de change.** (Open M-Sa 9am-4pm, Su 10am-4pm.) **Bank of Ireland** and its **ATM** are at 101 Upper George's St. (☎280 0273. Open M-F 10am-4pm, Th until 5pm.) The **Info Centre** can help with finding **work opportunities,** as can **Grafton Recruitment** on Upper George's St. (☎284 1818). Free **Internet** access is available at the **Dun Laoghaire Youth Info Centre,** in the church on Marine Rd. (☎280 9363; open M-F 9:30am-5pm, Sa 10am-4pm), and for a fee at **Net House,** 28 Upper George's St. (☎230 3085; open 24hr. €6 per hr.; students €5).

ACCOMMODATIONS

Dún Laoghaire is prime ground for B&Bs, few of which are modestly priced. Two hostels are also within walking distance, the best being **Belgrave Hall ❷** at 34 Belgrave Sq. From the Seapoint DART station, head left down the coast, then zigzag through the intersections: right on Belgrave Rd., left on Eaton Pl., right across from the blue and yellow doors, and left again across from Belgrave House. This top-tier hostel feels old but not run-down. Frolic with lovable Irish wolfhounds in a family-friendly setting. (☎284 2106. Free parking. Continental breakfast included. Laundry €7. F-Su 10-bed dorm €25, M-Th €20.) Head left out of the Salthill and Monkstown DART station to get to **Marina House ❷**, at 7 Old Dunleary Rd., next to the Purty Kitchen (see **Food and Pubs**, below). Young, energetic owners often mingle nightly with the guests. (☎284 1524 or 086 233 9283. Non-smoking bedrooms. Terrace BBQ. 6-bed dorms €16-19; 4-bed €18-21. Doubles €51.) Fall off the DART or ferry and you'll find **Marleen ❸**, 9 Marine Rd. Its convenient location attracts those in need of catching an early morning ferry. (☎280 2456. TV and tea facilities. Singles €35; doubles €60.) **Avondale ❸**, 3 Northumberland Ave., is around the corner from Dunnes Stores. A crimson carpet and a darling cocker spaniel (Oscar) lead guests to their big beds. (☎280 9628. Doubles €50.)

FOOD AND PUBS

Tesco sells groceries downstairs in the Dún Laoghaire Shopping Centre. (☎280 0668. Open M-W and Sa 8:30am-7pm, Th-F 8:30am-9pm, Su 11am-6pm.) Fast-food restaurants and inexpensive coffee shops line George's St. The best family restaurant in town is **Bits and Pizzas ❷**, 15 Patrick St. Go early or be prepared to wait. (☎284 2411. Pizzas and pasta €6-10; homemade ice cream €1.40. Open daily noon-midnight.) **La Strada ❸**, 2-3 Cumberland St. (☎280 2333), serves Italian dishes at a reasonable price (€7-14). For vegetarian fare in a bohemian setting, travel behind the blue door of **Old Cafe ❷**, 56 Lower George's St. (☎284 1024. Open M-Sa 9am-5pm.) Across the street at **Weir's ❸**, 88 Lower George's St., mahogany and brass elegance and a wrought-iron spiral staircase add style to your meal. (☎230 4654. Open M-F noon-10pm, Sa 10:30am-midnight, Su 5-8pm.) **Farrell's ❸** can be found upstairs in the Dún Laoghaire Shopping Centre; the panoramic coastal view looks just fine through a pint glass. The pub also serves sandwiches, fish, burgers, and salads from €8-12. (☎284 6595. Open M-W 10:30am-11:30pm, Th-Sa 10:30am-12:30am, Su 12:30-11pm.) Next door to the Marina Hostel, the stylish **Purty Kitchen** pub opens its loft to a nightclub with trad Tuesday and Thursday, and pop and jazz Friday through Sunday. (☎284 3576. Cover €10.) **Scott's Bar**, 17 Upper George's St., has music Wednesday through Sunday. (☎280 2657. F karaoke; Su trad.) Across the way, locals tear up the dance floor at **Nemos** on Thursdays.

SIGHTS AND ACTIVITIES

To get to the **James Joyce Tower** from the Sandycove DART station, turn left at either the green house or Eagle House, go down to the coast, turn right, and continue to the Martello tower in Sandycove; or take bus #8 from Burgh Quay in Dublin to Sandycove Ave. In September 1904, a young James Joyce stayed here for six tense days as a guest of Oliver St. John Gogarty, the surgeon, poetic wit, man-about-town, and first civilian tenant of the tower. Joyce later infamized Gogarty in the first chapter of *Ulysses*. The novel opens in and around the tower on the "snot-green" sea, with Buck Mulligan playing Gogarty. The tower's museum is a motherlode of Joycenalia: his death mask, love letters to Nora Barnacle, a draft manuscript page from *Finnegan's Wake*, and many editions of *Ulysses*. Upstairs, the **Round Room** reconstructs the author's bedroom; Joyce novices (see ***Ulysses* Pub Primer,** below) can enjoy views from the gun platform of "many crests, every ninth, breaking, plashing, from far, from farther out, waves and waves." (☎280 9265. Open Apr.-Oct. M-Sa 10am-1pm and 2-5pm, Su 2-6pm; Nov.-Mar. by appointment. €5.50, students €5.) At the base of the tower lies another Joyce-blessed spot, the **forty foot men's bathing place.** A wholesome crowd with a bevy of toddlers splashes in the shallow pool facing the road, but behind a wall, on the rocks below the battery and adjacent to the tower, men skinny-dip year-round.

The Dún Laoghaire harbor itself is a sight, full of boat tours, car ferries, fishermen, and yachts cruising in and out of the **new marina.** Frequent summer-evening **boat races** draw much of the town. On a clear day, head down to the piers—the setting for Samuel Beckett's *Krapp's Last Tape*—to soak up the sun or brood with extended alienated pauses. A number of outdoor and water activities are available in town. The **Irish National Sailing School & Club,** on the West Pier, offers beginner weekend and week-long sailing courses. (☎284 4195; www.inss.ie. Prices from €172-190.) The **Irish Canoe Union** has summer kayaking courses on area rivers (☎450 9838 or 087 245 7620). **Sea Thrill** will speed you around in inflatable boats (☎260 0949), and **Dublin Adventures** offers canoeing, kayaking trips, and rock climbing. (☎668 8047 or 087 287 3287; www.adventure-activities-ireland.com.) For indoor fun and dance, Dún Laoghaire's best *craic* can be had at the **Comhaltas Ceoltoiri Éireann** (COLE-tus KEE-ole-tori AIR-run), next door to the Belgrave Hall hostel. This is the national headquarters of a huge international organization for Irish traditional music, and it houses bona fide, non-tourist-oriented trad sessions *(seisiuns)*, as well as *céilí* dancing. (☎280 0295. July to mid-Aug. sessions M-Th at 9pm, with informal jam session after. €8-10. Year-round F night *céilí* €6.)

DAYTRIPS FROM DÚN LAOGHAIRE

DALKEY AND DALKEY ISLAND. A medieval heritage town, Dalkey draws a fine line between ritzy and quaint, complete with its own castle, island, and exceptional restaurants. Castle St. hosts most of the shops and restaurants, but there are a few hidden gems less than a block in either direction. At the far end of Castle St. (from the DART station) is **Dalkey Castle** (a.k.a. Goat Castle, after the coat of arms of a local medieval family) and its **Heritage Centre** *(☎285 8366; open M-F 9:30am-5pm, Sa-Su 11am-5pm. Tour at 3pm €4).* If you decide to stay overnight, you won't find a more beautiful B&B than **Tudor House ❺,** located just off Castle St. This stately, yellow mansion has an elegant pond out back and secluded grounds. *(☎285 1528. Singles €70; doubles €98-116.)* Excellent but expensive dishes can be found at **The Guinea Pig ❺,** Railroad St. *(☎285 9055. Early-bird special Su-F 6-7pm and Sa 6-7:30pm €20; mains begin at €22. Open daily 6pm-late.)* **P.D. Woodhouse ❹,** at 1 Coliemore Rd., just off Castle St. near the DART, cooks all of its dishes on an oak charcoal grill. Its early dinner (6-7pm, €12) is the best value in town. BBQ mains are €16-20. *(☎284 9399. Open M-Sa 6-11pm, Su 4-9:30pm.)* For a change of scenery and pace, trips to **Dalkey Island** are available by boat *(☎087 672 5647, talk to Aidan).* The island hosts **Martello Tower Number Nine,** one of the many towers built in anticipation of Napoleon's impending but unfulfilled invasion of the coast.

KILLINEY. Farther south from Dún Laoghaire, Killiney (kill-EYE-nee), Dublin's poshest suburb, may have the most gorgeous beach around. Pick up the Heritage map of Dún Laoghaire for details on seven Killiney-area walks. From the top of **Killiney Hill Park,** the views are breathtaking—that dark smudge on the horizon is

ULYSSES PUB PRIMER So you meant to read *Ulysses* but were intimidated by its 700-odd pages, thousands of cryptic allusions, and general screwiness. Despite ranking in the estimations of many as the greatest book of the 20th century, very few people have read the Modernist masterwork in its entirety. *Let's Go: Ireland*, a somewhat more accessible text, is here to help you: the factual fragments below should help you in even the most hoity-toity society.

The letter "s" both begins and ends the book. "S" stands for "Stephen" (Daedalus, one of the three main characters); "P" is for "Poldy" (nickname of Leopold Bloom, the second main character); and "M" for "Molly" (Poldy's wife, and the coolest of the three). Taken together, S-M-P stands for subject-middle-predicate, or logical sentence structure. The form (a syllogism) suggests a logical and narrative structure that readers can grasp, but which eludes the central characters.

By calling him "Poldy," Molly takes the "Leo," or lion, out of her husband, suggesting a theme of female domination, and yet the final words of the book, from her stream-of-consciousness monologue—"yes I said yes I will Yes" (remembering her response to Bloom's marriage proposal)—have drawn much critical attention as a moment of submission and affirmation. Another theory hinges on the final "Yes": in Molly's mind words are not capitalized, but on the page they are, thus granting supremacy to Joyce.

Ulysses uses 33,000 different words, 16,000 of which are used only once. William Shakespeare, in all his plays, only used 25,000. Joyce once said that he expected readers to devote nothing less than their entire lives to untangling his epic. For the less ambitious, this Primer should suffice.

called Wales. *(To reach the park from Castle St., turn left on Dalkey Ave. and climb Dalkey Hill, then take Burmah Rd. into the park.)* Before hitting the park, slip down to Torca Rd., where **Shaw's Cottage,** up the road on the left, once played home to young G. B. This is a private home; Shaw enthusiasts will have to make do with visiting his birthplace on 33 Synge St. in Dublin (see **Sights**, p. 113). Killiney hosts scattered B&Bs, and the best views, both inside and outside the house, are found at the **Druid Lodge ❺,** on Killiney Rd. Just follow the road to Dalkey and look for white boulders on the right; the lodge will be on the left. *(☎285 1632. Singles €65; doubles €90.)*

BRAY (BRÍ CHUALAIN) ☎01

Although officially located in Co. Wicklow, Bray functions as a suburb of Dublin: the DART and Dublin Bus trundle through the town regularly, bringing flocks of city folk to its beach. Well-tended gardens set against a slightly over-commercialized, cotton candy- and arcade-laden seafront are representative of Bray's compromise between beach crowd-serving and Victorian Ireland. However, the town clearly benefits from its mixed identities. Polished but not pretentious, Bray manages to stimulate the demanding tourist without sacrificing its small-town charm.

TRANSPORTATION AND PRACTICAL INFORMATION. Bray is a 40min. **DART** ride from Dublin's Connolly Station (€3.30 return). **Buses** #45 and 84 arrive from Eden Quay. Bray has good connections to Enniskerry, in Co. Wicklow: from the Bray DART station, bus #185 runs to Enniskerry (€2), as does **Alpine Coaches,** which also runs to Powerscourt Gardens, Powerscourt Waterfall, and Glencree. (☎286 2547. See tourist office for schedule.) **St. Kevin's Bus Service** shuttles from the town hall on Main St. to Glendalough. (☎281 8119. 1hr., 2 per day, €10 return.) To reach **Main St.** from the DART station, take **Quinsborough Rd.** or **Florence Rd.,** which run perpendicular to the tracks. **The Strand** runs along the beach, parallel to

Meath Rd. The Bike Rack, in the Boulevard Centre on Quinsborough Rd., **rents bikes.** (Open M-Sa 9am-6pm; €20 per day, €100 per wk.) Bray's **tourist office** is the first stop south of Dublin for Wicklow info. Sharing a building with the **heritage center,** the office is downhill on Main St. (☎286 7128. Open June-Sept. M-F 9am-5pm, Sa 10am-4pm; Oct.-May M-F 9:30am-4:30pm, Sa 10am-3pm. Closed M-F for lunch 1-2pm.) The **AIB Bank** has an **ATM** on Main St., near Quinsborough. (Open M-Tu and F 10am-4pm, W 10:30am-4pm, Th 10am-5pm.) Get online at the **Star Leisure Internet Cafe,** behind the Star Leisure arcade on the far end of the Strand. (☎286 1520. Open daily 10am-11:30pm. €2 per 15min.) And the **post office** is at 18 Quinsborough Rd. (☎286 2554. Open M-Sa 9am-5:30pm; closed Sa 1-2pm for lunch.)

ACCOMMODATIONS, FOOD, AND PUBS. B&Bs line the Strand, but cheaper ones are on Meath St. closer to the town center. Anne and Pat Duffy welcome guests to **Moytura ❸,** on Herbert Rd. The B&B is on the right just before the fork with King Edward Rd. The Duffys offer superb homemade bread, freshly squeezed orange juice, and chats on Irish history and literature. (☎282 9827. All rooms with bath. Singles €35; doubles €60.) **Bayview ❸,** on Meath Rd., is a small B&B with soaring ceilings. The owner, a master craftsman, has installed beautiful wood floors in the dining room. (☎286 0887. Singles €30; doubles €55.) **Ulysses ❹,** a green house in the middle of the Strand, is a 200-year-old house once operated as a B&B by Joyce's niece. (☎286 3860. Singles €40; doubles €74.)

SuperQuinn shelves groceries on Castle St., the continuation of Main St. downhill and across the bridge from the tourist office. (☎286 7779. Open M-Tu 8:30am-8pm, W-F 8:30am-9pm, Sa 8:30am-7pm.) At the other end of Main St., the historic **town hall** now sports a pair of golden arches, the international symbol for greasy fast food. But if it's *good* food you want, the best meal in town is at **Escape ❹,** Albert Ave., at the intersection with the Strand. A creative, vegetarian-friendly menu appears daily; the early-bird special (€17-19) is available weekdays from 4-7pm and Saturday 6-7pm. (☎286 6755. Mains €14. Open M-F 4-10:30pm, Sa 12:30-10:30pm, Su 12:30-8:30pm.) For lunch during the week try Escape's sister cafe, **Escapade ❷.** Continue down Albert Ave., go under the bridge, go left on Meath Rd., and it's on the left. (☎204 2696. Lunch €9 and under.) For meals of the carnivorous persuasion, head to **Seanchara ❹,** on the Strand between Convent Ave. and Sidmonton Ave. (☎204 1970. Mains €18-21. Open 5:30-10:30pm.) Back that up into the **Weary Ass Coffee Shop ❷,** 5 Quinsborough Rd., for omelettes and sandwiches. (☎286 2144. Open M-Sa 8am-5pm.) For nights out, try **Clancy's,** a dark, old-time pub with wooden plank tables, and trad on Tuesdays and Thursdays (☎204 0427).

SIGHTS. Along the beachfront, predictable arcade palaces cater to a crowd of Dublin beachgoers. The **National Sea Life Centre,** on the Strand, marks the dawning of the age of aquariums. (☎286 6939. Open daily 10am-5pm. €8, students and seniors €6, children €5.50.) Those un-thrilled by fenced-in fishies should head to the summit of **Bray Head,** high above the south end of the Strand and away from the neon lights. The trail begins after the short paved pedestrian walkway begins to curve up the hill. On the right, past the picnicking area, a set of steps launches one of several winding trails to the top. The hike is very steep and requires some climbing over rocks. Aim for the cross atop the hill and in about 30min. you'll be enjoying incredible views of the Wicklow Mountains and Bray Bay. Just outside of town, **Killruddery House and Gardens** has gardens as beautiful as those of the not-too-distant Powerscourt Estate. Its Elizabethan-Revival house with fancy-dancy rooms and a unique 20 ft. pendulum clock await. (☎286 2777. Gardens open Apr.-Sept. 1-5pm. House open May-June and Sept. 1-5pm. Call for tour times. House and Gardens €6.50; students and seniors €4.50, children €2.50.)

DAYTRIPS FROM BRAY

POWERSCOURT ESTATE. Lordly Powerscourt Estate sits near **Enniskerry** in Co. Wicklow, 5 mi. east of Bray. Built in the 1730s, the house has become an architectural landmark. Powerscourt was gutted by flames in 1974, but work has recently commenced to repair (gradually) the lost interior. Outside, the terraced gardens—displaying everything from Italian opulence to Japanese elegance—justify the high admission. Pointed Sugar Loaf Mountain admires from the distance, and furry friends rest in peace under the headstones of the pet cemetery in the back. Make time for the "long walk," which is roughly 1hr., depending on your degree of horticultural voyeurism. *(From Bray, take an Alpine bus to the garden entrance or #185 to Enniskerry; #45 runs direct from Dublin. Take the left fork as you face the town clock; the house and gardens are a few hundred yards beyond the gatehouse. ☎01 204 6000. Open daily 9:30am-5:30pm. Gardens and house €8, students and seniors €6.50; gardens only €6/€5.)*

POWERSCOURT WATERFALL. The 398 ft. plunge makes Powerscourt Ireland's tallest (permanent) waterfall—a record challenged by the temporary falls on Hungry Hill, in Co. Kerry (see **Adrigole,** p. 261). Although they're worth the visit during any season, the falls are by far most impressive in late spring and after heavy rains. A 40min. nature walk begins at their base and rambles through quiet, untended woods. *(The falls are 3½ mi. outside Enniskerry. Take a bus to Enniskerry and follow the somewhat cryptic signs from town. Open June-Aug. 9:30am-7pm; Sept.-May 10:30am to dusk. €2.50.)*

EASTERN IRELAND

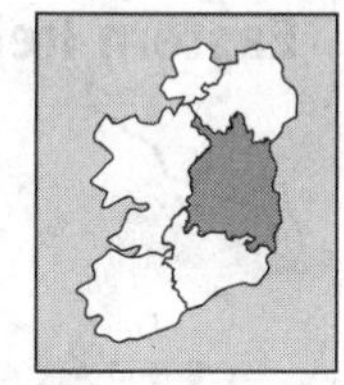

Woe betides the unfortunate soul whose exposure to eastern Ireland is limited to what he sees from inside a bus headed west from Dublin—the untouristed towns of the east hold many a marvel. The monastic city at Clonmacnois and the passage tombs (older than the pyramids) in Co. Meath continue to mystify archaeologists. The Wicklow Mountains offer spectacular views, and those too tired to continue hiking can head downhill to relax on the beautiful beaches. Farther north, the tiny lakeland towns of Co. Monaghan (actually a part of the Fermanagh Lake District in the North, see p. 543) harbor the warmest waters in the northern half of Ireland. And where else but Kildare (see p. 150) could you find a bog-themed theme park? The comprehensive delights of Co. Wicklow, Kildare, Meath, and Louth, most certainly deserve a closer look than daytrips from Dublin could ever allow.

COUNTY WICKLOW

Ladies and gentlemen, welcome to the glorious "Garden of Ireland." Exhausted of its gold in the Bronze Age, sacked by Vikings in the 9th century, and then crushed under the English thumb after the fracas of 1798 (see **Rebellion,** p. 59), Wicklow Town has a long-standing reputation of desirability. These days, the lush and mountainous county offers outdoor enthusiasts deserted back roads and seesawing ridges for bicycling. Wild as parts of it are, Wicklow is right in the capital's backyard; its major sights are accessible by bus from downtown Dublin, though moving about within the county is best accomplished by bike or car. Visitors flock to Wicklow's Historical Gaol, the monastic ruins at Glendalough, and the birthplace of political leader Charles Parnell near Rathdrum. The Wicklow Way, the first of Ireland's waymarked trails, is an excellent invitation to rough it for a week, and Brittas Bay's golden beaches validate the fine art of lounging in the sun.

WICKLOW COAST

The sparsely populated towns of the Wicklow coast seem a world away from jetsetting Dublin. The area lacks the heavy-hitting historical sights of the inland route through Glendalough and Kilkenny, but it also lets you skip the tourist glut. Those interested in catching a glimpse of the capital will find that towns like Wicklow or Arklow aren't too outrageously far to make a decent, cheaper base of operations.

WICKLOW TOWN (CILL MHANTÁIN) ☎0404

Touted both for its seaside pleasures and as a base camp for aspiring Wicklow mountaineers, Wicklow Town has a wide selection of restaurants and plenty of accommodations within walking distance of its pubs. An eager traveler can exhaust the sightseeing potential in the town itself fairly swiftly, but there are many afternoons' worth of hiking and cycling excursions in the hills.

EASTERN IRELAND

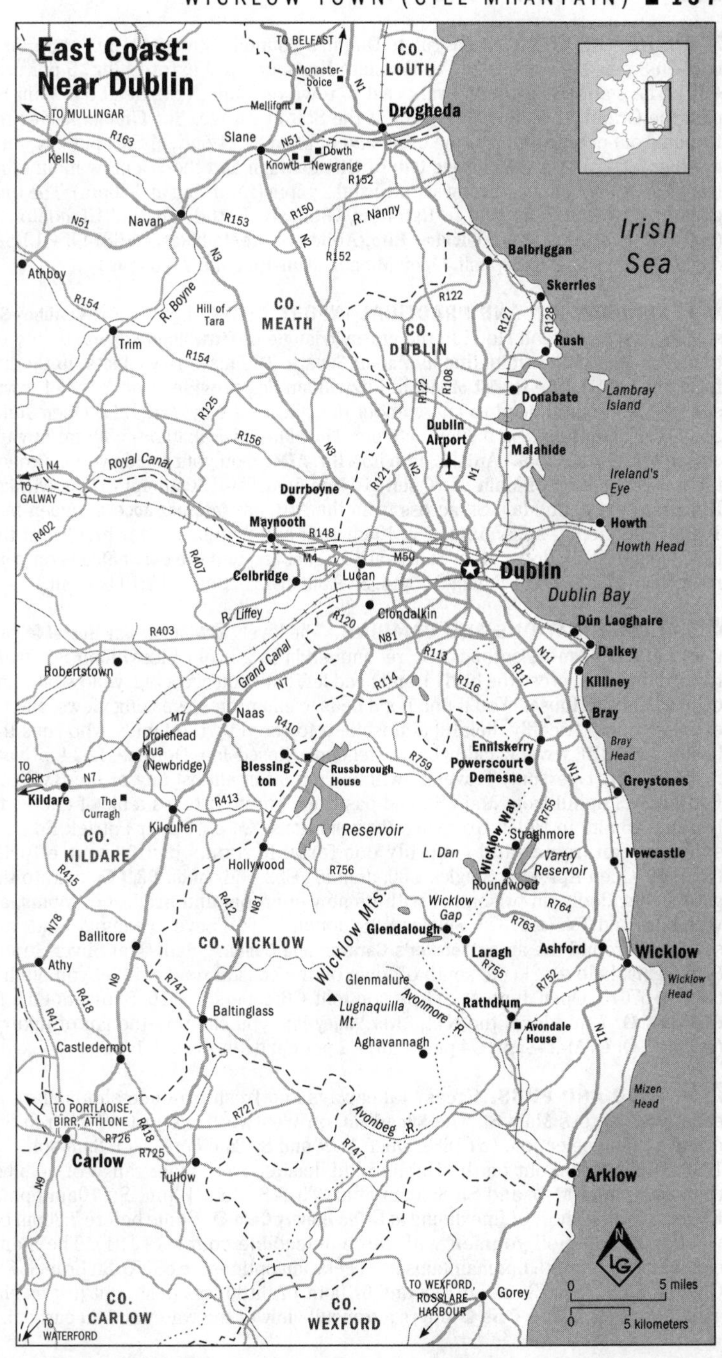

EASTERN IRELAND

TRANSPORTATION. **Trains** run to Dublin's Connolly Station (1¼hr.; M-Sa 4 per day, Su 3 per day; €9.50) and to Rosslare Harbour via Wexford (2hr., 3 per day, €19). The station is a 15min. walk east of town on Church St.; head out Main St. past the Grand Hotel and turn right at the Statoil garage. **Bus Éireann** leaves for Dublin from near the gaol at the other end of Main St. (1½hr.; M-Sa 9 per day, Su 6 per day; €6.20). A **guided driving tour** of Glendalough and the Wicklow mountains leaves daily at 10am (returning at 2pm) and 2:15pm (returning at 6:30pm). The tour goes through the Sally Gap to Rathnew, Glenealy, Rathdrum, and Glendalough (☎45152; call for prices). **Wicklow Hire,** Abbey St., **rents bikes.** (☎68149. €13 per day, €39 per wk. €40 deposit. Open M-Sa 8:30am-1pm and 2-5:30pm.)

ORIENTATION AND PRACTICAL INFORMATION. Long, narrow **Abbey St.** snakes past the Grand Hotel to the grassy triangle of **Fitzwilliam Square,** then continues as **Main St.,** terminating in **Market Square.** The historic **gaol** sits up the hill from Market Sq. The **tourist office,** in Fitzwilliam Sq., provides free maps of town, and can tell you all need to know about the Wicklow Way. (☎69117. Open June-Sept. M-F 9am-6pm, Sa 9:30am-5:30pm; Oct.-May M-F 9:30am-5:30pm; always closed for lunch 1-2pm.) An **AIB,** with its 24hr. **ATM,** is on your left as you approach the busiest section of Main St. (Open M 10am-5pm, Tu-F 10am-4pm.) The **Wicklow IT Access Centre,** on Main St. across from the AIB, has **Internet access.** (Open M-F 10am-1pm, 2-6pm, and 7-10pm; Sa 10am-1pm and 2-6pm. €6 per hr.) From the town center, walk down Main St. toward Market Sq., and the **post office** is on your right. (☎67474. Open M-F 9am-5:30pm, Sa 9:30am-12:50pm and 2:10-5:30pm.)

ACCOMMODATIONS AND CAMPING. The lovely **Wicklow Bay Hostel ❶** garners *Let's Go's* most enthusiastic recommendation. From Fitzwilliam Sq., walk toward the river, cross the bridge, and head left until you see a big, yellow building called "Marine House." You'll find good beds, clean rooms, amazing views, and an extraordinarily friendly, helpful atmosphere fostered by the family who runs the hostel. (☎69213; www.wicklowbayhostel.com. Closed Jan. Dorms €12-14; private rooms €16 per person.) Travelers will be content in almost any of the B&Bs on Patrick Rd., uphill from Main St. and past the church. It takes a bit of energy to hike the 15min. to Helen Gorman's **Thomond House ❸,** on Upper Patrick Rd., but splendid panoramas and superbly comfortable rooms justify your efforts. (☎67940. Open Apr.-Oct. Singles €36; doubles €52.) **Kilmantin B&B ❸,** next to the gaol, is decidedly un-prisonlike with its new sunroom and bright bedrooms, all with bath and TV. (☎67373. Singles €38; doubles €60.) Several campgrounds are scattered around the area. **Webster's Caravan and Camping Park ❶** at Silver Strand (see **Sights,** below), 2½ mi. south of town on the coastal road, will let you pitch a tent. (☎67615. Open June-Aug. 1-person tent €6; 2-person €10. Showers €1.) In **Redcross ❶,** 7 mi. down the N11, **River Valley** lets you camp in the lap of luxury. (☎41647. Open Mar.-Sept. €4 per adult, €2 per child. Showers €1.)

FOOD AND PUBS. Greasy takeaways and fresh produce shops glare at each other across Main St. The **SuperValu,** on Wentworth Pl. just off Church St., offers a grand selection. (☎61888. Open M-W and Sa 8am-8pm, Th-F 8am-9pm, Su 10am-7pm.) **Tesco,** out on the Dublin road, has an even wider range of edibles. (☎69250. Open M-W and Sa 8:30am-8pm, Th-F 8:30am-10pm, Su 10am-6pm.) Expect nothing short of fine dining at **The Bakery Cafe ❸.** Come before 7:30pm on weekdays and spoil yourself with three delectable courses (€21). The menu changes every month but maintains its vegetarian options. (☎66770. Su brunch €9. Open M-Sa 6-10pm, Su noon-4pm and 6-10pm.) A little less posh, but just as elegant, **Rugantino's River Cafe ❺** offers a tranquil view of the water and an early-bird special Monday through Thursday (6-7:30pm; €17). Later diners pay €18-22 for a variety of fishy mains. (☎61900. Open M-Sa 6-10pm, Su 1-3:30pm and 6-10pm.) **The Old Court Inn ❸,** Market Sq. (☎67680), serves a good plate of grub daily until 9pm. For a warm high, try the Guinness Hot Pot for €10. **Casapepe ❸** serves up no-frills Italian fare: pizzas €8-9; pastas, poultry, and fish €13-18. (☎67075. Open daily noon-midnight.) **Philip Healy's ❷,** Fitzwilliam Sq., serves food all day and doubles as a lively nocturnal hot spot on weekends. (☎67380. Open Su-W noon-11:30pm, Th-Sa noon-12:30am.) The **Bridge Tavern,** Bridge St., reverberates with the sweet sounds of trad, local chatter, and clinking pints. Tunes nightly at 10pm. (☎67718. Open M-W 10:30am-midnight, Th-Sa 11:30am-12:30am, Su 11:30am-11:30pm.)

SIGHTS AND FESTIVALS. Wicklow's premier attraction is **Wicklow's Historic Gaol.** The newly opened museum fills nearly 40 cells with audio clips, displays, and interactive activities relating to the gaol, its history, and the messy business of shipping convicts off to Australia. The canned wailing and moaning may seem a bit overblown, but the live actors keep it real. (☎61599. Tours every 10min. Open Apr.-Oct. daily 10am-6pm; last admission 5pm. €5.70, students and seniors €4.40, children €3.50.) The first left past Market Sq. leads to what remains of the **Black Castle.** The Normans built the castle in 1178, and the local Irish lords began attacking it almost immediately, finally destroying it in 1301. Since then, many assaults and changes in ownership have left only a few wind-worn stones, but the promontory offers a great vantage point over meadows and waves. At the other end of Main St., the ruins of a **Franciscan friary** hide behind a small gate and a run-down hut. The friary was built at the same time as the Black Castle and fell right along with it. It was subsequently rebuilt and became a place of retirement for both Normans and the native Irish, who considered it neutral ground.

A cliff trail provides smashing views while en route to **St. Bride's Head** (a.k.a. **Wicklow Head**), where St. Patrick landed on Travilahawk Strand in AD 432. The townspeople greeted him by knocking the teeth out of his sidekick, Mantan ("the toothless one" or "gubby"), who was later assigned to convert the same local hooligans. Either cut through the golf course from the Black Castle or head out the coastal road past the clubhouse and find the trailhead in the parking lot on the left. Hiking to St. Bride's Head takes over 1hr. Adventurous walkers can continue for 1½hr. to reach the isolated **lighthouse** at Wicklow Head. At Market Sq., Main St. becomes Summer Hill and then Dunbur Rd., the coastal road, from which beaches extend south to **Arklow.** From Wicklow, the closest strips of sun and sand are **Silver Strand** and **Jack's Hole,** though most people head to the larger **Brittas Bay,** halfway to Arklow. If you venture further to the town of Arklow, be sure to bring your fishing gear as you'll find excellent **angling opportunities** on the Avoca river and along the sea on both sides of the town. You'll also find the **longest stone bridge in Ireland** and its 19 very impressive arches (only 17½ of which are visible today).

Beginning the last week of July, Wicklow hosts its annual **Regatta Festival,** the oldest such celebration in Ireland. The two-week festivities feature hard-core skiff racing and a parade of whimsical homemade barges; join the spectators on the bridge and let loose with eggs and tomatoes! At night, amicable pub rivalries foster singing competitions and general revelry. The **Wicklow Gaol Arts Festival** livens up mid-July nights with plays and concerts. (☎69117; www.wicklowartsweek.com. Tickets €10-15.) Contact the tourist office for more information.

NEAR WICKLOW: AVONDALE HOUSE & RATHDRUM ☎0404

The birthplace and main residence of political leader Charles Stewart Parnell, **Avondale House** is now a museum devoted to the charismatic and ill-fated hero. The Parnell family study contains framed love letters from Charles to his mistress Kitty

IN RECENT NEWS

PRIESTLY PROGRAMS

It was inevitable that in a country with as rich a history of Catholicism as Ireland's, someone would eventually produce a television comedy starring priests. In fact, two tremendously popular shows have appeared in the last decade, each with a slightly different take on the lives of the holy brethren.

Ballykissangel (now syndicated in seventeen countries) is filmed in the green and hilly town of **Avoca** in Co. Wicklow. The show stars Father Damien Daly, a young British priest who alights in a small town in Ireland to minister to its parishioners. For six seasons this *Murder She Wrote* meets *Friends* detective-drama-comedy kept viewers across the world wondering who wouldn't make it to the next episode, and whether Father Daly was going to forsake his vows and finally jump into the sack with the lovely local barmaid.

Father Ted, a much darker comedy (blasphemy be damned!), features an anxious housekeeper and a set of three nun-hating, dysfunctional, Irish priests creating trouble on a fictional Craggy Island. This satirical masterpiece has Father Ted stealing the parish funds to gamble, the alcoholic Father Jack in a wheelchair and able to utter only four words ("drink, feck, girls, and arse"), and the simple, naive, and innocent Father Dougal going along for the ride. To cap the lampoon, the final episode makes a passing reference to its rival priestly program "Killybashangels."

O'Shea, while a small pantry off the impressive dining room is bedecked with political cartoons from the late 19th century. A 20min. video provides a celluloid glimpse into Parnell's life and his role in the development of Irish independence (see **Parnell,** p. 60). If your hunger for liberty turns out to be merely a craving for sausage rolls, the small **cafe** downstairs can help you out. (☎46111. House open daily 11am-6pm; closed W in winter. €4.45.) Floraphiles and hikers will fawn over the hundreds of acres of **forest** and **parklands** surrounding the house and spreading along the west bank of the **Avonmore River.** There are three hikes, each approximately 1hr. in length: the Pine Trail, the Exotic Tree Trail, and the River Walk.

Avondale House is on the road from Wicklow Town to **Avoca,** 1 mi. after **Rathdrum** and before the **Meeting of the Waters.** From Rathdrum, take Main St. heading toward Avoca and follow the signs. **Buses** arrive in Rathdrum from Dublin (2¾hr.; M-Sa 2 per day, Su 1 per day), as do **trains** (1hr., M-F 4 per day). Rathdrum is not easily visible from the train station; after exiting the station's driveway, turn left at the *Garda* station and stroll 200 yd. uphill to a path on your right—the path cuts through the Parnell National Memorial Park and up to Main St. The **tourist office,** in the Square at the center of town, offers pamphlets on hikes and area attractions. (☎46262. Open July-Aug. M-F 9am-5:30pm, Sa-Su 1-6pm. Sept.-May M-F 9am-5:30pm. Sometimes closed 1-2pm.) The **post office** (☎46211) is concealed within Smith's Fancy Goods on the Square, and the **Bank of Ireland** there has a 24hr. **ATM.**

In the center of town, **Stirabout Lane B&B ❸,** Main St., has beautifully decorated, doll-themed rooms and a lovely back garden. Ask the owner about all the best local fishing areas. (☎43142. Off-street parking. Singles €32; doubles €56.) Also in town, the **Old Presbytery Hostel (IHH) ❶** has a fairly luxurious setup in a 200-year-old stone building. To find it, continue past the tourist office, turn left after the grocery store, and then right at the top of the hill. (☎46930. June-Sept. dorms €12; Oct.-May €8.) Among the many B&Bs outside Rathdrum is the family-run **Woodland B&B ❹,** on the left as you head out to Avondale. (☎46011. Irish breakfast included. Singles €40; doubles €56.) For your nightly refreshment and daily dinner, you might want to check out the **Woolpack Pub ❸** in the Square. (☎46574. Main courses €7-19.) Hollywood geeks may recognize the upstairs from the film *Michael Collins.* The **Cartoon Inn** on Main St. is a pub with suitably wacky walls. (☎46774. Open M-W 10:30am-11:30pm, Th-Sa 10:30am-12:30am, Su 12:30-11:30pm.)

WICKLOW MOUNTAINS

Over 2000 ft. high, carpeted in fragrant heather and rushing with sparkling water, the Wicklow summits provide a happy home to grazing sheep and scattered villages alike. This region epitomizes the romantic image of pristine rural Ireland. Glendalough, a verdant, blessed valley renowned as a medieval, monastic village, draws a stream of coach tours from Dublin. Visitors also make it a point to see Ireland's tallest waterfall, near **Bray** (see p. 134). Public transportation is limited in this region, so driving is the easiest way to connect the scattered sights and towns. Those behind the wheel should be careful on the narrow and winding roads and expect to maneuver around hikers, bikers, tour buses, and the occasional flock of oblivious sheep. Everyone except hardcore wilderness demigods will find portions of the Wicklow Way challenging, but the effort is rewarded by the best-maintained trailpath in Ireland and its charming hostels. Stop by the tourist offices in Bray, Wicklow Town, Arklow, and Rathdrum for advice and colorful maps.

GLENDALOUGH (GLEANN DÁ LOCH) ☎0404

In the 6th century, a vision instructed St. Kevin to give up his life of ascetic isolation and set up one humdinger of a monastery. He offset the workaday austerity of monastic life by choosing one of the most spectacular valleys in Ireland in which to found Glendalough ("glen of two lakes"). More recently, the valley has become known for ruins, excellent hikes, and swarms of tourists. Glendalough, no longer a true town, consists of St. Kevin's habitat, a hostel, hotel, and roads barely wide enough for the convoy of tour buses that plague the valley. One mile up the road, the village of **Laragh** has groceries, food options, and plenty of B&Bs.

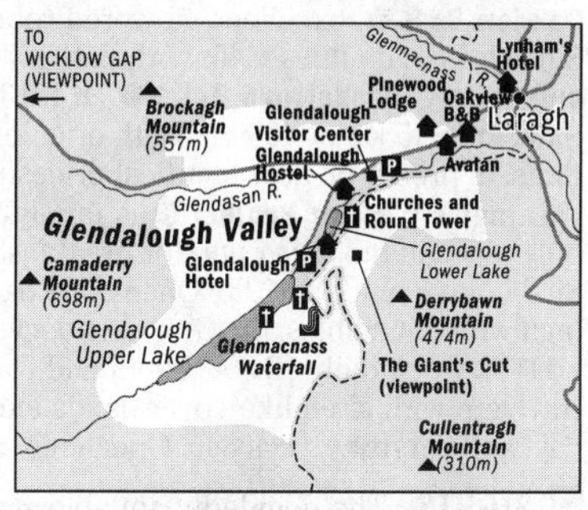

TRANSPORTATION. If you're not arriving on one of the countless charter bus tours, pilgrims come by **car** on R756, on **foot** along the Wicklow Way, or in **buses** run by **St. Kevin's Bus Service.** (☎01 281 8119. Buses leave from St. Stephen's Green in Dublin M-Sa 11:30am and 6pm, Su 11:30am and 7pm; €13 return.) Buses also leave from Bray, just past the Town Hall. (M-Sa 12:10 and 6:30pm, Su 12:10 and 7:30pm; €8 return.) **Bus Éireann** (☎01 836 6111; www.buseireann.ie) also runs **day tours** from Dublin's Busáras Station to Glendalough and through the mountains. (Apr.-Oct. daily 10:30am, return 5:45pm. €25, students and seniors €23, children €12.50.) Hitching to Glendalough is fairly easy from Co. Wicklow towns, but most Glendalough-bound traffic from Dublin is bus tours. Hitchers at the beginning of N11 in southwest Dublin hop to the juncture of N11 with Glendalough's R755. *Let's Go* still refuses to recommend hitchhiking.

PRACTICAL INFORMATION. Little Glendalough sits on a tributary of **R756,** just where the **Glenealo River** pools into its **Upper and Lower Lakes. Bike rental** is available at the Glendaloch Hostel. (See below; €10.20 for under 5hr., €15.25 per day. No deposit for hostel guests.) Road signs will lead you to the Bord Failté **tourist office,** located in a small trailer across from the Glendalough Hotel. (☎45688. Open from mid-June to Sept. M-Sa 10am-1pm and 2-6pm.) The considerably more glamorous **Glendalough Visitor Centre** (see **Sights,** below) is a wealth of both information and parking spaces. The **National Park Information Office,** between the lakes, is the best source for hiking information in the region. (☎45425. Open May-Aug. daily 10am-6pm, Apr. and Sept. Sa-Su 10am-6pm.) When the park office is closed, call the **ranger office,** located in nearby Trooperstown Wood (☎45800). **Laragh IT,** in the parking lot next to Lynham's pub, has **Internet access.** (☎45600. €6 per hr. Open M-F 9:30am-4:30pm and 7-10pm.) The Glendalough and Laragh **post office** is tucked into a row of B&Bs to the left of **Wicklow Heather** (see below).

ACCOMMODATIONS, FOOD, AND PUBS. **The Glendaloch Hostel (An Óige/HI) ❷**, a 5min. walk up the road past the Glendalough visitors center, on the left. Prices are a bit high, but good beds, excellent security, and an in-house cafe make it by far the best option in the area. The comparatively cramped Dublin hostels can't possibly compete with the grandeur of this establishment or the inspiring Wicklow Mountains backdrop. As with all the accommodations in the area, book ahead in the summertime. (☎45342. **Bike rental** and **Internet** both available. Wheelchair-accessible. Picnic lunch €4.50; full Irish €6.50; dinners €9.50. Towels €1.30. Laundry €5. Dorms €19.50; doubles €43. Off-season €2 less.)

B&Bs abound in neighboring Laragh. Tucked into the forest on the road up to St. Kevin's Church, **Pinewood Lodge ❸** offers excellent rooms furnished with, appropriately, pinewood. (☎45437. All rooms with bath. Singles €36-40; doubles €52-60.) Fall into the lush bedrooms of **Avalon ❹**, down the road to Glendalough from the Wicklow Heather restaurant, but try to avoid the mosquitoes that swarm the wooden swing in the backyard. (☎45331. Singles €40; doubles €56.) At nearby **Oakview B&B ❸**, excellent, flowered rooms are the rule. (☎45453. Open Mar.-Oct. Singles €35; doubles €46, with bath €50.) Hotel options include the established and stately **Glendalough Hotel ❺** (☎45135 or 45391) and the brand-new **Lynham's Hotel ❺** (☎45345 or 45398). Both offer similar facilities, including in-house restaurants, at premium, near-identical prices. (Singles €84-107; doubles €120-170.)

Laragh's **Wicklow Heather ❸** is family- and vegetarian-friendly and is about the only place in the area open for breakfast. (☎45157. Breakfast €5-8; mains €10-18; Su 3-course lunch €17.95. Open daily 8am-midnight.) **Lynham's ❸** also piles plates high with hot edibles; the Guinness beef stew (€11.50) is fabulous. (☎45345. Mains €11-15. Open daily 12:30-3:30pm and 5:30-9pm.) The attached **Lynham's Pub** lures travelers with siren-like cover bands and rock sessions every Wednesday, Thursday, and Saturday. (☎45345. Open daily until 11:30pm.)

SIGHTS. The decidedly amiable staff at the **Glendalough Visitors Centre** presents ample information on the valley's intriguing past. Your admission fee covers an exhibition, a tour of the ruins, and a 17min. audio-visual show on the history of Irish monasteries in general and St. Kevin's in particular. You'll learn that, in keeping with his ascetic image, St. Kevin would sometimes stand in one of the frigid lakes long enough for birds to make nests in his outstretched hands—before, of course, returning home to pray. (☎45325. Open June-Aug. daily 9am-6:30pm; Sept. to mid-Oct. 9:30am-6pm; mid-Oct. to mid-Mar. 9:30am-5pm; mid-Mar. to May 9:30am-6:30pm. Tours every 30min. during the summer. €2.50, students €1.20.)

The well-preserved ruins are free and always open, although only tour guides hold the keys to **St. Kevin's Kitchen.** The present remains reflect only a small part of what the monastery looked like in its heyday. A tiny 3 ft. base supports the 100 ft. **Round Tower** of Glendalough, which is one of the best-preserved in all of Ireland (see **Christians and Vikings,** p. 55) and the centerpiece of the monastery. It was built in the 10th century, primarily as a belltower, but also as a watchtower and retreat in tumultuous times. The entrance is a dozen feet above the ground; when Vikings threatened, the monks would climb the inside of the tower floor by floor and draw up the ladders behind them. The **cathedral,** constructed in a combination of Romanesque architectural styles, was once the largest in the country. In its shadow stands **St. Kevin's Cross,** an unadorned high cross that was carved before the monks had tools to cut holes clean through the stone. (We're talking *old.*) The 11th-century **St. Kevin's Church,** whose stone roof remains intact, acquired the misnomer "St. Kevin's Kitchen" because of its chimney-like tower. After 500 years of worshipful use, it has laid derelict except for a brief revival in the 19th century.

The **Upper and Lower Lakes** are a rewarding digression from the monastic site. Cross the bridge at the far side of the monastery and head right on the paved path for 5min. to reach the serene Lower Lake. Twenty-five minutes later, the path hits the National Park Information Office (see **Practical Information,** above) and the magnificent Upper Lake, where Mel Gibson wed his ill-fated bride in the film *Braveheart.* Drivers should continue past the hotel and park (€2) in the lot by the Upper Lake. The trail continues along the lakeside, passing **St. Kevin's Bed,** the cave where he prayed. Legend has it that when St. Kevin went there, his words ascended in a vortex of flame and light that burned over the Upper Lake's dark waters with such intensity that none but the most righteous monks could witness it without going blind. Before reaching the cave, look for the **burial grounds** at Reefert Church, where local chieftains found their eternal resting places.

THE WICKLOW WAY

Ireland's oldest marked hiking trail (est. 1981) is also its most spectacular. Stretching from **Marlay Park** at the border of Dublin to **Clonegal** in Co. Carlow, the 76 mi. Wicklow Way meanders north to south through Ireland's largest highland expanse. As you weave over heathered summits and through steep glacial valleys, yellow arrows and signs help you stick to the Way's various footpaths, dirt tracks, and even paved roads. Civilization is rarely more than 2 mi. away, but appropriate wilderness precautions should still be taken: bring warm, windproof layers and raingear for the exposed hills, and, although the terrain never gets frighteningly rugged, sturdy footwear is a must (see **Wilderness Safety,** p. 37). Water is best taken from farmhouses (with permission), not streams. Open fires are illegal within a mile of the forest and should be carefully monitored.

ORIENTATION AND PRACTICAL INFORMATION

Most tourist offices in the county sell the *Wicklow Way Map Guide* (€6.35), which is the best source of information on the trail and its sights—don't worry, you're not crazy, the map is orientated with North pointing down. Hiking from 7-8hr. each day for six days will carry you from one end to the other, though there are plenty of attractive abbreviated routes. Numerous side trails make excellent day hikes; *Wicklow Way Walks* (€8) outlines several of these loops. The northern 44 mi. of the Way—from Dublin to Aghavannagh—is the older section and, since it has the best scenery and all the hostels, attracts more people. An Óige publishes a pamphlet detailing 4-5hr. hostel-to-hostel walks (available at An Óige hostels in Co. Wicklow and Dublin). A trip touching on the highlights of the Way would run the 20 mi. from Powerscourt Waterfall near Enniskerry (see p. 134) to Glendalough, passing by the stupendous **Lough Dan** and the even more stupendous **Lough Tay,** and offering views as far away as Wales. For further information, contact the **National Park Information Office** (☎45425), located between Glendalough's lakes (see p. 142). Forestry lands are governed by **Coillte** (KWEEL-chuh; ☎01 201 1111), but much of the Way is simply on a right-of-way through private lands.

TRANSPORTATION

Several bus companies will drop happy packers at various spots along the trail. **Dublin Bus** (☎01 873 4222) runs frequently to Marlay Park in Rathfarnham (#15A and 15B from Trinity College) and Enniskerry (#44 or 185 from Bray), and less frequently to Glencullen (#44B). **Bus Éireann** (☎01 836 6111) comes somewhat near the Way farther south, with infrequent service from Busáras in Dublin to

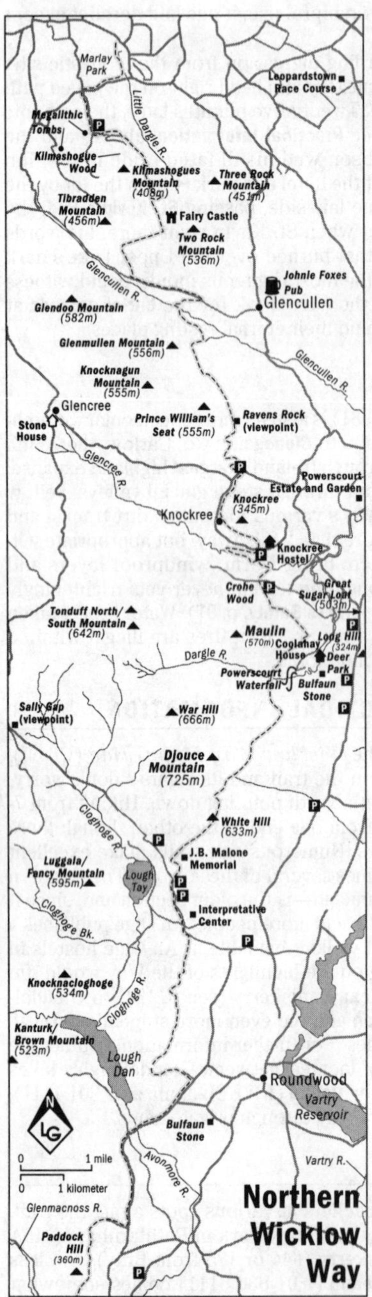

Aughrim, Tinahely, Shillelagh, and Hackettstown. **St. Kevin's** runs two shuttles daily between Dublin's St. Stephen's Green West, Roundwood, and Glendalough. (☎01 281 8119. €14 return.) To combat trail erosion, **bikes** are allowed only on forest tracks and paved sections, but many off-Way roads are equally stunning. For a particularly scenic route, take R759 to **Sally Gap,** west of the trail near Lough Tay, then head south on R115 past **Glenmacnass Waterfall** (roughly 15 mi.).

ACCOMMODATIONS

The splendor of the Wicklow Way isn't exactly a well-kept secret—many accommodations take advantage of the endless stream of bodies that trek the hike. **Camping** is feasible along the Way but requires planning ahead. Many local farmhouses allow you set up tent on their land; ask permission first. National Park lands are fine for low-impact camping, but pitching a tent in state plantations is prohibited.

HOSTELS

An Óige runs a cluster of hostels that lie close to the Way. All hostels include self-catering facilities, but only Glendaloch sells meals and boxed lunches; bring food along or expect to walk a few miles to a grocery store to purchase edibles. Except for the Glendaloch Hostel, all bookings are handled through the An Óige Head Office (☎01 830 4555). Hostels run from north to south in the following order:

Knockree (An Óige/HI), Lacken House, Enniskerry (☎01 286 4036), right on the Way. A reconstructed farmhouse 4 mi. from the village and 2 mi. from Powerscourt Waterfall. From Enniskerry, take the right fork of the road leading uphill from the village green and follow the signs to the hostel. Sheets €1.25. Lockout 10am-5pm. Dorms €11-12. ❶

Tiglin (An Óige/HI), a.k.a. **Devil's Glen,** Ashford (☎0404 40259), by the Tiglin Adventure Centre, 5 mi. from the main trail and a hilly 8 mi. from Powerscourt.

EASTERN IRELAND

From Ashford, take the Roundwood road for 3 mi., then follow the signs for the Tiglin turnoff and R763 on the right. Formerly a farm, recent renovations on the courtyard have brought a barbecue to the grassy front lawn. Basic, single-sex dorms. Curfew 11pm. Dorms €10-12. ❶

Glendaloch (An Óige/HI), a stone's throw from the Way (☎0404 45342), by the monastic ruins. An absolutely fabulous hostel, well worth a 2-3 day break from the Wicklow Way. Dorms €19.50; doubles €43. See **Glendalough,** p. 141. ❷

Glenmalure (An Óige/HI), Glenmalure. At the end of a dead-end road 7½ mi. along the Way south from Glendalough. By road, head from Glendalough to Laragh and take every major right turn. Back-to-nature lodging; doesn't even have a telephone or electricity (though they do have beds). Dorms €10-12. ❶

BED AND BREAKFASTS

Approved accommodations along the Way can be booked with a credit card through the **All-Ireland Room Reservation** service. (Freephone ☎00 800 668 668 66; www.ireland.travel.ie.) A number of B&Bs offer **camping** and pickup if you call ahead; the *Wicklow Way Map Guide* comes with a sheet that lists about 20. The following few will pick up hikers and allow camping.

Coolakay House (☎01 286 2423), 2½ mi. outside Enniskerry, next to the Powerscourt Waterfall. Small cafe and nice rooms bordering on hotel-esque. €33 per person. ❸

Hillview B&B, Tinahely in Knockananna (☎0508 71195). Sits one measly mile away. Singles €25; doubles €40. **Camping** €5-7 per person. ❸

Rosbane Farmhouse, Rosbane (☎0402 38100). A 7min. walk from the Way, near the summit of Garryhoe. €28 per person. **Camping** €7 per tent. ❸

Orchard House, Tinahely (☎0402 38264). Within earshot of the main trail. Relax by picking apples from the backyard orchard. **Internet** available. Singles €25-30. ❸

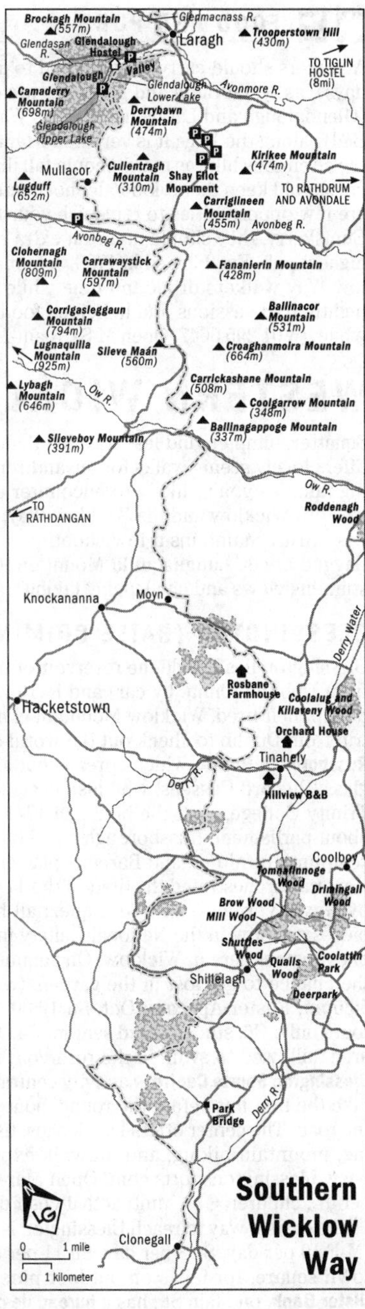

FOOD AND PUBS

All hikers should carry enough food to last through the length of the journey (5-6 days), as restaurants and groceries are only found in towns located off the Way (Glendalough and Laragh excepted). Water can be replenished at the hostels and B&Bs along the Way; it is very important for hikers to drink plenty of fluid during the strenuous hike as many people fall ill from dehydration. More importantly, hikers should keep their blood/alcohol content at an acceptable Irish standard. There are few opportunities to replenish your BAC, so when hikers reach Glencullen or Enniskerry, they should make an extra effort to climb to **Johnnie Fox's,** Ireland's highest pub. Established in 1798, Johnnie's is 1200 ft. above sea level. Here, Wicklow Way walkers drink and dine while enjoying the pub's excellent *craic*. The nightly trad sessions and delicious food (mains €9-18) make the journey worthwhile. (☎01 295 5647. Open M-Sa 10am-11:45pm and Su noon-11pm.)

WESTERN WICKLOW

Squatter, lumpier, and less traveled than the rest of the county, western Wicklow offers lovely scenic walks for misanthropic travelers looking to avoid the picnicking families you're likely to encounter elsewhere. It's possible to hike between western Wicklow and the Wicklow Way, but turn around if you see a red flag; the Irish Army maintains a few shooting ranges in the region. Hiking is safe in unflagged areas. Lungnaquilla Mountain, the highest peak in Co. Wicklow, offers stunning views and challenging hiking trails.

BLESSINGTON (BAILE COIMÍN) ☎045

Blessington lies beside the reservoir of the Liffey, close to the intersection of N81 from Dublin (30min. by car) and R410 from Naas (15min.). Hikers come here to put up their tired, Wicklow Mountain-exploring feet. Cultured types make the daytrip from Dublin to check out the world-class art inside the Palladian grandeur of **Russborough House,** which spreads out almost 2 mi. south on N81 toward Baltinglass. Richard Cassells, who also designed Dublin's Leinster House and much of Trinity College, built the house in 1741 for Joseph Leeson, an Anglo-Irish man-about-parliament. Russborough now houses an impressive collection of paintings, sculpture, furniture, and Baroque plaster-work. In 1986, the Dublin mobster "The General" orchestrated the theft of the 17 most valuable paintings, including works by Goya, Vermeer, and Velasquez; all but one have been recovered. The best pieces are now in the National Gallery in Dublin (see p. 112), but a few excellent ones remain here in Wicklow. On summer Sundays, a **life-size maze** offers visitors the chance to get lost in the garden. (☎865 239. Open May-Sept. daily 10:30am-5:30pm; Easter-Apr. and Oct. Su 10:30am-5:30pm. Admission by hourly 45min. tours only. €6, students and seniors €4.50, children €3.) Although you technically aren't allowed to swim in the reservoir, many activities take place on its waters. **Blessington Sports Centre** is activity central. From town, heading away from Dublin, take the first left before the roundabout and you'll find it on the left, ½ mi. down the road. The center offers kayak trips, fishing, windsurfing, and sailing. Quad biking, mountain biking, and hillwalk expeditions are also available. (☎865 092; www.blessingtonsports.com. Open Mar-Oct. daily 9am-6pm. Most activities €16 per hr., children €11. Multi-activity half days €45/€23; full day €70/€40.)

The easiest way to reach Blessington is by the #65 **bus** from Eden Quay in Dublin (M-F 10 per day, Sa 8 per day, Su 11 per day; €3). Turn to the **tourist office,** in the town square, for ideas on outdoor pursuits. (☎865 850. Open M-F 10am-5pm.) **Ulster Bank,** on Main St., has a **bureau de change** and an **ATM.** (☎865 125. Open M-F

10am-4pm, Th until 5pm.) **Halyon's House B&B ❸,** less than a 10min. walk out of town on the N81 to Dublin, across the road from the #65 bus stop, offers spacious rooms and a relaxed environment. (☎865 183. Singles €35, with bath €37; doubles €54/€58.) On the other side of town, 1 mi. out on the road to Naas, the friendly owners of the **Fairhill B&B ❸** provide excellent rooms for weary walkers of the Wicklow Way. (☎865 692. Singles €35; doubles €55.) Four miles out the road to Valleymount, **Baltyboys (An Óige/HI) ❶,** also known as the Blessington Lake Hostel, has excellent views and affordable rooms. (☎867 266; call ahead. Sheets €2. Lockout 10am-5pm. Open Mar.-Nov. daily; Dec.-Feb. F-Su. June-Sept. dorms €12, students €10; Oct.-May €10/€8.) For a quick bite to eat, try **The Courtyard Restaurant ❷** for large Irish breakfasts (€5.10) in the morning and tasty food throughout the day. (☎865 850. Open M and W-Sa 8:30am-7:30pm, Tu 8:30am-2pm, Sa 10am-7pm).

COUNTY KILDARE

The towns immediately west of Dublin in Co. Kildare are still well within the city's orbit; the best sights—Kildare's horses and Lullymore Heritage Park—make easy daytrips. From the 13th to the 16th century, the FitzGerald Earls of Kildare controlled all of eastern Ireland. Today, mansions and the big-money Irish Derby evoke Kildare's former prominence. The Irish National Stud rears horses that win the world's great derbies while the Curragh Racecourse, a few miles outside of Kildare town, hosts them. Farmhouse B&Bs are still the area's greatest attraction.

MAYNOOTH (MHAIGH NUAD) ☎01

Maynooth (ma-NOOTH) is a town of the erudite and the religious. In 1795, St. Patrick's College, the first Catholic seminary in Ireland, was opened with George III's permission—he was concerned priests educated in Revolutionary France would acquire dangerous notions of independence. Priests are still ordained here, but the 120 clerical students are far outnumbered these days by their 5000 peers in other disciplines. The serenely beautiful campus includes A.W. Pugin's Gothic **St. Mary's Square, College Chapel,** and the **Bicentenary Garden.** There is also the **National Science Museum,** displaying both scientific and ecclesiastical artifacts. (Open Tu and Th 2-4pm, Su 2-6pm. €1.30.) The **Visitor Centre,** under the arch of the first building on campus, provides a map and tours of the college. (☎708 3576. Open daily 8:30am-11pm. Tours €3 per person for groups of 15 or less, €2.50 per person for larger groups, students and seniors €1.) The FitzGerald family controlled its vast domain from **Maynooth Castle,** near the college but built earlier in 1176. Unfortunately, access to the castle is barred until renovations are complete.

Maynooth is 15 mi. west of Dublin on the M4. The **suburban rail** runs from Connolly Station in Dublin; **bus** #66 goes directly to Maynooth, and #67A runs via Celbridge, with both departing from Wellington Quay. The **Citizens Information Centre,** just around the corner farthest from St. Patrick's on Main St., is a volunteer-staffed center that answers questions about the area and hands out photocopied maps. (☎628 5477. Open M-F 10am-4:30pm.) **usit** has an office on Mill St., which runs perpendicular to Main. (☎628 9289. Open M-F 9:30am-5:30pm, Sa 10am-1pm.) **Internet access** is available at **Nikita Solutions Ireland** on Leinster St., off Main St. one block from St. Patrick's. (☎610 6454. Open daily 11am-10pm. €5 per hr., students €4.)

St. Patrick's College ❸ rents student apartments during the summer and a small number of rooms during the year; the fee includes access to the college swimming pool, weight room, tennis courts, and playing fields. The housing office shares space with the Visitor Centre. (Contact Bill Tinley, ☎708 6200; info@maynoothcampus.com. All rooms available early June to mid-Sept., limited availability Oct.-May. Singles €23-26, with breakfast €29.20-32.20; doubles from €39, with breakfast €51.38.) For food on a student budget, enjoy light fare and lots of baked goods (€1.20-3.80) at **Elite Confectionery ❶,** Main St. (☎628 5521. Open M-Sa 8:30am-6pm.)

Tiny **Celbridge** (SELL-bridge) lies 5 mi. south of Maynooth on Celbridge Rd. At the end of a long, lime-tree lined road is **Castletown House,** magnificent home of William Connolly. The richest man in 1720s Ireland, Connolly built this grandiose pad and touched off a nationwide fad for Palladian architecture. Comprehensive tours cover the origin of each painting, wall hanging, and piece of furniture. (☎628 8252. Open Apr.-Sept. M-F 10am-6pm, Sa-Su 1-6pm; Oct. M-F 10am-5pm, Su 1-5pm; Nov. Su 1-5pm. Admission by guided tour only. €3.80, seniors €2.50, students and children €1.50, families €9.50.) Connolly's "philanthropic" widow built an obelisk 2 mi. behind the estate to employ Famine-starved locals in 1740. Known as **Connolly's Folly,** its unruly stack of arches was used for the original plans of the Washington Monument. At the other end of Main St., the family-friendly grounds of **Celbridge Abbey** offer a small playground, model railway, and elegant gardens and walks. (☎627 5508. Open M-Sa 10am-6pm, Su noon-6pm. €3.80, seniors and children €2.50, families €9.50.) The Abbey's **Tea Room ❷** (admission not required) offers sandwiches, salads, and pastries from €1.10-5.70. If the weather is on your side, eat your treats outside in the gardens or make your own picnic with food from **Centra** on Main St. (☎628 8337. Open daily 7am-11pm.) **Buses** #67 and 67A run to Celbridge from Dublin. The **suburban rail** arrives roughly every hour at the Hazelhatch & Celbridge stop. A shuttle bus runs the distance between the station and town during peak hours; otherwise it's a €5 taxi.

KILDARE (CILL DARA) ☎045

Kildare is Ireland's horse-racing holy land. Carefully bred, raised, and raced right here, purebloods are the lifeblood of the town. The town's past is somewhat less equine-centric; it grew up around a church founded in AD 480 by St. Brigid. The sacred lass chose a site next to an oak tree that she saw in a vision, hence the town's Gaelic name, meaning "Church of the Oak." The center of town is a triangular square ("the Square," cleverly enough), which is scarred, unlike its calmer periphery, by ceaseless trucking traffic from the N7.

TRANSPORTATION AND PRACTICAL INFORMATION. Kildare straddles busy, harrowing N7 (Dublin-Limerick) and is connected to Heuston Station by **suburban rail** (40min., M-Sa every 30min. 6am-10:30pm). **Bus Éireann** heads for Dublin on its route from Limerick (1½hr., every hr. 10am-10pm, €10). **Rapid Express Coaches** (☎01 679 1549) offers a cheaper service between Dublin's Middle Abbey St. and Kildare (4-6 per day, €4). **The Bike Shop** offers **bike rental** on Claregate St. (☎522 309. €8.25 per day, €31.75 per wk. Open M-Tu and Th-Sa 9:30am-5:30pm.) The seasonal **tourist office** is in the Market House, on the Square. (☎521 240. Open May-Sept. M-Sa 10am-1pm and 2-5:30pm.) The same building houses the brand-new **heritage center,** which shows a short video about the town, hosted by the ghost of a monk from the local monastery. (☎530 672. Open M-Sa 9:30am-5:30pm. €3, students €2.50, children €1.50.) The **Bank of Ireland,** the Square, has a 24hr. **ATM.** (☎521 276. Open M 10am-5pm, Tu-F 10am-4pm.) For **work opportunities,** inquire at the Castleview Farm B&B (see below). **Internet access** is available at the **library,** in the Square. (☎520 235. Call for hours.) The **post office** is in a brick building on Dublin St., near the Square. (☎521 349. Open M and W-F 9am-5:30pm, Tu 9:30am-5:30pm, Sa 10am-1pm and 2:30-4pm.)

ACCOMMODATIONS, FOOD, AND PUBS. The only B&B in town is **Singleton's ❸**, 1 Dara Park. From the heritage center door, follow the road to the right; it's just before the Esso station and on the right. (☎521 964. All rooms with bath and TV. Singles €35; doubles €50.) Five miles out of town, on a working poultry farm, Julie and Colm Keane run the **Eagle Hill B&B ❸.** Call for pickup or take Tully Rd. out of town and follow the signs to top-notch rooms, all with bath. (☎526 097. **Bike rental** €10 per day. Singles €30.) Toward Monasterevin, 3 mi. from town, the 50 cows at **Castleview Farm and B&B ❸** produce milk for Bailey's Irish Creme. Ask farmer Ned about **work opportunities,** but be prepared to work long, hard dairy days. (☎521 816. Singles €37; doubles €60.)

If you're hungry enough to eat a horse… don't. Not in this town, mister. However, **Kristina's Bistro ❹,** Main St., serves large and delectable lunches (€8-10). The "big plate" main and appetizer is €14, and a la carte dinners run €14-22. (☎522 895. Lunch served daily 12:30-2:30pm; dinner M-F 6:30-10pm, Sa 6:30-11pm, Su 6:30-9pm.) Pubs are plentiful in Kildare, and most serve good grub. **The Silken Thomas ❷,** the Square (☎522 232), has locally renowned meals that range from sandwiches (€4-5) to bar lunches (€9-10; try the lamb with mint sauce), with pricier dinner mains (€12-19) available at night. The pub's name refers to "Silken Thomas" FitzGerald, who raised Dublin in revolt against the British in 1534. **Li'l Flanagan's,** behind Silken Thomas, is a delightfully scruffy old-time pub with dark, low ceilings, open peat fires, and an impressive matchbox collection hanging from the ceiling. (☎521 695. Live music most nights.) **Nolan's,** the Square, is a low-key joint that was once a hardware store—now the hammers and handsaws have been replaced by regular trad sessions. (☎521 528. Trad Tu and Th-Su.)

SIGHTS. The **Irish National Stud and Japanese Gardens,** just 1 mi. from the Square on Tully Rd., was founded by the eq-centric Colonel William Hall-Walker in 1900. The mystical son of a Scottish brewer, he cast each foal's horoscope at its birth—if the stars weren't lined up favorably, the foal would be sold, regardless of its lineage. These days, the Irish National Stud facilitates the rearing of thoroughbred racehorses; mating season kicks off on Valentine's Day, naturally. The Stud's small **Irish Horse Museum** tells the history of the horse through a few displays and the skeleton of Arkle, a bygone champion. **Tours** leave every hour to educate the ignorant about the world of stud farms and horseracing.

The **Japanese Gardens** allegorize the "life of man" through a beautiful, if phallocentric, semi-narrative trail. From the cave of birth to the hill of mourning, visitors experience learning, disappointment, and marriage in the media of caves, hills, and bridges. Hall-Walker designed the trail, and while he was clearly a few leaves short of a bonsai, it makes a worthy game. The newest addition to the Stud is the four-acre **St. Fiachra's Garden,** which opened for the new millennium. Peaceful St. Fiachra's blandly evokes "monastic spirituality" with quiet lakes, waterfalls, and a pit of Waterford Crystal. (☎521 617 or 522 693. Open mid-Feb. to mid-Nov. daily 9:30am-6pm; last admission 5pm. 35min. tours of the National Stud leave on the hour beginning at 11am. €8.50, students and seniors €4.) In town, the 10th-century **round tower,** just off the Square, is one of the few in Ireland that visitors can enter and climb; most others are lacking floors. (Open M-Sa 10am-1pm and 2-5pm, Su 2-5pm. €3, children €1.50.) Recently restored **St. Brigid's,** a Church of Ireland cathedral that lay derelict for over 200 years, lies in the shadow of the tower. The cathedral dates from the 12th century and sits on the site of a church founded by St. Brigid in AD 480. Brigid, one of the first and only powerful women in the Catholic Church, was accidentally ordained as a bishop by the scatter-brained Mel of Ardagh. (Open May-Oct. M-Sa 10am-1pm and 2-5pm, Su 2-5pm. Su services noon.) Next to the church is **St. Brigid's Fire Temple,** a pagan ritual site that St. Brigid repossessed for Christianity. Only female virgins were allowed to tend the fire, which burned continually for 1000 years. Archbishop George Browne of Dublin ended all of this nonsense—by extinguishing the flames, that is, not the virginity.

DAYTRIPS FROM KILDARE

THE CURRAGH. Between Newbridge and Kildare on the N7 lies the Curragh—5000 acres of what just may be the greenest fields in Ireland. Thoroughbred horses graze and train, hoping to one day earn fame and fortune at the **Curragh Racecourse,** which hosts the **Irish Derby** (DAR-bee) each year. The Derby is Ireland's premier sporting and social event and one of the most prestigious races in the world. In 2003, the Festival begins on June 27, and the gala Derby itself is on June 29. Hit the Curragh as early as 7:30am and watch scores of horses take their daily training run on one of the five gallops, each 1-1½ mi. long. Other races are held from late March through October, roughly every other weekend on Saturdays and Sundays at 2:15 or 2:30pm. *(☎441 205; www.curragh.ie. Race tickets generally start at €15, but run from €45 for the Derby. Train €20 from Heuston Station, includes admission. Bus Éireann serves the Curragh on race days, leaving from Busáras in Dublin.)*

PEATLAND WORLD AND LULLYMORE. The boglanders know whom to turn to in times of need: their friend Peat. Ten miles from Kildare in Lullymore, **Peatland World** explains this phenomenal flammable material. Located on a mineral island in the immense Bog of Allen, Peatland World features a museum and natural history gallery. On display are bog-preserved prehistoric artifacts, a model of an Irish cottage with a turf fire, and trophies from turf-cutting competitions. *(☎860 133. Open Apr.-Oct. M-F 9:30am-6pm, Su 2-6pm, Sa by appointment; Nov.-Mar. M-F 9:30am-5pm. €5, students €4, families €12.)* Two miles toward Allenwood, the **Lullymore Heritage and Discovery Park** shows what life in the boglands was like from the Mesolithic era through to the Famine. Visitors can also climb out onto the peat bog and watch peat mining in action. *(To reach Lullymore from Kildare, take R401 to Rathangan, and then R414 toward Allenwood. Buses go to Allenwood from Dublin roughly 8 times per day. ☎870 238. Open Apr.-Oct. M-F 9:30am-6pm, Sa-Su noon-6pm; Nov.-Mar. M-F 9:30am-4:30pm. Open other times by appointment. €5, families €12.)*

COUNTY MEATH

Meath is a hushed county, with a heavy blanket of history on its shoulders and ancient crypts lurking deep in its hills. The Hill of Tara was Ireland's political and spiritual center in Prehistoric times and retains an air of solemn mystery for today's visitors. The countryside, with its winding roads, rolling hills, and castle-laden towns, provides the perfect backdrop for a Sunday drive.

BOYNE VALLEY

The thinly populated Boyne Valley hides Ireland's greatest archaeological treasures. Massive passage tombs like Newgrange create subtle bumps in the landscape that belie their cavernous underground chambers. These wonders are older than the Pyramids and at least as puzzling. The Celtic High Kings once ruled from atop the Hill of Tara, leaving a healthy dose of mysterious folklore in their wake. The Hill's enduring symbolic significance and incredible views attract visitors aplenty, as do the well-preserved Norman fortifications in the town of Trim. According to legend, St. Patrick lit a flame atop the Hill of Slane that brought Christianity to Ireland. Every so often, farmers plow up artifacts from the 1690 Battle of the Boyne (see **The Ascendancy,** p. 58).

NEWGRANGE, KNOWTH, DOWTH ☎041

Along the curves of the River Boyne, between Slane and Drogheda, sprawls Brú na Bóinne ("homestead of the Boyne"). The Boyne Valley may not have all the passage tombs in the world, just the biggest and best—in this 2500-acre region there are some 40 passage tombs, all with more than five millennia of history behind them. Neolithic engineers constructed Newgrange, Dowth, and Knowth within walking distance of each other, possibly with future lazy travelers in mind.

No one really knows why the ancient settlers took on the immense projects to build the tombs, but any self-respecting tour guide will offer you his or her own pet theory. The standard assumption is that improvements in farming allowed more time for leisure, so the locals naturally decided to build mega-structures that would remain intact and waterproof for some 5000 years. Using a log rolling mechanism, the builders imported enormous kerbstones from miles away. The work was sluggish (it took 80 mega-men ten days to move one kerbstone), and the larger mounds took a half-century to build, when a decent lifespan was just 30 years.

The most impressive of the three main sights, for archaeologists if not for visitors, is **Knowth** (rhymes with "mouth"). Apparently there was a hunter-gatherer settlement here in 4000 BC, followed by an extraordinary number of subsequent dwellers: the Stone Age brainiacs who built the mound you see today; mysterious Bronze Age "beaker people," named for their distinctive urns; Iron Age Celts, whose many burials include two headless men with their gaming dice; and Christians as late as the 12th century. The enormous passage tomb, quite unusually, houses *two* burial chambers, back to back, with separate entrances east and west—possibly a nod to the Sun's movement across the horizon. Knowth's carvings are well preserved as prehistoric art goes, with unexplained spirals and etchings adorning the passage. Long-term excavations prevent the general public from entering, but the visitors center **tour** (see below) offers a peek.

Newgrange offers tourists the best glimpse at the structure and innards of a spectacular passage tomb. After about a thousand years of peaceful existence, the front of this one-acre circular mound collapsed and fell into disrepair. It stayed that way for four thousand years before it was rediscovered by landowner Charles Campbell in 1699. Unfortunately, Campbell left the tomb open and unsupervised and it remained so for the next two and a half centuries, gathering uncreative Renaissance graffiti (still visible) and succumbing to vandalism. In 1962, archaeologists began a fantastic real-life jigsaw puzzle as they pieced the outer wall back together again, one rock at a time. During the reconstruction, archaeologists discovered a roof box over the passage entrance. At dawn on the shortest day of the year (Dec. 21), 17 gilded minutes of sunlight shine through the roof box, reach straight to the back of the 60 ft. passageway, and irradiate the burial chamber. The tour provides a brilliant simulation of this experience, leaving visitors in awe. Those wishing to see the real event must sign up for a lottery, held every October. Ongoing excavations have kept **Dowth** (rhymes with "Knowth") closed to the public for several years. To gain admission, get a Ph.D. in archaeology.

To access Knowth and Newgrange, you must first pay admission to the **Brú na Bóinne Visitors Centre,** located near Donore on the south side of the River Boyne, across from the tombs themselves. Do not try to make your way directly to the sites—a guard minds the gate. Instead, head to the visitors center and immediately book a tour. The place is mobbed every day of the summer, and Sundays are especially manic. While you wait for your turn with the guide, check out the center's excellent exhibit on the lives of the gifted and talented stone-agers. Remember to dress appropriately when visiting—most of the tour takes place outside and Neolithic tombs lack central heating. (☎988 0300. Open June to mid-Sept. 9am-7pm, May 9am-6:30pm, late Sept. 9am-6:30pm, Mar.-Apr. and Oct. 9:30am-5:30pm, Nov.-Feb. 9:30am-5pm. Admission to the visitors center only €2.50, seniors €1.90, students and children €1.20, families €6.30; center and Newgrange tour €5/€3.80/€2.50/€12.70; center and Knowth €3.80/€2.50/€1.50/€9.50; center, Newgrange, and Knowth €8.80/€6.30/€4.10/€22.20. Last tour 1½hr. before closing. Last admission to center 45min.

before closing.) Downstairs you'll find a **tourist office,** which can give you a free area map. (☎980 305. Open daily 9am-7pm.) To reach the visitors center from Drogheda, turn left by the bus station and head straight on the uphill road. It's a pleasant 5 mi. bike ride, and hitchers report successful journeys, despite *Let's Go*'s fervent discouragement. **Bus Éireann** (☎836 6111) offers shuttles to the visitors center from **Dublin** (1½hr.; M-Sa every 15min., Su every hr.; €12.70 return), stopping at **Drogheda** (10min., €3.80 return). Several **bus tours** from Dublin include admission to the sights, including Bus Éireann (Sa-Th, €24.20).

NEWGRANGE FARM. Just down the road from Newgrange, **Newgrange Farm** has a coffee shop and a petting zoo for the kiddies. Farmer Bill will charm tykes and their parents with his tractor tour of the farm, including a small passage tomb and a bit of wildlife. There are usually scavenger hunts on Sundays, Teddy Bear Picnics on the June bank holiday, and Cadbury Easter-Egg Hunts on Easter weekend. *(☎24119. Open Easter-Aug. daily 10am-6pm; last admission 5pm. 30min. tour leaves Su 3 and 4pm, or when there's enough interest. Access to farm €4, invest another €2 for a tractor ride.)*

HILL OF TARA ☎046

Tara, deeply marked by a long and enigmatic history, awaits your visit with the serenity of the ages. From prehistoric times until the 10th century, **Tara** was the socio-politico-cultural heart of Ireland. Home to 142 former Irish Kings, the largest collection of Celtic monuments in the world, and a sacred site for ancient Irish religion, Tara beckons visitors to its flourishing green expanse. Many secrets are buried under the one hundred acres of grassy mounds called Tara, and the grounds are free and open to the public for casual perusal. Looking for secrets is allowed, just don't bring a shovel—in the early part of the 20th century, a misguided cult on a hunt for the Arc of the Covenant damaged the Mound of the Synods. Though the Arc remained elusive, they did manage to find a few ancient Roman coins. Located at Tara is the sacred *Lia Fail* ("Stone of Destiny"), an ancient phallus carved out of rock and used as a coronation stone; the rock was said to roar when the rightful king of Tara placed his hands upon it. The **Mound of Hostages,** the resident burial mound, dates to 2500 BC.

The enormous sight is about 5 mi. east of Navan on the N3. Take any **local bus** from Dublin to **Navan** (1hr.; M-Sa 37 per day, Su 15 per day; €7) and ask the driver to let you off at the turnoff, which is on the left and marked by a small brown sign. Then you've got about a mile of uphill legwork to enjoy. The actual buildings—largely wattle, wood, and earth—have long been buried or destroyed; what you'll see are concentric rings of grassy, windswept dunes. They are always open for exploration; to make sense of them, hit the **visitors center** in the old church. The center displays aerial photos and an audio-enhanced slideshow on Tara's history. After the film, your ticket entitles you to an excellent **guided tour** (35min., by request only; call ahead). The tour covers only the sights at the top of the hill, though Tara actually encompasses 100 acres of smaller mounds and ring forts. (☎046 25903. Center open mid-June to mid-Sept. daily 9:30am-6:30pm, May to mid-June and mid-Sept. to Oct. 10am-5pm. €1.90, seniors €1.20, students €0.70.)

TRIM (BAILE ATHÁ TROIM) ☎046

Jaded travelers looking for a break from Dublin should treat themselves to Trim, a little town lying just an hour outside of the capital. Ireland's largest Norman castle (and occasional Hollywood backdrop and set), surrounded by flocks of fat and happy sheep, overlooks this jewel of a heritage town located on the River Boyne.

ORIENTATION AND PRACTICAL INFORMATION. Bus Éireann stops in front of Trim Castle on its way to and from Dublin (1hr.; M-Sa roughly 1 per hr., Su 3 per day; €10.20). **Castle St.** intersects the central **Market St.**, which has most of the town's shops, then crosses the **River Boyne** under the alias **Bridge St.** The first left as you cross the bridge is **Mill St.** Bridge St. curves uphill on the far side, turning into **High St.** before splitting. The left fork becomes **Haggard St.** and the right becomes **Navan Gate St.**, the road to the nearby Newtown ruins. Signs direct you to the **visitors center** on Mill St., where you can get a useful map of Trim's sights. (☎37227. Open M-W and F-Sa 10am-5pm, Su noon-5:30pm.) The **tourist office** is temporarily located on Emmett St. **Bank of Ireland,** replete with an **ATM,** is on Market St. (☎31230. Open M 10am-5pm, Tu-F 10am-4pm.) The **library,** on High St., has **Internet access.** The **post office** is up the street from the tourist office where Market St. turns into Emmet St. (☎31268. Open M-F 9am-5:30pm, Sa 9am-12:30pm.)

ACCOMMODATIONS, FOOD, AND PUBS. The **Bridge House Tourist Hostel ❷,** tucked down a driveway as you turn from either High St. or the bridge onto Mill St., just before the tourist office, offers a mixed bag of coed rooms ranging from cramped to luxurious. The TV lounge is a funky converted medieval wine cellar. (☎31848. 4-bed dorms €15; doubles with bath €36.) Trim's B&B options are, on the whole, excellent. **Highfield House ❸,** a spectacular stone mansion overlooking Trim Castle and the river, offers the most luxurious stay in town, at a reasonable price. From the bus station, walk away from the bridge and it is on the right just before the roundabout. (☎463 6386. Breakfast included. Singles €38; doubles €64; triples €90.) The folks at sunny, spacious, and fastidiously clean **White Lodge ❹** will pick you up at the bus stop if you have a reservation. Otherwise, from the roundabout, cross the bridge onto High St., stay right onto Navan Gate St., walk between the posts, and it is on the other side of the cross street. (☎36549. Breakfast included. Singles €38-44; doubles €50-60, with bath €56. €4 less per person without breakfast.) In the heart of town, **Brogan's ❹,** High St., offers top-notch rooms with TV, showers, coffee/tea facilities, and telephones. At the in-house pub and beer garden, you can enjoy good eats and frequent live music. (☎31237. Includes breakfast. Singles €40; doubles €64.) The Bounty Bar (see below) also has a **B&B ❷** for those who like their breakfast, and pints, in bed.

Get **SuperValu**-able groceries at the top of Haggard St. (☎31505. Open M-W 8am-7pm, Th-F 8am-9pm, Sa 8am-7:30pm, Su noon-6:30pm.) **The Pastry Kitchen ❶,** Market St., is a greasy spoon that serves a decent meal. (☎38902. Sandwiches from €2.20. Open M-Sa 7:30am-5:30pm, Su 10am-2pm.) Next door, **Watson's Elementary Café ❷** serves up an adequate and inexpensive breakfast and is the only eatery open at 8am on a Sunday. (Filled baguettes €2.75; omelettes €3.50-4. Open daily 8am-6pm.) New on Market St. is **The Boyne Bistro & Bakery ❶,** serving sandwiches on fresh bread (€3-5), wraps, and bakery treats. (Open M-Sa 8:30am-6:30pm, Su noon-5pm; closes at 3pm in winter). Cheerful **Bennini's ❷,** in the carpark next to Trim Castle, is known for diverse salads and homemade baked goods. (☎31002. Mains around €7.50-8.60. M-F 9:30am-5pm, Sa 10am-5:30pm, Su 11am-5pm.) One door down, under the same ownership, is the bright and welcoming **Franzini O'Brien's ❸,** which serves a wide range of mains (fish, pasta, noodles, etc.) for €11-20. (☎31002. Tu-Sa 6:30-9:30pm, Su 5-8:30pm.) The **Emmet Tavern,** Emmet St., left as you face the post office, has boisterous and mostly local customers. (☎31378. Generally serving until 11:30pm.) Bring your fiddle to old-fashioned, antique-laden **The Bounty,** on High St., where, in keeping with the true Irish spirit, open mic participation is encouraged. The bar also has a B&B upstairs. (☎31640. M-F 5pm-1am, Sa-Su 1pm-1am. B&B singles €25.40; doubles €38.)

FROM THE ROAD

CHANGING PUB TASTES

I came from arid lands to liquid-indulgent Ireland seeking the **Holy Pint.** I was told that Ireland and its pubs had been for hundreds of years strictly a land of whiskey and Guinness. Expecting a purity of consumption untainted by inferior brews, I came to realize a sobering fact: Budweiser is everywhere. And, more shockingly, I found that the headless wonder is quite popular on the island.

The younger generation of pub-goers these days seem to be bucking the distinctly Irish drinking traditions for those more trendy. Not only has Guinness become less popular, but drinking draft beer in general has become less fashionable. The cool thing for younguns these days is imported bottled beer. Fruity beverages like Smirnoff Ice and Bacardi Breezers have also taken off like wildfire. They deliver less punch per euro, but their neat appearance makes them status symbols.

I didn't actually realize this until my fifth or sixth night in the country. When it became clear to me, I felt a great deal of pressure, being young myself, to turn away from the "old man's drink." So, when I approached the bar, I was left with a choice: do I drink what I want, or do I let the trendy imposters impose their chemical concoctions upon me. A moment of truth arose, and I chose tradition over trend. So for the love of God and all things Irish, when you step up, I hope you'll also have the courage to order yourself a pint o' the black stuff!

—Jack Riccobono

SIGHTS AND ACTIVITIES. **Trim Castle,** built by Norman invader Hugh de Lacy in 1172 and now open to the public after a regal £3 million face-lift, presides over Trim. The castle was the hub of social life during the Middle Ages, when the town was powerful and populous, and supported seven monasteries. When Norman power collapsed, the castle lost nearly all its strategic importance and thus survived the centuries relatively untouched. The keep costs a little extra to see, but the renovations inside are extraordinarily well done and the views from the top are fabulous. If visiting the household doesn't inspire, see if you can recognize scenes from *Braveheart.* You can take the tour, but you'll never take his freedom. (☎38619. Open May-Oct. 10am-6pm; last tour 5:15pm. Admission with 35-45min. guided tour only. Tours every 45min.; sign up upon arrival in Trim. No tour needed for the grounds. Tour and grounds €3.10, students €1.20; grounds only €1.20.)

Across the river stands what remains of the 12th-century **Yellow Steeple,** a belltower named for its twilight gleam; the gleam left with the lichen that was removed during restoration. In its shadow, **Talbot's Castle,** adapted from the steeple's original abbey, was home to Jonathan Swift and the undefeated, jazzy Duke of Wellington (though not at the same time). Despite the "private house" sign, the current owner often provides tours of its motley interior upon request. To get there, take the first right after crossing the bridge; a right-of-way through the driveway leads to the Yellow Steeple and the **Sheep Gate,** the only surviving piece of the town's medieval walls. Ten minutes out on the Dublin road in the direction opposite the castle, you can halloo your name to the reverberating ruins of **St. Peter and St. Paul's Cathedral,** across the river from **Echo Gate.** The cathedral grounds contain a tomb with two figures mistakenly called the **Jealous Man and Woman.** The sword between them conventionally signified chastity, not resentment. Put a pin between the two figures; when the pin rusts, your warts should disappear.

Trim Visitors Centre, next to the tourist office, educates and frightens with a multimedia presentation and a dramatic slideshow. Displays describe decapitations, the lecherous behavior of sinewy Hugh de Lacy, and hideous plague rats—so much for a prim and proper Trim. (☎37227. Open M-W and F-Sa 10am-5pm, Su noon-5pm. Admission for the 35min. shows every 45min. €3.20, students and seniors €2.20.) Green thumbs will enjoy the **Butterstream Gardens,** a 15min. walk past the SuperValu. The several serene acres are especially beautiful in June. (☎36017. Open May-Sept. daily 11am-6pm. €6, students €3.)

Each June, the **Scurlogstown Olympiad Town Festival** fills Trim with animal shows, carnival rides, haymaking, trad, and the evening High Nellie Rally, in which men and women dress up in absurd costumes and ride black bikes around town. For the daytime festival, locals dress up in 19th century period attire, move into thatched huts on the outskirts of town, and show off traditional artifacts. During the rest of the year, **fishing** on the Boyne is quite excellent. Diligent **kayakers** should also try their paddles at the notoriously tricky river. Join up with one of the many local **canoeing** clubs to rent your transportation. If paddles aren't your thing, what about stirrups? Contact the **Bachelors Lodge** in Navan (☎046 21736) and the **Borallion Riding Centre** in Balreesk (☎046 73688) for horse-riding options near Trim. For more information on all activities in the Boyne Valley, contact the Trim tourist office or David Byrne at the **Navan Tourist Centre** (☎046 73426).

BEYOND THE VALLEY OF THE BOYNE

KELLS (CEANANNAS MÓR) ☎046

Two types of people enjoy Kells—those who appreciate monastic ruins and artifacts, and those who enjoy partaking of the devil's nectar. If you fall in the middle, consider leaving this one out of the itinerary. If you enjoy the latter, you'll find a sip about every other door; the former, and you'll be able to wow them back at the home parish with ancient tales of religious infighting and thievery. History lesson: in 559 St. Colmcille (colm-KILL) founded a monastery here before going on to establish the more significant settlement on Iona, an island west of Scotland. At Iona, the famous *Book of Kells*, an elaborately decorated version of the Gospel, was begun. It came to Kells at some stage of completion in 804, when the Columbans fled Iona. In 1007, the book was stolen, its gold cover ripped off and its pages buried in a bog. The book was rescued two months later and remained in Kells until 1661, when it was carted off to Trinity College, where it is now recovering. Like the rest of Ireland, Kells is sick of Dublin hoarding all of the loot, and is desperately trying to retrieve the artifact. Trinity finds this infinitely amusing.

TRANSPORTATION AND PRACTICAL INFORMATION. Bus Éireann runs frequently from **Dublin** (1hr.; M-Sa 2-4 per hr., Su 15 per day; €8.50) and stops in front of **Headfort Arms Hotel**. With the Headfort behind you, the outstanding **tourist office** and **heritage center** are to your left in the former courthouse at the fork in the road. Get free town maps and heritage booklets, explore a collection of replicated relics, and enjoy an audio-visual presentation for €4. You can also spend hours learning Book of Kells minutiae from an interactive computer terminal. (☎49336. Open M-Sa 10am-6pm, Su 1:30-6pm.) Take advantage of free **Internet access** at the **public library,** on Maudlin St. **AIB** bank, on John St., has a 24hr. **ATM** (☎40610; open M 10am-12:30pm and 1:30-5pm, Tu-F 10am-4pm), as does **Bank of Ireland,** by the Headfort Arms (open M-F 10am-12:30pm and 1:30-4pm). The **post office** is on Farrel St. (☎40127. Open M-Sa 9am-5:30pm.)

ACCOMMODATIONS AND CAMPING. Kells Hostel ❷ sports a newly renovated kitchen, pool table, two **bikes to rent** (€10 each per day), and decent facilities. The giant hand-painted map in the common room is cheesy but incredibly helpful, pointing out sights, restaurants, and pubs. From the center of town, wind your way uphill on Carrick St. When you see the SuperValu on your left, look right (beside Carrick House) for the big blue letters. The bus from Dublin will stop across the street. (☎49995. Laundry €8. Reception 9am-noon and 5-10pm. Access code needed after hours. 15-bed dorms €13; private 2- to 4-bed rooms with baths €16 per person. **Camping** €8.) B&Bs in town are pricey but worth it. You can't beat

White Gables ❹, Headfort Pl., across from the tourist office. Enjoy exceptionally clean rooms, white linen beds, and abundant flowers both inside and out. And if that isn't enough to turn Martha Stewart green, the owner is a former chef. (☎40322. Singles €40; doubles €60.) Just down the road is the **Avalon B&B ❹,** 5 Headfort Park, offering homestyle luxury. (☎41536. Singles €40; doubles €58.)

FOOD AND PUBS. SuperValu grocery store can be found across the street from the hostel. (Open M-W and Sa 8am-7:30pm, Th-F 8am-9pm, Su 9am-6:30pm.) Many places in Kells shut down for lunch from 12:30-1:30pm—be a follower and grab your grub then too. Get one hell of a meal at **Dante's ❷,** Market St., which somehow manages to be both divinely elegant and carnally casual. Specialty pizza, pasta, and chicken are €10-14, fish and steak a sinful €15-19. (☎41630. Lunch €6.35-9. Open M-Th noon-11pm, F-Sa noon-midnight, Su 1-11pm; closed daily 3-6pm.) Dishin' out vegetarian-friendly delights, as well as carnivorous fare, and pumpin' 70s funk, **The Ground Floor ❹,** Bective Sq., manages to serve a triple-layer chocolate cake called "R.I.P." *and* be endorsed by the Irish Heart Association. Beat that. (☎49688. Mains €15-22. Open M-Sa 5:30-11pm, Su 5:30-10pm.) Brand-spanking new and duly proud of its fresh ingredients and eclectic world menu, **Vanilla Pod ❹,** next to Headfort Arms Hotel, is a restaurant not to be missed. (☎40084. 3-course early-bird special €16. Reservations recommended. Open M-F 5:30-10pm, Sa-Su 5:30-11pm.) **Pebbles ❷,** Newmarket St., is a popular coffee shop in Kells, serving up salads, shepherds pie, and the like. (☎49229. Lunch €7-9. Open M-Sa 8am-5:30pm.) **Tower Grille ❷** on Farrell St. is the place for takeaway grease: southern fried chicken, kebabs, burgers, spring rolls, and other fried balls of wonder are €3-6. (☎40314. Open M-Tu and Th-Sa noon-1am, Sa open until 2am.)

O'Shaughnessy's, on Market St., has pub grub by day for €8.50-12.50, raucous locals celebrating or seething over the most recent soccer game by night, and live trad on the weekends (☎41110. Food served noon-3pm.) At **The Blackwater Inn,** Farrell St. (☎40386), get more one-man-band trad on Wednesday and Friday. No food, just stick to the black water—Guinness, that is. Join the drunk, loud, and smoky crowd at **Chasers,** Cross St. (☎49293), where students play pool and read quotes on the walls until 12:30am. You'll find a pair of nightlife winners with **The Kelltic Bar** and **Vibe.** The Kelltic rocks with trad on Tuesday, DJ on Thursday, karaoke on Friday, and live bands every Sunday. (☎40063. Open M-F 4pm-midnight, Sa-Su noon-12:30am.) Vibe is the only dance club in Kells; fairly small but modern, attracting a young crowd. Occasional bands start around 11pm, otherwise don't bother showing up before midnight. (☎40063. 18+, ID required. €8-10. Ladies free before 12:30am Su. Open F-Sa until 2:30am, Su until 2am.)

SIGHTS. Thanks to its position as a center of Christian learning, the **monastery** at Kells was a favorite target for monkish rivalries. With the exception of the 12th-century bell tower, the current structure dates back as far as the 1700s. Most points of interest lie up the street from the new tourist office and heritage center. Inside the **heritage center** there's a replica *Book of Kells*, with copies of selected pages enlarged for your viewing pleasure. The grounds of **St. Columba's Church** hosts four **high crosses** covered with Biblical scenes; the west cross is little more than a stump, but the south cross, with its instructional depictions of crucifix-making, remains intact. Go upstairs inside the church for detailed explanations of each drawing and for more Book of Kells information and photos. A 12th-century wall encircled the church until 1997, when the County Council decided to build a path alongside it, undermining its foundations (and the walls came tumbling down). The nearby 100 ft. **round tower** never succeeded in protecting anything: its monks were torched, its book and saintly relics stolen, and would-be High King Murchadh Mac Flainn was murdered there in 1076. (Church grounds open dawn to dusk, church open M-Sa 10am-1pm and 2-5pm; Su for services only at 11:30am.)

Time has been kinder to **St. Colmcille's House,** across Church Ln., an awe-inspiring oratory where the *Book of Kells* just may have been completed. Pick up the key from amiable and retired Mrs. Carpenter, who often escorts visitors up the hill (groups preferred). Find her in her brown house at 10 Church View, then head up 600 ft. to the unmistakably oratory-like structure. The place looks almost exactly as it would have in St. Colmcille's day, except that the current doorway enters into the basement, which was originally connected by a secret tunnel to the church. Climb up the extremely steep staircase to walk around the tiny attic if you dare (if you are over four feet tall, you'll have to crouch).

Two miles down Oldcastle Rd., within the People's Park, is the **Spire of Loyd,** a 150 ft. mock-lighthouse viewing tower erected by the old Headfort landlords at the end of the 18th century. (☎47840. Group bookings of 10 or more only.) Coupling the adorable and the morbid, the spire is flanked by a public playground and the recently restored **Pauper's Graveyard,** where the area's impoverished buried their dead in mass graves during the Famine.

COUNTY LOUTH

On its way between the pulsing capitals of Dublin and Belfast, the N1 shoots through Lough, a county filled with smaller towns, crumbling ruins, and soaring mountains. History buffs will appreciate Drogheda, which lies 3 mi. east of where William and James battled on the Boyne and 5 mi. south of the religious one-two punch of Monasterboice and Mellifont Abbey. Dundalk is not only a convenient place to cross into the North, but it's also responsible for brewing your Harp. The hills and seacoasts of the Cooley Peninsula, meanwhile, command the affections of hikers, bikers, and ancient bards.

DROGHEDA (DROICHEAD ÁTHA) ☎041

The description perhaps best suited to this mid-sized industrial town is 'potential.' Convenient to Newgrange, Dowth, and Knowth, as well as Monasterboice, Mellifont, and Slane, Drogheda (DRAW-head-ah) is an ideal jumping-off point for many of eastern Ireland's historic sights. With a skeleton of crumbling medieval walls and gates, there is considerable history to be explored. For the less morbid of curiosities, plenty of friendly pubs line the streets in the town itself.

TRANSPORTATION

Trains: Station on the Dublin road east of town (☎983 8749). Follow John St. south of the river. To **Belfast** (2hr.; M-Sa 7 per day, Su 4 per day; €26.60) and **Dublin** (1hr., express 30min.; M-Sa 20 per day, Su 7 per day; €10.20).

Buses: John St. at Donore Rd. (☎983 5023). Inquiries desk and **luggage storage** open M-F 9am-6pm, Sa 8:30am-5:30pm. To: **Athlone** (2½hr., 1 per day, €10.70); **Belfast** (2hr.; M-Sa 7 per day, Su 6 per day; €9-10); **Dublin** (1hr.; M-Sa every 30min., Sun every hr.; €7.40); **Galway** (4hr., 1 per day, €25); **Mullingar** (2hr., 1 per day, €17.10).

Bike Rental: Quay Cycles, 11 North Quay (☎983 4526). €12 per day; ID deposit. Open M-Sa 9am-6pm.

YOU CAN'T KEEP A HARDMAN DOWN

In the town of Drogheda there's a wild story surrounding the affluent Anne Hardman, of Hardman Gardens, who died in 1844 after living a respectable 71 years. Legend has it that she was buried according to the customs of the day, in a tomb rather than a grave. Unfortunately—or fortunately, as it turns out—Mrs. Hardman had a selfish little servant who went to her tomb to plunder her jewelry the very night of her burial. "Why should the old hag get to rot with all those pounds?" he reasoned. After eagerly helping himself to her necklaces, earrings, and bracelets, he couldn't resist going for the prized rings as well. So impassioned was he in this mission that when he couldn't get the rings off her swollen hands he resolved to take them anyway, fingers and all. Much to his surprise, after a few successful hacks, Mrs. Hardman began to move! Understandably frantic, the servant ran straight down the hill to St. Mary's bridge and promptly boarded the next vessel for Liverpool. (Upon arrival his hair was completely white.) Meanwhile, poor rich Mrs. Hardman had awakened to find herself in a cold tomb, wrapped in shrouds. She was, well, a little upset. The situation became all the more distressing when she returned home and her superstitious family refused to admit her "ghost" into the house. Finally, her husband—the bravest and most coolheaded of the lot—realized that a ghost wouldn't be bleeding and allowed her inside. She died again twenty years later. This time, her condition was terminal.

PRACTICAL INFORMATION

Tourist Offices: Main branch in the bus station (☎983 7070). Offers a regional and Drogheda town map. Open M-Sa 9:30am-5:30pm, Su noon-5pm. A superior 2nd office is the **Information Point** at Millmount Museum (☎984 5684); head to the Martello tower on the big hill. Open M-F 9:30am-1pm and 2-5pm.

Banks: Cross St. Mary's Bridge and take the 2nd left to find numerous banks lining West St. **AIB** (☎983 6523; open M-F 9:30am-5pm, Th until 7pm) and **Permanent TSB** (☎983 8703; M-F 10am-5pm, Th until 7pm) both have **ATMs.**

Work Opportunities: The **Green Door Hostel** (see **Accommodations,** above) hires international staff to work at the hostel, bar, and adventure center. A minimum stay of 2 months is preferred. Contact owner Gavin in advance for availabilities.

Laundry: FM Laundry, 13 North Quay (☎983 6837). Turn right across St. Mary's Bridge. Self-service €6.50. Open M-Sa 9am-6pm.

Emergency: ☎999; no coins required. **Police** (*Garda*): West Gate (☎983 8777).

Hospital: Our Lady of Lourdes, Cross Lanes (☎983 7601).

Post Office: West St. (☎983 8157). Open Tu-Sa 9am-5:30pm, W open 9:30am.

ACCOMMODATIONS

Green Door Hostel, 47 John St. (☎983 4422; www.greendoorhostel.com), 1 block from the bus station. A young, friendly staff combined with a convenient location and joyously clean bathrooms more than compensate for the small kitchen and common area. The addition of more rooms by owner Gavin, as well as a bar that will serve food, should make the hostel even more fun in 2003. Bike storage and carpark. **Internet access.** Laundry €5.50. June-Sept. 10-bed dorms €13.50; doubles €42; family rooms €53. Oct.-May dorms €12; doubles €19.50; family rooms €47. ❶

Harpur House (IHO), William St. (☎983 2736). Follow Shop St. from the bridge up the hill, continue up Peter St. and take a right onto William St.; the hostel is the last house

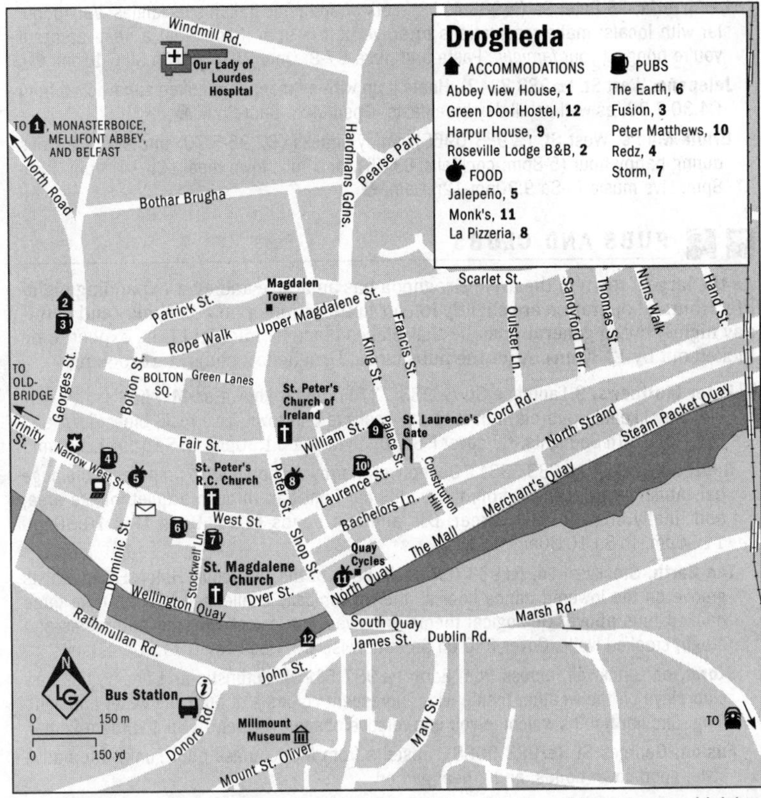

on the right. Drogheda's older hostel/B&B. Ask for a key if you'll be out past midnight. Full Irish breakfast €5. Laundry €4. 10-bed dorms €13.50; private rooms €17.50. ❶

Abbey View House, Mill Ln. (☎983 1470). From the bus station, go left on John St., and cross the river at the second bridge; take the first left and left again. Well kept and backpacker-friendly. Sitting pretty on the River Boyne, the house has free parking, big rooms with patchwork quilts, and an alleged tunnel to Monasterboice. Doubles €45. ❹

Roseville Lodge B&B, Georges St. (☎983 4046). Amiable Denis offers good-sized, sweet-smelling rooms, all with bath. Singles €32; doubles €55; family rooms €70. ❸

FOOD

An **open-air market** has been held in Bolton Square every Saturday since 1317, while the newer **Dunnes Stores** (☎983 4211) and **Tesco** (☎983 7063) on West St. sell groceries all week. (Both open M-W 9am-6pm, Th-F 9am-9pm, Sa 8:30am-7pm, Su noon-6pm.) West St. is the place for fast food to satisfy your late-night munchies.

Monk's, 1 North Quay (☎984 5630). A shiny cafe with breakfasts and lunches that are anything but ascetic. Yummy, unusual sandwiches include an avocado, crushed pineapple, and goat cheese bruschetta (€6.30), while a breakfast of chunky French toast would justify a vow of silence. Open M-Sa 8:30am-6pm, Su 10:30am-5pm. ❷

EASTERN IRELAND

La Pizzeria, 38 Peter St. (☎983 4208). Lots of authentic Italian specialities. Very popular with locals; make reservations or arrive before 9pm if you want a seat—earlier if you're bringing your *famiglia.* Pasta and pizza €7-8. Open M-Tu and Th-Su 6-11pm. ❷

Jalepeño, West St. (☎983 8342). Heats it up with all manner of grilled sandwiches from €4.30-7.30, as well as all-day breakfasts. Open M-Sa 9am-6pm. ❷

Bridie Mac's, West St. (☎983 0965). Enjoy snacks (€2.86-5.70) and sexy cocktails during happy hour (5-8pm; cocktails €3.75), or a full-blown meal (€8-14) from 3:30-8pm. Live music Th-Sa 9:30pm-12:30am. ❷

PUBS AND CLUBS

As the largest town in the area, Drogheda has an active and ever-expanding nightlife. Hours of operation are slightly longer in the summer and on Friday and Saturday nights, but in general, assume that places close by midnight (i.e., expect to be kicked out by 12:30am). After the pubs close, Drogheda's clubs start rocking.

Peter Matthews, 9 Laurence St. (☎983 7371), better known as **McPhail's.** This very old, very likeable pub plays host to the best *craic* in town. Live rock, blues, jazz, and Latin M and Th-Sa nights. €2 cover F-Sa. Open M-W 1-11:30pm, Th-Sa 1pm-12:30am.

Redz, 79 West St. (☎983 5331). Deceptively narrow facade fails to prepare for the huge bar. Atmosphere changes from the traditional front bar, through a quiet lounge area, and finally into the clubby rear. DJs and live bands Th-Su. Open M-W 10:30am-11:30pm, Th-Su 10:30am-12:30am.

The Earth, Stockwell Ln. (☎983 0969), in back of the Westcourt Hotel. Exhibitionists groove on the lowered dance floor as the rhythmically challenged look on from three packed bars above. Geological theme is played out in rock-textured bathrooms and rough, crooked walls. Cover €10 on Sa, otherwise €6. Open Th-Su 11:30pm-3am.

Storm, on Stockwell, across from Earth (☎987 5170). Futuristic and flashy, this new club plays on the weather theme with fluorescent columns of bubbling water and lightning. Circular booths welcome you into relative obscurity. Open Th-Su 11:30pm-2am.

Fusion, Georges St. (☎983 0088), upstairs from McGuinness pub. Funky alternative style, good cover bands, and a beer garden.

SIGHTS

ST. PETER'S CHURCHES. Drogheda has two St. Peter's Churches, and both could satisfy even the most morbid of curiosities. Come face-to-face with the blackened, shriveled head of St. Oliver in the imposing, neo-Gothic St. Peter's Church on West St. Built in the 1880s, this St. Peter's safeguards what's left of the martyr Oliver Plunkett. A handful of his bones are on display, as is the door of his London prison cell. *(Open daily 8:30am-8:30pm. Free.)* The other St. Peter's Church (Church of Ireland) hoards bad luck up at the top of Peter St. The tower of the original timber structure was destroyed in a 1548 storm. Another wooden structure replaced it, only to be torched (with refugees inside) by Cromwell. The present church was built in 1752 and is being renovated after falling victim to another more recent fire. Mounted on the wall of the cemetery's far left corner are cadaver tombs, with brutally realistic carvings of the half-decayed bodies of a man and woman. Dating from 1520, they are two of only 19 such tombs in the world.

BATTLE OF THE BOYNE. The Battle of the Boyne raged at **Oldbridge,** 3 mi. west of Drogheda on Slane Rd. In 1690, William of Orange's momentous victory over James II secured for Protestants the English Crown and a good deal more than the eastern half of Ireland (see **The Ascendancy,** p. 58). For the slightly more ambitious

THE SIEGE OF DROGHEDA Cromwell's two-day siege of Drogheda in 1649 was the first time in the town's illustrious history that its walls were breached. Originally twin towns separated by the Boyne, Drogheda was well-entrenched on both sides, and only a retractable drawbridge connected the two halves. So how did Cromwell win so quickly? One of the Drogheda captains had a wooden leg, so Cromwell sparked a rumor that the limb was full of gold. The rumor worked: Cromwell's men tracked down the poor captain faster than you can say "greed" and immediately ripped off his prosthesis. Disappointed to find that the wooden leg was, in fact, merely wood, they consoled themselves by beating the captain to death with his own limb—no doubt one of the more ignoble deaths in military history. With the walls breached and no captain to lead them, the disillusioned—and obviously distracted—Drogheda citizens crossed from the south side of the river to the north, forgetting to raise the drawbridge behind them. Cromwell proceeded to raze and burn the town, churches and all.

traveler, the not-for-profit **Obelisk Centre** (located in a small trailer) offers visitors a view of the battle site. *(Head 1½ mi. down Slane Rd. to the Obelisk Bridge; it's on the right. ☎984 1644. Open M-Th 9am-1pm and 2-5pm, F 9am-1pm and 2-4pm.)* Those with little imagination should stay home, since there's not much to see anymore. Still interested but no car? Get off your bum and walk the 45min. from town. Dúchas runs the **Battle of the Boyne Oldbridge Estate Center,** offering an informative 30min. tour recreating the Battle on the old battlefield. On Sundays it hosts a **living history program,** complete with cannons and live cavalry *(2 mi. north of Donore Village, on the right. ☎988 4343. Open daily 9:30am-5:30pm. Free.)*

MILLMOUNT MUSEUM. The recently reconstructed Martello tower dominates the Drogheda skyline. Inside, the **Millmount Museum** displays antique household appliances, a rock collection, and artifacts from the Civil War period (see **Independence and Civil War,** p. 62), including grenades with names etched in (for that personal touch). The museum also offers tours of the tower, shelled during the Civil War but repaired at long last. The tours run roughly 25min. and whiz through Drogheda's copious military and industrial history. *(☎983 3097. Open M-Sa 10am-6pm, Su 2:30-5:30pm. Museum €3; students €2.50; seniors and children €2; families €7. Tower only €2.50/€2/€1.50/€5. Museum and tower tour €4.50/€3/€2.50/€11.50.)*

TOURS AND OTHER SIGHTS. For an entertaining history that's at least 98% true, try the **Walking Tours of Historical Drogheda.** Or be a lonestar and complete the walk on your own with the guidance of the *Drogheda Heritage Route* pamphlet or the *Local Story* booklet, both free at the Millmount Information Point and at the tourist office. *(☎984 5684. Tours 1½hr. leave Tu-Sa at 10:20am and 2:20pm from the bus station tourist office. €1.90, seniors €1.30.)* At the end of West St. you'll find the four-story twin towers of **St. Laurence's Gate,** a 13th-century outer gate. And at the top of the hill on Peter St., the 14th-century **Magdalen Tower** is all that remains of the Dominican Friary that once stood on the spot.

 DAYTRIPS FROM DROGHEDA

MONASTERBOICE AND MELLIFONT ABBEY

Both ruins are signposted off the Drogheda-Collon road. Cyclists head 5 mi. north on the N1 until the Dunleer exit. At the bottom of the ramp, turn left and follow the Monasterboice signs. When that road ends, turn right and veer left when you meet the larger Drogheda-Collon road to get to Mellifont. If you decide to take a taxi, establish a charge at the start—it should cost no more than €20. The Monasterboice Information Office is open July-Aug. M-Sa 10am-6pm. The Mellifont Abbey Information Office (☎982 6459; open daily 10am-6pm) offer tours for €2; seniors €1.20, students €1. The site is free after hours.

What were once two of the most important monasteries in Ireland stand crumbling 5 mi. north of Drogheda. The grounds of **Monasterboice** (MON-uh-ster-boyce) include a round tower and some of the most detailed high crosses in existence, while also serving as the oldest working cemetery in Europe. The monastery was one of Ireland's most wealthy from its founding around AD 520 until the Vikings sacked it in 1097. An **information office** is on site, offering impromptu tours and information on the crosses. **Muireadach's Cross,** the first you'll see upon entering the grounds, sports an array of Biblical scenes and Celtic designs. On one side, Satan pulls down his side of the Judgment scales and kicks 14 souls to hell. At a height of nearly 21 ft., the **West Cross** is the tallest high cross on the whole island. The intricacies of its detail work make it arguably the finest cross of its kind (that is, Irish and high). And while it is an impressive religious monument, it's not without zanier touches—note the two old men trying to pluck out each other's beards. For more fun, go to the cross at the northeast corner of the graveyard—the nook below the sundial was purportedly used as a wart remover. *Let's Go* does not recommend rubbing your warts on crosses (at least not around other tourists). Another cross, right in front of the tower, was chipped away at by emigrants who wanted to take a piece of the Old Country with them during the Famine.

As the monastery at Monasterboice fell, the Cistercians planted their first foothold for Rome just a few miles away. **Mellifont Abbey,** founded in 1142, quickly became one of Ireland's wealthiest monasteries, in the process hosting a number of tragedies. The 1152 Senate of Mellifont weakened the independent Irish monastic system and sent their traditions of scholarship into decline. Three years later, Cistercian Pope Adrian IV granted the English King authority to "correct" Ireland, thereby putting his seal of approval on the Norman invasion of the 1170s. In 1603, the last of the proud O'Neills surrendered to the English at Mellifont and then fled Ireland for the Continent (see **Feudalism,** p. 56). Most of the ruins now lack both grandeur and basic substance, since the sight's stones were plundered between 1727 and 1880 for use in nearby buildings. The delicate Romanesque octagon of the **lavabo,** where monks once cleansed themselves of sins and grime, offers a sense of the original structure's impressiveness and intricacy of detail. The **visitors center** houses a small exhibition on the sight's history and offers a hand-drawn map of the area and a good tour of the site.

THE HILL OF SLANE, SLANE CASTLE, AND THE SLANE CONCERT

To get to the town of Slane, take bus #183, 70, or 188 from Drogheda (once every hr.), or bus #32 or 33 to Letterkenny from Dublin (once every 2hr.). Entrance to the Hill of Slane is free. Admission to Slane Castle (☎988 4400; www.slanecastle.ie) is by tour only. Tours last 30min. €7, students and seniors €4. For info and tickets to Slane Concert, call The Soundshop (☎983 1078), located in town. The concert takes place on the last Sa in Aug. Tickets cost €50-200. Slane Farm Hostel (☎982 4390) has rooms for €16 per person.

The tiny town of Slane, which hosts a riotous **Samba Festival** in the second week of July, lies about 10 mi. northwest of Newgrange. For truly spectacular views of County Meath, climb your way up the **Hill of Slane,** where, in AD 433, St. Patrick lit a large celebration fire to oppose the druid fires on hills nearby. He was brought before the druid king Laoghaire, who refused to be converted but spared St. Patrick's life and allowed him to preach in his kingdom. Buses will bring you into town, unless you can convince the driver to drop you off next to the hill. When you arrive at the peak, climb the ancient and diminutive stone spiral staircase in the **tower** to see why St. Patrick thought it was such a magical location.

In the town you'll find **Slane Castle,** recently reopened to the public after renovations following the horrific 1991 fire that burned down half of the building. Built in 1785, Slane Castle is a spectacular example of the Gothic Revival style. The castle tour takes about 1hr. and details the minutiae of over twenty rooms, including the dining room and its amazing neo-Gothic ceiling, which was saved during the fire by two firemen who doused the room with water for over eight hours. Each August, the castle opens its doors to the likes of U2 and the Red Hot Chili Peppers for the annual **Slane Concert.** The concert is one of Ireland's most magnificent and popular, drawing crowds nearing 100,000. If the accommodations at the castle prove too expensive, inquire at the nearby **Slane Farm Hostel ❷,** where Paddy Macken and his herds of sheep and cattle offer comfy beds at a cheap price.

DUNDALK TOWN (DÚN DEALGAN) ☎042

Dundalk, home of the Harp Brewery, is located at the mouth of Dundalk Bay, halfway between Dublin and Belfast. Recently, the town has made an effort to establish itself in the tourism industry as a source of information about the history and mythology of the Cooley Peninsula. Unfortunately, the criss-crossing streets of this mid-size town suffer from big-city congestion during the day. At night, Harp flows freely at Dundalk's 141 pubs, though the brewery itself is closed to visitors.

TRANSPORTATION. The N1 zips south to Dublin and north to Belfast, becoming A1 at the border. The **train station** (☎933 5526) is on **Carrickmacross Rd.** From Clanbrassil St., turn right on Park St., then right again on Anne St., which becomes Carrickmacross. Trains run to Belfast (1hr.; M-Sa 7 per day, Su 4 per day; €13.90) and Dublin (express 1hr., regular 1hr. 20min.; M-Th 10 per day, F 11 per day, Sa 12 per day, Su 5 per day; €14.60). **Buses** stop at the Bus Éireann station (☎933 4075) on Long Walk and run to Belfast via Newry (1½hr.; M-Sa 7 per day, Su 5 per day; €11.50) and Dublin (1½hr.; M-F 16 per day, Sa 13 per day, Su 7 per day; €8.85).

ORIENTATION AND PRACTICAL INFORMATION. Dundalk's main street is **Clanbrassil St.; Park St.** is the runner-up. Dundalk's streets change names often; Clanbrassil becomes **Market Sq.** and then **Earl St.** as it heads south. Earl St. intersects **Park St.;** if you head left from Earl St., Park becomes **Francis St.,** then **Roden Pl.,** then **Jocelyn St.** To the right, Earl St. becomes **Dublin St.** It's worth picking up the free *Dundalk Town Guide*, which includes maps marked with the city's sights, from the **tourist office.** From the bus stop, walk down the Long Walk, turn right onto Crowe St., and continue until it becomes Jocelyn St.; the office is on the right after the cathedral. (☎933 5484. Open June to mid-Sept. M-F 9:30am-5:30pm, Sa 9:30am-1pm and 2-5:30pm; mid-Sept. to May M-F 9:30am-1pm and 2-5:30pm.) Many **banks** (including **AIB** and **Bank of Ireland**) with 24hr. **ATMs** are within a block of each other on Clanbrassil St. **A1 Cabs,** Crowe St. (☎932 6666), runs cabs all day and night. Additionally, many taxis stand in the Square. **Datastore,** 58 Dublin St., provides your daily dose of **Internet access** (☎933 1212. €4 per 30min., €6 per hr. Open M-F 10am-10pm, Sa noon-8pm, Su 2-8pm.) The **post office** is on Clanbrassil St. (☎933 4444. Open M and W-Sa 9am-5:30pm, Tu 9:30am-5:30pm.)

ACCOMMODATIONS, FOOD, AND PUBS. Dundalk's B&B offerings are extensive, but most lie outside the town center. If you are not traveling by car, make sure to ask carefully about locations. **Glen Gat House ❸,** 18-19 The Crescent, rests off Anne St. near the train station and cathedral, and around the corner from Dublin St. Its award-winning garden, beautiful antiques, and overall elegance make it the most attractive option. (☎933 7938. First floor rooms equipped with

CAFE METZ

Fifty-eight hours out of the week, Cafe Metz in Dundalk Town is exactly what its name would suggest: a modern cafe and coffee shop with a Mediterranean edge. The cafe's soups, sandwiches, and sweet, delicious cappuccino draw locals and tourists alike to lunch amidst the modern decor spanning two floors—connected by a cool, curved staircase—in this hip cafe. But on Wednesday through Sunday evenings, Cafe Metz surpasses its luncheon expectations, transcending its name to become a thing divine.

As top-notch chefs craft an exquisite a la carte menu, a fine meal might begin with a warm duck salad (€6.50); for a main, we recommend the tender fillet of chicken stuffed with sun-dried tomatoes and served over a bed of wild mushroom tagliatelle (€16.50). Skip the Guinness for a night and accompany your feast with one of the restaurant's carefully selected wines. If you still have room (and money), top it off with a warm chocolate brownie drizzled in chocolate sauce and smothered in peppermint mousse (€5.25). Our mouths water just thinking about it. While this gourmet dinner is certainly a splurge, families and couples often celebrate special occasions at this upscale and delectable restaurant. Now we ask: isn't a holiday in Ireland occasion enough?

Cafe Metz, Francis St., Dundalk Town (☎933 9106). Splurge-worthy dinner served W-Su 6-10:30pm. Open Tu-Su for lunch. Wheelchair-accessible. MC/V

wheelchair friendly bathrooms. Singles €30-35; doubles €55-60.) In town, **Oriel House ❷,** 63 Dublin St., has basic rooms, but is conveniently located and inexpensive. (☎933 1347. Singles €20; doubles €36; triples €54.) If you have transportation, **Krakow ❸,** at 190 Ard Easmuinn and signposted from the train station, is another good option. All rooms have TV, hair dryer, and hotpot, and those upstairs have skylights. (☎933 7535. Singles €39; doubles €54.)

Restaurants and late-night fast food joints cluster on the main streets in town. **La Cantina ❷,** 1 River Ln., just off Park St., is a local favorite for its quality Italian eats. (☎937 7970. Dinner only, call after 5pm for reservations.) The sign hanging in the window of **Deli Lites ❶** on Clanbrassil St. challenges the passerby: "Try our delicious sandwiches, no one likes a coward," though the cheap, healthy breakfasts and sandwiches (€3-4) hardly inspire fear. (☎932 9555. Open M-Sa 9am-6pm.)

With 141 pubs lining the streets, Dundalk has a ready pint at every turn. **M. Courtney's** central location at 43-44 Park St. combines with a friendly atmosphere to make it the focal point of any evening on the town. (☎932 6652. Open M-W 3-11:30pm, Th-Sa noon-12:30am, Su 12:30-11pm.) **The Spirit Store,** Georges Quay, is a new fave worth the long walk down Jocelyn, though a cab (€5) might be a better bet. Live music upstairs, from trad to alternative rock, draws crowds of 18-80 year olds. The **Windsor Bar,** Dublin St., is convenient to both Glen Gat and Oriel House and serves particularly tasty pub-eats for a cheap price. (☎933 8146. Sandwiches €2.50; full meals €7-8. Food served noon-3pm and 6-10pm daily.) **Jockey's,** on Anne St., tempts pedestrians with its alluring front and serves well-priced victuals during the day. (☎933 4621. Breakfast daily 10am, lunch M-Sa noon-3:30pm. Trad F 10pm.) On Saturdays, those over 21 soothe their lonely hearts at the **Imperial Hotel,** home of **Sgt. Peppers,** a late-night club. (☎933 2241. Bar open M-W 11:30am-11:30pm, Th-Sa until 12:30am, and Su until 11pm. Club open Sa 11:30pm-2:30am.)

SIGHTS. Gothic **St. Patrick's Cathedral,** Francis St., was modeled after King's College Chapel in Cambridge. The warm, peachy-pink interior makes it a spot of comfort and solace. (☎933 4648. Open daily 7:30am-5pm.) Next to the tourist office, the award-winning **County Museum** caters to those interested in the history of County Louth, from the Bronze Age to the present. However, even those short on time and money can check out its most fun exhibit: the **Heinkel Bubble Car.** Visible from the entrance, this Dundalk-made, 60s era vehicle is the only car manufactured in the Republic. With three wheels and a single, front-opening door, the Bubble makes you wonder why. (☎932 7056. Open Tu-Sa 10:30am-5:30pm, Su 2-6pm. €3.80, students and seniors €2.50, children €1.25, families €10.15.) Past the far northwest corner of town, about 3 mi. out N51, the 12th-century **Cúchulainn's Castle** supposedly stands on the birthplace of the Ulster Cycle's most famous hero (see **Legends and Folktales,** p. 71). The seven-story **Seatown Windmill,** on Seatown Place, was once the largest in Ireland, but the wind was taken out of its sails when they were removed in 1890. Beaches beckon from **Blackrock,** 3 mi. south on R172.

COOLEY PENINSULA

The numerous trails in the mountains surrounding the Cooley Peninsula are a hiker's paradise, and Carlingford Lough has the warmest waters in the northern half of the island. Several ancient Irish myths are set in this dramatic landscape, among them the epic *Táin bo Cuailnge*, "The Cattle Raid of Cooley" (see **Legends and Folktales,** p. 71). Remarkably well-preserved stone remnants of medieval settlements are scattered across the peninsula.

CARLINGFORD (CARLINN) ☎042

The fresh, earthy scent of the mountains mingles with the salty breeze rising off the lough in the quiet village of Carlingford. While Slieve Foy, the nearest and highest of the Cooley Mountains, makes for rewarding hiking, many never leave the narrow alleys and tidy buildings below.

TRANSPORTATION AND PRACTICAL INFORMATION. **Buses** (☎933 4075) stop at the waterfront on their way to Dundalk (50min., M-Sa 6 per day, €4.25) and Newry (20min., M-Sa 5 per day, €3.10). The **tourist office** is right by the bus stop. (☎937 3033. Open Apr.-Sept. M-F 10am-5:30pm, Sa-Su 11am-5:30pm; Oct.-Mar. daily 11am-5pm.) A 24hr. **ATM** is on Newry St. For **taxis,** call **Gally Cabs** (☎937 3777). Those with solid aquatic or outdoors experience may find **work opportunities** among the international staff of **Carlingford Adventure Center** (see **Accommodations**). A minimum two-month stay is requested; contact ☎937 3100 for more information. **Murphy's Laundry** (☎938 3812; open M-Sa 9am-6pm; €9) is next to the **post office** (☎937 3171; open M-F 9am-1pm and 2-5:30pm, Sa 9am-1pm) on Dundalk St.

ACCOMMODATIONS, FOOD, AND PUBS. On Tholsel St., one block inland and left of the bus stop, **Carlingford Adventure Centre and Hostel (IHH)** ❷ provides small dorms on the first floor, while the new second floor has much nicer rooms with bath for just €5 more. The hostel is often filled with school groups; call ahead in May and June. (☎937 3100; www.carlingfordadventure.com. Open Feb.-Nov., all year for groups. Internet €1 per 16min. Downstairs: 8-bed dorms €15; 4-bed €17; bunked doubles €18; singles €19.)

Carlingford seems to have as many B&Bs as people, and nearly all are posh and pricey. Savvy travelers will *hora* to the **Shalom B&B** ❸, Ghan Rd., well-signposted from the waterfront. Tastefully eclectic decorations, a "passion suite," and **Internet access** make this one of Carlingford's nicest places to stay. (☎937 3151. Singles €38.50; doubles €52.) **Viewpoint** ❸, Omeath Rd., just off the waterfront beyond King John's Castle, provides large, bright motel-style rooms with baths and private entrances. (☎937 3149. Weekdays €30; weekends €35.) Past Shalom on Ghan Rd., the highly regarded **Beaufort's Guest House** ❹ is the sailor's best bet.

EASTERN IRELAND

Inquire about boat charters from owner Michael Caine. (☎937 3879. Singles €45; doubles €64-78.) In the center of town, **Belvedere House ❸** on Newry St. has painstakingly decorated, themed rooms, all related to the legend of Cúchulainn. Sing songs of joy in the double-powered showers. (☎937 3731. €35-40 per person.)

Though Carlingford contains only a handful of pubs and eateries, they offer up everything from traditional Irish hospitality to supernatural phenomena. Particularly strong *craic* is on tap at **PJ O'Hare's,** otherwise known as **The Anchor Bar.** It's only slightly bigger than a breadbox, but optimists will note that tight quarters make for close friendships. Inside, the publicans proudly display the clothes of a leprechaun caught in the nearby hills several years ago (see **The Leprechaun of Slieve Foy,** below). The backyard provides an alternative setting in which to slurp oysters (€7 for six) and drink with locals. (☎937 3106. Open Su-Th 11am-11:30pm, F-Sa 11am-12:30am.) Catty-corner to the Anchor Bar, **Carlingford Arms,** on Newry St., serves snacks from 12:30-9:30pm, and hearty meals (mains €11) after 5pm. (☎937 3418. Folk music F-Sa nights and Su 4-7pm.) Vegetarians might be better off next door at **Captain Corelli's Mandolin ❹,** where the Italian chef offers up fine pastas (€10-11), seafood (€13-17.50), and meats. (☎938 3848. Open M and W-Su 6-9:30pm.) For daytime fare, follow the signs to **Georgina's Bakehouse ❶,** where tasty sweets and light lunches are served in a homey atmosphere. (☎937 3346. Soups, salads, sandwiches, and desserts about €3 each. Open daily 10:30am-6pm.)

SIGHTS. The **Holy Trinity Heritage Centre** is housed in a renovated medieval church squeezed between several more recent centuries' buildings. The center's staff educates visitors on the history and local lore of Carlingford from the 9th century to the present using a small exhibition. (☎937 3454. Open M-F 10am-12:30pm and 2-4:30pm. €2, children €1.) The nearby ruins of the **Dominican Friary** have retained some of their high walls and dramatic arches and are open for exploration. Carlingford's three other surviving pre-Renaissance buildings provide interesting scenery for a stroll through town, but their interiors are closed to visitors. **King John's Castle,** by the waterfront, is the largest and most foreboding of Carlingford's medieval remains. It was built in the 1190s and named for King John, who visited briefly in 1210. **Taaffe's Castle,** along the quay, was built during the 16th century as a merchant house and contains classic Norman defensive features. In a tiny alley off Market Sq., the turret-laden 16th-century **Mint** is notable for its ornate limestone windows. At the end of the street, one of the old 15th-century town gates, the **Tholsel** (TAH-sehl), creates a narrow passageway for cars entering town. Although Carlingford is normally known for its quiet serenity, a weekend-long **folk festival** in September draws musicians from all over the Republic.

THE LEPRECHAUN OF SLIEVE FOY One misty morn about a decade ago, PJ (the late owner of PJ's Anchor Bar) was going about his usual morning work—painting murals over the windows of abandoned houses—when he heard a high-pitched yell. On his way to investigate the noise, he encountered a schoolteacher who had also heard it. The men's keen ears soon led them to the origin of the commotion—about halfway up Slieve Foy was a "faery ring" of trampled grass and at its center were bones and a wee leprechaun suit. Our heroes picked up the leprechaun remains and returned to Carlingford with their amazing discovery in hand. Subsequent "scientific" investigation determined that the bones were from a sheep—however, as PJ later commented, everyone knows that leprechauns are changelings, and this one, all bones though he was, had probably turned into a sheep as the men approached. The story soon reached the ears of national and international reporters, and for a short time afterwards, Carlingford was known worldwide as the town that had seen a leprechaun.

THE MIDLANDS

The Irish Midlands are traditionally composed of six counties: Cavan, Monaghan, Laois, Offaly, Longford, and Westmeath. These central counties are often passageways rather than destinations. Co. Monaghan and Cavan's friendly wee villages beckon calmer travelers who are looking for a convenient rest-stop on their way to the Northwest. The 19 lakes of Co. Westmeath have earned it the buttery nickname "Land of Lakes and Legends." Farther south in famously soggy Co. Offaly, small towns and the impressive ruins of Clonmacnois civilize the peatland. The Slieve Bloom Mountains, shared between Offaly and Laois, are splendid and under-appreciated. Co. Longford is calm and collected, but hardly exciting.

MONAGHAN TOWN (MUINEACHÁN) ☎047

Like many Midlands towns, Monaghan has undergone dramatic changes in recent years. The administrative center of its county, Monaghan has been the major beneficiary of the boomin' EU's euros. The effect on the fabric of the community is striking—chic boutiques and trendy bars now lie behind deteriorating limestone facades. With new names and glammed-up interiors, pubs and restaurants are trying with all their might to cater to the newly affluent populace.

TRANSPORTATION AND PRACTICAL INFORMATION. The **bus depot** is 5min. north of Market Sq. To reach the center of town from the station, walk against traffic up North Rd. (☎82377. Open M-Sa 8:30am-8pm.) Buses run to **Belfast** (1½hr.; M-Sa 5 per day, Su 2 per day; €8.25) and **Dublin** (2hr.; M-Sa 7 per day, Su 3 per day; €8.90). **ABC** (☎71500) runs 24hr. **taxis.** The roads in Monaghan are organized in a loop around the old courthouse and the enormous modern shopping center. From **the Diamond** in the northeast, **Dublin St.** heads south to **Broad St.,** which heads west to **Park St.,** which heads north to **Market Sq.** Visitors looking to cross town can save time by cutting through the shopping center. The **tourist office** is currently relocating to an undisclosed location, so call ahead. (☎81122. Open June-Sept. M-Sa 9am-5:30pm; call for off-season hours.) **AIB** has and **ATM** on the Diamond. Book ahead for 45min. of free **Internet access** at the **library,** North Rd. (Open M-F 11am-1pm and 2-5pm; also 6-8pm on M, W, and F.) The **post office** lies just north of Church Sq. on Mill St. (☎81342. Open M-F 9am-5:30pm.)

ACCOMMODATIONS, FOOD, AND PUBS. Centrally located **Ashleigh House ❸,** 37 Dublin St., provides rooms, all with bath, off a warren of narrow hallways. (☎81227. Singles €35; doubles €60.) **Hildene House ❸,** Canal St., also provides rooms and breakfast. (☎83297. From €25 per person.) **Tesco,** in the central shopping center, is a well-lit warehouse disguised as a grocery store. (☎71525. Open M-W and Sa 8:30am-8pm, Th-F 8:30am-10pm, Su noon-6pm). There's also a **SuperValu** on Church Sq. (☎81344. Open M-W and Sa 9am-7pm, Th-F 9am-9pm.) **Pizza D'Or ❷,** 23 Market St., behind the tourist office, is a late-night town institution. (☎84777. Pizzas from €6.35. Open M-F 5pm-1am, Sa-Su 5pm-3am.) **Mediterraneo ❸,** on Dublin St., makes decadent pasta and gourmet pizza. (Pastas and pizza €10-12; meat dishes €16-25. Open M and W-Sa 5:30-10:30pm, Su 4:30-10pm.) **Paramount Restaurant ❺,** affiliated with **Cooper's Bar,** Market St., serves delicious seafood and meat dishes in an elegant setting. Although it's a brand-new restaurant, locals are already buzzing about the cuisine. (☎72877. Prix-fixe dinner €35; a la carte dishes €20-22. Open daily 5-10pm.) If you're looking for good *craic,* Monaghan town offers plenty of pubs to quench your thirst. Young and old alike head

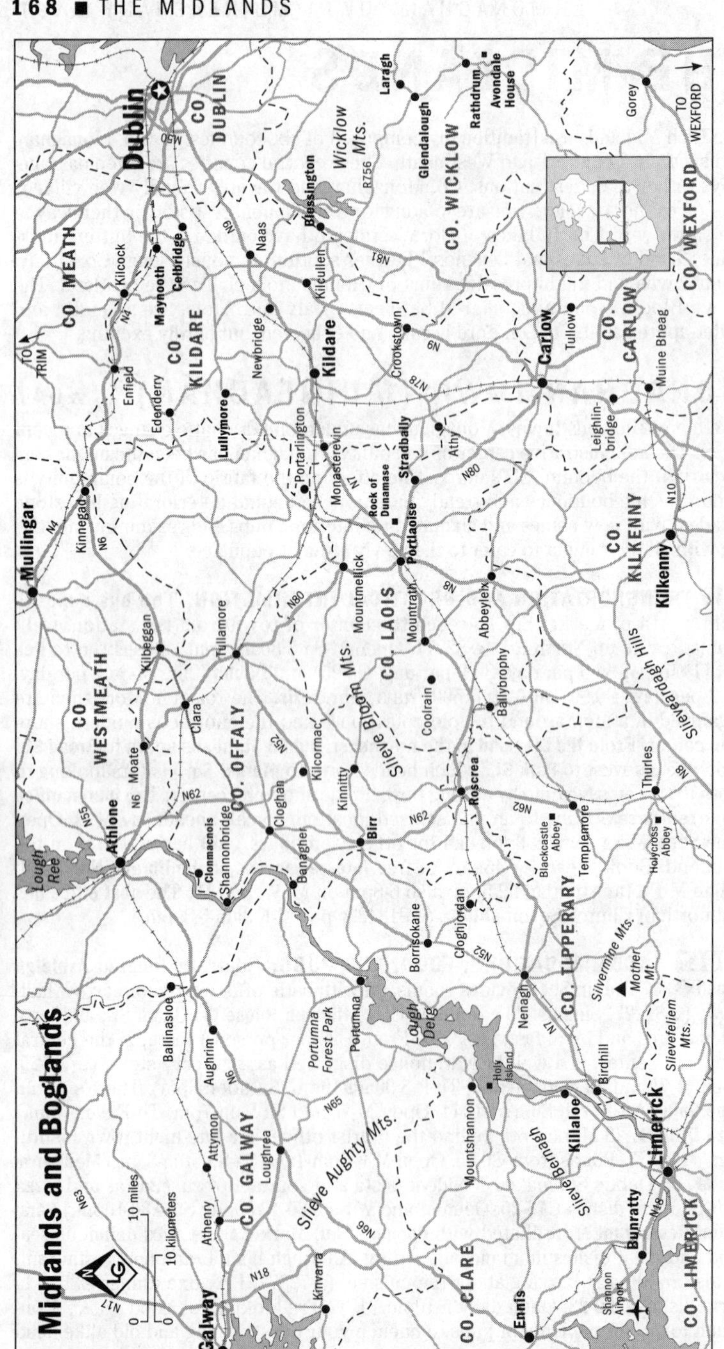
Midlands and Boglands
0 10 miles
0 10 kilometers
Galway
Athenry
Attymon
Loughrea
Kinvarra
CO. GALWAY
Slieve Aughty Mts.
Ennis
CO. CLARE
Shannon Airport
Bunratty
Limerick
CO. LIMERICK
Mountshannon
Holy Island
Killaloe
Slieve Bernagh
Birdhill
Slievefeliem Mts.
Aughrim
Ballinasloe
Portumna Forest Park
Portumna
Lough Derg
Nenagh
CO. TIPPERARY
Silvermine Mts.
Mother Mt.
Borrisokane
Cloghjordan
Templemore
Blackcastle Abbey
Holycross Abbey
Thurles
Slieveardagh Hills
Lough Ree
Athlone
Clonmacnois
Shannonbridge
Banagher
Cloghan
Birr
Kinnitty
Kilcormac
Roscrea
Coolrain
Ballybrophy
Moate
Clara
Kilbeggan
CO. WESTMEATH
CO. OFFALY
Slieve Bloom Mts.
Tullamore
Mountmellick
Mountrath
CO. LAOIS
Abbeyleix
Portlaoise
Rock of Dunamase
Stradbally
Portarlington
Monasterevin
Athy
Mullingar
Kinnegad
Edenderry
Lullymore
Enfield
TO TRIM
CO. KILDARE
Kildare
Newbridge
Kilcock
Maynooth
Celbridge
CO. MEATH
Naas
Kilcullen
Blessington
Dublin
CO. DUBLIN
Wicklow Mts.
Laragh
Glendalough
CO. WICKLOW
Rathdrum
Avondale House
Gorey
TO WEXFORD
CO. WEXFORD
Carlow
Crookstown
Tullow
CO. CARLOW
Muine Bheag
Leighlinbridge
CO. KILKENNY
Kilkenny
EASTERN IRELAND

to **The Squealing Pig,** the Diamond, for pints and reasonably priced food amidst torch lamps and exposed brick. (☎84562. Bar food around €6, served daily noon-10pm.) The wooden decor and comfy stools at **Terry's** (☎81149) are particularly conducive to conversation; a somewhat older crowd listens to folk on Monday nights. **Master Deary's,** on Market St. next to the Cooper Bar, is another new entry to the town's nightlife; early reviews are full of praise. Wooden booths, nice lighting, and flowing alcohol are sure to keep the locals and tourists coming.

SIGHTS AND ACTIVITIES. The comprehensive **St. Louis Heritage Centre,** Market Rd., occupies a red-brick building on the grounds of a convent school. Its exhibits trace the history of the St. Louis Order of nuns. (☎83529. Wheelchair-accessible. Open M-Tu and Th-F 10am-noon and 2:30-4:30pm, Sa-Su 2:30-4:30pm. €1.30.) On Hill St. across from the tourist office, the **Monaghan County Museum** chronicles the county's history. (☎82928. Open Tu-Sa 11am-1pm and 2-5pm. Free.) Monaghan's most impressive building lies on the south side of town—the 1895 **St. Macartan's Cathedral** offers stunning views. Monaghan abounds with activities for the adventurous. Perfect your riding skills or just enjoy a jaunt in the countryside at the **Greystones Equestian Centre** (☎047 88100) or the **Carrickmacross School of Equitation** (☎042 966 1017), which are both open year-round. Work on that chip shot on the several challenging **golf** courses in the area, including **Rossmore Golf Club** (☎047 71222). Dodge your friends and peg your enemies in a game of **paintball** in the Rossmore Forest Park with **Escarmouche Paintball** (☎0044 7774 636254).

DAYTRIP FROM MONAGHAN: LOUGH MUCKNO

Lough Muckno is in Castleblaney, 20 mi. southeast of Monaghan on the N2. ***Buses*** *on their Dublin route run 4-5 times per day. To get to the park from town, follow the main street north to the bottom of the hill, make a right, and head through the tall metal gates.*

Castleblaney, southeast of Monaghan, is home to the lovely **Lough Muckno Leisure Park.** Muckno means "Swimming Pig," but there is nothing squalid about these 900 acres of forest and lake. The park contains the grounds of **Hope Castle,** which once housed the owners of the **Hope Diamond.** In a Marxian turn of events, the castle is now over-run by immigrants fleeing the environmental catastrophe at Chernobyl. Hydrophobic park visitors can tour the trails of the **Black** and **White Islands,** while aquatic daredevils enjoy watersports at the **Adventure Centre,** next to the castle. (☎087 249 1305. Windsurfing €25 per 4hr.; tennis €2.50 per hr. Also sailing, horse-riding, bowling, and golf. Open Mar.-Oct. Tu-F 2-7pm, Sa-Su noon-7pm.)

ATHLONE (BAILE ÁTHA LUAIN) ☎0902

Settled on the flatlands on the border of counties Roscommon and Westmeath, Athlone is in the center of everything and the middle of nowhere. Holding down the fort at the intersection of the Shannon River and the Dublin-Galway road, it is *the* transportation hub. A 13th-century Norman castle dominating Athlone's waterfront further attests to the city's former strategic importance. The scenic Shannon offers enough fishing and boating to fulfill any waterlover's dream, and the monastic ruins at nearby Clonmacnois are reachable by road or boat. Athlone hosts a surprising number of standout accommodations, restaurants, and pubs, and its central but remote location means few tourists make the worthwhile journey.

TRANSPORTATION. Athlone's **train** and **bus depot** is on Southern Station Rd., which runs parallel to Church St. (☎73322. Tickets M-Sa 9am-5:30pm.) **Trains** leave for Dublin (1¾hr.; M-Sa 8 per day, Su 6 per day; €13-19) and Galway (1¼hr.; 4-5 per day; €10-15). This is the nerve center of **Bus Éireann** services; on their map, all roads lead to Athlone. There's at least one bus per day to almost all major cities,

EASTERN IRELAND

including Belfast, Cork, Derry, Waterford, Tralee, and Killarney (€14.60). The main route from Dublin to Galway trundles through frequently (14-15 per day; Dublin €9.50, Galway €10). **Nestor Buses** (☎091 797 244) also serves the region; for their routes and schedules, call them or stop by the Royal Hotel on Church St.

ORIENTATION AND PRACTICAL INFORMATION. The River Shannon splits Athlone into the **left bank** and **right bank.** The former is more hip and claims the castle, while the latter holds the shops and eateries. **Church St.** cuts through the right bank, while most of the action on the left bank takes place on **High St.** The besieged **tourist office,** in the castle, counterattacks with an arsenal of orientation ammunition; ask for the *Athlone and District Visitors Guide.* (☎94630. Open Easter-Oct. M-Sa 9am-6pm, Su 10am-5pm.) **Bank of Ireland** (☎92747) and **AIB** (☎75810), on Church St., have **ATMs.** (Both open M 10am-5pm, Tu-F 10am-4pm.) **Internet access** is splendid and cheap at **Techstore.ie,** Paynes Ln., a bit away from the river off Church St. (☎78888. €5 per hr., students €4. Open daily 9am-10pm.) The **post office** is by the castle on Barrack St. (☎83544. Open M-Sa 9:30am-5:30pm.)

ACCOMMODATIONS AND CAMPING. For a lively locale, look no farther than **The Bastion ❸,** 2 Bastion St., a spectacular B&B right in the middle of the Shannon's funkier left bank. An eclectic blend of art and tapestries adds a touch of chic. (☎94954. Fantastic continental breakfast. Singles €35-45; doubles €50-55.) The **Lough Ree Lodge ❷,** 25min. from the town center on the Dublin road, is Athlone's lone hostel. To get there, walk out Church St. past the shopping center, take the right fork, cross the bridge, and keep going until the college. **Bus Éireann** shuttles between the hostel and the Golden Island shopping mall (5min., every 15-20min. 9am-6pm, €1). A cut above your typical hostel, the biggest dorms at Lough Ree have four beds and all rooms have TVs, but resist the temptation of passivity—instead, mingle in the superbly clean kitchen or shoot pool in the common area. (☎76738. Wheelchair-accessible. Continental breakfast included. **Internet access.** Laundry €10. Dorms €15.50; singles €25; doubles €40.) **The Thatch ❸,** a bar and hotel opposite the castle, has palatial rooms equipped with all sorts of amenities and a good deal of noise from the bars below; quieter rooms are pricier, but have bathtubs. (☎94981. **Internet access** €1 per 8min. Singles €35; doubles €54-70.) **Higgins' ❹,** 2 Pierce St., on the left bank, has decent rooms at the top of a steep staircase and friendly, down-to-earth owners. (☎92519. Singles €38-42; doubles €60.) Over on the right bank, get one of the three cozy rooms at the petite and sufficient **Shannon View ❸,** 3 Shannon Villas, a few blocks up Church St. from the church. (☎78411. €30 per person.) The closest tent-land is at **Lough Ree East Caravan and Camping Park ❶,** staked out 3 mi. northeast on N55 (the Longford road) by a pleasant inlet on Lough Ree. Follow signs for the lough. (☎78561 or 74414. Open Apr.-Sept. Tents €2.50; caravans and cars €7; motorhomes €5. Laundry €7.)

FOOD. Head downstairs to **Dunnes,** Irishtown Rd., to fulfill your grocery needs. (☎75212. Open M-W and Sa 9am-7pm, Th-F 9am-9pm, Su noon-6m.) **Manifesto ❹,** Church St., just after the bridge on the right bank, is relaxed but elegant, and the fantastic food is served on giant plates. (☎73241. Mains €14-20. Open M-F 4:30pm-"late," Sa-Su 12:30pm-"late.") **The Left Bank Bistro ❹,** Bastion St., has been named one of the 100 best restaurants in Ireland. The lunches are affordable and filling; try the steak sandwich with potatoes and salad for €8-10. (☎94446. Lunch noon-5pm; dinner 6-9:30pm.) Three cheers for local favorite **Tribeca ❸,** hidden off High St. on the left bank and in one of Athlone's oldest buildings. Excellent pasta and pizzas are the order of the day. (☎98805. Mains €9-16. Open M-W 5-10pm, Th-F 5-11pm, Sa 4-11pm, Su 2-10pm.) The **Bonne Bouche ❷,** 21 Church St., serves a small variety of plate-filling, palate-pleasing meals in an atmosphere cluttered with Emerald Isle memorabilia. (☎72112. Mains €9. Open daily 10am-7pm.)

PUBS AND CLUBS. No one likes to be all athlone when the sun goes down—look to the town's lively pubs for companionship and a spot of music. *The Westmeath Independent* has entertainment listings, as does the *B-Scene* magazine that appears fortnightly at local cafes. Sawdust lines the floor and fishing rods decorate the ceiling at **Sean's Bar** (☎92358), behind the castle on Main St. It claims to be Ireland's oldest inn, established in AD 900, but the building holds up well to raucous school-night trad. She went through a phase as The Hooker, but **Gertie Brown's Costume Place** now entertains more regulars than ever. (☎74848. M trad.) Check your crown at the door of **The Palace,** Market Sq. (☎92229), for inter-generational mingling and occasional live music. There's no clowning around at **BoZo's,** in the basement of Conlon's on Dublingate St., just the usual boogying to chart-topping music. (☎74376. Cover €8. Open Th-Sa 11:30pm-2:30am.) At **Club Ginkel's,** above Manifesto, the crowd spiffs up to match the leopard-skin decor and purple roof. (Cover W-Sa €8. Open Th-Sa 11:30pm-2:30am, M and W 11:30pm-2am.)

SIGHTS AND FESTIVALS. Athlone's historical fame can be traced back to one single, crushing defeat. Orange Williamite forces besieged **Athlone Castle** in 1691, and, with the help of 12,000 cannonballs, they had little trouble crossing the river and sweeping up. The defending Jacobites, unskilled soldiers at best, suffered countless casualties; the attackers lost fewer than 100 of their 25,000 (see **The Ascendancy,** p. 58). The castle is free for all to wander, and provides some grand Shannon views. (Open May-Sept. daily 9:30am-6pm.) Inside, the **visitors center** tells a 45min. audio-visual tale of the battle, and marches on (without the slightest hint of transition) through Athlone history to relate the stories of home-grown tenor **John McCormack** and the river Shannon. The **museum** inside the visitors center has, among other things, gramophones and uniforms from the Irish Civil War. (☎92912. Open May-Sept. daily 10am-4:30pm. €4.55, students and seniors €2.65. Museum only €3/€1.50.) The two master crafters at **Athlone Crystal Factory,** 29-31 Pearse St., invite you to drop in and discover the fascinating details of crystal-making; covet their final products in the factory shop. (☎92867. Open M-Sa 10am-1pm and 2-6pm. Free.) **Viking Tours** sails a replica Viking ship up the Shannon to Lough Ree and, depending on demand, to Clonmacnois. The Clonmacnois ride includes a guided tour of the monastic ruins. (☎73383 or 086 262 1136. 1½-4hr. voyages depart from the Strand across the river from the castle. 2 or more per day. €8, students and children €5. Clonmacnois tour €13/€8.) If you'd like to spend your holiday floating self-guided down the Shannon, the happy sailors at **Jolly Mariner Marina** (☎72892 or 72113) will **rent cruisers** that berth up to eight people. (Rates vary by season. 3-berth cruiser €435-890 per wk.; 8-berth €1015-2390.) They also hire **outboards** (€65 per wk.; €65 deposit) and **bicycles** (€40 per wk.).

The last week in June brings the **Athlone Festival** with all its parades, exhibitions, and free concerts. Athlone hosts the **John McCormack Golden Voice Conference,** named for the town's famous songbird (see **Music,** p. 74), in late autumn. There is also a celebration for the Irish novelist **John Broderick** the first weekend in May, replete with guest speakers, poetry readings, and a general to-do about the man. Contact the tourist office (☎94630) or the Athlone Chamber of Commerce (☎73173) for further information on this and other summertime merriment.

CLONMACNOIS (CLUAIN MHIC NÓIS) ☎0905

Fourteen isolated miles southwest of Athlone, the monastic ruins of Clonmacnois (clon-muk-NOYS) keep watch over Shannon's boglands. St. Ciaran (KEER-on) founded his monastery here in AD 548; the settlement grew into a city and important center for religion and brainiactivity. Monks wrote the precious **Book of the Dun Cow** here around 1100, on vellum supposedly from St. Ciaran's cow. The holy heifer traveled everywhere with the saint, and miraculously produced enough milk for the whole monastery. The cows munching their way across the landscape today have ordinary udders, but the grandiosity of the sight still incites the imagination. The ruin's **cathedral** has seen its share of attacks over the course of its thousand years. One of its doorways is known as the **whispering arch;** even quiet sounds will travel up one side over to the other. **O'Connor's Church,** built in the 12th century, has Church of Ireland services from June through August on Sundays at 4pm. Peaceful **Nun's Church** is beyond the modern graveyard behind the main site, about ¼ mi. down the path. Its finely detailed doorways are some of the most impressive Romanesque architecture in Ireland.

If you have a car, the easiest way to reach Clonmacnois from Athlone or Birr is to take N62 to **Ballynahoun** and follow the signs from there. The town is accessible by bike, but cycling there involves a 14 mi. gauntlet of hilly terrain. Access to the monastery is through the **visitors center** and their displays, which include a 23min. audio-visual show. (☎74195. Open June to mid-Sept. daily 9am-7pm; mid-Mar. to May and mid-Sept. to Oct. 10am-6pm; Nov. to mid-Mar. 10am-5pm. €4.40, students €1.90, seniors €3.10. The center, unlike the sites, is wheelchair-accessible.) The **tourist office,** at the entrance to the Clonmacnois carpark, sells various guides to the city. (☎74134. Open Mar.-Nov. daily 10am-6pm.) **Paddy Kavanagh** runs a **minibus tour** that hits the monastery, a local pub, and the **West Offaly Railway,** which runs through a peat bog. Paddy accommodates almost all schedules and connects with incoming buses and trains. He will pick up sightseers from their accommodations if they're eager enough to call ahead. The tour is engaging and offers several "surprises," as Paddy shows off his Ireland with heart and charm. (☎0902 74839 or 087 240 7706. Clonmacnois €17; Clonmacnois and West Offaly Railway €22. Site admission fees an additional €14.)

One outstanding B&B is **Kajon House ❸,** on Shannonbridge Rd. near the ruins. Mrs. Kate Harte is a lovely ball of fire, and will gladly pick you up in Athlone if you call ahead. She and her husband, a chef, also make a fabulous dinner (€17-19) or snack (€7-10), and greet you with delicious homemade scones. (☎74191; www.kajonhouse.cjb.net. Singles €35-39; doubles €46, with bath €51. Stuffed animals included.) **Mr. and Mrs. Augustin Claffey ❷,** on Shannonbridge Rd. a few hundred yards before Kajon House, let rooms in an adorable cottage that dates from 1843. Two double beds, a lambskin rug, and a peat fire complement all the modern conveniences you could want, minus central heating. (☎74149. Self-catering. Open Apr.-Oct. €15 per person.) **Meadow View B&B,** half a mile in the other direction from Clonmacnois, has modern rooms, a sunny dining room, and a dog that is all bark and no bite. (☎74257. Singles €33; doubles €46-50, half-price if under 12.) The area's camping is 3 mi. east, at the **Glebe Touring Caravan and Camping Park ❶.** (☎0902 30277. Open Easter-Oct. €2 per person; €5 per tent. Laundry €4.)

THE SLIEVE BLOOM MOUNTAINS

Though less than 2000 ft. at their highest point, the Slieve Bloom Mountains burst lustily from the rolling plains between **Birr, Roscrea, Portlaoise,** and **Tullamore.** The mountain terrain is a combination of forest and energy-rich bogland. The 43 mi. circular **Slieve Bloom Way** takes hikers through and around the mountains. For all the details you'll need, pick up the *Slieve Bloom Way Map Guide* (€5) from the Portlaoise tourist office. The mountains' greatest asset, contrary to what a tourist office might tell you, is their lack of tourist-oriented activity—there's nothing to do but relax. The towns surrounding the mountains, bastions of rural Ireland's small-town lifestyle that they are, help you in your quest for peace and quiet.

Transportation can be very tricky. Two of the best towns for entry to the mountains are **Kinnitty,** to the northwest, and **Mountrath,** to the south; getting from one to the other should pose no problems for the automotive-blessed. Travelers reliant on public transportation, however, are considerably handicapped. The most important thing is to talk to people; ask how to get places, where to go, and who else to talk to. The **tourist offices** of the surrounding towns are good starting points; the **Portlaoise** branch (☎0502 121 178) can provide a handy list of Co. Laois residents who have been trained as tour guides. Noreen Murphy, for instance, is a mountain specialist and owns **Conlán House ❸,** one of the few B&Bs near the mountains. This cozy lodge sits atop a small hill and overlooks part of the walk 1¼ mi. away. (☎0502 32727. Singles €40; doubles €30-40; children half-price.) **Roundwood House ❺,** a gorgeous 16th-century house with two resident peacocks, is also fairly near the mountains: 3 mi. out R440 from Mountrath. (☎0502 32120. Singles €80; doubles €130.) The owners of the modern **Farren House Hostel ❶** can give you a lift out to their place from **Ballacolla,** a town reached twice a day by bus from Portlaoise. The hostel rooms are large and comfy, and the old farm junk sculptures in the driveway will force a smile. (☎0502 34032. Wheelchair-accessible. Continental breakfast €3.50. Laundry €4. Dorms €12.50. **Camping** €5.)

The *craic* can be mighty in Slieve Bloom villages, but it's all about the timing. When the pubs have trad sessions, they're not looking to impress the shamrock-seeking hordes. On Thursday nights, the **Thatched Village Inn** (☎0502 35277) in **Coolrain** gets the locals together for some infectiously fun set dancing. If you'd rather have your fancy-footin' outside, in a bog and on a mountain, then the **Fraughan Festival** is the event for you: ten days of music and dancing inspired by Lughnasa, a pagan sun-worshipping fete whose name sounds delightfully similar to "lunacy." (Late July or early Aug. Consult www.laoistourism.ie.) The **Irish Music and Set Dancing Festival** jigs into Coolrain on the first weekend in May. Contact Micheál Lalor (☎086 260 7658) for information on either festival.

BIRR (BIORRA) ☎0509

William Petty named Birr *"Umbilicus Hiberniae,"* the belly button of Ireland, though the town's non-too-central location leads *Let's Go* to suspect that old Will may have been speaking from behind a pint glass. Mislabeling aside, Birr's castle at least is well worth a visit. The rest of town is pleasant if unremarkable, and does a good job packing visitors off to the Slieve Bloom Mountains. The peaks don't start until **Kinnitty,** 9 mi. east; if you're not driving, bike; a dearth of cars makes thumb-travel impractical in addition to risky.

TRANSPORTATION.

Buses stop at the post office in Emmet Sq. **Bus Éireann** runs to: Athlone (50min.; M-Sa 3-5 per day, Su 1 per day; €7); Cahir (2hr., 1 per day, €11.10); Dublin (2½hr.; M-Sa 4 per day, Su 2 per day; €9); and Limerick (M-F 4-5 per day, Su 1 per day; €11.90). **Kearns Coaches** offer better fares to Dublin and Galway; get a schedule at Square News in Emmet Sq.

ORIENTATION AND PRACTICAL INFORMATION.

The *umbilicus* of Birr is **Emmet Sq.** Most shops and pubs are in the Square, or south down **O'Connell St.** The areas to the north and west, down **Emmet St.** and **Green St.,** are primarily residential. The **tourist office** is down Main St. from the Square on your right. (☎20110. Open May-Sept. daily 9:30am-1pm and 2-5:30pm.) They have some maps of the Slieve Blooms and can put you in touch with the Slieve Bloom Rural Development Society (☎37299). **P.L. Dolan,** Main St., **rents bikes.** (☎20006. €9 per day, €40 per wk.; deposit €50.80. Open M-W and F-Sa 9:30am-1pm and 2-6pm.) The **Bank of Ireland** in Emmet Sq. (☎20092) has an **ATM.** Get your daily dosage of (expensive) **Internet** at **The Book Mark,** Connaught St. (☎21988. €1.50 per 10min., €7 per hr.) The post office is in Emmet Sq. (☎20062. Open M-F 9am-5:30pm, Sa 9am-1pm.)

ACCOMMODATIONS, FOOD, AND PUBS. It would appear that Birr's navel-status, albeit dubious, is enough to hike up the price of a night's stay. Luckily, the town's B&Bs seem to justify the splurgitude. **Kay Kelly's B&B ❸** sits atop her toy store on Main St. in a three centuries-old Georgian house that has a fireplace in one of the bathrooms (those silly Georgians). In addition to her comfortable rooms, affable Kay offers a carpark, spacious TV room, and Victorian garden out back. (☎21128. All rooms with bath. Singles €30; doubles €52.) **Spinners Town House ❸,** Castle St., has crisp decor and roomy rooms; framed documents from Birr's past deck the walls. There's a charming **bistro** downstairs, where breakfast options include scrambled eggs with smoked salmon. (☎21673. All rooms with bath. Singles €35; doubles €65; deluxe—but not worth it—"medieval room" €89.) For cheaper singles, try **Maltings Guest House ❹** on Castle St., where you can indulge in lots of amenities, including those glorious little soaps. (☎21345. Singles €40; doubles €64.) The attached **restaurant ❷** (one of the few in town) serves decent vegetarian-friendly meals (and others) for €9-10.

A **SuperValu** hawks grocer-goods on O'Connell St. (☎20015; open M-Th and Sa 8am-7:30pm, F 8am-8pm, Su 9am-6pm); **Londis,** in the other direction from Emmet Sq., stays open until 9pm every day (☎21250). Locals will point you to **Kong Lam ❷,** Main St., for cheap Chinese takeaway. (☎21253. Mains €7-10. Open Su-M and W-Th 5pm-12:30am, F-Sa 5pm-1:30am.) Spend a few more pence on lunch at the **Coachhouse Lounge ❸,** in Dooly's Hotel on the Square. (☎20032. Lunch €4-7; dinner €13-16.) **Melba's,** the nightclub in Dooly's, stays open until 2am Friday through Sunday and demands a €7 cover. **Whelehan's,** on Connaught St. (☎21349), is owned by members of the Offaly hurling team, and is the liveliest place in town.

SIGHTS. You're welcome to tread on the Earl of Rosse's turf at **Birr Castle,** which remains his private home. The 120-acre demesne has babbling brooks, the tallest box hedges in the world, and paths perfect for aimless wandering. For those who like their romanticism without all the walking, **Declan Cleer** offers 30min. horse-and-carriage rides through the gardens. (☎21753 or 087 6693 237. €7 per person, minimum 4 people; 8 students €30.) The **Historic Science Centre,** inside the castle, showcases the noteworthy astronomy and photography that took place in the castle in the 19th century. The Third Earl of Rosse discovered the Whirlpool Nebula with the **Leviathan,** an immense telescope whose 72 in. mirror was the world's largest for 72 years. In order to build the telescope he had to invent metal alloys strong and shiny enough to give his mirrors a clear surface. You can still observe the Leviathan (outside in a stone enclosure) in action today, but only if the weather is cooperating. (☎20336. Castle open daily 9am-6pm. Leviathan tours 5 days per wk., around noon and 1pm. Wheelchair-accessible. €7, students €5.)

ROSCREA (ROS CRÉ) ☎0505

Picturesque Roscrea (ross-CRAY), actually in Co. Tipperary, strikes a pose 10 mi. south of Birr, to the southwest of the Slieve Blooms. Practically the only reason to make a stop in Roscrea sits on Castle St., and is—you guessed it—a **castle.** Of the 13th-century variety, the castle sports a fine vaulted ceiling, a drawbridge, and some pretty gruesome stories. The designers really must have liked their boiling oil—they fitted special stone machicolations (rectangular boxes where oil-tippers stand) on both sides of the castle keep, in case someone broke through the wall and tried to attack the keep from inside; the one inside is also fitted slightly off-center to allow for prevailing winds. The impressive counterbalanced **drawbridge** and spiked portcullis (lifting gate) don't work today, although **tours** offer a glimpse at a miniature version that shows the whole procedure. While waiting for the tour, be sure to check out the Victorian formal **gardens** at the far end of the grounds.

(☎21850. Open mid-May to Sept. daily 10am-6pm; last admission 5:15pm. €3.10, students €1.20.) Inside the castle grounds sits **Damer House,** built in 1722 when John Damer came along and purchased the entire town of Roscrea (including the castle). The house claims to rotate exhibits, but the rotation period seems to be a decade or so; an exhibit on the **Monastic Midlands** and a millennium-old chunk of **Bog Butter** are the current highlights. A small **tourist office** in Damer House has the free and useful *Roscrea Heritage Walk* map. (Open June-Aug. daily 10am-5:15pm.) The people of Roscrea chose pragmatism over creativity when naming their streets—a 12th-century Romanesque **church** facade overlooks Church St. A **round tower** sits nearby; its belfry was demolished in 1798 after a sharp shooter standing inside picked off a British soldier—the Brits returned fire, and then some.

Bus Éireann coaches stop at Christy Maher's pub on Castle St., downhill from the castle. Buses go to and from Athlone (1½hr., 3 per day); Cork (3hr., 1 per day); Dublin (2hr., 13 per day); and Limerick (1½hr., 13 per day). **Rapid Express Coaches** (☎056 31106) leave from the Rosemary Square fountain, following similar routes at better prices. The **Bank of Ireland** on Castle St. sports a 24hr. **ATM.** (☎21877. Open M-F 10am-4pm, Th until 5pm.) Mrs. Fogarty takes good care of her visitors in the elegant rooms of the lavender and lime **White House ❸,** on Castle St. next to the castle; enter through the restaurant. (☎21996. €30 per person.) Groceries abound at **Tesco,** in the shopping center. (☎22777. Open M-W and Sa 8:30am-7pm, Th-F 8:30am-10pm, Su noon-6pm.) **Freshfields,** Main St., vends fruits and veggies. (☎22384. Open M-Sa 9am-6pm.) Supper options in town are grim; hungry diners will make the effort to get to Birr or Athlone. Pints flow freely however; **Mick Delahunty's,** Main St., offers bar snackables, an arcade, pool table, and lots of TV sports. Those looking for live music will need to bring their own voice/guitar/pennywhistle. (☎22139. Food served 10:30am-6pm.)

PORTLAOISE (PORT LAOISE) ☎0502

If you ask the folks at the tourist office what there is to do in Portlaoise (port-LEESH), it's a safe bet that you'll be pointed outwards. The one worthwhile sight in close range is the **Rock of Dunamase.** To get there, take the Stradbally road east for 4 mi. and follow the sign at the big red church to Athy/Carlow; the Rock is on your left. This ancient fortress was the very model of impregnability until Cromwell impregnated it with iron balls some 400 years ago. Modern visitors can scramble among its ruins and nab great photos of the Slieve Bloom Mountains.

James Fintan Lawlor Ave. runs parallel to **Main St.** Lawlor Ave. is a four-lane highway that opens onto Portlaoise's several shopping centers, the most prominent of which is **Lyster Square.** To get to Main St., take a right after **Kellyville Park.** The **train station** is at the curve on **Railway St.,** which follows **Church St.** from Main St. (☎21303. Open daily 6:45am-10pm.) Trains run to Dublin and most points south (1hr.; 11-13 per day, Su 6 per day; €14.60). **Bus Éireann** stops on Lawlor Ave. on its way to Dublin (1½hr., 13 per day, €7.80). **Rapid Express** (☎067 26266) also serves Carlow (2 per day) and Dublin (5-6 per day) from Lawlor Ave. Super-friendly Liz at the **tourist office** in Lyster Sq. has tons of info on the area. (☎21178. Open June-Sept. M-Sa 9:30am-2pm and 3-5:30pm, Oct.-May closed Sa.) **AIB** (☎21349) graces Lawlor Ave. with an **ATM,** as does the **Bank of Ireland.** (☎21414. Open M-F 10am-4pm, Th until 5pm.) The **library** offers **Internet access.** (☎22333. €2.50 per 30min.) The regional **post office** is inside the shopping center on Lawlor Ave. (☎74220. Open M and W-F 9am-5:30pm, Tu 9:30am-5:30pm, Sa 10am-1pm and 2-5pm.)

Affordable accommodations in Portlaoise are limited. **Donoghue's B&B ❸,** 1 Kellyville Park, is in a beautifully kept house with breathtaking flower gardens. (☎21353. Singles €38; doubles €60, with bath €65.) **No. 8 Kellyville ❹** at, of all places, 8 Kellyville Park, offers basic and rather small rooms on the far side of cheap—must be the old-fashioned coverlets. (☎22774. Private carpark. Singles €44; doubles €63.50.) If you've had enough with affordability and just want luxury, try to book a room at **Ivyleigh ❺**, on Bank Pl. near the train station. Chandeliers glisten in the dining and sitting rooms in this historic house that dates back to 1850. (☎22081. Singles €70; doubles €105.) For groceries, head to **Tesco,** inside the mall on Lawlor Ave. (☎21730. Open M-Tu and Sa 9am-7pm, W-F 9am-9pm, Su noon-6pm.) Dinner options are limited, but competing Indian and Chinese restaurants on Main St. offer an ethnic flavor. Local favorite **Jim's Kitchen ❷,** in Hynes Sq. off Main St., serves the best meals in town; too bad it's only open until 5:30pm. A great selection of salads complements the mains, which start at €8.25. (☎62061. Open M-Sa 9am-5:30pm.) In addition to plentiful pubbly-grubbly options, brilliant coffee and a touch of class percolate at the **Cafe Latte** branch in the sparkling and fabulous **Dunamaise Arts Centre.** The cafe offers delectable lunches; the Arts Centre is home to a well-designed 250-seat theater. (☎63355. Cafe open M-F 9:30am-5:30pm, Sa 9:30am-1pm and 2-5pm. **Internet access** €2.50 per 30min.)

DAYTRIP FROM PORTLAOISE: EMO COURT AND GARDEN.

About 4 mi. out the N7 toward Dublin. ☎0502 26573. Open mid-June to Sept. M-Sa 10:30am-5pm, Su 10:30am-6pm. Court admission by guided tour only. Tours every hr. €2.50. Gardens open during daylight hours for free; tours given July-Aug. Su at 3pm.

With panoramic views of the **Slieve Bloom Mountains** and beautiful gardens out back, **Emo Court** is one of James Gandon's finer creations. Famous for his work on the Four Courts and Custom House in Dublin, Gandon designed the house in the 1780s for the first Earl of Portarlington. Work progressed somewhat slowly, however, and Emo Court wasn't completed for nearly 84 years. Gandon's obsession with perfection and fetish for symmetry can be seen throughout the house—in the foyer, two of the four stately doors are for decoration only. The house was originally set on 11,500 acres of land, but the Irish Land Commission bought it in 1920 and divvied it up, selling the house to the Jesuits in 1929 for use as a student-priest seminary. After dismantling several of the rooms, including the spectacular rotunda with its extremely detailed carved wood floor, the Jesuits sold the house to the government in 1969; in the mid-1990s the Heritage Foundation dutifully rebuilt the floor and patched together the rest of the house for visitors to enjoy.

SOUTHEAST IRELAND

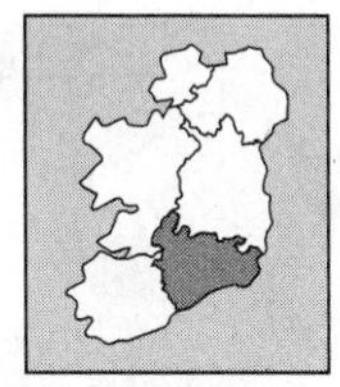

A power base for the Vikings and then for the Normans, this region has town and street names that ring of the Norse or Anglo-Saxon, rather than the Gaelic. The Southeast's most fruitful tourist attractions are its beaches, which draw native admirers to the coastline stretching from Kilmore Quay to tidy Ardmore. Kilkenny is a charismatic town, packed with historic sights and convenient to many of the region's finest attractions, while Waterford has resources, nightlife, and the grit of a real city. Cashel boasts a superbly preserved castle and cathedral complex perched on a giant rock; Fethard and Carrick-on-Suir are tiny enclaves of medieval charm. Continue your hunt for raging nightlife in Wexford, Carlow, and Waterford; the daylight hours are most enjoyably spent exploring the pretty paths through Glendalough, the Wicklow Mountains, Enniscorthy, and Wexford. The region is most easily seen by automobile and best seen by bicycle, but buses and trains make most of the cities and towns reachable for the wheel-less.

COUNTIES KILKENNY AND CARLOW

Northwest of Counties Wexford and Waterford and southwest of Dublinopolis, Counties Kilkenny and Carlow consist of lightly populated hills, small farming villages, and scattered medieval ruins. The medieval city of Kilkenny, a popular destination for both international tourists and the young Irish, is the bustling exception to the seemingly endless string of provincial towns. The town of Carlow, though much smaller, manages to produce a fair buzz on weekend nights.

KILKENNY CITY (CILL CHAINNIGH) ☎056

In a sense, Kilkenny is like a miniature version of Dublin—it has its own river, a renowned medieval namesake castle, excellent shopping, a tremendous selection of pubs, fantastic *craic*, and its own brewery. What it doesn't have are Dublin's headaches: the traffic is bearable, everything is walkable, it's impossible to get lost, and the hordes of tourists go to the castle and then disappear.

The city cemented itself in the history books in 1172 when Strongbow built the first rendition of Kilkenny Castle to command the crossing of the River Nore. His son-in-law later replaced the original structure with sturdier stone and incorporated the town in 1204; today, the refurbished castle rakes in tourists from around the world. The town wall, part of which still stands today, once designated the border between "English Town," inside the gates and governed by the Normans, and "Irish Town," governed by the local bishop. The two governments were apt to quarrel, and Kilkenny's nickname, "the fighting cats," is garnered from their behavior (see **Entertainment,** below). Today, a casual walk down its handsome streets—

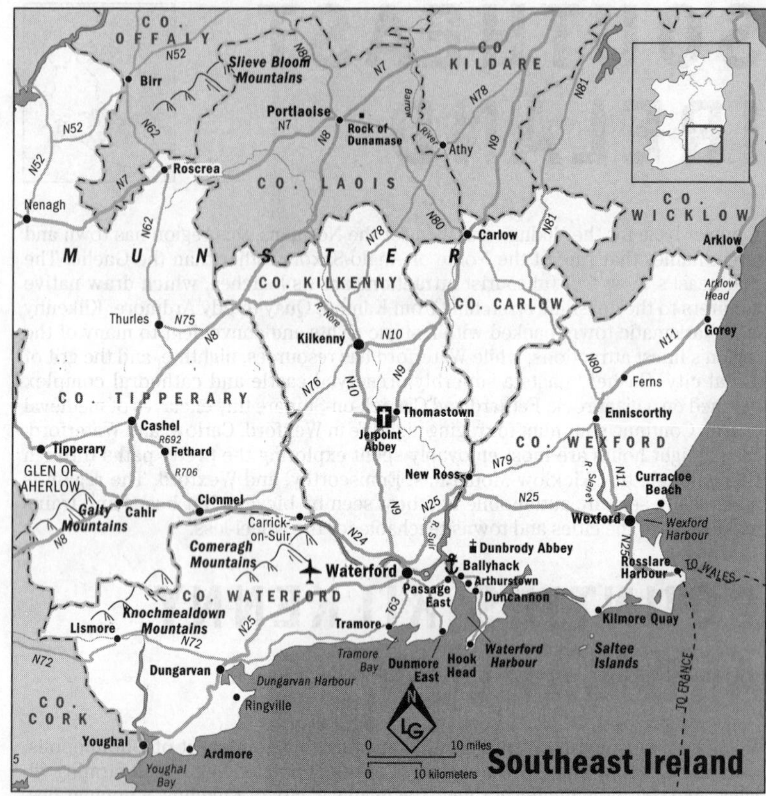

amidst churches, cafes, pubs, and restaurants—reveals Kilkenny's attempt to recreate its 15th-century charm; visitors to the town cannot help but notice the polished limestone adorning all the city's buildings. Storefronts have done away with tacky neon—even fast-food joints have hand-painted facades. These efforts are reaping their touristic reward: two Tidy Town awards are glinting on the mantel, and the city's population of 25,000 doubles during the high season.

TRANSPORTATION

Trains: Kilkenny MacDonagh Station, Dublin Rd. (☎22024). Open M-Sa 7am-8:15pm, Su 9am-1pm and 2:45-9pm. Always staffed, though the ticket window is open only at departure time. Kilkenny is on the main **Dublin-Waterford** rail route (3-5 per day). Trains to: **Dublin** (2hr.); **Thomastown** (15min.); **Waterford** (45min.). Connections to the west can be made at **Kildare Station,** 1hr. north on the Dublin-Waterford line.

Buses: Kilkenny Station, Dublin Rd. (☎64933 or 051 879 000), as well as a stop in the city center at **The Tea Shop,** Patrick St.; buy tickets at either location. Buses to: **Clonmel** (1¼hr., 6 per day, €6); **Cork** (3hr.; M-Sa 3 per day, Su 2 per day; €15.20); **Dublin** (2hr., 5-6 per day, €9); **Galway** via **Athlone** or **Clonmel** (5hr.; M-Sa 5 per day, Su 3 per day; €19); **Limerick** via **Clonmel** (2½hr.; M-Sa 5 per day, Su 1 per day; €13.30); **Rosslare Harbour** via **Waterford** (2hr.; M-Sa 5-6 per day, Su 3 per day; €7);

ACCOMMODATIONS
The Bailey & The Witness Box, **22**
Bregagh B&B, **3**
Daly's B&B, **12**
Demsey's B&B, **21**
Foulksrath Castle Hostel, **1**
The Kilford Hotel, **9**
Kilkenny B&B, **2**
Kilkenny Tourist Hostel (IHH), **4**

FOOD
Dunnes Supermarket, **17**
Italian Connection, **5**
La Creperie, **11**
Langton's, **8**
Lautrec's, **16**
M.L. Dore, **19**
Pordylo's, **18**
Ristorante Rinuccini, **13**
The Tea Shop, **14**
The White Oak, **7**

SERVICES
Brett's Laundrette, **6**
J.J. Wall Cycle, **10**
The Laundry Basket, **20**

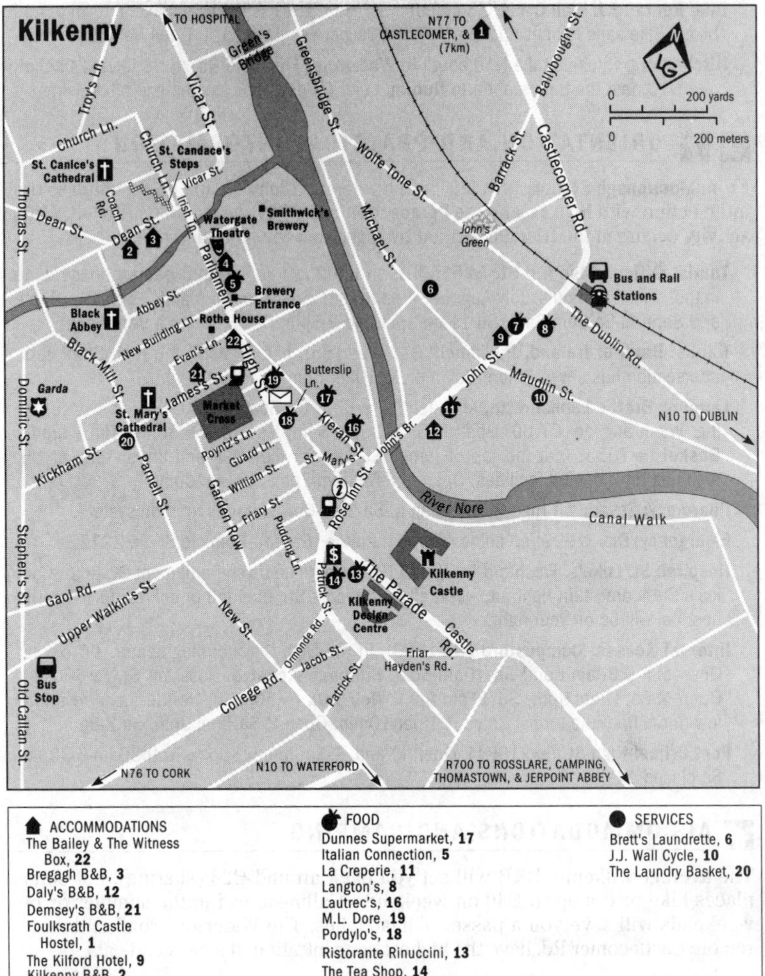

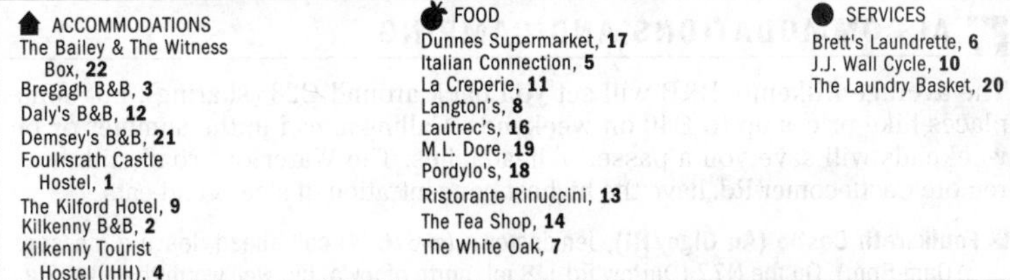

Waterford (1½hr.; M-Sa 2 per day, Su 1 per day; €6.35). **Buggy's Coaches** (☎41264) run from **Kilkenny** to **Ballyragget** (30min., M-Sa 2 per day) and **Castlecomer** (15min., M-Sa 2 per day, €1.30) with stops at the **An Óige hostel** (15min.) and **Dunmore Cave** (20min.). Buggy's also runs **local bus tours. J.J. Kavanagh's Rapid Express** (☎31106) has prices that beat Bus Éireann's (Dublin: M-Sa 4 per day, Su 2 per day; €5.70).

Taxi: All companies have a €5.10 min. charge, plus an additional €1.50 per mi. after 3-4 mi. **O'Brien's Cabs** (☎61333); **Kevin Barry** (☎63017); **Kilkenny Cabs** (☎52000). **Castle Cabs** (☎61188) also **stores luggage** for €1.30 per day.

Car Rental: Barry Pender, Dublin Rd. (☎65777 or 63839). 23+. Compact €63.50 per day, €317.40 per wk. Open M-F 9am-5:30pm, Sa 9am-1pm.

Bike Rental: J.J. Wall Cycle, 88 Maudlin St. (☎21236), is the only place in town to rent bikes. Bike sans helmet €12 per day or €65 per wk. ID deposit. Open M-Sa 9am-6pm.

Hitchhiking: Hitchers take N10 south to **Waterford,** Freshford Rd. to N8 toward **Cashel,** and N10 past the train station to **Dublin.** *Let's Go* does not recommend hitchhiking.

ORIENTATION AND PRACTICAL INFORMATION

From **MacDonagh Station,** turn left onto burgeoning **John St.** and go downhill to the intersection with **High St.** and **the Parade,** dominated by the castle on the left. Most activity occurs in the triangle formed by **High, Rose Inn,** and **Kieran St.**

Tourist Office: Rose Inn St. (☎51500), on the 2nd fl. of a 1525 pauper house. Free maps. "Flexible" hours. July-Aug. M-Sa 9am-7pm, Su 11am-1pm and 2-5pm; Apr.-June and Sept. M-Sa 9am-6pm, Su 11am-1pm and 2-5pm; Oct.-Mar. M-Sa 9am-5pm.

Banks: Bank of Ireland, Parliament St. (☎21155), has an **ATM**; the High St./Parade intersection has several more. All open M 10am-5pm, Tu-F 10am-4pm.

Laundry: Brett's Launderette, Michael St. (☎63200). Soap €1.30. No self-service drying. Wash and dry €7.60. Open M-Sa 8:30am-8pm; last wash 6:30pm. **The Laundry Basket** (☎70355), at the top of James St. Full service wash and dry starting at €5. Also has dry-cleaning facilities. Open M-F 8:30am-7pm, Sa 9am-6pm.

Pharmacy: Several on High St. All open M-Sa 9am-6pm; Sunday rotation system.

Emergency: Dial ☎999; no coins required. **Police** (*Garda*): Dominic St. (☎22222).

Hospital: St. Luke's, Freshford Rd. (☎51133). Continue down Parliament St. to St. Canice's Cathedral, turn right and veer left onto Vicars St., then left onto Freshford Rd. The hospital will be on your right.

Internet Access: Compustore (☎71200), in the High St. shopping center. €6 per hr. Open M-F 9:30am-6pm, Sa 10am-6pm. **Kilkenny e.centre,** Rose Inn St. (☎60093). Open M-Sa 10am-9pm, Su 11am-8pm. **Web Talk** (☎50366), beside e.centre and a few doors from the tourist office. €1 per 10min. Open M-Sa 9am-9pm, Su 2-8pm.

Post Office: High St. (☎21891). Open M and W-Sa 9am-5:30pm, Tu 9:30am-5:30pm, Sa closed 1-2pm.

ACCOMMODATIONS AND CAMPING

The average Kilkenny B&B will set you back around €28 (sharing), but some places hike prices up to €40 on weekends. Calling ahead in the summer or on weekends will save you a passel o' headaches. The Waterford road and more remote Castlecomer Rd. have the highest concentration of sleeps-and-eats.

Foulksrath Castle (An Óige/HI), Jenkinstown (☎67674; call ahead, leave a message 10am-5pm). On the N77 (Durrow Rd.), 8 mi. north of town, but well worth the hike. Turn right at signs for Connahy; the hostel is ¼ mi. down on the left. Buggy's Buses run from the Parade M-Sa twice a day (20min., call hostel for times, €2). Housed in a 15th-century castle, Foulksrath is literally a royal accommodation. Grand views from the roof, a common room with a fireplace, and paintings by the wonderful and artistic warden make up for the less-than-great bathrooms. Dorms €12-14; under 16 €1 less. ❶

Kilkenny Tourist Hostel (IHH), 35 Parliament St. (☎63541). Near all the popular pubs and next to Smithwick's Brewery. Brightly colored rooms brim with activity: people bustle about in the kitchen, lounge on couches, and sip Guinness on the front steps. Fun, and in a great location. Great town info posted in the front hall. Non-smoking. Kitchen with microwave open 7am-11pm. Laundry €5. Check-out 10am. 6- to 8-bed dorms €12-13; 4-bed €13.50-14.50. Doubles €31-33. ❶

Demsey's B&B, 26 James's St. (☎21954). A little old house by the Superquinn supermarket, off High St. Delightful proprietors rent out spacious, well-decorated, TV-blessed rooms. Parking €1 per night. Singles €28-30; doubles with bath €60-64. ❸

The Bailey, 13 Parliament St. (☎64337). Excellent B&B rooms located above and beside the Witness Box pub (see **Pubs,** below). Convenient, if a bit loud during music sessions below. €30 per person. ❸

Bregagh House B&B, Dean St. (☎22315), the first B&B on the left as you turn off High St. Clean rooms, all with bath, handsome wood furniture, and firm beds. Tolerable television room. Singles €40-46; doubles €64-80. ❸

Daly's B&B, 82 Johns St. (☎62866). Immaculate and nondescript rooms. Singles €38; doubles €64. Slightly reduced rates in the off season. ❸

Kilkenny B&B, Dean St. (☎64040). In operation for 33 years with an eccentric owner and basic, clean rooms. Rates vary; higher on weekends and bank holidays. Singles about €40; shared rooms €20-34 per person. ❸

The Kilford Arms Hotel, John St. (☎61018; www.travel-ireland.com/irl/kilford.htm). New hotel between Ó'Faolaín's bar and the White Oak restaurant (see **Food** and **Pubs,** below). Nice rooms, all with bath. Check out the Bengal tiger in the lobby. F-Sa singles €70; doubles €120. Su-Th €40/€70. ❺

Nore Valley Park (☎27229 or 27748). 7 mi. south of Kilkenny between Bennetsbridge and Stonyford, marked from town. Take the New Ross road (R700) to Bennetsbridge; take the signposted right just before the bridge. A class act, with hot showers, TV room, and a play-area for the kiddies. Crazy golf course (€2), peddle go carts (€1.50), picnic and barbecue areas. Wheelchair-accessible. Open Mar.-Oct. Backpackers €5; 2-person tent €11. Laundry €5.70. ❶

Tree Grove Caravan and Camping Park (☎70302). 1 mi. past the castle on the New Ross road (R700). 2-person tent €12. Free showers. ❶

FOOD

Dunnes Supermarket, Kieran St., sells housewares and food. (☎61655. Open M-Tu and Sa 8:30am-7pm, W-F 8:30am-10pm, Su 10am-6pm.) **Superquinn,** in the Market Cross shopping center off High St., has a slightly smaller selection. (☎52444. Open M-Tu and Sa 9am-7pm, W-F 9am-9pm.) Everything in Kilkenny's restaurants is great except the prices, which all hover somewhere in the lower stratosphere. Below are some reasonable options; otherwise, hit the pubs.

Pordylo's, Butterslip Ln. (☎70660), between Kieran and High St. One of the best eateries on the island. Zesty dinners (€10-23) from across the globe, many of which love vegetarians. Reservations recommended. Open daily 6-11pm. ❹

La Creperie, 80 John St. Sweet and savory crepes and sandwiches, all for a great price (crepes €3.60-5.10, sandwiches €2.45-4.50). Open M-F 10am-7:30pm, Sa 10am-8:30pm, Su 11am-6:30pm. ❶

Langton's, 69 John St. (☎65123). The eccentric owner has earned a gaggle of awards for his ever-changing highbrow restaurant. Full lunch menu with an Irish twist (€8-11) served daily 12:30-3:30pm; sophisticated dinner (€19-23) 6-10:30pm. ❹

Ristorante Rinuccini, 1 the Parade (☎61575), opposite the castle. Couples enjoy authentic Italian delights and romantic music in this glittering first-rate establishment. Lunch (€8-11) served noon-2:30pm; dinner (€15-19) served 6-10:30pm. ❹

The Tea Shop, Patrick St. (☎70051). An excellent little cafe in the city center where you can grab tasty breakfasts (€6) or sip herbal teas (€1.40) before catching the bus outside. Open M-F 8am-6pm, Sa 8am-5:30pm. ❷

Italian Connection, 38 Parliament St. (☎64225). Decked out in mahogany and carnations, and but not too fancy-shmancy. Lunch specials (€7.50-8.25) served noon-3pm. Dinner €11.50-19. Open daily noon-11pm. ❸

Lautrec's, 9 Kieran St. (☎62720). Loosen your belt and your wallet for good, quick Italian dinners. Open Su-Th 5:30-10pm, F-Sa 5:30-11pm. ❸

M.L. Dore, High St. (☎63374). Entrance on High and Kieran St. Sandwiches for €3.95 and light mains for €8.85-10.15, served in a clean, fresh cafe atmosphere. Open M-Sa 8am-10pm, Su 8am-9pm. ❷

The White Oak, John St. (☎61018). Traditional Irish food served in a glowing orange room. The interior is decked out with bizarre carved wooden chairs and oak branches attached to the ceiling. Weekend dinners €22 per person, weekdays €15. ❹

PUBS

Kilkenny, "The Marble City," is also known as the "Oasis of Ireland"—its watering holes have a range of live music on most nights, especially in the summer. *Let's Go* has picked twenty of the best and now proudly presents the very first **Kilkenny Pub Crawl.** We suggest starting your crawl at either the top of John St. or the end of Parliament St.—the former if you want to wind the night down slowly, the latter if you

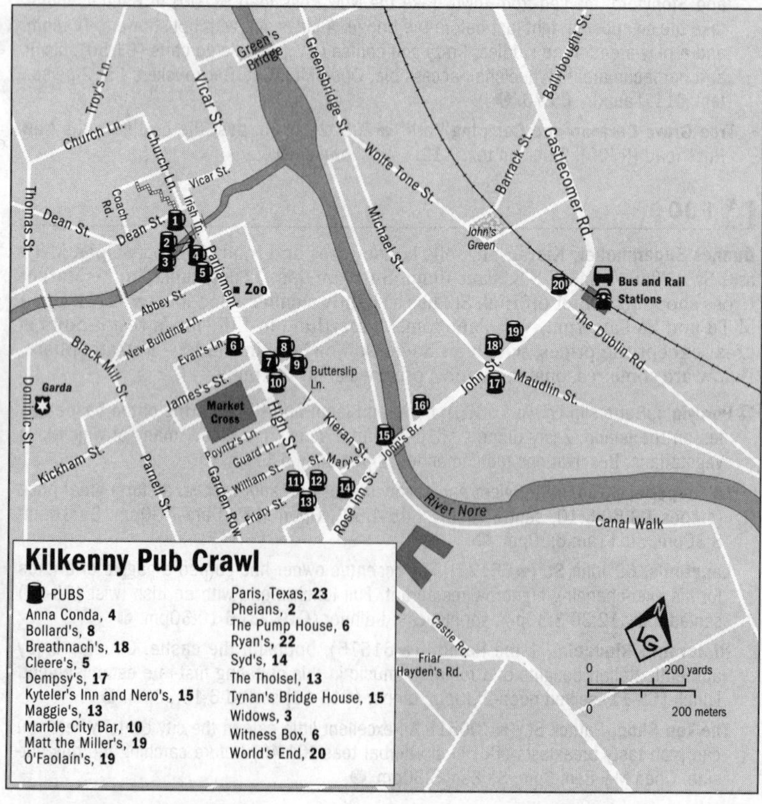

need a late-night fix and want to keep throwing down the Smithwick's well into the night. Alternatively, you could start at 3pm in the **Smithwick's Brewery** and begin your buzz on the house (tickets required, see **Sights** below).

Ó'Faolaíns, John St. (☎61018). Throbbing new bar with 3 floors, a 25 ft. high ceiling, and a rebuilt Welsh church crafted into the walls. Late bar (W-Sa until 2:30am, Su-M until 2am) and dance club (cover €5-10) make for a great place to end the night.

World's End, 34 John St. (☎22302). A drinking man's pub, hardcore with music W-Su.

Breathnach's Steak and Ale House, John St. (☎56737). Large, multi-floor pub with a few bars and a terrific grill (steaks €12.60-15.90).

Dempsey's, 61 John St. (☎21543). Examine the musty tomes in the big bookcase on the wall. This is as traditional as it gets.

Matt the Miller's, 1 John St. (☎61696), at the bridge. Huge, thronged, and magnetic. Pilgrims are sucked in and forced to dance to silly Europop or a bizarre trad/reggae mix. M rock music and late bar until 2am; cover €5. Th and Sa DJ; Tu and F bands.

Tynan's Bridge House Bar (☎21291), just around the corner from the tourist office, on the river. Double award-winning and the most original bar in Kilkenny. Extremely tiny, but terrific atmosphere.

Syd's, 25 Rose Inn St. (☎22134), just down from the tourist office. One of the few pubs in town with a snooker table (€1 per game).

The Tholsel, 8 High St. (☎21652). "Tholsel" means "house of taxes," but the only thing taxed is your eyesight, thanks to the psychedelic stained-glass window in the back.

Paris, Texas, High St. (☎61822). Cool Parisians crowd themselves in like cattle at this extremely popular bar; hipster cowpokes shimmy and smoke themselves a good time.

Ryan's, Friary St.(☎62281), just off High St. No frills, just a good crowd and a beer garden just past the rude bathroom signs. Th trad; Sa mongrel mix of trad, blues, and sweet, sweet soul.

Marble City Bar, 66 High St. (☎61143). Modern pub tucked in between High and Kieran St. Excellent meals including the "joint of the day" (usually stews or roasts) for €8.

Kyteler's Inn, Kieran St. (☎21064). The oldest pub in Kilkenny and the 1324 house of Alice Kyteler, Kilkenny's witch, whose husbands (all 4) had a knack for poisoning themselves on their 1st wedding anniversaries. The food and drink have since become safer. Trad fills the air twice a week. F-Su fiddle away the evening at **Nero's,** a nightclub that burns down the house. Cover €8-12. Open 11pm-2am.

Bollard's, 31-32 Kieran St. (☎21353). Run of the mill pub with a decent restaurant out back (dinner €10). Trad Tu and Th from 9:30pm.

Maggie's, Kieran St. (☎62273). Crowds bury themselves in this smoky wine cellar. Lunch (€7.30) served noon-2:30pm. Dinner €13-20. Tu-Th trad, rock on summer weekends. Cover €5-7.

The Witness Box, Parliament St. (☎64337), across the street from the Kilkenny Tourist Hostel and run by the owners of The Bailey (see **Accommodations,** above). Lots of local flavor and live music Th-M. Trad W.

The Pump House, 26 Parliament St. (☎63924). Remains a favorite among locals and hostelers. Loud, conveniently located, and packed. Ultra-hip upstairs enclave will make you wish you packed some Prada. M-Th summer trad, Su rock and blues.

Cleere's, 28 Parliament St. (☎62573). Thespians from the Watergate Theatre across the street converge here during intermission. A black-box theater in back hosts vivacious musical and theatrical acts (occasional cover up to €20). Trad M.

Widows, Parliament St. (☎52520). Find your future husband amongst the young crowd or in the Mexican restaurant upstairs (lunch Tu-F and Su; dinner Tu-Sa 6-10pm).

Phelans, Parliament St. (☎21647). In the same family for 130 years, this older man's pub has a 70s decor complete with glowing happy- and sad-face lights.

Anna Conda, Parliament St. (☎71657), near Cleere's. Outstanding trad fills the pub from the low ceilings in front to the high rafters in back. New beer garden overlooks the ducks on the Suir. M and F-Sa music. No cover.

SIGHTS

KILKENNY CASTLE. Although Kilkenny city is a sight in itself, 13th-century **Kilkenny Castle,** the Parade, is just plain and simply the bee's knees. It housed the Earls of Ormonde from the 1300s up through 1935, and many rooms have been restored to their former opulence. The 50 yd. **Long Galley,** a spectacle reminiscent of a Viking ship, displays portraits of English bigwigs, giant tapestries, and a beautiful Italian double fireplace. The basement houses the **Butler Gallery** and its modern art exhibits. You'll also find a **cafe** in the castle's kitchen, home of the castle's ghost. *(☎21450. Castle and gallery open June-Sept. daily 9:30am-7pm; Oct.-Mar. 10:30am-12:45pm and 2-5pm; Apr.-May 10:30am-5pm. Castle access by guided tour only. €4.40, students €2.)* The 52-acre **park** adjoining the castle provides excellent scenery for an afternoon jaunt. *(Open daily 10am-8:30pm. Free.)* Across the street, the internationally known **Kilkenny Design Centre** fills the castle's former stables with expensive Irish crafts. *(☎22118. Open Apr.-Dec. M-Sa 9am-6pm, Su 10am-6pm; Jan.-Mar. M-Sa 9am-6pm.)*

SMITHWICK'S BREWERY. Rumor has it that 14th-century monks, known to be a crafty bunch, once brewed a light ale in the **St. Francis Abbey** on Parliament St. Though the abbey is in ruins, their industry survives in the yard, at the **Smithwicks Brewery.** Commercial use started in 1710, making it the oldest brewery in Ireland—it has fifty years on its black cousin, although Guinness has the last laugh as it recently purchased Smithwick's Brewery (and, to add insult to injury, now brews Budweiser on site). Every day 50 free admission tickets are given out at the security guard station; take a right after the Watergate Theatre, and the gate is straight ahead. Collect your ticket and show up at 3pm outside the green doors on Parliament St. for an audio-visual tour, followed by **two free pints** in the private pub below the factory. *(☎21014. Tours given July-Aug. M-F.)*

ST. CANICE'S CATHEDRAL. Thirteenth-century St. Canice's sits up the hill off Dean St. The name "Kilkenny" itself is derived from the Irish *Cill Chainnigh,* meaning "Church of St. Canice." The 100 ft. **round tower** next to the cathedral was built in pre-Norman, pre-scaffolding times, and still stands tall on its 3 ft. foundation. With €2 and a bit of faith, you can climb the six steep ladders to a panoramic view of the town and its surroundings. *(☎64971. Open Easter-Sept. M-Sa 9am-1pm and 2-6pm, Su 2-6pm; Oct.-Easter M-Sa 10am-1pm and 2-4pm, Su 2-4pm. Donation requested.)*

THE BLACK ABBEY. Just off Abbey St., Black Abbey was founded in 1225 and got its name from the habits of its Dominican friars—outside, you'll see a row of coffins used to contain bodies struck by the Plague. Artifacts are routinely found buried around the grounds, most of which were originally hidden for fear of invaders. The heavy silence inside is probably due to the awe generated by the wall-size stained glass depicting the fifteen mysteries of the rosary. Gaze on the dark heights of nearby **St. Mary's Cathedral,** constructed during the Famine.

ROTHE HOUSE. Rothe House, Parliament St., was a Tudor merchant house when it was built in 1594, and now it's a small museum of local archaeological finds and Kilkennian curiosities. The dry, 15min. video and 1850-1990 period costumes are skippable, but the museum and house are worth the visit.*(☎22893. Open Apr-Oct. M-Sa 10:30am-5pm, Su 3-5pm; Nov.-Mar. M-Sa 1-5pm, Su 3-5pm. €3, students €2, children €1.)*

WALKING TOUR. If you're interested in Kilkennalia, including the down-and-dirty on folkloric tradition, take a **Tynan Walking Tour.** Besides spinning some animated yarns, the tour is the only way to see the **old city gaol.** Tours depart from the tourist office on Rose Inn St. *(☎65929 or 087 265 1745; www.tynantours.com. 1hr. tours Mar.-Oct. M-Sa 6 per day, Su 4 per day; Nov.-Feb. Tu-Sa 3 per day. €5, students and seniors €4.50.)*

ENTERTAINMENT

The tourist office provides a bi-monthly guide to the town's happenings; *The Kilkenny People* (€1.30) is a good newsstand source for arts and music listings. **The Watergate Theatre,** Parliament St., stages drama, dance, and opera year-round. (☎61674. Tickets €10-20, student discounts available. Box office open M-F 10am-7pm, Sa 2-6pm, Su 1hr. before curtain.) Each August, Kilkenny holds its **Arts Festival,** which has a daily program of theater, concerts, and readings by famous European and Irish artists. (☎52175. Event tickets up to €15.25; student and senior discounts vary by venue. Sold at the Eircom shop on Parliament St. or by phone.) The city's population increases by more than 10,000 when the **Cat Laughs** (☎63837); this **festival,** held the first weekend of June, features international comedy acts. The cat in question is the Kilkenny mascot of nursery rhyme fame: "There once were two cats from Kilkenny/ Each thought there was one cat too many/ So they fought and they fit/ And they scratched and they bit/ 'Til excepting their nails and the tips of their tails/ Instead of two cats there weren't any."

SPORTS AND ACTIVITIES

Activities in and around Kilkenny are plentiful, especially for outdoors enthusiasts. The **Kilkenny Anglers Club** (☎65220) can set you up with **fishing** on the Nore and sells permits to make it legal. If you'd prefer to paddle over the fish, call **Go with the Flow River Adventures** (☎087 252 9700) to **kayak** on the river Barrow. Those with an equestrian desire can choose from **Grange Equine Centre** (☎56205) for "half-day adventure trail blazing," **Kilkenny Top Flight Equestrian Centre** (☎22682) to ride along the banks of the Nore, or the pricier **Mount Juliet** (☎73044) for trail rides on a country estate. For a petrol-powered trip through the hills, call **Country ATVs** (☎33328) to hire a quad bike. The **Kilkenny Golf Course** (☎65400), out Castlecomer Rd., is an 18-hole championship course open to non-members. If you'd rather watch than participate, go see the "Fighting Cats" in a **hurling match** in Nowlan Park, near the train station (ticket info ☎65119; kilkenny.gaa.ie). In **Gowran Park** (☎26225), on the N9, **horseracing** thrills the fans.

DAYTRIPS FROM KILKENNY

THOMASTOWN AND JERPOINT ABBEY

***Bus Éireann** stops at **Jerpoint Inn** in **Thomastown** on its way from Waterford to Kilkenny (4-7per day). The folks at the Inn have a schedule for **Rapid Express** (☎31106), a private bus running between Dublin and Tramore. **Trains** run through Thomastown desperately seeking Dublin (M-Sa 5 per day; Su 3 per day) and Waterford (daily 4-5 per day). The **train station** is a 10min. walk out of town on Marshes Rd. Jerpoint Abbey: ☎24623. Open June-Sept. daily 9:30am-6:30pm; Oct. and Mar.-May 10am-5pm; Nov. 10am-4pm. €2.50.*

Thomastown, a tiny community on the Nore River south of Kilkenny, is the gateway to impressive **Jerpoint Abbey,** 1½ mi. away and a great afternoon trip from town. The strict Cistercian order founded Jerpoint in 1158. Though they stressed simplicity, somewhere along the line the monks cut loose and decorated their home with beautiful stone carvings of their favorite saints. The artistic trend caught on, and it seems that if it was made of stone, someone carved on it; virtually every pillar and wall is decorated with a figure. Tours discuss the life of medieval monks and give insights into the meanings behind much of the stonework and paintings. In town, at one end of Market St., rest the 13th-century remains of **Thomastown Church.** A trilogy of curiosities lie amongst the church's gravestones: an ancient ogham stone, a Celtic cross, and a weathered 13th-century effigy.

DUNMORE CAVE

*Buggy's Coaches (☎41264) stops at the Cave between Kilkenny and Castlecomer. From the drop-off point, the route is well signposted. (20min., M-Sa 8 per day, €2.50.) By **car,** take N78 (the Dublin-Castlecomer road) from Kilkenny; the turnoff for Dunmore is on the right after the split with N77 (Durrow Rd.). ☎67726. Open June-Sept. daily 9:30am-6:30pm; Oct.-Nov. and Mar.-May daily 9:30am-5:30pm; Dec.-Feb. Sa-Su and holidays 9:30am-5:30pm. Last admission 45min. before closing. €3.50, students €2.50.*

Six miles north of Kilkenny on the road to **Castlecomer,** the massive and eerie **Dunmore Cave** sulks underfoot. Known affectionately as "the darkest place in Ireland," the cave has a particularly strange history. Human bones recently unearthed from its limestone entrails show that 100 people died underground here in AD 928; whether the Vikings had anything to do with it is anyone's guess. A few years back, a couple of tourists who strayed outside the marked boundaries discovered a Viking stash of silver thread, coins, and other spoils, further confounding archeologists. 35min. tours, available on demand, point out all the important stalactites and stalagmites in the caves and accompany visitors up and down all 352 steps.

CARLOW TOWN (CEATHARLACH) ☎0503

The small, busy town of Carlow adorns the eastern side of the River Barrow on the N9 between Dublin and Waterford. Although you'd never guess it from the town's placid demeanor, in past centuries Carlow hosted several stunningly gruesome battles between Gael and Pale. During the 1798 Rebellion, 640 Irish insurgents were ambushed in the streets; a part of the gallows from which they were hanged is on display in the county museum. The rebels were buried across the River Barrow in the gravel pits of Graiguecullen (greg-KULL-en). Today's crowds have less of the insurgent flavor about them, in part, perhaps, because Carlow's surprisingly good nightlife offerings keep morale high. Raises the question: how many rebellions could have been avoided with the implementation of a decent pub crawl?

TRANSPORTATION. **Trains** run through Carlow from Dublin's Heuston Station on their way to Waterford (1¼hr.; M-Sa 5 per day, Su 3 per day; €15.20). The cheapest **buses** to Dublin depart from Doyle's, by the Shamrock D.I.Y.—you make it to the Custom House and back for as little as €5. **Bus Éireann** leaves from the corner of Barrack and Kennedy, in a little bus turnabout. Buses go to Athlone (2¼hr., 1 per day, €12.70), Dublin (1¾hr.; M-Sa 7 per day, Su 4 per day; €7.60), and Waterford (1¼hr.; M-Sa 7 per day, Su 6 per day; €7.60). **Rapid Express Coaches,** Barrack St. (☎43081 or 056 31106), run a Tramore-Waterford-Carlow-Dublin route (M-Sa 8-10 per day, Su 7-8 per day); they have timetables to a variety of Midland destinations at their office. For a **taxi,** call **Carlow Cab** (☎40000).

ORIENTATION AND PRACTICAL INFORMATION. From the train station, it's a 15min. walk to the center of town; head straight down **Railway Rd.,** turn left onto the **Dublin road,** and make another left at the Court House onto **College St.** The

tourist office is on College St., just off Tullow St. behind the public library. (☎31554. Open M-F 9am-1pm and 2-5pm, Sa 10am-5:30pm.) The **AIB** on Tullow St. offers a 24hr. **ATM** and a **bureau de change.** (☎31758. Open M 10am-5pm, Tu-F 10am-4pm.) For lovers of the **Internet** and the imperative, **Communicate Now** connects in the Carlow Shopping Centre between Tullow St. and Kennedy Ave. (☎43700. €1.50 per 10min., €6 per hr. Open M-W and Sa 10am-6pm, Th-F 10am-9pm.) The **post office** officiates post from the corner of Kennedy Ave. and Burrin St. (☎31773. Open M-Sa 9am-5:30pm, Tu open 9:30am.)

ACCOMMODATIONS, FOOD, AND PUBS. A stuffed otter in the hallway welcomes guests to the 200-year-old Georgian **Otterholt Riverside Lodge ❶**, a hostel near the banks of the River Barrow. It's half a mile from the center of town on the Kilkenny road; if you don't feel up to walking, the Kilkenny bus will stop there upon request. Saturday nights are popular, so reserve ahead. (☎30404. Laundry €5. Dorms €10-14; doubles €36. **Camping** €7.) The **Redsetter Guesthouse ❸** is at 14 Dublin St., next to the Royal Hotel in the center of town. Look no further to find that plush sitting room and those spacious, pedigreed bedrooms you've been dreaming of. (☎41848. Parking available. Singles €35, with bath €40; doubles €60-65.) Pricier, but in the heart of the entertainment center of town, **Dinn Rí ❹** has nice hotel rooms, and a stay gets you into the nearby **nightclub** (see below) for free. (☎33111. Singles €47, not available Sa; doubles €90-110; triples €115-150.)

It's a bird, it's a plane, no, it's **Superquinn,** in the Carlow Shopping Centre. (☎30077. Open M-Tu and Sa 8:30am-7pm, W-F 8:30am-9pm, Su noon-6pm.) Quinn faces off with **SuperValu** on Tullow St. for grocery supremacy. (☎31263. Open M-W 9am-7pm, Th-F 9am-9pm, Sa 9am-6pm, Su noon-6pm.) **La Napoletana ❷**, 63 Tullow St., serves piles of pasta (€8-12) at delicious prices. (☎40951. Open daily noon-3pm and 5:30-11pm.) Do it cafeteria-style at **Bradbury's** (a.k.a. **Strada**) **❷**, 144 Tullow St., where lunchtime mains are €6-7. (☎40366. Open M-Sa 8:30am-6pm.) **Sambodino's ❶**, on Tullow St., calls themselves "the sandwich specialists," and they're not kidding—five bread choices and lots of fillings make the difference. (☎34389. Sandwiches €2-3. Open M-Sa 8:30am-5pm.) **Teach Dolmain ❷** (CHOCK DOL-men), 76 Tullow St., has plates *teach*-full of award-winning grub. (☎30911. Lunch €7; dinner €9-17. Open daily noon-9pm.)

The hipsters of Carlow visit the **Dinn Rí,** an über-pub spanning the entire block between Tullow St. and Kennedy Ave., attached to the hotel of the same name (see **Accommodations,** above). It's been named Black and White Pub of the Year three of the past four years, and has plenty of seats to go around for the Sunday trad sessions. Its two nightclubs combine on Saturday nights, admitting a crowd larger than the populations of most Irish towns. Of the two, **The Foundry** is rumored to be the coolest, but **The Towers** has the live music. (☎33111. Expansive carvery lunch €6.65-7.75 noon-2:30pm. Nightclub open F-Su until 2:30am. Cover F and Su €5, Sa €10.) Carlow grooves to live rock and tributes at the surprisingly large **Scragg's Alley,** 12 Tullow St. (☎42233. Music on weekends.) Most Thursday nights, the music continues upstairs at the **Nexus** nightclub. **Tully's,** 149 Tullow St., pulls in the young and stylish (☎31862; F-Sa DJ).

SIGHTS AND FESTIVALS. In the middle of a field 2½ mi. from Carlow lies the **Brownshill Dolmen.** Marking a 6000-year-old burial site, the granite capstone is, well, big. "Big" meaning the largest of its kind in Europe, tipping the scales at no fewer than 150 tons. No one has a clue how those brawny neolithic lads managed to heft it up there, though *Let's Go* is not ruling out the possibility of intergalactic assistance. Dolmen-seekers: follow Tullow St. through the traffic light and keep going straight until the roundabout pointing to Dublin. Go left, then right at the next roundabout and follow the signs. **Carlow Castle** hunkers down behind the storefronts on Castle St.; it's in serious disrepair but visitors can still walk around its base and peer at the rubble. The castle's current condition can be blamed on one Dr. Middleton, who required larger windows and thinner walls. To make his modifications, he used the delicate touch of Acme dynamite. The good doctor, incidentally, was trying to make the castle into an insane asylum.

The best time to visit Carlow is during June, when the town hosts **Éigse** (AIG-sha, "gathering"), a ten-day festival of the arts. The gifted and talented from all over Ireland gather to present visual, musical, and theatrical works; only some events require tickets. For more information, check with the festival office on College St. (☎40491; www.itc-carlow.ie/eigse).

COUNTY TIPPERARY

In southern Tipperary, the towns of Clonmel, Cahir, and Cashel rest amid a sprawl of idyllic countryside and medieval ruins. The north of the county is far from the beaten tourist track, and for good reason: this fertile region has more spud farmers than visitors centers. South of the Cahir-Cashel-Tipperary triangle stretch the Comeragh, Galty, and Knockmealdown Mountains. Lismore, though located in Co. Waterford, is covered here in Co. Tipperary with the Knockmealdowns.

TIPPERARY TOWN (THIOBRAID ARANN) ☎062

Goodbye Piccadilly,
Farewell Leicester Square!
It's a long long way to Tipperary
But my heart lies there.

Tipperary is perhaps less enchanting for today's travelers than this WWI marching song would imply. In fact, the tune was written in 1912 by an Englishman who had never been to Tipperary. "Tipp Town," as it's affectionately known, is primarily a market town for the fertile Golden Vale farming region. Compared with the surrounding hills and the **Glen of Aherlow** to the south, Tipp Town doesn't have a particularly star-studded collection of sights. However, this doesn't stop happy Tippers from singing its praises each July during the **Pride of Tipperary Festival,** which features bands, sporting events, and old-fashioned fun.

Buses make the trip from Tipp's **Abbey St.** to Limerick (M-Th and Sa 7 per day, F 8 per day, Su 6 per day). The **tourist office,** on Mitchell St. in the Excel Centre, a large orange building that also houses the **Interpretive Centre** and a cineplex, is a useful resource for trips into the Glen and the nearby mountains. Glen of Aherlow trail maps go for €1. (☎51457; www.tipperary.ie. **Internet access** €1 per 15min. Entrance to the interpretive center €3. Open M-Sa 9:30am-5:30pm.) **AIB** is on Main St., along with its arch-rival **Bank of Ireland.** Each offers the convenience of an **ATM.** (Both open M-F 10am-4pm, Th until 5pm.) The **library** on Davis St. provides one free hour per day of **Internet access**—call or stop by in advance to put yourself on the waiting list. (☎51761. Open Tu and F-Sa 10am-1pm and 2-5:30pm, W-Th 2-5:30pm and 6:30-8:30pm.) The **post office** is on Davis St. (☎51190. Open M and W-F 9am-5:30pm, Tu 9:30am-5:30pm, Sa 9am-1pm and 2-5:30pm.)

The Royal Hotel ❸, on Bridge St., has adequate hotel rooms at a reasonable price, all with phone, TV, and bath. (☎33244. €40 per person.) The attached disco, **Hunters,** fires on until 2am. The aptly named **Central House B&B ❸,** 45 Main St., has a welcoming owner and free bike lockup. (☎51117. Singles €38; doubles €60.) Other B&Bs are on **Emly Rd.,** about ½ mi. west of town off Main St. Tipp features a full-scale **SuperValu** on Main St. (☎51901. Open M-F 8am-9pm, Sa 8am-7pm, Su

9am-6pm.) For simple bistro fare, you're sure to get lucky at the bright and colorful **Shamrog ❸,** Davis St., which dishes out everything from sandwiches to steaks. (☎82847. Lunch €8-12, dinner €9-15. Open M-Th 9am-5:30pm, F-Sa 9am-8:45pm, Su 12:30-7:45pm.) For a bit more elegance, try the **The Brown Trout ❸** on Bridge St., one block down from Main St., where a framed fish tank on the wall entertains diners. (☎51912. Dinner €10-14. Open daily 12:30-3pm and 6-9:30pm.) For a family-friendly, home-cooked meal, head to **Cranley's ❷,** 7 St. Michael's St. (☎33917. Burgers and lasagna €7-8. Open M-F 8am-6pm, Sa 9am-6pm.) Enjoy how sweet it is to watch others sweat and grunt while you sit back with your Guinness and watch the game on the big screen at **Tony Lowry's,** 46 Main St., next to Central House B&B. (☎52774. Lunch served noon-3pm. Live music Th nights.) If you think you're a better athlete than any up on the telly, stumble across the road to **T.C. Ryan's** to prove it with a game of pool or darts. When in doubt, another pint is sure to correct your aim. (☎51465. Su live country-western music. **Internet access** €1 per 12min.)

CASHEL (CAISEAL MUMHAN) ☎062

The town of Cashel lies tucked between a series of mountain ranges on the N8, 12 mi. east of Tipp Town. Legend has it that the devil furiously hurled a rock from high above the Tipperary plains when he discovered a church was being built in the town. The assault failed to thwart the plucky citizens, and today the town sprawls defiantly at the base of the 300 ft. Rock of Cashel. With a splendid hostel and a convenient location, Cashel is as fitting a base for the backpacker as it was for the medieval religious orders that scattered the region with ruins.

TRANSPORTATION AND PRACTICAL INFORMATION. All but one of Cashel's **buses** leave from the Bake House on Main St., across from the tourist office; the Dublin bus departs from Rafferty's Travel a few doors down. **Bus Éireann** (☎62121) serves: Cahir (15min., 6 per day, €3.35); Cork (1½hr., 6 per day, €12); Dublin (3hr., 6 per day, €15); Limerick (1hr., 5 per day, €12). **Main St.** is where it's at. All of it, except the rock. Cashel's **tourist office** splits rent with the **heritage center** in the City Hall on Main St. (☎61333. Open July-Aug. M-Sa 9:15am-6pm, Su depending on demand; Apr.-June and Sept. M-Sa 9:15am-6pm.) **McInerney's,** 3 doors from the SuperValu, **rents bikes.** (☎61225. €9 per day, €35 per wk. Open M-Tu and Th-Sa 9:30am-6pm.) The **AIB** has an **ATM.** (Open M-F 10am-12:30pm and 1:30-4pm, Th until 5pm.) The **post office** rocks the Cashel on Main St. (☎61418. Open M-F 9am-1pm and 2-5:30pm, Sa 9am-1pm.)

ACCOMMODATIONS AND CAMPING. A 5min. walk from Cashel on Dundrum Rd., and just a few hundred yards from the ruins of Hore Abbey, lies the stunning **O'Brien's Farm House Hostel ❶.** O'Brien's is deserving of several gold stars for its incredible view of the Rock, cheerful rooms, and extremely courteous hosts. (☎61003. Full-service laundry €8-10. Dorms €13-15; doubles €40-45. **Camping** €6; car and 5 adults €15.) Just steps from the Rock in a quiet residential neighborhood on Dominic St., you'll find a bargain at the quaint **Rockville House ❸.** (☎61760. Singles €38; shared rooms €25 per person.) **Rahard Lodge ❸,** ¾ mi. up Dualla Rd., is a modern farmhouse with tourist-attracting gardens. (☎61052. Singles €38; doubles €60.) **Thornbrook House ❸,** less than 1 mi. up Dualla Rd., shimmers with elegant chandeliers and sparkling bathrooms. All rooms have tea and coffee, TV, and hair dryer. (☎62388. Singles €40, with bath €50; doubles €55.)

FOOD AND PUBS. SuperValu has a large selection of groceries at its Main St. location. (☎61555; open M-Sa 8am-9pm, Su 8am-6pm). While waiting for the bus, enjoy decadent sweets at **The Bake House ❶,** across from the tourist office. Coffee and light meals are served in pseudo-elegance upstairs. (☎61680. Open M-Sa 8am-

7pm, Su 9am-6pm.) The superior pubmunch (€7) at **Ó'Suilleabáin ❷** (O'Sullivan's), Main St., makes it the local lunchtime haunt. (☎61858. Food served M-Sa noon-2:30pm.) You'll find inexpensive soup and sandwiches at **Spearman ❶,** behind Main St., near the tourist office. (☎61143. Open daily 12:30-2:30pm and 6-9pm.) **Pasta Milano ❸,** on Lady's Well St., has loads of affordable cuisine and flavorful wines to complement an outgoing Italian vibe. (☎62729. Pasta and pizza €8-15. Open daily 11:30am-midnight.)

Cashel's pub crawl is a straight shot down Main St. Start the night at **Feehan's** (☎61929), where the atmosphere is timeless. Head left out the back door to get to **Moor Lane Tavern** (☎62080), where you can shoot some darts, play snooker, or bust a move; a DJ spins Thursday through Sunday. If the stars are out, move next door to the multi-level beer garden at wheelchair-accessible **Mikey Ryan's** (☎61431). Cross over Main St. for some singing, joke-telling *craic* at **Davern's** (☎61121; music M and W), and finally, end the night down the street at **Dowling's,** where bartenders make it their one and only business to pour the best pint in town.

SIGHTS. Smart visitors head to the **Heritage Center,** in the same building as the tourist office on Main St., before making the trek to **The Rock of Cashel** (see below). The center features temporary exhibits and permanent installations such as "The Rock: From the 4th to 11th Century" and its much-anticipated sequel, "The Rock: 12th-18th Century." (☎62511. Open May-Sept. daily 9:30am-5:30pm; Oct.-Apr. M-F 9:30am-5:30pm. Free.) The **GPA-Bolton Library,** John St., displays a musty collection of books and silver that once belonged to Theophilus Bolton, an Anglican archbishop of Cashel. The library harbors ecclesiastical texts and rare manuscripts, including a 1550 edition of Machiavelli's *Il Principe*, the first English translation of *Don Quixote*, and what is (locally) reputed to be the **smallest book in the world.** (☎61944. Open Mar.-Oct. Tu-Sa 9:30am-5:30pm, Su 12:30-5:30pm; Nov.-Feb. M-F 9:30am-5:30pm. Tours M-Sa 9:45am-4:45pm, Su 12:45-4:45pm. €2; students, seniors, and children €1.50.) The internationally-acclaimed **Brú Ború Heritage Centre,** at the base of the Rock, hosts wonderful traditional music and dance. Afterwards, the musicians invite the audience to the bar for a round of informal trad. (☎61122. Performances mid-June to mid-Sept. Tu-Sa at 9pm. €13, with dinner €35.) In the town of **Golden,** 5 mi. west of Cashel on the Tipperary road, stand the ruins of lovely **Althassel Abbey,** a 12th-century Augustinian priory founded by the inappropriately-hued Red Earl of Dunster.

MCCARTHY'S...HOTEL?

The outrageously unique McCarthy's Hotel in Fethard was established by Richard McCarthy in the 1850's as a hotel, restaurant, liquor store, grocer, draper, hackney service, undertaker, and china shop. To the delight of many a weary traveler, the treasure behind the yellow and green facade still offers at least three of those original services. Indeed, the good folks at McCarthy's promise to "wine you, dine you, and bury you," all with the same warm, family care.

The Pub. Perhaps the biggest draw to McCarthy's (though the competition from its other services is quite deadly) is its historic Irish pub, which has served the likes of Éamon de Valera and Michael Collins. Andrew Lloyd Weber, whose castle is nearby, is a regular, and is rumored to have written an episode for the British sitcom *Blackadder* while sitting at the bar. The pub was recently featured favorably in Pete McCarthy's pub-guide, *The Road to McCarthy.*

The Restaurant(s). The surprisingly upscale but extremely popular **'s Restaurant** offers fresh, classic cuisine, including baked fillet of salmon with cucumber hollandaise, and a vegetarian stir-fry. (☎052 31176. Mains €16-22. Open W-Sa 6-10pm, Su 12:30-2:30pm and 6-9pm.) McCarthy's also runs **G&T's Restaurant,** next door, which offers tasty and reasonably priced sandwiches, pastries, and full meals. (☎052 32050. Mains €5-12. Open M-Sa 9am-6pm.)

THE ROCK OF CASHEL. Welcome to the Rock. You'll notice it on the horizon from miles away—that huge limestone outcropping topped with medieval buildings is the **Rock of Cashel,** sometimes called **St. Patrick's Rock.** The Rock is attached to a number of legends, some historically substantiated, others more dubious. St. Patrick almost certainly baptized the king of Munster here around AD 450; whether or not he accidentally stabbed the king's feet in the process is debatable. Periodic guided tours are informative, if a bit dry; exploring the buildings while in earshot of the guide is a more attractive option. The bi-steepled **Cormac's Chapel,** consecrated in 1134, holds semi-restored Romanesque paintings, disintegrating stone arches, and an ornate but barely visible sarcophagus once thought to be the tomb of King Cormac. The 1495 burning of the **Cashel Cathedral** by the Earl of Kildare was a highlight of Cashel's illustrious history. When Henry VII demanded an explanation, Kildare replied, "I thought the Archbishop was in it." As any Brit worth his blue blood would, the King made him Lord Deputy. However, the 13th-century cathedral survived the Earl, and today's visitors can inspect its vaulted Gothic arches. Next to the cathedral, a 90 ft. **round tower,** built just after 1101, is the oldest part of the Rock. The **museum** at the entrance to the castle complex preserves the 12th-century **St. Patrick's Cross.** A stirring film on medieval religious structures is shown every hour or so. (Rock open mid-June to mid-Sept. daily 9am-7:30pm; mid-Sept. to mid-Mar. 9:30am-4:30pm; mid-Mar. to mid-June 9:30am-5:30pm. Last admission 45min. before closing. €4.40.) Down the cow path from the Rock lies the promiscuous wreck of **Hore Abbey,** built by Cistercian monks who were fond of arches, and presently inhabited by nonchalant sheep. You'll make goodspeed to the abbey masonry if you jog down the hill next to the Rock.

NEAR CASHEL: FETHARD (FIODH ARD) ☎052

Within cycling distance from Cashel and Clonmel, and built on the River Clashawley, the tiny medieval town of Fethard is protected by an impressive intact stone wall dating from the 13th to 15th centuries. Behind the wall, the medieval **Holy Trinity Church** (not to be confused with the modern Holy Trinity Church at the opposite end of Main St.) looms over the surrounding graveyard. Pick up the key to the churchyard from the XL Stop & Shop on Main St.; the church is a block down on the left. For a peek into the church itself, talk to someone in the **Community Office** (☎31000; www.fethardonline.com)

The Undertaker. Perfect for when you've had just a little too much to eat and drink. Services provided by the undertaker include the funeral home, hearse and casket, coordination with the clergy, arrangement of death notices, preparation of the deceased for viewing, cremation, grave site preparation, repatriation to or from Ireland, and catering. Contact Annette McCarthy or Vincent Murphy ☎052 31149.

The multi-talented owners are also world-class **jockeys,** and horse-racing fans the likes of George Foreman have stopped in for a pint and to chat with the owners. Not surprisingly, with all the drunk and dead people floating around, McCarthy's also supposedly houses one or two resident **ghosts**—talk about *hidden* deal. Strangely enough, we still haven't figured out where the *hotel* part of McCarthy's Hotel comes in. Either way, it's a fabulous deal, though you hopefully won't have to take advantage of *all* their services any time soon.

McCarthy's Hotel, 2 Main St., Fethard (mccarthyshotel.com).

on Barrack St., where you can also get more general **tourist information** and pick up a guide to the town's sights. Another architectural sight of note is the **Town Hall** building, next to the churchyard's entrance. This nondescript building dates to the 17th century and is one of the oldest urban buildings of its type in Ireland. For those seeking medieval porn, Fethard is also host to two **Sheela-na-gig,** bizarre 15th-century exhibitionist stone carvings of nude women doing very un-Irish things. One of the two is adjacent to the Watergate Bridge; the other is next to the **Augustine Friary,** past the gate on the far end of town. Just outside town, toward Cashel, the **Fethard Folk Museum** holds thousands of items from the 19th and early 20th centuries, including farm tools, cooking utensils, bicycles, and a horse-drawn carriage. On Sundays, hundreds of people flock to the grounds for the biggest **car boot sale** in Ireland. (☎31516. Museum and boot sale Su 11:30am-5pm, museum open other times by request. €1.50, children €1.)

Travelers usually flock to the **Gateway B&B ❷,** Rocklow Rd., for its sunny breakfast room, soft, welcoming beds, and gregarious owner, Paddy. (☎31701; www.gatewaybandb.com. €25-28 per person.) After your brief foray with voyeurism, you'll probably need a pint—head down Coleen St., around the corner from the main square, to the **Wishing Well** ('the Well;' ☎31053), the town's resident provider of Guinness and good cheer. On Main St. you'll find the more welcoming and more traditional **Lonergans ❷.** In addition to pulling pints, Lonergans also offers pub grub throughout the day. (☎31447. Mains €9.) For lighter fare, go to **Bert's Bistro ❷** at the end of Main St. (☎30871. Open Tu-Sa 6-10pm, Su 12:30-3:30pm.)

CAHIR (AN CATHAIR) ☎052

The small town of Cahir (CARE) sits on the edge of the Galty Mountains and offers the hiker decent accommodation and pub choices that make up for the limited food options. Tourists will enjoy the well-preserved castle and the seemingly misplaced Swiss Cottage, a nice walk from town down the River Suir.

TRANSPORTATION. **Trains** leave from the station off the Cashel road just past the church, heading out to Limerick and Waterford (M-Sa 2 per day). **Bus Éireann** runs from the tourist office to: Cashel (15min., 6-7 per day, €3.20); Cork (1½hr., 7 per day, €11.70); Dublin (3hr., 6-7 per day, €15.90); Limerick via Tipperary (1hr., 5-7 per day, €9.30); Waterford (1¼hr., 6-7 per day, €10.30). Hitchers to Dublin or Cork position themselves on N8, a 20min. hike from the center of town. Those hitching to Limerick or Waterford wait just outside of town on N24, which passes through the town square. *Let's Go* does not recommend hitchhiking.

PRACTICAL INFORMATION. The **tourist office** on Castle St. offers many goodies: the *Southeast Guide*, which includes a map (free); Discovery Maps #74 and 75, which cover fantastic hill walks in the area (€6.30); Galty Mountains Walks (€0.50-1); and one of Ireland's best collections of postcards. (☎41453. Open daily 9am-6pm.) **AIB,** just up the street, has an **ATM** (☎41735); just a bit farther down, across from the Cahir House Hotel, is **Bank of Ireland** (☎41299; both open M-F 10am-4pm, W until 5pm). Backpackers can take advantage of the free **luggage storage** available at the **Crock O' Gold,** across from the tourist office. The **post office** is on Church St. (☎41275. Open M-F 9:30am-1pm and 2-5:30pm, Sa 9:30am-1pm.)

ACCOMMODATIONS, FOOD, AND PUBS. **The Rectory ❸,** on the Cashel road just past the railway tracks, provides old-fashioned rooms in a stately manor. You'll be hard pressed to find as outstanding a family as the one that runs these heavenly accommodations. (☎41406. Open May-Sept. Singles €30; doubles €50-55.) In town, the modest exterior of **Tinsley House B&B ❸** is a gateway into splendid, spacious, TV- and bath-equipped rooms. Proprietor Liam Roche is an encyclopedia of local history. (☎41947. Doubles €50.) Out Ardfinnan Rd., across from the **Swiss Cottage,** is **Scaragh B&B ❸.** Large rooms with wood floors in a quiet setting make for a comfortable and classy stay. (☎42105; www.welcomingyou.co.uk/scaraghhouse. Singles €38; doubles €56.) There are two hostels relatively close to Cahir. **Lisakyle Hostel (IHH) ❶,** 1 mi. south on Ardfinnan Rd., is the more accessible; from the bus station, walk up the hill and make a right at Cahir House. The exterior is bedecked with flowers, and the rooms are rustic but adequate. (☎41963. 6- to 8-bed dorms €10.50; 4-bed €12. Private rooms €14 per person. **Camping** €7.) **The Kilcoran Farm Hostel (IHH) ❶** offers an education in rural living, hosted by a garrulous chorus of sheep. From Cahir, either call for pickup or take the Cork road for 4 mi., turn left at the Top Petrol Station, and after ¼ mi., make a right at the T-shaped junction. This 25-acre organic farm at the foot of the mountains has no bunk beds and no breakfast, but there is a playground for the kiddies. (☎41906 or 086 344 9406; call ahead. €13 per person.)

For groceries, try **SuperValu,** on Bridge St. across the bridge from the castle. (☎41515. Open M-W 8:30am-6:30pm, Th 8:30am-8pm, F 8:30am-9pm, Sa 8:30am-7pm, Su 9am-1pm.) The **Galtee Inn ❸,** the Square, is a local favorite. Lunches are small and cheap (€8), but dinners swell in size and price, up to €12. (☎41247. Food served M-Sa until 10pm, Su until 9:30pm.) At the **Castle Arms ❷,** Castle St., you'll find cheap chow in an atmosphere that could only be called "pub." You can expect an older crowd at night. (☎42506. Mains around €8.) Next door, **Irwin's,** an old fashioned pint-puller, has cheap sandwiches (€4) and a rowdier crowd during the day than at night. Cannons once aimed toward the castle from the site of **J. Morrissey's,** Castle St.—these days sieges are staged around the bar. (☎42123. W trad.)

SIGHTS. Cahir's most famous landmark is **Cahir Castle.** It's exactly what every romantic envisions a castle to be—heavy on the battlements and decked out in a vibrant palette of grays. (Perhaps this is why it was deemed the ideal site for the 1981 flick *Excalibur.*) Built in the 13th century to be all but impregnable to military attack, the castle's defenses couldn't hold out after the implementation of gunpowder. In 1599, the Earl of Essex forced its surrender by lobbing a few cannonballs its way, one of which is still visibly stuck in the wall. Note the 11,000-year-old preserved head of the long-extinct Irish Elk; the noble beast's antlers span just about the whole wall. (☎41011. Open mid-June to mid-Sept. daily 9am-7:30pm; mid-Sept. to mid-Oct. and mid-Mar. to June 9:30am-5:30pm; mid-Oct. to mid-Mar. 9:30am-4:30pm. Last admission 30min. before closing. 30min. tour and 15min. audio-visual presentation. €2.50, seniors €1.90, students €1.50.)

The broad **River Suir** that flows into Waterford Harbour is but a wee stream in Cahir. A wild, verdant **river walk** starts at the tourist office and leads past the 19th-century **Swiss Cottage,** a ½ mi. walk from town. A charming jumble of architectural styles, the cottage was built so that occupants of Cahir Castle could fish, hunt, and pretend to be peasants. Gorgeously restored, it is a delight for anyone who fancies building, decorating, or being fabulously rich. (☎41144. Open May to mid-Oct. daily 10am-6pm; Apr. Tu-Su 10am-1pm and 2-6pm; mid-Oct. to Nov. Tu-Su 10am-1pm and 2-4:30pm; Mar.-Apr. and Oct.-Nov. closed M except on bank holidays. Last admission 45min. before closing. €2.50, students €1.30, seniors €1.90.) **Fishing** opportunities line the river walk past the Swiss Cottage. Fishing licenses (€19 per day) are the first step, and can be obtained at the Heritage Cornerstone on Church St. (☎42730. Open daily 7am-11pm.)

The **Mitchelstown Caves** are 8 mi. off the Cork road, halfway between Cahir and Mitchelstown in the hamlet of **Burncourt.** A 30min. tour takes you deep into a series of rippled subterranean chambers filled with fantastic mineral formations. (☎67246. Open daily 10am-6pm; last tour 5:30pm. €4.45.)

NEAR CAHIR: GALTY MOUNTAINS AND GLEN OF AHERLOW

South of Tipperary Town, the river **Aherlow** cuts through a richly scenic valley called the Glen of Aherlow. West of Cahir, the **Galty Mountains** rise abruptly along the south edge of the Glen—this purplish, lake-splotched range boasts **Galtymore Mountain** (3018 ft.), Ireland's third-highest peak. The Glen and mountains are ideal settings for both picnicking and full-fledged trekking. Serious hikers should invest in #66 and 74 of the *Ordnance Survey Discovery Series*, available at tourist offices and bookstores in Tipperary and Cahir (€6.60). The Tipp Town tourist office sells a series of trail maps of varying difficulty (€1). **Glenbarra** is also a popular base camp, reached by driving west from Cahir toward Mitchelstown.

The **Glen of Aherlow (Ballydavid Wood) Youth Hostel (An Óige/HI) ❶,** 6 mi. northwest of Cahir off the Limerick road, is a renovated hunting lodge that makes a good starting point for cavorting in the Galtees. (☎062 54148. June-Sept. €12, under 18 €8; Oct.-May €10/€7.) Dedicated hikers make the 10 mi. sojourn across the mountains to the **Mountain Lodge (An Óige/HI) ❶** in Burncourt, another hunting lodge in the middle of the woods (this one gas-lit and Georgian). From Cahir, follow the Mitchelstown road (N8) for 8 mi., turn right at the sign, and continue another 2 mi. on the unpaved path. (☎052 67277. June-Sept. €12, under 18 €10; Oct.-May €10/€8.) The **Kilcoran Farm Hostel** is a convenient stop on the hike back (☎052 41906; see **Cahir,** p. 192). The staff of the **Ballinacourty House ❶,** an excellent campsite in the Aherlow valley, provides detailed information on the Glen. (☎062 56230. Meals and cooking facilities available. Open Easter to Sept. €2 per adult, €1 per child. €10-11.50 per tent.) They also operate a pricey **restaurant** and a pleasant **B&B ❹.** (Dinners €27. Singles €39; doubles with bath €54-58.) To reach Ballinacourty House, take R663 off the Cahir-Tipperary road (N24) in **Bansha** and follow it for 8 mi. to the signposted turnoff.

CLONMEL (CLUAIN MEALA) ☎052

This medieval town on the banks of the River Suir (SURE) sweetens in the fall, when locally-produced Bulmer's Cider infuses the air with hints of apple. As Co. Tipperary's economic hub, Clonmel offers visitors returning from a day in the Comeragh Mountains all the comforts of modern life.

TRANSPORTATION

Trains: Prior Park Rd. (☎21982), less than 1 mi. north of the town center. Trains chug to **Limerick** (50min., M-Sa 2 per day, €12) and **Waterford** en route to **Rosslare Harbour** (1¼hr., M-Sa 1 per day, €8.20).

Buses: Bus info is available at the tourist office and train station. Coaches leave from in front of the train station to: **Cork** (2hr., 3-4 per day, €12.10); **Dublin** (3¼hr., 4-6 per day, €10.50); **Galway** (3¾hr., 4-6 per day, €15.80); **Kilkenny** via **Carrick-on-Suir** (5 per day, €6); **Limerick** via **Tipperary** (5-7 per day, €7.35); **Rosslare** (3½hr., 2-3 per day, €13.30); **Waterford** (1hr., 6-8 per day, €7.85). **Rapid Express** (☎29292) also runs their own bus to **Dublin** via **Kilkenny** (3hr.; M-Sa 3-4 per day, Su 2 per day; €8).

ORIENTATION AND PRACTICAL INFORMATION

Clonmel's central street runs parallel to the **Suir River.** From the station, follow **Prior Park Rd.** straight into town. Prior Park Rd. becomes businesslike **Gladstone St.,** which intersects the main drag, known successively as **O'Connell, Mitchell,** and **Parnell St.,** and then **Irishtown. Sarsfield St.** and **Abbey St.** run off the main street toward the riverside quays.

Tourist Office: Sarsfield St. (☎22960), across from Clonmel Arms Hostel. Pick up the 6 self-guided walking tours of the Knockmealdown Mountains (€1) or the free Heritage Trail map. Open July-Aug. M-Sa 9:30am-5:30pm; Sept.-June M-F 9:30am-5pm.

Banks: AIB (☎22500) and **Bank of Ireland** (☎21425) are neighbors on O'Connell St. Both have **ATMs** and are open M 10am-5pm, Tu-F 10am-4pm.

Pharmacy: Joy's, 68 O'Connell St. (☎21204). Open M-Sa 9am-6pm.

Emergency: ☎999; no coins required. **Police** (*Garda*): Emmet St. (☎22222).

Hospital: St. Joseph's and St. Michael's, Western Rd. (☎21900).

Internet Access: Circles, 16 Market St. (☎23315). Snooker club (€6 per hr.) and Internet cafe (€5.70 per hr.) all in one. Open daily 11am-11pm. The **library,** Emmet St. (☎24545), provides free web access in 50min. slots. Open M-Tu 10am-5:30pm, W-Th 10am-8:30pm, F-Sa 10am-5pm.

Post Office: Emmet St. (☎21164), next to the library. Open M-Sa 9am-5pm.

Work Opportunities: Employment Services, 2-3 Emmett St. (☎23486), has listings for work opportunities and training. Open M-F 9am-1pm and 2-5pm, closes F at 4:45pm.

ACCOMMODATIONS AND CAMPING

Clonmel caters to the hotel and B&B crowd, and is not the most backpacker-friendly town in Ireland. The area along the Cahir road past Irishtown is dotted with B&Bs, which run about €28-45 per person. If you're willing to walk a mile or two from town, your options multiply.

Brighton House, 1 Brighton Place (☎23665; www.tipp.ie/brighton.htm). From the train/bus station, walk toward town—it's on the left at the 1st set of lights. From town, walk out Gladstone St. This classy 1823 Georgian guest house has beautiful rooms and a garden with a working well. Singles €38; doubles €75. ❸

Riverside House, New Quay (☎25781). Close to downtown, guests watch swans swim by from the large windows of their expansive rooms. This stately house has been overlooking the Suir for more than a century. TVs in every room. €25 per person. ❸

Trasses (☎41459 or 42518). An apple farm turned campsite halfway between Clonmel and Cahir on the N24. Mid-June to Sept. €4.50 per person, €2.50 per child; Oct. to mid-June €4/€2.50. Electricity for caravans €2. Free showers. ❶

Powers-the-Pot Camping & Caravan Park, Harney's Cross (☎23085). Well outside town. Follow Parnell St. east out of town, turn right at the 1st traffic light (not N24), cross the Suir, and continue for 5½ mi. of arduous mountain road to the signposted turnoff. Only camping is available while renovations are under way on their hostel. Owners Niall and Jo can answer all your hillwalking questions and provide maps and guides for the Munster Way. 2-person tent €11; each additional adult €6, child €1.50. ❶

FOOD

The local outpost of the **Tesco** supermarket empire is on Gladstone St. (☎27797. Open M-Tu and Sa 8:30am-7pm, W-F 8:30am-9pm, Su 11am-6pm.) **The Honey Pot,** 14 Abbey St., sells health foods, bulk grains, organic veggies, and exquisite "free-trade" crafts from co-ops in India and Nepal. (☎21457. Open M-Sa 9:30am-6pm.)

Angela's Restaurant and Coffee Emporium, Abbey St. (☎26899), off Mitchell St. Remarkably fresh and boldly creative. Warm, soft buns make Angela's a local favorite for all to enjoy. Sandwiches and specials €5-7.60. Open M-Sa 9am-5:30pm. ❷

Niamh's (NEEVS), Mitchell St. (☎25698), at Gladstone St. Specialty coffees, hot lunches, sandwiches, and all-day brekkie (delicious meatless sausage option available) in a deli-style restaurant. Menu also caters to specific diets. Breakfast €4-6.70, sandwiches €3.55-6.50. Open M-F 9am-5:45pm, Sa 9am-5pm. ❷

IN RECENT NEWS

WORLD CUP DOMINATION

Gaelic sports, specifically **hurling** and **Gaelic football,** have been played in Ireland for thousands of years. Though they remain as popular now as they ever have been in the past, the widely televised and hugely commercialized FIFA World Cup event has produced a crop of rising Irish athletes who are choosing to forego their heritage sports to compete in soccer instead.

When the **Gaelic Athletic Association (GAA)**–the group that administers Gaelic sports and is as much a political organization as an athletic one–started purchasing and building stadiums in the early 20th century, they ruled that only Gaelic sports could be played on their grounds. Many Gaelic fans want to keep it that way, but there is a contingent of sports enthusiasts who argue that gigantic mega-stadiums, such as **Croke Park,** should be utilized for more than the 75 Gaelic games currently played there each year.

Though the GAA has relaxed its rules to allow special sporting events and exhibitions, as well as concerts and other non-sporting events, it still refuses to let soccer onto the fields. With Ireland's recent admirable performance in the **2002 World Cup,** Irish soccer fans will undoubtedly pressure the GAA to reconsider its stance. If they do, many hurling and Gaelic football devotees worry that it will help to further erode the small base of patriotic players who forego international sports and fame to pick up the hurley instead.

O Tuamas Cafe, 5-6 Market Pl. (☎27170). A filling meal, hot or cold (under €8), in a brightly-colored, upbeat environment. Finish with a mouthwatering dessert. Open M-Th 9am-5:30pm, F 8:30am-8pm, Sa 8:30am-5:30pm. ❷

Catalpa, Sarsfield St. (☎26821), next to the tourist office. Italian feasts in a former bank vault. Popular with the locals; call ahead. Pizza and pasta €6-10, meat dishes €9.50-18. Open Tu-Su 12:30-2:30pm and 6:30-11:30pm. ❸

Tom Skinny's Pizza Parlor, Market St. (☎26006). Pizza made fresh before your eyes. Glorious aromas, a shiny jukebox, and a portrait of Marilyn Monroe make this a scrumdiddlyumptious stop. Pizzas €6.80-13.50. Open daily noon-midnight. ❷

PUBS

For entertainment listings, check the *Nationalist* (€1.30) at newsagents or pick up a free copy of *South*, which lists local events, including pub happenings.

John Allen's (☎21261), next to St. Mary's in Irishtown. Surprisingly spacious and bright; lures a jolly all-ages crowd. Full meals (€8.50) served M-Sa noon-4pm. Sa trad.

Mulcahy's, 47 Gladstone (☎25054). Enormous and elaborate, with a curious combination of decorative themes and a whole lotta snooker tables. W night trad. Th-Su hosts **Danno's,** an 18+ disco (cover €4-8).

Barry's, O'Connell St. (☎25505). A classic, popular hang-out. Check out Tom Ryan's framed jersey from the 1962 All-Ireland hurling championship. Tom still stops by sometimes for a pint. **Cosmo,** the disco upstairs, rocks Th-Su 11pm-3am (cover €7).

SIGHTS

The Heritage Trail map, free at the tourist office, will point you to a good time in Clonmel. Stops along the way include the **West Gate** (at the western end of O'Connell St.), an 1831 reproduction of the medieval gate that separated Irishtown from the more prosperous Anglo-Norman area. The 84 ft. octagonal tower of **Old St. Mary's Church,** Mary St., stands near the remnants of the town wall that failed to rebuff Cromwell's advances in 1650. Just inside the door of the **Franciscan Friary** on Abbey St. are the 15th-century tomb effigies of a knight and lady of the Butler family. Clonmel's history as a hub o' transport is celebrated at the **Museum of Transport,** off Emmett St., in a converted mill packed to the ceiling with antique cars and classic road signs. (☎29727. Open June-Aug. M-Sa 10am-6pm, Su 2:30-6pm; Oct.-May closed Su.

€3.50.) The **Tipperary S.R. County Museum,** the Borstan, next to the swimming pool, tells the story of the county's history since the Stone Age and hosts small traveling exhibitions. (☎25399. Open M-Sa 10am-5pm. Free.) The tourist office's glossy leaflets *Clonmel Walk* #1 and 2 describe several **walks** in the area and nearby **Nire Valley.** See **Comeragh Mountains** (below) for day hike info.

THE EAST MUNSTER WAY

The East Munster Way begins as a gentle footpath through the lowland hills of **Carrick-on-Suir, Kilsheelan,** and **Clonmel,** and extends to a perch on the **Comeragh Mountains,** then runs full-force into the **Knockmealdowns,** ending 43 mi. later in **Clogheen.** Walkers pass a variety of tranquil scenes along the way, including the **Kilsheelan Woods,** the glistening River Suir, and the impressive vistas in the Comeragh Mountains. In Clogheen, ambitious hikers can follow the **Druhallow Way,** which connects with the **Kerry Way** (see p. 276), or take **Blackwater Way** into isolated Araglin Valley.

The best maps to use are #74 and 75 of the *Ordnance Survey Discovery Series.* The *East Munster Way Map Guide* (€6.20), available at the tourist office in Clonmel, provides a written guide and an accurate but less detailed map—though it does point out all the pubs along the way. For specific information on the East Munster Way, contact the Tipperary Co. Council in Clonmel (☎052 25399); **Powers-the-Pot Campground** (see p. 195) is your best bet for information on hikes in the Comeragh and Knockmealdown Mountains.

THE COMERAGH MOUNTAINS

The only sierra mountains in Ireland, the Comeraghs are distinctly wave-shaped, which means that they vary greatly in difficulty depending on the direction of your approach. The terrain ranges from perpetually soft and wet to exciting and difficult areas like the rocky *coums.* Irish for "mountain hollows," *coums* often house lakes. (The Welsh equivalent is *cwms,* which Scrabble buffs will recognize as the only word in the English language without a vowel.)

The Comeragh terrain includes marshy plateaus that are manageable for city folk in sneakers. *Nire Valley Walks* #1 through 12 (€1 each, at the Clonmel tourist office and Powers-the-Pot) are excellent waterproof maps illustrating fairly easy 2-4hr. day hikes from Clonmel. There are, of course, much more challenging treks to be found in this region. One such option begins from Powers-the-Pot, ½ mi. off the Munster Way (see **Clonmel,** p. 195). With your *Ordnance Survey #75* in hand, head east from the campsite and follow the ridges south. The land is mostly open and it's relatively hard to get lost in good weather, but make sure that someone knows you're out there. Guided walking is also available; ask Niall at Powers-the-Pot (☎052 23085). You might also consider seeing the Comeragh Mountains from atop a rented equine. **Melody's,** in Ballymacarbry, runs guided horse-riding tours that skirt the mountains. (☎052 36147. 2hr. treks €35; full day treks €80.)

THE KNOCKMEALDOWN MOUNTAINS

The Knockmealdown Mountains are a stunning collection of roughly contoured summits straddling the Tipperary-Waterford border 12 mi. south of Cahir. *Knockmealdown Walks* #1 through 4 (€1 each) are available at local tourist offices, including those in Clonmel and Clogheen. All four start at Clogheen; walks #2 and 4 leave from the nearby carparks. Many hikers prefer to begin in the town of **Newcastle,** where tiny but locally renowned **Nugent's Pub** stands. For guided **tours,** contact Helen McGrath—her tours depart at noon on Sundays from the Newcastle Carpark. (☎052 36359. €5-8. M-Sa tours available by request.) One sight of particular interest is the spectacular **Vee Road,** which runs south from Clogheen to the **Knockmealdown Gap,** erupting with purple rhododendrons in May and June. Just before the Vee Rd., in the town of **Graigue,** thirsty pilgrims can stop in at thatch-roofed **Ryan's Pub,** a charming, little building in the middle of a farmyard. At the mountain pass about two-thirds of the way up the Gap, pines give way to heather and bracken, and a parking lot marks the path up **Sugarloaf Hill.** This walk, roughly 1hr. long, challenges hikers to describe the landscape without using the words "patchwork" or "quilt." From there, you can continue on to the **Knockmealdown Peak,** the highest in the range (2609 ft.). On the road back down to Lismore, you'll pass the beautiful (and supposedly bottomless) **Bay Loch.**

The affable and decidedly unofficious **tourist office** in Clogheen, across from the turnoff for the Vee Road, serves generous portions of maps with a side of local lore. (☎052 65258. Open M-Sa 9am-5pm.) **Parsons Green,** 5min. from the village on the Cahir road, is a garden-campsite-activity center medley, offering **river walks, boating trips,** and **pony rides.** (☎052 65290. Pony rides €1 per person. **Camping** €3 per person, €2 per child; €5 per small tent, €6.50 per family tent. Laundry €6.)

LISMORE (LIOS MÓR) ☎058

Lismore's incongruously grand castle and glorious cathedral remind visitors that the sleepy little town was once a thriving monastic center. Although it sits next to the Blackwater River in Co. Waterford, Lismore is included here because it makes a convenient base for exploring Co. Tipperary's Knockmealdown Mountains.

TRANSPORTATION AND PRACTICAL INFORMATION. **Bus Éireann** stops across from the tourist office and runs to Cork (1¼hr., F 1 per day, €9.30) and Waterford via Dungarvan (1¼hr., M-Sa 1 per day, €10.20). A particularly nice way to reach Lismore from Clogheen is by way of the Vee Road. Hitchers wishing to get to Cork first ride east to **Fermoy,** then south on N8. Hitching to Dungarvan is also common, but never recommended by *Let's Go*. The eager-to-please **tourist office** and the **heritage center** share the old courthouse building. (☎54975. Both open June-Aug. M-Sa 9:30am-5:30pm, Su noon-5:30pm; Apr.-May and Sept.-Oct. M-Sa 9:30am-5:30pm.) Quasi-free **Internet access** is available at the **library** on Main St. with the purchase of a €2.50 membership card. (Open M, W, and F 11:30am-1pm and 2-6pm, Tu and F 1-4:30pm and 5:30-8pm.) The **post office** is located on E. Main St. (☎54220. Open M-F 9am-1pm and 2-5:30pm, Sa 9am-1pm.)

ACCOMMODATIONS, FOOD, AND PUBS. Accommodations in Lismore are sparse, but warm B&Bs can be found on either side of the town; you just need to know where to look—inquire at the tourist office for help. From the tourist office, take a right at the statue and head up the hill out of town to get to **Beechcroft ❸** (☎54273) and **Silver Birches ❸** (☎53405), both with gorgeous wood floors and electric blankets, and run by a friendly mother-daughter team. (Singles €30; doubles €55.) On the other side of town (head left from the tourist office and left at the fork in the road), **Pine Tree House ❸** has a nice front lawn and a horse in the attached paddock. Oh, and rooms for rent. (☎53282. Singles €36; doubles €53.)

Food in Lismore is good and plentiful. **SuperSave** on E. Main St. has groceries. (☎54122. Open M-W 9am-6pm, Th 9am-7:30pm, F 9am-8pm, Sa 9:30am-8:30pm.) **Eamonn's Place ❸**, E. Main St., serves tasty meals in a gorgeous beer garden. Try the chicken Maryland with banana and pineapple (€10) or the fish specials snagged right out of the Blackwater. (☎54025. Lunch from €7, served M-F 12:30-2:30pm; dinners €10-14, served daily 6-9pm.) **Madden's Bar,** E. Main St., serves soup and sandwiches at reasonable prices, and many a pint, accompanied by the refined Mr. Billy Hogan on the piano. (☎54148. Lunch €3.50, served 12:30-2:30pm.)

SIGHTS. Stunning **Lismore Castle** looms over the Blackwater River, swathed in foliage and aristocratic grandeur. Once a medieval fort, then a bishop's residence, the building was also home to Sir Walter Raleigh and the birthplace of 17th-century science guy Robert Boyle (of PV=nRT fame). Remodeled with great imagination in the 19th century, the castle is now privately owned by the English Duke of Devonshire, who sometimes takes in guests for an estimated €11,000 per week (yeah, that's a ❺). In 1814, the Lismore Crozier and the *Book of Lismore*, priceless artifacts thought to have been lost forever, were found hidden in the castle walls. You may wish to take a tour of the **gardens,** or just scamper across the bridge for a free peek. (☎54424. Open mid-Apr. to Sept. daily 1:45-4:45pm. Garden tours €4, children under 16 €2.) The bridge is also the starting point for peaceful **Lady Louisa's Walk** which runs along the tree-lined Blackwater.

Locals claim that a secret passage connects the castle to **St. Carthage's Cathedral,** on Deanery Hill. A number of tombs in the cathedral's ancient graveyard are sealed with heavy stone slabs, relics of Lismore's past as a hotspot for body-snatching. The cathedral did a better job retaining historical markers—a collection of 9th- and 10th-century engraved commemorative stones are set into one of its walls. Lismore's **heritage center,** housed with the tourist office in the town square, includes a 30min. video presentation and a cursory exhibit highlighting the 1000-year-old *Book of Lismore*. A new science room is dedicated to the life and works of Robert Boyle. (☎54975. Open June-Aug. M-Sa 9:30am-5:30pm, Su noon-5:30pm; Apr.-May and Sept.-Oct. M-Sa 9:30am-5:30pm. €4, seniors and students €3.50.) The center also runs **guided tours** of town (€6) and sells self-guided tour booklets (€2). Two miles from Lismore is a carpark for the **Towerswalk,** beloved by many a local. From the castle, cross the bridge and turn left; Towerswalk will be on your right after 3 mi. Keily-Ussher, a local landlord in the mid-1800s, began the tower and entrance gate to what was to be a grand castle; today the woodsy, 1hr. walk runs to "the Folly."

COUNTIES WEXFORD AND WATERFORD

Wexford and Waterford may be just a little too welcoming for their own good—Ireland's invaders, from Vikings to Christians to modern backpackers, have all tended to begin their island-conquering here. Away from the salty pubs and crowded streets of Wexford Town, beaches stretch thin in dismal, highly trafficked Rosslare and pop up again at the county's southwest edge, along idyllic Waterford Harbour. Waterford City is the commercial and cultural core of the southeast, famous for its crystal and sporting the oldest heritage in the country. New Ross, with its fine hostels and urban amenities, is a good base for exploring the southeast. **Slí Charman** (SHLEE KAR-man), usually referred to as "An Slí," is a pathway that runs 135 mi. along Co. Wexford's coast, from the Co. Wicklow border, through Wexford and Rosslare, all the way to Waterford Harbour. Major roads in the region are the east-west N25 (Rosslare-Waterford), the north-south N11 (Wexford-Dublin), and the N79 (Enniscorthy-New Ross).

ENNISCORTHY (INIS COIRTHAIDTH) ☎054

Fourteen miles north of Wexford, the handsome town of Enniscorthy lies among the hills that straddle the River Slaney. The town takes great pride in its part in the nationalist struggle—mention the year '98 to locals, and they'll assume you mean the Rebellion of 1798, when a local priest led an uprising at nearby Vinegar Hill and held the British at bay for 12 days (see **Rebellion,** p. 58). A sparkling new museum

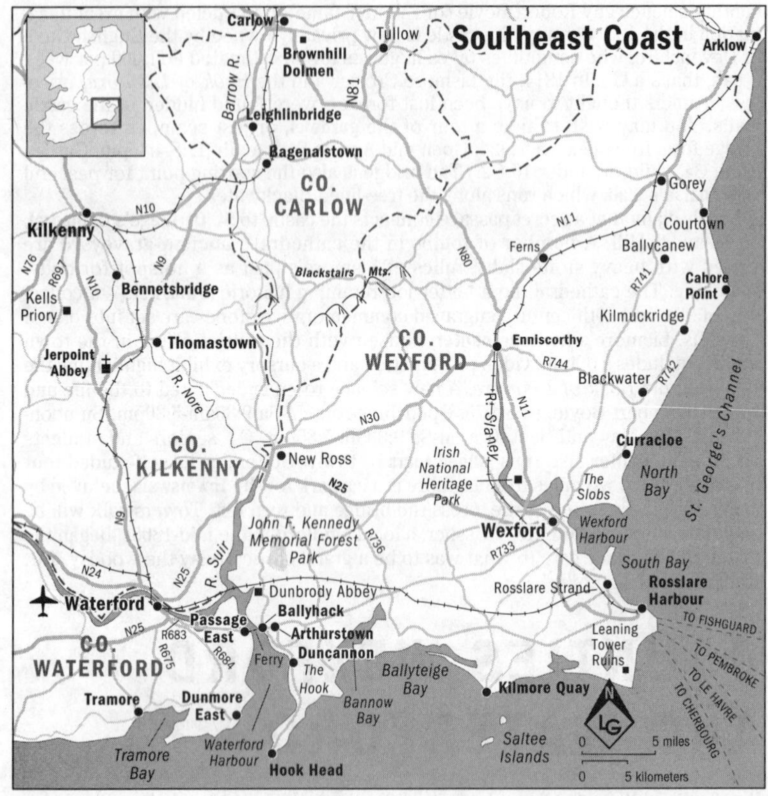

has been built specifically to chronicle the events of 1798. Hot-headed Enniscorthy was also one of the only towns to join Dublin in the 1916 Easter Rising, and it was the last to surrender (see p. 61). A history lesson on Ireland's political conflicts may be a sobering experience, but Enniscorthy's 20-odd pubs greatly diminish the chances of lingering grimness.

TRANSPORTATION. N11 passes through Enniscorthy, heading south to Wexford and north to Arklow, Wicklow, and Dublin. **Trains** run to Dublin (2½hr., 3 per day, €14.60) and Rosslare (50min., 3 per day, €9). **Buses** stop outside the Bus Stop Shop on Templeshannon Quay (between the 2 bridges and across the river from the Squares) on their way north to Dublin via Ferns (5-7 per day, €12.70), and south to Waterford (8-10 per day, €12.70) and Wexford (9-12 per day, €12.70). For **taxis,** call ☎37222, 33975, 36666, or 37888.

ORIENTATION AND PRACTICAL INFORMATION. From the railway station, take Templeshannon and cross the River Slaney into the center of town; turn left for **Abbey Square,** one of the main shopping areas, or continue uphill to bustling **Market Square.** The moderately well-informed **tourist office** is in the castle off Castle Hill. (☎34699. Open M-Sa 10am-6pm, Su 2-5:30pm; shorter hours in winter.) For further Enniscorthian lore, see the divine Maura Flannery in the **souvenir shop**

across the street. (☎36800 or 086 816 2301.) Several banks have 24hr. **ATMs,** among them **AIB** (☎33163; open M 10am-5pm, Tu-F 10am-4pm) and **Irish Permanent Bank,** Market Sq. (☎35700; open M-F 9:30am-5pm, W open 10:15am). A **post office** (☎33226) is by the Abbey Sq. roundabout.

ACCOMMODATIONS. Treasure every moment of your stay at **Valeview Farmhouse ❸,** adjacent to Ringwood Park, a modern farm bungalow 1½ mi. out of town on Slaney Dr. Tea or coffee, homemade treats by the chef/owner (who will also make you dinner for €25-30), and snuggly electric blankets await you in the winter. (☎35262. €25-30 per person.) At **Adelmar ❷,** Summerhill, Mrs. Agnes Barry's hospitality and delightful company do the trick. Go out to the Shell station on N11 toward Dublin, take a left, and follow the signs. (☎33668. Open June-Oct. €23 per person.) Just off Market Square is **P. J. Murphy's B&B ❸,** 9 Main St., across the street from the hotel and directly above Murphy's Pub. The rooms are comfy-cozy and the guest room is full of plump cushions. (☎33522. €25 per person.) Ten minutes out of town, **The Summerhill B&B ❸** sports cheerful dishware and brightly colored linens. Follow Duffry St. past the cathedral, take a right at the signpost, walk past St. Aidan's school, and turn the corner; Summerhill is on your left. (☎34219. €26 per person.)

FOOD AND PUBS. Caulfield's SuperValu, in the shopping center on Mill Park Rd., sells groceries and small edibles. (☎34541. Open M-Tu and Sa 8am-8pm, W 8am-9pm, Th-F 8am-10pm, Su 8am-6pm.) Vegetarians, and those seeking large portions, head to **The Baked Potato ❷,** 18 Rafter St., for cheap, hot food. (☎34085. Open M-Sa 8am-6pm.) For delicious meals of a similar persuasion, visit the equally praiseworthy **Cozy Kitchen ❷,** at 11 Rafter St., where hot scones and tea make a cheap and filling start to the morning. (☎36488. Bakery items around €2; most mains €4-6. Open M-W 8:30am-6pm, Th-Sa 8:30am-7pm.) In a land where food is largely devoid of taste and spice, **Tandori Restaurant's ❸** traditional Indian cuisine offers a welcome change. (☎38111. Dishes €10-14.50. Sunday buffet 1-3:30pm; €14.95. Open daily 12:30-2:30pm and 6pm-midnight.) **The Antique Tavern,** 14 Slaney St., is a pub that lives up to its name, with Enniscorthy artifacts and worldwide antiques brought in by devoted patrons. (☎33428. Open M-W 10:30am-11:30pm, Th-Sa 10:30am-12:30am, Su noon-11:30pm; bar menu noon-3:30pm.) With a little more room and live music on Wednesdays, **Rackards,** 23 Rafter St., is among the hippest spots in town. A zesty, vegetarian-friendly lunch is served from noon to 3pm. (☎33747. Open M-W 10am-11:30pm, Th-Sa 10:30am-12:30am, Su 10am-11pm.) **Shenanigan's** is the mischievous newcomer in Market Sq. Munch your grub and check out the mosaics. (Late bar Th-Sa; disco Th-F.)

SIGHTS AND FESTIVALS. The **National 1798 Visitor Centre,** a 5min. walk from town on Mill Park Rd., is an impressive multimedia barrage examining the Rebellion of 1798 and the Battle of Vinegar Hill. One room presents the conflict as a chess problem with larger-than-life pieces. There's also a 14min. film with all the battle violence you could want. If you're up for a 2½ mi. walk (or drive), head across the river to the summit of **Vinegar Hill** itself—the site offers a fantastic battle's-eye view of the town below. For a more intimate perspective, Maura Flannery's **Walking Tour of Enniscorthy** can't be beat. The 1hr. trek reveals the dirty little secrets of the town's past. Find out about the time, in 1649, when Enniscorthy women got Cromwell's soldiers drunk and killed them; or learn why, after flagrantly kissing up to Queen Elizabeth with *The Faerie Queene*, poet Edmund Spenser declined her offer to accept the local castle. (Info available at the tourist office, see above. Call a day ahead to reserve a tour. Offered in English or French; check to see if tours are already scheduled. €3.80, children €1.90.)

The **Wexford County Museum** fills the bulk of the **Norman Castle** on Castle Hill, chronicling Wexford's collective stream of consciousness and providing a fresh take on the tired historical narrative. The exhibition rooms display the original letters and belongings of principal players in the Rebellions, both 1798 and 1916. Since the museum's sad days as a 13-object display back in 1960, the curators have stuffed it from dungeon to eaves with odd bits like ship figureheads and a collection of international police patches. (☎35926. Open M-Sa 10am-6pm, Su 2-6pm. €3.80, seniors and students €2.50, children €0.65.)

St. Aiden's Cathedral, on Cathedral St. uphill from Murphy's Hotel, has been lovingly restored up to its star-specked roof. Original construction began in 1843 under the close supervision of architect Augustus Pugin, who littered the whole of Britain with his neo-Gothic creations. Something of a wonderkid, Pugin also made jewelry, textiles, and metalworks, and at the ripe old age of 14 he designed all of the furniture in Windsor Castle. In Market Sq., a statue commemorates **Father Murphy,** who fanned the flames of rebellion in 1798. (Got an afternoon to kill? Try walking around and counting the number of times you see the word "Murphy.") The priest had been something of a Loyalist before an angry mob threatened to burn down his church. He promptly installed himself at the head of the United Irishmen (see **Rebellion,** p. 59) and led the pikemen of Enniscorthy into battle.

If you're around in late June, check out the annual **Strawberry Fair's** 10 days of festivities and fructose. Pubs host literati-laden theater performances, and music plays on into the night. The **Blues Festival** in mid-September brings three days of entertainment by local and internationally renowned musicians.

WEXFORD (LOUGH GARMAN) ☎053

Incessant fighting between Gaels, Vikings, and Normans gave birth to Wexford's labyrinth of narrow, snaggling streets; sidewalks here are so small that cars along Main St. must yield to a convoy of baby carriages that march down its middle. No worries, though: park the car and pound the pavement to visit Wexford's main attractions—its quality pubs and restaurants. These line the stone passageways that were built in the 12th century when the Normans conquered the Viking settlement of Waesfjord. Today, fishing trawlers line the harbor in the water. One street back, crowds filter down Main St. and enjoy the many shops, restaurants, and traffic-dodging that give this unique, historical town its down-home charm.

TRANSPORTATION

Trains: O'Hanranhan (North) Station, Redmond Sq. (☎22522). With your back to the water at Crescent Quay, turn right, and walk for 5min. If the office is closed, buy tickets on the train. Info available from 7am until around 7:40pm. Trains hustle to Connolly Station in **Dublin** (2¾hr., 3 per day, €17) and to **Rosslare** (15min., 3 per day, €2.50).

Buses: Buses stop at the train station. If the station office is closed, check the Station Cafe (☎24056) across the street for info. Buses run to **Dublin** (2¾hr., 8-10 per day, €10) and **Rosslare** (20min., 9-12 per day, €3.35). Buses to and from **Limerick** (4 per day, €16) connect with **Irish Ferries** and **Stena-Sealink** sailings.

Taxi: Walsh Cabs (☎41449 or 087 256 7489); **Noel Ryan** (☎24056); **Wexford taxis** (☎46666). A list of additional taxi companies is posted in the train station.

Bike Rental: Hayes Cycle Shop, 108 South Main St. (☎22462). Rents touring bikes. 1-way rentals possible. €20 per day, €75 per wk. €75 or ID deposit. Open M-Sa 9am-6pm; bikes available by arrangement on Su.

Hitchhiking: The odds of getting a ride are highest around noon or from 5-7pm when the boats come in and traffic is heavier. Hitchers to Dublin (via N11) stand by the Wexford

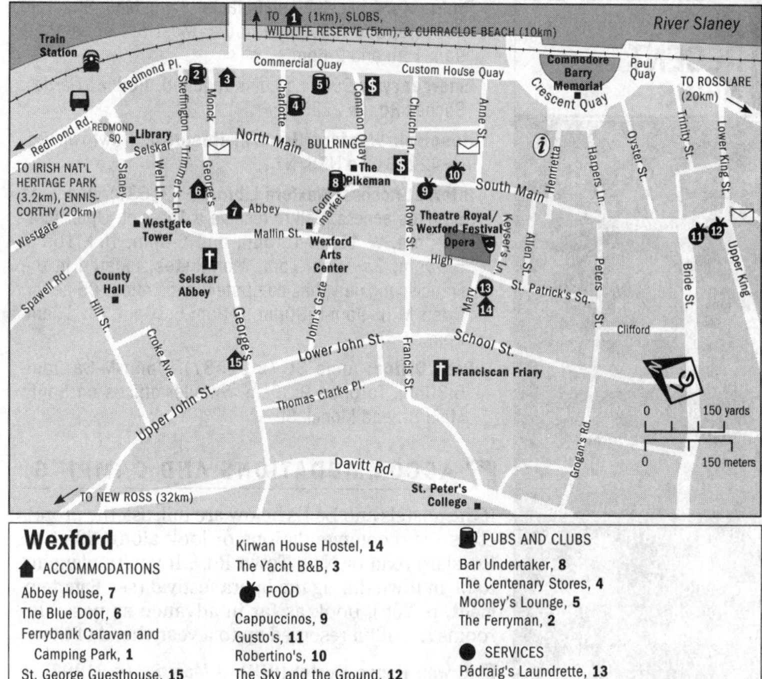

Bridge off the quays; those bound for Rosslare will head south along the quays to Trinity St., just past the Talbot Hotel. For Cork, New Ross, or Waterford, thumbing types continue down Westgate and turn left onto Hill St. then right onto Newtown Rd. (N25). N11 and N25 merge near the city; savvy hitchers make a point of specifying either the Dublin road (N11) or the Waterford road (N25). *Let's Go* does not recommend hitchhiking.

ORIENTATION AND PRACTICAL INFORMATION

Most of the town's action takes place one block inland, along the twists and turns of **Main St.** A plaza called the **Bullring** is near the center of town, a few blocks from where North Main St. changes to South. Another plaza, **Redmond Square,** sits at the northern end of the quays near the train and bus station. Two steeples and a number of other towers—including the Franciscan Friary at the top of the hill—define the town's skyline, but are less prominent to viewers walking its narrow streets.

Tourist Office: Crescent Quay (☎23111), facing the backside of Commodore Barry's statue. Scars on the windowsills attest to centuries of knife-sharpening sailors. Pick up *Discover Wexford* (€2), *Front Door to Ireland* (free map), or *Welcome to Wexford* (free, includes maps). Open Apr.-Sept. M-Sa 9am-6pm; Nov.-Mar. M-F 9:30am-5:30pm.

Banks: 24hr. **ATMs** are available at **TSB,** 73-75 Main St. (☎41922; open M-F 9:30am-5pm, Th until 7pm); **AIB,** South Main St. (☎22444); and **Bank of Ireland,** at the Bullring (☎21365; both open M 10am-5pm, Tu-F 10am-4pm).

Laundry: Pádraíg's Launderette, 4 Mary St. (☎24677), next to the Kirwan Hostel. No self-service. Wash €4, dry €1 per 5min. Open M-F 9:30am-6pm, Sa 9am-9pm.

SOUTHEAST IRELAND

IN RECENT NEWS

WHERE HAVE ALL THE HOSTELS GONE?

Recently, budget travelers have been arriving in the larger Irish cities only to find few hostels left that can take them in. Two main factors seem to be causing this trend: the first is the general down-turn in tourism over the last year, which has weakened the travel industry and closed businesses in Ireland and throughout Europe. A second, more salient explanation accounts for why those hostels that do remain open no longer take in travelers.

For the first time in its history, Ireland is experiencing a population influx. Each year, thousands of refugees fleeing persecution in their native countries arrive in Ireland seeking political asylum. Unable to suitably house all of these immigrants, the government has turned to hostels to solve the housing crunch. Many hostels throughout the country are now being offered three- to four-year contracts in which they agree to only house refugees and asylum seekers; the owners are not allowed to take in tourists during that time. In return they are paid as though their hostel is full each night.

However, rumor has it that some hostel owners, particularly in the southeast, have become greedy, ignoring this important caveat and allowing unknowing tourists to stay despite the governmental restrictions. When booking accommodations in the area then, be sure to check with the local tourist office to see which hostels can legally take you in.

Pharmacy: A gaggle of pharmacies along Main St. rotate Su, late, and lunchtime hours. Most are open M-Sa 9am-1pm and 2-6pm.

Emergency: ☎999; no coins required. **Police** (*Garda*): Roches Rd. (☎22333).

Hospital: Wexford General Hospital, Newtown Rd. (☎42233), on N25/N11.

Internet Access: Wexford Library (☎21637), Redmond Sq. Free access. Call to reserve a 1hr. slot. Open Tu 1-5:30pm, W 10am-4:30pm and 6-8pm, Th-F 10am-5:30pm, Sa 10am-1pm. **Megabytes,** located in the Franciscan Friary, has computers and coffee. €5 per hr. Open M-Th 9am-9:30pm, F 9am-5:30pm, Sa 10am-2pm.

Post Office: Anne St. (☎22587). Open M-Sa 9am-5:30pm, Tu open 9:30am. Smaller offices on South Main St. and Monck St.

ACCOMMODATIONS AND CAMPING

If the hostels and B&Bs below are full, ask the proprietors for recommendations or look along N25 (the Rosslare road or New Town Rd.). If you're planning to be in town during the opera festival (see **Entertainment,** p. 206), book as far in advance as possible; rooms are often reserved up to a year ahead of time.

Kirwan House Hostel (IHH), 3 Mary St. (☎21208). A refurbished 200-year-old Georgian house right in the heart of town. Some slants and creaks in its wooden floors, a BBQ-friendly patio out back, and loads of local info from the staff. Laundry available next door. Dorms €12-12.50; doubles €32; triples €48. ❶

The Blue Door, 18 Lower George St. (☎21047). Look for the crisp white building with flower baskets and, you guessed it, a blue door. View the castle from your room, or head downstairs for veggie-friendly meals. €30-40 per person. ❸

Abbey House, 34 Abbey St. (☎24408). This family-run B&B flaunts a central location, comfy quarters, and a sitting room with cushy seats and an electric fireplace. Singles €32-35; doubles with bath €52-56. ❸

St. George Guesthouse, Georges St. (☎24814). 4min. uphill from North Main St. in a regal yellow and white house. Bright and clean with an abundance of glass and mirrors. Free parking. TVs and phones in rooms. No smoking in bedrooms. €35 per person. ❸

The Yacht B&B, 2 Monck St. (☎22338). Above the Yacht Pub, ideal for those who like their stumbles short. Relaxed atmosphere. Call ahead. €25 per person. ❸

Ferrybank Caravan and Camping Park (☎44378). On the eastern edge of town; cross the bridge and go straight. Clean sites with striking ocean views. Open Easter-Oct. 1-person tent €7.60; 2-person €10.20. Showers €1.30. Laundry €1.90. ❶

FOOD

Dunnes Store on Redmond Sq. has everything from groceries to clothes to lampshades. (☎45688. Open M-Tu 9am-8pm, W 9am-9pm, Th-F 9am-10pm, Sa 9am-7pm, Su 10am-7pm.) The **L&N SuperValu** is on Custom House Quay. (☎22290. Open M-Tu and Sa 9am-6pm, W-F 9am-9pm.) Find **Tesco** in Lowney's Mall on Main St. (☎24788. Open M-Tu, and Sa 9am-7pm, W-F 9am-9pm, Su 11am-6pm.)

The Sky and the Ground, 112 South Main St. (☎21273). Lots of Guinness ads and old-time memorabilia make this a good stop for lunch. Scaled-down versions of the pricier fare served by the late-night restaurant upstairs (**Heavens Above;** mains €14-21) are served here until 6pm. Lunch is so good they occasionally sell out the entire menu. Most main courses €8.50-10. Su-Th live music, typically trad. ❸

Gusto's, 106 South Main St. (☎24336). Gusto's is to be relished. Its small, cafe-like appearance belies high-quality breakfasts, sandwiches, and soups, and a slightly arty-sophisticate vibe. The panini are a warm treat (€4). Breakfast €3.20-5.10. Open M-F 8:30am-5:30pm, Sa 8:30am-5pm. ❶

Robertino's, 19 South Main St. (☎23334). Eat delicious open-faced sandwiches or veggie-friendly fare at this restaurant decked out with Roman statues and murals. Mains €8-10. Open M-Sa 10am-11pm, Su noon-11pm. ❸

Cappuccino's, 25 North Main St. (☎23669). Aching for a bagel? Ache no longer—you've found the place. Sandwiches (€3.50 and up) and ciabatta melts (€7.15) round out the menu. Open M-Th 8am-6pm, F-Sa 8am-6:30pm, Su 10am-6:30pm. ❷

PUBS AND CLUBS

Mooney's Lounge, Commercial Quay (☎21128), by the bridge. Wexford's hot late-night venue. One side opens up for a disco bar after 9:30pm while the other continues as a pub. All sorts of live music Th-Su. Impressive television. 18+. Occasional cover (€7) for larger gigs. Open M-W until 11:30pm, Th-Su until 2:30am.

The Centenary Stores, Charlotte St. (☎24424), off Commercial Quay. A classy crowd flocks to this stylish pub and dance club situated in a former warehouse. Patio for those sunny afternoon pints. Excellent trad Su mornings and M and W nights. DJ spins techno and top-40 on a black-lit dance floor Th-Su 10:30pm-2am. Nightclub cover €8.

The Ferryman, 12 Monck St. (☎23877), on the corner of Redmond Pl. facing the water. Large and bright with ample skylights and faux torches. Carvery lunch served 12:30-3pm. Open M-W 10:30am-11:30pm, Th-Sa 10:30am-12:30am, Su 10:30am-11pm.

Bar Undertaker, next to the Pikeman (☎22949). As the evening wears on at this little pub, the drinkers morph into serious jazz fans. Music Th, Sa, and Su until 1am.

SIGHTS AND ACTIVITIES

The remains of the Norman **city walls** run the length of High St. **Westgate Tower,** near the intersection of Abbey St. and Slaney St., is the only one of the wall's original six gates that still stands. The tower gate now holds the **Westgate Heritage Centre,** where an excellent 30min. audio-visual show recounts the history of the town. The center is staffed by volunteers whose sporadic bouts of do-goody intentions make for erratic hours—contact the tourist office for more information (☎46506). Next door, the peaceful ruins of **Selskar Abbey**—site of Henry II's extended penance for his role in Thomas Beckett's murder—act as a flower-bed for glorious weeds. (Enter through the wicket gate by the Centre. Open M-F 10am-4pm. Free.)

An open area between North and South Main St. marks the **Bullring.** In 1621, bull baiting was inaugurated by the town's butcher guild as a promotional device—the mayor got the hide and the poor got the meat. **The Pikeman,** a statue of a stalwart peasant fearlessly brandishing his homemade weaponry, commemorates the 1798 uprising (see **Rebellion,** p. 59). A statue of **Commodore John Barry,** native son and founder of the US Navy, stands facing the sea. The **Friary Church,** in the Franciscan Friary on School St. (☎22758), houses the "Little Saint" in the back corner of the nave. The wax effigy of young St. Adjutor shows the bloody gash inflicted by the martyr's Roman father. The peaceful fellows gadding about in brown robes are Franciscan monks of an order that has lived in town since 1230. If you're looking for company, the **historical society** (☎21637) runs evening **walking tours** (free), depending on weather and interest—call ☎22663 after 5pm. If not, *Welcome to Wexford* (free at the tourist office) details a self-guided "Magical History" tour.

Wexford's hilly countryside and beaches make for excellent horseback riding. **Shelmalier Riding Stables,** 4 mi. away at Forth Mountain, has riding for novices and experts (☎39251; booking essential). **Boat trips** from Wexford Harbour are another way to explore the area and are perfect for those seeking close-up pictures of the **seals** at Raven Point. (☎40564. 30min. tour €7.)

ENTERTAINMENT

For detailed information on events throughout the county, pick up *The Wexford People* (€1.50) from any local newsstand or pub. The funky **Wexford Arts Centre,** Cornmarket, presents free visual arts and crafts exhibitions. Evening performances of music, dance, and drama take place here throughout the year. (☎23764. Tickets generally €9-10. Center open M-Sa 9am-6pm.) The **Theatre Royal,** High St., produces shows throughout the year, culminating in the internationally acclaimed **Wexford Opera Festival,** held in late October and early November. The festival rescues three obscure but deserving operas from the artistic attic and performs them in an intimate setting. (☎22400; box office ☎22144; www.wexfordopera.com. Box office open May-Sept. M-F 11am-1pm and 2-5pm; Oct.-Nov. M-F 9:30am-5:30pm.)

DAYTRIPS FROM WEXFORD

THE SLOBS AND CURRACLOE BEACH

The Wildfowl Reserve is on the North Slob, 2 mi. north of Wexford. Take Castlebridge/ Gorey Rd. to well-signposted Ardcavan Ln. (a €5 cab ride), or hike through the Ferrybank caravan park and along the increasingly sandy beach for 40min. Reserve Centre: ☎23129. Open mid-Apr. to Sept. daily 9am-6pm, Oct.-Apr. 10am-5pm. Free.

Wexford worked hard to get its Slobs, and it was worth it—they're now quite a sight to behold. Originally boglands, in the late 1840s the Slobs were filled to create more land for agriculture. Today, 420 of these acres are reserved for **The Wexford Wildfowl Reserve,** a safe haven for rare birds from around the world. Ten thousand of Greenland's white-fronted geese (one-third of the entire species) descend on the Sloblands between October and April, cohabiting with other honkers from as far away as Siberia and Iceland. Resident Irish birds arrive in the summer to mate along the channels. The **Reserve Centre** has a new wing that details the creation of the Slobs, highlights wildlife, and displays a water-based cannon formerly used to take out dozens of birds at a time.

If you continue along the coast for 6 mi. you'll soon reach broad **Curracloe Beach,** where Spielberg filmed the D-Day landings in *Saving Private Ryan*. Curracloe makes a fabulous cycling or walking daytrip; the beach is lined with dune bluffs whose stature rivals the steeples on the far side of the Slaney. To get there by bike, follow Castlebridge/Gorey Rd. beyond the turnoff for the Slobs to a signposted right turn for Curracloe Town. Cycle past the fields of sheep, and turn right in Curracloe Town at the post office (35min. from the bridge; 10min. by car).

THE IRISH NATIONAL HERITAGE PARK

The park is 3 mi. outside Wexford on the N11; cabs cost about €6. ☎20733. Open Mar.-Nov. daily 9:30am-6:30pm, last admission 5pm; Oct.-Feb. call for hours. €6.35, students €5.50.

The Irish National Heritage Park allows you to stroll through a Stone Age campsite, an early Norman tower, and reconstructions of old Irish homesteads, tombs, and fortifications that archaeologists have discovered across Ireland—over 9000 years of Irish history, all told. The guided tours, included in the price of admission, are an excellent way to explore the park. If you get hungry afterwards, hop over to the park's restaurant, **Fulacht Faidh** (open daily 12:30-5:30pm; mains €7-8).

ROSSLARE HARBOUR (ROS LÁIR) ☎053

Rosslare Harbour, best viewed from the deck of a departing ship, is a decidedly pragmatic seaside village whose primary function is welcoming voyagers and bidding them *bon voyage* as they depart for France or Wales. Unlike the seaports of popular imagination, Rosslare does not play host to international intrigue, spies, or casinos; it doesn't even have many good pubs or restaurants.

TRANSPORTATION. **Trains** run from the ferryport to: **Dublin** (3hr., 3 per day, €14.50); **Limerick** (2½hr., 1-2 per day, €13.35) via **Waterford** (1¼hr., €8.25); and **Wexford** (15min., 3 per day, €2.50). The rail office (☎33592) is open daily from 6am-10pm. The same office also houses the bus station (☎33595). Most **buses** stop by the Kilrane Church and the Catholic church and go to: **Dublin** (3hr., 10-12 per day, €12.70); **Galway** via **Waterford** (4 per day, €22); **Killarney** (M-Sa 5 per day, Su 3 per day; €20.50) via **Cork** (€17.10) and **Waterford** (€11.70); **Limerick** (M-Sa 5 per day, Su 3 per day; €17.10); **Tralee** (M-Sa 4 per day, Su 2 per day; €13); **Wexford** (20min., 13-17 per day, €4). **Stena Line** (☎61567; 24hr. info ☎61505) and **Irish Ferries** (☎33158) both serve the port. **Ferries** shove off for Britain (1 per day) and France (1 every other day). For further info see **By Ferry,** p. 27. Trains and buses often connect with the ferries; **Irish Rail** (☎33114) and **Bus Éireann** (☎051 879 000) have desks in the terminal. An office in the ferry terminal offers **Europcar** (☎33634), **Hertz** (☎33238 or 33511), and **Budget** (☎33318) rentals. Daily prices hover around €100 for 1-2 days. Only Europcar rents to drivers under 24. For a **taxi** out of town, call Dermot O'Hagan (☎33777), Jimmy Ferguson (☎33355), or Michael Brown (☎087 294 7883).

ORIENTATION AND PRACTICAL INFORMATION. To get from the ferryport into town, climb the ramp or walk the steps up the cliff; the path will bring you to the N25 which cuts through town. The Rosslare-Kilrane **tourist office** is 1 mi. from the waterfront on the Wexford road in Kilrane. (☎33622 or 33232. Open daily 10:15am-8pm.) If you need help in the ferry terminal, head to the **port authority desk** (☎33114). Exchange currency at the **Bank of Ireland,** on St. Martin Rd. past the supermarket. (☎33304. Open M-F 10am-12:30pm and 1:30-4pm. 24hr. **ATM** available.) The **post office,** in the SuperValu supermarket, has a **bureau de change.** (☎33201. Open M-F 9am-1pm and 2-5:30pm, Sa 9am-1pm.)

ACCOMMODATIONS, FOOD, AND PUBS. Exhausted ferry passengers often take what they can get in town, while good B&Bs and accommodations in Wexford and Kilmore Quay are often overlooked. B&Bs swamp N25 just outside of Rosslare. **Mrs. O'Leary's Farmhouse ❷,** off N25 in Kilrane, a 15min. drive from town, stands out far from the rest of the rabble. Open since 1955 and set on a glorious 100-acre farm right by the seaside, Mrs. O'Leary's well-kept home is a holiday unto itself. A grassy lane leads past dunes of wildflowers to a secluded beach. Call for pickup from town. (☎33134. €23 per person, with bath €25.50.) Pristine quarters with lots of space await at the **Oldcourt House B&B ❸,** on St. Martins Rd., about a 4min. walk past the SuperValu on the left. (☎33895. Singles €30-35; doubles €50-60.) If the ferry ride makes you desperate for a more luxurious rest, the modern amenities of the **Tuskar House Hotel ❹** on St. Martins Rd. should more than suffice. (☎33363. B&B shared rooms €39-49 per person; 2 nights plus breakfast and 1 dinner €99-125 per person.) To get to the **Rosslare Harbour Youth Hostel (An Óige/HI) ❶,** Goulding St., take a right at the top of the cliff, then head left around the far corner of the Hotel Rosslare; the hostel is past the supermarket to the left. Not the most luxurious accommodations in town, though they do have brand new mattresses. The cinder-block walls are compensated for by the courtyard out back. (☎33399. **Internet access** €1 per 10min. **Luggage storage** €1 per day. Check-in 5pm. Dorms €12-15.)

The restaurants in Rosslare Harbour tend to be expensive—your best bet is to grab some groceries and cook for yourself. The **SuperValu,** to your right on the way to the hostel, has a substantial selection. (☎33107. Open M-F 8am-7pm, Sa 8am-6pm, Su 9am-1pm.) If chippers are your thing, you'll be right at home in Rosslare, land of quick fried fish. You might also try the **Portholes ❷,** which combines meals with a maritime mini-museum and tables for pool sharks. (☎33110. Mains €9-13; food served 12:30-2:30pm and 6-9pm.) **Tuskar House Hotel ❸,** on St. Martins Rd. overlooking the ferryport, hosts two Chinese restaurants. (☎33363. Mains €8-15.) The Tuskar also houses a small hotel bar and the larger, residential **Punters Bar.** The best pub in Rosslare, however, is **Mac Faddens,** on the N25 about 1 mi. out of town. The *craic* here is as good as you'll get in Rosslare, so it's well worth the walk. (☎33590. Open Su-W 10:30am-11:30pm, Th-Sa 10:30am-12:30am.)

SIGHTS AND ACTIVITIES. On the way off or onto your boat, you'll walk across the gangplank over the waters of Rosslare Harbour. Look down as you walk across, as the **Harbour** is Rosslare's only sight. Though a transportation hub for thousands of visitors each year, the town has yet to invest in tourist attractions of any sort. For entertainment of any kind, head to the Tuskar House Hotel, which arranges **golf** outings and **sea angling** trips for guests of the hotel.

NEAR ROSSLARE HARBOUR

KILMORE QUAY AND THE SALTEE ISLANDS ☎053

Thirteen miles southwest of Rosslare Harbour on Forlorn Point, the small fishing village of Kilmore Quay (pop. 550) sings a siren song of thatched roofs and white-washed seaside cottages. In early July you'll find the entire town on *craic* for the annual family-oriented Seafood Festival, but during the rest of the year, the salty air keeps everything moving at a slow, dream-like pace. Kilmore Quay provides the ideal escape destination—it's where you come to get away from it all and write a novel on your romance with the sea. No, really, it is.

ORIENTATION AND PRACTICAL INFORMATION. To reach Kilmore Quay from Rosslare Harbour, take the Wexford road to Tagoat and turn left; from Wexford, take the Rosslare road, turn right on R739 near Piercetown, and continue for 4 mi. **Bus Éireann** runs between Wexford and Kilmore Quay (M-Sa 3 per day, €5.10), and **Doyle's Hackney & Bus Hire** (☎29624 or 087 472 959) shuttles a bus into Wexford on Tuesdays, Thursdays, and Fridays, leaving at 11am and returning at 2pm. Doyle's is also available for 24hr. hackney ("taxi") service. In town, two streets diverge from the harbor: **Wexford Rd.** and **"the back road."** A small beach lies to the left of the water, and the 7 mi. **Ballyteigue Beach** is also nearby. **Tourist information** is available at the **Stella Maris Community Centre** on the Wexford road, which also has private showers for €2 and **Internet access** for €4 per 30min. (☎29922. Center open M-Sa 8am-8pm, Su 9am-8pm.) The **post office** is on the Wexford road, on the way out of town. (☎29641. Open M-F 9am-12:30pm and 1:30-5:30pm.)

ACCOMMODATIONS, FOOD, AND PUBS. Thrifty and rustic lodging is available at the **Kilturk Independent Hostel ❷**, but not until May 2003, when it finally reopens after months of renovations. The hostel, which used to be an old schoolhouse, is located 1½ mi. from town on the Wexford road between Kilmore Quay and Kilmore Town. The buses between Wexford and Kilmore Quay will stop at the hostel by request; otherwise call the hostel for pickup. (☎29883. Dorms €15.) Among the town's many B&Bs is **The Haven ❸**, 100 yd. down from the first right after the post office. You'll delight in the ocean view, tea and coffee, and the elegant and friendly Betty Walsh. (☎29979. Singles €30; doubles €50.) May Bates's pleasant **Harborlights B&B ❸**, New Ross Rd., has a lush lawn, roomy quarters, and a good view of the Saltee Islands. It's right in the middle of town across from the Silver Fox restaurant, just to the left of the driveway. (Singles €35; doubles €56.)

The wonderful **Bird's Rock ❷** coffee shop, housed in the Stella Maris Community Centre (see above), serves huge dishes for €4-6. (☎29922. Open M-F 9:30am-5pm, Sa-Su 9am-1pm.) Reel in the best meal around at the **Silver Fox ❹**, across from the Maritime Museum. The super-fresh seafood is served in morbidly ironic fish-shaped dishes. Everyone knows it's good, so call ahead for reservations. (☎29888. Mains €15-22, vegetarian mains €15. Open M-Sa 5-9:30pm.) **The Wooden House ❷**, to your left as you head up from the Maritime Museum, serves pub food (€7-8) and sates thirsty fishermen. (☎29804. Open M-W until 11:30pm, Th-Sa until 12:30am, Su until 11pm.) Head to **James Kehoe's Pub**, on the Wexford road directly across from St. Peter's Church, for your fill of swills and gills. (☎29830. Mains €13-14; served until 8:30pm. Live music every Sa night. Open M-Sa until 12:30am, Su until 11pm.)

SIGHTS AND FESTIVALS. Kilmore Quay runs daily boat trips out to the **Saltee Islands**, formerly a pagan pilgrimage site and now Ireland's largest **bird sanctuary**. The winged population numbers near 50,000, and sings loudly on the rocks and in every crevice of the cliff banks. You'll find little more than salt and feathers in this refuge for puffins, razorbills, and grey seals, but it's an ideal place for a long picnic. Prominent granite monuments and a throne in the middle of one of the islands provide reminders that the Saltees once belonged to absentee landlord Prince Michael Salteens. A narrow ridge of rock is thought to have connected the smaller island to the mainland in ancient times. This land bridge, called **St. Patrick's Causeway**, was used for driving cattle to pasture on the islands. The beginning of St. Pat's bridge is visible at low tide. To get there, take the road to Kilmore town and turn right at the signpost, roughly 1 mi. from town; or scramble over rocks and tide-pools on the beach—turn left, it's a 20min. walk from the harbor. **Boats** leave the mainland each morning, weather permitting. **Declan Bates** makes the 30min. trip daily at around 11am and returns at 4pm. (☎29684 or 087 252 9736. €14, children €4.) **Dick Hayes** will bring you aboard for **deep-sea angling** and **reef-fishing**; call ahead to arrange a time or to ask about renting equipment. (☎29704 or 087 254 9111. Full day boat rental €300; evening rental 4:30-8pm €200. Rods €10.)

The village floats its **Maritime Museum** in the lightship *Guillemot*, once anchored near the harbor and now cemented into it. Climb into the hold and view Irish naval artifacts and marine accessories, then learn the tragic stories of local shipwrecks.

You can trigger wall speakers to give short audio explanations of the room's contents, available in French, German, or English. (☎29655. Open June-Aug. daily noon-6pm; May and Sept. Sa-Su noon-6pm. €4; students, seniors, and children €2.) Through town and just around the corner, the **Millennium Memorial Hiking Trail** winds its way along Forlorn Point. A stone ship overlooking the majestic ocean pays tribute to local sailors lost at sea, and a giant rib-bone from a fin whale that recently washed ashore is on display nearby. The **Kilmore Seafood Festival** hauls in seafood, music, and games for ten raucous days in mid-July.

NEW ROSS (ROS MHIC TREOIN) ☎051

New Ross makes an ideal rest from your tour of Ireland's southeast corner; Waterford, the Hook, Wexford, and Kilkenny all lie within easy reach of this fair hamlet. The town has a tidy little list of sights, most involving the Irish exodus and beloved great-grandson John F. Kennedy. The *Dunbrody*, a coffin ship replica from the Famine era, is a powerful must-see.

ORIENTATION AND PRACTICAL INFORMATION. Most goings-on in New Ross take place on a strip of waterfront known simply as **the Quay.** Other major thoroughfares are **Mary St.,** which extends uphill from the bridge, and **South St.,** which runs parallel to the Quay one block inland and later changes its name to **North St.** as it crosses Mary St. New Ross is on N25 (to Wexford and Waterford) and N30 (to Enniscorthy); hitchers find plenty of rides on either, especially in the morning and late afternoon. *Let's Go* does not recommend hitching at any time of day. **Bus Éireann** runs from the Mariners Inn on the Quay to; Dublin (3hr., 3 per day, €9); Rosslare Harbour (1hr.; M-Sa 4 per day, Su 3 per day; €9); and Waterford (25min.; M-Sa 8 per day, Su 4 per day; €4.70). A bus driven by a man called "The Sage" heads directly to Kilkenny from the train station. (1 per day; €5. Call the tourist office for details.) The New Ross **tourist office,** in the **Dunbrody Centre** next to the famine ship, has useful maps in the free *New Ross Town and Area Guide* and *A Guide to New Ross.* (☎421 857; www.newrosschamber.ie. Open daily 9am-6pm.) Banks with 24hr. **ATMs** abound: **Bank of Ireland,** the Quay (☎421 267), is just steps away from the bus stop and tourist office; **AIB** (☎421 319) and **TSB** (☎422 060) are across from each other on South St. The **post office** signs, seals, and delivers on Charles St., just off the Quay. (☎421 261. Open M-Sa 9am-5:30pm.)

ACCOMMODATIONS, FOOD, AND PUBS. The **Mac Murrough Farm Hostel ❶** is reason enough to visit New Ross. Follow Quay St. to Mary St. uphill to its end, turn left, then right, then left at the traffic lights (the SuperValu will be on your left) onto the Ring road. Take a right at the Statoil Station; the remaining mile to the hostel is signposted. Confused? Call for pickup. The delightfully down-to-earth owners make this the place to stay, the sheep give a rowdy greeting, and with dogs named Floozie and Trollop you just can't go wrong. (☎421 383; www.macmurrough.com. **Internet access** €2.50 per hr. Dorms €12-14; doubles €28-32.) For a bed in town and a bigger dent in your wallet, try **Riversdale House ❷,** William St. Follow South St. all the way to William St. and turn left up the hill. The owners take pride in their snazzy rooms and commanding view of town. (☎422 515. Singles €40; doubles €52-56.) **Inishross House ❷,** 96 Mary St., is closer, a good deal cheaper, but not quite so spiffy. (☎421 335. Singles €28; doubles €50.)

L&N SuperValu, generic grocer par excellence, is on the Quay. (☎421 392. Open M-Tu 8am-7pm, W 8am-8pm, Th 8am-9pm, F 8am-10pm, Sa 8am-7:30pm, Su 9am-6pm.) On South St., the friendly staff at **Il Primo ❸** dishes out large portions of Italian fare late into the night. (☎425 262. 18-21 South St. Mains €11.35-16.45. Open daily noon-11pm.) Down the street, **The Tea Rooms ❷** serve a nice breakfast and inexpensive sandwiches. (Mains €2-7. Open M-Sa 9am-6pm). Dine in transit aboard **The Galley** (☎421 723), which runs restaurant cruises from New Ross into Waterford Harbour. Choose your meal: lunch (2hr.; 12:30pm; €20, cruise only €10), tea (2hr.; 3pm; €10/€8), or dinner (2-3hr.; 6 or 7pm; €30/€15).

SIGHTS. During the **Great Famine,** thousands of emigrants searching for a better life stepped into the dank, dreary, and crowded holds of wooden sailboats to make the torturous 52-day journey across the ocean to America. Many left from New Ross, and one of the ships that carried the hopeful souls was called *The Dunbrody*. The original ship sank off the coast of Canada after her days as a famine ship were complete, but a brand new 410-ton, 176 ft. oak replica sits in New Ross, inviting visitors to see the conditions both first class and "steerage" passengers had to endure. Tours start with a 10min. video highlighting the making of the new **Dunbrody,** and then actors lead ticket-holders into the ship to relive the ordeal. The ship also has a computerized database for investigating coffin ship passengers. (Open July-Aug. daily 9am-6pm; Oct.-Mar. noon-5pm. €6, students €5, seniors €4.50.) For landlubbers, there's 13th-century **St. Mary's Church,** off Mary St. Mrs. Culleton, four doors down at 6 Church St., can provide the key and a booklet on the significance of the stone structures inside. Protestant masses are held in a new annex on Sundays. The roots of Camelot run deep in Co. Wexford—the **John F. Kennedy Arboretum** lies 7 mi. south of New Ross on the Ballyhack road (R783). Stroll around 623 gorgeous acres and nearly 6000 species dedicated to Ireland's favorite Yankee Prez. The small **cafe** doubles as gift shop. (☎388 171. Open May-Aug. daily 10am-8pm; Apr. and Sept. 10am-6:30pm; Oct.-Mar. 10am-5pm. Last admission 45min. before closing. €2.50, seniors €1.90, children €1.20.)

THE HOOK PENINSULA

Southeast of New Ross, the Hook is a peaceful peninsula noted for its historic abbeys, forts, and lighthouses. Sunny coastlines draw deep-sea anglers to Waterford Harbour and Tramore Bay, while the pubs on the oceanfront keep the midnight oil burning long past midnight. Unfortunately, public transportation does not reach this burgeoning vacation region, so itinerant travelers are dependent on cars or bikes. Those who make it here are rewarded with a quiet and relaxing place in which to enjoy the sanctity of being away from it all. You can approach the peninsula by an inland route from New Ross, or by crossing Waterford Harbour on the Ballyhack-Passage East ferry (every 20min., pedestrians €1.50). The Hook is best explored by car; hitching short rides is generally easy, although we at *Let's Go* do not recommend it. Plan ahead by checking out www.thehook-wexford.com.

BALLYHACK AND ARTHURSTOWN ☎051

Ten miles south of New Ross, **Ballyhack** threatens its cross-channel neighbor, Passage East, with a profile dominated by 15th-century **Ballyhack Castle.** Although the Castle fails to strike fear into the hearts of current invaders, it was built around 1450 by William Marshall (Strongbow's heir; see **Christians and Vikings,** p. 55) to protect his precious port at New Ross. Marshall wanted to make sure the job was done right, so he hired the Crusading Order of the Knights Hospitallers, who were known for their valor in battle and compassion for the sick. Tours lead visitors up the castle tower and take special delight in displaying the ghastly methods of self-defense employed by the "charitable" knights. The 500-year-old intact wicker ceilings will inspire new faith in your patio furniture. (☎389 468. Open mid-June to Sept. M-F 10am-1pm and 2-6pm, Sa-Su 10am-6pm. €1.20, students €0.50.)

Two miles north of Ballyhack on the New Ross road lurks **Dunbrody Abbey,** a magnificent ruin that was originally home to a late 12th-century Cistercian monastic order. The abbey is almost wholly intact, and you can wander through its little rooms with considerable freedom. Just across the road, the **visitors center** and a **cafe** sit among the rubble of a **castle** once associated with the abbey. The center features a doll-house replica of what the castle would have looked like whole and fully furnished. An impressive **hedge-row maze,** planted in 1992, began with 2 ft. high yew trees that once confounded only Lilliputians. They're now strapping 6 ft. adolescents, and will eventually reach 15 ft. (☎388 603. Center open July-Aug. 10am-7pm; May-June and Sept. 10am-6pm. Abbey €2. Castle and maze €3.)

The Ballyhack-bound will find lodgings in **Arthurstown,** where the Hook's budget accommodations are at their best and brightest. Take a right from the landing area of the Ballyhack ferryport and follow the **Slí Charman** (SHLEE KAR-man) coastal path; the village lies half a mile up the trail. Arthurstown has a pub and opulent views of water; water everywhere, but nary a bite to eat, so cook your own or head to Ducannon, a few miles away. Back in Ballyhack, the only edibles in town are found at **Byrne's ❷,** a small food store and pub right by the ferryport. The pub offers sandwiches (€3.50), but the store has a more extensive grocery selection. (☎389 107. Store open M-Sa 9:30am-9:30pm, Su noon-2pm and 4-7pm.) Coming from Ballyhack, the first left leads to the driveway of **Arthurstown Youth Hostel (An Óige/HI) ❶,** which was built 200 years ago to the uncompromising specifications of the English Coast Guard. The weathered interior hides a decent arrangement of dorms and a fantastic kitchen with broad pine tables, candles, and an upbeat communal air. (☎389 411. Lockout 10:30am-5pm. Dorms €12; doubles €34-40; quads €52.) Switch from rustic to elegant and treat yourself to the B&B located right next to the hostel. **Marsh Mere Lodge ❹** has a spectacular view from the patio deck and a treasure-trove of superb artwork and antiques. (☎389 186 or 087 222 7303; www.marshlodge.com. €40-50 per person.) Alternatively, head to **Glendine House B&B ❹,** a large Georgian manor up Duncannon Hill; look for the horses on the front lawn. The rooms are huge and beautifully decorated. (☎389 258; www.glendinehouse.com. **Internet access** available. Singles €40-50; doubles €70-80.)

DUNCANNON (DÚN CANANN) ☎051

The scenic Hook Head Peninsula truly begins after the village of Duncannon, south of Arthurstown. The area is popular as a weekend vacation spot, but during the week its rolling landscape shakes lose the bedlam and makes for pleasant jaunts among a bizarre assortment of medieval ruins and summer-time bungalows. The peninsula's circuit is best covered by car, but brave bikers should be up to the challenge. From Arthurstown, go east on the Duncannon Rd. and look for the sharp right turn with a sign marked "Duncannon"; the town is 1 mi. down the road.

Duncannon Fort, which holds down the cliffs at the edge of the village, has long failed to meet public expectations. From the moment it was built in the 1580s, people complained that it was too easy to conquer by land, and in the 17th century it surrendered to both Cromwell and William of Orange. Tours are given upon request. A small **cafe** provides shelter from the wind and an assortment of hot and cold eats for around €5. (☎389 454 or 389 188. Open daily 10am-5:30pm. €2.50, seniors €2.) For groceries in Duncannon, look to **Strand Store.** (☎389 216. Open daily 9am-10pm.) More substantive food options can be found in the center of Duncannon. Pub grub can be found at **Roches Bar ❷** (☎389 188; food from 12:30pm), which serves sandwiches (€3-6) and mains (€6-8). Next door and under the same ownership, brand new **Sqigl ❹** complements its mouthwatering dishes with an extensive wine list. (☎389 188. Mains €16-25. Open summer Tu-Th 7-10pm, F-Sa 7-11pm, Su 7-9:30pm; winter Tu-Th until 9:30pm, F-Sa until 10:30pm.)

HOOK HEAD

This tiny hamlet at the tip of the peninsula possesses the area's biggest attraction. A little under 5 mi. down the road from Templetown, a sign warns: "Great care must be taken near the water's edge: freak waves and slippery rocks." The **Hook Lighthouse,** a stout medieval tower founded by St. Dubhan, is the oldest operating beacon in the British Isles. Tours run up its 115 13th-century steps to reach panoramic views of the peninsula and neighboring Waterford Harbour. During the ascent, visitors are treated to a hearty dose of history and lighthouse lore. The top room is a recent addition—that is, it only dates back to 1800. (☎397 055. Lighthouse open Mar.-Oct. daily 9:30am-5:30pm. Guided tours every 30min. €4.75, students and seniors €3.50.) On the eastern side of the peninsula is Ireland's own gloriously secluded **Tintern Abbey,** founded in the 13th century, and the perfect place for an early evening picnic. (☎562 650. Open June-Sept. 9:30am-6:30pm. Wander freely or take a tour for €1.90.) The abbey is 3 mi. from the Ballycullane stop on the Waterford-Rosslare rail line. Call the tourist office in nearby **Fethard** for more information on the Hook region. (☎397 502. Open July-Aug. M-F 9:30am-5:30pm, Sa-Su 11am-3pm; Sept.-June M-F 9:30am-5:30pm.)

WATERFORD HARBOUR

Waterford Harbour straddles the Waterford-Wexford county line east of Waterford City. It is here that Oliver Cromwell coined the phrase "by hook or by crook": he had plotted to take Waterford City from either Hook Head or the opposite side of the harbor at Crooke. Both sides of the harbor host historic ruins, fishing villages, and stunning ocean views. Through most of the region, travelers should expect peace and quiet, but not convenience. To cross the harbor, either drive up 37 mi. and around through New Ross or take the **Passage East Car Ferry** between Ballyhack and Passage East. (☎382 480 or 382 488. Continuous sailings Apr.-Sept. M-Sa 7am-10pm, Su and holidays 9:30am-10pm; Oct.-Mar. M-Sa 7am-8pm, Su and holidays 9:30am-8pm. Cars €6, cyclists €2.50, pedestrians €1.30.) Unless you're looking for total rest and relaxation, the town of **Passage East** is best passed through. The journey from Waterford to Passage East and then around the Hook Peninsula affords some spectacular views, but be advised that Waterford is the only place in the harbor where you can rent a bike. The roads outside Waterford are hilly and windy, and a long bike journey will test the stamina of even the most ferocious cyclist. From Wexford, follow signs for Ballyhack to reach the ferry.

DUNMORE EAST (DÚN MÓR) ☎051

Vacationing Irish families have made little Dunmore East their summertime mecca. In good weather, you'll have to be careful not to squash any of the children swarming underfoot on the beaches. When you're not watching for urchins, look out to sea—the calm harbor, stunning cliffs, and distant Hook make for spectacular views. Dunmore's **beaches** are great for swimming, especially at several points where trails descend into isolated coves. Kittiwakes (small gulls) throng the coastline, building their nests in cliff faces unusually close to human habitation—you'll see hundreds of them on the cliffs of **Badger's Cove.** Wave after mesmerizing wave crashes into the rocks at the less fowl precipices, which are accessible via the dirt road past Dock Rd. For offshore thrills, the **Dunmore East Adventure Centre** on the docks will teach you to snorkel, surf, kayak, canoe, or rock-climb. Bring a towel and swimsuit; they'll provide the rest. (☎383 783. €30 per half-day activity.)

The **Suirway** bus service (☎382 209; 24hr. timetable ☎382 422) runs the 9½ mi. from Waterford to Dunmore East (30min., M-Sa 3-4 per day, €2.30). Wait outside the Bay Cafe, or just flag it down anywhere on its route. The town is spread along two areas: **the Strand,** and **Dock Rd.,** which leads uphill and to the docks. There's **no ATM** in Dunmore, but any of the small groceries along Dock Rd., including **Dingley's** (☎383 372; open 7:30am-10pm) should have a **bureau de change.**

Church Villa ❸ is an immaculate B&B with bright rooms and a sunny owner to match. Ask for the french toast, served with real maple syrup, for breakfast. (☎383 390. Singles €29.) **Creaden View B&B ❸,** on Dock Rd., has a nice garden and rooms overlooking the bay. (☎383 339. Singles €38-45.) **Springfield B&B ❸,** a signposted 200 yd. from the beach, has airy bedrooms and a conservatory breakfast room. (☎383 448. Open Mar.-Nov. Doubles €51-56.) Past the Anchor pub on the hill from the beach lies **Queally's Caravan and Camping Park ❶,** where the assorted Queally's will let you squeeze a tent among their trailers. (☎383 001. €13 per tent.)

Groceries are plentiful at **Londis Supermarket,** Dock Rd., on the right after you pass the Ocean Hotel. (Open summer M-F 9am-8:30pm, Sa-Su 9am-10pm; shorter off-season hours.) **The Melting Pot Cafe and Craft shop ❸,** on Dock Rd. near the post office, simmers with yummy smells and fantastic bay views. Indulge in their many tasty mains, such as pan-fried cod in herb butter, chips, and salad for €11.50. (☎383 271. Lunch €7.50; dinner €13. Open Su-W 11am-5pm, F-Sa 11am-4pm and 7-9:30pm.) The **Bay Cafe ❷,** also on Dock Rd., serves homemade food for sit-down or takeaway. (☎383 900. Sandwiches €3-6. Open M-Th 9am-6pm, F-Su 9am-9pm.) In the evening, denizens of Dunmore gather to enjoy live music at the **Anchor** (☎383 133) or **Power's Bar,** on Dock Rd. across from the post office (☎383 318; music Su).

TRAMORE (TRÁ MHÓR) ☎051

Those crazy Celts had an eye for the obvious—*Trá Mhór* is Irish for "big beach." Every summer, Tramore (Tra-MORE) draws enormous numbers of tourists to its smooth 3 mi. strand, many of whom are looking to take advantage of what is arguably the best surf in Europe. Despite the tacky amusements found at seaside resorts the world over, Tramore retains something of its small-town character. The cliffs rising above the beach are great places to roost and gape at the views.

TRANSPORTATION. Many buses connect Tramore to Waterford. **Bus Éireann** runs two routes: one takes you around the beach (12-16 per day) and the other goes via the race course (6-9 per day); both cost €2 and take 40min. **Rapid Express Coaches** (☎872 149) sends buses from the station to Waterford every two hours (7 per day, €2.50), and to Dublin. Call **Tramore Cabs** for a taxi. (☎391 500).

ORIENTATION AND PRACTICAL INFORMATION. Tramore can be difficult to get around, as few streets keep their names for longer than a block and undulating hills confound even the most homesick of homing pigeons. The bus station is on the **Waterford road** (technically **Turkey Rd.**), a block from the intersection of **Strand St.** (which becomes **Main St.** then **Summer Hill**) and **Gallwey's Hill** (which joins **Church Rd.** up the cliff). The **tourist office** moves all over, and was last seen next to the Tramore Cab station. (☎381 572. Open June-Aug. M-Sa 10am-1pm and 2-6pm, Su 11am-1pm and 2-6pm.) **AIB** (☎381 216) is on Strand St., and the **Bank of Ireland** (☎386 611) lies farther up; both have 24hr. **ATMs.** Inquire at the **library,** on Market St. (☎381 479), about free **Internet access.** The **post office** is on Main St. (☎390 196. M-F 9am-1pm and 2-5:30pm, Sa 9am-1pm.)

ACCOMMODATIONS AND CAMPING. Tramore is bursting with B&Bs—the cheapest are along the Waterford road and the best are along Church Rd. The most competitive rates and the best views in Tramore are at **The Cliff ❸,** Church St., a first rate Christian Guest House owned by the YWCA. The Cliff provides bed, breakfast, parking, and, for a little extra, an evening meal. (☎381 363; www.iol.ie/~thecliff. Singles €28-35; doubles €50-56. Only Christian groups can book in the winter, summer is non-denominational.) **Ard More House ❸,** Doneraile Dr., gazes at the water over town-house rooftops. Head up Church Rd. and take your first left. (☎381 716. Open Apr.-Sept. €26-32 per person.) **Venezia ❸,** on Church Road Grove and signposted off Church Rd., has top-notch beds. (☎381 412. Doubles €58-62.) Take a sharp right on Church Rd. at the top of Gallwey's Hill to find **Turret House ❹.** It's stylish, chic, and somewhat expensive, but huge rooms with bigger windows—some with ocean views—make the climb worthwhile. (☎386 342. €40 per person.) **Clonleen B&B ❹,** on Love Ln., lives up to its address with romantic rooms and a pair of friendly dogs. (☎381 264. Open Mar.-Oct. Singles €45; doubles €60.) If all the B&Bs in town are full, try **Seacrest ❸,** at the top of a hill on the main road out to Waterford. (☎381 888. Singles €30, with bath €38; doubles €56.) A mile and a half out Dungarvan Coast Rd., between the golf course and the Metal Man monument to shipwreck victims, the family-style **Newtown Caravan and Camping Park ❶** is the best of several nearby campsites. (☎381 979 or 381 121. Open Easter-Sept. €5-14 per tented person, depending on season. Showers €1.)

FOOD AND PUBS. Up Main St., **L&N SuperValu** awaits your wandering taste buds. (☎386 036. Open summer M-F 8am-10pm, Sa 8am-9pm, Su 9am-8pm; winter M-W 8am-8pm, F 8am-9pm, Sa 8am-8:30pm, Su 10am-8pm.) Schools of frying fish are as ubiquitous in Tramore as in any other Irish sea town. **Apple Brown Betty ❶,** in a wee octagonal hut on the beach directly across from the lifeguard station, has splendid ocean fare. (☎391 680. Giant crepes €3-5.50. Open 10am-7pm.) Trot on over to the **The Sea Horse ❷** on Strand St. for pub chow, fancy coffee, and a friendly atmosphere. (☎386 091. Mains €7; "mixed grill" meat and veggies €11. Food served noon-9pm.) If you're thinking "fancy" for dinner, head to **Asila ❸**, 2 Market St., but book ahead. (☎330 807. Lunches €7.50; vegetarian dinners €14; meatier dinners €15-19. Open Tu-F 10am-3pm and 6:30-9pm, Sa-Su 6:30-9pm.) For drinks and dance, the three floors of **The Victoria House ("The Vic"),** Queens St., get younger, louder, and more crowded as you descend. (☎390 338. Live pop Su afternoons.) A young set also fills **The Hibernian ("Hi B"),** or, as the late bar is dubbed, **The Cellar,** at the intersection of Gallwey's Hill and Strand St. (☎386 396. Carvery menu €8.50, served noon-7pm. Open M-W 11am-11:30pm, Th-Sa 11am-12:30am, Su 11am-11pm.) After the nightly live music at the bar ends, everyone hops next door to the pop chart-happy **Hi B Disco,** where tunes blast across a packed floor. (Disco W-Su. Cover €6.35. Doors close at 1am.)

ACTIVITIES. Surfing? In Ireland? Dude. The Emerald Isle boasts some of the best surf in Europe, and the **Tramore Bay Surf Centre** provides top-of-the-line day-time and evening fun. The friendly staff rents surfboards, bodyboards, wetsuits and other surfing accessories that could even make doggy-paddling look cool. They also offer individual and group lessons that help you in your quest to become the Irish Big Kahuna. Call ahead to check the variable surf. (☎391 297; www.surf-bay.com. Complete surf package €13 per hr. Open daily 9:30am-6:30pm; call ahead for bookings.) The waterfront promenade offers all sorts of entertainment, including the **Splashworld** indoor waterpark, an assortment of rides, pools, and screaming, neglected children. (☎390 176. Open M-F 7am-10pm, Sa-Su 9am-9pm. €8.50, students €6.50.) Just outside town the **cliffs** get *really* spectacular, and the tourist office can provide you with a list of historic and scenic walks along them. The best is the **Doneraile Walk,** a path that stems off of Church Rd.—follow the little, red markers away from Tramore and into a land of cliff, ocean, and cloud. About 1 mi. out, you can give **Guillamene Cove** a swim. Ignore the "Men Only" sign—a smaller one underneath explains that it's been "retained merely as a relic of the past." *Let's Go* does not recommend foolish diving or other acts of machismo.

DUNGARVAN (DUN GARBHÁN) ☎058

Filled with fishermen, market-goers, ocean breezes, and rollicking pubs, Dungarvan is far more endearing than most transportation hubs. Nestled a short distance from the Comeragh Mountains on a harbor with especially large tides, pub-goers on Davitt's Quay can sip their pints while watching the harbor boats ground themselves as the water slowly ebbs. Shopping is plentiful in the active square, and those hankering for another castle tour will delight in the towns Castle.

TRANSPORTATION AND PRACTICAL INFORMATION. **Buses** (☎051 879 000) leave from Davitt's Quay. They run east to Waterford (1hr.; M-Sa 16-17 per day, Su 13 per day; €7.35), west to Cork (13 per day, €11.60), and north to Lismore (M and Th-F 1 per day, €4.25) and Dublin (M-Sa 5 per day, Su 6 per day; €11.40). You can purchase bus tickets in advance from the **John Lynch Vegetable Shop,** next to **Davitt's Pub. Main St.,** also called **O'Connell St.,** runs through the town's central square; **Emmet St.,** or **Mitchell St.,** runs parallel to Main St. one block uphill and is home to the hostel and several B&Bs. The **Cork Rd.** veers off Emmet St. at the *Garda* station. The helpful **tourist office,** just outside the Square in the Courthouse building, has free maps and music listings for area pubs. (☎41741. Open M-Sa 9am-6pm.) **Bank of Ireland,** the Square, has a 24hr. **ATM,** as does the **AIB** on Meagher St. (Both open M 10am-5pm, Tu-F 10am-4pm.) Free and speedy **Internet access** is available at the **library** on Davitt's Quay. (☎41231. Open Tu-Sa 10am-5pm, also W-Th 6-8pm.) The **post office** sits on Bridge St., outside the Square. (☎41176. Open M-F 9am-5:30pm, Sa 9am-3pm.)

ACCOMMODATIONS, FOOD, AND PUBS. **Alwin House ❸,** O'Connell St., a bit down and across from the movie theater, is run by an extremely friendly family and has spacious rooms. (☎45994; www.cablesurf.com/alwin. Singles €40; doubles €60.) More expensive but with even bigger rooms, great views, and a gorgeous dining room, is **Mountain View House ❹,** just off O'Connell St. down from the theater. (☎42588. Singles €50-55; doubles €80-90.) The **Dungarvan Holiday Hostel (IHH) ❶,** on the Youghal road (Rice St.) just off Emmet St. opposite the *Garda* Station, is housed in a former Christian Brothers friary. (☎44340. Wheelchair-accessible. **Bike rental** €7.60 per day. Dorms €11.50; private rooms €13 per person.)

The immense **SuperValu** is on Main St. (☎45333. Open M-W 8am-9pm, Th-F 8am-10pm, Sa 8am-7:30pm, Su 9am-6pm.) Laid-back **Ormond's Cafe ❶,** on the Square, a few doors down from the tourist office, serves meals (€6-9) and outstanding desserts in a stone-walled, family-oriented, skylit cafe. (☎41153. Open M-Sa 8am-6pm.) Settle into the bizarre oversized wood furniture at **Interlude ❸,** on Davitt's Quay, next to the castle. Outdoor seating overlooking the water is brilliant on sunny days, but well-prepared meals and desserts are good at any time. (☎45898. Dinners €11-16. Open Tu-W 10:30am-9pm, Th-Sa 10:30am-9:30pm, Su 10:30am-5:30pm.) For authentic bagels with cream cheese and excellent coffee, walk down a little alley off of O'Connell St. to find **Broadway Bagels ❶.** (☎23843. Bagel sandwiches €4. Open M-Sa 8:30am-7:30pm, Su noon-5pm). At the far end of Darvitt's Quay, right near the castle, **Moorings Bar and Restaurant ❹** has a nautical feel, tasty meals, and a spacious beer garden. (☎41461. Food served noon-9:30pm. Dinner mains €16-20.) **Davitt's Pub,** Davitt's Quay, is huge, fabulous, and usually packed. A crowd of 18- to 80-year olds finds everything from intimate booths to tranquil tables overlooking the river to a large dance floor that opens as the night tears on. (☎44900. Disco Th-Su 11:30pm-2:30am.) In true seaside form, Dungarvan has its own **Anchor Bar** (☎41249), on Davitt's Quay. Small but sprightly and done up in hip primary colors, the Anchor hosts rock and trad bands most weekends. **Bridie Dee's,** 18 Mary St. (☎44588), has trad on Thursday through Monday nights.

SIGHTS AND FESTIVALS. **Dungarvan Castle,** presiding over Davitt's Quay, fell into disrepair a few years ago, at the beginning of the 14th century. The Provi-

SOUTHEAST IRELAND

sional IRA didn't much help matters when they set the joint on fire in 1922. The *Garda* took control of the building and used it as barracks until 1987, when it was vacated for renovations. A short video and the tour take visitors through the castle's turbulent history and all of its reconstructions. (☎48144. Tours leave on the hour. Open M-F 10am-5pm.) The **deep-sea fishing** in Dungarvan is excellent, though nearby waters do have a reputation for sharks. Fishing licenses are distributed at the tourist office. Capt. John Tynan leads expeditions on the *Avoca*. (☎42657 or 41327. €40 per day with rod and tackle.) The *Chaser V* can also be chartered at a similar price (☎41358). **Baumann's Jewellers,** 6 St. Mary St. (☎41395), has semi-precious tackle and a wealth of free information.

Dungarvan's **Féile na nDéise** (FAY-la nah ne-DAY-sya, "local area festival") packs the Square with free concerts during the first weekend in May, while in early July, the **Motorsport Weekend** pulls in vintage and race car enthusiasts.

ARDMORE (AIRD MHÓR) ☎024

St. Declan christianized Ardmore in the 4th century; the town's claim that it is the oldest Christian settlement in Ireland is well-supported by its ruins. Ardmore's must-do is the **cliffwalk,** a windy, 3 mi. path steeped in great ocean views and sprinkled with stops at all of the town's historic sights. A free map is available at the tourist office and the hostel. At one end of the walk is Ardmore's **cathedral,** built piecemeal on the site of St. Declan's monastery between 800 and 1400. The Deckster himself is said to be buried here, and the faithful swear that soil from the saint's grave cures diseases. In addition to its own collection of carvings, the cathedral houses two **ogham stones** (see **Ancient Ireland,** p. 54). Nearby you'll see a 97 ft. **round tower** whose door is the standard twelve monk-protecting feet above the ground (see **Glendalough,** p. 141). **St. Declan's Stone** is perched at the water's edge, on the right from Main St. along the shore. This intrepid lil' stone *floated* from Wales after the holy man visited. Down past the Cliff House hotel, at the other end of the cliffwalk, is **St. Declan's Well,** which contains water that is said to cure all afflictions. Hardy hikers can jump on the 56 mi. **St. Declan's Way,** which starts in town and runs up to Cahir in Co. Tipperary.

Buses run to Cork (1½hr.; M-Sa 3 per day, Su 1 per day; €10.10) and to Waterford via Dungarvan (2hr.; M-Th and Sa 2 per day, F 3 per day; €10.30). Ardmore is a 3 mi. detour off the Cork-Waterford road (N25). Hitching from the junction can be slow, and is not recommended by *Let's Go*. The excellent **tourist office,** housed in what appears to be a demonic sandcastle in the carpark by the beach, has information about the local beaches and an excellent leaflet outlining a **walking tour** of town. (☎94444. Open June-Aug. M-Sa 11am-1pm and 2-5pm, Su 2-5pm.) The **post office** is on Main St. (☎94191. Open M-F 9am-1pm and 2-5:30pm.)

The simple comforts of the **Ardmore Beach Hostel ❷,** which include beach access, are at the bottom of Main St., a hop, skip, and a jump away from the sand and surf. (☎94166. Dorms €13-14; private rooms €17 per person.) **Byron Lodge ❸,** Middle Rd., has literary aspirations and rooms with sunny alcoves. From Main St., take the street that runs uphill at the thatched cottage. (☎94157. Open Apr.-Sept. Singles with bath €32; doubles €54, with bath €56.) To find out about **camping** at the nearby but not immediately accessible **Goat Island** (free, no showers) ask at the tourist office. Ardmore's food offerings are tasty rather than extensive. **Quinn's Foodstore** is in the town center. (☎94250. Open June-Aug. daily 8am-9pm; Sept.-May 8am-6pm.) The local favorite restaurant is the **Cup and Saucer ❷,** Main St., which has a delightful flower garden out back, a distinctive homemade goodness, and meals for €5-7. (☎087 268 2403. Open daily 10am-6pm.) Vast **Paddy Mac's,** Main St. (☎94166), has pub grub on reserve from 12:30-8:30pm and a variety of weekend music. **Keever's Bar,** Main St. (☎94141), where the only sustenance available is liquid, is another fave of the older Ardmore crowd.

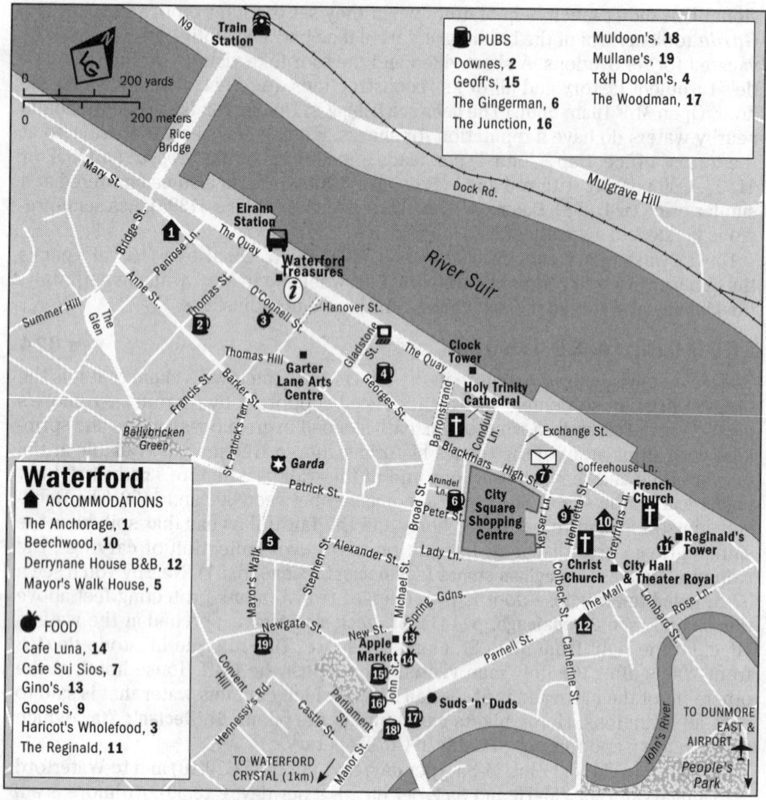

WATERFORD (PORT LÁIRGE) ☎051

A skyline of huge metal silos and harbor cranes greet the visitor to Waterford. Fortunately, behind this industrial facade lies a city with ten centuries of fascinating history. The grandson of the Viking Ivor the Boneless founded Vadrafjord around AD 914 to harbor his longships, making it the oldest city in Ireland. Long considered mere brutes, the Vikings have recently gained recognition for their suave contributions to the development of this mercantile hub (see **Christians and Vikings,** p. 55). Traces of early Vadrafjord persist in Waterford's streets, despite the massive freighters that have since replaced the longships.

TRANSPORTATION

Airport: ☎875 589. Served by **Euroceltic** (www.euroceltic.com). Follow the Quay, turn right at Reginald's Tower, then left at the sign. 20min. from town.

Trains: Plunkett Station, across the bridge from the Quay (call ☎317 889 M-F 9am-6pm; ☎876 243 for 24hr. timetable). Staffed M-Sa 9am-6pm, Su at departure times. To: **Dublin** (2½hr., M-F 5-6 per day, €17-21); **Kilkenny** (40min., 3–5 per day, €7); **Limerick** (2¼hr., M-Sa 2 per day, €14); **Rosslare Harbour** (1hr., M-Sa 2 per day, €8).

Buses: ☎879 000. The station is on the Quay, across the street from the tourist office. Office open M-Sa 8:15am-6pm. To: **Cork** (2½hr., 10-13 per day, €13.30); **Dublin** (2¾hr.; M-Sa 10-12 per day, Su 6 per day; €9); **Galway** (4¾hr., 5-6 per day, €17); **Kilkenny** (1hr., 1 per day, €7); **Limerick** (2½hr.; M-Th and Su 6 per day, F 7 per day; €13); **Rosslare Harbour** (1¼hr., 3-5 per day, €11.60). **City buses** leave from the Clock Tower on the Quay. €1 for most areas. **City Imp** minibuses (€1) also cruise the town.

Bike Rental: Altitude, 22 Ballybricken St. (☎870 356), past the *Garda* station at the far side of the green. €20 per day; includes helmet. Free delivery to local accommodations.

Taxis: A piece of cake to find, 24hr. a day. Either go to the **cab stand** on Broad St. or try: **7 Cabs** (☎877 777); **Five-O Cabs** (☎850 000); **Rapid Cabs** (☎858 585).

Hitching: Waterford's few hitchers place themselves on the main routes, away from the tangled city center. To reach N24 (Cahir, Limerick), N10 (Kilkenny, Dublin), or N25 (New Ross, Wexford, Rosslare), they head over the bridge toward the train station. For the N25 to Cork, they continue down Parnell St.; others take city buses out to the Crystal Factory before sticking out a thumb. *Let's Go* does not recommend hitching.

ORIENTATION AND PRACTICAL INFORMATION

Modern Waterford sits on the ruins of the triangular Viking city. The horned ones must have had a knack for urban planning, because the area between **the Quay, Parnell St. (the Mall),** and **Barronstrand St. (Michael and Broad St.)** is still hopping, even without the sweet music of falsterpibes filling the air.

Tourist Office: On the Quay (☎875 823), across from the bus station. From the train station, cross Rice Bridge and turn left. Open July-Aug. M-Sa 9am-6pm and Su 11am-5pm; Sept.-Oct. and Apr.-June M-Sa 9am-6pm; Nov.-Mar. M-Sa 9am-5pm.

Banks: 24hr. **ATMs** line the streets. On the Quay, they're at **AIB** (☎874 824), by the clock tower, and **Bank of Ireland** (☎872 074). Both open M 10am-5pm, Tu-F 10am-4pm.

Luggage Storage: Plunkett Station. €1.30 per item. Open M-Sa 7:15am-9pm.

Pharmacy: Gallagher's Pharmacy, Barronstrand St. (☎878 103). An oasis of pharmaceutical care in the city center. Open M-Sa 8:15am-10pm, Su 10am-7pm.

Work Opportunities: The friendly people at the **Youth Information Centre,** 130 the Quay (☎877 328), will help with finding short-term work. They also offer info on work, travel, health, and on a variety of support groups (including **gay and lesbian**).

Emergency: Dial ☎999 or 112; no coins. **Police** *(Garda)*: Patrick St. (☎874 888).

Hospital: Waterford Regional Hospital (☎873 321). Follow the Quay east to the Tower Hotel. Turn left, then follow signs straight ahead to the hospital.

Internet Access: Voyager Internet Cafe, 85 the Quay (☎843 843). €1.20 per 15min. Open M-Sa 10am-7pm. Also at the **Youth Information Centre** (see above).

Post Office: The Quay (☎874 321). The largest of several letter-dispensaries. Open M and W-F 9am-5:30pm, Tu 9:30am-5:30pm, Sa 9am-1pm.

ACCOMMODATIONS

Most B&Bs in the city center are nothing to write home about; those outside town on the Cork road are better. All Waterford's hostels have gone the way of the dodo.

The Anchorage, 9 the Quay (☎854 302). Upscale accommodations, right on the Quay. Each room at this hotel-esque B&B has a TV, phone, and tea/coffee-making facilities. Summer singles €40, doubles €75. winter singles €35, doubles €65. ❸

Beechwood, 7 Cathedral Sq. (☎876 677). From the Quay, go up Henrietta St. Mrs. Ryan invites you into her charming home, located on a quiet pedestrian street. Windows look directly out at Christ Church Cathedral. Doubles €42. ❷

Derrynane House, 12 the Mall (☎875 179). Watch noisy Wexfordians walk by through the B&Bs fantastic floor-to-ceiling windows. Clean but not sparkling, Derrynane is showing its age with out-dated rugs and ceiling lights that require tugs on dangling ropes. €25 per person. ❸

Mayor's Walk House, 12 Mayor's Walk (☎855 427). A 15min. walk from the train station. Quiet, subdued rooms at a simple price. The amiable Ryders offer advice, biscuits, and a bottomless pot of tea. Open Feb.-Nov. Singles €25; doubles €44. ❸

FOOD

Satisfy your piggy cravings by picking up some cheap groceries at **Dunnes Stores** in the City Square Mall. (☎853 100. Open M-W 9am-7pm, Th-F 9am-9pm, Sa 9am-6pm, Su noon-6pm.) **Treacy's,** on the Quay between the Granville Hotel and the tourist office, has a small deli and a large selection of food-stuffs. (Open daily 8am-11pm.)

Haricot's Wholefood Restaurant, 11 O'Connell St. (☎841 299). Healthy, innovative dishes, sociable staff, and vegetarian-friendly meals—eat here as often as you can. The menu is constantly changing and everything is made from scratch (including the *craic*). Mains €8-10. Open M-F 9am-8pm, Sa 9am-6pm. ❷

Cafe Luna, 53 John St. (☎834 539). A late-night cafe serving pasta, salads, and sandwiches with a creative twist. Homemade soup and half a sandwich for €4.15. Most mains €5-7. Open M-W until midnight, Th-Su until 3:30am. ❷

Goose's Barbecue and Wine House, 19 Henrietta St. (☎858 426). Eat delicious skewer-grilled dishes with your vino at this stone-wall, eclectically decorated establishment. Vege-friendly. Mains €14-18. Open Tu-Sa 6-11pm. ❸

Gino's, John St. (☎879 513). A busy, bright, family restaurant that serves pizza prepared right before your eyes. Call in for takeaway orders. Individual pizzas €4.10. Homemade ice cream. Open daily until 10:45pm (sit-down) or 11pm (takeaway). ❷

Cafe Sui Sios, 54 High St. (☎841 063). The Gaelic phrase "Sui Sios" means to "Take a seat." Good advice in this popular and intimate cafe. Big portions and fine desserts lighten the concrete walls. Open Su-Th and Sa 8:30am-6pm, F 8:30am-8:30pm. ❷

The Reginald, 2-3 the Mall (☎855 087). Eat with your back to a section of the actual Norman wall that defended 14th-century Waterford. A bar, restaurant, and "Knight Club" with rich, delicious food and a classy (if rather touristy) environment. The menu changes daily. Salad buffet daily noon-3pm, bar menu 3-7pm, dinner 6-10:30pm. ❸

PUBS AND CLUBS

The Quays are flooded with pubs, and the corner of John and Parnell St. has its share as well. The good times continue past pub closings at 12:30am, when late bars and weekend discos kick it into high gear.

T&H Doolan's, George's St. (☎841 504). Doolan's has been serving for a respectable 300 years, in an awe-inspiring building with low, low ceilings that have been standing for over 800. Ask about Sinead O'Connor, who crooned here during her college days. The crowd is split between natives and imports. Trad nightly at 9:30pm.

Downes, Thomas St. (☎874 118). After you peer into the working well and play some snooker (€6 per hr.), finish up your pint and play a few games of squash on one of the two courts up the back steps (€5 per 40min.). Cool down with another pint in one of the quiet, relaxing nooks. Open Su-Th until 11:30pm, F-Sa until 1:30am.

The Gingerman, Arundel Ln. (☎875 041). Trad sessions jam at the front tables, and the good times spill into the dramatic dark wood and mirrors rear. Fortify yourself with *calcannon* (deluxe mashed potatoes) and ribs (€8.80). Food served noon-6pm.

Geoff's, 8 John St. (☎874 787). Most locals will tell you that Geoff's is the place to see and be seen. Bring a cell phone and a group of friends, slurp your pint, and laugh a bit too loudly. Deceptively spacious. Open until 12:30am on weekends.

The Woodman, at Parnell and John St. (☎858 130). A small traditional pub. Shuts down at 12:30am on weekends, so click those heels and head to the adjoining **Ruby's Nightclub,** which throbs with chart hits until 2:30am. Get your pre-boogie buzz in the pub's front lounge before 10pm to evade the €7-8 cover.

Mullane's, 15 Newgate St. (☎873 854), off New St. Sessions as hardcore as this aren't easy to come by. Older regulars with a sprinkling of young and a dash of tourist–the perfect mix. Call ahead for session times (usually W-Th and Sa-Su 9:45pm-12:15am); the pub is almost empty when there isn't one.

The Junction, at Parnell and John St. (☎844 842). With jams athumpin', a billiard table, large telly, and faux-train car to snuggle in, the Junction keeps a younger breed of pub-ber-clubbers scattered throughout its mega-space. Late bar throughout the week.

Muldoon's, John St. (☎873 693). **Merlin's** dance club, next door, casts a late-night spell on Muldoon's, your basic sports fan drinking hole.

SIGHTS

You can cover all of Waterford's sights in a day, but only if you are as swift as a Viking raider and as organized as a Norman invader. Buying the **City Pass** from **Waterford Tourism,** 1 Arundel St. (☎852 550), or at the Waterford Crystal Factory, Waterford Treasures, and Reginald's Tower, will get you into all three for €9.20.

THE WATERFORD CRYSTAL FACTORY. What do fancy dinner sets, the Times Square Millenium Ball, and all major sporting trophies (made from glass) have in common? They were all handcrafted at the spectacular Waterford Crystal Factory, 2 mi. from the city center on N25 (the Cork road). Watch master craftsmen transform molten goo into sparkling crystal or admire the finished products—and their astronomical prices—in the gallery. To get there, catch the City Imp outside Dunnes on Michael St. and request a stop at the factory (10-15min., every 15-20min., €1) or take city bus #1 (Kilbarry-Ballybeg, €1.10), leaving across from the Clock Tower every 30min. *(☎373 311 or 332 500. 1hr. tours every 15min.; audio-visual shows on demand. Tours €6. Mar.-Oct. daily 8:30am-4pm; Nov.-Jan. M-F 9am-3:15pm. Gallery open Mar.-Dec. daily 8:30am-6pm; Jan. M-F 9am-5pm; Feb. daily 9am-5pm.)*

WATERFORD TREASURES. To touch up on the 1000-year history of Waterford, head to Waterford Treasures at the Granary, connected to the tourist office. Named the **1999-2000 Ireland Museum of the Year,** the €4.5 million museum is well worth a visit. While the kids entertain themselves with the multimedia displays, parents can check out the amusing (and gory) cartoons that line the walls. An audio-visual handset lets you learn more about the historical oddities you find particularly interesting. The actual artifacts, such as the town's written charters, make quite an impressive show. *(☎304 500. Open June-Aug. M-F 9am-9pm, Su 10am-9am; May and Sept. M-F 9:30am-6pm; Oct.-Apr. M-F 10am-5pm. €6.)*

REGINALD'S TOWER. Hulking down at the end of the Quay, Reginald's tower has guarded the city's entrance since the 12th century. Its virtually impenetrable 10 ft. thick Viking walls have housed a prison, a mint, and the wedding reception of Strongbow and Aoife (see **Christians and Vikings,** p. 55). Tiny models illustrate the contributions Vikings, Normans, and English kings have made to Waterford's growth. *(☎873 501. Tours on demand. Open June-Sept. daily 9:30am-6:30pm; Oct.-May 10am-5pm. €1.90, seniors €1.20, students €0.70.)*

OTHER SIGHTS. The Walking Tour of Historic Waterford helps you to sort out the city's mongrel lineage. Included in the tour is a visit to a part of the original Viking walls. *(☎873 711 or 851 043. 1hr. tours depart from the Granville Hotel on the Quay and the Granary museum. Tours Mar.-Oct. daily at 11:45am and 1:45pm. €5.10.)* Many of Waterford's more recent buildings were the brainchildren of 18th-century architect John Roberts. The **Theatre Royal** and **City Hall,** both on the Mall, are his secular masterpieces. He's also responsible for the Catholic **Holy Trinity Cathedral** on Barronstrand St. and the Church of Ireland **Christ Church Cathedral** in Cathedral Sq. (up Henrietta St. from the Quay), making Waterford the only city in Europe where Catholics and Protestants worship in buildings designed by a common architect.

ENTERTAINMENT AND FESTIVALS

The tourist office can provide an annual list of major events in town, and any local newspaper, including the free *Waterford Today*, should have more specific entertainment listings. Keep your eyes peeled for posters as well. The seasonal **Waterford Show** at City Hall offers an entertaining performance of Irish music, stories, and dance. Ticket cost €12, and include a glass of Baileys or wine at the show. (☎358 397 or 875 788; after 5pm try ☎381 020. May-June and Sept. Tu, Th, and Sa 9pm. July-Aug. Tu-Th and Sa 9pm. Call for reservations or inquire at the tourist office.) The **Garter Lane Arts Centre,** 22a O'Connell St., supports all different forms of art inside its old Georgian brick. Visual exhibits adorn the walls and are usually free. Musical concerts cost less than €15, and dance and theater productions grace its stage year-round. (☎855 038. Center and box office open M-Sa 10am-6pm; performance nights until 9pm. €3-5 student and seniors discount.) Waterford's largest festival is the **Spraoi** ("spree"), held during the August bank holiday weekend. A celebration of life or something, the Spraoi attracts bands from around the globe and culminates in a sizeable parade. (☎841 808; www.spraoi.com.)

SOUTHWEST IRELAND

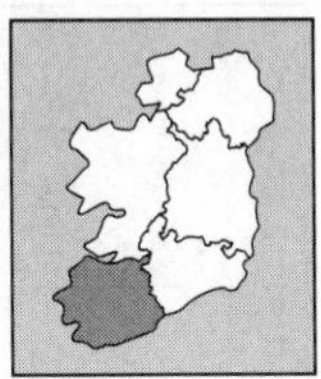

With a dramatic landscape ranging from lush lakes and mountains to stark, ocean-battered cliffs, Southwest Ireland is rich in storytellers and history-makers. Outlaws and rebels once lurked in hidden coves and glens now frequented by visitors and lorded over by publicans. The urban activity of Cork City and the area's frantic pace of rebuilding and growth contrast with the ancient rhythm of nearby rural villages. The Ring of Kerry draws huge numbers of visitors every year, and no place in Ireland has as many multilingual real estate signs as Killarney—the land in west Cork is steadily being snapped up by investors, the French, and the occasional movie star. If the tourist mayhem is too much for you, you can always retreat to the placid stretches along the Beara Peninsula and Cork's southern coast.

EASTERN COUNTY CORK

Historically, the superb harbors along the eastern coast of Co. Cork have made the area into a prosperous trading center. Its distance from Dublin and the English Pale, however, saved the area from total domination during the 1600s, and afforded local Irishmen much freedom from the invasive British. Consequently, Cork was seething with patriotic activity during the 19th and 20th centuries. Headquarters of the "Munster Republic" controlled by the anti-Treaty forces during the Civil War, the county produced patriot Michael Collins, as well as the man who assassinated him in 1922 (see **Independence and Civil War,** p. 62). Today, Cork City is a hotbed of industry and culture, while the seaside towns of Kinsale and Cobh gaily entertain tall ships and stooped-over backpackers. Ireland's rich archaeological history is particularly accessible from Cork, with Celtic ring forts, mysterious stone circles, and long-ruined abbeys dotting the nearby sheep-speckled hills.

CORK CITY (AN CORCAIGH) ☎021

In its capacity as Ireland's second-largest city, Cork (pop. 150,000) orchestrates most of the athletic, musical, and artistic activities in the Irish southwest. The river quays and pub-lined streets reveal architecture both grand and grimy, evidence of Cork's history of ruin and reconstruction. Indeed, what few pre-industrial charms smokestacks didn't blacken, the English blighted. The old city burned down in 1622, Cromwell expelled half its citizens in the 1640s, the Duke of Marlborough laid siege in 1690, and Cork was torched again in 1920 during the Irish War for Independence. Wise visitors will exploit the city's resources more politely: Cork is a place to eat, drink, shop, and sleep while exploring the exquisite scenery of the surrounding countryside. Within the city limits, time is best filled by taking in the vibrant street scene, or meandering across the campus of University College Cork.

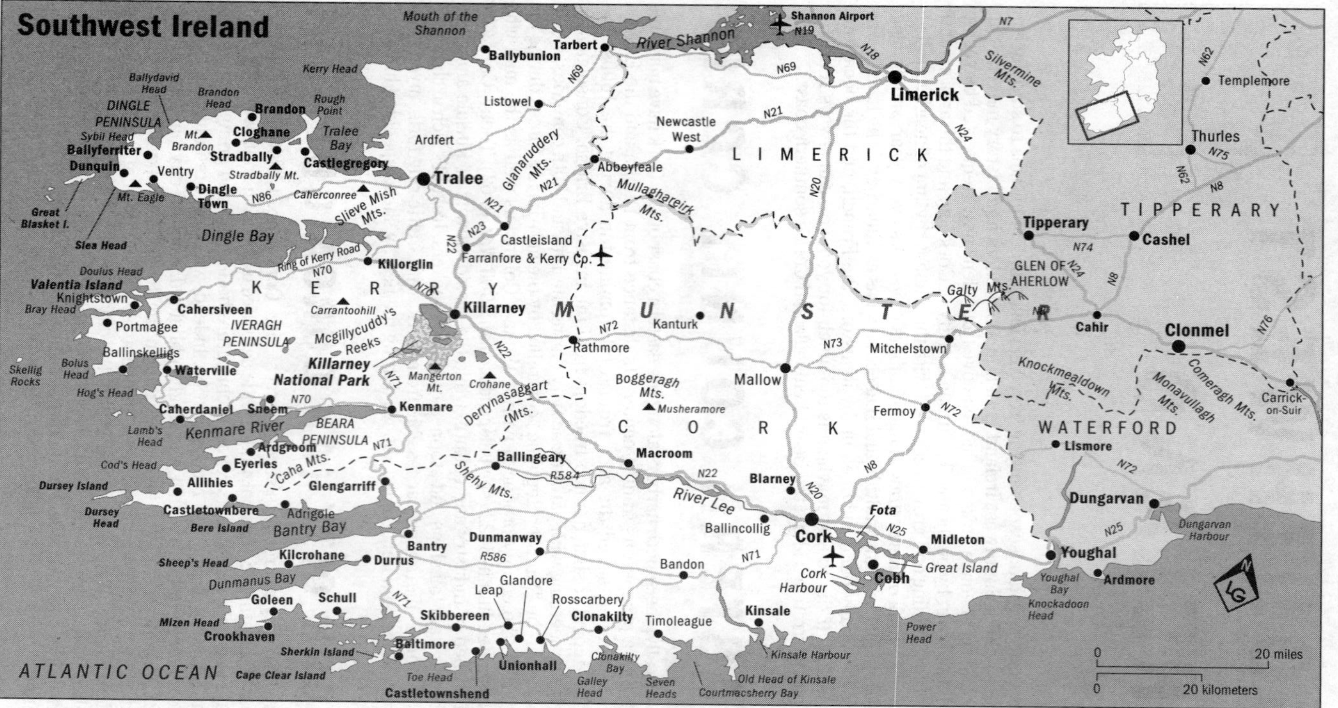
Southwest Ireland
TIPPERARY
LIMERICK
KERRY
CORK
MUNSTER
WATERFORD
ATLANTIC OCEAN
Limerick
Shannon Airport
River Shannon
Mouth of the Shannon
Tarbert
Ballybunion
Listowel
Abbeyfeale
Newcastle West
Tralee
Tralee Bay
Castlegregory
Brandon
Cloghane
Stradbally
Dingle Town
Dingle Bay
DINGLE PENINSULA
Ventry
Dunquin
Ballyferriter
Slea Head
Great Blasket I.
Valentia Island
Knightstown
Portmagee
Cahersiveen
IVERAGH PENINSULA
Waterville
Ballinskelligs
Skellig Rocks
Killorglin
Killarney
Killarney National Park
Mcgillycuddy's Reeks
Carrantoohill
Kenmare
Kenmare River
Sneem
Castletownbere
Bere Island
Bantry Bay
Bantry
Glengarriff
BEARA PENINSULA
Dursey Island
Dunmanus Bay
Schull
Goleen
Crookhaven
Mizen Head
Cape Clear Island
Sherkin Island
Baltimore
Skibbereen
Castletownshend
Union Hall
Glandore
Rosscarbery
Clonakilty
Timoleague
Kinsale
Old Head of Kinsale
Bandon
Macroom
River Lee
Ballincollig
Blarney
Cork
Cork Harbour
Cobh
Fota
Midleton
Great Island
Youghal
Youghal Bay
Ardmore
Dungarvan
Dungarvan Harbour
Lismore
Mallow
Kanturk
Fermoy
Mitchelstown
Cahir
Tipperary
GLEN OF AHERLOW
Galty Mts.
Knockmealdown Mts.
Cashel
Clonmel
Comeragh Mts.
Monavullagh Mts.
Carrick-on-Suir
Thurles
Templemore
Silvermine Mts.
Farranfore & Kerry Co.
Castleisland
Rathmore
Boggeragh Mts.
Mullaghareirk Mts.
Ballingeary
Dunmanway
Shehy Mts.
Caha Mts.
20 miles
20 kilometers

INTERCITY TRANSPORTATION

Airport: Cork Airport (☎431 3131), 5 mi. south of Cork on the Kinsale road. **Aer Lingus** (☎432 7155), **British Airways** (☎800 626 747), and **Ryanair** (☎01 609 7800) connect Cork to Dublin, Paris, and several English cities. A taxi (€9-10) or bus (16-18 per day, €3.15) will deliver you from the airport to the bus station on Parnell Pl.

Trains: Kent Station, Lower Glanmire Rd. (☎450 6766; www.irishrail.ie), in the northeast part of town across the river from the city center. Open M-Sa 6:35am-8:30pm, Su 7:50am-8pm. Train connections to: **Dublin** (3hr.; M-Sa 7 per day, Su 5 per day; €44.40); **Killarney** (2hr.; M-Sa 7 per day, Su 4 per day; €17.70); **Limerick** (1½hr.; M-Sa 7 per day, Su 4 per day; €17.70); **Tralee** (2½hr., 3 per day, €22.80).

Buses: Parnell Pl. (☎450 8188), 2 blocks east of Patrick's Bridge on Merchant's Quay. Inquiries desk open daily 9am-6pm. **Bus Éireann** goes to all major cities: **Bantry** (2hr.; M-Sa 7 per day, Su 4 per day; €11.80); **Dublin** (4½hr.; M-Sa 6 per day, Su 5 per day; €19); **Galway** (4hr.; M-Sa 7 per day, Su 4 per day; €15.80); **Killarney** (2hr.; M-Sa 13 per day, Su 10 per day; €11.80); **Limerick** (2hr., 14 per day, €12.10); **Rosslare Harbour** (4hr., 3 per day, €17.10); **Sligo** (7hr., 5 per day, €21.10); **Tralee** (2½hr., 12 per day, €12.70); **Waterford** (2¼hr., M-Sa 13 per day, €13.30).

Ferries: Ringaskiddy Terminal (☎427 5061), 8 mi. south of the city, sends ferries off to Roscoff, France (14hr. €46-96). Call **Brittany Ferries** (☎437 8401) or stop by their office on the Grand Parade, by the tourist office. Bus Éireann (☎450 8188) makes the 30min. trip to the ferry, leaving from the Cork bus station. Buses leave 1¼hr. prior to ferry departure from bay #10. **Swansea-Cork Ferries** sends daily ferries on the 10hr. trip to Swansea, Wales. (☎427 1166; €30-43.) For more info, see **By Ferry,** p. 27.

ORIENTATION

Cork's compact city center wasn't always an island. Before being diverted to create its modern moat, the River Lee's present north and south channels once ran straight through the city in grand Venetian fashion. The pavement of horseshoe-shaped **St. Patrick St.** was laid directly over the waterflow, thus the inspiration for its unconventional U-shape. St. Patrick St. ends its horseshoe and becomes **Grand Parade** to the West; to the north it crosses **Merchant's Quay,** home of the bus station. North across St. Patrick's bridge, **McCurtain St.** runs east to **Lower Glanmire Rd.** and the train station, before becoming the **N8** to Dublin, Waterford, and Cobh. Downtown action concentrates on the vaguely parallel **Paul, St. Patrick,** and **Oliver Plunkett St.** Their connecting north-south avenues are shop-lined and largely pedestrian. Heading west from Grand Parade, **Washington St.** becomes **Western Rd.** before reaching **University College Cork** and the **N22** to Killarney.

LOCAL TRANSPORTATION

Bus: The main bus station (☎450 8188) at Parnell Pl. offers free timetables for the **city buses.** From downtown, catch the buses (and their schedules) at the bus station on Merchant's Quay, across from the Father Matthew statue. **Bus #8** runs down Western Rd. toward UCC and the An Óige hostel. Downtown buses run M-Sa every 10-30min. 7:30am-11:15pm, with reduced service Su 10am-11:15pm. Fares from €0.95.

Car Rental: Budget Rent-a-Car, Tourist Office, Grand Parade (☎427 4755). €45 per day, €250 per wk. 23+. **Great Island Car Rentals,** 47 McCurtain St. (☎481 1609). €70 per day, €250 per wk.; add €13 per day for drivers under 25. 23+.

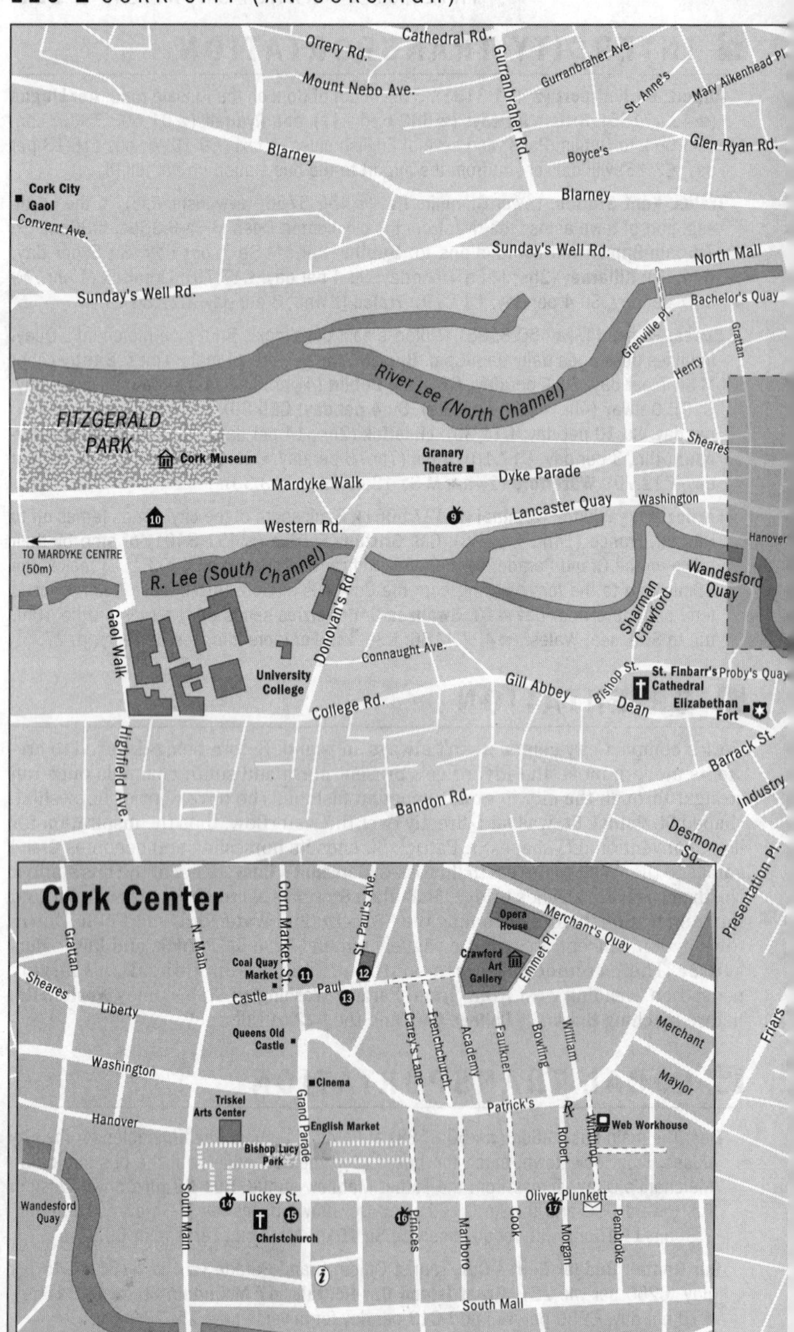

SOUTHWEST IRELAND

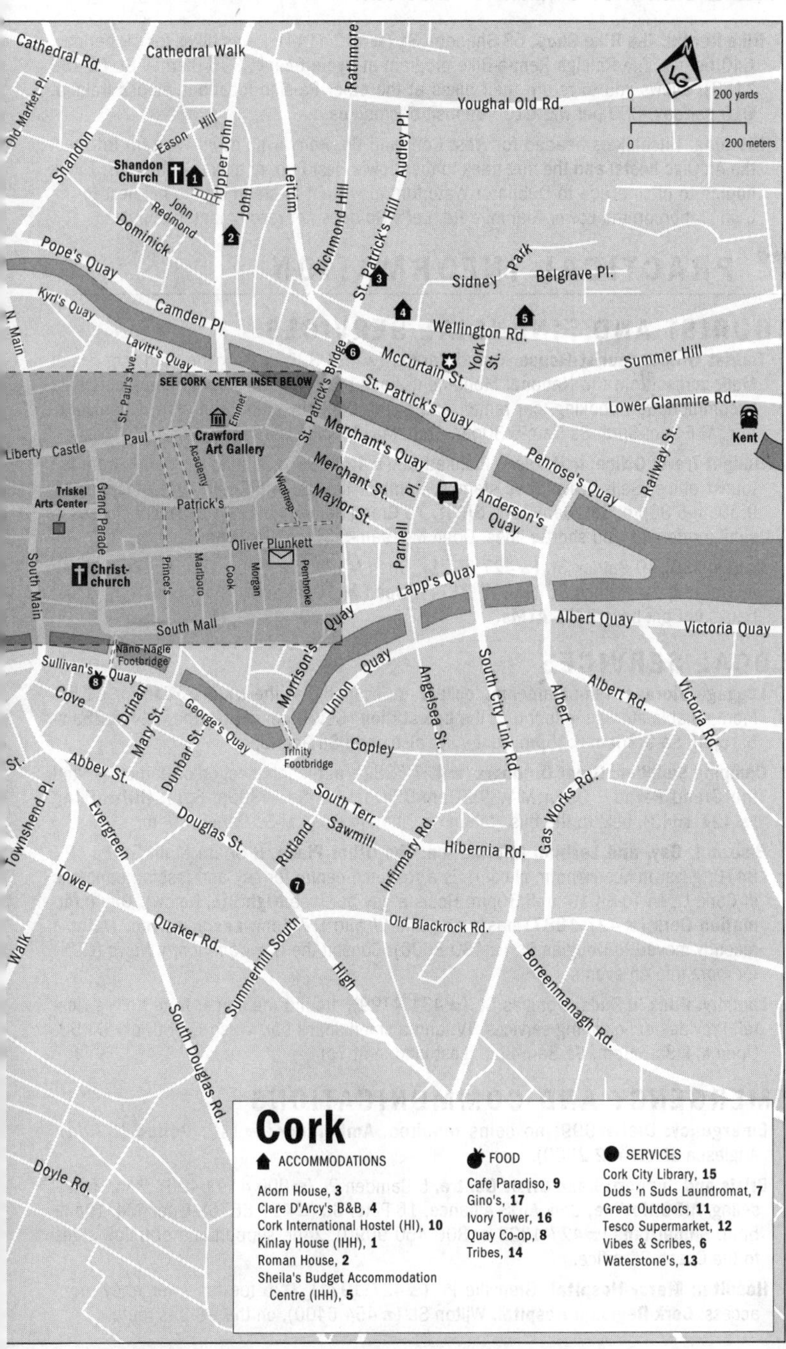
Cathedral Rd.
Cathedral Walk
Rathmore
Youghal Old Rd.
200 yards
200 meters
Old Market Pl.
Shandon
Eason Hill
Upper John
Shandon Church
John Redmond
Dominick
John
Leitrim
Audley Pl.
Richmond Hill
St. Patrick's Hill
Pope's Quay
Kyrl's Quay
Camden Pl.
Sidney Park
Belgrave Pl.
Wellington Rd.
N. Main
Lavitt's Quay
St. Patrick's Bridge
McCurtain St.
York St.
Summer Hill
SEE CORK CENTER INSET BELOW
St. Paul's Ave.
Emmet
St. Patrick's Quay
Lower Glanmire Rd.
Kent
Paul
Crawford Art Gallery
Liberty
Castle
Academy
St. Patrick's
Merchant's Quay
Merchant St.
Penrose's Quay
Railway St.
Triskel Arts Center
Grand Parade
Patrick's
Winthrop
Maylor St.
Pl.
Anderson's Quay
Oliver Plunkett
South Main
Christchurch
Prince's
Marlboro
Cook
Morgan
Pembroke
Parnell
Lapp's Quay
South Mall
Quay
Albert Quay
Victoria Quay
Nano Nagle Footbridge
Sullivan's Quay
Morrison's
Union Quay
Angelsea St.
South City Link Rd.
Albert
Albert Rd.
Victoria Rd.
Cove
Drinan
Mary St.
George's Quay
Dunbar St.
Trinity Footbridge
Copley
St.
Abbey St.
Townshend Pl.
Evergreen
Douglas St.
South Terr.
Sawmill
Infirmary Rd.
Hibernia Rd.
Gas Works Rd.
Rutland
Tower
Old Blackrock Rd.
Quaker Rd.
Summerhill South
Walk
High
Boreenmanagh Rd.
South Douglas Rd.
Doyle Rd.
Cork
ACCOMMODATIONS
Acorn House, 3
Clare D'Arcy's B&B, 4
Cork International Hostel (HI), 10
Kinlay House (IHH), 1
Roman House, 2
Sheila's Budget Accommodation Centre (IHH), 5
FOOD
Cafe Paradiso, 9
Gino's, 17
Ivory Tower, 16
Quay Co-op, 8
Tribes, 14
SERVICES
Cork City Library, 15
Duds 'n Suds Laundromat, 7
Great Outdoors, 11
Tesco Supermarket, 12
Vibes & Scribes, 6
Waterstone's, 13

Bike Rental: The Bike Shop, 68 Shandon St. (☎430 4144). Rents bikes for €9 per day, €40 per wk. The Raleigh Rent-a-Bike program at **Cycle Scene,** 396 Blarney St. (☎430 1183), allows you to return their bikes at the other Raleigh locations across Ireland. €15 per day, €80 per wk. €100 deposit or credit card.

Hitching: Hitchhikers headed for West Cork and Co. Kerry walk down Western Rd. past the An Óige hostel and the dog track to the Crow's Nest Pub, or they take bus #8. Those hoping to hitch a ride to Dublin or Waterford may want to stand on the hill next to the train station on the Lower Glanmire Rd. *Let's Go* does not recommend hitchhiking.

PRACTICAL INFORMATION

TOURIST AND FINANCIAL SERVICES

Tourist Office: Tourist House, Grand Parade (☎427 3251), near the corner of South Mall, across from the National Monument along the River Lee's south channel. Offers accommodation booking, car rental, and a free Cork city guide and map. Open June-Aug. M-F 9am-6pm, Sa 9am-5:30pm; Sept.-May M-Sa 9:15am-5:30pm.

Budget Travel Office: usit, Oliver Plunkett St. (☎427 0900), around the corner from the tourist office. Sells **TravelSave** stamps, Rambler tickets, and Eurail tickets. Open M-F 9:30am-5:30pm, Sa 10am-2pm. **SAYIT,** 76 Grand Parade (☎427 9188), specializes in similar offerings and shorter lines. Open M-F 9am-5:30pm, Sa 10am-4pm.

Banks: TSB, 40 Patrick St. (☎427 5221). Open M-F 9:30am-5pm, Th until 7pm. **Bank of Ireland,** 70 Patrick St. (☎427 7177). Open M 10am-5pm, Tu-F 10am-4pm. Most banks in Cork have 24hr. **ATMs.**

LOCAL SERVICES

Luggage Storage: Temperamental lockers are available at the **train station** for €1.50. More reliable storage is found at the **bus station** (€1.90 per item). Open M-F 8:35am-6:15pm, Sa 9:30am-6:15pm; June-Aug. also open Su 9am-6pm.

Camping Supplies: Great Outdoors (☎427 6382), at the intersection of Patrick St. and the Grand Parade. Open M-W 9:30am-5:30pm, Th-Sa 9:30am-6pm. **Hillwalking** (☎427 1643), next to the bus station on Clontarf. Open M-Sa 9am-5:30pm.

Bisexual, Gay, and Lesbian Information: The Other Place, 8 South Main St. (☎427 8470; gayswitchcork@hotmail.com), is a resource center for gay and lesbian concerns in Cork. Open Tu-Sa 10am-5:30pm. Hosts a gay bar (see **Nightlife,** below). **Gay Information Cork** (☎427 1087) has a helpline W and F 7-9pm. **Lesbians Inc. (L.Inc.)** recently moved to Douglas St. (☎480 8600). Consult the *Gay Community News* (GCN) for more info on events.

Laundry: Duds 'n Suds, Douglas St. (☎431 4799), around the corner from Kelly's Hostel. Provides dry-cleaning services, TV, and a small snack bar. Wash €2.50, dry €3.50. Open M-F 8am-9pm, Sa 8am-8pm. Last load in at 7pm.

EMERGENCY AND COMMUNICATIONS

Emergency: Dial ☎999; no coins required. **Ambulance:** ☎112. **Police** *(Garda)*: Anglesea St. (☎452 2000).

Crisis and Support: Rape Crisis Centre, 5 Camden Pl. (☎800 449 6496). 24hr. counseling. **AIDS Hotline,** Cork AIDS Alliance, 16 Peter St. (☎427 6676). Open M-F 10am-5pm. **Samaritans** (☎427 1323 or 800 460 9090). 24hr. support line or follow signs to the Coach St. office.

Hospital: Mercy Hospital, Grenville Pl. (☎427 1971). €25 fee for emergency room access. **Cork Regional Hospital,** Wilton St. (☎454 6400), on the #8 bus route.

Pharmacies: Regional Late Night Pharmacy, Wilton Rd. (☎434 4575), opposite the Regional Hospital on bus #8. Open M-F 9am-10pm, Sa-Su 10am-10pm. **Phelan's Late Night,** 9 Patrick St. (☎427 2511). Open M-Sa 9am-10pm, Su 10am-10pm.

Internet Access: Web Workhouse, Winthrop St. (☎434 3090), connecting Patrick and Oliver Plunkett St. Near the post office. Lofty converted warehouse hums with high-speed computers. Smoking and non-smoking sections. Tea and coffee available. 8am-noon €3 per hr.; noon-5pm €4-5; 5pm-3am €2.50; Su €2.50 per hr. all day. Open M-Th and Su 8am-3am, F and Sa 24hr. **Cork City Library** (☎427 7110), across from the tourist office. €1.30 per 30min. Open Tu-Sa 10am-1pm and 2-5pm.

Post Office: Oliver Plunkett St. (☎427 2000). Open M-Sa 9am-5:30pm.

ACCOMMODATIONS

Cork's international youth hostels stand like student-populated fortresses at three ends of the city. All three are excellent, and popular, so call ahead. A few terrific B&Bs populate **Patrick's Hill;** the best ones congregate nearer **Glanmire Rd. Western Rd.,** leading out toward University College, is knee-deep in pricier B&Bs.

Sheila's Budget Accommodation Centre (IHH), 4 Belgrave Pl. (☎450 5562), at the intersection of Wellington Rd. and York Street Hill. Sheila's is centrally located and offers a big kitchen and summertime barbecues in a secluded backyard. All rooms non-smoking and with bath. The 24hr. reception desk doubles as a general store and offers breakfast for €3.20. **Sauna** €2. **Bike rental** €12. **Internet access** €1 per 15min. Free luggage storage. Check-out 10:30am. Dorms €15-16; singles €30; doubles €40-50. ❷

Clare D'Arcy B&B, 7 Sidney Place, Wellington Rd. (☎450 4658; www.darcysguesthouse.com). From St. Patricks bridge, start up St. Patricks Hill, turning right onto Wellington road; look for the blue sign on the left. The most authentically luxurious guesthouse in Cork. Elegant Parisian-style interior: chandeliers, wide staircase, original paned glass windows. Rooms #5 and 6 have panoramic views of the city; the enormous arched window of room #7 looks out over garden. Freshly squeezed OJ and smoked salmon for breakfast. Doubles €80; shared rooms €35-45 per person. ❹

Kinlay House (IHH), Bob and Joan Walk (☎450 8966; www.kinlayhouse.ie), down the alley to the right of Shandon Church. Kinlay House's bright colors and warm atmosphere offset its large, motel-like layout. Recent renovations have brought wonderful family-sized rooms to the house. Video library and game room available to all. Continental breakfast included. **Internet access** €1 per 15min. Laundry €7. Free parking. 10- to 14-bed dorms €14. Singles €25-30; doubles €40-44. Family-sized rooms €70. ❷

Roman House, 3 St. John's Terr., Upper John St. (☎450 3606), in a muted red building with a black front door. Cross the North Channel by the opera house, make a left on John Redmond St., then bear right onto Upper John St. Located across from Kinlay House. Colorfully decorated in decadence, Roman House is Cork's only B&B catering specifically to gay and lesbian travelers (though any and all are welcome). Walls display artist/proprietor's original work. Bath, TV, oversized armchairs, and coffee-making facilities in every room. Vegetarian breakfast option. Singles €40; doubles €60. ❷

Cork International Hostel (An Óige/HI), 1-2 Redclyffe, Western Rd. (☎454 3289), a 15min. walk from the Grand Parade. Bus #8 stops across the street. Immaculate and spacious rooms with high ceilings in a stately brick Victorian townhouse. All rooms with bath. Continental breakfast €2.50. **Internet** €1 per 10min. Check-in 8am-midnight. 10-bed dorms €14; 6-bed €15; 4-bed €15. Doubles €41. Reduced prices if under 18. ❷

Acorn House, 14 St. Patrick's Hill (☎450 2474; www.acornhouse-cork.com). Fresh, understatedly elegant Georgian townhouse. 15 ft. french windows with tie-back scarlet curtains. €45 per person, negotiable in low season. ❹

FOOD

Downtown Cork is blessed with an array of delicious restaurants and cafes; the lanes connecting Patrick St., Paul St., and Oliver Plunkett St. are particularly appealing. The **English Market,** accessible from Grand Parade, Patrick St., and Oliver Plunkett St., displays a wide variety of meats, fish, cheeses, and fruits fresh from the farms and fisheries of West Cork. Cork's local specialties include *crubeen* (pig's feet), *drisheen* (blood sausage; its texture is a hybrid of liver and Jell-O), and Clonakilty black pudding (an intriguing mix of blood, grain, and spice). The **Tesco** on Paul St. is the biggest grocery store in town. (☎427 0791. Open M-W and Sa 8:30am-8pm, Th-F 8:30am-10pm.)

Quay Co-op, 24 Sullivan's Quay (☎431 7660). Large townhouse-style windows enliven the vibrant colors and youthful intellectual buzz. A vegetarian and vegan's delight, and no chore for carnivores either. Excellent soups and desserts. Apricot and yogurt flan €2.50. Specials €6.50. Open M-Sa 9am-9pm. Store open M-Sa 9am-6:15pm. ❷

Tribes, Tuckey St. (☎427 6070). Continue past the fountain ending Oliver Plunkett St., keeping the Bishop Lucy park to your left. The only late-night coffee shop serving full cafe food until the wee hours. Crunchy low-light college java shop with south islander theme. Global spectrum of coffee blends (Jamaican to Ethiopian €1.65). Teas from black currant to wild strawberry nettle (€1.80). Hawaiian bagel sandwich €5.40; bronx burger €5.40. Open M-W noon-1am, Th-Sa noon-4am. ❶

Ivory Tower, Princes St. (☎427 7939), upstairs in the old exchange building. Escapes pretension by a hair's breadth; dark wood paneling, gold tapestry cushions, and large bay windows. Try the handmade gnocchi with wild mushrooms, the aphrodisiac of tropical fruits, and finish with the blood-orange sorbet. 5-course dinner €50. A la carte €23-30. Dinner only Tu-Su 6-10pm. ❺

Gino's, 7 Winthrop St. (☎427 4485), between Patrick and Oliver Plunkett St. Primo pizzas. Lunch special includes pizza and homemade ice cream for €7.50. Beware the throngs of noon-time school kids. Open M-Sa noon-10:30pm, Su 1-10:30pm. ❷

Café Paradiso, 16 Lancaster Quay (☎427 7939). Award-winning vegetarian meals bordering on gourmet. Cool-colored Mediterranean feel, and popular with the laid-back jet-setting crew. Watermelon, feta, and cucumber salad €7. Lunch €7-13; dinner €9-18. Open Tu-Sa 12:30-3pm and 6:30-10:30pm. ❸

PUBS

Cork's pub scene has the variety of music and atmosphere you'd expect to find in Ireland's second-largest city. There are more pubs than you can shake a stick at along Union Quay, Oliver Plunkett, and South Main St; to guide you on your tipsy quest, *Let's Go* offers our first ever Cork City **Pub Crawl.** The city is especially proud of its own **Murphy's,** a thick, creamy stout that some say rivals Guinness. (Some others say that those who say are only saying rubbish.) A cheaper stout, **Beamish,** is also brewed here. Nearly all pubs stop serving at 11:30pm.

The Lobby, 1 Union Quay (☎431 9307). Arguably the most famous venue in Cork; has given some of Ireland's biggest folk acts their first shining moments. 2 floors overlook the river. Live music nightly, from trad to acid jazz. Come early to the parlor-sized upstairs room for more popular acts. Occasional cover €2.50-6.35.

An Spailpín Fánac (on spal-PEEN FAW-nuhk), 28 South Main St. (☎427 7949), across from the Beamish Brewery. One of Cork's more popular pubs as well as one of its oldest (est. 1779). Intermingled crowd of visitors and locals come for the live trad offered most nights; storytelling last Tu of every month.

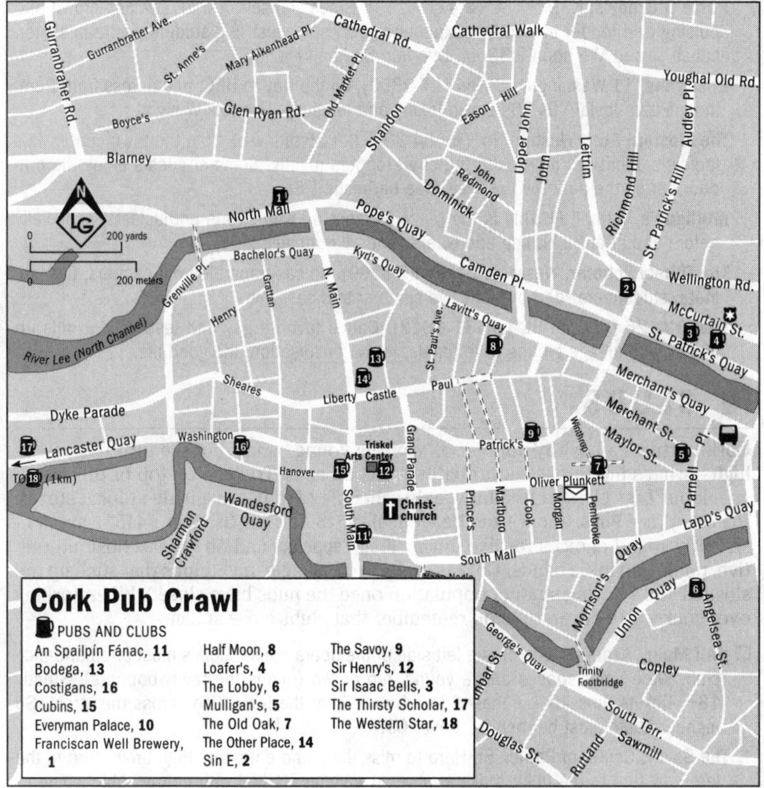

Bodega, 46-49 Cornmarket St. (☎427 2878), off the northern end of Grand Parade and the western end of Paul St. Stone front, wood floors, and a stratospheric hall ceiling. An artsy cafe by day, it transforms at night into an upscale, classy club. Great wine selection and an intimate balcony. Sharp dress.

The Old Oak, Oliver Plunkett St. (☎427 6165), just across from the grand old General Post Office. Year after year it wins a "Best Traditional Pubs in Ireland" award, and with good reason. Packed and noisy; each section has its own particular vibe. Bar food served M-F noon-3pm. Bar closes F-Sa 1:45am.

Sin E, 8 Coburg St. (☎450 2266), just left of McCurtain St. after crossing St. Patrick's bridge. Mosaic glass exterior. Has some of Cork's best live music, especially Th nights. Mixed crowd, mellow (though still noisy) atmosphere.

Sir Isaac Bell's, North Quay of the Lee's north channel, next to the Gresham Metropole Hotel. Tiny, cozy pub with a great selection of beers. Easy to strike up a conversation with the person next to you.

Franciscan Well Microbrewery, 14b North Mall (☎421 0130), along the North Quay, just east of Sundays Well Rd. Fantastic local brews, with a great Belgian selection. The home-brewed Blarney Blonde and Rebel Red come highly recommended. Backyard beer garden in summer. Packed venue for **Oct. Belgian Beer Festival.**

Rosie O'Grady's, N. Main St. (☎427 8253). Brace yourself. A wild, swelling crowd and pulsing trad render the Rosie's experience Cork's liveliest. Big student scene in winter. Lunch served M-F noon-2:30pm. Live trad Su-M and W.

Costigans, 11 Washington St. (☎427 3350), on the way to UCC, and across from Dominoes Pizza. Jovial 20s-30s crowd joking and laughing. Live folk W night.

The Western Star, Western Rd. (☎454 3047). A 25min. walk from the town center, this largely student bar rocks with the chart-toppers nightly. Summer guests enjoy the outdoor bar on the patio by the river. Free barbecue F-Sa.

Mulligan's, Parnell Pl. This is the place to meet up with sports enthusiasts, especially before and after Su hurling and Gaelic football matches.

The Thirsty Scholar, Western Rd. (☎427 6209). An easy stumble from campus, this intimate, student-crowded pub has live summer trad sessions.

Loafer's, 26 Douglas St. (☎431 1612). Cork's favorite gay and lesbian pub fills up nightly with all age groups. Live bands, lively conversation, the good life.

CLUBS

Cork nurtures a healthy number of aspiring young bands, but the turnover rate is high—what's hip this week probably won't be next. To keep on top of the scene, check out *List Cork*, a free bi-weekly schedule of music available at local stores. **The Lobby** (see **Pubs,** above) and **Nancy Spain's,** 48 Barrack St. (☎431 4452), are consistently sound choices for live music. **Fred Zeppelins** and **An Phoenix** host alternative, punk, and indie bands. Cork is also full of swingin' nightclubs that suck up the sloshed and swaying student population once the pubs have closed. When forking over your €5-10 cover, though, remember that clubs close at 2am.

Half Moon, Academy Ln., on the left side of the opera house. Cork's most popular dance club. Wide open spaces and a young, hip crowd (minus the teeny-boppers). Strictly 18+. Tickets must be purchased in advance from the box office across the street. Su nights are the most happening. Cover €9.

The Savoy, Center of Patrick St. Hard to miss the grand entrance. High brow. Turn to the left, now turn to the right, strike a pose, now vogue. "Filled with untouchable women," laments Simon the bartender. Cover €6.

Sir Henry's, S. Main St. (☎427 4391). One of Cork's most intense dance experiences. Prepare to be wedged between sweaty, semi-conscious bodies on the 3 dance floors.

Fast Eddie's (☎425 1438), off S. Main St. Busy. Young. Thumping. Shaggy. A bit of a visual marketplace–you'd probably better go check it out. Strictly 18+. Cover €8.

Cubins, Hanover St. (☎427 9250). The wall paintings of Cork's newest club insist ancient Rome is where it's at. Even a cover charge hovering around €8 and a long wait in line can't cramp the style of local patrons breaking down to 90s dance hits.

Everyman Palace, 15 McCurtain St. (☎450 3077). Theater also houses a late-night blues and jazz club on weekends. Open F-Su 10pm-2am, as well as show nights.

The Other Place (☎427 8470), in a lane off South Main St. Cork's gay and lesbian disco rocks F and Sa 11:30pm-2am. Dance floor and a bar/cafe upstairs (opens earlier). Highly appreciated by Cork's gay population, especially the younger set, on weekend nights. Cover €5, free before 10pm.

SIGHTS

Cork's sights can be loosely sorted into three areas: the Old City, on the island in the center of town; the Shandon neighborhood, to the north of the River Lee; and the western part of the city, around the university. All can be reached on foot, a sensible approach in such a pedestrian-friendly city. For guidance, pick up *The Cork Area City Guide* at the tourist office (€1.90).

THE OLD CITY

TRISKEL ARTS CENTRE. The small but dynamic Triskel Arts Centre maintains two small galleries with rotating exhibits. It also organizes a wide variety of cultural events, including music, film, literature, theater, and the visual arts. *(Tobin St. ☎427 2022; triskel@iol.ie. Open M-Sa 10am-5:30pm. Gallery free; films €5.)*

ST. FINBARR'S CATHEDRAL. Looming over Proby's Quay, St. Fin's is a testament to the Victorian obsession with neo-Gothic bombast. Finbarr allegedly founded his "School of Cork" here in AD 606, but no trace of the early foundation remains. The present cathedral was built between 1735 and 1870, and now houses contemporary art exhibits in the summer. *(Bishop St. ☎496 3387. Open M-Sa 10am-5:30pm. €2.50 requested donation.)*

KEYSER HILL. On a nice day, you can get a decent view of Cork—and a much too good view of Beamish Brewery—from Keyser Hill. At the top of the stairs leading up the hill is the **Elizabethan Fort,** a star-shaped and ivy-covered remnant of English domination. To access the fort's impressive view, climb the stairs just inside the main gate. *(Follow South Main St. away from the city center, cross the South Gate Bridge, turn right onto Proby's Quay then left onto Keyser Hill. Always open. Free.)*

CHRIST CHURCH. The area around steeple-less Christ Church provides a quiet spot to rest in a city center otherwise lacking green space. The site, scattered with eclectic statues, suffered the Protestant torches three times between its 1270 consecration and the construction of the final version in 1729. *(Off the Grand Parade just north of Bishop Lucy Park. Walk down the Christ Church Ln., keeping the park on your left, until you emerge on South Main St. To the right is the church. Always open. Free.)*

SHANDON AND EMMET PLACE

ST. ANNE'S CHURCH. Commonly called Shandon Church, St. Anne's sandstone- and limestone-striped steeple inspired the red and white "rebel" flag still flying throughout the county. Like most of Cork, the original church was ravaged by 17th-century pyromaniacal English armies; construction of the current church began in 1722. Clocks grace each of the four sides of Shandon's tower. Notoriously out of sync and usually just plain wrong, the clocks have been held responsible for many an Irishman's tardy arrival at work and have earned the church its nickname, "the four-faced liar." *(Walk up Shandon St., take a right on unmarked Church St., and continue straight; the church overlooks Kinlay House. ☎450 5906. Open June-Sept. M-Sa 9:30am-5:30pm. €4, students and seniors €3.50, family €12. Group rates available.)*

OTHER SIGHTS. The monstrous cement **Opera House** was erected two decades ago after the older, more elegant opera house went down in flames. *(Emmet Pl. Over the hill from Shandon Church and across the north fork of the Lee. ☎427 3377. Gallery open M-Sa 10am-5pm. Free.)* **Cork Butter Museum** comes closer than one might think to making Cork's commerce history, and preserved butter, interesting. *(Church St. ☎430 0600. Open May-Sept. M-F and Su 10am-1pm and 2-5pm. €4, students and seniors €3.)* **Crawford Art Gallery** runs a program of temporary exhibitions, both Irish and international. The striking main gallery room is filled with marble ghosts of the Venus de Milo and Michelangelo, among others of artistic fame. *(Off Paul St. ☎427 3377. Open M-Sa 10am-5pm. Free.)* At the **Shandon Craft Centre,** potters, crystal-blowers, and other artisans ply and sell their trades and wares. *(Church St., across from the church.)*

READING MATERIAL

If you're traveling alone, or traveling with someone you wish you had left at home, you'll probably want to immerse yourself in a book. Lucky for you, as some of the best in Ireland reside in Cork City:

New Books. If you just can't find what you're looking for among the used books, a few of the new bookstores in Cork offer reasonable alternatives. The two best are: The monstrously huge **Waterstone's,** 69 Patrick St. (☎427 6522), open M-Th and Sa 9am-7pm, F 9am-9pm, Su noon-7pm; and **Mercier Bookstore,** 18 Academy St. (☎427 5040), off Patrick St., open M-Sa 9am-5:30pm.

Used Books. **Vibes and Scribes,** 3 Bridge St. (☎450 5370), just over St. Patrick's Bridge, is one of the best used bookstores, in Cork and otherwise. It offers an outstanding Irish interest selection and second-hand basement. Open Tu-F 10am-6:30pm, Sa-M 12:30-6:30pm. A pipe-smoking professor-like proprietor runs **Connolly's Bookstore,** Paul St. Plaza (☎427 5366). Browsing music often includes Ella Fitzgerald in this intimate academic-flavor shop.

Specialty Books. Creepy but cool **Mainly Murder,** Paul St. (☎427 2413), next door to the teddy bear store, specializes expressly in crime novels. The pleasant elderly proprietress is straight out of an Agatha Christie mystery.

WESTERN CORK CITY

UNIVERSITY COLLEGE CORK (UCC). Built in 1845, UCC's campus is a collection of brooding Gothic buildings, manicured lawns, and sculpture-studded grounds, all of which make for a fine afternoon walk or a picnic along the River Lee. One of the newer buildings, **Boole Library,** celebrates number-wizard George Boole, mastermind of Boolean logic and model for Sherlock Holmes's arch-nemesis Prof. James Moriarty. *(Main gate on Western Rd. ☎490 3000.)*

FITZGERALD PARK. Rose gardens, playgrounds, and a permanent parking spot for the ice cream man are all found within the park. Also present are the befuddlingly esoteric exhibitions of the **Cork Public Museum,** which feature such varied goodies as 18th-century toothbrushes and the clothes of James Dwyer, Sheriff of Cork. *(From the front gate of UCC, follow the signposted walkway across the street. ☎427 0679. Museum open M-F 11am-1pm and 2:15-5pm, Su 3-5pm. M-Sa free; Su €1.50.)*

CORK CITY GAOL. If your time in Cork is tight, make sure to see the Cork City Gaol. The museum is a reconstruction of the gaol (pronounced 'jail') as it appeared in the 1800s. Descriptions of Cork's social history accompany tidbits about miserable punishments, such as the "human treadmill" that was used to grind grain. *(Sunday's Well Rd. From Fitzgerald Park, cross the white footbridge at the western end of the park, turn right onto Sunday's Well Rd., and follow the signs. ☎430 5022. Open Mar.-Oct. daily 9:30am-6pm, Nov.-Feb. 10am-5pm. Last admission 1hr. before closing. €5, students and seniors €4, family €14. Admission includes audio tour.)*

ENTERTAINMENT

The lively streets of Cork will make your search for amusement an easy one. If you tire of the pub scene, take advantage of the music venues, dance clubs, theaters, and sports arenas, or just explore the innumerable cafes and bookshops.

THEATER AND FILM

Everyman Palace, McCurtain St., hosts the big-name musicals, plays, operas, and concerts. (☎450 1673. Tickets €10-23. Box office open M-F 9am-6pm, Sa 10am-5:30pm, until 8pm on show nights.) The **Opera House,** Emmet Pl., next to the river, presents an extensive program of dance and performance art. (☎427 0022. Open M-Sa 9am-5:30pm.) The **Granary,** Mardyke Quay (☎490 4275), stages performances by local and visiting theater companies. **Triskel Arts Centre,** Tobin St. (☎427 2022), simmers with avant-garde theater and hosts regular concert and film series. **The Firken Crane Centre,** Shandon Court, houses two theaters dedicated to developing local dance talent. Performance dates vary throughout the year. (☎450 7487. Tickets €9. Call for details.) For Hollywood celluloid and the occasional art-house flick, head to the **Capitol Cineplex** at Grand Parade and Washington St. (☎427 2216 or 427 8777; www.film-info.net. €6.35, students €4.45; matinees €4/€3.81.)

SPORTS

Cork is sporting-mad. Its soccer, hurling, and Gaelic football teams are perennial contenders for national titles (see **Sports,** p. 77). From June through September, **hurling** and **Gaelic football** take place every Sunday afternoon at 3pm. For additional details contact the Gaelic Athletic Association (☎439 5368; www.gaa.ie) or consult *The Cork Examiner.* Be cautious when venturing into the streets on football game days, especially during championships—screaming, jubilant fans have been known to mow tourists down, or, even more dangerous, force them to take part in the revelry. Tickets to big games run €17-20 and are scarce, but Saturday, Sunday, and Wednesday evening matches are cheap (€1.50-5) or free. You can buy tickets to these local games at the **Pairc Uí Chaoimh** (park EE KWEEV), the GAA stadium. Take the #2 bus to Blackrock and ask the driver to let you off at the stadium. The newly opened **Mardyke Arena** provides a break from the Irish rain. The massive complex holds three training gyms, a lap pool, basketball courts, and climbing walls. (☎490 4751. Day passes €10. Call ahead.)

FESTIVALS

Big-name musicians play for free in local pubs and hotels during the three-day **Guinness Cork Jazz Festival** (☎427 8979) in October. Anyone coming to town during that weekend should book rooms well ahead. The week-long **International Film Festival** (☎427 1711), in early October at the Opera House and the Triskel Arts Centre, is another popular choice. The **Cork Midsummer Festival** (☎427 0022; www.corkfestival.ie) promises to enchant from mid-June through the beginning of July. In April, the **International Cork Choral Festival** (☎430 8308) fills city hall, churches, and outdoor venues with voices from across the globe. **The Irish Gay and Lesbian Film Festival** is in mid-October. Call The Other Place (see **Nightlife,** above) for details.

DAYTRIP FROM CORK: BLARNEY

Bus Éireann runs buses from Cork to Blarney M-F 15 per day, Sa 16 per day, Su 10 per day; €4.10 return. Arrive by 9:30am (5min. wait), or wait for up to 3hr. when the buses roll in.

In the middle of the idyllic countryside stands Ireland's tourism epicenter, **Blarney Castle,** resting place of the celebrated **Blarney Stone.** The prevailing myth of the stone's origin holds that it is a chip of the Scottish Stone of Scone that was presented to the King of Munster in gratitude for support during a rebellion in 1314. (Any excuse to do battle with the Brits.) Today it stands as just another slab of limestone among so many others in the castle wall. Still, with everyone else doing it, you might just find yourself bending over backwards to kiss the stone in hopes of acquiring the legendary eloquence bestowed on the smoocher. The term "blarney" refers to the supposedly Irish talent of stretching, or even obstructing, the truth. Queen Elizabeth I allegedly coined it during her long and tiring negotiations over control of the castle. The owner, Cormac McCarthy, Earl of Blarney, followed the rules of 16th-century diplomacy, writing grandiose letters in praise of the Queen, but he never relinquished the land. Ruffling her royal feathers, Her Majesty was heard to say, "This is all blarney—he never says what he means!" The Irish consider the whole thing a bunch of blarney; they're more concerned with the san-

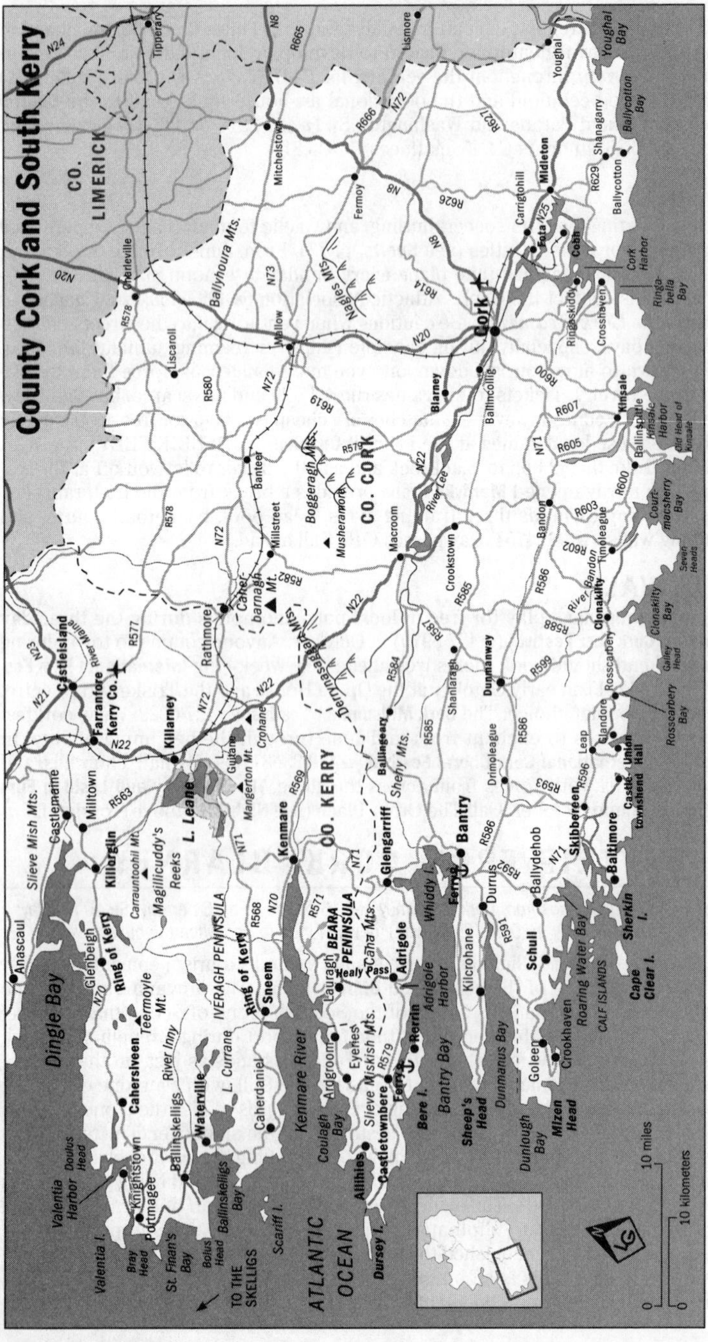
County Cork and South Kerry
CO. LIMERICK
CO. CORK
CO. KERRY
ATLANTIC OCEAN
Dingle Bay
Bantry Bay
Kenmare River
Dunmanus Bay
Dunlough Bay
Roaring Water Bay
CALF ISLANDS
Cork
Cork Harbor
Cobh
Fota
Midleton
Carrigtohill
Youghal
Youghal Bay
Ballycotton
Ballycotton Bay
Shanagarry
Ringaskiddy
Crosshaven
Ringabella Bay
Kinsale
Kinsale Harbor
Old Head of Kinsale
Ballinspittle
Courtmacsherry Bay
Timoleague
Bandon
River Bandon
Seven Heads
Clonakilty
Clonakilty Bay
Galley Head
Rosscarbery
Rosscarbery Bay
Glandore
Leap
Union Hall
Castletownshend
Skibbereen
Baltimore
Sherkin I.
Cape Clear I.
Schull
Ballydehob
Crookhaven
Goleen
Mizen Head
Durrus
Kilcrohane
Sheep's Head
Drimoleague
Dunmanway
Bantry
Whiddy I.
Glengarriff
Adrigole
Adrigole Harbor
Rerrin
Bere I.
Castletownbere
Allihies
Dursey I.
Eyeries
Ardgroom
Lauragh
Healy Pass
Caha Mts.
BEARA PENINSULA
Slieve Miskish Mts.
Coulagh Bay
Kenmare
Sneem
Ring of Kerry
IVERAGH PENINSULA
Caherdaniel
L. Currane
Waterville
Ballinskelligs
Ballinskelligs Bay
Bolus Head
Scariff I.
TO THE SKELLIGS
St. Finan's Bay
Bray Head
Valentia I.
Valentia Harbor
Portmagee
Knightstown
Doulus Head
Cahersiveen
Teermoyle Mt.
River Inny
Glenbeigh
Killorglin
Carrauntoohil Mt.
Magillicuddy's Reeks
Mangerton Mt.
L. Leane
Killarney
Crohane
Farranfore
Kerry Co.
Castleisland
River Maine
Milltown
Castlemaine
Slieve Mish Mts.
Anascaul
Rathmore
Caherbarnagh Mt.
Millstreet
Banteer
Boggeragh Mts.
Musheramore
Derrynasaggart Mts.
Ballingeary
Shehy Mts.
Shanlaragh
Macroom
Crookstown
River Lee
Ballincollig
Blarney
Mallow
Liscaroll
Ballyhoura Mts.
Charleville
Nagles Mts.
Fermoy
Mitchelstown
Lismore
Tipperary
10 miles
10 kilometers

itary implications of so many people kissing the same hunk o' rock. Unless stone-smooching is highlighted in your itinerary, roll over to the castle itself, built in 1446. Other stone-boycotters head left through the archway to explore the more authentic **Druid Gardens**—intrepid travelers will tag along with a passing tour group for an explanation of the garden's intriguing mythological history. *(☎438 5252. Open June-Aug. M-Sa 9am-7pm, Su 9:30am-5:30pm; Sept. M-Sa 9am-6:30pm, Su 9:30am-sundown; Oct.-Apr. M-Sa 9am-6pm or sundown, Su 9:30am-5pm or sundown; May M-Sa 9am-6:30pm, Su 9:30am-5:30pm. Last admission 30min. before closing. Castle and grounds €4.50, seniors and students €3, children €1.50.)*

NEAR CORK CITY: MIDLETON ☎021

Sweet, sweet Jameson is distilled in Midleton *(Mainstir na Corann)*, where visitors learn why Queen Elizabeth once called Irish whiskey her one true Irish friend. Pilgrims in search of the "water of life" (a literal translation of the Gaelic word for "whiskey") come to Midelton for the **Jameson Heritage Centre.** The center rolls visitors through a 1hr. tour that details the craft of whiskey production and includes a glass of the potent stuff at the end—for demonstration purposes only, of course. After all, "the story of whiskey is the story of Ireland." (☎461 3594. Wheelchair-accessible. Open Mar.-Oct. daily 10am-6pm. Tours every 30-45min., last tour 4:30pm. Open Nov.-Feb. by tour only, M-F at noon and 3pm, Sa-Su at 2 and 4pm. €6, students and seniors €5, children €2.50. Tours in French, German, and Italian by request.) Whisk away to Midleton on a **bus** from Cork (30min.; M-F 18 per day, Sa 13 per day, Su 4 per day; €4.88) or drive from Cork or Cobh on the main Cork-Waterford highway (N25).

Whether or not you've had a drop too much at the tour, it'd be a good idea to stay over at **An Stór (IHH) ❶.** From Main St., turn onto Connolly St. and then take your first left onto Drury's Ave. This hostel lives up to its Irish name ("the treasure") with cozy beds, a spacious kitchen, and a wealth of information. (☎463 3106. Laundry €3.50. Dorms €11.50; doubles €16.50.) Get your groceries at **Tesco** on Main St. (☎463 1530. Open M-W and Sa 8:30am-7pm, Th-F 8:30am-9pm, Su 12:30-6pm.) Delicious meals are cooked daily by Eleanor O'Sullivan at **The Granary Foodstore ❷** in Roxboro Mews, an alley off Main St. (☎461 3366. Meals €5-8. Open M-Sa 9am-6pm.) Otherwise, Main St. offers multiple options for pub grub or simple takeaway to soak up the whiskey. Head to **The Meeting Place** and the adjoining **Rory Gallagher's Bar,** Connolly St., for pints and excellent live music on most nights. (☎463 1928. Tu Irish Folk Club night. Occasional €3 cover.)

KNOW YOUR WHISKEY Anyone who drinks his or her whiskey as it's meant to be drunk—"neat," or straight—can tell you that there's a huge difference between Scotch whiskys (without an e), American whiskeys, and Irish whiskeys (Bushmills, Jameson, Power and Son, and the like). But what makes an Irish whiskey *Irish?* The basic ingredients in whiskey—water, barley (which becomes malt once processed), and heat from a fuel source—are always the same. It's the quality of these ingredients, the way in which they're combined, and the means of storage, that gives each product its distinctive flavor: American whiskey is distilled once and is often stored in oak; bourbon is made only in Kentucky; scotch uses peat-smoked barley; Irish whiskey is triple distilled. After this basic breakdown, individual distilleries will claim that their further variations on the theme make their product the best of its class. The best way to understand the distinctions between brands is to taste the various labels in close succession to one another. Line up those shot glasses, sniff, and then taste each one (roll the whiskey in your mouth like a real pro), and have a sip of water between each brand.

COBH (AN CÓBH) ☎021

Little more than a slumbering harbor village today, Cobh (KOVE) was Ireland's main transatlantic port until the 1960s. For many of the emigrants who left between 1848 and 1950, the steep hillside and multicolored houses comprised their final glimpse of Ireland. In keeping with Irish tradition, Cobh has some sad stories to tell. In 1912, the city was the *Titanic's* last port of call four days before the "unsinkable" ship went down. Just a few years later, when the Germans torpedoed the *Lusitania* during World War I, most survivors and some of the dead were taken back to Cobh in lifeboats. Today, with its recently revamped waterfront and a superb museum, Cobh is anything but tragic. Nearby Fota Island hosts a fantastic wildlife park where animals from all over the world roam in open (though fenced off) splendor. Both Cobh and Fota Island are easily accessible by train or car, and they make excellent daytrips or overnight stays from Cork.

TRANSPORTATION AND PRACTICAL INFORMATION. Cobh is an easy trip by **rail** from Cork (25min.; M-Sa 19 per day, Su 8 per day; €4 return). Drivers take N25, then R624. The **tourist office** occupies the restored site of the Royal Cork Yacht Club, built in 1854 and reputedly the **world's first yacht club.** Located on the water to the right coming out of the train station, the office gives out free maps, guides, and advice. (☎481 3301; www.cobhharbourchamber.ie. Open M-F 9:30am-5:30pm, Sa-Su 11:30am-5:30pm.) The **library,** underneath the bridge across from the bus stop, has free **Internet access** for members; the cost of membership is €2.50 (☎481 1130; Internet available Tu-Sa 11am-5:30pm). **Atlantic Bar** has a cybercafe upstairs as well. (☎481 1489. Open M-Sa 11am-8pm. €3 per 15min.)

ACCOMMODATIONS, FOOD, AND PUBS. Should you decide to anchor in Cobh, hurry on over to **The Vega B&B ❸,** located above the Voyager pub. The rooms are brand new and sparkling, and the pancakes are a welcome change from the greasy breakfasts served in other B&Bs. (☎481 4161 or 086 230 4424. Singles €55; doubles €90.) Another option in town is the **Beechmont House Tourist Hostel ❶.** Go past the Cathedral's main doors and take a right at the Quarry Cock Pub; the house is at the top of the hill. Comfortable beds make up for the slight griminess. (☎481 2177. Call ahead. Dorms €12.50.) Pubs, restaurants, and more B&Bs face Cobh's harbor from Beach St.; the **SuperValu** lives up to its name on the same thoroughfare. (☎481 1586. Open M-Tu 9am-6pm, W-F 9am-9pm, Sa 9am-6:30pm.) Dine in first-class luxury at **The Titanic Queenstown ❹,** a bar, bistro, and restaurant located in the building and adjoining pier from which the *Titanic's* passengers last set sail. Lottery winner Vincent Keaney purchased the site and spared no expense in creating an exact replica of the cafe *Parisienne*, the first-class smoke-room and deck of the doomed ship. Order bar food downstairs or stop by in the evening for live bands and *céilís* on the deck. (☎485 5200.) **The River Room ❷,** on West Beach, grills large and tasty ciabatta sandwiches (€5.40), and lunchtime quiche. (☎481 5650. Open M-Sa 8:30am-6pm, Su 10am-4:30pm.) Cobh holds its own in the pub count. The DJs and rock acts at the **Voyager** pack in a young horde nightly. (☎481 4161. M-Tu 4-11:30pm, W-Sa noon-11:30pm, Su noon-2pm and 4-11pm.) **The Ship's Bell** (☎481 1122) attracts a more seasoned, local crowd for pub grub and live trad on weeknights.

SIGHTS AND ACTIVITIES. Cobh commemorates its eminent but tragic history with class and style at **The Queenstown Story,** a heritage center adjacent to the railway station. The museum's flashy multimedia exhibits trace the port's past, with sections devoted to emigration, the *Lusitania*, the *Titanic*, and the peak of transatlantic travel. Resolve your confusion over the town's three names over the years—the original Cove, Victoria-inspired Queenstown, and finally Gaelicized Cobh. (☎481 3591. Open daily 10am-6pm, last admission 5pm. €5, students €4.) Towering over Cobh, the ornate Gothic spire of **St. Colman's Cathedral** dominates the town's architectural landscape. The spire itself is closed to visitors, who will have to content themselves with the view of the harbor from the hill. Completed in 1915, the cathedral boasts the largest carillon in Ireland, consisting of 47 bells weighing over 7700 lb. (Open daily 7am-8pm. Free.)

Visitors interested in creating their own ocean adventure can contact **International Sailing,** based on East Beach. Dinghy, windsurfing, and power boat lessons are available here (from €45), as are canoes for €7 per hr. (☎481 1237. Open M-Th 9:30am-9pm, F-Sa 9:30am-6pm, Su 10:30am-5:30pm.) If self-paddled boats don't appeal, Marine Transport Services, at the harbor, offers **Harbour Cruises** that take roughly 1hr. (☎481 1485. Tours leave daily at noon, 2 and 3pm, and also Su 4 and 5pm. €5, children €3.) If you've vowed to remain on dry land after learning of the town's sobering history, you can take a guided walking tour or minibus ride on the **Titanic Trail,** which offers interesting tidbits about the town's history. (☎4815 211. 1¼hr. walking tour daily at 11am from the Titanic Queenstown, afternoons by request. May-Sept. €7.50 includes a cup of coffee. 1hr. minibus tour daily at 3pm from the Waters Edge Hotel. May-Sept. €8.)

DAYTRIP FROM COBH: FOTA ISLAND.

Fota is an intermediate stop on the train from Cork to Cobh; if you buy a ticket from Cork to Cobh or vice versa, you can get off at Fota and re-board for free.

Ten minutes from Cobh by rail lies Fota Island, where penguins, peacocks, cheetahs, and giraffes roam, largely free of cages, in the **Fota Wildlife Park.** This may well be the closest you'll ever come to a ring-tailed lemur or Chilean flamingo. The park has as many species as acres—70—with animals from South America, Africa, and Asia. (☎481 2678. Open Apr.-Oct. M-Sa 10am-6pm, Su 11am-6pm. Last admission 5pm. €7; seniors, students, and children €4.20.) A **snack bar** in the park serves sandwiches and burgers (€2-4). The **Fota Arboretum,** about a mile from the station but adjacent to the park, cares for plants and trees as exotic as the beasts next door. (Gates close at 5:30pm. Free.)

YOUGHAL (EOCHAILL) ☎024

Thirty miles east of Cork on the N25, beach-kissed Youghal (YAWL) has been basking in the notoriety garnered after it was chosen for the filming of *Moby Dick* starring Gregory Peck. A popular beach and remarkably narrow streets have kept Youghal interesting even after its fifteen minutes of fame.

TRANSPORTATION AND PRACTICAL INFORMATION. **Buses** stop on Main St. in front of the public toilets and across from Dempsey's Bar. They travel to Cork (50min., 17-19 per day, €9) and Waterford via Dungarvan (1½-2hr., M-Su 14 per day, €15.20). Hitching to Cork or Waterford along N25 is possible, but hitchers should always consider the potential risk involved. The outstanding **tourist office,** Market Sq., on the waterfront behind the clocktower, distributes a useful "tourist trail" booklet and a monthly calendar of events (both free), and can point you toward the trad action. (☎20170. Open July-Aug. M-F 9am-7pm, Sa 9:30am-5:30pm, Su 11am-5pm; June and Sept. M-F 9am-5:30pm, Sa-Su 11am-5pm; Oct.-May M-F 9am-5:30pm.) The **library,** on Church St. off Main St., provides free **Internet access** with a €2.50 membership to Cork County libraries. (☎93459. Open Tu-Sa 10am-1pm and 2-5:30pm.)

ACCOMMODATIONS, FOOD, AND PUBS. Finding lodgings in Youghal might take a little legwork; the tourist office can give you a pamphlet with a list of Bord Fáilte-approved accommodations. You might try the majestic **Avonmore**

House ❸, South Abbey, where fully equipped rooms are kept tidy by a capable and helpful staff. (☎92617. Singles €34-40; doubles €58-66.) Alternatively, many tourists are drawn to **Attracta ❸,** across the street, with slightly closer beach access. (☎92062. Singles €32-38; doubles €56-62.)

The town's eateries tempt a wide range of taste buds and budgets. As always, there's the foraging-for-yourself option: **Pasley's SuperValu** is in the town center on Main St., by the tourist office (☎92150; open M-W 9am-7pm, Th and Sa 9am-8pm, F 9am-9pm, Su 10am-6pm), and **L&N SuperValu** lies up the road on N. Main St. (☎92279; open M-W 9am-6pm, Th-Sa 9am-9pm, Su 9am-6pm). The best breakfast in town is in **O'Fóglu's ❷,** next to the clock tower. They also serve delicious food all day long. (☎20903. Breakfast €5.55; sandwiches €3-4.) For huge scones (and some of the cleanest bathrooms in all of Ireland), go to **The Red Stone Pub & Restaurant ❸,** 150-151 N. Main St. (Scone and coffee €3.20; mains €12-13. Breakfast served 10:30am-12:30pm; carvery lunch until 2:30pm; dinner 5:30-9:30pm.)

Music fills each cranny twice a week at the popular **Nook Pub,** which celebrated its 100th year under the ownership of the Treacy family in early 2001. (☎92225. Open M-W 10:30am-11:30pm, Th-Sa 10:30am-12:30am, Su 12:30-11:30pm.) Young'uns head to **The Clock Tavern,** S. Main St., where dark recesses echo with the tick-tock of rock six nights a week. (☎93052. Cover for big-namers €5. Open M-W and Su noon-11:30pm, Th-Sa noon-12:30am.) Tourists have a whale of a time at **Moby Dick's,** in Market Sq., which is filled with nautical murals and some guy named Herman. The pub-folk have a somewhat, well, monomaniacal obsession with Gregory Peck and John Huston. (☎92099. Ballads F.)

SIGHTS. The huge **Clockgate,** built in 1777, straddles crowded Main St. From here you can see the old **city walls,** built on the hill sometime between the 13th and 17th centuries. The tower served as a prison and makeshift gallows (prisoners were hanged from the windows). On Church St., **St. Mary's Church** and **Myrtle Grove** stand side-by-side. The former may be the oldest operating church in Ireland; parts of it date back to the original Danish-built structure, constructed in 1020. One corner of the church holds the elaborate grave of Robert Boyle, first Earl of Cork. Myrtle Grove was the residence of Sir Walter Raleigh when he served as mayor of Youghal in 1588-89. Though the house is now privately owned, you can at least see the very window where Raleigh's buddy Edmund Spencer is said to have finished his hefty epic *The Faerie Queen.* For a condensed version of Youghal's history since the 9th century, drop by the tourist office's **heritage center.** (☎20170. Same hours as tourist office. €2.) Across the street from the center and up a little alley, the **Fox's Lane Folk Museum** is the place to discover the surprisingly interesting history of razor blades and sewing machines. (Open Tu-Sa 10am-1pm and 2-6pm. Last admission 5:30pm. €3.)

WESTERN COUNTY CORK

Western Cork, the southwestern third of the county, was once the "badlands" of Ireland; its ruggedness and isolation rendered it lawless and largely uninhabitable. Ex-hippies and antiquated fishermen have replaced the roving, cave-dwelling outlaws, and they do their best to make the villages hospitable to tourists. Roaringwater Bay and wave-whipped Mizen Head mark Ireland's land's end. The lonely beauty here is a stately solitude unmarred by the tourist-approved shamrocks planted elsewhere in Ireland. From Cork City you have two choices for your westward rambles—an inland or a coastal route. A **coastal bus** runs from Cork to Skibbereen, stopping in Bandon, Clonakilty, and Rosscarbery (M-Sa 8 per day, Su 6 per day). An **inland bus** travels from Cork to Bantry, via Bandon and Dunmanway (M-

Sa 7 per day, Su 4 per day). **Hitchers** are reported to have few problems finding a ride in these parts, but should always consider the dangers involved.

THE INLAND ROUTE

Those looking to avoid the tourist crowds should consider one of the scenic inland routes that move westward from Cork. Winding like the serpents that St. Paddy expelled years ago, these roads are not for saving time, but for savoring the scenery. Popular choices include Cork-Macroom-Killarney, Cork-Macroom-Ballingeary-Bantry/Glengarriff, and Cork-Dunmanway-Bantry/Skibbereen. The rocky faces of the Shehy Mountains, between Dunmanway and Ballingeary, have some of Ireland's most well-preserved wilds—best explored by foot or bike.

DUNMANWAY (DÚN MÁNMHAI) ☎023

Located in relative isolation at the intersection of R586, R587, and R599, **Dunmanway** is a hidden treasure, one of the few Irish towns that truly prizes tradition over tourism. No red carpets for visitors here---Dunmanway lets its scenery speak for itself. Over the mountains to the northwest, quiet **Ballingeary** (*Béal Athán Ghaorthaídh)* is the failing heart of one of West Cork's declining *gaeltachts*. Lacking accommodations and restaurants, visitors have no choice but to base themselves in Dunmanaway and cycle over to take advantage of Ballingeary's scenic offerings.

TRANSPORTATION AND PRACTICAL INFORMATION. **Bus Éireann** voyages eastward from Cork to Dunmanway (M-Sa 6 per day, Su 4 per day; €8); buses depart from in front of Tom Twoney's jewelers on the main square. The **library** ('An Leabharlann') offers the town's lone **Internet access.** (€2.50 Cork library membership gains you free access. Open Tu 2-8pm, W-F 2-5:30pm, Sa 10:30am-1pm and 2-5:30pm.) To reach Ballingeary from Dunmanway, take R587 northwest to R584. It's on the Macroom to Bantry/Glengariff road. A true *gaeltacht,* signs are posted in traditional script and only in Ballingeary's Irish name (Béal athán Ghaorthaídh).

ACCOMMODATIONS, FOOD, AND PUBS. Located in the hills 3 mi. from town, **Shiplake Mountain Hostel (IHH)** ❶ is a perfect example of Dunmanway's unassuming dignity. Shiplake's luckiest guests stay in one of the three colorful **gypsy caravans,** equipped with heat, electricity, and breath-taking views of the surrounding Shehy mountains. A wood stove cozifies the farmhouse common room and cookie jar brownies (€0.60 each) ameliorate all other ailments. Call for a free ride from Dunmanway, or follow Castle St. from the corner of the main square (Gatsby's Nightclub) toward Coolkelure, turning right at the small hostel sign. (☎45750; www.shiplakemountainhostel.com. **Bike rental** €9 per day. Breakfasts €2.50-5; bag lunches €5; vegetarian mains €7-10. Dorms €11; caravans €12.50-13.50 per person. **Camping** €6 per person.)

Central **Centra** stocks victuals (☎45778; open M-Sa 8am-9pm, Su 8:30-6pm). Overlooking the main square, newly converted **Upstairs at the Merchants** ❸ serves serious three-course lunches and delicious dinners. (☎55556. Wild salmon €15. Open daily noon-4pm and 7-10pm.) Dunmanway's 8500 residents support 23 pubs, most of which serve food. Owned and operated by a sixth-generation O'Donovan, **The Shamrock** ❷ (☎45142) has a traditional atmosphere (as well it should after 250 years) and rollicking Sunday afternoons. Enjoy a true Irish meal (€6.50-9) and discuss your ancestors with owner Mike, whose own forefathers adorn the walls. Main Street **An Toísín** serves a mellow meal by day and diverse music at night. (☎45076. DJ Sa.) **The Arch Bar** (☎45155) packs in the football-watching crowd.

THE MUSTARD SEED AT ECHO LODGE

Once a hilltop convent, Ballingarry's charming Echo Lodge country hotel now houses 17 high-ceilinged rooms and suites, each exquisitely decorated to a unique cultural theme. Crisp white linen, well-fluffed pillows, and original pane glass windows mark each room, while bold, classic colors provide background to the house's museum quality art collection. Guests of the lodge also have access to a small fitness room, massage room, and a sauna.

Owner Daniel Mullane and head chef David Norris welcome guests and non-guests to the elegant dining room of the even more enticing **Mustard Seed restaurant** downstairs. The award-winning gourmet food—made from fresh herbs and vegetables grown in the gardens out back—matches the tasteful decor and friendly staff. Splendid four-course dinner menu, from grilled goat's cheese to steamed salmon, is around €47 per person. The food can also be prepared to meet specific dietary requirements. This is an all-around world-class dining experience.

The Mustard Seed, Echo Lodge, Ballingarry (☎069 68508). From the top of Adare village, take the N21 toward Killarney for ½ mi., and turn left for Ballingarry. Follow signs for Rathkeale, then Ballingarry. Wheelchair-accessible. Restaurant open daily 7-9:45pm. Bed and breakfast open year-round. Doubles €165-254. AMEX/MC/V.

SIGHTS AND ACTIVITIES. Seven miles beyond the Shiplake hostel turnoff lies soup-bowl **Lake Cullenagh.** Its pine-wooded paths and shaded picnic areas offer a day's worth of welcome distraction; inquire with the folks at the Shiplake Hostel for information on hiking and biking routes in the area. Closer to town, **Lake Coolkellure** hides its own miniature beach and provides prime brown-trout **fishing.** Over in Ballingeary, the entrance to **Gougane Barra Forest** lies open. From the road though the forest, visitors can see the River Lee's pure source streams flow together. A **church** marking the site of **St. Finbarr's monastery** lies at the base of the mountains, next to a lake. Sweeping views reward those willing to climb the wooded trails to the ridgeline. East of Ballingeary on R584 toward Cork, the Creedon family of **Inse Géimhleach Gaelic School** welcomes students of all nationalities to an intensive week of Irish text and translation seminars, choral workshops, poetry readings, lectures, and music sessions. Students are welcome to attend the full week, a full day, or just a morning class. (Contact Mr. Creedon ☎49012. Language seminars at 11am, choral workshops 7pm, lectures 9pm, sessions 11pm.)

SOUTHERN COAST

From Cork, N71 runs its asphalt course all the way to Clonakilty via Bandon. Past Clonakilty, the population starts thinning out. Mountains rise, craggy ridges replace smooth hills, and rocky shoals proliferate as Ireland's southern coast begins to look more like its western one. The islands in the stretch of ocean between Baltimore and Schull may be the fiercest, most outlandish places in all of southern Ireland. High cliffs plunge into the sea, earning the islands a legacy of shipwrecks. The intrepid O'Driscoll clan (pirates, *arr*) informally ruled the bay for centuries, sallying into the Atlantic for raids, off-loading brandy from Spanish galleons, then speeding home through secret channels between the islands. These days, crossroads along N71 link mellow tourist towns and hardworking fishing villages. "Blow-ins," expatriates from America and Northern Europe, have settled in the area, replacing the area's dwindling native population. These kick-back expats are drawn to Western Cork's leisurely pace and extraordinary scenery, but are shaping its culture to their own tastes.

KINSALE (CIONN TSÁILE) ☎021

Every summer the population of upscale Kinsale temporarily quintuples with a flood of tourists. Visitors come to swim, fish, and eat at Kinsale's 12 famed and expensive "Good Food Circle" restaurants. Connoisseurs of culture, dreamy beachcombers, and high-speed aquatic daredevils also find their fix in Kinsale—as do the millionaires who helicopter onto the links at the Old Head for a quick nine holes once or twice a year. Kinsale's pleasant present barely recalls the grimmer roles the town has played in history: the victory of Elizabethan England at the 1601 Battle of Kinsale cleared the way for several centuries of colonialism (see **Feudalism,** p. 56); 80-odd years later, deposed Catholic King James II came here for a last failed attempt to claim his throne; then, in 1915, the *Lusitania* was sunk just off Kinsale's Old Head. These days, boats from Great Britain come loaded with vacationers eager to fill the town's coffers.

ORIENTATION AND PRACTICAL INFORMATION. Kinsale lies at the base of a U-shaped inlet, a 30min. drive southwest of Cork on R600. Facing the water, **Charles Fort** and the **Scilly Walk** (pronounced "silly") are to the left; the piers, **Compass Hill,** and **James Fort** are to the right; the town center is behind you. **Buses** to and from Cork stop at the Esso station on the Pier (40min.; M-Sa 10-11 per day, Su 5 per day; €6.50 return). The **tourist office,** Emmet Pl., in the black-and-red building on the waterfront, distributes free maps. (☎477 2234. Open July-Aug. daily 9am-6pm, Mar.-Nov. M-Sa 9am-6pm.) The **Bank of Ireland,** Main St., has a 24hr. **ATM.** (☎477 2521. Open M 10am-5pm, Tu-F 10am-4pm.) At 8 Long Quay, **Mylie Murphy's** painted sign displays a plump fish riding a bicycle. Clever man. (☎477 2703. **Bike rental** €12 per day, €65 per wk. **Fishing poles** €10 per day, €60 per wk. **Fresh bait** €2-6. Deposit or credit card required. Open M-Sa 9:30am-6pm, call ahead Su in summer.) Access the **Internet** at **Finishing Services,** also on Main St. (☎477 3571. €2.50 per 15min., €6 per hr. Open M-F 9am-5:30pm.)

ACCOMMODATIONS AND CAMPING. Kinsale's hotels and plush B&Bs cater to an affluent crowd—budget-orientated beds can be found at **Guardwell Lodge ❷,** Guardwell St., as can self-catering kitchens and modern, cheerful top-floor rooms. (☎477 4686. Dorms €17; private rooms €15-25 per person. 10% discount with the mention of *Let's Go.*) Just up the road, **O'Donovan's B&B ❸** sports delightfully simple and comfortable rooms. (☎477 2428. €24-28 per person.) The can't-miss-it-canary yellow facade of **The Gallery ❸** speaks volumes for the quirkiness that lies within. The proprietor is a jazz musician (hence the white baby grand), his wife is a painter, and the award-winning salmon breakfasts are sometimes accompanied by heaping scoops of ice cream—who knew? (☎477 4558. €34-43 per person.) For authentic Georgian elegance, **The Old Presbytery ❹** offers luxurious self-catering apartments. Each comes complete with a sitting room, fireplace, full kitchen, and claw-footed porcelain tub; some even have a jacuzzi. The owners also rent bedrooms to more budget-minded travelers. (☎477 2027; www.oldpres.com. 4-5 person apartments €155 per night; 3-night minimum stay. 2-4 person bedrooms €95-140.) For those who brought their own accommodations, plots of land can be rented at the **Garrettstown House Holiday Park ❷,** 6 mi. west of Kinsale in Ballinspittle on the R600. (☎477 8156. Open May-Oct. One adult with tent €12.)

FOOD AND PUBS. If you're looking for gourmet, look no further—locals claim that Kinsale is the only town in Ireland with more restaurants than pubs, though good food often comes at a price. Budget visitors fill their baskets at the always present and always affordable **SuperValu** on Pearse St. (☎477 2843. Open M-Sa 8:30am-9pm, Su 10am-9pm.) At **Patsy's Corner ❶,** Market Sq., locals pack in behind the wraparound corner window for homemade cakes and tortes teetering with fruit and cream. (☎086 865 8143. Soup and gourmet brown bread €3. Open daily 9am-5:30pm.) On Main St., **The Mad Monk ❶** supplies dependable pub grub and music on most nights. (☎774 602. Meals €5-8.) The best of the best changes weekly; inquire at your B&B for the tastiest meal in town.

A proper pub crawl will take you well out of Kinsale's small maze of streets. **The Spaniard** (☎477 2436), atop the hill on the Scilly Peninsula, is well worth the trip. With its thick stone walls, low-beamed ceilings, and dark wood paneling, this little pearl lures fishermen and other locals to foot-tapping trad sessions held several nights a week. To get to the pub, follow the signs to Charles Fort for ¼ mi. (☎477 2436. Mains €7-14.) Those who make the hike to Charles Fort are rewarded with a pint of Irish black gold at the picturesque **Bulman Bar** (☎477 2131). The long walk home is sure to sober you up.

SIGHTS. A 30min. trek up **Compass Hill,** south of Main St., brings wide views of the town and its seascapes. Even more impressive is the vista from **Charles Fort,** the classic 17th-century star-shaped fort that was a British naval base until 1921. The battlements and buildings overlook the water and offer nearly limitless opportunities for climbing and exploration. You can reach Charles Fort by following **Scilly Walk** (30min.), a sylvan path along the coast that starts at the end of Pearse St. (☎477 2263. Open mid-Mar. to Oct. M-F 10am-6pm; Nov. to mid-Mar. Sa-Su 10am-5pm, M-F by appointment. €4, seniors €2.50, students and children €1.50.) Across the harbor from Charles Fort, the ruins of similarly-starry **James Fort** tempt explorers with secret passageways and panoramic views of Kinsale. To reach this fort, follow the pier away from town, cross the Duggan bridge, then turn left. After scrambling through the ruins and the rolling heath, descend to Castlepark's hidden arc of **beach** behind the hostel. (Always open. Free.)

Back in town, on Cork St., **Desmond Castle** broods over its rather gloomy history. The 15th-century custom house served as an arsenal during the 100-day Spanish occupation of 1601 and as a naval prison during the 17th century. Inside the castle, the **International Museum of Wine** douses visitors with the chronicle of Kinsale's history as a wine port. (☎477 4855. Open mid-June to early Oct. daily 10am-6pm; mid-Apr. to mid-June Tu-Sa 10am-6pm. Last admission 45min. before closing. €2.50, seniors €2, students and children €1.50.) In 1915, a trigger-happy German U-boat torpedoed the British ocean liner *Lusitania* off the Old Head, a promontory south of Kinsale. The fury provoked at over 1000 civilian deaths hastened the United States' entrance into WWI. Hearings on the *Lusitania* case took place in the **Kinsale Courthouse,** Market Sq., which now contains a regional **museum.** Up the hill from Market Sq., check out the restored west tower of the 12th-century **Church of St. Multose,** the patron saint of Kinsale. The ancient graveyard is also worth a peek. (☎477 2220. Church open until dusk. Graveyard always open. Free.)

CLONAKILTY (CLOCH NA COILLTE) ☎023

Once a linen-making town with a workforce of over 10,000 people, Clonakilty ("Clon") lies between Bandon and Skibbereen on N71. Henry Ford was born nearby, but the favorite son is military leader, spy, organizational genius, and real Irish hero Michael Collins. The wily Collins returned home during the Civil War, because "they surely won't kill me in my own country." So much for nationalist bravado—he was ambushed and murdered 25 mi. from town. Most visitors, being more interested in relaxation than revolution, head to nearby Inchydoney Beach. During the second week of July, there is much feasting at the Black and White Pudding Festival (see **Food and Drink,** p. 67); prizes are given out for the best recipe and the most pudding consumed—not for the faint of heart, or stomach.

ORIENTATION AND PRACTICAL INFORMATION. Clonakilty's main drag begins at the tourist office on **Ashe St.** and continues along the road, eventually turning into **Pearse St.** and finally **Western Rd.** A stone tribute to axe-wielding rebel Tadgh an Astna serves as a central point. To the statue's left, **Rossa St.** runs into **Connelly** near the Wheel of Fortune water pump. **Astna St.** angles off the statue toward the harbor and **Inchydoney Beach** (bear right.) **Buses** from Cork (3-4 per day, €8.50) and Skibbereen (M-Th and Sa-Su 2 per day, F 3 per day; €5.50) stop in front of Lehane's Supermarket on Pearse St. You can walk the 3 mi. to Inchydoney or **rent a bike** at **MTM Cycles** on Ashe St. (☎33584. €10 per day, €45 per wk.) The **tourist office,** 25 Ashe St., hands out maps and advice. (☎33226. Open July-Aug. M-Sa 9am-7pm, Su 10am-5pm; June M-Sa 9am-6pm; Mar.-May and Sept.-Nov. M-Sa 9:30am-5:30pm.) **AIB** and **Bank of Ireland** cash in on Pearse St.; each has a 24hr. **ATM.** (Both open M 10am-5pm, Tu-F 10am-4pm.) If you become a member of the Co. Cork **library** (€2.50), you can access the **Internet** at the Clon branch in the Old Mill on Kent St. (☎34275. Open Tu-Sa 10:30am-6pm.) The Gothic **post office** addresses town from Bridge St. (Open M-F 9am-5:30pm, Sa 10am-4pm.)

ACCOMMODATIONS, FOOD, AND PUBS. The **Old Brewery Hostel ❶,** Emmet Sq., also known as the Clonakilty Hostel, has a super kitchen area and comfortable beds. Coming from Lehane's, head down Pearse St., make a left at the Roman Catholic church, then a right at the park in Emmet Sq. (☎33525. **Bike rental** €9 per day. Wheelchair-accessible. Dorms €12; doubles €30.) A 5min. walk from town and a right turn after the museum leads you to **Nordav ❸,** 70 Western Rd. Removed from the road by a well-groomed lawn and splendid rose gardens, this family-style B&B features gloriously spacious suites and smaller but lovely doubles. (☎33655. €26-33 per person.) **Desert House Camping Park ❶** is connected to a dairy farm half a mile southeast of town on the road to Ring Village. (☎33331. Open May-Sept. €1 per person; small tent €7; family tent €9. Showers €0.65.)

Clonakilty's culinary fame (and infamy) comes from its style of **black pudding,** a sausage-like concoction made from beef, blood, and grains. Those eager to try it, or its pasty **white pudding** sister (made with pork minus the blood), should head to the award-winning butcher at **Twomey's.** (☎33365. Open M-Sa 9am-6pm.) Most local restaurants also offer it, generally for breakfast. But fear ye not—Clon has many other options for daily sustenance. Brown-bag it at **Lehane's Supermarket** on Pearse St. (☎33359. Open M-Th 8am-6:30pm, F 8am-8pm, Sa 8am-7pm, Su 9am-1:30pm.) **Betty Brosnans ❶,** 58 Pearse St., serves the best cafe lunch in town. (☎34011. Chicken and avocado baguette €4; fresh milkshakes €2.50. Breakfast all day. Open M-Sa 9am-6pm.) Pass under the vine-covered arches at **Gearoidins ❷,** 18 Pearse St., for great values any time of day. (☎34444. Most meals €6-10. Open M-Th 9:30am-6pm, F-Sa 9:30am-9pm, Su 11am-8pm.)

There's music aplenty in Clonakilty, regarded as the diamond in the rough of Western Cork's otherwise less-than-remarkable trad scene. The hugely popular **De Barra's** on Pearse St. draws big-name acts with its superb sound system and ideal set-up. The nightly folk and trad can be enjoyed anywhere in the huge venue—in the main room, small nooks, beer garden, or upstairs on the balcony. (☎33381. Occasional €4 cover.) Around the corner, **Shanley's,** 11 Connolly St. (☎33790), does music every night of the summer, juggling folk, rock, and the occasional nationally-known star. Through the arched Recorders' Alley off Pearse St., **An Teach Beag** is Clonakilty's center for storytelling and set dancing.

SIGHTS. To fill the hours before the pubs pick up, join the locals at **Inchydoney,** one of the nicest beaches this side of Malibu. On Inchydoney Rd. you'll pass the **West Cork Model Railway Village,** where Kinsale, Bandon, and Clonakilty of 1940 are reborn in miniature. (☎33224. Open Feb.-Oct. M-F 11am-5pm, Sa-Su 1-5pm. €4, students €2.50.) Back in town, the **West Cork Museum,** Western Rd., displays an early 20th-century beer-pouring machine, the christening shawl of patriot O'Donovan Rossa, and other assorted historical baubles. (Open May-Oct. M-Sa 10am-6:30pm. €3, students €1.50, children free.) While in Clon, don't miss your opportunity to learn about the heroic **Michael Collins.** Tours of various sights relating to his life and death can be arranged through the tourist office or through Timothy Crowley (☎46107). Two miles east you'll find the **Lios na gCon Ring Fort,** which has been "fully restored" based on excavators' guesses at its 10th-century form. It is the only ring fort in all of Ireland reconstructed on its original site.

UNION HALL (BREANTRA) ☎028

Between Clonakilty and Skibbereen, just across the water from the cute and harmless hamlet of **Glandore,** sits the fishing village of **Union Hall.** Set amidst rolling green pastures and forested land too rocky for farming, the town was once a semi-permanent hangout for **Jonathan Swift.** Travelers passing between Union Hall and Skibbereen often pause to picnic in the shady seaside groves of **Rennin Forest. Knockdrum Fort,** just west of town, demonstrates just what becomes of Iron Age Celtic forts over the centuries. Three miles out of town, tourists flock to the pterodactyl teeth, dinosaur droppings, stone-age calendars, and Easter Rising rifles of the **Ceim Hill Museum.** The museum's proprietress, who you will probably find even more interesting than her collection, found all the artifacts in her backyard. (☎36280. Open daily 10am-7pm. €4.) For more interactive distractions, consult the folks at **Atlantic Sea Kayaking** (☎21058), who provide guided water-borne transportation to the area's nearby islands and sea caves. They also run **overnight camping trips** to an uninhabited island and run a spectacular **moonlight paddle.** (☎21058. Half-day trip €35, full day €60. Overnight camping trip €100. Moonlight paddle €38.) For **fishing trips** and **whale-watching expeditions,** call Capt. Colin Barnes (☎086 327 3226), who has a blessed knack for spotting seals and whales.

The town is also home to legendary **Maria's Schoolhouse Hostel (IHH) ❶.** Once the Union Hall National School, Maria's hostel has been redecorated in Brobdingnagian style—the huge common room was refitted with a cathedral ceiling and big skylights were installed in the dorm. This hostel is more than reason enough for a detour en route to Skibbereen. To get to Maria's, turn right after the bridge into the village center, bear left at the church, then take the first right (marked by a small sign). Or call for a lift—from the Skibbereen-Clonakilty bus, ask the driver to let you off in **Leap** (LEP) and call the hostel. (☎33002. 3-course dinner with occasional musical accompaniment F-Sa €22. Laundry €7. Dorms €12; doubles €38-50.) Back in town, **Centra** provides the basics (☎34955. Open M-Sa 8am-9pm, Su 8am-2pm), and **Dinty's Bar ❷** serves up monster portions of ocean-centric victuals. (☎33373. Mains €7-8. Food served 12:30-2:30pm and 6-9pm.) Fresh seafood or less expensive pub grub awaits at the waterside patio/beer garden of **Casey's Bar ❷.** (☎33590. Mains €6.50-12. Food served daily noon-8:30pm.) The jovial atmosphere and billiard tables at **Maloney's** (☎33610) draw a young crowd. **Nolan's Bar** (☎33758) supplies a few bites and spirited trad.

SKIBBEREEN (AN SCIOBAIRIN) ☎028

The biggest town in Western Cork, Skibbereen ("Skib") is a convenient stop for travelers roaming the coastal wilds. Skib was established in 1631 by refugees fleeing Baltimore, where a bunch of marauding Algerian pirates were up to their old city-sacking tricks. In more recent times, Skib has evolved into a market town for local farmers, whose big-wheeled vehicles and big-time smell still rumble through town on a regular basis. Many stores in Skibbereen close on Thursdays around noon to recover between market days (W, F, and Sa). If you don't want to join in the farm fun, the town is in perfect striking distance for daytrips to seaside destinations like Baltimore, Schull, and Castletownshend.

ORIENTATION AND PRACTICAL INFORMATION. Skibbereen is laid out in an L-shape, with **North St.** as the base, supporting **Main St.** and **Bridge St.** (Main St. turns into Bridge St. at the small bridge). The clock tower, post office, and stately "Maid of Erin" statue are at the elbow. Hitchers typically stay on N71 to go east or west but switch to R595 to go south. **Buses** stop at Calahane's Bar on Bridge St. and run to Baltimore (year-round M-F 5 per day, June-Sept. also Sa 4 per day; €2.80); Clonakilty (M-Sa 8 per day, Su 3 per day; €5.65); Cork (7 per day, €11.30); and Killarney (2 per day, €14). **Roycroft Cycles,** on Ilen St. off Bridge St., **rents bikes.** They also participate in Raleigh's One-Way Rent-A-Bike program and, new for 2003, they will begin an **airport pickup service;** call for details. (☎21235. €14.50 per day, including helmet. Deposit €65. Open M-Sa 9:15am-6pm.) The **tourist office** is next to the Town Hall on North St. (☎21766. Open July-Aug. daily 9am-7pm; June M-Sa 9am-6pm; Sept.-May M-F 9:15am-5:30pm.) **AIB** has an **ATM** at 9 Bridge St., and **Bank of Ireland** has one in front of the SuperValu on Main St; the bank itself is on Market St. (☎21388 and 21700. Both open M-F 10am-4pm, W until 5pm.) There's an interesting **Fine & Rare Book Shop** across from the post office on Market St. (☎22115. Open June-Aug. daily 11am-5pm; Sept.-May by appointment.) Scrub your duds at **West Cork Dry Cleaners,** across from the bus stop on Bridge St. (☎21627. €5 per load. Open M-Sa 10am-6pm.) There are two affiliated **pharmacies** facing each other on Main St. (☎21543. M-Sa 9am-6pm. After-hours emergency ☎086 858 8957.) Two computers with **Internet access** are available at the **library,** across from the Arts Centre on North St., which participates in the Co. Cork Library's one-time membership fee (€2.50) granting unlimited free access to their web connections. (☎22400. Open Tu-Sa 10am-5:30pm.) Many more computers with fast access are available at the **Flexible Learning IT Center,** on the 3rd floor of the Arts Centre building. (☎21011. Less than €1 per hr. Open M-F 9:30am-1pm and 2-5pm.) The **post office** is on Market St. (☎21002. Open M-Sa 9am-5:30pm, Tu open 9:30am.)

ACCOMMODATIONS AND CAMPING. **Russagh Mill Hostel and Adventure Centre (IHH) ❶,** about 2 mi. out of town on the Castletownshend road, features a **climbing wall,** and runs camps for groups of children and adults, but also welcomes the simple hosteler. This renovated 200-year-old mill only has basic dorms, but its glassed-in sunroom is a marvel. (☎22451. Check-out 11am. Open mid-Mar. to Nov. Dorms €11; private rooms €15 per person.) The proprietress of **Bridge House ❸,** Bridge St., could be a set designer for Victorian period films; as she puts it, "My house is my stage!" True to spirit, each room is decorated with a theatrical sense of humor. (☎21273. €25-27 per person.) **Dalton's ❷,** on North St., provides the most basic beds in town, with TV and bath, but breakfast is not included. Rooms come in single, double, and family-sized. (☎23881. €22 per person.) The **Hideaway Campground ❶,** Castletownshend St., is the place for campers and caravaners. (☎22254. Kitchen facilities available. Tent €10; with car €11.50. Showers €0.65.)

FOOD AND PUBS. The cafes along Main St. and North St. offer a number of inviting options. Field's **SuperValu,** Main St., struts its stuff as a supermarket and also houses a cafe. (☎21400. Open M-Sa 9am-7pm.) At **Kalbo's Bistro ❸,** 48 North St., cool jazz and excellent, innovative mains go hand in hand. Try the delicate marinated monkfish over lime couscous. (☎21515. Lunch €6-9; dinner €11.50-18. Open M-Sa 11:30am-4:30pm and 6:30-9:30pm, Su noon-2:30pm and 6:30-9:30pm. Reserve ahead in July and Aug.) **The Wine Vaults ❷,** on Bridge St., has tasty, freshly baked pizza, as well as typical pub standards. (☎23112. Pizzas €6.50-11, mains €11.50. Food served mid-July to Aug. M-Sa noon-9pm; Sept. to mid-July M-Sa noon-7pm.) Scones and hearty breakfasts are served up at **The Stove ❷,** on Main St.

(☎22500. Meals €6-9. Open M-Sa 8am-6pm.) Find blues, folk, and a young crowd at the **Wine Vaults** (see above), where locals and tourists crush a happy cup together. **Seán Óg's,** Market St. (☎21573), hosts contemporary folk and blues several nights a week, a Tuesday trad session, and a nightly outdoor beer garden. **Kearney's Well,** 52-53 North St. (☎21350), attracts lively locals, while the more comfortable digs at **Bernard's** off Main St., are all the better to converse in.

SIGHTS AND ACTIVITIES. Newly opened in the old gasworks building on Upper Bridge St., the **Skibbereen Heritage Centre** leads visitors through interactive displays highlighting the natural beauty and biological wealth of **Lough Hyne** (also spelled Ine; see **Baltimore,** p. 248), and educates well-fed visitors about the devastation of the Famine. (☎40900; www.skibbheritage.com. €4, students and seniors €3, children €2, families €9. Open mid-May to mid-Sept. daily 10am-6pm; mid-Mar. to mid-May and mid-Sept. to Oct. Tu-Sa 10am-6pm. Last admission 5:15pm.) The **West Cork Arts Centre,** North St., rotates exhibits of Irish modern art. (☎22090. Gallery open M-Sa 10am-6pm. Free.) Get wired into the local arts scene with *Art Beat*, free at the center. Pick up a copy of the *The Skibbereen Trail* map at the tourist office (€1.75) and take a self-guided tour of the town's major sights. Included on this tour is the **Abbeystrewery Cemetery,** where between 8000 and 10,000 Famine victims are buried. The gardens at **Liss Ard Experience,** down the Castletownshend road toward the hostel, promise to "induce new perceptions of light and sky." Created as a unique attempt at conservation, the Experience's 50 acres include a waterfall garden, a wildflower meadow with over 100 species of butterflies, and the surreal "Irish sky garden" designed by American artist James Turrell. (Open May-Sept.) Based about 8 mi. from Skib, Jim Kennedy at **Atlantic Sea Kayaking** offers paddle daytrips, as well as night paddles in Lough Hyne and Castlehaven Bay. (☎21058 or 086 606 5973. €38 per person.) The **Atlantic Boating Services'** shack on Bridge St. sells wet suits, flippers, and other water accessories. (☎22145. Open July-Aug. daily 10am-6pm, Sept.-June Tu-W and F-Sa 10am-5pm.)

BALTIMORE (BAILE TAIGH MÓR) ☎028

The tiny fishing village of Baltimore (pop. 200) has traded its pirates for tourists and is now a center for aquatic sport and a point of departure for the Sherkin and Cape Clear Islands. In the center of town is the stone wreckage of Dún na Sead ("The Fort of the Jewels"), one of nine regional 16th-century castles belonging to the prolific O'Driscoll clan. O'Driscolls from near and far congregate here every June to elect a chieftain and to stage a family gathering, complete with live music, jammed pubs, and convivial inebriation. Artists and tourists flock to Baltimore with almost equal enthusiasm to enjoy its bright, dramatic seascapes.

TRANSPORTATION AND PRACTICAL INFORMATION. It's difficult to miss anything in Baltimore. The main road from Skibbereen passes along the waterfront before running 1½ mi. out of town to the milk bottle **Beacon,** a cliff-top lighthouse that once guided ships between the mainland and Sherkin Island. Inside the small **general store** below O'Driscoll castle, the **post office** (☎20101; open M-F 9am-5:30pm, Sa 9am-1pm) displays a **Bus Éireann** schedule; buses run to Skibbereen regularly (M-Sa 3-4 per day, fewer in winter; €3). For information on ferries to Cape Clear or Sherkin, see p. 249. The small **tourist office** (☎20441), in the blue harbor-side craft center, is non-Bord Fáilte and keeps sporadic hours.

ACCOMMODATIONS, FOOD, AND PUBS. A delightful German family runs the popular **Rolf's Hostel (IHH) ❶**, a 300-year-old complex of stone farmhouses just 10min. from the waterfront. Walking from the pier, start back up the

Skibbereen road, then turn left at the signposted turnoff. The comfortable pine beds (brass in private rooms) and stunning views are hard to resist. (☎20289. **Bike rental** €12 per day. **Internet access** €0.75 per 6min. Laundry €5. Dorms €12-13; doubles €35; family rooms €47.) Hallway candles light the way through the stone walls of **Fastnet B&B ❸**. Ask for the secluded back double room for the best ocean views, or the upstairs triple for plum curtains and room enough to do cartwheels. (☎20515. Doubles €52-64. Children half-price.) On the waterfront, the Diving & Watersports Centre welcomes budget-seeking guests to the **Baltimore Holiday Hostel ❷**. Follow the signs downhill from the post office and look for the red sign that says "Le Bistro." (☎20300. **Bike rental** €10 per day. Laundry €7. Dorms €15.)

Provisions for extended island stays can be found at **Cotter's Gala,** on the main road facing the harbor. (☎20106. Open June-Aug. daily 9am-9pm; Sept.-May 9am-7:30pm.) The **Cafe Art and Restaurant ❷,** at Rolf's Hostel (see above), is famous for its fresh Mediterranean salads. Candles and wine goblets separate the cafe from the restaurant. (☎20289. Open Tu-Su 8am-9pm. Sandwiches €4-5. Mains €12-14.) Front and center **La Jolie Brise ❸** peddles the tastiest pizzas (€6-10) in town. (☎20600. Open 8:30am-11pm; closes 9pm in winter.) Shying away from the front-row hubbub, **Mews Restaurant ❺** is decked out in forest greens and glossed pinewood floors that whisper of an Irish Martha Stewart. The restaurant is also known to serve the best food (Duck Confit €25) in town. (☎20390. Open June-Sept. 6-10pm.) Baltimore's pub stride of ten to twelve paces begins at lively **McCarthy's,** famous for its trad and folk bands (F and Sa in summer), and its mid-May **fiddle festival** that attracts the likes of Christie Moore. (☎20159. Bar food noon-10pm. Occasional cover €3-13.) The intense maritime theme continues in **Bushe's Bar** (☎20125), and, just around the corner, at the well-cushioned **Algiers Inn** (☎20145).

SIGHTS AND ACTIVITIES. Most of Baltimore's best sights are found underwater; wrecked U-boats, galleons, and many other subaquatic curiosities await the more amphibious visitors. To arrange dives or equipment rentals, contact the **Baltimore Diving & Watersports Centre,** located in the Baltimore Holiday Hostel. (☎20300. 1hr. snorkel dive €12.50, including equipment; course and dive for the inexperienced €40.) **Atlantic Boating Service,** located at the end of the pier, offers all manner of aquatic fun. (☎22734. **Waterskiing** from €40. **Boat rental** €14-20 per hr., €65 per day.) Explorers equipped with bicycles or cars should head east to circular **Lough Ine** (sometimes spelled Hyne), Northern Europe's only saltwater lake, where clear rapids change direction with the tide. The lough, originally freshwater, was converted by rising sea levels following the last Ice Age. These days Ine is a stomping ground for marine biologists searching for the dozens of sub-tropical species it shelters. **Walking trails** wind through the woods around the lake, and the steeper climbs lead to incredible views. A few miles back toward Skib, the well-groomed **Creagh Gardens** face off with their rustic woodland setting. (☎22121. Open daily 10am-5pm. €3.80, children €1.90.)

CAPE CLEAR ISLAND (OILEÁN CHLÉIRE) ☎028

The scenery visible from the ferry landing is desolate and foreboding; the landscape of patchwork fields separated by low stone walls hasn't changed much since Spanish galleons stopped calling here hundreds of years ago. The main industry on this wild and beautiful island is farming—be sure to ask locals about the legendary banana plantation (but resist offers of employment as a harvester at all costs).

TRANSPORTATION AND PRACTICAL INFORMATION. Capt. Conchúr O'Driscoll (☎39135) runs ferries to and from Baltimore (2-6 per day; €11.50, children €5.50). For ferries direct to Schull, speak to Capt. Molloy. (☎28138. 45min.

June 1 per day, July-Aug. 3 per day. €11.50 return.) Contact Capt. Cierán O'Driscoll about **ferry loops** from Cape Clear to Baltimore, Schull, and back. (☎28138. Daily departures from Cape Clear Island mid-June to mid-Sept. 9am and 12:15pm. Single €8; full-loop, including lunch voucher €13.) Life here is leisurely and hours are approximate—for current opening hours and general island information head to the **information office** in the Pottery Shop, on the left just up from the pier. (☎39100. Open July-Aug. 11am-1pm and 3-6pm; June and Sept. 3-6pm.) There are no banks or ATMs on the island, but a temporary **library** is housed in the green box trailer on the far side of the pier. (Open W and Th-Sa 2-4pm.)

ACCOMMODATIONS, FOOD, AND *CRAIC*. **Cléire Lasmuigh (An Óige/HI) ❶**, the Cape Clear Island Adventure Centre and Hostel, is a 10min. walk from the pier; follow the main road and keep left. The hostel is in a picturesque stone building with killer views of the harbor. Irish students lodge here in the summer, so call ahead. (☎39198. Check-in strictly 3:30-8pm. Dorms €9-11.) Opposite from Ciarán Danny Mike's (see below), the **Cluain Mara B&B ❷** has sunny rooms with harbor views. (☎39153. €22-25 per person; self-catering apartment €32.) Up the (very) steep hill past the hostel, well-flowered **Ard Na Gaoithe ❸** has spacious doubles, family rooms, and a filling breakfast buffet. (☎39160. €25 per person.) **Cuas an Uisce Campsite ❶**, on the south pier, is a 5min. walk from the harbor. Start uphill from the harbor, bear right before colorful Ciarán Danny Mike's, and it's just 400 yd. up to the left. Pete the warden takes to the sea by day—leave a note or check in at the pubs. (☎39136. Open June-Sept. €5 per person, under 16 €2.50, children free. Tent rental €5. Showers €1.)

Basic groceries are available at **An Siopa Beag** (☎39099) on the pier. The shop also has a small **coffee dock** that peddles takeaway pizzas on some summer evenings (June F-Sa 5-7pm, July-Aug. daily 6-8:30pm). Dinner options on Cape Clear are limited to the island's two pubs. Multi-generational **Ciarán Danny Mike's** is Ireland's southernmost pub and restaurant. Ciarán (son), Danny (father), and Mike (grandfather), serve slurpalicious soups and tempting dinners. (☎39172. Soup €3; sandwiches €3; mains €8-15.) Closer to the pier, **Cotter's Bar** also serves bar necessities—pub grub and Guinness. (☎39102. Open daily noon-9pm.) Tip: what Cape Clear's pub scene lacks in variety it makes up for in stamina. Without a resident island *Garda* to regulate after-hours drinking, the fun often rolls on past 3am.

SIGHTS AND ACTIVITIES. A steep 25min. hike up the narrow hill above the harbor sits the Cape Clear **heritage center,** packed with everything from a family tree of the ubiquitous O'Driscolls to a waterlogged deck chair from the *Lusitania.* (Open June-Aug. daily 2-5:30pm. €2, students €1.50.) On the road to the center, after the hill, in the second house on the left, **Cléire Goats** (☎39126) is home to some of the best-bred furry beasts in Ireland. For €1.50 you can test the owner's claim that his **goat's milk ice cream** is richer and more scrumptious than the generic bovine variety. Cléire Goats also runs half-day to week-long courses for those who want to blend the theory and practice of goat-keeping. (Bookable only through www.emara.com.) From many of the island's hills you can gaze out at the ruins of the **O'Driscoll castle** (near the North Harbour), and the **old lighthouse** (to the south, beyond the hostel). Though the castle remains on private property, the lighthouse is open for exploration. The **bird observatory,** a white farmhouse in the North Harbour, is one of the most important in Europe. (☎39189. Only die-hard ornithologists roost here; €14 per night.) Three miles off the east shore is **Fastnet Rock Lighthouse;** for a closer look contact Capt. Cierán O'Driscoll (☎39153; Wed. 7:30pm sailings in summer). Capt. Cierán also runs **whale and dolphin watching** excursions and **ocean bird watching** trips with resident experts like Pete the warden. (☎39172.

€15 per person.) For **sea-kayaking** and **diving** trips, contact the **Roaringwater Bay Centre.** (Kayaking €12 per hr., snorkeling €10 per hr.) Swallow a hefty dose of island lore in early September at Cape Clear's annual **International Storytelling Festival,** which features puppet workshops, music sessions, and a weekend's worth of memorable tales. (☎39157. €7 per event, €30 entrance to all weekend events.)

SHERKIN ISLAND (INIS ARCAIN) ☎028

Just 10min. across the water from Baltimore, Sherkin Island (pop. 100) lures visitors with its sandy, cliff-enclosed beaches, wind-swept heaths, over-abundance of cows, and absence of people. The first thing you'll see as you step off the ferry are the ruins of a 15th-century **Franciscan abbey,** founded by the infamous Fineen O'Driscoll. Vengeful troops from Waterford sacked the abbey in 1537 to get back at the O'Driscolls for stealing their wine. Unimpressive **Dún-na-Long Castle** ("fort of the ships"), also built by the buccaneer clan and also sacked in the '37 raid, lies in a crumpled heap north of the abbey and behind Islander's Rest. Continue on the main road from the ferry dock and you'll pass blue-green **Kinnish Harbour** and the Sherkin **Art Exhibition Community Hall.** (☎20336. Open June-Sept. 9am-6pm.) To get to Sherkin's best beaches, continue down the main road to the east side of the island, where you'll find the glorious **Silver Strand.** Nearby lie **Cow Strand** and **Trabawn,** which are more secluded and great for swimming. For particularly breathtaking views from the island's east side, turn left at the signs for **Horseshoe Harbour** and its defunct **lighthouse.** Sherkin is liveliest each July during the annual **regatta.**

Ferries arrive from Baltimore ten times a day in the summer and thrice in the winter (€7 return). Ferry schedules are posted outside the **Islands Craft Office** in Baltimore (see p. 248) and on the back of the ubiquitous Sherkin brochure; Capt. Vincent O'Driscoll (☎20125) can also provide information. Ferries run by Capt. Kieran Molloy (☎28138) run from Schull (1hr., June-Sept. 1-3 per day, €11.50 return). The friendly family at **Windhoek Cottages and B&B ❷** have converted their old stone stables into self-catering cottages, all equipped with kitchen, bath, and heating—a steal for families or groups of four to five. They also rent warm B&B rooms that fit up to three. Follow signs straight on from the ferry dock toward Silver Strand beach. (☎20275 or 086 608 4428. Cottages €60 per night, €380 per wk. B&B €50 per room.) If you're traveling alone, a tranquil treat awaits at **Cuinne House ❷** (KWEENA), where each spacious, wood-paneled room is blessed with an ocean view. To reach the B&B, take the road behind the Jolly Roger pub. (☎20384. Evening meals €16. €24-26 per person.) Central **Abbey Store,** on the main road, visible from the pier hill, stocks the basics and houses a small **post office.** (☎20181. Open M-Sa 9am-6pm, Su noon-6pm; closes early on Su in winter.) The amiable **Jolly Roger ❸** (☎20379) has periodic trad sessions during the summer and serves dependable pub grub from noon to 7pm. Their heaping bowls of fresh-herbed **Sherkin mussels** (€6) are reason enough to visit the island. If you'd rather eat closer to the beach, grab a sandwich (€2-3) at **Cuisin Snack Bar ❶** (☎086 238 4228), on the road between Silver and Cow Strands.

MIZEN HEAD AND SHEEP'S HEAD

The serene southwestern tip of Ireland is comprised of two narrow peninsulas. Sheep's Head, to the north, extends out into the ocean like a skinny finger along Bantry Bay; just across Dunmanus Bay to the south, Mizen Head reaches as far to the southwest as the borders of Ireland allow. Both make for excellent day-long cycling trips, perhaps best for the cycling-fit, but the endless isolated coves and windswept beaches along the coast may entice more careful exploration.

SCHULL (AN SCOIL) ☎028

An ideal base for forays onto Mizen Head and ferry trips to nearby Cape Clear and the Sherkin Islands, the seaside town of Schull ("skull") is situated 4 mi. west of **Ballydehob,** on R592, off good ole N71. Schull provides the last stronghold of culture and commerce before sheep society begins to edge out human. With its first-rate hostel, surprisingly sophisticated eateries, and bike and boat rental options, it is the perfect spot for enjoying the rare Irish sunshine. Be warned that many other travelers are wise to Schull's charms; holiday cottages and B&Bs draw droves during the summer months, when the town's population explodes from 300 to 3000.

TRANSPORTATION AND PRACTICAL INFORMATION. **Buses** to Cork via Skibbereen (M-Sa 2-3 per day, Su 1-2 per day; €12.10) and Goleen (M-Sa 2 per day, Su 1-2 per day; €3.10) stop in front of the **AIB** on Main St. Check the schedule posted on the corner or call the Cork bus station (☎021 450 8188); Schull does not have a local **Bus Éireann** agent. **Ferries** connect Schull to Cape Clear and the Sherkin Islands (June 1 per day, July-Aug. 2-3 per day; €12 return; contact Capt. Molloy ☎28138 or inquire at the pier) and to Baltimore (June to mid-Sept. 3 per day; €8 return; contact Capt. O'Driscoll ☎39135). For lovely jaunts to Barley Cove Beach or along the Dunmanus road on the northern side of the peninsula, **rent bikes** at **Freewheelin',** located in Cotter's Yard Sweater Shop on Main St. (☎28889 or 28165. Open M-Sa 10am-11pm. Call ahead. €10 per day, €50 per wk. Pickup before 10:30am is preferable.) Pick up the detailed *Schull Guide*, which has good suggestions for walking and cycling in the area, in any store (€2), or peruse one of the hostel's copies. Make money appear out of thin air at the 24hr. **ATM** at **AIB** on Upper Main St. (☎28132. Open M-F 10am-12:30pm and 1:30-4pm.) There's a **pharmacy** on Main St. (28108. Open M-Sa 9:30am-1:15pm and 2:15-6pm.) Restaurants up and down Main St., such as Adele's Bakery (☎28459), have been known to offer travelers summer **work opportunities** waiting tables and in the kitchen. Pay is usually about €6 per hr., plus tips. The **post office** on Main St. doubles as a photography shop. (☎28110. Open M-F 9am-1pm and 2-5:30pm, Sa 9am-1pm.)

ACCOMMODATIONS, FOOD, AND PUBS. Schull's appeal to budget travelers can be traced to the **Schull Backpackers' Lodge (IHH) ❶** on Colla Rd. From the bus stop, walk up Main St. and bear left; walk down past the old church and take a right down the marked and very long driveway. The wooden lodge is clean and friendly, offering fine dorms with fluffy comforters and lots of information on local walks and rides. The in-house **English language school** keeps the hostel lively with long-term guests in summer, but beds are also booked by groups, so call ahead in July and August. The lodge also **rents bikes** (€11 per day), has **Internet access** (€1 per 15min.), and may offer short term **work opportunities** in the summer season. (☎28681; www.schullbackpackers.com. Laundry €4.50. Key deposit €2. June-Aug. dorms €11.50; singles €16; doubles €33, with bath €37. Low season a bit less.) **Adele's B&B ❸,** Main St., above the restaurant of the same name, has three small but cozy doubles with dark wooden floors. (☎28459. Tasty continental breakfast included. Shared bathroom. €25.50 per person.) Three miles toward Goleen, **Jenny's Farmhouse ❷** is a quiet place to stable for the night. (☎28205. Call for pickup from Schull. €14 per person, with breakfast €15.50-18.)

Those who are tiring of traditional Irish stew and fried chips will delight in the surprising variety of fine food available in Schull. For standard supplies, head to **Spar Market** (☎28236; open July-Sept. daily 7am-9pm, Oct.-June M-Sa 7am-8pm, Su 8am-8pm) or smaller **Hegarty's Centra** (☎28520; open daily 7am-10pm), just across from each other on Main Street. **The Courtyard ❷,** also on Main St., caters to those with more discerning taste buds; its delicious fruit scones with currants, raisins, and lemon zest (€0.55) make for a lovely breakfast, while sandwiches (€7-9.50) such as ciabatta with bacon, smoked cheese, and tomato relish (€9.50) are superb for lunch. (☎28390. Open M-Sa 9:30am-6pm.) Just up the street, **Adele's** ❷ also bakes up fresh breakfast treats and a variety of fancy pastries for tea time. (☎28459. Sandwiches €6-9. Open Easter-Nov. Tu-Sa 9:30am-6pm, Su 11am-6pm.) Several Schull pubs have thrown off the culinary yoke of standard fried Irish fare in favor of much more creative offerings. One such spot is **Hackett's Bar** ❶, on Main St., which has a great range of affordable options on its lunch menu, from a hummus and salad plate (€4.45) to mussels in white wine and cream (€4.45). This joint also features live rock bands on weekends throughout the year. (☎28625. Food served daily noon-3pm.) Another spot for relatively inexpensive fine food is the classy **Courtyard Pub & Restaurant** ❷, located behind its sister gourmet shop on Main St. The spicy salmon cakes with lemongrass and corriander dip (€12.50) are a favorite. The pub also features excellent live trad and folk several nights a week. (☎28390. Mains €9-12.50. Food served noon-9pm. See posters outside for music nights and hours.) The portions at **The Waterside Inn** ❷ are sure to satisfy, with classic Irish and seafood standards served in the pub; live music follows on most nights. A much more upscale menu (mains €18-25) is available at the adjacent **restaurant** ❺. (☎28203. Pub meals €8-12, served daily 12:30-9:30pm in the summer; winter weekends only.) Cozy **An Tigín** (☎28830), at the top of Main St., caters to local Gaelic football fans, hosts live music by the hearth most Fridays, and has a funny little beer garden out back.

SIGHTS AND ACTIVITIES. The **Schull Planetarium,** Colla Rd., offers extraterrestrial diversions for rainy days and occasional lecture series on such topics as "Creation." (☎28552. 45min. star shows usually at 4 or 8pm, but call ahead for schedule. €4.50.) Schull invites you to take a break from historical hype and explore the **walking** and **biking trails** snaking along the water and up into the hills. Inquire at the Backpacker's Lodge for maps and information. While Schull's many shipwrecks belie the calm harbor and beckon the curious diver, there is sadly no full service dive shop. However, the **Watersports Centre** on the pier rents wetsuits, scuba tanks, and fishing gear, and also offers **kayak and sailing courses.** (☎28554. Open Apr.-Oct. M-Sa 9:30am-6pm. Dinghies €40 per half-day. Motorboats €80 per day. Half-day kayak trip €45. 2½hr. sailing course €80.)

GOLEEN, CROOKHAVEN, AND MIZEN HEAD ☎028

The Mizen becomes more scenic and less populated west of Schull. The peninsula's native population thins out, but European house-buyers have answered the call for reinforcements. As such, the Mizen is mobbed during peak-season weekends, when sun-loving vacationers pack sandy beaches. The most reliable transit is **Betty Johnson's Bus Hire,** which will take you on a tour of the Mizen via the scenic northern coast road. The tour includes bits of local history and runs to the Mizen Vision (see below). Call Betty for her schedule; she will make a run any day when there are at least six people interested (☎28410; about 3hr.; €12). **Bus Éireann** only goes as far as **Goleen** (2 per day on the Cork-West Cork line; inquire in Schull or Ballydehob for a detailed schedule). **Hitching,** while always risky, is possible in the peak-season, with hitchers often perching at the crossroads on the Goleen Rd. just outside of town. Confident **cyclists** can make a daytrip to Mizen Head (36 mi. return from Schull); less confident cyclists can tackle less taxing jaunts—the Backpackers' Lodge includes a good **bike map** with rental.

The block-long town of **Goleen** *(Goilin)* is a nice spot for ice cream on the way to more southwesterly points. **The Green Kettle** specializes in antiques and homemade scones served in its rear garden. (☎35033. Open June-Aug. daily 10am-6pm,

Sept.-May Sa-Su 10am-5pm.) About a mile up the hill just outside of town is **The Ewe,** a strange little "art retreat" that offers pottery classes and zany art gifts from its gallery/shop. For €2.50, visitors can stroll the low-growing sculpture garden, a short person's paradise. (☎35492. Open daily 10am-6pm. Half-day pottery courses €32, children €20; "paint-a-bowl" €12.) Those seeking a quiet place for rest and relaxation can head to **Heron's Cove B&B ❸,** down the hill from Goleen on the water. (☎35225. All rooms with bath and TV. €35 per person.) The **restaurant ❹** downstairs serves a delicious pan-fried lemon sole (€19.50), as well as other excellent seafood. (☎35225. Open June-Aug. daily 5:30-9:30pm. Booking required Sept.-May.) For maps, postcards, currency exchange, accommodations listings, and cheap **Internet access** (€1.50 per 10min.), head to the **Mizen Tourism Cooperative Society** sub-office, back on Goleen's main street. (☎35255. Open M-F 10am-6pm.)

Slightly longer than the main road, and tremendously worthwhile, is the coast road, which winds past **Barley Cove Beach** and continues on to Mizen Head. Tiny **Crookhaven** (*An Cruachan;* pop. 37), a 1 mi. detour off this road, is perched at the end of its own peninsula. Meet half of the population at **O'Sullivan's ❷,** which serves sandwiches, soups, and cold pints on the water's edge. (☎35319. Food served daily noon-8pm.) The other half will be at the **Crookhaven Inn ❷,** which provides similar fare in a lovely outdoor cafe overlooking the bay. (☎35309. Sandwiches €3, meals €7-10. Food served daily noon-8pm.) **Barley Cove Caravan Park ❶,** 1½ mi. from Crookhaven, offers **camping** adjacent to Mizen's most celebrated strand, and includes **tennis** and **pitch-and-putt** facilities. (☎35302. Open Easter-Sept. Mini-market and takeaway. **Bike rental** €15 per day; deposit €50. €14 per 2-person tent. Laundry €10.) Campers have a short walk to the warm, shallow waters of Barley Cove Beach, a sandy retreat for those not ready to brave the frigid sea.

Three miles past Barley Cove, Ireland comes to an abrupt end at spectacular **Mizen Head,** whose cliffs rise 700 ft. above the waves. **Mizen Head Lighthouse,** built in 1909, was recently automated and electrified, and the nearby buildings were turned into a small museum, the **Mizen Vision.** To get to the museum, you'll have to cross a suspension bridge only slightly less harrowing than the virtual shipwreck that waits inside. The museum illuminates the solitary lives of lighthouse keepers and the lighthouses they keep. Its small, windy viewing platform is the most southwesterly point in Ireland. Return via the 99 steps (or take the ramp) to the newly opened **Visitor Centre,** to peruse more exhibits or indulge in pricey items from the **cafe.** (☎35115. Open June-Sept. daily 10am-6pm; mid-Mar. to May and Oct. 10:30am-5pm; Nov. to mid-Mar. Sa-Su 11am-4pm. €4.50, students €3.50, under 12 €2.50, under 5 free.) Those on wheels can return to Schull via Dunmanus along the locally renowned coastal road, which runs the northern coast of the peninsula.

BANTRY (BEANNTRAI) ☎027

According to the big *Book of Invasions*, Ireland's first human inhabitants landed just 1 mi. from Bantry (see **Legends and Folktales,** p. 71). In the grand tradition of British invasion, 17th-century English settlers arrived in the bay and drove the Irish out. In 1796, Wolfe Tone and a band of Irish patriots made an ill-fated attempt to return the favor with the help of the French Armada. These days, the invasion racket has died down considerably, but Bantry still has plenty to plunder for the eager explorer. Amidst the distinctly untouristy and unfrilly feeling of a working town, Bantry's pubs and live music provide authentic *craic* every night. The town's main attraction is the incredibly elegant Bantry House and gardens, which should not be missed. For daytrips out onto the Sheep's Head peninsula or to Whiddy Island, this is the best place to anchor for the night.

TRANSPORTATION. Buses stop outside Julie's Takeaway in Wolfe Tone Sq. **Bus Éireann** heads to Cork via Bandon and Bantry (M-Sa 8 per day, Su 4 per day; €10) and to Glengarriff (M-Sa 3 per day, Su 2 per day; €3.25). From June to September, buses go to Killarney via Kenmare (2 per day) and Tralee (2 per day), and to Skibbereen (2 per day). **Berehaven Bus Service** (☎70007) also stops here on its way to and from Cork. **Bike rental** is available from **The Bicycle Shop,** formerly Kramer's, on Glengarriff Rd., Newtown, near the Independent Hostel. (☎52657. €12.15 per day, €50 per wk.; helmet included. ID or credit card deposit. Open June-Aug. M-Sa 9:30am-6pm; Sept.-May M-Tu and Th-Sa 10am-5pm.)

ORIENTATION AND PRACTICAL INFORMATION. Bantry lies at the eastern end of **Bantry Bay.** With your back to the water, **New St.** leads straight into town, out of **Wolfe Tone Sq.,** while **William St.** branches off to the right. From the left corner of the Square, **Marino St.** splits into **Old Barrack Rd.** and **Glengarriff Rd. Main St.** runs perpendicular to the Square, intersecting New St., which turns into **Bridge St.** Sheep's Head stretches due west; the Beara Peninsula is northwest. Cars, cyclists, and hitchers stay on N71 to get in or out of town. The **tourist office,** Wolfe Tone Sq., has a **bureau de change,** maps of Bantry and Sheep's Head, and an uncommonly stern staff. (☎50229. Open July-Aug. daily 9am-6pm; Apr.-June and Sept.-Nov. M-Sa 9:30am-5:30pm.) **AIB,** Wolfe Tone Sq. has an **ATM,** as does the neighboring **Bank of Ireland.** (☎50008 and 51377. Both open M 10am-5pm, Tu-F 10am-4pm.) Travelers looking for short-term **work opportunities** in Bantry might find odd-jobs at **The West Cork Chamber Music Festival,** the last week of June and the first week of July. Inquire at Bantry House (☎50047) or at the festival box office (☎52788). **Coen's Pharmacy** peddles potions in the Square. (☎50531. Open M-Sa 9:30am-1pm and 2-6pm.) The **police** *(Garda)* can be found in the Square (☎50045). **St. Joseph's Bantry Hospital,** Dromleigh Rd. (☎50133), is ¼ mi. past the library. The **library,** at the top of Bridge St., provides **Internet access** to Co. Cork library cardholders; purchase a card for €2.50 at any participating branch. (☎50460. Open Tu-W and F-Sa 10am-1pm and 2:30-6pm, Th 10am-6pm.) **fast.net business solutions** on Main St. also has web access. (☎51624. €1 per 10min. Open M-F 9am-6pm, Sa 10am-5pm.) The **post office** is at 2 William St. (☎50050. Open M-Sa 9am-5:30pm, Tu open 9:30am.)

ACCOMMODATIONS AND CAMPING. Bantry Independent Hostel (IHH) ❶, on the former Bishop Lucey Pl. in Newtown, is the more comfortable and relaxed of Bantry's two hostels. To get there from the Square, head away from town on Glengarriff Rd.; take the left fork, walk up the slight hill, down the street, and around the far bend (about 8min.). If you're coming in by bus on Glengarriff Rd., save yourself the walk and ask the driver to let you off at O'Mahoney's Quickpick Food Store. From there, walk up the hill across the road and take a right around the bend. The hostel has decent bunks, formidable security, and a secluded setting. (☎51050. Laundry €5. Open mid-Mar. to Oct. 6-bed dorms €10; doubles €24.) The **Harbour View Hostel ❶,** on Harbour View, to the left of the fire station along the water, is signposted from the Square as a "small independent hostel." These are drearily basic, cramped accommodations. (☎51140. Dorms €10; singles €12; private rooms €10 per person.) For more upscale rooms right on the Square, check out the **Bantry Bay Hotel ❹.** (☎50062. Singles €50-60; doubles with breakfast, TV, and bath €90-100. Live music nightly July-Aug.) Four miles from town, on Glengarriff Rd. in Ballylickey, the **Eagle Point Camping and Caravan Park ❶** has a private beach, tennis courts, TV room, and free showers. (☎50630. Open May-Sept. €6.50 per person. Laundry €5.)

FOOD AND PUBS. SuperValu, New St., stocks an exhilarating variety of foodstuffs. (☎50001. Open M-Th 8:30am-7pm, F 8:30am-9pm, Sa 8:30am-6:30pm.) **Organico,** on the Glengarriff Rd., has a surprising variety of health and whole foods, including freshly baked organic bread. (☎51391. Open M-Sa 10am-6pm.) The Square is lined with tourist-drawing, pricey restaurants, but those off the Square, as well as most of the pubs, offer cheaper options. For delicious toasted sandwiches (€3-4) and a great choice of sweet treats, turn off New St. onto Main St. and follow your nose to **Floury Hands Cafe and Bakery ❶.** (☎52590. Open M-Sa 8am-5:30pm.) Family-owned and operated **O'Siochain ❶,** Bridge St., offers tasty homemade Irish standards in a comfy, kitschy coffeehouse. (☎51339. Sandwiches €3.50, mains from €9. Open June-Aug. daily 9am-10pm, Sept.-May 9am-6pm.) Vegetarians need not apply at **Peter's Steak House ❷,** a no frills diner-style joint on New St. (☎50025. Most mains €11-12, sirloin steak €16.50, omelettes €7. Open July-Aug. daily 10am-11pm; Sept.-May 10am-10pm.) **Chin Fong Chinese Restaurant & Takeaway ❶** fries up food late into the night on Main St. (☎52811. Mains €6.50-9, veggie dishes €5.50. Open Su-Th 5:30pm-1am, F-Sa 5:30pm-2am.)

Bantry's pubs have real homegrown spirit and character; the locals work hard during the week and drink hard on weekends. **Anchor Bar,** New St. (☎50012), is usually the liveliest, luring the locals with a pub disco atmosphere on weekends and live music during the summer (Th). **The Schooner,** Barrack St. (☎52115), has a cargo of mixed music on weekends. Ballad-lovers get their fill from frequent sessions at **J.J. Crowley's** (☎50027) in the Square. After the pubs shut, the young'uns head to the **disco** in the Bantry Bay Hotel (see **Accommodations,** above). (Cover €7. Open June-Aug. F-Sa until 2am.) Lonely Yanks used to find solace at the **Kilgoban** (☎50649) on Marino St., which was won by an American couple in the Guinness "Win your own pub in Ireland" contest. The outsiders recently sold the place; visitors now arrive to find company you'd more expect at any native pub.

SIGHTS AND ENTERTAINMENT. Bantry's main tourist attractions lie a 10min. walk from town up a long and shady driveway off the Cork road. **Bantry House and Gardens,** a Georgian manor with magnificently restored grounds dramatically overlooking the Bay, is a lovely sight not to be missed. Full admission allows visitors to wander freely around the manicured gardens and gain access to the house, with an ornate interior decorated to match its elaborate grounds. The former seat of the Earls of Bantry, the house was used as a hospital during Ireland's Civil War and again during "the Emergency" (neutral Éire's term for WWII. The current residents are the somewhat-less-wealthy descendants of the Earls, who, over the last twenty years, received enough grants and donations to restore the property to its current elegant condition.

The Earls had a bit of scrambling to do when Irish rebel **Theobald Wolfe Tone** harnessed a bit of France's anti-English sentiment for his own nationalist insurrection (see **Rebellion,** p. 59). Wolfe Tone's campaign, as well as the 1980s discovery of an Armada ship that had been scuttled in the harbor, is thoroughly documented in the **1796 Bantry French Armada Exhibition Centre.** Enjoy the irony of its location next to Bantry House, former residence of Richard White, the man who mobilized British resistance to Wolfe Tone's invasion. **Refreshments** (coffee and cakes €2-3) are available in the Armada center. (☎50047. House open mid-Mar. to Oct. daily 9am-6pm; exhibition 9am-5pm. Garden and exhibition €4. House, exhibition, and gardens €9.50, students and seniors €8. Accompanied children free.)

If doomed missions and grandiose nobles don't pique your interest, you might take a cruise on one of the **sea trips** that circumnavigate the harbor and drop you at **Whiddy Island,** where quiet beaches attract birds and their watchers. (☎51739. Trips depart July-Sept. daily at 2:30, 4, and 6pm, as well as M, W, F at 9:30 and 11am. €7 return.) Bantry hosts the **West Cork Chamber Music Festival** during the last week of June and early July. The **RTE Vanburgh String Quartet** is joined by scores of other international performers. Performances take place in the elegant rooms of Bantry House. (☎52788. 1-show tickets from €12; full-wk. tickets €160-345; workshops free.) The Chamber Music Festival includes the spin-off **Literary Fringe,** which offers readings and workshops held at the Bantry Library and Bantry House, and awards the prestigious Fish Short Story Prize. (Workshops €25-160, readings and discussions free.) Flex your fervor for seafood during the annual **Bantry Mussel Fair,** held the second weekend in May.

NEAR BANTRY: SHEEP'S HEAD (MUINTIR BHAIRE)

Although largely ignored by tourists passing through Skibbereen and Bantry en route to more publicized peninsulas, Sheep's Head is a pleasant alternative for those eager to evade the company of camera-toters and the exhaust of tour buses (which aren't allowed here). Visitors already impressed by the gentle southern coves and craggy northern cliffs may also marvel at the prevalence of bovine beasts over the peninsula's woolly "namesake." (English-speaking cartographers flagrantly misinterpreted the Irish name for the peninsula, which actually meant "the people of Baire.") Hitchers may find it difficult to catch rides to or from this least populated part of West Cork. Many **walkers** and **cyclists** take advantage of the peaceful roads and the well-plotted **Sheep's Head Way.** Maps and guides of the Way are available in the Bantry tourist office (see **Bantry,** above). Criss-crossing paths provide endless options for those on foot. The road circling Sheep's Head sticks to the coast, making for easy cycling with constant vistas. Aside from the climb connecting the village of **Kilcrohane** to the northern road, which rewards with stunning views from **Finn MacCool's Seat,** the counterclockwise route feels downhill most of the way.

Sheep's Head is a manageable cycling daytrip from Bantry for the extremely fit (40 mi. return), but those who prefer a more leisurely pace will find peaceful lodging at any of the B&Bs speckling the peninsula or at the tiny **Carbery's View Hostel ❶** in Kilcrohane. The hostel is conveniently signposted from the western end of town and is perfectly situated over the bay. (☎67035. €10 per person.) If you decide to stay in Kilcrohane, pick up limited supplies at **O'Mahoney's Shop** on the main road (☎67001; open M-Sa 9am-9pm, Su 10:30am-1pm and 7-9pm), which also houses the **post office.** Head to **Fitzpatrick's ❶** (☎67057) for a pint, then wash it down with a sandwich or two (€2). In Ahakista, 5 mi. to the east, **The Tin Pub** rattles with *craic* and redefines "beer garden," with its splendid view of the bay, shaded paths to the sea, public barbeque, and Sunday trad. Check postings in the window for **free guided walks** of the area. (☎67337. Open at noon. **Internet access** €1 per 10 min.)

BEARA PENINSULA

Beara Peninsula's rugged and desolate landscape offers a haunting canvas for the lonely explorer. Fortunately, the tourist mobs circling the nearby Ring of Kerry usually skip the Beara altogether, but in doing so they ironically miss out on some of the best views of the Iveragh from across the bay. Thus, this is the place for unspoiled scenery and solitude; if you're looking for pubs, people, and other signs of civilization, you might be happier on the Iveragh or Dingle Peninsulas. The spec-

FROM THE ROAD

B&B BRAWLERS

During my travels for *Let's Go*, I happened upon two B&Bs in Ireland pitted against each other in an actual B&B War. The two establishments involved in said war operated their B&Bs directly across the street from one another; both were listed in our guidebook. Having enjoyed the town and the research thus far, I stopped in at the first B&B and met *Mary* (name changed). Mary politely offered me coffee and biscuits, which I gratefully accepted. Her rowdy kids pounced all over me as she paid no mind, and between sorting out payments with guests, fixing her computer with a neighborly old man, and telling me that her mother's B&B had been in Irish guide books since 1979, she also managed to craftily bad-mouth the B&B across the way. "The woman over there has had a mental breakdown. She says the most inappropriate things to her guests," she carefully explained. The example offered up for confirmation of this was that the woman had reportedly said to a guest "You look really sexy in those pajamas." After an hour of similar stories, I was thoroughly convinced that I was going to soon be meeting a lunatic, so I decided to do pub research before going back to the second B&B.

When I finally made my way there, I was greeted by *Sally* (name changed) who also offered me coffee and raisin bread. Like Mary, Sally went to great lengths to assure me that business was "fantastic" and repeated comments from her own guests. Sprinkled in every sentence,

tacular **Caha** and **Slieve Miskish Mountains** march down the center of the peninsula, separating the Beara's rocky south from its lush northern shore. West Beara remains remote—travelers wander treacherous single-track roads along the stark Atlantic coastline, picking their way though mountains, rocky outcrops, and the occasional herd of sheep. The dearth of cars west of Glengarriff makes **cycling** the 125 mi. of **The Beara Way** a joy, but for hitchhikers, the town marks the point west of which they'll find themselves admiring the views for longer than sanity can bear. *Let's Go*, in favor of sanity, does not recommend hitchhiking.

GLENGARRIFF (AN GLEANN GARBH) ☎027

A midday stroll through Glengarriff may leave you wondering if anyone actually lives there full-time; the town's position as gateway to the Beara Peninsula and its prominence in the wool industry draw hordes of tourists in the summer months. But that shouldn't stop you from enjoying the lovely walks in the nearby nature reserve or the unusual gardens on Garinish Island.

TRANSPORTATION. Bus Éireann stops in front of Casey's Hotel on Main St. Buses run to Glengarriff from Bantry (25min.; M-Sa 3-5 per day, Su 2-3 per day; €3.45), Castletownbere via Adrigole (45min., 2-3 per day, €3.10), and Cork (2hr., 3 per day). From June to mid-September, a route runs twice a day to: Kenmare (45min.), Killarney (1¾hr.), and Tralee (3hr.). **Berehaven Bus Service** (☎70007) also serves Bantry (M 2 per day, Tu and Th-Sa 1 per day; €3.80), Castletownbere (M-Tu and Th-Sa 2 per day, €5.10), and Cork (2hr., M-Tu and Th-Sa 3 per day, €10.40). **Rent bikes** from **Jem Creations,** an art gallery just down from the main intersection on Main St. (☎63113. Open daily 9:30am-7pm. €10 per day, €50 per wk.)

PRACTICAL INFORMATION. Glengarriff is graced with two friendly, map-dispensing **tourist offices.** The **Bord Fáilte** office is on the Bantry road on the edge of town. (☎63084. Open May-Oct. M-Tu and Th-Sa 9:30am-1pm and 2-5:30pm.) The other, privately-run office is next to the public bathrooms on the main road, just down from the bus stop. (☎63201. Open July-Aug. daily 9am-9pm; Sept.-June 9am-6pm.) There are several **bureaux de change** (in tourist offices and B&Bs) but **no bank** or **ATM** in Glengarriff, so stock up on cash before you arrive. The **Eccles Hotel** may offer travelers summer **work opportunities.** The **post office** is inside O'Shea's Market on Main St. (☎63001. Open M-F 9am-1pm and 2-5:30pm, Sa 9am-1pm.)

ACCOMMODATIONS, FOOD, AND PUBS. There's little need to stop by either tourist office if you stay at **Murphy's Village Hostel ❶**, in the middle of town on Main St. Peruse readily available maps and discuss your plans for Beara adventure with Mr. Murphy while munching one of Mrs. Murphy's banana chocolate-chip muffins. (☎63555. **Internet access** €6.50 per hr. Laundry €6.50. Dorms €11; doubles €29.) Just up Main St. and marked by a mermaid, **Wanda's Hostel ❶** provides a laid-back atmosphere and soft beds. (☎63595. Laundry €3.50. 24hr. reception. Dorms €12.50; doubles €25.) The **Hummingbird Rest ❶** (☎63195), a 10min. walk from town along the Kenmare road and right near the entrance to the nature reserve, offers little singles and doubles (€12 per person), free laundry, and excellent **camping** (€5 per person). Back in the center of town, **Maureen's B&B ❷**, on Main St. behind a craft and sweater shop, offers comfortable rooms for a good value but is slated to undergo massive renovations, reopening anew by Easter 2003. Maureen has claimed she'll keep her same great prices post-renovation; time will tell. (☎63201. €25.50 per person; without breakfast €20.) Two **campsites** are neighbors on the Castletownbere road 1½ mi. from town: **Dowling's** (☎63154; open Apr.-Oct.; €5 per person) and **O'Shea's** (☎63140; open mid-Mar. to Oct.; €6 per person with or without car).

Groceries can be had in town from **O'Shea's Market** on Main St. (☎63346. Open M-Sa 8am-9pm, Su 9am-7pm.) Restaurants in Glengarriff are touristy but decent. Abundant and affordable options await at **The Village Kitchen ❷**, attached to the Murphys' hostel, which serves a breakfast menu all day, including vegetarian sausage and pancakes with maple syrup (€7.60), and also has **Internet access** for €6.50 per hr. (☎63555. Vegetarian tortilla with semi-unappealing refried beans €7.25. Omelettes from €3.25. Open Mar.-Oct. 8am-6pm.) **Johnny Barry's** (☎63315) and **The Maple Leaf** (☎63021), both on Main St., serve standard pub fare at standard prices until around 8:30pm daily. Both host live music on weekends through the year: everything from disco to country at Johnny Barry's; trad at the Maple Leaf.

SIGHTS AND ACTIVITIES. Hike through giant rhododendrons and moss-encrusted evergreens at the lush **Glengarriff National Nature Reserve and Ancient Oak Forest.** Trails range from pebbled paths for curious, scone-snarfing pedestrians to rugged climbs for serious, granola-munching hikers. *Walking Around Glengarriff* (€0.10), available at hos-

however, were insults about Mary and her business. "She over-charges people," and "the Americans who stayed there last week were so disgusted that they demanded their money back and were telling everyone in town about their horrible stay. She's even being reported to the tourist board."

Though neither Mary nor Sally had known I worked for a travel guide company (anonymity is a virtue in this game), both women had leapt at the chance to plug their own establishment while pulling the rug out from the others'. I thought it quite sad when I left Sally's, realizing that in an effort to undercut each other, they had actually undercut themselves. When I returned later that day for some more practical information, and revealed to Sally that I worked for *Let's Go,* she hurried to remind me how long she had been in the book, and how surprised she was that our book would lower ourselves so much by including an establishment like Mary's. I'd like to believe that she found me such a powerful figure in the travel guide industry that she thought I was worth all this effort, but I have the funny feeling that I was just another listener/potential sympathizer for each of the two sides of this ongoing B&B war.

—Kira Whelan

tels in town and at the tourist office, outlines several walks in the park; for those with a good pair of boots and a yearning for hilly thrills, there are more detailed maps available. A popular walk with a panoramic view of water, mountain, and forest is the path leading to **Lady Bantry's Lookout** (45min. return). Glengarriff is also a good starting point for the Beara Way.

Bountiful lakes, rivers, and inlets around Glengarriff are perfect territory for the hook-weilding fisherman. Try to wrap your tongue around the name of **Lake Eekenohoolikeaghaun** (ISH-na-hoo-lick-a-gone) as you wait for a tug on your line. Upper and Lower Lough Avaul are well-stocked with trout, but you'll need a permit (available at the Maple Leaf Pub, €7.50 per day) to hunt them. **Fishing** in Barley Lake, nearby rivers, and the ocean is permissible for the permitless. Fish fanatics can pick up *Fishing in Glengarriff* (€0.10) at the tourist office. (For more info, ask at the piers or call the regional Fisheries Board ☎026 41222.)

Gardening connoisseurs and picnic fans will delight in **Garinish Island,** an islet in Glengarriff Harbour. Garinish was a rocky outcrop inhabited by a thriving society of gorse bushes until 1900, when English financier Annan Bryce acquired the island from the War Office and dreamed up a fairyland for his family. A million hours of labor and countless boatloads of topsoil later, he had his elaborately designed exotic garden; plans for a mansion were completed but never put into action. Bryce's diplomat son bequeathed their blooming island to the Irish people in 1953, and it has been considered a national treasure ever since. (☎63040. Open July-Aug. M-Sa 9:30am-6:30pm, Su 11am-6:30pm; June M-Sa 10am-6:30pm, Su 11am-6:30pm; May and Sept. M-Sa 10am-6:30pm, Su noon-6:30pm; Apr. M-Sa 10am-6:30pm, Su 1-4:30pm; Mar. and Oct. M-Sa 10am-4:30pm, Su 1-5pm. Last landing 1hr. before closing. Guidebook €2. €3.10 adults, children and students with ID €1.20, seniors and groups €2.20, families €7.60.) Three boats run trips to the island. **Blue Pool Ferry** leaves from the pier in town, next to the public bathrooms; the other boats depart from the Eccles Hotel. (8min., about every 20min. €7 return with same boat. Blue Pool offers €1 discounts for Murphy's hostelers.) You're likely to catch a glimpse of seals lounging on the seaweedy rocks along the way.

THE HEALY PASS

According to the proprietor of a Bantry pub, a patron once remarked in passing "that something ought to be done about the path from Adrigole to Lauragh." Tim Healy, the listener, must have remembered those words when he became Lord Governor of Ireland, and anyone who travels across the pass that bears his name will be grateful he did. R574 winds up between some of the highest peaks in the **Caha Mountains,** connecting the two tiny towns of Adrigole and Lauragh over the border between counties Cork and Kerry. The curvaceous pass is best explored by car, and to enjoy the full effect of the breathtaking views you'll want to travel from south to north. Begin in Adrigole near the Hungry Hill Hostel (see **Adrigole,** below), and thread your way through rocky terrain and particularly plump sheep to reach **Don's Mountain Cabin** and its excellent selection of local-interest books. The choice of frozen treats from Don's gas-powered fridge is less extensive, but still hits the spot. (☎027 60033. Open daily 10am-6pm.) Fifty yards beyond, the verdant sweep of Co. Kerry opens like a dream. The ride down may be slightly harrowing, but after the views of Glanmore Lake, Kenmare Bay, and the distant mountains of the Iveragh Peninsula, you'll be stunned into silence. Hit the pub in Lauragh for a few pints to quiet the mind. The challenge of **biking** the pass intimidates all except the most robust cyclists, but hitchers judge the panoramic payoff to be worth the wait for a lift, despite the risks involved.

ADRIGOLE (EADARGOIL) ☎027

Before taking the pass north to Lauragh, spend a night or three in Adrigole. The spacious dorms and extensive facilities at the **Hungry Hill Hostel ❶,** along the Castletownbere road, make it an ideal base for outdoor expeditions. The hostel will outfit you with whatever you need for land or sea, and after a day of hiking or boating you can relax in the attached **restaurant.** (☎60228. **Bike rental** €8 per day. **Boat rental** €80 per day. Diving compressor available. **Internet access** €0.65 per 6min. **Laundry** €2.50. Dorms €11; doubles €28-35; family rooms €45. **Camping** from €6.) Roughnecks can attempt to tackle the 2245 ft. **Hungry Hill,** where a mountaintop lake overflows on rainy days to create Ireland's tallest (temporary) **waterfall.** (For the permanent record, see p. 134.) Also nearby, the **West Cork Sailing Centre** offers courses ranging from a 3hr. half-day lesson to a week-long course. (☎60132; www.westcorksailing.com. Half-day lesson July-Aug. €55 per person for group of 2, off-season €45. Week course July-Aug. €304 per person, off-season €236. **Kayak rental** July-Aug. €10 per hr., off-season €6. Open St. Paddy's Day through Oct.)

LAURAGH (AN LAITHREACH) AND GLANMORE LAKE ☎064

The R574 rejoins the Ring of Beara road at **Lauragh,** where awestruck travelers wishing to rest their awestruck heads can find peaceful accommodation and a hearty meal. Lauragh itself consists of little more than **post office,** pub, and tiny **shop** (open 10am-9pm in summer and afternoons the rest of the year), but nearby Glanmore Lake is an idyllic spot. Three miles from the main road and well-marked by signs, the **Glanmore Lake Youth Hostel (An Óige/HI) ❶** feels more like an Alpine retreat than an Irish hostel. Housed in a stately former schoolhouse, it's perfect for fishing, hiking, and swimming. (☎83181. Continental breakfast €5; Irish breakfast €6.50; soup and sandwiches €6. Towels €1. Open Easter-Sept. Dorms €12.)

The only full meals served in these parts are at **Josie's Lakeview Restaurant and B&B ❷,** 1 mi. from the hostel and signposted from every direction. The huge portions of home-cooked food won't disappoint, and the view from the glassed-in dining room must be seen to be believed. (☎83155. Lunch €6-8, dinner from €9. Food served noon-8pm.) Trad usually spills out of **An Síbin** on Friday nights. Take in the local *craic* and pay no mind to the booted leg dangling in the fireplace. (☎83106. Near the junction of the Healy Pass road and R571. Soup and sandwiches €2-3.) If the natural landscape hasn't stated your scenic appetite, wander through the evergreens, treeferns, and massive rhododendrons at **Derreen Gardens,** a ½ mi. north of Lauragh on the coastal road to Kenmare. (☎83588. Open Apr.-Sept. daily 10am-6pm. €4, children and students €2.)

CASTLETOWNBERE (BAILE CHAISLEAIN BHEARRA) ☎027

Castletownbere sits on the southern edge of the peninsula west of Adrigole. One of Ireland's largest fishing ports, this commercial hub attracts rigs from as far away as Spain. Cyclists often speed through en route to villages farther west and north, and the town occasionally fills with nirvana-seekers heading to the nearby Buddhist center. The town's energetic pubs and can't-get-fresher-than-this fish restaurants revitalize weary trekkers on their way around the rest of the peninsula.

TRANSPORTATION. Bus Éireann offers a year-round service to Cork via Glengarriff (3hr., 1-2 per day, €17.80) and a summer route between Castletownbere and Killarney via Allihies, Ardgroom, and Kenmare (M-Sa 2 per day, €11.20 to Killarney). Two **minibuses** operate between Cork and Castletownbere via Bantry and Glengarriff; they will take interested groups on tours of the Beara. Phone **Har-**

rington's (☎74003) or **O'Donoghue's Berehaven** (☎70007) for reservations. (Leaves Cork M-Tu and Th-Sa 6pm; Castletownbere M-Tu and F-Sa 8am, Th 7:30am. To Cork €11.50, Glengarriff €5.30, Bantry €6.50. Tours €25-30.) You can **hire bikes** at **SuperValu** (☎70020; €10 per day; open M-Sa 8am-9pm, Su 9am-9pm) or at **Beara Cycles,** Main St., just up from the Square. (☎086 101 2026. Rental includes helmet, map, and lock. €9.50 per day, €55 per wk. Open M-F 9am-6pm, Su 10am-6pm.)

ORIENTATION AND PRACTICAL INFORMATION. The Castletownbere action all happens on one main street—**Main St.** The molehill-sized **tourist office** shares a frazzled office with **Beara Action** (see below) in the main square. (☎70054. Open June-Sept. M-F 10am-5pm.) The **AIB** across the Square has the **only ATM** on the peninsula. (☎70015. Open M 10am-5pm, Tu-F 10am-4pm.) For **laundry,** head to **O'Shea's Laundrette** on Main St. near the SuperValu. (☎70966. €9 per load. Open M-Sa 9am-6pm.) The *Garda* toward the end of Main St. can be reached at ☎70002 or 50045. Free emergency numbers are ☎999 or 112. **Beara Action,** under the same roof as the tourist office, provides **Internet access.** (☎70880. €1 per 15min., €5.50 per hr. Open M-F 9:30am-5:30pm, July-Aug. Sa 10am-6pm, Su noon-6pm.)

ACCOMMODATIONS, FOOD, AND PUBS. Six miles west of town, on the Allihies road, is **Garranes Farmhouse Hostel (IHH) ❶.** The sea views from this intimate cottage are worth the trek, or the €9 cab, from Castletownbere. Sometimes the attached Buddhist center (see below) occupies all the rooms, so phone ahead. (☎73147. Laundry €10. Dorms €10; singles €20; doubles €25-28.) **Castletown House ❷,** on Main St. above the Old Bank Seafood Restaurant, offers fine rooms, all with bath and TV, and lots of advice. Be sure to show the friendly owner your *Let's Go* guide. (☎70252. **Internet** €2.50 per hr. for guests. €22.50-25.75 per person.) The **Harbour Lodge Hostel ❶,** located behind the church in a former convent (head up the church steps and around to the right), provides decent rooms and unconventional gym facilities for those dying to work out. (☎71043. Wheelchair-accessible. Gym €6.75. Sauna €4. Use of kitchen €3. **Laundry** €6.35. Dorms €13; doubles with bath €40; family rooms €60. **Camping** €8 per 2-person tent.)

Spar, the Square, supplies cheap, snacky options. (☎70057. Open all year M-Sa 8am-10pm, Su 9am-10pm.) Seafood lovers should head to **The Lobster Bar ❸,** the Square, for its homemade bread, potato salad, and seafood platters (€10-12) practically large enough for two. Maria's secret-recipe banoffee pie is sensational. (☎70031. Main menu served June-Aug. only noon-9pm.) **Jack Patrick's ❷** and his patrons in-the-know get meat fresh from the butcher of the same name next door. (☎70319. Lunches €7. Dinner mains €7-10. Open M-Sa 11am-9pm, July-Aug. Su 1-9pm.) The less-epicurean **Cronin's Hideaway ❷** serves cheap food, fast and fresh. (☎70386. Mains €4.50-10. Open M-Sa 5-10pm, Su 12:30-10pm; takeaway open daily 5:30pm-midnight.) When the fishing boats are in, most of the pros spend their land time touring from pub to pub; if you're lucky, you might hear a tall tale from the sea. For a pint, repast, or provisions, join the locals at **MacCarthy's.** (☎70014. Sandwiches under €3. Food served 10:30am-7pm. Trad and ballads Tu and weekends.) **O'Donoghue's** (☎70007), the Square, lures a sporty crowd with its big-screen TV, sunny (or starry) tables outside, and live bands most Saturdays. Trad on summer Fridays keeps the feet tapping at **Twomey's Ivy Bar** (☎70114).

SIGHTS AND ACTIVITIES. A 5min. walk up North Rd. from the church, a brand new museum offers visitors a break from outdoor adventures, overgrown ruins, and the ubiquitous smell of fish. With interactive exhibits on two floors, **Call of the Sea: The Beara Experience** covers the main topics of the peninsula's history and illuminates the lesser-known exploits of smugglers and slavers. (☎70835. €4, students and seniors €3, family €9. Open May to mid-Sept. M-Sa 10am-5pm, Su 1-

5pm; last admission 4:15pm. Call ahead in low season.) Six miles west of town, the **Dzogchen Buddhist Centre** (☎73032; phones answered Tu-Th 2:30-5:30pm, otherwise leave a message) is in the same cliff-perched compound as the Garranes Farmhouse Hostel (see **Accommodations,** above). The view from the meditation room is inspiration itself. A very respected Tibetan Buddhist teaching site, the center offers a daily program with meditation and compassion exercises.

Two miles southwest of Castletownbere on the Allihies road, a donation of your choice buys admission to the two-piece ruins of **Dunboy Castle.** Cows graze the grounds of the enormous, crumbling, Gothic-style halls of the **19th-century mansion.** A quarter-mile past the mansion, the 14th-century fortress **O'Sullivan Bere** is in far worse shape. The original owner accidentally blew up the fort in 1594 (oops!), and English armies finished the job eight years later. The road that runs by the castle becomes a shady trail and passes a number of sheltered coves. A small detour off the Allihies Road (bear right at the fork on the way out of town) leads you to conveniently proximate examples of three archeological spectacles characteristic of West Cork and Kerry. The first is a **stone circle,** at Derrintaggart West, with a dozen of the original 15 stones still standing. (Think Stonehenge. Now think less impressive.) At Teernahillane, about 1 mi. farther along, you'll find a raised **ring fort** 30 yd. in diameter and 2 yd. high. Just beyond that is a small **wedge grave.**

Castletownbere's seat at the foot of hefty **Hungry Hill** (2245 ft.) makes it a fine launch pad for daytrips up the mountain. (Inquire at the tourist office; see **Adrigole,** p. 261.) For those who prefer to while away the time splashing about in the harbor, Frank Conroy at **Beara Watersports** arranges **kayak** excursions and offers **sailing lessons.** (☎70692 or 086 309 8654; www.seakayakingwestcork.com. Kayak daytrip including small lunch €57 per person. 3hr. morning sail instruction €35 per person. Groups considerably cheaper.)

DAYTRIPS FROM CASTLETOWNBERE

BERE ISLAND

Two ferries chug to Bere Island. Murphy's Ferry Service (☎027 75014; www.murphysferry.com) leaves from the pontoon 3 mi. east of Castletownbere off the Glengarriff road but lands you much closer to the island's "center" at Rerrin Village. (30min.; June-Aug. 8 per day, Sept.-May 4 per day; €6 return, children free; with car €20 return including passengers.) The other company, Bere Island Ferry (☎027 75009), leaves from the center of Castletownbere and drops you inconveniently on the western end of the island, near the walking paths, ruins, and the island's other pub. (June 21-Sept. M-Sa 7 per day, Su 5 per day; €4 return, with car €20 return.) Phone ahead during the off season.

The spectacular ferry ride to the tiny fishing community of Bere Island makes for a lovely daytrip. Visit the friendly folks and take in the beautiful scenery and quirky run-down cars on the island—old autos now get transported from the mainland to Bere. There are no *Garda* on the island, so be aware that the absence of law enforcement leads to much drunk driving. The island used to be a British naval base—forts and military remnants are still scattered across it—and the Irish Army now uses it for training. Across the harbor from Rerrin, the masts of a fishing ship protrude from the sea like giant iron toothpicks. The ship burned in 1982 under mysterious circumstances after her owner ran out of money to pay the crew.

The least expensive accommodations on Bere are at **The Admiral's House Hostel/B&B ❷,** a 7min. (well-signposted 300 yd.) walk from Rerrin. Rooms are basic but comfortable. (☎027 75213 or 75064. 6-bed dorms with bath €15; singles €30; doubles €40.) **Kitty Murphy's Cafe ❷,** by the Murphy ferry landing in Rerrin, serves affordable food all day. (☎027 75996. Sandwiches €2.50, mains €6.50-12. Open M-Sa 12:30-4:30pm and 6:30-9pm.) The attached **shop** furnishes supplies. (☎027

75004. Open M-Sa 9am-4:30pm and 7-9pm.) Gaze at maps or chat with locals next door at **Desmond O'Sullivan's** pub. **The Hotel** pub is 3 mi. down the main road, about a 15min. walk from the Bere Island Ferry pier. (☎ 027 75018. Sandwiches €2-3.)

DURSEY ISLAND

Just off the tip of the Beara, accessible by Ireland's only cable car. The cables begin 5 mi. out from Allihies, off the Castletownbere road. Car runs M-Sa 9-10:30am, 2:30-4:30pm, and 7-7:30pm; Su hours vary depending on which church has Mass that day. €4 return, children €1. For cable car info, call the Windy Point House. (☎ 73017; see below.)

A copy of the 91st Psalm adorns the wall of the cable car out to Dursey—you may find yourself calling upon "the Lord your defender" as you dangle above the Atlantic. The 10min. aerial trip out is the most thrilling aspect of the island, whose enchanting tranquility and sweeping panoramas may inspire poetic musings but are unlikely to set your heart racing. Walks around the island expose you to a stark combination of sea, sky, land, and sheep. The English army laid waste to **Dursey Fort** in 1602, but only after raiding the unarmed garrison and callously tossing soldiers over the cliffs to their doom. A trip to the western tip provides a stunning view over sea cliffs and a chance to observe the island's much-vaunted flocks of migrant birds, who at any given time have the edge in numbers over Dursey's seven human residents. If you stop for lunch at **Windy Point House ❷**, near the base of the cable car on the mainland, you may be tempted to spend the night. Windy Point provides a full midday menu, luxurious accommodations, and views of Dursey Sound. (☎ 027 73017. Food served 11am-6pm. B&B €23.50 per person, with bath and sea view.) **Camping** on the island is legal.

NORTHERN BEARA PENINSULA

Past Castletownbere, the Beara Peninsula stretches out into the Atlantic, the landscape becoming rocky and harsh; yet sojourners find fulfillment in the lonely beauty of the cliff-lined coast and distant wee villages. The isolation of this part of the southwest both attracts and frustrates hitchers, who report finding rides mainly during mid-afternoon beach traffic in July and August. Despite some steep hills, **biking** is a lovely way to tour the area, with the road hugging the coastline for most of its route. The solitary adventurer can take to the hills along the **Beara Way.** And while the barren beauty of the Beara cannot be fully experienced from behind the glass of a car window, motoring around the peninsula will come close enough.

ALLIHIES (NA HAILICNI) ☎027

Set between the Slieve Miskish mountains and the rolling sea, Allihies's abandoned cottages nearly outnumber its inhabitants. Fenced-off mine shafts, empty buildings, and a carved-up hillside testify to what was once a booming copper-mining town. Even **Ballydonegan Strand** is a by-product of the mines: the sand is ground-up mountain extract. Although some might call Allihies desolate, visitors in a tranquil state of mind will delight in gorgeous sunsets over glistening beaches. More pristine and secluded are the white sands of **Garinish Strand,** which lies a few miles down the road toward Dursey; follow the signs to the right at the fork. At the turnoff to Dursey, look for the largest **wedge tomb** on the Beara peninsula—it consists of two sidestones and a single capstone. The road to the Dursey cable car, off the Castletownbere road, passes **Lehanmore Ring Fort,** which remains an impressive remnant even if its crumbling walls can barely keep the cows out these days.

Pamphlets and maps are available at the **tourist information** hut on Main St., which is open sporadically, mostly afternoons in summer. **O'Sullivan's** can fill your shopping bag or picnic basket. (☎ 73004. Open M-Sa 9am-8pm.) After a long day of hiking, sink into a sofa in the cavernous sitting room of the recently-renovated **Village Hostel (IHH) ❶,** next to the very red O'Neill's pub on Main St. (☎73107. Open May-Oct. Dorms €12.50-13; singles €18; doubles €36; family room €50-55.) The **Allihies Youth Hostel (An Óige/HI) ❶** lies 1 mi. south of the village (12min. walk) and is well-marked from the road. (☎73014. Sheets €1. Open June-Sept. Dorms €12.50, hostel members €10.50; under 18 €9/€7.) **Anthony's ❶** is well equipped for **camping** all year, with hot showers and scenery to spare. Take the road all the way to the beach, turn right, and look for signs that say "campground;" it's about a 10min. walk from town. (☎73002. 1 person with tent €4.50. Showers €1.) Allihies's four pubs cater mostly to locals. Usually one—seemingly chosen by tacit consensus among the villagers—is lively each night. **O'Neill's ❷** hosts trad and ballads on Wednesdays and Sundays in the summer; it's also the best bet for a meal, even for the vegetabley-inclined. (☎73008. Sandwiches €2.50-6, evening menu from €9. Food served noon-9pm, with more options after 6pm.) Music fills **O'Sullivan's** (☎73165) on weekend nights most of the year. **The Lighthouse** (☎73000) and the **Oak Bar** (☎73110) also see their share of action; both have occasional trad.

EYERIES AND ARDGROOM ☎027

Venture across the craggy coast, home to none but the hardiest of sheep, to reach the hamlet of Eyeries *(Na Haorai)*. A 5min. walk east of the village, the **Ard Na Mara Hostel's ❶** view of Kenmare Bay makes for a soothing stay. (☎74271. Dorms €10. **Camping** €5.) Three miles outside of Eyeries, on the main road to Allihies, is the **Urhan Hostel ❶,** housed in an old schoolhouse along with a **post office** and a **general store.** This clean, no-frills hostel meets all your basic needs, but has been booked solid in July-Aug. for the next three years by Belgian schoolchildren. Damn those Belgians and their schoolchildren. The hostel is still available the rest of the rainy year. (☎74005. Dorms €10; private rooms €12 per person. **Camping** €5.) The affiliated **Urhan Inn Pub** (☎74088), right next door, makes for ridiculously easy stumbles home. Within Eyeries village, culinary options are limited. **O'Sullivan's** vends general provisions on Main St. (☎74016. Open daily 8:30am-9pm.) Several pubs, including **O'Neill's** (☎74009), **O'Shea's** (☎74025), and **Causkey's** (☎74161), serve sandwiches and grub. Only Causkey's might throw in some music on the side.

For fuller menus and lively *craic*, head down the road to the smaller village of **Ardgroom** (a-GROOM; *Dha Dhrom*). Basic, pleasant rooms are available at **O'Brien's B&B ❷** (☎74019; open May-Sept.; €20 per person, doubles €50), right by **The Village Inn Bar and Restaurant ❷,** which serves up hearty meals from seafood to pasta. (☎74067. Lunch €3-7; dinner from €7.50. Food served daily noon-3pm and Tu-Su 6-9pm.) **The Holly Bar,** one door down, keeps patrons as happy as children on Christmas morning with frequent summertime trad. Around the corner at the gas station, provision yourself at **Harrington's General Store.** (☎74003. Open daily 8:30am-10pm.)

Several mysterious ancient sights lie along the much longer—and much hillier—scenic coastal route between Eyeries and Ardgroom. At **Ballycrovane,** the tallest *ogham* stone in Ireland remembers the good ol' (really ol') days (see **Christians and Vikings,** p. 55). This 17 ft. stone is on private property, but it is well signposted; the landowners collect €1.50 from each visitor. Further on in Kilcatherine sits the **Hag of Beara,** a bizarre rock formation that, according to legend, is the petrified remains of an ancient woman. It's hard to see, but some say that the outline of the hag's face is on one side. Nearby, off the Allihies road, skulk the 18th-century ruins of **Kilcatherine Church;** an unusual stone carving of a cat's head adorns the entrance door. Also look for the **Mass Rock,** which was used as an altar by Catholics forced to hide their religion. (See **The Ascendancy,** p. 58.)

COUNTIES LIMERICK AND KERRY

The imagined Ireland of small wee villages, enchanted green mountains, and jagged coastal cliffs can be discovered in Co. Kerry. Arguably the most beautiful region on the Emerald Isle, there is no doubt that it is the most touristed; each summer, tiny towns open their doors to infusions of visitors. The Iveragh Peninsula, home of the picturesque and well-traveled Ring of Kerry, is anchored at its base by the mountainous Killarney National Park, and extends all the way out to tranquil Valentia Island at its tip, and beyond to the mysterious monastic settlement on the Skellig Islands far off its western shore. The Dingle Peninsula's popularity is growing rapidly, but skinny roads help preserve the ancient sights and traditional feel of Slea Head, the West Dingle *gaeltacht*, and the haunting Blasket Islands. Further North, in Co. Limerick, rich green pastures dotted with ancient castle ruins characterize the landscape. Now known for its dairy cattle and the gentle Galtee Mountains, the area once played host to a number of important monasteries. Resting at the foot of the Shannon River, the historic poverty of Limerick City has been recently erased with the help of the EU and the raging Celtic Tiger. Convenient to Shannon Airport and pretty little Adare, the city now attracts visitors like pubbers at last call. In the summer, buses are readily available to most areas in these counties, but public transportation dries up in the off-season.

IVERAGH PENINSULA

As the Southwest's most celebrated peninsula, the Iveragh's picturesque villages, fabled ancient forts, and rough romantic scenery often adorn the photographs and postcards handed around back home. The peninsula's majestic views rarely disappoint the droves of tourists that cruise through on private tour buses. The busbound tend to know the area only as "The Ring of Kerry," but travelers who take the time to explore the rugged landscape will find that there is much more than the views glimpsed through windows at 50mph. The Kerry Way walking trail, which sweeps its pilgrims up above the asphalt Ring and lays the best views at their feet, is one such detour; another is the Skellig Ring, which swings through Ballinskelligs and Portmagee along the westernmost tip of the peninsula.

KILLARNEY (CILL AIRNE) ☎064

Only a short walk away from some of Ireland's most extraordinary scenery, Killarney manages to celebrate its tourist-based economy without offending the leprechaun-loathing travelers out there. You'll find all you need in town, including lots of trinkets to weigh down your pack, but all that fades to dust in the face of the glorious national park only a few minutes away.

TRANSPORTATION

Airport: Kerry Airport, Farranfore (☎976 4644), halfway between Killarney and Tralee on the N22. 20min. from Killarney; cabs and buses go back and forth to town. **Ryanair** (☎01 609 7800; www.ryanair.com) flies to **London Stanstead** (2 per day); **Aer Arann Express** (☎1890 462 726; www.aerarannexpress.com) goes to **Dublin** (4 per day).

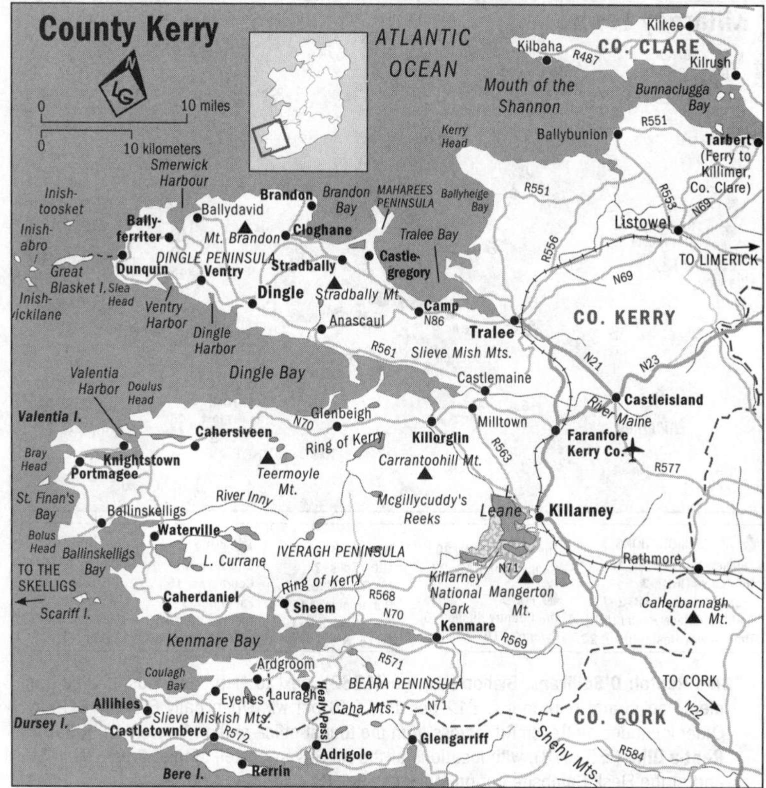

Trains: Killarney Station (☎31067, recorded info ☎1890 200 493, inquiries ☎1850 366 222). Off East Avenue Rd. near the intersection with Park Rd. Open M-Sa 7am-12:30pm and 2-6pm, Su 30min. before departures. 4 trains per day to: **Cork** (2hr., €17.80); **Dublin** (3½hr., €45); **Limerick** (3hr.; €19.70).

Buses: Park Rd. (☎30011), connected to the outlet mall. Open mid-Sept. to June M-Sa 8:30am-5pm; July to mid-Sept. 8:30am-6pm. Buses to: **Belfast** (3-4 per day, Su 2 per day; €25); **Cork** (2hr., 10-14 per day, €12); **Derry,** via **Sligo** and **Donegal,** (7½hr.; 2-3 per day; €24); **Dingle** (2hr.; M-Sa 7 per day, Su 4 per day; €11.60); **Dublin** (6hr., 5-6 per day, €19); **Farranfore/Kerry Airport** (10-17 per day, €3.10); **Galway,** via **Tarbert Ferry,** (6-7 per day, €17.10); **Kenmare** (40min., 2-3 per day, €6.35); **Kilkenny** (2-3 per day, €17.10); **Limerick** (2hr., 6-7 per day, €12.40); **Shannon Airport** (3hr., 6-7 per day, €13.90); **Skibbereen** (1 per day, €12.40); **Tralee** (10-17 per day, €5.80); **Waterford** (9-12 per day, €17.10). Buses leave June-Sept. daily on the **Ring of Kerry Circuit,** stopping in **Killorglin, Glenbeigh, Kells, Cahersiveen, Waterville, Caherdaniel, Sneem,** and **Moll's Gap.** (Book tickets at hostel; students €15.25 return with 1-night stop.) **Bus Éireann** runs a no-frills Ring of Kerry loop in the summer (2 per day; see **Ring of Kerry,** p. 276). The **Dingle/Slea Head** tour hits **Inch, Anascaul, Dingle, Ventry, Slea Head, Dunquin,** and **Ballyferriter** (June to mid-Sept. M-Sa 2 per day, €12.40).

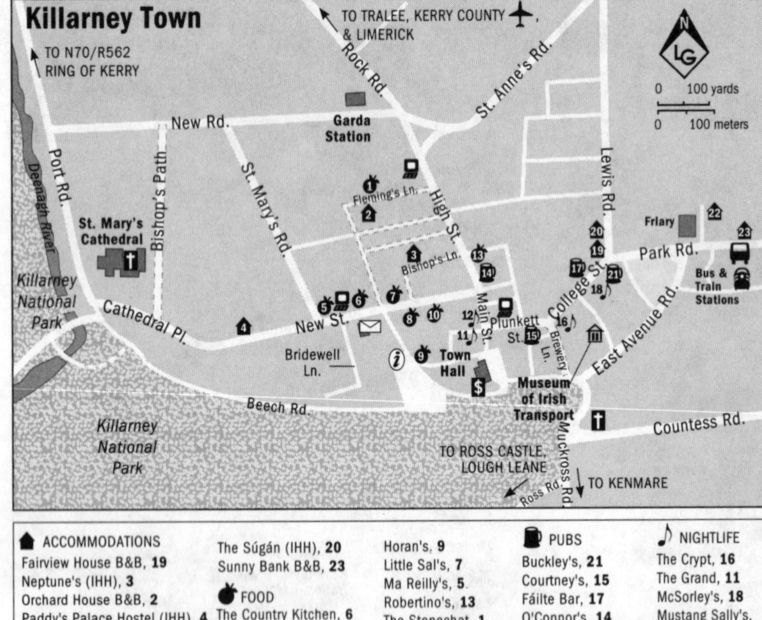

Bike Rental: O'Sullivans, Bishop's Ln. (☎31282), next to Neptune's Hostel. Free panniers, locks, and park maps. €12 per day, €70 per wk. Open daily 8:30am-6:30pm. Other locations on Beech Rd. across from the tourist office and on Brewery Ln. **Killarney Rent-a-Bike** (☎32578), with locations at the An Súgán hostel, Market Cross, Main St., and at the Flesk Campsite out on Muckross Rd. €12 per day, €60 per wk.

ORIENTATION AND PRACTICAL INFORMATION

Most of Killarney is packed into three crowded streets. **Main St.,** in the center of town, begins at the **Town Hall,** then becomes **High St. New St.** and **Plunkett St.** both head in opposite directions from Main St.—New St. goes west toward Killorglin, and Plunkett becomes **College St.** then **Park Rd.** on its way east to the bus and train stations. **East Avenue Rd.** connects the train station back to town hall, meeting **Muckross Rd.,** which leads to the Muckross Estate and Kenmare.

Tourist Office: Beech St. (☎31633). Exceptionally helpful and deservedly popular. Open July-Aug. M-Sa 9am-8pm, Su 10am-1pm and 2:15-6pm; June and Sept. M-Sa 9am-6pm, Su 10am-1pm and 2:15-6pm; Oct.-May M-Sa 9:15am-1pm and 2:15-5:30pm.

Banks: AIB, Main St. (☎31922), next to the town hall. Open M-F 10am-4pm, W until 5pm. **Permanent TSB,** 23-24 New St. (☎33761). Open M-F 10am-5pm, Th until 7pm. Both have **ATMs;** others are scattered throughout the town.

American Express: East Avenue Rd. (☎35722). Open M-F 9am-1pm and 2-5pm, Sa 11am-1pm and 2-5pm.

Laundry: J. Gleeson's Launderette (☎33877), on Brewery Ln. off College St. Self-service €5.90; full service €7. Open M-W and Sa 9am-6pm, Th-F 9am-8pm.

Pharmacy: Sewell's Pharmacy, Main St. (☎31027), at New St. Open mid-July to mid-Aug. Tu-F 9am-9pm, M and Sa 9am-6:30pm; mid-Aug. to mid-July M-Sa 9am-6:30pm.

Emergency: Dial ☎999; no coins required. **Police** *(Garda)*: New Rd. (☎31222).

Hospital: District Hospital, St. Margaret's Rd. (☎31076). Follow High St. 1 mi. from the town center. Nearest emergency facilities are in Tralee.

Internet Access: Cafe Internet, 18 New St. (☎36741), next to the Country Kitchen. €1 per 10min. Open June-Aug. M-Sa 9:30am-11pm, Su 11am-11:30pm; Sept.-May M-Sa 9:30am-10pm, Su 10am-10pm. **Web-talk,** 53 High St. Also €1 per 10min. Open May-Sept. M-F 9am-10pm, Sa 9am-9pm, Su noon-9pm; Oct.-Apr. M-F closes at 10pm. Discount international phone calls.

Post Office: New St. (☎31051). Open M and W-Sa 9am-5:30pm, Tu 9:30am-5:30pm.

ACCOMMODATIONS AND CAMPING

With every other house a B&B, it's easy enough to find cushy digs in Killarney. Cheap digs, on the other hand, will require more work—call ahead. Camping is not allowed in the National Park, but there are excellent campgrounds nearby.

IN TOWN

Neptune's (IHH), Bishop's Ln. (☎35255), the first walkway off New St. on the right. Immense and immaculate with superb showers and numerous amenities. Staff is friendly and professional. Ideal location and a model hostel all others should look to imitate. **Tour booking:** Dingle €17, Ring of Kerry €16.50, Gap of Dunloe €24. **Internet access** €2 per 30min. Wheelchair-accessible. Breakfast €2.50. Free luggage storage; €10 locker deposit. Laundry €7. Curfew 3am. 8-bed dorms €11; 6-bed €11.50; 3- to 4-bed €12. Doubles €34. 10% ISIC discount. ❶

The Railway Hostel (IHH), Park Rd. (☎35299). The first right as you head toward town from the bus station. Big, modern building with sunny rooms and a pool table. Rather than numbers, dorms have names like Disney, Porcupine, Oyster, and Robin, making your quarters much easier to remember after you've had a few pints. **Internet access** €1 per 8min. Curfew 3am. Dorms €11.50; singles €21; doubles €34. ❶

The Súgán (IHH), Lewis Rd. (☎33104), 2min. from the bus or train station. Make a left onto College St.; Lewis Rd. is the 1st right. Small, ship-like bunk rooms blur the distinction between intimacy and claustrophobia; exuberant staff and impromptu storytelling and music around the fire-lit common room provide a happy escape. **Bike rental** discount at Killarney Rent-a-Bike €10 per day. 4- to 8-bed dorms €12; singles €14. ❶

Paddy's Palace Hostel (IHH), 31 New St. (☎35388), a block past the post office. Cramped bunks aren't as palatial as the name implies, but a relaxed atmosphere and proximity to the Park help offset the aesthetic offenses. Continental breakfast included. Free luggage storage. **Tour booking:** Dingle €19, Ring of Kerry €15. **Internet** €1.30 per 10min. 4- to 6-bed dorms €14; doubles €35-40. ❶

Orchard House B&B, Fleming's Ln. (☎31879), off High St. Down a quiet lane right in the center of town. An unbeatable bargain that will make you want to extend your stay—commence nesting with TV, tea, coffee, and hair dryer in each immaculate room. Consult with the proprietors about activities in the area. Individually-tailored breakfasts. Singles €25-30; doubles and triples €45-60. ❸

Sunny Bank B&B, Park Rd. (☎34109), across from the bus station. Cheerful and downright luxurious; glassed-in breakfast room starts the day on a sunny note (should Ireland ever in fact be blessed by sun). June-Sept. doubles €58; Oct.-May €52. ❸

Fairview House B&B, College St. (☎34164), next to An Súgán. Hotel-equivalent luxury for B&B prices. You'll feel like a king rather than a weary traveler in this plush establishment filled with fluffy beds, TVs, and an elegant dining and sitting room (€25-45 per person). If that's not enough, go for rooms at the extra-luxurious annex, **The Copper Kettle** (€25-35 per person), or **Rosslands** (€22.50-35 per person), out near the Park. **Tours** can be arranged upon request. ❸

OUTSIDE TOWN

Peacock Farms Hostel (IHH), Gortdromakiery, (☎33557), 7 mi. from town. Take the Muckross road out of town, turn left just before the Muckross post office, then go 2 mi. and follow the signposts up a steep hill; or call for a ride from the bus station. Brave rough and narrow roads for cheap, clean, and cheerful digs with an unsurpassed view overlooking Lough Guitane. Free daily buses to town at 9am and 6:30pm. Wheelchair-accessible. Organic breakfast €3.50. Open Apr.-Oct. Dorms €10-12; doubles €28. ❶

Killarney Hostel (An Óige/HI), Aghadoe, (☎31240), 3 mi. west of town on the Killorglin road. Call for a ride to and from the bus and train stations. Well-equipped hostel in a stone mansion. Kitchen, TV room, occasional barbecues. **Tours:** Ring of Kerry €16.50, Gap of Dunloe €21. **Bike rental** €10 per day; deposit €10. **Internet access** €1 per 7min. Continental breakfast €3.50; dinner €7.60. Laundry €5. Reception 7am-midnight. Dorms €12; doubles €44; quads €82. Sept.-June €1.30-2.50 cheaper. ❶

Black Valley Hostel (An Óige/HI), Beaufort, (☎34712). 14 mi. from town on the Gap of Dunloe road, a few miles from Lord Brandon's Cottage. Conveniently located on the Kerry Way hiking route. A dearth of street signs requires you to call for directions in advance. Buses stop 6 mi. away in Beaufort Bridge. This spare but spotless hostel was one of the last buildings in Ireland to receive electricity. Friendly owners also have a small shop that sells groceries. Sheets €1.30. Midnight curfew. Peak season dorms with membership €11, without €13. Off-season €2 cheaper. ❶

Kiltrasna Farmhouse, Loughguittane Rd. (☎31643). Off Muckross Road. 2nd road on the left after the Gleneagle Hotel. 6 bedrooms, all with bath, including one wheelchair-accessible room, are tastefully decorated with colorful bedspreads. Woodbacked and cushioned chairs in the elegant dining room look out the huge windows to the hills and the farm's sheep. In the visitors book, previous occupants laud the peacefulness and tranquility. Open Mar. to mid-Oct. €26 per person; inquire about group rates. ❸

Fleming's White Bridge Caravan and Camping Park (☎064 31590). On the Ballycasheen road. A second site is in Glenbeigh, near the beach. An award-winning site many times over, the campsite offers laundry, TV lounge, a shop for essentials, and modern shower facilites. The kids will enjoy the game room and the enticing grassy stretches begging for a football match. €4.50-5.50 per person with tent. ❶

FOOD

Food in Killarney is affordable at lunchtime, but prices skyrocket when the sun goes down. A number of fast-food joints and takeaways stay open until 3-4am, fulfilling their humanitarian mission to satisfy your post-Guinness munchies. **Tesco,** in an arcade off New St., has groceries. (☎32866. Open M-W 8:30am-8pm, Th-F 8:30am-9pm, Sa 8:30am-7pm, Su 10am-6pm.) For organic foods, hit up **Horan's,** in Innisfallen Centre near the tourist office carpark. (☎35399. Open M-W and Sa 8:30am-6:30pm, Th 8:30am-8pm, F 8:30am-9pm.)

The Stonechat, Fleming's Ln. (☎34295). Hanging plants and a painted copy of *Starry Starry Night* adorn the inside of this cozy quiet cottage. Specializes in veggies meals, though chicken and fish dishes are also available. Lunch €5.35-7.60, dinner €10.20-13. Open M-Sa 11am-5pm and 6-10pm. ❸

Cyrano's, Innisfallen Centre (☎35853). Cyrano's knows variety, including tasty meatless feasts. Sate that silver tongue with dessert and cappuccino. Lunch specials €7.40. Open M-Sa 9:30am-6pm. ❷

Little Sal's, New St. (☎36344). The walls of this cafe are lined with red bricks and mirrors. A variety of cheap but tasty meals awaits. Burgers and lasagna (€7.95), pizzas (€7.95-9.50), and a range of baguette sandwiches (€3.25-4.95). ❷

The Country Kitchen, 17 New St. (☎33778). Delicious odors waft onto the street. Glorious baked goods, well-crafted sandwiches, and hot evening meals. Worth a visit just for dessert. Lunch (€5.10-6.35) served until 5pm; dinner €7.60-11.50. Open July-Aug. M-F 8am-8pm, Sa 9am-6pm; Sept.-June M-Sa 9am-6pm. ❷

Ma Reilly's, 20 New St. (☎39220). Irish stew and other hot treats in a popular little joint. Gaze upon black and white photos of Killarney past while the friendly staff takes your order. Open M-Sa 9am-10pm, Su 9am-9pm. ❷

Robertino's, High St. (☎34966). The perfect place to come for an Italian dinner, a date, or hey, how about both! Italian music serenades and candles complete the mood. Frescoes and statues will transport you to Italia as you savor pastas (€11.80-12.90), pizzas (€14.70-19.75), and meat dishes (€17-23.80). Open daily 4-10:30pm. ❹

PUBS AND CLUBS

Trad is a staple in Killarney's pubs on summer nights, but herds of lumbering tourists looking for the next great jig have made for a crowded, noisy drinking experience. Several nightclubs simmer from 10:30pm until 3am; most charge €6-8 cover but often offer discounts before 11pm. Check out the free and widely available *Red Turkey Guide to Killarney*, published biweekly, for events listings.

O'Connor's Traditional Pub, 7 High St. (☎31115). Patrons both foreign and domestic mingle in an upbeat, comfortable atmosphere. Traditional Irish food available from 12:30-9:30pm (try the Irish stew or the chowder). M and W-Th trad 9:30-11:30pm.

The Grand, High St. (☎31159). Locals and tourists alike start the night early (open at 7pm) but stick around late for the fantastic live music. Extremely popular club for young tourists. Follow its nightly progression from trad (9-11pm) to Irish rock (11pm-1am) to a disco in the back (midnight-3am). Arrive before 11pm and dodge the €5-8 cover.

Courtney's Bar, Plunkett St. (☎32689). Join in with locals for Th and Su night open sessions, or just unwind in good company with hearty stout.

Buckley's Bar, College St. (☎31037). Classy and traditional, a quiet place with lots of dark wood and leather, where the older crowd enjoys a pint and good conversation. Nightly trad in the summer.

Fáilte Bar, College St. (☎33404). All are welcome to relax with the locals at this dark and woody pub. DJs spin the hits Th-Su nights. **Internet** €0.65 per 6min.

The Crypt, College St. (☎31038), next to the Killarney Towers Hotel. Looks gothic but attracts neatly-dressed trendy types. Mixed dance music. Cover €7-9

McSorley's, College St. (☎39770). Locals and tourists get intimate on 2 dance floors to the tune of chart and hip hop hits. Offers a pool table and comfy seats when things slow down. M drink promo (pints €1.90), Tu live music, W R&B, Th comedy, F-Sa live band, Su Ladies Night. DJs M and Th-Su. Cover €6.50-9.

Mustang Sally's, Main St. (☎35790). The Blues Brothers greet you on the way into this massive pub. Huge menu variety is sure to please any palate. (Lunch 12:30-3pm; dinner 5-9pm. €8.50-16.50 a la carte. 4-course early-bird meal €12.95.) Several TVs assure you don't miss the action of the match, and you can always work off that meal on the pub's 2 dance floors. Cover €7. DJ spins the hits 9pm-12:30am Th-Su.

SIGHTS AND ACTIVITIES

Congested with bureaux de change, souvenir shops, and disoriented foreigners, Killarney plays second fiddle to the glorious National Park just beyond the city limits. Still, Killarney has a charm of its own. The neo-Gothic **St. Mary's Cathedral** on New St. has three huge altars and can seat 1400 within its rough limestone walls. Very peaceful and very beautiful, you'll find yourself coming here quite often to repent for all the sinful drinking you're sure to do at Killarney's tempting pubs. (Always open. Free.) At the **Museum of Irish Transport,** located down a lane between College St. and East Avenue Rd., relics live out their dust-collecting dreams. Turn-of-the-century cars and a horse-drawn fire engine from 1842 impress the nostalgic, but weary cyclists will definitely count their blessings at the sight of the 1820s hobby horse, an early pedal-less bicycle that could only be propelled a la Fred Flintstone. (☎34677. Open Apr.-Oct. daily 10am-6pm; last admission 5pm. €4, students and seniors €2.50.) The Killarney area has excellent **salmon and trout fishing,** especially in August and September. Unrestricted trout-hunting is allowed in nearly all of Killarney's lakes, but fishing in rivers and Barfinnihy Lake requires a permit (€3.80 per day). Contact **O'Neill's Fishing Shop,** Plunkett St. (☎31970), for details. **Trailways,** College St. (☎39929), rents rods for €8 per day.

Trailways is also your one-stop shop for tours of the National Park. They'll book **boat and riding tours** free of charge and advise you on how best to see the National Park. **O'Donoghue's** (☎35593) offers a **pony and cart trip** through the mountains to a picnic site, followed by a **boat tour** through the lake systems. The **Lily of Killarney Watercoach** (☎31068) has five daily sailings leaving from Ross Castle. Tours cover the Park, accompanied by commentary infused with history and folklore in the comfort of a heated vessel. If you're not sure about your sea legs, try **Quad Safari** (☎066 947 4465). Tours from 3½ to 6hr. long. If 4-legged quad bikes aren't your bag, 4-legged gentle beasts are available from the **Killarney Riding Stables** (☎31686; €20-50 per person) and **Rocklands** (☎32592; €16.50 per hr.).

You're in luck if you swing through town during one of Killarney's festivals; locals take them quite seriously and always make a great showing. In mid-May and mid-July, horses gallop in the **Killarney Races** at the race course on Ross Rd. (Tickets available at gate, €3.80-6.35.) The **Killarney Regatta,** the oldest in Ireland, draws rowers and spectators to Lough Leane the first Sunday in July. For the 4th of July weekend, Killarney celebrates American Independence Day, Irish style, with the **Irish-American Music Festival.**

KILLARNEY NATIONAL PARK

Glaciers sliced up the Killarney region, scooping out a series of lakes and glens and scattering silk-smooth rocks and precarious boulders across the terrain before continuing their march toward the next defenseless landscape. As a result, Killarney National Park makes for preternaturally dazzling hiking, biking, and climbing. The park, stretched across 37 sq. mi. of prime Kerry real estate, between Killarney to the northeast and Kenmare to the southwest, incorporates a string of forested mountains and the famous **Lakes of Killarney:** huge **Lough Leane (Lower Lake),** medium-sized **Muckross (Middle) Lake,** and the small **Upper Lake,** 2 mi. southwest of the other two and connected by a channel. An indigenous but elusive herd of 850 red deer is reported to be at large in the glens that surround the lakes.

The Kenmare road curves along the southeastern shores of the lakes, passing the park sights but missing some of the woodland paths. With many more tourists than locals driving these sections, hitching can be difficult besides being risky. **Bikes** are a great means of exploring (see **Practical Information,** p. 268). Walkers

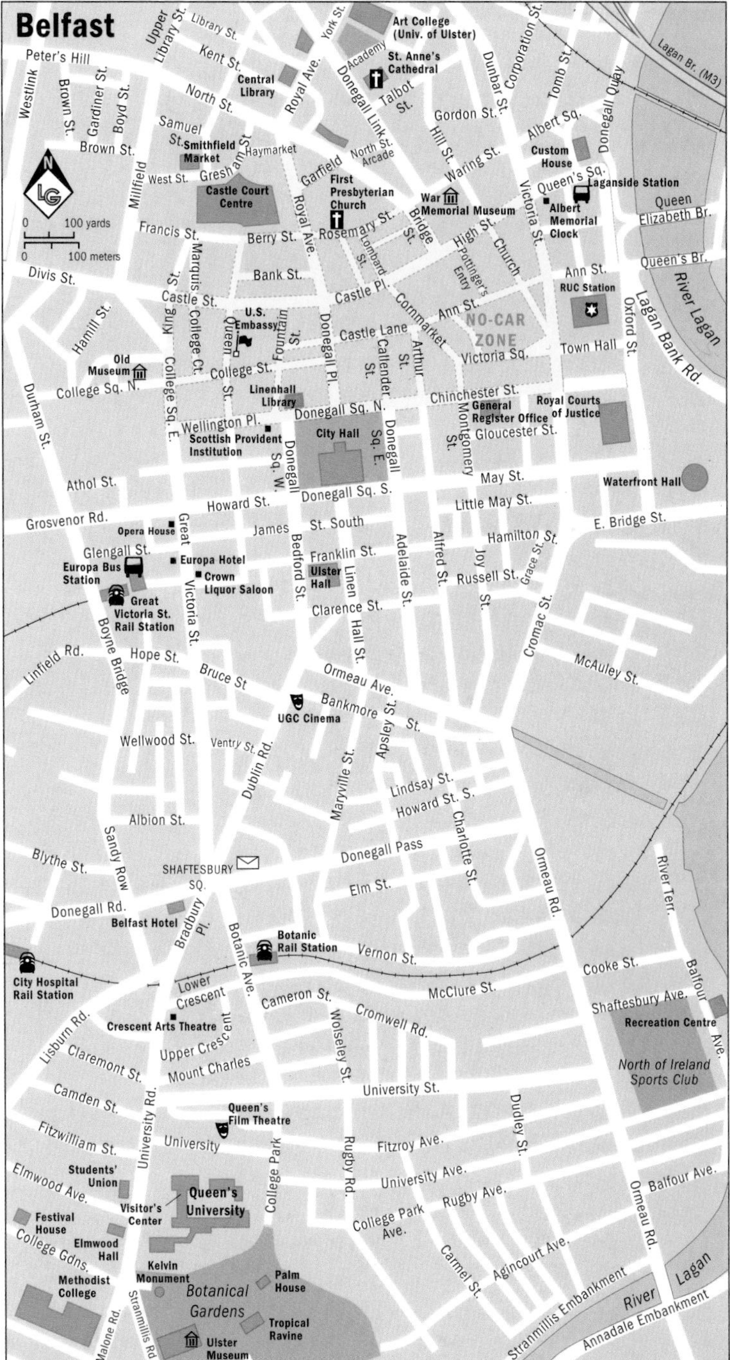
Belfast
0 100 yards
0 100 meters
Art College (Univ. of Ulster)
St. Anne's Cathedral
Central Library
Smithfield Market
Castle Court Centre
First Presbyterian Church
War Memorial Museum
Custom House
Laganside Station
Albert Memorial Clock
RUC Station
NO-CAR ZONE
Town Hall
U.S. Embassy
Old Museum
Linenhall Library
General Register Office
Royal Courts of Justice
Scottish Provident Institution
City Hall
Waterfront Hall
Opera House
Europa Hotel
Europa Bus Station
Crown Liquor Saloon
Ulster Hall
Great Victoria St. Rail Station
UGC Cinema
SHAFTESBURY SQ.
Belfast Hotel
Botanic Rail Station
City Hospital Rail Station
Crescent Arts Theatre
Recreation Centre
North of Ireland Sports Club
Queen's Film Theatre
Students' Union
Queen's University
Visitor's Center
Festival House
Elmwood Hall
Methodist College
Kelvin Monument
Botanical Gardens
Palm House
Tropical Ravine
Ulster Museum
River Lagan
River Lagan
Lagan Br. (M3)
Queen Elizabeth Br.
Queen's Br.

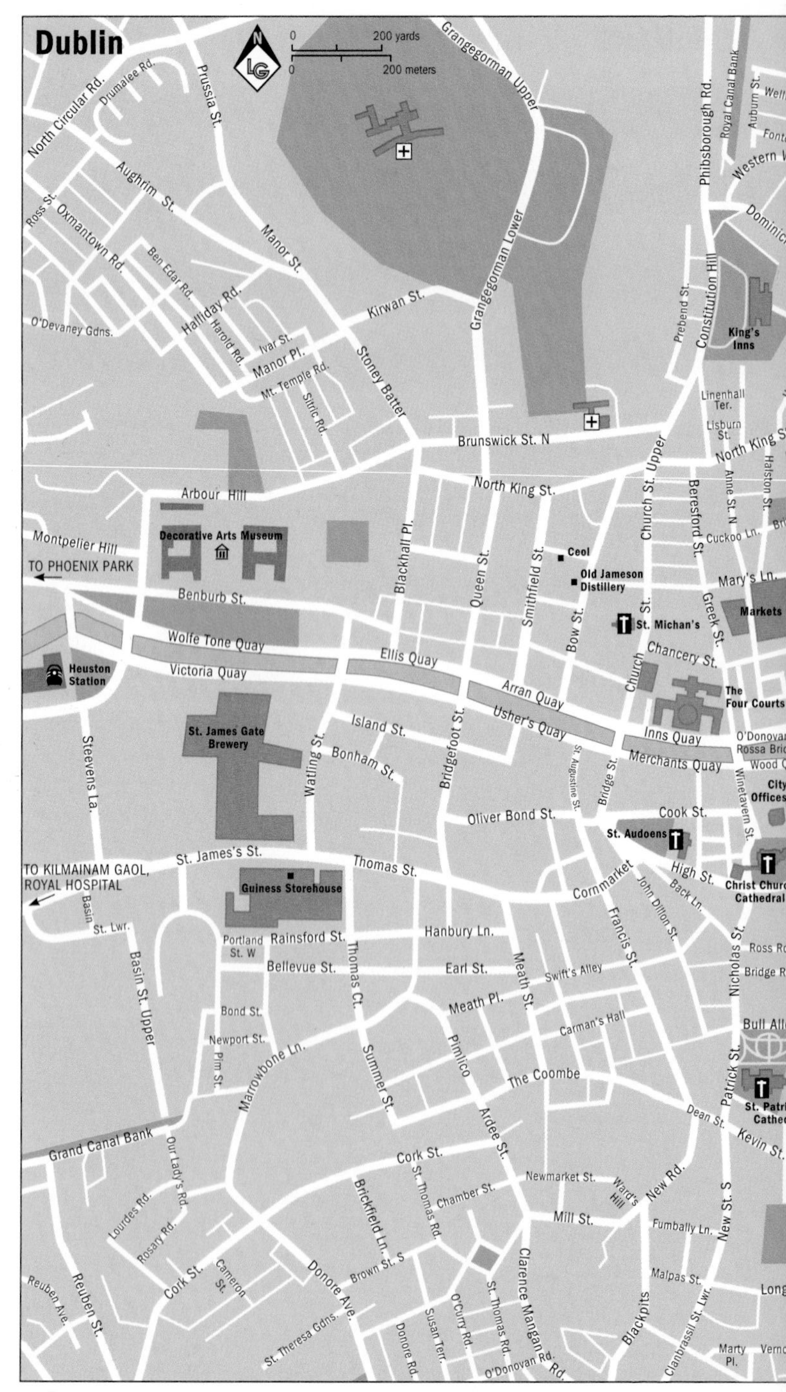

Dublin
0
200 yards
0
200 meters
Grangegorman Upper
Grangegorman Lower
North Circular Rd.
Drumalee Rd.
Prussia St.
Aughrim St.
Ross St.
Oxmantown Rd.
Manor St.
Ben Edar Rd.
Halliday Rd.
Harold Rd.
Kirwan St.
O'Devaney Gdns.
Ivar St.
Manor Pl.
Mt. Temple Rd.
Sitric Rd.
Stoney Batter
Brunswick St. N
North King St.
Arbour Hill
Decorative Arts Museum
Montpelier Hill
TO PHOENIX PARK
Benburb St.
Blackhall Pl.
Queen St.
Smithfield St.
Ceol
Old Jameson Distillery
Bow St.
St. Michan's
Church St. Upper
Beresford St.
Prebend St.
Constitution Hill
Phibsborough Rd.
Royal Canal Bank
Auburn St.
Western Way
Dominick
King's Inns
Linenhall Ter.
Lisburn St.
North King St.
Anne St. N
Halston St.
Cuckoo Ln.
Mary's Ln.
Markets
Greek St.
Chancery St.
The Four Courts
Wolfe Tone Quay
Ellis Quay
Victoria Quay
Heuston Station
Arran Quay
Usher's Quay
Inns Quay
Merchants Quay
O'Donovan Rossa Bridge
Wood Quay
City Offices
Winetavern St.
Steevens La.
St. James Gate Brewery
Island St.
Watling St.
Bonham St.
Bridgefoot St.
St. Augustine St.
Bridge St.
Oliver Bond St.
Cook St.
St. Audoens
TO KILMAINAM GAOL, ROYAL HOSPITAL
St. James's St.
Thomas St.
Guiness Storehouse
Cornmarket
High St.
Back Ln.
John Dillon St.
Christ Church Cathedral
Basin St. Lwr.
Portland St. W
Rainsford St.
Hanbury Ln.
Francis St.
Nicholas St.
Ross Rd
Bridge Rd
Basin St. Upper
Bellevue St.
Thomas Ct.
Earl St.
Meath St.
Swift's Alley
Bond St.
Meath Pl.
Carman's Hall
Newport St.
Pim St.
Marrowbone Ln.
Summer St.
Pimlico
The Coombe
Bull Alley
Patrick St.
St. Patrick's Cathedral
Dean St.
Kevin St.
Grand Canal Bank
Our Lady's Rd.
Ardee St.
Cork St.
St. Thomas Rd.
Newmarket St.
Ward's Hill
New Rd.
Brickfield Ln.
Chamber St.
Lourdes Rd.
Rosary Rd.
Mill St.
Fumbally Ln.
New St. S
Cork St.
Cameron St.
Donore Ave.
Brown St. S
Malpas St.
Reuben Ave.
Reuben St.
Clarence Mangan Rd.
St. Thomas Rd.
O'Curry Rd.
Susan Terr.
Donore Rd.
St. Theresa Gdns.
Blackpits
Clanbrassil St. Lwr.
O'Donovan Rd.
Marty Pl.
Long

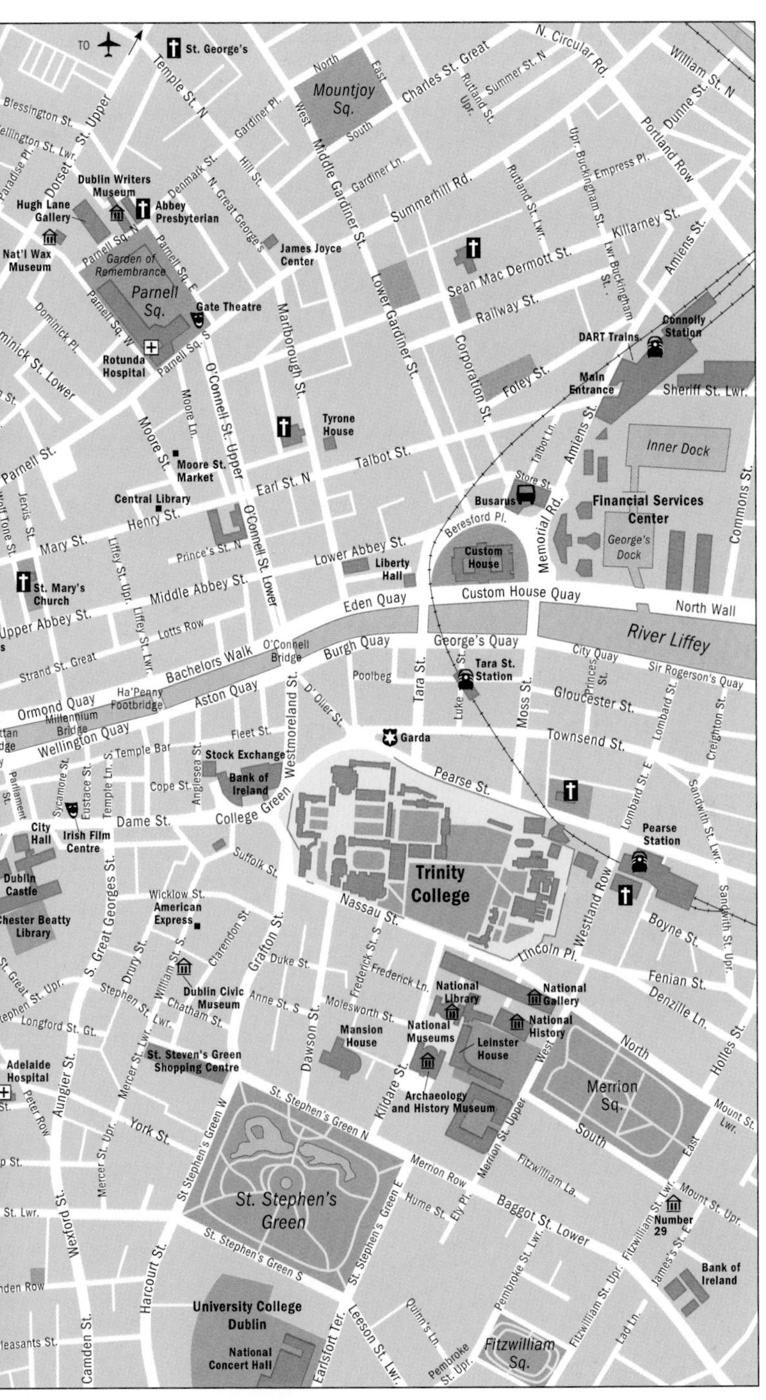

TO
St. George's
Mountjoy Sq.
N. Circular Rd.
William St. N
Dunne St.
Portland Row
Charles St. Great
Rutland St. Upr.
Summer St. N
Temple St. N
Blessington St.
Wellington St. Lwr.
Dorset St. Upper
Paradise Pl.
Gardiner Pl.
Hill St.
Middle Gardiner St.
Gardiner Ln.
Summerhill Rd.
Rutland St. Lwr.
Upr. Buckingham St.
Empress Pl.
Killarney St.
Amiens St.
Dublin Writers Museum
Hugh Lane Gallery
Abbey Presbyterian
Nat'l Wax Museum
Parnell Sq. N
Garden of Remembrance
Parnell Sq.
Parnell Sq. E
Parnell Sq. W
Parnell Sq. S
Denmark St.
N. Great George's
James Joyce Center
Gate Theatre
Rotunda Hospital
Dominick Pl.
Dominick St. Lower
Lower Gardiner St.
Sean Mac Dermott St.
Lwr Buckingham St.
Railway St.
Connolly Station
DART Trains
Main Entrance
Sheriff St. Lwr.
Foley St.
Corporation St.
Marlborough St.
O'Connell St. Upper
Moore Ln.
Moore St.
Tyrone House
Parnell St.
Moore St. Market
Talbot St.
Talbot Ln.
Inner Dock
Store St.
Busarus
Financial Services Center
George's Dock
Commons St.
Memorial Rd.
Beresford Pl.
Earl St. N
Central Library
Henry St.
Wolf Tone St.
Jervis St.
Mary St.
Prince's St. N
O'Connell St. Lower
Lower Abbey St.
Liberty Hall
Custom House
Custom House Quay
North Wall
Liffey St. Upr.
Middle Abbey St.
St. Mary's Church
Upper Abbey St.
Eden Quay
Lotts Row
Liffey St. Lwr.
Bachelors Walk
O'Connell Bridge
Burgh Quay
George's Quay
River Liffey
City Quay
Princes St.
Sir Rogerson's Quay
Strand St. Great
Poolbeg
Tara St.
Tara St. Station
Luke St.
Moss St.
Gloucester St.
Lombard St.
Creighton St.
Ormond Quay
Ha'Penny Footbridge
Aston Quay
Westmoreland St.
D'Olier St.
Millennium Bridge
Wellington Quay
Fleet St.
Garda
Townsend St.
Temple Bar
Stock Exchange
Sycamore St.
Eustace St.
Temple Ln. S
Anglesea St.
Bank of Ireland
Pearse St.
Lombard St. E
Sandwith St. Lwr.
Parliament St.
Cope St.
Dame St.
College Green
City Hall
Irish Film Centre
Suffolk St.
Trinity College
Pearse Station
Westland Row
Dublin Castle
Chester Beatty Library
S. Great Georges St.
Wicklow St.
American Express
Clarendon St.
Grafton St.
Nassau St.
Frederick St. S
Boyne St.
Sandwith St. Upr.
Lincoln Pl.
Drury St.
William St. S
Duke St.
Frederick Ln.
National Library
National Gallery
Fenian St.
Denzille Ln.
Stephen St. Upr.
Stephen St. Lwr.
Dublin Civic Museum
Chatham St.
Anne St. S
Molesworth St.
National History
Longford St. Gt.
Mansion House
National Museums
Leinster House
West
North
Holles St.
Merrion Sq.
Adelaide Hospital
Aungier St.
Mercer St. Lwr.
St. Steven's Green Shopping Centre
Dawson St.
Kildare St.
Archaeology and History Museum
Peter Row
York St.
St. Stephen's Green N
Merrion St. Upper
South
East
Mount St. Lwr.
St. Stephen's Green W
Mercer St. Upr.
Merrion Row
Fitzwilliam La.
Mount St. Upr.
St. Stephen's Green
Hume St.
Ely Pl.
Baggot St. Lower
Number 29
St. Stephen's Green E
Fitzwilliam St. Lwr.
James's St. E
Wexford St.
St. Stephen's Green S
Pembroke St. Lwr.
Fitzwilliam St. Upr.
Bank of Ireland
Camden Row
Harcourt St.
University College Dublin
Quinn's Ln.
Lad Ln.
Camden St.
Pleasants St.
National Concert Hall
Earlsfort Ter.
Leeson St. Lwr.
Pembroke St. Upr.
Fitzwilliam Sq.

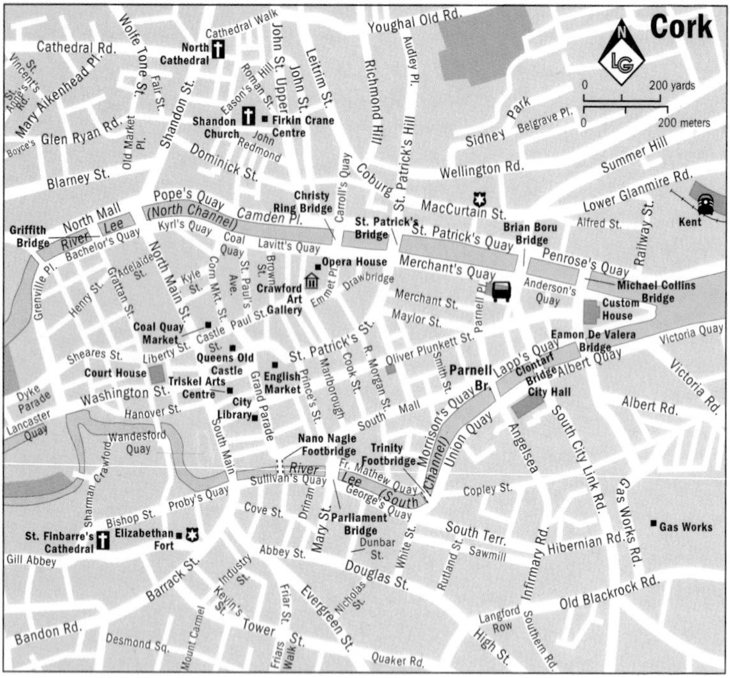

Cork

N
LG
0 200 yards
0 200 meters

Cathedral Walk
Cathedral Rd.
North Cathedral
St. Vincent's
St. Anne's Rd.
Mary Aikenhead Pl.
Wolfe Tone St.
Fair St.
Shandon St.
Eason's Hill
Roman St.
John St. Upper
John St.
Leitrim St.
Richmond Hill
Audley Pl.
St. Patrick's Hill
Youghal Old Rd.
Sidney Park
Belgrave Pl.
Summer Hill
Shandon Church
Firkin Crane Centre
John Redmond
Boyce's
Glen Ryan Rd.
Old Market Pl.
Dominick St.
Blarney St.
Carroll's Quay
Coburg St.
Wellington Rd.
Lower Glanmire Rd.
Pope's Quay
Christy Ring Bridge
MacCurtain St.
Kent
North Mall
(North Channel)
Camden Pl.
St. Patrick's Bridge
Brian Boru Bridge
Alfred St.
Railway St.
Griffith Bridge
River Lee
Kyrl's Quay
Bachelor's Quay
Coal Quay
Lavitt's Quay
St. Patrick's Quay
Penrose's Quay
Opera House
Merchant's Quay
Michael Collins Bridge
Grenville Pl.
Adelaide St.
North Main St.
Kyle St.
Corn Mkt. St.
St. Paul's Ave.
Brown St.
Crawford Art Gallery
Emmet Pl.
Drawbridge
Anderson's Quay
Custom House
Henry St.
Grattan St.
Merchant St.
Parnell Pl.
Maylor St.
Coal Quay Market
Castle St.
Paul St.
Eamon De Valera Bridge
Victoria Quay
Liberty St.
Queens Old Castle
St. Patrick's St.
Oliver Plunkett St.
Smith St.
Sheares St.
Court House
R. Morgan St.
Cook St.
Marlborough
Prince's St.
Grand Parade
English Market
Parnell Br.
Lapp's Quay
Clontarf Bridge
Albert Quay
Victoria Rd.
Dyke Parade
Washington St.
Triskel Arts Centre
City Library
South Mall
City Hall
Albert Rd.
Lancaster Quay
Hanover St.
Morrison's Quay
Union Quay
Angelsea
South City Link Rd.
Wandesford Quay
South Main
Nano Nagle Footbridge
Trinity Footbridge
(South Channel)
Crawford
Sharman Crawford
River Lee (South)
Sullivan's Quay
Fr. Mathew Quay
George's Quay
Copley St.
Gas Works Rd.
Proby's Quay
Bishop St.
Cove St.
Drinan St.
Mary St.
Parliament Bridge
White St.
South Terr.
Gas Works
St. Finbarre's Cathedral
Elizabethan Fort
Dunbar St.
Rutland St.
Sawmill
Infirmary Rd.
Hibernian Rd.
Gill Abbey
Abbey St.
Douglas St.
Barrack St.
Industry St.
Old Blackrock Rd.
Nicholas St.
Evergreen St.
Kevin's St.
Tower St.
Friar St.
Langford Row
Southern Rd.
High St.
Bandon Rd.
Desmond Sq.
Mount Carmel
Friars Walk
Quaker Rd.

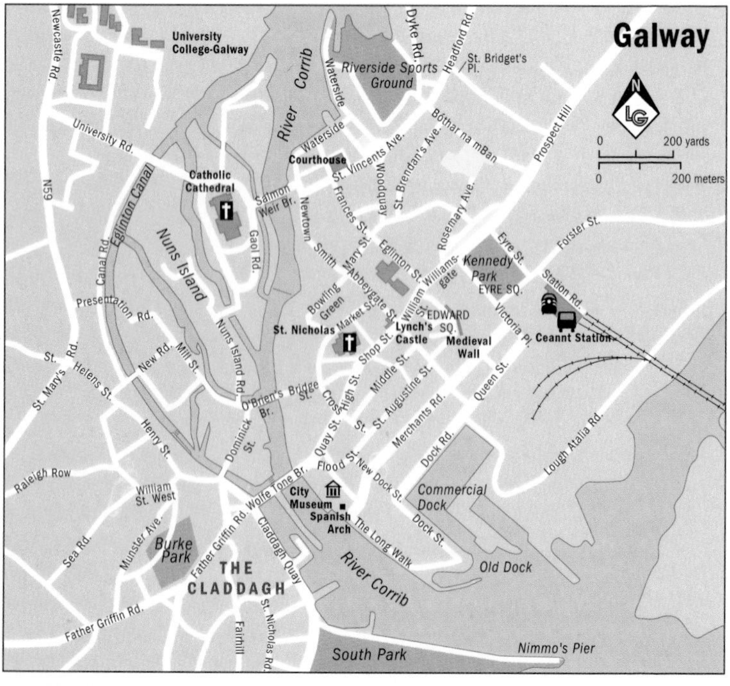

Galway

N
LG
0 200 yards
0 200 meters

Newcastle Rd.
University College-Galway
Dyke Rd.
Headford Rd.
St. Bridget's Pl.
River Corrib
Waterside
Riverside Sports Ground
Bóthar na mBan
Prospect Hill
University Rd.
Courthouse
St. Vincents Ave.
Woodquay
St. Brendan's Ave.
Catholic Cathedral
Salmon Weir Br.
Eglinton Canal
N59
Newtown Smith
St. Frances St.
Rosemary Ave.
Forster St.
Gaol Rd.
Nuns Island
Canal Rd.
Mary St.
Eglinton St.
Kennedy Park
Eyre St.
EYRE SQ.
Williams-gate
William St.
Station Rd.
Abbeygate St.
Bowling Green
Presentation Rd.
Market St.
EDWARD SQ.
Victoria Pl.
St. Nicholas
Lynch's Castle
Medieval Wall
Ceannt Station
Shop St.
St. Mary's Rd.
St. Helens St.
New Rd.
Mill St.
Nuns Island Rd.
Middle St.
St. Augustine St.
Queen St.
O'Brien's Bridge
Br.
St.
High St.
Cross St.
Merchants Rd.
Dock Rd.
Lough Atalia Rd.
Henry St.
Dominick St.
Quay St.
Flood St.
New Dock St.
Raleigh Row
William St. West
Wolfe Tone Br.
City Museum
Commercial Dock
Spanish Arch
Dock St.
Munster Ave.
Sea Rd.
Father Griffin Rd.
Claddagh Quay
The Long Walk
Burke Park
THE CLADDAGH
River Corrib
Old Dock
St. Nicholas Rd.
Fairhill
Nimmo's Pier
South Park

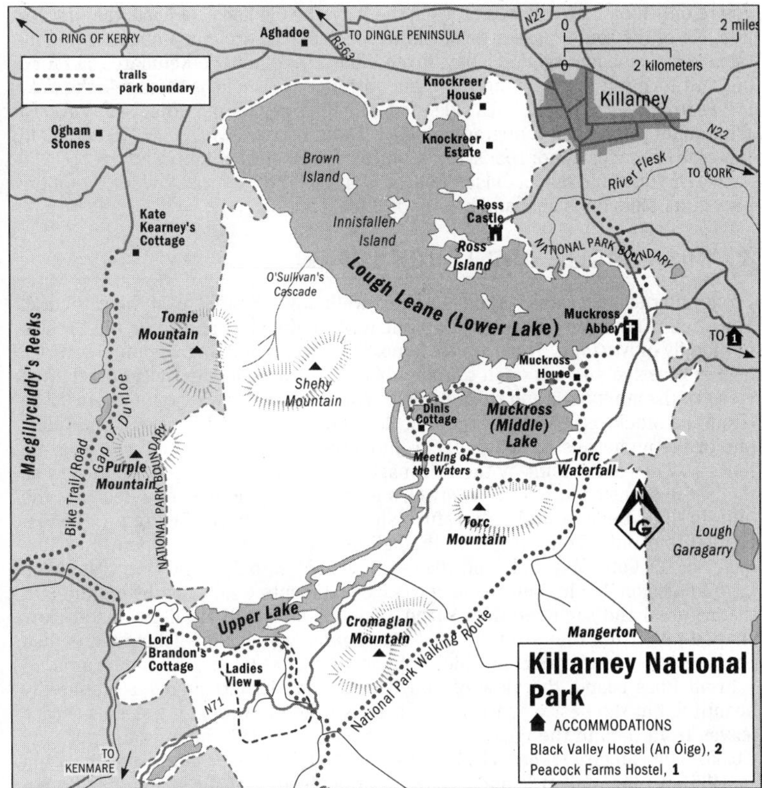

can't cover as much ground, but they have more freedom to climb the off-road trails. Unfortunately for both bikers and hikers, many visitors choose to admire the woods from horse-drawn carriages (€20-30). Unlike bikers and hikers, horses leave behind *cac capall* (Gaelic for the substance whose smell will be your constant companion). The park's size demands a map; as luck would have it, maps are available at the Killarney tourist office or the Park's **Information Centre,** behind Muckross House. (☎31440. Open July-Sept. daily 9am-7pm.)

The park's most popular destinations are **Ross Castle** and **Lough Leane, Muckross House** on **Middle Lake,** and the **Gap of Dunloe,** just west of the park area and bordered on the southwest by **Macgillycuddy's Reeks,** Ireland's highest mountain range. Visits to most of these sights can be managed in several hours or stretched out over a full day, depending on your mode of transport. Hikers and bikers should take the necessary precautions, and maybe a few unnecessary ones just for kicks (see **Camping,** p. 36). As always, watch out for both domestic and foreign crazy drivers.

If you're on foot, the **Gap of Dunloe** (see below) demands more than a casual day excursion. However, biking from Killarney—stopping to explore Muckross and Torc—is an enjoyable way to see a good chunk of the park in one day. If you aren't the type to stomach 14 mi. of cycling, there are several short, well-marked and well-paved walking trails closer to Killarney. The park is also a perfect starting point for those rugged few who plan to walk the 129 mi. **Kerry Way** (see p. 276). If you're only looking to dip your toes in the Way, the **Old Kenmare Road,** the first (or last) leg of the route, passes through the spectacular Torc and Mangerton Mountains and can be managed in a day. From Killarney, follow the Kenmare road for 4 mi. and turn left just beyond the main entrance to Muckross House—the Way leaves from the carpark on this side road. The Killarney tourist office sells a *Kerry Way* guide, which has topographic maps. The *Ordnance Survey* (#78 and 83 in this case) includes minor roads, trails, and archaeological points of interest (€6.60 each). Or you could take a **Guided Walk** (☎ 064 33471) for €7 that covers 2hr. of the park and points out sights and history of the region.

ROSS CASTLE AND LOUGH LEANE

From Killarney, **Knockreer Estate** is a short walk down New St. past the cathedral. The original mansion housed the Catholic Earls of Kenmare and, later, the Grosvenor family of *National Geographic* fame. The current building, built in the 1950s, is unimpressive and not open to the public, but nearby **nature trails** afford great views of the mountains and roaming deer. You can drive or walk out to **Ross Castle** (from the Muckross road turn right on Ross Rd. 2 mi. from Killarney), but taking one of the numerous footpaths from Knockreer (15min.) will be a more scenic journey. The castle, built by the O'Donaghue chieftains in the 14th century, was the last in Munster to fall to Cromwell's army. During the past two decades, the building has been completely refurbished in 15th-century fashion. (☎35851. Guided tour only. Tours begin on the half hour and last 40min. Open June-Aug. daily 9am-6:30pm; May and Sept. 10am-6pm; mid-Mar. to Apr. and Oct. 10am-5pm. Last admission 45min. before closing. €3.80, students €1.60.) Paths continue to the arboreal and secluded **Ross Island,** which is no island at all. A lobster-claw shaped peninsula that stretches out into Lough Leane, Ross Island's greenish pools testify to many years in which copper mining has taken place in the area.

From Ross island, the view of Lough Leane and its mountains is admittedly beautiful, but the best way to see the area is from the water. A **waterbus service** leaves from behind the castle for lake cruises. (☎31068. Summer 5-6 per day. €6.35.) You can hire **rowboats** by the castle (€2.50 per hr.), or take a **motorboat trip** (☎34351) to Innisfallen Island (€3.50), to the Meeting of the Waters via Lough Leane and Muckross Lake (€6.35), or to the Gap of Dunloe via Lough Leane, Muckross Lake, and Upper Lake. (€9.50, return €12. Bikes ride free.)

On Innisfallen Island the stoic remains of **Innisfallen Abbey** remain stoic. The abbey was founded around AD 600 by St. Finian the Leper; then in the Middle Ages it became a university and opened its doors to student rabble. The *Annals of Innisfallen,* now entombed in similarly filthy Oxford, recount world and Irish history. The annals were written in Irish and Latin, circa 1326 by circa 39 monastic scribes. At the abbey's center is a yew tree; yew and oak groves were sacred to the Druids, and resolutely non-Druidic abbeys were often built among and around them. The separate **Augustinian Abbey** is so ruined that even experts in Augustiniology might have a hard time identifying the body.

MUCKROSS AND THE MEETING OF THE WATERS

The crumblings of **Muckross Abbey,** built in 1448, lie 3 mi. south of Killarney on the Kenmare road. The abbey's grounds contain a modern graveyard full of expired locals. (Always open. Free.) From the abbey, signs direct you to **Muckross House,** a massive Victorian manor whose garden blooms brilliantly in early summer. The house, completed in 1843, oozes staid aristocracy and commands a regal view of the lakes and mountains. Its elaborate furnishings and decorations include justifiably angry-looking deer mounted on the walls. Upon first visiting Muckross House, the philosopher George Berkeley proclaimed: "Another Louis XIV may make another Versailles, but only the hand of the Deity can make another Muckross." Outside the house lie the **Muckross Traditional Farms,** a living history museum designed to depict rural life in early 20th-century Kerry. Help costumed demonstrators whip up traditional cuisine and crafts, or just lounge on the lawns. (☎31440. House open July-Aug. daily 9am-7pm; Sept.-Oct. and mid-Mar. to June 9am-6pm; Nov. to mid-Mar. 9am-5:30pm. Farms open June-Oct. 10am-7pm; Mar.-May 10am-6pm. House or farms each €5.10, students €2; joint ticket €7.60/€3.50. Last admission 1hr. before closing.)

From Muckross House, a path leads along the water to the 60 ft. drop of **Torc Waterfall.** The waterfall is also the starting point for several short trails along **Torc Mountain.** Walking among the moss-jacketed trees affords some of the park's best views. It's a 2 mi. stroll in the opposite direction to the **Meeting of the Waters**—walk straight down the front lawn of Muckross House and follow the signs. The paved path is nice, but the dirt trail through the **Yew Woods** is more secluded and not accessible to bikes. The Meeting of the Waters is a quiet spot where channels from the Upper Lough introduce themselves into the Middle, which then offers its watery handshake to the Lower. The weary, however, may be more happy to meet sandwiches and cold drinks at **Dinis Cottage.** (☎31954. Open mid-May to Sept. daily 10:30am-6pm.) Park explorers should note that there's no direct route from the Muckross sights to Ross Castle; those wishing to conquer both in one day must return to Killarney, making for a total trip of 10 mi.

GAP OF DUNLOE

A visit to the Gap of Dunloe is a many-splendored thing—pilgrims can expect both misty mountain vistas and significant caloric expenditure. **Organized treks** to the Gap can be booked from area hostels or the Killarney tourist office. (☎31633; see **Practical Information,** p. 268. About €25 per person.) Such treks, which combine a guided walking tour with a boat trip, shuttle visitors to the foot of the Gap, eliminating the 7 mi. hike from town. Foresighted travelers pack their lunches, though after walking over the Gap and down to **Lord Brandon's Cottage ❶,** a warm meal or a cold pint may be hard to resist. (☎34730. Sandwiches €2.50 and soups €2.20. Open May-Oct. daily 10am-6pm.) From there, trippers meet a boat that takes them across the lake to Ross Castle. (Open June-Sept. daily 9am-6pm.) A bus returns them, at long last, to Killarney. Attempting the Gap on foot using this route, however, is a trek up the long side of the mountain. It is far easier, and potentially less expensive, to attack by bike from the opposite direction. Bring your wheels on the scenic **motorboat** trip from Ross Castle to the head of the Dunloe Gap. (1½hr. €12 per person, €12 for the bike. Book ahead at the Killarney tourist office or hostels.) From Lord Brandon's Cottage, turn left over the stone bridge and continue for 2 mi. to the hostel and church. Hang a right onto a hairpin-turn-laden road that winds up to the top of the Gap (1½ mi.). What follows is a well-deserved 7 mi. downhill coast through the park's most magical scenery.

At the foot of the Gap, you'll pass **Kate Kearney's Cottage ❷.** Kate was an independent mountain-dwelling woman famous for brewing and serving a near-poisonous *poitín* (see **Love Poitín #9,** p. 416). Her former home is now a pub and restaurant that sucks in droves of tourists. (☎44146. Sandwiches €2.30-7; hot dishes €6.35-7.60. Food served 9am-9pm. Summertime trad W, F, and Sa.) The 8 mi. ride back to Killarney passes the entirely ruined **Dunloe Castle,** an Anglo-Norman stronghold demolished by Cromwell's armies. You may also notice a set of *ogham* stones from about AD 300. To return home to Killarney, click your heels, bear right after Kate's, turn left on the road to Fossa, and turn right on the Killorglin road.

RING OF KERRY AND THE KERRY WAY

The term **"Ring of Kerry"** is generally used to describe the entire Iveragh Peninsula, but it more correctly refers to a particular set of roads: N71 from Kenmare to Killarney, R562 from Killarney to Killorglin, and the long loop of N70 west and back to Kenmare. If you don't like the captivity of the prepackaged private bus tours that run out of Killarney, **Bus Éireann** offers a regular summer circuit through all the major towns on the Ring (☎064 30011; mid-June to Aug., 2 per day). Buses travel around the Ring counterclockwise, from Killarney to Killorglin, along Dingle Bay, east by the Kenmare River, and north from Sneem back to Killarney. Another bus runs year-round in the mornings, traveling clockwise from Waterville back to Killarney (1 per day). **Bikers** may find themselves jammed between buses and cliffs on the narrow, bumpy roads, though traffic can often be avoided by doing the Ring clockwise. Additionally, cycling clockwise lets you face the eye-candy, rather than leaving it behind. A new bike route, which avoids most of the main roads and has better views, is signposted. Drivers must choose between lurching behind large tour buses and meeting them face-to-face on narrow roads.

Those wishing to avoid the tour bus superhighway that is the Ring of Kerry road need not write off the Iveragh Peninsula entirely; just a step from the N70, solitude and superior scenery reward walkers along **The Kerry Way.** This well-planned route traverses a wide variety of terrain, from rugged inland expanses to soaring coastal cliffs. Described as an "inner" ring of Kerry, the Way brings walkers above the road, to higher ground and better views. Its 135 mi. route follows a smorgasbord of paths—from pastures to old "butter roads," to ancient thoroughfares between early Christian settlements—and crosses the main road just often enough to make daytrips convenient from almost anywhere on the Ring. Look for the wooden posts marked with a yellow walking man and you won't be far off. Those who like their landscapes stark and a little rough around the edges will enjoy the dramatic stretch from Kenmare through Killarney and northwest to Glenbeigh. An especially inspiring stretch of the Way runs between Waterville and Caherdaniel, filled with views known to elicit a tear or two from even the gruffest pint-puller.

KILLORGLIN (CILL ORGLAN) ☎066

Killorglin lounges along the banks of the River Larne, 13 mi. west of Killarney and in the shadow of Iveragh's mountainous spine. Tourists tend to pass through on their way west to the showier scenery, but what the town lacks in sights it more than makes up for with its annual festival dedicated to he-goats. In mid-August, the ancient **Puck Fair** transforms the town, as thousands of visitors flock in for three riotous days culminating in the coronation of a large mountain goat as King Puck. Pubs stay open until 3am, then close for an hour so publicans can rest their pint-pulling arms. Be aware that the town's hostel and B&Bs book up as early as a year in advance of the revelry; aspiring Pucksters should call ahead.

ORIENTATION AND PRACTICAL INFORMATION. The Ring of Kerry **bus** from Killarney (June-Sept. 2 per day, €4.25) stops in Killorglin on Mill Rd., just down from the tourist office, and goes on to Cahersiveen (50min., €6.35), Waterville (1¼hr., €7.50), and Sneem (3hr., €8.40). An eastbound Cahersiveen bus goes to Killarney (July-Aug. M-Sa 4-6 per day; Sept.-June M-Sa 2-4 per day). Killorglin's **Main St.** runs up from the river and widens into **the Square.** At the top of the Square and to the right, **Upper Bridge St.** climbs to the tourist office and intersects **Iveragh Rd.** For a **taxi,** call **Killorglin Cabs** (☎087 274 0269). **O'Shea's,** at the bottom of Main St., **rents bikes.** (☎976 1919. €10 per day, €50 per wk. Open M-Sa 9am-6pm.) The spiffy **tourist office** hands out information. (☎976 1451. Open July-Aug. M-Sa 9am-5:30pm; Sept.-June W 10am-3:30pm, Tu and F 10am-5pm.) **AIB,** on Main St., has an

ATM. (☎976 1134. Open M-F 10am-4pm, Tu until 5pm.) Clean up at **Laune Dry Cleaners and Launderette,** Upper Bridge St. (€7 per load. Open M-Sa 9am-6pm; Oct.-June closes W at 1pm.) **Mulvihill Pharmacy** is halfway up Main St. (☎976 1115. Open M-Sa 9am-6:30pm. After-hours call ☎976 1387.) Get 50min. of fast, free **Internet access** at the **library,** set back from Iveragh Rd. near the tourist office. (Open Tu-Sa 10:30am-1:30pm and 2:30-5:30pm.) The **post office** is a bit further down on Iveragh Rd. (☎976 1101. Open M-F 9am-1pm and 2-5:30pm, Sa 10am-1pm.)

ACCOMMODATIONS, FOOD, AND PUBS. The bright and bountiful **Laune Valley Farm Hostel (IHH) ❶,** 1¼ mi. from town off the Tralee road, beds guests alongside its more permanent population of cows, chickens, dogs, and ducks. The farm-fresh milk and eggs for sale make whipping up scrambled eggs for breakfast too tempting to resist. (☎976 1488. Wheelchair-accessible. Dorms €12-14; doubles €31-35.60. **Camping** €5 per person.) **Orglan House B&B ❸,** a 5min. walk from town down the Killarney road, has grand views from immaculate rooms and will relieve you from brown bread delirium with a delicious, individually tailored breakfast—even the elusive pancake (scarce in Ireland) is available. (☎976 1540. Singles €36; doubles €46-54.) **Laune Bridge House B&B ❸** is a few doors closer to town than Orglan House. (☎976 1161. Singles €35; doubles €50-60.) Tent up at **West's Caravan and Camping Park ❶,** 1 mi. east of town on the Killarney road in the shadow of **Carrantoohill,** Ireland's tallest peak. Fishing, table tennis, and a tennis court are available for use. (☎976 1240. Open Easter to mid-Oct. Adult and tent €4.50; car, tent, and 2-adults €13.50. 2 night mobile home rental €75. Showers €2. Laundry €4.)

SuperValu serves up deli sandwiches in the Square. (☎976 1117. Open M-Sa 9am-9pm.) An organic cornucopia is available at **Broadbery's Irish Food Hall ❷,** a gourmet deli/restaurant also in the Square. Enjoy delicious platters of local farm cheese, smoked wild salmon, homemade liver and pork pate, and bread baked on the spot. (☎976 2888. Sandwiches €5; meals €7-9. Open M-Sa 9am-10pm.) **Bunker's ❷,** across from the tourist office, covers all the bases—it's a restaurant and coffee-shop with a pub next door and takeaway across the street. (☎976 1381. Mains €7-12. Open daily 9:30am-10:30pm; takeaway until late.) On Mill Rd., across from the tourist office and above the fast food joint on the corner, **Harmony** fries up excellent Chinese food ❷. (☎976 2588. Lunch specials €5.80-8.50; dinners €9-14. Open M-F noon-2pm and 5pm-midnight, Sa-Su 3:30pm-midnight.) Frugality comes at the price of ambience at the **Starlite Diner ❷,** the Square. (☎976 1296. Burgers €4.50; all-day breakfast €7.50. Open daily 9:30am-11pm.) Locals meet their Guinness needs at the **Old Forge,** a lively stone pub on Main St. (☎976 1231. Trad some nights in summer, disco Th-Sa.) An older, more subdued crowd watches football at the **Laune Bar,** Lower Main St., on the water. The Laune Rangers football club began here in 1888. (☎976 1158. Trad Th.) DJs, cocktails, and karaoke (F night) lure youngsters to **The Shamrock,** Main St. (☎976 2277).

SIGHTS AND ACTIVITIES. If you're visiting Killorglin outside the three-day reign of King Puck, you can catch up on what you missed at the **The Basement Museum,** just past the church down Mill Rd. Though the exhibits primarily focus on the festival, a private collection of circus posters can also be found. (☎976 1353. Open noon-9pm, or thereabouts.) If it's wildlife you're looking for, take a trip to the **Haven World of Reptiles,** self-proclaimed as "One of Europe's Largest Reptile Houses." Just off the Square on Langford St., the zoo has an interesting variety of scaly creatures, including transforming axolotls. (☎979 0844. Open June-Sept. M-Sa 10am-6pm, Su 1-6pm; Oct.-May closed M. €7.50, children €6.50.) Five miles from town off the Killarney road, **Ballymalis Castle** rests on its 16th-century laurel, dozing on the banks of the Laune in view of Macgillycuddy's Reeks. **Cromane Beach** lies 4 mi. west of Killorglin; follow the N70 (toward Glenbeigh) and branch off to the right at the signs. **Cappanalea Outdoor Education Centre,** 7 mi. to the southwest off the Ring of Kerry road, offers canoeing, rock-climbing, windsurfing, sailing, hill-walking, and fishing. (☎976 9244. Open daily 10am-5pm. Day course with any 2 activities €33, teenagers €20; any 1 activity just €17/€10. Individual booking July-Aug. only; group booking with a minimum of 6 people is available all year.)

CAHERSIVEEN (CATHAIR SAIDBHIN) ☎066

Best known in Ireland as the birthplace of patriot Daniel O'Connell (see **Rebellion,** p. 59), Cahersiveen (CAH-her-sah-veen) serves as a useful base for exploring nearby archaeological sites and for short trips to Valentia Island and the Skelligs. With a cozy hostel, excellent restaurant, Internet cafe, and plenty of local pub charm, this little hamlet leads many to pause on their way around the Ring.

TRANSPORTATION AND PRACTICAL INFORMATION. The Ring of Kerry **bus** stops in front of Banks Store on Main St. (mid-June to Aug., 2 per day) and continues on to Killarney (2½hr., €11.50) via Waterville (25min., €4), Caherdaniel (1hr., €4.25), and Sneem (1½hr., €8). Another bus heads directly east to Killarney (M-Sa 1 per day, in the morning, all year). The town revolves around one street, the N70 **Ring of Kerry Rd.,** which takes on the names **Church, Main, West Main,** and **New St.** as it passes through. **Casey's,** on Main St., **rents bikes.** (☎947 2474. €10 per day, €50 per wk.; helmet and lock included. Open July-Aug. M-Sa 9am-6pm, Su 10:30am-12:30pm; Sept.-June M-Sa 9am-6pm and by appointment.) Cahersiveen's **tourist office** is across from the bus stop, next to the post office. (☎947 2589. Open June to mid-Sept. M-F 9:30am-1pm and 2-5:30pm.) A map and walking guide to the **Heritage Trail** (€1.30) is sold at the Barracks Heritage Centre (see **Sights,** below). Main St. is home to an **AIB** with an **ATM.** (☎947 2022. Open M 10am-5pm, Tu-F 10am-4pm.) **Internet access** is free at the **library** on Main St. Anyone over 18 is allowed two 50min. sessions a week. (☎947 2287. Open Tu-Sa 10:30am-1:30pm and 2:30-5pm.) Fast computers and an extensive **video game collection** are available at the island-themed **Java Cybercafe,** upstairs on West Main St. (☎947 2116. Internet €3 per 20min., €7 per hr. Open July-Aug. M-Sa 11am-9pm, Su 2-6pm; Sept.-May M-W, F-Sa 11am-8pm, Th 5-8pm, Su 2-6pm.) The **post office** is on Main St. (☎947 2010. Open M-F 9:30am-1pm and 2-5:30pm, Sa 9:30am-1pm.)

ACCOMMODATIONS, FOOD, AND PUBS. The **Sive Hostel (IHH) ❶,** 15 East End, Main St., has a welcoming and well-informed staff, comfortable beds, and a third-floor balcony. For those lacking the private transport necessary to reach Portmagee, from which most of the ferries to the **Skellig Islands** leave, the hostel can also arrange boat trips to the Skelligs for just €32. (☎947 2717. Sheets €0.65. Laundry €5.10. Dorms €10.50; doubles €25-32. **Camping** €5 per person.) Next to the post office, **O'Shea's B&B ❸** has comfortable rooms, some with impressive castle and mountain views. (☎947 2402. Vegetarian breakfast option. Singles €25-30; doubles €50.) Campers revel in **Mannix Point Caravan and Camping Park ❶,** at the west end of town. The site adjoins a nature reserve and faces the romantic ruins of Ballycarbery Castle across the water. The common area is complete with turf fire and antique piano. (☎947 2806. Open mid-Mar. to Oct. €5 per person. Showers €1. Laundry €2 wash, dry €2.)

Centra sells colossal scones and other necessities. (☎947 2583. Open M-F 8am-10pm, Sa-Su 8am-9:30pm.) The freshest seafood available can be found at **QC's Chargrill Bar & Restaurant ❹,** Main St. The colorful, modern restaurant is a bit pricey, but the fish and steaks grilled on its unique Basque-style barbecue are worth the price. The delicious fresh crab claws, courtesy of the chef's father, who owns the local fish shop, are served with garlic and chilis. (☎947 2244. Mains €15-

22. Food served 12:30-3pm and 6-9:30pm.) Casual **Cupán Eile ❷,** Main St., cooks up filling sandwiches and breakfasts (€4-7); vegetarian options available. (☎947 3200. Mains €5-7. Open M-F 9am-6pm, Sa 9am-5pm.) For classic dishes with international flair, try the **Red Rose ❸,** Church St. (☎947 2293. Day menu €6-9, served W-M 12:30-6pm. Evening menu €11.50-16.50, served daily 6-9:30pm.)

The pubs on Main St. harken back to the tradition of the early 20th century, when establishments served as both watering holes and the proprietor's "main" business, be it general store, blacksmith, or leather shop. **Mike Murt's** (☎947 2396) brims with town characters and ancient tools. Prepare to tell your life story to the pint-clutching ensemble. The **Anchor Bar** (☎947 2049), toward the west end of Main St., sells Guinness alongside fishing tackle. Come after 10pm and take your drink into the kitchen for friendly conversation. Locals speak lovingly of **Sceilig Rock** (☎947 2305), where pop and trad take turns shaking the wooden floor. Modernity has hit **Fertha Bar** (☎947 2023), where trendy rock bands frequently appear on weekends—Fridays are a good bet. **The Shebeen** (☎947 2361) has trad and set dancing on Thursdays. And youth from around the Ring head to **The Harp Nightclub.** (☎947 2436. Open F-Sa until 3am, and sometimes Su in the summer. Cover €7.)

SIGHTS AND FESTIVALS. O'Connell's Church in Cahersiveen is the only house o' worship in Ireland named for a layperson. "The Liberator" and other high points of Irish history are celebrated at the **Old Barracks Heritage Centre,** a block down Bridge St. (☎947 2777. Open May to mid-Sept. M-Sa 10am-5pm, Su 1-5pm. €4, students and seniors €3.50, families €9.) Though the center's exhibits are well done and could have you reading all day long about the rise and fall of the town's fishing industry, the building itself may be of more interest—its bizarre architecture has inspired a local rumor that confused officials had accidentally built a colonial outpost, while a proper barracks was erected somewhere in India.

Past the barracks and across the bridge, a wealth of fortifications huddle together. Turn left past the bridge, and left again off the main road to reach the ruined 15th-century **Ballycarbery Castle,** once owned by O'Connell's ancestors. Two hundred yards past the castle turnoff stand a pair of Ireland's best-preserved stone forts. You can walk atop the 10 ft. thick walls of **Cahergall Fort,** or visit the small stone dwellings of **Leacanabuaile Fort,** the best-preserved of Ireland's 40,000 ring forts. A few minutes' walk beyond the second fort is **Cuas Crom Beach,** known for its fine swimming. If you continue on past the turnoff to Cuas Crom and take the next left, you'll arrive at **White Strand Beach,** another popular swimming area. Turn right after passing over the bridge and you will be on your way to **Knocknadobar Mt.,** which holds 14 stations of the cross and a holy well at its base. The map and the manager at the Sive Hostel can help plot the way. During the first weekend in August, Cahersiveen hosts a **Celtic Music Weekend,** which features street entertainment, fireworks, pub sessions, and numerous free concerts.

VALENTIA ISLAND (DAIRBHRE) ☎066

A welcome escape for travelers sick of dodging tour buses and those that ride them, Valentia Island's removed location offers stunning views of the mountains on the mainland. The island's tranquility was compromised over a century ago with the installation of the first transatlantic cable, which connected Valentia to Newfoundland; important characters from all over the world, including Queen Victoria, came to test it out. Things have since died down, and the island's tiny, winding roads are perfect for biking or hiking. The locals' reputation for being amusingly off the mark keeps the *craic* flowing, in spite of its isolated locale. Bridge and ferry connections to the mainland are at opposite ends of the island, but there's no public transit to or on Valentia.

GREEN ROOTS It seems that *homo sapiens* isn't the only species with an ancestral stake in the Emerald Isle. In 1992, Swiss geologist Ivan Stossel discovered a track of small footprints on the rocky shore of Valentia Island. After analyzing layers of volcanic ash in the groove-like prints, scientists concluded that they were stamped out 385 million years ago, making them the oldest fossilized footprints in the Northern Hemisphere. They are believed to be those of a "Devonian tetrapod," a creature that predates the dinosaurs. The prints are currently unmarked and unprotected, but the government is taking steps to preserve this and other important archaeological sites. Until then, fossil fanatics can ask locals for directions.

TRANSPORTATION AND PRACTICAL INFORMATION. A comically short **car ferry** trip departs during the summer from **Reenard Point,** 3 mi. west of Cahersiveen, just off the Ring of Kerry road. **Taxis** from Cahersiveen cost about €7. The ferry drops passengers at **Knightstown,** the island's population center. (☎947 6141. Ferries depart every 8min. May-Oct. M-Sa 8:15am-10pm, Su 9am-10pm; cars €7 return, pedestrians €2, cyclists €3.) Most cars are headed for the pier, making thumbing it pretty easy, but *Let's Go* never recommends hitchhiking. The bridge connecting Valentia to the mainland starts at **Portmagee,** 10 mi. west of Cahersiveen. To get to Portmagee, head south from Cahersiveen or north from Waterville, then west on R565. Hitching in this area is difficult and not recommended by *Let's Go*. Enthusiastic bikers can follow the gorgeous **Skellig Ring,** an offshoot of the Ring of Kerry that branches from Waterville and runs along the coast through Ballinskelligs and Portmagee, rejoining the main Ring road at Cahersiveen. For a **taxi** on the island, call Teddy (☎947 6183 or 087 264 8646).

ACCOMMODATIONS AND FOOD. Valentia has a surprising variety of budget accommodations in and around Knightstown, including the lovely **Coombe Bank House ❷.** This spacious hostel and B&B occupies a grand stone house set among the farm fields, about a 15min. walk from the ferry landing. To get there, bear right at the pier, walk through town on the main street, and head right where the road forks, following the signs for the stone quarry and keeping the ocean on your right. Take your first left when you see the sign for Coombe Bank; the large house is set back from the road, surrounded by tall evergreens. (☎947 6111. Call ahead in the evening as the house is often locked until the owner returns home around 5pm. Continental breakfast €4. Free laundry. Dorms €16; family rooms available. B&B €25 per person, without breakfast €20.) The large **Royal Pier Hostel (IHH) ❷** in Knightstown once hosted Queen Victoria, and its stately sitting room and dining area still exude grandeur. (☎947 6144. Wash and dry €8. Dorms €15; singles €20, with breakfast €30.) A 30min. walk down the main road from Knightstown lies tiny **Chapeltown,** home to the **Ring Lyne Hostel and B&B ❶,** which offers basic double and triple rooms above a **restaurant** that serves meals between noon and 10pm (€6.50-10), and a pub. (☎947 6103. Dorms €14; B&B €25-27.) Back in Knightstown, halfway up the main street and then down to the right on Peter St. (follow the brown signs depicting a hut and tree), the **Valentia Island Youth Hostel (An Óige/HI) ❶** is housed in an old coast guard station overlooking the bay. Don't let its rough exterior fool you; the neat dorms are a bargain. Unfortunately, new arrivals are left waiting for the manager who also doesn't return home until around 5pm. (☎947 6154. Sheets €1.50. Open June-Sept. Dorms €13.) **Altazamuth House ❸,** to the left on Peter St., has pretty bedrooms, a sunny breakfast room, and a brand-new sunroom—should the sun ever dare show its face in Ireland. (☎947 6300. Open Apr.-Oct. **Bike rental** €10 per day. €25 per person.)

Limited supplies are available at the **store** a block up from the water to your left along the main street. (Open M-Sa 9am-8pm, Su 9:30am-2pm.) **Knightstown Coffee ❷** is a pleasant cafe with outdoor tables and excellent espresso, soup, and scrumptious desserts. It's on your right as you walk up the main street. (☎947 6373. Sandwiches €2.50-6.35. Open Easter-Sept. daily noon-6pm.) **Boston's,** on the main road out of Knightstown, serves quality pub dishes. (☎947 6140. Specials €7.70; sandwiches €2.50-6.50. Food served daily noon-8pm.) Two new restaurants next to Boston's should be open for the 2003 summer season. The **pub** attached to the Royal Pier has pub grub, a pool table, and comfortable chairs that look out onto the harbor. (☎947 6144. Meals €7-15. Food served noon-9pm.)

SIGHTS AND ACTIVITIES. The road from town to the **old slate quarry,** which runs past the turnoff to the Coombe Bank House, offers Valentia's best views across Dingle Bay. Try to arrive at the quarry (a 1hr. hike from Knightstown) just before sunset. Slate from this massive dig roofed the British Parliament, and the hollowed-out cliffside now houses a "sacred grotto." At the opposite end of the island, hike up to **Bray Head,** where the ruins of a Napoleonic lookout tower offer great views of the Skelligs. On the way there from Knightstown you'll pass the turnoff for **Glanleam Subtropical Gardens,** which feature such attractions as the 50 ft. tall Chilean Fire Bush. (☎947 6176. Open daily 11am-5pm. €4, students €2.50.)

The Royal Pier hostel will arrange **sea angling** for €25 per hour and **boat trips** for €35 per person. (☎947 6144 or call boatman Owen Walsh directly at ☎947 6327 or 087 283 3522.) **Moriarty's Dive Center** (☎947 6204), just down from the pier, offers a one week certification course Easter to October, all equipment included (€380 per person), and **evening harbor boat trips** from July to August for just €15.

WATERVILLE (AN COIREAN) ☎066

Wedged between crashing Atlantic waves and the quiet waters of Lough Cussane, Waterville was built as a telecommunications portal by the English, who then inundated it every summer as they came to vacation on its scenic shores. Nowadays, Waterville's human traffic comes from the tour bus hordes who are released for a seaside lunch before rumbling on to Sneem for sweater shopping. Those who remain might take a surf lesson or splurge on a meal at one of the peninsula's best restaurants. The meditative traveler is left to amble along the isolated shore, which Charlie Chaplin once treasured for the liberating anonymity it granted him.

TRANSPORTATION AND PRACTICAL INFORMATION. The Ring of Kerry **bus** stops in front of the Bay View Hotel on Main St. (June to mid-Sept. 2 per day), with service to Caherdaniel (20min., €2.80), Sneem (50min., €5.45), and Killarney (2hr., €11.50). The eastbound **Bus Éireann** travels to Cahersiveen in the morning once per day, year round, while en route to Killarney. The **tourist office** is on the beach, across from the Butler Arms Hotel. (☎947 4646. Open June-Sept. M-Sa 10am-6pm.) There is no **ATM** in town, but the **Bank of Ireland** opens a sub-office facing the water once a week. (Open W 10:45am-1pm.) A small **pharmacy** resides in the town center. (☎947 4141. Open M-Sa 9:30am-6pm, and Su 9am-1pm for newspaper and candy only.) **Web connections** are available at the new **Internet Cafe** on the southern end of town, next to the Peter's Place hostel. (☎947 8992. Open June-Sept. daily 9:30am-10pm. €3 per 30min.) The **post office** is just across from the tourist office. (☎947 4147. Open M-F 9am-2pm and 3-5:30pm, Sa 9am-1pm.)

ACCOMMODATIONS, FOOD, AND PUBS. B&Bs line the length of Main St. (prices run €25-32), but the only hostel in Waterville is **Peter's Place ❶.** On the southern end of town facing the water, cheap rates and a candlelit sitting

THE BIG SPLURGE

SHEILIN SEAFOOD RESTAURANT

The warm, family-run **Sheilin Seafood Restaurant** in **Waterville** serves unbelievably fresh fruits from the sea with exquisite taste and simplicity. Fresh local lobster, salmon, scallops, and crab are featured on the menu nightly, and are prepared in unpretentious fashion by owner/chef Marie Courtney. The perfect meal, as recommended by Ms. Courtney herself, would begin with the avocado and crab starter (€7), served hot or cold, followed by the inventive and tasty soup o' fish–chock full of mussels, salmon, squid, and cockles (€4). For a main, the black sole, simply grilled and buttered and served with fresh vegetables, is the house specialty (€17). Finally, the delectable blackberry tart, made from freshly picked berries (seasonal from Aug.-Nov.), makes for a scrumptious dessert. The fine seafood, friendly atmosphere, and creative menu at Sheilin's truly speaks for itself and is well worth the price. Your taste buds won't believe they're still in Ireland.

Sheilin's Seafood Restaurant and Wine Bar, Waterville (☎947 4231), just down from the Centra and P. Murphy's grocery store. Dinner nightly 6:30-9:30pm. Book in advance July-Aug., especially Th-Sa. Call ahead in winter. MC/V.

room make up for stiff mattresses and a little bathroom. Inquire with Peter about **work opportunities** available between March and October. (☎947 4608. **Skellig boat trips** €35. Dorms €10; doubles €12.50. **Camping** €5.) Next to the tourist office, luxurious, long-term lodgings can be found at **The Huntsman ❷**, which rents deluxe apartments overlooking the sea, each with its own sauna, jacuzzi, and fireplace. If you're staying a few days with a couple of friends, this is your best option. (☎947 4124. Sleeps 4 people. €650 per wk. Book in advance.)

Between **Centra** (☎947 4257; open May-Sept. 7am-11pm, Oct.-Apr. 8am-9:30pm) and the neighboring **P. Murphy's** (☎947 4253; open June-Sept. 7:30am-11pm, Oct.-May 7:30am-10pm), all your grocery needs will be met. **The Chedean ❷,** across from the Butler Arms Hotel, has small town ambience and delicious home-baking. Peruse the wacky selection of secondhand books on sale for charity (€2) and the Skellig-inspired puffin paintings (€20-65) over a slice of frosted coffee cake or fresh quiche. (☎947 4966. Food €2.50-6. Open late Apr.-Oct. 10am-6pm.) Across the street from the post office, choose from the selection of takeaway at the **Beach Cove Cafe ❶;** there are several tables inside, but it's best to take your food down to the water, weather permitting. (☎947 4733. Pizza, burgers, and sandwiches €2-5. Open M-Th 10am-11pm, F-Su 9:30am-1am.) Gaelic football legend Mick O'Dwyer lends his name to **O'Dwyer's: The Villa Restaurant & Pub ❷,** at the corner of Main St. and the Ring of Kerry Rd. Enjoy a pint or some homemade cottage pie (€6.75) with the local crowd. (☎947 4248. Meals €6.50-10. Food served daily noon-4pm and 6-9pm.) Mick also runs the **Piper 2000** nightclub at the Strand Hotel down the road. (☎947 4436. Open June-Sept. W and Sa-Su. Cover €7.) **The Bay View Hotel** pours pints in two bars and throws a Friday night disco in July and August. (☎947 4122. Cover €7.) On Main St., the **Lobster Bar and Restaurant** (☎947 4629 or 947 4183) attracts tourists with a Guinness-grasping lobster on its sign and a variety of live music and events including trad, karaoke, and theme nights—check what's happening with the tourist office. **The Fishermen's Bar** (☎947 4144) once poured pints for the Little Tramp. No live music, but serves food daily noon-3pm and 6-8:30pm.

SIGHTS AND ACTIVITIES. Lough Currane's waters lie about 2 mi. inland from town; keeping the ocean on your right, follow the lake road then turn left, or just head inland along the smaller streets. Locals claim that a submerged castle can be seen in times of low water, but outsiders seem to have better luck with the ruins of a monastery on Church

Island. **Quad Safari** on Main St. leads adventurers around the mountains and lakes on mountain bikes and all-terrain 4-wheelers. (☎947 4465; www.actionadventurecentre.com. 3hr. guided bike trek €55.) These folks also arrange bookings for **horseback riding** (€25 per hr.), **Skellig jaunts** (€32), and **"war games"** (€50 per 4hr.). If it's **fishing** you crave, head to the folks at the **Tackle Shop** down Main St., who can outfit you with lures, rods, boots, and nets. (☎947 4433. Open mid-Jan. to Oct. daily 9am-7pm.) For lake and sea angling **boats for hire** and **salmon & seatrout fishing** opportunities, contact John Murphy (☎947 5257 or 086 399 1074). Perhaps the waves are calling your name; if you wanna learn how to catch one, try the **Surf School** next to Peter's Place, in the same spot as the new Internet cafe. They use a gentle break at the other end of Ballinskelligs Bay on the sandy **Reena Rua Beach,** named for the red grass that grows along the dunes, to teach beginner lessons. (2hr. lesson €30. Open daily 9:30am-9pm.)

The Irish-speaking hamlet of **Ballinskelligs,** across the bay from Waterville, probably isn't worth a special trip. But if you're there to catch a Skellig-bound boat or passing through by bike or car on the scenic and bus-free **Skellig Ring,** check out the ruins of **Ballinskelligs Monastery,** near the pier. The monks of Skellig Michael (see **The Skelligs,** below) retreated here after 11th-century storms made journeys to the island increasingly treacherous. **Prior House Youth Hostel (An Óige/HI)** ❶ offers basic hostel accommodations, a convenient general store, and close proximity to **Ballinskelligs Beach.** (☎947 9229. Store open 9am-9pm. Open Apr.-Sept. Dorms €8-10.) Two miles south of Ballinskelligs, the dead-end road to **Bolus Head** affords great views of the Skelligs and St. Finan's Bay. As it heads around the bay through the lovely area known as **The Glen,** the Skellig Ring passes popular **surfing spots** and climbs to a summit that's straight vista-licious.

THE SKELLIG ROCKS ☎066

About 8 mi. off the shore of the Iveragh Peninsula, the stunning Skellig Rocks rise abruptly from the sea. More than just masses of natural rubble, these islands awe visitors who, like George Bernard Shaw, often find them "not of this world, but a place you dream of." While the multitudes rush around the Ring of Kerry, those who detour to the Skelligs are rewarded with an encounter unforgettable for bird-lovers and the ornithologically indifferent alike. As **Little Skellig** comes into view, the jagged rock pinnacles appear snow-capped; increased proximity reveals that they are actually covered with 24,000 pairs of crooning gannets—the largest such community in Europe. Boats dock at the larger **Skellig Michael,** where daytrippers have 2-3hr. to picnic, explore, and cavort with hundreds of peculiar puffins and nearby seals. Climb the vertigo-inducing 630 stone steps past kittiwakes, petrels, and many more gannets and puffins, to reach an ancient **monastic settlement.** Sixth-century Christian monks carved out an austere community along the craggy faces of the 714 ft. high rock to escape the secular scourges of the mainland. Their still-intact beehive-like dwellings are fascinatingly explained by guides from *Dúchas*, the Irish Heritage service, though the dark interiors and stark surroundings alone speak eloquently of the monks' severe spiritual path. There is no toilet or shelter on the rock, and the Ministry of Tourism does not recommend the trip for young children, the elderly, or those who suffer from serious medical conditions.

The fantastic and sometimes soggy **ferry voyage** takes about 1hr. (depending on conditions, point of departure, and boat) and costs €32-35. Most boats depart around 10am from Portmagee, the straightest shot out to the Skelligs, but some pick up passengers beforehand from Reenard Point and Valentia Island. Many boats return to the dock by around 3pm. The Sive hostel and the campsite in **Cahersiveen** (see p. 278), as well as Peter's Place in **Waterville** (see p. 281), will arrange trips that include a ride to the dock for no extra cost. Joe

Roddy and Sons (☎947 4268 or 087 284 4460) and Sean Feehan (☎947 9182) depart from **Ballinskelligs;** Michael O'Sullivan (☎947 4255) and Mr. Casey (☎947 2437 or 087 239 5470) leave from **Portmagee.** Seanie Murphy picks up passengers in **Reenard** and Portmagee (☎947 6214 or 087 236 2344). Roddy and O'Sullivan will pick you up from Waterville, and Casey will collect you from Cahersiveen. Ferries run from April to October, depending on the weather; call ahead for reservations and to confirm departures.

The grass-roofed **Skellig Experience Visitors Centre** is just across the Portmagee Bridge on Valentia Island. Videos and models engulf visitors in virtual Skellig; for an extra (steep) charge you can sail from the center to the islands themselves, although the boats do not dock. The video is a relaxing diversion, provided you ignore its dramatic rhetorical questions. (☎947 6306 or 947 9413. Open July-Aug. daily 9:30am-6:15pm; Apr.-June and Sept. 10am-6pm. €5.50, students with ID and seniors €4; with cruise €25/€20.)

CAHERDANIEL (CATHAIR DONAL) ☎066

There's little to attract the Ring's droves of travel coaches to Caherdaniel. However, the hamlet (that is, two pubs, a grocer, a restaurant, and a takeaway) does lie near **Derrynane National Park,** which contains the ancestral home of patriot Daniel O'Connell (see **Rebellion,** p. 59), and miles of beaches ringed by sparkling dunes.

TRANSPORTATION AND PRACTICAL INFORMATION. The Ring of Kerry **bus** stops in Caherdaniel twice a day at the junction of the Ring of Kerry Rd. and Main St., picking up passengers for Sneem (30min., June-Sept. 2 per day, €4) and Killarney (1½hr., June-Sept. 2 per day, €9.30). The eastbound buses come through once a day in the morning all year, heading to Waterville, Cahersiveen, and Killarney. The **tourist office** is 1 mi. east of town at the Wave Crest Camping Park. (Open mid-Mar. to Oct. daily 8am-10pm.)

ACCOMMODATIONS, FOOD, AND PUBS. Guests have the run of the house at **The Travelers Rest Hostel ❶,** across from the gas station near the crossroads. A relaxed sitting room with a fireplace and small dorms makes this hostel look and feel more like a B&B. (☎947 5175. Continental breakfast €4. Dorms €12; private rooms €15 per person.) Just down from the Blind Piper Pub & Restaurant (see below), roomy accommodation awaits weary trekkers at the **Kerry Way B&B ❸.** The managers can also arrange **diving trips** for €45. (☎947 5277. All rooms with bath. €25 per person.) Campers perch over the beach 1 mi. east of town on the Ring of Kerry Rd. at **Wave Crest Camping Park ❶.** The well-stocked shop and self-service laundry are handy, even for non-campers. (☎947 5188. Laundry €5 per load. Shop open 8am-10pm. Site open mid-Mar. to Oct. and off-season by arrangement. €5 per person including tent. Showers €1.)

Caherdaniel's grocery and pint needs are met at **Freddy's Bar and Grocery** on the main corner. (☎947 5400. Grocery open daily 9am-8pm or thereabouts; pub has standard hours.) The **Courthouse Restaurant ❷** serves sit-down and takeaway Irish food with homespun charm. (☎087 928 1179. Sandwiches under €2.50; takeaway under €3.80; sit-down meals, including all-day breakfast, €6-9. Open July-Aug. daily 9am-1:30am; Sept.-June 10am-11:30pm.) The **Blind Piper Pub and Restaurant ❹** is a popular local hangout—outdoor tables by the stream are perfect for enjoying your pub vittles. Music drowns out the babbling brook in July and August, with trad on Fridays and discos Saturday and Sunday. The candlelit restaurant upstairs serves pricey options, including dishes with Balinese flare. (☎947 5126. Pub food €5-10, served noon-8pm; restaurant food €13-20, served Th-Su 6:30-8:30pm.)

SIGHTS. A trip to Caherdaniel would be incomplete without a visit to **Derrynane National Park,** 1½ mi. along the shore from the village and well signposted. The highlighted attraction, **Derrynane House,** was the residence of Irish patriot Daniel "The Liberator" O'Connell, whose election to Parliament and inability to take his seat as a Catholic inspired the movement that culminated in the Catholic Emancipation Act of 1829 (see **Rebellion,** p. 59). Inside the house, you can check out the dueling pistol that O'Connell used to kill challenger John d'Esterre, as well as the black glove he wore to church for years afterwards to mourn his victim. The 30min. film on O'Connell presents an engrossing and refreshingly textured image of the acerbic barrister. (☎947 5113. Open May-Sept. M-Sa 9am-6pm, Su 11am-7pm; Apr. and Oct. Tu-Su 1-5pm; Nov.-Mar. Sa-Su 1-5pm. Last admission 45min. before closing. €3, students and children €1.50.) A few trails lead from the house through dunes and gardens down to the beach. Worth the 15min. walk, **Abbey Island**—only a true island during exceptionally high tides—extends into the water to the southwest. There, the **Abbey of St. Finian** shows the wear and tear of 1300 years and enchants explorers with its creepy graveyard.

If you're game for hiking or pedaling 6 mi. uphill, the pre-Christian **Staigue Fort,** west of town and marked with large signs, will make you feel tall and powerful. The largest stone fort in Ireland, Staigue surveys the sea from high on a hill, and keeps an eye out for any pesky Pictish invaders. (☎947 5288. Fort always open. Free.) For a close look at the watery side of Caherdaniel, contact **Activity Ireland,** housed in the Kerry Way B&B. (☎947 5277. Diving €45.) They will also help direct you to the horse-riding options available at the **Eagle Rock Equestrian Centre** (☎9477 5145) and toward **Bealtra Boats** (☎9477 5129) for fishing and Skelligs trips.

SNEEM (AN TSNAIDHM) ☎064

The hordes tend to make Sneem their first or last stop along the Ring, and the town is well prepared to receive them. Canned Irish music rolls out of the shops on the South Sq. between the clutter of postcard stands. Two public squares and a unique sculpture collection make Sneem a browser's paradise, and once the crowds have thinned, the view from the bridge turns out to be not unimpressive.

TRANSPORTATION AND PRACTICAL INFORMATION. The Ring of Kerry **bus** travels straight to Killarney (1hr., June-Sept. 2 per day, €7.50), and another bus connects to Kenmare (mid-June to Aug. M-Sa 2 per day). The eastbound bus from Killarney stops once a day before continuing all the way around the Ring. The **tourist office** is housed in the Joli Coeur Craft Shop near the bus stop. (☎45270. Open mid-Mar. to Nov. daily 11am-5pm.) **Bike rental** is available at **M. Burns Bike Hire,** in the North Sq. (☎45140. €12 per day, €60 per wk. Open M-Sa 9:30am-7pm.) Eeexxcellent. **Internet** is available at the **Goosey Island Campsite** (see below). Jockey for a position with postcard-wielding warriors at the **post office** a few doors down. (☎45110. Open M-F 9am-1pm and 2-5:30pm, Sa 9am-1pm.)

ACCOMMODATIONS, FOOD, AND PUBS. The **Harbour View Hostel ❶,** an 8min. walk from town on the Kenmare road, used to be a motel; with ranch-style units in a gravel lot, it's hard to forget. Basic dorms are cramped walk-throughs, but the more expensive dorms and doubles are quite roomy. (☎45276. Sheets €0.65. Laundry €6. Dorms €10-14; doubles €44. **Camping** €7 with tent.) Sneem's oldest and arguably nicest B&B is **The Bank House ❸,** North Sq., where the chatty owner will help you navigate the local attractions with the assistance of his aerial map. (☎45226. Open Mar.-Nov. €25 per person.) The **Old Convent House ❸,** Pier Rd. (take a right off the South Sq. just after Erin Co. Knitwear), is an old stone house with magnificent views; redone rooms are comfy but lack soul. (☎45181.

€25-30 per person.) With its excellent location in the town center, **Goosey Island Campsite ❶** lets you lay your tent along the grassy river bank. (☎45577. **Internet** €6 per hr. Open Apr. to mid-Oct. €6.50 per person; bunks €10. Showers €1.)

You may want to take off your hiking boots and slide on a pair of fancy loafers before entering **Sacre Coeur ❹,** just above the North Sq. Steak, seafood, and chicken dishes for €12.50-18.50 are served in a somewhat imposing dining room. (☎45186. Open Easter-Oct. daily 6-10pm, Su prix-fixe 3-course lunch €15, served 12:30-2:30pm.) Or throw on a pair of dirty sneakers and gallop down to the **Hungry Knight ❶** for fish and chips or a game of pool with young Sneemen. (☎45237. Burgers from €1.70. Open July-Aug. daily noon-3:30am, Apr.-June and Sept. daily noon-11:30pm.) Just north of the bridge, **The Village Kitchen ❷** serves seafood and sandwiches in a cafe setting. (☎45281. Sandwiches €3-4; house specials €5.50-8.50. Open June-Sept. daily 9:30am-6pm, Oct.-May 10am-5pm.) Massive pub meals are served at **The Blue Bull** by the post office. Stick around for ballad sessions on Saturday nights in the summer (☎45382; food daily noon-8pm). At the **Fisherman's Knot** (☎45224), across the bridge on the Caherdaniel Rd., locals tap their toes to trad or discos a few nights a week in summer. **O'Shea's** (☎45515), in the North Sq., reverberates with old-fashioned sessions on Sundays and Wednesdays in the summer.

SIGHTS. Charles de Gaulle visited Sneem in 1969, and the town was so honored it erected a monument to commemorate the event—they mounted a bronze sculpture of de Gaulle's head on a boulder of local stone. Thus a tradition was born. Today, Sneem's **sculpture park** celebrates the late President Cearbhaill O'Dalaigh, the Egyptian goddess Isis, wrestling champ "Crusher" Casey, and an odd set of cave buildings. It's difficult to decide which is more bizarre, the sculptures themselves or their collective name, "The Way the Faeries Went." Get a *Sneem Guide* in the tourist office for an abbreviated tour (€0.65).

KENMARE (NEIDIN) ☎064

A bridge between the Ring of Kerry and the Beara Peninsula, Kenmare has adapted to a continuous stream of visitors. Everything you'd expect of a classic Irish town is here (yes, we're talking about colorful houses and misty mountain views and the like). Tourists fresh off the bus may dilute Kenmare's appeal, but pleasant surroundings overshadow the sweater stalls and postcard stands. Its convenient location along the Kerry Way makes Kenmare a common stop for trekkers.

TRANSPORTATION

Buses: From Brennan's Pub on Main St. to **Castletownbere** via **Ardgroom** and **Eyeries** (40min., June-Aug. M-Sa 2 per day); **Cork** via **Glengarrif** and **Skibbereen** (June-Sept. daily 2 per day); **Killarney** (1hr.; M-Sa 3 per day, Su 2 per day; only 2 per day in winter), where connections are available to **Tralee** and **Cork; Sneem** (35min., June-Aug. M-Sa 2 per day), where connections are available to the **Ring of Kerry** bus during the summer. Significantly fewer routes and times in the off-season (Oct.-May); check with the tourist office for current schedules or call the bus station in Killarney (☎34777).

Taxis: Kenmare Koach & Kab (call Declan Finnegan ☎41491 or 087 248 0800). Also offers bus tours around the Rings of Beara and Kerry (€20 per person) and to Glengarrif and Killarney (€15 per person) during the summer.

Bike Rental: Finnegan's (☎41083), corner of Henry and Shelbourne St. €12 per day, €75 per wk. Open June-Aug. M-Sa 9:30am-9pm; Sept.-May M-Sa 9:30am-6:30pm.

ORIENTATION AND PRACTICAL INFORMATION

Kenmare's main streets form a triangle: **Henry St.** is the lively base, while **Main St.** and **Shelbourne St.** connect on either side. The intersection of Henry St. and Main St. forms **the Square,** which contains a small park and the tourist office. Main St. then becomes N71, heading toward **Moll's Gap** and **Killarney;** N70 to **Sneem** and the **Ring of Kerry** also branches off this road. From Kenmare, savvy travelers take N70 west (rather than N71 north) to do the Ring clockwise and avoid tour bus traffic.

Tourist Office: the Square (☎41233). Friendly staff hands out a *Heritage Trails* map and houses the free **Heritage Center** (see **Sights,** below). Open May-June M-Sa 9am-1pm, 2-5:30pm; July-Oct. M-Sa 9am-6pm, Su 10am-5pm.

Bank: AIB, 9 Main St. (☎41010), on the corner of Henry St., and **Bank of Ireland,** the Square, both have an **ATM.** Banks open M 10am-5pm, Tu-F 10am-4pm.

Work Opportunities: Kenmare has plenty of restaurants hiring summer cooks and wait staff, such as **An Leath Phingin,** 35 Main St. (☎41559). Several sizeable hotels will hire travelers, including the **Landsdowne Arms** (☎41368), at the top of Main St.

Bookstore: The Kenmare Bookstore, Main St. (☎41578). Bestsellers and Irish classics. Open June-Aug. M-Sa 9:30am-9pm, Su 11am-6pm; Sept.-May M-Sa 9am-6pm.

Laundry: O'Sheas, Main St. (☎41394). Wash €2.50, dry €0.75 per 10min. Open M-F 8:30am-6pm, Sa 9:30am-6pm.

Pharmacy: Sheahan's, Main St. (☎41354). Open M-Sa 9am-6pm. **Brosnan's,** Henry St. (☎41318, same number after hours). Open M-Sa 9am-6:30pm, Su 12:30-1:15pm.

Emergency: ☎999; no coins required. **Police** *(Garda)*: Shelbourne St. (☎41177).

Hospital: Old Killarney Rd. (☎41088). Follow the signs on Railway Rd.

Internet Access: Web World Internet Cafe (☎41368), inside the Landsdowne Arms Hotel, at the corner of Main and Shelbourne St. Fast connections. €1 per 10min., €5 per hr. Open June-Aug. M-F 9am-9pm, Sa 9am-10pm; Sept.-May M-Sa 9am-6pm.

Post Office: Henry St. (☎41490), at the corner of Shelbourne St. Open June-Sept. M-F 9am-5:30pm, Sa 9am-1pm; Oct.-May M-F 9am-1pm and 2-5:30pm, Sa 9am-1pm. Also has **Internet access:** €1 per 10min.; students €1 per 15min. Cheaper 6-8pm. Computers available June-Aug. 8am-8pm, Sept.-May 8am-6pm.

ACCOMMODATIONS AND CAMPING

Fáilte Hostel (IHH) (☎42333), at the corner of Henry and Shelbourne St. Proprietress Maureen runs a tight ship at this excellent and immaculate hostel. The fully-equipped kitchen, TV room, and great location often persuade guests to stay another night. Curfew 1am. Open Apr.-Oct. Dorms €12; doubles €32-40; triples €42; quads €56. ❶

Hawthorn House, Shelbourne St. (☎41035; www.hawthornhousekenmare.com). Friendly owner helps you feel at home with her 8 comfortable, recently redone rooms. Open year-round. Book ahead July-Aug. All rooms with bath and TV. Doubles €60-70. ❸

Keal Na Gower House B&B, the Square (☎41202), near the tourist office. A small B&B with a lovely patio overlooking a babbling brook. One room has a bathtub; the other 2 have brook views. €28-30 per person. ❸

Rose Cottage, the Square (☎41330), next door to Keal Na Gower House. A pretty stone house set back behind a lovely green garden. Enjoys very marginal historical significance as the temporary home of Abess Mary O'Hagan, sister to Ireland's first Catholic Chancellor, Thom O'Hagan. June-Sept. €32 per person; Oct.-May €30. ❸

The Coachman B&B, Henry St. (☎41311). Basic double and triple rooms above the bar. €15-20 per person, with bath €20-25. €3 discount without breakfast. ❷

Ring of Kerry Caravan and Camping Park, Sneem Rd. (☎41648), 3 mi. west of town. Overlooks mountains and a bay. Kitchen, TV room, and small shop. Open Apr.-Sept. 1 person with tent €7, 2 with car and tent €16.50. Shower €0.50. Laundry €3.50. ❶

FOOD

Food is plentiful but pricey in Kenmare, especially for dinner. Try the smaller cafes for snacks, and check the pubs for cheap lunches. **SuperValu** is on Main St. (☎41307. Open M-Th 8am-8pm, F 8am-9pm, Sa 8am-7pm, Su 9am-5pm.) **The Pantry,** Henry St., has a limited selection of organic stock. (☎42233. Open M-Sa 9:30am-6pm.) Takeaway is always a cheap option; there are several on Main St., including the late-night **Ferrari,** serving fried fish, burgers, and chips for under €3. (☎42045. Open June-Sept. daily 3pm-3am, Oct.-May Su-Th 3pm-1am, F-Sa 3pm-3am.)

An Leath Phingin, 35 Main St. (☎41559). Gaelic for "The Half Penny." Enjoy a taste of Italy in an old stone townhouse. Start with king prawns (€8.50) or homemade pork sausage (€7.50) grilled over an oak fire, followed by baked salmon (€17.90). Pizza and pasta €13-16. Book ahead July-Aug. Open Mar.-Nov. M-Tu and Th-Su 6-9:30pm. ❹

Jam (☎41591). Kerchiefed town belles serve up bakery and deli delights. Try a tomato and cheese scone topped with poppy seeds (€1) or construct your own toasted sandwich masterpiece (€3.30). Open M-Sa 8am-5pm. ❶

The Purple Heather Pub, Henry St. (☎41016). Has served very tasty lunches and snacks transcending that of the average pub since 1964. Sample assorted local farm cheeses (€6.50) or the special potato, cheddar, onion, and thyme omelette served with organic greens (€6.70) in a cozy red leather booth. Open M-Sa 11:30am-6:30pm. ❷

Mickey Neds Bar & Restaurant (☎40200), just off the Square, across from the tourist office. Offers creative and experimental combinations from the kitchen, like grilled turbot with green-pea mash and orange chive butter (€23). Slick, modern lounge is lovely for an after-dinner drink. Food served Tu-Sa noon-3pm and 6-9pm, Su noon-3pm. ❹

The Coachman's Inn, Henry St. (☎41311). A popular wood-paneled pub that serves Irish standards like roast Kerry lamb with mint sauce (€8.25). Lunch menu €6-8 served noon-5:30pm, dinner menu €12.50-14 served 5:30-9:30pm. Trad F-Sa at 9:30pm. ❸

PUBS

Kenmare's pubs attract a hefty contingent of tourists, making live music easy to come by in summer. And the locals still hold their own at most watering holes.

O'Donnabháin's, Henry St. (☎42106). A favorite among permanents and temporaries of all ages, with a beer garden out back.

Moeran's Bar, in the Landsdowne Arms Hotel (☎41368), at the top of Main St. Wise visitors follow the locals here. Trad every night June-Sept.; varies the rest of the year.

Atlantic Bar, the Square (☎41094). Relaxed local joint with a lot of character. Serves breakfast 9:30-11:30am, lunch 12:30-3pm, and dinner 5-9pm. Live trad Su. Disco Sa.

Crowley's, Henry St. (☎41472) Poses the question: "With frequent trad, why bother with interior decorating?" Trad not quite as frequent anymore—sessions about once a week; more often in winter.

The Wander Inn, (☎42700). A classic joint in leather and mahogany. Live music usually F-Su in summer.

SIGHTS

There are plenty of good hikes in the country around Kenmare, but few sights in the town itself. To reach the **Kerry Way,** walk along the street that runs past the tourist office and take the little stone bridge that crosses over the brook; brown signs will point the way to the Way, which heads up and over the surrounding green hills of farmland. Picnic among local herds of goat and cow while absorbing wonderful views of the peninsula and distant coastline. Closer to town, the ancient **stone circle,** a 2min. walk down Market St. from the Square, is the largest of its kind (55 ft. diameter) in southwest Ireland. (Always open. €1.50.) The stone circle is one stop on Kenmare's **tourist trail** (maps at the tourist office), a well-marked route that leads visitors over historic bridges and past a small tower known as **Hutchin's Folly.** The new **Heritage Centre,** in the back of the tourist office, has a model of the stone circle and other historical exhibits, as well as puzzling attempts to connect the town to Margaret Thatcher and Confederate general P.G.T. Beauregard. (Open May-June M-Sa 9am-1pm and 2-5:30pm; July-Oct. M-Sa 9am-6pm, Su 10am-5pm. Free.) **The Kenmare Lace and Design Centre,** above the tourist office, has demonstrations of the Kenmare lace-making technique, invented in 1862 by local nuns and once on the cutting edge of lace technology. (☎42636. Open Mar.-Sept. M-Sa 10am-1pm and 2-5:30pm. Free.) **Seafari Cruises** explores Kenmare Bay and its otter and seal colonies, with the off-chance of a whale sighting. (☎83171 for reservations. 2-3 per day. €18, students €14, teens €10, children €8, families €45.) The cruises depart from the pier. Take Henry St. out of town and follow the Glengarriff road; turn right just before the bridge. For fishing gear, permits, and info, head to **John O'Hare Fishing Tackle** on Main St. (☎41499. Day permit for fly fishing €5. Open M-W and F-Sa 9:30am-1pm and 2-6pm, Th 9:30am-1pm.)

DINGLE TOWN (AN DAIGEAN) ☎066

Although the *craic* is still home-grown, ever-expanding hordes of tourists (looking to catch a glimpse of Fungi the Dolphin) smother the docks and pubs of this bayside town. To be fair, Dingle does have fantastic hostels, a swingin' music scene, and easy access to its namesake peninsula's more isolated hideaways.

TRANSPORTATION

Buses: Buses stop by the harbor, on the Ring road behind Garvey's SuperValu. Information available from the Tralee bus station (☎712 3566). **Bus Éireann** runs to: **Ballydavid** (Tu and F 3 per day, €4 return); **Ballyferriter** (M and Th 3 per day, €3.20); **Dunquin** (M and Th 4-5 per day, Tu-W and F-Sa 1-2 per day; €3.15); **Tralee** (1¼hr.; M-Sa 6 per day, Su 4 per day; €7.90). June-Sept. additional buses tour the south of the peninsula from Dingle (M-Sa 2 per day).

Bike Rental: Paddy's Bike Shop, Dykegate St. (☎915 2311), rents quality bikes. €10 per day, students €8; €50 per wk., €40. Panniers €2 per day. Open daily 9am-7pm.

Cabs: Cooleen Cabs (☎087 248 0008) and **Dingle Co-op Cabs** (☎915 1000).

ORIENTATION AND PRACTICAL INFORMATION

The **R559** heads east to Killarney and Tralee, and west to Ventry, Dunquin, and Slea Head. A narrow road runs north through Conor Pass to Stradbally and Castlegregory. In downtown Dingle, **Strand St.** runs next to the harbor along the

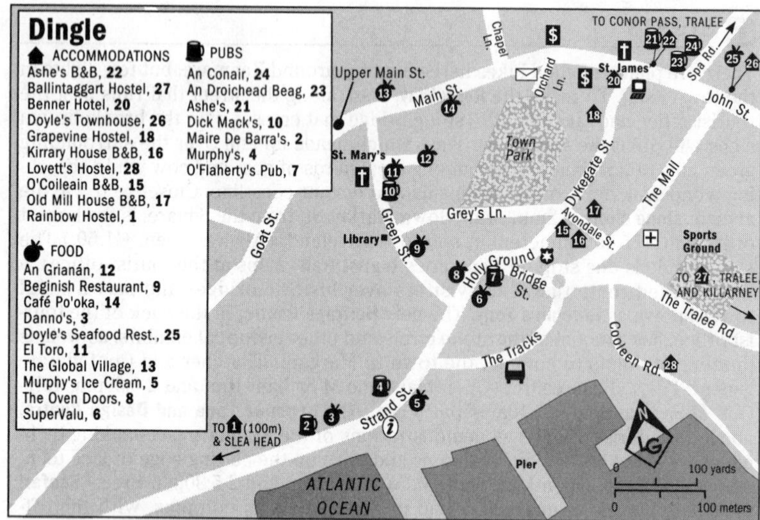

marina, while **Main St.** is its parallel counterpart uphill. **The Mall, Dykegate St.,** and **Green St.** connect the two, running perpendicular to the water. In the eastern part of town, a roundabout splits Strand St. into **The Tracks,** which continue along the water, **The Holy Ground,** which curves up to meet Dykegate St., and the **Tralee Road.**

Tourist Office: Strand St. (☎915 1188). Vies for attention with scores of dolphin-crazy tourists. Open July-Aug. M-Sa 9am-7pm, Su 10am-5pm; Sept.-Oct. and mid-Mar. to June M-Sa 9:30am-6pm, Su 9:30am-5pm.

Banks: AIB, Main St. (☎915 1400). Open M 10am-5pm, Tu-F 10am-4pm. **Bank of Ireland,** Main St. (☎915 1100). Same hours. Both have multi-card tolerant **ATMs.**

Camping Equipment: The Mountain Man, Strand St. (☎915 2400). Offers 2½hr. bus tours to Slea Head (€12). Sells the very informative *Guide to the Dingle Peninsula*, which includes walking and cycling maps for specific regions of the peninsula. No tent rental. Open July-Aug. daily 9am-9pm; Sept.-June 9am-6pm.

Laundry: Níolann an Daingin, Green St. (☎915 1837), behind El Toro. Wash and dry €9 per load. Open M-Sa 9am-1pm and 2-5:30pm.

Work Opportunities: Dingle's many pubs, restaurants, and takeaways could all use a helping hand. Many restaurants on and around Strand St. will hire travelers as short-term employees, especially during the summer. Technically, only EU residents are eligible to work in Ireland without a costly permit, but more informal arrangements are common.

Emergency: ☎999; no coins required. **Police** *(Garda)*: The Holy Ground (☎915 1522).

Pharmacy: O'Keefe's Pharmacy Ltd. (☎915 1310), on The Holy Ground next to the SuperValu. Open M-W and F-Sa 9:30am-6pm, Th 9:30am-1pm, Su 10:30am-12:30pm.

Internet Access: At the **library** (☎915 1499). 50min. free each day, but call to arrange a time. Open Tu-Sa 10:30am-1:30pm and 2:30-5pm. **Dingle Internet Cafe,** Main St. (☎915 2478). Leather chairs and cyber space. €2.60 per 20min., €6 per hr. Open May-Sept. M-Sa 10am-10pm, Su 2-6pm; Oct.-Apr. daily 10am-6pm.

Post Office: Upper Main St. (☎915 1661). Just the place for mailing Fungi postcards. Open M-F 9am-5:30pm, Sa 9am-1pm.

ACCOMMODATIONS AND CAMPING

Most of Dingle's hostels are great, but only some are close to town. Accommodations in town and along Dykegate and Strand St. fill up fast—always call ahead.

Grapevine Hostel, Dykegate St. (☎915 1434), off Main St. Smack in the middle of town and just a brief stagger from Dingle's finest pubs. Friendly folks guide you through the musical, cushy-chaired common room to close but comfy bunk rooms. The Dingle Internet Cafe is but a short stride away. 8-bed dorms €10.80-12; 4-bed €12-13.35. ❶

Rainbow Hostel (☎915 1044). Take Strand St. west out of town and continue straight through the roundabout for ¼ mi. Jackson Pollock-style interior decor and fierce camaraderie in the cavernous kitchen. Free lifts to and from town all day in the Rainbow-Mobile. **Bike rental** €6 per day. **Internet access** €1 per 10min. Laundry €7. 5- to 12-bed dorms €12; private rooms €14 per person. **Camping** €6.50. ❶

Ballintaggart Hostel (IHH), on N86 (☎915 1454). A 25min. walk east of town on the Tralee road; the Tralee bus will stop here on request. Built in 1703 as a hunting lodge and used as a soup kitchen during the Famine, this grand stone mansion witnessed the strangling of Mrs. Earl of Cork after a poisoning attempt went awry. Her ghost supposedly haunts the enormous bedchambers, enclosed cobblestone courtyard, and elegant, fire-heated common rooms. Free shuttle to town 3-5 times per day. Laundry €6 and ironing necessities available. 8- to 12-bed dorms €12.50; 4-bed €15. Doubles €43; family rooms €65. **Camping** €11 per small tent and €13 per van. ❶

Ashe's B&B, Lower Main St. (☎915 0989). Look out onto Main St. with unrivaled views or choose to be creepy and gaze upon the old graveyard. The 4 rooms are tastefully decorated with soft cream colors and antique bureaus. All rooms with bath and TV. The closest B&B to the pub downstairs. €30 per person. ❸

O'Coileain B&B, Dykegate St. (☎915 1937), on the corner of Avondale St. At this ideal retreat right in the center of town, the young proprietors and their wee helpers show guests to handsome rooms, all with bath. Tea and coffee facilities are available in the sitting room. **Bike rental** €7.60 per day. Private rooms €28-30 per person. ❸

Kirrary House B&B, Avondale St. (☎915 1606), off Dykegate St. With pride and good cheer, Mrs. Collins puts up guests in delightful rooms. Book whirlwind **archaeological tours** with Sciúird Tours, operated by Mr. Collins (see **Sights,** below), or lounge in the garden with tea and cake. **Bike rental** €7.60 per day. Private rooms €30 per person. ❸

Old Mill House B&B, Avondale St. (☎915 1120 or 915 2349), across from Kirrary House. You could save a few euros by skipping breakfast–if it weren't for those amazing crepes. All rooms with comfy pine beds, bath, TV, and hair dryer. **Bike rental** €6 per day. Private rooms €20 per person, with bath €24.50. ❷

Lovett's Hostel, Cooleen Rd. (☎915 1903). Turn opposite the Esso station past the roundabout. This small, low-key hostel relaxes on the outskirts of Dingle's hustle 'n bustle. Sheets €1. Dorms €11; doubles and triples €28-30. ❶

Benner Hotel, Lower Main St. (☎915 1638). Four-poster beds, antique wood furniture, and chandelier lighting await the weary traveler at this plush, centrally located hotel. Each room has a fireplace, phone, and coffee-making necessities. Bathrooms are blessed with large tubs. Enjoy a meal at the connected restaurant or meet a fellow traveler for a drink at the bar. Wheelchair-accessible. €76 per person. ❺

Doyle's Townhouse, John St. (☎915 1174). Decorated with antique flair and stripped pine furniture, bedrooms come with all the modern conveniences one could desire (including satellite TV). Victorian-style drawing room is a perfect place to read the paper as the grandfather clock chimes the hour. Open mid-Feb. to mid-Nov. Singles €55. ❺

FROM THE ROAD

A BREAKFAST OF CHAMPIONS

Travel coincidences are common, especially in a small country like Ireland. You invariably bump into the same tourists in different places—at accommodations, on tours, or even in that local restaurant down the alley hidden behind the church that no one knows about except the locals. As a *Lets Go* researcher-writer, such run-ins were common for me, but the best was the day I ate breakfast with the competition. I arrived one morning in the dining room of a medium-sized B&B just as everyone was filing in for breakfast. As I sat down, I placed my copy notes on the table next to another, similar set of paperwork. I eyed the man across the table, just as he looked at my notes and up at me with a questioning grin. The introductions commenced and we quickly realized that the inevitable had occurred—I was working for *Let's Go* and he was a writer for a useful, yet rival guide; our paths had finally crossed. We laughed and set about the diplomatic duty of swapping notes without disclosing too much of our own careful research. It was a battle of the wits. We shared stories, joked about how tiring it is to check the post office hours in every town, and laughed at the parallel lives we had both led in Ireland in the last months, but we remained cautious. After breakfast, we went our separate ways—two opposing soldiers having shared a brief cease-fire in the fierce war of research-writing.

—Chris Gregg

FOOD

Dingle is home to a wide range of eateries, from doughnut stands to gourmet seafood restaurants. **SuperValu,** The Holy Ground, stocks a SuperSelection of groceries and juicy tabloids. (☎915 1397. Open June-Aug. M-Sa 8am-10pm, Su 8am-9pm; Sept.-Apr. M-Sa 8am-9pm, Su 8am-7pm.) **An Grianán,** on Green St., on the side street before El Toro and Dick Mack's, vends crunchy wholefoods and organic vegetables. (☎915 1910. Open M-F 9:30am-6pm, Sa 10am-6pm.)

Murphy's Ice Cream, Strand St. (☎915 2644). American brothers Kieran and Sean set up shop a few years back, and visitors and locals alike are sure glad they did. The former New Yorkers scoop Ireland's only truly homemade ice cream (from €2). Cappuccinos only €2.50. These guys deserve the superlatives you'll exclaim. Open June-Sept. 10:30am-6pm and 7:30-10pm; mid-Mar. to May 10:30am-6pm. ❶

Danno's, Strand St. (☎915 1855). The railroad theme may not toot your whistle, but for hearty burgers (€7.60-9) and cold pints, this popular pub can't be beat. Watch the match on one of the two TVs or warm yourself by the stone fireplace. Food served Tu-Su 12:30-2:30pm and 6-9pm. ❸

El Toro, Green St. (☎915 1820). The only Spanish and Italian specialists in town. Dine on homemade gourmet pizzas (€7.30-11.50) or *paella* while soft Italian music flows over you. Look out on the hills or admire the owner's talent for oil painting as your tastebuds enjoy his talent for cooking. Dinner 6-10pm daily. ❸

The Oven Doors, The Holy Ground (☎915 1056), across from SuperValu. Crispy pizzas (€5.85-9), spectacular sundaes (€4.65), and incredible cakes (€3) draw mobs to this art-bedecked cafe. Try the apple crumble upstairs in the doily-covered Tea Room. Open May-Sept. daily 9:30am-10pm, mid-Mar. to Apr. and Oct.-Jan. 10am-7pm. ❸

The Global Village, Main St. (☎915 2325). Offers a fantastic variety of meals from around the world, several of them veggie-oriented. Swap travel stories with the owner, who collected many of the recipes himself, or enjoy an intimate candlelit dinner with a date. Dinner €13.95-21.50. Open mid-Mar. to mid-Nov. 6-10pm. ❹

Cafe Po'oka, Main St. (☎915 0773). Swish through the beaded curtain into a Bohemian wonderland. Feast like a local on crepes (€3.50-7) or all-day breakfasts (€3.50-6.50), and listen to the cheerful staff clutter dishes and croon along to everything from spicy Latin beats to funky down-home blues. Open 11am-6pm, or thereabouts. ❷

Beginish Restaurant, Green St. (☎915 1321). In its third season, Beginish is a gorgeous option for a quiet and intimate dinner. Candles set the mood in the main dining room, and the tender lamb specialty (€24.50) or black sole (€25.50) give your tastebuds the sense that they, too, are in heaven. Open Tu-Su, dinner 6-10pm (dinner generally runs €35 per person. Set menu €28.50). ❺

Doyle's Seafood Restaurant, John St. (☎915 1174). Doyle's serves up delicious dishes from the sea (€27.50-38) and has pictures of celebrities like Dolly Parton and Tom Cruise, who have sampled the cuisine and attested to their delight. The wooden kitchen tables and stone walls create a cozy atmosphere that welcomes boisterous groups and quiet couples alike. M-Sa dinner from 6-10pm. ❺

PUBS

Dingle has 52 pubs for 1500 people, and, not surprisingly, many of them cater to tourists. Don't fret—there's still plenty of *craic* to be found in town.

An Droichead Beag (The Small Bridge), Lower Main St. (☎915 1723). The most popular pub in town unleashes 401 sessions of trad a year–9:30pm every night and the odd afternoon as well. Numerous nooks nurture conversation, and the disco upstairs opens W, F, and Sa nights. The pool table lets you establish rivalries of your own, while the big screen TV lets you cheer for those more established during the Su matches.

An Conair, Spa Rd. (☎915 2011), off Main St. Word has it that it hosts the most authentic trad sessions in town. Subdued local crowd enjoys exceptional trad and lusty ballads. M set dancing; W-Sa trad starting at 9:30pm, Su 5-7pm in July and Aug.

Ashe's, Lower Main St. (☎915 098). A mite sick o' the trad? Youngsters and old'uns alike gather here for live jazz on Th nights. Sample non-traditional pub food (salads €7.50-9.90, sandwiches €5.20, and wraps €5.95) from 10am-6pm.

O'Flaherty's Pub, The Holy Ground (☎915 1983), a few doors up from the traffic circle. Trad masters have the pub filled with tourists by 9:30pm nightly in summer and 3-4 times per wk. in winter.

Maire De Barra's, Strand St. (☎915 1215). A mixed-age, largely tourist crowd looking to hear great folk and modern trad. Music nightly in summer and weekends in winter.

Murphy's, Strand St. (☎915 1450). Ballads and trad resound from this classic pub by the marina. Listen or chat in cozy corners. Music nightly Apr.-Oct.; Sa only Nov.-Mar.

Dick Mack's, Green St. (☎915 1960), opposite the church. The proprietor leaps between the bar and leather-tooling bench at "Dick Mack's Bar, Boot Store, and Leather Shop." Shoeboxes and whiskey bottles line the walls. Though heavily touristed, frequent spontaneous sing-alongs indicate enduring local support.

SIGHTS AND ACTIVITIES

When **Fungi the Dolphin** was first spotted in 1983, the townspeople worried about the effect he would have on the bay's fish population. To say he is now welcome is an understatement, as he single-fipperedly brings in droves of tourists and plenty of cash to his exploiters. **Dolphin Trips** leave to see him from the pier between 10am and 7pm in the summer. (☎915 2626. 1hr. €10, children under 12 €5, free if Fungi gets the jitters and doesn't show.) Watching the antics from the shore east of town is a cheaper, squintier alternative. To get there, walk 2min. down the Tralee road, turn right at the Skellig Hotel, and follow the sand away from town for about 10min. The small beach on the other side of a stone tower is often crowded with Fungi-fanatics. Anti-dolphinites can be coaxed along by the promise of great views on the walk. **Dingle Ocean World,** Strand St., has smaller critters yanked from the sea for your viewing pleasure. Observe fish in an underwater tunnel or pet the skates in the touch tank. (☎915 2111. Tours and feeding shows. Open July-Aug. daily 9am-8:30pm; May-June and Sept. 10am-6pm; Oct.-Apr. 10am-5pm; last admission 30min. before closing. €7.50, students €6, seniors €5.50, children €4.50.)

You can **rent a wetsuit** from **Flannery's** on Cooleen Rd., just east of town off the Tralee road. They also run **swimming trips** from 8-10am. (☎915 1967. Wetsuits day rental €20; swim trips €15.) Take advantage of the nearby beaches and try your hand at **surfing,** courtesy of **Finn McCool's,** Green St. (☎915 0833). Or rent a surf board (€20 per day), body board (€20 per day), or wetsuit (€20 for adults). **Dingle Marine Eco-Tours** offers two trips that head in opposite directions along the peninsula coast, dispensing insights on bay life and views of archeological sites (☎086 285 8802; tours 2-2½hr.). If you'd like to check out the **Blasket Islands,** board the *Peig Sayers*, named for one of the island's most famous residents, at the Dingle pier at 11am, 1, or 3pm (€30; inquire at Dolphin Trips). The trip to the islands takes 40min., and you'll have a couple of hours to hike before being evacuated like the islanders before you. **Deep-sea angling** trips leave daily in the summer. (☎915 9947. €30 per half-day, includes equipment and skippered boat.)

The Mountain Man camping store (see **Orientation and Practical Information,** above) sells *The Easy Guide to the Dingle Peninsula* (€6.35), which includes walks, cycling tours, history, and a map. **Sciúird Archaeology Tours** will take you on a whirlwind bus tour of the area's ancient spots. (☎915 1606 or 915 1937. 3hr. tours. 2 per day, €15. Book ahead.) There are several **Slea Head Tours,** 2hr. minibus trips highlighting the peninsula's scenery and historic sights. **Moran's Tours** (☎915 1155 or 086 275 3333) depart daily at 10am and 2pm; **O'Connor's Tours** head to the Head at 11am. (☎087 248 0008. Both tours leave from the pier. €10.20.) Tired of watchin' Fungi? **Dingle Horse Riding** offers the chance to canter on mountain trails and gallop on local beaches. (☎915 2199. €25-115.) Summer festivals periodically set the town a reelin'. The **Dingle Regatta** hauls in salty dogs on the third Sunday in August. In mid-August, try your luck at the **Dingle Races.** During early September, the **Dingle Music Festival** lures big-name trad groups and other performers from across the musical spectrum. (☎915 1983; www.iol.ie/~dingmus.)

VENTRY, SLEA HEAD, AND DUNQUIN ☎066

Glorious Slea Head presents to the world a face of jagged cliffs and a hemline of frothy waves. Green hills, interrupted by rough stone walls and occasional sheep, suddenly break off into the foam-flecked sea. Hollywood chose these parts to satisfy its craving for classic Irish beauty and filmed *Ryan's Daughter* and *Far and Away* here, successfully exploiting the scenery's tendency toward the highly dramatic. The most rewarding and unforgettable way to see Slea Head and Dunquin in a day or less is to bike along the predominantly flat Slea Head Drive (R559).

VENTRY (CEANN TRÁ). Less than 4 mi. past Dingle Town toward Slea Head on R559, the village of Ventry contains little more than a sandy beach and the hillside bric-a-brac of **Rahinnane Castle.** While this small ruin is hardly worth peeping into, the **Celtic and Prehistoric Museum,** 2 mi. farther down the road, is a must-see. Once you've greeted the puzzling robotic sheep, trek over slabs of fossilized sea worms from the Cliffs of Moher and past a nest of dinosaur eggs to the main collection, which is illuminated by guidebooks available in eight languages. The 50,000-year-old, fully restored skull and tusks of "Millie," recently recovered off the coast of Holland, will make you grateful that the last woolly mammoth has shuffled off to that great glacial meadow in the sky. (*☎915 9931. Open Mar. to mid-Nov. daily 10am-5pm; other months call ahead. Adults €5, students €3.50, children €3.*) Near the old castle, **Ballybeag Hostel's** ❷ marvelous new facilities and secluded-yet-convenient location make this an ideal place to recharge your battery before exploring the treasures at the western end of the peninsula. To reach the hostel's massive beds and soothing sitting room, follow signs up from the inland turn just past the beach, or hop on one of the seven daily shuttles from Dingle Town. Ballybeag was built by an Italian tourist who never ended her vacation to Ventry—you'll understand her decision completely. *(☎915 9876. Bike rental €7 per day. Laundry €2. Wheelchair-accessible. €20 per person.)*

SLEA HEAD (CEANN SLÉIBHE). Slea Head Drive continues on past several Iron Age and early Christian rocks and ruins. Clustered on hillsides over the cliffs, **Dunbeg Fort** and the **Fahan** oratories (beehive-shaped stone huts built by early monks) can be explored for €2, but are visible for free from the road. Slea Head looks out onto the resplendent **Blasket Islands** (see p. 295). Try to pick out the **Sleeping Giant's** profile from among the scattered group. For the best views, locals advise hiking to the top of **Mount Eagle,** which is an easy jaunt from the Ballybeag Hostel (see **Ventry,** above). If rough seas keep you from visiting the Blaskets, or even if they don't, check out the outstanding exhibits at the **Great Blasket Centre,** just outside of Dunquin on the road to Ballyferriter. Thoughtfully designed, the museum evokes the islanders' lost way of life, bringing visitors physically and emotionally closer to the Great Blasket as they descend the long corridor to a glassed-in viewing point. There is also a **cafe** *(open 10am-5pm)* for sandwiches and light lunch. *(☎915 6444. Open July-Aug. daily 10am-7pm; Easter-June and Sept.-Nov. 10am-6pm. Last admission 45min. before closing. €3.10, students €1.20.)*

DUNQUIN (DÚN CHAOIN). North of Slea Head, the scattered settlement of Dunquin consists of stone houses, a pub, the guttural music of spoken Irish, and no grocery store—stock up in Dingle or in Ballyferriter. Along the road to Ballyferriter across from the turnoff to the Blasket Centre and right on the **Dingle Way,** the **An Óige Hostel (HI) ❶** offers ocean views from the bunks and limited supplies from the mini-general store. *(☎915 6121. Continental breakfast €3. Sheets €1.30. Reception 9-10am and 5-10pm. Lockout 10am-5pm. May-Oct. 8- to 10-bed dorms €11.50-12.50; 4- to 6-bed €13-14; doubles €30-32. Jan.-Apr. and Nov.-Dec. €1.30-2.50 cheaper.)* Back toward the pier, the ferry captain's home doubles as the delightful **Gleann Dearg B&B ❸.** Try to tear your eyes away from the Great Blasket long enough to appreciate the homey, spacious rooms and conservatory dining room. Also serves up a splurge-worthy three-course lobster and crab dinner for €30 (weather permitting to bring in the catch). The four-person family suite is a rare find. *(☎915 6188. Open Apr.-Oct. €25 per person.)* **Kruger's ❸,** purportedly the westernmost pub in Europe, features pub grub, spontaneous music sessions, and superlative views. *(☎915 6127. Mains €6.35-12.70. B&B €25 per person.)* Just past the pier, indulge in the sandwiches and divine homebaked delicacies of **Caife Dún Chaoin ❶.** The strawberry gateau is in a category of its own, and the view takes its place with the rest of panoramific Dunquin. *(☎915 6194. Sandwiches €3.25, quiche €6, cakes €3.35. Open Feb.-Nov. 9am-7pm.)*

BLASKET ISLANDS (NA BLASCAODAÍ) ☎066

Whether bathed in glorious sunlight or shrouded in impenetrable mist, the islands' magical beauty and aching sense of eternity explain the disproportionately prolific literary output of the final generation to reside there. Six islands comprise the Blaskets: Beginish, Tearaght, Inishnabro, Inishvickillane, Inishtooskert, and Great Blasket. **Great Blasket Island** once supported an austere but proud community of poet-fishermen and storytellers, peaking at 176 inhabitants during the First World War. However, the collapse of the fish export market on which islanders depended resulted in a tide of emigration, and the village's future became bleak: as one resident reluctantly predicted, "after us, there will be no more." The islands were evacuated in 1953, after their population dropped below a safely sustainable level.

Mainlanders attempted to preserve the dying tradition by sponsoring the autobiographies of Blasket storytellers. The resulting **memoirs** bemoaned the decline of *gaeltacht* life; among them are Maurice O'Sullivan's *Twenty Years A-Growing*, Thomas O'Crohan's *The Islander*, and Peig Sayers's *Peig*. Mists, seals, and occasional fishing boats continue to pass through the Blaskets, but the unique way of life that once thrived there has faded into an inky memory.

A day on Great Blasket cannot be spent better than in uninterrupted rumination. Wander along the white strand, follow grass paths across all four of the island's miles, explore silent stone skeletons of houses clustered in the village, and observe the puffins and seals that populate the shores. The isolated Blaskets have no public litter system; kindly pack out all rubbish packed in.

Blasket Island Ferries bridge the gap between the Blaskets and Dunquin in about 20min. (☎915 6422. Apr.-Oct. daily every 20min. 10:30am-6pm, weather permitting. €17.80 return, students €15.25.) Keep in mind that if the weather is bad, the boats don't run; people have been stuck here for three weeks during gales. Of course, this may mean coordinating your trip to match a likely gale—we don't blame you. Another boat—the *Peig Sayers*—leaves the **Dingle Marina** every 2hr., arriving at Great Blasket Island in 35min. (☎915 1344 or 087 672 6100. €30, children €15.)

A warm bed and a hot drop are available at the **Blasket Island Hostel and Cafe ❶,** up the hill at the top of the old village. The cafe serves basic sandwiches (€3.80-5.10), soup, and sweets whenever the ferries run or guests are staying. Full meals can be had by prior arrangement. Hostelers should expect unparalleled tranquility and simplicity in the unaltered former home of Peig Sayers herself. (☎086 848 6687 or 086 852 2321; www.greatblasketisland.com. Sheets €2.50. Open Apr.-Oct. Dorms €12-18.) You can camp on Great Blasket, but like the hostelers, come prepared for the rigors of island life as the settlers before you did.

BALLYFERRITER (BAILE AN FHEIRTÉARAIGH) ☎066

Ballyferriter is western Dingle's closest approximation to a town center. The surrounding settlement is an unpolluted *gaeltacht*—you ought to have memorized those Guinness signs by now. The **Chorca Dhuibhne Museum,** in the center of town, brims with photos and text relating to the area's wildlife, archaeology, and folklore. (☎915 6333. Open daily 9:30am-5pm. €1.90, students €1.30.) The museum represents a noble attempt to make the area's history accessible, and it's a good starting point for visiting nearby ancient sights. Speaking of which, from the hostel at the western end of Ballyferriter, you can follow the signs to the Iron Age **Dún An Óir** ("Fort of Gold"), where, in 1580, the English massacred over 600 Spanish, Italian, and Irish soldiers engaged in a rebellion against Queen Elizabeth. Along the main road back to Dingle, the historico-architecturally inclined will find several diversions. Closest to Ballyferriter is **Riasc,** a puzzling monastic sight with an engraved standing slab. Heading east, follow signs to **Gallarus Oratory,** a mortarless yet watertight masterpiece of 8th-century stonework that was used for worship. Continue straight on the dirt road to view the sight for free at any hour, or turn left at the signs for the **visitors center** if you'd rather begin with the 15min. video tour of Dingle's ancient places. (☎915 5333. Oratory always open. Free. Visitors center open Apr. to mid-Oct. daily 9:30am-8pm. €2.50, students €2, children free.)

For greater grandeur uncorrupted by hype, take the longer route back to Dingle Town, which passes through **Murreagh** to **Kilmalkédar Church.** The church (*Cill Mhaoilchéadair* in Irish) is a remarkably intact 7th-century specimen with blended Romanesque and traditional Irish architectural features. Among the graves overlooking Smerwick Harbour, look for the **ogham stone** (see **Christians and Vikings,** p. 55) and a mysterious **sundial.** Local legend holds that you can ensure your entrance to heaven by passing through the rear window of the old church three times consecutively. (You've gotta go all the way around, don't cut through the side window—God doesn't like a cheater.)

Five minutes outside town on the Dunquin road, behind a shop of the same name, **An Cat Dubh ❶** crosses your path in a tacky but friendly way. (☎915 6286. €12 per person. **Camping** €4 per person.) There are several Ballyferriter B&Bs: the one next door to the hostel, **An Spéice ❸,** provides quiet rest and a varied brekkie menu. (☎915 6254. All rooms with bath. €25 per person.) For a more raucous time, try the **B&B ❸** at the Tigh'n tSaorsaigh Pub (see below). Groceries are available at **O Shúilleaghán Market** (O'Sullivan's), on Main St. (☎915 6157. Open May-Sept. daily 9am-11pm; Oct.-Apr. 9am-6pm.) Upon landing in town, many visitors head straight for **Tigh Pheig ❸** (Peig's Pub), on Main St. Frequent evening trad sessions in the summer, appetizing meals, and two pool tables keep the locals coming too. (☎915 6433. Daily lunch specials €7.50, dinner mains from €8.90.) Across the street, **Tigh Uí Mhurchú** (Murphy's), with its cushioned stools and attentive bartender, is a perfect place to watch the matches or hear music several times a week. (☎915 6224. Lunch 12:30-3pm, dinner 6-9pm.) Locals also flock to **Tigh Uí Chathain** for the lunchtime rush and return for lively banter in the evening. (☎915 6359. Mains €6-9.50. Lunch noon-2:30pm, dinner 6-8:30pm. Closed W.) Stop for pints or a filling meal (mains €5.50-9) at **Tigh'n tSaorsaigh** and you may find yourself staying the night at the connected **B&B ❸**. (☎915 6344. Open daily 1-9pm. Doubles €50-60.)

NORTHERN DINGLE ☎066

Hikers and beach junkies alike can get their fix on the peninsula's northern shore, far from the tourist bonanza to the south and west. Jaw-dropping views from the mountains motivate casual ramblers to make the daytrip from Dingle Town, while the more serious packers following the Dingle Way enjoy the solitude. The seaside villages, though not destinations in themselves, are all pleasant places to get a meal, a pint, or a night's rest. On Fridays, **Bus Éireann** runs a bus from Tralee to Castlegregory and on to Cloghane. Hitchhiking over the Conor Pass is reportedly common during the tourist season, but one should always consider the risks.

From Dingle Town, a winding cliff road runs north through the **Conor Pass,** which at 1500 ft. is the highest mountain pass in Ireland. Buses won't fit on the narrow road, but cars squeeze through, and superstar bikers and walkers huff-and-puff it past valley views on 3 mi. of continuous incline. The road crests at **Brandon Ridge,** and your tribulations are rewarded with dazzling views that will blow you away—if the high winds haven't already. On clear days, you can gaze awestruck at lakes thousands of feet below, even at distant Valentia Island (see p. 279) off the south coast across the peninsula and the **Maharee Islands** to the north. As the road twists down, a small waterfall and a few picnic tables mark the base of **Pedlars Lake,** named in honor of a traveling tradesman who lost his wares (and his life) to a gang of brigands. These days, you're more likely to encounter geologists than bandits roaming the glacier-sliced lakes and boulder-pocked landscape.

CLOGHANE (AN CLOCHÁN) AND BRANDON (BRÉANAINN). Beyond the lake, the road heads downhill to the sea. Signs point out the westward fork to **Cloghane** (Claw-hane) and its even smaller northern neighbor, **Brandon.** These quiet hamlets are good starting points for hiking up the 3127 ft. **Mt. Brandon** or tackling the seldom-trod but magnificent region to the north that culminates in **Brandon Point.** You can pick up maps of the area in the **tourist office** on the main road in Cloghane. *(☎713 8277. Open June to mid-Sept. Hours limited and vary yearly; call ahead or go to the post office down the street.)* Each July 25, the devout head up the "Saint's Road" on Mt. Brandon, which was misnamed in honor of alleged trailblazer and Holy Wandering Spirit St. Brendan. The rest of the year, the **Pilgrim's Route,** which forks off the Dingle Way just west of Ventry and rejoins it in Cloghane, attracts hikers who prefer ancient Christian sites and inland ridges to coastline rambles.

Whether you've just conquered the mountain, are preparing for the trek, or prefer to savor a good novel or film from a perch by the sea, **Mount Brandon House Walking Lodge ❶** leaves little (or nothing) to be desired. Stretch those weary legs in the glassed-in sitting room and watch the tide recede, or curl up on the massive couch and pop in a video from the small but excellent collection. *(☎713 8299. Wheelchair-accessible. Laundry €4. Family rooms available. 3- to 6-bed dorms €14; doubles €33.)* The lively **Tigh Tomsi ❷** pub serves hot meals next door *(☎713 8301. Open M-Sa noon-1am, Su noon-11pm; music W, Sa, and Su in summer, weekends in winter)*, while **The Coffee Shop ❶**, attached to the front of the hostel, dishes up delightful soups, sandwiches, snacks, and breakfast *("open 9am-5ish")*.

STRADBALLY (STRAID BAILE). Six miles back east in Stradbally, the friendly **Conor Pass Hostel (IHH) ❶** has a few small but welcoming beds. *(☎713 9179. Open mid-Mar. to mid-Oct. €12 per person.)* The hostel makes a good base for hikes in the **Slieve Mish Mountains** to the east. The 2713 ft. ascent to **Cáherconree** culminates with a lookout over the Shannon Estuary, the Iveragh, and the Atlantic. Stradbally is also an excellent place from which to embark on the **Loch a'Duín** nature and archaeology walk *(map guides available in area tourist offices and gift shops)*. Stradballyans stock up at **Tomásin's Pub and Restaurant ❸**, across the street from the hostel. *(☎713 9179. Lunch €4.50-9, served noon-3pm; dinners €10.20-16.50, served 6-9pm.)* For a surprisingly varied selection of whole foods and organic produce, hit up **An Siopa** 100 yd. down the road to the west. *(☎713 9483. Open mid-Mar. to mid-Oct. Tu-Sa 10am-7pm.)* Take your picnickables down to Stradbally's **beach;** the strand beyond the dune is especially magnificent at low tide.

CASTLEGREGORY (CAISLEAN CHRIARE). In Castlegregory, 1½ mi. north of the main road, you'll find the only real grocery store in northern Dingle and more than a fair share of the excitement. Residents (and furriners) take advantage of the unrelenting winds along the narrow, sandy **Maharees Peninsula** stretching into the sea north of the village, where wetsuited windsurfers show off for sunbathers. The conditions here so pleased competitors in the 2000 **Windsurfing World Championships** that the event seems to have settled on a permanent venue, returning to Castlegregory each October. Strive to stay afloat with gear rented from **Jamie Knox** *(☎713 9411)* or **Waterworld** *(☎713 9292)*, both located on the waterfront and offering similar services at similar prices. *(Wetsuits €5 per hr.; kayaking and canoeing €6; windsurfing €15; surfing €12-15; snorkeling €6 per hr.; ski and wakeboarding €40 for ½ hr.)* Gallop (on a horse) through the surf of the Maharees beaches courtesy of **O'Connor's Trekking** *(☎066 713 9216)*, or lower your handicap at the lovely golf course of **Castlegregory Golf and Fishing Club** *(☎713 9444; €25 for 18 holes, clubs €6; no credit cards)*. The **Maharees Regatta** hits the waves in early July, and a week or two later the **Summer Festival** shakes up the town with parades and dances.

A bus connects Castlegregory to Tralee *(€5.10)*. The small but informative **tourist office** is next to Spar Market. *(☎713 9422. Open M-F 9:30am-5pm. Oct.-Mar. usually closes by 3pm.)* For a night's rest, straight up (read: bring your own sheets), try **Fitzgerald's Euro-Hostel ❶**, above the pub at the junction between the main road and the route up to Maharees—not to be confused with the town's other two pubs with the same name. *(☎713 9133. Dorms €12; doubles €24.)* For a more luxurious experience, treat yourself like royalty at **Castle House B&B ❸**, 50 yd. down the Maharees road from the village. Soak in the bath or stroll down their private beach before choosing from the extensive breakfast menu. *(☎713 9183. All rooms with bath and TV. €28 per person.)* Pitch your tent just steps from the popular watersports spots at **Sandy Bay Caravan Park ❶**. *(☎713 9338. €7.60 per small tent.)* **Spar Market** is an oasis in otherwise grocery-free terrain. *(☎713 9433. Open M-Sa 8:30am-9pm, Su 8:30am-7:30pm.)* In a restored stone cottage on Main St., **Milesian Restaurant ❷** hosts frequent music and poetry readings and an ever-changing menu with vegetarian options. *(Mains €7-11. Open Easter-Nov. and winter weekends 5-9:30pm.)* Just before the Spar Market, **Barry's Village Bistro ❷** is a great place to stop in for a burger or pizza, topped off with homemade apple pie. *(☎713 9214. Burgers €6.50, fish and chicken from €8.50.)* **Ned Natterjack's,** named for the rare and vocal Natterjack toad that resides in this area, presents various genres of music and has a hoppin' beer garden. *(☎713 949. Music F-Su.)*

TRALEE (TRÁ LÍ) ☎066

Tralee lacks true village charm. As the economic and residential capital (pop. 20,000) of Kerry, it offers little appeal to the long-term visitor. Still, large storefronts line the city's main streets, and quality pubs serve up bar food and trad. Ireland's second-largest museum, detailing the history of Kerry, stands out, but no tourist development could possibly top the city's famed gardens. The annual **Rose of Tralee** is a centuries-old pageant that has Irish eyes glued to their TVs in August.

TRANSPORTATION

Airport: Kerry Airport, in **Farranfore** (☎976 4966), off N22 halfway between Tralee and Killarney. (See **Killarney,** p. 266.)

Trains: Oakpark Rd. (☎712 3522). Ticket office open daily before departures. Trains tie Tralee to: **Cork** (2½hr.; M-Sa 4 per day, Su 3 per day; €22.90); **Dublin** (4hr.; M-Sa 4 per day, Su 3 per day; €45.10); **Galway** (5-6 hr., 3 per day, €45.10); **Killarney** (40min., 4 per day, €7.50); **Rosslare Harbour** (5½hr., M-Sa 1 per day, €21.60); **Waterford** (4hr., M-Sa 1 per day, €16.50).

Buses: Oakpark Rd. (☎712 3566). Open June-Aug. M-Sa 8:30am-6pm, Su 8:30am-4pm; Sept.-May M-Sa 9am-5:15pm. To: **Bantry** (2½hr., June-Sept. 2 per day, €12.45); **Cork** (2½hr.; M-Sa 14 per day, Su 10 per day; €12.70); **Dingle** (1¼hr.; July-Aug. M-Sa 8 per day, Su 5 per day; Sept.-June M-Sa 4 per day, Su 2 per day; €7.90); **Galway,** via **Tarbert Ferry,** (M-Sa 11 per day, Su 9 per day; €17.10); **Killarney** (40min.; June-Sept. M-Sa 14 per day, Su 12 per day; Oct.-May M-Sa 5 per day, Su 6 per day; €5.85); **Limerick** (2¼hr., 7-8 per day, €12.20); **Skibbereen** (3hr., June-Sept. 2 per day, €14.60).

Taxi: Lee Cab (☎712 0555). Cabs also park at the intersection of Denny St. and the Mall. €1.30 per mi., less for long distances.

Bike Rental: O'Halloran, 83 Boherboy (☎712 2820). €10 per day, €50 per wk. Helmet €1.30 per day. Open M-Sa 9:30am-6pm.

ORIENTATION AND PRACTICAL INFORMATION

Tralee's streets are hopelessly knotted; in-the-know travelers arm themselves with free maps from the tourist office. The main avenue—variously called **the Mall** (as it passes by **the Square), Castle St.,** and **Boherboy**—has many stores and restaurants along its roughly east-west path. **Edward St.** connects this main thoroughfare to the train and bus stations. Wide **Denny St.** runs south to the tourist office and park.

Tourist Office: Ashe Memorial Hall (☎712 1288), at the end of Denny St. From the station, head into town on Edward St., turn right on Castle St., then left onto Denny St. Well-informed staff provides free maps and the such. Open July-Aug. M-Sa 9am-7pm, Su 9am-6pm; May-June and Oct. M-Sa 9am-6pm; Nov.-Apr. M-F 9am-5pm.

Banks: AIB, Denny St. (☎712 1100), at Castle St. Open daily 9am-6pm. **Bank of Ireland** (☎712 1177), a few doors down. M 10am-5pm, Tu-F 10am-4pm. Both have **ATMs** throughout town.

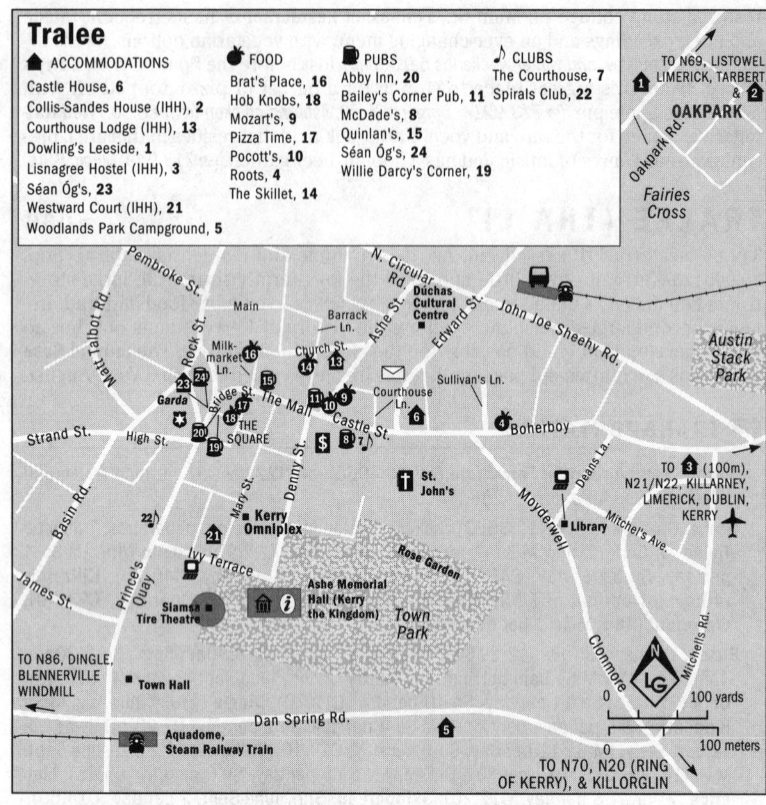

Camping Equipment: Call of the Wild, Ivy Terr. (☎712 3820). Has the widest selection of outdoorsy gear in town. Open M-Sa 9:30am-6pm. **Landers,** Courthouse Ln. (☎712 6644). No tent rental. Open M-F 9am-6pm.

Laundry: The Laundry, Pembroke St. (☎712 3214). Open M-Sa 9am-6pm.

Emergency: ☎999; no coins required. **Police** *(Garda)*: High St. (☎712 2022).

Pharmacy: Kelly's, the Mall (☎712 1302). Open M-Sa 9am-6pm.

Counseling and Support: Samaritans (☎712 2566), 44 Moyderwell. 24hr. hotline.

Hospital: Tralee County General Hospital (☎712 6222), off the Killarney road.

Internet Access: Library, Moyderwell St. (☎712 1200). Book by phone or in person. Open M, W, and F-Sa 10am-5pm; Tu and Th 10am-8pm. **Millennium Computer College,** Ivy Terr. (☎712 0020). €1 per 10min. Open M-Sa 10am-6pm.

Post Office: Edward St. (☎712 1013), off Castle St. Open M and W-Sa 9am-5:30pm, Tu 9:30am-5:30pm.

ACCOMMODATIONS AND CAMPING

Tralee's several scattered but decent hostels can barely contain the rosy festival-goers in late August. Rows of pleasant B&Bs line the area where Edward St. becomes Oakpark Rd.; others can be found along Princes Quay, close to the park.

Courthouse Lodge (IHH), 5 Church St. (☎712 7199), off Ashe St. Centrally located but buffered by a quiet street. You'll find a clean bed, shower, kitchen, and TV room with VCR in this new-ish hostel. All rooms with full bath. **Internet access** €1 per 10min. Top sheets and towels €1 each. Laundry €6. Dorms €14; doubles €32. ❶

Collis-Sandes House (IHH), Oakpark Rd. (☎712 8658). Near-perfect, but far from town and sometimes booked solid. Follow Oakpark Rd. (N69) 1 mi. from town, take the first left after Spar Market, and follow signs another ½ mi. to the right; or call for pickup. Magnificent high ceilings and Moorish arches lend grandeur to this ex-convent. Free rides to town 5 times per day. Continental breakfast €2.50. Laundry €4.50 wash, €4.50 dry. Wheelchair-accessible. 14-bed dorms €11.50; 8-bed €13; 6-bed €12-15; 4-bed €13-15. Singles €25; doubles €38. **Camping** €6.50 per person. ❶

Seán Óg's, 41 Bridge St. (☎712 8822). An ideal location with 14 rooms, this B&B is also home to a traditional pub downstairs. Exceptionally friendly service and an easy crawl to bed after several pints. €25 per person. ❸

Dowling's Leeside, Oakpark Rd. (☎712 6475). About ½ mi. from the town center on Edward St. Pamper yourself at this cheerful B&B decorated with antique Irish pine furniture and cushy chairs. The lovely hostess and friendly cocker spaniel will make you want to move in. All rooms with showers. Singles €25; doubles €51. ❸

Lisnagree Hostel (IHH), Ballinorig Rd. (☎712 7133). 1 mi. from town, near the train station. Follow Boherboy St. out of town—it's on the left fork after the traffic circle. Relaxed, family-run hostel great for couples and kids, but slightly remote for those hitting the pubs at night. Dorms €11; singles €18; doubles €28; family room €12 per person. ❶

Westward Court (IHH), Mary St. (☎718 0081). Follow Denny St. to the park; turn right, then right again at the Ivy Terrace Diner. Spotless, uniform dorms off a hotel-like corridor. All rooms with bath. Continental breakfast included. Wheelchair-accessible. Laundry €6.35. Curfew 3am. 4-bed dorms €16; singles €24; doubles €44. ❷

Castle House, 27 Upper Castle St. (☎712 5167). Watch satellite TV in your fully-loaded room and listen to the traffic go by. Ideally located for pub crawls; morning pancakes ease even the worst hangovers. Singles €40; doubles €65. ❹

Woodlands Park Campground, Dan Spring Rd. (☎712 1235), a ¼ mi. past the Aquadome. National award-winner. Game room and shop. Laundry €6. Open Apr.-Sept. €15 for two people in a tent. Showers €1. ❶

FOOD

True gourmands may be disappointed with the culinary landscape of Tralee, but pub grub and fast food are readily available. If they don't sell it at the massive **Tesco** in the Square, you probably shouldn't be eating it. (☎712 2788. Open M-W and Sa 8:30am-8pm, Th-F 8:30am-10pm, Su 10am-6pm.) Across the street, **Seancar** peddles wholefoods and organic produce. (☎712 2644. Open M-W and Sa 9am-6pm, Th 9am-8pm, F 9am-9pm.)

Pocott's, 3 Ashe St. (☎712 9500). Quality homemade Irish food; fast, fresh, and cheap. Lunches are especially popular (around €6.35, served noon-3pm), and small Irish breakfasts are a steal (€4-6.50). Most dinner mains €6-8. Open July-Sept. M-Sa 9am-9:30pm, Su noon-7pm; Oct.-June M-Sa 9am-7pm, Su noon-7pm. ❷

Mozart's, 4 Ashe St. (☎712 7977). A range of well-prepared delights—bagel sandwiches (€3.20) in the morning, wraps (€3.80-5.10) in the afternoon, stir-fries and steaks (€8.25-16.50) in the evening. Open M-Th 9am-6:30pm, F-Sa 9am-9:30pm. ❸

Brat's Place, 18 Milk Market Ln., down a pedestrian walkway off the Mall. A veg-head's dream. Lunch on local and organic ingredients in a pleasant, private setting. Soup €3, mains €7, desserts €3.50. Open M-Sa 12:30-2:30pm, later if the food lasts. ❷

The Skillet, Barrack Ln. (☎712 4561), off the Mall. Traditional decor matches the stew and other native specialties. Lunches run €7.50-9.50; dinner is pricier (steak from €14.50). Open M-Sa 10am-10pm; Apr.-Sept. also Su 1-10pm. ❸

Hob Knobs, the Square (☎712 1846). This low-key cafeteria brushes elbows with tasty breakfasts (large Irish €5) and shoots the breeze with decent lunches (€4.45-6). Open M-Sa 8am-5pm; July-Aug. open until 10pm. ❷

Roots, 76 Boherboy (☎712 2665). An ever-changing but limited menu of gargantuan vegetarian dishes. Watch your meal be prepared or relax at one of the 5 tables in this cozy establishment. Open M-F 11am-3:30pm. ❷

Pizza Time, the Square (☎712 6317). No pretense, just high quality chow at low prices. Pizzas €7-10, pasta €8-9, burgers €5.75. Delivery available Su-Th 6pm-midnight and F-Sa 6pm-12:30am. Open M-Th and Su noon-midnight, F noon-2am, Sa noon-4am. ❷

PUBS AND CLUBS

Seán Óg's, 41 Bridge St. (☎712 8822). Plenty of room to chat up other patrons in this traditional pub. Mike and JP serve as your personal drinking consultants while offering toasted sandwiches and snacks between pints of the black stuff. Impressive fireplace (hand-built by the owner) keeps you warm on those long winter nights. Trad Tu, W, F, and Su. You may find it hard to leave the conversation; no need--the B&B upstairs offers comfy beds after a long night at the bar (see **Accommodations** above).

Abbey Inn, Bridge St. (☎712 3390), across from Seán Óg's. Edgy crowd comes to hear live rock most weekends. Bono swept here—when U2 played the Abbey in the late 70s, the manager made them sweep the floors to pay for their drinks because he thought they were so bad. The late night crowd is young; they spend more time scoping each other out for a possible evening encounter than drinking or dancing. Th live music, DJ other nights. Open M-Sa until 2:30am, Su live band until 1am. Food 9am-9:30pm.

Willie Darcy's Corner (☎712 4343), the Square. Just over 2 years old and pure class. All ages meet here over candlelit tables. Genial conversation takes the place of music. Soups and sandwiches served from 12:30-2:30pm

Bailey's Corner Pub (☎712 6230), at Ashe and the Mall. Kerry's rugby legacy adorns the walls, and current players join an older crowd at the bar. Munch on sandwiches and a variety of hot food (€3-6.50) while you watch the matches. Trad M-W and Su.

McDade's, Upper Castle St. (☎712 1877). Part of the Quality Tralee Hotel, the immense, polished wood pub attracts a slightly older, touristy crowd. Fills up late when folks come to grind out back in the club **The Courthouse** (see below).

Quinlan's, (☎712 1027), the Mall. Step back in time a few hundred years in this classic joint, which closes at 6pm and doesn't open at all on Su. Food 10:30am-5:30pm.

Spirals, Princes Quay (☎712 3333), located in the Brandon Hotel. One of Tralee's two nightclubs, Spirals spins the disco ball every Sa night. Cover €8.

The Courthouse, Upper Castle St. (☎712 1877), behind McDade's Pub. The second of Tralee's two nightclubs, the Courthouse keeps the crowds groovin' each F and Sa night. Cover €6-8. For information on other local goings-on, get a copy of *The Kerryman* (€1.10), available from almost any newsagent.

SIGHTS AND FESTIVALS

Tralee is home to Ireland's second-largest museum, **Kerry the Kingdom,** in Ashe Memorial Hall on Denny St. One of the perennial favorites for museum awards, the Kingdom marshals all the resources of display technology to tell the county's story from 8000 BC to the present. Budding historians will find themselves rooted in front of vivid dioramas and videos on everything from Kerry's castles to her greatest Gaelic football victories. Downstairs, "Geraldine Tralee" takes you through a superbly assembled recreation of medieval city streets, as seen from a small moving cart. Enjoy the shouts and clamor of yesteryear as life-size townspeople carry on daily activities of the time period. The museum puts on a special exhibition with contributions from museums around the world each year—look for a fantastic and thorough French Revolution exhibit in 2003. (☎712 7777. Free audio tours in French and German. Open mid-Mar. to Oct. daily 10am-6pm; Nov. noon-4:30pm. €8, students €6.50, children €5.) Across from the museum, another from the ranks of Ireland's "second-largests"—**Town Park,** in this case—blooms each summer with the **Roses of Tralee.** Nearby, gray carpeting in **St. John's Church,** Castle St., dampens the echo and the Gothic mood, but the stained glass is worth a look.

Just down the Dingle road is the **Blenneville Windmill and Visitors Centre,** the largest operating windmill in the British Isles. The small museum recalls Blenneville during the Famine, when it was Kerry's main port of emigration, focusing on the "coffin ships" that carried Ireland's sons and daughters to distant shores. A 10min. audio-visual presentation covers the history of the region and the windmill's restoration. In the future, visitors will be able to search databases to discover when their ancestors migrated on those infamous "coffin ships." (☎712 1064. Open Apr.-Oct. daily 10am-6pm. €4, students €2.50.) The building on the Princes Quay traffic circle looks like a cross between a Gothic castle and a space-age solarium, but it's actually Tralee's €6-million **Aquadome,** complete with whirlpools, steam room, sauna, and gym. Waterslides and a unique mini-golf course should captivate even the most demanding little urchins. (☎712 8899. Open daily 10am-10pm. June-Sept. €8, children €7; Oct.-May €6.35, €5.10. Aquagolf €5.70, students €3.20.) **Tralee & Dingle Railway,** restored to its days of wine and roses, runs the 2 mi. between the Aquadome and the Blenneville complex. (☎712 1064. Trains leave the Aquadome every hour on the hour and leave the windmill on the half. Closed M. July-Aug. 10:30am-5:30pm; May-June and Sept. 11am-5pm. €4, students €2.50.)

The **Siamsa Tíre Theatre,** at the end of Denny St. next to the museum, is Ireland's national folk theater. It mounts brilliant summer programs depicting traditional Irish life through mime, music, and dance. October through April hosts various touring productions. (☎712 3055; www.siamsatire.com. Performances July-Aug. M-Sa; May-June and Sept. M-Th and Sa. May-Sept. shows start at 8:30pm, Oct.-Apr. 8pm. Box office open May-Sept. M-Sa 9am-10pm; Oct.-Apr. before curtain. Tickets from €20.) The **Dúchas Cultural Centre,** Edward St., also does the singing-and-dancing stuff. (☎ 712 4083. Shows July-Aug. Tu 8:30pm. Tickets €5.)

Lovely, marriageable lasses of Irish descent descend upon the town during the last week of August for the beloved **Rose of Tralee Festival.** A maelstrom of entertainment surrounds the main event—a "personality" competition to earn the coveted title "Rose of Tralee." Rose-hopefuls or spectators can call the Rose Office in Ashe Memorial Hall (☎712 1322). As if the live music on every street corner and a four-day-long party wasn't enough, the festival is followed by the **Tralee Races.**

TARBERT (TAIRBEART) ☎068

A tiny and peaceful seaside spot on the N69 in Kerry, Tarbert is home to an incredible hostel and a convenient ferry service running between Counties Kerry and Clare. The boat ride will save you an 85 mi. coastal drive through Limerick. **Bus Éireann** stops outside the hostel on its way from Tralee to Doolin and Galway (5hr.; mid-June to Sept. M-Sa 3 per day, Su 2 per day; Galway to Tralee €19). During the rest of the year, the nearest stop to Tarbert is in **Kilrush. Shannon Ferry Ltd.** makes the 20min. Shannon crossing between the port a mile from Tarbert and Killimer.

(☎065 905 3124. June-Aug. every 30min.; Apr.-Sept. 7:30am-9:30pm and Oct.-Mar. 7am-7:30pm every hour on the half-hour from Tarbert and on the hour from Killimer; Su year-round from 10am. €12.50 per carload, €3 per pedestrian or biker.) A **bus** leaves from the Tarbert ferry terminal and goes to Kilrush; check at the hostel for a schedule (☎36500; M-Sa 2-3 per day, Su 2 per day). The **tourist office** is in the carefully restored 1831 Bridewell Jail and Courthouse; walk down the street from the hostel and turn right onto the road toward the ferry.There is also a small coffee shop in the old jail, with coffee, scones, and a gift shop with postcards. (Open Apr.-Oct. daily 10am-6pm. Tours €5, students €3.50.) Be sure to get cash before you come; the nearest **ATM** is 15 mi. away in Listowel.

A few hundred yards from the ferry stands **Tarbert House,** which has been home to the family of Signeur Leslie of Tarbert since 1690. The recently restored exterior rivals the period pieces and priceless art it protects. (☎36198. Open daily 10am-noon and 2-4pm. €2. Tours given by Mrs. Leslie herself.) The hour-long **Tarbert House Woodland Walk** takes ramblers through Leslie's Wood, with views of the River Shannon, Tarbert Old Pier, and Tarbert Bay. The path is marked and begins next to the tourist office. The **Ferry House Hostel ❶** is the four-year-old occupant of a 200-year-old building in the center of town. The friendly owners spent a year traveling and taking detailed notes on the best and worst of the world's hostels before opening their own. The success of their study is evident in the most comfortable bedding found anywhere, excellent showers, and a cafe. (☎36555. Sheets €1.30. Laundry €5.10. Wheelchair-accessible. Open year-round. Cafe open June-Sept. Reception May-Sept. 8am-7pm. Dorms €8.90; doubles €25-33.) **Coolahan's** is the most notable of Tarbert's five pubs, a little establishment with regulars speaking English and Irish at the bar. Drop down to **The Anchor,** on the street perpendicular to the hostel, for a light seafood chowder and live music Saturday nights.

LIMERICK (LUIMNEACH) ☎061

Despite a thriving trade in off-color poems, Limerick City has long endured a bad reputation. Although its 18th-century Georgian streets and parks are both regal and elegant, 20th-century industrial and commercial developments cursed the city with a featureless urban feel. During much of the 20th century, economic hardship spawned poverty and crime, earning the city the nickname of "Stab Town." What little attention Limerick received seemed to focus on squalor—a tradition exemplified by Irish-American author Frank McCourt's celebrated memoir *Angela's Ashes.* But despite the historical stigma, Limerick is now a city on the rise. A large student population fosters an intense arts scene, adding to a wealth of cultural treasures that have long gone unnoticed. In addition, the Republic's third largest city boasts top quality museums and a well-preserved 12th-century cathedral.

TRANSPORTATION

Trains: (☎315 555) Inquiries desk open M-F 9am-6pm, Sa 9am-5:30pm. Trains from Limerick to **Cork** (2½hr.; M-Sa 6 per day, Su 5 per day; €17.70); **Dublin** (2hr.; M-Sa 10 per day, Su 9 per day; €33.10); **Ennis** (M-Sa 2 per day, €6.90); **Killarney** (2½hr.; M-Sa 4 per day, Su 3 per day; €19.60); **Rosslare** (3½hr., M-Sa 1 per day, €30.60); **Tralee** (3hr.; M-Sa 6 per day, Su 3 per day; €19.60); **Waterford** (2hr.; M-Sa 2 per day in summer, 1 per day in winter; €22.80).

Buses: Colbert Station, just off Parnell St. (☎313 333; 24hr. talking timetable ☎319 911.) Open June-Sept. M-F 8:10am-6pm, Su 9am-6pm; Oct.-May M-Sa 8:10am-6pm, Su 3-7pm. **Bus Éireann** sends buses to **Cork** (2hr., 14 per day, €12.10); **Derry** (6½hr., 3 per day, €22.80); **Donegal** (6hr., 4 per day, €20.20); **Dublin** (3½hr., 13 per day,

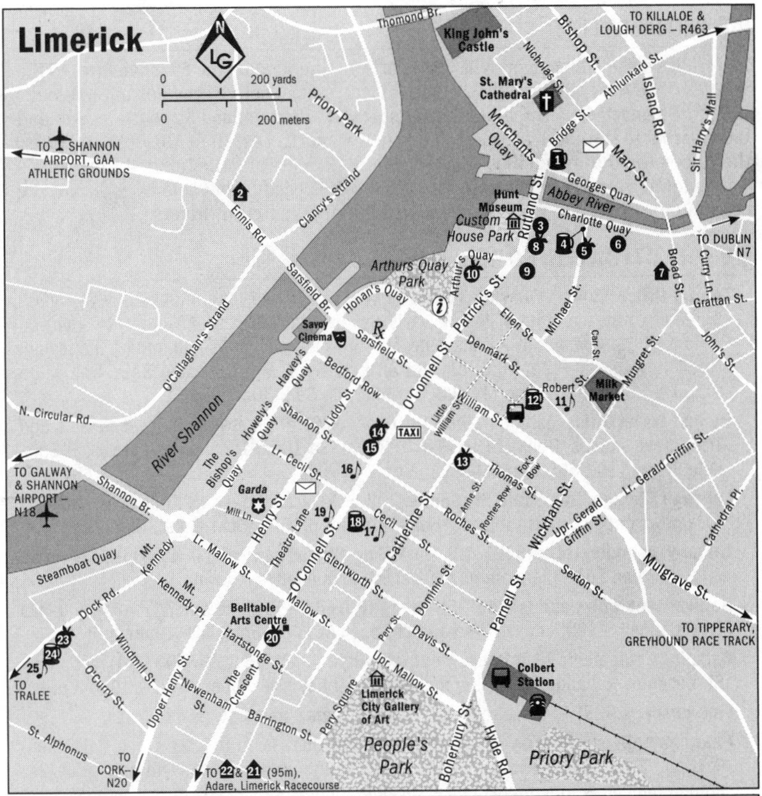

Limerick

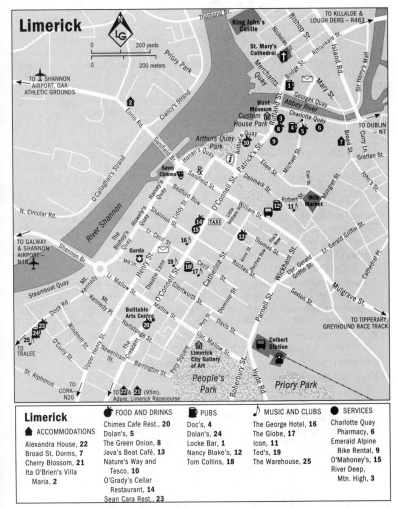

ACCOMMODATIONS
- Alexandra House, **22**
- Broad St. Dorms, **7**
- Cherry Blossom, **21**
- Ita O'Brien's Villa Maria, **2**

FOOD AND DRINKS
- Chimes Cafe Rest., **20**
- Dolan's, **5**
- The Green Onion, **8**
- Java's Beat Café, **13**
- Nature's Way and Tesco, **10**
- O'Grady's Cellar Restaurant, **14**
- Sean Cara Rest., **23**

PUBS
- Doc's, **4**
- Dolan's, **24**
- Locke Bar, **1**
- Nancy Blake's, **12**
- Tom Collins, **18**

MUSIC AND CLUBS
- The George Hotel, **16**
- The Globe, **17**
- Icon, **11**
- Ted's, **19**
- The Warehouse, **25**

SERVICES
- Charlotte Quay Pharmacy, **6**
- Emerald Alpine Bike Rental, **9**
- O'Mahoney's, **15**
- River Deep, Mtn. High, **3**

€13.30); **Ennis** (45 min., 14 per day, €6.70); **Galway** (2hr., 14 per day, €12.10); **Kilkenny** (1½hr., 2 per day, €13.30); **Killarney** (2½hr.; M-Sa 6 per day, Su 3 per day; €12.40); **Tralee** (2hr., 7 per day, €12.10); **Waterford** (2½hr., 6-7 per day, €13.30); **Wexford** and **Rosslare Harbour** with some buses timed to meet the departing ferries (4hr., 3-4 per day, €15.20). A **local bus** network runs from the city center to the suburbs (M-Sa 2 per hr. 7:30am-11pm, Su 1 per hr. 10:30am-11pm; €0.95); #2 and 8 access the university; #6 follows the Ennis road.

Taxi: Top Cabs (☎417 417). Takes you to most places in the city for under €3.80 and to the airport for about €25.

Bike Rental: Emerald Alpine, 1 Patrick St. (☎416 983). €20 per day, €70 per wk. Deposit €50. Return to any participating Raleigh location. Open M-Sa 9:15am-5:30pm.

ORIENTATION

Limerick's streets form a no-frills grid pattern, bounded by the **Shannon River** to the west and the **Abbey River** to the north. The city's most active area lies in the blocks around **O'Connell St.** (which becomes **Patrick St.,** then **Rutland St.** to the north, and **the Crescent** to the south). Follow O'Connell St. north past Hunt Museum and cross the Abbey River to reach **King's Island,** where St. Mary's Cathedral and King John's Castle loom over the landscape. The city itself is easily navigable by foot, but the preponderance of one-way streets makes it a nightmare for drivers.

PRACTICAL INFORMATION

Tourist Office: Arthurs Quay (☎317 522; www.shannon-dev.ie), in the space-age glass building. From the station, follow Davis St. as it becomes Glentworth; turn right on O'Connell St., then left at Arthurs Quay Mall. Has free city maps and info on the region. Open July-Aug. M-F 9am-6:30pm, Sa-Su 9am-6pm; May-June and Sept.-Oct. M-Sa 9:30am-5:30pm; Nov.-Apr. M-F 9:30am-5:30pm, Sa 9:30am-1pm.

Budget Travel Office: usit (☎415 064), O'Connell St. at Glentworth St., issues ISICs and **TravelSave** stamps. Open M-F 9:30am-5:30pm, Sa 10am-1pm. **Budget Travel,** 2 Sarsfield St. (☎414 666). Open M-F 9am-6pm.

Luggage Storage: Bus/Train Station (☎202 513). €2.50 per day. 24hr. limit. Open M-F 8am-6pm and 6:30-8:45pm, Sa 8am-6pm and 6:30-7:45pm, Su 9:30am-7pm.

Laundry: Launderette (☎312 712), on Mallow St. Full service from €8. Open M-F 9am-6pm, Sa 9am-5pm. There are no self-service launderettes in town.

Banks: Bank of Ireland (☎415 055) and **AIB** (☎414 388) are among the many banks on O'Connell St. Both have **ATMs** and are open M 10am-5pm, Tu-F 10am-4pm.

Camping Equipment: River Deep, Mountain High, 7 Rutland St. (☎400 944). O'Connell St. becomes Rutland St. as it approaches the Abbey River. Open M-Sa 9:30am-6pm.

Emergency: ☎999; no coins required. **Police** *(Garda)*: Henry St. (☎414 222).

Pharmacy: Charlotte Quay Pharmacy, Charlotte Quay (☎400 722). Open daily 9am-9:30pm. **Sarsfield Pharmacy** (☎413 808), at the corner of Sarsfield and Liddy St., around the corner from tourist office, has later hours.

Hospital: Regional (☎301 111). Follow O'Connell St. south past the Crescent.

Internet Access: Surfers Cafe, 1 Upper William St. (☎440 122), just uphill from O'Connell St. Tea and coffee available. Internet €7.50 per hr., students €6.30. Calls to UK, Europe, Australia, Canada, and US €0.10 per minute.

Post Office: Lower Cecil St. (☎315 777), just off O'Connell St. Open M-Sa 9am-5:30pm, Tu open 9:30am.

ACCOMMODATIONS

Limerick suffered from a series of hostel-closures in 2002. Lured by government funding, those still operating have filled their rooms with long-term residents (most political asylum seekers), and hung a permanent "no vacancies" sign on their door. Smaller private budget accommodations are beginning to fill the gap, including a promising row of mid-market B&Bs on southern O'Connell St. and some more rural options lining Ennis road (over Sarsfield bridge).

Alexandra House B&B, O'Connell St. (☎318 472), several blocks south of the Daniel O'Connell statue. Red brick townhouse with a pleasantly pastel interior and sun-lit upstairs bedrooms. One of the better B&B values found in the city center. All rooms come with TV and tea-making facilities. Full Irish breakfast. Great deals for families. Student concessions. Singles €26; shared rooms €24-32 per person. ❸

Cherry Blossom Budget Accommodation, O'Connell St. (☎318 472), next to Alexandra House. Limerick's newest kid on the block; the energetic proprietress aims to fill the gap created when the city's hostels fled town. Wild color scheme may sometimes require sunglasses. Dorms €14-15; doubles €32-38. ❶

Ita O'Brien's Villa Maria, 27 Belfield Park (☎455 101), up Ennis Rd. from Sarsfield Bridge, opposite Jury's Hotel. Enough porcelain to remind you of grandma's house. "Cockles and Mussels, alive, alive-o" on the piano downstairs. Petite breakfast. No smoking. Singles €30; doubles €46; triples available (negotiable). ❷

Broad St. Dorms, Broad St. (☎317 222). Vigilant security and cleaning staff attempt to compensate for the impersonal feel of this quasi-dormitory. Wheelchair-accessible. Continental breakfast included. Laundry wash €1.50, dry €1.50. Free parking. 3-bed dorms €16.50; singles €19; doubles with bath €44. ❷

FOOD

Inexpensive and top-notch cafes around Limerick's center offer refreshing alternatives to fast food and pub grub. Forage for groceries at **Tesco** in Arthurs Quay Mall. (☎412 399. Open M-W and Sa 8:30am-8pm, Th-F 8:30am-10pm, Su noon-6pm.) **Nature's Way,** also in the mall, has a limited selection of natural foods and veggie basics. (☎310 466. Open M, W, and Sa 9am-6pm; Th 9am-7pm; F 9am-8pm.)

Dolans, 4 Dock Rd. (☎314 483). Friendly little pub doubles as a spirited restaurant out back. Quoth John, the patron: "Best damn seafood chowder this side of the Atlantic." Limerick's best choice for an evening pre-pub meal. Next stop: here, of course. Lunch menu €5-9 all day, pub hours. ❷

Sean Cara Restaurant, 3 Dock Rd., adjacent to Dolans. Intimate and candlelit, with stone masonry walls and finished plank wood floors. Live harpist on weekends. Vegetarian options and an excellent wine selection. Oven-baked wild Shannon Salmon (€15.20); chargrilled 12oz. sirloin prime Irish beef (€17.70); melon and wild berries (€4.50). Most dishes generous enough to feed 2. Dinner 6-10pm. ❹

The Green Onion, Rutland St. (☎400 710). Limerick's vegetarian headquarters. Converted library building with loft and high molded ceilings. Bold and dramatic interior, just over the artsy border. After 6pm, dinner prices fly high (€13-20), but the "all-day" lunch menu offers simpler and cheaper options (€7-9). Open M-Sa noon-10pm. ❸

Chimes Cafe Restaurant, 61 O'Connell St. (☎087 266 5946), in an intimate space below the Belltable Arts Centre. Relaxed intellectual vibe and percolating conversation await within. Home-baked scones and cakes (€0.85-3). Soups, sandwiches, salads, vegetarian dishes (€3-8). Open 8am-5:30pm. ❶

O'Grady's Cellar Restaurant, O'Connell St. (☎418 286). Look for the little, green awning. This subterranean spot serves as a midday refuge from the bustling streets. Irish cuisine anchors the menu. Meals €6.50-9. Open daily 9:15am-10:30pm. ❷

Java's Beat Cafe, 5 Catherine St. (☎418 077). Flavored coffees and herbal teas combat Limerick's drear. Enjoy a salad, sandwich, or bagel (€2.50-7) upstairs in the hearth side hammock. Open M-Th 9am-midnight, F-Sa 9am-3am, Su 10:30am-midnight. ❶

PUBS

A wide range of musical options caters to the city's diverse pub crowd and its immense student population. Trad-seekers can certainly get their nightly fix, though the chase may be a bit more challenging than in other Irish cities. After a few weeks of "Wild Rover," however, Limerick may be just the place to sample some accordion-free tunes.

Dolan's, Dock Rd. (☎314 483). Worth a Shannon-side walk from the city center to hear the nightly trad played for rambunctious local patrons. The **Warehouse** nightclub is part of the building (see **Clubs,** below).

Locke Bar and Restaurant, Georges Quay (☎413 733). Join the classy crowd on the quay-side patio, or head inside where owner Richard Costello, a former member of Ireland's national rugby team, joins in trad sessions several nights a week.

Nancy Blake's, Denmark St. (☎416 443). The best of both worlds—an older crowd huddles in the sawdust-floored interior for trad M-W nights, while boisterous students take in nightly rock in the open-air "outback." No cover.

Doc's, Michael St. (☎417 266), at Charlotte's Quay in the Granary. The outdoor beer garden, complete with palm trees and a waterfall, heals ale-ing young folks. College bands often play during the term, and DJs bust out chart-toppers most weekend nights.

Tom Collins, 34 Cecil St. (☎415 749). Do your best to blend in with the locals at this cozy establishment. Ordering a Guinness will earn you a nod.

CLUBS

Limerick's insatiable army of students keeps dozens of nightclubs thumping from 11:30pm until 2am nightly. Cover charges can be steep (€6.35-10.20), but keep an eye out for promotions.

The Globe, Cecil St. (☎313 533). 2 floors of manic clubbery, with suggestive artwork and flashing video screens. The Cranberries are known to stop by to sip fine champagne in the upstairs lounge, which is usually restricted to members. Cover €7.

The Warehouse (☎314 483), behind Dolan's on Dock Rd. Draws big-name bands and rising stars, with something for all ages. Authentic reggae on Th, ABBA tribute periodically. Cover €7-12, higher for well-known acts.

Icon, Cornmarket Row, Denmark St. Limerick's newest nightclub and currently *the* hotspot for 20-somethings. Central dance floor suits groovers and onlookers alike. Cover €7-9.

The George Hotel, O'Connell St. (☎414 566). Pick your decade: Th for 70s, F for 80s, and Sa for 90s. The circular dance floor and balcony are always packed. Cover €8-9.

Ted's, O'Connell St. (☎417 412). Pure pop for the older set, who aren't impressed by flashy shows and fog machines. Cover €6.50-9.

SIGHTS

THE HUNT MUSEUM. This fascinating museum houses Ireland's largest collection of art and artifacts outside the National Museum in Dublin, spanning from the Stone Age to the 20th century. The collection includes one of Leonardo da Vinci's four "Rearing Horse" sculptures, a gold crucifix given by Mary Queen of Scots to her executioner, and a coin reputed to be one of the infamous 30 pieces of silver paid to Judas by the Romans. When browsing, open any drawer to find surprises like one of the **world's smallest jade monkeys,** or ask for a guided tour if you're hungry for details. The just plain hungry will surely be satisfied by the ravishing desserts and selection of sandwiches available at the museum **cafe.** *(Custom House, Rutland St. extension of O'Connell ☎312 833. Open M-Sa 10am-5pm, Su 2-5pm. €7, seniors and students €4.)* The nearby **Limerick City Gallery of Art,** Perry Sq., contains a densely packed collection of Irish paintings and international exhibits. *(☎310 633. Open M-F 10am-6pm, Sa 10am-1pm. Free.)* Abstract and experimental pieces fill the small **Belltable Arts Centre,** O'Connell St. *(☎319 866. Open M-F 9am-6pm, Sa 10am-6pm. Free.)*

KING JOHN'S CASTLE. The visitors center has vivid exhibits and a video on the castle's gruesome past. Outside, the **mangonel** is a particularly convincing testament to perverse military tactics: repopularized by *Monty Python's Quest for the Holy Grail*, the mangonel was used to catapult pestilent animal corpses into enemy cities and castles. *(Nicholas St. Walk across the Abbey River and take the 1st left after St. Mary's Cathedral. ☎411 201. Open Mar.-Dec. daily 9:30am-5:30pm. Last admission 4:30pm. €6.50, students and seniors €5, families €16.)*

ST. MARY'S CATHEDRAL. The rough exterior of St. Mary's, near King John's Castle, was built in 1172 on the site of a Viking meeting place. The little fold-down shelves built into the wall next to the altar display elaborate carvings depicting the struggle between good and evil. These carvings are called *misericordia*, Latin for "acts of mercy," and were used by choir members for relief during long services during which sitting was prohibited. *(☎416 238. Open daily 9:15am-5pm. Free.)*

LIMERICK RACECOURSE. Newly opened in 2002, Limerick's €15 million Greenmount track is located 12 mi. from the city center, in the countryside near Patrickswell village. Thoroughbreds race 2-3 days per month in March, May, June, July, October, and December. *(☎320 0000. Follow O'Connell St. south of the city toward Adare. Keep straight at all roundabouts, following signs for Patrickswell. Day prices and race days vary.)*

WALKING TOURS. Tours cover either the northern, sight-filled King's Island region or the more downtrodden locations described in Frank McCourt's *Angela's Ashes*. *(☎318 106. King's Island tour daily at 11am and 2:30pm; Angela's Ashes tour daily at 2:30pm. Both depart from St. Mary's Action Centre, 44 Nicholas St. €5.50.)*

ACTIVITIES AND ENTERTAINMENT

The **Belltable Arts Centre,** 69 O'Connell St. (☎319 866), stages big-name productions year-round. (Box office open M-Sa 9am-6pm and prior to performances. Tickets €10-20.) The **Theatre Royal,** Upper Cecil St. (☎414 224), hosts the town's largest concerts. The **University Concert Hall,** on the UL campus, showcases opera and music. (☎331 549. Tickets €9-25.) For a more casual evening, catch a film at **Savoy** on Bedford Row (☎411 611; €7, before 6pm €5, students €3.50 M-F before 6pm), or try your hand at **billiards** or **snooker** at **Stix** on King's Island, 28 Nicholas St. (☎410 170. Open M-Su 9am-10pm. Pool €5 per hr., snooker €6 per hr.)

DAYTRIPS FROM LIMERICK

BUNRATTY CASTLE AND FOLK PARK

***Buses** running between Limerick and Ennis stop outside the Fitzpatrick Hotel in Bunratty, 8 mi. northwest of Limerick along the Ennis road (16 per day; from Limerick €2.95, from Ennis €4.70). The castle and folk park draw legions of tourists; avoid the fanny-packed crowds by arriving early and heading straight for the castle. There's an **ATM** across the street from the hotel in the Village Mills shopping complex.*

Up the road to the right of the four-star Fitzpatrick Hotel, **Bunratty Castle and Folk Park** has a jumbled collection of historical attractions from all over Ireland. Built in 1425 by the MacNamara clan, the castle shines amidst its surroundings in the otherwise forgettable park. It is allegedly the most complete medieval castle in Ireland, and impresses even jaded tourists with superbly restored furniture, tapestries, and stained-glass windows. Don't miss the **Earl's bedroom,** where the ornate, enormous posts and canopy dwarf the pathetically tiny bed, bringing new meaning to the term "king size." Crowds of visitors clog the castle's narrow stairways during summer months, but you may find the view from the battlement worth the spiraling climb. **The Great Hall** of the castle comes to life twice nightly with **medieval feasts** for deep-pocketed tourists, as local damsels in full wench-regalia and accompanied by medieval music serve meals and bottomless glasses of wine to would-be chieftains. (☎800 269 811. 4-course meal with wine €45.50. Book a week in advance.) The **folk park** originated in the 60s, when builders at Shannon Airport couldn't bear to destroy a quaint cottage for a new runway. Instead, they moved the cottage, now labeled the **Shannon Farmhouse,** to Bunratty, and since then, reconstructions of turn-of-the-century houses and stores from all over Ireland have been added. Peat fires blaze in the cottages, lit each morning by inhabitants in period attire. In some of the buildings, period tasks and crafts are demonstrated on a rotating basis. Most appealing is the baking that goes on in the **Golden Vale Farmhouse,** where you can watch apple pies (€3) and biscuits made the old-fashioned way before following the finished products to the **Tea Rooms** for a taste test. (Open daily 9am-6pm, last admission 4pm. €9.50, students €8, family €25.) If too much period fever leaves you with a headache, head back to the main road for oysters (€8.50) or a sandwich (€3-8.50) on the balcony at **Durty Nelly's** (☎364 861). The original proprietress earned her name in 1620 by serving Bunratty's soldiers more than just beer, if you know what we mean.

NEAR LIMERICK: ADARE (AN DARE) ☎061

The well-preserved medieval architecture and meticulous rows of tiny thatched cottages have earned Adare a reputation as one of the prettiest towns in Ireland. With that distinction comes a legion of tourists, who infiltrate the town's pricey restaurants and fancy hotels daily. The four major historical sights of note are the 13th-century **Trinitarian Abbey** on Main St., the 14th-century **Augustinian Priory,** the **Franciscan Friary,** and **Desmond Castle.** Though it's officially private, visitors who ask are often granted permission to explore the grounds of **Adare Manor.** Formal French gardens, the wandering Maigue river, and magnificent mature trees (some over 300 years old) cover the sprawling 840 acre estate. Stay for **afternoon tea,** or move on to polish your polo skills at the **Clonshire Equestrian Centre** (☎396 770), on the A21; alternatively, come in October to check out the **International Horse Show.**

Buses arrive in Adare from Limerick (25min., 8 per day, €5) and Tralee (1¾hr., 8 per day, €12). After getting off the bus, head down Main St. to the sky-lit **heritage center** complex, home of the local **tourist office.** (☎396 255. Open June-Oct. M-F 9am-7pm, Sa-Su 9am-6pm; May M-Sa 9am-6pm; Nov.-Dec. and Mar.-Apr. M-Sa 9am-5pm. Closed 1-2pm.) **AIB,** near Texaco, has an **ATM.** (☎396 544. Open M-F 10am-4pm.) The **library** by the tourist office offers Adare's only **Internet access,** available by appointment and with the purchase of a €2.50 membership card. (Open Tu and F 10am-1pm, 2-5:30pm, and 6:30-8:30pm; W-Th and Sa 10am-1pm and 2-5:30pm.)

Although it has no hostel, Adare offers several reasonably priced accommodations. Station Rd., the street beginning to the right of the heritage center, is lined with B&Bs that cost around €30 per person. Just 200 yd. up the N21 to Killarney, **Ardmore House B&B ❸** offers fresh linened rooms with plenty of light and pine-wooded floors so smooth you could glide across. (☎396 167. Doubles €50.) A short trek to Manorcourt, **Riversdale's ❸** tastefully decorated rooms are modern and tidy. (☎396 751. Singles €27; doubles €55.) To reach **Adare Camping and Caravan Park ❶,** bear left onto N21 at the uptown fork, turn left at Ivy Cottage toward Ballingeary, and follow the signs. A family of horses welcomes visitors to this grassy site. (☎395 376. **Hot tub** €5. Tent €13; caravan €17. Laundry €8.) Twelve miles out of town on the N69, nature trails wind through **Curraghchase Forest Park.** Extensive grounds include an arboretum and the ruins of the home of 18th-century poet Aubrey DeVere. The more intrepid can camp in summer (May-Sept.) at the **Curraghchase Caravan Park ❶.** (☎396 349. Open field tent spot. Showers, kitchen, groceries. Tent €8; caravan €13. Laundry €5.)

Budgeteers can stock up on picnic foods at **Centra** on Main St. (Open M-Sa 7:30am-7pm, Su 9am-1pm.) **The Blue Door ❷,** a 200-year-old thatch-roofed, rose-fronted cottage, offers reasonable lunches and pricey dinners. (☎396 481. Lunches €7-10. Open M-F 11am-3pm and 6:30-9:30pm, Sa noon-3pm and 6:30-9:30pm.) **The Arches Restaurant ❸** offers similar lunchtime values—a main course and coffee hovers around €9. (☎396 246. Open M-Sa noon-3pm and 5-9:30pm, Su 5-8:30pm.) Whatever sort of pub you're looking for, Adare has a Collins for you: **Pat Collins Bar** (☎396 143), next to the post office on Main St., opens early and serves cheap grub in a relaxed atmosphere, while around the corner, **Sean Collins Bar** (☎396 400) rollicks with trad on Sunday and Tuesday evenings.

Western Ireland
LG
0
20 miles
0
20 kilometers
ATLANTIC OCEAN
Donegal Bay
DONEGAL
TYRONE
Donegal Town
Ballyshannon
Bundoran
Lower Lough Erne
Lough Melvin
FERMANAGH
Enniskillen
Drumclif
Manorhamilton
Sligo Bay
Sligo
Dromahair
CAVAN
Ceide Fields
Killala Bay
Easky
Belmullet
Ballycastle
Inishcrone (Enniscrone)
Killala
Ballysadare
Collooney
SLIGO
Riverstown
Bangor
Ballina
Tobercurry
Ballymote
Lough Allen
Drumshanbo
Blacksod Bay
Lough Conn
Boyle
LEITRIM
Carrick-on-Shannon
Keel
Achill Island
MAYO
Clew Bay
Clare Island
Castlebar
ROSCOMMON
Inishturk
Roonah Quay
Louisburgh
Westport
Knock
Castlerea
Longford
Claremorris
CONNACHT
Inishbofin
Lough Mask
Leenane
Ballinrose
Roscommon
LONGFORD
Inishshark
Cleggan
Letterfrack
Cong
GALWAY
Lough Ree
CONNEMARA
Clifden
Lough Corrib
Tuam
WESTMEATH
Roundstone
Oughterard
Athlone
Rossaveel
Ballinasloe
Inveran
Barna
Galway
Carraroe
Spiddal
Aran Islands
Galway Bay
Inishmore
Loughrea
OFFALY
Inishmaan
Inisheer
Kinvara
Ballyvaughan
Portumna
Gort
Birr
Doolin
Lisdoonvarna
LAOIS
Cliffs of Moher
Corofin
Roscrea
Lahinch
CLARE
Lough Derg
Milltown Malbay
Ennis
Nenagh
Shannon Airport
Sixmilebridge
R. Shannon
TIPPERARY
Kilkee
Kilrush
Thurles
Killimer
Limerick
Mouth of the Shannon
Tarbert
MUNSTER
Rathkeale
LIMERICK
Cashel
Listowel
Newcastle West
Tipperary
Abbeyfeale
Kilmallock
Clonmel
Tralee Bay
Tralee
Dingle Peninsula
Kanturk
WATERFORD
Dingle Bay
Killarney
Mallow
Fermoy
Dungarvan
KERRY
CORK
Killarney National Park
N15
N56
A47
A46
A35
N16
A4
A32
A509
N4
N59
N17
N26
N58
N5
N61
N84
N60
N63
N55
N6
N65
N62
N52
N64
N67
N18
N85
N7
N68
N19
N69
N75
N24
N8
N74
N21
N20
N73
N23
N22
N72
N70
N71
N25

WESTERN IRELAND

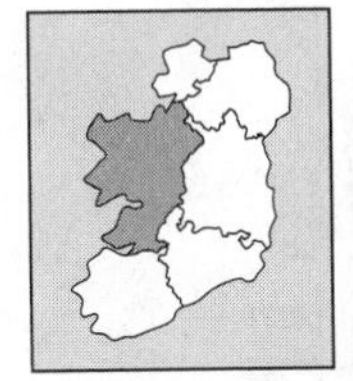

Ask the gentleman sitting next to you at the pub—he will probably agree that the west is the "most Irish" part of Ireland. Yeats once said (and he could have been on a barstool at the time), "For me, Ireland is Connacht." For less privileged Irish in recent centuries, it was mostly poor soil and emigration. When Cromwell uprooted the native Irish landowners in Leinster and Munster and resettled them west of the Shannon, the popular phraseology for their plight became "To Hell or Connacht." The Potato Famine (see p. 60) that plagued the entire island was most devastating in the west—entire villages emigrated or died. Today, every western county has less than half of its 1841 population. Though wretched for farming, the land from Connemara north to Ballina is a boon for hikers, cyclists, and hitchhikers who enjoy the isolation of boggy, rocky, or strikingly mountainous landscapes. Western Ireland's gorgeous desolation and enclaves of traditional culture are now its biggest attractions.

Galway is a different story: the city has long been a successful port and is currently a haven for young ramblers and music lovers of every ilk. Farther south, the Cliffs of Moher, the mesmerizing moonscape of the Burren, and a reputation as the center of the trad music scene attract travelers to Co. Clare. The Shannon River, the longest in all of Britain and Ireland (214 mi.), pools into holiday-haven Lough Derg and runs south through the city of Limerick, sketching the eastern boundary of the rugged, rocky west. To the north, the farmland of the upper Shannon spills into Co. Sligo's mountains, lakes, and ancient monuments.

COUNTY CLARE

Wedged between the tourist metropoli of Galway and Kerry, Co. Clare is largely free of the traveling hordes. What tourists do venture into the county, flock to the area's premier attraction, the Cliffs of Moher. As they rise 700 ft. from the ocean's surface, waves crash upon the rocks and seagulls circle below its skyscraper-high ledges. Elsewhere, Co. Clare unfurls other geologic wonders: fine sands glisten on the beaches of Kilkee and 100 sq. mi. of exposed limestone form Ireland's most peculiarly alluring landscape, the Burren. On the coast, charmismatic seaside villages line the strands while farming communities dot the stark and empty inland.

ENNIS (INIS) ☎065

Growing fast but slow to lose its charm, the capital of Clare combines city-calibre nightlife and shopping with the familiarity of a small town. Quaint overlapping streets belie the Ennis that, by winning the title "Information Age Town," earned each of its households a free computer a few years back. The constantly dividing River Fergus flows around much of Ennis, fully enclosing a large area just north of today's town center—this is the "island" from which Ennis draws its name. The town is best experienced on a Saturday, when the pubs and clubs are hopping and

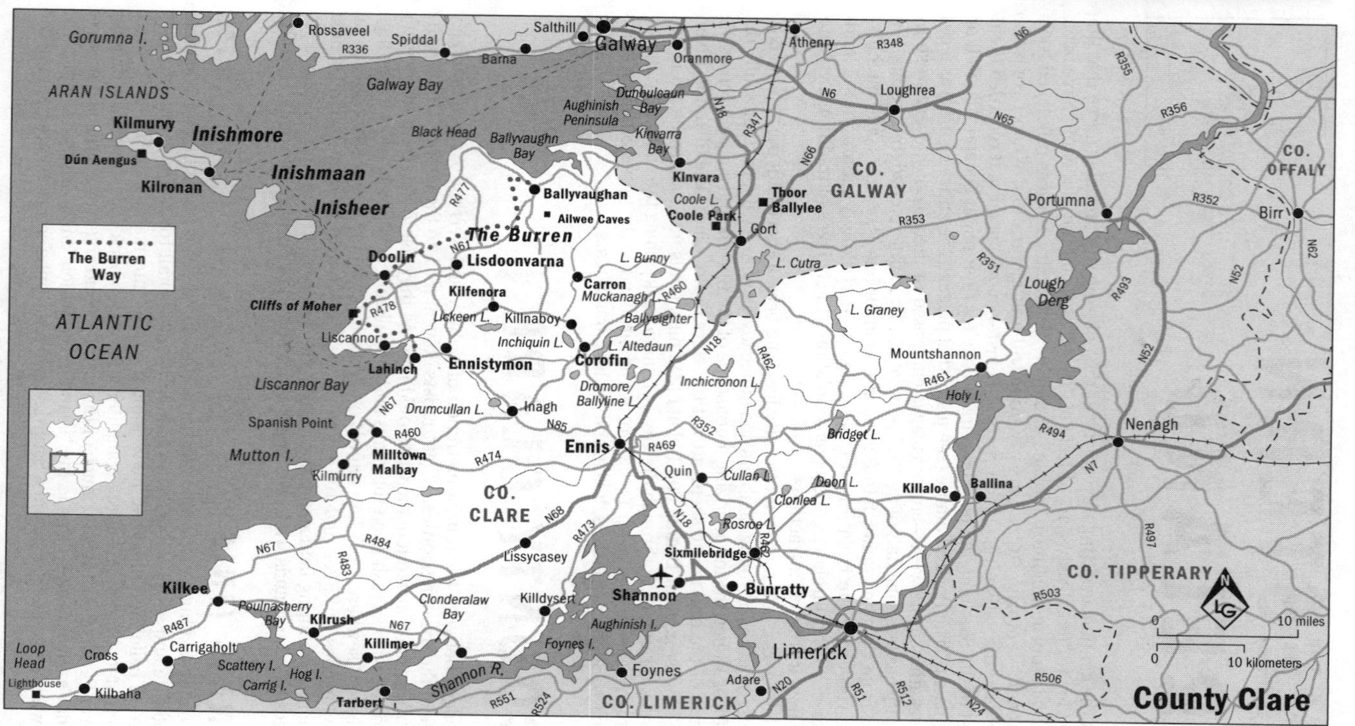
County Clare
10 miles
10 kilometers
The Burren Way
ATLANTIC OCEAN
ARAN ISLANDS
Gorumna I.
Kilmurvy
Inishmore
Dún Aengus
Kilronan
Inishmaan
Inisheer
Rossaveel
Spiddal
Barna
Salthill
Galway
Oranmore
Athenry
Galway Bay
Dunbulcaun Bay
Aughinish Peninsula
Black Head
Ballyvaughn Bay
Kinvarra Bay
Kinvara
Coole L.
Coole Park
Thoor Ballylee
Gort
CO. GALWAY
Loughrea
Portumna
Birr
CO. OFFALY
Lough Derg
Ballyvaughan
Aillwee Caves
The Burren
Doolin
Lisdoonvarna
Cliffs of Moher
Kilfenora
Carron
Muckanagh L.
L. Bunny
L. Cutra
Lickeen L.
Killnaboy
Ballyeighter L.
Inchiquin L.
L. Altedaun
Liscannor
Lahinch
Ennistymon
Corofin
Dromore/Ballyline L.
Inchicronon L.
L. Graney
Mountshannon
Holy I.
Liscannor Bay
Drumcullan L.
Inagh
Spanish Point
Milltown Malbay
Mutton I.
Kilmurry
Ennis
Quin
Cullan L.
Bridget L.
Doon L.
Clonlea L.
Rosroe L.
Killaloe
Ballina
Nenagh
CO. CLARE
Lissycasey
Sixmilebridge
Shannon
Bunratty
CO. TIPPERARY
Kilkee
Poulnasherry Bay
Kilrush
Clonderalaw Bay
Killdysert
Killimer
Aughinish I.
Foynes I.
Limerick
Loop Head
Cross
Carrigaholt
Scattery I.
Hog I.
Carrig I.
Lighthouse
Kilbaha
Tarbert
Shannon R.
Foynes
Adare
CO. LIMERICK

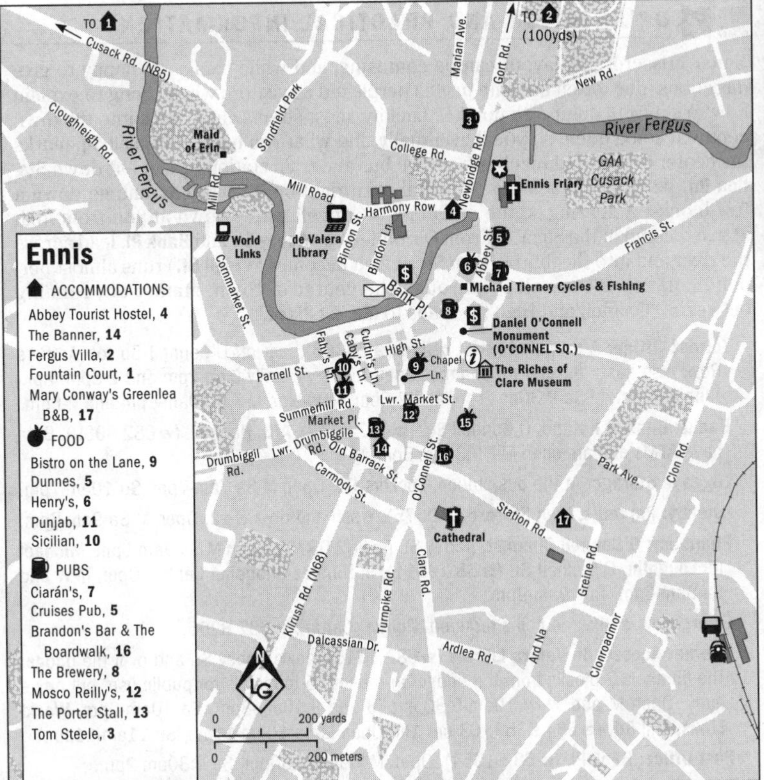

a makeshift produce market springs up in Market Square. Ennis's proximity to Shannon Airport and the Burren make it a common stopover for tourists, who can enjoy a day of shopping followed by a night at the musical pubs.

TRANSPORTATION

Trains: The station (☎684 0444) is a 10min. walk from the town center on Station Rd. Open M-Sa 6:15am-5:30pm, Su 15min. before departures. Trains leave for **Dublin** via **Limerick** (M-Sa 2 per day, Su 1 per day in the evening; €26.60).

Buses: The bus station (☎682 4177) is beside the train station. Open M-Sa 7am-5:15pm. Between 7:20am and 7:20pm, hourly departures head to: **Cork** (3hr., €13.90); **Dublin** via **Limerick** (4hr., €13.30); **Galway** (1 hr., €9.95); **Limerick** (40min., €6.70); **Shannon Airport** (40min.). Buses head less regularly to **Doolin** (1hr., 2 per day, €4.70) and **Kilkee** (1hr.; M-Sa 3 per day, Su 2 per day; €9.20). The West Clare line (4-7 per day) goes to combinations of **Doolin, Ennistymon, Kilkee, Kilrush, Lahinch,** and **Lisdoonvarna.** The crowded post bus runs from the post office to **Liscannor** and **Doolin** (M-Sa 2 per day, €3.50); arrive early to get a seat.

Bike Rental: Michael Tierney Cycles and Fishing, 17 Abbey St. (☎682 9433, after 6pm ☎682 1293). Dispenses info on bike routes and fishing expeditions. Bikes €10 per afternoon, €20 per day, €80 per wk. Deposit €50. Open M-Sa 9:30am-6pm.

ORIENTATION AND PRACTICAL INFORMATION

Ennis' crisscrossing layout can be confusing, and while locals are happy to give directions, they often become just as perplexed as visitors when trying to explain how to get from point A to point B. Luckily, most streets curve back into the town center at some point, so you'll eventually find what you need. **O'Connell Sq.** marks the center of town; to reach it from the bus and train stations, head left down **Station Rd.** When you reach the cathedral, turn right on **O'Connell St.** and go down a few blocks. A soaring statue of Daniel O'Connell stares down at you from high atop a column in the Square. From O'Connell Sq., **Abbey St.** and **Bank Pl.** lead across the river and into the 'burbs. **High St.** (which becomes **Parnell St.**) runs almost perpendicular to O'Connell St. through the center of town. **Market St.**, running between O'Connell and High St., leads to **Market Place.**

Tourist Office: A friendly **tourist office** (☎28366), just off O'Connell Sq. on Arthur's Row. Also has a **bureau de change.** Open July-Sept. daily 9am-1pm and 2-6pm; Apr.-June and Oct. M-Sa 9:30am-1pm and 2-6pm; Nov.-Mar. M-F 9:30am-1pm and 2-6pm.

Banks: Bank of Ireland, O'Connell Sq. (☎682 8777). **AIB,** Bank Pl. (☎682 8089). Both have **ATMs** and are open M-F 9:30am-5pm.

Luggage Storage: At the bus station. Lockers €1. Open M-Sa 7am-7pm, Su 10am-7pm.

Laundry: Parnell's, High St. (☎682 9075). Wash and dry €8-12. Open M-Sa 9am-6pm.

Pharmacy: O'Connell Chemist, Abbey St. (☎682 0373). Open M-Sa 9am-6pm. **Michael McLoughlin,** O'Connell St. (☎682 9511), in Dunnes Shopping Centre. Open M-W and Sa 9am-6pm, Th-F 9am-9pm.

Emergency: ☎999; no coins required. **Police** *(Garda):* ☎682 8205.

Internet Access: de Valera Library (☎682 1616), down Abbey St. and over the bridge. The library is 2 blocks from the bridge on the left. 5 terminals for public use, but arrive early. Open M and W-Th 10am-5:30pm; Tu and F 10am-8pm, Sa 10am-2pm. **World Links,** Mill Rd. (☎684 9759. €3 per 1hr. Open M-Sa 10am-11pm, Su 11am-11pm.)

Post Office: Bank Pl. (☎682 1054). Open M-F 9am-5:30pm, Sa 9:30am-2pm.

ACCOMMODATIONS

Abbey Tourist Hostel, Harmony Row (☎682 2620; www.abbeytouristhostel.com). A freshly painted exterior overflows with flowers, and rooms and bathrooms are clean and comfortable. Friendly, young owners give advice on town and Burren exploration and run **minibus trips** to Doolin and the Cliffs of Moher. Curfew Su-W 1:30am, Th 2:30am, F-Sa 3am. Dorms €12-15; singles €25; private rooms €19 per person. ❶

Mary Conway's Greenlea B&B, Station Rd. (☎682 9049). Between the cathedral and the station, a 5min. walk from the heart of town. Excellent value for singles and couples alike. Rooms are clean and equipped with TVs. Open Mar.-Oct. €20 per person. ❷

The Banner (☎682 4224), at Old Barrack St. and Market Pl. Hotel-esque accommodations atop a pub for a reasonable price. All with bath, TV, stylish telephone, and windows overlooking the town. Breakfast €4. €24-28 per person. ❸

Fergus Villa, Gort Rd. (☎682 4981 or 086 211 0085), 2min. north of the town center. A sparklingly clean B&B run by an incredibly energetic family of athletes and musicians. All rooms with TV and hairdryer. Singles €40; shared rooms €30 per person. ❸

Fountain Court, the Lahinch road (☎682 9845), 2 mi. out of town. Comfortable, if a little pricey. All rooms include bath, TV, and CD player. Guests lounge in the big sitting room and enjoy a generous breakfast menu. €32.50-45 per person. ❸

FOOD

Enormous **Dunnes,** in the mall on O'Connell St., offers enough inexpensive food and beverages to feed all of Clare. (☎684 0700. Open M-Tu and Sa 9am-7pm, W 9am-9pm, Th-F 9am-10pm, Su 11am-7pm.)

Henry's (☎682 2848), by the Abbey St. carpark. Scrumptious, overfilled baps and salads bring locals in the know to this hidden gem tucked between the carpark and the river. Ham, salami, provolone, green olives, and olive oil on a plump bap €4.70. All-natural, homemade ice cream is the Ennis dieter's menace (one scoop €1.30). ❶

Punjab, Parnell St. (☎684 4655). Excellent Balti and tandoori meals at good prices, especially as most will suffice for dinner tonight and lunch tomorrow. A group of 4 can enjoy a complete meal for €44, while 2 vegetarians can have it all for €25. Takeaway prices about €1 less. Delivery within a 3 mi. radius €2.50. Open daily 5-11pm. ❸

Sicilian (☎684 3873), the corner of Cabey's Ln. and Parnell St. Surprisingly bright and cheerful behind the Venetian blinds. One of the biggest bangs for your euro, with pizza (from €6.35) and pasta (€10) to spare. Open daily 5-11pm. ❷

Bistro on the Lane, Chapel Ln. (☎684 0622), off Lower Market St. Gourmands will find this little stone bistro worth the splurge—the well-traveled chef combines local produce to create a small but inventive and delightful menu. Salad with mozzarella, bacon, and peaches €7; noissettes of lamb €18. Cheaper veggie options. Open 6-10pm. ❸

PUBS

With over 60 pubs to its name, Ennis has no shortage of nightlife. Most host trad sessions that help uphold Clare's reputation as a county of musical excellence. Good pubs line the streets—just stop and listen for a moment. For music listings, get *The Clare Champion* (€1.35) in just about any shop.

Cruises Pub, Abbey St. (☎682 1800), next to the Friary. A high-class restaurant fills the back, and quality Mediterranean grub sneaks through into the lively front pub until session time (9:30pm). The 1658 birthdate makes it one of the oldest buildings in Co. Clare, and much of the original interior remains intact. International music star Maura O'Connell once lived upstairs. Now, local music stars appear nightly for cozy sessions.

Ciarán's (☎684 0180), off O'Connell St., opposite the Queen's Hotel. Traditional music within a contemporary space. Locals turn out in droves when owner Ciarán takes out his bodhrán to join in the top-notch sessions 3 nights a week. Trad with or without the drummer boy every night but Tu.

Brandon's Bar, O'Connell St. (☎682 8133). Regulars gobble up huge plates of spuds, meat, and veggies (mains €7-8) alongside their pints. M trad, Th open mic, F-Sa live rock. On weekends, **The Boardwalk,** a popular nightclub, opens upstairs. More interesting are sing-a-long club nights every alternate W. Cover Th-Sa €6-8.

Tom Steele, Newbridge Rd. (☎682 1238). Fewer tourists make it to this side of the river, where the young and chic congregate for frequent live jazz and acoustic sets. Weekends bring DJs to the clubbier 2nd fl.

The Brewery, 2 Abbey St. (☎684 4172). Packed with people slurping their pints and distilling conversation. Especially popular on weekends, when drink promos and DJs crank things up a notch.

Mosco Reilly's, Market St. (☎682 9413). Upright drinkers on stools lean their elbows on upright beer barrels. Two airy rooms leave more than enough space for live bands on weekends and raucous Gaelic football watching on Sunday afternoons.

The Porter Stall, Market Pl. (☎087 682 1322). DJs and drink promos draw a rowdy young crowd of 20-somethings to this impressively sized bar.

SIGHTS AND FESTIVALS

The Riches of Clare Museum, attached to the tourist office, traces the history of Co. Clare from the Bronze Age to its present state through concise explanations and audio-visual exhibits. The uppermost floor focuses on the recent achievements of Clare's residents, displaying such gems as James Devine's recent award for the world record in tap dancing speed—a searing 38 taps per second. (☎682 3382. Open M-Sa 9:30am-5:30pm. €3.50; students €2.50; children €1.50.) Two blocks along Abbey St. away from O'Connell Sq. rest the ruins of the 13th-century **Ennis Friary,** second only to the Clare hurling team in the local esteem it demands. In 1375 the seminary became one of Ireland's most important theological schools. In the entrance to the south transept, there is a small inset depicting the crucifixion of Christ. Legend has it that Judas's wife, while cooking chicken soup, attempted to comfort her husband by telling him that Christ was as likely to rise from the grave as the chicken she was cooking was to rise from its pot. Well the cock rose, as seen in the lower right corner of the inset. Another unusual feature is the ecclesiastical **jail cell** behind the gate in the sacristy. Here young scholars who engaged in wine-induced revelry were sent to think about what they'd done. (☎682 9100. Open June to mid-Sept. daily 10am-6pm; Apr.-May and mid-Sept. to Oct. Tu-Su 10am-5pm. Last admission 45min. before closing. €1.20, students €0.50.) Across from the Friary, a block of sandstone is inscribed with part of Yeats's "Easter 1916" (see **Easter Rising,** p. 61).

Perched nobly on his monument in his central square, **Daniel O'Connell** watches over today's town. A 10min. walk from the town center on Mill Rd. leads to the **Maid of Erin,** a life-sized statue remembering one of the **"Manchester Martyrs,"** three nationalists hanged in Manchester in 1867 (see also **Kilrush,** p. 321). She stands proudly with her left hand on a Celtic cross; an Irish wolfhound to her side looks up for guidance. Saturday is **Market Day** in Market Sq., where all conceivable wares are sold beneath a statue of crafty Daedalus. A 30min. walk winds along the trout-filled **River Fergus;** directions (and lists of other varmints to watch for) are posted in the parking lot between the river and Abbey St. Walking along the Fergus in the easternly direction will bring you to Cusack Park, where Ennis's much beloved **hurling** team stages matches most weekends. Check local papers or local fanatics for game times and buy your ticket at the park (most tickets €3-10). Several miles out of town lies **Dromore Wood,** a beautiful nature reserve around a lake where the stillness is broken only by the occasional youngster reveling in the delicious freedom of a bicycle and summertime. (Open daily until 9pm. Free.)

While most locals enjoy the free music at pubs, tired tourists head to the new, state-of-the-art **Glor Music Centre** to hear their fill earlier in the evening. The venue is not just for tourists, though; it serves as a regional arts center and plans to expand its repertoire to incorporate a diverse mixture of contemporary film, theater, and music, along with the more tourist-oriented performances of traditional music and dance. (☎684 3103; www.glor.ie. Box office open M-Sa 9:30am-5:30pm. Traditional performances Su-Th. Tickets €12-22, student concessions often available.) The last weekend in May, Ennis takes its musical inclinations for the full ride during the **Fleadh Nua Music and Culture Festival,** when sessions and other festivities spill out of pubs and into the streets.

THE SHANNON VALLEY AND LOUGH DERG

Northeast of Limerick, the River Shannon widens into the lake region of Lough Derg. Affluent middle-aged tourists powerboat between the small towns of Killaloe and Ballina, Mountshannon, and Portumna, while younger and vehicle-free travelers are rarer here than they are in regions to the south and west. Lough Derg's summertime watersport culture provides a good workout but little to see in the way of archaeological interest. Travelers lured into the deceptively sleepy Sixmilebridge on their way to or from the airport are in danger of falling in love and never leaving again.

SIXMILEBRIDGE (DROICHEAD ABHANN Ó GCEARNAIGH) ☎061

Halfway between Shannon and Limerick, this sleepy town has a spectacular hostel and makes a perfect stop on the way to or from the airport. **Buses** hit Sixmilebridge twice daily coming from Shannon Airport and four times from Limerick. There is a **bureau de change** at the **Credit Union** on Main St., but **no ATM** machine in town. The **pharmacy** is on the corner as you come into town. (Open M-F 9:15am-1:30pm and 2:30-6:15pm, Sa 9:30am-1:30pm.) On the first street on your right as you head up Main St., enjoy free **Internet** for up to 1hr. at the gorgeous **Kilfinaghty Public Library,** housed in an 18th-century stone church recently refurbished with the financial support of poet laureate Seamus Heaney. (☎369 678. Open Tu-F 10am-1pm and 2-5:30pm, Tu and Th also from 6-8pm, and Sa 10am-2pm.)

After a night in Sixmilebridge's hostel, **The Jamaica Inn ❶,** you'll likely find yourself extending your travel plans. Head downhill from the bus stop at the center of town and cross the bridge, which, at a distance of exactly six old Irish miles from Limerick, gave the town its name. Take the first left and follow the signs—a short walk from town past the Duck Inn near the old mill pond. Retriever/collie twins Bob and Marley welcome you to this spotless hostel, which offers every possible amenity in the most serene of settings. The tiny "tourist information point" at the edge of the bridge will rarely open its doors, but the hostel staff will cheerfully supply all the guidance you could need. (☎369 220. **Bike rental** €15. Laundry €8. Dorms €13-14; singles €26-28; doubles €22-24.) The Jamaica Inn also runs an in-hostel **restaurant ❸,** serving breakfast from 8:30am-2pm, lunch Monday through Friday noon-2pm, and dinner Wednesday through Saturday 6:30-8:30pm. (Breakfast €2-6, lunch €6.50, dinner €9-15.) Sixmilebridge doesn't offer much else in the restaurant department, but **John and Seppie Crowe's Supermarket** on Main St. supplies you with everything you need to cook up a storm, and has a little coffee shop as well. (☎369 176. Open M-Sa 7:30am-9pm, Su 7:30am-8:30pm.) You could also try the **Village Diner ❷,** on Main St., for breakfast, burgers, and chips. Take your food outside to enjoy the view of the sea god statue in the water by the bridge. (Open M-Th noon-midnight, F-Sa noon-2am, Su 5pm-1:30am.) The town's six pubs quench the thirst worked up by a long day of hiking. **The Mill Bar** (☎369 145) offers snacks with your drinks, while hurling enthusiasts populate **Casey's** (☎369 215).

The beauty of the Shannon Valley begs for exploration. Hostel co-owner Michael is a wealth of information on scenic walks, the most rewarding leading up to **Gallows** and **Woodcock Hills,** where visitors endure breathtaking views. Icthyophiles might pass the time trying to hook dinner 2 mi. north of town at **Castle Lake.**

KILLALOE AND BALLINA ☎061

A flowery bridge connects twin towns Killaloe (Kill-a-LOO; *Cill Dalua*) and Ballina *(Beal an Átha)* across the base of Lough Derg, 15 mi. northeast of Limerick City. Residents celebrate the rich history of this, King Brian Boru's old residence, though weary city-dwelling visitors are more interested in the area's present tranquility, broken only by the purr of powerboats and trailing waterskiers.

TRANSPORTATION AND PRACTICAL INFORMATION. Tiny twins that they are, transportation to one town serves for both. Local buses run between Killaloe and Limerick (4 per day; €7.80), depositing riders at the school 400 yd. outside town. **Bikes** are available for rent from **Mountshannon Harbour.** (☎9927 950. Delivery available. €30 per wk.) The **tourist office,** in the former Lock House on the Killaloe side of the medieval bridge that links the towns, provides information on walks in the area. (☎376 866. Open May-Sept. daily 10am-6pm.) An **ATM**-blessed **AIB** sits on Main St. (☎376 115. Open M-F 10am-4pm, Tu until 5pm.) Heal your pains at **Grogan's Pharmacy,** on Main St. in Killaloe. (☎376 118. Open M-F 9:15am-6:30pm, Sa 9:15am-1:30pm.) The **library,** in the same building as the tourist office, provides free **Internet access.** (☎376 062.) The **post office** is up the hill on Main St. (☎376 111. Open M-F 9:30am-12:30pm and 1:30-5:30pm, Sa 9:30am-12:30pm.)

ACCOMMODATIONS, FOOD, AND PUBS. Killaloe is a manageable daytrip from Limerick, but several nice B&Bs near town make it a pleasant stopover. The Kellys of **Mount Bernagh ❸,** 1¼ mi. north along the Killaloe side of the river, are quite possibly two of the nicest people in Ireland. Their warmth and hospitality will renew your faith in humanity, while their comfortable rooms and electric blankets maintain the warm fuzzy feeling through the night. (☎375 461. Singles €30; shared rooms €25 per person.) Right in town, **Derg House B&B ❸** offers well-appointed rooms with soothing, sea-green bedspreads; all rooms have bath and TV and look onto the river. (☎375 599. Singles €38; shared rooms €32 per person.) The very hospitable **Kincora House ❸,** Main St., across from Crotty's Pub, is filled with antiques and serves a healthy breakfast with vegetarian options. (☎376 149. Singles €38; shared rooms €32 per person.)

Purchase basic groceries at **McKeogh's,** on Main St. in Ballina. (☎376 249. Open M-Th 8am-7:30pm, F-Sa 8am-8pm, Su 8:30am-7pm.) Most restaurants are on the Ballina side of the river, though **Crotty's Courtyard Bar ❸** is defiantly Killaloean. Hearty grub is served here on a patio decorated with antique ads. (☎376 965. Lunch €6, served noon-3pm; dinner €8-12, served 5-10pm.) The mini-grocery and **butcher shop** next door also fall under Crotty's jurisdiction. Crossing over into Ballina, you'll find a few tasty options. To the immediate left is **Galloping Hogan's ❹,** where diners can choose between sitting outdoors and sitting almost outdoors, in the glassed-in front room. Highly regarded meals run €13-20, while pastas and vegetarian options are slightly cheaper. (☎376 162. Call ahead for dinner. Lunch served daily noon-6pm, dinner 6-9pm.) Straight up from the bridge, **Molly's** serves quality pub grub with lake views on the side and has plans to open the rooftop for seating by 2003. (☎376 632. Mains €8-12; food served 11am-10pm.)

SIGHTS AND ACTIVITIES. At the base of the town on Royal Parade lies **St. Flannan's Cathedral,** built around 1200 and still in use today. Inside, the **Thorgrim Stone** is inscribed with a prayer for the conversion of the Viking Thorgrim to Christianity, in both Scandinavian runes and the monks' *ogham* script (for those of you whose Old Norse is a bit rusty). Market Sq. may have once held the **Kincora palace** of legendary Irish High King BrianBorú, grandpappy to the O'Brien clan, who ruled here in 1002. The other candidate for the site ofBorú's palace is the abandoned fort known as **Beal Ború** (now a subtle circular mound in a quiet forest glade), 1½ mi. out of town toward Mountshannon. **St. Lua's Oratory** was built on Friar's Island in the 9th century. When the Shannon hydroelectric scheme required a total submersion of the island, the oratory was moved to its present location at the top of Church St. In mid-July, the **Féile Brian Ború** celebrates Killaloe's most famous resident with four days of music, watersports, and various Ború-ish activities. The final night brings pageantry and banquets—raid your pack for that perfect Viking t-shirt. Immediately following is the **Killaloe Music Festival** (☎202 620; tickets €10-30), featuring the **Irish Chamber Orchestra.**

The **Lough** has been attracting people to Killaloe and Ballina for centuries. An option for today's visitor is a relaxing, hour-long cruise on the *Derg Princess*, leaving from the heritage center daily at 2:30pm. (☎376 159. 1-2 daily. €8 fare includes admission to the heritage center exhibit.) **Whelan's** also runs a cruise with historical narration on its *Spirit of Killaloe* twice daily. (☎086 814 0559. €7.50.) The same company rents out **motorboats** for fishing or cruising. (☎376 159. €15 first hr., €10 second hr., and €5 per hr. thereafter. Check to see if they have fishing rods available. Open daily 10am-8pm.) Rent or buy **fishing gear** at **T.J.'s** in Ballina. (☎376 009. Open M-Su 8am-10:30pm. Rod and reel €10 per day. Deposit €40.) A boat (and a bit of navigational prowess) lets you access the eminently picnicable **Holy Island** (a.k.a. **Iniscealtra**), and the remains of five **churches** dating to the 6th century, as well as a **round tower.** For more guidance, try the **Holy Island Boat Trip,** which departs from Mountshannon Harbour. (☎921 615. €8. Call for times.) A few miles north of Killaloe, indulge in an afternoon of watersports at the **University of Limerick Activity and Sailing Centre.** (☎376 622. Windsurfing €15 per hr., kayaking €8 per hr., sailboats €15-25 per hr.) Get out of the water and into the saddle at **Carrowbaun Farm Trekking Centre** (☎376 754; €13 per hr.).

CLARE COAST

The Cliffs of Moher form the most famous part of the Clare coastline, where limestone walls soar 700 ft. over the Atlantic. However, the spectacular scenery is not isolated to this single tourist-laden spot; the majority of the western coastline in Clare is composed of similarly thrilling cliffs, and scenic walks and drives delight the travelers who trek past the typical tour bus route to discover their own favorite ledges, islands, and coves. At several places, the cliffs seem to have lost the battle with the Atlantic, and sandy beaches at Lahinch and Kilkee sit low within the rocky landscape. The southern border of Clare looks across the River Shannon at Kerry from small maritime towns. Those traveling between Co. Clare and Co. Kerry may want to take the 20min. **Tarbert-Killimer car ferry** across the Shannon estuary, avoiding the 85 mi. inland drive by way of Limerick. (☎065 905 3124. €11.50 per car, €2.50 for pedestrians and bikers.)

KILRUSH (CILL ROIS) ☎065

In spite of its size, tiny Kilrush is home of the coast's principal marina. The first permanent settlement here began in the 12th century, when monks from nearby Scattery Island built a church in a mainland meadow. Seven hundred years later, Famine-stricken tenants banded together to withhold rent from their absentee landlords; "Boycott" was the name of the debt collector who was the first to be refused. Today, music, boating, and the opportunity to see the dolphins bring small but steady numbers of travelers to town.

TRANSPORTATION AND PRACTICAL INFORMATION. **Bus Éireann** (☎682 4177) stops in Market Sq. on its way to **Ennis** (1hr., 2-5 per day, €7.80) and **Kilkee**

(20min., 1-4 per day, €2.55). Pricey **bike rental** is available at **Gleesons,** Henry St., through the Raleigh Rent-A-Bike program. (☎905 1127. €20 per day, €80 per wk. Deposit €80.) The **tourist office,** with its **bureau de change,** is currently on Frances St., but moves frequently; call for the latest location. (☎905 1577. Open May-Sept. M-Sa 10am-6pm.) **AIB** on Frances St. has an **ATM.** (☎905 1012. Open M 10am-5pm, Tu-F 10am-4pm.) **Anthony Malone's pharmacy,** on the right side of Frances St., has all you need for a quick fix. (☎905 2552. Open M-Sa 9am-6pm, Su 11am-1pm.) One hour of free **Internet access** comes compliments of **Kilrush Library,** on O'Gorman St. (☎905 1504. Open M-Tu and Th 10am-1:30pm and 2:30-5:30pm; W and F 10am-1:40pm and 2:30-8pm; Su 10am-2pm.) The **Internet Bureau,** beside the marina, also provides access. (☎905 1061. €4 per 20min. Open daily; call for hours.) The **post office** is on Frances St. (☎905 1077. Open M-F 9am-5:30pm, Sa 10am-4:30pm.)

ACCOMMODATIONS, FOOD, AND PUBS. **Katie O'Connor's Holiday Hostel (IHH) ❶,** on Frances St. next to the AIB, provides clean quarters in rooms that date back to 1797. Hostelers enjoy an open hearth and the warmest of welcomes from kindly owners Mary and Joe. (☎905 1133. Kitchen open all night. Check in at the store next to the sign for the hostel. Dorms €11; doubles €25; quads €46.) **The Kilrush Creek Lodge ❸,** in the blue and red building across from the marina and next to the Adventure Centre, is art deco and popular with youth and business groups. (☎905 2595. Some rooms with balconies. Wheelchair-accessible. Laundry €4. Singles €39; shared rooms €30-35 per person.) Irish, American, and Canadian flags fly high by **The Grove ❸** on Francis St. Inside this guesthouse are spacious rooms with tables and desks for dashing out those long-neglected postcards; out back, guests volley on the tennis courts. (☎905 1451. Singles €35; doubles €50.)

A gargantuan **SuperValu** sells groceries at the marina end of Frances St. (☎905 1885. Open M-W and Sa 8:30am-7pm, Th-F 8:30am-9pm, Su 9am-6pm.) The incredible aroma of bread floating down Frances St. comes from **Cosidines ❶.** (☎905 1095. Soda loaf €1.30. Open M-Sa 8am-6pm.) For a quick lunch, the **Quayside ❶** restaurant and coffee shop offers soups and sandwiches from behind baskets of homemade scones. (☎905 1927. Toasted sandwich €3. Open M-Sa 9:30am-6pm.) For dinner there are three choices: pub grub, fast food, or Chinese. **Chan's Chinese ❷,** the Square, is the most elegant of the bunch; the house special is Szechaun is €10. (☎905 1200. Open daily 4pm-midnight. Takeaway €1-2 less.) Of Kilrush's 15 or so pubs, at least one is sure to have music on any given night. **Crotty's Pub,** Market Sq., is where concertina player Mrs. Crotty helped repopularize trad in the 1950s, as evinced by the pub's inspirational tributes to the legendary lady. Today, cozy Crotty's is the place to be for the hottest trad in town and even crazier *craic.* (☎905 2470. Trad Tu-Th, Sa.) **Charlie Martin's,** next to the hostel, reopened in 2002 after a ten-year hiatus. Older locals reminisce about its older days, while the younger crowd celebrates the new generation of entertainment. (Trad Sa-Su.)

SIGHTS AND ACTIVITIES. Kilrush's real attractions lie offshore, and most visitors head straight for the marina. The Shannon Estuary is home to Ireland's only known resident population of **bottlenose dolphins.** Climb aboard the *M.V. Dolphin Discovery* for a 98% chance of cruising alongside the playful swimmers. (☎905 1327. 2-2½ hr. May-Sept. 3 per day; call during off-season. Book ahead on weekends. €14; children €7.) The eco-cruise passes by **Scattery Island,** the site of a 6th-century monastic settlement. The island's resident population took off for the mainland back in the 70s, leaving behind the rubble of monastic ruins, churchyards, and a 120 ft. circular tower. **Scattery Island Ferries** sails regularly in summer from the marina (May-Sept. 3-4 per day; €8 return, children €6) and irregularly in other seasons. Transportation can be arranged with Gerald Griffins (☎905 1327) or at the marina. More active aquatic exploration starts at the **Kilrush Creek Adventure**

Centre, in the red and blue building at the end of Francis St. Instructors lead hour-long sessions of **sailing, kayaking, canoeing, archery,** and **windsurfing** for €15, and half- or full-day multiactivity sessions for €30 and €50 respectively. Call ahead for schedules. (☎905 2855; www.kcac.nav.to. Open Apr.-Sept. daily.) On the mainland, the small but interesting **Scattery Island Centre,** Merchant's Quay, can give you oodles of insights on the island's history and ecology. (☎905 2139. Open mid-June to mid-Sept. daily 10am-6pm. Free.) In the center of town, a monument facing the town hall remembers the Manchester Martyrs of 1867 (see **Ennis,** p. 313). Just outside town on the ferry road, the dirt paths of the 420-acre **Kilrush Forest Park** lead to the **Vandeleur Walled Garden,** where small patches of flowers shine between stretches of serene lawn. Many find the free park more beautiful than the gardens. Follow signs from the ferry road for the walled garden; it's a 20min. walk from town. (Open summer 10am-6pm; winter 10am-4pm. €2.50, children €1.30.)

The **Éigse Mrs. Crotty Festival** ("Rise up, Mrs. Crotty!") celebrates the glory of the concertina (see **Music,** p. 74) with lessons, lectures, and non-stop trad in the pubs and on the streets for a weekend in mid-August. Contact Rebecca Brew of Crotty's Pub (☎905 2470) for more info, or check out the website www.eigsemrs-crotty.com. In late July, Kilrush celebrates its finned friends with the new, family-oriented **Shannon Dolphin Festival,** which includes live music in the Square, kiddie rides and dolphin fun-facts by the marina, and an aquatic-themed parade. Contact the Festival Office (☎905 2522) for more information.

KILKEE (CILL CHAOI) ☎065

From the first weekend in June through the first weeks of September, Kilkee is an Irish holiday town. Families fill the pastel summer homes, the teens working resort jobs party until early morning, and the less-gainfully employed beach bums fill the swimming holes along the shore. But the crescent-shaped town overlooking a half-circle of soft sand has a quieter side that emerges when the holiday-makers leave, the population drops from 25,000 back down to 2300, and the countryside is once again green and quiet.

TRANSPORTATION AND PRACTICAL INFORMATION. Bus Éireann (☎682 4177 in Ennis) leaves from Neville's Bar (confusingly, the sign reads Kett's and there is no bus sign), around the corner from the tourist office. Buses head to **Galway** with a stop at the **Cliffs of Moher** (4hr., summer 2 per day) and to **Limerick** (2hr., 3-4 per day) via **Ennis** (1hr.). The **tourist office** is next to the Stella Maris Hotel in the central square. (☎56112. Open June-Sept. daily 10am-6pm.) The **ATM** at the **Bank of Ireland,** O'Curry St., dishes cash. (☎56053. Open M-F 10am-12:30pm and 1:30-4pm, M until 5pm.) Across the street is **William's,** a hardware store and **pharmacy** that happens to **rent bikes.** (☎56041. Open M-Sa 9am-6pm. Bikes €9 per day, €45 per wk. Deposit €40.) **Internet access,** limited to one golden hour per day, happens at the pink **Kilkee Library,** on O'Connell St. (Free. Open M and W 1:30-5:30pm, Tu and Th-F 10am-1pm and 2-5:30pm.) After hours, head to **The Myles Creek Pub,** where use of the **Internet** terminal costs €1 per 8min. (☎905 6771). Go **postal** on O'Connell St. (☎56001. Open M-F 9am-5:30pm, Sa 9am-12:30pm.)

ACCOMMODATIONS, FOOD, AND PUBS. The friendly folk at the **Dunearn ❸,** a 10min. walk out of town up the left coastal road, welcome backpackers with open arms. (☎905 6545. Open June-Sept. Singles €33; shared rooms €26 per person.) Neighboring **Duggerna B&B ❸** offers the same spectacular views of cliffs and sea, and similarly comfortable rooms. (☎905 6152. Open May-Sept. Singles €38; shared rooms €26 per person.)

Gala vends victuals on the corner of O'Curry St. and Circular Rd. (☎905 6446. Open summer M-F 9am-11pm, Sa 9am-10pm, Su 9am-9pm.) **The Pantry ❷,** O'Curry St., is a culinary oasis in a desert of fast food. Because "Life's too short to drink bad wine," they stock a large selection, with gourmet food to further please the palate. (☎905 6576. Lunches €8. Open May-Sept. daily 9:30am-7:30pm.) The **Country Cooking Shop ❶,** in the alley behind its parent Pantry, bags the same quality fare for considerably cheaper takeaway and makes desserts for the decadent traveler. (Carrot cake €6.) At night, grab some tasty lo mein (€6) from **Gold Sea ❷** and picnic beneath the stars. (☎908 3847. Open M-Sa 1pm-1am, Su 1pm-1:30am.)

After a day spent frolicking or snoring on the beach, you can fritter away even more time by drinking your way through the dense strip of pubs along O'Curry St. **Naughton's** is a pretty pub that gets very packed—get there early for a seat, or join the jumble of locals and vacationers that flood the floor. **The Myles Creek Pub** (☎905 6771) features a different live band every night in the summer to accompany its 18-25 crowd. The **Central Bar** (☎905 6103) has plenty of seating, pool tables, and dark wood to go with the dark pints. It's also a good bet for weekday music, with trad, folk, and country bands performing M-Th. The **Old Bistro** (☎905 6898) is a rough-hewn gem rebuilt several years ago by a handy Limerick chef and his wife, and the **Strand Bar** (☎905 6177) is a great place to end your crawl—a high-heel's throw from the beach, the Strand has live music and dancing on most nights.

SIGHTS AND ACTIVITIES. The spectacular **Westend Cliff Walk** begins at the end of the road left of the seacoast and makes a gentle climb along the tops of the cliffs, which are nearly as impressive as those of Moher, and far less touristed. The long grasses extending to the cliffs' edges are as intriguing as the cliffs themselves, as the wind has swirled them into tufts like so much tousled hair. The Cliff Walk intersects with the similarly scenic **Loop Head Drive** after passing the Diamond rocks, where bits of *Ryan's Daughter* were filmed. The drive passes unusual, plateau-like islands just off the cliffs, which rise straight out of the water with near perfect verticality, and sport flat, grassy tops. To the right, the photogenic drive runs through small villages, ruined farmhouses, hippie enclaves, and plenty of pasture to the **Loop Head Lighthouse,** at the tip of Co. Clare. On the way, it passes through **Carrigaholt,** a village 7 mi. south of Kilkee on the Shannon Estuary. The Loop Head Drive can be biked (30 mi.), though the return trip has some steep moments. To the left, the road leads back to Kilkee.

If the tide is out, scramble out onto the rock formations in front of the carpark of the Cliff Walk—the three **Pollock Holes** should be exposed. The first and easiest to reach is traditionally called the Children's Hole, the second, the Women's Hole, and the third, the Men's Hole (where women are now allowed, but men still dip nude). Dry off over a relaxed game of **pitch-and-putt;** the 18-hole course starts on the other side of the carpark. (☎906 6152. Open daily in the summer 10am-8:30pm. €6.) Those in search of über-relaxation can lounge at the **Kilkee Thalassotherapy Centre,** across from the bus stop. Seaweed baths in the 160-year-old porcelain tub (€16 per 25min.) are the center's specialty. (☎905 6742. Open mid-June to mid-Sept. M-Sa 10am-7pm, Su noon-6pm; shorter hours mid-Sept. to Jan. and Mar. to mid-June.) For a change of locomotion, commandeer a set of hooves at the **Kilkee Pony Trekking & Riding Centre.** (☎906 0071. €15 per hr.) If underwater is more your style, you're in luck—Kilkee is famous for its **diving.** Jump in at the **Kilkee Diving Centre,** a 5min. walk down the shore road from town. The center also rents out **kayaks** for €5 per 30min. (☎905 6707. Open daily June-Sept.; call for off-season hours. 2hr. beginner lesson €65. Experienced divers can rent equipment; €52 per dive.)

LAHINCH (LEACHT UI CHONCHUIR) ☎065

In the 1880s, small, lively Lahinch became a summer haven for the well-to-do; the arcades and fast food spots that now outnumber establishments of fine dining are evidence of the town's wider appeal today. While the moneyed still come to Lahinch for its championship-level golfing and mile-long beach, surfers and teens are the more visible contingent of the summer population, descending on the town to ride the waves by day and dance their remaining energy away come nightfall.

TRANSPORTATION AND PRACTICAL INFORMATION. **Buses** stop near the golf course 2-3 times a day during the summer, coming from Cork, Doolin, Dublin, Galway via Ennis, and Limerick. Gerard Hartigan runs a **taxi** service (☎086 278 3937); see below for his Burren tours. The nearest **bike rental** is **Griffin's,** in Ennistymon. (☎707 1009. €10 per day, €50 per wk. ID deposit. Opens at 9am; bikes can be returned any time to the bar next door.) The **Lahinch Fáilte** tourist office, at the bottom of Main St., organizes tours and books accommodations. (☎708 2082. Open summer 9am-9pm; winter 9am-6pm.) An **ATM** is next door. **Medicare,** on Main St., is the only **pharmacy** in town, and takes advantage of its monopoly with hiked-up sunblock prices. (☎708 1999. Open M-Sa 9:30am-1:30pm and 2-5:30pm.) **Mrs. O'Brien's Kitchen and Bar,** Main St., has **Internet access** until late. (☎708 1020. Open daily 9am-11pm. €9 per hr.) A **bureau de change** is at the bottom of Main St. (☎708 1743; open M-Su 9am-10pm), and the **post office,** Main St., also changes money (☎708 1001; open M-F 9am-1pm and 2-5:30pm, Sa 9am-1pm).

ACCOMMODATIONS, FOOD, AND PUBS. **St. Mildred's B&B ❸,** next to the hostel on Church St., is not just the oldest B&B in Lahinch, it's also the oldest house; no signs of wear are evident though, as the delightfully friendly and hospitable owners keep it in top condition. The sitting room, and most of the bedrooms, have expansive views of the beach. (☎708 1489. Singles €25; shared rooms with bath €25 per person.) The **Lahinch Hostel (IHH) ❷,** on Church St., at the end of Main St. away from the tourist office, has good-sized 4-bed dorms, and somewhat tight 6-bedders. Luckily, all are immaculate and remarkably free of surfers' sand tracks. (☎708 1040. Laundry €6. Dorms €15; private rooms €17 per person.) Walk 10min. up N67, past the sign for the campground, to get to the **Cois Farraige B&B ❸.** This serene house has beautiful rooms with light wood paneling and views of the sea and the family's horses out back. Ask for an upstairs room. (☎708 1580. A June-Sept. singles €35; doubles €53. Off-season €30/€50.) The **Lahinch Caravan & Camping Park ❶,** also on N67, provides space for campers amidst a well-entrenched set of caravans. (☎708 1424. Open Easter-Sept. Reception summer daily 9am-9pm; off-season 9am-5pm. €6 per person. Laundry €5.)

Lahinch's dining options are less than tantalizing, making the shelved food of the **Centra,** Main St., look particularly appealing. (☎708 1636. Open June-Sept. daily 8am-10pm, Oct.-May 8am-8pm.) **The Spinnaker Restaurant and Bar ❷,** next to Lahinch Fáilte, has a spacious purple and blue Chinese restaurant upstairs and a denser pub/club below. (☎708 1893. Meals €5-10. Tu, W folk; Th glam rock; Sa DJ. No cover.) **O'Looney's,** on the Promenade, features a perfectly located deck from which to survey the waves while filling up on grub o' th' pub. Party it up with the surfing crowd on weekends—this is one of the town's hottest nightclubs. (☎708 1414. Food served until 9:30pm. Nightclub open May-Aug. Th-Sa. 18+. Cover €8.) **Flanagan's,** Main St. (☎708 1161), is a popular pub that draws people of all ages with its eclectic mix of live music—everything from reggae, to jazz, to acoustic, trad, and pop gets a turn within these cozy confines. Sharply dressed clubbers pack into the modern space of **Coast** on weekends; during the week cool cats sip their cocktails in the front bar before a brilliant backlit fishtank (F-Sa cover €8).

WILLIE WEEK

For the better part of the year, the quiet town of **Milltown Malbay** *Scraid Na Catharach*), 10 mi. south of Lahinch, doesn't have much to offer he ordinary traveler. Accommoda-ions and transportation are scarce; he main street has a few pubs and ots of cars puttin' it in reverse when hey realize they've missed the turnoff o the Cliffs of Moher. But beginning he first Saturday in July, the town ights up with the excitement of **Willie Veek,** a huge–and affordable–music estival hosted by the **Willie Clancy School of Traditional Music** (☎065 '08 4148). Throughout the week, housands of musicians, instrument-nakers, fans, tourists, and *craic*-ieads flock here from all corners of he globe to celebrate the famous rish piper and Milltown's native son. Participants pay only **€90 for an entire week** of lectures, lessons, and ecitals (the trad sessions in the own's packed pubs are free). On the inal Saturday a monster concert of nternational artists closes out the fes-ivities; an event not be missed.

Accommodations in Milltown–ncluding the sprawling **Station House** (☎065 708 4008) and the conveniently located **O'Loughlin's Ocean View B&B** (☎065 708 4249; both around €25 per person)–are usually booked months in advance, but the trip to Milltown can be easily made from accommodations in Lahinch. In town, marvelous sand-wiches can be had at **Baker's Cafe** ☎065 708 4411); **Cleary's, Clancy's,** and **O'Malley's** are the most happening pubs.

ACTIVITIES. Visitors to **Lahinch Seaworld & Leisure Centre,** at the far end of the promenade, can watch baby lobsters take their first unsure steps, bringing to mind the miraculous cycle of life and death and butter sauce. The last laugh, however, goes to **"Lobzilla"**—this 11 lb. behemoth eluded lobster nets for approximately 50 years before Thomas Galvin pulled him from the depths. (☎708 1900. Open M-F 10am-10pm, Sa-Su 10am-8pm. Aquarium or pool only €5.90, students €4.90; combined admission €9.90/€7.90.) Catch fish in their natural habitat on a fishing trip with **O'Callaghan Angling.** (☎682 1374. Boats run June-Sept. Evening trips 6-9:30pm €30; full-day trips 9am-6pm €70.) Lahinch is world-renowned for its **golfing,** sometimes being referred to as the Saint Andrews of Ireland. But fame costs: a trip to the links starts at €50 for the **Castle course** and a whopping €110 for the **Championship course,** and reservations should be made three months in advance (☎708 1003). John McCarthy, of **Lahinch Surf School,** seeks out the breakers. A 2hr. lesson with all equipment costs those over 16 €25 and youngsters €18, while a weekend **surf "camp"** (€55) will give you a more comprehensive start. If you'd prefer to go it alone, you can also rent equipment for fairly cheap. (☎960 9667. 2hr. surfboard rental €8; bodyboard €5; wetsuit €8.) Surf's up? Call the **Surf Report** to find out (☎081 836 5180). **Arcades** along the beach are mostly glutted with those in the 7-16 age. Gerard Hartigan offers entertaining minibus **tours** of the Burren and Cliffs of Moher. Please take the proper precautions—his enthusiasm is infectious. (☎086 278 3937. 4½hr. €14 per person.)

DOOLIN (DUBH LINN) ☎065

Something of a national shrine to Irish traditional music, the little village of Doolin draws thousands of visitors every year to its three pubs for nights of *craic* that will go straight from your tappin' toes to your Guinness-soaked head. Walk 15min. up Fisher St. to see crashing waves or a few minutes out of town for rolling hills crisscrossed with stone walls. You'll want to be back in time for dinner—several of Doolin's restaurants have won the coveted Bridgestone award for the best food in Ireland. Most of Doolin's 200-odd permanent residents run its four hostels, countless B&Bs, and pubs. The remaining locals farm the land and, in their spare time, wonder how so many backpackers end up in their small corner of the world.

TRANSPORTATION

Buses: Stop at the Doolin Hostel and Nagle's Camping Ground; advance tickets can be purchased at the hostel. Route #15 to **Kilkee** or to **Dublin** via **Ennis** and **Limerick** (2 per day). #50 to the **Cliffs of Moher** (15min.) and to **Galway** (1½hr.) via other towns in the Burren (summer M-Sa 5 per day, Su 2 per day; off-season M-Sa 1 per day).

Ferries: Boats to the **Aran Islands** leave from the town's pier, about 1 mi. from the town center along the main road, but those from Galway and Rossaveal are cheaper under almost all circumstances. See **Aran Islands,** p. 336.

Bike Rental: The **Doolin Bike Store** (☎707 4260), outside the Aille River Hostel. €10 per day. Open daily 9am-8pm.

ORIENTATION AND PRACTICAL INFORMATION

Doolin could be divided into two villages about a mile apart from each other, though many locals ignore such distinctions. Close to the shore is the **Lower Village,** with **Fisher St.** running through it from the pier. Fisher St. traverses a stretch of farmland and B&Bs on its way to the **Upper Village,** where it turns into **Roadford.** Virtually all of Doolin's human and commercial life resides on this main road. The 8 mi. paved and bicycle-friendly segment of the **Burren Way** links Doolin to the **Cliffs of Moher.** Pedestrians will find the route an exhausting but manageable half-day trip; the steep climb along the road from Doolin to the Cliffs lets cyclists coast the whole way back, saving energy for a night of foot-stomping fun at the pubs.

Banks: A traveling bank comes to the Doolin Hostel every Thursday at 10:30am. The nearest ATM is in Ennistymon, 5 mi. southeast.

Internet: Available at the Aille River Hostel. Nonresidential rate is €8 per hr.

Post Office: There may or may not be a **post office** in 2003, depending on whether someone chooses to run it; no one has stepped up since the previous postman died.

ACCOMMODATIONS AND CAMPING

Tourists pack Doolin in the summer, so book early if you have a real preference. Locals know where the money is: almost every house on the main road is a B&B.

Aille River Hostel (HIH), Main St. (☎707 4260), halfway between the villages. Friendly, laid-back atmosphere in a gorgeous location. The Aille River gurgles around a tiny island out front that overflows with wildflowers; an unofficial beer garden sets up on the island just before hostelers head to the pubs for the nightly session. Musicians often stop by Aille to warm up before gigs. **Internet access** €6 per hr. for guests. Washer free, dryer €2. Dorms €11-11.50; private rooms €13.50 per person. **Camping** €6. ❶

Westwind B&B (☎707 4227), Upper Village, behind McGann's, in the same driveway as the Lazy Lobster. The rooms are sunny and immaculate. The french toast is breakfast happiness. Quentin Tarantino stayed here in '95, but nobody really noticed because Co. Clare had just won the All-Ireland Hurling Championship. The owners give helpful advice to spelunkers and other Burren explorers. €25 per person. ❸

Doolin Cottage (☎707 4762), next door to the Aille. The friendly young proprietress keeps her rooms spotless and brightly decorated. Vegetarians savor natural yogurt and honey for breakfast; so do meat-eaters if they know what's good for them (but the full fry is also available). Open Mar.-Nov. All rooms with bath. €22 per person. ❷

Doolin Hostel (IHH), Fisher St. (☎707 4006; www.doolinhostel.ie), Lower Village. This, the oldest hostel in town, is Doolin's bus station, occasional bank, and unofficial town hall; bright-faced owner Paddy is the kind overseer. Hostel includes a small shop, **bureau de change, Western Union** office, and bus ticket sales. Laundry €4. Reception 7:30am-9pm. Large-ish dorms €11.50; 4-bed with bath €12.50. Doubles €33. ❶

Rainbow Hostel (IHH), Toomullin (☎ 707 4415), Upper Village. Just steps from pubs-of-legend McGann's and McDermott's. Wooden interior reminiscent of a ship's, with cheery and comfy pastel rooms. Free guided **Burren walking tours; Burren slideshows** given upon request. Laundry €4. Dorms €11; doubles €26. ❶

Flanaghan's Village Hostel (IHH), Toomullin (☎ 707 4564), a 5min. walk up the road from the Upper Village (away from Lower Village). This new hostel offers spacious sunny rooms, a sitting room with leather couches, and a back garden with farm creatures. Laundry €6. 6-bed dorms €11; doubles €25. ❶

FOOD AND PUBS

Doolin's few restaurants are excellent though pricey; first prize (and perhaps a small fortune!) goes to the entrepreneur who opens an affordable restaurant in this four-hostel town. Until then, be grateful that all three pubs serve quality grub.

The Doolin Deli (☎ 707 4633), Lower Village. The only place to go for food under €8. Packs overstuffed sandwiches (€2.50), bakes scones (€0.90), and stocks groceries. Take-out only. Open June-Sept. M-Sa 8:30am-9pm, Su 9:30am-9pm. ❶

The Doolin Cafe (☎ 707 4795), Upper Village, just past McDermott's. The "cafe" part refers to the comfortably casual atmosphere, not the excellent, upscale food. The early-bird special (5:30-7pm) is still pricey but nonetheless an outstanding value, with 4 gourmet courses for €22. Dover sole with fennel and crab sauce €19. Vegetarian options. Open for dinner daily 5:30-10pm, lunch Sa-Su noon-3pm. ❹

Bruach na hAille (☎ 707 4120). Has a working antique phonograph and delicious, creative, home-grown dishes. Lunchtime paninis (served with salad) are tasty, if somewhat overpriced (€8.95). Arrive before 7pm to score the 3-course early-bird special €18.50. Open daily noon-4pm and 5:30-10:30pm. ❸

McDermott's (☎ 707 4328), Upper Village. Local foot-traffic heads this way around 9:30pm nightly, and remains at a standstill 'til closing; a 9:20pm arrival may win you a seat (not to mention smirking rights). Serious sessions prove that Doolin's trad is more than a tourist trap. Grub until 9:30pm.

O'Connor's (☎ 707 4168), Lower Village. The busiest and most touristed of the three, with drink and song nightly at 9:30pm all year.

McGann's (☎ 707 4133), Upper Village. Music nightly at 9:30pm in the summer and Th-Su at 9:30pm in the winter.

DAYTRIP FROM DOOLIN: THE CLIFFS OF MOHER

The cliffs are 6 mi. south of Doolin on R478. ***Bus Éireann*** *clangs by on the summer-only Galway-Cork route, sometimes cooling her heels at the Cliffs for 30min. (2-3 per day), while the local Doolin-Limerick bus rounds out the public transport options with an additional 3 buses per day. In winter, a bus originating in Galway leaves Doolin at noon and deposits riders at the Cliffs for 1hr. before retracing its route. The well-signposted 20 mi. Burren Way and several trails weave through limestone and wildflowers from Doolin and Liscannor. Hitchers report some difficulty finding rides here. Parking €2.50.*

The **Cliffs of Moher,** members of an elite group of Ireland's über-touristy attractions, draw more gawkers on a good July day than many counties see all year. Although cliffs compose much of Clare's coast, this stretch has been targeted for tourism because the cliffs are at their highest here, where 700 ft. of sheer verticality is battered by Atlantic waves. Touristy they may be, but with good reason—the views are breathtaking, and unquestionably among Ireland's most dramatic. To the north, the **Twelve Pins of Connemara** form dark and mysterious silhouettes against the skyline; to the west lie the limestone stitched Aran Islands; to the south more cliffs jut from the sea along the route to Loop Head, while the Kerry Mountains peak across the River Shannon. Finally, the view straight down is exhilarating—gulls whirl several hundred feet beneath your shoes, and farther down still the overmatched waves explode against unrelenting limestone. **O'Brien's Tower** is a viewing point just up from the carpark; don't fall for its illusion of medieval grandeur—it was built in 1835 as a tourist-trap-tower by Cornelius O'Brien, an early tour-promoter. You'll do just as well to stick to the ground view—what's another dozen feet compared to the several hundred provided by Mother Nature? (Tower open Apr.-Oct. daily 9am-7:30pm. €1.50, students €0.80.) Most tour groups cluster around the tower, experiencing the exhilaration of the drop through telephoto lenses and binoculars. The more adventurous climb over the stone walls and head left, trekking along a clifftop path (officially closed) for more spectacular views and a greater intimacy with the possibility of falling. (Winds blow a few tourists off every year; *Let's Go* does not recommend falling off a Cliff as it would hurt, greatly.) The seasonal **tourist office** beside the parking lot houses a **bureau de change** and a **tea shop** amidst hundreds of postcards. (☎065 708 1171. Open May-Sept. daily 9:30am-5:30pm.) **Liscannor Ferries** operates a fantastic cruise from Liscannor that sails directly under the cliffs. (☎065 708 6060. 1¾hr, 2-3per day, €20.)

THE BURREN

Entering the Burren's magical 100 sq. mi. landscape is like happening upon an enchanted fairyland. Lunar limestone stretches end in secluded coves, where dolphins rest after a long day of cavorting with the locals. Mediterranean, Alpine, and Arctic wildflowers announce their bright, microcosmic contours from cracks in mile-long rock planes, while 28 of Ireland's 33 species of butterfly flutter by. Geologists have no explanation for why such a variety of animalian and botanic species coexists in the area, except that it has something to do with the end of the Ice Age. (Excellent work, "geology.") Disappearing lakes and proud prehistoric tombs—including the 5500-year-old **Poulnabrone Tomb,** one of Ireland's most touristed and photographed sights—add to the mystery and the expectation that witches, faeries, or ogres might come ambling across the rocks at any moment.

The best way to see the Burren is to **walk** or **cycle,** but be warned that the dramatic landscape makes for exhausting climbs and thrilling descents. Check your brakes *before* you set out. Tim Robinson's meticulous maps (€6.35) detail the **Burren Way,** a 26 mi. hiking trail from Liscannor to Ballyvaughan; *The Burren Rambler* maps (€2.55) are also extremely detailed. Sarah Poyntz's *A Burren Journal* gives a sense of life in the Burren today. **Bus** service in the Burren is some of the worst in the Republic. Bus Éireann (☎065 682 4177) connects Galway to towns in and near the Burren a few times a day during the summer but infrequently during the winter. Every summer weekday (June-Oct.) some of those buses continue to Killimer and the Shannon Car Ferry (to Killarney and Cork). **Buses stop at:** the Doolin Hostel in Doolin (p. 332), Burke's Garage in Lisdoonvarna (p. 331), Linnane's in Ballyvaughan (p. 330), and Winkle's in Kinvara (p. 334). Other infrequent but year-round buses run from individual Burren towns to Ennis. **Full-day bus tours** from Galway are another popular way to see the Burren (see p. 336). Based in Lahinch, Gerard Hartigan gives a more thorough **minibus tour** (see p. 325). Hitching in these parts requires patience and, as always, entails some risk.

An interview with Willie Daly, the .isdoonvarna "matchmaker."

LG: How long have you been with he matchmaking festival?

WD: I've been with the festival ince I was 24. My father was in it and ne grandfather was in it. Farmers vould come to them about getting narried. I had no curiosity in it and lidn't expect to fall into it, but I think t's an important service.

LG: So people fill out a form and hen they receive phone numbers?

WD: Aye, they do. They give us the orm and we give them the names of eople we think would be suitable.

A few minutes into the interview he phone rings...

WD (into phone): ... yes, I'll take he details. I'll send you a form and ou can put in a little bit about yourself. And write down the sorts of hings that you desire in a woman. ınd we put that in a file, and it's very confidential, it's just me daughter and neself, and we're very private. Ah, ou will. I'll send you off a list of ıames. Yeah. When did you get the ast one, John, when did you get the ast one? And was there not anything n it that was suitable for you, then? Hmmm. Have you got a pen with you, ınd I'll give you the name of a nice irl I have now. What age are you ohn?...*the phone cuts off.*

LG: So how do you decide which eople are good for one another?

WD: I give each person a questionıaire to fill out, explaining about hemselves and what they look for in a nate. Then they call up and I give hem names and numbers of people n my file for them to call and meet.

BALLYVAUGHAN (BAILE UÍ BHEACHÁIN) ☎065

Along the jagged edge of Galway Bay, about 8 mi. northeast of Lisdoonvarna on N67, the Burren's desolation is suddenly interrupted by the little oasis of Ballyvaughan. The town center is just minutes from caves and castles, making it a frequent stopover for spelunkers and old-bone fiends.

TRANSPORTATION AND PRACTICAL INFORMATION. **Buses** come to Ballyvaughan from Galway, Doolin, and the Cliffs of Moher (M-Sa 4 per day, Su 2 per day). The **tourist office,** inside the Spar Market on Main St., stores a healthy collection of pamphlets and gives information on walks and accommodations. (☎707 7077. Open June-Sept. daily 9am-6pm; Oct.-May 9am-5pm.) **Bike rental** and **laundry** services are found at **Connoles,** up the road toward N67. (☎707 7061. Open M-Sa 9am-6pm. Bikes €12.70 per day, €50 per wk. Deposit €20 and ID. Laundry €10.)

ACCOMMODATIONS, FOOD, AND PUBS. B&Bs rule the roost at Ballyvaughan—you'll find several on the road into town and almost every other door seems to be one as well. **Gentian Villa B&B ❸,** on the Main Rd. toward Kinvara, has clean, comfortable rooms and a friendly proprietress. (☎707 7042. All rooms with bath. Open Easter-Oct. Doubles €50.) **O'Briens B&B ❸,** above the pub and restaurant on Main St., has pleasing rooms, a constellation of cozy fireplaces, and a hearty Irish breakfast. (☎707 7003. Doubles €60-70, all with bath and TV.) Popular **Seaside Oceanville ❺,** next to Monk's Pub on the pier, has gorgeous views and beautiful rooms for families and couples. (☎707 7051. Open Mar.-Oct. €54-57.)

Spar sells various foodstuffs. (☎77077. Open M-Sa 8:30am-8pm, Su 9:30am-5:30pm.) **An Féar Gorta ❷** ("the Hungry Grass") has tea, tasty cakes, and a garden setting to enchant. Deep-cushioned chairs test the potency of the tea's caffeine. (☎707 7157. Sandwiches €6-7. Open June-Sept. M-Sa 11am-5:30pm.) The sunny little **Tea Junction Cafe ❷** has sandwiches and vegetarian mains, but tempts you to ruin your appetite with their rhubarb pie. (☎707 7289. Vegetarian chili €6. Open June-Sept. daily 9am-6pm; Oct.-May 10am-5pm.) **Monk's Pub and Restaurant ❷** holds its Guinness seminary by the sea—have the mussels outside on a sunny day. Tourists crowd around the huge stone fireplace for the trad, while locals gravitate toward the bar. (☎707 7059. Famous seafood chowder €5. Music 2 nights a week.) Back in town, **Greene's** is a small, card-playing locals' pub—the older crowd who knows where the Guinness runs best. (☎707 7147. Open M-Sa 6pm-midnight.)

SIGHTS. **Burren eXposure,** a mile out of Ballyvaughan on N67 toward Kinvara, gives a soaring audio-visual introduction to the Burren landscape through three films shown on a wall-to-wall screen almost as expansive as Limestone Land itself. (☎707 7277. €5, children €2.50.) Also on N67 is the turnoff for **Newtown Castle and Trail,** where you can find the restored 16th-century home of the O'Loghlens, the Princes of the Burren. An hour-long **guided tour** covers about half a mile of beautiful hillside terrain, discusses the geology of the Burren, and visits a Victorian folly "gazebo" (a miniature children's castle), as well as an 18th-century military waterworks system. (☎77216. Open Easter-early Oct. daily 10am-6pm. Castle free but donations appreciated. Trail tour €2.50.) Newtown Castle is right beside the **Burren College of Art** (☎707 7200; www.burrencollege.com), which offers year-round and summer courses. Several weekend workshops are offered in the summer, focusing on painting the Burren landscape or learning more about the botany of the area. On the way to Ballyvaughan, find peace and solitude interrupted only by the birds chirping at the **Corcomroe Abbey.** Founded in 1194 as a monastery by the Cistercian Order, the foundation actually dates back to 1182. The impressive walls and arches house centuries-old graves while the cemetery outside is still in use. Prehistoric bears once inhabited the two million-year-old **Aillwee Cave** (EYEL-wee), 2 mi. south of Ballyvaughan and almost a mile into the mountain. Since caves are the same temperature year-round, bears felt their way inside and scratched out cozy beds. Anyone scared of the dark should avoid the tour, as should experienced spelunkers. (☎707 7036. Open July-Aug. daily 10am-7pm; mid-Mar.-June and Sept.-early Nov. 10am-4pm. Parking €2. €7.50.) Those itching to do serious **spelunking** should contact the Speleological Union of Ireland (SUI; www.cavingireland.org) or the Burren Outdoor Education Centre (☎707 8066).

LISDOONVARNA (LIOS DÚN BHEARNA) ☎065

The locals call it "Lis-doon," but for everyone else in Ireland, its name is synonymous with its **Matchmaking Festival.** The month-long September *craic*-and-snogging fest has drawn the likes of Jackson Browne and Van Morrison to its all-day music stages. Amidst the hullabaloo, farm boys and girls of all ages—their crops safely harvested, but with wild oats yet to sow—gather together to pick their mates. Local celebrity and professional matchmaker Willie Daley from Ennistymon presides over the event. No one is really saying how successful the festival is in making

LG: Have any marriages resulted?

WD: Well, I get invited to some but I don't attend in case it embarrasses them, since people know what I do.

LG: So, what is the most important advice you have for people looking to get married?

WD: A woman needs to be treated with respect. She needs be made to feel important and wanted. You can't take her for granted. That's the key.

The phone rings again...

WD (into phone): Hello? Sorry, okay John. Now this is the name of a very nice woman. She's somewhere around 60, she's just 60. Her name is Kathleen.* She has her own house. What? No, I can't give out her last name, she only wants her first name given out. Now there's another girl. Now what age are you again John? Ah, you're not that well on. But that girl I was going to say, Mona,* is in her 70s. So here's another number for you John... Best of luck with you now. They're both nice women. Oh now you're right. You have a very good attitude, now. Now there is another girl, who doesn't want to see anyone young. Her name is Christine.* Now, she is somewhere in her 50s now and she doesn't want a young fella. Now don't be afraid of that now. You've got a good attitude, you'll be fine. Well you have the number now, so you have no excuse. Now try those three now, and if it doesn't work out, don't worry, we have thousands of others. Okay John, good luck. Good luck. You're welcome. It's not a problem, I do this all the time. It's me job.

* names have been changed.

matches that last longer than a six-pint hangover, but as one Lisdoon local puts it, "Everything works if you want it to." For more info on the festival, or on matchmaking in general, contact the **Hydro Hotel** and stay for their nightly music. (☎707 4005. Wheelchair-accessible. Open Mar.-Oct.) In the 1700s, Lisdoon saw carriage upon carriage of therapy-seekers rolling in to try the curative wonders of sulfur and copper. You can still give it a whirl at the **Spa Wells Health Centre,** Sulfur Hill Rd., at the bottom of the hill south of town. Loosen up with a massage or sulfur bath before the big evening at Ireland's only operational spa. (☎707 4023. Sulfur bath €25; full massage €35. Open June-Sept. M-F 10am-6pm, Sa 10am-2pm.)

Buses travel 4 mi. to Doolin and on to Lahinch daily from the main square during the summer (1-3 per day). A **tourist office,** next to the Spa, provides ample information on the town and region. (☎707 48011. Open June-Sept. M-F 10am-6pm, Sa 10am-2pm.) **Rent a bike** at the Esso filling station. (☎707 4022. Open M-Sa 9am-7pm, Su 10am-6pm. €8 per day, €45 per wk. Deposit €60 or ID.) In the ninth circle of hell that is the Burren's public transportation system, Peter Mooney's **cab hire** is a welcome relief. (☎707 4663 or mobile ☎087 206 9019.) There is no hostel in Lisdoonvarna, but the B&Bs are more than accommodating. Dermot of **Dooley's Caherleigh House ❷,** right up the hill from the Spa, makes every guest feel pampered with tea and cookies, crackling fires, and superb breakfasts. (☎707 4543. All rooms with bath. €23 per person.) Those staying at **Mrs. O'Connor's Roncalli B&B ❸** can visit the lovingly kept garden or bathe in the natural light that floods the rooms. It's a 7min. walk from the town center; keep going past the Esso station, the Smokehouse, and the next filling station. (☎707 4115. Apr.-Oct. All rooms with bath. €25 per person.) Enjoy the perks and comforts of a three-star hotel at the **Carrigann Hotel ❹.** Owner and chef Mary Howard leads visitors to cozy rooms with beautiful garden views and then cooks up bar food or a delightful dinner to suit their taste. (☎707 4036. Mar.-Oct. €40-60 per person.) Guests can book **Burren Walking Holidays,** 3-6hr. walks with Shane Connolly, a charming in-house guide who expertly brings the Burren to life through fun facts and stories.

The smoked trout salad (€9) from the **Roadside Tavern and Restaurant ❷,** on the Doolin Rd., is enough to feed two. The pub itself is dimly lit and decorated with shellacked postcards from around the world. Ghostly old photos of trad sessions past form a backdrop to their living version. (☎707 4084. Food served daily 12:30-4pm. Trad Mar.-Sept. nightly at 9:30pm, Oct.-Feb. Sa only.) The **Smokehouse** next door is your one-stop shop for the salmon of knowledge, the trout of truth, and the eel of eternity. (☎707 4432. Tours €2.60, students €2. Open M-Su 9am-6pm.)

KILFENORA (CILL FHIONNÚRACH) ☎065

The village of Kilfenora lies 5 mi. southeast of Lisdoonvarna on R478; its **Burren Centre** and several grocers make it an ideal departure point for trekkers and bicyclists heading into the limestone wonderland (that is, if you already have a bike: there are no rental agencies in town). However, visitors would be wise not to miss the non-geological sights—**seven high crosses, numerous wedge tombs,** and a **cathedral.** The town also has one of the most overlooked trad scenes in the county.

The **Burren Centre** provides a comprehensive guide to the nearby stony stretches; a 3D model of the relatively flat Burren and lectures on the natural history of the region are featured. (☎708 8030. Open Mar.-May daily 10am-5pm; June-Aug. 9:30am-6pm; Sept.-Oct. 10am-5pm. €5, children €3.) Next to the Burren Centre, Church of Ireland services are still held in the nave of the **Kilfenora Cathedral.** (1st and 3rd Su of the month at 9:45am.) Although the structure itself dates from 1190, the site has been church-ridden since the 6th century. West of the church is the elaborate 12th-century **Doorty Cross,** one of the "seven crosses of Kilfenora." Although time and erosion have taken their toll, carved scenes of Christ's entry into Jerusalem are still visible among odd birds and menacing heads.

In the yellow house across from the Burren Centre, **Mary Murphy ❷** greets arriving guests with tea and coffee. Rooms are basic but include bath; price also includes a sizzling morning fry. (☎708 8040. Open Feb.-Oct. Singles €25; doubles €44.) Kilfenora's pub trifecta hums with so much music and dancing it could make you miss your bus…if Kilfenora had buses that is. **Vaughan's ❶** offers trad sessions nightly, set dancing in the adjacent thatched cottage on Thursday and Sunday nights, and weekend BBQs, weather permitting. (☎708 8004. Sandwiches €3-4.50, superb seafood chowder €4. Food served from 9am-9pm.) Kitty Linnane and her *céilí* band of '54 put Kilfenora on the musical map; **Linnane's,** affectionately called "Kitty's Corner," still hosts lively trad sessions in a familial environment and has won various awards for its food and music. (☎708 8157. Sessions nightly in summer, weekends in off season; year-round W supersession.)

COROFIN (CORA FINNE) ☎065

Seven lakes and the River Fergus make the village of Corofin lush, even though it's only a few miles away from the craggy Burren. If you have more than a sneaking suspicion that your ancestors emigrated from hereabouts, the **Clare Heritage and Genealogical Research Centre,** Church St., can help you trace your roots. (☎683 7955; www.clareroots.com. Open M-F 9am-5:30pm.) A **Heritage Museum,** across the street in a decaying Protestant church, houses artifacts from the Famine, emigration, and landowner days. (€2.50.) A **history trail** that stays within 2 mi. of the village center leads you to local sights, such as the well-preserved 12th-century **St. Tola's Cross** and the battlefield where, in 1318, Conor O'Dea's victory put off English domination for another two centuries (oh happy Dea). Three miles south of Corofin, **Dysert O'Dea Castle and Archaeology Centre,** housed in a restored 15th-century tower, uncovers the more distant past. (☎683 7722. Open May-Sept. daily 10am-6pm. €3.20.) The **Dromore National Nature Reserve** and its peaceful, swan-inhabited lakes are about 8 mi. west of Corofin. Follow signs to Ruan Village; the reserve is signposted from there. (Tour center open June-Sept.) Those eager to try their luck fishing can call **Burke's** (☎683 7677) and hire boats (€20).

Buses travel to and from Ennis (M-Sa 1 per day, €7.60) and Lahinch (M-Sa 1 per day, €5.30). The **tourist office,** Church St., is in the **Clare Heritage Centre.** (☎37955. Open June-Sept. daily 10am-6pm.) **Spar Market,** Main St., houses the **post office** and sells fruits, veggies, and staples. (Open daily 9am-9pm. Post office open M-F 9am-1pm and 2-5:30pm, Sa 9am-1pm.) The **Corofin Country House B&B ❸** lies just outside of town on the way to Ennis and is easily identified as the only big red house on the road. The beautiful wood floors and furniture welcome you inside, and the comfortable beds assure a good night's sleep. (☎683 7791. Open Apr.-Nov. €27 per person.) The **Corofin Village Camping Park ❶,** on Main St., offers clean, modern facilities including free showers and a game room with pool table. (☎683 7683. Wheelchair-accessible. Laundry €8. €5.70 per person, €14.60 per family.) At the **Corofin Arms Pub ❷** you can get good pub grub garnished with friendly service and conversation. (☎683 7373. Sandwiches with fries €5. Food noon-9:30pm.)

CARRON (AN CARN) ☎065

A pub, a hostel, and a mile-wide, 5 yd. deep puddle in the midst of a limestone landscape is the sum total of Carron. Sure enough, its dimensions constitute a mind-boggling figure; this is **Europe's largest disappearing lake.** If you go 4 mi. northwest of Carron, you too can see the **Poulnabrane Dolmen,** Ireland's second-most popular and photogenic rock group. About 5000 years ago, over 25 people were put to rest with their pots and jewels under the five-ton capstone, only to be dug up by intrepid archaeologists in 1989. Two miles east of the village, Ireland's only **perfumery** creates scents from the Burren's moss and lichens; the wildflowers are now

THE BIG SPLURGE

DUNGUAIRE CASTLE BANQUET

Step back in time and dine medieval banquet style at Dunguaire Castle. When you arrive at the castle, you are greeted by a butler in medieval dress. A harpist and singers serenade you as you mingle with the night's other guests. After a brief history of the castle, your table upstairs awaits. Starters of smoked salmon and brown bread whet your appetite for future courses. Next, slurp leek and potato soup out of the bowl, but don't worry, you do get utensils for the hot chicken dish and the delicious apple tart and cream dessert. Banter with the medieval servants that cater to your every desire, and feel free to refill your cup from the jugs of red or white wine (or water for the kiddies). The Lord and Lady of the feast are selected from the largest booked party and these two new-found celebrities preside over the evening by lighting the Candle of Poetry. After you've had your fill of food, enjoy a 40min. literary pageant based upon the Irish poets W.B. Yates, Sean O'Casey, and more, interspersed, of course, with song and harp. At the end of the evening, as you prepare to reenter the present century, sip coffee downstairs before departing with a unique memory.

Dunguaire Castle (☎091 637 108), 10min. from Kinvara along the Galway road. Seatings 5:30 and 8:45pm nightly, book early. Banquets last 2½hr. €42 per person, children ages 10-12 €31.50, ages 5-9 €21, under 5 free.

protected and can no longer be distilled for their aromas. (☎89102. Open Mar.-June and Sept.-Oct. 9:30am-5pm; July-Aug. 9am-7pm.)

The village lies off a small road connecting Bellharbor to Killnaboy; to get there, **drive** (8min.) or **hike** (1½hr.) south from Bellharbor. It's also possible to **bike** from Kilfenora, but the climbs on the small roads are exhausting. Hitching odds approach nil, which is how much *Let's Go* recommends this form of transport. A single magnificent hostel overlooking the giant lough houses half the town's population—**Clare's Rock Hostel ❶** has comfortable dorms with baths, tasteful decor, and cheerful management. (☎89129. Laundry €7. Reception 5-10pm. Open June-Oct. Dorms €10.50; singles €13; doubles €30.) Across the way, **Croide Na Boirne ❷** offers gorgeous views, a crackling fire, a pool table, and **goat burgers.** (☎89109. Mint-embalmed kidburger €6.40. Food served Apr.-Dec. noon-9pm.)

KINVARA (CINN MHARA) ☎091

Just across the bay from the tourist hordes of Galway, this small harbor town of floating swans and passing hookers (boats!) can get surprisingly lively on weekends. The perfect place to come and relax after weeks of touristing, Kinvara offers some of the best pubs outside of Galway and the friendliest B&Bs in the region.

TRANSPORTATION AND PRACTICAL INFORMATION. Buses connect Kinvara to Galway City and nearby Doolin (€5) three times a day from Flatley's Pub (see **Pubs,** below). **Bike rental** can be found at McMahon's Hardware on Main St. The **post office** is just off Main St. (☎637 101. Open M-F 9am-5:30pm, Sa 9am-12:30pm.) There are no laundry, Internet, or banking facilities in town.

ACCOMMODATIONS, FOOD, AND PUBS. All visitors to Kinvara should hit up **Fallon's B&B ❸,** in the center of town on Main St. Sweetheart Maura Fallon and family offer lovely rooms ranging from spacious singles to doubles and family rooms. (☎637 483. Irish breakfast €8-10. Singles €40; doubles €60. All with bath, TV, and snacks.) Located on the Quay, **Cois Cuain B&B ❸** is a quaint B&B with clean, bright rooms perhaps best suited to couples. (☎637 119. Open Apr.-Nov. Doubles €54, all with bath.) The more upscale **Merriman Hotel ❺,** across from Fallon's, has 32 rooms, each with a bath, TV, and phone. Two rooms accommodate disabled travelers, and the hotel has its own restaurant, **The Quilty Room,** with 3-course meals for €30, and bar, **M'Asal Beag Dubh,** to boot. (☎638 222. June-Sept. singles €75; doubles €115; Oct.-May €60/90.)

Food of the supermarket variety can be had at the **Londis** on the main road (☎637 250). **Rosaleen's** ❶ wood floors and blue tablecloths provide a cafe-like atmosphere for intimate converstation over coffee and sandwiches. (☎637 503. Open mid-June to Sept. daily 5:30-9:30pm, lunch on weekends; Mar. to mid-June Th-M 5:30-9:30pm.) Inside **Keogh's** ❷, a restaurant that doubles as a bar, a humorous sign requests: "If you're drinking to forget, please pay in advance." (☎637 162. Breakfast €5-6.50, sandwiches €7-9.) For a more elegant dinner in a candlelit atmosphere, head to the **Pierhead** ❹ for its seafood menu and quay views overlooking the water. (☎638 188. Starters €7-9, mains €16-22; bar menu available. Open June-Aug. daily 11am-midnight, Sept.-May 5pm-midnight.)

Kinvara's pub scene is the most active thing in town—all are located within seconds of each other on Main St., making for a very convenient pub crawl. A 20-something crowd flocks to **The Ould Plaid Shawl,** named after the Frances Fahy poem (Fahy was born in this very building in 1854). Tuesday nights are devoted to dart competitions (€2 to enter), but patrons can take advantage of the jukebox and pool table anytime in the week. (Th trad. Open Th-Sa 5pm-12:30am, M-W 5-11:30pm, Su 5-11pm.) The older set of locals head to **Greene's** for Guinness and spontaneous trad sessions. Reportedly the place to be for music on Monday nights, tiny Greene's has been passed down through generations of daughters and remains one of the few Irish bars owned and run by females. (☎637 110. Th-Sa 10:30pm-1am, M-W 10:30pm-midnight, Su 10:30-11:30pm.)

SIGHTS AND FESTIVALS. Dunguaire Castle, 10min. from town on the Galway Rd., is actually a tower house—a popular type of dwelling for 16th-century country gentlemen. The narrow, winding staircase leads to expansive views of town, sea, and countryside. (☎637 108. Last admission 4:30pm. Open May-Sept. daily 9:30am-5pm. €4, students €3.50.) The first weekend in May, Kinvarans go crazy at the **Cuckoo Fleadh,** welcoming over 200 musicians to their town, and in mid-August they celebrate the **Cruinn Iú Na mBá,** "the gathering of the boats." Enjoy your own boat ride courtesy of **Galway Hooker Trips** (☎087 231 1779). For a cheap hooker ride, set sail with skipper Mehall on the *An Traonach.* Alongside Kinvara, **Doorus Peninsula** reaches out into Galway Bay. For those not enamored of nature, it's probably best to stay in Kinvara, but for hikers, bikers, or families with cars, Doorus is righteous. Many of its sights are detailed in *Kinvara: A Rambler's Map and Guide*, available throughout town.

COOLE PARK AND THOOR BALLYLEE ☎091

Two of W. B. Yeats's favorite retreats, both of which he eulogized, lie about 20 mi. south of Galway near **Gort,** where N18 meets N66. **Coole Park** is now a ruin and a national park; **Thoor Ballylee** has been restored to appear as it did when Yeats lived there. The sights are best accessible by car, but biking is another option. (Be warned—high winds can make biking the 4 mi. from Kinvara a painful struggle.)

The **Coole Park** nature reserve was once the estate of Lady Gregory, a playwright and friend of Yeats (see **The Irish Literary Revival,** p. 71). To Yeats, Coole Park represented the aristocratic order being destroyed in the 1920s by industrialism and war. Although the house was ruined in the 1922 Civil War (see p. 62), the yew walk and garden have survived. In the picnic area, a great copper beech known as the **"autograph tree"** bears the initials of several important historic figures, including George Bernard Shaw, Sean O'Casey, Douglas Hyde (the first president of Ireland), and Yeats himself. The **Coole Park Visitors Centre** offers a 30min. film on Yeats, as well as an ample book collection on local rocks, trees, and wildlife. The best guide to Coole Park is *The 7 Woods Trail and Family Trail* (€1.20), available at the visitors center. (☎631 804. Open mid-Apr. to mid-June Tu-Su 10am-5pm; Easter to Aug. daily 9:30am-6:30pm; Sept. 10am-5pm. Last admission 1hr. before closing for the audio program and 15min. for the Centre. €2.50, students €1.20.) A mile from the garden, **Coole Lake** is where Yeats watched "nine-and-fifty swans... all suddenly mount/ And scatter wheeling in great broken rings/ Upon their clamorous wings." **Whooper** and **mute swans** still gather here in winter; in summer, they are replaced by cows lumbering down to the beach.

Three miles north of Coole Park, a mile-long stretch of road runs from the Galway road to **Thoor Ballylee,** a tower built in the 13th and 14th centuries. In 1916, Yeats bought it for £35 (€44.50!) and renovated it; he lived here with his family off and on from 1922 to 1928. While cloistered here to write his "Meditations in Time of Civil War," Republican forces blew up the bridge next to the tower. In Yeats's account, they "forbade us to leave the house, but were otherwise polite, even saying at last 'Good-night, thank you.'" The **visitors center** plays a 30min. film on Yeats's life and boasts a nice gift shop and rather extensive book selection. (☎631 436. Open Easter-Sept. M-Sa 10am-6pm. €5, students €4.50.)

The **Kilartan Gregory Museum** greets visitors in a large stone house situated on the road from Kinvara at the turnoff to N18. The building was once the national school where Lady Augusta Gregory started one of the first branches of the early Irish government, the **Gaelic League.** It now houses a charming reproduction of a traditional Irish schoolroom, complete with actual posters and books from the turn of the century. (☎631 069 or 632 346. Open June-Aug. daily 10:30am-5:30pm; Sept.-May Su 1-5pm. €2.50, students €1, families €6.)

COUNTY GALWAY

The third-largest county in Ireland, Galway is also its most varied. The day and night, never-ending *craic* of Galway City draws more musicians and travelers than any other city outside Dublin. Twenty miles offshore lies the ancient silence of the Aran Islands' stacked limestone walls. The rugged mountain landscape of the county's coastline offers daytripping hikers the opportunity to commune with grazing cattle while providing shade for the exquisite beaches that lie in between each ridge. Connemara is a largely Irish-speaking region with a harsh rocky interior and even hardier locals; Clifden, its largest city, has abandoned the native tongue in favor of homogeneous tourism. Nearby, isolated Inishboffinand Inishturk provide intense doses of island nothingness.

GALWAY CITY (GAILLIMH) ☎091

In the past few years, Co. Galway's reputation as Ireland's cultural capital has brought flocks of young Celtophiles to Galway City (pop. 70,000). Mix the over 13,000 students from Galway's two major universities, a large transient population of twenty-something Europeans, and waves of international backpackers, and you have a college town on *craic;* Galway is the fastest-growing city in Europe, and it has the energy to prove it. Street performers dazzle with homegrown tricks while locals, tourists, and wandering spirits lounge in outdoor cafes during that contemplative stretch of time between the *craic* that's been had and the *craic* that will soon be upon them. Fast-walking hipsters dish out flyers, entrance keys to the night's most exuberant live music. Follow them down the rabbit hole and become another strange face in Galway's mesmerizing pub universe. In the summer, a series of excellent festivals quickens the city's already frenetic pace.

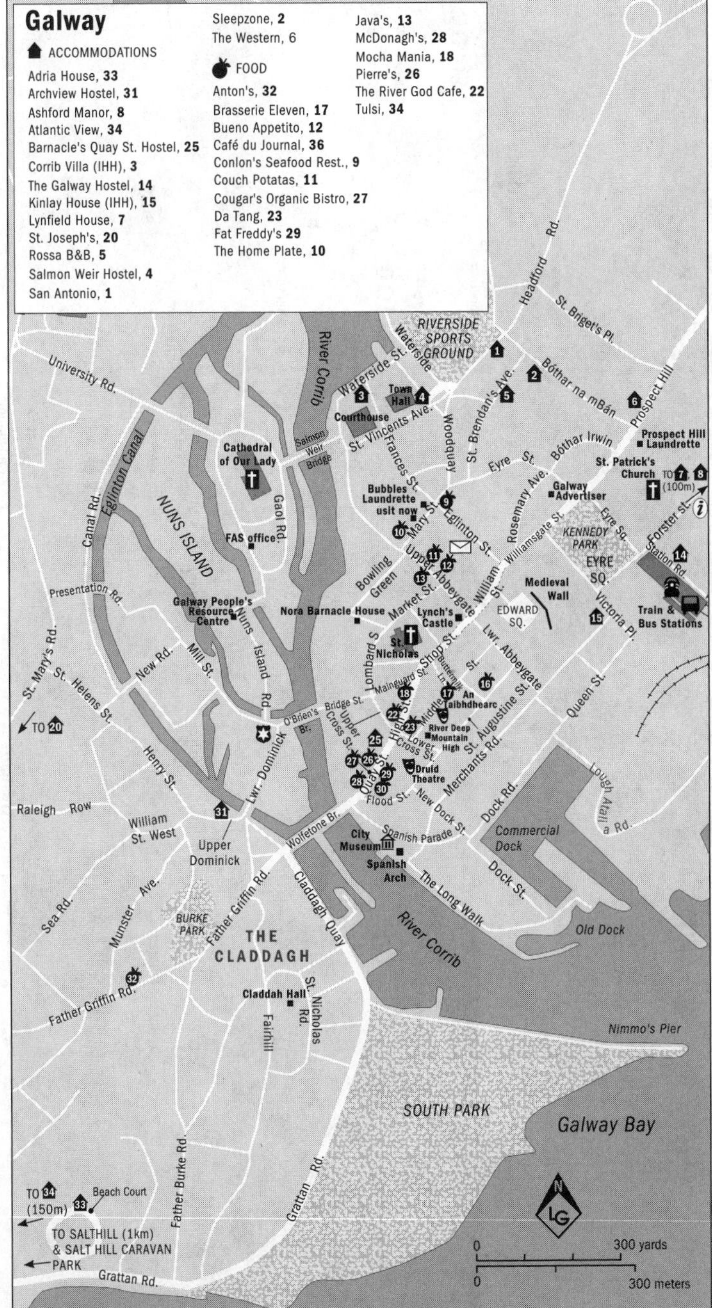

Galway
ACCOMMODATIONS
Adria House, 33
Archview Hostel, 31
Ashford Manor, 8
Atlantic View, 34
Barnacle's Quay St. Hostel, 25
Corrib Villa (IHH), 3
The Galway Hostel, 14
Kinlay House (IHH), 15
Lynfield House, 7
St. Joseph's, 20
Rossa B&B, 5
Salmon Weir Hostel, 4
San Antonio, 1
Sleepzone, 2
The Western, 6
FOOD
Anton's, 32
Brasserie Eleven, 17
Bueno Appetito, 12
Café du Journal, 36
Conlon's Seafood Rest., 9
Couch Potatas, 11
Cougar's Organic Bistro, 27
Da Tang, 23
Fat Freddy's 29
The Home Plate, 10
Java's, 13
McDonagh's, 28
Mocha Mania, 18
Pierre's, 26
The River God Cafe, 22
Tulsi, 34
RIVERSIDE SPORTS GROUND
River Corrib
University Rd.
Waterside St.
Waterside
Town Hall
Courthouse
Headford Rd.
St. Briget's Pl.
Bóthar na mBán
St. Brendan's Ave.
Prospect Hill
Prospect Hill Laundrette
Woodquay
St. Vincents Ave.
Salmon Weir Bridge
Cathedral of Our Lady
Frances St.
Eyre St.
Bóthar Irwin
St. Patrick's Church
TO 7 8 (100m)
Eglinton Canal
Canal Rd.
NUNS ISLAND
Gaol Rd.
Bubbles Laundrette usit now
Mary St.
Eglinton St.
Rosemary Ave.
Galway Advertiser
Williamsgate St.
KENNEDY PARK
Eyre Sq.
Forster St.
Station Rd.
EYRE SQ.
FAS office
Bowling Green
Upper Abbeygate
William St.
Medieval Wall
Presentation Rd.
Galway People's Resource Centre
Nuns Island Rd.
Market St.
Nora Barnacle House
Lynch's Castle
EDWARD SQ.
Victoria Pl.
Train & Bus Stations
Lombard St.
St. Nicholas
Shop St.
Lwr. Abbeygate
St. Mary's Rd.
St. Helens St.
New Rd.
Mill St.
Mainguard St.
Buttermilk Ln.
An Taibhdhearc
St. Augustine St.
Queen St.
TO 20
O'Brien's Br.
Bridge St.
Upper Cross St.
High St.
Middle St.
River Deep Mountain High
Lower Cross St.
Merchants Rd.
Henry St.
Lwr. Dominick
Quay St.
Druid Theatre
Flood St.
New Dock St.
Dock Rd.
Lough Atalia Rd.
Raleigh Row
William St. West
Upper Dominick
Wolfetone Br.
City Museum
Spanish Parade St.
Spanish Arch
Commercial Dock
The Long Walk
Dock St.
Sea Rd.
Munster Ave.
BURKE PARK
Father Griffin Rd.
Claddagh Quay
River Corrib
Old Dock
THE CLADDAGH
Claddah Hall
St. Nicholas Rd.
Fairhill
Nimmo's Pier
SOUTH PARK
Galway Bay
Father Burke Rd.
Grattan Rd.
TO 34 (150m)
Beach Court
TO SALTHILL (1km) & SALT HILL CARAVAN PARK
0
300 yards
0
300 meters

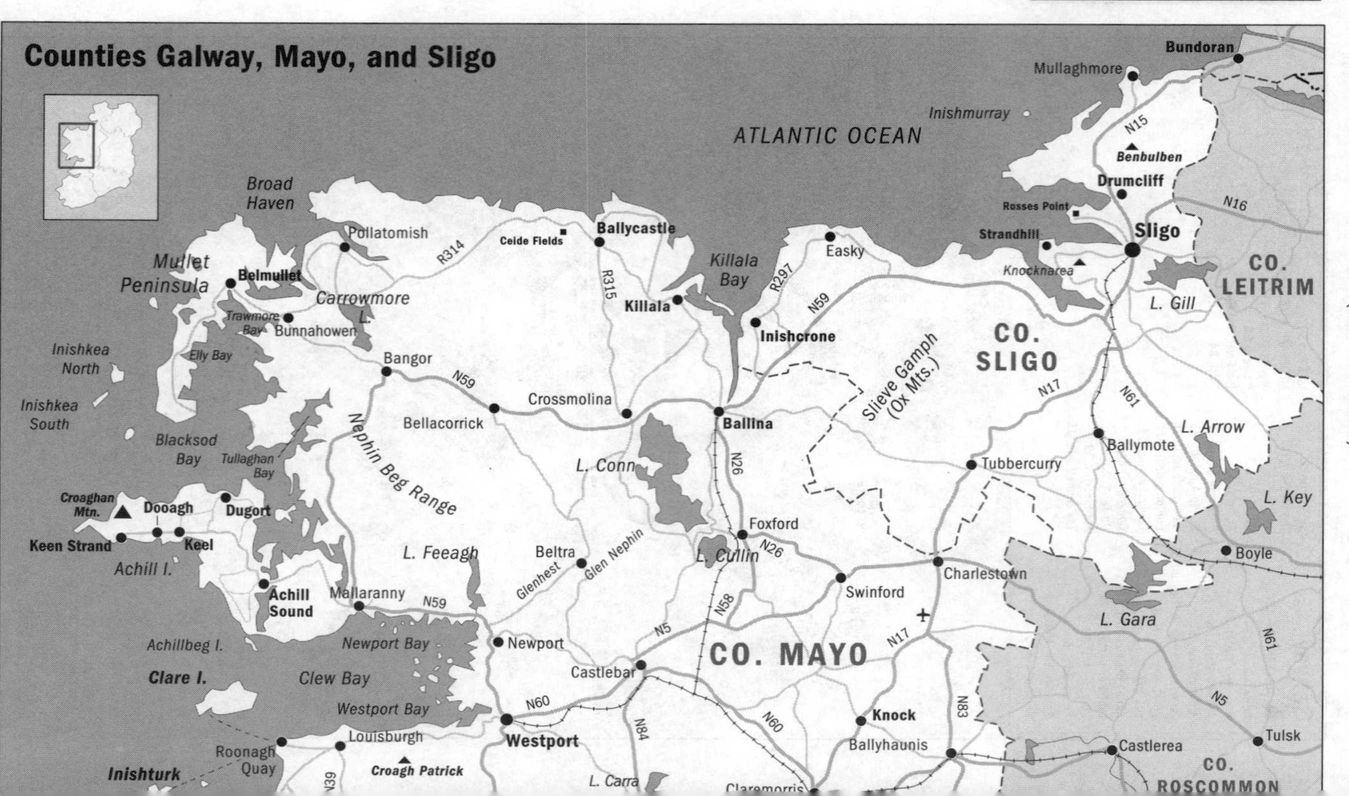
Counties Galway, Mayo, and Sligo
ATLANTIC OCEAN
Bundoran
Mullaghmore
Inishmurray
N15
Benbulben
Drumcliff
Rosses Point
Sligo
Strandhill
Knocknarea
N16
CO. LEITRIM
L. Gill
CO. SLIGO
Slieve Gamph (Ox Mts.)
N17
N61
L. Arrow
Ballymote
Tubbercurry
L. Key
Boyle
Broad Haven
Pollatomish
R314
Ceide Fields
Ballycastle
R315
Killala Bay
Killala
Easky
R297
N59
Inishcrone
Mullet Peninsula
Belmullet
Carrowmore L.
Trawmore Bay
Bunnahowen
Inishkea North
Inishkea South
Elly Bay
Bangor
Crossmolina
Bellacorrick
Ballina
N26
Blacksod Bay
Tullaghan Bay
Nephin Beg Range
L. Conn
Croaghan Mtn.
Dooagh
Dugort
Keen Strand
Keel
Achill I.
Foxford
L. Feeagh
Beltra
Glenhest
Glen Nephin
L. Cullin
Achill Sound
Mallaranny
Swinford
Charlestown
L. Gara
N58
N5
Achillbeg I.
Newport Bay
Newport
CO. MAYO
Clare I.
Clew Bay
Castlebar
N60
Westport Bay
Westport
N84
Knock
N83
Ballyhaunis
Roonagh Quay
Louisburgh
Croagh Patrick
Inishturk
N39
L. Carra
Claremorris
Castlerea
Tulsk
CO. ROSCOMMON

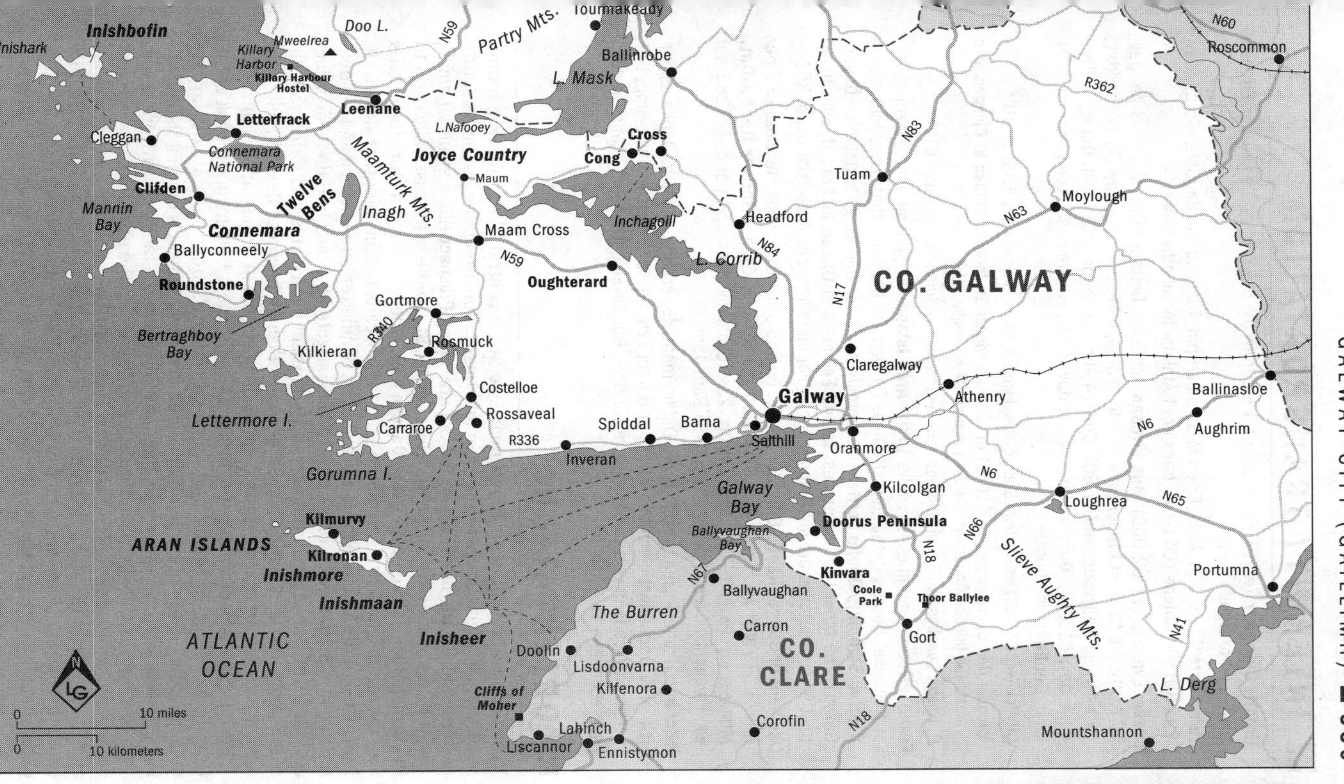
Inishbofin
Inishark
Doo L.
N59
Partry Mts.
Tourmakeady
Killary Harbor
Mweelrea
Killary Harbour Hostel
Ballinrobe
L. Mask
Leenane
Letterfrack
Cleggan
L.Nafooey
Cross
Cong
Joyce Country
Maamturk Mts.
Maum
Connemara National Park
Clifden
Twelve Bens
Inagh
Mannin Bay
Connemara
Ballyconneely
Maam Cross
N59
Oughterard
Inchagoill
L. Corrib
Roundstone
Bertraghboy Bay
Gortmore
R340
Rosmuck
Kilkieran
Costelloe
Lettermore I.
Carraroe
Rossaveal
R336
Inveran
Spiddal
Barna
Salthill
Galway
Gorumna I.
Kilmurvy
ARAN ISLANDS
Kilronan
Inishmore
Inishmaan
Inisheer
ATLANTIC OCEAN
Doolin
Lisdoonvarna
Kilfenora
Cliffs of Moher
Lahinch
Liscannor
Ennistymon
The Burren
Carron
CO. CLARE
Corofin
N18
N67
Ballyvaughan
Ballyvaughan Bay
Galway Bay
Doorus Peninsula
Kinvara
Coole Park
Thoor Ballylee
Gort
N18
N66
Slieve Aughty Mts.
Kilcolgan
Oranmore
Claregalway
Athenry
N6
Loughrea
N65
Aughrim
Ballinasloe
Portumna
N41
L. Derg
Mountshannon
Headford
N84
N17
Tuam
N83
CO. GALWAY
N63
Moylough
R362
Roscommon
N60
0
10 miles
10 kilometers

INTERCITY TRANSPORTATION

Airport: Carnmore (☎755 569), about 3 mi. from the city center. 5 small **Aer Éireann** planes jet to **Dublin** daily.

Trains: Eyre Sq. (☎561 444). Open M-Sa 9am-6pm. Trains to **Dublin** (3hr., 4-5 per day, €21-30) via **Athlone** (€11-14); transfer at Athlone for all other lines.

Buses: Eyre Sq. (☎562 000). **Bus Éireann** heads to: **Belfast** (7hr., M-Su 2-3 per day, €27.50); the **Cliffs of Moher** (late May to mid-Sept. M-Sa 3-4 per day, Su 1-2 per day; €11.40) via **Ballyvaughan** (€7.80); **Cork** (4½hr., 13 per day, €15.80); **Donegal** (4hr., 4 per day, €15.20); **Dublin** (4hr., 14 per day, €12). Private coach companies specialize in **Dublin**-bound busery.

Citylink (☎564 163) leaves from Supermac's, Eyre Sq. (9 per day, last bus 5:45pm; €10).

Michael Nee Coaches (☎095 51082) drives from Forster St. through **Clifden** to **Cleggan,** and meets the **Inishboffin** ferry (M-Sa 2-4 per day; €7.80 single, €11.20 return).

P. Nestor Coaches (☎797 144) leaves from the Forster St. carpark (5-7 per day, €10).

Ferries: Three companies ferry folks to the **Aran Islands;** in general, the best prices are at the ticket booths in the tourist office. Be warned, however, that the Doolin-based **O'Brien Shipping/Doolin Ferries** is extremely unreliable and tough to get info about in Galway. The other two companies, **Island Ferries** and **Queen of Aran II,** with ticket booths all over town, are more dependable. For more info, see **Aran Islands,** p. 351.

Car Rental: Budget Rent-a-Car, 12 Eyre Sq. (☎566 376). 23+. Economy class €55 per day, €379 per wk. Open M-F 8am-6pm, Sa-Su 9am-6pm. **Windsor Rent-A-Car,** Monivea Rd. (☎770 707). Free pickup. 23+. Economy class €58 per day, €286 per wk. Frequent weekend deals. Open M-Sa 9am-4pm.

Hitching: Hitchers usually wait on the Dublin road (N6) scouting rides to Dublin, Limerick, or Kinvara. Most catch bus #2, 5, or 6 from Eyre Sq. to this main thumb-stop. University Rd. leads drivers to Connemara via N59. But haven't you heard? *Let's Go* does not recommend hitchhiking.

ORIENTATION

Buses and trains will deposit you near **Eyre Sq.,** a central block of lawn, monuments, and lounging tourists; the train and bus station are up the hill on its southeastern side. To the northeast of the Square, along **Prospect Hill,** a string of small, cheap B&Bs await your business, while **Forster St.,** to the southeast, takes you to the **tourist office** before turning into **College Ave.,** where larger and more lush B&Bs are clustered. The town's commercial zone spreads out in the other direction. Northwest of the Square, **Woodquay** is an area of quiet(er) commercial and residential activity. **Station Rd.,** a block east of **Williamsgate St.,** leads into the pedestrian-only heart of Galway, where many of its most popular cafes and pubs *craic*kle with activity day and night. **Shop St.** becomes **High St.** becomes **Quay St.,** but without the passing traffic it feels like a single, long stretch of street-carnival fun.

Fewer tourists venture over the bridges into the more bohemian **left bank** of the Corrib, where great music and some of Galway's best pubs await, largely untapped. Just south of the left bank is the **Claddagh,** Galway's original fishing village. A road stretches west past the quays to **Salthill,** a tacky beachfront resort with row-houses and skyrocketing property values. To the north of the west bank are the university areas of **Newcastle** and **Shantallow,** quiet suburbs where students and families live. Galway's Regional Technical College is a mile east of the city center in suburban **Renmare,** which dozes peacefully by its bird sanctuary. The few pubs along **the docks** in the southeast of the city are largely fishermen hangouts that close up and clear out early in the night. When weather permits, guitar players and lusty paramours lay on the lawn by the river along the **Long Walk.**

LOCAL TRANSPORTATION

With its many pedestrian-only and one-way streets, little Galway lends itself best to walking. Other forms of transport are of use mostly to those staying out of the city center or planning excursions from the city.

Buses: City buses (☎562 000) leave from the top of Eyre Sq. (every 20min., €0.95). Buses to every neighborhood: #1 to **Salthill,** #2 to **Knocknacarra** (west) or **Renmare** (east), #3 to **Ballybrit,** #4 to **Newcastle,** and #5 **Rahoon.** Service M-Sa 8am-11pm, Su 11am-11pm. Commuter tickets €12 per wk., €40 per month. Students €10/€32.

Taxis: The biggest companies are **Big O Taxis,** 21 Upper Dominick St. (☎585 858), and **Cara Cabs,** Eyre Sq. (☎563 939). 24hr. taxis can usually be found around Eyre Sq. and near the tourist office. **Black Cabs** are considerably cheaper than taxis due to differences in licensing and fixed-price service, but they can't be hailed on the street; they are run by **MGM** (☎757 888), **Claddagh** (☎589 000), and **Eyre Square** (☎569 444).

Bike Rental: Europa Cycles, Hunter Buildings, Earls Island (☎563 355), opposite the cathedral. €7 per day, €40 per wk. Deposit €40. Open M-Sa 9am-6pm, Su 9am-noon and 4-6pm. **Mountain Trail Bike Shop,** Middle St. (☎569 888). €10 per day, €75 per wk. €40 deposit. Open daily 9:30am-5:45pm.

PRACTICAL INFORMATION

TOURIST AND FINANCIAL SERVICES

Tourist Office: Forster St. (☎537 700). A block south of Eyre Sq. A big and busy office, where little comes free; you must specifically ask for the free *Galway Tourist Guide* if you don't want to pay for your info. **Bureau de change** available. Books accommodations upstairs. Open July-Aug. daily 9:30am-7:45pm; May-June and Sept. daily 9am-5:45pm; Oct.-Apr. M-F and Su 9am-5:45pm, Sa 9am-12:45pm. The **Salthill** office (☎520 500) is in an odd, round, metallic building next to the aquarium, visible from the main beach. Open May-Sept. daily 9am-5:45pm.

Travel Agency: usit now, Mary St. (☎565 177). Sells the ever-important **TravelSave** stamps (a well-spent €10). Also books student and youth-rate flights. Open May-Sept. M-F 9:30am-5:30pm, Sa 10am-3pm; Oct.-Apr. M-F 9:30am-5:30pm, Sa 10am-1pm.

Banks: Bank of Ireland, 19 Eyre Sq. (☎563 181), and **AIB,** Lynch's Castle, Shop St. (☎567 041), both have 24hr. **ATMs** and are open M-F 10am-4pm, Th until 5pm.

LOCAL SERVICES

Camping Equipment: Forget your raingear? Visit **River Deep Mountain High,** Middle St. (☎563 968). Open M-Th and Sa 9:30am-6pm, F 9:30am-7:30pm.

Bookstores: Charlie Byrne's Bookshop, Middle St. (☎561 776). A massive stock of secondhand and discounted books, neatly organized by subject. Open July-Aug. M-Th and Sa 9am-6pm, F 9am-8pm, Su noon-6pm; Sept.-June M-Th and Sa 9am-5pm, F 9am-8pm. **Kenny's** (☎562 739), between High and Middle St., has an enormous collection of Irish interest books and an art gallery. Open M-Sa 9am-6pm.

Library: St. Augustine St. (☎561 666). Open M 2-5pm, Tu-Th 11am-8pm, F-Sa 11am-1pm and 2-5pm. Don't expect an oasis of calm—the children's wing can be quite noisy.

Bisexual, Gay, and Lesbian Information: Galway Gay Helpline, Eglinton St., P.O. Box 45 (☎566 134). Recorded info on meetings and events Tu and Th 8-10pm. The ***Gay Community News*** is available at Charlie Byrne's Bookshop (see above).

Laundry: The Bubbles Laundrette, 18 Mary St. (☎563 434). Wash and dry €8. Open M-Sa 9am-6pm. **Prospect Hill Launderette,** Prospect Hill (☎568 343). Self-service wash and dry €6. Open M-Sa 8:30am-6pm; last wash 4:45pm.

Work Opportunities: See **Long-Term Stays,** p. 344.

EMERGENCY AND COMMUNICATIONS

Emergency: ☎999; no coins required. **Police** *(Garda)*: Mill St. (☎538 000).

Counseling and Support: Samaritans, 14 Nun's Island (☎561 222). 24hr. phones. **Rape Crisis Centre,** 3 St. Augustine St. (☎1850 355 355). Limited hours.

Pharmacies: Pharmacies abound in the city; all keep similar hours. **Flanagan's,** Shop St. (☎562 924). Open M-Sa 9am-6pm. **Matt O'Flaherty's,** Shop St. (☎566 670).

Hospital: University College Hospital, Newcastle Rd. (☎524 222).

Internet Access: Celtel e.centre, Eyre Sq., is conveniently located. €4.80 per hr., 10% student discount. Open daily 8am-10pm. **Fun World,** Eyre Sq. (☎561 415), above Supermac's, can be noisy but has great night deals. €5 per hr.; 8-11pm €3 per hr. Open M-Sa 10am-11pm, Su 11am-11pm. **Hotlines,** right in the middle of Quay St., offers early-bird discounts. Otherwise, €5 per hr. Open M-F 9:30am-10pm, Sa-Su 10:30am-10pm. **Neatsurf,** 7 St. Francis St. (☎533 976). The fastest and cheapest at €0.75 per 10min. Open M-Sa 9am-11pm, Su 11am-11pm.

Post Office: Eglinton St. (☎562 051). Open M and W-Sa 9am-5:30pm, Tu 9:30am-5:30pm.

ACCOMMODATIONS

In the last few years, the number of accommodating beds in Galway has tripled; it now approaches one thousand. Nevertheless, it is wise to call at least a day ahead in July and August and on weekends. Hostels are spread throughout the city and come in all shapes and sizes; almost all are well run and conscientious. Most B&Bs can be found in Salthill, but there are also a few closer to the city center.

HOSTELS AND CAMPING

Salmon Weir Hostel, 3 St. Vincent's Ave. (☎561 133). Not as impressively stacked or spacious as some of its brethren, but extremely homey, with a friendly, laid-back vibe. Don't be surprised to find members of the staff strumming away in the stairwell, or travelers communing out back over their beverages of choice. Free tea and coffee. Laundry €6. Curfew 3am. 12-bed dorms €9-10; 6-bed €13-14; 4-bed €14-15. Doubles €35. ❶

Sleepzone, Bóthar na mBán (☎566 999; www.sleepzone.ie), northwest of Eyre Sq. Extremely accommodating, if somewhat inconveniently located; takes the "s" out of "hostel." Big, beautiful, new, and fully loaded—huge kitchen, common room with flatscreen TV, carpark, **Internet access** (€4.50 per hr.), and a peaceful terrace. Wheelchair-accessible. Laundry €6. 8- to 10-bed dorms €16.50; 6-bed €18; 4-bed €20. Singles €40; doubles €54. Weekends €1.50-10 more, Nov.-Apr. €2-17 less. ❷

Kinlay House (IHH), Merchants Rd. (☎565 244), half a block off Eyre Sq. A surprisingly huge, well-located hostel with all manner of rooms and services, including a foosball table. **Aran Island Ferry bus** departs from out front. Discounts when you book with their other locations in Cork and Dublin. **Bureau de change.** Wheelchair-accessible. Small breakfast included. Laundry €7. 8-bed dorms €15; 4-bed €16, with bath €19. Singles €27; doubles €40, with bath €48. Oct.-June €0.50-1.50 less. ❷

The Galway Hostel, Eyre Sq. (☎566 959), right across from the station. Burren Shale tiles lead up past soft yellow walls to tight dorms and clean bathrooms. Busy and hospitable. Light breakfast included. **Internet access** (€5 per hr.). 24hr. reception. Large dorms €15; 4-bed €19, with bath €22. Doubles €45-50. ❷

Barnacle's Quay Street Hostel (IHH), Quay St. (☎568 644). Bright, spacious rooms in the eye of the Quay St. storm. Über-convenient for post-pub crawl returns, but that same convenience can make front rooms quite noisy. Light breakfast included. No alcohol allowed on premises. Excellent security. Big dorms €15; 8-bed €16.50; 6-bed €19; 4-bed €20. Singles €50; private rooms €25 per person. Rates lower in off-season. ❷

Archview Hostel, Dominick St. (☎586 661). Religion isn't the opiate of the masses—the Archview is. Laid-back, with long-termers laying about like (friendly) dirty laundry (fear not, short-term dorms are cleaner). A longer walk from the station (about 15min.) is compensated for by the hostel's location in Galway's bohemia. A bit worn, but at these prices, who cares? **Internet** €5 per hr. Dorms €10. Long-term stays €45 per wk. ❶

Corrib Villa (IHH), 4 Waterside (☎562 892), past the courthouse. Georgian townhouse with high ceilings, a fresh coat of purple paint, clean rooms, and beds of varying comfort. Laundry €5. 6- to 12-bed dorms €15. ❷

Salthill Caravan and Camping Park (☎523 972). Beautiful location on the bay, about ½ mi. west of Salthill. A good hour walk along the shore from Galway. Open Apr.-Oct. €6 per hiker or cyclist. ❶

BED AND BREAKFASTS

St. Martin's, 2 Nun's Island Rd. (☎568 286), on the west bank of the river at the end of O'Brien's Bridge. The gorgeous back garden spills into the river. Located near Galway's best pubs, and just across the river from the main commercial district. All rooms with bath. Singles €32; doubles €60. Large family room €25 per person. ❸

Adria House, 34 Beach Court (☎589 444; www.adriaguesthouse.com). On a quiet cul-de-sac off Grattan Rd., between the city center and Salthill. Home to a dynamic duo of owners—one is a former chef and the other a former member of the tourist board who now works for a rental car agency. €20-55 per person, with prices highest July-Aug. ❹

Lynfield House, 9 College Rd. (☎567 845), just past the tourist office. Only a few blocks from Eyre Sq. and the bus/train station. Another deluxe B&B run by the same family as Adria, with the same room configurations and fluctuating rates. ❹

Ashford Manor, 7 College Rd. (☎563 941), by Lynfield House. A classy, if pricey B&B, complete with TVs, direct dial phones, and hair dryers in every room. Ample parking. Big breakfast selection. €45-48 per person. ❹

San Antonio, 5 Headford Rd. (☎564 934), a few blocks north of Eyre Sq. Rooms with multiple single beds are backpacker-friendly, as are the owners. With breakfast €25 per person; without €20. ❷

The Western, 33 Prospect Hill (☎562 834; www.thewestern.ie), just past Eyre Sq. A large B&B that is well priced and convenient to the stations, Eyre Sq., and the pub downstairs. Rooms are simple but have cable TV and hotpot. Free parking. July-Aug. singles €40; shared rooms €35 per person. Oct.-May €30-32.50 per person. ❸

Atlantic View, 4 Ocean Wave (☎582 109), off Grattan Rd. A fully loaded B&B with relatively easy access to both Salthill and Galway City. Some 2nd fl. rooms open onto a balcony that commands a great view of the ocean. Luxurious room number 3 features a double, a single, and a jacuzzi. Some rooms wheelchair-accessible. Late July-Aug. €45-75 per person; June to mid-July and Sept. €35-50; Oct.-May €35. ❹

Rossa B&B, 21 St. Brendan's Ave. (☎562 803). On a small, busy street, but more convenient than staying outside the city. June-Sept. €25 per person; Oct.-May €20. ❸

St. Joseph's, 24 Glenard Ave. (☎522 147), Salthill. Small B&B with the lowest prices around. €17 with continental breakfast, €20 with full Irish breakfast. ❷

LONG-TERM STAYS

Galway has a large population of youthful transients who visit, fall in love, find jobs, stay for a few months, and move on. Most share apartments in and around the city, where rents run €50-75 per week. Those staying for less than a month are best off at one of the hostels, such as the Archview (see above), that have cheap weekly rates (€45). The best place to look is the *Galway Advertiser*. Apartment hunters line up outside the *Advertiser*'s office at the top of Eyre Sq. at around 2pm on Wednesdays; when the classified section is released at 3pm they high-tail it to the nearest phone box (in Eyre Sq.). An ideal time to start looking for housing or jobs is just before the university lets out, in the second or third week of May.

Jobs are also relatively attainable in Galway, with most **short-term work** found in the service industry—simply ask around at local pubs and restaurants. A four-month student visa or other work permit helps a great deal by making you legal, although the situation isn't entirely hopeless without it. The Thursday morning *Galway Advertiser* has a long list of various job vacancies. Galway also has two centers which aid the introduction to productive society. **FAS,** in Island House to the left of the cathedral, posts vacancies for everything from service to managerial to research positions, and can get you in touch with recruiters. (☎534 400; www.fas.ie. Open M-F 9am-5pm.) The friendly folk at the **Galway Peoples' Resource Centre,** in Canavan House on Nun's Island Rd., provides free guidance services through all aspects of the job search. (☎564 822 or 562 688. Open M-F 9am-5pm.) If you want to secure something before you arrive, see **Alternatives to Tourism,** p. 47, for other job-placement services in and around Ireland.

FOOD

The east bank has the greatest concentration of restaurants; the short blocks around Quay, High, and Shop St. are filled with good values, especially at the cafes and pubs. **SuperValu,** in the Eyre Sq. mall, is for those who want to cook or stock up on fruit and cereal. (☎567 833. Open M-W and Sa 9am-6:30pm, Th-F 9am-9pm, Su noon-6pm.) **Evergreen Health Food,** 1 Mainguard St., has all the healthy stuff. (☎564 215. Open M-Sa 9am-6:30pm. Additional location in the Galway Shopping Centre on Headford Rd. is open W-F until 9pm.) On Saturday mornings, an **open market** sets up cheap pastries, ethnic foods, and fresh fruit, as well as jewelry and artwork, in front of St. Nicholas Church on Market St. The crepes are a steal—€3.50 for Belgian chocolate, banana, and Bailey's. (Open 8am-5pm.)

Anton's (☎582 067). Just over the bridge near the Spanish Arch and a 3min. walk up Father Griffin Rd. Self-consciously hip eateries on the other side of the river could learn a lot from this hidden treasure where they let the food do all the talking. Scrambled eggs with smoked salmon €5. Open M-F 8am-6pm, Sa 10am-5pm. ❶

Java's, Abbeygate St. (☎567 400). Hip, dimly lit cafe. The craving and the raving flock here at all hours to satisfy hunger and various other pangs. The New York-style bagels are excellent (€4.75), as are the brownies. As reliable as Irish rain—only closes early Christmas Eve. Open daily 10:30am-3am. ❶

McDonagh's, 22 Quay St. (☎565 001). Fish and chips madness—locals and tourists alike line up and salivate at this century-old institution. Certificates and newspaper clippings lining the wall attest to its international acclaim. Takeaway fish fillet and chips €5.65. Open daily noon-midnight; takeaway M-Sa noon-midnight, Su 5-11pm. ❷

The Home Plate, Mary St. (☎561 475). Diners enjoy massive helpings on tiny wooden tables. Quaint and vegetarian-friendly, with curry dishes and sandwich variations big enough to share (but good enough to make you want one for yourself). The vegetarian wrap (€8.85) is fantastic. Mains €7-10. Open M-Sa noon-9:30pm. ❷

The River God Cafe, High St. (☎565 811). French and Asian flavors combine in subtle seafood curries and tofu dishes. The champagne sorbet (€3.95) makes bubbly heavenly. Mains €10-14. Open daily 5-10pm. ❸

Tulsi, Buttermilk Walk (☎564 831), between Middle and High St. This award-winning restaurant serves Ireland's best Indian food. The lunch (€6.95) is better and almost as cheap as the fast food joints around the corner. Open daily noon-3pm and 6-10pm. ❷

Cougar's Organic Bistro, Quay St. (☎569 600). A chance for vegans to leave the kitchen and let someone else cater to their diet; meat-eaters won't mind joining them—there are many diverse and tasty options for everyone. Roasted pumpkin paella €8.20; goat-cheese ravioli €8.50. After 6pm head upstairs to the **Claddah Loft,** where similarly inventive meals are excellent, if more expensive. Open daily noon-10pm. ❸

Da Tang, Middle St. (☎561 443). Businessmen and hipsters crowd together in this busy Chinese noodle house. Some of the best food in town. Pickled mustard mixes with shredded pork in broth (€9). Takeaway available. Open M-Th 12:30-3pm and 5:30-10pm; F-Sa 12:30-3pm and 6-11pm; Su 6-10:30pm. ❷

Couch Potatas, Upper Abbeygate St. (☎561 664). Locals eat huge portions until dizzy. Try the Sir Walter Raleigh—potato with chicken breast and curry—€8.55; not even the staff knows where that name came from. Open M-Sa noon-10pm, Su 1-10pm. ❷

Bueno Appetito, Upper Abbeygate St. (☎538 166). The rarely found pizza-by-the-slice is available here for those who don't want a whole pie (meat or veggie €2.50). Pastas (€6.30) are about the cheapest in town. Open daily 10:30am-10:30pm. ❷

Café Du Journal, Quay St. (☎568 426). Enter and relax instantly. Bookshelves and regulars line dark, multi-colored walls, while sun-seekers sit out on Quay. Grab a newspaper, coffee, and a gourmet sandwich. Specials €5-8. Open daily 9am-10pm. ❷

Fat Freddy's, Quay St. (☎567 279). Galway's youth give high marks to the large pies rolling down the pipe at this pizza joint, although the wait can be a drag. Large pizza €8.60. Open daily noon-11:30pm. ❷

Pierre's, 8 Quay St. (☎566 066). If you're going to break the bank, it ought to happen at this oasis of quiet amidst the din of Quay St. Save room for dessert—the raspberry mousse floating in a chocolate cup is divine. 3-course meal €21. Open 6-10:30pm. ❹

Brasserie Eleven, 19 Middle St. (☎561 610). A good spot for an upscale, pre-theater meal, with an enticing range of meat, seafood, and vegetarian options. Tomato and basil lamb with salad and garlic bread €14.50. Open daily 12:30-10:30pm. ❸

Mocha Mania, Mainguard St. (☎566 146). Smokeless *craic.* A bright, friendly, cigarette-free coffee shop with dozens of coffee concoctions. Lovely apple tarts. Tasty panini (€5). Espresso €1.70; desserts €3.50. Open M-Sa 8am-6pm, Su noon-5pm. ❶

Conlon's Seafood Restaurant, 3 Eglinton St. (☎562 268). If you're not in the mood to wait through the lines at McDonagh's, this friendly, casual spot is a good alternative. Choose from some 20 varieties of fish and chips (€7.50), or feast on the seafood salad bar (€14.50). Dozen oysters €15.75. Open M-Sa 11am-11:30pm. ❸

PUBS

Christmas is coming early this year, kids, and under the tree is the first (but certainly not the last) *Let's Go* **Galway Pub Crawl.** So hydrate, line your stomachs with soda bread, pull on your runners, and get going. With approximately 650 pubs and 70,000 people, Galway maintains a healthily low person-to-pub ratio (100:1, if you do the math). Indeed, the city's intricate constellation of pubs is its number one attraction. Music is alive and well every night, whether as the latest alternative rock, live trip-hop, or some of the best trad in the country. Very broadly speaking, Quay St. and Eyre Sq. pubs cater more to tourists, while locals stick to the more trad-oriented Dominick St. pubs. Look for flyers for specific dates, or check the *Galway Advertiser*, freely available at their office at the top of Eyre Sq.

DOMINICK STREET

Roisin Dubh ("The Black Rose"), Dominick St. (☎586 540). Intimate, bookshelved front hides one of Galway's hottest live music scenes. Largely rock and singer-songwriters, but folk and blues put in appearances, and sessions are quite frequent. Marvel at the musicians pictured on the walls—they've all played the Roisín. Cover M-Tu €5-20.

Zulus, Dominick St. (☎581 204). Galway's first gay bar. Approximately 95% male, but all are welcome to join in the fun at this friendly little place. Lively local banter and laughter ricochet off the walls until late into the night.

The Blue Note, William St. West (☎589 116). Where all the cool kids go. Twenty-something hipsters amass on lush couches, getting up to mingle or dance. Galway's best bet for turntable music, with top-notch guest DJs. Occasional indie films in the winter.

The Crane, 2 Sea Rd. (☎587 419), a bit beyond the Blue Note. A friendly, musical pub that is well known as the place to hear trad in Galway. Enter through the side door and hop up to the 2nd fl. loft. 2 musicians quickly become 6, 6 become 10, 10 become 20. Trad every night and all day Su. Set dancing Tu.

Stranos, William St. West (☎588 219). A mixed lesbian and gay bar/club/meeting house with a pool room on the 3rd fl. Frequent theme nights; check out the GCN at Charlie Byrne's for current listings. DJs Th.

Monroe's, Dominick St. (☎583 397). Trad in a veritable *craic* warehouse. One of Galway's finest for Irish music. Nightly sessions from 9:30pm weekdays. Tu Irish dancing. Cheap pizzas from the joint next door are served until midnight.

Mossimo's, William St. West (☎588 239). Modern, sleek bar with comfy couches and a young crowd. Nightly DJs have a jazzy slant.

Aras Na nGael, Dominick St. (☎526 509). A bar for Irish speakers, this club nonetheless welcomes all sorts (well, kind of). Come F or Sa night and absorb the rhythms of the Irish language as you quietly nurse your Guinness.

THE QUAY

The King's Head, High St. (☎566 630). Like visitors to the city itself, pubbers come into King's Head expecting to spend the night, but fall in love and end up living there instead. There's certainly enough room for it, with 3 floors and a huge stage devoted to nightly rock. Upstairs music varies. Su jazz brunch 1-3pm.

Busker Browne's (☎563 377), between Cross St. and Kirwin's Ln. in an old nunnery. Get thee to this upscale, 20-something bar that packs a professional crowd onto wall-to-wall couches. If the first 2 floors leave you unimpressed, head to the fantastic 3rd floor **"Hall of the Tribes,"** easily the most spectacular lounge in Galway. Su morning excellent live jazz downstairs.

Seaghan Ua Neachtain (a.k.a. **Knockton's**), Quay St. (☎568 820). The oldest pub in Galway, dating back to 1894. Afternoon pint-sippers munch sandwiches and study the streams of pedestrians from street-corner tables. Nightly trad.

The Quays, Quay St. (☎568 347). Popular with tourists, the younger crowd, and scamming yuppies, or any combination of the above. The massive, multi-floored interior was built with carved wood and stained glass from an old church; it's worth a visit just to see the interior. Forget your camera? Try the bathrooms, where disposables are thoughtfully sold to capture moments of fleeting sobriety. Cover €3-9. Open 10pm-1:30am.

The Front Door, Cross St. (☎563 757). Beams of light criss-cross the dark interior of this pub. More rooms open as it gets busier, filling 3 maze-like stories. Get lost with that special someone, but don't expect any privacy—rowdy young pubbers fill in quickly.

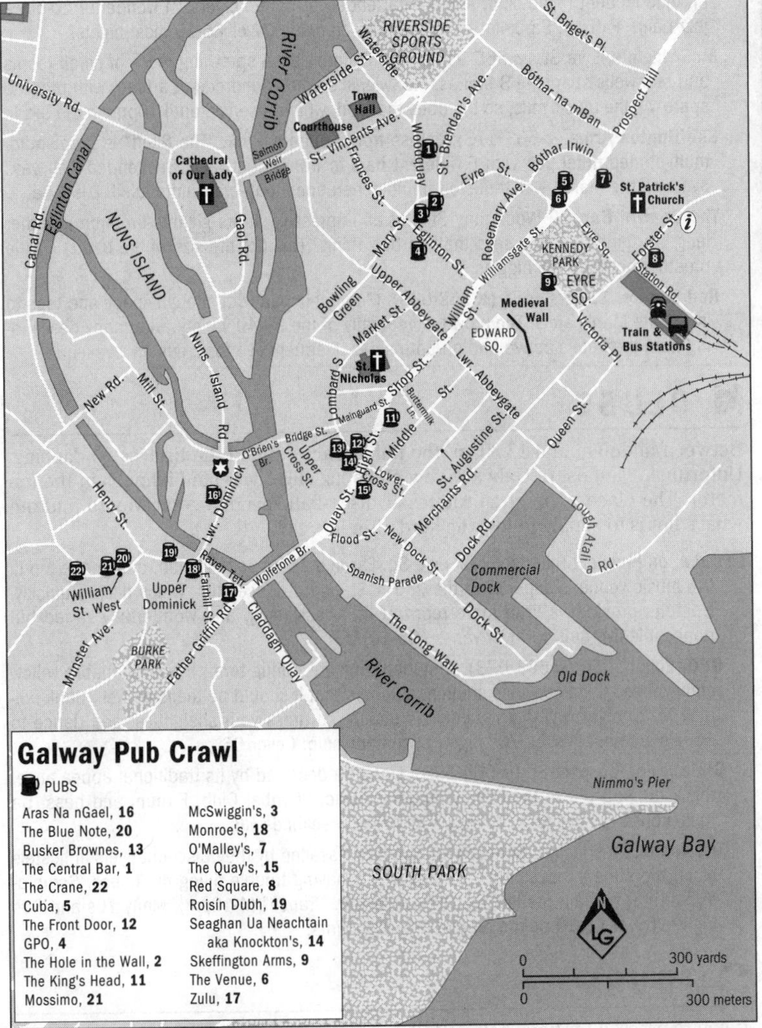

Bazaar (☎534 496), across from the Arch and lit with purple lights. A lush, Moroccan-themed bar popular with the smartly dressed. No trad here, but jazz on W and DJs F-Sa.

EYRE SQUARE

The Hole in the Wall, Eyre St. (☎565 593). This surprisingly large pub fills up fast with college-age singletons year-round. An ideal meet-market with booths for intimate groups, 3 bars for mingling, and tables to dance on. Flirtation spills into the small beer garden. Quality of music varies, but *craic* is a constant.

Cuba, Prospect Hill (☎565 991). Conveniently located under the club and live music venue (see **Clubs,** below), this colorful bar liberates itself on weekends and becomes an independent rogue club. Ask the bartender for Cuban cigars. M wonderful 20-piece jazz band, F disco, Sa ballads, Su stand-up comedy. Cover €5-10 most nights.

McSwiggin's, Eyre St. (☎568 917), near Eglinton St. A sprawling mess of small rooms and stairwells spanning 3 stories, McSwiggin's holds hundreds at a time, with room to spare. As the music rolls, so too does the food, which is served until 10pm on the 3rd fl.

Skeffington Arms (☎563 173), across from Kennedy Park. "The Skeff" is a splendid, multi-storied hotel pub with 6 different bars to wander between. Suspended walkways overlook the rear. A well-touristed, multi-generational pub crawl unto itself. DJs F-Sa.

The Central Bar, 32 Woodquay St. Not as impressive as its giganto-brethren in either length or girth, but who says that's a bad thing? (It's not the size of the bar...) A little breather between the biggies.

Red Square, 11 Forster St. (☎569 633). Monolithic pub with enough space and taps to intoxicate Mao's army. The crowd is generally of the 30-40 variety, with many descending from the hotels above and on both sides. Frequent live rock; DJs on weekends.

CLUBS

Between midnight and 12:30am, the pubs drain out and the tireless go dancing. Unfortunately, most of Galway's few clubs lag slightly behind its pubs in the fun factor. The place to be often rotates at disco-ball speed; a good way to find out what's hot is to simply follow the herd after last call.

Cuba, on Prospect Hill, right past Eyre Sq. Far and away the best club, though the top fl. live-music venue is superior to the 2nd fl. standard dance club, which fills up quickly. Upstairs provides a little more room, a little less flash, and wonderfully varied but danceable live music. Cover varies (€5-10).

GPO, Eglinton St. (☎563 073). A student favorite during term; the inescapable yellow smiley faces try to convince summer clubbers that it should be theirs as well. Bank holiday M "Sheight Night" gives you the chance to dress your sheightiest and dance to Abba's greatest hits. Tu 70s night, W comedy club. Cover €6.

O'Malley's, Prospect St. (☎564 595). Don't be deceived by its traditional appearance, this club/pub blasts thoroughly modern music. W Tribal Club, F drum and bass, Sa funk/house, Su live rock. Cover €3 midweek, weekends €6.

The Venue, Prospect St. Chances are you'll be assailed by their discount flyers in hostels or on the streets, assuming that they're still having trouble filling the house. Scrub-a-dub-dub at W foam parties. Su afternoons 6hr. "trance" (4-10pm). Many 70s and 80s nights. Cover €5-10 before promotional discounts.

TOURS

If you're pressed for time, half- or full-day group tours may be the best way to see the sights of Galway, the Burren, and Connemara. Some offer excellent values, with lower prices than bus tickets. Hour-long tours in and around the city seem largely unnecessary, as Galway is central and walkable, but they might be a good option on a rainy day. These hop on, hop off **buses** line up outside the tourist office (most €9, students €8). Several lines depart from the tourist office, bus station, and Merchant's Rd. (by Kinlay House) once a day for both Connemara and the Burren (€20-25, students €15-20): **Bus Éireann** (☎562 000), **Healy Tours** (☎770 066), **Lally Tours** (☎562 905), and **O'Neachtain Tours** (☎553 188). The ***Corrib Princess*** (☎592 447) sails from Galway's Woodquay and tours north-lying Lough Corrib (1½hr., June-Aug. daily 2:30 and 4:30pm, €9).

SIGHTS

EYRE SQUARE. If you're traveling by bus or train, Eyre Square will undoubtably be the first sight you stumble upon, and you won't be alone—visitors and locals alike gather on this centrally located square of grass for picnics, sunbathing, and basic downtime. Although the park was rededicated with the official name **John F. Kennedy Park,** you might get confused looks if you refer to it as anything but Eyre Square. Around its grassy commons, a collection of monuments speak for various interests. **The Browne Doorway** was transferred from the ruins of an ornate 17th-century home to serve as the Square's gate in 1904; it now looks strangely out of place without the fence that enclosed the park until 1965. The big rusty sculpture in **Quincentennial Fountain** celebrates the **Galway Hooker;** while the nearby statue portrays the Irish-speaking poet **Pádraig Ó'Cónaire.** On the south side of the Square is the **Eyre Square Shopping Centre,** a large indoor mall that encloses a major section of Galway's 13th-century **medieval town wall.**

CLADDAGH. Until the 1930s, this area was an Irish-speaking, thatch-roofed fishing village. Stone bungalows replaced the cottages, but a bit of the small-town atmosphere persists in this predominantly residential area. The famous **Claddagh rings,** traditionally used as wedding bands, are today's mass-produced reminders. The rings depict the thumb and forefingers of two hands holding a crown-topped heart. The heart should be turned outward until marriage; once the heart is turned inward, the wearer's heart is no longer available. *(Across the river, south of Dominick St.)*

LYNCH'S CASTLE. The Lynch family ruled Galway from the 13th to the 18th century. Their elegant 1320 mansion now houses the Allied Irish Bank. The bank's small displays relate a dubious family legend: in the late 1400s, Lynch Jr. killed a Spaniard whom he suspected of eyeing his girl. Junior, sentenced to hang, was so beloved by the populace that no one would agree to be the hangman. Lynch Sr., the lord of the castle, was so determined to administer justice that he hanged his own son before a horrified yet admiring public. As various versions of the episode passed along, the term **Lynch's Law** came to refer to execution without legal authority—strange, since this execution was carried out for the purpose of following the law. *(Exhibit room open M-F 10am-4pm, Th until 5pm. Free.)*

NORA BARNACLE HOUSE. The little home of James Joyce's life-long companion has hardly changed since its famous-by-association inhabitant left. Original love letters and the table where he composed a few lines arouse followers of the literary great. *(8 Bowling Green; the house with the maroon split-door. ☎564 743. Open mid-May to mid-Sept. W-F 10am-1pm and 2-5pm. Times vary; call ahead. Mid-Sept. to mid-May by appointment only. €2.50.)*

CHURCH OF ST. NICHOLAS. Your prayers will be answered here—St. Nicholas is the patron saint of travelers. A stone marks the spot where Columbus supposedly stopped to pray before bursting onto the New World scene. Note the three-faced clock on the exterior; local folklore claims that the residents on the fourth side neglected to pay their church taxes. Glorious stained glass and relics from the Connacht Rangers provide further distraction. Don't miss the **farmer's market** outside on Saturdays. *(Market St., behind the castle. Open May-Sept. daily 9am-5:45pm. Free.)*

CATHEDRAL OF OUR LADY ASSUMED INTO HEAVEN AND ST. NICHOLAS. The enormous yet dull exterior of Galway's Catholic cathedral provides no hint of the controversy that assailed its eclectic design a quarter-century ago: the interior consists of dark and imposing Connemara stone walls decorated with elaborate mosaics, as well as green Connemara marble floors. *(Beside the Salmon Weir Bridge at* *the intersection of Gaol and University Rd. Open M-F 9am-6pm. Organ practice most weekdays 3:30-5:30pm. Open for mass M-F and Su at 9, 11am, and 6pm.)*

MENLO CASTLE. Depending on the amount of *craic*-induced adrenaline in your system, **hire a boat** and drift, row, or zoom up Lough Corrib to visit the ruined seat of the Blake family. **Frank Dolan's** fleet of boats will take you away from the crowd and up Galway's gorgeous stretch. *(13 Riverside, Woodquay. ☎565 841. €4 per hr.)*

GALWAY CITY MUSEUM. Old photographs of the Claddagh, a knife-sharpener by a peat fire, and some fishy statistics form the bulk of this small exhibit, which could benefit from fuller, clearer labeling. Though the patio area above the Spanish Arch does provide a nice view of the sea, river, and the plebs stretched out below. *(In the tower house next to the Spanish Arch. ☎567 641. Open May-Oct. daily 10am-1pm and 2:15-5pm; check at the tourist office for Nov.-Apr. opening times. €2, students €1.)*

ATLANTAQUARIA. Recently opened as the National Aquarium of Ireland, the museum features all things aquatic, with a particularly interesting tank filled with rays and ridiculous-looking "dabs." Like big eyes? A wax paper-covered jar upstairs holds the gigantic peeper of a fin whale. *(☎585 100. Open 10am-8pm.)*

OTHER SIGHTS. Across the University Rd. bridge from the cathedral is the **National University of Ireland at Galway.** The university was built 157 years ago, during the Famine, as the Tudor-style Queen's College Galway. Today, the university enrolls some 12,000 students each year. The **Long Walk,** by the river, makes a pleasant stroll that brings you to the **Spanish Arch,** which was built in 1584 as a defensive bastion and is now one of the city's finest surviving medieval structure.

ACTIVITIES

From the Claddagh, the waterfront road leads west to **Salthill,** where the coast alternates between pebbles and sand; when the ocean turns sunset red, it's time for some serious beach frolicking. Casinos, swimming pools, and a mini amusement park join the unappealing facades of new hotels that dominate the esplanade. (**Leisureland swimming pool** ☎521 455. Open daily 8am-10:30pm. Call for lane times. €7, children €4.80. **Summer carnival** open daily noon-11pm. Most rides €2-3.) A 15min. walk along the coast from Salthill will bring you to **Rusheen Riding Centre,** where you can rest your feet while on a horseback ride over the beach or countryside. (Barna Rd. ☎521 285. Call for reservations. Most rides €20-25 per hr., 10% student discount.) The nearest **golf course** to the city is **Galway Bay Golf and Country Club,** which is beautifully surrounded by the ocean on three sides (☎790 500; €55-60 per person). There is also a **GAA Stadium** in Salthill (Pearse Stadium; Dr. Manix Rd.).

ENTERTAINMENT

ARTS, THEATER, AND FILM

The free *Galway Advertiser* provides listings of events and is available at the Galway Advertiser office at the top of Eyre Sq. For tickets to big concerts and events throughout Ireland, make your way to **Zhivago** on Shop St. (Ticket hotline ☎509 960. Open June-Sept. M-Sa 9am-9pm, Su 10am-6pm; Oct.-May M-W and Sa 9am-6pm, Th-F 9am-9pm, Su noon-6pm. €1.90 booking fee.)

SIAMSA NA GAILLIMHE. At Claddah Hall, dancers, singers, musicians, and actors stun audiences with their showcase of traditional Irish performances. *(On Nimmos Pier, off Claddagh Quay. ☎755 479; www.homepage.eircom.net/~siamsa. Performances July M-F 8:45 pm. Tickets €10-18.)*

TOWN HALL THEATRE. Presents everything from Irish-themed plays and original Irish films to international hit musicals. Responsible for the summer **Film Fleadh** and **Arts Festival.** *(Courthouse Sq. ☎569 777. Programs daily in summer; most performances 8pm. Tickets €6.50-20; student discounts often available.)*

AN TAIBHDHEARC. An Taibhdhearc (an TIVE-yark), a mostly Irish-language theater, was founded in 1928 by a group of academics from Galway University, and has launched quite a few Irish actors into the limelight. Poetry readings and musicals alternate with full-blown plays. *(Middle St. ☎562 024. Box office open M-F 10am-6pm, Sa 1-6pm. Tickets €8-12, student discounts often available.)*

DRUID THEATRE. Internationally renowned performances of contemporary Irish plays, all in English. *(Chapel Ln., between Quay and Flood St. Performances nightly 8pm. Tickets €15-20, students €12-15.)*

GALWAY ARTS CENTRE. Hosts rotating art and photography exhibits and frequent workshops on dance, printing, and painting, as well as occasional poetry readings. *(47 Dominick St. ☎565 886; www.galwayartscentre.ie. Open M-Sa 10am-6pm. Free.)*

FESTIVALS AND EVENTS

Festivals rotate through Galway all year long, with the greatest concentration during the summer months. Reservations for accommodations during these weeks, especially Race week, are key.

GALWAY RACES. The gates go up at the end of July. The attending masses celebrate horses, money, and stout, not necessarily in that order. The grandstand bar at the 23,000-seat-capacity **Ballybrit track** measures over 70 yd., making it the **longest bar in Europe.** The major social event is Ladies' Day, when those with the best hats and overall dress are officially recognized. *(☎753 870; www.iol.ie/galway-races. Tickets €15-20 at the gate or by advance purchase.)*

GALWAY ARTS FESTIVAL. For two crazed weeks in mid-July, the largest arts festival in Ireland reels in famous trad musicians, rock groups, theater troupes, and filmmakers. Unofficial performers flock to the streets, which are only cleared for parades. *(General information ☎583 800; www.galwayartsfestival.ie. Box Office, Victoria Pl. ☎566 577. Open M-Sa 9:30am-5:30pm.)*

GALWAY POETRY AND LITERATURE FESTIVAL. Also known as the Cúirt, this festival gathers the very highest of the nation's brows in the last week of April. Past guests have included Caribbean poet and Nobel Prize winner Derek Walcott and reggae star Linton Johnston. Performances take place all over the city, but the main events are held in Town Hall. *(☎565 886.)*

GALWAY FILM FLEADH. Filmmania. Ireland's biggest film festival is a jumble of films, lectures, and workshops. The Fleadh features independent Irish and international filmmakers and screens its stuff in early July, right before the Arts Festival. *(☎569 777; www.galwayfilmfleadh.com.)*

GALWAY INTERNATIONAL OYSTER FESTIVAL. Galway's last big festival of the year takes place in late September. Street theater, parades, and free concerts surround this 49-year-old Galway tradition, which culminates in the **Guinness World Oyster Opening Championship.** *(☎527 282; www.galwayoysterfest.com.)*

ARAN ISLANDS ☎099

On the westernmost edge of Co. Galway, isolated from the mainland by 20 mi. of swelling Atlantic, lie the spectacular Aran Islands *(Oileán Árann)*. The green

THE HIDDEN DEAL

AER ÁRANN

Have you ever noticed how expensive it can be to travel to an island? Because islands' secluded yet inconvenient locations blatantly preclude all notions of driving, walking, or biking, enterprising ferry companies develop veritable monopolies on the island-transit business, and therefore charge whatever they please. The three ferries that travel to the islands charge between €19-35 round-trip—a high price for budget travelers to pay. At these prices, however, the €44 round-trip air journey offered by Aer Árann suddenly becomes a hidden deal. For only €9-24 more than the ferry, travelers can enjoy the luxury of flying to and from the magnificent isles. It's double the fun and takes just a fraction of the time, and it's especially attractive considering how unreliably the ferries run. And you know there's nothing like seeing an island from the sky! Better yet, a combined flight/sail option (€37) satisfies those who can't decide on one mode of locomotion.

Aer Árann (☎01 814 1458; within Ireland ☎1890 46 27 26; www.aerarann.ie). Flights to all three islands leave from the small airport in Inverin, 19 mi. west of Galway, and can be booked over the phone or at the Galway tourist office. To Inishmore: 10min.; 8 per day; €44 return, students €37. Shuttle bus to the Airport leaves from Kinlay House in Galway 1hr. before departure, €6.

fields of Inishmore, Inishmaan, and Inisheer are hatched with a maze of limestone walls—the result of centuries of farmers piling the stone that covered the islands to clear the fields for cultivation. The landscape is as moody as the Irish weather and tends to adopt its disposition, from placid blue calms to windy torments. The majestic, mythical Arans have continually sparked the imaginations of both Irish and foreign alike. We know little of the earliest islanders, whose tremendous but mysterious cliff-peering forts seem to have been constructed by the secret designs of the limestone itself. Early Christians flocked here seeking seclusion; the ruins of their churches and monasteries now litter the islands.

TRANSPORTATION

Three ferry companies—**Island Ferries, Queen of Aran II,** and **O'Brien Shipping/Doolin Ferries,** operate boats to the Aran Islands. They depart from three main points: **Doolin** (40min. to Inisheer), **Galway** (2hr. to Inishmore), and **Rossaveal,** the main departure point, several miles west of Galway (40min. to Inishmore). If the ferry leaves from Rossaveal, the company making the trip will provide a shuttle bus from Galway City to Rossaveal for an additional fee. The Island Ferries and Queen of Aran ferries serving Inishmore are reliable and leave daily—if the one you've booked cancels for weather, check with the others, as some are more trepidatious than others. Traveling from Galway and Doolin to the Aran Islands, or between the islands themselves, can be difficult, to say the least— purchase all of your tickets before setting sail.

Island Ferries (☎091 561 767 or 568 903, after-hours ☎572 273; www.aranislandferries.com), has main offices in the Galway tourist office and on Forster St., close to Eyre Sq. One ferry sails to **Inishmore** (Apr.-Oct. 3 per day, Nov.-Mar. 2 per day) and another to **Inishmaan** via **Inisheer** (2 per day); both depart from **Rossaveal** (€20 return, students €16.50). A bus runs from Galway's Kinlay House B&B to the ferryport (departs 1½ and 1hr. before sailings; €6, students €5).

Queen of Aran II (☎566 535 or 534 553). The only ferry company based on the islands; also has a ticket booth in the Galway tourist office. Only goes to **Inishmore.** (4 departures daily. €19 return, students €12.) Boats leave from **Rossaveal,** with a bus departing from Kinlay House (1¼hr. before sailings; €6, students €5).

O'Brien Shipping/Doolin Ferries (Doolin ☎065 707 4455; Galway ☎091 567 676; after-hours ☎065 707 1710). Somewhat daily service in the summer, off-sea-

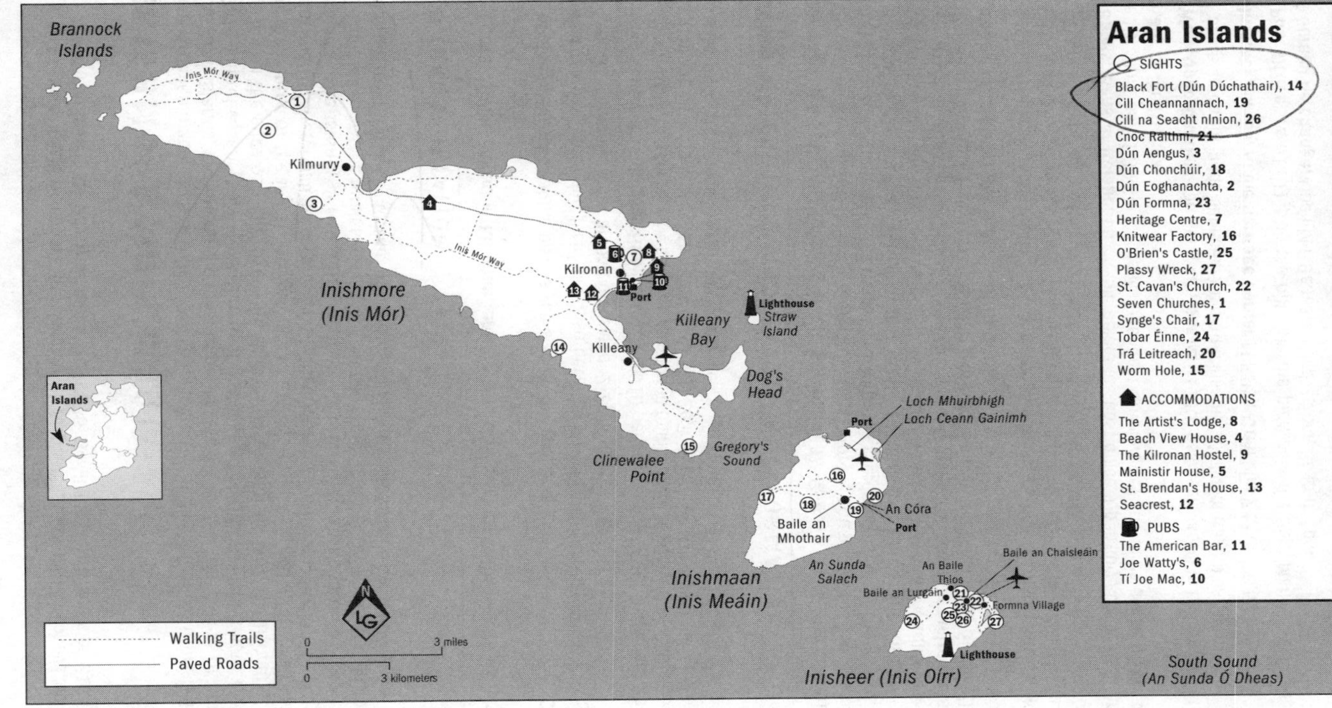
Aran Islands
SIGHTS
Black Fort (Dún Dúchathair), 14
Cill Cheannannach, 19
Cill na Seacht nInion, 26
Cnoc Raithní, 21
Dún Aengus, 3
Dún Chonchúir, 18
Dún Eoghanachta, 2
Dún Formna, 23
Heritage Centre, 7
Knitwear Factory, 16
O'Brien's Castle, 25
Plassy Wreck, 27
St. Cavan's Church, 22
Seven Churches, 1
Synge's Chair, 17
Tobar Éinne, 24
Trá Leitreach, 20
Worm Hole, 15
ACCOMMODATIONS
The Artist's Lodge, 8
Beach View House, 4
The Kilronan Hostel, 9
Mainistir House, 5
St. Brendan's House, 13
Seacrest, 12
PUBS
The American Bar, 11
Joe Watty's, 6
Tí Joe Mac, 10
Brannock Islands
Inis Mór Way
Kilmurvy
Inishmore (Inis Mór)
Kilronan
Port
Killeany
Lighthouse
Straw Island
Killeany Bay
Dog's Head
Clinewalee Point
Gregory's Sound
Aran Islands
Loch Mhuirbhigh
Loch Ceann Gainimh
Port
An Córa
Port
Baile an Mhothair
An Sunda Salach
Inishmaan (Inis Meáin)
Baile an Chaisleáin
An Baile Thios
Baile an Lurgain
Formna Village
Lighthouse
Inisheer (Inis Oírr)
South Sound (An Sunda Ó Dheas)
Walking Trails
Paved Roads
0 3 miles
0 3 kilometers
N

son 3 times per wk. **Galway** to any island €20-25 return. **Doolin** to **Inishmore** €32 return, to **Inishmaan** €28 return, and to **Inisheer** €25 return. ISIC discount €5 (not available if bought on board). **Galway-Aran-Doolin** about €35. Unreliable **inter-island** trips €10.

INISHMORE (INIS MÓR)

The archaeological sites of Inishmore (pop. 900), the largest and most touristed of the Aran Islands, are among the most impressive in Ireland. Of the dozens of ruins, forts, churches, and holy wells, the most dazzling is the Dún Aengus ring fort, teetering on the edge of a cliff over the Atlantic. Crowds disembark at Kilronan Pier at the center of the island, spread out to lose themselves amid stone walls and stark cliffs, then coalesce again around major sights. Minivans and "pony traps" traverse the island, encouraging anyone on foot to climb aboard and pay up, though bikes are the most scenic way to get around. Exactly 437 kinds of wildflowers rise from the rocky terrain and over 7000 mi. of stone walls divide the land.

TRANSPORTATION

Ferries: Boats unload in **Kilronan,** arriving from **Galway** and **Doolin.** See **Transportation, p. 352**.

Minibus: Minibuses at the pier as you step off the boat offer identical tours. 2hr. €10.

Pony Traps: Ponies and their carts also hover by the gangplanks, offering more picturesque, if bumpier, rides around the island. 2-2½hr. 4 adults €60.

Bike Rental: Aran Bicycle Hire (☎61132). €10 per day. Deposit €10. Open daily 9am-5pm. **B&M Bicycle Hire** (☎61402), next to the tourist office. €10 per day, €60 per wk. Deposit €10. Open Mar.-May 9am-5pm; May-Sept. 9am-7pm. Bike theft is a problem after dark–either lock it up or don't leave it.

ORIENTATION AND PRACTICAL INFORMATION

The majority of human life hangs out in **Kilronan** *(Cill Rónáin)*, a cluster of buildings that makes up the island's main village, although houses and a few restaurants also huddle below Dún Aengus. Kilronan is the only place on the island to buy supplies, so stock up. The **airstrip** is on Inishmore's east end, while Kilmurvey, Dún Aengus, and most of the major sights are on the west. Anyone spending a few days on the Arans should invest in the Robinson map (€6.35), which meticulously documents every rock on all three islands, though a free map from one of the bike rentals might suffice for basic exploration.

Tourist Office: Kilronan (☎61263). Changes money, helps find accommodations, and has limited **luggage storage** (€1) during the day. Also sells the *Inis Mór Way* (€1.90). Open July-Sept. daily 10am-6:45pm; Oct. 10am-5pm; Nov.-Mar. 10am-4pm.

Banks: Bank of Ireland, up the hill before the post office. Open July-Aug. W-Th 10am-12:30pm and 1:30-3pm. Plastic-dependent travelers beware: there are **no ATMs on any of the Islands.**

Work Opportunities: The American Bar (☎61130) has been known to hire travelers for short-term work in the summer. 1-month minimum. Minimum wage plus tips.

Internet Access: At the **heritage center** M-F 9am-1pm and 2-5pm. €6.50 per hr.

Post Office: (☎61101), up the hill from the pier, past the Spar Market. Also has a **bureau de change.** Open M-F 9am-1pm and 2-5pm, Sa 9am-1pm.

ACCOMMODATIONS

Many minibuses make stops at hostels and B&Bs that are farther away; call the individual accommodations or ask at the tourist office for more information.

Mainistir House (IHH), Main Rd. (☎61169), 1 mi. from "town" on the road that begins between the American Bar and the sweater stores. Once a haven for musicians and writers, this sprawling hostel still attracts expatriots to its magazine-filled sitting room, where big windows look onto the sea. Cook Joel prepares a legendary dinner (see **Food,** below) and tasty breakfast biscuits. **Bike rental** €10 per day. Laundry €6. Dorms €12; singles €20; private rooms €16 per person. ❶

The Kilronan Hostel (☎61255), visible from the pier and adjacent to Tí Joe Mac's. 4-bed dorms are small, but bright and immaculate. Central location near all the important liquids—a 2min. walk from the pier and close to the taps of Joe Mac's pub. Helpful, knowledgeable staff will point you toward the island's wonders. €1 sheets are essential if you prefer not to sleep on plastic mattresses. **Bike rental** €10. Dorms €13, all with bath. ❶

The Artist's Lodge (☎61457). Take the turnoff across from Joe Watty's pub on the main road, continue straight down the path, and look right at the end. Cozy and inviting, with 3 good-sized, 4-bed dorms. Lodgers sip free tea and peruse the hostel's video collection by a crackling fire, or head out to the picnic table in the yard. Dorms €10. ❶

St. Brendan's House (☎61149). Take an immediate left off the entrance to the main road. An ivy-covered house with character across the street from the ocean. Full Irish breakfast included. Apr.-Oct. €20 per person, with bath €25; Nov.-Mar. €18/€20. €2 less with continental breakfast. ❷

Beach View House (☎61141), 3½ mi. west of Kilronan, on the main road near Kilmurvey. A great base for hiking. Some rooms have inspiring views of Dún Aengus, and all have beautifully warm quilts. Open May-Sept. Singles €36; doubles €48.50. ❸

Seacrest (☎61292), before St. Brendan's. A bright, spacious B&B close to the pier. **Jetski hire** can be arranged for €20 per 15min. with Amanda (☎087 298 6114). All B&B rooms with bath. Shared rooms €28 per person. ❸

FOOD AND PUBS

The **Spar Market,** past the hostel in Kilronan, functions as an unofficial community center. (☎61203. Open summer M-Sa 9am-8pm, Su 10am-6pm; winter M-Sa 9am-8pm, Su 10am-5pm.)

Mainistir House (see **Accommodations,** above). Dinner here is far and away the best deal on the island. Fill up for days on magnificent, mostly vegetarian buffets. 8-person tables are arranged to encourage conversation with fellow travelers or locals in search of epicurean bliss. BYO-wine. Dinner 8pm, reserve beforehand. €12. ❸

Tigh Nan Phaid (☎61330), in a thatched building at the turnoff to Dún Aengus. A nice resting spot after a morning of trekking. Specializes in home-cooked bread with home-smoked fish. Whiskey-cured Aran smoked salmon €5.95. Open daily 11am-5pm. ❷

The Ould Pier (☎61228), up the hill from the town center. Serves up fresh fish-and-chip configurations, burgers, and sandwiches. Eat inside or outside on sturdy picnic benches adorned with fresh flowers. Fish and chips €8.70. Open June-Sept. daily until 7pm. ❷

The Man of Aran Restaurant (☎61301), located just past Kilmurvey Beach to the right. For wonderful organic (if upscale) lunches in a historic setting. Toasties €3.20. Lunch daily 12:30-3:30pm; dinners in summer. ❷

Tí Joe Mac (☎61248), overlooking the pier. Locals and hostelers savor their pints on the terrace and their music in the back room. Sessions W.

American Bar (☎61130). Despite the name, an Irish pub true and true. The 2 sides the bar attract different clientele—young islanders and tourists stick to the left by the ol table, while older locals chew the fat on the right. Music most summer nights.

Joe Watty's (☎61155), west of the harbor on the main road. You've used it for orientation, why not use it for intoxication? Weekends usually bring bands and trad.

SIGHTS AND ENTERTAINMENT

The time-frozen island, with its labyrinthine stone wall constructions, rewards the wandering visitors who take the day to cycle or walk around its hilly contours. The **Inis Mór Way** is a mostly paved route that makes a great bike ride, circling past a majority of the island's sights. The graveled portion of the path leading from Dún Árran to Kilmurvy offers exhilarating views and bumpy, but fun, riding. The tourist office's maps of the Inis Mór Way (€2) purportedly correspond to yellow arrows that mark the trails, but the markings are frustratingly infrequent and can vanish in fog; it is best to invest in a Robinson map for serious exploring or content yourself with following the crowds and hoping for the best.

If you only have a few hours, high-tail it to the island's deservedly most famous monument, **Dún Aengus,** 4 mi. west of the pier at Kilronan. The **visitors center** below guards the stone path leading up to the fort. (☎61008. Open May-Sept. 10am-6pm, Oct.-Apr. 10am-4pm. €2.50; students €1.20.) One of the best-preserved prehistoric forts in Europe, Dún Aengus opens its 4000-year-old concentric stone circles onto the seacliff's 300 ft. drop, leaving the modern visitor awed and thoroughly humbled. Controversy continues as to whether it was built for defensive or ceremonial reasons. Many visitors are fooled by the occasional appearance of an island on the horizon—a vision so realistic that it appeared on maps until the 20th century. **Be very careful:** strong winds have been known to blow tourists off the cliffs.

A 30min. path to the left of the fort offers tremendous views of the cliff from below. Another 10min. farther along, there is a small freshwater stream. If the wind and light are just right, glinting droplets of water become suspended in the air in an upside-down waterfall. A few minutes beyond the stream is a view of the **Worm Hole,** named such for a sea serpent that was believed to dwell in this saltwater lake. The bases of the surrounding cliffs have been hollowed by mighty waves to look like **pirate caves.** If you follow the cliffs to the left of Dún Aengus for about 1 mi., you can climb down into the tidal pool and walk back beneath the cliffs to the Worm Hole. The walk is thrilling at high tide, but is more accessible at low tide. The sound of the waves crashing under the rock is worth the 30min. trek.

The road leading to the fort from Kilronan splits near Dún Árann. Either way will get you to Dún Aengus; turning left up the big hill will bring you to Dún Árann, and then down through a windy, gravel path to Kilmurvey, where it will rejoin the flatter, paved coastal route. Most tourists decide that the **Dún Árann Heritage Park,** at the top of the hill, is not worth the €3.50 admission fee. With sights such as cow dung and edible seaweed, they're probably right, though the lighthouse does provide a nice view from high atop the island. Inishmore's best beach is at **Kilmurvey,** with a sandy stretch and cold, cold water. Half a mile past the beach, a left turn leads to **Dún Eoghanachta,** a huge circular fort with 16 ft. walls. To the right past Eoghanachta are the misleadingly named **Seven Churches**—there were never more than two; the other buildings were likely monks' residences.

Uphill from the pier in Kilronan, the new, expertly designed **Aran Islands Heritage Centre** provides a fascinating introduction to the islands' monuments, geography, history, and peoples. The center also screens *Man of Aran* several times a day. (☎61355. Open June-Aug. 10am-7pm; Apr.-May and Sept.-Oct. 11am-4pm. Exhibit or film only €3.50, students €3. Combined admission €5.) The **Black Fort** *(Dún*

Dúchathair), 1 mi. south of Kilronan across eerie terrain, is larger than Dún Aengus, a millennium older, and greatly underappreciated. Finish off your day on Inishmore with **Ragus,** performed at the Halla Rónáin (down the street from the Aran Fisherman Restaurant)—an hour-long jaw-droppingly energetic display of traditional Irish music, song, and dance that receives rave reviews and costs almost twice as much in Dublin. (Tickets available at the door or from the **Aran Fisherman Restaurant,** ☎61104. Shows at 2:45, 5, and 9pm. €13.) On summer Saturday nights, the first steps of a ***céilí*** begin at midnight at the dance hall (cover €6).

INISHMAAN (INIS MEÁIN)

Seagulls circle the cliffs and goats chew their cud, but there's little human activity to observe in the limestone fields of Inishmaan (pop. 300). With the rapid and dramatic changes that have taken place on the other two islands over the last few years, Inishmaan remains a fortress, quietly avoiding the hordes of barbarians invading from the east via Doolin and Galway. Even residents of Inishmore report that stepping onto Inishmaan is like stepping back twenty years into the past.

For those who find beauty in solitude, a walk along the rocky clifftop is sheer bliss. The *Inishmaan Way* brochure (€2) describes a 5 mi. walking route that passes all of the island's sights. The thatched cottage where John Synge wrote much of his Aran-inspired work is a mile into the island on the main road. Across the road and a bit farther down is **Dún Chonchúir** (Connor Fort), an impressive 7th-century ring fort. At the western end of the road sits **Synge's Chair,** where the writer came to think and compose. The view of splashing waves and open seas is remarkable, but an even more dramatic landscape awaits a bit farther down the path where the coastline comes into view. To the left of the pier, the 8th-century **Cill Cheannannach** church left its rubble on the shore; islanders were buried here until the mid-20th century under stone slabs. A mile north of the pier, **Trá Leitreach** is Inishmaan's safest, most sheltered beach. Entering the **Knitwear Factory,** near the center of the island, is uncannily like stepping into a Madison Ave. boutique. The company sells its sweaters internationally to all sorts of upscale clothiers, but visitors get them here right off the sheep's back at nearly half the price—expect to pay €90 for an Aran sweater. (☎73009. Open M-Sa 10am-5pm, Su 10am-4pm.)

For **tourist information,** as well as the chance to buy a variety of local crafts, try the **Inishmaan Co-op** (☎73010; open M-F 8:30am-5pm). Take the turnoff for the knitwear factory, continue straight, then make a right turn after the factory. The **post office** (☎73001) is in **Moore Village,** Inishmaan's tiny population center. **Mrs. Faherty** runs a **B&B ❸,** signposted from the pier, and will fill you up with an enormous dinner. (☎73012. Open mid-Mar. to Nov. Dinner €12. Singles €30; doubles €50.) **Tigh Congaile ❸,** on the right-hand side of the first steep hill from the pier, is a gorgeous B&B. (☎73085. Singles €35; shared rooms €30 per person.) Its **restaurant ❸** concentrates on perfecting seafood. (Lunch under €6.80, dinner from €16. Open June-Sept. daily 10am-7pm.) The **An Dún Shop** (☎73067) sells food at the entrance to Dún Chonchúir. **Padraic Faherty's** thatched pub is the center of life on the island and serves a small selection of grub until 6:30pm.

INISHEER (INIS OÍRR)

The Arans have been described as "quietness without loneliness," but Inishmaan can get pretty damn lonely, and Inishmore isn't always quiet. Inisheer (pop. 300), the smallest Aran, is the perfect compromise. On clear days, when the island settles into an otherworldly peacefulness, daytripping visitors wonder if these few square miles don't hold the key to the pleasures of a simpler life.

PRACTICAL INFORMATION. Rothair Inis Oírr rents **bikes.** (☎75033. €8 per day, €50 per wk.) Free **Internet access** is available at the **Inisheer Co-op Library,** a nondescript beige building up the road from the pier, past the beach (☎75008. Open Tu, Th, and Sa 2:30-5pm). The **post office** is farther up to the left of the pier, in a turquoise house. (☎75001. Open M-F 9am-1pm and 2-5:30pm, Sa 9am-1pm.)

ACCOMMODATIONS, FOOD, AND PUBS. The **Brú Hostel (IHH) ❶,** visible from the pier, is spacious and promises great views. The upper rooms have skylights for star-gazing, but the lower rooms have bigger windows. Call ahead in July and August. (☎75024. Continental breakfast €4, Irish breakfast €6.50. Laundry €5. 4- to 6-bed dorms €12; private rooms €16 per person.) **The Mermaid's Garden ❷,** signposted from the airstrip, on the other side of the beach, rents out a lovely, big room in their family home and serves a wonderful selection of breakfasts. (☎75062. €25 per person; €60 per family.) **Sharry's B&B ❸,** behind the Brú Hostel, promises views and high ceilings. (☎75024. Singles with bath €32, without €25; shared rooms €25 per person.) For campers who don't mind chilly ocean winds, the **Ionad Campála Campground ❶** stretches its tarps near the beach. (☎75008. Open July-Aug. €5 per tent, showers included.)

Tigh Ruairí, an unmarked pub and shop in a white building up the road running perpendicular to the beach, is your best bet for Inisheerie groceries. (☎75002. Shop open July-Aug. daily 9am-8pm; Sept.-June M-Sa 10am-6pm, Su 10:30am-2pm.) **Fisherman's Cottage ❷** serves amazing, organic, mostly island-grown meals. They've also been known to offer "Food for Healing" courses in April, May, and September. (☎75053. Soup and bread €2.50, dinners €12.70. Open daily 11am-4pm and 7-9:30pm.) **The Mermaid's Garden** (see **Accommodations,** above), will please steak lovers and tree-huggers alike with its impressive menu. (Vegan sandwich with hummus, roasted peppers, aubergine, and olives, €8.50.) **Cafe na Trá ❷** ("Cafe on the Beach") is, as its name implies, just off the sand. The decor is summery with Mediterranean hues, and the fish is fresh and tasty. (Cod and chips €7.50. Open June-Aug. 10:30am-6pm.) **Tigh Ned's** pub, next to the hostel, caters to a younger crowd, while the pub at the **Ostan Hotel** (☎75020), just up from the pier, is more dim, and as crowded as a place on Inisheer can get.

SIGHTS AND HIKING. You can see the sights of the island on your own by foot or bike, or with guidance on a **Wanderly Wagon** (☎75078) or **pony cart tour** (☎75092; both €7 per 45min.). The **Inis Oírr Way** covers the island's major attractions on a 4 mi. path. The first stop is in town, at **Cnoc Raithní,** a bronze-age tumulus (stone burial mound) that is 2000 years older than Christianity. Walking along the **An Trá** shore leads to the romantic overgrown graveyard of **St. Cavan's Church** *(Teampall Chaomhain)*. On June 14, islanders hold mass in the church's ruins in memory of their saint; a festival has recently been added. Cavan's nearby grave is said to have great healing powers. Below the church, a sandy beach stretches back to the edge of town. Farther east along the water, a grassy track leads to majestic **An Loch Mór,** a 16-acre inland lake brimming with wildfowl. The stone ring fort **Dún Formna** is above the lake. Continuing past the lake and back onto the seashore you'll find the **Plassy Wreck,** a ship that sank offshore and washed up on Inisheer in 1960. The wreck has been taken over by buttercups, crows' nests, and graffiti. Ironically enough, the **lighthouse** is quite visible from the wreck. The walk back to the island's center leads through **Formna Village** and on out to **Cill na Seacht nInion,** a small monastery with a stone fort. The remains of the 14th-century **O'Brien Castle,** razed by Cromwell in 1652, sit atop a nearby knoll. On the west side of the island, **Tobar Einne,** St. Enda's Holy Well, is believed to have curative powers, and is still a place of pilgrimage for the islanders. **Aras Eanna** is a huge, double-winged building sitting atop one of the island's highest points as peacefully as the nearby clouds. The left wing of the building houses visiting artists, whose Aran-inspired work is then displayed in the right wing. The center also screens films on Inisheer and runs **Irish language courses** (beginner, intermediate, and advanced; week-long course €150). Its cafe serves up delectable scones for just €1. One night a week, the center's theater becomes Aran's only **cinema,** while other nights see the occasional concert. (☎75150. Films €3, concerts €7. Gallery free. Open 10am-5pm.)

LOUGH CORRIB

Three hundred and sixty-five islands dot Lough Corrib, one for every day of the year. The lough, Ireland's largest, has enough elbow room for all of them. The eastern shores of Lough Corrib and Lough Mask stretch quietly into fertile farmland. The west slips into bog, quartzite scree, and the famously rough Connemara country. The island of Inchagoill, in the middle of the lough, contains the site of the second-oldest existing Christian monuments in Europe, while nearby Inisheanbó's luxurious and secluded digs have delighted Bob Hope and two of the Rolling Stones. Lough Corrib is considered one of Europe's best spots for salmon and trout angling, the principal activity on shore and boat.

OUGHTERARD (UACHTAR ÁRD) ☎091

A small population center along the N59 between Galway and Clifden, Oughterard (OOK-ter-rard) watches most touring vehicles blink briefly in its direction before heading to bigger and better-known attractions. But this little town draws Galway natives and those in the know to its quiet shores for weekend reprieves, and the city-weary traveler might do well to follow their lead. Hikers use Oughterard as a base from which to stage hikes into the Maamturk Mountains, while the less energetic prefer to angle in Lough Corrib's salmon-rich waters. Aughnanure Castle, a few miles from town, is worth a visit even for those just passing through.

TRANSPORTATION AND PRACTICAL INFORMATION. Bus Éireann stop on Main St. in Oughterard (July-Aug. M-Sa 6-9 per day, Su 2 per day; Sept.-June 1 per day) on their way from Galway via Clifden. Hitchers report easy going in summer between Galway and anywhere west. *Let's Go,* as you well know, does not recommend hitchhiking. A helpful independent **tourist office** sells the useful *Oughterard Walking & Cycling Routes* handbook for around €3. (☎552 808. Open May-Aug. M-F 9:30am-5:30pm, Sa-Su 10am-5pm; Sept.-Apr. M-F 9:30am-5pm.) The **Bank of Ireland** on Main St. has an **ATM.** (☎552 123. Open M-F 10am-12:30pm and 1:30-4pm, Th until 5pm.) **Flaherty's Pharmacy** mends from Main St. (☎552 348. Open M-Sa 9:30am-1pm and 2-6pm.) Also on Main St. (detect a theme?) is the **post office.** (☎552 201. Open M-F 9am-1pm and 2-5:30pm, Sa 9am-1pm.)

ACCOMMODATIONS, FOOD, AND PUBS. Cranrawer House (IHH) ❶, a 10min. walk down Station Rd. off Main St., is a beautiful hostel with big windows looking out on its generous expanse of land. The owner is a professional casting instructor and guides day expeditions to the lough, at a cost. (☎552 388. **Bike rental** €10 per half-day, €15 per day, €70 per wk. Fishing trips €25 per hr., full day €100. Laundry €8. Common room lockout midnight-8am. Open Feb.-Nov. 8- to 12-bed dorms €11; 5-bed family room with bath €13 per person for groups of 4 or 5. Private rooms with bath €15 per person.) The large lawn of **Corrib View House ❸**, about 6 mi. down the Aughnanure Castle road off N59, descends to the lake's edge, from which angling can be arranged. Guests also have full use of the tennis court. (☎552 345. All rooms with bath. €32 per person.)

Keogh's Grocery, a.k.a. **Spar,** sells food and fishing tackle from its location at the bend in Main St. The photo of Bob Hope buying snacks is not for sale. (☎552 583. Open summer M-Sa 8am-10pm; winter M-Sa 8am-8pm, Su 9am-9pm.) Great pub grub and brilliant *craic* flow from **The Boat Inn ❷,** across from Spar, and spill onto the tables that line the sidewalk. (☎552 196. Sandwiches and stews €4-7. Food served 11:30am-10pm. Live music F-Su.) Thatched **Power's Bar,** a few doors down, is the local Guinness tap. (☎557 222. Music Th and Su, disco Sa.) Across the street at **Keogh's Bar,** you can try your unsteady hand at drunk emailing. (☎552 222. Th disco, summer Sa-Su live rock or trad. **Internet access** €6.35 per hr.)

SIGHTS AND ACTIVITIES. A mile south of town, a turnoff from N59 leads to Oughterard's top attraction, 16th-century **Aughnanure Castle.** Here a river, red with peat, curves around the impressively preserved fortified tower that was once home to the O'Flaherty clan. The secret chamber and murder hole are highlights of the optional 40min. tour. Watch your footing and your head—the O'Flaherty's were not a tall people, and they intentionally built their spiral staircases imperfectly in the hopes that ascending attackers would be tripped up. (☎82214. Open mid-June to mid-Sept. daily 9:30am-6:30pm. €2.50, students €1.20.) The 19th-century silver- and lead-yielding caverns of **Glengowla Mines,** 2 mi. west of town off of N59, are the only show mines in all of Ireland. (☎552 360. Open Mar.-Nov. daily 9:30am-6pm. Call for off-season hours.) Glann Rd. covers the 9 mi. from Oughterard to the infamous **Hill of Doon,** where the pre-Celtic Glann people annually sacrificed a virgin to the panther goddess Taryn. It is said that the practice continued in secret until the 1960s, when they ran out of virgins. The 16 mi. **Western Way Walk** begins where Glann Rd. ends and threads through mountains, loughs, and Connemara coastline affording gorgeous views of the **Twelve Bens** and **Maamturks.**

Closer to home than many of the town's other sights, local sports enthusiasts swarm the **Gaelic pitch,** near the intersection of Pier Rd. and Main St., where they cheer on the local boys for €5 in the spring, though prices approach €20 as September's championships near. **Angling** on Lough Corrib is easily the most popular activity in Oughterard, and is arranged for visitors almost entirely through the town's accommodations. Surpisingly enough, golfing is generally less expensive than fishing; the **Oughterard Golf Club,** at the turnoff to Aughnanure Castle, is a beautiful 18-hole course with fine facilities. (☎552 131. €25 per person.)

Following the hatch of the 'mayfly,' a myriad of **angling competitions** tangle Lough Corrib with lines in—you guessed it—May, while competitors from all over Ireland assemble in June for the **Currach Racing Championships.** A family-oriented festival atmosphere accompanies the **Oughterard Pony Show** in late August.

DAYTRIP FROM OUGHTERARD: INCHAGOILL.

The Corrib Queen (☎092 46029) sails daily from Lisloughrea Quay on Cong's Quay Rd. (see p. 370), Ashford Castle, and the Quay road in Oughterard; it offers a brief but enlightening tour of the island (1½hr., June-Aug. 4 per day, €12-14 return). Those interested in more extensive exploration should take a morning ferry out and return in the afternoon.

Inchagoill (INCH-a-gill), reputed to mean "the Island of the Stranger," has been uninhabited since the 1950s. Aside from a few ancient monastic ruins and some toppled gravestones, there's little to see on the island. Still, at the right time of day, Inchagoill's eerie beauty and solitude can make it as captivating as any of its more touristed island cousins. Two churches, about which very little is known, lie just down the right-hand path from the pier. **St. Patrick's Church,** built in the 5th century, is now only a crumbling, heap-like heap. The famous **Stone of Lugna,** which supposedly marks the gravesite of St. Patrick's nephew and navigator, is 3 ft. tall and stands among the other stones surrounding the church. Its inscription means "stone of Luguaedon, the son of Menueh." (Good thing we cleared *that* u the earliest known example of the Irish language written in Roman scrip second-oldest known inscribed Christian monument in Europe (the olde catacombs of Rome). The second Church, the **Church of the Saint,** only d to the 12th century and therefore bears less discussion.

CONNEMARA (CONAMARA)

Connemara, a thinly populated region of northwest Co. Galway, extends a lacy net of inlets and islands into the Atlantic Ocean. The rough gang of inland mountains, desolate stretches of bog, and rocky offshore islands are among Ireland's most arresting and peculiar scenery. Driving west from Galway City, the relatively tame and developed coastal strip stretching to Rossaveal suddenly gives way to the pretty fishing villages of Roundstone and Kilkieran. Farther west, Clifden, Connemara's largest town, draws the largest crowds and offers the most tourist services. Ancient bogs spread between the coast and the rock-studded green slopes of the two major mountain ranges, the **Twelve Bens** and the **Maamturks.** Northeast of the Maamturks is **Joyce Country,** named for a long-settled Connemara clan. Ireland's largest *gaeltacht* is also located along the Connemara coastline, and Irish-language radio (Radio na Gaeltachta) broadcasts from Costelloe.

Cycling is a particularly rewarding way to absorb the region. The 60 mi. routes from Galway to Clifden (via Cong) and Galway to Letterfrack are popular despite fairly challenging dips and curves toward their ends. The seaside route through Inverin and Roundstone to Galway is another option. In general, the dozens of loops and backroads in north Connemara make for beautiful and worthwhile riding. **Hiking** through the boglands and along the coastal routes is also popular—the **Western Way** footpath offers dazzling views as it winds 31 mi. from Oughterard to Leenane through the Maamturks. **Buses** serve the main road from Galway to Westport, stopping in Clifden, Oughterard, Cong, and Leenane. N59 from Galway to Clifden is the main thoroughfare; R336, R340, and R341 make more elaborate coastal loops. **Hitchers** report that locals are likely to stop; *Let's Go* does not recommend taking advantage of locals' generosity. Connemara through the tinted windows of a tour bus (see **Galway,** p. 348) is better than no Connemara at all.

ROUNDSTONE (CLOCH NA RÓN) ☎095

Roundstone is a one-street fishing village that, like many of its neighbors along the Coast road, could do well in a quaint little Irish town contest. That withstanding, the striking surroundings and surprising variety of cultural offerings make Roundstone worthy of a brief visit. In the distance beyond the bay, a few prominent Bens rise into the clouds. The 2hr. hike up **Errisbeg Mountain,** which overlooks Roundstone's main street, culminates in a panoramic view of the entire region. Two miles along the coast beyond Roundstone, the beaches between Dog's Bay and Gorteen Bay fan out to a small knobby island.

The town is home to the famed **Roundstone Musical Instruments,** the only full-time *bodhrán* maker in the world (see **Traditional Music,** p. 74). Instruments built here have been used across the world by famous Irish musicians, including the Chieftains. The owners have taken advantage of this fame and its attendant attendance by opening a veritable trad megastore with attached Irish kitsch warehouse. (☎35875. Open daily 9am-6pm.) Roundstone's primary cultural event is its annual **arts festival,** held in July. For information on the festival, check with the town's ever-informative **Information Centre.** (☎35815. Open M-F 10am-1pm and 2-3pm.)

After (or before) drumming yourself into a frenzy, head to **Espresso Stop ❶** for coffee and cafe fare at the cheapest prices in town. (€4-7. Open daily 10am-6pm.)

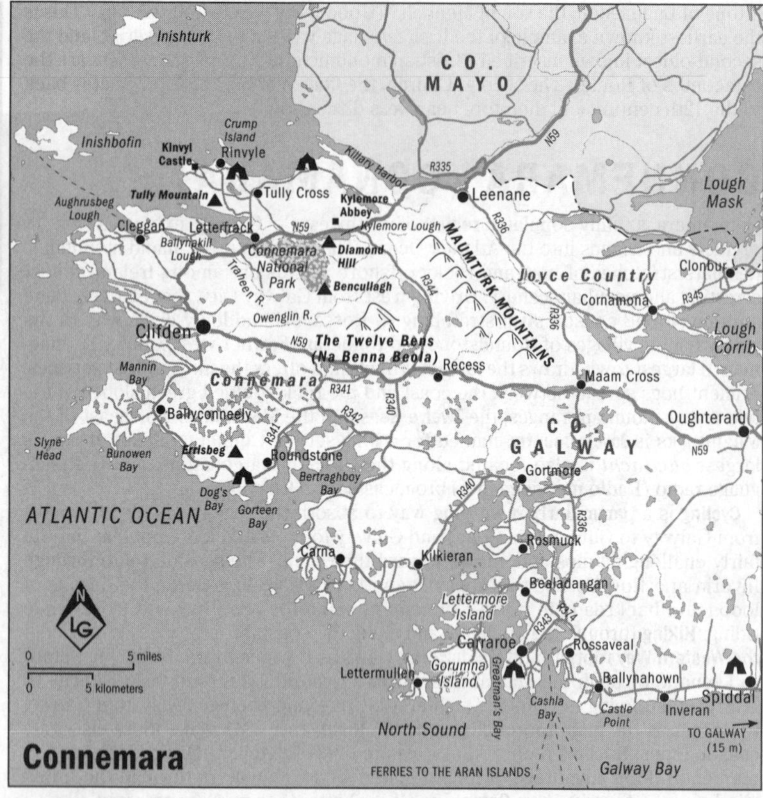

Vegetarians might prefer to venture a few doors down to **O'Dowd's ❸**, where mains are more expensive (€9-15) but explicitly non-carnivorous options are readily available. Finish off the day with a pint in the attached pub, then sleep off your merrymaking at **Wit's End B&B ❸**, where an ever-attentive proprietress maintains cozy and immaculately coordinated rooms. (☎35951. Open June-Sept. €28 per person.) Travelers more interested in thrift than comfort should seek out the **Gorteen Bay Caravan and Camping Park ❶**, 6 mi. west of Roundstone on the R341. (☎35882. No kitchen. Hot showers €1. Plots of land €6 per person.)

CLIFDEN (AN CLOCHÁN) ☎095

The town proper is a cluster of touristically directed buildings resting between a small cliff and a pair of modest peaks. Socially, Clifden serves as a buffer between the built-up southern half of Co. Galway and pristine northern Connemara. During the off season (Sept.-May), the town is relatively quiet, but tourists flood in during the summer months. Outdoors outfitters and other upscale amenities cater to this crowd; budget accommodations have become increasingly scarce in recent years.

TRANSPORTATION

Buses: Bus Éireann (☎091 56200) rolls from the library on Market St. to **Galway** via **Oughterard** (2hr.; mid-June to Aug. M-Sa 6 per day, Su 2 per day; Sept.-May 1-3 per day; €9) and **Westport** via **Leenane** (1½hr., late June-Aug. M-Sa 1 per day). **Michael Nee** (☎51082) runs a private bus from the courthouse to **Cleggan** (mid-June to Aug. 3 per day, Sept.-May 3 per wk.; €6) and **Galway** (2hr., 2 per day, €11).

Taxi: C&P Hackney Service (☎21309 or 086 859 3939). **Shannon Cabs** (☎51123 or 087 667 1738). **Joyce's** (☎21076 or 22082) is based out of the Clifden Town Hostel.

Bike Rental: Mannion's, Bridge St. (☎21160, after hours 21155). €9 per day, €60 per wk. Deposit €20. Open M-Sa 9:30am-6:30pm, Su 10am-1pm and 5-7pm.

Boat Rental: John Ryan, Sky Rd. (☎21069). Fishing trips and excursions. €50 per day. Open year-round. Call anytime.

ORIENTATION AND PRACTICAL INFORMATION

Most local traffic comes in on N59 from Galway (1½hr. to the southeast), which curves at the Esso Station and heads northeast to Letterfrack, Connemara National Park, Westport, and all other points north. **Market St.,** where the bus stops, runs parallel to **Main St.,** and the two meet at **the Square; Bridge St.** connects these main arteries near the Esso station. **Church Hill** runs up steeply from the Square, and **Sky Rd.** and **Clifden Beach** are on the far side of town. Reportedly, hitchers find rides at the Esso station on N59.

Tourist Office: Galway Rd. (☎21163). Extensive info on Connemara, including transportation schedules and lists of restaurants and activities in the area. Open June M-Sa 10am-6pm; July-Aug. M-Sa 9am-6pm and Su noon-4pm; Sept.-Oct. M-Sa 10am-5pm; Mar.-May M-Sa 10am-5pm.

Banks: AIB, the Square (☎21129). **Bank of Ireland,** Sea View (☎21111). Both have **ATMs;** both open M-F 10am-12:30pm and 1:30-4pm, W until 5pm.

Laundry: The Shamrock Washeteria, the Square (☎21348). Wash and dry €6 per load. Open M-Sa 9:30am-6pm. **Hillview Laundrette** (☎21836). Wash and dry €6.20 per load. Open M-Sa 9am-6pm.

Pharmacy: Clifden Pharmacy, Main St. (☎21821), just off the Square. Open M-F 9:30am-6:30pm, Sa 9:30am-6pm.

Emergency: ☎999; no coins required. **Police** *(Garda)*: ☎21021.

Hospital: ☎21301 or 21302. On the right as you enter Clifden from Galway.

Internet Access: Two Dog Cafe, Church Hill (☎22186). Cafe amenities run the gamut from creative bistro fare and tasty sandwiches (€6.50) to weekly poetry readings (Su 8-10pm), discount international calling, and computers with speedy connections. €1.30 per 15min. Food served M-Sa 10:30am-5pm. Internet available M-Sa 10:30am-7pm.

Post Office: Main St. (☎21156). **Currency exchange** at just 1.5% commission. Open M-F 9:30am-5:30pm, Sa 9:30am-1pm.

ACCOMMODATIONS & CAMPING

B&Bs litter the streets; the going rates are €25 per person and up. Reservations are necessary in July and August.

Clifden Town Hostel (IHH), Market St. (☎21076). Great facilities, spotless rooms, helpful owner, quiet atmosphere, and close to the pubs. Behind the modern decor, stone walls remind you that the house is 180 years old. Open year-round, but in Nov.-Feb. call ahead. Dorms €12-15; doubles €32-34; triples €32; quads €56-60. ❶

Shanaheever Campsite, Westport Rd. (☎21018 or 22150), a little over 1 mi. outside Clifden. The tranquility of this spot compensates for its distance from the pubs. Game room and hot showers included. Laundry €6. Open year-round, but May-Sept. call ahead. €12 per person for tent or trailer. ❶

Brookside Hostel (IHH), Hulk St. (☎21812), head straight at the bottom of Market St. Clean, roomy dorms look over fat, innocuous sheep loitering in the backyard. Super-knowledgeable owner will painstakingly plot a hiking route for you. Laundry €6. Wheelchair accessible. Open Mar.-Oct. Dorms €11.50; doubles €30. ❶

White Heather House, the Square (☎21655). Great location, and most rooms have panoramic views. Prices include a full Irish breakfast. Singles €25-30; doubles €50. ❸

Foyles Clifden Bay Hotel, Main St. (☎21801). Pretty rooms right in the center of town. All with bath and breakfast. July-Aug. doubles €55-60; Sept.-June €37-45. ❸

FOOD

Clifden has a surprising variety of culinary options, ranging from family-run kitchens to pub fare, aspiring gourmet cooking to Chinese and fast food. For those who prefer cooking for themselves, **O'Connor's SuperValu,** Market St., provides supermarket standards. (Open M-F 9am-7pm, Su 10am-6pm.)

Cullen's Bistro & Coffee Shop, Market St. (☎21983). Family-run establishment that cooks up hearty meals (thick Irish stew €12.50) and temptingly delicious homemade desserts (rhubarb crisp with fresh cream €3.90). Open daily 11am-10pm. ❸

Walsh's, Market St. (☎21283). A busy bakery with a large seating area, Walsh's serves up morsels including soups and sandwiches, baps, and fresh pastries, all for €2-5. Open June-Sept. M-F 8:30am-6pm, Sa-Su 9am-6pm; Oct.-May M-Sa 8:30am-6pm. ❶

Connemara Diner, the Square. Burgers (beef, fish, or bean) and other takeout tasties served up hot and fast, all night long, baby. Open daily 6pm-1am. ❷

E.J. King's, the Square (☎21330). Crowded pub serves excellent food on exceptionally old wood furniture. Fish and chips €9. Food served daily noon-9pm. The official restaurant upstairs serves the same food at higher prices until 10pm. ❷

Derryclare Restaurant, the Square (☎21440). Candlelit dining room with an ambitious menu that strives toward fine dining. Tasty steamed mussels in a white wine and cream sauce (€14.50), fresh Connemara oysters (€9 for half-dozen), Coquille St. Jacques (€22.25), and vegetarian curry (€14). Open Mar.-Nov. daily noon-10pm. ❹

Jasmine Garden, Church Hill (☎21174). Walk up the steep hill from the Square and bear to the right. Standard Chinese selections with plenty of veggie options. Mains €6.50-10. Open M-F 5:30-11:30pm, Sa-Su 5:30pm-midnight. ❷

PUBS

Malarkey's, Church Hill (☎21801). Pool table, poetry readings, open mic nights, and good impromptu music. Revelers sit on the floor when the chairs and pool table fill up. As the sign out front proclaims: "The *Craic* Begins at 6pm!"

Mannion's Bar and Lounge, Market St. (☎21780). Bring your own instrument, or just pick up some spoons when you get there. Music nightly in summer, F-Sa in winter.

E.J. King's, the Square (☎21330). Edgar Allen Poe lighting with a spacious interior. Live music in the summer starts at 10pm. Opens at 10am.

King's, the Square (☎21900). A quiet pub with an older (masculine) local crowd. The town's best pint by consensus. Open daily from 10:30am.

O'Toole's, Bridge St. (☎21222), offers a pub disco some F-Sa nights for the dancing types and local young 'uns. Open year-round from noon.

SIGHTS AND ACTIVITIES

The 10 mi. long **Sky Rd.** provides a lovely route for hiking, biking, or a scenic drive. Starting just past the Square, it loops around the little peninsula to the west of town, paving the way to beautiful views of green hills and some legitimately dizzying coastline cliffs. Although good for bicycling, there are a few strenuous climbs to reach the highest vistas. The whole loop will take about 4-5hr. to hike. A mile down Sky Rd. stands what's left of **Clifden Castle,** once home to Clifden's founder, John D'Arcy. Farther out, a peek at the bay reveals the spot on a bog near Ballyconnelly where US pilots John Alcock and Arthur Brown landed the first nonstop trans-Atlantic flight in 1919. One of the nicer ways to acquaint yourself with Connemara is to hike south to the **Alcock and Brown monument,** situated just off the Ballyconnelly road 3 mi. past Salt Lake and Lough Fadda.

Open yourself to the magic of the bog by joining one of the inspiring tours led by Michael Gibbons, the critically acclaimed archaeologist-raconteur of the **Connemara Walking Centre** on Market St. The tours explore the history, folklore, geology, and archaeology of the region, and investigate bogs, mountains, and the Inishbofin and Omey islands. The center also sells wonderful maps and guidebooks. Though closed for renovation for the 2002 season, it should be reopened for 2003. (☎21379 or 22278; www.walkingireland.com. Open Mar.-Oct. M-Sa 10am-6pm. Call ahead. Full-day or 2 half-day boat tours Easter-Oct. daily; call for a schedule. €19-32.)

Clifden Town Hall, at the base of the Square on Seaview Rd., erupts with performances of trad, dance, and song every Tuesday in July and August at 9pm. In late September, during the annual **Clifden Arts Week** (☎21295), dozens of free concerts, poetry readings, and storytellings summon even larger hordes of well-heeled tourists. Famous guests have included the Nobel Prize-winning Irish poet Seamus Heaney. On the third Thursday of August, attractive and talented equine contenders come to Clifden from miles around to compete for top awards at the **Connemara Pony Show,** held in the backyard of the Brookside Hostel.

INISHBOFIN ISLAND (INISH BÓ FINNE) ☎095

Inishbofin, the "island of the white cow," has gently sloping hills (flat enough for pleasant cycling) scattered with rugged rocks, an excellent hostel, and near-deserted sandy beaches. Living as they do 7 mi. from the western tip of Connemara, the 200 rough-and-tumble islanders keep time according to the ferry, the tides, and the sun; visitors can easily adapt to their system. There's not much to do on the island except for scrambling up the craggy hills, sunbathing on the sand, communing with the seals, watching birds fish among the coves, and sleeping under a blanket of bright stars. It's a rough life, but somebody has to live it.

TRANSPORTATION AND PRACTICAL INFORMATION. **Ferries** leave for Inishbofin from **Cleggan,** a tiny village with stunning beaches 10 mi. northwest of Clifden. Two ferry companies serve the island. Malachy King operates the *Island Discovery* and the *Galway Bay,* which comprise the larger, steadier, and faster of the two fleets. (☎44642. 45min.; July-Aug. 3 per day, Apr.-June and Sept.-Oct. 2 per day; €15 return, children €7.50. Tickets available at the pier, in Clifden, or on the boat.) The *M.V. Dún Aengus/Queen of Aran* is operated by Paddy O'Halloran year-round. (☎45806. 45min.; July-Aug. 3 per day, Apr.-June and Sept.-Oct. 2 per day, Nov.-Apr. 1 per day; €12.70 return. Tickets purchased most conveniently on the ferry.) Stock up at the **Spar** before you go, especially if you're taking a later ferry. (☎44750. Open daily 9am-10pm.) **Bike rental** is available at the Inishbofin pier (☎45833) for €7 per day, but the island's hills and narrow roads are best explored on foot. To sort out your stay, call ahead or visit the **Community Resource Centre** (☎45909) to the left of the pier on the main road. The pleasant staff provides maps (€1.20-4.50), updated information on services, and limited **Internet access.**

ACCOMMODATIONS, FOOD, AND PUBS. Kieran Day's excellent **Inishbofin Island Hostel (IHH)** ❶ is a 15min. walk from the ferry landing. Take a right at the pier and head up the hill; bear right at the top and the hostel is in the unmistakably yellow building. Visitors are blessed with a large conservatory, swell views, and bits of poetry from disparate sources. (☎45855. Sheets €1. Laundry €5 for wash and dry, €2.50 for wash. Dorms €10. **Camping** €5 per person.) The **Emerald Cottage** ❷, a 10min. walk west from the pier to the left, welcomes guests with home-baked goodies. (☎45865. Singles €20; doubles €40.) **Horseshoe Bay B&B** ❷, on the east end of the island, is still famous for a visit from Nicholas Cage (or a reasonable facsimile thereof) several years back; somehow, remarkably, the place remains pleasantly isolated. (☎45812. Doubles €42.) **Lapwing House B&B** ❷ (☎45996), up the road behind the Community Center, is run by Mary Day-Louvel; she offers doubles for €30 and will feed her guests through the winter.

The Dolphin Restaurant ❹, next to the island hostel, provides an unexpected high cuisine alternative and gets rave reviews from the locals. (☎45992. Mains €16-19. Open June-Aug. 7-9pm.) The island's nightlife is surprisingly vibrant with frequent trad performances in the summer. Close to the pier, **Day's Pub** (☎45829) serves food from noon to 5pm, and stays open later for pool playing, drinking, and occasional evenings of music. **Cloonan's Store** is behind the pub and sells picnic-applicable items year-round. (☎45829. Open M-Sa 11am-1pm and 3-5pm, Su noon-3pm.) The smaller and more sedate **Murray's Pub,** a hotel-bar 15min. west of the pier, is great for conversation, slurred or otherwise. The pub also serves food.

SIGHTS. Days on Inishbofin are best spent meandering through the rocks and wildflowers of the island's four peninsulas. Paths are scarce, but rambling through the hills is rewarding. Each peninsula warrants about a 3hr. walk. Most items of historical interest are on the southeast peninsula. East of the hostel lie the ruins of the 15th-century **Augustinian Abbey,** built on the site of a monastery founded by St. Colman in 667. A **well** and a few **gravestones** remain from the 7th-century structure. East of the abbey, a conservation area encompasses pristine beaches and a small village. Spectacular views reward those who scramble up nearby **Knock Hill. Bishop's Rock,** a short distance off the mainland, becomes visible at low tide. On the other side of the island, to the west of the pier, is the **Cromwellian Fort,** which was used to hold prisoners before transporting them to the West Indies.

The ragged northeast peninsula is fantastic for **bird watchers:** gulls, cornets, shags, and a pair of peregrine falcons fish among the cliffs and coves. Inishbofin provides a perfect climate for vegetation hospitable to the corncrake, a bird that's near extinction everywhere except in Seamus Heaney's poems; two pairs of corncrakes presently call Inishbofin home. Fish swim in the clear water off two massive blowholes, while small land masses called **The Stags** tower offshore. The tidal causeway that connects The Stags to the mainland during low tide is extremely dangerous—stick to the shore proper. **Trá Gheal** (Silvery Beach) stretches along the northwest peninsula, but swimming here is dangerous. Off to the west is Inishark, an island inhabited by sheep and seals; the seals are most visible during their date-and-mate season in September and October. Inspirational archaeologist Michael Gibbons, of the **Connemara Walking Centre** in Clifden, offers tours focusing on Inishbofin's history, archaeology, and ecology. Leo Hallissey's fantastic **Connemara Summer School** (☎43443) studies the island's archaeology and ecology.

INISHTURK ISLAND (INIS TOIRC) ☎098

Inishturk (pop. 90), a small, rounded peak rising 600 ft. out of the ocean between Inishbofin and Clare Island, has more spectacular walks and views than either of its more populated neighbors. Consult locals for directions to the **Sea Cliffs,** a 30min. hike that will not disappoint. You would never guess it now, but before the Famine, the island teemed with a population of nearly 800. These days, Inishturk seems virtually undiscovered. John Heanue's two **boats,** the *Caher Star* and the *Lady Marlyn*, make the bumpy passage to the island twice a day. (☎45541 or 086 202 9670. Departures from **Cleggan** Tu-Th, and from **Roonah Quay** F-M. €20 return; buy tickets on the boat.) For transport to and from Roonah Quay, check with **Port Cabs** (☎087 220 2123). Those attempting an expedition to Inishturk should treat it as such: bring adequate supplies and a good book. There are no budget restaurants on the island, but the three B&Bs serve ginormous home-cooked meals. **Concannon's B&B ❷** is a colorful house just off the pier with vibrant rooms and a flower garden. (☎45610. Dinner upon request €25. Doubles €50.) **Teach Abhainn ❸** lies far from the pier but close to the most striking scenery on the island. (☎45510. Dinner €25. Singles €30; doubles €50.) Guests at the Heanue's **Ocean View ❷,** up the road from Concannon's, heartily applaud fantastic meals and decadent rooms. (☎45520. Doubles €25.) A 15min. walk up from the pier, **The Community Centre** (☎45655) serves as the town **pub** and hosts traditional dancing, singing, and music sessions. It also houses the island's **Annual Trad Festival,** featuring nationally known musicians, every second weekend of June. For **tourist information,** call island manager Danny Kirrane (☎45778 or 45862).

LETTERFRACK (LEITIR FRAIC) ☎095

Perched at the crossroads of N59 and the Rinvyle road, Letterfrack boasts three pubs and a legendary hostel, but little else to speak of. The **Galway-Clifden** bus (mid-June to Aug. M-Sa 11 per wk.; Sept. to mid-June M-Sa 4 per wk.) and the summertime **Clifden-Westport** bus (M and Th 2 per day, Tu-W and F-Sa 1 per day) stop at Letterfrack. Though **hitchers** report short waits on N59, and although there's nothing we like more than a nice, short wait, *Let's Go* will not recommend hitchhiking.

The **Old Monastery Hostel ❶,** a sharp right and up the hill from the crossroads, is one of Ireland's finest. Sturdy pine bunks, desks, and couches fill the spacious high-ceilinged rooms, a peat fire burns in the lounge, and framed photos of jazz greats hang in the cozy basement cafe. Owner Steve Gannon cooks buffet dinners of the vegetarian and (mostly) organic style during the summer (buffet €9, plate €7; call by 5pm); he also provides fresh scones and porridge for breakfast. **Work opportunities** are sometimes available; inquire with Steve when you arrive. (☎41132. Breakfast included. **Bike rental** €9 per day. **Internet access** available. Laundry €5. 6- and 8-bed dorms €10; 4-bed €12. Doubles €15. **Camping** €6.) Fine pub grub, gourmet groceries, and friendly locals are all in evidence at **Veldon's ❷,** which fills at 10:30am and empties late, sometimes after a trad session. (☎41046. Shop open June-Aug. daily 9:30am-9pm; Sept.-May 9am-7pm.) **The Bard's Den** (☎41042), across the road, casts its net with a skylight, an open fire, and a big screen TV for sports fans. (Opens at 12:30pm; music on F nights from July-Aug.)

Visitors in the mood for a morsel of fishy camp should head to Derryinver's **Ocean's Alive,** 1½ mi. north of Letterfrack on the Rinvyle road. If touch tanks leave you cold—or if they just leave you hungry for more fishy fun—head to the dock. Ocean's Alive's own *Connemara Queen* cruises out seven times a day for a 1hr. **seal- and deserted island-viewing expedition.** According to local legend, the ship's captain can be induced to play his accordion. **Fishing trips** can also be arranged on demand. (☎43473. Open May-Sept. 10am-6pm; Oct.-Apr. 10am-4pm. Museum €5, students €4. *Queeny* cruise €13/€10. Fishing trip €32/€28.) During **Bog Week** (the last week in Oct.) and **Sea Week** (the first week in May), respected environmentalists gather to discuss bog- and sea-related issues while musicians jam amongst the peat. (Check www.connemara.net for more information.)

The road from Letterfrack to Leenane passes by **Kylemore Abbey,** a castle set in the dramatic shadow of a rocky outcropping. Built in 1867 by an English industrialist, the castle was sold to a group of Benedictine nuns in 1920 to pay off the Duke of Manchester's gambling debts. The same Benedictine sisters have lived there ever since, and they will cheerfully chat with interested tourists. There's more to see at the small neo-Gothic **church** a few hundred feet down from the abbey. A rocky path clambers its way up to a ledge above the castle that affords a beautiful view of the lake. (☎41146. Abbey open Apr.-Oct. 9am-6pm; Nov.-Mar. 10am-4pm; Jan.-Feb. 10am-5pm. €5, students €3.50.) The newly restored six-acre **Victorian Walled Garden** is worth a gander if you have nature-taming fantasies or if you liked *The Secret Garden.* The immaculately trimmed plot of local and tropical plants presents a lovely anachronism amongst the looming mountains nearby. (Open Easter-Nov. Garden entry €6.50, students €4. Garden and abbey €6.50/€5.)

CONNEMARA NATIONAL PARK ☎095

Connemara National Park occupies 8 sq. mi. of mountainous countryside and is home to a number of curiosities, including hare runs, orchids, and roseroot. The far-from-solid terrain of the park is composed of bogs thinly covered by a screen of grass and flowers. Be prepared to muddy your legs and raise your pulse. Guides lead free walks through the bogs (July-Aug. M and F at 10:30am) and offer several children's programs on Tuesdays and Thursdays. The **Visitors Centre** and its adjoining museum team up with perversely funny anthropomorphic peat and moss creatures to teach visitors the differences between hollows, hummocks, and tussocks. Follow this with the dramatic 25min. slide show about the park, which elevates the battle against opportunistic rhododendrons to epic scope. (☎41054. Open June daily 10am-6:30pm; July-Aug. 9:30am-6:30pm; May and Sept. 10am-5:30pm. €2.50, students €1.25.)

The **Snuffaunboy Nature** and **Ellis Wood Trails** are easy 20min. hikes. The Snuffaunboy features alpine views while the Ellis wood submerges walkers in an ancient forest; both teem with wildflowers. A guidebook mapping out 30min. walks (€0.60) is available at the visitors center. For the more adventurous, trails lead from the back of the Ellis Wood Trail and 10min. along the **Bog Road** onto **Diamond Hill,** a 2hr. hike that rewards climbers with views of bog, harbor, and forest, or, depending on the weather, impenetrable mist. (Diamond Hill was closed in 2002 for erosion control; call ahead to confirm opening.) More experienced hikers may head for the **Twelve Bens,** a rugged range that stretches to heights of 2400 ft. There are no proper trails, and the range is not recommended for novice hikers, but Jos Lynam's guidebook, available at the visitors center (€6.35), meticulously plots 18 short hikes through the Twelve Bens and the Maamturks. Hikers often base themselves at the **Ben Lettery Hostel (An Óige/HI)** ❶, which overlooks postcard-quality stretches of scenery in Ballinafad. The turnoff from N59 is 8 mi. east of Clifden. (☎51136. Dorms €10-12.) A hike from this remote but friendly hostel through the park to the Letterfrack hostel can be made in a day. A tour of all twelve Bens takes hardy walkers 10hr. **Cycling** the 40 mi. loop through Clifden, Letterfrack, and Inagh valley is breathtaking, but only appropriate for strong bikers.

LEENANE (AN LÍONÁN) ☎095

Farther east along N59, **Killary Harbour,** Ireland's only fjord, slices through coastal mountains and continues inland to the wilderness outpost of Leenane (pop. 47). Wrapped in the skirts of the **Devilsmother Mountains,** this once-populous region was reduced to a barren hinterland during the Famine. Today, the crumbled remnants of farms cover surrounding hills. *The Field* was filmed here in 1989 and no one in town will ever forget it. Those who rank among the legions of *Field* enthusiasts will be the only people excited to learn that Aasleagh Falls served as the backdrop for the murder scene. At the **Leenane Cultural Centre,** on the Clifden-Westport Rd., spinning and weaving demonstrations expose the grisly fate of wool. (☎42323. Open Apr.-Oct. daily 10am-6pm. €2.35, students €1, family €7.) The **coffee shop ❶** in the Cultural Centre has cheap lunches. (Sandwiches and sweets €2-5.)

For adventure and excitement, head to **Killary Adventure Company,** a few miles outside Leenane. Operating since 1980, they are Ireland's leading adventure company. They offer everything from rock climbing to water skiing, windsurfing to helicopter rides. Archery, clay-pigeon shooting, and kayaking are other options. They also offer accommodations if you're too tired to walk into town. (☎43411; www.killary.com. Half-day of activities starts at €32, full day €58.)

Killary Harbour Hostel (An Óige/HI) ❶ perches on the fjord's edge 7 mi. west of Leenane; the turnoff from N59 is marked. Aside from its unbeatable waterfront location, this hostel's claim to fame seems to be that Ludwig Wittgenstein (he of logical positivism fame) lived there for several months back in 1947. The building's hall windows and front door are no match for harsh Harbour winds, so pack warm clothes and supplies. (☎43417. Lockout 10am-5pm. Curfew 11:30pm. Sheets €1.25. Open on weekends Mar.-May; all week June-Sept. Dorms €12-13.) If the hostel-*craic* has become a bit much, cloister yourself in **The Convent B&B ❸,** on the northern side of town along N59. The dining room retains stunning stained windows from its previous life as a chapel. (☎42240. Open Easter-Nov. Doubles €50.)

COUNTY MAYO

Ancient, boggy plains and isolated settlements typify the dramatic countryside of Co. Mayo, but its enormous inland loughs and curved coastline also provide a wealth of memorable scenery, including scads of majestic islands and quaint harbor towns. Westport is lively and popular; these days, Ballina is as famous for nightlife as it is for its salmon fishing; and intriguing former sea resorts, such as Achill Island and Enniscrone, call out to post-resort travelers from the seaboard. In 1798, "The Year of the French," a certain General Humbert landed at Kilcummin. The good general ill-advisedly formed a combined force of French soldiers, Irish revolutionaries, and rural secret societies, and launched an attack, only to be foiled at Ballina and Ballinamuck by the wily Brits.

SOUTHERN MAYO

Southern Mayo is not oft-overlooked, like many of Ireland's most beautiful areas, nor is it offensively touristy, like many others. Plenty of people come here, but aside from the anomalously popular one-trick ponies that is Cong, it seems like a destination between destinations, a place for in-the-know backpackers to recharge (Westport) or explore (Achill Island), but not to linger (Kathmandu). The area itself is rural and quiet, except for the brief moments of summer tourism insanity, and public transport at all times can be very difficult.

CONG (CUNGA FEICHIN) ☎092

Just over the border from County Galway is little, deep-green Cong (pop. 300). Bubbling streams and shady footpaths criss-cross the forests surrounding the town, and a ruined abbey crumbles at their edge. Nearby, majestic Ashford Castle towers over the choppy waters of Lough Corrib. In the past century, main roads were built to bypass this little hamlet; were it not for two recent events, Cong might have slumbered into obscurity. In 1939, Ashford Castle was turned into a $300/€zillion per night luxury hotel, bringing the rich and famous to Cong from around the world. And, in 1951, John Wayne and Maureen O'Hara shot *The Quiet Man* here. Thousands of fans come each year to find the location of every scene, providing locals with a popular combination of bemusement and profit.

TRANSPORTATION AND PRACTICAL INFORMATION. **Buses** leave for Clifden from Ryan's Hotel (M-Sa 1 per day), Westport from Ashford gates (M-Sa 1-2 per day), and Galway from both locations (M-Sa 2-3 per day; all are €8-9). Because of infrequent transportation, some hitchhikers find rides at the nearby bus stop at Ballinrobe. **O'Connor's Garage,** Main St., **rents bikes.** (☎46008. Open daily 7am-9pm. €10 per day, ID deposit.) The town's **tourist office,** Abbey St., will point you toward Cong's wonders, listed in *The Cong Heritage Trail* (€2.35). *Cong: Walks, Sights, Stories* (€3.59) describes good hiking and biking routes and, unlike hitchhiking, is highly recommended. (☎46542. Open Mar.-Nov. daily 10am-1pm and 2-6pm.) Across from the tourist office you will find **pay phones** and public toilets. Get your fix at **Daly's Pharmacy,** Abbey St., by the tourist office. (☎46119. Open M-F 10am-6pm.) Got mail? The **post office** is on Main St. (☎46001. Open M-Tu and Th-Sa 9am-1pm and 2-5:30pm, W 9am-1pm.)

ACCOMMODATIONS AND CAMPING. The **Cong Hostel (IHH) ❶,** on Quay Rd., 1 mi. down the Galway road near the entrance to Ashford Castle, is an immaculate compound with every imaginable facility. The playground, picnic area, game room, and huge TV room are sure to keep you entertained. The tremendous camping area sprouts its own little village every summer. (☎46089. Continental breakfast €3.50, full Irish breakfast €6. Sheets €1. 14-bed dorms €10; 4-bed €13.50. Doubles with bath €32. **Camping** with facilities €6. Showers for campers €0.70.) **The Quiet Man Hostel (IHH) ❶,** on Abbey St. across from Cong Abbey, is owned by the same gracious family that operates the Cong Hostel. Central, spotless, and sociable, those suffering from *Quiet Man* fever will shiver to learn that all the rooms are named after the film's characters. Like the Cong Hostel, the Quiet Man also screens the "legendary" film nightly, offers **bureaux de change, rent bikes** (€10 per day, €6 per half-day) and **boats** (rowboats €20 per day, motorboats €40 per day), and lends guidebooks and **fishing rods** for free with a small deposit. (☎46089. Continental breakfast €4, Irish breakfast €6. Dorms €14, private rooms with bath €15 per person.) Other options provided by the family include **Mary Kate B&B ❷,** offering rooms with bath and TV (☎46089; €20 per person), and 4-person **cottages** in town. For more information, inquire with the owners at Cong Hostel. The **Courtyard Hostel (IHH) ❶,** on Cross St. in the small village of **Cross,** east of Cong, provides peace of mind several miles off the beaten track. Although it has perhaps seen better days, the hostel maintains the rustic charm of a farmhouse, with ducks and chickens roaming the yard. (☎46203. Dorms €10; doubles €30. **Camping** €5.) Within town, B&B's are mostly of the above-pub variety. For more peaceful roosts, look along the main road between Cong and Cross. The star of this stretch is **Ballywarren Country House ❺.** Two of the three rooms come equipped with VCR and bidet; all have large baths, telephones, flower-topped beds, and complimentary sherry and chocolates. (☎46989; www.ballywarrenhouse.com. Award-winning candlelit dinners €35. Doubles €112-136.) **Inchagoill Island** provides a free and eerie **camping** venue, though it'll still cost you a bit to get there (see p. 360).

FOOD, PUBS, AND CLUBS. Cooks can go crazy at **O'Connor's Supermarket,** Main St. (☎46485. Open M-Sa 8am-9pm, Su 9am-8pm.) At **Danagher's Hotel and Restaurant ❷,** on Abbey St., young locals and Ashford Castle staffers down mammoth meals and countless pints. (☎46028. Mains around €9.25; toasties €3.50. Sa rock, Su DJ; occasional karaoke.) **The Quiet Man Coffee Shop ❶,** Main St., is obviously obsessed. A bright, cheery street-front counter rides in tandem with a dark dining room overlooking a river; both are freckled with black- and white- film memorabilia. (☎46034. Sandwiches €2.80. Open mid-Mar. to Nov. daily 10am-6pm.) **Lydon's** Main St. (☎46053), across the street and around the corner from the Spar, is the place to attend trad sessions; they begin at around 10pm on Wednesdays and Saturdays. The nearest nightclub, **The Valkenburg,** is in Ballinrobe; a bus picks groups up outside Danagher's on weekend nights around 11:30pm and drops them back at 3am. (Bus €2; varying cover centers around €10.)

SIGHTS. Lord and Lady Ardilaun, former heirs to the Guinness fortune, were more interested in the scenery of Mayo than the brewing of beer; accordingly, they spurned Dublin for **Ashford Castle,** where they lived from 1852 to 1939. Much of *The Quiet Man* was shot on its grounds, though the castle itself was used as cast housing, not scenery. The castle is only open to guests, but visitors can gape at and stroll through the **gardens** for €5. Oscar Wilde once informed Lady Ardilaun that she could improve what he called her "dull" gardens by planting petunias in the shape of a pig, the family crest. Sadly, she never complied. A walk from the castle along Lough Corrib leads to a public **swimming beach.**

The sculpted head of its last abbot keeps watch over the ruins of the 12th-century **Royal Abbey of Cong,** near Danagher's Hotel. (Always open. Free.) Ruairi ("Rory") O'Connor, the last High King of a united Ireland, retired to the abbey for his final 15 years of life, after multiple losses to Norman troops. At the other end of the abbey grounds, a footbridge spans the **River Cong.** To the left is the **Monk's Fishing House,** a 12th-century structure with a hole in the floor through which the monks held a net to catch fish swimming downstream. After the fishing house, the path becomes pocked with caves, including **Pigeon Hole; Teach Aille,** a 4000-year-old burial chamber; **Giant's Grave;** and the **Ballymaglancy caves.** (Hostels lend out detailed cave maps.) The caves are often wet and slippery, and are obviously not for the claustrophobic. Spelunkers, however, should enjoy exploring the dark depths. Essential spelunking safety gear consists of waterproof clothing, at least one flashlight, and a friend who knows when to expect you back.

The Quiet Man Heritage Cottage, Cong's thatch-roofed replica of Hollywood's studio replica of a Cong thatch-roofed cottage, provides a dose of fun for postmodernists and for *Quiet Man* enthusiasts. Upstairs, there is a brief yet thorough timeline of the pre-John Wayne Cong, as well as a 6min. video on the film. (☎46089. Open daily 10am-5pm. €3.75, students €3.) **Lough Corrib Cruises** runs a nightly cruise on the Lough with on-board live trad. (☎46029. €13, students €10.)

WEBB-DEFEAT Of the many caves in Cong Forest, none has as sinister a history as Captain Webb's. In the 18th century, a deformed and mentally disturbed Captain "Webb" Fitzgerald led 12 women to the cave, forced them to strip, and pushed them over the abyss to their deaths. The 13th victim fared better: she asked Webb to turn around in the name of decency while she disrobed, and once he did, the wily woman gave him a taste of his own medicine. When any woman in Cong is done harm, it is said Webb's cry can be heard from his resting place deep underground.

WESTPORT (CATHAIR NA MART) ☎098

In the lovely town of Westport, palm trees and steep hills lead down to quaint, busy streets, where tourists and locals alike duck into brightly-colored pubs, cafes, and shops. Small arched bridges span the still, mirror-like Carrowbeg River, which spills out into Westport Harbor. Visitors would be well-advised to follow the river's lead and head to the Quay, have a pint outside, and watch the wide, blue water become red, then blue again, as the sun sets. Hustle back to Bridge St. for pure, unadulterated *craic*. Book your accommodations in advance or you might have some trouble; tourists flock to Westport like hungry seagulls to harbor feed.

TRANSPORTATION

Trains: Trains arrive at the **Altamount St. Station** (☎25253 or 25329), a 5min. walk up the North Mall. Open M-Sa 9:30am-6pm, Su 2:15-6pm. Train service to **Dublin** via **Athlone** (M-Th and Sa-Su 3 per day, F 2 per day; €21-23).

Buses: The **Bus Éireann** counter is housed in the tourist office. Buses leave from Mill St. and head to: **Achill** (2hr., 1-3 per day, €7.35); **Ballina** (1hr., 2-6 per day, €8.50); **Castlebar** (20min.; M-Sa 11-15 per day, Su 6 per day; €3.35); **Galway** (2hr.; M-Sa 7-8 per day, Su 4 per day; €11.60); **Louisburgh** (40min., M-Sa 2-3 per day, €4.25).

Taxis: Brendan McGing, Lower Peter St. (☎25529).

Bike Rental: Sean Sammon, James St. (☎25471). €8 per day; includes lock and pump on request. Open M-Sa 10am-6pm, Su by prior arrangement.

ORIENTATION AND PRACTICAL INFORMATION

The tiny **Carrowbeg River** trickles through **Westport's Mall; Bridge St.** and **James St.,** the town's parallel main drags, extend south. **Shop St.** connects the **Octagon,** at the end of James St., to the **Town Clock** at the end of Bridge St. **High St.** and **Mill St.** lead out from the town clock, the latter into **Altamount St.,** where the Railway Station lies beyond a long stretch of B&Bs. Westport House is on **Westport Quay,** a 45min. walk west of town along **Quay Rd.** The original site of the town before it expanded down the river, the Quay is now a kind of miniature Westport. The N60 passes through Clifden, Galway, and Sligo in addition to Westport. Hitchers report finding rides easily, although there is always some risk involved.

Tourist Office: James St. (☎25711). Free town maps. Open July-Aug. M-Sa 9am-6:45pm, Su 10am-6pm; Apr.-June and Sept.-Oct. M-Sa 9am-5:45pm.

Banks: Bank of Ireland, North Mall (☎25522), and **AIB,** Shop St. (☎25466), both have **ATMs** and are open M-F 10am-4pm, Th until 5pm.

Laundry: Westport Washeteria, Mill St. (☎25261), near the clock tower. Full service €6, self-service including detergent €5. Open M-Sa 9:30am-6pm.

Pharmacy: O'Donnell's, Bridge St. (☎25163). Open M-Sa 9am-6:30pm. Rotating Su openings (12:30-2pm) posted on the door.

Work Opportunities: Several of the accommodations in town (see below) will hire travelers for short-term work, usually for a minimum of 2-3 months. Most offer free housing and stipend in exchange for reception, cleaning, or pub duties, and some prefer prior experience. Specifically, inquire at: **Old Mill Holiday Hostel** (contact Aoife Carr, ☎27045; oldmill@iol.ie), **Club Atlantic** (contact Anne McGovern and Oliver Hughes, ☎26644 or 26717), **Dunning's Pub and B&B** (contact Mary, ☎25161).

Emergency: ☎999; no coins required. **Police** *(Garda)*: Fair Green (☎25555).

Internet Access: Dunning's Cyberpub, the Octagon (☎25161). A Guinness with your email? €1.30 per 10min., €7.60 per hr. Open daily 9am-11:30pm. **Gavin's Video and Internet Cafe,** Bridge St. (☎26461). Not much of a cafe to speak of (no food or drink allowed), but cheaper than Dunning's. €1 per 10min. Open daily 10am-10pm. **Staunton's Music and Games,** Bridge St. (☎28431), claims to have the fastest connection in Westport. €1.30 per 10min., €6 per hr. Open daily 9:30am-6pm, later in summer.

Post Office: North Mall (☎25475). Open M-Sa 9am-5:30pm.

ACCOMMODATIONS AND CAMPING

Westport has hostels to suit every taste; its B&Bs cluster on Altamount Rd. off the North Mall, with more farther off near the Quay. Most charge €25-32 per person.

The Granary Hostel (☎25903), a 25min. walk from town, at the bend in Quay Rd. This converted granary includes a conservatory and a serenely removed garden. Amenities are basic, with showers and toilets a few steps outdoors, but the lovingly placed stones and the tree pushing through the wall of the conservatory lend it an otherworldly calm. Cooking facilities and showers 8am-10:30pm. Open Apr.-Sept. Dorms €10. ❶

Altamont House, Altamont St. (☎25226). Award-winning Irish breakfasts and hospitality have kept travelers coming back for 36 years. Cheerful owner Mary acts as your mother-away-from-home, but don't worry, she's more likely to light you a fire and make a cup of tea than ask you to do the dishes and keep curfew. €25 per person, with bath €27. ❸

Old Mill Holiday Hostel (IHH), James St. (☎27045), through an archway next to the tourist office. Character, comfort, and convenience in a renovated mill and brewery. Sheets €1.50. Laundry €6. Kitchen/common room lockout 11pm-8am. Dorms €12. ❶

Club Atlantic (IHH), Altamont St. (☎26644 or 26717), across from the train station and a 5min. walk up from the Mall. Popular with youth organizations, this massive complex has a game room, shop, and an elephantine kitchen. Dorms are quiet and comfortable. **Camping** space is beside a forest and bubbling river. **Sauna** and **pool** use at the nearby Westport Hotel €6. 4- to 6-bed dorms €10-11.50; doubles €26-31. Camping €6. ❶

Roscaoin House, Altamont St. (☎28519). The chandeliers in the foyer are your first indication of the luxury level at this B&B, which features well-appointed rooms with bath, a beautiful back garden, and free **Internet.** Doubles €60-75. ❸

Dunning's Pub and B&B, the Octagon (☎25161). Centrally yet quietly located above a bustling pub and convenient Internet cafe. Guests lounge with their pints and pizzas at sidewalk tables out front, surveying all the Westport action. €30 per person. ❸

FOOD

The **country market,** by the town hall at the Octagon, vends farm-fresh vegetables, eggs, baked-goods, rugs, and crafts. (Open Th 9am-1pm.) The **SuperValu** on Shop St., by contrast, has abundant supplies of processed goodies. (☎27000. Open M-Sa 8:30am-9pm, Su 10am-6pm.) Restaurants, which are primarily clustered around Bridge St. and the Octagon, cater to yuppie tourists, and are generally crowded and expensive; book ahead for tables after 6:30pm on weekends.

McCormack's, Bridge St. (☎25619). An upstairs hideaway with creative dishes and local art adorning the walls. Ravenous locals and tourists feast on huge sandwiches, salads, and hot specials. Several veggie options, not including warm brie and bacon salad (€6.30). Hot breakfast baguette €3.80. Open M-Tu and Th-Sa 10am-5pm. ❷

Sol Rio, Bridge St. (☎28944). Romantically lit, lovingly prepared Italian. The tempting dinner mains will set you back a few thousand *lira* (or €15), but the delicious lunches are reasonably priced (€4-8). The most interesting of the several vegetarian options are the appetizers, which are available as main courses upon request—the Mushroom Ripinne makes an excellent meal. Open daily noon-3pm and 6-10pm. ❸

Antica Roma, Bridge St. (☎28778). Striking a compromise between fast food and finer dining, this Italian restaurant/burger joint may not have the fanciest decor in town, but it does serve the cheapest meals you'll find after the 6pm cafe closing time. Pizzas €4.25-7.25, burger and chips €3-5. Open Tu-Sa noon-10pm, Su 4-10pm. ❶

Gavin's Cafe, Bridge St. (☎087 932 8463). Look for the emerald-green everything. Cheap sandwiches (€2.80-3.20) and tasty pastries (€1). Open M-Sa 9am-6pm; take-away after 5:30pm. ❶

The Lemon Peel (☎26929), just up the hill from the Octagon, quietly located off from the main restaurant glut. Rolls tide over hungry diners as they peruse the short but impressive menu, which includes veggie options. The barbary duck (€18) is highly recommended. Open June-Aug. daily 6-9:30pm; Sept.-May Tu-Sa 6-9:30pm. ❹

The Cove, Bridge St. (☎27096). Seafood takes priority at this local favorite, though a sirloin steak (€17.50) should please those who prefer their meat land-side. Open daily for breakfast (10am-noon); lunch (noon-3:30pm); dinner (M-Sa 6-9:30pm). ❸

The Urchin, Bridge St. (☎27532). Modern cuisine and sunny, yellow walls. Specializes in fresh seafood, but serves interesting and filling meals to the resident vegetarian as well. Vegetarian crepes €12.90; seafood-stuffed sole €17.80. Open daily 6-10pm. ❹

PUBS AND CLUBS

Westport's excellent pub scene tends to be overrun by tourists seeking great local *craic;* lucky for them, their cravings are often fulfilled.

Matt Molloy's, Bridge St. (☎26655). Owned by the flautist of the Chieftains. All the cool people (and apparently everyone else) go here. Officially, trad sessions occur nightly at 9:30pm; in reality, any time of the day is deemed appropriate. Go early if you like yours sitting down. Open Th-Sa 12:30pm-12:30am, M-W 12:30-11:30pm, Su 12:30-11pm.

Henehan's Bar, Bridge St. (☎25561). A run-down exterior hides a vibrant pub. The beer garden in the back is ripe for people-watching; 20-somethings fight 80-somethings for space at the bar. Music nightly in summer, weekends only in winter.

Cosy Joe's, Bridge St. (☎28004). Despite its 3 floors and 2 bars, the place still manages to live up to its name. Tightly packed with the young and happy. Th-Sa DJ. Open M-W and Su 10:30am-11:30pm, Th-Sa 10:30am-1am.

The Towers, the Quay (☎26534), 1 mi. from the town center; follow Quay Rd. from the Octagon. Fishing nets and excellent grub reel in the customers; scenic beer garden peers into the harbor. Most food €7-9, served noon-9:30pm. Music F-Su in summer, F-Sa in winter. Open Tu-W and Su noon-11:30pm, Th-Sa noon-12:30am.

McHale's (☎25121), just up Quay Rd. from the Octagon. Its excellent sessions are often overlooked by tourists, but not by friendly locals. Trad W, F, and Sa, country Su. Open Su-W noon-11:30pm, Th-Sa noon-12:30am.

Hoban's, the Octagon (☎27249). A cozy local fave, with handshakes and hugs at every turn. Trad Th-Sa. Open M-Sa 12:30-11:30pm, Su 12:30-11pm.

Kelly's, Castlebar St. (☎28834), off the Mall. An alternative pub where an eclectic set of young locals lounge and listen to frequent live music. DJs Sa. Open "late."

Wits, Mill St., in the Westport Inn. Upscale bar becomes Westport's number one down-and-dirty nightclub on weekends. 18+. Cover €8. Open F-Su midnight-2:30am.

Castlecourt Hotel, Castlebar St. Multi-leveled dance club with inspired lighting effects and a younger crowd than Wits. 18+. Cover €8. Open Th-Su midnight-2:30am.

SIGHTS AND ACTIVITIES

Westport House's current state of commercial exploitation must be a bitter pill to swallow for Lord Altamont, its elite inhabitant and the 13th great-grandson of Grace O'Malley. The small **zoo, train ride, paddle swan boats,** and **log flume** may entertain younger children, but the overcrowded and slightly faded house struggles to hold the attention of older visitors, especially as entry to most of the rooms is closed off. The **grounds,** on the other hand, are beautiful and free. All this supposed fun is a 45min. stroll from town along the main roads—from the Octagon, ascend the hill and bear right, then follow the signs to the Quay. (☎25430 or 27766. Open July-Aug. M-F 11:30am-5:30pm, Sa-Su 1:30-5:30pm; June house and zoo only M-Sa 1:30-5:30pm, everything Su 1:30-5:30pm; Apr.-May house and rides only Su 2-5pm; Sept. house only daily 2-5pm. Full admission €19, house only €9; students €13/€6; children €12/€6.) More interesting is the **Clew Bay Heritage Centre** at the end of the Quay. A veritable garage sale of history, this charmingly crammed center brims with scraps from the past, including a pair of James Connolly's gloves, a sash belonging to John MacBride, and a stunning original photograph of the not-so-stunning Maud Gonne. The Centre also provides a **genealogical service.** (☎26852. Open July-Sept. M-F 10am-5pm, Su 2:30-5pm; Oct.-June M-F 10am-2pm. €3, students €1.50, under 15 free.) The manager of the Heritage Centre also leads **historical walks** from the town clock in July and August (1½hr.; Tu and Th at 8pm; €5, children free). In town is the more basic **Westport Heritage Centre,** housed in the tourist office (see **Orientation and Practical Information,** above). The Centre details the history of the town's development and has an **interactive scale model** of Westport just as precious as the real thing. (€3.)

Conveniently located behind the tourist office is **Westport Leisure Park,** where you can work off your pints in the **fitness suite,** swim laps in the large **pool,** and reward yourself after in the **sauna** or **jacuzzi.** (☎29160. Open M-F 8:30am-10pm, Sa-Su 10am-8pm. Swim and spa facilities €5.20, students €4; fitness suite €6.40/€5; combined €7.50/€6.) Just out of town is the **Carrowholly Stables & Trekking Centre,** from which horse rides to the banks of Clew Bay originate. (☎27057. €20 per hr.) In late August, celebrate the **Westport Arts Festival** (☎66502) with a week of free concerts, poetry readings, and plays, or check out all things equine at the **Westport Horse and Pony Fair Competitions** in late September (☎25616).

DAYTRIP FROM WESTPORT: CROAGH PATRICK

***Murrisk Abbey** is several mi. west of Westport on R395 toward Louisburgh. **Buses** go to Murrisk (July-Aug. M-F 2-3 per day; Sept.-June M-Sa 1-2 per day), but if you're traveling with a friend, a **cab** (☎27171) would be cheaper and more convenient. Biking is another option, although it might not be palatable to those climbing the mountain. **Ballintubber Abbey** (☎094 30709) is about 6 mi. south of Castlebar on N84, and 22 mi. from Croagh Patrick. The **Croagh Patrick Information Centre** (☎64114) foots the mountain on the Pilgrim's Path off R395, and has shower and locker facilities.*

Conical **Croagh Patrick** rises 2510 ft. over Clew Bay. The summit has been revered as a holy site for thousands of years; it was considered most sacred to Lug, the Sun God, and one-time ruler of the Túatha de Danann (see **Legends and Folktales,** p. 71). After arriving here in AD 441, St. Patrick prayed and fasted for the standard 40 days and 40 nights, argued with angels, and then banished the snakes from Ireland. Another tale holds that the pagan Celtic god Crom Dubh resided at Croagh Patrick until St. Paddy himself threw him into a hollow at the mountain's base. Faithful Christians have climbed the mountain in honor of St. Paddy for nearly 1400 years. The barefoot pilgrimage to the summit originally ended on St. Patrick's feast day, March 17th, but the death-by-thunderstorm (an act of god, no doubt) of 30 pilgrims in AD 1113 moved the holy trek to Lughnasa—**Lug's holy night** is on the last Sunday in July, when the weather is slightly more forgiving. Others climb the mountain just for the exhilaration and incredible views. The hike takes 4hr. roundtrip, but be forewarned: the terrain can be quite steep, and the footing unsure. Well-shod climbers start their excursion from the 15th-century **Murrisk Abbey;** pilgrims and hikers also set out for Croagh Patrick along the Tóchar Phádraig, a path from **Ballintubber Abbey.** The new and useful **Croagh Patrick Information Centre** offers tours, showers, luggage storage, food, and directions to the summit.

NEAR WESTPORT: CLARE ISLAND ☎098

Although only a ferry ride away, Clare Island occupies a world entirely different from bustling, heavily touristed Westport. Sheep calmly rule this desolate but beautiful island, intently grazing and wholly indifferent to the dramatic green climbs and rugged cliff descents of their kingdom. Grace O'Malley, known locally as Granuaile, ruled the 16th-century seas west of Ireland from her castle above Clare's little but lovely Blue Flag **beach.** Granuaile died in 1603; supposedly, she was laid to rest under the ruins of the **Clare Island Abbey,** near the shop. Granuaile's legacy is maintained by the island's residents, at least half of whom are O'Malleys.

The main activity on the island is **hiking,** with paths, appropriate for both walking and biking, running to all of the major sights, and mountains that provide more challenging terrain. A leaflet detailing five walks is available at the hotel or at the ferry ticket counters. The cliffs of **Knockmore Mountain** (1550 ft.) rise from the sea on the western coast, where the ruins of a Napoleonic **signal tower** stand crumbling. A 2hr. walk runs along the east side of the island to the **lighthouse.** Just 10min. before the lighthouse is the **Ballytougheny Loom Shop and Demonstration Centre,** a short walk up a path to the left of the road. The family of weavers that reside here spin their own wool and dye it using lichens and onions; sometimes they even let visitors take a hand at the spinning wheel. For those who want a full introduction to the trade, longer workshops are offered. (☎25800. Open Apr.-Oct. M-Sa 11am-5pm, Su noon-4pm; Nov.-Mar. call ahead.) **Andrew O'Leary,** of bike hire fame (see below), gives **minibus tours** of the island. (Inquire at bike shop. 1¼hr. €30 flat rate.) After a few hours of trekking, relax on the harbor's pristine sandy beach and contemplate becoming the island's 155th inhabitant.

To get on and off the island, take either **O'Malley's Ferry** (☎25045; July-Aug. 8 per day, May-June and Sept. 3 per day, Oct.-Apr. call ahead; bikes free; €15 return, students €10, children €7.50) or the **Clare Island Ferry** (☎26307; 20min. July-Aug. 5 per day, May-June and Sept. 3-5 per day, Oct.-Apr. call ahead; bikes free; €15 return, students €12), which both offer free tea and coffee on board. Both leave from **Roonah Pier,** 4 mi. beyond Louisburgh and 18 mi. from Westport. Those without wheels can take the Bus Éireann/Clare Island Ferry **daytrip,** which departs from the tourist office at 10am and returns by 6pm (€25 for bus and ferry combined). Once islandside, take advantage of **O'Leary's Bike Hire,** near the harbor (€10 per day); if no one's there, knock at **Beachside B&B ❸** (☎25640), where the same family rents out clean rooms (with baths) for €25. Just past the beach, the hospitable **Sea Breeze B&B ❸** (☎26746) offers comfortable rooms for the same price. Those who want to get to know Clare's natural charms can pitch their tents at the **Clare Island Camp Site ❶** on the beach. (☎26525. Showers and toilet facilities across the road at the Community Center. €4 per person.) Two miles along the west road from the harbor, **O'Malley's Store** has food staples. (☎26987. Open daily 11am-6pm.) A little before O'Malley's is the **Wavecrest Restaurant ❸,** an in-home restaurant that serves scones so moist and flavorful you'll push the butter and jam aside. (☎26546. Scones €1.30; crab salad sandwiches €10. Open daily 11am-5:30pm and 7:30-9:30pm for €22 set menu dinner.) To the right along the coast from the harbor, the **Bay View Hotel** (☎26307) houses Clare's only pub and source for alcohol.

ACHILL ISLAND (ACAILL OILÉAN)

Two decades ago, Achill (AK-ill) Island was Co. Mayo's most popular holiday destination. Its popularity has inexplicably dwindled, but Ireland's biggest little island remains one of its most beautiful and personable. Ringed by glorious beaches and cliffs, Achill's interior consists of a couple of mountains and more than a few bogs. **Cycling** the Atlantic drive is another great way to see the island. During the first two weeks of August, Achill hosts the **Scoil Acla** (☎45284), a festival of trad and art where local musicians return to the island and offer music lessons and free concerts to all. The **Achill Seafood Festival** goes down the second week in July—mussels, oysters, and fish, oh my!

Buses run infrequently over the bridge linking Achill Sound, Dugort, Keel, and Dooagh to Westport, Galway, and Cork (June-Aug. M-Sa 5 per day, Sept.-May M-Sa 2 per day), and to Sligo, Enniskillen, and Belfast (June-Aug. 3 per day, Sept.-May 2 per day). If the buses are too infrequent, call for a **taxi,** "no matter how short the trip." (☎087 243 7686.) Hitchhiking is relatively common during July and August, as is cycling. The island's **tourist office** is beside the Esso station in Cashel, on the main road from Achill Sound to Keel. (☎098 47353. Open M-F 10am-5pm.) There is an **ATM** in Achill Sound but no bank on the island, though **currency exchange** is available at Achill Sound's post office.

ACHILL SOUND (GOB A CHOIRE) ☎098

Achill Sound's strategic location at the island's entrance accounts for the high concentration of shops and services, but practicality isn't the only reason to stop here; come for the **ATM** and stay for the internationally famous stigmatic and faith healer who holds services at **Our Lady's House of Prayer.** The OLHOP is about 20 yd. up the hill from the town's main church and is open for services daily 9:30am-6pm. The healer draws thousands to the attention-starved town each year, but local opinions remain polarized—some profess a great deal of faith in the faith healer, while others express only skepticism. (This latter feeling no doubt subverts the entire premise of faith healing; what a conundrum.) About 6 mi. south of Achill Sound—turn left at the first crossroads—two ruined buildings stand in close proximity. The ancient **Church of Kildavnet** was founded by St. Dympna after she fled to Achill to escape her father's incestuous intentions. Nearby, a crumbling 16th-century tower house with memories of better days calls itself the remains of **Kildavnet Castle.** Grace O'Malley, Ireland's favorite medieval pirate lass, once owned the castle.

Achill Sound has a **post office** with a **bureau de change** (☎45141; open M-F 9:30am-12:30pm and 1:30-5:30pm), a **SuperValu** supermarket (open M-Sa 9am-7pm), a **Bank of Ireland ATM,** and a **pharmacy** (☎45248; open July-Aug. M-Sa 9:30am-6pm; Sept.-June M-Sa 9:30am-6pm). **Bike rental** is sometimes available at the **Achill Sound Hotel.** (☎45245. €9 per day, €40 per wk. Deposit €50. Open daily 9am-9pm.) **The Wild Haven Hostel ❶,** a block past the church on the left, positively glows with polished wood floors and antique furniture. The sunny conservatory doubles as a swank ivy-walled dining room. (☎45392. Sheets €1.30. Laundry wash €2.50, dry €3. Dorms €13; private rooms €17-19 per person. **Camping** €5.) If that doesn't work out, try the **Railway Hostel ❶,** just before the bridge to town. The hostel is housed in a former rail station—the last train pulled out about 70 years ago—and is bursting with recently renovated dorm-style rooms. The proprietors can be found at the **Mace Supermarket** in town. (☎45187. Laundry €3. Dorms €10; doubles €25.) Opposite the Railway Hostel, **Alice's Harbour Bar** flaunts gorgeous views, a stonework homage to the deserted village, and a boat-shaped bar, as well as a brand-new disco that spins top-40 hits on summer weekends. (☎45138. Bar food €5-8; served noon-8pm. Cover for disco €7.)

KEEL (CAOL) ☎098

Keel is an old-fashioned resort town at the bottom of a wide, flat valley. The sandy and cliff-flanked **Trawmore Strand** sweeps eastward for 3 mi. Stimulated by a government tax scheme, hundreds of holiday developments have sprung up like subsidized mushrooms over the past three years. Happily for locals who prefer their hills green, that pro-development plan has now ended. Two miles north of Keel on the road that loops back toward Dugort sits **Slievemore Deserted Village,** which (being deserted) is now populated only by the stone houses used by cattle ranchers until the late 1930s. Resist the temptation to crawl up and around the existing structures: not only are many of them dangerously unstable, but doing so will incur the wrath of blood-thirsty archaeologists, who wander the site between June and September searching for ancient artifacts when the **Archaeological Summer School** hits town. (Call Theresa McDonald at the Achill Folklife Centre for details: ☎43569 or 087 677 2045; www.achill-fieldschool.com.) Along the same road as the abandoned village is **Giant's Grave,** a megalithic multichambered tomb.

O'Malley's Island Sports center **rents bikes** and sells groceries, fishing tackle, and ammunition. (☎43125. Bikes €12 per day, €65 per wk. Open M-Sa 9am-7pm, Su 10am-2pm.) Guests at the **Wayfarer Hostel (IHH) ❶,** on the outskirts of town near the caravan park, take in views of Keel Strand within unusually secure surroundings. (☎43266. Laundry €4. Open mid-Mar. to mid-Oct. Dorms €10; private rooms €9-10 per person.) There are indeed opulent vistas at the **Richview Hostel,** at the far end of Keel, which offers a taste of the laid-back, friendly, and slightly disheveled life. (☎43462. Dorms €10; private rooms €13 per person.) Everyone deserves some extravagance now and then—Mrs. Joyce's **Marian Villa ❹** is a 20-room hotel/B&B with thoughtfully decorated rooms and a veranda that looks out over the sea. (☎43134. Singles €44.50; doubles €63.50.) Directly on the beach, the **Keel Sandybanks Caravan and Camping Park ❶** provides a sandy spot to pound your tent stakes, conveniently located near the pubs. (☎43211. July-Aug. €8.25 per tent; late May-June and Sept. €6.50. Electricity €1.50. Laundry €4.)

Price Cutters Market sells crisps and biscuits. (☎43125. Open M-Su 9am-8pm.) Keel has numerous chippers; more nutritious food and (less nutritious) sweaters are available at **Beehive Handcrafts and Coffee Shop ❶.** Salads, sandwiches, and home-baked goodies delight—the apple-rhubarb pie is orgasmic. (☎43134 or 43018. Open daily 11am-6:30pm.) **Calvey's ❸,** next to Price Cutters, whips up hearty meals. (☎43158. Catch of the day €12.50. Open daily 11:30am-4:30pm and 5:30-9:30pm.) Inspired drinking is encouraged and music is applauded at the very vinyl **Annexe Inn.** (☎43268. Nightly sessions July-Aug.) On weekends, thangs are shaken and grooves gotten on at the **Achill Head Hotel,** the randiest party in all Achill. (☎43108. 18+. Su cover €6.35.) The **Shark's Head Bar** in the hotel serves up pints until 12:30am, after which people retire to the back-room nightclub to dance until the cows come home (assuming the cows come home around 2am).

DOOAGH (DUMHACH) ☎098

Corrymore House, 2 mi. up the road from Keel in Dooagh (DOO-ah), was one of several Co. Mayo estates owned by Captain Boycott, whose mid-19th-century tenants went on an extended rent strike that verbified his surname. **The Pub,** Main St. (☎43109), serves soup and sandwich fare and is lovingly maintained by the mistress of the house. Across the street is a monument to Don Allum, the first man to row across the Atlantic in both directions. A similarly grueling ride over the cliffs (by bike, not boat) to the west of Dooagh leads to **Keem Bay** beach, the most beautiful spot on the island. Wedged between the sea and woolly, green walls of weed, rock, and sheep, the Bay was once a prime fishing hole for Basking sharks.

A river of amethyst runs under the Atlantic and comes up for air in **Croaghaun Mountain,** west of Keem Bay. Most of the accessible crystals have been plundered, but local old-timer Frank McNamara still digs out the deeper veins with a pick and shovel and sells his haul at his store in Dooagh (☎43581). The mountains, climbable from Keem Bay, provide bone-chilling views of the **Croaghaun Cliffs,** hot contenders in the ongoing intra-Ireland competition for recognition as the highest sea cliffs in Europe (see **Slieve League,** p. 413). Dooagh is also home to the **Achill Folklife Centre** (☎43564), which runs the Archaeological Summer School and offers special exhibitions and lectures on subjects ranging from the Irish Ring Fort to Maritime Life. Special exhibits change each season. (€2.50. **Weekend archaelogical course,** with accommodation, €314 per person. Open June-Sept. M-Sa 9:30am-5:30pm.)

DUGORT (DUMHACH GORT) ☎098

A right turn after Cashel leads to the northern part of the island, where the tiny hamlet of Dugort waxes anachronistic atop a sea cliff. Dugort slept through much of the 20th century and will likely sleep through the 21st. Mist-shrouded **Slievemore Mountain** looms to the east. Cemeteries and abandoned buildings west of Dugort are the result of an ill-fated effort in the mid-1800s to convert the islanders to Protestantism by sending in Irish-speaking missionaries. Boats leave for the **seal caves** daily between 11am and 6pm from the pier down the road from the Strand Hotel. Passengers are treated to views of frolicking seals. **McDowell's Hotel and Activity Centre** rents surfboards, kayaks, canoes, and other equipment, and offers day- and week-long activities. (☎43148. Half-day activities €20, full day €35.)

A soft pillow awaits your head at **Valley House Hostel ❶.** The striking facade of this 100-year-old house has only improved with age, and travelers will appreciate its spacious interior. Additionally, residents enjoy the services of a **pitch-and-putt** (€3.80, kiddies €2.50) overlooking the lovely and **fishable lake** (€10 per day including gear). An in-house pub helps visitors banish the hobgoblin of sobriety. (☎47204. Showers €0.65. Laundry €2.50. Open Easter-Oct. Dorms €10; private rooms €14 per person. **Camping** €1.50 site fee and €4 per person.) The brutal maiming of the woman who once owned the house was part of the inspiration for Synge's play *Playboy of the Western World* (see **The Revival,** p. 71). **Seal Caves Caravan and Camping Park ❶** lies on a windy stretch of turf between Dugort Beach and Slievemore Mountain. Check in up the road at the blue house/shop. (☎43262. July-Aug. €5 per person; Apr.-June and Sept. €4. Showers €0.65. Laundry €3.)

NORTHERN MAYO

Northern Mayo's twin claims to fame could not look more different. The Mullet Peninsula is one of the most remote and sublime destinations outside of Donegal and Northern Ireland; Ballina has the feel of the commercial and social center of a large, remote area, which is exactly what it is.

BELMULLET (BÉAL AN MHUIRTHEAD) AND THE MULLET PENINSULA ☎097

Located on the isthmus between Broad Haven and Blacksod Bays at the beginning of the Mullet Peninsula, Belmullet withstands cold Atlantic winds and the constant threat of rain, providing a sheltered base for the intrepid traveler. Not many tourists make it to the Mullet; peak-season crowds are mostly youths attending the Irish language summer schools farther down the peninsula. As a result, visitors mostly come to enjoy the cultural immersion and the solitude afforded by this region's isolation. The beaches are mostly empty, as is the soggy moorland covering the peninsula's western half. Nevertheless, fishing holes and friendly pubs are abundant. Some travelers might find all this less than thrilling, but for those with their sights set on authenticity and rustic relaxation, the Mullet can't be beat.

TRANSPORTATION AND PRACTICAL INFORMATION. An infrequent **bus** service departs from Ballina and runs the length of the peninsula (July-Aug. M-Sa 2 per day, Sept.-June 1 per day; €9.55). The **Erris Tourist Information Centre** on Barrack St. is amazingly helpful. (☎81500. Open for walk-ins July-Aug. M-Sa 10am-6pm; phones open all year M-F 9am-4pm.) **Bank of Ireland** has an **ATM.** (☎81311. Open M-F 10am-12:30pm and 1:30-4pm, Th until 5pm.) **Belmullet Cycle Centre,** located 2 mi. outside of Belmullet in Binghamstown, **rents bikes.** (☎086 237 7069. €10 per day. Open M-Sa 10:30am-6pm.) **Enternetwest,** the Square, links you to the Information Superhighway. (☎20937. €1.30 per 15min. Open June-Aug. M 1-9pm, Tu-Sa 11am-9pm; Sept.-May M-Sa 1-9pm.) The **post office** is at the end of Main St. (☎81032. Open M and W-Sa 9am-2pm and 3-5:30pm, Tu 9:30am-5:30pm.)

ACCOMMODATIONS, FOOD, AND PUBS. There are no budget accommodations on the Mullet itself. Fortunately, the village of **Pollatomish** (PO-lah-to-MUS), 15 mi. northeast on the coast road, features two high-quality hostels. Vegetarians and meatheads alike will enjoy fresh, organic ingredients in the home-cooked meals prepared at clean and cozy **Kilcommon Lodge Hostel ❶.** Bunnies and ducks wander around while the owners advise guests on hiking routes. (☎84621. Breakfast €5; dinner €10. Dorms €9.50; private rooms €11 per person. **Camping** €6.50 per person.) Despite its name, **The Old Rectory Holiday Hostel ❶** brings a strictly modern aesthetic to hostel decor. Each room is expertly decorated, from vibrant wallcoverings to funky lamps. (☎84115. Open Apr.-Oct. Dorms €15.) For a bed that's actually *in* Belmullet, hit up the **Western Strands Hotel ❸,** Main St., which is centrally located and provides breakfast and bath for all. (☎81096. Singles €32-38; shared rooms €26-31 per person; discounts for families and children.)

Erris Superstore, the Square, peddles groceries somewhat late into the night. (Open daily 9am-10pm.) **The Appetizer ❷** posits several solutions to the potato problem—the lunch specials here feature copious helpings of fried, mashed, and saladed spuds. Potatoes with a side of meat can be had for €9. (☎82222. Open M-F 9:30am-2pm.) Belmullet's pub scene is pure, home-grown *craic.* Impromptu good cheer can be found at **McDonnell's,** Barrack St. (☎81194), any early evening of the week. A more restrained time can be had at **Lavelle's** (☎81372), where crowds come for Belmullet's best pints and stay for the weekend karaoke sessions. In an otherwise macho pub scene, the **Anchor Bar,** on Barrack St., provides a more tender option; the ladies of Belmullet flock to this pub before hitting its late-night disco. (☎81007. Cover €7. Disco open F-Sa midnight-2am.) On the other end of the spectrum, the testosterone-rich **Lenehan's** (☎81098) and **Clan Lir** (☎82360), both on Main St., are popular with patriarchs and football rowdies, respectively.

SIGHTS AND ACTIVITIES. The **Ionad Deirbhle Heritage Centre,** at the end of the peninsula in Aughleam, explores locally significant items, including the histories of the whaling industry and the Inishkey (*Inis Gé*) islands. The guides also provide info on day hikes and boat rides at the southern end of the peninsula. (☎85728. Open Easter-Oct. 10am-6pm. €3.) Josephine and Matt Geraghty also run **boat trips** to the islands off the peninsula's southern coast, as well as **sea angling** excursions. (☎85741. Open May-Sept. Call ahead. Island junket €20 per person; 6-person minimum. Fishing trips €215 for the whole boat.) **Fly fishing** from both shore and boat abounds in nearby **Cross Lake;** for details, contact **George Geraghty** (☎81492) or the **Fishing Supply Store** on American St. (☎82093). The **Belmullet Sea Angling Competition** (☎81076), in mid-July, awards €2.55 per lb. for the heaviest halibut. The **Feille Iorras** (FAY-la ER-is), a peninsula-wide music festival, is held during the last weekend in July (☎81500; www.belmullet.net).

BALLYCASTLE, KILLALA, AND THE CEIDE FIELDS ☎096

Along R314 north of Ballina lies a series of towns and sights, the grandest of which is Ballycastle *(Baile an Chaisil)*, a strip of shops and pubs surrounded by holiday cottages and rolling hills of rugged bog. Ballycastle's main attraction is the **Ballinglen Arts Foundation,** which provides grants for international artists to spend five- to six-week periods of residency in Ballycastle. In return, each artist leaves behind a work for the Foundation's archive. Each set of paintings reveals a distinct experience of Northern Mayo, making the variety and quality of these works overwhelmingly diverse and thought-provoking. The foundation building is only open to the public during July and August. (☎43189.) **Bus Éireann** runs a service from Ballycastle to **Ballina** and **Killala** (M-Sa 1 per day, €6.35). **Ulster Bank** opens Tuesdays from 10am to noon.

A 25min. walk away from town on R314 will take you to the **Keadyville B&B ❸,** whose spacious accommodations and glass-walled dining room are plush enough for an afternoon of exquisite loafing. (☎43288. Singles €33; doubles €47.) **McNamee's Supermarket** sells all the simple essentials. (☎43057. Open daily 8am-9pm.) **Mary's Bakery and Cottage Kitchen ❷** whips up authentic baked goods and scrumptious lunch specials complete with Mayo, naturally. (☎43361. Open June-Oct. daily 10am-6pm; Nov.-Dec. and Feb.-May M-Sa 10am-6pm.)

The **Ballycastle Resource Centre** sells a small brochure (€0.25) outlining nice walks in the area. (☎43407. Open July-Sept. M-W 10am-4pm, Th-Sa 11am-3:30pm, Su 11:30am-4pm.) One of these walks makes its pleasant way on down to the ocean, the **Dun Briste** sea stack, and stoic **Downpatrick Head** (see below). Five miles west of Ballycastle on R314, the **Ceide Fields** (KAYJ-uh feeldz) excavation site has finally been opened to the public. A futuristic four-story glass, steel, and peat ziggurat built around a 5000-year-old pine tree, the center elegantly articulates—through exhibits, tours, and an audio-visual presentation—the dynamic relationship between Northern Mayo's first settlers and its environment. (☎43325. Open June-Aug. daily 10am-6pm; Sept. 9:30am-5:30pm; Oct. and Mar.-May 10am-5pm; Nov. 10am-4:30pm. Tours every hr.; film every 30min. €3.10.) If all the bog is bringin' you down, the 350-million-year-old **Ceide Cliffs** rear up nearby and can be viewed dramatically from the observation deck atop the pyramid-shaped center.

Eight miles south of Ballycastle, along the Ballina road, is **Killala** *(Cill Alaidh)*, a charming seaport best known as the site of the French Invasion of 1798 (see **Rebellion,** p. 59). That year, at the peak of international revolutionary fervor, one thousand and sixty-seven French soldiers landed at Killala to join the United Irishmen under Wolfe Tone in a revolt against the English (see **Bantry,** p. 254). Instead of a well-armed band of revolutionaries, the Frenchies found a rag tag band of pure-of-heart (as well as impoverished, Irish-speaking, and poorly equipped) peasants. Undeterred, the combined forces pressed on, winning a significant victory at Castlebar before being soundly hammered by British forces at Ballnamuck. Aside from the Ballina road, Killala and Ballycastle are also connected by the **Coast Road,** a scenic expanse of highway with views of dramatic blowholes and unique geological formations such as **Downpatrick Head,** an isolated spire separated from the sea cliffs by erosion. This multilayered rock formation supposedly broke off from the mainland during a dispute between St. Patrick and a pagan king.

BALLINA (BÉAL AN ÁTHA) ☎096

Ballina (bah-lin-AH) is a fisherman's mecca. Armies in olive-green waders invade the town each year during the salmon season (Feb.-Sept.). Ballina has at least one non-ichthyological attraction, though: every Saturday night, almost everyone in a 50 mi. radius, from sheep farmers to students, descends on the town like a stampeding herd of lemmings. These weekly influxes ruffle the feathers of the humble hub, but leave it slightly hipper for the wear. Many pubs forsake trad for modern rock and blues; restaurants supplement pub grub with stir-fry, fajitas, and calzones. These many developments can turn a layover in Ballina into an incongruous cross-cultural experience. Former Irish President Mary Robinson grew up in Ballina and refined her political skills in the town's pubs (see **Current Issues,** p. 64).

TRANSPORTATION

Trains: Station Rd. (☎71818), near the bus station. Open M-Sa 6:45am-6pm, Su 10am-6pm. Service to **Dublin** via **Athlone** (M-Su 3 per day, €20.90). From the station, go left, bear right, and walk 4 blocks to reach the town center; several signs point the way.

Buses: Kevin Barry St. (☎71800). Open M-Sa 7:30am-9:30pm. Buses to: **Athlone** (1 per day, €15.20); **Donegal** (M-Sa 3 per day, Su 1 per day; €13.30); **Dublin** via **Mullingar** (4hr., 6 per day, €12.10); **Galway** via **Westport** (2hr.; M-Sa 6 per day, Su 5 per day; €11.50); **Sligo** (2hr., M-Sa 3-4 per day, €9.75).

Taxis: Lynott's Cabs (☎087 295 8787 or 086 295 8787) can drive you, or find a ride home at the **taxi stand** in the town center on O'Rahily St., near the post office.

Bike Rental: Michael Hopkins, Lower Pearse St. (☎21609). €10 per day, €45 per wk. Deposit €40. Open Apr.-Sept. M-Sa 9am-6pm.

ORIENTATION AND PRACTICAL INFORMATION

On the east bank of the **River Moy** is the cathedral and tourist office. A bridge crosses over to the west bank, where the commerical center is located; the bridge connects to **Tone St.,** which turns into **Tolan St.** This main strip intersects with **Pearse St.** and **O'Rahily St.,** which run parallel to the river, to form Ballina's center.

Tourist Office: Cathedral Rd. (☎70848), on the river just past St. Muredach's Cathedral. Open June-Aug. daily 10am-5:30pm; May and Sept. M-Sa 10am-1pm and 2-5:30pm. **Fishing Permits and Licenses** (€4-32) are available at the **Northwest Regional Fisheries Board** from John Baker, Angling Officer. (☎22788. Open daily 9:30-11:30am, or seek Mr. Baker at the river.)

Banks: Bank of Ireland, Pearse St. (☎21144). Open M and Th-F 10am-4pm, Tu 10am-5pm, W 10:30am-4pm. **Ulster Bank,** Pearse St. (☎21077). Open M-F 10am-4pm, Tu until 5pm. Both have **ATMs.**

Laundry: Gerry's Laundrette, Tone St. (☎22793). Laundry €7. Open M-Sa 9am-6pm.

Pharmacy: Molloy's, Garden St. (☎21375). Open M-Sa 9am-6pm.

Emergency: ☎999; no coins required. **Police** *(Garda)*: Walsh St. (☎21422).

Internet Access: Surf 'N' Train Internet Cafe, Hill St. (☎70562). Walking down Tolan St., take a right on James Connolly St.; it's two blocks down on your right. €1.50 per 10min. Open May-Aug. M-F noon-9pm, Sa noon-7pm; Sept.-Apr. M-F noon-7pm, Sa 1-7pm. **Moy Valley Resources** (☎70905), in the same building as the tourist office. Open M-Th 9am-1pm and 2-5:30pm, F 9am-1pm and 2-5pm. €8 per hr.

Post Office: Corner of Bury St. and O'Rahilly St. (☎21309). Open M-Sa 9am-5:30pm.

ACCOMMODATIONS AND CAMPING

B&Bs line the main approach roads into town, charging €27-35 per person.

Lismoyne House, Kevin Barry St. (☎70582), near the bus station. Newly renovated stately rooms with high ceilings and big bathtubs perfect for soaking away long hours of fishing or pubbing. The owner offers tips on angling. €35 per person. ❸

Ms. Corrigan's Greenhill, Cathedral Close (☎22767). Behind the tourist office and just a cast away from river, lake, and sea fishing. Bright, spacious rooms look onto rose gardens. Singles €33-39. €3-4 reduction with Continental instead of full Irish breakfast. ❸

Breda Walsh's Suncraft (☎21573), two doors down from Greenhill B&B. Yet another fine option. Singles €35; doubles €54. ❸

Belleek Camping and Caravan Park, Killala Rd. (☎71533). 2 mi. from Ballina toward Killala on R314, behind the Belleek Woods. Open Mar.-Oct. €5 per person with tent; camper with two people €13. Laundry €4. ❶

FOOD

Aspiring gourmets can prepare for a feast at the **Quinnsworth** supermarket on Market Rd. (☎21056. Open M-W and Sa 8:30am-7pm, Th-F 8:30am-9pm, Su noon-6pm.) Lard-soaked takeaway may be cheap, but it's not always a welcome treat. Fortunately, most Ballinalian restaurants are attached to pubs and serve similar menus in the pub at a cheaper price. (See **Pubs** for additional food info.)

Cafolla's (☎21029), just up from the upper bridge. One of the town's two unique Irish diners, open late and with milkshakes that tingle tongues. Everything from eggs and toast to curry burgers. Takeaway counter and restaurant open daily 10am-midnight. ❷

Chungs at Tullio's, Pearse St. (☎70815). Chinese and Italian cuisine, served on different sides of the restaurant. Mains €9-14. Open daily noon-2:30pm and 6-10pm. ❸

Dillon's, Dillon Terr. (☎72230). Head all the way down Pearse St.; it curves into Dillon Terr. The restaurant is through a stone archway on your left. Creative attempts at pizza and pasta using local ingredients—namely salmon, smoked salmon, grilled salmon, fried salmon, and dill (€8-11). Pub serves food M-Sa 3-9pm, Su 1-9pm; restaurant upstairs serves M-Sa 6-10pm, Su 1-10pm. Trad on W nights. ❸

The Bard, Garden St. (☎21894 or 21324), above Tone St. The haute cuisine option in Ballina, with Mexican and Thai selections, as well as warm goat cheese salad (€3.60) and a variety of pasta dishes (€12-14). Open M-Sa 5-9:30pm, Su noon-9pm. ❸

PUBS AND CLUBS

Gaughan's, O'Rahilly St. (☎70096). Pulling the best pint in town since 1936. No trad or TV—just great grub, homemade snuff, and friendly conversation with Pints O'Guinness.

The Parting Glass, Tolan St. (☎72714). Jolly, musical drinkers raise this Glass over and over again. Trad sessions weekly and live music most nights; call ahead for schedule.

Murphy Bros., Clare St. (☎22702), across the river, 3 blocks past the tourist office. The Brothers Murphy pour pints for twenty-somethings amongst dark wood furnishings. They also serve good if typical pubmunch. Food served noon-8:30pm.

Emmett's Treffpunkt, Tolan St. (☎21608). An appreciably funkier crowd packs in to down pints beneath a mural of venerable rock legends. This deceptively tiny pub manages to squeeze in legions of black-clad fans for live (alternative and hardrock) music each weekend, all without sacrificing its friendly atmosphere.

The Music Box (☎72379). Located in the rear of the Broken Jug. Top 40-lovin' folks arrive in herds when this, Ballina's most popular nightclub, opens its doors. Open W and F-Su 11:30pm-2:30am. Cover €7-9.

The Loft, Pearse St. (☎21881). Young and old mix like oil and water within the dark confines of this energetic club. Three floors. Live music Tu-F and Su.

Armada Bar, inside Belleek Castle. The castle itself is an expensive hotel, but this bar, built from an actual 500-year-old Spanish wreck, is quite affordable. Downstairs, another bar occupies a medieval banquet hall.

SIGHTS AND HIKING

Walking through the bird-rich **Belleek Woods,** which surround **Belleek Castle,** will elicit a series of emotions ranging from childlike wonderment to jaded skepticism. Faced with an almost-too-idyllic forest, visitors will wax nostalgic for Narnia, Sherwood, and the Forbidden Forest. To dull the pain of returning to the grown-up world of "rules" and "physical laws," stop in at the castle for a few drinks (see **Pubs and Nightlife,** above). If you want to brave the woods, from the tourist office cross over the lower bridge to the Western Shore, take the second right, and follow Nelly St. (which becomes Castle Rd.) for 1 mi. At the back of the railway station is the **Dolmen of the Four Maols,** known locally as "Table of the Giants." The dolmen, which dates back to 2000 BC, is said to be the burial site of four Maols who murdered Ceallach, a 7th-century bishop.

The lonely **Ox Mountains,** east of Ballina are eminently cyclable, with scads of dirt and asphalt trails criss-crossing their way up the slopes. The 44 mi. **Ox Mountain drive** traces the scenic perimeter of the mountains and is well signposted from **Tobercurry** (21 mi. south of Sligo on the N17). The **Western Way** footpath begins in the Ox Mountains and winds its way past Ballina through Newport and Westport, ending up in Connemara. The Western then meets the **Sligo Way,** which continues up toward Sligo. Tourist offices sell complete guides of both trails. At the **Ardchuan Lodge,** 5 mi. north of Ballina on the Sligo road, diminutive equines can be hired for group treks through the woods. (☎45084. €15 per person. Open M-Sa 8am-6pm.) The annual week-long **Ballina Street Festival** (☎79814) has been swinging through mid-July since 1964. Much of Co. Mayo turns up for the festival's **Heritage Day,** when the streets are closed off and life reverts to the year 1910. All the flashier aspects of traditional Irish life, including the greased pig contests, are staged.

SLAP THAT BRIDGE The remote bridge fording the Owenmore River in Bellacorick (18 mi. west of Ballina on the N59) may appear innocuous at first glance, but this is no ordinary arhythmic structure. Goodness, no. What you have here is an authentic *musical* bridge. Although it's not given to spontaneous choruses of *Dies Irae* as one might hope, the bridge will gladly live up to its name with a little help from a friend. Unusual markings run the length of the stone wall, and a pile of small stones sits on each end. All you need to do to play a tune is run from one side of the river to the other whilst dragging a stone along the top of the handrail. The way barflies tell it at the nearby pub, the bridge was cursed during its construction by the death of chief engineer William Bald. The aforementioned alkies warn that the same fate will befall anyone who tries to complete the construction, and speak of the near-death experience of a man who tried to place the final stone in its lodging fifty years ago. The man's son cast the offending stone into the water, saving his ailing father from the jaws of fate.

NEAR BALLINA: ENNISCRONE (INISHCRONE) ☎096

The strikingly gorgeous Enniscrone Strand stretches along the eastern shore of Killala Bay, 8 mi. northeast of Ballina on scenic Quay Rd. (R297). Sunny days see droves of Irish weekenders vying for towel space; most days, therefore, the miles of sand remain unpopulated. Across from the beach, the family-run **Kilcullen's Bath House** simmers—steam baths in cedar wood cabinets and cool seaweed baths will relax even the tensest of travelers. (☎36238. Seaweed bath €12.50, plus steam bath €15. 30min. massage by appointment €22.50. Open May-Oct. daily 10am-9pm; mid-Mar. to Apr. M-F noon-8pm and Sa-Su 10am-8pm; Nov. to mid-Mar. M-F noon-8pm and Sa-Su 10am-8pm.) The **tourist office** closed in 2001 but is rumored to be reopening soon; contact the Ballina tourist office (☎70848) in the meantime.

Gowan House B&B ❸, Pier Rd., is set just back from the sea; their big bedrooms are decorated in bright colors and finished off with Baltic Pine. (☎36396. Singles €34; doubles €56.) The biggest draw of Maura O'Dowd's **Point View House ❸,** Main St., may be its central location, but that does not eclipse Ms. O'Dowd's 50 years of experience in running the place. (☎36312. All rooms with bath. €25.50 per person.) **The Atlantic Caravan Park ❶,** on Main St. at the edge of town, has grass for tents of all sizes. (☎36132. Laundry facilities available. €6.50 per tent. Showers €0.65.) If it's victuals you want, head to **Tracey's ❶** on Main St. (☎087 682 3745). Run by Tracey herself, this cool little cafe specializes in all-day breakfast and other simple taste treats. (Open June-Aug. daily 9:30am-8pm; Sept.-May M-F 9:30am-5pm and Sa-Su 9:30am-7pm.) **Walsh's Pub,** also on Main St. near the bus stop at the top of the hill, serves great pubfüd all day and hosts weekly music sessions. Inquire here about **Internet access.** (☎36110. Lunch served 1-2:30pm.)

COUNTY SLIGO

Known best as the birthplace and poetic inspiration of William Butler Yeats, County Sligo is one of Ireland's most magical and underrated treasures. The near-symmetrical Knocknarea and "bare Ben Bulben" mountains dominate the faery-haunted landscape, which—besides being a geographical who's who of Yeats's verse—hides in its hills the oldest megalithic tombs in the country. Don't be surprised to see wetsuited surfers, boards on backs, headed out to shore; Sligo's Strandhill beach is renowned for its top-notch waves. The commercial center of the county, Sligo Town has the excited bustle of a city and the intimate, narrow passages of a welcoming hamlet. A fleet of high-quality hostels and a lively pub culture make it a good hub for daytrips around the area.

SLIGO TOWN (SLIGEACH) ☎071

A cozy town with the sophistication of a city, present-day Sligo often gets lost in a haze of Yeats nostalgia. On Rockwood Parade, street fiddlers play to indifferent swans egging their young along the Garavogue River, while locals nibble their lunches under restaurant canopies. Toward the city center, the pace picks up a bit, as drivers and pedestrians take turns crossing congested intersections and shoppers dart in and out of the many clothing and book stores. Later at night, the town's thriving nightlife is as diverse as any in Ireland—from traditional bars that relish their silence, to musical pubs that showcase nightly trad sessions, to modern and trendy clubs; expect a full range in Sligo. The Yeats Memorial Building and countless other landmarks remember the bygone days of the wordsmith.

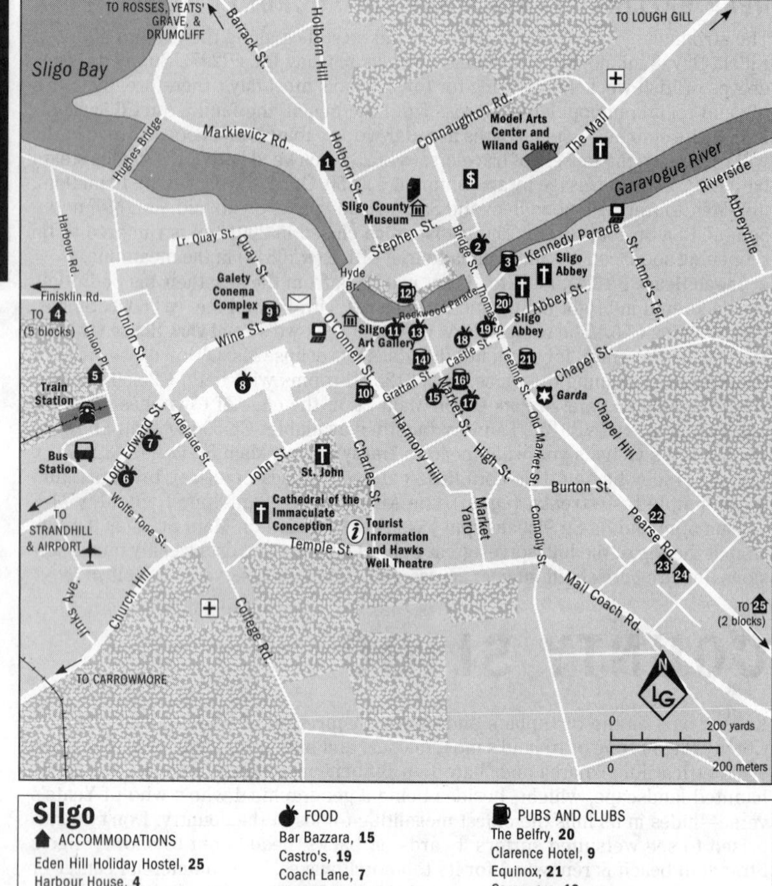

Sligo

ACCOMMODATIONS

Eden Hill Holiday Hostel, **25**
Harbour House, **4**
Lough Gill, **24**
Pearse Lodge, **22**
Railway Hostel, **5**
St. Ann's, **23**
The White House Hostel (IHH), **1**

FOOD

Bar Bazzara, **15**
Castro's, **19**
Coach Lane, **7**
Fiddler's Creek, **11**
Ho Wong, **17**
Hy-Breasil, **2**
Kate's Kitchen, **18**
The Loft, **6**
Pepper Alley, **13**
Tesco Supermarket, **8**

PUBS AND CLUBS

The Belfry, **20**
Clarence Hotel, **9**
Equinox, **21**
Garavogue, **12**
Hargadon Bros., **10**
McLaughlin's, **16**
Shoot the Crows, **14**
Toff's, **3**

TRANSPORTATION

Airport: Sligo Airport, Strandhill Rd. (☎68280). Open daily 9:30am-5:30pm. To **Dublin** (35min., 3-5 per day).

Trains: McDiarmada Station, Lord Edward St. (☎69888). Open M-Sa 7am-6:30pm, Su 20min. before each departure. Trains to **Dublin** via **Carrick-on-Shannon** and **Mullingar** (3hr., 4 per day, €19).

Buses: McDiarmada Station, Lord Edward St. (☎60066). Open M-F 9:15am-6pm, Sa 9:30am-5pm. Buses to: **Belfast** (4hr., 2-3 per day, €22); **Derry** (3hr., 4-7 per day,

€13.30); **Donegal** (1hr., 3-7 per day, €9.75); **Dublin** (3-4hr., 4-5 per day, €12.40); **Galway** (2½hr., 4-6 per day, €11.40); **Westport** (2½hr., 1-4 per day, €12.70).

Local Transportation: Frequent **buses** to Strandhill and Rosses Point (€3.80 return).

Taxis: Cab 55 (☎42333); **Finnegan's** (☎77777, 44444, or 41111). €5 for first 2½ mi.

Bike Rental: Flanagan's Cycles, Market Sq. (☎44477; after hours ☎62633). Rental and repairs. €15 per day, €60 per wk.; deposit €50. Open M-Sa 9am-6pm.

ORIENTATION AND PRACTICAL INFORMATION

Trains and buses pull into **McDiarmada Station** on **Lord Edward St.** To reach the main drag from the station, take a left on Lord Edward and follow him straight onto **Wine St.,** then turn right onto **O'Connell St.** at the post office. More shops, pubs, and eateries beckon from **Grattan St.,** a left turn off O'Connell St. To get to the river, continue down Wine St. and turn right just after the Yeats building onto idyllic **Rockwood Parade,** where plenty of swans and locals take their feed. From here, the bridge over the river takes you to (surprise!) **Bridge St.,** while a right turn on **the Mall** will take you to the gorgeous new **Model Arts Centre and Niland Gallery.**

TOURIST, FINANCIAL, AND LOCAL SERVICES

Tourist Office: Northwest Regional Office, Temple St. (☎61201), at Charles St. From the station, turn left along Lord Edward St. and follow the signs right onto Adelaide St. and around the corner to Temple St. Provides info on the whole of the northwest. Open June-Aug. M-Sa 9am-7pm, Su 10am-6pm; Oct.-May M-F 9am-5pm.

Bank: AIB, The Mall (☎42157). 24hr. **ATM.** Open M-W, F 10am-4pm, Th 10am-5pm.

Luggage Storage: Bus station. Open M-F 9:30am-1:30pm and 2:45-6pm. €1.90.

Bookstore: The Sligo Bookshop, O'Connell St. (☎47277). Fiction, Irish, travel, and the requisite Yeats. Open M-Sa 9am-6pm.

Laundry: Pam's Laundrette, 9 Johnston Ct. (☎44861), off O'Connell St. Wash and dry from €9.50. Open M-Sa 9am-6pm.

Camping Supplies: Call of the Wild, Stephen St. (☎46905). Supplies and info on camping, hiking, and surfing. Open M-F 9:30am-6pm, Sa 9am-6pm.

EMERGENCY AND COMMUNICATIONS

Emergency: ☎999; no coins required. **Police** *(Garda)*: Pearse Rd. (☎42031).

Crisis Line: Samaritans, 11 Chapel St. (24hr. ☎42011). **Rape Crisis Line** (☎1800 750 780; **24hr.** line ☎1800 778 888) M-F 10:30am-midnight.

Pharmacy: T. Hunter, O'Connell St. (☎42696). Open M-Sa 9am-6pm. Local pharmacies post schedules of rotating Su openings.

Hospital: On the Mall (☎71111).

Internet Access: Cygo Internet Cafe, 19 O'Connell Street (☎40082). €6.50 per hr., students €5.25. Open M-Sa 10am-7pm. For slightly cheaper, slightly farther late-night access, hit up **Galaxy Complex,** Riverside (☎40441). €6.40 per hr., students €4.50. Open daily 10am-midnight.

Post Office: Wine St. (☎59266). Open M and W-Sa 9am-5:30pm, Tu 9:30am-5:30pm.

ACCOMMODATIONS

There are plenty of high-quality hostels in Sligo, but they often fill up quickly, particularly in mid-August when the Yeats International Summer School is in session. If you're staying a few days with a group of people, getting a cottage can be cheaper; contact the tourist office for more info.

MARKREE CASTLE

For those seeking the royal experience, enormous Markree Castle provides travelers with the opportunity to live out the grandeur of a regal life, at least for a night. The magnificent castle, as it stands today, dates from around 1802, though the land itself has been in Cooper family hands since it was bestowed on Edward Cooper some 350 years ago for his military service to Oliver Cromwell. The caste fell into disuse following WWII, and its future remained uncertain until Charles and Mary Cooper turned the former family home into a hotel in 1989. This elegant guesthouse now exists as the only Irish castle still owned by direct descendants of the original family.

Today, awestruck travelers ascend the red-carpeted grand staircase to view an enormous stained-glass window featuring the Cooper family tree. Gorgeous, spacious rooms are filled with antique furniture, and grand windows look out onto either the River Unsin or the beautiful parks and gardens that surround the castle. Breakfast is served in a gilded, chandeliered dining room that makes room service look like punishment.

Markree Castle. (☎67800; www.markreecastle.ie.) 15 mi. southwest of Sligo on the N4. Breakfast included. Set dinner €37.50. ***Horseback-riding*** *from the castle's stables €17 per hr. May-Sept. singles €108; doubles €189.90; triples €227.90; Jan.-Apr. and Oct.-Dec. €98.50/ €169.40/€206. Children under 12 in parents room €19, under 4 free.*

Eden Hill Holiday Hostel (IHH), off Pearse Rd. A 20min. trek from the bus station, though those who came to hike the nearby mountains shouldn't mind. Follow Pearse Rd. and turn right at the Marymount sign just before the Esso station; take another quick right after one block. Fully renovated and restored in 2001, this hostel reopened in 2002 to reveal its original Victorian look, down to the in-room fireplaces (not for actual use). Clean and airy comfort with a laid-back, friendly staff. Showers are only hot for a few hours each morning and evening. Laundry facilities. Dorms €11. ❶

The White House Hostel (IHH), Markievicz Rd. (☎45160). Take the first left off Wine St. after Hyde Bridge; reception is in the brown house. Wonderfully convenient to the heart of town, with a view of the water to boot. Despite the name, the *brown* house (rather than the neighboring white one) is where the action is, as staff and travelers alike congregate over the large dining table. Key deposit €3. Dorms €10. ❶

Harbour House, Finisklin Rd. (☎71547). A 10min. walk from the bus station, *away* from town. A plain stone front hides a luxurious hostel with a classy TV lounge *and* additional TVs in some rooms. All rooms with bath. Limited kitchen hours. Year-round dorms €16; June-Aug. private rooms €18 per person, Sept.-May €17. ❷

Railway Hostel, 1 Union Place (☎44530). From the main entrance of the train station, take 3 immediate lefts and you're there. An 8-bed hostel with rooms of different configurations. Slightly run-down, but nonetheless homey, with a pleasant lounge with TV, stereo, and free tea and coffee. Dorms €10; doubles €26. ❶

St. Ann's B&B, Pearse Rd. (☎43118), 1½ blocks after the *Garda* Station. Looks like a charming bungalow and has the unusual perk of a swimming pool out back. Be forewarned fairweather swimmers—the unheated water is chilly most of the year. Singles €38; doubles €58. ❸

Pearse Lodge, Pearse Rd. (☎61090). Comfortable rooms, all with bath and equipped with hair dryers. Even more exciting is breakfast: a cornucopia of international breakfast options delights every palate. French toast and bananas, bagels with cream cheese, and the omnipresent full Irish are but a few of the enticing choices. Singles €35-44. ❹

Lough Gill, Pearse Rd. (☎50045). Ivy-laced exterior leads to small but tastefully decorated rooms. A basket of toiletries, digestives, and tissues for the Irish cold are thoughtful additions to every room. Singles €38; shared rooms €28 per person. ❸

FOOD

Little-known Yeats lyric: "For fresh fruits you can fondle/ for not too much dough/ head to O'Connell/ and go to Tesco." **Tesco Supermarket,** O'Connell St., has aisles worth of cheap food. (☎62788. Open M-Tu and Sa 8:30am-7pm, W-F 8:30am-9pm, Su 10am-6pm.) **Kate's Kitchen,** Castle St., offers sophisticated pâtés and other deli-cacies. (☎43022. Open M-Sa 9am-6:30pm.) The demands of international visitors have induced culinary development; pick up *Discover Sligo's Good Food*, free at most hostels and bookstores, for new listings.

Bar Bazzara, 34 Market St. (☎44749). An alternative spot to sip fantastic coffee concoctions. The Honey Bee (mocha with almond syrup and honey; €2.65) is most popular, but the Irish Cream milkshake (€2.80) is the true path to utopia. For the full experience, head to the cozy back room, where funky lanterns and board games predominate. Open M-Th 9:30am-6pm, F 9:30am-8pm, Sa 10am-8pm. ❶

Coach Lane, 1-2 Lord Edward St. (☎62417). Winner of the "Newcomer of the Year" award in 2000; it's easy to see why. Excellent service and amazing food unites local sensibilities with international flair. A venturesome meal might start with a goat cheese purse (€6), followed by monkfish sauteed in Chardonnay (€23), ending in tiramisu ladyfingers (€5.50). Hope you remembered your wallet! Open nightly 5:30-10pm. ❹

Castro's, 10-11 Castle St. (☎48290). A painting of Fidel that graces the cheery walls of this little Cuban-Irish cafe proves that the owners have no hang-ups about dictatorship and Communism. Spicy tortilla wraps (with salad, €6) make for a welcome break from standard sandwich fare. Open M-Sa 9am-6pm. ❷

Fiddler's Creek, Rockwell Parade (☎41866). New and popular 'pubstaurant.' Dinners are pricey (veggie menu €11, meats €14-20), but a casual atmosphere prevails. Lunch noon-3pm; dinner served daily 6-9:30pm. Pub 21+. open daily noon-1am. ❹

Hy-Breasil, Bridge St. (☎61180), just over the river. Coffee for the caffeine-addicts (€2), fresh-squeezed juice for the more healthy (€2.50), and various sweet crepes for the blissfully indulgent (€2.95). Mmmmm. Open M-F 9am-6pm, Sa 10am-6pm. ❶

The Loft, Lord Edward St. (☎46770), across from the bus station. Mexican meals sizzle but don't come cheap at this oft-recommended spot; prepare to pay for your fajitas (chicken €15.30). Veggie options. Open nightly 6-10:30pm, Su lunch 12:30-4pm. ❸

Ho Wong, Market St. (☎45718). Centrally located, offering inexpensive Cantonese and Szechuan takeaway with an Irish flair. Mains €5-9. Open M-Th 5pm-12:30am, F-Sa 5pm-1:30am, Su 5pm-1am. ❷

Pepper Alley, Rockwood Parade (☎70720), along the river. Popular for its prices and location. Huge selection of sandwiches (€2.55-4.20)–you choose the toppings. Weekends offer more upscale Mexican dinners. Open M-W 8am-6pm, Th-Sa 8am-10pm. ❶

PUBS

Over 70 pubs crowd Sligo's main streets, filling the town with live music during the summer. Events and venues are listed in *The Sligo Champion* (€1.27). Many pubs post signs restricting their clientele to 21+, but you're really only stuck if you're under 18—those without proof won't be given the time of day.

Shoot the Crows, Grattan St. Owner Ronin holds court at this hippest destination for Sligo pint-seekers. Dark faery-folk dangle from the ceiling as weird skulls and crazy murals look on in amusement, though the welcoming atmosphere banishes any potential creepiness. No phone, so unnecessary ringing can't interrupt weekend revelry. Music Tu and Th 9:30pm.

McLaughlin's Bar, 9 Market St. (☎44209). A true musician's pub, where all manner of song may break out in an evening, from trad sessions to folky and/or grungy accoustics. Open M-W 4-11:30pm, Th-Sa 4pm-12:30am, Su 7am-11pm.

McLynn's, Old Market St. (☎60743). Three generations in the making, with the fourth up and coming, McLynn's is an excellent spot for weekend trad, with owner-cum-fiddler

Donal leading the music Th-Su. Lord of the Dance Michael Flatley's favorite pub. Open M-W 4-11:30pm, Th-Sa 4pm-12:30am, Su 7-11pm.

Hargadon Bros., O'Connell St. (☎70933). A pub worth spending the day in. Open fires, old Guinness bottles, and *poitín* jugs in a maze of dark and intimate nooks. Pints unfettered by modern audio-visual distractions; no music but for muffled sips and the clinking of glasses. Open M-W 10:30am-11:30pm, Th-Sa 10:30am-12:30am, Su 5-11pm.

Garavogue (☎40100), across the river from the footbridge. A modern pub combining a spacious 2-story wooden interior, a 20-something crowd, and palm trees beneath the skylights. Dress to impress. DJs Th and Sa. Open M-Sa 10:30am-midnight, Su 11:30am-11pm.

The Belfry, Thomas St. (☎62150), just off the bridge. Modern-medieval decor, with big bell and bigger chandelier. 2 floors, 3 bars, 30 Irish whiskeys—you do the math. Live bands F, DJ Sa. Open M-W 10:30am-11:30pm, Th-F 10:30am-12:30am, Sa 4pm-1am.

The Clarence Hotel, Wine St. An alternative for those tired of MTV remixes. DJs stay ahead of the game with cutting-edge sounds in the club and international jazz in the front bar. Not as big or popular as others, but draws a faithful and appreciative crowd (known to do some chandelier-swinging). Cover €4.50-8, with early birds catching discounts. Bar open Su-Th until 12:30am, F-Sa 'til late. Club Tu and Sa.

Equinox, Teeling St. (☎44721). A total renovation in Apr. 2002 has turned this into a modern, pulsating club. Navigate through its many dark bar rooms, dance in a central dance floor, or retreat to the bathrooms to watch music videos on flatscreen TVs (*Let's Go* is as bewildered as you are). 18+. Cover €5-10. Open W-M 11pm-2:30am.

Toff's, Kennedy Parade (☎62150), on the river behind the Belfry pub. A well-lit, crowded dance floor reveals that young local club-goers drink better than they dance. Th-Su Disco. 18+.Cover €7-10; €2 discount with card from the Belfry. Open 11pm-2:30am.

SIGHTS AND ACTIVITIES

In town you'll find the well-preserved and Yeats-free 13th-century **Sligo Abbey,** on Abbey St. The former Dominican Friary contains cloisters and ornate coupled pillars that, though old, can hardly be called ruined. Most of the walls and many of the ceilings are intact, meaning that you can spend an afternoon ducking in and out of various little rooms. Those who enjoy preaching to the (imaginary) choir can mount the stairs to the Reader's Desk to send forth their words of wisdom. (☎46406. Open Apr.-Oct. daily 10am-6pm; Nov.-Mar. call for weekend openings. Last admission 45min. before closing. Tours available on request. €1.90, students and children €0.70.) The 69 stained-glass windows of the 1874 **Cathedral of the Immaculate Conception** on John St. are best visited at dawn or dusk when the sun streams through. Farther down John St., the **Cathedral of St. John the Baptist,** built in 1730, has a tablet dedicated to Susan Mary, Yeats's mother. The fanciful **courthouse** on Teeling St. was built in 1878 on the site of its predecessor.

The Model Arts Centre and Niland Gallery, on the Mall, holds an impressive collection in an elegant and airy space. On wide, white walls hangs one of the country's—and thus, presumably, the world's—finest collections of modern Irish art, including a number of works by Jack Yeats, William's brother, and the contemporaneous Nora McGuinness and Michael Healy. The gallery also hosts frequent exhibitions of recent works. (☎41405. Open Tu-Sa 10am-5:30pm, and June-Oct. Su noon-5:30pm. Free.) The **Sligo County Museum** preserves small reminders of Yeats, including pictures of his funeral. The collection's highlights include first editions by the man himself, a few illustrated broadside collaborations between Papa Yeats and Baby Yeats, and Countess Markievicz's prison apron. (Open June-Sept. Tu-Sa 10:30am-12:30pm and 2:30-4:50pm; Oct.-May 10:30am-12:30pm. Free.) The **Sligo Art Gallery,** in the Y[ou-know-who]eats Memorial Building on Hyde Bridge, rotates innovative exhibits of contemporary Irish art with an annual exhibition on northwest Ireland in October. (☎45847. Open M-Sa 10am-5:30pm, except bank holidays.) Also in the **Yeats Memorial Building** is a small exhibit by The Yeats Society on their main man. Photos, writing snippets, and a brief history of Yeats are to one side; on the other runs a brief film coupling images of the nearby countryside with his poetic descriptions. (☎42693. Open daily 10am-4:30pm. Free.)

For a break from Yeats worshipping, head to the **Sligo Riding Centre** in Carrowmore, only 2 mi. from Sligo Town, offering horseback rides over the beaches and through the mountains. (☎61353. €18 per hr. Open daily 10am-10pm.) Swelter in the sauna or take a dip in the pool at the **Regional Sports Centre** (☎60539), near Doorly Park. Or dive in deeper with the **Sligo Sub Aqua Club.** (Contact Stuart Barker at ☎42241.) Dives normally take place Wednesday evenings and Sunday afternoons; a small donation is requested from visiting divers to offset costs.

ENTERTAINMENT

A monthly *Calendar of Events*, free from the tourist office, describes the festivals and goings-on in the northwestern Republic. **Hawk's Well Theatre,** on Temple St. beneath the tourist office, presents modern and traditional dramas, ballets, and musicals. (☎61526 or 61518. Box office open M-Sa 10am-6pm. Tickets €8-20, students and children €5-8.) The **Blue Raincoat Theatre Company,** Lower Quay St., is a traveling troupe that spends 16 weeks of each year performing "physical theatre" in its Quay St. factory space. (☎70431. Tickets for lunchtime performances €6.50, evening performances €10.) For more traditional fare, Hollywood style, try the **Gaiety Cinema Complex** on Wine St., which features seven screens of entertainment that is not trad. (☎74002; www.gaietysligo.com. Tickets €4.50-6.50, children €4-5.)

The ten-day **Sligo Arts Festival** (☎69802) takes place in early June and features music, art, theater, and children's events. During the first two weeks of August, the internationally-renowned **Yeats International Summer School** opens some of its poetry readings, lectures, and concerts to the public. International luminaries like Seamus Heaney are regular guests. (☎42693. 2002 fee was €450, not including housing. For an application, contact the Yeats Society, Yeats Memorial Building, Douglas Hyde Bridge. Office open M-F 9:30am-5:30pm.)

DAYTRIPS FROM SLIGO

Small brown quill and inkwell signs mark the **Yeats trail,** a driving route that hits most of the must-sees. **John Howe's** bus company (☎42747) runs coach tours from the tourist office through Yeats country (3½hr.) and to Lough Gill (3hr.). Call ahead to arrange times and prices. If aquatic exploration is your game, **Peter Henry's Blue Lagoon** will **rent boats.** (☎42530. Rowboat €30 full day, half-day €20; motorboat €60/€40.) The **Wild Rose Water-Bus** tours **Lough Gill** to the tune of Yeats' poetry, and includes a stop at **Parke's Castle.** (☎64266. June-Aug. 2 per day from the Blue Lagoon, a 10min. walk east from town along the Garavogue; 5 per day from Parke's Castle. €12, students €10, children €6. An additional lough cruise on F nights departs from Parke's Castle at 9pm.)

STRANDHILL PENINSULA, CARROWMORE, AND KNOCKNAREA

The turnoff to Carrowmore is on R292, which loops around the peninsula, about 1 mi. west of Sligo. To reach Carrowmore from town, follow the signs west from John St. ***Bus Éireann*** *departs from the Sligo bus station, bound for Strandhill and Carrowmore (M-F 7 per day, Sa 5 per day; €2.10).* ***Taxi Direct*** *(☎41444) services the peninsula; a taxi to Carrowmore costs €5.* ***Carrowmore Interpretive Centre*** *(☎61534) open May-Oct. daily 10am-6pm; last admission 5:15pm. Tours available. €1.90, students and children €0.70.*

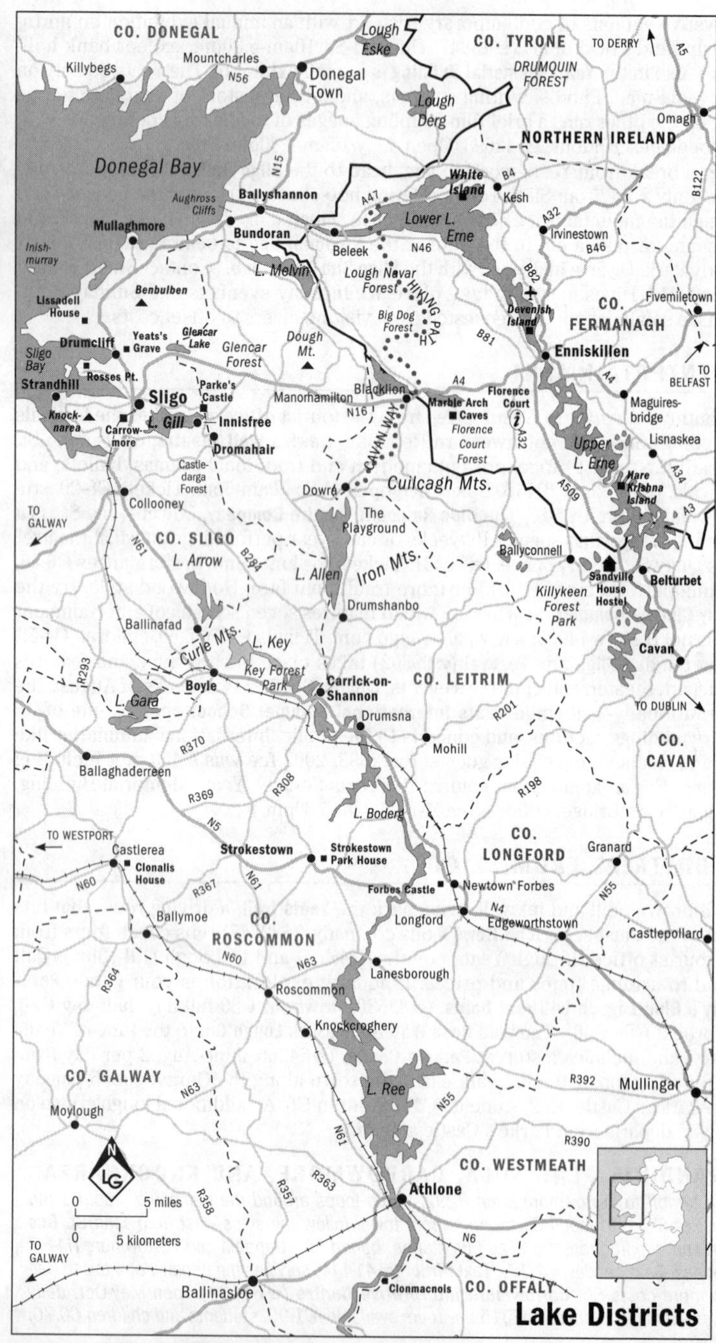

CO. DONEGAL
CO. TYRONE
DRUMQUIN FOREST
NORTHERN IRELAND
Donegal Bay
Lough Eske
Lough Derg
Donegal Town
Killybegs
Mountcharles
Omagh
Ballyshannon
Bundoran
Mullaghmore
Beleek
White Island
Kesh
Lower L. Erne
Irvinestown
L. Melvin
Lough Navar Forest
HIKING PATH
Big Dog Forest
Devenish Island
CO. FERMANAGH
Fivemiletown
Enniskillen
Benbulben
Lissadell House
Drumcliff
Yeats's Grave
Glencar Lake
Glencar Forest
Dough Mt.
Sligo Bay
Rosses Pt.
Strandhill
Sligo
Parke's Castle
Manorhamilton
Blacklion
Marble Arch Caves
Florence Court
Florence Court Forest
Maguiresbridge
Lisnaskea
TO BELFAST
Knocknarea
Carrowmore
L. Gill
Innisfree
Dromahair
Castledarga Forest
CAVAN WAY
Culcagh Mts.
Upper L. Erne
Hare Krishna Island
Collooney
Dowra
The Playground
TO GALWAY
CO. SLIGO
L. Arrow
L. Allen
Iron Mts.
Ballyconnell
Sandville House Hostel
Belturbet
Killykeen Forest Park
Drumshanbo
Ballinafad
Curlie Mts.
L. Key
Key Forest Park
Cavan
CO. LEITRIM
Boyle
Carrick-on-Shannon
L. Gara
Drumsna
Mohill
TO DUBLIN
CO. CAVAN
Ballaghaderreen
L. Boderg
CO. LONGFORD
TO WESTPORT
Castlerea
Clonalis House
Strokestown
Strokestown Park House
Granard
Forbes Castle
Newtown Forbes
Ballymoe
Longford
Edgeworthstown
CO. ROSCOMMON
Castlepollard
Lanesborough
Roscommon
Knockcroghery
CO. GALWAY
L. Ree
Mullingar
Moylough
CO. WESTMEATH
Athlone
0 5 miles
0 5 kilometers
TO GALWAY
Ballinasloe
Clonmacnois
CO. OFFALY
Lake Districts

Best known for its two miles of dunes, windy **Strandhill** ducks under the solemn Knocknarea Mountain at the southern edge of Sligo Bay. Surfing here is excellent for the wetsuited; swimming is dangerous for mere mortals. Hang ten with a 2hr. all-inclusive lesson from the optimistically named **Perfect Day Surf School.** (☎68464. Located right on the beach, by the bus stop. €25 per lesson, under 18 €15.) If you prefer your seaweed heated, indulge in a **Celtic Seaweed Bath,** the ideal cure for damp bones, sore feet, and aching backs. (☎68686. Open May-Oct. M-F 10am-9:30pm, Sa-Su 10am-8:30pm; Nov.-Apr. M-F 11am-9pm, Sa-Su 10am-6:30pm. 1hr. steam and bath €14; 2 sharing €20.) At low tide, a causeway connects the beach to **Coney Island,** but don't get stuck—there ain't no rollercoaster out there.

An assortment of passage graves spooks visitors at **Carrowmore,** 3 mi. southwest of Sligo. The site had over 100 tombs and stone circles before modern folks quarried and cleared many away, but it's still the largest megalithic cemetery in Ireland. About 30 of the 70 remaining tombs remain open to the public; some of these date as far back as 5400 BC. Ongoing excavation turns up one or two new formations each year. The small but interesting **Interpretive Center** does its best to explain their meaning based on the scant information available.

The 1078 ft. **Knocknarea** ("hill of the moon") perches above the southwestern shore of Sligo Bay. The 30min. climb to the summit rewards pilgrims with stunning views of misty bays, heathered hills, and the mighty Benbulben Mountain. Queen Mebdh (or Maeve), the villain of the *Táin bo Cuailnge* (see **Legends and Folktales,** p. 71), is reputedly interred in the 30 ft. high, 160 ft. wide **cairn** on the summit; she stands upright, facing her Ulsterside enemies. Sheep bleat mere yards away while layers of peat reluctantly give way underfoot. The **forested park** on Knocknarea's eastern slopes is criss-crossed by trails; there are several ways up, though on rainy days it's best to stick with the graveled paths, as it can get quite slick otherwise.

LOUGH GILL

The forested 24 mi. road around Lough Gill, just southeast of Sligo, runs past woody nature trails, Yeatsian haunts, a castle, and several small towns. It's flat enough to make a wonderful bike trip from Sligo, but be sure to get an early start. Take Pearse Rd. and turn left at the Lough Gill signs. The ***Wild Rose Water Bus*** *(see* ***Daytrips from Sligo,*** *above) is another popular way to tour the lough.* ***Parke's Castle*** *(☎64149) open mid-Mar. to Oct. daily 10am-6pm; last admission 5:15pm. 25min. tours available on request. €2.50, students and children €1.20, families €6.30.*

Beautiful Lough Gill, dotted with some 80 tiny islands, is bordered on one side by gnarled mountains, while thickly wooded hills cut through farmlands on the other—the striking outline of Benbulben Mountain, rising from beyond, completes the scene. Legend has it that the bell from Sligo Abbey is buried in its depths; only the chosen (or delusional) can hear it ring from below the waves.

The first stop on the round-lough route is **Holywell,** a leafy, flower-strewn shrine resting near a well and waterfall. During the Penal Law years, secret masses were held at this site; if the British military happened to approach, the congregation would disband and pretend to be enjoying a football game. The main road then reaches **Dooney Rock,** on the south shore of Lough Gill near Cottage Island. Here, Yeats's "Fiddler of Dooney" made "folk dance like a wave of the sea." Nature trails around the rock lead to views of **Innisfree,** a perfectly round island in the lake that the young Yeats wistfully wrote about from the hustle-bustle of 1893 London: "I will arise and go now, and go to Inisfree..."

The next town past the Inisfree turnoff is **Dromahair,** which still shelters the **Creevelea Friary.** Founded in 1508 as the Friary of Killanummery, its frying days ended in 1650 when Oliver Cromwell expelled the monks and confiscated their house. Since 1721, it has been used as a burial site. Dromahair is the farthest point on the route; from here, turn left onto R286 to head back to Sligo Town.

On the road back stands **Parke's Castle,** a recently renovated 17th-century manor house-cum-fortress. Built by Anglo Captain Robert Parke in 1609 to protect himself from dispossessed Irish landowners, the castle stands on the still-visible foundation of an earlier O'Rourke family stronghold. The remains of a moat are also still visible, though it was filled in long ago when the family could no longer endure the stench of the surrounding waste and excrement. Two miles from town, a left turn leads to **Hazelwood,** the park where Aengus wandered "among long dappled grass" in "The Song of Wandering Aengus." Its **sculpture trail** makes for an artistic ramble and excellent picnicking spot.

DRUMCLIFFE AND BENBULBEN: YEATS, YEATS, YEATS

Buses from Sligo to Derry stop at ***Drumcliffe.*** *(10min. Summer M-Sa 7per day, Su 3 per day; winter M-Sa 3 per day. Returns tougher, as it is a request-only stop–make sure to flag down the bus. €4 return.) Hitching is reportedly painless, but* Let's Go *does not recommend it. Glencar Lake is signposted about 1 mi. north of Drumcliffe on N15. The* ***Drumcliffe Church Visitors Centre*** *has given way to a more commercial enterprise: sandwiches and Guinness magnets replace tourist information, though a free pamplet is available.* ***Lissadell House*** *(☎63150) open June to mid-Sept. M-Sa 10:30am-1pm and 2-5pm; last tour 45min. before closing. €5, children €2.50. Grounds free.*

Yeats composed the epitaph that was to be placed on his gravestone a year before his 1939 death in France; "Under Bare Ben Bulben's head/ In Drumcliffe churchyard Yeats is laid.../ By his command these words are cut:/ Cast a cold eye/ On life, on death/ Horseman pass by!" Georgia, his wife, didn't get around to carrying out his dying wish (to be buried in France, disinterred a year later, and then buried next to Benbulben) until nine years later, which is sort of creepy, but not nearly so creepy as the dying wish itself. (Another creepy funfact: When the two married, he was a venerable 52 years, while she was an innocent 15.) The road Yeats refers to is now N15, where noisy trucks and motorcycles pass by daily; his grave is in **Drumcliffe's** churchyard, 4 mi. northwest of Sligo, just to the left of the church door. In response to yet another of Yeats's dying requests—My final resting station/ should be near film animation—the church also projects an informative animated feature on Drumcliffe's pre-Yeatsian significance as a 6th-century Christian site, of which the **ancient cross** and **round tower** across N15 are remnants (☎63125; call ahead for film). A few miles northeast of Drumcliffe, **Glencar Lake** and its majestic **waterfall,** mentioned in Yeats's "The Stolen Child," provide a venue for further excursions.

Farther north of Drumcliffe, **Benbulben Mountain,** rich in mythical associations, protrudes from the landscape like the keel of a foundered boat. St. Colmcille founded a monastery on the peak in AD 547, and it continued to be a major religious center until the 16th century. The 1729 ft. climb is inevitably windy, and the summit can be extremely gusty. If you can keep from being blown away, standing at the 5000 ft. drop at the mountain's edge can be a humbling and beautiful experience. (*Let's Go* does not recommend the overzealous pursuit of humbling experiences.) Signs on Drumcliffe road guide travelers to Benbulben; for detailed directions to the trails, ask at the Drumcliffe gas station.

Eva Gore-Booth and her sister Constance Markievicz entertained Yeats and his friends 4 mi. northwest of Drumcliffe at **Lissadell House.** (Countess Connie was the first woman elected to the *Dáil* and was second in command for the Easter Rising; see p. 61.) The house's current restoration reflects an attempt to return the house to the grandeur of those heady times. Former man of the manor Henry Gore-Booth was an avid hunter, but the real trophy on display—a formerly ferocious and quite dead brown bear—was actually shot by the butler. To reach the house from Drumcliffe road, take the first left after Yeats Tavern Hostel and follow the signs.

COUNTIES ROSCOMMON AND LEITRIM

Rivers and lakes (and a significant number of fast-moving highways) meander through the untouristed counties of Roscommon and Leitrim, which span a diamond-shaped area between Sligo and Centre O'Ireland. Carrick-on-Shannon teems with pubs but nevertheless manages to remain relaxed, while Boyle is an excellent festival hostess with a soaring abbey. Motor vehicle is the *modus transportis* of choice in this region. Because of traffic that is predominantly fly-by and non-local, Roscommon and Leitrim don't always make for easy hitching. **Parke's Castle, Dromahair,** and **Crevelea Abbey** are in Co. Leitrim, but are covered in Sligo (see p. 385).

CARRICK-ON-SHANNON (CORA DROMA RÚISC) ☎078

Coursing slowly through the green hills of Leitrim on its way to the sea, the Shannon River pauses when it reaches the rows of white yachts moored at Carrick-on-Shannon's marina. Life is low-key here in this proud seat of Ireland's least populous county—anglers fish for pike during the day, and in the evening merry drinkers fill the pubs with song. The town's few sights won't sustain an energetic visitor, but the parks and lakes nearby make good daytrips. A bridge spans over the Shannon and into town from Co. Roscommon, leading to the clock tower and Main St.

TRANSPORTATION AND PRACTICAL INFORMATION. Elphin Road Station (☎20036) is a 10min. walk southwest of town. **Trains** leave from here for Dublin (2¼hr., 3-4 per day, €16) and Sligo (1hr., 3-4 per day, €10.10). **Buses** (☎071 60066) leave from Coffey's Pastry Case for: Boyle (12min., 3-4 per day, €4.20); Dublin (3hr., 3-4 per day, €10.35); and Sligo (1hr., 3-4 per day, €8.70). For a **taxi,** call **P. Burke,** on Bridge St. (☎088 256 1311). **Geraghty's** on Main St. **rents bikes.** (☎21316. Open daily 9:30am-7pm. Weekly rentals only. €30 per wk.) The amazingly friendly and accommodating staff at the **tourist office,** on the Marina, will help you with everything you need, and probably more. (☎20170. Open June-Aug. M-Sa 9am-6pm, Su 10am-2pm; Apr.-May and Sept. M-F 9am-1pm and 2-5pm. Contact Northwestern Tourism in Sligo the rest of the year at ☎071 61201.) The **AIB** bank on Main St. has an **ATM.** (☎20055. Open M 10am-5pm, Tu and Th-F 10am-4pm, W 10:30am-4pm.)Also on Bridge St. are **Cox's pharmacy** (☎20158; open M-Th 9:30am-6pm, F-Sa 9:30am-6:30pm) and **Gartlan's Cyber Cafe,** where you can access the **Internet.** (☎21735. €6 per hr. Open M-Sa 9:30am-5:30pm.) The **post office** is on St. George's Terr. (☎20020. Open M-Sa 9am-5:30pm.)

ACCOMMODATIONS, FOOD, AND PUBS. Campers can pitch their tents by the riverbank for free, but the **Lough Key Campground ❶**, 4 mi. northwest of town on the road to the lake, is a more enticing option with clean facilities and piping hot showers. (☎079 62212. €12 per tent, €14 for vehicles.) **An Óige Hostel ❷**, Bridge St., is sparklingly tidy, despite its location above a veterinary clinic. The cleanliness may be due in part to the shortage of dorm-dirtying backpackers in these parts. Weekdays see little traffic, though the hostel is often booked with groups and rowers on weekends. (☎21848. Dorms €15.) **The Four Seasons B&B ❸**, on Main St. in the hub of town, is large and conveniently located, offering big rooms, all with bath. (☎21333. €30 per person.) Other B&Bs line the Dublin road, Station Rd., and the manicured lawns of St. Mary's Close.

Cheap dinners are hard to come by in this town; **Londi's Supermarket,** Bridge St., is a good place to stock up on raw materials. (Open M-Sa 8am-10pm, Su 8am-8pm.) The popular **Chung's Chinese Restaurant ❷** on Main St. cooks up a storm. Book dinner well in advance to avoid long waits, or save big by ordering takeaway. (☎21888. Takeaway around €7.60; sit-down €10. Open daily 6-11pm.) An intimate eatery serving up some of the best Italian in town, **La Belle Vita ❸,** Main St., offers pizza, pasta, and various meat and fish dishes. (☎20333. Most pastas €8.50; meat or fish around €15. Open Tu-Su noon-3pm and 5-10:30pm.) **Coffey's Pastry Case ❶** on Bridge St. serves up sandwiches (€3) and sit-downs, but the wealth of pastries—served with a dollop of rich cream—truly require a taste; the meringues (€1) are lighter than air. (☎20929. Open M-Sa 8:30am-7:30pm, Su 9:30am-7pm.)

The Anchorage, on Bridge St., is the town's most popular and venerable pub, offering a traditional feel and a mixed crowd. (☎20416. Open Su-W noon-11:30pm, Th-Sa noon-12:30am.) Just across the town bridge, the glorious, grassy beer garden at **Ging's** entices tourists to sit and relax with a glass. (☎21054. Open Su-W 1-11:30pm, Th-Sa 1pm-12:30am.) Carrick's nearest nightclub, **Rockin' Robbins,** 1 mi. from the town center, pulls in 21+ partiers from the whole of the county. Minibuses (€2) leave from The Anchorage on weekends. (Open F-Su. Cover €5-9.)

SIGHTS AND ACTIVITIES. At the intersection of Main St. and Bridge St., teeny tiny **Costello Memorial Chapel** is, at 16x12 ft., reputedly the second-smallest church in the world, though no one in town seems to know what it's second to. Edward Costello had the chapel built as a monument to his wife after she died in 1877; the coffins of the loving couple are on display beneath fogged plexiglass on either side of the aisle. The **Angling and Tourism Association** (☎20489) gives the line on rentals, sights, and fishing-oriented associations. To really go native, head to the 12,000-seat **football pitch** just outside town on a Sunday afternoon and watch Leitrim battle other counties in Gaelic football. (Tickets €20, students €8; pay at the field.) Pick up the *Leitrim Observer* at any newsagent for other local listings.

Four miles northwest of Carrick-on-Shannon on the road to Boyle, the 850 acres and 33 forested islands of **Lough Key Forest Park** burst with rhododendrons in spring, but are worth exploring at any time of year. The park was once the center of the **Rockingham Estate,** which covered most of the surrounding area. The estate's classical mansion burned down in 1957, though the less impressive stables, church, and icehouse were spared the wrath. Numerous signposts won't let you miss the **round tower, faery bridge,** and **wishing chair,** all of which are on the Green Walk. (☎079 62363. Map and brochure available from the Carrick-on-Shannon tourist office. Park always open. Admission €2.55 per car 10am-6pm.) **Lough Key** and the diminutive castle-topped **Castle Island** just offshore can be explored in group fashion on a **Lough Key Boat Tour** (☎20252). The same company also rents boats to those who prefer to chart their own routes. Also nearby is the **Lough Key Campground** (see **Accommodations,** above). North of the lough lies the site of Ireland's most important pre-human battle, in which the Túatha De Danann defeated Ireland's indigenous demons, the Formorians (see **Legends and Folktales,** p. 71).

DAYTRIP FROM CARRICK-ON-SHANNON: STROKESTOWN

Strokestown is 15 mi. south of Carrick-on-Shannon, where R368 meets N5 from Longford. ***Strokestown Park House*** *rises above Strokestown's Main St. ☎33013. Open Mar.-Oct. daily 10am-5:30pm, Dec.-Feb. by previous arrangement. House accessible by guided* *tour. House, garden, or Famine Museum each €5, students €3.80, children €2; combination of any two €8.50/€7/€4; all three €12/€10/€5.20.*

This Palladian-style house was designed in the 18th century by Richard Cassells, the architect of Dublin's Leinster House, as a gentleman's country home for the prestigious Mahon family. The Mahon family and their descendants lived here until 1979, and the house has hardly changed since the turn of the century. The upstairs **playroom** houses an eerie collection of toys of the pre-Playstation variety; pedal-powered play cars and a tea set with dolls arranged to partake are reminders of childhoods past. Outside, the recently restored **Pleasure Garden** features the longest herbacious border in Ireland, which is abloom with vibrant colors during the summer months. **The Famine Museum,** in the old stables next to the house, tells the plight of the former plantation laborers, presenting a stark contrast to the wealth and privilege of the house. When the Famine hit Strokestown, Major Denis Mahon evicted over 3000 of the workers, who ended up emigrating on what became known as the "coffin ships." By 1847, the remaining tenants, having had enough of Mahon's downsizing, killed the Major with the gun that is on display in the museum. The detailed exhibit explores the history of the Potato Famine as well as its connection with present-day social problems elsewhere in the world.

BOYLE (MAINISTIR NA BÚILLE) ☎079

Settled on a river and squeezed between two lakes, hilly Boyle was once used by clans and troops as a strategic base of operations. The present-day town was founded as a strategic base of the capitalist, rather than militant, variety, as enterprising shopkeepers hoped to take advantage of its convenient location and the lure of its well-preserved **Boyle Abbey** and **King House.** The modern explorer would do well to follow their example—Boyle contains numerous interesting historical sights and offers convenient access to nearby mountains, lakes, and parks.

TRANSPORTATION AND PRACTICAL INFORMATION. Trains (☎62027) run from Boyle to Dublin (3hr., 3-4 per day, €15.80) and Sligo (30min., 3-4 per day, €6.30). **Buses** stop outside the Royal Hotel on Bridge St. and also run to Dublin (3½hr., 3-4 per day, €12) and Sligo (30min., 3-4 per day, €7.35). **Bikes** are yours for the renting at **Riverside Cycle,** on Riverside. (Open M-Tu and Th-Sa 10am-1pm and 2-6pm. €10 per day, lock included.) Boyle's **tourist office,** inside the gates of King House on Main St., will book accommodations and provide pamplets, but is not authorized to do much else. (☎62145. Open May-Sept. daily 10am-1pm and 2-6pm.) **National Irish Bank,** at the intersection of Bridge St. and Patrick St., has an **ATM.** (☎62058. Open M 10am-5pm, Tu-F 10am-4pm; closed 12:30-1:30pm.) **Ryan's pharmacy** is at the intersection of Patrick St. and Main St. (☎62003. Open M-Sa 9am-6pm.) For **Internet access,** surf down to the **Boyle Library,** in King House. (See **Sights,** below. ☎62800. "Free" with €3.80 membership fee. Open Tu and Th 1-8pm, W and F-Sa 10am-1pm and 2-5pm.) The **post office** is on the Carrick road. (☎62029. Open M and W-F 9am-5:30pm, Tu 9:30am-5:30pm, Sa 9am-1pm and 2-5:30pm.)

ACCOMMODATIONS, FOOD, AND PUBS. The nearest budget digs are found at the hostel in Carrick-on-Shannon (see p. 395). More lavish beds, however, abound in Boyle's B&Bs. Every visitor to the 170-year-old **Abbey House ❸,** on Abbeytown Rd., is housed in an elegant, antique-laden room. The sitting areas are spacious and have views of an authentic, dyed-in-the-wool babbling brook, while some of the rooms look onto Boyle Abbey next door. Self-catering family cottages for four are also available. (☎62385. All rooms with bath. €28 per person; cottage prices available on request.) Cheery **Cesh Corran ❸,** across from the abbey (see

Sights, below), welcomes visitors with a turquoise hallway. The rooms are equally bright and vibrant and come stacked with hair dryers and chocolates, in addition to the usual amenities. (☎62247. Singles €35; shared rooms €30 per person.)

Londi's Supermarket, Bridge St., is the place to stock up on sundries. (☎62112. Open M-F 8am-8pm, Sa 8am-7pm, and Su 8am-2pm.) The **Stone House Cafe ❶,** on Bridge St., is an old stone tower gone intimate cafe. (☎64861. Veggie options daily. Sandwiches from €2. Open M-F 9am-6pm, Sa 10am-6pm.) **King House Restaurant ❷,** within the gates of King House (see **Sights,** below), offers breakfasts (€5) and lunches (€6) both tasty and convenient. (☎64805. Open daily 9am-6pm.) An excellent view of the river accompanies the Asian-Irish meals of **Chung's Restaurant ❸** at the Royal Hotel on Bridge St. (☎62390. Dinners €9-18.) For perfect pints and rousing trad, everyone heads to **Kate Lavin's** on Patrick St. (☎62855).

SIGHTS AND ENTERTAINMENT. At the bottom of Main St.'s hill, gothic arches curve over the green lawns of magnificent **Boyle Abbey.** Although the Abbey was built by Cistercian monks, its impressive high arches and intricate Celtic carvings suggest the monks were not as strict with their building guidelines as they were with their prayer schedule. (☎62604. Open Apr.-Oct. daily 10am-6pm. Tours every hour. €1.20. Key available from Mrs. Mitchell at the Abbey House B&B.) In the early 1990s, the Roscommon Council voted to raze **King House,** Main St., to make room for a carpark. Luckily for visitors, the pavement-happy were thwarted by the building's sturdy architectural base—and so it remains, a tribute to its own history. Built by Sir Henry King circa 1730 to impress his young bride, the Georgian mansion has served as a family home for 40 years and army barracks for 140 years. Within the mansion is the **Boyle Civic Art Collection,** which houses contemporary Irish sculpture and paintings. (☎63242. Open Apr.-Sept. daily 10am-6pm; last admission 5pm. €4.) **Frybrook House,** a 5min. walk from the bridge, was built in 1752 and restored to shininess in 1994. Although it is now a family home, most of the house's furniture is Georgian or Victorian. (☎63513. Appointment only.)

July is a busy time for Boyle. Early in the month, visitors can enroll in crash courses in everything from the button accordion to the tin whistle at the **Dr. Douglas Hyde Summer School of Traditional Irish Music and Dance** in nearby Ballaghaderreen. (Contact Paddy McGray ☎086 850 8605; www.ballaghaderreen.com. €55, under 18 €40.) The month's final week rings in the **Boyle Arts Festival,** and with it, a series of recitals, workshops, and exhibitions that render art aficionados delirious. (☎63085 or 64069; www.boylearts.com. Most tickets €3-5.)

NORTHWEST IRELAND

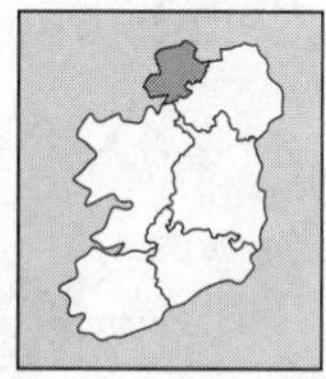

Northwest Ireland is comprised entirely by Co. Donegal. Among Ireland's counties, Donegal (DUN-ee-gahl) is second to Cork in size and second to none in glorious wilderness. The landscape here offers a sharp contrast to that of Southern Ireland, replacing lush, smooth hillsides with jagged rock and bald, windy cliffs. Cottage industries, fishing boats, and tweed factories occupy the locals' time by day, while a pure form of trad keeps them packed in the pubs at night. Donegal's *gaeltacht* is a storehouse of genuine, unadulterated Irish tradition, left largely untouched by the Irish tourist machine; be assured that you'll encounter fewer camera-toting tourists here than anywhere else in the country. In its 13th year, the Earagail Arts Festival in Co. Donegal (☎074 29186; www.donegalculture.com) still manages to distinguish itself from other arts festivals in Ireland in its scope and its remarkable selection of artists, musicians, and performers. Hitchhikers report that drivers in Donegal provide the most rides in all of Ireland. Easy or hard, *Let's Go* does not recommend hitchhiking.

COUNTY DONEGAL

Although its name means "fort of the foreigner," visitors are still likely to feel out of place in this most remote and least Anglicized of Ireland's "scenic" provinces. Donegal escaped Ireland's widespread deforestation; vast wooded areas engulf many of Donegal's mountain chains, while the coastline alternates beautiful beaches with craggy cliffs; the tallest sea-cliffs in Europe are near Slieve League. The remote Inishowen Peninsula provides excellent coastal driving and cycling. And, in between its larger pockets of civilization, distance from all things English has preserved the biggest *gaeltacht* in Ireland.

TRANSPORTATION

Donegal has the public transportation to get you where you want to go, but only if you're willing to wait. There is no **train** service in the county, and **buses** tend to hit smaller towns only once or twice per day, often in the early morning or late at night. Only major towns like Letterkenny, Donegal Town, and Dungloe—and a select few smaller towns—**rent bikes.** Hitchers report short waits and friendly drivers on major roads, particularly those north of Donegal Town, although some risk is always involved in hitching. Byways are largely devoid of drivers.

When you hop on a bus, ask if student, child, or senior fares are available. **Bus Éireann** (Dublin ☎01 836 6111; Letterkenny ☎074 21309; Sligo ☎071 60066; Strabane ☎074 31008; www.buseireann.ie) connects Donegal Town with Dublin (4¼hr., 5 per day) and Galway (4hr.), and Letterkenny to Galway (4¾hr.; M-Sa 5 per day, Su 3 per day) and Donegal Town (4hr.), and some of the smaller villages in the southern half of the region. Private buses take the place of Bus Éireann for most of the major routes in Donegal. Their prices are reasonable and their drivers more open to persuasion if you're looking to be let off on the doorstep of a

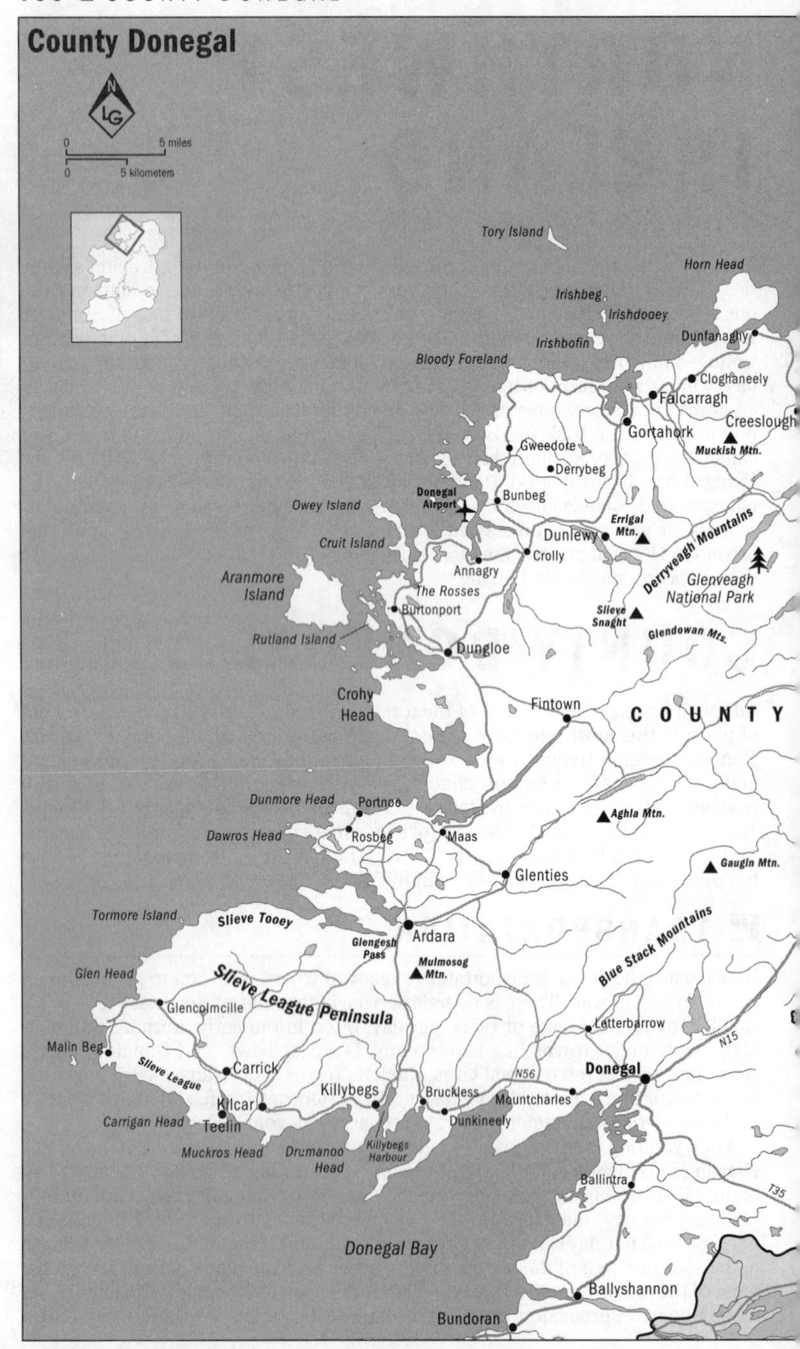
County Donegal
N
LG
0 5 miles
0 5 kilometers
Tory Island
Horn Head
Irishbeg
Irishdooey
Irishbofin
Dunfanaghy
Bloody Foreland
Cloghaneely
Falcarragh
Creeslough
Gortahork
Muckish Mtn.
Gweedore
Derrybeg
Donegal Airport
Bunbeg
Owey Island
Errigal Mtn.
Dunlewy
Derryveagh Mountains
Cruit Island
Crolly
Annagry
Aranmore Island
The Rosses
Glenveagh National Park
Burtonport
Slieve Snaght
Glendowan Mts.
Rutland Island
Dungloe
Crohy Head
Fintown
COUNTY
Dunmore Head
Portnoo
Aghla Mtn.
Dawros Head
Rosbeg
Maas
Gaugin Mtn.
Glenties
Tormore Island
Slieve Tooey
Blue Stack Mountains
Ardara
Glengesh Pass
Mulmosog Mtn.
Glen Head
Slieve League Peninsula
Glencolmcille
Letterbarrow
N15
Malin Beg
Slieve League
Carrick
N56
Donegal
Killybegs
Bruckless
Mountcharles
Kilcar
Carrigan Head
Teelin
Dunkineely
Muckros Head
Drumanoo Head
Killybegs Harbour
Ballintra
T35
Donegal Bay
Ballyshannon
Bundoran

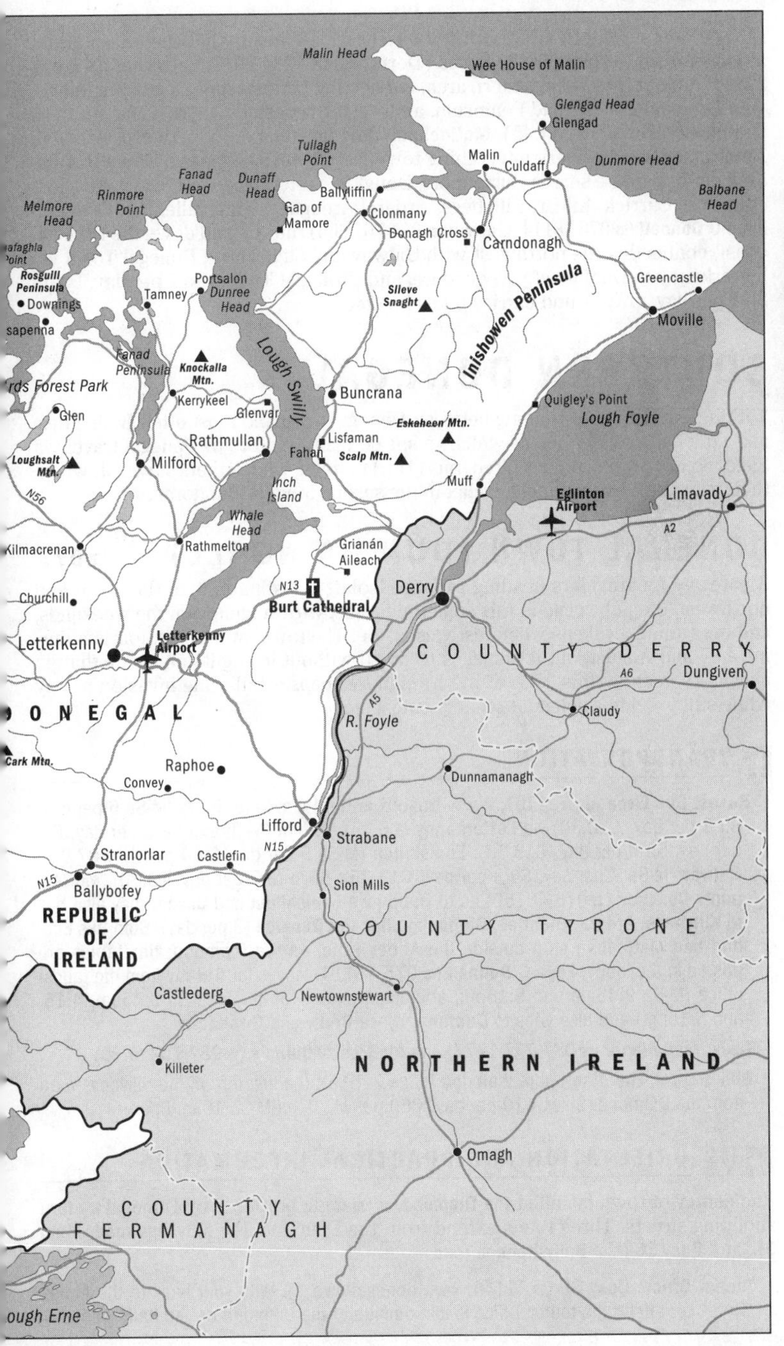

Malin Head
Wee House of Malin
Glengad Head
Glengad
Tullagh Point
Malin
Culdaff
Dunmore Head
Fanad Head
Dunaff Head
Ballyliffin
Balbane Head
Rinmore Point
Melmore Head
Gap of Mamore
Clonmany
Donagh Cross
Carndonagh
Rosguill Peninsula
Downings
Portsalon
Tamney
Dunree Head
Slieve Snaght
Inishowen Peninsula
Greencastle
Moville
Fanad Peninsula
Knockalla Mtn.
Lough Swilly
Buncrana
Kerrykeel
Glenvar
Quigley's Point
Lough Foyle
Glen
Rathmullan
Lisfaman
Eskaheen Mtn.
Fahan
Scalp Mtn.
Loughsalt Mtn.
Milford
Muff
N56
Inch Island
Whale Head
Eglinton Airport
Limavady
A2
Kilmacrenan
Rathmelton
Grianán Aileach
N13
Derry
Churchill
Burt Cathedral
Letterkenny
Letterkenny Airport
COUNTY DERRY
Dungiven
A6
A5
DONEGAL
R. Foyle
Claudy
Cark Mtn.
Raphoe
Convey
Dunnamanagh
Lifford
Strabane
N15
Stranorlar
Castlefin
N15
Ballybofey
Sion Mills
REPUBLIC OF IRELAND
COUNTY TYRONE
Castlederg
Newtownstewart
Killeter
NORTHERN IRELAND
Omagh
COUNTY FERMANAGH
Lough Erne

remote hostel. The flexibility of their routes also means that the buses aren't always on time. **Lough Swilly Buses** (Derry ☎028 7126 2017; Letterkenny ☎074 22863) fan out over the northern area, connecting Letterkenny, Derry, the Inishowen Peninsula, the Fanad Peninsula, and western coastal villages as far south as Dungloe (fares €5.85-11.45). **McGeehan's Bus Co.** runs daily between Donegal, Dublin, and almost every intervening town. (☎075 46150. Donegal Town to Dublin 2 per day; route serves Burtonport, Dungloe, Lettermacaward, Glenties, Glencolmcille, Carrick, Kilcar, Killybegs, Ardara, Ardaghey, Enniskillen, and Cavan.) **Feda O'Donnell** (☎075 48114; Galway ☎091 761 656) runs up and down the Donegal coast, connecting the northwest with Galway and Sligo (from Donegal Town via Letterkenny to Dunfanaghy, Gweedore, and Crolly; M-Th and Sa 2 per day, F and Su 3 per day; €7.60), and carries bikes for free.

SOUTHERN DONEGAL

With infrequent buses running between Donegal town and most other Irish cities, and no local train service of which to speak, many visitors to Donegal travel via Sligo. Some travelers take a direct bus (1hr.) to town, while others slow it down on their way north by stopping to relax in the surfing town of Bundoran.

DONEGAL TOWN (DÚN NA NGALL) ☎073

A gateway for travelers heading to more isolated destinations to the north and northwest, the pub scene in this sometimes sleepy town ignites on the weekends, and everything awakens when festivals arrive. The town swells with tourism during July and August, but it manages to do so without losing its unique, lethargic charm—somehow this "fort of the foreigner" keeps a full-scale invasion at bay while still providing splendid scenery, and a smile.

TRANSPORTATION

Buses: Bus Éireann (☎21101; www.buseireann.ie) leaves to: **Derry** (M-Sa 6 per day, Su 3 per day; €10.30) via **Letterkenny** (€6.35); **Dublin** (M-Th and Sa 5 per day, F 7 per day, Su 6 per day; €13.35); **Enniskillen** (M-Sa 5 per day, Su 4 per day; €7.90); **Galway** (M-Sa 4 per day, Su 3 per day; €13.35); **Sligo** (3-7 per day, €9.80). **McGeehan's Coaches** (☎075 46150) go to **Dublin** via **Enniskillen** and **Cavan;** they also bus to **Killybegs, Ardara, Glenties, Glencolmcille,** and **Dungloe** (3 per day). Both Bus Éireann and McGeehan stop outside the Abbey Hotel on the Diamond; timetables are posted in the lobby. **Feda O'Donnell** (☎075 48114) leaves for **Galway** from the tourist office (M-Sa 9:45am and 5:15pm; additional times F at 1:15pm, Su 9:45am, 4:15, and 8:15pm) and also goes to **Dunfanaghy** via **Crolly** and **Gweedore.**

Taxis: McCallister (☎087 277 1777) and **McBrearty Quinn's** (☎087 762 0670).

Bike Rental: The Bike Shop, Waterloo Pl. (☎22515), the first left off the Killybegs road from the Diamond. Bikes €10 per day, €60 per wk. Open M-Sa 10am-6pm.

ORIENTATION AND PRACTICAL INFORMATION

The center of town is called **the Diamond,** a triangle bordered by Donegal's main shopping streets. Three roads extend from the Diamond: the **Killybegs road, Main St.,** and **Quay St.** (the **Ballyshannon road**).

Tourist Office: Quay St. (☎21148; www.donegaltown.ie). With your back to the Abbey Hotel, turn right; the tourist office is just outside of the Diamond on the Ballyshannon/

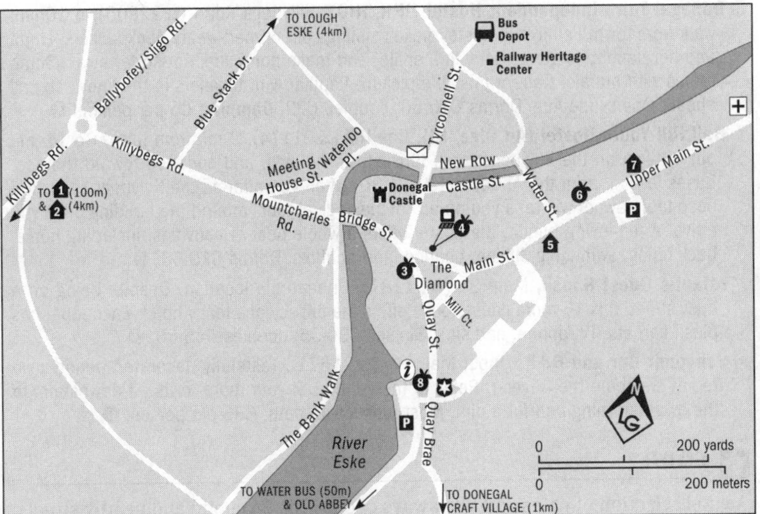

Donegal Town

ACCOMMODATIONS
- Atlantic Guest House, **5**
- Ball Hill Youth Hostel, **2**
- Donegal Town Independent Hostel, **1**
- The Schooner Bar and B&B, **7**

FOOD
- The Blueberry Tea Room, **4**
- Coffee House & Deli Bar, **3**
- Dom Breslin's Restaurant, **8**
- Donegal's Famous Chipper, **6**

Sligo road, next to the quay. Brochures galore on Co. Donegal, a free town map, and reservations for accommodations throughout the Republic. There are few tourist offices in the county; it's wise to stop here before heading north. Open July-Aug. M-Sa 9am-6pm, Su noon-4pm; Sept.-Oct. and Easter-June M-F 9am-5pm, Sa 10am-2pm.

Banks: In the Diamond you'll find an **AIB** (☎21016), **Bank of Ireland** (☎21079), and **Ulster Bank** (☎21064); each with 24hr. **ATMs.** All open M-F 10am-4pm, Th until 5pm.

Laundry: Dermó's Launderette & Dry Cleaning, Millcourt Suite 8, the Diamond (☎22255). Large wash and dry €13, shared load €10. Open M-Sa 9am-7pm.

Pharmacy: Begley's Chemist, the Diamond (☎21232). 1hr. photo processing. Open M-Sa 9:15am-6pm.

Emergency: ☎999; no coins required. **Police** *(Garda)*: ☎21021.

Hospital: Donegal Hospital, Main St. (☎21019).

Internet Access: The Blueberry Tea Room has a cyber-cafe on its 2nd floor (see **Food,** below). €3.50 per 30min. €6 per hr. Open M-Sa 9am-7pm.

Post Office: Tyrconnell St. (☎21007), past Donegal Castle and over the bridge. Open M-Sa 9am-5:30pm.

ACCOMMODATIONS AND CAMPING

Donegal Town has some of the most welcoming hostels in the country. If you're looking for the full fry in the morning, the tourist office will provide you with a list of B&B options. During the high season, beds are in demand, so plan and call ahead. Of course, you will probably want to book extra nights when you get there.

Donegal Town Independent Hostel (IHH/IHO), Killybegs Road (☎22805), a 10min. walk from town. Family-run hostel makes siblings out of road-weary backpackers. Linda and her daughters greet you with a smile, and make home feel not so far away. Some rooms with murals. Call for possible pickup. Popular with travelers in the know, so call ahead. Open June-Aug. Dorms €10.50; doubles €22. **Camping** €6 per person. ❶

Ball Hill Youth Hostel (An Óige/HI), Ball Hill (☎21174), 3 mi. from town. Go 1½ mi. out of town on the Killybegs road, turn left at the sign, and continue toward the sea. Buses leaving from the Abbey Hotel (€1.30) often go as far as the Killybegs road. The hospitable owner will take you on an "archaelogical tour" around the building once you arrive. A fun-loving bunch, the hostel offers a whole host of activities, including horse-back riding, swimming, hiking, boating, and bonfires. Dorms €10.50. ❶

Atlantic Guest House, Main St. (☎21187). Unbeatable location. Despite being on a busy street, this 16-room guest house offers the privacy of a fancy hotel. Each room has plush carpets, TV, phone, and sink. Singles €30-35; doubles €45-60. ❸

Schooner Bar and B&B, Upper Main St. (☎21671). Tastefully decorated period-style rooms welcome the traveler. Relax in the comfort of your room, or head downstairs to the award-winning pub for a pint. Most rooms with bath. €35 per person. ❸

FOOD

A good selection of cafes and takeaways occupy the Diamond and nearby streets. For groceries, head to the **SuperValu,** minutes from the Diamond down the Sligo road. (☎22977. Open M-W and Sa 9am-7pm, Th-F 9am-9pm, Su 10am-6pm.) **Simple Simon's,** the Diamond, sells fresh baked goods, local cheeses, and homeopathic remedies for the hippie in you. (☎22687. Open M-Sa 9:30am-6pm.)

The Blueberry Tea Room, Castle St. (☎22933), on the corner of the Diamond that leads to the Killybegs road. Justifiably popular, with food that could be described as home-cooked if your mother knew how to cook. Sandwiches, daily specials, and all-day breakfast. Mains around €6.50. Open M-Sa 9am-7pm. Houses a cyber-cafe upstairs. ❷

Dom Breslin's Restaurant and Bar, Quay St. (☎22719), next to the Tourist Office. Decorated with sailing memorabilia—you'll receive your food from "The Galley," but don't feel bad if you're in the "Third Class" or "Steerage" section, your meal will be first class all the same. Specializes in steaks (€12-19) and seafood (€13-17). Lunch 12:30-4pm; dinner and a la carte from 4-9:30pm. Trad nightly July-Aug. and Sept.-June F-Sa. Nightclub open July-Aug. W and Sa. ❹

Donegal's Famous Chipper, Main St. (☎21428). The quintessential takeaway. Any guess as to what's on the menu? Around €3.95 for the day's catch, plus any kind of potatoes you want (as long as it's chips). Open M-Tu and Th-Su 4:30-11:30pm. ❶

The Coffee House and Deli Bar, the Diamond (☎21014), attached to the Abbey Hotel. Try a sandwich (€2.55-3.20) or the satisfying 2-course "Plate of the Day" with veggies and potatoes (€6.35). Open 9am-5:30pm. ❷

PUBS AND CLUBS

Donegal's pubs are well-equipped to deal with a town's worth of thirsty visitors. To guide you through its 'limited' collection, we present you with the **Donegal Town Pub Crawl.** If it's on the map, you'll want to be there.

The Schooner Bar and B&B, Upper Main St. (☎21671). A great mix of hostelers and locals gather in this lantern- and candlelit James Joyce Award-winning pub. The best trad and contemporary sessions in town take place here on weekends from June-Aug. Sa nights summon trendy DJs.

The Olde Castle Bar and Restaurant, Castle St. (☎21062). Stone walls and corbel windows, for that recently-renovated medieval feel. The atmosphere is low-key; this is the place to have a soulful conversation with that lad or lass you've been eyeing. Bar food noon-3pm. Open June-Aug. M-Th 'til 11:30pm, F-Su 'til 12:30am; Sept.-May 'til 11pm.

Charlie's Star Bar, Main St. (☎21158). Well-lit and spacious. Sip your Guinness around the huge horse-shoe shaped bar. Folks gather here for GAA games and for ballads.

McGroarty's, the Diamond (☎21049). The biggest bar in town packs in a well-mannered crew of locals and tourists for blues and ballads on the weekend. Food M-F noon-4pm.

The Voyage Bar, the Diamond (☎21201). This pub keeps its patrons happy, but ask the jovial proprietor about its name and a tear glints in his eye: "Everyone has a voyage to make in life." Younger crowd. Rock music on weekends.

The Coach House, Upper Main St. (☎22855). Spontaneous sing-alongs are known to break out at any time of day in this wood-beamed local hangout. Downstairs, the **Cellar Bar** opens its doors nightly at 9:15pm for trad and ballads. Confident musicians and singers are encouraged to join in. Cover €2.

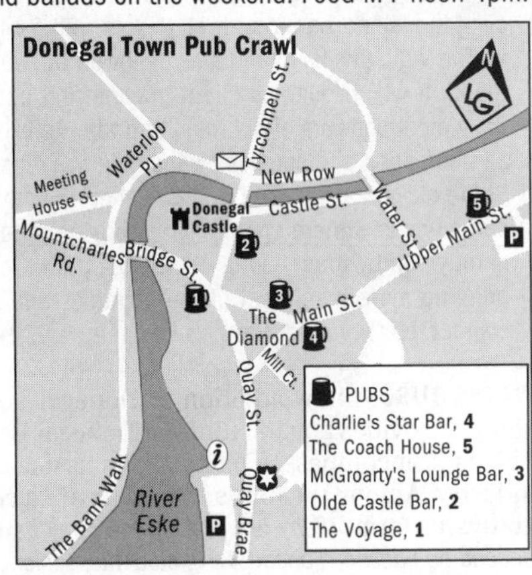

SIGHTS AND FESTIVALS

DONEGAL CRAFT VILLAGE. Six craftspeople open their workshops to the public in Donegal's craft village. The innovative work of a potter, a jeweler, a painter, an ironsmith, and two sculptors make great gift alternatives to the legions of mass-produced leprechauns sold elsewhere. *(About 1 mi. south of town on the Sligo road. ☎22225. Open July-Aug. M-Sa 10am-6pm, Su noon-6pm; Sept.-June call ahead.)*

DONEGAL CASTLE. Originally the seat of several chieftains, Donegal was torn apart by Irish-English conflict during the 17th century. Evidence of this turmoil remains at Donegal Castle, the former residence of the O'Donnell clan and, later, various English nobles. The recently refurbished ruins of the O'Donnell clan's castle of 1474 stand adjacent to the manor built by English rulers in 1623. *(Castle St. ☎22405. Open Mar.-Oct. daily 10am-5:15pm; Nov.-Feb. Sa-Su 10am-5:15pm. Guided tours on the hour. €3.80, students and children €1.50, seniors €2.50, families €9.50.)*

OLD ABBEY AND ST. PATRICK'S CHURCH. The stones and doorways of Donegal Castle's grand manor were taken from this ruined 15th-century Franciscan Friary. The remains of the original building—stairways and wall fragments—mingle with those of humans, evidence of the site's later incarnation as a cemetery. The abbey was destroyed in an explosion in 1601; a quartet of dispossessed monks went on to write the *Annals of the Four Masters*, the first narrative history of Ireland and the source of many still-extant myths. An **obelisk** built on the Diamond in 1937 pays homage to the holy men, as does **St. Patrick's Church of the Four Masters,** a stolid Romanesque church about half a mile up Main St. *(Old Abbey is a short walk from the tourist office along the south side of town. St. Patrick's open M-F 9am-5pm. Free.)*

STATION ISLAND Station Island in County Donegal's **Lough Derg** is the site of one of Ireland's most arcane and interesting Christian rituals. In AD 554, the priest soon to be known as St. Patrick arrived on Station Island and prepared to shut himself in a cave for 15 days. According to legend, he experienced a series of hellish visions during his cavely meditations. Every summer since, hosts of pilgrims have come to Station Island to emulate the Original Paddy's saintly lifestyle. The pilgrimage, which can be undertaken in June or July, comprises a three-day orgy of fasting, praying, and circling the island barefoot. It all begins with 24 hours of uninterrupted meditation known as The Vigil; this is immediately followed by two days of "Stations," a Celtic-Christian tradition in which pilgrims chant prayers and perform preordained movements. The only daily meal consists of dry toast and tea. An expurgated version of the ritual that forgoes all the fasting and shoeless wandering has recently begun to grace the menu-free menu. Some old-schoolers scoff at this "softer" pilgrimage, forgetting that the modern three-day ceremony is a mere shadow of its original fifteen-day self, which involved none of this namby-pamby toast eating. Whichever path the contemporary pilgrim chooses, he need bring no more then a set of warm clothes and a repentant heart. *(For more information, contact the Prior of St. Patrick's Purgatory ☎ 072 61518; www.loughderg.org.)*

WATERBUS. A new addition to Donegal Town's tourism machine, the Waterbus shuttle provides aquatic tours of Donegal Bay. The tour is at once scenic and morbid, as it encompasses many sights associated with the Famine-era "coffin ship" industry. Among the tour's highlights are a colony of seals, a shore-side castle, and an oyster farm. *(Ferry leaves from the quay next to the tourist office. ☎ 23666. Departures depend on tides; call ahead. €10; students, seniors, and children €5.)*

ACTIVITIES. Donegal Guided Town and Country Walks offers a historical exercise of the mind and legs from June-Aug. daily at 5:30pm. The guides will enlighten you on the town's history or delight you with tours through the surrounding countryside. The experienced guides are also available year-round to help you plan your attack on the Slieve League, Bluestacks, Errigal, and Derryveagh Mountains. (*☎ 35967 or info@northwestwalkingguides.com.*) Those less inclined to use their own feet to explore the countryside can rent four from **Deane's Open Farm.** The farm has horse trekking and pony rides. Kids also get the chance to feed and nurse a variety of animals. (*☎ 37160. From Donegal Town, drive 12 mi. on N56 toward Killybegs and follow the signposts.)*

FESTIVALS. The **Donegal Summer Festival,** held the last weekend in June, brings to town such diverse activities as craft and antiques fairs, air-sea rescue displays, clay-pigeon shoots, and the Bonny Baby show, as well as plenty of live bands and trad sessions. To join in on the three-day party, be sure to call ahead for a room—the town doubles in size for the weekend. *(Contact the tourist office at ☎ 21148.)* For two weeks in July, the **Earagail Arts Festival** rages throughout County Donegal. Twenty towns and over 40 venues host 100 events including music and dance, theater and comedy, open air performances, exhibitions, and special activities for the kids. Tickets vary from free to €25. Tourist offices are the best place to get your booklet to guide you through the daily happenings. *(Ticket Hotline ☎ 074 29186.)*

DAYTRIP FROM DONEGAL TOWN: LOUGH ESKE

The hike to the lough and back takes 2hr. Follow signs for "Harvey's Point" (marked from the Killybegs road). After about 3 mi., you'll come to half of a metal gate supported by a single stone pillar. Turn right at the gate and follow the path to reach the remains of Lough Eske Castle. Drivers can reach the 15 mi. loop around the lough by following signs to Lough Eske from the Mountcharles road.

The most worthwhile of Donegal Town's sights actually lies a few miles outside of town at Lough Eske ("fish lake"), an idyllic pond set among a fringe of trees and ruins. The crumbling but majestic **Lough Eske Castle,** built in 1861, lies loughside, its slightly overgrown grounds and seriously decrepit buildings providing a gorgeous site for picnics and afternoon rambles. Continue following the path around front to find a **Celtic high cross** (see **Christians and Vikings,** p. 55) surrounded by breathtaking gardens that contain the burial site of the castle's former master.

BUNDORAN (BUN DOBHRÁIN) ☎072

At the mouth of the Dobhran River, Bundoran is the first stop in Donegal for visitors coming from Sligo or Leitrim. In 1777, Bundoran was the summer residence of Viscount Enniskillen, but it has since fallen into the hands of the plebeian masses. Beautiful beaches, fishing, and some of the best surf in Ireland have made this a popular destination for tourists from across both the Republic and Northern Ireland. In recent years, taxbreak-fueled development has been rapid and haphazard—the population of the town swells from 2000 to 20,000 during the summer. During the day, tourists stroll the mile-long shore road; at night, youngsters party in the town's many pubs, saloons, and nightclubs. The touristic flair means that Bundoran has many amusements to offer, such as a new six-screen Cineplex, a bowling alley, a strip of arcades, and souvenir shops that only a true kitschophile could love. These attractions offer welcome diversions to the rural-weary traveler and, combined with the magnificent waves crashing against the ragged cliffs, make Bundoran a pleasant weekend stop on the way north into Donegal.

TRANSPORTATION AND PRACTICAL INFORMATION. Catch **Bus Éireann** (☎51101) at the Main St. depot for: Donegal (7 per day); Dublin (3 per day); and Galway, via Sligo (M-Sa 4 per day, Su 3 per day). **Ulsterbus** runs to Enniskillen (summer M-Sa 7 per day, Su 3 per day; off-season M-Sa 3 per day, Su 1 per day). **Feda O'Donnell** (☎075 48356) serves Galway and Letterkenny. The **tourist office,** just over the bridge on Main St., provides brochures of Donegal's attractions. (☎41350. Open June-Aug. M-Sa 9am-6pm, Su 10am-6pm; off-season daily 9am-5pm.) **AIB,** on Main St., has an **ATM.** (☎41222. Open M 10am-5pm, Tu-F 10am-4pm.) **Goodwin's Hire and Sell** rents **bicycles** and **fishing equipment** from the blue shed behind the Sand Dune B&B on Sea Rd. (☎41526. Bikes €10 per day, €35 per wk.; deposit €30. Fishing rods €8 per day. Open M-Sa 8:30am-6pm.) **Donegal Adventure Centre** (see **Accommodations,** below) also rents bikes. Short-term **work opportunities** can be found at La Sabbia restaurant, attached to the Homefield Hostel (see **Accommodations,** below.). Direct inquires to the owner/chef at the hostel (☎42277) or at the restaurant (☎42253). For **Internet access,** head to **CyberZone,** Station Rd., just off Main St. near the Railway Bar. (☎29428. €1.60 per 15min.)

ACCOMMODATIONS, FOOD, AND PUBS. Every third house in Bundoran seems to be of the B&B persuasion; the cheaper and quieter ones are farther down Main St., away from the bridge. **Homefield Hostel (IHH) ❷,** Bayview Ave., is off Main St.; head left up the hill between the Church of Ireland and the Bay View Guest House. One wing of the huge building, which happens to be the former summer residence of that famous Viscount Enniskillen, connects to a surprisingly great Italian restaurant (see **La Sabbia,** below), while the other cradles a high-ceilinged parlor. The bunks are a bit creaky but rooms here are reasonably comfortable and well-maintained. (☎41288. Continental breakfast included. Dorms €16; doubles €25. Renovations are being done in the off-season, so call ahead.) A few steps further up from the hostel is the **Donegal Adventure Centre ❶,** which caters specifically to youth groups but also offers backpackers comfortable rooms, very nice facilities, and adventure sports like **mountain biking** and **surf lessons.** The friendly manager Niamh (NEEV) will set you up with all sorts of info. (☎42418. Surf lessons from €20. Free laundry. Curfew 3am. Dorms €12; private rooms €20. Mar.-Oct. 3-day activity weekend over bank holidays, 1 per month, €150.) **Thalassa House ❷**, W. Main St., is an orange-red B&B offering sunny and comfortable rooms. (☎41324 or 41685. All rooms with bath. Singles €25-35.)

The best restaurant in town is **La Sabbia ❷**, an Italian bistro connected to the Homefield Hostel. Enjoy impeccable food in a cozy but cool cosmopolitan atmosphere. (☎42253. Gourmet pizzas and pasta dishes €7-11. Open June-Aug. Th-Tu 7-10pm, Sept.-May Th-Su 7-10pm, but call ahead.) **McGarrigle's Restaurant ❸** serves dishes with a bit more panache than its neighbors on the Main St. strip, and often at lower prices. (☎42060. Breakfast served all day. Mains €11-17. Open June-Sept. daily 10am-10pm, Oct.-May 10am-3pm and 6-10pm.) The **Ould Bridge Bar,** Main St., just over the bridge, manages to combine the spirits of local pub and surfer bar while retaining a friendly, casual buzz. A favorite of the Homefield/Adventure Center crowd. (☎42050. Food until 9pm; bar open 8am-late.) The **Railway Bar** (☎41196), further up the hill on Main St., serves up fine pints to the local wisemen, including the mayor. Huge crowds of over a thousand have been reported at the edge of town in **The Dome,** Bundoran's own superclub. (☎42430. Open Sa-Su nights. Cover €8 on Sa, €7 on Su.)

SIGHTS AND ACTIVITIES. A stroll past the Northern Hotel affords an impressive view of the mighty Atlantic waves to your left. Curious sights include the **Faery Bridges,** the **Wishing Chair,** and the **Puffing Hole,** where water spouts up through a bed of rocks. The **Aughross Cliffs** ("Headlands of the Steeds") were once a pasture for warhorses. At the western end of town, down the hill from Thalassa House, there is a bathing pool built onto the smooth rock face. In the center of town is the small **Bundoran Beach,** which suffers terribly in comparison to the golden sand of its neighbor, **Tullan Strand.** In fact, the beaches in this area are better for **surfing** than they are for swimming. There are several accessible breaks adjacent to town, including a reef break called the Peak at Bundoran Beach and a shore break on the Tullan Strand. **Fitzgeralds Surfworld,** Main St. (☎41223; www.surfworldireland.com), reports conditions and serves as the friendly local surf oracle. Rentals and lessons are available from the **Donegal Adventure Centre** (see **Accommodations,** above.) **Bundoran's Water World** provides a heated environment for summertime splashing, with a pool and two large water slides. (☎41172. Open summer daily 10am-6pm. €7, children and seniors €5.) Parents can retreat to the adjacent **Aqua Mara Spa** for a Seabath Steam (€15 per hr.) or a spin in the Relaxarium (€8), which combines music, murals, artificial sunsets, and aromatherapy into a 15min. extravaganza. (☎41173. Open W-Su 10am-8pm; call ahead if possible.) **The Homefield Hostel's Equestrian Centre** will have you galloping across dunes and beaches. (☎41288. Open Apr.-Oct. Lessons €20 per hr.) The brand new six-screen **Cineplex** offers standard Hollywood fare nightly, as well as the occasional wee Irish flick. Turn off Main St. away from the sea at the Railway Bar; the building will soon come into view. (☎29999; €6.50; weekly schedule posted around town.) The annual **Bundoran Music Festival,** held over the October bank holiday weekend, attracts big names in trad, bands, and the occasional hypnotist.

BALLYSHANNON (BÉAL ÁTHA SEANAIDH) ☎072

Quainter and quieter than its touristically rowdy neighbor Bundoran, Ballyshannon twiddles its thumbs by the River Erne, which splashes over the Falls of Assaroe (*Ess Ruaid*) just west of the bridge. The falls are one of Ireland's oldest pagan holy sites, but there's little to see now other than water and Christians.

TRANSPORTATION AND PRACTICAL INFORMATION. **Allingham's Bridge** connects the town's two halves and honors Ballyshannon poet William Allingham, who inspired Yeats to study the mythic traditions of Co. Sligo. Most of the town lies north of the river, where **Main St.** splits halfway up a hill. This hill, named **Mullach na Sidh** ("hill of the fairies"), is believed to be the burial site of legendary High King Hugh, who supposedly drowned in the Assaroe falls. **Buses** (☎074 31008) leave the depot just beside the bridge for Donegal Town (25min., 8-10 per day, €4.55) and Sligo (1 hr.; M-Sa 8 per day, Su 4 per day; €7.25.) If you need cash ASAP, hit the **ATM** at **AIB,** Castle St. (☎51169. Open M-F 10am-4pm, Th until 5pm), or the **Bank of Ireland** on Main St. (☎54153. Open M-F 10am-4pm, Th until 5pm.) The **post office** is on Market St. in the main triangle where Market splits from Main St. (☎51111. Open M-F 9am-1pm and 2-5:30pm, Sa 9am-1pm.) **Internet access** can be found at **The Engine Room,** in the rear of the shopping center across from the Cineplex. (☎52960. €4 per 30min. Open M-F 9am-2pm and 2:30-5:30pm.)

ACCOMMODATIONS, FOOD, AND PUBS. Duffy's Hostel (IHH) ❶ is a small bungalow-turned-hostel just 5min. from town on the Donegal road. The gregarious owners maintain one treasure trove of a second-hand bookshop out back. (☎51535. Open Mar.-Oct. Laundry €2. Dorms €10. Camping €5.) Ten minutes down the Belleek road, the Assaroe Lake Side Caravan & Camping Park ❶ has a beautiful location and brand-new facilities, including sports fields and a playground. (☎52822. 2-person tent €10, 4- to 6-person tent €14. Laundry €2.) Shannon's Corner B&B ❸, at the top of Main St., has sunny rooms upstairs. (☎51180. €25 per person) Downstairs they run a bistro ❷ normally crowded with locals clawing for the open prawn sandwich at just €7. (Open M-Sa 9am-5pm). The new Mace Supermarket offers fruits and veggies. (☎58144. Open M-Tu 8:30am-7pm, W and Sa 8:30am-7:30pm, Th-F 8:30am-8pm, Su 9:30am-2pm.) Finn McCool's, on Main St., is the most popular pub in town and is reputed to have the best trad sessions in Donegal. Get here early; the pub is tiny and Guinness bottles take up as much space as the people. (☎52677. Trad every other night in the summer at 10pm.) The Cellar (☎51452), 5min. down the Bundoran Rd. below Sweeny's White Horse, has live trad every Friday starting around 9:30pm.

SIGHTS AND FESTIVALS. From the left fork of Main St., a left turn past the Imperial Hotel leads to **St. Anne's Church,** where William Allingham is buried with all his kit and kin. Around June, a fish ladder in the river near the power station allows tourists to point and laugh at salmon and trout struggling upstream to spawn. The 12th-century Cistercian **Abbey of Assaroe** peacefully sits by the placid river. From town, take the left fork of Main St. past the Thatched Pub and take the second left. The Cistercians put a canal in the river, harnessing its hydraulic power for a still-operational water mill. A tiny path outside leads to the **Abbey Well,** which, unlike you, was blessed by St. Patrick. Pilgrims bless themselves with its water each year on August 15. To the right of the bridge and 120 yd. down the riverbank, a tiny cave harbors a **mass rock** used during Penal Days and two hollow stones that once held holy water (see **The Ascendancy,** p. 58). Things in town heat up during the first weekend in August, when the annual **Ballyshannon Music Festival** (☎51088) brings a combination of Irish folk music and Irish folk to the area. When wandering around, keep an eye out for tourist information bulletin boards, which always list sights of interest and local history.

SLIEVE LEAGUE PENINSULA

Just west of Donegal Town, the Slieve League Peninsula's rocky cliffs jut imposingly out of the Atlantic. The cliffs and mountains of this sparsely-populated area harbor coastal hamlets, untouched beaches, and some of the most dramatic scenery in all of Ireland. R263 extends along the peninsula's southern coast, linking each charming village to the next. Backpackers and cyclists navigating the hilly terrain are advised to work their way westward, then northward, toward Glencolmcille. Stunning coastal vistas, pleasant inland paths, and windy and cottage-speckled fields of heather are hidden along the bends and twists of this road, so it pays to take your time. **Ardara** and **Glenties** make pleasant stops along the inland route back, and also make fine points of departure for your trek north, deeper into Donegal. Although most easily covered by **car,** the peninsula is a spectacular opportunity for **cycling** (you can expect to walk your bike on frequent, serious hills). Despite recent improvements in service, **buses** to area hostels remain infrequent. Hitchers report finding rides in Slieve.

SOUTHEASTERN SLIEVE LEAGUE ☎073

A handful of single-street villages skitter along the coast road between Donegal Town and Slieve League. For those fierce and furious **cyclists** willing to endure such demanding grades, the route offers rewarding views of the coast. **The Art Gallery,** on the coast road to Killybegs, features the work of local artists. (☎35675. Open Mar.-Oct. W-Su 11am-7pm.) About 12 mi. outside of Donegal Town—10 mi. past the tiny village of **Mountcharles**—is *very* tiny **Dunkineely,** which is surrounded by megalithic tombs, holy wells, and small streams, all of which are accessible by round-trip walks of less than 4 mi. More information on these walks is available at the **Gallagher Farm Hostel (IHH) ❶,** which sits about quarter of a mile off the main road in the town of **Bruckless,** about 1½ mi. beyond Dunkineely. This original 17th-century barn has been converted into a wonderfully clean, well-equipped hostel, with lots of kitchen space, a huge fireplace, and a ping-pong table. (☎37057. Laundry €4. Dorms €11.50. **Camping** €6.50.) Between the hostel and Dunkineely, a turnoff leads to **St. John's Point,** which has views across to the Sligo coastline.

KILLYBEGS (NA CEALA BEAGA) ☎073

The first thing you'll notice about Killybegs is its odor, which rises with alarming ardor from one of the largest fish processing factories in Ireland. Once you've gotten over the town's... ambience, you'll be free to enjoy its busy harbor, fresh-to-the-point-of-twitching seafood, and lively pubs. The residents of Killybegs work hard and play hard—many local pubs have late-night licences, so last call isn't until 1am, and most people don't leave until 2am.

TRANSPORTATION AND PRACTICAL INFORMATION. The **Bus Éireann** (☎21101) route from Donegal Town to Glencolmcille stops in Killybegs (July-Sept. M-Sa 3 per day, Su 1 per day; Oct.-June M-Sa 1 per day). **McGeehan's Coaches** (☎075 46150) also has service (July-Sept. 2 per day; Oct.-June M-Th 1 per day, F-Su 2 per day) to Donegal Town and Dublin from Dungloe, Ardara, Glenties, Glencolmcille, and several other towns on the peninsula. Your friendly local **tourist office,** on Conlin Rd. between Main St. and Shore Rd. at the western end of town, provides maps of nearby day hikes and contact information for local fishing outfits. (☎32346. Open Mar.-Nov. daily 9:30am-5:30pm.) Killybegs has the only **banks** and **pharmacies** in the area. Both **Bank of Ireland** and **Ulsterbank** are on Main St. at the western end of town, and both have 24hr. **ATMs.** (Both open M-F 10am-4pm, Th until 5pm.)

McGee's Pharmacy, Main St., sells a full cargo of medicines and toiletries. (☎31009. Open M-F 9:30am-6pm.) The **post office** sorts mail on Main St. (☎31060. Open M-F 9am-1pm and 2-5:30pm, Sa 9am-1pm.)

ACCOMMODATIONS. Mrs. Tully puts up guests a mile east of the town center in **Tullycullion House ❸.** To get there, head south off N56; boat-shaped signs point the way. Unsurpassed panoramic views of Killybegs Harbour and comfortable rooms await; as do Mrs. Tully's two pet donkeys. Inquire here about the availability of self-catering cottages on the beach 3 mi. away. (☎31842. €26 per person.) **Banagh House ❸,** on Fintra Rd., is a 5min. walk from town. The beautiful yellow house overlooks the Harbour and promises luxurious rooms with every amenity. In the morning, breakfast is served with ocean views. (☎31108. €28 per person.)

FOOD AND PUBS. The taste of fish in Killybegs's air provides only a hint of the excellent seafood to be found in its eateries. **Melly's Cafe ❷,** on Main St. across from the Diamond, serves up what may well be Ireland's best fish and chips, all for just €7.50. (☎31093. Open M-Th 8:30am-10:30pm, F-Sa 8:30am-4am, Su 2-10:30pm.) If grease has burned you in the past, the **Atlantic Fresh Seafood ❶** trailer right by the main dock will nurse your wounds with a slew of fresh and smoked critters pulled right out of the water. (Open daily 9am-6pm.) Sick of fish? Too bad; **Kitty Kelley's ❸,** halfway between Killybegs and Kilcar, also serves fresh seafood dishes, along with innovative Mediterranean fare, in a 200-year-old cottage. (☎31925. Dijon mackerel €12.10. Open nightly 5-9:30pm.)

Whether or not you've come to Co. Donegal to hear fiddling, a stop at the **Sail Inn** (☎31130), at the far end of Main St. from the pier, is a must. Locals gather here for GAA matches and above-average bar chow. Renowned musicians often turn up for frequent sessions. **The Harbour Bar,** across from the pier on the west side of the Diamond, is notorious for its jolly late hours. (☎31049. Rock and ballads summer Tu-Su.) **Hughie's Bar,** on the northern end of Main St., hops with frequent impromptu music sessions and a weekend disco. (☎31095. Open until 2am. Disco cover €5.)

KILCAR (CILL CHARTHAIGH) ☎073

A breathtaking 8 mi. down R263 from Killybegs is the village of Kilcar, the gateway to Donegal's *gaeltacht* and commercial base for many Donegal weavers. The main street, also known as the scenic coast road that runs east to Killybegs and north to Carrick, passes Kilcar's main attraction—its superlative accommodations.

TRANSPORTATION AND IMPRACTICAL INFORMATION. The **Bus Éireann** (☎21101) route from Donegal Town to Glencolmcille stops in Kilcar (July-Sept. M-Sa 3 per day, Su 1 per day; Oct.-June M-Sa 1 per day). **McGeehan's Coaches** (☎075 46150) also has service (July-Sept. 2 per day. Oct.-June M-Th 1 per day, F-Su 2 per day) to Donegal Town and Dublin from Dungloe, Ardara, Glenties, Glencolmcille, and other towns on the peninsula. The nearest **bank, pharmacy,** and **civilization** are in Killybegs. However you get **Internet access** at the newly renovated **Áistan Cill Cartha** (see **Sights;** €6 per hr.).

ACCOMMODATIONS AND CAMPING. Located 1½ mi. out the Carrick coast road from Kilcar and only 5min. from the beach, Shaun of the **Derrylahan Hostel (IHH) ❶** is a warm and welcoming wellspring of local information and myth. His 200-year-old former church doubles as a hostel and a working farm. Call for pickup from Kilcar or Carrick. Booking ahead in July and August is a good idea; visiting in the beginning of April, during lambing season, is an even better one. (☎38079. Laundry €7. Dorms €10; private rooms €14 per person. **Camping** €6,

FROM THE ROAD

"UNSETTLED WEATHER"

One month into my Irish travels, I hadn't had a single day in which there was not at least a brief spell of rain. I had long since given up on checking the forecast: the weather in Ireland is terminally "unsettled," as the meteorologists euphemistically label the reliable mixture of rain and rain. I had nearly forgotten what my skin looked like, as my raincoat had become the quintessential fixture of my wardrobe. When my editors back in sweltering Boston asked if I had been renting bikes to get around I scoffed, "you do realize that you can't hold an umbrella and ride a bike at the same time?" Nor did those in Ireland offer any solace, as the daily reminders that this was the worst summer they had seen in three, five, even 50 years did little to buoy my spirits (though they might offer the 2003 reader more hope!). What I wanted to hear was that the clouds would somehow "run out" of rain, and that the remainder of my summer would be bone dry. No such luck; I instead was told that rainy Junes precede rainy Julys.

With this in mind, I was less than excited by the approach of the 4th of July, the American day of independence that is typically celebrated with cookouts, fireworks, and trips to the beach. My plan for the 4th did include a trip to the beach–Bundoran–but a beach in 50° weather is somehow not quite the same. I was also scheduled to check out the somewhat nearby Errigal Mountain. Decision one was somewhat embarrassing:

with separate showers and kitchen.) Less then a mile from Kilcar, **Dún Ulún House ❶** offers a remarkable range of luxurious accommodations: from B&B-style rooms with baths to camping plots on individual hedged terraces overlooking ringfort ruins to self-catering cottages that can be rented for groups of six to ten or as dorms. These options are dizzying, but they can't hold a candle to the *blitzkrieg* of information you'll receive from the energetic owners—if you blink too long, they will have traced your ancestry to Donegal and settled you in for an extended stay. (☎38137. 6- to 10-bed cottage dorms around €10 per person; B&B-style rooms €23.50 per person, cheaper without breakfast or bath. **Camping** €5 per person.)

On the scenic road from Killybegs to Kilcar that becomes Main St., **Inishduff House B&B ❸** sits next to Blue Haven restaurant. Ethna welcomes you with tea and biscuits before showing you to one of the six luxurious rooms—all with bath—that might well win the "largest B&B rooms in Ireland" contest. Your massive accommodations boast incredible views of the bay and ocean. If the large rooms and coastal views aren't enough to induce you to stay longer, the food will: guests have begged to stay another night just for the morning delights that often include smoked salmon. (☎38542. All rooms with TV and bath. €32 per person.)

FOOD AND PUBS. **Spar Market** on Main St. sells groceries and fishing tackle. (Open M-Sa 9am-9:50pm, Su 9:30am-1:30pm and 7-10:30pm.) **The Rendezvous Coffee Shop ❷**, set behind a convenience store, serves sandwiches for €2.25 and lasagna for €6. (☎38344. Open M-Sa 9:30am-4:30pm.) Kilcar's best meal by far is at **Teach Barnai ❸** on Main St. Ann and Michael Carr's restaurant has a rustic feel, and serves fare from lamb to *colcannon*, a traditional Irish vegetarian dish. (☎38160. Mains €10.15-16.50. Open nightly 6-10pm.) Just down the street, **John Joe's** (☎38015) hosts nightly trad. The **Piper's Rest Pub,** Main St. (☎38205), has recently changed hands; the new hands stripped the stone walls of their musical instruments, so the *craic* has yet to be established. Expect a mixed, younger crowd.

SIGHTS AND FESTIVALS. **Studio Donegal** sells handwoven tweeds fresh off the loom. Visitors are invited to watch the yarn being spun, the cloth being woven, and the jackets being sewn. (☎38194. Open M-F 9am-5:30pm, June-Sept. also open Sa 9:30am-5pm.) In the same building, on the same floor as Studio Donegal, is **Áistan Cill Cartha** (ASH-lahn kill KAR-ha). This community organization provides genealogical information, compendiums of residents' oral histories, and local history collections. The center also has a gym, a library, Internet access, and films for children that show regularly during the summer. Locals (like your hostel or B&B owner) can direct you to the **prehistoric and natural wonders** that surround Kilcar, including the Megalithic tombs, old graveyards, and the Spanish church. If you're interested in **deep-sea fishing,** inquire at your hostel or B&B for help in setting up an appropriate venture, or you can contact *Nuala Star* in Teelin (☎39365). Kilcar's **International Sea Angling Festival** casts off during the first weekend in August. (Contact Cara Boyle ☎38341.) It's directly followed by the **Kilcar Street Festival,** a week of sport, art, and tomfoolery. (Contact Joe McBrearty ☎38135.)

CARRICK AND TEELIN ☎073

From Kilcar, the coast road passes the villages of **Carrick** *(An Carraig)* and **Teelin** *(Teileann)*. The two villages are about 2 mi. apart; take the left in the village of Carrick to continue on to Teelin and the **Slieve League Cliffs.** For most of the year, these mighty mites are but brief stopping points for travelers on their way to Slieve League Mountain (see below) or the larger villages on the peninsula. During the last bank holiday weekend in October, though, the village scene is transformed by the annual **Carrick Fleadh,** where barrels of creamy, foaming refreshment are accompanied by bushels of trad. **Fishing** is the other main attraction, and it manages to bait a goodly number of visitors each year. The *Nuala Star* in Teelin offers day-long, half-day, hourly, or evening trips, as well as **diving charters** (☎39365 or 087 628 4688). Dropping lines is especially rewarding around **Teelin Bay,** particularly in an area called **Salmon Leap.** Salmon fishing requires a permit (€15 per day), available in Teelin from Frank O'Donnell (☎39231) or at the **Teelin Bay B&B** ❸ right across from the river. In addition to pescredentials, Kathleen and Patrick offer tidy room and board for fishermen and other travelers. (☎39043. Singles €25; doubles €45.) The **Glen River** is best for trout; tackle can be bought at the **Spar** in Kilcar. For food that won't try to get away, head 3 mi. up the Ardara road to **Bialann Na Sean Scoile** ❷ for homecookin' and mashed potatoes stacked as high as Slieve League. (☎39477. Mains €5-10, dinner specials €6. Open daily 10am-10pm.) To engage in the part of fishing that involves drinking, turn left off of Carrick's Main St. and head up the Teelin road to **Cúl A' Dúin** (☎39101). Formerly known as the Rusty Mackerel, this pub was recently purchased by international trad megastars and native Teelinites Altan. When not touring, they sometimes hold court in this back-to-basics house.

I decided that I would see *Spiderman* (which I had heard contained moments of sentimental American patriotism) at night, after eating at McDonald's (which I don't even particularly like). Decision two was that I would actually climb Errigal Mountain, rain or shine.

Waking up to rain (surprise!) that morning, I decided to splurge a bit and take a taxi to Dunlewy. As I hiked through the village, the rain continued unabated, and as I set out for Errigal, with water beginning its ascent from my soaked-jean legs, I wasn't entirely sure I would resist calling the cab again if I ran across a pay phone. Luckily, my hour and a half stroll afforded me no such "wuss out" opportunities, and by the time I reached the foot of the mountain, my resolve to reach its pinnacle was strong. I knew that it probably wasn't entirely wise to climb a mountain by myself on a rainy day; *Let's Go* would certainly not recommend doing so. But with each step I took, pressing into the wet wind, I felt better and better, and there was no way that I was turning back before reaching the top. Halfway up my umbrella busted entirely, having flipped inside out too many times. I laughed out loud as suspicious sheep eyed the wet and wild-haired madwoman I had become. No more would I fight or fear the rain, I loved it. And when I reached the summit and circled the cairn, my head literally in the clouds I had so often cursed, I had to marvel at the beauty of having that moment to myself, on top of the world.

—Abby Shafroth

THE SLIEVE LEAGUE WAY ☎073

Slieve League Mountain lays claim to the hotly-contested title of having the highest sea cliffs in Europe. The face of its sheer, 2000 ft. drop really is spectacular—on a clear day, a hike over the cliffs will move you to marvel at the infinite expanse of the Atlantic and the compact hamlets along the inland portion of the peninsula. To reach the mountain, turn left halfway down Carrick's Main St. and follow the signs for Teelin. A right turn at the Cúl A' Dúin pub (see **Carrick and Teelin,** above) will put you on the inland route to Slieve League. The more popular route involves hanging a left at the pub and following the coastal route to **Bunglass** (a 1½hr. walk from Carrick), where there is a carpark at the head of the cliff path. From here, the trail heads north and then west along the coast. One hour along the path from the carpark, the mountaintop narrows to 2 ft., becoming the infamous **One Man's Pass.** On one side of this pass, the cliffs drop 1800 ft. to the ocean below. No worries, though—the rocky floor on the other side is only 1000 ft. down. There are no railings here, and those prone to vertigo generally opt to lower their centers of gravity by slithering across the 33 yd. platform. After near-certain death, the path continues along the cliffs all the way to **Rossarrell Point,** 6 mi. southeast of Glencolmcille. The entire hike from the Teelin carpark to Rossarrell Point takes about 4-6hr., depending on frequency of stops; length of legs; and sudden, life-threatening, and random weather conditions. Other, shorter routes involving loop-like figures can also be plotted. (For advice and in the interest of safety, discuss your plans with a hostel owner and carry the *Ordnance Survey Discovery Series #10.*)

One possible itinerary for backpackers would start in Kilcar at the Derrylahan Hostel and devote 6 or 7hr. to hiking over the Slieve League Way to the Malinbeg Hostel in **Malinbeg.** Following a short jaunt across the Silver Strand (see **Glencolmcille,** p. 416), packer rats can continue north and east to the Dooey Hostel in Glencolmcille. This route takes you past three great hostels and some of Ireland's most stunning scenery, but it's not obligatory—other attractive options abound; hostel owners, for instance, may provide pickups at an appointed time.

Never go to Slieve League in poor weather; in suboptimal weather, the cliffs at Bunglass are a safer option. Use extreme caution if you plan to cross the pass; it is not a necessary part of the hike across Slieve League. (You can also enjoy a steep climb by walking along the inland face of the mountain.) People have died here in the past, and by all indications, they will continue to do so. Hikers are blown off the pass by gusts of wind which, in a peculiarly gust-like manner, arise unexpectedly; people slip at moments of poor visibility. Keep in mind that weather at high elevations is *not* always the same as weather at low elevations, and that the former is given to rapid and drastic change. It's always a good idea to ask a local expert for advice and to tell someone reputable when you expect to return so that you will be missed. If you hike alone, *Let's Go* will scold you mercilessly.

GLENCOLMCILLE (GLEANN CHOLM CILLE) ☎073

Wedged between two sea-cliffs at the northwestern tip of the Slieve League peninsula, **Glencolmcille** (glen-kaul-um-KEEL) is actually a parish—a collection of several tiny, Irish-speaking villages that have come to be regarded as a single entity. "The Glen," as it is affectionately known, was named after St. Colmcille, who founded a monastery here. This sometime pilgrimage site centers around the street-long village of **Cashel,** which lies just off R236 along the aptly-named Cashel St. The road leads past the village's several storefronts and down to the coast, where most of the area's accommodations and attractions are located. Buses of tourists roll in for the Folk Village (see **Sights,** below), but few venture to the desolate, wind-battered cliffs that lie just beyond.

TRANSPORTATION AND PRACTICAL INFORMATION. The **Bus Éireann** (☎21101; www.buseireann.ie) funmobile leaves from the village corner to Donegal Town, stopping in Killybegs and Kilcar (July-Sept. M-Sa 3 per day, Su 1 per day; Oct.-June M-Sa 1 per day). **McGeehan's** buses leave from Biddy's Bar bound for Carrick, Kilcar, Killybegs, Ardara, Glenties, Fintown, and Letterkenny (July-Sept. 2 per day; Oct.-June M-Th 1 per day, F-Su 2 per day). Glencolmcille's tiny **tourist office** is on Cashel St. (☎30116. Open July-Aug. M-Sa 10am-7:30pm, Su 11am-6pm; Apr.-June and Sept. to mid-Nov. M-Sa 10am-6pm, Su 11am-1:30pm.) The nearest **banks,** and, consequently, the nearest **ATMs,** are in Killybegs and Ardara. A **bureau de change** can be found at the Folk Village and at the **post office,** which is east of the village center. (☎30001. Open M-F 9am-1pm and 2-5:30pm, Sa 9am-1pm.)

ACCOMMODATIONS, FOOD, AND PUBS. A trip to Donegal, or even to Ireland, wouldn't be complete without a visit to old Mary and her not young son Leo at the **Dooey Hostel (IHO) ❶**, the original Irish independent hostel. To get there, turn left at the end of the village and follow the signs uphill for almost a mile. It's a hike, but the view is spectacular, and the building follows suit; it's built into the hillside overlooking the sea, and a garden's worth of flowers grows out of the rocky face that is the hostel's corridor. The vibrance of the atrium is matched only by that of its owners' personalities. Simply put, don't miss this one—it has been the high-point of many a traveler's journey. (☎30130. Wheelchair-accessible. Dorms €9.50; doubles €21. **Camping** €5.50.) Mrs. Ann Ward's **Atlantic Scene ❸**, the next house after the hostel, lives up to its name. The beds are soft, but you'll stay awake just to admire the view. Tasty breakfasts ensure you won't sleep late. (☎30186. Open May-Sept. €25-30 per person.) More B&Bs surround the Folk Village (see **Sights,** below). Five miles southwest of Cashel lies Malinbeg, and in it you'll find the welcoming arms of the **Malinbeg Hostel ❶.** Run by Frank and Kathleen, the hostel combines more bells and whistles than any hostel in the area, and offers superlative views of Raithlin O'Byrne Island's lighthouse. The hostel is a 5 mi. hike from Glencolmcille, but the owners will pick up those who phone ahead. (☎30006 or 30965. Dorms €10; doubles €24-28. Family rooms are available.)

Byrne and Sons Food Store, Cashel St., supplies basic nutritive and printed matter. (☎30018. Open M-Sa 9am-10pm, Su 9am-1pm and 6-9pm.) **An Chistin ❸** (AHN KEESHT-ahn; "the kitchen"), at the Foras Cultúir Uladh (see **Sights**), is especially affordable for lunch. (☎30213. Mains €6.50-15. Open May-Sept. daily 9am-9pm; Apr. and Oct. noon-9pm.) The **teashop ❶** in the Folk Village tempts with delicious sandwiches (€1.90) and Guinness cake (€1). The town's three pubs have a dark, dusty 1950s Ireland feel to them: imagine spare rooms with plastic-covered snugs and, for once, a minimal amount of wood paneling. The pubs are primarily a haven for locals, which could be either bad or good; regardless, they develop an affinity for visitors during July and August. Most famous among them is the unassuming 120-year-old **Biddy's,** at the mouth of Carrick Rd. A favorite of the older crowd, this is the place to meet all those Irish speakers you've been dreaming of. (☎30016. Trad 3 times a week during the summer.) **Roarty's** (☎30273), the next pub down Cashel St., welcomes guests with trad several times a week. Last on the road is **Glen Head Tavern** (☎30008), the largest of the pint-peddling trio. Practically the whole village could fit into its recently redone lounge, which hosts legendary trad sessions. Though the three pubs offer cold drinks and warm smiles, Donegal Town is still where most travelers and locals go for their nightly dose of trad and drink.

LOVE POITÍN #9 The county may be more famous for fiddling and tweed, but there is another, lesser-known craft that denizens of Donegal have practiced with similar single-mindedness and mythological resolve: the distillation of *poitín* (pah-CHEEN). Generation after generation, elusive bootleggers of hill and bog pass down the secret of bottling lightning. Despite years of legal persecution, bottles of powerful *poitín* are stashed under sinks and in broom closets all across Donegal. It is said that the poet Dylan Thomas moved to the valley next to Port in an attempt to isolate himself and cleanse the alcohol from his system, but that he was foiled by the availability of *poitín*. The drink is a part of the regional folklore, a symbol of the silent resistance to authority that is so central to the Donegal character.

Poitín is a 140-proof kick in the face. Culled from potatoes steeped in a mixture of apples, berries, and barley, then thrice-distilled in a gigantic copper worm, this gift of the gods arrives clear, with a bouquet reminiscent of paint thinner. The traditional method for determining the quality of a batch is to pour a bit into a saucer and set it ablaze. Like arsenic, the stuff should burn bright blue. If it doesn't, it may blind you. If it does, it may blind you. **Beware:** Because of its high alcohol content and über-dodgy mode of preparation, poitín is simultaneously illegal and dangerous. It is not served in pubs or brought out in polite company.

SIGHTS. Glencolmcille's craft movement began in the 1950s under the direction of the omnipresent **Father James McDyer,** who was also responsible for bringing in electricity, founding the Folk Village, and building the local football field. Today, the town is renowned for its handmade products—particularly its sweaters, which are on sale at numerous "jumper shops" on the roads surrounding the town. Close to town is the **Foras Cultúir Uladh** (FOR-us KULT-er UH-lah; "The Ulster Cultural Institute"), which runs the **Oideas Gael institute** for the preservation of the Irish language and culture. Foras offers regular courses of varied lengths on such pursuits as hiking, painting, pottery, local archaeology, traditional music, and Irish language. You can also buy trad recordings and books on Ireland, or see concerts, performances, and frequently changing exhibitions on local history. (☎30248. Open June-Aug. daily 9am-6pm; Sept.-May M-F 9am-5pm.)

A bit past the village center is Father McDyer's **Folk Village Museum and Heritage Centre,** the town's attraction for non-hiking, non-Irish speaking tourists. The museum is housed in thatch-roofed stone cottages, which date from 1700, 1850, and 1900; the 1850s schoolhouse is open to the general public, and guided tours describe the furniture and tools from each of these eras in Irish history. A short nature trail from the village leads up a hill past various reconstructed remains, including a Mass rock, a sweat house, and a lime kiln. The **sheeben** (the old name for an illegal drinking establishment) sells whiskey marmalade. (☎30017. Open Easter-Sept. M-Sa 10am-6pm, Su noon-6pm. Tours July-Aug. every 30min., Apr.-June and Sept. every hr. Tour costs €2.50.) The two-day **Glencolmcille Folk Festival,** a lively and occasionally raucous celebration, occurs during the first or second weekend of August. (Contact Ellen McGinley ☎30053 or Gerry Gilespie ☎30111.)

Fine beaches and cliffs make for excellent hiking in all directions. A 5 mi. walk southwest from Cashel leads to **Malinbeg,** a winsome hamlet at the edge of a sandy cove that now has its own hostel (see **Accommodations,** above). This coastal area was once notorious for smuggling *poitín* through tunnels (see **Love Poitín #9,** above), some of which may still be in use. When a sunny day happens to grace Donegal, a trip to the **Silver Strand** will be rewarded with stunning views of the gorgeous beach and surrounding rocky cliffs. From the strand, you can start a long-distance trek along the Slieve League coastline (see **Slieve League Way,** p. 414). A sandy beach links the cliffs on the north and south sides of Glencolmcille. An hour's walk north of town through land dotted with prehistoric ruins (including St. Colmcille's stations of the cross), **Glen Head** is easily identified by the Martello tower at its peak. The tourist office and the hostel both have maps showing the locations of major sights. A third 3hr. walk from town begins at the Protestant church and climbs over a hill to the ruins of the ghostly "Famine village" of **Port,** in the valley on the other side. Supposedly haunted by crying babies, this eerie village has been empty since its last, hunger-stricken inhabitants emigrated. The only current resident, according to local rumor, is an eccentric artist who lives by the isolated bay without electricity or water. The gargantuan **phallic rock** sticking out of the sea is just what it appears to be: the only part of the Devil still visible after St. Colmcille banished him into the ocean.

The road east from Glencolmcille to Ardara passes through the spectacular **Glengesh Pass.** Nine hundred feet above sea level, the road scales the surrounding mountains using such secret weapons as hairpin turns. **Biking** is common in these parts, but be warned that the steep and winding pass offers a challenging ride suitable for only the most intrepid cyclists. Hitching is a tough task along this unfrequented road.

ARDARA (ARD AN RÁTHA) ☎075

The historic center of the Donegal tweed industry, Ardara (ar-DRAH) now tends to attract tweed fiends with high credit limits. The town is one of the cheapest sources of locally-produced knit and woven articles, though better deals can often be found at small "craft centers" in surrounding villages. Today, Ardara's heritage center plays an important role in the movement to revive traditional hand-weaving techniques and silversmithing, as well as a local arts consciousness. During the first weekend of June's **Weavers' Fair,** weavers from all over Donegal congregate in Ardara to flaunt their weft, while musicians make their own contribution to the festivities. Visitors uninterested in merchandise and vexed by crowds can escape to the spectacular scenery along the Maghera Caves Road.

TRANSPORTATION AND PRACTICAL INFORMATION. **Bus Éireann** (☎074 31108) stops in Ardara in front of O'Donnell's on a circular route running from Donegal Town to Glenties (M-F 2 per day). **McGeehan's Coaches** (☎46150) stop on the Diamond as part of the Dublin-Donegal Town-Dungloe route. (July-Sept. M-Sa 2 per day, Su 1 per day; Oct.-June M-Sa 2 per day.) **Feda O'Donnell's** (☎48114) service between Donegal and Galway stops in Ardara once a day (Su and M only) with further stops throughout the *gaeltacht.* The **Ardara Heritage Centre** has craft-oriented tourist information. (☎41473. Open Jan.-Nov. daily 9:30am-5pm.) **Ulster Bank,** the Diamond (☎41121), has a 24hr. **ATM.** (☎41121. Open M-F 10am-12:30pm and 1:30-4pm, Th until 5pm.) **Don Byrne's,** past town on the Killybegs road, provides maps and brand new **rent-a-bikes** loaded with gizmos. (☎41658 or 41156. €15 per day, €60 per wk. Open June-Sept. M-Sa 9:30am-6pm, Su 10:30am-12:30pm; call ahead in the winter.) The **Ardara Medical Hall,** Front St., next to the heritage center, is just a glorified **pharmacy.** (☎41120. Open M-Sa 9am-1pm and 2-6pm.) The **post office** is on Main St. (☎41101. Open M-F 9am-1pm and 2-5:30pm, Sa 9am-1pm.)

ACCOMMODATIONS. **The Green Gate (An Geata Glás) ❹,** 1 mi. outside of town, is a reason in itself to visit Ardara. From the Donegal road west of town, ascend the hill to the north and follow the signs, or call to be picked up in a 1950 Citroën. The owner, Paul Chatenoud, traded his musical bookshop and apartment overlooking Notre Dame for this trio of 200-year-old cottages overlooking the bay in order to write a book about "love, life, and death." Visitors are the happy beneficiaries of his literary quest—the same artistic vision has furnished the room interiors and surrounding gardens with antique lamps, hand-painted records of French operas, and a library of Freud and Proust. Sample these delights at your peril, though; one night in this Epicurean sanctuary could easily become many. (☎41546. Book in advance. Singles €45; shared rooms €30 per person.) If the Green Gate is full, try the **Holly Brook B&B ❸**, on the Killybegs road near the outskirts of town. The rooms are sunny and immaculate, but the owner's family is what makes this place special: Peter Oliver, a famed local musician, runs the Corner Bar (see **Food and Pubs,** below), and his even more famous daughters have won national prizes in Irish step-dancing—one of them currently stars in Riverdance. (☎41596. €25 per person.) The **Drumbarron Hostel and B&B (IHO) ❶**, the Diamond, has rooms that are clean, well-lit, and covered with signs enumerating the establishment's many rules. Its central location guarantees easy access to the pubs—assuming you can get back before the 1am curfew—and plenty of morning traffic noise. Drumbarron also offers a B&B option across the street. (☎41200. Breakfast €7. Dorms €10; doubles €21. B&B €22.50, with bath €23.)

FOOD AND PUBS. There is a **Spar** market on Main St. (☎41107. Open M-Sa 8:30am-9pm, Su 8:30am-1pm.) **L'Atlantique Restaurant ❹,** below Triona Design on Main St., serves delicious French seafood in a dining room that somehow manages to make a ceiling full of fishing nets seem classy. Mains are expensive for budget travelers (€12.60-25.90), but you'd pay ten times as much for the same meal in Paris; the prix-fixe menu is more reasonable at €17. (☎41707. Open nightly 6:30-9:30pm. Reservations recommended.) On Main St., the **Nesbitt Arms Hotel ❷** serves excellent pub grub. (☎41103. Food €3-9. Open noon-9pm.) The attached restaurant serves snazzier fare. **Charlie's West End Cafe ❷,** halfway up Main St., lacks the trendy atmosphere its name suggests, but the service is quick and the prices are low. (☎41656. Enormous lunch specials €4.75, sandwiches €1.90. Open M-Sa 10am-11pm, Su 5-10pm.) There are 13 pubs in Ardara, lucky you. Decked out in bright copper kettles and warm woolen mittens, **Nancy's Bar,** Front St., just might become one of your favorite things. Come for the seafood or the weekend trad sessions. (☎41187. Mussels €5; food served noon-9pm.) Local musician Peter Oliver, he of the Holly Brook B&B, has returned to the publican business with his purchase of the **Corner Bar** (☎41736). The place is filled with tourists, but for good reason—the nightly summertime trad sessions are worth the crowd.

SIGHTS. The **Ardara Heritage Centre,** the Diamond, tells the story of the centuries-old Donegal tweed industry. Hand-loom demonstrations show the dexterity required to create the richly varied textiles that, these days, are sold in mass quantities throughout the world. The center has recently become a sort of craft village; several weavers, a silversmith, and a sculptor all ply and hawk their trades and wares. (☎41473. Open Jan.-Nov. daily 9:30am-6pm. Free.) Next door in the same building, **The Loom House** offers food for those weaving-weary. (Open Jan.-Nov. daily 9:30am-9:30pm.) Beautiful walks are there for the taking in the area surrounding Ardara. From town, head south toward Glencolmcille and turn right toward **Loughros Point** (LOW-crus) at the "Castle View" horse-riding sign. At the next horse-riding sign, either turn right for a beautiful view of Ardara Bay, or continue straight to reach stupendous views of the sea at the Point (1hr. walk). One mile from town on the Killybegs road, a sign points the way to the coastal **Maghera Caves,** which housed weapons during the Irish War for Independence. The British eventually found the guns and, pursuant to one of their most consistently successful revolution-crushing procedures, killed the rebel owners. After the caves turn-off, follow the signs several miles west on small roads, some of the most beautiful in Ireland. The six caves vary in size and depth; all require a flashlight. At low tide you can enter the Dark Cave, once the refuge of *poitín*-makers. The road that passes the caves continues across a mountain pass to Dungloe. Independent and guided **horse rides** start from **Castle View Ranch,** 2½ well-posted miles from Ardara off Loughros Point Rd. (☎41212. €20 per hr., €75 per day.)

Only the most steel-willed tourist can resist the purchase of a hand-knit sweater. Fortunately, Ardara has three shops with superior stock and (relatively) reasonable prices. The **John Molloy Factory Shop**, half a mile out of town on the Killybegs road, has tons to choose from, and if you ask nicely, they'll show you the factory floor in back. The tour will give you a whole new respect for the art of knitting and weaving, dispelling any notions of old women clustered together in rocking chairs. (☎41133. Open M-Th 9am-6pm, F 9am-5pm, Sa 10:30am-5pm, Su 1-5:30pm.) **Kennedy,** Front St. (☎41106), near the top of the hill, offers garments whose designs are so contemporary that they *almost* challenge the more staid looks at other stores. Wild. The town's other manufacturers are **Triona Design** (☎41422), at the entrance of town on the Killybegs road, and **Bonner's** (☎41303), Front St.

GLENTIES (NA GLEANNTA) ☎075

Glenties's proudest moment came in the mid-90s, when it won a string of victories in the "Ireland's Tidiest Town" contest. This Golden Age has passed, and the town is now most often experienced as a relatively tidy blur seen through the window of a moving vehicle. In its defense, Glenties has several short hikes and other amenities that make it a pleasant stop on the route through northwest Donegal, and every Saturday night it hosts one of the largest discos in the area.

TRANSPORTATION AND PRACTICAL INFORMATION. **Bus Éireann** (☎074 31008) stops in front of the post office on its route to Donegal Town via Ardara (M-F 2 per day). **McGeehan's** (☎46150) also runs a summertime Letterkenny-Glencolmcille bus that stops in almost all of the Slieve League Peninsula villages (M-Sa 2 per day). **Feda O'Donnell's** (☎48114) service between Donegal and Galway stops in Glenties once a day (Su and M only) on a route that hits many towns to the northwest. In town, the **Bank of Ireland,** Main St., has one of the area's few **ATMs.** (☎51124. Open M-F 10am-12:30pm and 1:30-4pm, Th until 5pm.) **Glenties Medical Hall,** Main St., provides pharmaceuticals. (☎51289. Open M-Tu and Th-F 9:30am-1pm and 2-6pm, W 9:30am-1pm.) Inquire at the Donegal Organic Farm (see **Accommodations,** below) about **work opportunities.** The **post office** is on Main St., snuggled inside a newsagent. (☎51101. Open M-F 9am-1pm and 2-5:30pm, Sa 9am-1pm.)

ACCOMMODATIONS, FOOD, AND PUBS. **Campbell's Holiday Hostel (IHH) ❶,** around the bend at the far end of Main St. toward Ardara, provides spare, clean rooms decorated in primary colors. The common space has a fireplace, satellite TV, and two fully equipped kitchens. (☎51491. Wheelchair-accessible. Sheets €2. Laundry €4. Open Mar.-Oct. Dorms €12; private rooms €14 per person.) The most convenient and best-priced B&Bs in the area are on the far side of town, at the western end of Main St. **Andros B&B ❸** has plush-carpeted rooms and suites for up to four. (☎51234. All rooms with bath and TV. €25 per person.) **Marguerite's B&B ❸,** next door in a nearly identical house, is distinguished by its hardwood floors. (☎51699. All rooms with bath. €25 per person.)

The **Donegal Organic Farm** sells unadulterated veggies. (See **Sights,** below. Open M-Sa 9:30am-8pm.) On Main St. there is a wholefoods shop called **Good Earth** (☎51794; open M-Sa 9:30am-6pm) and a **Spar** supermarket (☎51131; open daily 8am-10pm). For a sit-down meal, the bar in the **Highlands Hotel ❷** is a tasty option. (☎51111. Sandwiches €2.55, lunch €5.70, mains €6.70-11.10.) The **Nighthawks Cafe**

❶, Main St., provides comfort food at all hours. (☎51389. Open M-Th 10am-midnight, F 10am-2am, Sa 10am-4am, Su 3pm-1am.)

Like everything else in town, the pubs are on Main St. **Paddy's Bar** (☎51158) draws youngish locals and hostelers, with rock and trad performances every night during the summer. The big screen TV serves well for the televised matches on Sunday. **Keeney's Food Pub** (☎51920), on the opposite side of the street, dishes up pub grub from 12:30-9pm, though the pints flow until late. The **Limelight** "entertainment complex" dominates the Glenties social scene from behind a faded and cracked facade at the eastern (Dungloe) end of Main St. This is your typical small-town nightclub, with top-40 and dance music on separate floors and an entire rural county's worth of drunken folk. (☎51118. F alcohol-free for ages 15-18, cover €5; Sa 18+, €8. Su live music. Open 10pm-2am.)

SIGHTS AND HIKING. Next to the hostel, **St. Connell's Museum and Heritage Centre** is a good starting point for exploration of the surrounding countryside. Student staffers will work hard to find information for curious visitors. An assortment of exhibits and videos mostly concern St. Connell and the remaining markers of his 6th-century missionary; it also has a "study room" for genealogy. (€2.50, children €1. Open Apr.-Sept. M-Sa 10am-5pm, closed for lunch 1-2pm.)

The countryside around Glenties contains a number of attractive short hikes, many of which are signposted from the crossroads next to the heritage center. One of the most satisfying routes takes you to **Inniskeel Island,** 8 mi. past Glenties toward Dungloe; signs point the way from a carpark at **Narin Beach.** The island, where the ruins of **St. Connell's** 6th-century church lie, is accessible only when the tide is out; check the *Irish Independent* or other newspapers for tidal information. Another series of trails leads into the foothills south of town.

South of Glenties on N56, there is an uphill turnoff marked "organic farm"; 2 mi. up that road is indeed Thomas Becht's **Donegal Organic Farm,** a sort of hillside *mélange* of forestry plantation, hydroelectric power plant, and vegetable garden. In addition to peddling veggies, the place offers tree-sponsorship programs, ECO-Working camps for adolescents, and longer-term opportunities for individuals with serious (not ha-ha) interests in sustainable agriculture or forestry. (☎51286; www.esatclear.ie/~tbecht. Open M-Sa 9:30am-8pm.) A **nature trail** at the farm guides visitors through the forest and connects to the longer trail bound for **Lough Anney,** the reservoir for Glenties. Farther uphill is a waterfall and Special Area for Conservation (SAC) that makes a nice picnic-spot. The entire walk is 8 mi. round-trip. A shorter option is the 2½ mi. walk along the **Owenrea River** leading to **Mullantayboyne;** from town, head down Main St. toward Glencolmcille and turn right at the Meenahall sign. The river lies ahead on the right side of the road. The *Ordnance Survey Discovery Series #11* is the best map for walking the area.

The **Harvest Fair** used to be an annual celebration of local agriculture, industry, and beer; the former two have since fallen by the wayside to make more room for the latter. Gee, imagine that. The first weekend in October, fiddlers from across the globe descend on Glenties for **Fiddler's Weekend.**

THE NORTHWEST GAELTACHT

The four parishes in Co. Donegal's northwest corner comprise the largest *gaeltacht* in the Republic. Though the Rosses, Gweedore, Gartan, and Cloghaneely all maintain distinct identities, they are united by their intensely traditional Irish culture, which has flourished unperturbed in the *gaeltacht*'s geographic isolation. Donegal's distinct dialect of Irish and the county's famous style of fiddling, both cultural forms that serve as showpieces in other parts of Ireland, are here living parts of daily routines. There are few visitors to the area, and locals often feign incredulity about its appeal. Do not let them fool you—whether it be the solitude of hikes through the Derryveagh Mountains or the raucous *craic* of a great trad session, there will always be plenty to discover in the isolated north.

THE ROSSES

Extending from northward from Dungloe, the Rosses are part of a linguistic buffer zone known as the "broken" *gaeltacht;* locals here regularly employ both the English and Irish language in everyday conversation. While the N56 rides along the spectacular midwest coast from Glenties to Dungloe, expansive, sandy beaches lie isolated by the eerie stillness of the Derryveagh Mountains. A stay among the Rosses's bogs and hills is an excellent primer for journeys deeper into the *gaeltacht;* this is also the northernmost outpost of information and supplies.

DUNGLOE (AN CLOCHÁN LIATH) ☎075

Dungloe (dun-LO) may be the capital of the Rosses, but it's still a one-horse town; the largest attraction is an annual festival at the end of July featuring local-born crooner Daniel O'Donnell. Dungloe is also near Crohy Head, which boasts hours of hiking and cycling along a beautiful beach. More importantly, this town contains the last official tourist office for visitors continuing northwest.

TRANSPORTATION AND PRACTICAL INFORMATION. Dungloe is a stopping point for **Bus Éireann** (☎073 21309) on its way to Donegal Town thrice daily in July and August. The following private bus lines also serve Dungloe: **Doherty's** (☎21105) to Larne via Letterkenny and Derry; **Feda O'Donnell** (☎48114) to Galway (Su-M only) via Glenties, Ardara, Killybegs, Donegal Town, and Sligo; **McGeehan's** (☎46150) to Dublin via Glenties, Ardara, Donegal Town, and Enniskillen (July-Sept. M-F 3 per day, Sa 2 per day, Su 1 per day; Oct.-June M-Sa 2 per day); **Swilly** (☎22863) to Derry via Burtonport, Annagry, Crolly, Bloody Foreland, Falcarragh, and Letterkenny (M-F 3 per day). **Brennan** (☎22633 or 086 261 0888) and **Joyce** (☎087 222 4967) provide **taxi** services for the area. The Dungloe **tourist office,** on a well-marked side street off Main St. toward the shore, is the only such office for northern Donegal. (☎21297. Open May-Sept. M-Sa 10am-6pm, Su noon-4pm.) Main St. sports a **Bank of Ireland** with a 24hr. **ATM** (☎21077; open M-F 10am-12:30pm and 1:30-4pm, Th until 5pm), as well as **O'Donnell's Pharmacy.** (☎21386. Open M-Sa 9am-6pm.) For the web-savvy, the **library,** housed in the chapel on Chapel St., offers **Internet access.** (☎22500. €2.50 per 30min. Open 2-5:30pm.) The teeny **post office** is on Quay Rd. (☎21067. Open M-F 9am-1pm and 2-5:30pm, Sa 9am-1pm.)

ACCOMMODATIONS, FOOD, AND PUBS. Greene's Independent Holiday Hostel (IHH) ❶, Carnmore Rd., is right off Main St. heading away from the water. Mr. Greene's basic hostel offers a comfy common room and a kitchen. (☎21943. **Bike rental** €6.50 per day for guests; others €7.60. Dorms €11; private rooms €12-14 per person.) **Dungloe Camping and Caravan Park ❶** is right behind Greene's hostel. (☎21943. €6 per person; €13 per car or caravan. Laundry €5.) A 10min. walk down the Burtonport road, **Ard Crone House ❸** welcomes guests into its curiously red halls. (☎21153. Singles €38; shared rooms €26 per person.) **Ostán na Rosann ❺** sits on the hill toward Burtonport, just outside of town. In addition to its spacious rooms, this upscale hotel offers a top-notch leisure and fitness center with a pool, gym, jacuzzi, and sauna. What's more, you don't have to leave the grounds for a meal—enjoy bar food or a full dinner menu while gazing out at the bay. (☎22444. B&B singles €57-63; doubles with dinner €125-138.)

GAELTACHT PUBSPEAK *Let's Go,* ever by your side, has assembled a course on navigating a potential conversation that may arise in a *gaeltacht* pub. When you enter a pub, you will most likely be greeted with a friendly "*Cen chaoi an bhfuil sibh*?" (ken QUEE on WILL shiv; "How's it going?") to which you would reply, "*Beidh mé go-brea ma tagann tu Guinness domsa!*" (BAY may GO-bra ma TA-gin to Guinness DUM-sa; "I'll be fine if you give me a Guinness!") As the night proceeds you may need to use the facilities–just ask "*Cá bhfuil an leithreas le'dthoil?*" (ka WILL on le-RUSS le-the-HULL; "Where's the toilet?") And if you're deep in the *gaeltacht,* you'll likely hear "*Amach ansin*" (a-MOCK on-SHIN; "Outside"). Later in the night, when you spot a young lass or lad, steel yourself and ask "*Ar mhaith leat a bheith ag damsha?*" (err WA lat a VE-egg DOWSA-a; "Would you like to dance?") When the time is right, and you and Seamus/Molly are staring soulfully at each other through your pint glasses, you might slip in an oh-so-subtle "*Ar maith leat a beith ag dul a codladh liomsa?*" (err MA lat a VE-egg DULL-a COLL-ah LUM-sa; "Would you like to sleep with me?") If you receive a *bos* in the *aghaidh,* blame it on pronunciation. For more fun with the mother tongue, see the **Glossary,** p. 559.

If you're cooking, stop by the **Cope Supermarket,** Main St. (☎21022. Open M-Sa 9am-6pm, F until 7pm.) **SuperValu** is about half a mile down Carnmore Rd. (☎21006. Open M-Th 9am-6:30pm, F 9am-8pm, Sa 9am-7pm.) **Doherty's ❷** provides a variety of consistently cheap dishes in a voluminous cafe/takeaway. (☎21654. Pizza €5.50-7.60; mains from €4.50. Open M-Th 9am-11pm, F-Sa 9am-midnight, Su 1-9pm.) At the **Riverside Bistro ❸,** patrons can expect slightly snazzed-up versions of traditional cuisine, served at somewhat inflated prices under Parisian surrealist photographs. Vegetarian mains begin at €8.30 and meaty meals run from €13-19. (☎21062. Lunch specials €6.30. Open daily 12:30-3pm and 6-10pm.) **Beedy's,** Main St. (☎21219), no longer offers trad, but this many-splendored bar still rocks out with local bands on weekends and has a beer garden perfect for those occasional sunny days. For the not-so-sunny days (welcome to Ireland), establish your prowess at the pool table. **Bridge Inn** hosts a Saturday disco, and-packs crowds in for GAA games on summer nights. (☎21036. Disco cover €6.35.) When the nightclub isn't open, idle youngsters congregate across the street at the **Atlantic Bar** (☎22166) to watch live bands on weekends year-round.

SIGHTS. Party animals flock to Dungloe during the last week of July, when the population swells to 80,000 for the 10-day-long **Mary from Dungloe Festival.** The highlight of the festival is when the new "Mary from Dungloe" is crowned, although most attendees would argue that it's the three concerts that Daniel O'Donnell performs during the week that really make the festival. Strange as it may seem to the outside observer, tickets for the songster go on sale in January and sell out almost immediately. Interested parties should join in the madness with similarly lemming-esque enthusiasm. For festival information and ticket bookings, call the **Festival Booking Office** next to the tourist office. (☎21254. Open M-Sa 10am-6pm.) For sea-angling and boat tours, visitors should contact Neil and Ann Gallagher at **West Donegal Sea-Angling Charters** (☎48403 or 087 833 2969; www.donegalseaangling.com). For information on inland fisheries or inland boat hire in the Rosses, the pertinent organization is **Rosses Anglers Association.** (☎21163, 42124, or 42167. Day permit €6.35; boat fee €12.70.)

The **Crohy Head** (*Ceann na Cruaiche*) peninsula, 6 mi. southwest of Dungloe, is surrounded by a slew of oddly shaped rock formations that extend from its jagged coast. The **Crohy Head Youth Hostel (An Óige/HI) ❶,** in an old coast guard station, offers stupendous views of these formations and of the Atlantic beyond.

Come prepared for wind and cold, as the building sits as it did 30 years ago. (☎21950. Call ahead; warden may be off-site. July-Sept. €10.) To reach Crohy Head from Dungloe, turn onto Quay Rd. (toward Maghery) halfway down Main St. and follow the bumpy road along the sea for 3½ mi., about 1 mi. past Maghery.

BURTONPORT AND ENVIRONS (AILT AN CHÓRRAIN) ☎075

About 5 mi. north of Dungloe, the fishing village of Burtonport is less a town than a few pubs clustered around a pier. The ferry to Arranmore Island docks here, and the village also makes a good base for **fishing** and **boat trips** to the many uninhabited islands in the area. **Bus**-wise, **Feda O'Donnell's** (☎48114) service between Donegal and Galway stops in Burtonport once a day (Su-M) on its rambles throughout the *gaeltacht*. The **O'Donnell Trans-Ulster Express** (☎48356) speeds through Burtonport on its way to Belfast via Letterkenny and Derry. **Swilly** (☎21380) has daily stops in Burtonport on its Derry-Letterkenny-Dungloe route.

More salmon land here than in any other spot in the British Isles. Intense **sea angling competitions** take place during July and August—call the Dungloe tourist office for details. **Sea anglers** can book trips from the shop on Burtonport Pier. (☎42077 or 086 833 2969. Open daily 10am-5pm. Fishing trips €30; rod rental €6.50.) The **Burtonport Festival** rouses up locals the week preceding the Mary from Dungloe Festival in July with a similar program of endemic trad, dance, and sport. The **post office** is at the start of town, about 200 yd. from the pier. (☎42001. Open M-F 9am-1pm and 2-5:30pm, Sa 9am-1pm.)

Call ahead from Dungloe to the big yellow **Cois na Mara Hostel ❶**, about a 10min. walk from town on the main road. This former B&B ("Erin House") has now become a sort of hostel-guesthouse, complete with high ceilings, custom-made bunk beds, and breakfasts of scones and oatmeal. Owner Tim, a well-traveled trad fan, directs guests to the best local sessions. (☎42079. Breakfast included. **Internet access** €3.50-4.50 per hr. **Laundry** €4. Dorms €12; doubles €30.) The **Cope,** at the top of the town, is the largest **grocery** on either side of the water, so stock up before boarding the Arranmore ferry. (☎42004. Open M-Sa 9am-6pm.) The James Joyce Award-winning **Lobster Pot ❸,** on Main St. beside the harbor, attracts the biggest crowds in town—hey, the place serves good food, what can we say? Try to make like DiCaprio and tackle the Titanic Seafood Platter (€25.50). Wall-hangings include Irish soccer jerseys and a Jaws head clutching a nail-polished hand in its teeth. (☎42012. Sandwiches from €2.50; mains €6.35-14. Restaurant open daily 6-9:30pm; bar food 1-6pm.) All of Burtonport's pubs squat around the harbor, and most sport a maritime theme. Try the scrumptious steak baguette (€8.95) at **Skipper's Tavern,** which teems with nets, skippers' hats, and nautical knots. (☎42234. Bar food all day. Trad and ballads most summer nights.) Across from the pier at **O'Donnell's Bar** (☎42255), landlubbers escape the salt air at Burtonport's oldest pub. The **Harbour Bar** (☎42321), next to the pier, serves beer.

Five miles north of Burtonport on the coast road is the little village of **Kincasslagh** (*Cionn Caslach*), birthplace of singer Daniel O'Donnell, and the site of his **Viking House Hotel ❺.** Big, beautiful, and clearly king of the hill, the Viking House is a mecca for those desiring creature comforts—and Golden Girls on O'Donnell pilgrimages. (☎43295. B&B singles €57; doubles €85; triples €121.) A minor road heads west to the beaches and thatched cottages of **Cruit Island** (actually a peninsula masquerading as an island). At the end of this imposter island, you'll find a **golf course** (☎43296). Farther north, the magnificent sandy stretch known as **Carrickfinn Strand** is marred only by the presence of tiny **Donegal Airport** (☎48284). To find this beautiful beach, take the left turn leading to the airport and continue to the carpark at the edge of the beach; from here you're just a stroll away from sandy stretches (where swimming is restricted to only the most shallow of areas).

ARRANMORE ISLAND (ÁRÁINN MHÓR) ☎075

Although one side of Arranmore Island (pop. 600) is primarily Irish-speaking and shows relatively little influence from the mainland, the other was, for a time, well-known for its riotous partying into the wee hours. Alas, community complaints resulted in an increased *Garda* presence on the island during summer weekends. There are those who claim that this development has only forced revelers out onto the beach in search of *craic*, but the fact remains that every pub is now swept out at 1am. Fortunately, scenic walks have not yet been restricted, and these can be found in abundance merely by leaving the bustling area around the docks.

TRANSPORTATION AND PRACTICAL INFORMATION. The **ferry office,** next to the pier, sends boats to Burtonport. (☎20532. Office open daily 8:30am-8:30pm. 25min. July-Aug. 7-8 per day; Sept.-June M-Sa 6 per day, Su 4 per day. Bicycles €3. Tickets €9; students €8, children €5, seniors free with ID.) Although Arranmore has no official tourist office, the ferry office serves as an unofficial source of information, and maps of the island (€3) can be purchased at most off-shore stores and B&Bs. A guide to the Arranmore Way (€1.05) is available at Teac Phil Bán's store (see **Accommodations, Food, and Pubs,** below). By day, **O'Donnell's** (☎087 260 6833 or 087 780690) will provide **taxis.** The **post office** is just off the pier on the main road. (☎20301. Open M-F 9am-1pm and 2-5:30pm, Sa 9am-1pm.)

ACCOMMODATIONS, FOOD, AND PUBS. Along the shore to the left of the ferryport stretches a string of pubs and houses. Down the street from the ferry lies the newly renovated **Arranmore Hostel ❶,** a clean, modern building in an excellent seaside location visible from the quay. Call ahead to let the owners (who live off-site) know when you're coming and to book the popular sea-view dorm. (☎20737, 20015, or 20515. Wheelchair-accessible. July-Aug. dorms €13; private rooms €14.50 per person; family rooms €47. Rates reduced in Sept. and June.) The house closest to the ferry is the **Boat House ❸,** where life-long islanders offer clean rooms and expert advice on exploring Arranmore. (☎20511. All rooms with bath. €26 per person.) Located at the top of the hill almost directly across from the ferry landing is **The Glen Hotel ❸.** This beautiful, family-run establishment has been part of the island's history since the mid-1800s, with affordable prices and a bar and restaurant on-site. (☎20505. Breakfast included. Open Apr.-Oct. Singles €30-34; shared rooms €31-33 per person.)

Although the tradition of late-night drinking has been curtailed by constant police scrutiny, there are still plenty of fine (standard-hours) pubs on Arranmore. Make **Early's Bar** (☎20515), 50 yd. up the hill from the landing, your first stop when you arrive on the island; a nice, hot whiskey will strip away any lingering chill. Crooner Daniel O'Donnell earned his first gig at this pub, and he gives an annual concert on-island (bringing the supplicating hordes with him) as a token of thanks for Arranmore's early support. (☎20515. Trad on summer weekends.) To the left of the ferry dock as you step off the boat is **Teac Phil Bán's.** At high tide the ocean laps against the restaurant's foundations; at the attached grocery store, visitors can buy items from books on Arranmore genealogy (€6.35) to *dulce*, a local seaweed delicacy. (☎20908. Open M-F 11am-11pm, Sa-Su 11am-1pm.) **Bonner's Ferryboat Restaurant,** a coffee shop attached to the Arranmore Ferry Office, also functions as an **amusement center.** Imagine all of the rollercoaster rides, cotton candy, and things you love about Disneyland…now forget it. Here you'll find gambling, a pool table, and some video games. Late afternoon sees an influx of youngsters from Irish-language programs. (Sandwiches €2-5.50; mains €5.50-14. Open daily 9am-8:30pm.) **Pally's** (☎20584) is a mile past the ferry dock; turn left off the main road toward the sea, and turn left at the sign for a pint atop 150-year-old tiles stolen from a church.

Neily's (☎20509), half a mile more down the main road, is a local watering hole that has been globalized by the installation of a satellite TV. **O'Donnell's** (☎20918), overlooking a small bay, is the farthest pub out on the inhabited portion of the island.

SIGHTS AND ACTIVITIES. **The Arranmore Way** is the main attraction on this little island. This well-marked footpath runs the circumference of the island and offers three possible hiking paths. A full perambulation of Arranmore Way takes a good 6hr. The longest of the three trails goes to the **lighthouse** at the far tip of the island, high above cliffs and crashing water. Along the way you'll pass **The Old Mill,** the **Old Coastguard Station,** the inner-island **lakes,** a **mass rock,** and all the sights of the town's main road. For those who have seen one lighthouse too many, on the second walk (about 4hr.) you'll still encounter the town's main sights, including the **craft shop** and the **Glen Hotel,** and you'll also pass **The Bridge,** with an amazing view of the islands and the Donegal coastline. Sticking mainly to the southeastern part of the island and never leaving habitation, the third hiking option, only 5 mi. long (about 2hr.), brings you to easily accessible views of the island, perfect for the faint of heart or fatigued of foot. All three trails are detailed in the *Siúlóid Árainn Mhóir* (€1.05), available at Teac Phil Bán's (see **Food,** above).

Those who wish to devote their summers to self-edification will run to the Foghlaín.com Irish Language and Culture Center, offering **Gaelic-language courses** on Arranmore Island. A typical day in this one-week summer program would consist of classes in conversational and practical Gaelic, workshops on various aspects of Irish culture, and guided historical walks around the island. Evening activities include trad sessions, poetry readings, and set dancing. You'll leave Arranmore smarter than the average tourist and be able to confidently chat up that Irish lad/lass you've been eyeing in the *gaeltacht* (☎21593; 1-week cultural course €165).

RANAFAST AND ITS ANNAGRY (ANAGAIRE) ☎075

In the heart of the Donegal *gaeltacht*, the village of **Annagry,** about 6 mi. past Burtonport on R259, marks the beginning of the **Ranafast** area, famous for its storytelling tradition. Usually an eerily still coastal hamlet, Annagry is upended each summer by flocks of young people from across the island piling in to attend Irish-language camps. Travelers seeking luxury B&B pampering in Annagry should head to **Danny Minnie's ❹.** All rooms come complete with bath and gorgeous antique furniture, creating a comfortable and cozy temporary abode. (☎48201. €40 per per-

LET'S GO DOES NOT RECOMMEND HITCHHIKING (UNLESS IT'S WITH A FRIDGE...)

Ireland has no shortage of great literature, extending from the stories of Cúchulainn in the 8th century to James Joyce's *Ulysses* in the 20th. Now, relative newcomer Tony Hawks has made quite a name for himself with his 1998 book *Round Ireland With a Fridge.* The basic premise: during a night of Guinness-induced revelry, a friend bets Tony £100 that he cannot hitchhike the circumference of Ireland, in one month, with a fridge. From this wager, the author embarks on his circuit and is discovered by the Irish media, who promptly elevate him to folk-hero status. Dubbed "Fridge Man," he meets kings (of Tory Island), nuns (who bless him), spoons players, and wacky local characters, who take his small fridge (which he also uses as a suitcase) horseback-riding and surfing. Oh, and he drinks a lot. He's since written another book, *Playing the Moldovans at Tennis,* also the product of a Guinness-goggled gamble. So while we at *Let's Go* do not recommend hitchhiking, we admit that undertaking this activity with a household appliance may, at one point, have had its benefits.

son.) Downstairs, enjoy a superb candlelit meal in the hotel's **restaurant ❺**, while admiring the elegant dining room (mains €20-35). In addition to their storytelling and fine dining, the outskirts of Annagry hold some well-respected trad institutions. About 500 yd. south of the village, on top of a hill to the left of the road, is **Teác Jack's** (☎48113) pub and restaurant. Although better known for genre-defying pub food, Jack's also hosts congregations of talented local musicians on weekend nights in the summer. Closed for renovations in 2002, a newer, larger pub of the same name should be up and running smoothly in 2003. Three miles west of town is the (in)famous **Leo's Tavern** (☎48143). Leo is the father of voice guru **Enya** and the family group **Clannad,** and he's certainly not shy about it—beyond hanging their silver, gold, and platinum records from the walls, Leo has cobbled together an entire lounge act centered around his role as humble *paterfamilias*. Leo plays his enormous electric piano-accordion on stage and leads sing-alongs for daytime tour groups, nightly audiences, and his own amusement. On Thursday nights in July and August a large company of musicians gather at Leo's for "real" trad sessions. For a more feasible (and surprisingly impressive) musical experience, head to **Teác Tessie,** across the street, where a rotating cast of locals and musical pilgrims gathers for fine trad on Sunday nights. (☎48124. Food served 11am-8pm.)

GWEEDORE (GAOTH DUBHAIR)

The coastal parish of Gweedore serves as a gateway to the inland mountains that guard its border with Cloghaneely. Errigal Mountain, the legendary Poison Glen, and the Bloody Foreland are the most famous sights in this beautiful expanse of bog, rock, and sea. Because it is situated between the Rosses to the southwest and Cloghaneely to the east, Gweedore fulfills another, more socially relevant role as the weekend amusement center for *gaeltacht* youth, who flood Derrybeg's discos on weekend nights. Tory Island, off Gweedore's northern coast, *is* a world apart from Ireland, with its own elected king and freedom from Irish taxes.

DUNLEWY AND ERRIGAL MOUNTAIN ☎075

A mile north of the small town of **Crolly,** N56 and the coastal road diverge. N56 turns inland and reaches R251 after about 5 mi. This road leads east through the village of **Dunlewy** *(Dún Lúiche)*, past the conical **Errigal Mountain,** and on to **Glenveagh National Park.** Dunlewy, which straddles the border of Gweedore and Cloghaneely parishes, makes a great base for exploring the pristine heaths of the **Derryveagh Mountains.** Trails for hikers of varying abilities extend over the region like an interlocking web of…walking paths. These are often hard to follow, even with a map; hikers should get themselves the *Ordnance Survey Discovery Series #1* and *6*, and always inform someone of their plans before setting off. The town itself offers its own set of scenic trails, including the ascent to Errigal, a ramble through the **Poison Glen,** and the numerous paths in Glenveagh National Park (see p. 427).

Buses only come as close as Crolly, 1 mi. south. **Feda O'Donnell** (☎48114) provides a daily coach service to and from Galway and Donegal Town; **John McGinley Coaches** (☎074 35201) makes Crolly its starting point for a Dublin journey; **O'Donnell Trans-Ulster Express** (☎48356) goes by on its way to Belfast via Letterkenny and Derry; and **Swilly** (Dungloe ☎21380, Derry ☎7126 2017) passes through on its Dungloe-Derry route. To get from Crolly to Dunlewy, you'll have to grab a taxi: **Charlie Mac** (☎087 26037) and **Popeye's** (☎075 32633) can help you on your way.

The two hostels in Dunlewy are along R251. The warden of the **Errigal Youth Hostel (An Óige/HI) ❶,** only 1 mi. from the foot of Errigal, has modernized the facilities of this aging hostel. As it stands, the place is clean but basic, perfect for backpackers with their minds on the trail. (☎31180. Lockout 10am-5pm. Curfew 1am. June-

Sept. dorms €11; bunked private rooms €14.50 per person. Oct.-May €9.50/€13.) A few hundred yards down the road to the west, in the shell of the old Dunlewy Hotel, is the **Backpackers Ireland Lakeside Hostel ❶.** Though the hot showers are in the chilly basement, this relatively new hostel is another good option for weary hikers and one without the regulations of its neighbor. (☎32133. Dorms €10; private rooms €12 per person.)

A few minutes up the road is a turnoff to **Dunlewy Lake** and the **Poison Glen.** Within the glen is the former **manor** of an English aristocrat. In an open spot next to the lake stands his **abandoned church;** its decaying, roofless exterior makes a spooky addition to the myth-laden surroundings. If you continue along the paved road around a few curves, you'll reach an unmarked carpark that signals the beginning of the trail up the side of **Errigal Mountain** (at 2466 ft., Ireland's 2nd-highest peak). Expect your scramble through loose scree and over a narrow ridge to take the 3hr. round-trip. Be sure to keep an eye on the clouds—they've been known to congregate suddenly around the mountaintop, and if visibility drops too much, your trip back down could be shortened by several hours, in a very bad way.

Back in Dunlewy proper, just before the hostel, the **Ionad Cois Locha Dunlewy,** or **Dunlewy Lakeside Centre,** offers boat tours on Dunlewy Lake, weaving demonstrations, a craft shop, a playground, pens containing red deer, enough info on the area to stand as a tourist office, and a fire-warmed cafe. (☎31699. Open Easter-Oct. M-Sa 10:30am-6pm, Su 11am-7pm. Boat trip or weaving cottage tour €4.50; students and seniors €4, children €3.25, families €9. Combined ticket €7/€6/€5/€18. Playground €3, children €2.50, families €9.) The center also provides an excellent packet of walks in Dunlewy; all interested ramblers should take advantage. There are two routes through the Errigal Mountains: the "tourist route" (3 mi., ascending 1716 ft.; 2-2½hr.) and the more rugged northwest ridge route (2 mi, 1860 ft.; 2-2½hr.); each route will bring you to the summit (which is, incidentally, the smallest in the country at only a few feet across). The center also offers trad concerts on Tuesdays in the summer (tickets €10-13) and music workshops all year.

NORTHWEST IRELAND

DAYTRIPS FROM DUNLEWY

On the eastern side of the Derryveagh Mountains, **Gartan Parish** is the most rural of the *gaeltacht* parishes. As a result, there are few towns and even fewer accommodations. Nevertheless, Gartan is home to some of the *gaeltacht*'s greatest attractions. Aesthetically-minded visitors will find much to treasure here, whether in the scenic beauty of **Glenveagh National Park** or the eclectic collection of **Glebe House.** Most travelers base themselves in Dunlewy or daytrip out of Letterkenny via **Bus Éireann's** "Hills of Donegal" Tour. (☎074 21309. €7.60 return.)

GLENVEAGH NATIONAL PARK. From the hostels in Gweedore, it's an easy hike into Glenveagh National Park's 37 sq. mi. of forest glens, bogs, and mountains. One of the largest herds of red deer in Europe roams the park; deer-watching is best at dusk and in the winter, when the deer come down to the valley to forage. Despite Glenveagh's status as the second most popular national park in Ireland, you probably won't be aware of any other human animals within its pristine confines—make sure to hold on to that map. Park rangers lead **guided nature walks** and more strenuous **hill walks.** The **visitors center** has information about these as well as self-guided routes, and can prepare you for your hike with several exhibits, a 25min. video on the park's wildlife and history, and a meal at its cafeteria-style **restaurant.** The Park Guide (€6.35) and *Ordnance Survey #6* (€4.95) are both available at the visitors center, which is on R251 east of Dunlewy *(☎074 37090. Park and center open Mar.-Nov. daily 10am-5pm. Call ahead for info or to schedule a walk.)*

FROM THE ROAD

OF TRACTORS AND TRAVELERS

In Ireland, you'll always find a helpful hand from the locals—this is something I've learned all too well. One day, while on my way to Tory Island, I found myself on a somewhat perilous, unmarked single-car road. After about 3 mi. of unposted driving, I lost faith in the Irish transit authorities, as one is wont to do when faced with a dearth of signs encouraging you along your uncertain way. As fate or karma would have it, I soon paid for my lack of faith when my trusty Nissan Micra became stuck in a veritable ditch. After 20min. of wheel-spinning, mud flying, and some ingenious attempts at self-extraction via plywood planks, I was almost resigned to a roadside fate and a night in the car. Beaten, but not broken, I instead hiked back to the nearest farmhouse only to have a family greet me with excited, knowing smiles. Apparently, I was not the first casualty of this road. The previous week they had pulled out some Slovakians from the very same ditch, and the year before was a record one, with nearly a dozen such stranded visitors. It was decided that the car would not budge from mere pushing, so another local was called, and he brought with him the might of a tractor. I took pictures of the extraction and promised to send a shot back to my saviors. They declined my offer of monetary payment, wisely acknowledging that I could someday return the favor if they ever found themselves in a ditch in California.

—Kira Whelan

Summertime tourists can take the minibus from the park's entrance to **Glenveagh Castle,** 2½ mi. away. Despite its relative youth, Glenveagh Castle looks like a medieval keep with its thick walls, battle-ready rampart, turrets, and round tower. *(Minibus from park entrance runs every 10-15min.; last departure 1½hr. before closing. Adults €2, students €1. Castle open for guided tours only; last tour 1¼hr. before closing. €2.50, students €1.20.)* The surrounding **gardens** brighten up the bleak history that surrounds the castle; they were designed by a later owner, American Henry McIlhenny, who left the estate to the government at his death. Consider taking the free **tour** of the grounds. *(Depart castle courtyard July-Aug. Tu and Th 2pm.)* A mile up the incline behind the castle is **View Point,** which provides a glimpse of the park's vast expanse.

GLEBE GALLERY AND GLEBE HOUSE. The delicately manicured 20-acre plot on the northern shore of Gartan Lough, 11 mi. east of Dunlewy, was bequeathed to the state in 1981 by the English-cum-Irish painter Derek Hill. The site houses two radically different spaces for the presentation of art. The **Glebe Gallery,** formerly Hill's own display space, hangs different exhibitions of contemporary art throughout the year in a gallery with wood floors, track lighting, and all the other modern trappings. **Glebe House,** Hill's former residence, is another beast altogether. The house contains over 300 paintings and an assortment of craft objects, all preserved as they were when Hill lived there. Hill's friend Henry McIlhenny, owner of the Glenveagh castle (see above), gave Hill the only Georgian piece of furniture in this Georgian house: of the Tiffany lamp he is rumored to have commented, "I think it is rather vulgar, but it fits quite well with the rest of the house." Judge for yourself. The collection lies somewhere between the ridiculous and the sublime—how could anyone find fault with a space that hangs works by Renoir and Picasso with the same obvious pride that parents reserve for children's drawings on a refrigerator? Works by Hill's contemporaries (including the **Tory Island "primitive" painters**) round out this cluttered collection. Both the Glebe Gallery and Glebe House are on R251, 5 mi. southeast of the visitors center in Glenveagh National Park. *(☎074 37071. Open Easter week and late May to late Sept. M-Th and Sa-Su 11am-6:30pm; last tour 5:30pm. €2.50, students and children €1.20, seniors €1.90.)*

ST. COLMCILLE HERITAGE CENTRE. St. Colmcille (AD 521-597), famed for bringing Christianity from Ireland to Scotland, once resided near the shores of Gartan Lough. The countryside around the lough is punctuated with Colmcillian ruins. The newly opened St. Colmcille Heritage Centre, across Gartan Lough from Glebe House, is devoted to his legacy, and has permanent exhibits about the development of Christianity in Donegal, with a focus on Colmcille's life and martyrdom in Iona, Scotland. *(☎074 37306 or 37021. Open Apr.-Sept. M-Sa 10:30am-6pm, Su 1-6pm. €2, students €1.50, children €1, seniors €1.50.)* It also functions as an unofficial tourist office; documents provide lucid directions to other saintly sights, including **Colmcille's Birthplace** and **Abbey,** as well as the **Bed of Loneliness.** This giant stone slab, on the southeastern corner of the lake, was the site where ol' Col' meditated and slept the night before he began his exile in Scotland. Since then, prospective emigrants have lain on the stone overnight to ward off future loneliness.

BUNBEG AND DERRYBEG ☎075

Where N56 moves inland to Dungloe, R257 continues along the coast to Bunbeg *(An Bun Beag)*. Since there's little traffic, this scenic stretch of road is perfect for cyclists. Hitchers tend to stay on N56, where cars are more common. **Bunbeg Harbour,** the smallest enclosed harbor in Ireland, was a main exit and entry point during the height of British occupation, and relics from that period—military barracks, grain stones, look-out towers—line the harbor. The mile of R257 between Bunbeg and **Derrybeg** *(Doirí Beaga)* is facetiously referred to by locals as "the Golden Mile"; unlike the rest of the region, this stretch has not escaped the roaming hand of tourism. Those who have grown tired of beautiful hikes and remote wilderness are sure to find some relief in Derrybeg's suburban splendor.

TRANSPORTATION AND PRACTICAL INFORMATION. To reach Derrybeg by **bus,** try **Swilly's** (☎074 22863), whose Donegal-Derry service hits the town daily. Derrybeg's streets have several banks, but only the **AIB** has both a **bureau de change** and an **ATM.** Across the street, **Bank of Ireland** has only a **bureau de change.** (☎31193. Both banks open M-F 10am-12:30pm and 1:30-4pm, Th until 5pm.) **Gweedore Chemists** (☎31254) is housed in a white building across the street and a few yards up from Hudi Beag's pub. The local **post office** is... well... a post office. (☎31165. Open M-F 9am-1pm and 2-5:30pm.)

ACCOMMODATIONS, FOOD, AND PUBS. There are no longer any budget accommodations in Bunbeg or Derrybeg; these are primarily stop-by-and-stock-up towns for the budget traveler. However, there are several reasonable and lovely B&Bs in town, as well as a couple of hotel options. The left immediately after the AIB leads to **An Teach Bán ❸,** run by amiable owners Linda and Paul, who serve the best Irish breakfast around. Clean and cheerful rooms offer beautiful views of the bay, and the new, nearly completed conservatory make this B&B worth a night's stay or two. (☎31569. Singles €23-28; shared rooms €26 per person.) A few yards up on the left is **Teac Campbell Loístín ❸.** This large B&B is elegantly decorated and provides all the amenities you could desire in your room (☎31545; €26 per person). **Seaview Hotel ❹** (☎31159; singles €45.50-50; doubles €80-90) and **Ostan Radharc an Eargail ❹** (☎31355; singles €45; doubles €75) provide more luxurious bed and breakfast options, along with a multitude of on-site services. The **Bunbeg House ❺** (☎31305), on the waterfront, offers a steep prix-fixe dinner (€30 per person), as well as a **B&B ❸** (€35 per person).

At the west end of Derrybeg is **Teach Niocáin,** which is not only a **grocery** with a fantastic hot bar and sandwich shop, but also a **laundrette.** (☎31065. 5 sausage rolls for €1.30. Wash and dry €6.35. Open daily 8am-10pm.) Visitors to Derrybeg in search of late-night snacks or basic toiletries can always hit the **Shopping Basket.** (☎31485. Open daily 9am-10pm.) Derrybeg's best option for takeaway is **Machaire an Chlochair Cafe ❶** (formerly Sgt. Peppers), which has a wide selection of the three basic food groups—pizza, ice cream, and deep-fried. (☎31110. Open daily noon-12:30am.) The **Tabhairne Hughie Tim** ❷ in the Seaview Hotel serves up bar food (€7.90-18.50) from 3-9:30pm, while next door, the hotel's restaurant **Gola Bistro** ❺ offers more upscale fare (mains €18.50-22.50). The irresistible **Hudi Beag's** pub (☎31016), a two-story white building at the western entrance to town, is the epicenter for half of Derrybeg's musical tradition. On Monday nights, only the truly tone-deaf could pass up the intense session taking place inside. (Think 10-25 musicians at a time from 10pm-1am!) The youth of Derrybeg and every other village within driving distance congregate on weekends to go to the disco at the **Millennium Club,** in the Seaview Hotel (cover €7; F-Su 10:30pm-2am).

SIGHTS AND ACTIVITIES. Bunbeg's harbor is one of two docking places for **Donegal Coastal Cruises** (a.k.a. **Turasmara;** ☎35061 or 31991), the ferry service for Tory Island, which departs from R257 at the edge of town once a day at 9am (see **Transportation,** p. 431). Boats also sail from Bunbeg to **Gola Island,** a nearer but not larger land mass that claims deserted beaches and beautiful views. (☎32487 or 087 293 4895. 25min. 6 per day. €10.15, under 12 €6.35.) Halfway between Bunbeg and its harbor, a single stone pillar marks a rough path that leads to the banks of the **Clady River,** where salmon fishers fish for salmon. **Teach Tomáis** (☎31054), the oldest shop in the parish, specializes in Irish books and crafts, but also offers a small and brilliantly-selected collection of English-language works. (Open M-F 10am-6pm. If shop is locked, knock at the kitchen door to its right.)

North of Derrybeg on R257, the **Bloody Foreland,** a short length of rough scarlet rock, juts out into the sea. At sunset on clear evenings, the sea reflects the deep red hue of the rocks and sea, thereby composing one of Ireland's most famous views. An old legend holds that the sea is colored with the blood of sailors who perished in the wrecks of Spanish galleons. Farther west, the headland at **Meenlaragh (Magheraroarty)** offers miles of unspoiled beaches. A **holy well** remains full of fresh water despite tidal rushes twice a day. This is also the other landing for Tory Island ferries (see **Transportation,** below).

For those of the watersport persuasion, check out the **sailing center** (☎31305) at Bunbeg Harbour. The center offers **dinghy sailing** for beginners and experienced skippers; boats and "weather gear" are provided—you will get wet. You can also call about **speedboat, waterskiiing,** and **island trips** (☎31305). Back on land, children can enroll in modern and ballet **dance lessons** through **Gweedore Dance** (☎60947; €30 per wk.) and adults can take week-long **Irish language courses** through **An Chrannóg** (☎32188; €150 per wk.).

TORY ISLAND (OILEÁN THORAIGH) ☎074

Bare Tory Island, only 8 mi. off the coast, is visible from the Bloody Foreland. Named for its many *tors* (hills), the island provides minimal footing for the weather-beaten cottages and eccentric local characters that fill the town. The island gained mythical status as the home of the demonic Formorians—the original Tory Island pirates who regularly invaded the mainland. Its age-old reputation as a haven for pirates prompted people to equate the word "Tory" with "pirate" or "rascal." The use of "Tory" to mean "Conservative" derives from this Irish slang. (A Whig, incidentally, was originally a Scottish horse thief.) Tory's reputation for swashbuckling and buccaneering was accurate as recently as last century, when the island thrived on illegal *poitín* production; the inaccessibility of the island thwarted British efforts to control its trade (see **Love Poitín #9,** p. 416). All six layers of the island's turf were burned in *poitín* production; as a result, today's Tory appears more sandy and grassy than the mainland. Only one tree survives in the harsh conditions of the small island's sea-exposed area; please stop by and give it a hug. The eastern end of the island breaks apart into a series of jagged sea cliffs.

The small Irish-speaking community has managed to maintain a strong sense of independence. Islanders refer to the mainland as "the country," and still elect a **"Rí na nóileán"** (king of the island) to a lifetime position that usually entails him becoming the island's PR man—he'll greet you when you get off the boat and tell stories of the island's past. Many of Tory's unusual traditions remain intact, including a superstition that deters fishermen from rescuing drowning boatsmen.

TRANSPORTATION AND PRACTICAL INFORMATION. **Donegal Coastal Cruises** (a.k.a. Turasmara; ☎075 31320 or 075 31340; see Bunbeg and Derrybeg, p. 430) runs boats from **Bunbeg** (1½hr.; June-Aug. 1 per day, Oct.-May less frequent) and, more frequently, from **Meenlaragh** (a.k.a. Magheroarty) beyond **Bloody Foreland** on R257 (1hr., June-Aug. 2 per day). Be sure to call ahead to check departure times. The crossing is choppy on the clearest of days, and storms have stranded travelers here for days in summer and even weeks in winter. (Bunbeg dock ☎075 31991, Meenlaragh ☎074 35061. All crossings €19 return, students €16, under 15 €10, under 5 and bicycles free.) On the island, **bikes** can be hired next to the hostel from Patrick Rodgers. (Open all day June-Sept. €7-8 per day, deposit €6.35.)

ACCOMMODATIONS, FOOD, AND PUBS. Tory tourists have several options for accommodations, the cheapest of which is the newly reopened **Tory Hostel (Bru Thoraigh) ❶,** 200 yd. west of the quay, whose spare facilities and thin, foam mattresses provide shelter from the wind. It's the unmarked, white house with green trim just after the seawall—better yet, call in advance. (☎65145. Open June-Sept. 3-bed dorms €12.) **Eilish Rodger's B&B ❷** provides slightly more comfortable digs immediately to the right of the pier (€20 per person). For travelers in need of more creature comforts, the **Óstan Thóraig ❹** has hotel rooms with bath and TV, and the knowledgeable staff makes up for the island's lack of tourist office. (☎35920. Open Apr.-Oct. Singles €50-57; shared rooms €38-44.50 per person. Inquire for specials.) The hotel's **restaurant ❺** is expensive (open 6-9pm; mains €18.50-23), but its **bar ❷** has both daytime and evening menus (food served 12:30-3pm and 6-8:30pm; mains €7.25-10.50), an enormous stained-glass panel of aquatic life, and satellite TV. The island manages to support a takeaway, **Cafe an Chreagain** (KRAY-gun), during peak season. (☎35856. Open 10am-11pm.) **Club Thoraighe** (☎65121 or 35502) features Tory Island trad, which has a slightly stronger rhythmic emphasis than mainland music, and *céilís* (KAY-lees), probably the most popular nighttime option…maybe the only nighttime option.

SIGHTS. East of the pier, **Gailearai Dixon** (Dixon Gallery) showcases the work of the Tory Primitives, a group of local artists promoted by Derek Hill of Glebe House fame (see p. 428). The "primitive" or "naive" moniker derives from the fact that the artists lack formal training. The group's work usually depicts the natural scenery of the island in color-drenched pigments, evoking the living fury of the sea around Tory and the shadowy ruins of its medieval religious past. (☎35011 or 65428. Interested aesthetes should call ahead.) The island's interesting historical sights include the **ruins** of the monastery that St. Colmcille founded in the 6th century, the **Tau Cross** close to the town center, and a **phallic torpedo** erected in the middle of the road; all three contribute to Tory's quirky and alien feel.

Island legend claims that a stone on one of Tory's hills has the power to fulfill wishes. If you throw three pebbles onto the stone, which sits on the east end of the island on an unapproachable perch, your wish will come true. In addition to the **wishing stone,** the island features a **cursing stone.** (The location of the latter has been concealed by local elders to prevent its misuse.) The cursing stone has been credited with the 1884 shipwreck of the aptly named *HMS Wasp* which British officials had sent to collect taxes. The islanders still pay no taxes.

CLOGHANEELY

East of Gweedore lies the parish of Cloghaneely. White sand beaches lure countless tourists here during the two-month high season in July and August, but the area's natural beauty remains year-round. Horn Head and the Ards Forest Park provide the best scenic bargains in all of Ireland; investing even a small amount of time and energy into exploration yields expansive and breathtaking returns.

FALCARRAGH (AN FÁL CARRACH) ☎074

Amidst the silvery strands that stretch along the coast northeast of the Bloody Foreland, and the rocky and pocked landscape found further inland, rests one of the busiest little Irish-speaking towns in the *gaeltacht*. Falcarragh, like many of the settlements in this region, offers little to do in the town itself; it does, however, serve as a colorful rest stop for those heading to the beaches beyond Dunfanaghy. The towering sand dunes at **Ballyness,** 3 mi. out of town, are Falcarragh's primary attraction; to reach them, follow the signs for "Trá" (beach) at south end of town.

Several private **bus** companies stop in Falcarragh: **Feda O'Donnell** (☎48114) traces the West Coast, running from Crolly through Donegal Town to Sligo and Galway; **McGinley** (☎35201 or 01 451 3809) passes through on a Donegal-Dublin trek; **O'Donnell Trans Ulster Express** hits Falcarragh as it cuts a swath from Dungloe to Belfast via Letterkenny and Derry; and **Swilly** (☎22863) drops in on its way from Donegal to Derry. Hitching is reportedly quite common in this area. For travel over shorter distances, **Joe's Taxi** is ready to help (☎65017 or 63018). The **Bank of Ireland** provides both an **ATM** and a **bureau de change.** (☎35484. Open M and W-F 10am-12:30pm and 1:30-4pm, Th until 5pm.) The anonymous **Laundrette** on Main St. keeps odd hours but also cleans clothes. (☎35794. Open M-Tu and F-Sa 10am-5pm with breaks for lunch, dinner, and tea.) **Flynn's Pharmacy** sells the expected glut of medicines. (☎35778. Open M-F 9:30am-6pm, Sa 10am-6pm.) Falcarragh's **post office,** Main St., delivers mail. (☎35110. Open M-F 9am-1pm and 2-5:30pm, Sa 9am-1pm.)

The **Shamrock Lodge Hostel (IHH) ❶,** above the pub on Main St. (☎35959), was gutted by fire last year and remains closed as of press time. Call ahead. Next to the post office, **Loistin Oiche ❷** offers bed and breakfast in a modern abode with mountain views. (☎35145. €19 per person.) **Centra** provides a better than average selection of produce, and alcoholic libations in its off-license. (☎35529. Open M-Sa 8:30am-9pm, Su 9am-7pm.) The focus at **John's Cafe ❶,** at the top of Main St., is the delicious food they serve. Cramped benches and plain white walls conceal better-than-average chipper fare. (☎65613. Mains €5-6. Open M-Sa 10am-7pm; summer also open Su 1-7pm.) The **Gweedore Bar ❷,** Main St., curries favor with lunching local businessmen. (☎35293. Lunch specials €5.50; served 12:30-2:30pm.)

Visitors to the **Shamrock Lodge** (*Lóistín na Seamróige*), in the center of town, are greeted by cartoon paintings of Celtic warriors on the pub's facade, and it just gets weirder from there. The front room (for oldster Ulsters) is a traditional pub, complete with GAA paraphernalia and a *céilí* room for trad performances. In the back, you'll find a pool room, a beer garden, a younger clientele, and a "Mexican" saloon bar with authentic swinging doors. (☎35859. Th rock and country, Sa trad.) On Ballyconnell Rd., just off Main St. at the northern end of town, the cave-dark **Loft Bar** presents a collection of old mugs and flowery upholstery, with colorful regulars to match. (☎35992. Sporadic music in the summer.)

DUNFANAGHY (DÚN FIONNACHAIDH) ☎074

Seven miles north of Falcarragh, Dunfanaghy is a pleasant beach town with a distinctly Anglicized character. In the past, it functioned as an administrative center for the occupying government; now it serves as a summer refuge for Northern

Irish tourists seeking to avoid marching season back home. Transportation into Dunfanaghy is as sparse as it is in the rest of the region. Buses serving the area include **Feda O'Donnell's** (☎48114) route from Donegal south to Galway and Sligo and **McGinley's** (☎35201) service between Donegal and Dublin.

Just over 1 mi. south of Dunfanaghy, the **Corcreggan Mill Hostel (IHH, IHO)** ❶ sits by the side of the road in a complex that consists of a kiln house and a railway car. Owner Brendan has converted an old train into comfortable 4-bed dorms and private doubles with mahogany floors and walls. There are also bunks and loft doubles available in the former kiln house. Three kitchens—two for hostelers, one for campers—have been redone using recycled materials. Almost every bus stops right at the door. Hostelers usually team up to hire a local minibus to travel to and from the pubs. (☎36409. Laundry €4 with line dry. Kiln house dorms €10; loft doubles €30. Railway dorms €13; doubles €30. **Camping** €6.) The **Corcreggan Mill House B&B** ❸ is run by a separate group that leases the central buildings from the hostel. The modernized facilities include conference rooms, **a restaurant** (early-bird 3-course prix-fixe €15, mains €17-30), an outdoor *céilí* dance floor, and a wine bar. (☎36900. Weekly *céilí*, weather permitting. B&B doubles €60.) In town, the 3-star **Carrig Rua Hotel** ❹ has excellent B&B accommodations for those seeking a more upscale alternative. (☎36133. €45-58 per person.)

At **Ramsay's Store,** at the parking lot in the center of town, travelers should have no trouble piecing together their own meals. (☎36120. Open M-Sa 7:30am-9:30pm, Su 8am-10:30pm.) **Danny Collins's** ❷ bar is open from 11am until whenever the *Garda* come to shut it down. Though the upstairs restaurant is expensive, the pub's food is cheap and superlative. (☎36205. Soup €1.50; crepes, meat, and vegetarian mains €6.95. Bar food 1-7pm. Restaurant open 6-9:30pm.) Across the street, **Muck n' Muffins** ❶ is a purveyor of pottery and light meals. Let pastry and tea help you enjoy the bay views. (☎36780. Open M-Sa 10am-5pm, Su 11am-5pm.) The **Carrig Rua Hotel** ❸ contains a bistro of the same name, as well as the elegant Sheephaven Fine Dining Room. (☎36133. Bistro mains €5-7; open daily 12:30-9pm. Sheephaven Dining Room mains €12.95-21; open daily 7-9pm.)

The **Dunfanaghy Workhouse Heritage Centre** is a few hundred yards southwest of town. This former poorhouse has undergone a miraculous transformation from Famine days, when it offered prison-like accommodations and rations to the destitute. The curators have created an exhibit on the effects of the Great Hunger in Northwest Donegal that is both grisly and deeply moving. The centerpiece of the collection is a series of life-size dioramas following the life of a local woman named Hannah, who survived both the Famine and the workhouse. A small **coffee house** and a **craft shop** are attached. (☎36540. Open Mar.-Oct. M-Sa 10am-5pm, Su noon-5pm. €4, seniors €2.85, children €2, families €10.)

Between Dunfanaghy and Falcarragh is a maze of small roads and boggy hills. You can easily walk, cycle, or drive, and hitching is common to any of the natural attractions within a 5 mi. radius of either town. The helpful *Walking Donegal: Dunfanaghy* (€3) is available throughout the region. **Horn Head,** signposted on the way into Dunfanaghy, invites long rambles around its pristine beaches, megalithic tombs, and gorse-covered hills. Those tireless hikers who make the 3½hr. (8½ mi.) trek to the northern tip of Horn Head from Dunfanaghy will experience some of the most spectacularly high sea cliffs in Ireland. Some argue that this is the lazy man's Slieve League (see p. 414), but there is clearly something to be said for a hike with equally impressive scenery and a lower mortality rate. The truly lazy can drive all but the last 1½ mi. **Ards Forest,** a couple of miles past Dunfanaghy on N56, features a number of nature trails ranging in length (1½-8 mi.). Adjacent to the forest are pristine beaches accessible only on foot. (Open July-Aug. daily 10:30am-9pm; Easter-June and Sept. Sa-Su 10:30am-4pm. Parking €4.) About 5 mi. south of town on N56, **New Lake**—so called because it was formed in 1912 after a massive storm blocked up an estuary—features a world-famous ecosystem and lots of frisky otters. Turning your back to the sea anywhere in Dunfanaghy will bring the expanse of **Muckish Mountain** into view.

Those interested in climbing Muckish Mountain have two options. The first, more difficult route takes 4hr. and covers 7 mi. It's best to bring along *Ordinance Map #2* (€6.35) and a compass for this hike. To get to where the path begins, drive from Dunfanaghy in the direction of Creeslough, turn right when you see the graveyard on your left, and continue for 3 mi. to where the grassy track crosses the road. Park here and walk uphill on the road to the two foundations. Walk to the upper one, and to its right, across a narrow stream, the path begins. When you reach the quarry later on in the hike, the path to the summit is to the right. For those with less time, or less energy, the second and easier route to the summit takes only 2hr. Drive to Muckish Gap (marked by a shrine), follow the path northeast for half a mile, then turn northwest to reach the summit. If the only walking that interests you is over greens, you can trek the links (oh, and **golf** them, too) at the **Dunfanaghy Gold Club** (☎36335). Created in 1905 by six-time British Open champion Harry Vardon, the course is an 18-hole true links course.

FANAD PENINSULA

The Fanad Peninsula, which juts into the Atlantic between Lough Swilly and Mulroy Bay, offers a striking contrast between the verdant fields of its interior and the clean, sandy beaches running along its edges. Most visitors stick to the eastern coastal villages of **Rathmelton, Rathmullan,** and **Portsalon,** which contain colorful old houses and sweeping views across Lough Swilly. These villages may lack the nightlife and cultural offerings of their (relatively) more cosmopolitan neighbors, but wanderers who need those wide-open spaces know what a treasure the Fanad is. Backpackers will enjoy several gentle hikes, either along the northeastern coast or into the **Knockalla Mountains.** The Fanad Peninsula presents a challenge for the car-less—buses are infrequent and the road conditions are not ideal for cyclists. Those willing to venture into this northern coastal projection however, will enjoy lush scenery and a level of isolation not available on the more touristed Inishowen (see p. 439). The Swilly bus only runs as far as Portsalon once per day; without a car, you had better plan on spending the night.

RATHMELTON (RÁTH MEALTAIN) ☎074

At the nape of the peninsula sits venerable 17th-century Rathmelton (also spelled Ramelton). Resting on the shores of the Leannan Estuary, the town is a rest stop for travelers continuing north toward points not yet explored. Those who visit the town itself have usually come to learn about their Irish roots at the **Donegal Ancestry Centre,** which rests on the quay. (☎51266. Open M-Th 9am-4:30pm, F 9:30am-3:30pm. Assessments €63.) If you lack Irish in your blood (poor thing), you can brush up on your Rathmelton history with **The Rathmelton Story** exhibit, housed in the same renovated factory as the Ancestry Centre. (☎51266. Open Apr.-Sept. 10am-5:30pm; last admission 5pm. €3.80.) Both the well-established and rootless alike flock to the **Lennon Festival** in mid-July, when a carnival comes to town.

The **National Irish Bank,** the Mall, has a **bureau de change** but **no ATM.** (☎51028. Open M-F 10am-12:30pm and 1:30-3pm, Th until 5pm.) **Bridge Launderette,** the Mall, takes its name from its location. (☎51333. Open M-Sa 9am-6pm.) **Murray and Sons Pharmacy** is also on the Mall. (☎51080. Open M-Sa 9am-6pm, W until 1pm.) The **post office** is on Castle St. (☎51001. Open M-F 9am-5:30pm, Sa 9am-1pm.)

The rooms of the **Lennon Lodge Hostel** ❷ blur the distinction between hostel and B&B. Downstairs is a bar, and upstairs is a large common room in which you can sit back and relax, tapping your feet to the sounds of the trad sessions playing at the pub below. (☎51227. Laundry and kitchen facilities. Shared rooms €22 per person.) Just off the Mall and right along the Swilly bus route, **Crammond House ❸,** Market Sq., is a 1760s townhouse with expansive rooms and high ceilings. (☎51055. Open Easter-Oct. €23 per person, with bath €25.50.) **Whoriskey's/Spar Supermarket** sells DIY meals. (☎51006. Open M-Sa 8:30am-10pm, Su 8:30am-9pm.) At the top of town on the road to Milford, well-established **Bridge Bar** (☎51119) knows how to please its mature clientele—with live music three nights a week. (☎51119. Music W and F-Sa.) **Conway's** (☎51297), an old thatched cottage at the bottom of the hill down Church St., pours proper pints. Fans of televised sports hustle over to **O'Shaughnessy's** (☎51342), down the hill from the Mall.

RATHMULLAN (RÁTH MAOLÁIN) ☎074

The town of Rathmullan sits 5 mi. north of Rathmelton along the main coastal road. Its claim to fame? In 1607, the last powerful Gaelic chieftains, Flighty Earls Hugh O'Neill and Red Hugh O'Donnell, fled from Ireland after suffering numerous defeats to British invaders. They and 99 of their closest friends set sail from Rathmullan for Spain to gather military support from the Catholic King Phillip II (see **Feudalism,** p. 56). In more recent Anglo-Irish struggles, Wolfe Tone, champion of Irish independence, was arrested here in 1798 (see **Rebellion,** p. 59). The town's past is kept very much alive at the **"Flight of the Earls" Heritage Centre,** housed in a particularly foreboding Martello tower in the town center. A helpful staff uses artwork, literature, and wax models to recount Rathmullan's history in detail. (☎58229. Open Apr.-Sept. M-Sa 10am-1pm and 2-5pm, Su noon-5pm. €3, students and seniors €2, children €1.) Around the corner, the remains of the **Rathmullan Priory,** a 14th-century Carmelite monastery, lie shrouded in ivy.

Tourist information of the printed variety is happily dispensed at the heritage center (see above). **Mace Supermarket,** on the coastal road into town, supplies basic gastronomic needs. (☎58148. Open daily 8am-10pm.) Off Main St., hidden from the raucous downtown hustle and bustle, the **Knoll B&B ❸** shelters itinerants with a huge protected estate and modern amenities. (☎58241; call ahead. Shared rooms €25 per person.) Next door to the heritage center, the **Beachcomber Bar ❷** offers beach access and pub grub, some of which is vegetarian. One wall is consumed by a gigantic ocean view, and a sandy beer garden opens out back in the summer. (☎58125. Meals €7-10. Food served in summer daily noon-9pm.)

While in town, those interested in **fishing** can beam aboard the *Enterprise 1* full- and half-day excursions. Contact Angela Crerand (☎58131 after 6pm) or Niall Doherty (☎58129 or 087 263410) for more information. And **Golden Sands Equestrian Centre,** on the Portsalon road, offers the less sea-sturdy an opportunity to trek across the countryside atop grand equine beasts (☎58124).

NORTHERN AND WESTERN FANAD ☎074

North of Rathmullan, the road narrows, winding and dipping at the whim of the increasingly wild landscape. These remote roads are discouraging to pedestrians and all but the fittest bikers; hitching is nearly impossible here. The "towns" in this region are generally little more than a group of holiday cottages centered around a post office, but this is also where the peninsula's only budget accommodations can be found. Along the coast a little over halfway from Rathmullan to Portsalon and just north of the village of **Glenvar,** a signposted lane leads from the main road to the remote **Bunnaton House Hostel (IHO) ❶.** Perched on a cliff in the restored shell of an 1813 coast guard station, the hostel has an incredible view to the east, providing some consolation to travelers who have undertaken the arduous journey there. (☎50122. Breakfast €4-6. Dorms €11; singles €19;

doubles €30.) Continuing north, the main road becomes both mind-bogglingly steep and breathtakingly beautiful. Just before Portsalon, the road crests a hill where the northern tip of the peninsula and **Stocker Strand,** rated the second best in the world by a British "beach expert," suddenly appear. Next to the strand and 3 mi. south of Portsalon, the enormous **Knockalla Holiday Centre ❶** buzzes in the summer with an army of campers and caravans. (☎59108. Open Mar.-Sept. €11 per tent. Showers €1 per 5min.)

Portsalon (port-SAL-un), which was a resort town until its hotel burned down three years ago, now has just three shops and a few residences along the water. The scenic riches that justify the trials of visiting the peninsula lie just north of town—within 5 mi., you'll reach **Fanad Head,** where the **Great Arch of Doaghbeg** keeps the **Fanad Lighthouse** company. The arch, a mass of rock over 80 ft. wide detached from seaside cliffs, is visible from above, though not from the main road. (Cyclists are advised to approach these sights from the west, on the newer, smoother road.) Arch-lovers should follow the unmarked walking trail that begins in the six-acre **Ballydaheen Gardens,** a seaside array of Japanese and English gardens designed to blend into the natural landscape; this trail is also the only way to reach a series of coastal caves known as the **Seven Arches.** (☎59091. Open May-Sept. M-Sa 10am-3pm. €4.) From Fanad Head, the route down the western side of the peninsula winds in and out of the inlets of **Mulroy Bay.** Mrs. Borland's **Avalon Farmhouse ❷,** on Main St. in tiny **Tamney** (also known as Tawney)—also reachable by a road that cuts across the peninsula from Portsalon—has homemade jam and an attractive decor. (☎59031. Open Easter-Sept. €25 per person.)

LETTERKENNY (LEITIR CEANAINN) ☎074

Letterkenny is the commercial center of Donegal. More importantly for travelers, it's also the region's primary transportation hub. Though its heavy traffic may be a civil engineer's nightmare, the town is a surprisingly cosmopolitan breeze in an otherwise rustic atmosphere—the large student population supports a number of hipster cafes and pubs. Most tourists still arrive only for travel connections, but the appeal of a short stay here should not be overlooked.

TRANSPORTATION

Buses: The almighty **Bus Depot** is on the eastern side of the roundabout at the junction of the Port (Derry) road and Pearse Rd., in front of the shopping center.

Bus Éireann (☎21309) runs a "Hills of Donegal" tour, going to **Dungloe, Glenveigh National Park,** and **Gweedore** (M-Sa 1 per day, €16.50). Regular service to: **Derry** (30min.; M-Sa 6 per day, Su 3 per day; €6.35); **Dublin** (4½hr., 5-6 per day, €12.70); **Galway** (4¾hr., 4 per day, €15.25) via **Donegal Town** (50min., €6.35); **Sligo** (2hr.; M-Sa 5 per day, Su 4 per day; €11.50).

Doherty's Travel (☎075 21105). Buses for **Dungloe** and **Burtonport** depart from Dunnes Stores daily at 5pm (€6.35).

Feda O'Donnell Coaches (☎075 48114 or 091 761 656). To **Crolly** (2 per day, €6.35) via **Dunfanaghy** and **Galway** (2-3 per day, €12.70) via **Donegal Town** (€6.35).

Lough Swilly Buses (☎22863). To: **Derry** (M-Sa 9 per day, €5.60); **Dungloe** (M-Sa 4 per day, €10.20); **Fanad Peninsula** (M-Sa 2 per day, €8.90); **Inishowen Peninsula** (M-F 4 per day, Sa 3 per day) via **Buncrana** (€5.70), **Cardonagh** (€6.35), and **Moville** (€7).

McGeehan's (☎075 46150). 2 per day to **Glencolmcille** (€11.50) and **Killybegs** (€8.90).

McGinley Coaches (☎35201). 2 per day to **Dublin** (€14) and to **Gweedore** via **Dunfanaghy.**

Northwest Busways (☎077 82619) sends buses around Inishowen (M-F 4 per day, Sa 3 per day), making stops in **Buncrana** (€5.70), **Carndonagh** (€6.35), and **Moville** (€7).

Bike Rental: Church St. Cycles (☎26204), by the cathedral. €20 per day. €80 deposit. Open M-Sa 10am-6pm.

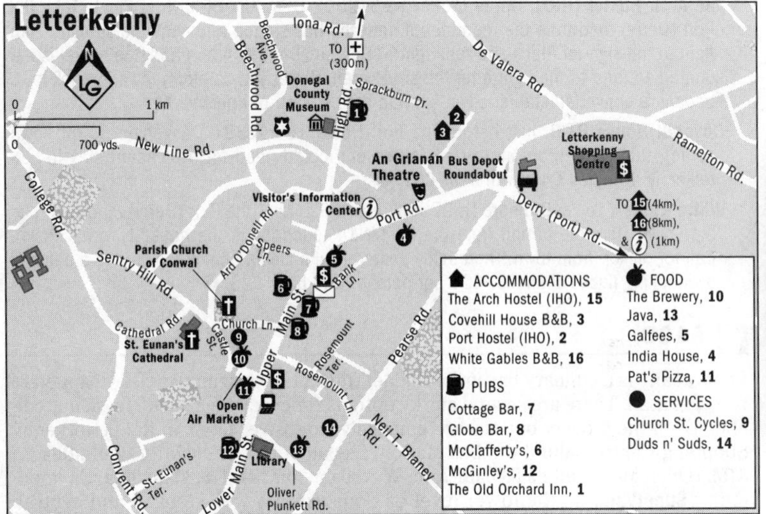

PRACTICAL INFORMATION

Tourist Offices: Bord Fáilte (☎21160), off the rotary at the intersection of Port (Derry) Rd. and Blaney Rd.; ¾ mi. out of town past the bus station. Info on Co. Donegal and accommodations bookings. Open July-Aug. M-Sa 9am-8pm, Su 10am-2pm; Sept.-June M-F 9am-5pm. **Chamber of Commerce Visitors Information Centre,** 40 Port Rd. (☎24866), is closer with a slightly smaller selection of info. Open M-F 9am-5pm.

Banks: AIB, 61 Upper Main St. (☎22877). **Bank of Ireland,** Lower Main St. (☎22122). **Ulster Bank,** Main St. (☎24016). All are open M-F 10am-4pm, Th until 5pm. AIB and Bank of Ireland both have 24hr. **ATMs.**

Bookstore: Bookmark, High Rd. Eclectic mix of used books. Open M-Sa 11am-5:30pm.

Laundry: Duds n' Suds, Pearse Rd. (☎28303). Load €8.50. Open M-Sa 8am-7pm.

Hospital: Letterkenny General (☎25888), north off High Rd. past the roundabout.

Pharmacy: Magee's Pharmacy, Main St. (☎21409 or 21419). Open M-W and Sa 9am-6:30pm, Th-F 9am-8pm.

Internet Access: Cyberworld, Main St. (☎20440), in the basement of the Four Lanterns takeaway. €6.35 per hr., students €4.45. Open M-Sa 10:30am-9:30pm. **Letterkenny Central Library,** Main St. (☎24950). Open M, W, and F 10:30am-5:30pm; Tu and Th 10:30am-8pm; Su 10:30am-1pm. Book in advance.

Post Office: Halfway down Main St. (☎22287). Open M and W-Sa 9am-5:30pm, Tu 9:30am-5pm.

ACCOMMODATIONS

The Port Hostel (IHO), Orchard Crest (☎25315). In a sheltered glade up the hill from the An Grianán Theatre, with easy access to the city center. In addition to ever-important bus schedules, the proprietress offers a variety of directed fun, including barbecues, pub crawls, and roadtrips to the beach and Glenveagh (dependent on interest; €7.60). Some rooms have balconies. Laundry €4.45. Dorms €12; private rooms €13-16 per person. ❶

The Arch Hostel (IHO), Upper Corkey (☎57255), 6 mi. out of town in Pluck. Take the Port (Derry) road from the roundabout near the bus station and continue straight. Turn right at the sign for Pluck and fork right at Seamus Doherty Auto Parts; the hostel is the unmarked farm to the right after the stone arch. Better yet, call from town for pickup. 6 beds in a converted stable loft–a spartan dream. €10 per person. ❶

Covehill House B&B, just before The Port Hostel (☎21038). Convenient to the town center, this B&B offers all the amenities one could need for a pleasant stay in Letterkenny. Doubles €46, with bath €52. ❷

White Gables, Lower Dromore (☎22583). Head 3 mi. out the Port (Derry) road and take the Lower Dromore turnoff from the N13/N14 roundabout; the house is ½ mi. down. Call for pickup from town. Thoroughly pastoral, with clean, cheery rooms and a balcony overlooking flocks of sheep. €20 per person, with bath €25. ❷

FOOD

Letterkenny is a culinary haven for budget travelers, particularly if they happen to be vegetarian. There are several quirky options for cheap meals with fresh ingredients. Even the grocery options are unusually extensive. **Tesco,** in the Letterkenny Shopping Centre behind the bus station, has all you could ask for, including an **ATM.** (Open M-Tu and Sa 8:30am-7pm, W 8:30am-8pm, Th-F 8:30am-9pm, Su noon-6pm.) **SuperValu,** on the lower level of Courtyard, is well-stocked and central. (☎25738. Open M-W and Sa 8:45am-6:15pm, Th-F 8:45am-9pm.) Around the corner, **Simple Simon Living Food,** Oliver Plunkett Rd., has an admirable selection of organic and vegetarian foods. (☎22382. Open M-Sa 9am-6pm.)

Java, 3-4 Oliver Plunkett Rd. (☎29808), at the end of Main St. across from the library. Full breakfasts, desserts, and sandwiches (€2.50-5) in an often-frantic and always-funky coffee shop decked in wrought-iron lamps and tile prints. Takeaway available. Open M-F 8:30am-5:30pm, Sa until 6pm, Su 11am-5pm. ❶

Galfees, 63 Main St. (☎28535), near the High Rd. fork. Most evening mains €5-7. Open 9am-7:30pm; cheaper evening menu served from 5pm. A 2nd branch is in the basement of the Courtyard Shopping Centre (☎27173), where Irish illustrations and wooden walls transcend the mall ambience. ❷

India House, Port Rd. (☎20470), across from the Theatre. Though this sit-in restaurant is expensive, takeaway promises vegsters and meat-eaters alike a variety of flavor at moderate prices. Meat dishes €9-15, vegetarian €6-9. Open Tu-Su 5:30-11pm. ❸

Pat's Pizza, Main St. (☎21761). Hearty takeaway for the budgeteer. Sit-down meals in the tiled interior. Always crowded at night. Delivery available. Pizza about €5, kebab special €6.30. Open M-W 5pm-12:30am, Th-Sa noon-1am, Su 4pm-12:30am. ❶

The Brewery, Market Sq. (☎27330). Enjoy better-than-average pub food in the downstairs bar, or sit down for the a la carte dinner meal upstairs from 5:30-10:30pm (€15-22.50). Carvery lunch M-F noon-3pm. Bar food M-F 3-7pm, Sa-Su noon-7pm. ❹

PUBS

McGinley's, 25 Main St. (☎21106). Hugely popular student bar in the chapel-like upstairs; older-but-still-hip crowd on the Victorian ground floor. W-Su rock and blues.

Globe Bar, Main St. (☎22977). Fuchsia facade; gaggles of hipsters within. Drink promotions (M-Th) lure the kids in, and DJs keep them there. Join the crowd on the dance floor, or establish your supremacy at the pool table. Live band Tu and Th, karaoke F.

Cottage Bar, 42 Main St. (☎21338). A kettle on the hearth, animated conversation around the bar, and nuns drinking Guinness in the corner. W trad.

McClafferty's, 54 Main St. (☎21581). Daytime patrons are an older, more conte tive set; the night is young. Karaoke Su.

The Old Orchard Inn, High Rd. (☎21615). Despite the encroaching popularity of n establishments, good Ol' Orchard remains the weekend bar-to-be, sporting 3 perpetually-packed floors of logwood furniture. A cellar bar hosts occasional trad and other live music (Th-F and Su). Bar food daily 12:30-10pm. The disco on the top floor is a local-magnet. Disco open W-Su until 2am. Cover €7-8.

SIGHTS AND ACTIVITIES

St. Eunan's Cathedral, perched high above town on Church Ln., looks like the heavenly kingdom when it's lit up at night. (Church Ln. is on your right up Main St. away from the bus station.) Proposed as a "resurrection of the fallen shrines of Donegal," the cathedral's construction took 11 years—all of them years of economic hardship and depression. The story of St. Colmcille is beautifully carved in the arch at the junction of the nave and transept. (Open daily 8am-5pm, except during Su masses 8-11:15am and 12:30pm. Free.) Across the way, the Church of Ireland's smaller **Parish Church of Conwal** shelters a number of tombstones, some of which date from circa 1600. (Su services 8 and 10:30am.)

Renovated during the summer of 1999, the **Donegal County Museum,** High Rd., displays exhibits of anything and everything having to do with Co. Donegal. (☎24613. Open M-F 10am-12:30pm and 1-4:30pm, Sa 1-4:30pm. Free.) Entering its third year, the **An Grianán Theatre** serves as the primary venue of the **Earagail Festival** (see **County Donegal,** p. 399) and puts on an eclectic program of music, dance, and visual art. (☎20777; www.angrianan.com. Open M-F 9:30am-6pm.)

Anglers can drop line in a number of the nearby lakes that overflow with salmon. Call **Letterkenny Anglers** for more details (☎21160). Golfers of all ages can perfect their short game at the 18-hole **Letterkenny Pitch & Putt** (☎25688 or 26000). Those looking to hit the long ball should try the **Letterkenny Golf Club** (☎21150). If you tire of walking the links, hop on a horse and rest your feet at the **Black Horse Stables** (☎51327) or **Ashtree Riding Stables** (☎53312). Both offer trekking and lessons for all levels of experience. If horses fail to meet your need for speed, rev up at the **Letterkenny Indoor/Outdoor Karting Centre** and take to the road a la Mario Andretti. (☎29077. Open M-Sa 1-11pm.) After it all, relax in the sauna, swimming pool, and whirlpool at the **Letterkenny Leisure Centre** on High Rd. (☎25251).

INISHOWEN PENINSULA

Brochures trumpet the Inishowen Peninsula as the "crown of Ireland." Indeed, it would be a shame to leave Ireland without seeing this region, which offers characteristically Donegalien landscape combined with uncharacteristic accessibility and proximity to major sights, including the transcendently beautiful **Malin Head.** During the week, Inishowen is a relatively unpopulated mosaic of mountains, forests, meadows, and white-sand beaches. Two towns, **Buncrana** and **Carndonagh,** are connected by a winding road that affords sublime views. Sadly, *Let's Go* is not the only organization to have noted these attractive qualities—signs of development abound on the until-recently-untouristed peninsula. Hordes of holiday-makers from Derry and elsewhere in the North rush in on summer weekends, and construction sites for luxury apartments and cottages have begun to crop up along the coast. Despite all of this, the peninsula's attractions merit several days of exploration; visitors traveling by public transportation have no choice but to spend at least this long, and those with cars will hardly want to do otherwise.

The nearest commercial center to Inishowen is Derry. **Lough Swilly Buses** (Derry office ☎028 7126 2017, Buncrana ☎077 61340) runs buses from Derry to points on the Inishowen: Buncrana (35min.; M-Sa 12-14 per day, Su 3 per day; UK£2.50/€4); Moville and Greencastle (50min., M-Sa 5-6 per day, UK£3.50/€5.50); Carndonagh (1hr., M-Sa 4 per day, UK£4/€6.40); Malin (1hr.; M, W, F 2 per day, Sa 3 per day; UK£5/€8); Malin Head (1½hr.; M, W, F 2 per day, Sa 3 per day; UK£5/€8). Swilly also connects Buncrana directly to Carndonagh (50min., M-Sa 3 per day), and offers an eight-day "Runabout Ticket" (UK£20/€32, students UK£12/€19) and student rates; their return fares are considerably cheaper than two one-way tickets. **Northwest Buses** (Moville office ☎82619) runs from Moville through Culdaff, Carndonagh, Ballyliffin, Clonmany, Buncrana, Fahan, and on to Letterkenny (M-Sa 3 per day, €6.35); from Shrove to Derry via Moville (1hr., M-Sa 2 per day, €4.70); from Derry to Culdaff (M-Sa 2 per day, €2.50); a Moville-Letterkenny express bus (M-Sa 2 per day, €6.35); and from Carndonagh to Derry (M-Sa 3-4 per day, €4.70).

Drivers follow the well signposted **Inish Eoghain 100** road that navigates the peninsula's perimeter over the course of almost exactly 100 mi.—hitchers report having an easy time finding rides on this road. Ambitious **bikers** will enjoy miles of smooth, if sometimes inclined, roads; cycling can be particularly difficult near the **Gap of Mamore,** due to ferocious northwesterly winds and hilly terrain. The map published by the Inishowen Tourism Society, available at the Carndonagh tourist office, and the *Ordnance Survey Discovery Series #3*, are both effective tools for navigating the peninsula; the former is more schematic and makes for easier reading, while the latter provides more detailed topographical information and is best for people on foot.

BUNCRANA (BUN CRANNCHA) ☎077

Long Slieve Snaght looms over Buncrana, at Inishowen's southeastern edge. While not terribly exciting in itself, the town is the peninsula's most common entry point, offering beds and conveniences to northbound explorers. While slow most of the year, the town swells with revelers who come for the town's Music Festival in July.

PRACTICAL INFORMATION. A **tourist office,** on Main St. at the southern edge of town, offers peninsular information, including a book of waymarked hikes. (☎62600. Open M-F 9am-5pm, Sa 10am-2pm, Su noon-3pm.) **AIB,** 8 Market Sq. (☎61087; open M-F 10am-12:30pm and 1:30-4pm, Th until 5pm), and **Bank of Ireland,** Main St. (☎61795; open M-F 10am-4pm, Th until 5pm), both have 24hr. **ATMs. ValuClean,** Lower Main St., promises to wash your dirty clothes. (☎62570. Laundry from €8. Open M-Sa 9am-6pm.) **E. Tierney Chemist's,** 42 Lower Main St., is the local pharmacy. (☎62412. Open M-F 9:30am-6:30pm, Sa 9:30am-6pm.) Get **connected** at **Job Club** on St. Oran's Rd. (☎61376; open M-F 9:30am-4:45pm; €3.60 per hr.), or at the town's **library** (☎61941) on Lower Main St. The **post office,** Main St., is also a newsagent. (☎61010. Open M-F 9am-1:15pm and 2:15-5:30pm, Sa 9am-1pm.)

ACCOMMODATIONS, FOOD, AND PUBS. Tudor House ❸, Causeway Rd., off Main St. on the northern end of town, has large rooms with TV, bath, polished wood cabinets, and lovely pastel duvets. (☎61692. €25 per person, children €12.) **O'Donnell's Supermarket,** also at the north end of Main St., sells sundry staples. (☎61719. Open daily 7am-11pm.) **Food for Thought** sells health food and raw materials for a bitchin' ethnic feast. (☎63550. Open M-Sa 10am-6pm.) **O'Flaitbeartais ❷** (o-FLAH-her-tees), Main St., looks like a hunting lodge but attracts a varied crowd for noontime feedings and weekend music. (☎61305. Lunch served noon-3pm; most dishes €5. W trad.) The black-clad waitresses of the **Town Clock Restaurant ❷** contrast sharply with the home-style fare on the menu, which includes local favorites from toasties to kebabs. (☎63279. Most dishes €5. Open daily 8:15am-9pm.) Upstairs is the **Town Clock B&B ❷,** which offers simple rooms at a simple price. (☎62146. €23 per person.) The **West End Bar,** Upper Main St. (☎61564), has a copper bar that shines like a lucky penny, and a low-lit lounge in back. The mostly-local crowd arrives on weekends by around 10pm.

SIGHTS AND ACTIVITES. Buncrana's primary attractions all lie on a long stretch of open space along the river. Behind a youth activity center, peaceful, pretty **Swan Park** is overlooked by two castles: stately Queen Anne-era **Buncrana Castle,** in which Wolfe Tone was imprisoned after the French "invasion" of 1798 failed (see **Rebellion,** p. 59), and the 1430 **O'Doherty Keep,** a not-quite-Arthurian castle that looks more like a derelict mansion. Both are closed to the public. To reach the park, walk up Main St. toward the shorefront and follow Castle Ave. from the roundabout next to the West End Bar and Cinema. The park is beyond the Castle Bridge, which arcs 100 yd. to the right. A **coastal walk** begins at Castle Bridge, goes past the keep, turns left at the castle, and then ascends the hill. **Ned's Point Fort,** also along the coast, built in 1812, is surprisingly (but not pleasantly) modern-looking. The path passes **Porthaw Bay** and culminates in sandy **Sragill Strand. Friar Hegarty's Rock,** beyond the beach, witnessed the friar's murder during Penal Times.

Outside the north edge of the park on Dunree Rd. (a continuation of Main St.) is the community-owned and operated **Tullyarvan Mill.** This renovated corn mill presents a mixture of exhibits on textile history, tracing Buncrana's transition from hand-weaving in 1739 to Fruit-of-the-Looming in 1999. The mill also houses a **craft shop** and **coffee shop,** and its riverside benches make a nice spot for picnicking. (☎ 61613. Open M-Sa 10am-5pm.) Those looking to golf rather than sew should head to the **Buncrana Golf Club** (☎ 62279) for a relaxing game or four.

DAYTRIP FROM BUNCRANA

GRIANÁN AILIGH. At the bottom of the peninsula, 10 mi. south of Buncrana and 3 mi. west of Derry (see p. 513), the hilltop ringfort Grianán Ailigh (GREEN-in ALL-ya) is an excellent place to start or finish your tour of Inishowen. This site—which provides 360° views of the surrounding countryside—has been a cultural center for at least 4000 years: first as a Druidic temple at the grave site of Aedh, the son of The Dagda, divine king of the Túatha De Dannan; then as a seat of power for the northern branch of the Uí Néill clan, who ruled Ulster and moved here after their chieftain married Princess Aileach of Scotland; and finally as a Mass rock where Catholics worshipped in secret during the time of the Penal Laws. Much of the present stone structure is a 19th-century reconstruction, but the bottom section of the circular wall is original. Beyond the fort, a cross marks the site of a **healing well,** holy since pre-Christian times and supposedly blessed by St. Patrick.

Grianán Ailigh is just west of the junction of R238 and N16; the 300-year-old **Burt Woods** are right alongside. From Buncrana, follow the Inish Eoghian 100 south to Burnfoot, continue onto Bridgend, and follow the signs to Burt Woods; the ringfort is just a mile to the southeast. To reach the fort from Letterkenny, follow N13 past the turnoff for R265 and R237, and follow the signs that point the way. Two miles down N13 from Bridgend is the Catholic **Burt Circular Chapel,** a replica of the ancient fort. To reach the fort from the Chapel, take the 2 mi. road to the top of the hill. Just past the Chapel is the **Grianán Ailigh Heritage Centre,** inside a former Church of Ireland. The center can prepare you for the 2 mi. journey with mind-bending displays of wax figures and stomach-bending Irish food. *(☎ 077 68000. Lunch specials €7; served noon-3pm. Restaurant open daily noon-10pm; center closes 6pm. €3.50.)* No public transport comes near, so the carless have to cycle or walk. Travelers who hitch say drivers here are helpful.

GRIANÁN AILIGH: MYTHS AND LEGENDS

Gather 'round, kids; *Ma Go*'s gonna larn you some history... Grianán Ailigh figures into many legends and tales, including the naming of Inishowen ("the Island of Owen"). Owen was the son of **Niall of the Nine Hostages,** the semi-legendary ancestor of the Uí Néills. One story claims that Niall slept with an old hag to gain sovereignty over Ireland. Once in charge, he captured young St. Patrick over in Scotland and brought him to Ireland as a slave. Having escaped captivity and begun his missionary work, St. Pat baptized Niall's son Owen at this very same hillfort, consecrating the Uí Néill fortress as a Christian holy site. The prominence of Grianán Ailigh as the home of rulers ended in the 11th century, but the symbolic identity of the fort survived past its physical destruction; after the Flight of the Earls in 1607, Red Hugh O'Neill swore he'd return to Grianán Ailigh as high ruler of Ireland. Legend has it that Red Hugh's soldiers still lie slumbering in a cave near the fort, each with one hand on the hilt of his sword and the other on the reins of his also-sleeping horse. They won't wake until the new ruler of Ireland lands on the island. Shhh.

WESTERN INISHOWEN

From Buncrana, the Inish Eoghain 100 runs through Dunree Head and the Mamore Gap, while R238 cuts through the interior directly to Clonmany and Ballyliffin. Spectacular beaches, marvelous mountainsides, and complete isolation await the traveler who dares to venture this deep into the peninsula.

DUNREE HEAD AND THE MAMORE GAP ☎077

Fort Dunree and the Mamore Gap were the last area of the Republic occupied by the British, who handed over the fort keys to the Irish army in 1938. **Dunree Head** pokes out into Lough Swilly 6 mi. northwest of Buncrana. Salt-and-peppered peaks rise up against the ocean, buffered by the occasional bend of sandy, smooth beach. At the tip of the head, **Fort Dunree** hides in the jagged sea cliffs. Today the fort holds a military museum and is a superb vantage point for admiring the sea-carved landscape of the Inishowen and Fanad peninsulas. One of the six **Guns of Dunree,** built during the 1798 Rebellion to defend Lough Swilly against Napoleonic invaders, is among the museum's displayed weaponry. The exhibits also include copies of German Intelligence maps of the Inishowen Peninsula from World War II. The fort's location overlooking Lough Swilly is a boon for birdwatchers. (Open June-Sept. M-Sa 10am-6pm, Su 1-6pm. Fort and walks €4; students €2.)

Farther north along Inish Eoghain 100 toward Clonmany, a sign points left up a hill to the edge of the **Mamore Gap.** 800 ft. above sea level, the pass meanders between Mamore Hill and Urris. Otherworldly views over the mountains to the Atlantic can be seen from the pass's eastern face. The sharply inclined road through proves difficult but worthwhile for hikers and cyclists. It's only a 30min. climb uphill; most bikers will be forced to walk. It's easier to drive, although the hairpin turns over the sea are sometimes quite frightening. Queen Mebdh of Connacht, Cú Chulainn's diva archenemy (see **Legends and Folktales,** p. 71), is supposedly buried here (and at Knocknarea, Co. Sligo, and a few other places).

The road descends from the gap onto wave-scoured northern beaches. The Inish Eoghain 100 proceeds to **Urris, Lenan Head,** and inviting **Lenan Strand.** Once known for its prodigious—even for Donegal—*poitín* production (See **Love *Poitín* #9,** p. 416), Urris was the last area in Inishowen to relinquish spoken Irish. The subdivided flat-bed farms along the road reveal the enduring influence of Famine-era farming practices. Heading north, the road passes over **Dunaff Head,** through **Rockstown Harbour,** and ends at a stunning beach (the aforementioned Lenan Strand).

CLONMANY, BALLYLIFFIN, AND DOAGH ISLAND ☎077

North of the Gap, the two tiny villages of **Clonmany** *(Chuain Maine)* and **Ballyliffin** *(Baile Lifin)* are separated by a single mile. Travelers with the resources to hire a car and stay in a B&B will find them a restful spot to spend the night; Clonmany provides the pubs, while Ballyliffin has plenty of accommodations and long stretches of sandy beach.

Ballyliffin's highlights are its three long miles of golden sands on **Pollen Strand** and its world-famousg **golf course;** both Nick Faldo and Fred Daly are among the many pros who have played the greens of the **Ballylifin Golf Club.** Grassy dunes connect the village with **Doagh Island,** where **Carricksbrahy Castle,** a former seat of the MacFaul and O'Donnell clans, is a wave-crashed ruin at the end of a 2½ mi. beach walk. Area signs with the curious imperative "Visit My Famine Village!" point the way to Doagh Island and the **Doagh Visitors Centre,** which houses a collection of exhibits discussing poverty and starvation in Ireland. With green shamrocks on the walls of thatched cottages, a Famine village juxtaposed with a petting zoo, and light wordplay, this attraction might initially appear to be in poor taste. However, the well-meaning museum ultimately manages to provide a balanced bit of edutain-

IN RECENT NEWS

MOVING HOUSE

An unconventional memorial to the survivors of the Irish Famine has appeared on the New York City skyline—or, rather, below it. Removed stone by stone and shipped across to the US, a ruined 1820s Northwest Irish stone-brick cottage has been reconstructed in Battery Park as Manhattan's **Irish Hunger Memorial,** "a field forever Ireland." The memorial features the authentic cottage upon a rolling green hill of imported gorse and heather, which stands in stark contrast to its urban-industrial surroundings in downtown New York.

The name for the Irish Hunger Memorial comes from the Gaelic term for the Famine: "An Gorta Mór," or "the Great Hunger," which lasted from 1845-1852 and wiped out millions of the nation's population. The memorial serves to raise public awareness on the tragic history of Ireland and the events that led to the Famine, offering American descendants of Irish immigrants a sense of connected cultural memory. At the dedication in July 2002, New York Governor George Pataki and city Mayor Michael Bloomberg unveiled the memorial to Irish president Mary McAleese. Mr. Pataki declared: "The Irish Famine Memorial will serve as a reminder to millions of...Americans who proudly trace their heritage to Ireland of those who were forced to emigrate during one of the most heartbreaking tragedies in the history of the world."

ment—children laugh while their elders are presented with much food for thought. (☎78078. Open daily 10am-5:30pm. €4; students and seniors €3.)

Many of the golfer-types visiting Ballyliffin stay at **Rossaor House ❹,** near the entrance to town. Though more expensive than other B&Bs, Rossaor pampers guests with a garden, fantastic views of the Strand and Malin Head, and smoked salmon and scrambled egg breakfasts. (☎76498. Singles €45; doubles €70.) Alternatively, wanderers can stay in the spacious, well-furnished rooms of **Castlelawn House ❸,** just behind the Strand Hotel. (☎76977. All rooms with bath and TV. €30-33 per person.) Also look next door at the **Carrickabraghey House ❸,** owned by the sister of Castlelawn's proprietress. (☎76600. €30-33 per person.) In Clonmany, your best and possibly only bet for a bite to eat is the **Village Diner ❷,** an unrepentant chipper and takeaway with all-day Irish breakfast (€5) and late hours. (☎78887. Open M-W 9am-10pm, Th 9am-10:30pm, F and Su 9am-midnight, Sa 9am-1:30am.) Weekend country music and occasional trad fill the air in and around **McFeeley's,** on Main St. (☎76122). During the first full weekend in August, all the pubs in the Square are saturated with trad for the **Clonmany Festival.**

NORTHERN INISHOWEN

From the southeastern coast, R240 cuts straight up the middle of the peninsula to commercial Carndonagh, an important stocking-up point. North of Carndonagh, R238 veers east to Culdaff. Going north on R242 leads to Malin Head, the northernmost tip of the island. The northern half of the Peninsula is the most friendly to budget travelers, containing the largest tracts of unspoiled scenery and the region's only hostels, all of which happen to be superlative.

CARNDONAGH (CARN DOMHNACH) ☎077

Two miles south of Trawbreaga Bay, Cardonagh ("Carn") is Inishowen's main market town—the peninsula's farmers swarm on here alternate Mondays to hawk their hoofed creatures. Predictably, commercial Carn has but one sight to offer: the old Church of Ireland that hulks 10min. down Bridge St. Outside its walls, **Donagh Cross,** a 7th-century Celtic cross, is all that remains of the monastery founded by St. Patrick when he brought Christianity to the peninsula. Two shorter pillars flank the cross: one depicts David playing his harp, and the other displays Christ's crucifixion. The **church's bell** supposedly came from the Spanish Armada ship *Trinidad de Valoencera,* which went down in **Kinnagoe Bay.**

Carn Cabs, the Diamond (☎74580), provides taxis for late-night jaunts. **McCallion's Cycle Hire,** 3 mi. from town on the Ballyliffin road, will collect and deliver bikes anywhere on the peninsula. (☎74084. €9 per day, €40 per wk.) **Inishowen Tourism,** Chapel St., just off the Diamond, is non-Bord Fáilte approved but remarkably helpful with information on the entire peninsula and accommodations bookings. (☎74933; www.visitinishowen.com. Open June-Aug. M-F 8:30am-6pm, Sa 10am-6pm, Su noon-6pm; Sept.-May M-F 9:30am-5:30pm.) **AIB,** the Diamond, is the only bank in town with a 24hr. **ATM.** (☎74388. Open M-F 10am-12:30pm and 1:30-4pm, M until 5pm.) At the eastern end of town on the Moville road, **The Book Shop** offers used books and a huge selection for Irish history enthusiasts. (☎74389. Open Su-Tu and Th-F 2-6pm, Sa 11am-6pm.) **ValuClean,** Bridge St., washes and dries for €5.40. (☎74150. Open M-Sa 9am-6pm.) **McAteer's,** the Diamond, is the local **pharmacy.** (☎74120. Open M-Sa 10am-6pm.) The **post office** meters mail on Bridge St. (☎74101. Open M-F 9:30am-1:30pm and 2:30-5:30pm, Sa 9:30am-1pm.)

Less than a 5min. walk from the Diamond, Chapel St. turns into Millbrae as it passes **Dunshenny House B&B ❸,** where dainty-flowered wallpaper sets a dainty-flowered mood. (☎74292. All rooms with bath. Singles €30; shared rooms €25 per person.) Just down Chapel St. from the church, the house of **Oregon B&B ❷** has stood since 1911; except for the addition of a few modern fixtures, it hasn't changed much. (☎74113. Shared rooms €21 per person.) **G&S Coscutters,** in the Cardonagh Shopping Centre on Bridge St., sells an array of foods. (☎74124. Open M-Sa 9am-9pm, Su 10am-7pm.) The **Sandwich Mill ❶** at the **Arch Pub** sells sandwiches on baps, panini, and ciabatta. (☎73029. Open M-Sa 10:30am-6pm.) **The Quiet Lady,** Main Rd., gets noisy at night when she plays hits for a local crowd of fancy-footers. During the day she offers filling meals, including roasted meats and vegetables for €5. (☎74777. Food served 10:30am-9pm. W and Sa-Su live music.)

NORHTWEST IRELAND

CULDAFF (CÚI DAPBHCHA) ☎077

The area around Culdaff on the eastern side of the peninsula holds a variety of ancient monuments. The "Bronze Age triangle" above the Bocan Parochial House, a mile from Culdaff toward Moville, includes the **Bocan Stone Circle,** the **Temple of Deen,** and **Kindroyhead,** where there is evidence of a prehistoric field and fort system. A 12 ft. **high cross** stands next to the **Cloncha Church,** which is signposted 1½ mi. from Culdaff toward Moville. The village also hosts the annual **Charles Macklin Festival** (☎79104) during the second weekend in October, with performances of the 17th-century playwright's plays, poetry competitions, and a slew of trad sessions. **Culdaff Strand,** an outstanding stretch of beach best seen at daybreak or dusk, is a short walk to the east.

The Pines ❶, about a mile down Bunagee Rd. and marked by a small sign, is an independent hostel found in a spiffy house with immaculate, recently renovated rooms. (☎79060. Dorms €10.) For more upscale lodging, head to **McGrory's ❹.** This family-run guesthouse has rooms outfitted with every amenity and comfort available. (☎79104. Singles €55; shared rooms €45 per person. Call for special deals.) Almost half the town comes to the hotel's **restaurant ❷** downstairs for dinner and lunch. Stone walls, a blazing fire, and better-than-average pub grub make for a relaxing and comfortable meal. (☎79104. Meals €4-13.) Out back, **Mac's Backroom Bar** has live music that attracts throngs from around the peninsula. The music venue has hosted up-and-comers Atlan, among others, and boasts frequent concerts. (Trad Tu and F. Live music W and Sa.)

MALIN HEAD (CIONN MÁLAINN) ☎077

Inishowen's most popular attraction is Malin Head, the northernmost peninsula of Ireland. Aside from its latitude, the stretch is remarkable for its rocky, wave-tattered coast and sky-high sand dunes. Inish Eoghain 100 continues east from Carndonagh to Malin Head, passing through the tiny, tidy town of **Malin** on its way. Five miles from Culdaff, R242 coincides with the Inish Eoghain 100 and winds toward Lagg, where the five standing rocks of **Five Fingers Strand** jut into the ocean. The water looks tempting but is icy cold and dangerous for swimming. The sand dunes here are reputedly the highest in Europe, towering over 100 ft. in some places. Turn left above the little, white church and look for the signs. High above the beach, the **Knockamany Bens** provide fantastic views of the whole peninsula and even as far as Tory Island on a clear day. Meteorologists have repeatedly recorded Malin Head as the **sunniest spot in Ireland.** Yes, sunshine and Ireland can coexist.

The scattered town of **Malin Head** includes **Bamba's Crown,** a tooth of dark rock rising up from the ocean spray, noteworthy for being the peninsula's most northern tip. Until the 19th century, Malin Head was the site of an annual pilgrimage in which young men and women "frisked and played in the water all stark naked" to celebrate the sea god's affair with the goddess of the land. On a clear day, the Head offers a view of Scotland, and perhaps an opportunity to hear the call of the **corncrake,** a near-extinct bird indigenous to the area. Written in white-washed stones on a nearby lower cliff, and readable from thousands of feet above, "S. S. EIRE" (*Saor Stát Éire*; "Irish Free State") identified Ireland as neutral territory to Nazi would-be bombers. People have removed many of the stones to announce their own identities, but "EIRE" is still intact. A path to the left of the carpark skirts the cliff face and leads to **Hell's Hole,** a 250 ft. chasm that roars with the incoming tide. Farther down the coast you'll find the (super) naturally formed **Devil's Bridge.** The **raised beaches** around Malin Head (the result of glaciers that ripped through the region millions of years ago) are covered with semi-precious stones; walkers sifting through the sands may find jasper, quartz, small opals, or amethysts. The **Atlantic Circle** is a 5 mi. circuit of the Inish Eoghain 100 that tours the peninsula's tip.

The area around Malin Head teems with affordable accommodations. To reach the **Sandrock Holiday Hostel (IHO/IHH) ❶**, Port Ronan Pier, take the left fork off the Inish Eoghain 100, just before the Crossroads Inn (also a bus stop). This hostel is right on the water with huge views and potential opportunities to see passing seals and dolphins. The owners make great company and are extremely willing to help plan your attack on the town or the nearby walking trails. (☎70289; www.carndonagh.com/sandrock. Sheets €1.35. Laundry wash €4, dry €2. 10-bed dorms €10.) Five miles past Malin on the way into Malin Head, **Druin Doo B&B ❷** has a wonderful loft for weary travelers. (☎70287. €24 per person.) On the Inish Eoghain 100, after the phone booth and across from the post office, the **Malin Head Hostel (IHO/IHH) ❶** welcomes guests with an open fire, reflexology (€35), aromatherapy (€45), and carraigan moss jam (made from a local seaweed). The rooms are impeccably clean, and Mary's garden yields fresh, cheap veggies for hostelers' consumption. (☎70309. Wash €3.50, dry €2.50. 5-bed dorms €12; doubles €30.) Both Malin Head and the Sandrock hostel can provide **rental bikes** from **McCallion's Cycle Hire** in Carn. (☎74084. €9 per day.) Half a mile south of the Crossroads Inn, across the street from the phone box, Mrs. Doyle at **Barraicín ❷** tends a friendly, comfortable B&B, a beautiful garden, and a bulletin board with maps and photos of local sights. If you're traveling by bus, get off at Malin Head's only phone booth, which stands a bit before the post office. (☎70184. €22 per person, with bath €22.)

All of Malin Head's pubs have licensed fisherman's late hours and sell groceries. Country-rock, fishing tackle, and revitalizing brew are all available at **Farren's,** Ireland's northernmost pub. (☎70128. Music nightly July-Aug.) **Seaview Tavern and Restaurant** (☎70117), commonly referred to as "Vera Dock's," pours your pint in its 12x12 ft. space beneath shelves full of corn flakes and motor oil. It opens at 8am and closes (or is supposed to close) at 1am. The **restaurant ❷** next door serves tasty, local seafood and takeaway. (Food from €6.30; served 10am-9:15pm.)

EASTERN INISHOWEN

Though overshadowed by its northern neighbor Malin Head, **Inishowen Head** draws hundreds of beach-bathers to the natural beauty of its **Shroove Strand.** On the most northern beaches, which look over Lough Foyle, small crowds gather on the handful of hot days in an Irish summer. A delightful "shore walk" runs about 6 mi. between the small thumb of Inishowen Head and Moville. Any local can direct you to **Port a Doris,** a delightful little cove accessible only at low tide and littered with semi-precious Shroove pebbles. **Tunn's Bank,** a huge sandbank a few hundred yards offshore, is reputedly the resting place of Manannan McLir, the Irish sea god whose children were turned into swans.

MOVILLE AND GREENCASTLE ☎077

Tiny Moville *(Bun an Phobail)* is located at the intersection of R239 (from Derry) and R238 (from Culdaff). Even smaller Greencastle *(An Caislean Nua)* hides 3 mi. north along R239. During the summer, both towns are swamped with upscale Derryites searching for the beach and a game of golf. In Moville, an **AIB** with a 24hr. **ATM** is on Main St. (☎82050. Open M-F 10am-12:30pm and 1:30-4pm, Th until 5pm.) **Ulster Bank,** Main St., also has a 24hr. magic cash box. **Foyle's,** Main St., works it as only a **pharmacy** can. (☎82929. Open M-Sa 9:30am-6pm.) Get connected at **Computer Warehouse** (☎85944; €1.30 connection fee plus €1 per 15min.; open Tu-F 10am-5pm, Sa 10am-2:15pm) or surf the **Internet** for free at the **library** on Main St. The **post office** is on Malin Rd. where it intersects Main St. (☎82016. Open M-F 9am-1pm and 2-5:30pm, Sa 9am-1pm.)

For a good night's rest, try Mrs. McGuinness's **Dunroman B&B ❸,** off the Derry road across from the football field, where breakfast is served in a sunny conservatory overlooking the River Foyle. Green plants and murals painted by the eldest McGuinness daughter complete the splendid setting. (☎82234. Singles €30; shared rooms €25 per person.) **Mace Grocery,** Main St., will sell you all the groceries you require. (☎82045. Open daily 7am-9pm.) The local budget traveler's haven is at the **Barron's Cafe ❷,** Main St., which serves heaps of food cooked in the kitchen of the family house behind the storefront. (☎82472. All-day breakfast €5, burgers around €3, mains €5-11. Open daily 9:30am-8pm.) Fishermen and bikers keep each other company at the **Hair o' the Dog Saloon ❷,** at the Lower Pier behind Main St. Not-so-common pub grub includes juicy, American-style hamburgers on homemade kaiser buns for €2.50-5 and pizza for €3.80-6.35. (☎82600. Live music weekends. Food served noon-9pm.) **Eggman's,** on Main St., gathers an older, local crowd in its front rooms and a younger set in the back room. (☎82183. Open M-F 10:30am-1am, Sa-Su 10:30am-1:30am. W and F-Su disco; no cover.)

From Inishowen Head, the road leads south to **Greencastle,** a village that throws some spice (or sea salt, at least) into the one-street Irish-village mix. Greencastle's **castle,** built by the Red Earl of Ulster, is now an ivy-covered ruin. The Irish government maintains a center for training professional fisherfolk next to the ruins. Relics of life on the seas are in the spotlight at the **Greencastle Maritime Museum** on the shorefront. Housed in an old coast guard station, the museum's impressive collection includes a traditional but newly built Fanad *curragh*, an Armada room, a 19th-century rocket cart for rescuing passengers of wrecked ships, ship models, and photographs, as well as a brand new **planetarium** with weekend laser light shows. (☎81363. Open June-Sept. M-Sa 10am-6pm, Su noon-6pm; call ahead for off-season hours. €4; students, seniors, and children €2; families €10. Combined museum-planetarium pass €8/€4/€20. F-Sa nights laser light shows; €6.)

In a secluded mansion overlooking Lough Foyle, Mrs. Anna Wright warmly welcomes guests to the high-ceilinged, aristocratic **Manor House ❸.** From Main St., head out of town in the direction of the castle. Turn right at the first road after the town, following the sign to the castle and the fort. Pass both and fork right at the bottom of the hill, following the signs to the B&B. (☎81010. €30 per person.) Next to the Maritime Museum, the **Brooklyn Cottage** ❸ is a modest whitewashed house with modern amenities and a wall-to-wall loughview from its conservatory. (☎81087. Open Mar.-Nov. Singles €30; doubles €50.) If it's *really* fresh fish you want, head to **Greencastle Seafoods Ltd.**, next to the Maritime Museum, where a whole salmon can be bought for about €3.20 per lb. (☎81605. Open M-F 8:30am-5pm.) For the lazy-inclined, **Seamy's Fish and Chips** ❸ serves fried fish from its spic 'n' span kitchen that sits behind an inviting neo-Georgian storefront. (☎81379. All meals under €4. Open M-F noon-1am, Sa-Su 2pm-1am.) The **Greencastle Fort** ❸, next to the castle, was once a Napoleonic sea fort that housed 160 redcoats, 30 bluecoats, and nine cannons, and it has served the likes of Kaiser Wilhelm and the emperor of Japan. Today it protects an inn and a pub with affordable grub and spontaneous trad sessions most summer weekend nights. (☎81044. Meals €7.60-10.20; served daily in summer noon-9:30pm.) Up the street from Greencastle Seafoods, the **Ferryport Bar** is a second home for most of the youth in Greencastle (☎81296. Summer Th-Su chart or trad-type music.) **The Drunken Duck** (☎81362), 3 mi. north of Greencastle, is a friendly pub named for a local woman whose beer leaked into her poultry feeding troughs.

NORTHERN IRELAND

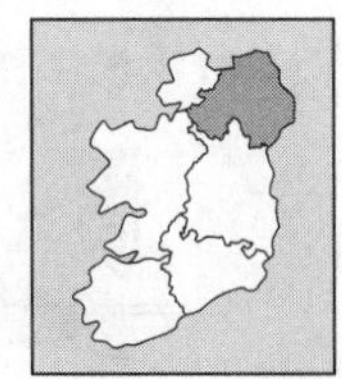

The calm tenor of life in the North has been overshadowed overseas by media headlines screaming about riots and bombs. But acts of violence and extremist fringe groups are less visible than the division in civil society that sends Protestants and Catholics to separate neighborhoods, separate stores, separate pubs, and often separate schools, with separate, though similar, traditional songs and slang. The split is often hard for an outsider to discern, especially in rural vacation spots. On the other hand, it would be nearly impossible for a visitor to leave Northern Ireland without seeing street curbs in both cities and villages painted with the colors of their residents' sectarian identity. The 1998 Good Friday Agreement, granting Home Rule and hoping to lead the North out of its struggles, has been struggling itself. Home Rule was suspended and reinstated in February 2000, and by the summer of 2001 a lack of progress on paramilitary promises to "put weapons beyond use" brought the Good Friday government to a frustrated halt. London took the reins again, if only briefly, and both sides renewed their efforts to make their country as peaceful as it is beautiful. And Northern Ireland *is* beautiful.

Thatched-cottage fishing villages dot the strands of the Ards Peninsula, leading to the rounded peaks of the Mournes and the national park retreats of Newcastle. To the west lie the easily-accessible Sperrin Mountains and the tidy-walled farms of the Fermanagh Lake District. Industrial Enniskillen rests just north, though travelers would do well to continue onward to Derry, a city rich in both political and historical significance. Nearby lies the world's eighth wonder of the world, the Giant's Causeway, a volcanic staircase that extends out to the Atlantic. Hillside forts and castles loom on the cliffs above. On the way to bursting nightlife of Belfast you'll pass through the waterfalls and valleys of the glorious Glens of Antrim.

ESSENTIALS

MONEY

Legal tender in Northern Ireland is the British pound. Northern Ireland has its own bank notes, which are identical in value to English and Scottish notes of the same denominations but not accepted outside Northern Ireland. Both English and Scottish notes, however, are accepted in the North.

BRITISH POUND		
	AUS$1 = £0.35	£1 = AUS$2.73
	CDN$1 =£0.42	£1 = CDN$2.18
	NZ$1 = £0.30	£1 = NZ$3.34
	ZAR1=£0.09	£1 = ZAR11.74
	US$1 = £0.71	£1 = US$1.42
	€1= £0.62	1 = €1.61

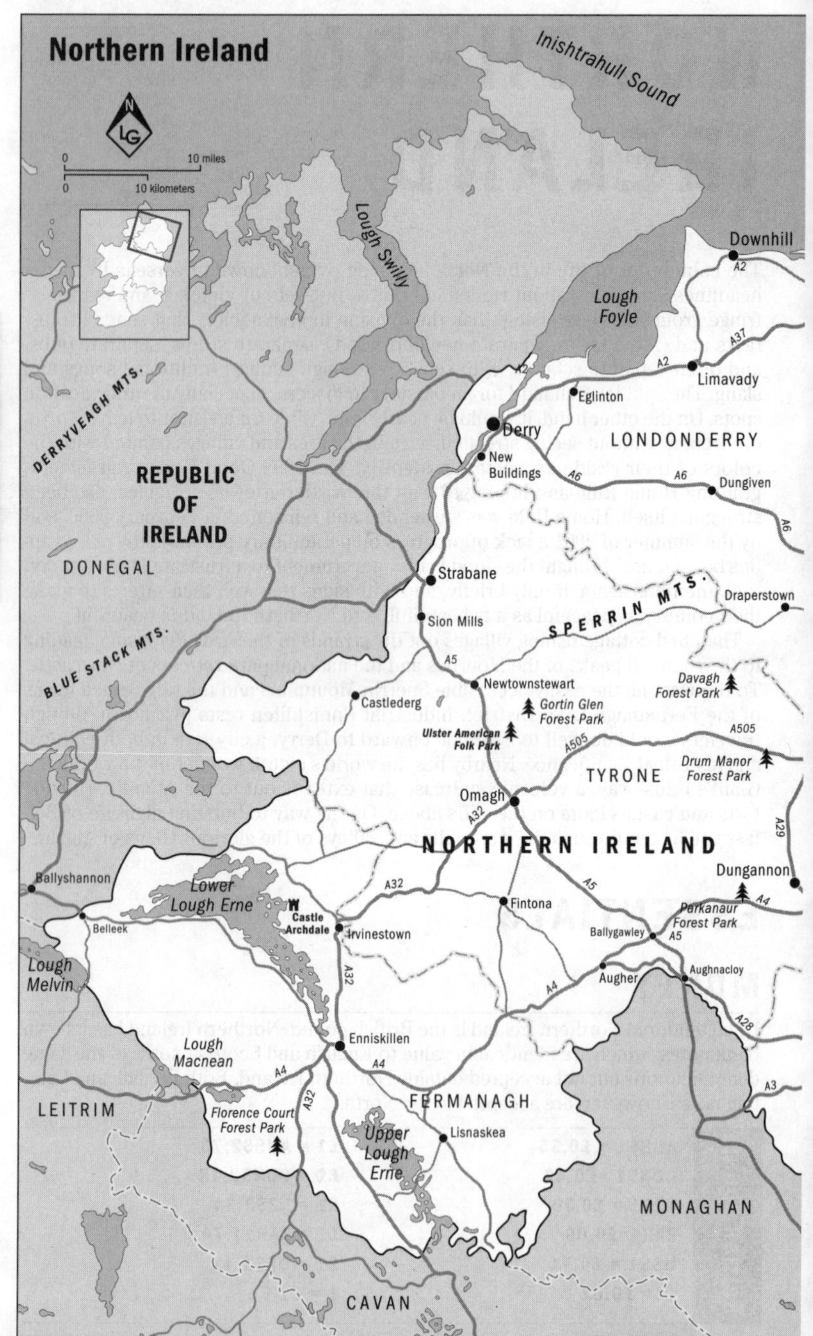

Northern Ireland
0
10 miles
0
10 kilometers
Inishtrahull Sound
Lough Swilly
Lough Foyle
Downhill
Limavady
Eglinton
Derry
LONDONDERRY
New Buildings
Dungiven
DERRYVEAGH MTS.
REPUBLIC OF IRELAND
DONEGAL
Strabane
Sion Mills
SPERRIN MTS.
Draperstown
BLUE STACK MTS.
Newtownstewart
Castlederg
Gortin Glen Forest Park
Ulster American Folk Park
Davagh Forest Park
Drum Manor Forest Park
TYRONE
Omagh
NORTHERN IRELAND
Dungannon
Ballyshannon
Lower Lough Erne
Castle Archdale
Irvinestown
Belleek
Fintona
Parkanaur Forest Park
Ballygawley
Aughnacloy
Augher
Lough Melvin
Enniskillen
Lough Macnean
LEITRIM
FERMANAGH
Florence Court Forest Park
Upper Lough Erne
Lisnaskea
MONAGHAN
CAVAN

SCOTLAND
Rathlin Island
North Channel
Giant's Causeway
Ballintoy
Carrick-a-rede
Portrush
Bushmills
Ballycastle
Portstewart
Coleraine
Cushendun
ANTRIM HILLS
Cushendall
Glenariff
Ballymoney
Glenariff Forest Park
Carnlough Bay
Dunloy
Carnlough
Garvagh
Kilrea
Drains Bay
Ballygalley
Cullybackey
Ballymena
Larne
ANTRIM
Castledawson
Ballyclare
Whitehead
Randalstown
Magherafelt
Carrickfergus
Antrim
Greenisland
Belfast Lough
Helen's Bay
Moneymore
Belfast International Airport
Newtownabbey
Craigavad
Bangor
Donaghadee
Cookstown
Holywood
Millisle
Lough Neagh
Crumlin
Belfast
Newtownards
Dundonald
Stewartstown
Castlereagh
Ards Peninsula
Dunmurry
Comber
Ballywater
Belvoir Park Forest
Coalisland
Lisburn
Carryduff
Kirkcubbin
Ballygowan
Moygashel
Strangford Lough
Saintfield
Portavogie
Lurgan
Hillsborough
Craigavon
Portadown
Waringstown
Dromore
Crossgar
Ballyahinch
Portaferry
Ballyleny
Richhill
Gilford
DOWN
Strongford
Tandragee
Saul
Armagh
Downpatrick
Banbridge
Gosford Forest Park
Castlewellan Forest Park
Markethill
Ardglass
Castlewellan
Rathfriland
Keady
ARMAGH
Dundrum Bay
Tollymore Forest Park
Newcastle
Bessbrook
Newry
MOURNE MTS.
Slieve Gullion Forest Park
Warrenpoint
Kilbroney Forest Park
Annalong
Rostrevor
Crossmaglen
Carlingford Lough
Kilkeel
NORTHERN IRELAND

Euros are generally not accepted in the North, with the exception of some border towns which will calculate the exchange rate and add an additional surcharge. UK coins come in denominations of 1p, 2p, 5p, 10p, 20p, 50p, and £1. Most banks are closed on Saturday, Sunday, and all public holidays. On "bank holidays," occurring several times a year in both countries, most businesses shut down. Usual weekday bank hours in Northern Ireland are M-F 9:30am to 4:30pm.

For more comprehensive travel information, see **Essentials,** p. 7.

The information in this book was researched in the summer of 2002. Inflation and the Invisible Hand may raise or lower the listed prices by as much as 20%. You can find up-to-date exchange rate information in major newspapers or on the web at www.oanda.com.

SAFETY AND SECURITY

Although sectarian violence is dramatically less common than in the height of the Troubles (see p. 455), some neighborhoods and towns still experience turmoil during sensitive political times. It's best to remain alert and cautious while traveling in Northern Ireland during **Marching Season,** from July 4 to 12 (**Orange Day;** see p. 453). The twelfth of August, when the **Apprentice Boys** march in Derry (see p. 530), is also a testy period during which urban areas should be avoided or traversed with much circumspection. The most common form of violence is property damage, and tourists are unlikely targets (beware of leaving your car unsupervised, however, if it bears a Republic of Ireland license plate). In general, if you are traveling in the North during marching season, be prepared for transport delays, and for some shops and services to be closed. Vacation areas like the Glens and the Causeway Coast are less affected by the parades. In general, use common sense in conversation, and, as in dealing with any issues of a culture not your own, be respectful of locals' religious and political perspectives. Overall, Northern Ireland has one of the lowest tourist-related crime rates in the world.

Border checkpoints have been removed, and armed soldiers and vehicles are less visible in Belfast and Derry. Do not take **photographs** of soldiers, military installations, or vehicles; your film will be confiscated and you may be detained for questioning. Taking pictures of political murals is not a crime, although many people feel uncomfortable doing so in residential neighborhoods. Unattended luggage is always considered suspicious and worthy of confiscation. It is generally unsafe to hitch in Northern Ireland. *Let's Go* never recommends hitchhiking.

Northern Ireland is reached by using the UK **country code 44;** from the Republic dial **048.** The **phone code** for every town in the North is **028.**

HISTORY AND POLITICS

Throughout its turbulent history, Northern Ireland has remained steadfast in its determination to remain a divided society. The frustrations of the recent peace talks only prove how important it is for Northerners to retain their individual cultural identities, even at the cost of lasting peace. They continue to defend the lines that define their differences, whether ideological divisions across the chambers of Parliament or actual streets marking the end of one culture and the beginning of the next. The 950,000 Protestants are generally **Unionists,** who want the six counties of Northern Ireland to remain in the UK; the 650,000 Catholics tend to identify with the Republic of Ireland, not Britain, and many are **Nationalists,** who want the six counties to be part of the Republic. The extremist problem-children on either side are known as **Loyalists** and **Republicans,** respectively, groups who tend to prefer defending their turf with rocks and petrol bombs. In December 1999, the world felt a stirring of optimism after the reinstatement of Home Rule in the North, but continued tensions over disarmament of the extremist factions ("You put your guns down." "You put 'em down first.") and recent political victories by hardliners have kept peace a sweet but distant dream.

For more information about Ireland before the break between the North and South in 1920, see **Life and Times,** p. 54.

A DIVIDED ISLAND: IT STARTS

The 17th-century **Ulster Plantation** saw thousands of English and Scottish settlers come to Ireland. Protestants fleeing rosary-laden France initially sought refuge in Ulster, bringing with them commercial skills to the small linen manufacturing industry already present. Over the following two centuries, merchants and working-class immigrants from nearby Scotland settled in northeast Ulster. Institutionalized religious discrimination may have limited Catholic access to land ownership and other basic rights, but made it quite an attractive destination for Scots Protestants, who profited from the cheap land options. The British brought the smokestacks of progress to Counties Antrim and Down while the rest of the island remained agricultural. By the end of the 19th century, Belfast was a booming industrial center with thriving textile mills and ship-building factories, most of which refused to hire Catholic workers.

In the late 19th century, while the excitables down south were whirling themselves into a Republican frenzy, the picture looked much different in the northeast. During its 300-year tenure, the Ulster Plantation had created a working- and middle-class population in Ulster that identified with the British Empire and did not support Irish Home Rule. The **Orange Order,** named after William of Orange, who had been victorious over arch-nemesis Catholic James II in the 1690s (see p. 58), organized Protestants into local lodges, with ritualistic behaviors such as oaths of loyalty and ceremonial midnight leprechaun sacrifices. They ordained July 12th as a holiday—**Orange Day**—on which to hold parades celebrating William's victory at the **Battle of the Boyne.** The Order's constituency and radicalism continued to grow despite legislative disapproval—it quietly gained momentum, culminating in its explosive opposition to the first Home Rule Bill in 1886 (see p. 61).

Lawyer and politician **Edward Carson,** with trusty sidekick **James Craig,** advocated against Home Rule and sought to make the British elite better understand the arguments against it. In 1912, when Home Rule seemed more possible, Carson held a mass meeting, and Unionists signed the Ulster Covenant of Resistance to Home Rule. In 1914, Home Rule appeared even more likely, so the Unionist **Ulster Volunteer Force** (**UVF;** see p. 455) armed itself by smuggling guns in through Larne—an act

1609
English and Scottish settlers set up the Ulster Plantation in Counties Donegal, Derry, Tyrone, Armagh, Cavan, and Fermanagh.

1613
Derry incorporated as Londonderry on March 29.

1641
An uprising (ostensibly for Charles I) begins in Ulster, spreads south, and massacres thousands of Protestants.

1689
Jacobites (followers of James II) lay siege to Protestant Derry. Thousands die of starvation and disease.

1717
Beginning of mass migration of Ulster-Scots to the American colonies.

1795
Protestant Orange Order founded in Armagh.

1798
United Irishmen rebellion begins.

1801
Act of Union creates "United Kingdom of Great Britain and Ireland" and "United Church of England and Ireland."

that prompted Nationalists to sneak their own guns in through Howth. WWI gave Unionists more time to organize and made British leaders realize that the imposition of Home Rule on Ulster would bring havoc: the UVF would pair off against the **Irish Republican Army** (**IRA;** see p. 62) who in turn would fight the governing body. In addition to fearing for the safety of the Anglo-philes in Ireland, the British government also sought to keep control of the North's strategic and profitable harbors. Responding to these concerns, the **1920 Government of Ireland Act** created two parliaments for the North and South; it went nowhere in the south and was quickly superseded by the **Anglo-Irish Treaty and Civil War** (see p. 62), but the measure (intended to be temporary) became the basis of the Northern government until 1973. The new Parliament met at **Stormont,** near Belfast.

The baby-statelet of newly constituted Northern Ireland, included only six of the nine counties of Ulster, leaving predominately Catholic Donegal, Monaghan, and Cavan to their own devices. This arrangement suited the one million Protestants in the six counties, yet it threatened the several hundred thousand Protestant Unionists living elsewhere on the island and the half-million Catholic Nationalists living within the new Ulster. Carson and Craig had helped orchestrate these odd borders, hoping to create the largest possible area in which a permanent Protestant majority resided. Craig, the North's first Prime Minister, his successor **Sir Basil Brooke,** and most of their Cabinet ministers thought in terms, as Brooke put it, of "a Protestant state for a Protestant people." Orange Lodges and other strongly Protestant groups continued to control politics, and the Catholic minority boycotted elections in protest of their "imprisonment within the north." Anti-Catholic discrimination was widespread. The **Royal Ulster Constabulary (RUC),** the new and Protestant police force in the North, filled its ranks with part-time policemen called Bs and **B-Specials,** a major source of Catholic casualties. The IRA continued sporadic campaigns in the North through the 20s and 30s with little result. In the Irish State, the IRA was gradually suppressed.

The 1930s sent the Northern economy into the dumps, requiring more and more British subsidies, while the Stormont Cabinet aged and withered. **WWII** gave Unionists a chance to show their loyalty—the Republic stayed neutral and stayed out, but the North welcomed Allied troops, ships, and airforce bases. The need to build and repair warships raised employment in Belfast and allowed Catholics to enter the industrial workforce for the first time. The Luftwaffe firebombed Belfast toward the end of the war, making it one of the UK's most damaged cities and earning Churchill's public commendation.

Over the following two decades, a grateful British Parliament poured money into loyal little Ulster. The North's standard of living stayed higher than in the Republic, but discrimination and joblessness persisted, especially for Catholics. The government at Stormont neglected to institute social reform, and parliamentary districts were painfully and unequally drawn to favor Protestants. Religious rifts reinforced cultural divides between and even within neighborhoods. After a brief, unsuc-

1845
Great Irish Famine begins.

1870
Filibustering Isaac Butt seats himself as head of the new Home Rule League.

1886
First Home Rule Bill, attempting to return autonomy to Ireland, defeated.

1892
Ulster Convention at Belfast opposes Home Rule Parliament.

1893
2nd Home Rule Bill finds defeat in British House of Lords.

1905
Sinn Féin and Ulster Unionist Council both formed.

1912
Over 500,000 Protestants in the North sign a pledge to oppose Home Rule by all means necessary.

1914
Home Rule Bill passed by England but suspended because of WWI.

1916
Easter Rising.

1920
IRA kills 14 British secret agents. British soldiers retaliate, killing 12.

1920
Government of Ireland Act partitions country into North and Republic.

cessful attempt at school desegregation, Stormont ended up granting subsidies to Catholic schools. As the Republic gained a surer footing, violence (barring the occasional border skirmish) receded on the island. In 1962 the *New York Times* bid the IRA a formal, eulogistic farewell. **Capt. Terence O'Neill,** who became the third Stormont Prime Minister in 1963, tried to enlarge the economy and soften discrimination, meeting in 1965 with the Republic's Prime Minister, Sean Lemass. O'Neill summed up the liberal Unionist view when he said, "If you treat Roman Catholics with due kindness and consideration, they will live like Protestants."

THE TROUBLES

The economy grew, but the bigotry festered along with the Nationalist community's resentment at their forced unemployment and lack of political representation. The American civil rights movement inspired the 1967 founding of the **Northern Ireland Civil Rights Association (NICRA),** which worked to end anti-Catholic discrimination in public housing. NICRA leaders tried to distance the movement from constitutional concerns, although many of their followers didn't get the message. Protestant extremists included the acerbic **Rev. Ian Paisley,** whose **Ulster Protestant Volunteers (UPV)** overlapped in membership with the illegal, resurrected, paramilitary UVF. The first NICRA march was raucous but nonviolent. The second, held in Derry in 1968, was a bloody mess disrupted by Unionists and then by the RUC's water cannons. The Troubles had begun.

Catholic **John Hume** and Protestant **Ivan Cooper** formed a new civil rights committee in Derry but were overshadowed by Bernadette Devlin's radical, student-led **People's Democracy (PD).** The PD encouraged, and NICRA opposed, a four-day peaceful march from Belfast to Derry starting on New Year's Day, 1969. Paisleyite harassment along the way was nothing compared to the RUC's physical assault on Derry's Catholic Bogside once the marchers arrived. After that, Derry authorities agreed to keep the RUC out of the Bogside, and this area became **Free Derry.** O'Neill, granting more civil rights concessions in the hopes of calming everyone down, was deserted by more of his hard-line Unionist allies. On August 12, 1969, Catholics based in Free Derry threw rocks at the annual Apprentice Boys parade along the city walls. The RUC attacked the Bogside residents, and a two-day siege ensued. Free Derry retained its independence, but the violence showed that the RUC could not maintain order alone. The British Army arrived to regain order.

O'Neill resigned in 1969. Between 1970 and 1972, leaders alternated concessions and crackdowns to little effect. The rejuvenated IRA split in two, with the "Official" faction practically fading into insignificance as the new **Provisional IRA,** or **Provos** (the IRA we talk about today), took over with less ideology and more guns. British troops became the their main target. In 1970, John Hume founded the **Social Democratic and Labor Party (SDLP),** with the intention of bringing about social change

1939
The North joins WWII while the Republic remains neutral.

1967
Northern Ireland Civil Rights Association (NICRA) founded.

October 1968
Derry riots over the NICRA's march; unofficial start to the Troubles.

January 1969
People's Democracy student-led march meets violent RUC opposition in Derry. RUC banned from Bogside, known as "Free Derry."

July 1969
Further riots break out during Marching Season.

August 1969
British Army arrives to maintain order.

1970
IRA divides, with the more violent Provos taking charge.

August 1970
Moderate Social Democratic and Labor Party (SDLP) founded.

January 1972
"Bloody Sunday" in Derry. 14 Catholics killed. British embassy in Dublin burned down in retaliation.

May 28, 1974
Direct British rule from Westminster begins after failed power-sharing experiment.

1970-1976
Strife brings an average of 275 deaths per year.

March 1981
Bobby Sands leads Nationalist prisoners in hunger strike.

November 1985
Anglo-Irish Agreement signed; grants Republic a "consultative role" without legal authority in governance of North.

March 1993
IRA bomb in Warrington kills 2 children and provokes public outcry.

August 1994
IRA announces a ceasefire, but refuses to disarm.

January 1995
British army ends daytime patrols in Belfast.

February 1995
"Joint framework" proposal opens up talks with Sinn Féin, IRA's political arm.

January 1996
US diplomat George Mitchell proposes surrender of all guerilla weaponry.

February 1996
IRA breaks ceasefire with London office bombing.

through the support of both Catholics and Protestants; by 1973, it had become the moderate political voice of Northern Catholics. British policies of **internment without trial** outraged Catholics and led the SDLP to withdraw from government. The pattern was clear: any concessions to the Catholic community might provoke Protestant violence, while anything that seemed to favor the Unionists risked an explosive IRA response.

On January 30, 1972, British troops fired into a crowd of non-violent protesters in Derry; the famous event, known today as **Bloody Sunday,** and the ensuing reluctance of the British government to investigate, increased Catholic outrage. Fourteen Catholics were killed—the soldiers claimed they had not fired the first shot, while Catholics said the soldiers shot at unarmed, fleeing marchers. Only in 1999 did official re-examination of the event begin; the inquiry will likely take several years.

On February 2, 1972, the British embassy in Dublin was burned down. Soon thereafter, the IRA bombed a British army barracks. After further bombings in 1973, Stormont was dissolved and replaced by the **Sunningdale executive,** which split power between Catholics and Protestants. This policy was immediately crippled by a massive Unionist work stoppage, and a policy of **direct British rule** from Westminster began. A referendum that year, asking if voters wanted Northern Ireland to remain part of the United Kingdom, showed that voters supported the Union at a rate of 90 to 1—Catholics had boycotted the polls. The verdict didn't stop the violence, which brought an average of 275 deaths per year between 1970 and 1976.

In 1978, 300 Nationalist prisoners in the Maze Prison in Northern Ireland began a campaign to have their special category as political prisoners restored. The campaign's climax was the 10-man H-Block **hunger strike** of 1981. Leader **Bobby Sands** was the first to strike—he was elected to Parliament from a Catholic district in Tyrone and Fermanagh as he starved to death in prison. Sands died after 66 days and became a martyr; his face is still seen on murals in the Falls section of Belfast (see p. 484). The remaining prisoners officially ended the strike on October 3, seven months and two days after it began.

Sands's election was no anomaly. The hunger strikes galvanized Nationalists, and support for **Sinn Féin,** the political arm of the IRA, surged in the early 80s. British Prime Minister Margaret Thatcher and Taoiseach Garret FitzGerald signed the **Anglo-Irish Agreement** in 1985. The Agreement granted the Republic of Ireland a "consultative role" but no legal authority in the governance of Northern Ireland. It improved relations between London and Dublin but infuriated extremists on both sides. Protestant paramilitaries attacked "their own" RUC, while the IRA continued its bombing campaigns in England. In 1991 and 1992, the Brooke Initiative led to the first multi-party talks in the North in over a decade, but they managed, conveniently, to forget to invite Sinn Féin. The **Downing Street Declaration,** issued at the end of 1993 by Prime Minister John Major and Taoiseach Albert Reynolds, invited the IRA to participate in talks if they refrained from violence for three months.

1994 CEASEFIRE: FAT LADY?

On August 31, 1994, the IRA announced a complete cessation of violence. While Loyalist guerillas cooperated by announcing their own ceasefire, Unionist leaders bickered over the meaning of the IRA's statement; in their opinion, it did not go far enough—only disarmament could signify a commitment to peace. Nonetheless, **Gerry Adams,** Sinn Féin's leader, defended the statement and called for direct talks with the British government. The peace held for over a year.

In February 1995, John Major and Irish Prime Minister John Bruton issued the **joint framework** proposal. The document suggested the possibility of a new Northern Ireland Assembly that would include the "harmonizing powers" of the Irish and British governments and the right of the people of Northern Ireland to choose their own destiny. Subsequently, the British government began talks with both Loyalists and, for the first time, Sinn Féin. Disarmament was the most prominent problem in the 1995 talks—both Republican and Loyalist groups refused to put down their guns.

The IRA ended their ceasefire on February 9, 1996, with the bombing of an office building in London's Docklands. Despite this setback, the stalled peace talks, to be chaired by US diplomat **George Mitchell,** were slated for June 10. Ian Paisley, now leader of the extreme **Democratic Unionist Party (DUP),** objected to Mitchell's appointment, calling it a "dastardly deed," but did not boycott the talks. The talks proceeded sluggishly and precariously. Sinn Féin refused to participate because it did not agree to the **Mitchell Principles,** which included the total disarmament of all paramilitary organizations. Sinn Féin's popularity had been growing in Northern Ireland—in the May elections, they gathered 15% of the vote—but their credibility was seriously jeopardized on June 15, 1996, when a blast in a Manchester shopping district injured more than 200 people.

As the peace process chugged along, the Orangemen's July and August marches grew more contentious. Parades through Catholic neighborhoods incited violence by both residents and marchers. The government created a **Parades Commission** to oversee the re-routing of parades and encourage the participation of both sides in negotiations. Protestants believe the Commission's decisions infringe on their right to practice their culture. Catholics argue that the marches are a form of harassment and intimidation from which they deserve protection. **Orange Day 1996** saw another burst of violence after the Parades Commission banned an Orange Order march through the Catholic Garvaghy Rd. in staunchly Protestant Portadown. Unionists reacted by chucking petrol bombs, bricks, and bottles at police, who replied with plastic bullets. After four days of violence, police allowed the marchers to go through, but this time Catholics responded with a hail of debris. Similarly, the nightlife in Belfast and Derry consisted mostly of those rioting and those avoiding the rioters.

On October 7, the IRA bombed the British army headquarters in Belfast, killing one soldier and injuring 30 in Northern Ire-

July 1996
4-day clash between Catholics and Protestants in Portadown.

May 1997
Tony Blair elected Prime Minister of Britain. Sinn Féin-Sinn Féin wins more seats in Parliament but refuses to swear allegiance to Queen.

July 1997
Portadown riots after Marching Season; Orange Order cancels and re-routes several parades.

July 1997
IRA announces a 2nd ceasfire.

1998
Peace process delayed by violent outbursts from extremist groups.

April 11, 1998
Northern Ireland Peace Agreement drafted. A May 22 landslide vote confirms that even a majority of Protestants approve. 108-member Northern Ireland assembly assigned governing responsibilities.

June 1998
David Trimble and Seamus Mallon elected First Minister and Deputy First Minister, respectively.
June 1998
Tony Blair retains RUC, but appoints Chris Patten to review RUC record.
July 1998
Marching season disrupts the new-found peace.
August 15, 1998
Bombing in Omagh by "Real IRA" splinter group leaves 29 dead and 382 injured.
October 1998
Hume and Trimble receive Nobel Peace Prize.
1999
Northern Ireland Assembly fails to establish itself as politicians battle over disarmament and the release of political prisoners.

December 1999
London signs devolution bill; returns home rule to Northern Ireland. A power-sharing 12-member cabinet is formed.

January 2000
Trimble gives IRA an ultimatum to disarm. The IRA refuses.

February 2000
Inability to resolve disarmament issue leads Britain to suspend power-sharing experiment after 11 weeks.

land's first bombing in two years. In early 1997, the IRA tried to make the North an issue in the upcoming British elections by making issuing bomb threats, including one that postponed the Grand National horse race. The public was uninjured but thoroughly angered, and John Major condemned Sinn Féin.

In May of 1997, the Labour party swept the British elections and **Tony Blair,** riding high on hopes of peace, became Prime Minister. Sinn Féin made its most impressive showing yet: **Gerry Adams** and **Martin McGuinness** (who has recently admitted to being second-in-command of the IRA during Bloody Sunday) won seats in Parliament but refused to swear allegiance to the Queen and were barred from taking their places. In spite of this, the government ended its ban on talks with a still-uncooperative Sinn Féin. Hopes for a renewed ceasefire were dashed when the car of a prominent Republican was bombed; in retaliation, the IRA shot two members of the RUC.

GOOD FRIDAY AGREEMENT

The 1997 marching season gave Mo Mowlam, the British government's Northern Ireland Secretary, a rough introduction to her new job. The Orange Order started their "festivities" a week early in Portadown. More than 80 people were hurt in the ensuing rioting and looting, and Mowlam came under scrutiny for allowing the parade to go on without considering the consequences. On July 10, the Orange Order called off and re-routed a number of contentious parades, offering hope for peace. The marches turned out mostly peaceful—police fired a smattering of plastic bullets at rioters in Derry and Belfast, but there were no casualties. On July 19, the IRA announced an "unequivocal" ceasefire to start the following day.

In September 1997, Sinn Féin joined the peace talks. Members of the **Ulster Unionist Party (UUP),** the voice of moderate Protestants, joined shortly thereafter and were disparaged by Paisley and the DUP for sitting with terrorists. UUP leader **David Trimble** assured Protestants that he would not negotiate directly with Sinn Féin. Catholic Monica McWilliams and Protestant Pearl Sagar, co-founders of the recently formed, religiously mixed **Northern Ireland Women's Coalition,** brought a human rights agenda and a commitment to peace to the talks, and found themselves next in line for Paisley's derisive attacks.

The peace process, despite its noble aspirations, did not enjoy universal support. In January 1998, another dozen lives (mostly civilian and Catholic) were lost to sectarian idiocy. After two Protestants were killed by Catholic extremists in early February, Unionist leaders charged Sinn Féin with breaking its pledge to support only peaceful actions toward political change and tried to oust party leaders from the talks. Representatives from Britain, Ireland, and the US continued to push for progress, holding the group to a strict deadline in April. Mowlam expressed her commitment by visiting Republican and Loyalist prisoners in the maximum-security Maze prison to encourage their participation in the peace process.

After a long week of negotiations, the delegates approved a draft of the **1998 Northern Ireland Peace Agreement** in the wee small hours of Saturday, April 11—thus it's commonly called the **Good Friday Agreement.** The pact emphasized that change in the North could come only with the consent of its people. It declared that the "birthright" of the people is to choose whether to identify personally as Irish, British, or both; even as the status of Northern Ireland changes, the Agreement says, residents retain the right to hold Irish or British citizenship.

On Friday, May 22, in the first island-wide vote since 1918, residents of both the North and the Republic voted the Agreement into law. A resounding majority (71% of the North and 94% of the Republic) voted yes to the Agreement, which divided governing responsibilities of Northern Ireland into three strands. The new main body, a 108-member **Northern Ireland Assembly,** assigns committee posts and chairs proportionately to the parties' representation. Catholics see this as an opportunity for reclaiming the political power they were long denied. On June 25, the UUP and the SDLP won the most seats, while Sinn Féin garnered more support than ever before. Voices of moderation on both sides, David Trimble of the UUP and Seamus Mallon of the SDLP were elected First Minister and Deputy First Minister. The second strand of the new government, a **North-South Ministerial Council,** serves as the cross-border authority. At least 12 possible areas of focus were under consideration in 1998, including social welfare issues such as education, transportation, urban planning, tourism, and EU programs. The final strand, the **British-Irish Council,** approaches similar issues, but operates on a broader scale, concerning itself with the entire British Isles.

While many felt that a lasting peace was finally in reach, a few controversial issues remained unresolved. Sinn Féin called for disbanding the largely Protestant RUC, which had been cited by the UN for its policies of intimidation and harassment. Blair declared that the RUC would continue to exist, but appointed Chris Patten, the former governor of Hong Kong, to head a small one-year commission to review the RUC's recruiting, hiring, training practices, culture, and symbols.

And then it was marching season again. In the end of May 1998, a march by the Junior Orange Order provoked violence on Portadown's Garvaghy Rd., and area still smarting from the 1996 debacle. In light of this disturbance, the Parades Commission hesitated to grant the Orange Day marching permits. On June 15, the Parades Commission rerouted the Tour of the North, banning it from entering the Catholic Cliftonville Rd.-Antrim Rd. areas in Belfast. Aside from two short standoffs with the RUC, the parade proceeded without conflict. But the day after the assembly elections, Nationalists and policemen at a parade in West Belfast started the familiar dance of destruction. Early July saw a wave of violence that included hundreds of bombings and assaults on security forces as well as a slew of arson attacks on Catholic churches.

May 29, 2000
Britain restores power-sharing after IRA promises to disarm.

June 2000
IRA weapon caches are inspected for the first time.

June 30, 2000
Taoiseach Ahern wins an 84-80 "no-confidence" vote. He defends his party's role in the peace process and his questioned appointment of a disgraced former judge to a high financial post.

July 2000
Marching season concludes after 10 days of widespread riots, protests over marching routes, and at least 1 casualty. Belfast and Portadown are barricaded and shut down by the Orange Order.

July 28, 2000
Final political prisoners are released from Maze Prison near Belfast to both heroic welcomes and bitter disgust. The historic prison is scheduled to close by the end of the year.

Summer 2000
Royal Ulster Constabulary overhaul urged on by Catholics and opposed by Protestants.

Other parades passed peacefully, but a stand-off began over the fate of the July 4 **Drumcree** parade, which was forbidden from marching down war-torn Garvaghy Rd. Angered by the decision but encouraged by a history of indecision by the British government, thousands of people participated in a week-long stand-off with the RUC. Rioting occurred in Portadown and elsewhere, and Protestant marchers were angered by what they saw as the disloyalty of their own police force. Neither the Orangemen nor the Parade Commission would budge, and the country looked with anxiety toward July 12. On the night of July 11, however, a Catholic home in almost entirely Protestant Ballymoney was firebombed by local hooligans, and three young boys were killed. Marches still took place the following day; but instead of rioting against the Orangemen who passed though their neighborhoods, Catholics looked on at the marches in silent reproach. The **Drumcree standoff** gradually lost it numbers, and the Church of Ireland publicly called for its end. Although some tried to distance the boys' deaths from the events at Drumcree, the murders led to a reassessment of the Orange Order and to a new sobriety about the peace process.

Then, on August 15, a bombing in the religiously mixed town of **Omagh** left 29 dead and 382 injured. A tiny splinter group calling itself the **"Real IRA"** claimed responsibility for the attack. The terrorists' obvious motive for one of the worst atrocities of the Troubles was to undermine the Good Friday Agreement. Sinn Féin's Gerry Adams unreservedly condemned the bombing. The US has now outlawed the Real IRA and inducted them into the Terrorist Hall of Infamy, despite Sinn Féin's concern that criminalization will only attract more young lunatics.

In October of 1998, Catholic John Hume and Protestant David Trimble received the Nobel Peace Prize for their participation in the peace process. The coming year, however, was full of disappointments. The formation of the Northern Ireland Assembly, a fundamental premise from Good Friday, ended up in failure. Two major provisions of the Agreement caused (or, rather, highlighted) serious rifts between Catholic and Protestant politicians: the gradual decommissioning of all paramilitary groups' arms, and the early release of political prisoners. Disagreement over the **Northern Ireland (Sentences) Bill** fanned the flames and split the UK Parliament for the first time during the talks. The bill required the release of all political prisoners, including those convicted of murder, by May 2000. Dissenters feared that the bill did not sufficiently link the release of prisoners to their organizations' full disarmament, which was the greatest concern for most Unionists: the military wings of political parties, most notably Sinn Féin, were expected to disarm themselves in time for the June elections. The Agreement, unfortunately, lacked a time frame for decommissioning. During the summer of 1999, the deadline for the Assembly's inauguration was pushed farther back. Unionists refused to take seats with Sinn Féin, and Blair, Mowland, and Irish PM Bertie Ahern spent yet another round of long nights attempting to negotiate between sides. In July, First Minister Trimble failed to appear on the day that he was due to appoint the newly elected Assembly. Many interpreted Trimble's behavior as following the prerogatives of his own Unionist political party rather than the democratic will of the voters who approved the Peace Agreement. The Nationalist Deputy PM Seamus Mallon resigned the following day.

Orange Day 1999 came and went with little fanfare. The messy stuff didn't start until August 12, when the Apprentice Boys marched through Derry and Belfast. Catholics in Belfast staged a sit-down protest in the path of the marchers, only to be forcefully removed by the RUC. On the streets of Derry, petrol bombs and riot gear were once again in fashion.

CURRENT EVENTS

December 1999—London returns Home Rule to Northern Ireland after 27 years of British domination. A power-sharing government was formed under the leadership of Trimble and Mallon, but the IRA's hidden weapon caches remained a central conflict and threatened the collapse of the new assembly, whose four parties included the Democratic Unionist Party, the UUP, the Labour Party, and, to the tune of much controversy, Sinn Féin.

In late January 2000, Trimble gave the IRA an ultimatum to put its weapons "beyond use," and predicted a return to British rule if his demands were not met. The IRA's unwillingness to comply hamstrung the February peace talks, and just to make things a little more interesting, the dissident IRA Continuity group (still peeved at the "official" IRA's compromises) bombed a rural hotel in Irvinestown. Every Irish political group, including Sinn Féin, condemned the attack. Though the blast injured no one, it was an unwelcome reminder of the past in the midst of a stalled peace process. Britain suspended the power-sharing experiment just 11 weeks after its implementation and reintroduced direct British rule.

On midnight of May 29, 2000, Britain restored the power-sharing scheme after the IRA promised to begin disarmament. In June, they allowed two ambassadors to inspect their secret weapon caches. These advances did little to dispel conflict throughout the rest of the summer. In the Republic, "Teflon" **Bertie Ahern** of the Fianna Fail party scraped out an 84-80 "no-confidence" victory against the opposition Labour party. Marching season was, again, a nasty affair, although Tony Blair and Ahern expressed satisfaction over its containment. The Orange Order, reacting to the prevention of a march by the Parades Commission, shut down both Belfast and Portadown, barricading streets and rioting with police. The marching season concluded after 10 ugly days.

On July 28, the last political prisoners in **Maze Prison** walked free under the highly criticized Good Friday provisions, and by September 29 the Maze was completely empty of all prisoners. Supporters gave them heroes' welcomes, but other civilians and relatives of the deceased found the early release of convicted murderers, some carrying life sentences, appalling. Many of the released men expressed remorse and stated that their war was over, but others refused to apologize. Her Majesty has not yet declared what is to be done with Her Prison.

The story remains the same in the North—political squabbling at the negotiation tables and on the floors of various Parliaments continues, punctuated now and then by bombs or plastic bullets out on the streets. Both sides are making efforts to repair the past—the Bloody Sunday inquiry continues with testimony from British Military as well as IRA figures, and the European Court of Human Rights has recently awarded compensation to the families of 10 IRA fighters lost to the British government's "shoot to kill" policy. Meanwhile, the long slow path to disarmament points to a safer future—in the spring of 2001, the IRA was still dragging its heels, but allowed international diplomats a third visit to their secret arms dumps. The inspectors confirmed that the weapons (rumored to be enough to keep a small country in the war-making business for a decade) are unused. Loyalists were not satisfied. In the June 2001 elections, loyalist extremists were voted into Parliament in unprecedented numbers. It was suspected that violence would break once more; inflammatory leaders on both sides called for action. In July of 2001, in the Troubles-fraught Belfast area of Dayton, Catholic schoolchildren were targeted by Protestant protesters as they walked to their nearby school. The children suffered mental abuse and physical threats for several months before things calmed down. Then, in 2002, the IRA broke new ground when they destroyed a small payload of their weapons, marking the first time they had ever voluntarily destroyed any of their resources. Though the public's reaction was not as grand as they had hoped, the concession proved to be conducive to continued peaceful discussion.

BELFAST (BÉAL FEIRSTE)

Despite the violent associations conjured by the name Belfast, the North's capital feels more neighborly than most international, and even Irish, visitors expect. The second-largest city on the island, Belfast (pop. 330,000) is the focus of Northern Ireland's cultural, commercial, and political activity. For several hundred years it has been a cosmopolitan, booming center of mercantile activity, in brazen contrast to the rest of the island (that is, until the "Celtic Tiger" began roaring). Renowned writers and the annual arts festival maintain Belfast's reputation as a thriving artistic center. Luminaries such as Nobel Prize-winning Seamus Heaney and fellow poet Paul Muldoon roamed the halls of Belfast's esteemed Queen's College, giving birth to a modern, distinctively Northern Irish literary *esprit* that grapples with—and transcends—the difficult politics of the area. The Belfast bar scene, a mix of Irish-British pub culture and international trends, entertains locals, foreigners, and a student population as lively as any in the world.

Belfast was founded as the capital of the "Scots-Irish" Presbyterian settlement in the 17th century and was William of Orange's base during his battles against Catholic King James II (see **The Protestant Ascendancy,** p. 58). In the 19th century, Belfast became the most industrial part of Ireland, with world-famous factories and shipyards. By the turn of that century, Belfast had gathered enough slums, smoke, flax mills, Victorian architecture, and social theorists to look more British than Irish. The ship-building industry drew Scottish laborers across the channel for jobs, securing the region's allegiance to the UK. During the Troubles (see p. 455), armed British soldiers patrolled the streets, frequent military checkpoints slowed all traffic, and stores advertised "Bomb Damage Sales."

Those days are over now, and, due to extensive renovations of Belfast's downtown commercial district, the unobservant traveler could remain oblivious to the city's prior history. Indeed, the Belfast of today is really many cities in one: the City Centre, with stately City Hall as its hub, hums with hurried shoppers and briefcase-toters during the day; the industrial docks now hold The Odyssey, Northern Ireland's newest and most extravagant tourist-attraction complex; south of Shaftesbury Square, college-age hipsters idle the nights away in cafes and keep the streets alive while moving between clubs; West, and also East Belfast, where Catholics and Protestants divide themselves and paint their stories on the walls, make for fascinating, if sometimes grim, living history.

During the first week of July through around July 12, or "Marching Season" (also known by some locals as "the silly season"), these murals of anger and mourning seem to leap off the walls. This is when the "Orangemen," Protestants celebrating William's victory over James II, parade through Northern Ireland's streets wearing orange sashes and bowler hats. These marches are usually met with Nationalist (pro-Republic) protests, and violence can ensue. If you are in Belfast during this week, exercise common sense safety measures and expect delays in transportation and availability of services, as many restaurants and stores temporarily close.

INTERCITY TRANSPORTATION

Airports: Belfast International Airport (☎9448 4848) in Aldergrove. **Aer Lingus** (☎0845 973 7747), **British Airways** (☎0845 722 2111), **British European** (☎9045 7200), **BMI** (☎9024 1188), and **Easyjet** (0870 600 0000) land here. **Airbus** (☎9066 6630) runs to Belfast's Europa and Laganside bus stations in the city center (M-Sa every 30min. 5:45am-10:30pm, Su about every hr. 7:10am-8:45pm; £5, £8 return).

Belfast City Airport (☎9093 9093), at the harbor, is the destination of **Manx Airlines** (☎0845 7256 256) and **British European. Trains** run from the City Airport **(Sydenham Halt)** to Central Station (M-Sa 25-33 per day, Su 12 per day; £1).

Trains: For info on trains and buses, contact **Translink.** (☎9066 6630; www.translink.co.uk. Inquiries daily 7am-10pm.) All trains arrive at Belfast's **Central Station,** East Bridge St. Some also stop at **Botanic Station** on Botanic Ave. in the center of the University area, or at **Great Victoria Station,** next to the Europa Hotel. To: **Bangor** (33min.; M-F 39 per day, Sa 25 per day, Su 9 per day; £3); **Derry** (2hr.; M-F 9 per day, Sa 6 per day, Su 3 per day; £6.70); **Dublin** (2hr.; M-Sa 8 per day, Su 5 per day; £20); and **Larne** (M-F 12 per day, Sa 16 per day, Su 8 per day; £3.80). To get to Donegall Sq. from Central Station, turn left and walk down East Bridge St. Turn right on Oxford St., then left onto May St., which runs into Donegall Sq. A better option for those with luggage is the **Centrelink** bus service, free with rail tickets (see **Local Transportation,** below).

Buses: There are 2 main stations in Belfast. Buses traveling to and from the west, the north coast, and the Republic operate out of the **Europa Station** off Great Victoria St., behind the Europa Hotel (☎9066 6630; inquiries daily 7am-10pm). Buses to **Cork** (10hr., M-Sa 1 per day, £17.19); **Derry** (1¾hr.; M-Sa 19 per day, Su 6 per day; £7.50); **Donegal** (4hr.; M-Sa 6 per day, Su 1 per day; £11.25); **Dublin** (3hr.; M-Sa 7 per day, Su 5 per day; £10.31); **Galway** (7hr.; M-Th 6 per day, F 6 per day, Sa 4 per day, Su 2 per day; £15.63). Buses to and from Northern Ireland's east coast operate out of **Laganside Station,** off Donegall Quay (☎9066 6630; inquiries daily 7am-10pm). If you're on foot, take a left when you exit the terminal onto Queen's Square and walk past the clock tower. Queen's Square becomes High St. and runs into Donegall Pl.; a left here will get you to City Hall and Donegall Sq. (at the end of the street). The **Centrelink** bus connects both stations with the city center (see **Local Transportation,** below).

Ferries: To reach the city center from the **Belfast SeaCat terminal** (☎08705 523 523; www.seacat.co.uk), off Donegall Quay, you have 2 options. Late at night or early in the morning, a **taxi** might be your best bet, as the docks are rather isolated at these times. If on foot, take a left when you exit the terminal onto Donegall Quay. Turn right onto Albert Sq. about 2 blocks down at the Customs House (a large Victorian stone building). After 2 more short blocks, turn left on Victoria St. (not Great Victoria St.). Turn right again at the clock tower onto High St., which runs into Donegall Pl. Here, a left will lead you to the City Hall and Donegall Sq. (at the end of the street), where you can catch a **Centrelink** bus (see **Local Transportation,** below). **SeaCat** departs for: **Heysham** in England (4hr., Apr.-Nov. 1-2 per day); the **Isle of Man** (2¾hr.; M, W, F 1 per day Apr.-Nov.); and **Troon** in Scotland (2½hr., 2-3 per day). Fares £10-30 without car, cheapest if booked 4 wk. in advance. **Norse Merchant Ferries** (☎0870 600 4321; www.norsemerchant.com) run to **Liverpool** in England. **P&O Ferries** in **Larne** (☎0870 242 4777) run to **Cairnryan** in Scotland, and to **Fleetwood.** For information on ferries and hovercraft to Belfast from **England** and **Scotland,** see **By Ferry, p. 27**.

Car Rental: Budget, 96-102 Great Victoria St. (☎9023 0700). Economy £51 per day, £185 per wk. Ages 23-75. Open M-F 9am-5pm, Sa 9am-12:30pm. Other offices at **Belfast International Airport Office** (☎9442 3332; open daily 7:30am-11:30pm) and **Belfast City Airport Office** (☎9045 1111; open M-Sa 7:30am-9:30pm, Su 9am-9:30pm). At **Belfast International Airport** you'll also find **Alamo** (☎9442 2285), **Dan Dooley** (☎9445 2522), **Hertz** (☎9442 2533), and **Thrifty** (☎9442 2777). Dan Dooley is the only company who will rent to 21-23 year-olds. At **Belfast City Airport** you'll also find **Alamo** (☎9073 9400) and **Hertz** (☎9073 2451), among others.

Hitching: Hitchhiking is notoriously hard around Belfast and particularly inadvisable in the weeks around Marching Season. Most people take the bus out as far as Bangor or Larne before they stick out a thumb. But hey, *Let's Go* never recommends hitchhiking.

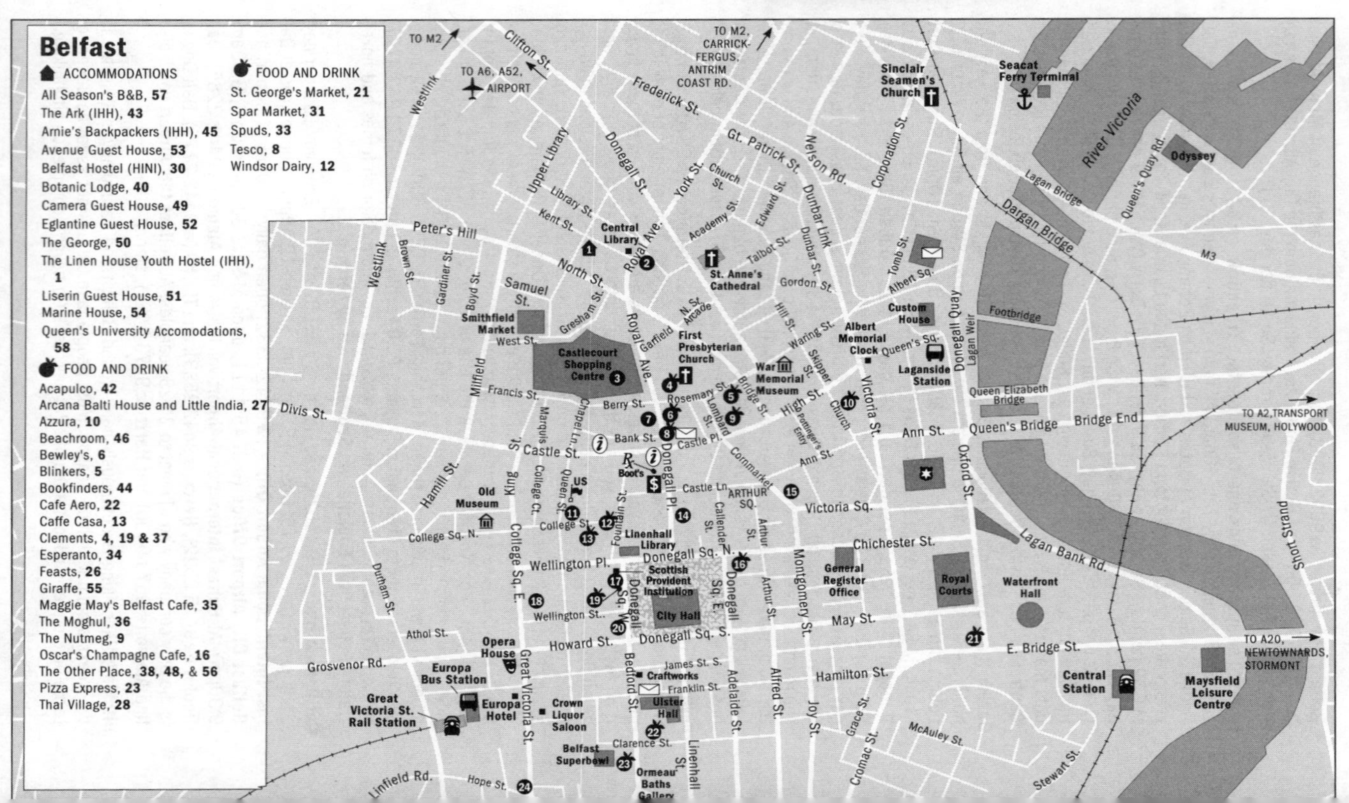
Belfast
ACCOMMODATIONS
All Season's B&B, 57
The Ark (IHH), 43
Arnie's Backpackers (IHH), 45
Avenue Guest House, 53
Belfast Hostel (HINI), 30
Botanic Lodge, 40
Camera Guest House, 49
Eglantine Guest House, 52
The George, 50
The Linen House Youth Hostel (IHH), 1
Liserin Guest House, 51
Marine House, 54
Queen's University Accomodations, 58
FOOD AND DRINK
Acapulco, 42
Arcana Balti House and Little India, 27
Azzura, 10
Beachroom, 46
Bewley's, 6
Blinkers, 5
Bookfinders, 44
Cafe Aero, 22
Caffe Casa, 13
Clements, 4, 19 & 37
Esperanto, 34
Feasts, 26
Giraffe, 55
Maggie May's Belfast Cafe, 35
The Moghul, 36
The Nutmeg, 9
Oscar's Champagne Cafe, 16
The Other Place, 38, 48, & 56
Pizza Express, 23
Thai Village, 28
FOOD AND DRINK
St. George's Market, 21
Spar Market, 31
Spuds, 33
Tesco, 8
Windsor Dairy, 12
TO M2
TO A6, A52, AIRPORT
Clifton St.
TO M2, CARRICKFERGUS, ANTRIM COAST RD.
Sinclair Seamen's Church
Seacat Ferry Terminal
River Victoria
Odyssey
Queen's Quay Rd.
Lagan Bridge
Dargan Bridge
M3
Westlink
Frederick St.
Gt. Patrick St.
Nelson Rd.
Corporation St.
Upper Library
Library St.
Kent St.
Donegall St.
York St.
Church St.
Academy St.
Edward St.
Dunbar Link
Dunbar St.
Talbot St.
Tomb St.
Albert Sq.
Peter's Hill
Brown St.
Gardiner St.
Boyd St.
Central Library
Royal Ave.
North St.
St. Anne's Cathedral
Gordon St.
Samuel St.
Smithfield Market
West St.
Gresham St.
N. St. Arcade
Garfield
First Presbyterian Church
Hill St.
Waring St.
Albert Memorial Clock
Queen's Sq.
Custom House
Laganside Station
Donegall Quay
Lagan Weir
Footbridge
Castlecourt Shopping Centre
Milfield
Francis St.
War Memorial Museum
Skipper St.
Rosemary St.
Bridge St.
High St.
Church
Victoria St.
Queen Elizabeth Bridge
Divis St.
Berry St.
Lombard St.
Pottinger's Entry
Queen's Bridge
Bridge End
TO A2, TRANSPORT MUSEUM, HOLYWOOD
Ann St.
Castle St.
Marquis
Chapel Ln.
Bank St.
Castle Pl.
Commarket
Oxford St.
Boot's
Donegall Pl.
Castle Ln.
ARTHUR SQ.
Hamill St.
Old Museum
King St.
College Ct.
Queen St.
US
Fountain St.
Victoria Sq.
Callender St.
Arthur St.
College St.
Linenhall Library
Chichester St.
Lagan Bank Rd.
Short Strand
College Sq. N.
College Sq. E.
Wellington Pl.
Donegall Sq. N.
Scottish Provident Institution
Montgomery St.
General Register Office
Royal Courts
Waterfront Hall
Durham St.
Wellington St.
Donegall Sq. W.
City Hall
Donegall Sq. E.
May St.
Athol St.
Opera House
Howard St.
Donegall Sq. S.
E. Bridge St.
TO A20, NEWTOWNARDS, STORMONT
Grosvenor Rd.
Europa Bus Station
Great Victoria St.
James St. S.
Craftworks
Bedford St.
Franklin St.
Adelaide St.
Alfred St.
Hamilton St.
Central Station
Mayfield Leisure Centre
Great Victoria St. Rail Station
Europa Hotel
Crown Liquor Saloon
Ulster Hall
Joy St.
Grace St.
Cromac St.
McAuley St.
Clarence St.
Belfast Superbowl
Linenhall St.
Stewart St.
Linfield Rd.
Hope St.
Ormeau Baths Gallery

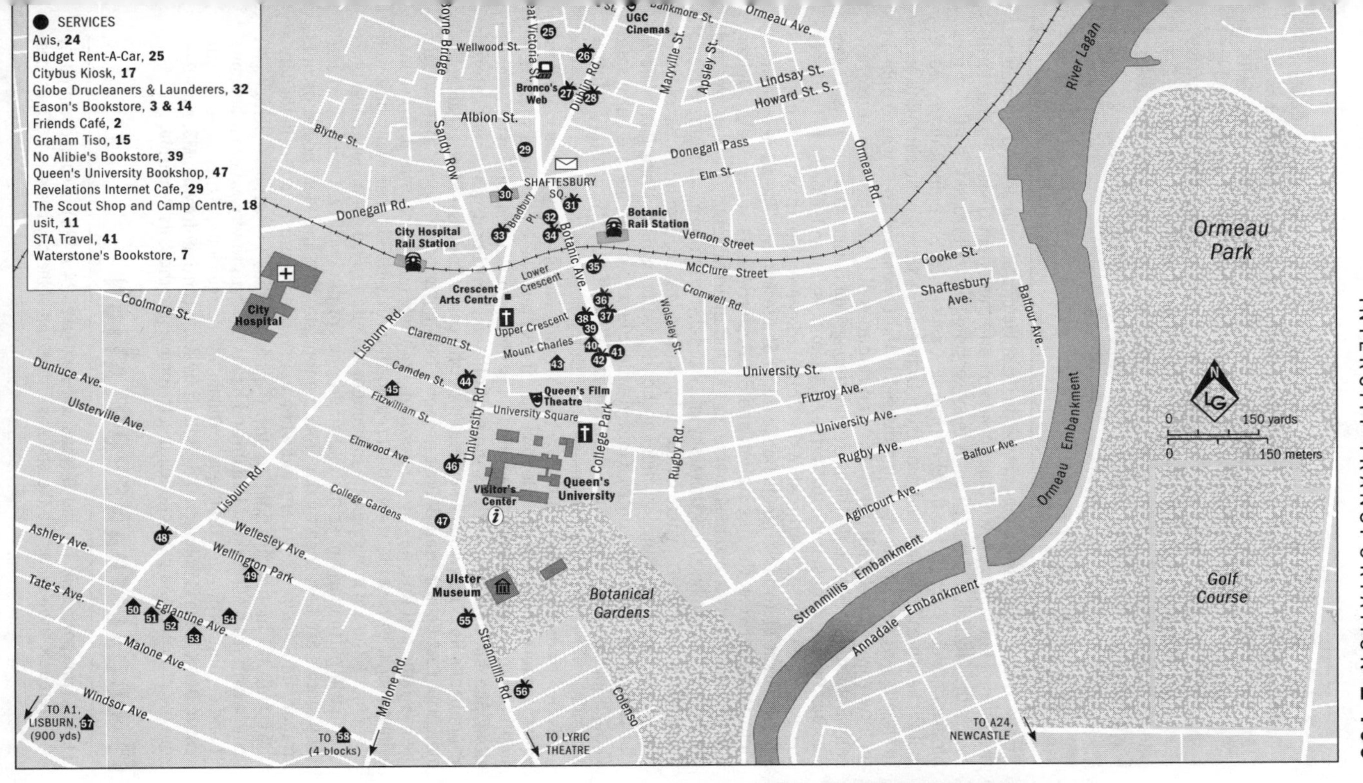

NORTHERN IRELAND

"THE RAPE OF THE FALLS" The area stretching from Divis Tower to Cavendish Sq. is known as the **Lower Falls.** This area was sealed off by the British Army for 35 hours in July, 1970, in an episode known as the **Rape of the Falls.** Soldiers, acting on a tip that arms were hidden in some of the houses, searched homes at random while residents were forbidden to leave the area, even for milk or bread. It is estimated that before this event, there were only 50 Republicans in the area. After the incident, however, over 2000 people turned to the IRA. Many regard this raid as the biggest tactical mistake ever made by the British army in Northern Ireland.

ORIENTATION

Buses arrive at the Europa bus station on **Great Victoria St.** near several landmarks: the Europa hotel, the Crown Liquor Saloon, and the Opera House. To the northeast is the **City Hall** in **Donegall Sq.** A busy shopping district extends north for four blocks between City Hall and the enormous Castlecourt Shopping Centre. Donegall Pl. becomes **Royal Ave.** and runs from Donegall Sq. through the shopping area. In the eastern part of the shopping district is the **Cornmarket** area, where pubs in their narrow **entries** (small alleyways) and centuries-old buildings of characteristically Belfastian design hold their ground amongst modern establishments. **Laganside Bus Centre,** with service to Northeast Ireland, is, indeed, alongside the River Lagan, on Queen's Sq., northeast of the Cornmarket area. South of the Europa bus station, Great Victoria St. meets **Dublin Rd.** at **Shaftesbury Sq.** The stretch of Great Victoria St. between the bus station and Shaftesbury Sq. is known as the **Golden Mile** for its highbrow establishments and Victorian architecture. **Botanic Ave.** and **Bradbury Pl.** (which becomes **University Rd.**) extend south from Shaftesbury Sq. into **Queen's University's** turf, where cafes, pubs, and budget accommodations await. In this southern area, the busiest neighborhoods center around **Stranmillis, Malone,** and **Lisburn Rd.** The city center, Golden Mile, and the university are quite safe. Though locals advise caution in the East and West of the city, central Belfast is generally safer for tourists than many other European cities.

Divided from the rest of Belfast by the Westlink Motorway, working class **West Belfast** is more politically volatile than the city center. There remains a sharp division between sectarian neighborhoods: the Protestant neighborhood stretches along **Shankill Rd.,** just north of the Catholic neighborhood, which is centered around **Falls Rd.** The two are separated by the **peace line.** The **River Lagan** splits industrial **East Belfast** from Belfast proper. The shipyards and docks that brought the city fame and fortune extend north on both sides of the river as it grows into **Belfast Lough.** During the week, the area north of City Hall is essentially deserted after 6pm. Although muggings are infrequent in Belfast, it's a good idea to use taxis after dark, particularly near the clubs and pubs of the northeast area. West Belfast's murals are best seen by day. Ask the tourist office and local hostel owners for more information on where and when to practice the most caution in the city.

M1 and M2 motorways join to form a backwards "C" through Belfast. A1 branches off from M1 around **Lisburn** and heads south to Newry, where it becomes N1 and continues through **Drogheda** to **Dublin.** M2 merges into A6 then heads northwest to **Derry. Larne** is connected to Belfast by A8. A third motorway, **M3,** runs east from the city, becoming A2 and leading to **Bangor** and the **Ards Peninsula.**

LOCAL TRANSPORTATION

Local Transportation: The red **Citybus Network** (☎9024 6485) is supplemented by **Ulsterbus's** "blue buses" to the suburbs. Travel within the city center £1.10, concessions 55p. Citysaver fares are available M-F 9:30am-2pm (90p, concessions 45p). Generally, Citybuses going south and west leave from Donegall Sq. East. Those going north and east leave from Donegall Sq. West. 4-journey tickets £3.40, concessions £1.70. 7-day "gold cards" allow unlimited travel in the city (£12.60). 7-day "silver cards" permit unlimited travel in either North Belfast, West/South Belfast, or East Belfast (£8.30). All transport cards and tickets can be bought from the kiosks in Donegall Sq. West (M-Sa 8am-6:25pm) and around the city. The **Centrelink** bus connects all the major areas of Belfast in the course of its cloverleaf-shaped route: Donegall Sq., Europa, Castlecourt Shopping Centre, Central train station, and Laganside Bus Stations. The buses can be caught at any of 24 designated stops (every 12min.; M-F 7:25am-9:15pm, Sa 8:36am-9:15pm; £1.10; free with bus or rail ticket). Late **Nightlink** buses shuttle the tipsy from Donegall Sq. West to various small towns outside of Belfast at 1 and 2am F-Sa. (£3, payable on board or at the Donegall Sq. W. kiosk.)

Taxis: 24hr. metered cabs abound: **Value Cabs** (☎9080 9080); **City Cab** (☎9024 2000; wheelchair-accessible); **Fon a Cab** (☎9023 3333); **Abjet Cabs** (☎9032 0000).

Bike Rental: McConvey Cycles, 183 Ormeau Rd. (☎9033 0322; www.mcconvey.com). Locks supplied. Open M-Sa 8:30am-6pm. £10 per day, £40 per wk., £20 from F-M. Deposit £50. Panniers £15 per wk.

NORTHERN IRELAND

PRACTICAL INFORMATION

TOURIST AND FINANCIAL SERVICES

Tourist Office: Belfast Welcome Centre, 47 Donegall Pl. (☎9024 6609). Has a great, free booklet on Belfast and info on surrounding areas. Books reservations throughout Northern Ireland and the Republic. Open June-Sept. M-Sa 9am-7pm, Su noon-5pm; Oct.-May M-Sa 9am-5:30pm. **Irish Tourist Board (Bord Fáilte),** 53 Castle St. (☎9032 7888). Provides info and makes reservations for accommodations "south of the border." Open June-Aug. M-F 9am-5pm, Sa 9am-12:30pm; Sept.-May M-F 9am-5pm.

Irish Cultural Centre: 216 Falls Rd. (☎9096 4180). Arts center celebrating the Irish language, including performances with English translation. Open daily 9am-5pm, later on performance nights.

Travel Agency: usit, College St., 13b The Fountain Centre (☎9032 7111), near Royal Ave. Sells ISICs, European Youth Cards, TravelSave stamps (£6), and virtually every kind of bus or rail pass imaginable. Books ferries and planes, and compiles round-the-world itineraries. Open M-F 9:30am-5pm. Additional office at Queen's University **Student Union** (☎9024 1830). Open M-F 10am-5pm. **StaTravel,** 92-94 Botanic Ave. (☎9024 1469), fulfills all the same duties from its convenient location. Open M-Tu and Th-F 9:30am-5:30pm, W 10am-5:30pm, Sa 11am-5pm.

Hostelling International Northern Ireland (HINI): 22 Donegall Rd. (☎9032 4733). Books HINI hostels free, international hostels for £2.80. Sells HI membership cards to NI residents (£10, under 18 £6).

Embassies: For an extensive list of embassies and consulates, see **Essentials,** p. 7.

Banks: Banks and **ATMs** are a dime a dozen in Belfast. The major players are: **Bank of Ireland,** 54 Donegal Pl. (☎9023 4334); **First Trust,** 1-15 Donegall Sq. North (☎9031 0909); **Northern Bank,** 14 Donegall Sq. West (☎9024 5277); **Ulster Bank,** Donegall Sq. East (☎9027 6000). Most banks open M-F 9am-4:30pm.

Currency Exchange: Thomas Cook, 10 Donegall Sq. W. (☎9088 3800). No commission on cashing Thomas Cook traveler's checks, others 2%. Open M-W and F 5:30am-10pm, Th 9am-6pm, Sa 10am-5pm. **Belfast International Airport office** (☎9444 7500). Open May-Oct. M-Th 5:30am-8:30pm, F-Sa 5:30am-11pm; Nov.-Apr. daily 6am-8pm.

Work Opportunities: The Ark (see **Accommodations,** below) regularly hires travelers to work at the hostel; workers often live in hostel's long-term housing. Flexible payment/accommodation arrangements. Those with catering experience may contact Sharon at **Azzura** (see **Food,** below). This friendly, eclectic restaurent hires workers for a min. 2 months. For a formally arranged temporary position, inquire at **Industrial Temps,** 87/91 Great Victoria St. (☎9058 9880), or **Adecco,** 38 Queen St. (☎9024 4660).

LOCAL SERVICES

Luggage Storage: For security reasons, there is no luggage storage at airports, bus stations, or train stations. The **Belfast Welcome Centre** (see above) will store luggage for 4hr. (£2). All 4 **hostels** will hold bags during the day for guests, and **the Ark** will hold bags during extended trips if you've stayed there (see **Accommodations,** below).

Bookstores: Waterstone's, 8 Royal Ave. (☎9024 7355) and 44-46 Fountain St. (☎9024 0159), has a large selection and a helpful staff. Open M-W and F-Sa 9am-6pm, Th 9am-9pm, Su 1-6pm. **Eason's,** Donegall Pl. and Castlecourt Shopping Centre (☎9023 5070). Large Irish section; lots of travel guides. Open M-W and F-Sa 8:30am-5:30pm, Th 9am-9:30pm. **Queen's University Bookshop,** 91 University Rd. (☎9066 6302), offers Irish history textbooks and a renowned collection of Beat generation manuscripts. Open M-F 9am-5:30pm, Sa 9am-5pm. For gumshoes-in-training, **No Alibies Bookstore,** 83 Botanic Ave. (☎9031 9607), specializes in crime, mystery, and American Studies. Open M 10am-4:30pm, Tu-Sa 10am-6pm. There are also dozens of 2nd-hand bookstores around; a walk in the university area is sure to turn up several.

Libraries: Belfast Central Library, 122 Royal Ave. (☎9050 9150). Open M and Th 9am-8pm, Tu-W and F 9am-5:30pm, Sa 9am-1pm. Belfast residents get 30min. free **Internet** per day. It's £1.50 per 30min. for non-residents, though this is not always strictly enforced. **Linen Hall Library,** 17 Donegall Sq. North, enter via 52 Fountain St. (☎9032 1707). Extensive genealogy and information on the Troubles. Free Irish language courses Sept.-May. Open M-F 9:30am-5:30pm, Sa 9:30am-4pm. (See **Sights, p. 477**.)

Women's Resources: Downtown Women's Group, 109-113 Royal Ave. (☎9024 3363).

Bisexual, Gay, and Lesbian Information: Rainbow Project N.I., 33 Church Ln. (☎9031 9030). Open M-F 10am-5:30pm. **Lesbian Line** (☎9023 8668). Open Th 7:30-10pm.

Disability Resources: Disability Action (☎9029 7880). Open M-F 9am-5pm.

Laundry: Globe Drycleaners & Launderers, 37-39 Botanic Ave. (☎9024 3956). About £3-4 per load. Open M-F 8am-9pm, Sa 8am-6pm, Su noon-6pm.

Camping Equipment: Graham Tiso, 12-14 Cornmarket (☎9023 1230), offers 3 floors of everything you could need to survive the great outdoors. Also has notice boards and flyers that sometimes advertise hiking, climbing, and water-related trips. Open M-W and F-Sa 9:30am-5:30pm, Th 9:30am-8pm. **The Scout Shop and Camp Centre,** 12-14 College Sq. East (☎9032 0580). Ring bell for entry. Vast selection. Open M-Sa 9am-5pm.

EMERGENCY AND COMMUNICATIONS

Emergency: ☎999; no coins required. **Police:** 65 Knock Rd. (☎9065 0222).

Counseling and Support: Samaritans (☎9066 4422). 24hr. **Rape Crisis Centre,** 29 Donegall St. (☎9024 9696, freephone 0800 052 6813). Open M-F 10am-6pm. **Contact Youth,** 139 Raven Hill Rd. (☎9045 7848; open 9:30am-5pm. Toll-free ☎0808 808 8000; line open M-F 4-9pm.) Offers one-on-one counseling appointments.

Pharmacy: Boot's, 35-47 Donegall Pl. (☎9024 2332). Open M-W and F-Sa 8:30am-6pm, Th 8:30am-9pm, Su 1-6pm. Also on Great Victoria St. and Castle Pl.

Hospitals: Belfast City Hospital, 9 Lisburn Rd. (☎9032 9241). From Shaftesbury Sq. follow Bradbury Pl. and take a right at the fork. **Royal Victoria Hospital,** 12 Grosvenor Rd. (☎9024 0503). From Donegall Sq., take Howard St. west to Grosvenor Rd.

Internet Access: The **Belfast Central Library** (see **Local Services,** above) offers email access at £1.50 per 30min.; web access £2 per hr. **Revelations Internet Cafe,** 27 Shaftesbury Sq. (☎9032 3337). £4 per hr., students and hostelers £3 per hr. Open M-F 10am-10pm, Sa 10am-6pm, Su 11am-7pm. **Bronco's Web,** 122 Great Victoria St. (☎9080 8081). £2 per hr. **Belfast Welcome Centre,** 47 Donegall Place, is most central. £1.25 for 15min., students £1. Open M-Sa 9:30am-7pm, Su noon-5pm. **Friends Cafe,** 109-113 Royal Ave. (9024 1096). £2 per hr. Open M-F 8am-5pm, Sa 9am-3pm.

Post Office: Central Post Office, 25 Castle Pl. (☎9032 3740). Open M-Sa 9am-5:30pm. *Poste Restante* mail comes here (see **Mail,** p. 38). **Postal code:** BT1 1NB. Branch offices: **Botanic Garden,** 95 University Rd., across from the university (☎9038 1309; **postal code:** BT7 1NG); 1-5 **Botanic Ave.** (☎9032 6177; **postal code:** BT2 7DA). Both open M-F 8:45am-5:30pm, Sa 10am-12:30pm.

ACCOMMODATIONS

Despite a competitive hostel market, Belfast's fluctuating tourism and rising rents have shrunk the number of available cheap digs. Nearly all are located near Queen's University, south of the city center; convenient to pubs and restaurants, and a short walk or bus to the city center, this area is by far the best place to stay in the city. If you have a lot of baggage you may want to catch **Citybus** #69, 70, 71, 83, 84, or 86 from Donegall Sq. to areas in the south. A walk to these accommodations takes 10-20min. from the bus or train station. Reservations are highly recommended in the summer, as hostels and B&Bs can be busy.

HOSTELS AND UNIVERSITY HOUSING

The Ark (IHH), 18 University St. (☎9032 9626). A 10min. walk from Europa bus station on Great Victoria St. The kind of place where people will ask you how your day was—and actually care. The amazing sense of community here may have to do with the somewhat small rooms, the always bustling, well-stocked kitchen (with free tea and coffee), and the number of backpackers who end up staying long-term to work in the city. Staff provides help in finding work, and offers more spacious long-term housing nearby (around £40 per wk.). Also **books tours** of Belfast (£8), in addition to Giant's Causeway excursions (single-day £16). **Internet access** £1 per 20min. Weekend luggage storage. Laundry £4. Curfew 2am. 4- to 6-bed dorms £8.50-9.50; doubles £32. ❶

Arnie's Backpackers (IHH), 63 Fitzwilliam St. (☎9024 2867). A short walk from Europa Bus Station on Great Victoria St. Relaxed, friendly atmosphere. Amusing triple-bunked beds in some rooms are, if nothing else, conversation starters. Impressively clean despite the presence of Jack Russell staffers Rosy and Snowy. Closer than the tourist office, the library of travel info here includes bus and train timetables. Key deposit £2 or ID. Luggage storage during the day. 8-bed dorms £7; 4-bed £8.50. ❶

Belfast Hostel (HINI), 22 Donegall Rd. (☎9031 5435; www.hini.org.uk), off Shaftesbury Sq. A foreboding, concrete exterior belies the hostel's clean and inviting innards. Simple, modern 2- to 6-bed rooms. Book ahead for weekends. Also **books tours** of Belfast and Giant's Causeway. Breakfast (£2) is served up in a Giant's Causeway themed lounge. Wheelchair-accessible. **Internet access** £1 per 20min. Laundry £3. 24hr. reception. Dorms £8.50-10.50; singles £17; triples £39. ❶

The Linen House Youth Hostel (IHH), 18-20 Kent St. (☎9058 6400; www.belfasthostel.com), bordering West Belfast. Across from the main entrance to City Hall, turn left onto Donegall Pl., which becomes Royal Ave. Take a left onto Kent St. just before the Belfast Library. This converted 19th-century linen factory now houses scores of weary travelers (about 160 beds). A new basement common room (open until 1am) with foosball and ping pong almost makes up for the impersonal feel. Downtown location is a mixed blessing, depending on the season and time of night. **Books tours:** black cab (£7); Giant's Causeway (£16). 24hr. secure parking £4. **Internet access** £2 per hr. Bike and luggage storage 50p. Towels 50p. Laundry £3. 18-bed dorms £6.50-7; 6- to 10-bed dorms £8.50-9. Singles £15-20; doubles £24-30. ❶

Queen's University Accommodations, 78 Malone Rd. (☎9038 1608; www.qub.ac.uk). Take bus #71 from Donegall Sq. East; otherwise, it's a 35min. trek on foot from Europa. University Rd. runs into Malone Rd.; the residence halls are down a long driveway on your left. Undecorated, institutional dorms provide spacious singles or twin rooms with sinks and desks. Open mid-June to Aug. and Christmas and Easter vacations. Free laundry. Singles for UK students £8.50, with bath £12; for international students £10/£14.50; for non-students £12.40/£17. ❶

BED AND BREAKFASTS

The B&B universe, just south of Queen's University between Malone and Lisburn Rd., is one of healthy competition and close (sometimes familial) camaraderie. Occupying every other house on the block, they tend to be surprisingly similar in price, quality, and decor. Calling ahead is generally a good idea; most owners, however, will refer you to other accommodations if necessary.

Camera Guesthouse, 44 Wellington Park (☎9066 0026). A beautiful, light-filled, family-run guest house. What really differentiates it is the breakfasts, which delight with a wide selection of organic options and herbal teas. Also caters to those with specific dietary concerns. Singles £25, with bath £37; doubles £50/£55. Lower rates in July. ❸

Botanic Lodge, 87 Botanic Ave. (☎9032 7682), on the corner of Mt. Charles Ave. B&B comfort surrounded by excellent eateries and a short walk to the city center. All rooms with sink and TV, some with bath. Singles £25, with bath £35; doubles £40/£45. ❸

Marine House, 30 Eglantine Ave. (☎9066 2828; www.marineguesthouse.com). A mansion that gracefully overcomes the alienating implications of its size. Having seen the airy inside of the house, *Let's Go* can almost assure you it's not haunted. Housekeeping standards as high as the ceilings. Singles £35; doubles £48; triples £66. ❹

All Seasons B&B, 365 Lisburn Rd. (☎9068 2814). Further out, this comfy roost is especially great for those with cars; secure parking is free. Amazingly hospitable family owners and super-strength showers round out the deal. Singles £25; doubles £40; triples £55. ❸

Avenue Guest House, 23 Eglantine Ave. (☎9066 5904). Large rooms with excellent beds, a modern decor, and expansive window views. All rooms with bath and direct dial phone. Singles £35; doubles £45. ❹

The George, 9 Eglantine Ave. (☎9068 3212). Renowned for its spotlessness. Amenities include fresh fruit at breakfast and saloon-appropriate leather couches in the common room. All rooms with bath. Singles £35; doubles £45. ❹

Eglantine Guest House, 21 Eglantine Ave. (☎9066 7585). Small but comfortable rooms for slightly less than the competition. Singles £22; doubles £40; triples £60. ❸

Liserin Guest House, 17 Eglantine Ave. (☎9066 0769). Comfy beds and huge, homey lounge make an inviting abode. Watch TV while taking a shower. Upper rooms are skylit. Coffee, tea, and biscuits available all day. £20 per person. ❸

FOOD

Dublin Rd., Botanic Ave., and the Golden Mile have the highest concentration of restaurants. Bakeries and cafes dot the shopping areas; nearly all close by 5:30pm, though on Thursdays most of the city center stays open until 8:45pm. For dinner in the city center, head to a pub for pub grub, or to a bar for more upscale fare. The huge **Tesco Supermarket** at 2 Royal Ave. (☎9032 3270) is one of the few groceries you'll find with a dome, and its prices are better than most of the city's convenience stores. (Open M-W and Sa 8am-7pm, Th 8am-9pm, F 8am-8pm, Su 1-5pm.) The **Spar Market** at the top of Botanic Ave. is open 24hr.; order your food through a service window at night. For fruits and vegetables, plunder the lively **St. George's Market,** East Bridge St., in the enormous warehouse between May and Oxford St. (Open Th 3-9pm and F 6am-1pm.) **The Nutmeg,** 9A Lombard St. (☎9024 9984), supplies organic foods and raw ingredients. (Open M-Sa 9:30am-5:30pm.)

QUEEN'S UNIVERSITY AREA

The University area is brimming with student-filled eateries of every kind—if you can't find what you want here, you never will.

Maggie May's Belfast Cafe, 50 Botanic Ave. (☎9032 2622). Hip dive with nostalgic murals of yesteryear's Belfast. Relax with a cuppa and newspaper, or any one of the floating arts publications; order when you feel like it. Also boasts some of the best breakfasts around (served all day). Toasted pancakes with maple syrup £1.75. Dinners £4-6. Heaps of veggie options. Open M-Sa 8am-10:30pm, Su 10am-10:30pm. ❷

Bookfinders, 47 University Rd. (☎9032 8269). Atmospheric bookstore/cafe with mismatched dishes, counter-culture paraphernalia, and the occasional poetry reading. If you push the right door, you may end up in Narnia. Art gallery upstairs features student work. Soup and bread £2.25, sandwiches £2.20-2.50; extensive vegetarian options, and even a few for the woebegone vegan. Open M-Sa 10am-5:30pm. ❶

The Other Place, 79 Botanic Ave. (☎9020 7200), 133 Stranmillis Rd. (☎9020 7100), and 537 Lisburn Rd. (☎9020 7300). Reasonably priced all-day breakfast menu with chalkboard-listed specials. Features huge servings and an array of ethnic foods. Open Tu-Su 8am-10pm. ❷

The Moghul, 62A Botanic Ave. (☎9032 6677), overlooking the street from 2nd floor corner windows. Outstanding Indian lunch Thali for carnivores or vegetarians M-Th noon-2pm (£2.99), or all-you-can-eat buffet F noon-2pm (£4.99). Open for dinner M-Th 5-11:30pm, F-Sa 5-11:45pm, Su 5-10:30pm. Take-out available. ❷

Acapulco, 75 Botanic Ave. (☎9058 5100). Tantalizing Mexican served within a sunflower-heavy interior. Fajitas £9.96-12.45. Open Tu-Su 5:30-10:30pm. ❹

Esperanto, 35 Botanic Ave. (☎9059 1222) and 158 Lisburn Rd. (☎9059 0888). Kebab Specialists. Budget protectors. Most meals £3. Botanic location open 11am-1am; Lisburn 4:30pm-1am. ❷

Beachroom, 1 Elmwood Ave. (☎9032 4803), in University Student Union. Cafeteria-style food served in–drum roll, please–a cafeteria. Beachroom is closed from mid-May to Sept., when **Cloisters** is open instead, serving basic paninis and sandwiches for £2. Both open M-F 8:30am-4:30pm. ❶

THE GOLDEN MILE AND DUBLIN ROAD

We at *Let's Go* always try to score you a classy meal, but when late-nite Guinness-induced munchies strike, Dublin Rd. is the place to go. Besides the establishments listed below, it has the highest density of takeaways in Belfast, ranging from Chinese to Mediterranean fare. Embrace Man's eternal search for fast food.

Pizza Express, 25-27 Bedford St. (☎9032 9050). Sounds like your typical franchise, but the spiral staircase and Tuscan decor suggest otherwise. Actually serves *real* pizza. 1- to 2-person pies £5-7. Open M-Sa noon-11:30pm. ❷

Feasts, 39 Dublin Rd. (☎9033 2787). Pleasant street-side cafe, serving Irish and international farmhouse cheeses in sandwiches (£3.95, take-out £2.95) and other dishes. Makes pasta on the premises (£5-7). Open M-F 9am-6pm, Sa 10am-6pm. ❷

Thai Village, 50 Dublin Rd. (☎9024 9269). One of the few, the proud, the only Thai restaurants in Northern Ireland. Serves tofu dishes (a rarity in these parts), as well as an excellent duck curry (£9.95) amidst white tablecloths. Two-course lunch £6.95. Open M-Sa noon-2:30pm and 6-11pm, Su 5:30-10pm. ❸

Arcana Balti House and Little India, 53 Dublin Rd. (☎9032 3713). Cozy Indian joint. Upstairs is the only Balti House in Belfast; downstairs is its only vegetarian Indian restaurant. Thankfully, such pioneering doesn't inflate the prices. Downstairs Thali special lunch £2.50, dinner £8.50; upstairs £4.95/£7.95 and up. Lunch served M-Sa noon-2pm; dinner M-Th 5-11:30pm, F-Sa 5pm-midnight, Su 5-10:30pm. ❸

Cafe Aero, 44 Bedford St. (☎9024 4844). Don't pass by thinking it's merely a place for coffee: real meals, most with international influences, are served here too. The surreal decor, with a wave-like ceiling and test tubes of flowers on the walls, is fun in and of itself. Lunches £5-8, dinners £7-10. Lots of veggie options. Open M-Sa 11am-11pm. ❸

Spuds, 23 Bradbury Pl. (☎9033 1541). What you always imagined Irish fast food to be. Get your spud stuffed with anything from bacon and cheese to chicken curry (most around £2.50). Open M-W 9am-2am, Th-Sa 9am-3am, Su 9am-1am. ❶

NORTH OF DONEGALL SQUARE

Lots of great places for lunch reside in the shopping district north of City Hall, but good luck finding a meal here after 5:30pm. You're better off walking along the Golden Mile, south of Donegall Square.

Azzura, 8 Church Ln. (☎9024 2444). This tiny cafe is about as good as it gets for the foodie—gourmet pizzas, pastas, soups, and sandwiches arrive warm from the oven for under £4. Like chili peppers in your dishes? Pick your own from the plant draping the door (the owners grow much of their own organic produce). Don't be surprised if seemingly psychic chef Sharon knows what you want before you do. Intriguing and delicious options abound for both veggies and meat-lovers. Open M-Sa 9am-5pm. ❷

Blinkers, 1-5 Bridge St. (☎9024 3330). An authentic diner—cluttered ashtrays and all—with authentic prices. A relief after the ultra-modern cafes that engulf the area. Quarter-pound burger £2.30. Open M-W 9am-7pm, Th-Sa 9am-9:30pm. ❶

Clements, 37-39 Rosemary (☎9032 2293), with additional locations at 4 Donegall Sq. W., 66-68 Botanic Ave., 131-133 Royal Ave., and 139 Stanmillis. Each has a uniquely modern and posh interior, but serves up the same selection of soups, bagels, paninis, and desserts for £1-4. Chocoholics will melt in huge bowls of fabulous hot chocolate (£1.80), and everyone can feel good about drinking the Fair Trade Coffee. Open F-W 8am-6pm, Th 8am-8pm. Botanic and Stranmillis locations open daily until midnight. ❶

Caffe Casa, 12-14 College St. (☎9031 9900). An early arrival in the new crop of swanky cafes, which claims to have the best coffee in Belfast. In good weather, the windows are opened, spilling tables onto the sidewalk. Sandwiches (£4), entrees (£4.50), and sumptuous desserts (£1-2.50). Open F-W 8am-5:30pm, Th 8am-7:30pm. ❷

Oscar's Champagne Cafe, 11 Chichester St. (☎9043 9400). Ultra-modern take on a Tuscan countryside cafe. Upscale and innovative menu. Wild boar foccaccia £4.50; steak bocata £5.25. Wine, beer, and champagne available. Open M-Sa 9am-5pm. ❸

Windsor Dairy, 4 College St. (☎9032 7157). This takeaway bakery delights with piles of pastries for 30-50p and daily specials for around £2. Open M-Sa 7:30am-5:30pm. ❶

Bewley's, Rosemary St. (☎9023 4955), just inside of the Donegall Arcade. For those missing Dublin, this Bewley's is a good replica of the original Japanese tea room (see p. 105). Newspapers and magazines upstairs. Carrying out will save you about a third of your moolah. Open M-Sa 8am-5:30pm. ❷

PUBS

Pubs were prime targets for sectarian violence at the height of the Troubles. As a result, most of the popular pubs in Belfast are new or restored, and those in the city center and university area are quite safe now. The *Bushmills Irish Pub Guide*, by Sybil Taylor, relates the history of Belfast's pubs (£6.99; available at local book stores). Once again, *Let's Go* proudly presents the **Belfast Pub Crawl** and Pub Crawl Map. Since the city center closes early and can feel pretty deserted late at night, we recommend beginning early in Cornmarket's historic entries, visiting the traditional downtown, then partying until closing time in the university area.

CORNMARKET

Here you'll find Northern Ireland's oldest and most inviting. Expect local crowds in most of the establishments, and authentic *craic* in all.

Morning Star Pub, 17-19 Pottinger's Entry (bar ☎9032 3976; restaurant 9023 3986), between Ann and High St. Look for the Victorian wrought-iron bracket above the entry. A classy old place with an excellent U-shaped bar and wooden snugs for closer chats. Most supplement their pints with the award-winning food, dabbling in exotic tastes like alligator and wild boar. Entrees £6-12. Open M-Sa 11:30am-11pm, Su 11:30am-7pm.

White's Tavern, 2-4 Winecellar Entry (☎9024 3080), between Lombard and Bridge St.; look for a left turn off High St. White's is Belfast's oldest tavern, serving drinks since 1630. An excellent stop for an afternoon pint. W gay-friendly night (£3 after 10pm). Live music Th-Sa. Open M-Tu 11:30am-11pm, W-Th 11:30am-3am, F-Su 11:30am-1am.

NORTH OF DONEGALL SQUARE

Although the patrons in pubs North of Donegall Sq. are as friendly as any other, this area does tend to get rather deserted at night; pub-crawlers should practice extra caution in these parts.

Queen's Cafe Bar, 4 Queen's Arcade (☎9032 1347), between Donegall Pl. and Fountain St. A buzzing yet friendly and low-pressure bar in a glitzy shopping arcade off Donegall Pl. Mixed, gay-friendly crowd. Open M-W 11:30am-9pm, Th-Sa 11:30am-11pm.

Hercules Bar, 61-63 Castle St. (☎9032 4587). This working man's pub pulls in the best musicians the local soil produces. Th-Sa trad sessions get up to 20 musicians going around 9:30pm. Owners can point you to more good music. Open M-W 11:30am-11pm, Th-Sa 11:30am-1am, Su noon-8pm.

Madden's, 74 Berry St. (☎9024 4114). Buzz to be let in. An old wooden bar with musical instruments on the walls. Attracts good-sized crowds with its traditional Irish bands (upstairs F-Sa) and traditional blues and folk (Sa). No cover. Open M and F-Sa until 1am, Tu and Th until 11:30pm, W until midnight.

Kelly's Cellars, 30 Bank St. (☎9032 4835), off Royal Ave. just after the Fountain St. pedestrian area. The oldest pub in Belfast that hasn't been fully renovated, with the downstairs unchanged since 1720. Owner often welcomes visitors with a pint on the house and a kiss on the cheek. Trad all day F-Sa, occasional live bands, including folk and rock. Open M-Th 11:30am-11pm, F-Sa 11:30am-2am.

THE GOLDEN MILE AND THE DUBLIN ROAD

The mecca for all things alcohol related. Drink up, and drink long.

Auntie Annie's, 44 Dublin Rd. (☎9050 1660). Entertaining live music on both floors and a relaxed atmosphere have won this bar a faithful following among all ages. M and Tu singer/songwriter, Th "Frisky Disco," F Pop scene. Downstairs open M-Sa noon-1am, Su 6pm-midnight; upstairs Th-Sa until 2am with £3 cover.

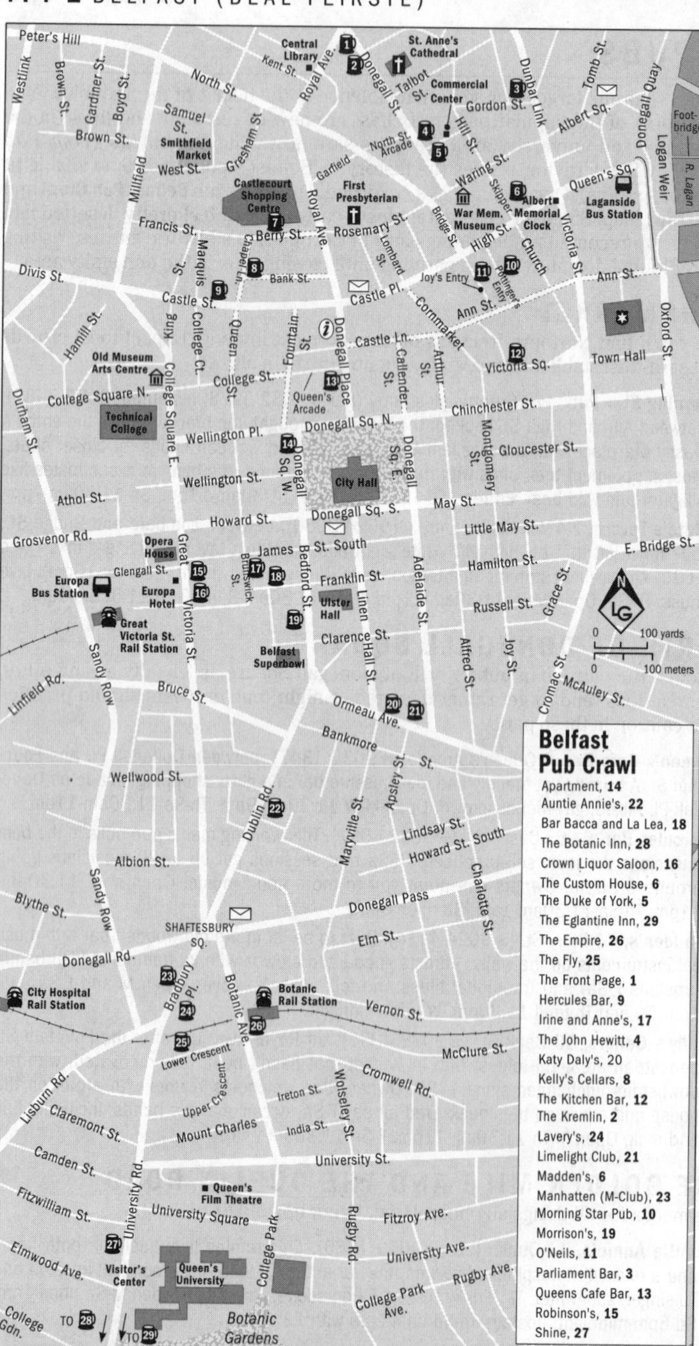
Belfast
Pub Crawl
Apartment, 14
Auntie Annie's, 22
Bar Bacca and La Lea, 18
The Botanic Inn, 28
Crown Liquor Saloon, 16
The Custom House, 6
The Duke of York, 5
The Eglantine Inn, 29
The Empire, 26
The Fly, 25
The Front Page, 1
Hercules Bar, 9
Irine and Anne's, 17
The John Hewitt, 4
Katy Daly's, 20
Kelly's Cellars, 8
The Kitchen Bar, 12
The Kremlin, 2
Lavery's, 24
Limelight Club, 21
Madden's, 6
Manhatten (M-Club), 23
Morning Star Pub, 10
Morrison's, 19
O'Neils, 11
Parliament Bar, 3
Queens Cafe Bar, 13
Robinson's, 15
Shine, 27
Peter's Hill
Central Library
St. Anne's Cathedral
Commercial Center
Smithfield Market
Castlecourt Shopping Centre
First Presbyterian
War Mem. Museum
Albert Memorial Clock
Laganside Bus Station
Foot-bridge
R. Lagan
Old Museum Arts Centre
Technical College
Queen's Arcade
City Hall
Town Hall
Opera House
Europa Bus Station
Europa Hotel
Great Victoria St. Rail Station
Ulster Hall
Belfast Superbowl
SHAFTESBURY SQ.
City Hospital Rail Station
Botanic Rail Station
Queen's Film Theatre
Visitor's Center
Queen's University
Botanic Gardens
TO
0
100 yards
100 meters
LG
N
Westlink
Brown St.
Gardiner St.
Boyd St.
North St.
Kent St.
Royal Ave.
Donegall St.
Talbot St.
Dunbar Link
Tomb St.
Donegall Quay
Logan Weir
Gordon St.
Albert Sq.
Hill St.
Samuel St.
Brown St.
Millfield
West St.
Gresham St.
Garfield
North St. Arcade
Waring St.
Skipper
Queen's Sq.
Francis St.
Berry St.
Chapel Ln.
Rosemary St.
Bridge St.
High St.
Church
Victoria St.
Lombard St.
Divis St.
Marquis St.
Bank St.
Joy's Entry
Pottinger's Entry
Ann St.
Castle St.
Castle Pl.
Cornmarket
Oxford St.
Hamill St.
King St.
College St.
Queen St.
Fountain St.
Donegall Place
Castle Ln.
Callender St.
Arthur St.
Victoria Sq.
College Square N.
College Square E.
College Ct.
Chinchester St.
Durham St.
Wellington Pl.
Donegall Sq. N.
Donegall Sq. W.
Donegall Sq. E.
Montgomery St.
Gloucester St.
Wellington St.
Athol St.
Howard St.
Donegall Sq. S.
May St.
Grosvenor Rd.
Little May St.
James St. South
E. Bridge St.
Great Victoria St.
Glengall St.
Brunswick St.
Bedford St.
Franklin St.
Hamilton St.
Adelaide St.
Linen Hall St.
Russell St.
Grace St.
Clarence St.
Alfred St.
Joy St.
Cromac St.
McAuley St.
Sandy Row
Linfield Rd.
Bruce St.
Ormeau Ave.
Bankmore St.
Wellwood St.
Dublin Rd.
Apsley St.
Maryville St.
Lindsay St.
Howard St. South
Albion St.
Charlotte St.
Blythe St.
Donegall Pass
Elm St.
Donegall Rd.
Bradbury Pl.
Botanic Ave.
Vernon St.
McClure St.
Lower Crescent
Upper Crescent
Cromwell Rd.
Lisburn Rd.
Claremont St.
Ireton St.
Wolseley St.
Mount Charles
India St.
Camden St.
University St.
University Rd.
Fitzwilliam St.
University Square
Rugby Rd.
Fitzroy Ave.
College Park
University Ave.
Elmwood Ave.
Rugby Ave.
College Park Ave.
College Gdn.

Crown Liquor Saloon, 46 Great Victoria St. (☎9024 9476). This, the only National Trust-owned pub, had its windows blown in from a bomb attack on the Europa Hotel, but you'd never know it; the stained glass, gas lamps, and impressive Victorian snugs, each with its own door, seem original. It's filled with tourists, though, and locals generally go elsewhere. Open M-F 8:30am-midnight, Su 12:30-10pm.

Robinson's, 38-40 Great Victoria St. (☎9024 7447). 4 floors of theme bars, but is most renowned for **Fibber McGee's** in the back, which hosts incredible trad sessions Tu-Su at 10pm, with an additional session Sa 5-7pm. Nightclubs on top 2 floors. F 80s night. Cover F £5, Sa £8. M-Sa 11:30am-1am, Su noon-midnight.

Lavery's, 12 Bradbury Pl. (☎9087 1106). 3 floors of unpretentious fun–you don't have to dress up to get noticed (but some do anyway). W live music in the 1st floor back bar. DJs on weekends; disco in the 2nd floor Gin Palace (£1-3 cover), or ascend to the 3rd floor "Heaven" club (£5 cover) F-Sa. Open until 1am; upstairs until 2am.

Apartment, 2 Donegall Sq. W. (☎9050 9777). Where Belfast's beautiful people, and occasionally their uncles, come for pre-clubbing cocktails. Spacious, modern layout (a see and be seen essential) is kept that way by restricting numbers, so arrive before 10pm on weekends and dress smart–jeans and sneakers are not allowed. Open M-F until 1am; Su until midnight. 21+ after 6pm.

Irine and Anne's, 12 Brunswick St. (☎9023 9123). Belfast's newest bar. An instant hit, drawing a standing-room only crowd that starts grooving as the night goes on (and drinks sink in). DJs from 9pm. 21+. Open M-Sa 11am-1am, Su noon-midnight.

Morrisons, 21 Bedford St. (☎9024 8458). Recently renovated from traditional pub to modern bar, with lots of high tables and stools. Friendly young atmosphere pulls in many couples on weekends, when there are mixed musical offerings. Cover £3-7. W Pub Quiz. Gay-friendly one F per month.

QUEEN'S UNIVERSITY AREA

Close the books and rally the troops—this is where the children come to play.

The Botanic Inn, 23 Malone Rd. (☎9066 0460). "The Bot" is a huge and hugely popular student bar, packed nightly from wall-to-wall. Pub grub £4-5. Su carvey meal £4.50, students £3.50. Trad W, no cover. Th-Sa DJs. Strictly 21+. Cover £2. Open until 1am.

The Empire, 42 Botanic Ave. (☎9024 9276). This 120-year-old building was once a church, but its 2 stories have been entirely revamped to resemble Belfast's Victorian music halls. Used to be a student only hang-out, but the cast of returning alums mixes things up. Sept.-June Tu comedy, Th-Su live bands. Cover F-Sa £3-7, M-Th and Su £3.

The Eglantine Inn, 32 Malone Rd. (☎9038 1994). Almost an official extra-curricular, "The Eg" is the admitted playground for those too young to get into The Bot. Satisfies munchies, too; entrees £3-7, served noon-8pm. W-Sa shake it upstairs with the DJ. Open M-Sa until 1am, Su until 6pm.

NORTH BELFAST

Given that the city center clears out after 6pm, pubs in this area should be your starting point. After dark, take a cab to the pubs near the docklands.

The John Hewitt, 51 Lower Donegall St. (☎9023 3768). A pub named after the late Ulster poet. Run by the Unemployment Youth Resource Centre, to which half the profits go, so drink up. Tu trad, Th live bands, F jazz. Music starts around 9:30pm. Open M 11:30am-11pm, Tu-Sa 11:30am-1am, Su 8pm-midnight.

The Duke of York, 7-11 Commercial Ctr. (☎9024 1062). Students make the long journey from Queen's for a reason–good *craic* and an old-timey, traditional feel make this one of the few pubs with a majority of young people. Th trad, F acoustic sessions. Open M-W 11:30am-midnight, Th-Sa 11:30am-1am.

The Kitchen Bar, 16 Victoria Sq. (☎9032 4901). A homey, family-owned bar that frequently hosts excellent trad. Homebaked food (around £5) served daily until 6pm, drawing in business lunchers. Open M-Th 11:30am-midnight, F-Sa 11:30am-1am.

O'Neils, Joy's Entry (☎9032 6711), off High St. A spacious pub during the wk.; on weekends it transforms into a wild club. Features "Digital Boogie," and some weekends drum and bass. 21+. Cover Th £5, F-Sa £7-8. Open M-Th noon-10pm, F-Sa noon-2am.

The Front Page, 106 Donegall St. (☎9032 4924), 2nd fl. The center of the universe to the locals who pack it nightly and the newsies who hover by day. Local rock bands W-Th are a student draw, and the odd punk night and monthly big name DJ keep things bouncing 'til late. Open M-W 11:30am-12:30am, Th-F 11:30am-3am.

The Northern Whig, 2 Bridge St. (☎9050 9888). Although the prominent statues in this spacious modern bar used to grace the top of the Communist Party Headquarters in Prague, the clientele is of more capitalistic leanings. Young professionals pack in during a hopping lunch hour and return by night to "give back" to the economic underdog that is alcohol. Lunch £6. Food 10am-6pm. Bar open M-Sa 10am-1am, Su 1pm-midnight.

CLUBS

For information on the city's nightlife, most clubbers consult *The List*, a biweekly newsletter available at the tourist office, hostels, and certain restaurants around town. To savor some history with your pints, take one of the very popular **historical pub tours** of Belfast (call ☎9268 3365 for info; £6 not including drinks). Ask the staff at the Queen's University Student Union about the latest night spots.

The Fly, 5-6 Lower Crescent (☎9050 9750). Popular with a young set of partiers. Extensive entomological decor geared toward its namesake (read: this place has a lot of big bugs; fake ones, that is). 1st floor bar for the pints, 2nd for mingling and dancing, and an Absolut lounge, featuring some 60 flavors of vodka—from garlic, to coffee, to Starburst—in test-tube shots on the 3rd. Tu Salsa (with lessons from 7:30-9:30pm). Frequent theme nights include Alice in Wonderland and Dance Wars. No cover.

Bar Bacca and **La Lea,** 48 Franklin St. (☎9023 0200), off Bedford St. A dark, Morroccan-themed bar that smells of incense and young professionals downstairs, with a 2-floor gay-friendly club upstairs continuing the theme W-Su. The unique atmosphere of the bar, complete with small open fires set in cubbies in the walls, helped it to win 2002 Bar of the Year honors for both Ireland and the UK. Homey, in an odd, mod kinda way. Bar open M-Sa until 1am, Su until midnight. DJ Su. 21+. Club 23+. Cover Th £5, F £5-7, Sa £10, Su £5-7 (less before 10pm).

Manhattan (M-Club), 23-31 Bradbury Pl. (☎9023 3131). Huge 3-story dance club packed with a younger crowd clad in Brit-pop fashions. Dress to impress. Th student night, F 70s night. No cover for 1st-floor bar; nightclub cover £4-6.

Katy Daly's Pub and **The Limelight,** 17 Ormeau Ave. (☎9032 5942). High-ceilinged, wood-paneled, antique pub, with strobe-filled nightclub next door. Draws a student-heavy mixed age crowd. Pub hosts local bands Tu, singer/songwriters W-Th and Sa. Club has Tu student night, F "Disco A Go-Go," Sa indie disco. Pub open M-Sa noon-1am; club open 10pm-2am. Cover £2-5.

Shine, Queen's University Student Union (☎9032 4803). Hot club spot, pulsating with top-notch DJ every Sa. Open Sa 10pm-3am. Cover £5-12.

GAY AND LESBIAN NIGHTLIFE

On Wednesday nights, **White's Tavern,** the oldest pub in Belfast, becomes one of the most progressive (see **Cornmarket,** above), and **Queen's Cafe Bar** always attracts a mixed crowd, gay and straight (see **North of Donegall Square,** above).

The Kremlin, 96 Donegall St. (☎9080 9700). Look for the imposing statue of Stalin above the entrance. Belfast's newest, hottest, and friendliest gay nightspot with too many different venues to list, from foam parties to internationally renowned drag queens. Tight security. F theme night. Bar open M-Th 6pm-3am, F-Su 1pm-3:30am. Club open Th-Su. Cover varies, but free Su, M, and before 9pm.

The Custom House, 22-28 Skipper St. (☎9024 5588), off High St. 1 block west of the Albert Memorial Clock. A more relaxed bar during the week that gets wild on weekends—Sa hosts a DJ, karaoke, and live band in separate rooms. Mixed-age crowd, mostly male. M bingo, F DJ. Sa £3 cover.

Parliament Bar, 2-6 Dunbar St. (☎9023 4520), corner of Dunbar and Talbot St.; Talbot is off Donegall St. Once the premier gay bar of Northern Ireland, still kicking with shows and themes nightly. M pool competition, Tu pub quiz, W Glitz Blitz, Th drag disco, Sa Spank, Su cabaret. Cover £5-10. Open M, W 11:30am-1am, Tu, Th 11:30am-2am, F-Su 'til late. Cover Th £2, F £4, Sa £5-10, the earlier the cheaper.

TOURS

BLACK CAB TOURS. If you do only one thing in this city, take a black cab tour of West Belfast. The tours provide a fascinating commentary highlighting the murals, paraphernalia, and sights on both sides of the Peace Line. Most drivers come from the communities and have been touched personally by their histories but make pains to avoid bias. Almost every hostel books these tours with their favored **black cab** operators, some their own, usually for £7-8. **Original Belfast Black Taxi Tours** give impassioned, yet even-handed commentary and will answer any question. *(☎0800 032 2003. £7.50 per person for groups of 3 or more.)* Michael Johnston of **Black Taxi Tours** has made a name for himself with his witty, objective presentations. *(☎0800 052 3914; www.belfasttours.com. £9 per person.)*

CITYBUS. Citybus provides several tours that hit the city's major sights, both glitzy and gritty. The **Belfast City Tour** introduces visitors to the landmarks of downtown Belfast. *(1½hr. May-Sept. M-Sa 11am. £9, students £8, seniors and children £6, families £23.)* **Belfast Living History Tour** is their answer to the numerous black cab tours of West Belfast. *(☎9045 8484. 1½hr. May-Sept. M-Sa 2:30pm. £9, students £8, seniors and children £6. All tours leave from Castle Place, in front of the post office.)*

SIGHTS

DONEGALL SQUARE

Donegall Square marks the northern boundary of the Golden Mile and the southern end of the pedestrian-only Cornmarket district. Belfast's old city center, the Square is dominated by City Hall, once a favorite target for IRA bombers.

BELFAST CITY HALL. The most dramatic and impressive piece of architecture in Belfast is appropriately its administrative and geographic center. Removed from the crowded streets by a grassy square, its green copper dome (173 ft.) is nonetheless visible from nearly any point in the city. Inside, a grand staircase ascends to the second floor, portraits of the city's Lord Mayors somberly line the halls, and glass and marble shimmer in three elaborate reception rooms. The **City Council's** oak-paneled chambers, only used once a month, are deceptively austere, considering the Council's reputation for rowdy meetings (fists are known to fly). Directly in front of the main entrance, an enormous marble **Queen Victoria statue** stares down at visitors with her trademark formidable grimace, while bronze figures representing Shipbuilding and Spinning kneel at her feet. A more sympathetic figure of womanhood stands on East grounds, commemorating the fate of the *Titanic* and her passengers. An inconspicuous pale gray stone column in front remembers the 1942 arrival of the US Expeditionary Force, whose soldiers were stationed here to defend the North from Germany; it was rededicated after President Clinton's visit to Belfast in 1995. The interior of City Hall is accessible only by guided tour. *(☎9027 0456. 1hr. tours June-Sept. M-F 10:30, 11:30am, and 2:30pm; Sa 2:30pm; also Aug.-Sept. Su 3:30pm Oct.-May M-Sa 2:30pm. Free.)*

OTHER SIGHTS. One of Belfast's oldest establishments is the **Linen Hall Library;** the red hand of Ulster decorates the top of its street entrance. The library contains a famous collection of political documents relating to Northern Ireland. Devoted librarians scramble to get their hands on every Christmas card, hand bill, and newspaper article related to Belfast's political history. *(Enter via 52 Fountain St. ☎9032 1707. Free tours available, but call ahead. Open M-F 9:30am-5:30pm, Sa 9:30am-4pm.)* Nearby, the **Scottish Provident Institution,** built in 1902, displays a decadent facade glorifying virtually every profession that has contributed to industrial Belfast. *(Across the street from City Hall, on the corner of Donegall Sq. North and East Bedford St.)* For a taste of Irish craftsmanship, head to **Craftworks.** Collections include leather goods, knitwear, ceramics, and jewelry. *(Bedford St. ☎9024 4465. Open M-Sa 9:30am-5:30pm.)*

CORNMARKET AND ST. ANNE'S CATHEDRAL

Just north of the city center, a bustling shopping district engulfs eight blocks around Castle St. and Royal Ave. Castle St. was named for the old city castle, whose place has been usurped by the Golden Arches. Although the Cornmarket area is dominated by modern buildings, relics of old Belfast remain in the tiny alleys, or **entries,** that connect the major streets.

ST. ANNE'S CATHEDRAL. Belfast's newspapers all set up shop around St. Anne's, also known as the **Belfast Cathedral.** This Church of Ireland cathedral was begun in 1899, but to keep from disturbing regular worship, it was built around a smaller church already on the site; upon completion of the new exterior, builders extracted the earlier church brick by brick. Each of the cathedral's ten interior pillars name one of Belfast's fields of professionalism: Science, Industry, Healing, Agriculture, Music, Theology, Shipbuilding, Freemasonry, Art, and "Womanhood." In a small enclave called the **Chapel of Peace,** visitors are asked to pray for the healing of world strife. *(Donegall St., a few blocks from the city center. Open M-Sa 10am-4pm.)*

THE ENTRIES. Between Ann and High St. runs **Pottinger's Entry,** which contains the **Morning Star Pub** and its award-winning food (see **Pubs,** p. 473). **Joy's Entry,** farther down Ann St., is where the Unionist *Belfast News Letter* was printed for over 100 years; the only establishment still in the entry, the **Globe Tavern,** is disappointingly modern inside. Off Lombard and Bridge St., **Winecellar Entry** is the site of Belfast's oldest pub, **White's Tavern,** serving since 1630 (see **Pubs,** p. 473).

OTHER SIGHTS. Though most of Belfast's buildings are young by European standards, the city's oldest public building, **The Old Stock Exchange,** sits on the corner of North and Waring St. Tireless Charles Lanyon designed a new facade for the building in 1845 when the original was deemed not grand enough. Just a block west, on Rosemary St., the **First Presbyterian Church of Belfast** is the city's oldest church, founded 1644. *(☎9032 5365. Su service 10:30am.)*

THE DOCKS AND EAST BELFAST

Although the docks were once the active heart of Belfast, continued commercial development made the area more suitable for industrial machinery than people. However, the **Odyssey,** on the east bank amidst reminders of the city's shipbuilding glory days, promises to bring back the hordes. The most famous of the shipyards is Harland & Wolff, whose magnum opus was, unfortunately, the *Titanic.* The shipyards figure in numerous poems and novels, notably at the end of Paul Muldoon's "7, Middagh St." Today the twin cranes **Samson** and **Goliath** towering over the Harland & Wolff shipyard are the most striking part of the docks' skyline.

ODYSSEY. Belfast's newest mega-attraction is a gigantic center that houses five distinct attractions. *(2 Queen's Quay. ☎9045 1055; www.theodyssey.co.uk.)* The **Odyssey Arena,** with 10,000 seats, is the largest indoor arena in Ireland. The venue is home to the Belfast Giants ice hockey team, and big name performers such as Destiny's Child house-sit when the players are away. *(Performance box office ☎9073 9074; www.odesseyarena.com. Hockey ☎9059 1111; www.belfastgiants.co.uk.)* The **W5 Discovery Centre** is a top-of-the-line science and technology museum that beckons geeks of all ages (as well as the suave and sophisticated *Let's Go* reader) to play with pulley chairs, laser harps, robots, and the Fire Tornado. *(☎9046 7700. Workshops run throughout the summer. Wheelchair-accessible. Open M-Sa 10am-6pm, Su noon-6pm; last admission 5pm. £5.50, students and seniors £4, children £3.50, families £15.)* The **Sheridan IMAX Cinema** shows both 2D and 3D films on its enormous 62x82 ft. screen, while **Warner Village Cinemas** shows Hollywood blockbusters on its 14 normal-sized screens. *(IMAX ☎9046 7000; www.belfastimax.com. £5, students M-Th £4.50, children M-Th £4. Multiplex ☎9073 9234. £5/£3.70/£3.20.)* A mall-esque **Pavilion** contains the usual shops, bars, and restaurants—including that tourist mecca, the Hard Rock Cafe. *(Hard Rock Cafe ☎9076 6990. Open M-Sa noon-1am, Su noon-midnight.)*

LAGAN LOOKOUT AND LAGAN WEIR. The £14-million weir was built to eliminate the Lagan's drastic tides, which used to expose stinking mud flats during ebb. Depending on the day and weather, you may or may not see the undertaking as fully successful. The Lookout, refurbished in 2002, has a near 360° view and a room of displays on the history of Belfast and the purpose of the weir. Both structures are part of a huge development project that includes the **Laganside Trail** along the far side of the river and **Waterfront Hall,** a concert hall with an uncanny resemblance to a sponge cake. *(Donegall Quay, across from the Laganside bus station. ☎9031 5444. Lookout open Apr.-Sept. M-F 11am-5pm, Sa noon-5pm, Su 2-5pm; Oct.-Mar. Tu-F 11am-3:30pm, Sa 1-4:30pm, Su 2-4:30pm. £1.50, students and seniors £1, children 75p.)*

SINCLAIR SEAMEN'S CHURCH. Who says Herman Melville was being silly when he wrote about his Nantucketers' nautical chapel? Here, the minister delivers his sermons from a pulpit carved in the shape of a ship's prow, collections are taken in miniature lifeboats, and an organ with port and starboard lights taken from a Guinness barge carries the tune. The exterior was designed by the prolific Charles Lanyon, who was also responsible for the Custom House and almost every other notable 19th-century building in Belfast—except the Albert Memorial Clock Tower. Boy, was he angry about that! *(Corporation St., down from the SeaCat terminal.)*

OTHER SIGHTS. The stately **Custom House,** Lanyon's 1857 baby, stands between Queen Sq. and Albert Sq. as you approach the river from the clock tower. Designed in an E-shape, it rests on an elaborate pediment of Lady Britannia, Salty Neptune, and Mercury, the god of trade. Belfast also has its own leaning tower of Pisa and Big Ben, in one compact piece: the **Albert Memorial Clock Tower.** Named for Victoria's prince consort and designed in 1865 by W. J. Barre, the tower slouches precariously at the entrance to the docks, where Oxford St. runs beside the Lagan.

THE GOLDEN MILE

"The Golden Mile" refers to a strip along Great Victoria St. that is encrusted with many of the jewels in Belfast's crown. Because it drew a number of powerful

Englishmen to its glittering establishments and was funded largely by the British-based government, The Golden Mile was once a target for IRA bombers. Today it occupies safe territory within the city center.

GRAND OPERA HOUSE. The city's pride and joy, the opera house was cyclically bombed by the IRA, restored to its original splendor at enormous cost, and then bombed again. Top opera and musical theater allow visitors today to enjoy the current calm in high fashion, while tours on Saturday allow a look behind the ornate facade. *(☎9024 0411. Tours begin across the street at the office Sa 11am. £3, seniors and children £2. Office open M-W 8:30am-8pm, Th 8:30am-9pm, F 8:30am-6:30pm, Sa 8:30am-5:30pm.)* See **Theatre,** p. 485.

THE CROWN LIQUOR SALOON. The National Trust restored this highly frequented pub to make it a showcase of carved wood, gilded ceilings, and stained glass. Doored snugs fit groups of two to 10 comfortably. Once upon a time you could order another round by hitting the buzzer in the booth, but now you have to get up and stagger to the bar. See **Pubs,** p. 473.

EUROPA HOTEL. Having suffered 32 attacks, the Europa has the dubious distinction of being "Europe's most bombed hotel." In March of 1993, the hotel installed shatterproof windows; luckily, they haven't been tested yet and likely won't be anytime soon. Enjoy your stay.

NORTHERN IRELAND

QUEEN'S UNIVERSITY AREA

Though the students largely empty out in the summer, their turf, with its city garden oasis, is fun to explore all year round. The walk from the city center only takes 15-20min., but Citybuses #69 and 71 will get you there as well.

QUEEN'S UNIVERSITY BELFAST. Charles Lanyon designed the beautiful Tudor-revival brick campus in 1849, modeling it after Magdalen College, Oxford. The **Visitors Centre,** in the Lanyon Room to the left of the main entrance, offers Queen's-related exhibits and merchandise. A new gallery keeps aesthetes on their toes with rotating shows. *(University Rd. Visitors Centre ☎9033 5252. Open May-Sept. M-Sa 10am-4pm, Oct.-Mar. M-F 10am-4pm. Gallery open M-F 9am-5pm, Sa 10am-4pm.)*

BOTANIC GARDENS. Birds do it, bees do it, and on warm days, the majority of the student population does it. You can do it with them, if you like. Bask in Belfast's occasional sun behind the university, that is. Meticulously groomed, the gardens offer a welcome green respite from the traffic-laden city streets. Inside the gardens lie two 19th-century greenhouses, the toasty **Tropical Ravine House,** and the more temperate Lanyon-designed **Palm House.** Summertime visitors should be sure to stop and smell Europe's most fragrant bloomers in the rose gardens. *(☎9032 4902. Open daily 8am-dusk. Tropical House and Palm House open Apr.-Sept. M-F 10am-noon and 1-5pm, Sa-Su 2-5pm; Oct.-Mar. M-F 10am-noon and 1-4pm, Sa-Su 2-4pm. Free.)*

ULSTER MUSEUM. This museum has developed a variety of disparate exhibits to fill its halls, including Irish and modern art, local history, dinosaur bones, and 18th-century fashion. Most popular are the blackened and shriveled Mummy of Takabuti and the treasure salvaged from the *Girone*, a Spanish Armada ship that sank off the Causeway Coast in 1588. *(In the Botanic Gardens, off Stranmillis Rd. ☎9038 3000. Open all year M-F 10am-5pm, Sa 1-5pm, Su 2-5pm. Free, except for certain exhibitions.)*

SOUTH BELFAST

Riverside trails, ancient ruins, and idyllic parks south of Belfast make it hard to believe that you're only a few minutes from the city center. The area can be reached by bus #71 from Donegall Sq. East, though it's still a bit of a hike from the drop-off. The **Belfast City Council Parks Section** can provide further information; they have a guide-map at most parks, the Welcome Centre, and Belfast Castle.

SIR THOMAS AND LADY DIXON PARK. The most stunning of the parks, sitting pretty on Upper Malone Rd., 20,000 rose bushes of every variety imaginable bloom here each year. The gardens were founded in 1836 and include stud China roses, imported between 1792 and 1824. *(Open M-Sa 7:30am-dusk, Su 9am-dusk.)*

GIANT'S RING. Four miles north along the tow path near Shaw's Bridge lies an earthen ring with a dolmen in the middle, remarkable for being older than dirt (birthdate 2500 BC or thereabouts). Little is known about the 600 ft. wide circle, but experts speculate that it was built for the same reasons as England's Stonehenge. Those clever experts quickly leave the room when it's mentioned that no one knows too much about Stonehenge, either. *(Always open. Free.)*

NORTH BELFAST

The sights of North Belfast are grouped in and around **Cave Hill Forest Park.** A sunny and unhurried day is best for visiting, as walking is the primary mode of transportation after taking Antrim Rd. or Citybuses #45-51 to the park.

BELFAST ZOO. Set in the hills alongside Cave Hill Forest Park, the zoo's best attribute is its natural setting, where animals from the world over struggle to look at home. The recommended route takes you past elephants, giraffes, camels, zebras, and the ever-entertaining, acrobatic spider monkey. *(5 mi. north of the city on Antrim Rd.; take Citybus #9 or any one between #45 and 51. ☎9077 6277. Open Apr.-Sept. daily 10am-5pm; Oct.-Mar. 10am-2:30pm. Apr.-Sept. £6, children £3, families £16.50. Oct.-Mar. £5/£2.50/£13. Seniors, children under 4, and the disabled always free.)*

BELFAST CASTLE. The Earl of Shaftesbury presented this building to the city in 1934, a few years after the castle-building craze had gone out of fashion. The castle lacks the history and majesty of older castles; nevertheless, its location, atop **Cave Hill,** long the seat of Ulster rulers, makes for fabulous views. The ancient King Matudan had his McArt's Fort here, where the more modern United Irishmen plotted rebellion in 1795. Marked trails lead north from the fort to five **caves** in the area, thought by historians to be ancient mines; only the lowest is accessible. For those on foot, the small path to the right of the gate makes for a much shorter and prettier walk than the road. *(Open M-Sa 9am-10:30pm, Su 9am-6pm. Free.)*

WEST BELFAST AND THE MURALS

The neighborhoods of West Belfast have historically been at the heart of political tensions in the North. The Catholic area (centered on **Falls Rd.**) and the Protestant neighborhood (centered on the **Shankill**) are separated by the **peace line,** a grim, gray, seemingly impenetrable wall. Along the wall, abandoned houses with boarded-up windows point to a troubled past and an uncertain future. Yet now, one bit of the peace line, near Lanark, contains peace paintings and signatures—painted mostly by tourists— indicating hope for the future. The Falls and Shankill embody both the raw sentiment that drives the Northern Irish conflict and the casual calm with which those closest to the Troubles approach daily life. West Belfast is not a tourist attraction in the traditional sense, though the walls and houses along the area's streets display political **murals** which speak to Belfast's troubled past. These murals are the city's most popular and interesting attraction.

Those traveling to these sectarian neighborhoods often take **black cabs,** community shuttles that whisk residents to the city center, picking up and dropping off passengers along their set routes. Some black cabs can also be booked for **tours** of

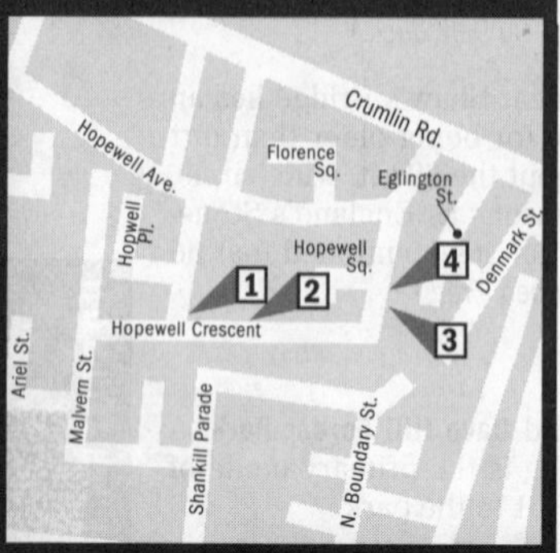

THE CATHOLIC MURALS

The murals of West Belfast are the city's most intriguing attractions. The following is a list of Catholic Belfast's more famous and important; also included are those buildings most related to the Troubles.

1. Mural illustrating the **Hunger Strikes of 1981,** during which several imprisoned Catholics died in protest of the conditions of their arrest and detainment. Look for it on the side of the library.
2. The old **Sein Féin office.** Once used as the national headquarters for the North; murals usually line the walls opposite the office.
3. Portrayal of **Bobby Sands,** found on Sevastopol St. on the side of the Sinn Féin Office. Sands was one of the first hunger strikers to die. He was elected to British Parliament during this time and is remembered as the North's most famous martyr.
4. Formerly known as **Northern Ireland's National RUC Headquarters,** this building has the honor of being the most bombed police station in England, the Republic, and the North. Its fortified, barb-wired facade is found on Springfield St.

the Falls or Shankill (see **Tours,** p. 477). This year, *Let's Go* offers two **neighborhood maps** (see **The Insider's City**) of the Protestant and Catholic murals, allowing those who lack the funds for a tour to explore the murals for themselves.

It is best to visit the Falls and Shankill during the day, when the neighborhoods are calmer and, more importantly, when the murals can be seen. The Protestant Orangemen's Marching Season, in the weeks around July 12, is a risky time to visit the area—the parades are underscored by mutual antagonism that can lead to violence (see **History and Politics,** p. 455). Because the area around the peace line is rather desolate, travelers are advised not to wander from one neighborhood over to the other, but to return to the city center between visits to Shankill and the Falls.

The murals in the Falls and Shankill change constantly, so the sections below and the neighborhood maps describe but a few. For a guide to the mural's iconography, consult our glossary of common mural symbols (see **The Mural Symbols of West Belfast,** p. 484). While it is tacky to gawk at and photograph these walls, they *are* partly intended as propaganda, and many tourists take snap-shots. However, before heading out with your camera, ask locals about the current political climate and cautions. Around the time leading up to Marching Season, tension sometimes builds, and picture-taking may not be well received. Photography is always acceptable on black cab tours, however, as drivers have agreements with the communities. But do not take photographs of **military installations,** as your film may be confiscated.

THE FALLS. This Catholic neighborhood is larger than Shankill and houses a younger, more vibrant population, and the city's best nightlife. On **Divis St.,** a high-rise apartment building marks the site of **Divis Tower,** an ill-fated housing development built by optimistic social planners in the 1960s. The project soon became an IRA stronghold and saw some of the worst of Belfast's Troubles in the 1970s. The British army still occupies the top floors, and Shankill residents snidely refer to it as "Little Beirut."

Continuing west, Divis St. turns into **Falls Road.** The **Sinn Féin** office is easily spotted: one side of it is covered with an enormous portrait of Bobby Sands (see **The Troubles,** p. 455, and **Belfast Murals,** p. 455) and an advertisement for the Sinn Féin newspaper, *An Phoblacht.* Continuing down Falls Rd. will take you past a number of murals, which are generally on side streets just off Falls Rd., on Beechmont. Murals in the Falls, unlike those of the Shankill, are becoming less militant in nature, though there are a few left in the Lower Falls that speak to days past.

The Falls road soon splits into **Andersontown Rd.** and **Glen Rd.,** the site of Ireland's only urban *gaeltacht.* On the left are the Celtic crosses of **Milltown Cemetery,** the resting place of many Republican dead. Inside the entrance, a memorial to Republican casualties is bordered by a low, green fence on the right; the grave of Bobby Sands can be found here. Another mile along Andersontown Rd. lies the street's namesake—a housing project that was formerly a wealthy Catholic neighborhood—and more murals. The Springfield Rd. Police Service of Northern Ireland station, previously named the RUC station, is the **most-attacked police station in Ireland and the UK;** its charred defenses are formidable, as are the directional video cameras and microphones that deck its eight-story radio tower.

SHANKILL. North St. turns into Shankill Rd. as it crosses the Westlink and then arrives in Protestant Shankill, once a thriving shopping district. Turning left (coming from the direction of North St.) on most side roads leads to the peace line. At Canmore St., a mural on the left depicts the Apprentice Boys "Shutting the Gates of Derry—1688" as the Catholic invaders try to get through (see **Rebellion, Reunion, Reaction,** p. 59). A little farther, also on the left and across a small park, a big, faded mural labeled "UVF—then and now" depicts a modern, black-garbed Protestant paramilitary man and a historical "B-Specials" soldier side-by-side. The densely decorated **Orange Hall** sits on the left at Brookmount St. McClean's Wallpaper, on the right, was formerly Fizzel's Fish Shop, where 10 people died in an October 1993 bomb attack. The side streets on the right guide you to the **Shankill Estate** and more murals. Through the estate, **Crumlin Rd.** heads back to the city center, passing an army base, the courthouse, and the jail. The oldest Loyalist murals are found here.

SANDY ROW AND NEWTOWNARDS RD. As the Shankill area steadily loses its middle-class residents, a growing Protestant population lives on **Sandy Row.** This stretch is a turn off **Donegall Rd.** at **Shaftesbury Sq.**—an orange arch topped with King William marks its start. Nearby murals show the Red Hand of Ulster, a bulldog, and William crossing the Boyne. While murals in the Falls and Shankill are often defaced or damaged, better-preserved and more elaborate art adorns the secure Protestant enclave of **East Belfast,** across the Lagan; be particularly careful when traveling in this area. A number of murals line **Newtownards Rd.** One likens the UVF to the ancient hero, Cúchulainn—Ulster's defender. In doing so, it unintentionally illustrates the overlap in the cultural authorship of both the British and the Irish.

THE INSIDER'S CITY

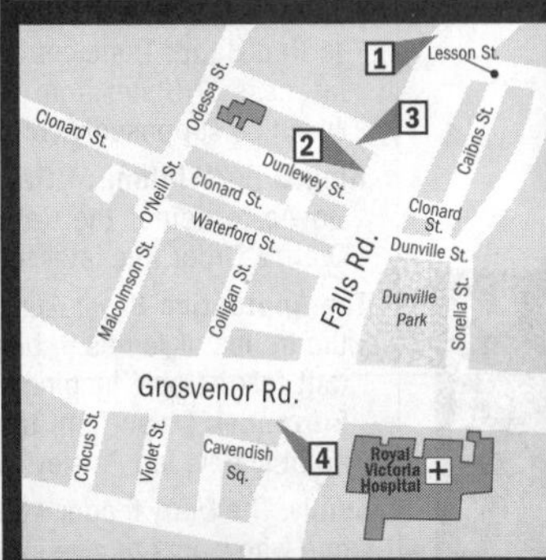

THE PROTESTANT MURALS

The Protestant murals found in the Shankill area of West Belfast tend to be of a more militant nature. The following is a guide to the area's more well-known. These murals are all found near Hopewell St. and Hopewell Cresent, to the north of Shankill Rd., down Shankill Parade. Best reached by going South from Crumlin Rd.

1. Painting of a **Loyalist martyr,** killed in prison in 1997. The mural remembers those who have died fighting for British-Ulster rule.

2. Depiction of the **Grim Reaper,** with gun and British flag. Beside him on the painting lie crosses with the names of three IRA men who set off a bomb in the Shankill area in 1993 and are still at large.

3. A collage of illustrations that represent Northern Ireland's Loyalist militant groups. Included are: the **UFF, UDU, UDU,** and the **UDA.**

4. Orange and yellow mural with a large black silhouette representing the **Scottish Brigade.** Captures the connection Protestant Loyalists feel to their brethren across the way.

THE MURAL SYMBOLS OF WEST BELFAST

PROTESTANT MURALS

Blue, White, and Red: The colors of the British flag; often painted on curbs and signposts to demarcate Unionist murals and neighborhoods.

The Red Hand: The crest of Ulster Province; used by Unionists to emphasize the separateness of Ulster from the Republic. Symbolizes the hand of the first Norse King, which he supposedly cut off and threw on a Northern beach to establish his primacy.

King Billy/William of Orange: Sometimes depicted on a white horse, crossing the Boyne to defeat the Catholic King James II at the 1690 Battle of the Boyne. The Orange Order was later founded in his honor.

The Apprentice Boys: A group of young men who shut the gates of Derry to keep out the troops of James II, beginning the great siege of 1689. They have become Protestant folk heroes, inspiring a sect of the Orange order in their name. The slogan **"No Surrender,"** also from the siege, has been appropriated by radical Unionists, most notably Rev. Ian Paisley (see **The Troubles,** p. 455).

Lundy: The Derry leader who advocated surrender during the siege; now a term for anyone who wants to give in to Catholic demands.

Scottish Flag: Blue with a white cross; recalls the Scottish-Presbyterian roots of many Protestants whose ancestors were part of the Ulster Plantation (see **Cromwell,** p. 58).

CATHOLIC MURALS

Orange and Green: Colors of the Irish Republic's flag; often painted on curbs and signposts in Republican neighborhoods.

Landscapes: Usually imply Republican territorial claims to the North.

The Irish Volunteers: Republican tie to the earlier (nonsectarian) Nationalists.

Saiorse: Irish for "Freedom"; the most common term found on murals.

Éireann go bráth: "Ireland forever"; a popular IRA slogan.

Tiocfaidh ár lá: (CHOCK-ee-ar-LA) "Our day will come."

Slan Abnaile: (slang NA-fail) "Leave our streets"; directed at the primarily Protestant RUC police force.

Phoenix: Symbolizes united Ireland rising from the ashes of British persecution.

Lug: Celtic god, seen as the protector of the "native Irish" (Catholics).

Green Ribbon: IRA symbol for "free our POWs."

Bulldog: Britain.

Bowler Hats: A symbol for Orangemen.

ARTS AND ENTERTAINMENT

Belfast's many cultural events and performances are covered in the monthly *Arts Council Artslink*, which is free at the tourist office. Daily listings appear in the daily *Belfast Telegraph* (which also has a Friday Arts supplement) as well as in Thursday's issue of the *Irish News*. For more extensive information on pub entertainment, pick up the biweekly two-page bulletin *The List*, available free at the tourist office, hostels, and many pubs. The **Crescent Arts Centre,** 2 University Rd., supplies general arts info, but mostly specific news about their own exhibits and concerts, which take place September through May. They also host three seasonal terms of eight-week courses in yoga, writing, traditional music, dance, theater, and drawing. (☎9024 2338. Open M-Sa 10am-10pm. Classes £36.) **Fenderesky Gallery,** 2

University Rd., inside the Crescent Arts building, hosts contemporary shows all year. (☎9023 5245. Open Tu-Sa 11:30am-5pm.) The **Old Museum,** 7 College Sq. North, is Belfast's largest venue for contemporary artwork. (☎9023 5053. Open M-Sa 9am-5:30pm.) Besides exhibits, it features workshops and a variety of dance, theater, and music performances. (Tickets ☎9023 3332. Most tickets £6-8, students and concessions £3.) A word of warning to summer travelers: July and August are slow months for Belfast arts; around July 12, the whole city shuts down.

THEATER

The truly **Grand Opera House,** 2-4 Great Victoria St. (☎9024 0411; www.goh.co.uk), shows a mix of opera, ballet, musicals, and drama. Tickets for most shows can be purchased either by phone until 9pm or in person at the box office, 2-4 Great Victoria St. (☎9024 1919; 24hr. info line ☎9024 9129. Tickets from £12.50, with occasional student concessions. Open M-W 8:30am-6pm, Th 8:30am-9pm, F-Sa 8:30am-6pm.) **The Lyric Theatre,** 55 Ridgeway St., mixes Irish plays and international works. (☎9038 1081; www.lyrictheatre.co.uk. Box office open M-Sa 10am-7pm. Tickets M-Th £10, F-Sa £12.50.) **The Group Theatre,** Bedford St., produces comedies and farces in the Ulster Hall from September to May. (☎9032 9685. Box office open M-F noon-3pm. Tickets £4-8.) The **Old Museum Art Centre,** 7 College Sq. North, presents avant-garde contemporary works. (☎9023 5053. Tickets £3-8.)

MUSIC

Ulster Hall, Bedford St. (☎9032 3900), brings Belfast everything from classical to pop. Try independent box offices for tickets: **Our Price** (☎9023 0262) or the **Ticket Shop** at Virgin (☎9032 3744). **The Grand Opera House** (see **Theater,** above) resounds with classical vocal music. **Waterfront Hall,** 2 Lanyon Pl., is one of Belfast's newest concert centers, hosting a series of performances from classical to pop throughout the year. (☎9033 4400. Tickets £10-35, student discounts usually available.) The **Ulster Orchestra** plays concerts at Waterfront Hall and Ulster Hall. (☎9066 8798; www.ulsterorchestra.org.uk. Tickets £5-23, with the cheapies behind the stage.)

FILM

There are two major movie theaters in Belfast, in addition to the new one at the Odyssey (see **Sights,** p. 479). Commercial films are shown at **UGC Cinemas,** 14 Dublin Rd.; most movies arrive a few months after their US release. (24hr. info ☎0870 155 5176. £4.40, students and seniors £2.75, children £2.55; before 5pm £2.75.) **Queen's Film Theatre,** in a back alley off Botanic Ave., draws a more artsy crowd. (☎9024 4857. £2-3.80. "Meal and movie" discounts for certain restaurants.)

FESTIVALS

QUEEN'S UNIVERSITY BELFAST FESTIVAL. Belfast reigns supreme in the art world for three weeks each November, during the university's annual festival. Over 300 performances of opera, ballet, film, and comedy invade venues across the city, drawing internationally acclaimed groups. Tickets for the most popular events sell out months ahead of time, though there's almost always something to see without planning ahead. *(☎9066 7687; www.belfastfestival.com. For advance schedules, write to: The Belfast Festival at Queens, 25 College Gardens, Belfast BT9 6BS. Tickets sold by mail and phone from mid-Sept. through the festival's end. Prices range from £2.50 to £25.)*

WEST BELFAST ARTS FESTIVAL (FÉILE AN PHOBAIL). This week-long series of events, held the second week of August, is the high point of the year for Falls residents. The Nationalist festivities celebrate Irish traditional culture, bringing in both big name trad groups and indebted rockers. *(☎9031 3440; www.feilebelfast.com.)*

SPORTS AND ACTIVITIES

The state-of-the-art **Belfast Superbowl,** 4 Clarence St. (☎9033 1466), doesn't offer football, but it does have 20 glow-in-the-dark bowling lanes. *(Open M-Sa 10am-midnight, Su noon-midnight.)* **Lagan Valley LeisurePlex,** Lisburn (☎9267 2121), 8 mi. from Belfast, is one of the biggest family-fun facilities in all of Ireland, and comes complete with a huge galleon, master-blasters, and thrilling water rides. Dominating the skyline just north of Belfast, **Cave Hill** offers adventure sports of a different kind. The **Cave Hill walk** starts from the parking lot of the **Belfast Zoo,** trails the Ulster Way for a short distance, and then branches off on its own on a straight shot up toward **McArt's Fort** (1100ft.), which sits at the summit. During the 3hr. climb, hikers pass **caves** that were carved into the hill years ago by Neolithic wanderers searching for shelter. Hikers will also be granted all-encompassing views of Belfast and its port. (Call ☎9032 1221 for more info.) On the 9 mi. **Lagan Valley Towpath Walk,** travelers also temporarily join with the Ulster Way for part of their journey along the canal towpaths to **Sir Thomas and Lady Dixon Park.** (☎9023 1221 for info.)

If you'd rather sit and watch than walk and run, take a cab to the **Odyssey Arena** to catch the **Harp Larger Belfast Giants** battle it out with county competitors (☎9059 1111). **Soccer** fanatics will be sure to nab a game or two at the **Windsor Park** pitch on Donegall Ave. (☎9024 4198). **Gaelic Footballers** will run to Andersonstown, West Belfast, to enjoy the Sunday afternoon matches. (Call the GAA at ☎9038 3815.) **Horseracing** goes down at the Maze, Lisburn (☎9262 1256). Located just 10 mi. from Belfast, the premier racecourse has a dozen meetings throughout the year, including the **Mirror May Day** fixture and the **Ulster Harp Derby** in June. **Rugby** can be viewed and played at **Ravenhill Stadium** (☎9064 9141).

NORTHERN IRELAND

DAYTRIPS FROM BELFAST

ULSTER FOLK MUSEUM AND TRANSPORT AND RAILWAY MUSEUMS

The Ulster Folk Museum and Transport and Railway Museums stretches across 176 acres in the town of Holywood. To reach it, take the Bangor road (A2) 7 mi. east of Belfast. Buses and trains stop here on the way to Bangor. ☎9042 8428. Open July-Sept. M-Sa 10am-6pm, Su 11am-6pm; Mar.-June M-F 10am-5pm, Sa 10am-6pm, Su 11am-6pm; Oct.-Feb. M-F 10am-4pm, Sa 10am-5pm, Su 11am-5pm. Folk Museum £4, students and seniors £2.50. Transport Museum £4/£2.50. Combined admission £5/£3.

Established by an Act of Parliament in the 1950s, the **Folk Museum** aims to preserve the way of life of Ulster's farmers, weavers, and craftspeople. The Folk Museum contains over 30 buildings from the past three centuries and all nine Ulster counties, including the usually overlooked Monaghan, Cavan, and Donegal in the Republic. All but two of the buildings are transplanted originals. All have been successfully integrated in the museum's natural landscape to create an amazing air of authenticity. While unobtrusive attendants stand nearby to answer questions, there are no cheesy historical scenes or written explanations to interrupt the visitor's own imaginative roleplay. In addition to the functional printer's press on Main St., period costumes with living villagers in them and a silent movie house will soon be added. The museum also hosts special events, including trad sessions, dance performances and workshops, storytelling festivals, and textile exhibitions.

The Transport Museum and the Railway Museum are across the road from the Folk Museum. Inside the **Transport Museum,** horse-drawn coaches, ship models, bicycles, and cars display the history of vehicles in motion. Their motorcycle exhibition is extensive, following the evolution of the genre from the ABC Skootamota,

BUT DOC, A CAR WITH GULL WINGS?!!!

In 1978, John Z. de Lorean, then the Vice President of General Motors, raised the hopes of many Belfastians by deciding to construct his new car factory just outside the city. With a pair of cowboy boots and a heap of great salesmanship, de Lorean gathered $200 million from investors and earned the status of savior among Northern Ireland's unemployed population. There was reason, however, not to believe the hype. In 1982, the factory shut down after producing just 10,000 cars, due to consistently high and unrealistic sales projections. Fast-talkin' de Lorean was arrested the same year on drug charges. His dream car—with its "gull wings" and sleek design—lives on in popular memory as Marty McFly's time-traveling vehicle in the *Back to the Future* series.

a 1919 gem, to Harley-mania with a life-size 1950s diner installation. Also included is the ill-fated history and a model of John de Lorean's car of the same name (see **But Doc...**, below). A *Titanic* exhibit includes original blueprints and traces the fate of the Belfast-built ship. The hangar-shaped **Railway Museum** stuffs in 25 old railway engines, including the largest locomotive built in Ireland.

NEAR BELFAST

ISLE OF MAN ☎01624

*The **Isle of Man Steam Packet Company** (☎646 645) runs ferries to **Douglas** from the SeaCat Terminal, Donegall Quay, in Belfast (2¾hr.; Apr.-Sept. 2 per week, usually M and F, July-Aug. also W; €33-38). Public transportation is run by **Isle of Man Transport** (☎663 366); the Travel Shop, by the Douglas bus station, has maps and schedules. (☎662 525. Open M 10am-12:30pm and 1:30-5:45pm, Tu-F 8am-5:45pm, Sa 8am-3:30pm.) Isle of Man Bus Tour Company, Central Promenade (☎674 301), in Douglas, operates the popular **"Round the Island"** tour (W and Su; £15).*

When the grit and grime of Belfast city proves too much, the Isle of Man offers a welcome retreat. Belfast and Dublin locals often vacation to the Isle to take advantage of its coastal vistas and isolated hiking opportunities. But be warned: Though it may appear as simply a droplet of land in the Irish Sea, the Isle of Man is actually its own tiny independent nation. It has its own currency, though Northern Irish currency can be used, and its international dialing code (44) is shared with Britain.

Douglas, the small island's capital city (town), is home to the **Manx Museum,** which chronicles Man's history. (☎648 000. Open M-Sa 10am-5pm. Free.) Past the Villa Marina Gardens on Harris Promenade sits the **Gaiety Theatre.** Designed in 1900 and recently restored, the theater shone during Douglas's seaside resort days. (☎615 001. 1½hr. tours leave Sa 10:15am; July-Aug. also Tu and Th 1:45pm. £3, children £1). For a place to stay, check with the friendly family at **Glen Mona ❸,** 6 Mona Dr. (☎676 755; singles £22; shared rooms £20 per person), or at the **Grandstand Campsite ❶** (☎621 132; open mid-June to mid-Aug. and Sept; £6 per pitch). At **Brendann O'Donnell's** pub, 16-18 Strand St., Guinness posters and Irish music point to the owner's loyalties. (☎621 566. Open Su-Th noon-11pm, F-Sa noon-midnight.) Paramount City, on Queens Promenade (☎622 447), houses the city's biggest and best nightclubs: **Director's Bar** and **Dark Room.** (Cover £3-4. Open F-Sa 10pm-3:15am.)

Peel is a fishing town on the west coast. **Peel Castle,** on St. Patrick's Isle, is reached by causeway. (Open Easter-Oct. daily 10am-5pm; winter hours vary. £3, children £1.50, families £7.50.) Across the harbor, the **House of Manannan** emphasizes the role of the sea in Manx history. (☎648 000. Open daily 10am-5pm, last admission 3pm. £5, children £2.50.) Buses (☎662 525) from Douglas come to the station on Atholl St. The **Tourist Centre** is in the Town Hall, Derby Rd. (☎842 341. Open M-Th

8:45am-5pm, F 8:45am-4:30pm.) Most travelers flock to **Kimberley House ❸**, 8 Marine Parade, for their comfy beds and amiable owners. (☎844 763. £23 per person).

Hiking on Man is excellent. The 90 mi. Raad ny Foillan ("Road of the Gull") trail winds around the island; the spectacular 12 mi. **Port Erin to Castletown route** highlights the south; and Bayr ny Skeddan ("The Herring Road") runs 14 mi. between Peel and Castletown, overlapping the Millennium Way, 28 mi. from Castletown to Ramsey along the 14th-century Royal Highway. All tourist centers on the island can provide you with the appropriate maps and guides.

The first two weeks of June turn Man into a motorcycling beast for the **T.T. (Tourist Trophy) Races;** the respected **International Cycling Week** occurs around the same time. The **Manx language** is heard when laws are proclaimed on July 5, during the **Manx Heritage Festival.** Find other events at www.isleofman.com.

COUNTIES DOWN AND ARMAGH

Locals flock to this sleepy but scenic area to take advantage of the seaside—the coast of Down and the Ards Peninsula are covered with fishing villages, holiday resorts, and 17th-century ruins. The Mourne Mountains, almost directly south of Belfast and just a *lough* away from the Irish Republic, rise above the town of Newcastle, the largest seaside resort in Co. Down. An inland county surrounded by rivers and lakes, Armagh is set on the rolling hills of Northern Ireland's Drumlin Belt. The best time to visit Co. Armagh is during apple blossom season in May, when the countryside, known as the "Orchard of Ireland," is covered in pink. Armagh town is an ecclesiastical center of great historical interest; traces of human habitation at Navan Fort date back to 5500 BC. Armagh's other population centers, Craigavon and Portadown, near Lough Neagh, are industrial centers of less interest to tourists, although Craigavon does host the Lough Neagh Discovery Centre's acres of feathered friends and wooded park land.

BANGOR (BEANNCHOR)

Bangor found a place on early medieval maps of Ireland with its famous Abbey, but this pious era ended in the 9th century, when the Vikings were running rampant. By the Victorian era, the town had become eminent again, this time as the seaside see-and-be-seen for Belfast residents. Today, hilly Bangor caters to families and older vacationers during the week, while its nightlife draws busloads of twenty-somethings on the weekends. Its location makes it an inevitable (and enjoyable) stop on the way down the Ards Peninsula.

TRANSPORTATION

Trains: Abbey St. (☎9127 1143), at the south end of town. To **Belfast** (30min.; M-F 29 per day, Sa 17 per day, Su 11 per day; £3).

Buses: Abbey St. (☎9127 1143), joined to the train station. To **Belfast** (45min.; M-Sa 33 per day, Su 8 per day; £2.55) and all **Ards Peninsula** towns, including **Donaghadee** (23min.; M-F 19 per day, Sa 15 per day, Su 5 per day; £1.80).

Taxi: A1 Taxi, 53 High St. (☎9147 7007). 24hr.

ORIENTATION AND PRACTICAL INFORMATION

The road from Belfast runs south-north through town, changing names several times along the way—**Abbey St.** becomes **Main St.,** which curves to the right at the waterfront to become **Bridge St.,** then **Quay St.,** and finally **Seacliff Rd.** Turning to

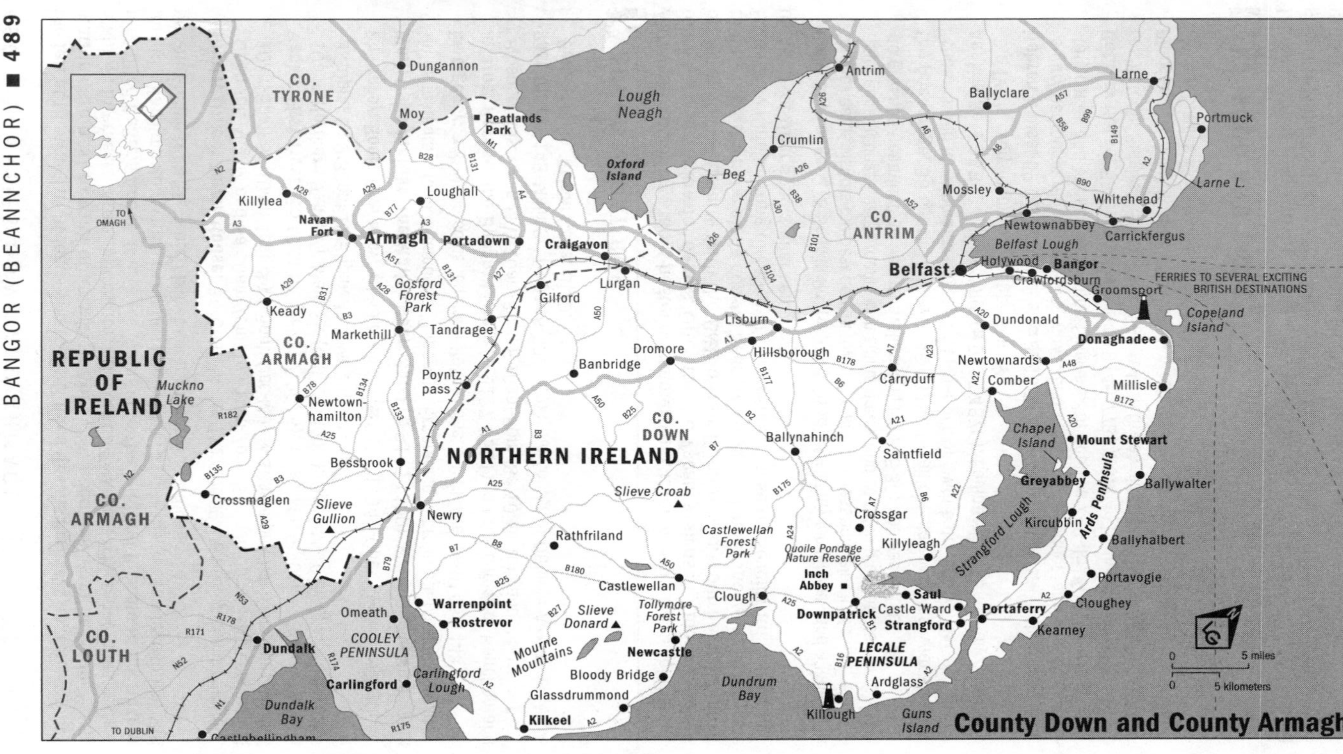
County Down and County Armagh
REPUBLIC OF IRELAND
NORTHERN IRELAND
CO. TYRONE
CO. ARMAGH
CO. ARMAGH
CO. LOUTH
CO. DOWN
CO. ANTRIM
Lough Neagh
Oxford Island
L. Beg
Muckno Lake
TO OMAGH
TO DUBLIN
Dungannon
Moy
Peatlands Park
Killylea
Navan Fort
Armagh
Loughall
Portadown
Craigavon
Lurgan
Gilford
Keady
Markethill
Gosford Forest Park
Tandragee
Poyntz pass
Newtown-hamilton
Bessbrook
Crossmaglen
Slieve Gullion
Newry
Omeath
COOLEY PENINSULA
Dundalk
Carlingford
Carlingford Lough
Dundalk Bay
Antrim
Crumlin
Ballyclare
Larne
Portmuck
Larne L.
Mossley
Whitehead
Newtownabbey
Carrickfergus
Belfast Lough
Belfast
Holywood
Bangor
Crawfordsburn
Groomsport
FERRIES TO SEVERAL EXCITING BRITISH DESTINATIONS
Copeland Island
Lisburn
Hillsborough
Dromore
Banbridge
Dundonald
Donaghadee
Newtownards
Carryduff
Comber
Millisle
Ballynahinch
Saintfield
Chapel Island
Mount Stewart
Greyabbey
Ards Peninsula
Ballywalter
Slieve Croab
Crossgar
Kircubbin
Strangford Lough
Ballyhalbert
Rathfriland
Castlewellan Forest Park
Quoile Pondage Nature Reserve
Killyleagh
Inch Abbey
Castlewellan
Saul
Portavogie
Clough
Castle Ward
Portaferry
Cloughey
Warrenpoint
Rostrevor
Slieve Donard
Tollymore Forest Park
Downpatrick
Strangford
Kearney
Mourne Mountains
Newcastle
LECALE PENINSULA
Bloody Bridge
Dundrum Bay
Ardglass
Glassdrummond
Killough
Guns Island
Kilkeel
0 5 miles
0 5 kilometers

the left at the waterfront leads you to B&B lined **Queens Parade.** The train and bus stations are next to each other where Abbey St. becomes Main St. From there, Main St. intersects three important roads: **Castle Park Ave.,** which becomes restaurant-filled **Dufferin Ave.** as it crosses Main St. to the left (and **Princetown Rd.** further inland); **Hamilton Rd.,** which becomes **Central Ave.** as it leads to Crawfordsburn; and pub-intensive **High St.,** which is between Bridge St. and Quay St.

Tourist Office: Tower House, 34 Quay St. (☎9127 0069). Books accommodations. Open July-Aug. M and Sa 10am-7pm, Tu-F 9am-7pm, Su noon-6pm; Sept. and June M 10am-5pm, Sa 10am-4pm, Su 1-5pm; Oct.-May M 10am-5pm, Sa 10am-4pm.

Banks: First Trust, 85 Main St. (☎9127 0628). Open M-F 9:30am-4:30pm, W open 10am. **Northern Bank,** 77 Main St. (☎9127 1211). Open M 10am-5pm, Tu-F 10am-3:30pm, Sa 9:30am-12:30pm. All have 24hr. **ATMs.**

Pharmacy: Boots Pharmacy, 79-83 Main St. (☎9127 1134). Open M-Sa 9am-5:30pm.

Work Opportunities: The Marine Court Hotel (☎9145 1100). Will hire travelers to work in its restaurant for a minimum of 2 months. Experience is preferred. Minimum wage.

Emergency: ☎999; no coins required. **Police:** Castle Park Ave. (☎9145 4444).

Internet Access: The **Bangor Library** (☎9127 0591), on the corner of Hamilton and Prospect Rds. Open M-W 10am-8pm, F 10am-5pm, Sa 10am-1pm and 2-5pm.

Post Office: 143 Main St. (☎9146 3000), on the corner of Dufferin Ave. Open M-Sa 9am-5:30pm. **Postal Code:** BT20.

ACCOMMODATIONS

Although Bangor is without hostel or campground, it teems with B&Bs; check the tourist office window for details. Often the 'No Vacancy' signs in windows are left up by mistake—inquire with the B&B owner if interested. Your best chance at finding a B&B will be along coastal Seacliff Rd. and inland Princetown Rd. where B&Bs lie within spitting distance of each other. Those on Seacliff Rd. are recommended for their spectacular sea views.

Cairn Bay Lodge, 278 Seacliff Rd. (☎9146 7636). A slightly longer walk and a little more money earns visitors the best deal in town. The place to rest and relax in Bangor, with elegant guest lounges, large rooms with sitting areas, and certified proprietress Jenny willing to give spa treatments to weary travelers. Singles £25-30; doubles £55-60. ❸

The Anchorage, 36 Seacliff Rd. (☎9146 1326). Small but stately rooms, with excellent showers and large breakfast plates. £17 per person, with bath £22.50. ❷

Anglers Rest B&B, 24 Seacliff Rd. (☎9127 4870). Equipped with a friendly owner and big TVs in every room. £15 per person. ❷

Hebron House, 59 Queens Parade (☎9146 3126). Marble fireplaces in the sitting area, sunny bedrooms with outstanding views, and a full-course dinner for £10. Complimentary coffee and tea served in front. Singles £30; doubles £40-45. ❸

Bethany House, 58 Queens Parade (☎9145 7733). Owned by the same friendly family as Hebron. Singles £30; doubles £40, £45 with sea view. ❸

Pierview, 28 Seacliff (☎9146 3381). An economical choice; the family room in front is lovely. Singles £18; doubles £40. ❷

FOOD AND PUBS

Like any great resort town, Bangor has no shortage of places to eat. Every third shop on Main St. has baked goods and sandwiches, and every pub in town serves grub. Pubs and clubs gather along High St. and the waterfront.

Piccola Pizzeria, 3 High St. (☎9145 3098). Kebabs, burgers, and the town's best take-away pizza for £2.90-4.70. Open daily 4:30pm-late. ❷

The Diner Cafe, 8 Dufferin Ave. (☎9146 4586). Provides filling, inexpensive food. All-day breakfast £2. Open M-Sa 8am-5:30pm, Su 10am-3:30pm. ❶

Brazilia Cafe, Bridge St. (☎9127 2763). Colorful decor reflects the Irish love for all things Brazilian, while the menu reflects their love for all things on baguette. Sandwiches £2.80-4.60. Open 9am-4:30pm. ❷

Ramsteins, 28 Dufferin Ave. (☎9147 4135). The newest addition to Bangor's lineup of culinary teases. Draws raves from locals for its diverse menu, vegetarian options, and inexpensive prices. Open Tu-Su 9am-8pm, Su 9am-noon. ❷

Wolseys, 24 High St. (☎9146 0495). Regulars enjoy cheap food in blue velvet snugs during the day, while nights take on a livelier character. Pub Quiz on M reminds the crowd why alcohol and testing don't mix. Meals £5-6. £3 cover F-Sa. Disco F-Sa. ❷

Bar Mocha, 18-20 Quay St. (☎9145 1100), on a little alley off Quay. Difficult to find but worth the search. 21+ age requirement generates a 25-35 crowd. £3 cover F-Sa. Open W-Sa, 8pm-late.

Jenny Watts, 41 High St. (☎9127 0401). Draws an older crowd, except during Su jazz. Low-ceilinged underpass leading to rear feels like the cave for which Jenny is famous (see **Jenny Did Watt?!,** below). Upstairs DJs spin at the 23+ club F-Sa from 10pm-1am. Cover £2. Bar open M 11:30am-11pm, Tu-Sa 11:30am-1am, Su 12:30pm-12am.

NORTHERN IRELAND

SIGHTS AND ACTIVITIES

North Down Visitors and Heritage Centre, adjoining Town Hall on Castle Park, is on the grounds where there once stood the castle of the Hamilton family, who, for a short time, owned all the land around Bangor. (☎9127 1200. Open July-Aug. Tu-Sa 10:30am-5:30pm, Su 2-5:30pm; Sept.-June Tu-Sa 10:30am-4:30pm, Su 2-4:30pm. Free.) The rest of the Hamilton Estate consists of 129 sometimes-wooded, sometimes-grassy acres that now comprise the public **Castle Park.** Nearby, 37-acre **Ward Park,** up Castle St. or Hamilton Rd. from Main St., entices with tennis courts, bowling greens, a cricket pitch, a pitch-and-putt, and a string of lakes harboring a wildlife sanctuary. (☎9145 7177 and 9145 8773. Tennis courts £3.80 per hr.; rackets £1.50. Bowls £4.55; children, students, and seniors £2.95. Pitch-and-putt £1.85/£1.10.) The **North Down**

JENNY DID WATT? An aura of mystery surrounds Jenny Watt, no matter which of the countless variations of her story is told. Inside Bangor's Jenny Watt's pub (see **Food and Pubs,** above), a banner dedicated to her life testifies to this confusion, posing questions that seek the truth about her dashing existence. But the basic consensus is as follows: she was a smuggler of tobacco, arms, and most everything else prior to the 1798 Rebellion. She was also famous for defying the genteel rules of her landed English aristocracy, both in her commercial dealings and in her love life. She fell for a man named Conn, who was the handsome young Chief of Conlig. Both her romantic and financial exploits eventually demanded that she avoid being seen, and to this end she hid in a Silurian fissure (on the coastal walk of Bangor) that now bears her name. However, some rumors claim that it was more than just a fissure: it was a series of caves connecting Bangor Abbey, Springhilt, Conlig, Little Glandeboye, and The Primacy. Such a cave undoubtedly would have contributed to the success of her smuggling operations and the length of her scandalous betrothal to Conn. Her luck eventually ran out, though—the tragic heroine drowned trying to save her lover at Brompton, who was fleeing from English soldiers.

GRACE NEILL'S PUB AND BISTRO

To say there are a lot of pubs in Ireland would be a pitiful understatement. It's no false stereotype that pints are the life-blood of many an Irish village, town, and city. Because there are so many, though, it can sometimes be tricky to weed out the good from the bad, and to make worthwhile distinctions between the often similar establishments. But Grace Neill's Pub and Bistro in Donaghadee stands out from the crowd as the **oldest pub in Ireland,** at least according to the *Guinness Book of World Records*. Originally opened as "The King's Arms" in 1611, and renamed for a former landlady just last century, Grace Neill's has allegedly catered to the likes of Peter the Great and Oliver Cromwell during its 390-year lifespan.

Luckily, a world-class chef keeps the award-winning menu in pace with the times—with nightly specialties ranging from Thai to Italian dishes—while still offering up more traditional Irish fare. Of course, it will cost you to dine amidst history: while the "pub" aspect of Grace Neill's may only set you back £3.30 for a pint, the "bistro" asks £21 for its tasty yet steep prix-fixe meal. Tempting treats include local artichoke soup, risotto of chorizo and squid, and baked mango and white chocolate cheesecake. The prices might be a lot to stomach, but think of the bragging rights!

Grace Neill's Bistro, 33 High St., Donaghadee (☎9188 4595; www.graceneills.co.uk).

Coastal Path forays 15 mi. along the bay's edge from Holywood through Bangor and Groomsport to Orlock Point. Along the way lie abandoned World War II lookouts, Helen's Bay (a popular bathing spot), Crawfordsburn Country Park, **Greypoint Fort** (an old fort with a massive gun), and a giant redwood. Bikes are not allowed on the path. The region is recognized for its colonies of black guillemots, more widely known as the Bangor penguins.

The path also passes through the picturesque village of Crawfordsburn, 3 mi. from Bangor and home to Ireland's oldest hotel. **The Old Inn,** Main St., dates from 1614 and maintains many of its original wood decorations. The Inn has been visited by celebrities ranging from Peter the Great of Russia to C.S. Lewis, and, more importantly, serves affordable food in its **Parlour Bar** (☎9185 3255; food served M-Sa noon-7pm, Su noon-9pm). The **Crawfordsburn Country Park,** off B20 (A2) at Helen's Bay, offers coastal paths, forests, and a waterfall. If you're walking, turn onto the easily missed footpath just before the Texaco station. (Park open Apr.-Sept. 9am-8pm; Oct.-Mar. 9am-4:45pm.) Inside the park, the **Visitors Centre** provides info on the area's natural history and trails. (☎9185 3621. Open M-Sa 9am-5pm, Sa-Su 10am-5pm.) The Bangor **bus** and **train** both run through Crawfordsburn.

Bangor claims to be the **festival** capital of Northern Ireland, hosting many events throughout the year, including the **Bangor Traditional Sail** in August, when old Irish fishing boats display their aged hulls. Later in the month, the **Wild August Bank Holiday Weekend** sweeps through town—£15 gains you access to foam machines, trapeze artists, and lots of DJs. In September, crowds gather for **Aspects,** one of Ireland's premier literary festivals. Seamus Heaney has been known to make an appearance. Contact the tourist office for details.

ARDS PENINSULA

The Ards Peninsula is bounded on the west by tranquil Strangford Lough; to its east lies the agitated Irish Sea. The shore of the lough from Newtownards to Portaferry is crowded with wildlife preserves, historic houses, crumbling ruins, and spectacular lake views. On the Irish Sea side of the Ards, each fishing village seems tinier and twice as nice as the one before.

Ulsterbus leaves Laganside Station in **Belfast** to traverse the peninsula, stopping in almost every town. **Trains** roll no farther than Bangor. From the south, a **ferry** crosses frequently between Strangford and Portaferry (see p. 494). **Biking** is another fairly painless way to see the Ards Peninsula.

DONAGHADEE (DOMHNACH DAOI)

The fishing villages along the coast south of Bangor consist of little more than one harbor and a few pubs apiece. The largest is Donaghadee (don-uh-guh-DEE), famous for its lifeboat and lighthouse. The musically inclined might be interested to learn that composer Franz Liszt spent three days here waiting for a ship to bring him to England.

A well-spent morning in Donaghadee would include a stroll along the marina to the first electrical (and still-operational) **lighthouse** in Ireland. Past the lighthouse, the town commons spread along the shore. At the other end of town, an old ruined *motte* (MOTE), with a romantic Disney-esque feel, towers above the village on Donaghadee's single hill. With a dearth of fair maidens in the area, the castle's most recent occupant was a 200 lb. block of ammunition, used to blast stone from the hill to build the harbor. Down at **Lemon's Wharf** is the spruced-up and well-loved **RNLB Sir Samuel Kelly.** In 1953, the *Samuel Kelly* rescued scores of passengers when the *Princess Victoria* sank offshore on its way to Scotland. Quinton Nelson at the marina skips passengers out to the **Copeland Islands,** a wildlife sanctuary just offshore. He also takes anglers out **deep-sea fishing.** (☎9188 3403. June-Sept.; fishing 10:30am-12:30pm, 7:30-9:30pm; £7, children £5; pleasure boating 2-5pm; £5/£2.50.)

Ulsterbus drives to Donaghadee via Groomsport from Bangor (23min.; M-F 19 per day, Sa 15 per day, Su 5 per day; £1.80) and Belfast (1hr.; M-F 19 per day, Sa 15 per day, Su 9 per day; £2.80). On High St. there is a **Northern Bank** with a 24hr. **ATM.** (Open M-F 10am-12:30pm and 1:30-3:30pm, M until 5pm.) Nearby is a **post office** (☎9188 2437; open M-Tu and Th-F 9am-12:30pm and 1:30-5:30pm, W 9am-1pm, Sa 9am-12:30pm). The **Donaghadee Health Centre,** 5 Killaughey Rd., is off High St. by the library. (☎9127 5511. Open daily 8:30am-1pm and 2-6pm.)

A handful of pubs and eateries are scattered along High St. and along the waterfront. One of the more notable gourmet options include **Pier 36 ❹,** located near the lighthouse. The restaurant won Guinness's seal of approval as Irish Seafood Bar of the Year in 2000, but veggies and land-lubbers need not fear—alternatives to tuna are also available. (☎9188 4466. Lunch 11:30am-2:30pm; dinner 7-11pm. Live music W and F.) For lighter and cheaper snacks, try **Robin's Nest ❶,** 16 New St., for panini (£3.50) and homebaked muffins. (☎9188 3177. Open Th-Tu 9am-8pm, W 9am-6pm.) **Kan Inn ❷,** 10 Bridge St., has Chinese takeaway. (☎9188 8863. Open W-M 5pm-midnight.)

South of Donaghadee, gnat-sized fishing villages buzz along the eastern shoreline. **Millisle, Ballywalter, Ballyhalbert, Portavogie, Cloughey,** and **Kearney** make good stops on an afternoon's drive, but none merits a special visit. **Portavogie** is famous for its prawns, and **Millisle** is home to the **Ballycopeland Windmill.** A2 runs the length of the shore, where hitching is reportedly easy, but *Let's Go* doesn't recommend it.

MOUNTSTEWART AND GREYABBEY

Fifteen miles southeast of Belfast on A20, roving pheasants greet you at **Mountstewart House and Gardens.** To reach Mountstewart from Belfast, take the Portaferry **bus** from Laganside Station and ask the driver to let you off at Mount Stewart (1hr.; M-F 16 per day, Sa 14 per day, Su 4 per day; £2.60). Held by a string of Marquesses of Londonderry, both house and garden are now National Trust property. They are worth a detour to see a striking contrast to the plebeian homes at the Ulster Folk Museum (see p. 486). Many of the trappings of the stately 18th-century **Mountstewart House** are faded and tattered, but the regal portraits, gilded ceilings, chandeliers, and china still manage to give the place an air of grandeur. The 22 chairs in the formal dining room held the arses of Europe's greatest diplomats at the 1814 Congress of Vienna, during the divvying-up of the post-Napoleonic continent. Lady Edith Londonderry had each seat embroidered with the coat of arms of its occupant and his country. (☎4278 8387. Open June-Aug. daily noon-6pm; May and Sept. W-M, including bank holidays, noon-6pm; Mar.-Apr. Sa-Su and bank holidays noon-6pm; and Oct. Sa-Su noon-6pm. Tours every 30min.; first tour at noon, last tour 5pm. House, garden, and temple £4.75.)

Mountstewart's **gardens,** covering 85 acres, are a more enticing attraction than the house itself; they are currently nominated as a UNESCO World Heritage Site. The estate comprises seven gardens and several woodsy walks, all designed by Lady Edith herself. Taking advantage of Ireland's temperate climate, Lady Edith imported flowers, trees, and shrubs from as far as Australia. Her **Dodo Terrace** contains a menagerie of animal statues representing the members of her upper-crusty social group, the Ark Club. The elite critters include Winston "the Warlock" Churchill and Nelson "the Devil" Chamberlain. The **Shamrock Garden,** whose name belies its shape, contains a Red Hand of Ulster made of begonias, and a topiary Irish Harp. An afternoon could easily be spent strolling through the gardens; ambitious ramblers, however, may explore the surrounding estate on one of the longer walks, such as the Lake Walk, Rock Walk, or Rhododendron Hill. The gardens also host the **Summer Garden Jazz Series** on the last Sunday of each month from April through September. (Open Mar.-Apr. daily 10am-6pm, May-Sept. 10am-8pm, Oct.-Feb. 10am-4pm. Garden £3.75, children £2, families £8.50.) Based on The Tor of the Winds in Athens, the **Temple of the Winds,** used by Mountstewart's inhabitants for "frivolity and jollity," sits atop a hill with a super view of Strangford Lough. To reach the temple from Mountstewart House, turn left on the main road and go about ¼ mi. (Open Apr.-Oct. Sa-Su and bank holidays 2-5pm.)

A few miles down from Mountstewart lies the town of **Greyabbey,** famous for its ruined Cistercian abbey. Founded in AD 1193 by Affreca, wife to Norman conqueror John de Courcey, the abbey was the first fully Gothic building in Ireland. The beautiful ruins have an adjoining cemetery and a medieval monastic "physick" garden, where healing plants were cultivated. (☎9054 3033. Open Apr.-Sept. Tu-Sa 10am-7pm, Su 2-4pm; Oct.-Mar. Sa 10am-4pm, Su 2-4pm. £1, children 50p.) After a hard day of touring, abandon the ascetic life and have a pint in Greyabbey's **Wildfowler Inn,** 1-3 Main St. (☎4278 8260). You can set your watch by the locals' comings and goings, and £6 buys you more than you can eat.

PORTAFERRY (PORT AN PHEIRE) ☎028

Portaferry lies on the southern tip of the Ards Peninsula and peers at Strangford town across the churning waters of Strangford Lough. Tourists stop in this beautiful seaside town to relax and check out its aquatic offerings, including Northern Ireland's largest aquarium. In addition, Portaferry's excellent hostel and pubs make it a base for daytrips into Strangford and the southernmost Ards villages.

TRANSPORTATION. To reach Strangford Lough from the bus stop, follow either **Ferry St.** or **Castle St.** downhill for about 100m. **Ulsterbuses** from Belfast drop off visitors at **The Square** in the center of town. (1½hr.; M-F 19 per day, Sa 16 per day, Su 9 per day; £4.50.) **Ferries** leave Portaferry's waterfront at 15 and 45min. past the hour for a 10min. chug to Strangford, returning on the hour and half-hour. (☎4488 1637. £1, seniors and children 50p, car and driver £4.20.)

PRACTICAL INFORMATION. To reach the Portaferry **tourist office** from the bus stop, take **Castle St.** toward the lough. The tourist office is on the corner of Castle St. and **The Strand.** In addtion to the usual plethora of brochures and a **bureau de change,** it also has a 12min. video on the medieval "tower houses" of Co. Down. (☎4272 9882. Open July-Aug. M-Sa 10am-5:30pm, Su 1-6pm; Easter-June and Sept. M-Sa 10am-5pm, Su 2-6pm.) The **Portaferry Health Centre,** 44 High St., is on the north side of town. (☎4272 8429. Open M-F 8:30am-6pm.) Near the bus station you'll find **Northern Bank,** The Square (☎4272 8208; open M 10am-5pm, Tu-W and F 10am-3:30pm, Th 9:30am-3:30pm; closed daily 12:30-1:30pm; 24hr. **ATM**), and the **post office,** 28 The Square (☎4272 8201; open M-W and F 9am-1pm and 2-5:30pm, Th 9am-1pm, Sa 9am-12:30pm). The **postal code** is BT22.

ACCOMMODATIONS, FOOD, AND PUBS. A peaceful stay awaits at the **Portaferry Barholm Youth Hostel ❶,** 11 The Strand, across from the ferry dock. Defying hostel stereotypes, Barholm is supremely accommodating and ideally located right on Strangford Lough, with single and double bedrooms, semi-private bathrooms, a greenhouse-like dining room, and great views. Because the hostel often hosts groups, weekend reservations are necessary. (☎4272 9598. Laundry £3. Wheelchair-accessible. Apr.-Sept. £11.50 per person; Oct.-Mar. £10.) If you want to stay closer to the pubs, you can't do better than the **Fiddler's Green B&B ❸,** located above the pub on Church St. (☎4272 8393. Singles £25, with bath £30; doubles £44/£54). A third option is **Adair's B&B ❷,** 22 The Square (☎4272 8412; £17 per person).

For a quick bite, **Ferry Grill ❶,** on High St. across from Spar Market, stays open until 1am on weekends and serves various burger-and-fries configurations. (☎4272 8568; food less than £2.50.) For locally preferred fish and chips, head to **Joe's Hot Spot ❷,** 18 The Square, or just call them up—they deliver. (☎4272 8868. Fish and chips £3.20. Open M 5-11pm, Tu-Th 12:30-2pm and 5-11pm, F-Sa 12:30-2pm and 5pm-1am, Su 4:30-7:30pm.) For dinner, wander down to the **Cornstore ❷,** Castle St., just before Exploris and the Portaferry castle. Well-cooked seafood, traditional plates, and a wealth of vegetarian options (peppers filled with BBQ risotto and mozzarella, £5.25) are served here between the yellow and salmon walls. (☎4272 9000. Open daily noon-9pm.) For homemade muffins and hot soup, duck into **The Shambles Coffee Shop ❶,** 3 Castle St., through the crafts shop. (☎4272 9675. Open M-F 10am-5pm, Sa-Su 10am-6pm.) There are also numerous fresh fruit and veggie **markets** and convenience stores scattered around High St. and The Square. Every Saturday from Easter through the end of September, the Market House in The Square welcomes a **country market** (10am-1pm).

At night, everyone stumbles to the **Fiddler's Green,** Church St., where publican Frank and his sons lead rowdy sing-alongs, encouraging musicians to join in the festivities. The amazingly friendly atmosphere stands testament to their plaque: "There are no strangers here. Just friends who have not yet met." (Open M-Sa 11:30am-11pm, Su noon-10pm.) Across the street, John Wayne memorabilia decks the walls of **The Quiet Man.** On weekends, the pub plays music ranging from disco to live bands, while weeknight patrons amuse themselves with occasional karaoke. (☎4272 9629. Open daily 11:30am-11pm; bar until 1am.) **M.E. Dumigan's,** Ferry St., is just up from the waterfront. This tiny pub is so crammed with locals that *craic* is guaranteed. (Open M-Sa 11:30am-midnight, Su 12:30pm-midnight.)

SIGHTS AND FESTIVALS. Portaferry's claim to fame is **Exploris,** Northern Ireland's only public aquarium and one of the UK's best. Located near the pier next to the ruins of **Portaferry Castle,** Exploris houses first-rate exhibits on local ocean and seashore ecology. Your journey begins in the shallow waters of Strangford Lough, proceeds through the Narrows, and ends in the depths of the Irish Sea, where the largest tank in Europe is home to a number of sharks and other large fish. The open tanks in the Aquarium's dimly lit corridors teem with everything from searays and nurse sharks to jellyfish and lumpsuckers; touch tank and interactive displays keep the kiddies occupied. Exploris also contains a seal sanctuary to welcome injured seals. (☎4272 8062. www.exploris.org.uk. Open Apr.-Aug. M-F

10am-6pm, Sa 11am-6pm, Su 1-6pm; Sept.-Mar. M-F 10am-5pm, Sa 11am-5pm, Su 1-5pm. £5.40, seniors and children £3.20, families £11-15, under 5 free.)

Another attraction in Portaferry is the **Seafood Festival** held in early September. After enjoying a massive town barbecue, crowds take to the streets for a weekend's fill of street theater, entertainment, and demonstrated cookery. Nightly live pub sessions keep the energy (and the eating) going. Book B&Bs well in advance. (For more info on the festival contact Mrs. Catherine Graham, ☎9045 2829.)

LECALE PENINSULA

Called by some "The Island of Lecale," the region spans the west coast of Strangford Lough from the village of Strangford to Downpatrick, then continues inland to Ballynahinch in the north and Dundrum in the west. It was once bound entirely by bodies of water, including the Irish Sea, Strangford Lough, and a series of streams and ponds. Industrialization passed Lecale by, even as it hit the surrounding areas of Co. Down, leaving the area culturally isolated. Today, agricultural production on its rolling green hills still supports the region, while beautiful parks, lavish estates, and St. Patrick-related sites/sightings draw visitors from afar.

STRANGFORD (BAILE LOCH CUAN)

This tiny harbor village lies just across the Lough from Portaferry, northeast of Downpatrick on A25 and north of Ardglass on A2. Strangford has limited accommodations; its tourist appeal lies in its proximity to the **Castle Ward House and Estate.** To get to the estate by car or bus (request to be dropped off there) from Strangford, take A25 toward Downpatrick. The entrance to the grounds is about 2 mi. up the road on the right (£3 per car). Pedestrians seeking a safe and pleasant shortcut should take the **Loughside Walk** (see below). This 18th-century estate, once owned by Lady Anne and Lord Bangor and now the property of the National Trust, lies atop a verdant hill with a spectacular view of the Lough. One wing of the house, built in 1768, is classical, which satisfied Lord Bangor; the other is Gothic, to suit Lady Anne's fancy. Alas, even exorbitant compromise was not enough, and they split up soon after the house was built. The 700-acre estate features a rectangular lake, a tower house, a restored corn mill, and a "Victorian Pastimes Centre" for children. Throughout the summer, the **Castle Ward Opera** (☎9066 1090) performs here. (☎4488 1204. House open July-Aug. daily noon-6pm; Mar.-Apr. Sa-Su noon-6pm; May M and W-F 1-6pm, Sa-Su noon-6pm; June daily 1-6pm. Last tours leave at 5pm. £4.70. Grounds open year-round dawn to dusk. £3 per person.)

The **Strangford Lough Wildlife Centre** is located on the estate and provides information on the natural environment of the lough, as well as fun with microscopes. If you are walking, follow A25 past the causeway and take an immediate sharp right, which brings you to the entrance to the Castle Ward Caravan Park (see below). Follow the driveway to the right fork and go through the brown gate on your right. This takes you to the **Loughside Walk,** a 30min. stroll along the coastline to the Centre. Watch your step, or risk stepping on one of the many birds scuttling across the path. (☎4488 1411. Open May M and W-Su noon-6pm; June-Sept. daily noon-6pm; Apr. and Oct. Sa-Su noon-6pm.)

Back in town, a small 16th-century tower house optimistically called **Strangford Castle** stands to the right of the ferry dock as you disembark. Wander into its dark, spooky interior and find a humbling view from the third floor. (Gate key available from Mr. Seed, 39 Castle St., across from the tower house's gate, daily 10am-7pm.)

Buses to **Downpatrick** leave from The Square (25min.; M-F 10 per day, Sa 5 per day; £2.20). **Ferries** leave for **Portaferry** every 30min. (M-F 7:30am-10:30pm, Sa 8am-11pm, Su 9:30am-10:30pm; £1, cars £4.80.) The **Castle Ward Caravan Park** ❶ lies on the Castle Ward National Trust property, off the road to Downpatrick. (☎4488 1680. Open mid-Mar. to Sept. £5 per small tent. Free showers.) At the cozy old **Cuan Bar and Restaurant ❹**, The Square, enjoy a warm welcome, quality pub grub, and a room-temperature Guinness. (☎4488 1222. Broccoli & walnut lasagna £6.25, 2-course meal £16. Open M-Sa noon-9:30pm, Su noon-9pm. Live music on weekends.) The Cuan pulls triple duty as the **Cuan B&B ❹**. (All rooms with bath and TV. Singles £35-40; doubles £60-70.)

DOWNPATRICK (DÚN PÁDRAIG)

Rumored to be the burial place of St. Paddy himself, Downpatrick is the county's administrative center and capital. Though nights here can be slow, by day the town's streets are filled with shoppers, school children, and heavy traffic, as young and old alike flock to town from nearby villages to do a day's shopping or learning. The surrounding countryside, peppered with St. Patrick-related religious and archaeological sites, is best seen in a daytrip by car or bike.

NORTHERN IRELAND

TRANSPORTATION

Buses: 83 Market St. (☎4461 2384). To: **Belfast** (1hr.; M-F 30 per day, Sa 12 per day, Su 6 per day; £3.90); **Newcastle** (30min.; M-F 21 per day, Sa 12 per day, Su 5 per day; £2.50); **Strangford** (25min.; M-F 9 per day, Sa 5 per day; £2.20).

Taxis: Downpatrick Taxis, 96 Market St. (☎4461 4515), runs early to late.

Bicycles: Down Discount Cycles, 45b Church St. (☎4461 4990), next to the Texaco station. Rentals £5 per day. Open M-Sa 9:30am-5:30pm.

ORIENTATION AND PRACTICAL INFORMATION

Market St., the town's main street, is flanked by the bus station at one end and connections to other significant streets at the other. From the station, the first right is **St. Patrick's Ave.** Farther on, Market St. meets **Irish St.** on the right and **English St.** on the left, spelling out the town's geopolitical divide. Market St. becomes **Church St.** and continues straight ahead. **Scotch St.** lies between Church St. and Irish St.

Tourist Office: 53a Market St. (☎4461 2233), in the **Heritage Centre.** Open July-Aug. M-Sa 9:30am-6pm, Su 2-6pm; Sept.-June M-Sa 10am-5pm.

Banks: Northern Bank, 58-60 Market St. (☎4461 4011). Open M 9:30am-5pm, Tu-F 10am-3:30pm. **Bank of Ireland,** 80-82 Market St. (☎4461 2911). Open M-Tu and Th-F 9:30am-4:30pm, W 10am-4:30pm. Both have 24hr. **ATMs.**

Laundry: Crawford's Dry Cleaners, 16 St. Patrick's Ave. (☎4461 2284). £5-6 per load. Open M-Sa 9am-5:30pm.

Pharmacy: Foy's Chemist, 16 Irish St. (☎4461 2032). Open M-F 9am-1pm, 2-5:30pm. **Deeny Pharmacy,** 30a St. Patrick's Ave. (☎4461 3807). Open M-Sa 9am-5:30pm.

Emergency: ☎999; no coins required. **Police:** Irish St. (☎4461 5011).

Hospital: Downe Hospital (☎4461 3311).

Internet Access: e-Learn Shop, 102 Market St. (☎4461 1500), across from the bus stop. £1 per hr. Open M and W 9am-9pm, Tu and Th-F 9am-5pm, and Sa 10am-1pm. **Downpatrick Library,** 79 Market St. (☎4461 2895), next to the bus stop. Internet £1.50 per 30min. Open M-Tu and Th 10am-8pm, W and F-Sa 10am-5pm.

Post Office: 65 Market St. (☎4461 2061), inside the SuperValu shopping center. Open M-F 9am-5:30pm, Sa 9am-5pm. **Postal code:** BT30.

ACCOMMODATIONS

With pricey B&Bs, often located on the outskirts of town, visitors to Downpatrick usually stay at one of Portaferry or Newcastle's hostels, or the caravan parks near Strangford. The closest campground is **Castle Ward,** near Strangford (see p. 496).

Dunleath House, 33 St. Patrick's Dr. (☎4461 3221). Turn off Market St. onto St. Patrick's Ave., take the first right onto St. Patrick's Dr., then left onto Mourne View Ct. Luxurious, with a superbly hospitable proprietress. Singles £24; doubles £40. ❸

Hillside B&B, 62 Scotch St. (☎4461 3134). Follow Market St. to its end and turn right after the Arts Centre. Comfortable rooms, convenient location, and relatively low prices await you at this large B&B. Singles £17, without bath £16; doubles £35/£32. ❷

Denvir's Hotel, 14-16 English St. (☎4461 2012). Has slept the likes of Jonathan Swift and Daniel Day Lewis. Breakfast included. Singles £30; doubles £50. ❸

FOOD AND PUBS

Downpatrick's eateries surpass those of many nearby towns in both quality and quantity. For picnic food from mom-and-pop shops, try the deli in **Hanlon's Fruit and Veg,** 26 Market St. (☎4461 2129. Open M-Sa 8am-5:45pm), or the supermarkets surrounding the bus station.

Daily Grind Coffee Shop, 21a St. Patrick's Ave. (☎4461 5949). Selection of tasty sandwiches (£2-3), salads (£3-4), and rich desserts (£2), served in a cheery yellow and blue cafe. Open M-Sa 10am-5pm. ❶

Abbey Cafe, 36 Market St. (☎4461 3039). Inexpensive lunches and themed breakfasts, such as the Abbey Belly-Buster (£5), help fill you for the day. Vegetarian options also available. Open M-Sa 9:30am-5:30pm. ❷

Oakley Fayre's, 52 Market St. (☎4461 2500). Full meals in a diner-esque seating area behind a bakery. Lasagna or cottage pie for just £4. Open M-Sa 9am-5:15pm. ❷

Denvir's Restaurant and Pub, 14 English St. (☎4461 2012). More substantial food at a more substantial price. Pub dates from 1642. United Irishmen fighting for Home Rule in the 1768 rebellion met here as a literary society (see p. 59). Restaurant serves pub food, and the pub hosts live music Th and Sa. Lunch (£3-5) served M-Sa noon-2:30pm. Dinner (£5-9) served M-Th and Su 7-8pm, F-Sa 7-9pm. ❸

Mullans Pub, 48 Church St. (☎4461 2227). A little out of the way, but trad on Su (5-9pm) and good *craic* on weekends justify the walk. Open daily noon-11pm.

Maginty's, 7 Church St. (☎4461 4170). Claims that a double-cooled tap makes its Guinness the best in town. The ghost of Tom Russell, one of the leaders of the 1803 Presbyterian rebellion for Home Rule, continues to haunt the place. Open M-W 11:30am-11pm, Th-Su 11:30am-12:30am.

SIGHTS AND ACTIVITIES

The state-of-the-art **Saint Patrick Center,** 53a Market St., tells you everything you always wanted to know about Ireland's patron saint but were afraid to ask. An interactive biographical tour takes you from St. P's early capture by Irish pirates up through his later teachings and enduring legacy. A rooftop garden, craft shop, and art gallery also await you, as does the local **tourist office.** (☎4461 9000. Open June-Aug. M-Sa 9:30am-6pm, Su 1-6pm; Apr.-May and Sept. M-Sa 9:30am-5:30pm, Su 1-5:30pm; Oct.-Mar. M-Sa 10am-5pm. Last admission 1hr. before closing. Exhibit £4.50, students and seniors £3, children £2.25. Garden and art gallery free.)

Down County Museum and Heritage Centre, at the end of English St., offers effusive regional history. Housed in the jail where Thomas Russell was hanged, the museum introduces you to Co. Down, St. Patrick, and a wax gang of 19th-century prisoners. Once you've caught up on your history, visit the courtyard for a game of gigantic chess or checkers. (☎4461 5218. Open M-F 10am-5pm, Sa-Su 1-5pm.) Beside the museum is the Church of Ireland **Down Cathedral** (☎4461 4922). A Celtic monastery until the 12th century, the cathedral went Benedictine under the Norman conqueror John de Courcey and later fell into ruin. Rebuilt in 1818, the present cathedral incorporates stone carvings from its medieval predecessor and houses the only private pew boxes still in use in Ireland. The entrance to the church proudly proclaims that it represents 1500 years of Christianity, beginning with St. Patrick's settlement in nearby Saul (see below). In the graveyard, a stone commemorates the **grave of St. Patrick;** he is joined by the remains of **St. Brigid** and **St. Colmcille** (a.k.a. St. Columba). Though it is uncertain whether the gravestone marks the correct site, it does bring visitors to a beautiful view of the city.

A similar view is afforded atop the **Mound of Down,** on the outskirts of town. This Bronze Age hill fort was once known as Dunlethglaise, or "fort on the green hill." Later, in the Iron Age, an early Christian town flourished on the mound until Anglo-Norman invaders under John de Courcey defeated the Irish chief MacDunleavy and his troops. Today, visitors will be hard-pressed to find signs of the fort or the city, but the green hill remains a lovely spot for a walk. For anyone who prefera watching others exert energy, a number of sporting events take place in and around Downpatrick. In town, you can occasionally catch **Gaelic** or **soccer matches** at Dunleath Park, just past the bus stop on Market St. And at the **Downpatrick Race Course** (☎4483 9630), a 1½ mi. down A25 toward Newcastle, crowds are drawn by the excitement of the races and the course's 300 year history.

NORTHERN IRELAND

DAYTRIPS FROM DOWNPATRICK

SAUL AND THE STRUELL WELLS

Follow the signs on the Saul road for 2 mi. past Downpatrick to reach Saul Church, on the site where St. Patrick is believed to have landed in the 5th century. The bus to Raholp stops there on request. Church (☎4461 4922) open daily until 5pm. Su services 10am.

Co. Down reveres anything touched by St. Patrick's sweet, sweet hands; **Saul** may be the most beloved sight of all. After being converted to Christianity, local chieftain Dichu gave Patrick the barn (*sabhal*) that later became the first parish church in Ireland. Replicas of an early Christian church and round tower commemorate Big Paddy's arrival from Scotland. A little over a mile further down Saul Rd., on the summit of Slieve Patrick, stands **St. Patrick's Shrine.** The monument consists of a huge granite statue of St. Patrick, bronze panels depicting his life, and an open-air temple. Even nonbelievers will appreciate the 360° view of the lough, the mountains, and, on a clear day, the Isle of Man. At the **Struell Wells,** southeast of Downpatrick on the Ardglass road (B1), water runs through underground channels from one well to the next, until it reaches 200-year-old bath houses. Belief in their curative powers originated long before Christianity arrived on the scene.

INCH ABBEY AND THE QUOILE PONDAGE NATURE RESERVE

The Abbey ruins lie just over 1 mi. from Downpatrick on the Belfast road (A7). The bus to Belfast will stop at nearby Abbey Lodge Hotel on request. The Nature Reserve is 1 mi. from Downpatrick off Strangford Rd. ☎4461 5520. Open Apr.-Aug. daily 11am-5pm; Sept.-Mar. Sa-Su 1-5pm.

The **Cistercian Inch Abbey,** the earliest standing Gothic ruin in Ireland, was founded in 1180 by the Norman conqueror John de Courcey to make up for his destruction of the Eneragh monastery a few years earlier. The Abbey, which was closed off to Irishmen for some 400 years until it closed in 1541, is near the marshes of the River Quoile. Though low foundation walls are all that remain, the Abbey's enchanting grounds, which are always open, make for an excellent picnic site. The **Quoile Pondage Nature Reserve** offers hiking and bird-watching around a manmade pond created in 1957 when a tidal barrier was erected to prevent the flooding of Downpatrick. The barrier has brought an unusual assortment of vegetation, fish, and insects to the area. The **Quoile Countryside Centre** provides a surplus of information.

NEWCASTLE (AN CAISLEÁN NUA)

The numerous arcades, joke shops, and waterslide parks of Newcastle's main drag stand in dramatic contrast to the majestic Mourne Mountains rising from the south end of town. On weekends, packs of kids prowl the streets in search of fun, while July and August bring the rest of the family to sunbathe on the beach. With its hostel and numerous B&Bs, Newcastle is often used by travelers as an inexpensive base from which to explore the nearby parks and the Mourne Mountains.

TRANSPORTATION

Buses: Ulsterbus, 5-7 Railway St. (☎4372 2296), at the end of Main St. farther away from the mountains. To: **Belfast** (80min.; M-F 19 per day, Sa 17 per day, Su 10 per day; £5); **Downpatrick** (40min.; M-F 15 per day, Sa 10 per day, Su 5 per day; £2.50); **Dublin** (3hr.; M-Sa 4 per day, Su 2 per day; £10.31); **Newry** (2hr.; M-F 12 per day, Sa 7per day, Su 2 per day; £5.40).

Taxi: Donard Cabs (☎4372 4100 or 4372 2823); **Shimna Taxis** (☎4372 6030).

Bike Rental: Wiki Wiki Wheels, 10b Donard St. (☎4372 3973), beside the Xtra-Vision building (left from the bus station). £10 per day, £50 per wk.; children £5 per day; ID deposit. Open M-Th and Sa 9am-6pm, F 9am-8pm, Su 2-6pm.

ORIENTATION AND PRACTICAL INFORMATION

Newcastle's main road runs parallel to the waterfront; initially called **Main St.** (where it intersects with **Railway St.**), its name subsequently changes to **Central Promenade** and then to **South Promenade** as it approaches the Mournes.

Tourist Office: 10-14 Central Promenade (☎4372 2222), 10min. down the main street from the bus station. Free map and visitor's guide. Mildly frustrating 24hr. touch-screen computer in front provides basic information about traveling in Northern Ireland. Open July-Aug. M-Sa 9:30am-7pm, Su 1-7pm; June and Sept. M-Sa 10am-5pm, Su 2-6pm.

Banks: First Trust Bank, 28-32 Main St. (☎4372 3476). Open M-F 9:30am-4:30pm, W open 10am. **Ulster Bank,** 115-117 Main St. (☎4372 3276). Open M-F 9:30am-4:30pm. Both have 24hr. **ATMs.**

Camping Equipment: Hill Trekker, 115 Central Promenade (☎4372 3842). Mourne trail maps, hiking tips, info on guided tours, and boot rentals (£1.50 per day; deposit £10). Open Tu-Su 10am-5:30pm.

Pharmacy: Gordon's, Railway St. (☎4372 2724). Open M-F 9am-6pm, Sa 9:30am-5pm. **Thornton's,** 49 Central Promenade (☎4372 3248). Open M-Sa 9am-6pm.

Work Opportunities: Anchor Bar (see **Hidden Deal**) will hire international waitstaff and bartenders willing to work for a minimum of 2 months. No experience necessary. Pays approximately £5 per hr. Call ☎4372 3344 for more info.

Emergency: ☎999. **Police:** South Promenade (☎4372 3583).

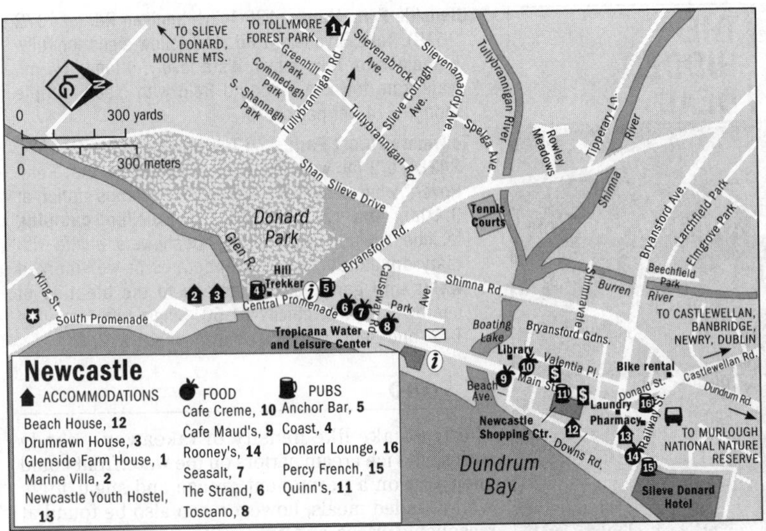

Internet Access: The **Anchor Bar** (see **Pubs,** below) has unlimited web access with purchase of a drink. If you've had drunk mailing experiences in the past that you don't care to repeat, use **Newcastle Library,** 141-143 Main St. (☎4372 2710), for £2 per hr.

Post Office: 33-35 Central Promenade (☎4372 2418). Open M-W and F 9am-12:30pm and 1:30-5:30pm, Th and Sa 9am-12:30pm. **Postal Code:** BT33.

ACCOMMODATIONS AND CAMPING

B&Bs crowd this seaside town like 13-year-old boys around a new arcade game. The tourist office will happily provide you with a list of them (the B&Bs, not the games). A lone hostel rounds out the accommodation portfolio; of the area's campsites, Tollymore Forest Park is probably the most scenic, but the Mournes themselves are a free and legal alternative.

Newcastle Youth Hostel (HINI), 30 Downs Rd. (☎4372 2133). Walking away from the bus stop, go left along Railway St. and take a right onto Downs Rd. at the Newcastle Arms. The central, waterfront location is about 45 seconds from the bus station, and though rooms are dim at night, big windows pull in the sun (when it's out). Large, well-furnished kitchen. Ask for a key if you plan to stay out late. Check-in 5-11:30pm. Lockers 50p. Laundry £2. Dorms £10, under 18 £9; 6-person family apartment £41. ❶

Marine Villa, 151 Central Promenade (☎4372 5030). Cozy B&B with elegant dining room and marvelous sea view. Slight distance (10min.) from busy shops and loud pubs of Main St. may be a perk. Singles £20, with bath £25; doubles £40. ❸

Beach House, 22 Downs Rd. (☎4372 2345). This B&B welcomes guests twice-over: from the smiling baker on the porch, to the acorns (symbolizing hospitality) intricately carved into the amazing staircase inside. The antique claw-foot bathtub uncovered by the discerning proprietress would cost thousands to purchase today. Singles June-Sept. £35; doubles £60. Oct.-May singles £30/£56. ❹

Drumrawn House, 139 Central Promenade (☎4372 6847), a few doors in from Marine Villa. A small Georgian townhouse with the same great sea view. £21.50 per person. ❸

THE ANCHOR BAR

Two fierce predators often eat away at the wallet of the typical budget traveler in Northern Ireland: the 'net and the pint. Internet access is the cheapest way to keep in touch, but it still commands a premium, while local pub-culture demands that visitors do as the locals do, which means doling out pounds to the blonde in the black skirt. But, at the Anchor Bar in Newcastle, one payment covers both costs: purchasing a pint (or glass, or even a cup of coffee) earns you *free* time online. How much time? How much do you want?–the friendly staff sets no limit, though courtesy calls for some restraint when others are waiting.

In addition to its fabulous drunk-emailing deals, Anchor has plenty of pints and past times to offer the patron less interested in surfing the web. The friendly bartenders and regulars alike watch football games on the huge flatscreen TV, while others engage in their own matches on the pool table. According to the young manager, the bar will soon be adding a beer garden out back. For even more of a great deal, stop by for a cheap, filling meal (£2-4) at the Anchor, served from noon to 7pm on weekdays, noon to 6pm on Saturday, and 2-7pm on Sundays.

The Anchor Bar. 9 Bryansford Rd., Newcastle (☎4372 3344). Open M-Sa 11:30am-12:30am, Su 2pm-midnight.

Glenside Farm House, 136 Tullybrannigan Rd. (☎4372 2628). Take Bryansford Rd. and follow signs for Tullybrannigan, or take a taxi; it's a lovely, if long, 1½ mi. walk from town. A standard B&B with clean, simple rooms. £14 per person. ❷

Tollymore Forest Park, 176 Tullybrannigan Rd. (☎4372 2428), a 2 mi. walk along A2 or 10min. on the "Rural Rover," which leaves the Newcastle Ulsterbus station at 9:10am and 12:25pm (£1.10). Excellent **camping** facilities include clean, piping hot showers, a cafe with tasty doughnuts, and 584 hectares of well-marked walks and gardens. Fall asleep to the bleating of nearby sheep. Electricity £1.50. Single tent May-June £12, and Sept. M-Th £8. Caravan space £12. ❷

FOOD

The fruitcake-like density of takeaways, candy stores, and ice cream parlors on the waterfront could keep you on a permanent grease and sugar high. Well-rounded meals, however, can also be found at reasonable prices, and two- or three-course set meals are often good values.

Seasalt, 51 Central Promenade (☎4372 5027). Local modern art fills this stylish (and delicious!) cafe. Create your dream panini from a wide selection of gourmet fillings (£3-4, served with salad), or go Epicurean with pate (£3.50) or local crab in spiced garlic butter (£6.50). On F-Sa nights, it transforms into a reservations-only 3-course bistro (£19.50) that must be experienced to be believed. Amenable to those with special dietary needs. Open Su-Tu 9am-6pm, W-Th 9am-10pm, F-Sa 9am-1am. Bistro begins 6pm. Closed M Sept.-May. ❷

Cafe Maud's, 106 Main St. (☎4372 6184). Order your large personal pizza (£4.95 with chips and drink), crepe (£2.50), or panini (£3) at the counter and enjoy it on the terrace overlooking the water. In the off-chance that it's rainy, lounge inside on a squishy couch while sipping coffee. Open M-Su 9am-9:30pm. ❷

Rooney's, corner of Railway St. and Downs Rd. (☎4372 3822). The chef's international experience infuses food with varied influences, from Australian to Thai. Seared shark (£11.50) and kangaroo loin (£13) tempt the adventuresome, while non-meat options delight vegetarians. Romantics should request table 105, which juts out from the 2nd floor, leaving lovers alone with the sea. Open Su-Th noon-9pm, F-Sa noon-10pm. ❹

Toscano, 47 Central Promenade (☎4372 2263). The front window of this upstairs restaurant spans the entire wall, offering an unobstructed ocean view. Meals range from standard fish and chips (£5) and individual pizzas (£5-7) to pricier entrees (steak £12). Fried-type food served 11am-11pm; pizza served after 6pm. ❸

Cafe Creme, 105 Main St. (☎4372 6589). Takes its coffee seriously, comparing it to Guinness, Chardonnay, and velvet pajamas. Contact the Coffee Police (www.coffeepolice.com) should your cup fall short of perfection. Coffee £0.85. Desserts £2. Open June-Aug. daily 8:30am-10pm; Sept.-May 8:30am-6pm. ❶

The Strand, 53-55 Central Promenade (☎4372 3472). Popular with locals, this bakery/restaurant serves filling dinners (£5-7), each with tea and a generous basket of scones. Open June-Aug. 8:30am-11pm; Sept.-May daily 9am-6pm. ❸

PUBS AND CLUBS

With a few exceptions, the pubs of Newcastle cater largely to the older set on all but karaoke night, when young thangs crowd in for their chance in the spotlight. Check signs in windows for karaoke nights so you know what to expect.

Quinn's, 62 Main St. (☎4372 6400). A 20s-style interior and an amorous young crowd. Cover bands F-Su. Open M-W 11:30am-12am, Th-Su 11:30am-1:30am.

Donard Lounge, Main St. (☎4372 2614), by the Donard Hotel. Karaoke is popular with 20-somethings Th night; an older crowd fills in other nights. Cover £2 after 11:30pm on Th. Open M-W 11:30am-11:30pm, Th-Sa 11:30am-1am, Su 12:30pm-12:30am.

Percy French (☎4372 3175), in the Slieve Donard Hotel where Railway meets the sea. Classier drinks and an older crowd. French was a popular Irish songwriter whose flowery lyrics still appeal to sentimentalists. Youngsters come for Tu karaoke. Cover bands F-Sa. Open M and W-Th 11:30am-11pm, Tu and F-Sa 11:30am-1am, Su 12:30-10pm.

Coast, 121 Central Promenade (☎4372 4100), behind O'Hare's Front Bar. The place to be F and Sa nights, Coast is the popular new kid on the clubbing block. Cover £5 after 11pm. Club open F (18+) and Sa (officially 21+) 10pm-1:30am Sept.-June, every night in July and Aug. Front Bar open daily 11:30am-1:30am.

SIGHTS AND ACTIVITIES

Hikers will find paradise in the majestic Mournes (see **Hiking: The Mourne Mountains,** below), while equestrians have a choice of beach or forest for riding. Three parks managed by the Department of Agriculture are just a hop, skip, and a jump from Newcastle. **Tullymore Forest Park** lies just 2 mi. west of town at 176 Tullybrannigan Rd. A magical entrance lined with gigantic, gnarled trees leads you toward ancient stone bridges, rushing waters, and well-marked trails. The **Shimna River** runs from east to west and cuts the park in half. From the four main trails, which range in length from 1 to 8 mi., hikers come across diverse wildlife including deer, foxes, badgers, and otters (if you're particularly quiet and well behaved.) The "Rivers Trail" hike (3 mi.) encompasses most of the park and is highly recommended, as is the hike (3½ mi.) to the viewpoint. (☎4372 2428. Open daily 10am-sunset. Adults £2.) The park is amply equipped with a campground (see **Accommodations,** p. 502), visitors center, cafe, and impressive outdoor arboretum. If you're not up for the rambling walk to Tollymore, take one of Ulsterbus's "Rural Rover" shuttles from the Newcastle bus station (15min., departs 9:10am and 12:25pm, £1.10).

Castlewellan Forest Park is spread over the hills just north and east of the Mournes. From the Newcastle bus station take Castlewellan Rd. into town, turn left on Main St. at the roundabout, and continue for 400m. The entrance is at the top of the main street in Castlewellan, and the campground is opposite the library. (☎4377 8664. Open daily 10am-sunset. £4 per car. Call M-F 9am-5pm for info and site booking. **Camping:** Single tent July-Aug. and Oct.-Apr. £10, May-June and Sept. M-Th £8. Caravan space £12. Electricity £1.50.) The park contains easily accessible attractions: a Scottish **baronial castle** (now a Christian Conference Centre not open to the public but viewable from across the park), an impressive **Sculpture Trail** (with sculptures made of natural materials), and the North's **National Arboretum.** The park's lake overflows with trout; fishing permits are available at the ranger station from April through mid-October. Buses run from Newcastle to Castlewellan (10min.; M-F 25 per day, Sa 16 per day, Su 6 per day; £1.20).

At the opposite end of town is the **Murlough National Nature Reserve,** on the Dundrum Rd. (A24) toward Belfast. Home to sand dunes and woodlands, Murlough boasts marvelous swimming (for the polar bear crowd), as well as seal-watching during the summer/fall moulting season. In July, upwards of 150 seals may be stretched out on the sands. Plenty of critters can be seen throughout the year, including badgers, foxes, skylark, meadow pipits, and the endangered European insect species of marsh fritillary (a checkered little bugger). To get there, take the Downpatrick or Belfast bus from Newcastle and get off at Murlough. (☎4375 1467. Beach and walks open in daytime. May-Sept. £3 per car; free other times.)

Mount Pleasant Riding and Trekking Center, a cozy, family-run riding center on 15 Bannonstown Rd. in Castlewellan, offers forest or beach trails for riders of all experience levels, ages 5 and up. (☎4377 8651; £11 per hr., helmet provided; open daily 10am-5pm.) More experienced riders can check out **Mourne Trail,** also in Castlewellan at 96 Castlewellan Rd., which offers rides in Tullymore Forest Park for those ages 10 and up. Advanced booking required. (☎4372 4351; £10 per hr.; open daily.) For the less equestrian, back in town, the **Tropicana Water and Leisure Center,** 10-14 Central Promenade, (☎4372 5034), has a heated outdoor swimming pool, water slides, swan boats, and a pitch-and-putt.

HIKING: THE MOURNE MOUNTAINS

Before heading for the hills from Newcastle, stop at the **Mourne Countryside Centre** and **Mourne Heritage Trust** (☎4372 4059), 91 Central Promenade. A friendly and knowledgeable staff leads hikes and offers a broad selection of guides to the mountains. Those planning short excursions can purchase *Mourne Mountain Walks* (£6), which describes 10 one-day hikes, while those planning to camp in the Mournes overnight should buy the *Mourne Country Outdoor Pursuits Map* (£4.95), a detailed topographical map. (Open year-round M-F 9am-5pm.) If the Centre is closed, get your maps at the Newcastle tourist office and your information at Hill Trekker (see **Practical Information,** p. 488). Seasoned hikers looking for company might want to join the **Mourne Rambling Group** (☎4372 2758), which sends gangs into the Mournes each Sunday. Shuttle buses run between Silent Valley and Ben Crom Reservoirs (☎4176 2817; June and Sept. Sa-Su 1 per day, July-Aug. 3 per day; £2.15). If you're around in late June, join in the **Mourne International Walking Festival** (contact Heather Wilson ☎4461 0800).

The **Mourne Wall,** built between 1904 and 1923, encircles 12 of the mountains just below their peaks. Following the length of the 22 mi. wall takes a strenuous 8hr.; many people break it up with a night under the stars. The Mournes' highest peak, **Slieve Donard** (850m), towers above Newcastle. The trail up is wide, well maintained, and paved in many places with flagstones and cobblestones (5hr. return). **Donard Park,** on the corner of Central Promenade and Bryansford Rd., provides the most direct access to the Mournes from Newcastle; it's convenient to both Slieve Donard and **Slieve Commedagh,** both 3 mi. from town. Carefully follow the dirt path at the back of the carpark as it crosses two bridges. It eventually joins the Glen River Path for about 1½ mi. to reach the Mourne Wall. At the wall, turn left for

Slieve Donard or right for Slieve Commedagh. Those seeking a more remote trek might try **Slieve Bernagh** (739m) or **Slieve Binnian** (747m), most easily accessed from **Hare's Gap** and **Silent Valley,** respectively. The two craggy peaks, both with tremendous views, can be combined into a 12 mi. half-day hike. Most of the land in and around the Mournes is privately owned. Visitors should bear this in mind and treat the environs with respect. Close those sheep gates!

Wilderness **camping** is legal and popular (contact Catherine McAleenan for more info at ☎417 69825). Common spots include the **Annalong Valley, Lough Shannagh,** and the **Trassey River. Hare's Gap** and the shore of **Blue Lough** at the foot of Slievelamagan are also good places to pitch a tent. While camping around the Mourne Wall is allowed, camping in the forest itself is strictly prohibited due to the risk of forest fires. Remember to bring warm clothing; the mountains get cold and windy at night, and Irish weather conditions are known to change suddenly. A local volunteer **Mountain Rescue** team (☎999) is available in case of emergencies.

WARRENPOINT (AN POINTE)

A few miles down the coast from Newcastle, on the north side of Carlingford Lough, is the harbor town of Warrenpoint. It first gained fame as a resort town in the 1800s, when merely having a half-decent beach was enough to satisfy tourists. Today, nearby Rostrevor is a large part of Warrenpoint's appeal. Rostrevor draws annual crowds to the area for the Fiddler's Green Festival, making Warrenpoint an important source of accommodations. Recently, the town has put money into beautifying the waterfront with a small but well-manicured promenade. Though the industrial harbor has hindered such efforts, the end of the pier provides an unparalleled view of the Cooley and Mourne Mountains.

ORIENTATION AND PRACTICAL INFORMATION. The bus drop-off is in **The Square;** facing the water, the Square becomes **Church St.** to your left and **Charlotte St.** to your right. Euphemistically named **"ferries"** (tiny motorboats) land at the other end of the waterfront. The **tourist office,** two blocks from the bus stop on Church St., offers a town map along with armloads of free glossy regional guides. **Ulster Bank,** 2 Charlotte St., **Northern Bank** on Queen St., and **First Trust** on The Square all have 24hr. **ATMs.** The **Red Star Passenger Ferry** (☎4177 3070) runs a sporadic service (weather and tides permitting) across the lough to Omeath, a town in the Republic. (June-Sept.; £3 return.) **Rent bikes** at **Stewart's Cycles,** 14 Havelock Pl., beside the Surgery Clinic on Marine Parade. (☎4177 3565. Also does repairs. £6 per day, £25 per wk. Open M-F 2-6pm.) **Walsh's Pharmacy** is at 25 Church St. (☎4175 3661. Open M-Sa 9am-6pm.) In an **emergency** dial ☎999, no coins required. The **post office** sits at 9 Church St. (☎4175 2225. Open M-Tu and Th 8:30am-5:30pm, W 8:30am-1pm, F 9am-5:30pm, Sa 9am-12:30pm.) The **postal code** is BT34.

ACCOMMODATIONS, FOOD, AND PUBS. Whistledown and Finn's ❹, 6 Seaview, offers hotel-quality rooms at B&B prices. In-room TVs with BBC2 are an additional bonus to those suffering from *Simpsons* withdrawal. The enormous Victorian townhouse, which also houses a modern bar and restaurant, is directly on the waterfront at the end of Church St. Talk to the bartender to book rooms. (☎4175 4174. Breakfast included. Singles £30; doubles £55.) Ask for a room that looks onto the Lough at the larger **Boathouse Inn ❹,** 1-3 Marine Parade, around the corner from the Square. (☎4175 3743. Breakfast included. Singles £40; doubles £60; family rooms £70.) **Lough View ❸,** 10 Osborne Promenade, has smaller rooms for a smaller price (☎4177 3067. Singles £25; doubles £40.)

Most of Warrenpoint's eateries have a take-out option, ideal for eating while dangling your feet from the pier. **Vecchia Roma ❷,** on the corner of the Square and

Marine Parade, offers carnivorous and vegetarian Italian fare under a decorative trellis. (☎4175 2082. Pizzas £4.45-7.45; other entrees £7-15. Open M-Th 5-10pm, F-Sa 5-11pm, Su 12:30-2:30pm and 5-9:30pm.) On Church St., **Jenny Black's ❶** combination of a coffee bar and art gallery eludes the trap of the self-consciously hip, offering simple hot sandwiches (£2-3.50) and desserts (£1-2.50) amidst up-and-coming local art. (☎4177 3775. Open M-Sa 9am-5:30pm.) The **Genoa Cafe ❶,** the Square, boasts that it has served fish and chips to Warrenpoint since 1910. Today the restaurant sports thoroughly modern decor, but the fish and chips are still battered in tradition. (☎4175 3688. Open daily noon-11pm.) **Diamonds Restaurant ❶,** the Square, is always packed with locals devouring burgers, seafood, pasta, and desserts. (☎4175 2053. Open M-Th 10am-7pm, F-Su noon-10pm.)

Though locals often go into Newry at night, Warrenpoint has quite a few pubs of its own. **Jack Ryan's** offers eats (most dishes £2-5) and live music Friday to Sunday, as well as karaoke on Thursday. (☎4175 2001. Food served M-F 12:30-2:30pm; Sa-Su 12:30-8pm.) At **The Square Peg,** 14 The Square, twenty and thirty-somethings pour in after 11:30pm. Live music Friday to Sunday nights. (☎4177 4077. Occasional weekend cover up to £7. Open M-Sa 11:30am-1am, Su 12:30pm-12:30am.)

SIGHTS AND FESTIVALS. While lough and mountain views are Warrenpoint's only sights in town, **Narrow Water Castle** is a 2 mi. walk or drive on the A2 toward Newry; bus drivers will stop on request. The 16th-century structure forms one of the best-preserved tower houses in Ireland and is thought to have been built for defense and toll collection. In the 19th century, it took on a new function as a dog kennel, leaving one to wonder who let the dogs out. In mid-August, thousands gather to witness the **Maiden of the Mournes Festival,** for which lasses from Ireland, Europe, and the US gather to display their personalities and prodigious talents.

ROSTREVOR (CAISLEAN RUAIRI)

The tiny village of Rostrevor, which lies 3 mi. from Warrenpoint along the A2, has a "downtown" of one sharply sloped block (the #39 bus from Newry to Kilkeel frequently makes the journey). At its bottom, a short bridge ends at **Fairy Glen,** a small park with bike path that runs along a pretty stream. A hundred yards further are the rolling hills of the much larger **Kilbroney Park.** In addition to a cafe and some wonderful climbing trees, Kilbroney contains **Rostrevor Forest,** one of the few remaining virgin Irish Oak forests in Ireland, as well as the usual assortment of wildlife, wild walks, and wild picnic facilities. *(Open daily dawn-dusk. Free.)* Aside from its idyllic parks, Rostrevor is known for its annual **Fiddler's Green Festival.** During this late July extravaganza, fans and performers gather to enjoy traditional Irish music, poetry readings, storytelling, and art. As a wee colleen, former President of the Republic Mary Robinson used to tip her half-pints at the **Corner House Bar,** the big, red barn-like building at the front of town. *(☎4173 8236. Tu trad, Sa-Su live music at 10pm. Open daily 11:30am-1am.)*

MY MONUMENT IS BIGGER THAN YOUR MONUMENT

Hidden in the tree line about halfway between Rostrevor and Warrenpoint stands a dull, massive gray spike. The unadorned monument stands in honor of Trevor Ross, who led the commandeering and burning of the United States White House in 1814. Seizing the President's home during an official banquet, General Ross evacuated the house and set it ablaze—but only after polishing off the meal with the help of his battallion. The General's hometown has honored him not only with the great pointer (whose uncannily phallic resemblance to the Washington Monument may or may not be intentional), but also by taking his name, Rostrevor.

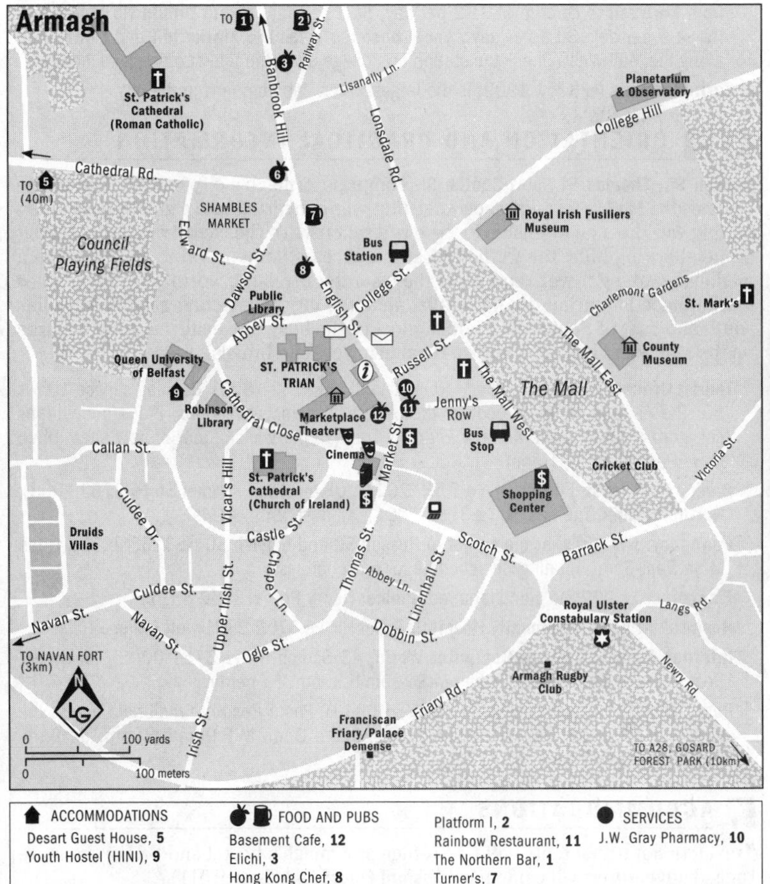

ARMAGH (ARD MACHA)

Armagh takes great pride in promoting itself as "The Christian Captial" of Ireland; if you haven't gotten your religious fill in the rest of the country, your cup just might runneth over here. In the 5th century, St. Patrick supposedly based his saintly mission on the hill known as *Druim Saileach*. Today, St. Patrick's Church of Ireland Cathedral rests where the original church was built in AD 445. Across the way on another hilltop, St. Patrick's Roman Catholic Cathedral also looks over town. Under the watch of these two stone behemoths, the town's population shops, enjoys the arts, and offers a lively pub scene and nightlife for visitors.

TRANSPORTATION

Buses: Ulsterbus station, Lonsdale Rd. Buses to **Belfast** (1hr.; M-F 22 per day, Sa 15 per day, Su 7 per day; £5) and **Enniskillen** via **Monaghan** (2hr.; Sept.-July 2 per day, Oct.-June M-Sa 1 per day; £5.50). Armagh is also a stop for the "Cross-Border Service" from **Portrush** to **Dublin** (M-Sa 2 per day, Su 1 per day) and to **Dublin** via **Monaghan** (M-Sa 6 per day, Su 3 per day). **Local buses** to areas like **Markethill** and **Newry** stop along the Mall West. Check the station on College St. or the tourist office for schedules.

Taxi: Eurocabs (☎3751 1900) is the largest 24hr. cab company in the city.

ORIENTATION AND PRACTICAL INFORMATION

English St., Thomas St., and **Scotch St.** comprise Armagh's city center. Just to the east lies **the Mall,** a former racecourse that was converted into a grassy park when betting was deemed offensive to the city's sanctity. To the west, two cathedrals sit on neighboring hills: the Catholic Cathedral rears its neo-Gothic spires, while a medieval-looking tower represents the Church of Ireland. North of the Shambles marketplace is a primarily **Nationalist area;** the city's **Protestant neighborhood** lies south and east of Scotch St. Though most of the busy city center is safe, the area on the Mall West has been known to spawn weekend brawls.

Tourist Office: Old Bank Building, 40 English St. (☎3752 1800). Booking service 10% + £2. The *Armagh Miniguide* covers the city's sights and attractions. Pious pedestrians can grab a guide to the *Armagh Pilgrim's Trail* (£1), a walking tour of holy sites. Open M-Sa 9am-5pm, Su 1-5pm.

Banks: First Trust, English St. (☎3752 2025); **Ulster Bank,** Market St. (☎3752 2053); **Northern Bank,** Thomas St. (☎3752 2004). All have 24hr. **ATMs.**

Pharmacy: J.W. Gray, at the corner of Russell St. and English St. (☎3752 2092). Open M-Sa 9am-6pm. Rotating Su schedule for prescriptions.

Emergency: ☎999; no coins required. **Police:** Newry Rd. (☎3752 3311).

Hospital: Armagh Community Hospital, Tower Hill (☎3752 2381), off College Hill.

Internet Access: Armagh Computer World, 43 Scotch St. (☎3751 0002), inside the Best Buy and up the stairs. Open M-Sa 9am-5:30pm. £3 per hr.

Post Office: 31 Upper English St. (☎3751 0313). *Poste Restante* mail held across the street at 46 Upper English St. (☎3752 2079). Open M-F 9am-5:30pm, Sa 9am-12:30pm. **Postal code:** BT6 17AA.

ACCOMMODATIONS

Travelers not toting tents will find refuge at Armagh's hostel and B&Bs; the more rugged adventurer will camp near **Gosford Forest Park** (see p. 511).

Armagh Youth Hostel (☎3751 1800), behind Queen's University campus. From the tourist office, turn left twice and follow Abbey St. for 2 blocks. Walk through the parking lot; the entrance to the hostel is in a small abbey. Huge and squeaky clean; excellent, under-used facilities. Excellent Security. Wash and dry £1.50 each. Reception 8-11am and 5-11pm. Dorms £12; private rooms £13.50 per person. Under 18 £2 less. ❷

Desart Guest House, 99 Cathedral Rd. (☎3752 2387), the 2nd left off Desart Ln. The building is a formidable mansion with sunny rooms and embalmed raptors on display in the halls. Singles £20; doubles £35. ❸

Maghnavery House, 89 Gosford Rd., Markethill (☎3755 2021). Located out of town and with only a few rooms, but the 19th-century farmhouse is in an ideal location to explore Armagh, Newry, and the Gosford Forest Park. Singles £25-30; doubles £40-50. ❸

Charlemont Arms Hotel, 57-65 English St. (☎ 3752 2028). In the heart of town and across the street from the tourist office, this family-run hotel has 30 large bedrooms complete with TV and tea/coffee amenities. The bar and restaurant will ensure that you don't go to bed hungry. Singles £45; doubles £60-65. ❺

FOOD

Finding affordable grub is a challenge. Your best bet is to get groceries at **Sainsbury's** in the Mall Shopping Centre, Mall West (☎3751 1050; open M-W and Sa 8:30am-8pm, Th-F 8:30am-9pm) or at **Emerson's** on Scotch St. (☎3752 2846; open M 9am-6pm, Tu-W 8am-8pm, Th-F 8am-9:30pm, Sa 8am-6:30pm).

The Basement Cafe, English St. (☎3752 4311), under the Armagh Film House. Cheap meals, chic setting. Sandwiches £1.90. Open M-Sa 9am-5:30pm. ❶

Elichi, Banbrook Hill (☎3751 8800). Promises Italo-Indo-European takeaway, or at least a respectable pizza. Open daily 5pm-midnight. ❷

Rainbow Restaurant, 13 Upper English St. (☎3752 5391). Buffet-style lunches in a cheery atmosphere. Lunch from £3. Open M-F 8:45am-5:30pm, Sa 8:45am-9pm. ❷

Our Ma's Cafe, 2 Lower English St. (☎3751 1289). Cheap, delicious, and a little on the punny side. 3-course lunch £3.75. Open M-Sa 9am-5:30pm, Su 9am-3:30pm. ❷

Hong Kong Chef, English St. (☎01 8615 11047). Tasty Chinese takeaway until late. Curry chicken £3.70. Open Su and Tu-W 5pm-midnight, Th noon-2pm and 5pm-midnight, F-Sa noon-2pm and 5pm-1am. ❷

PUBS

Armagh's nightlife is a strange beast—like the rest of the town scene, it's segregated along sectarian lines. Visitors should orient themselves with the help of locals (such as hostel workers) before hittin' the town.

Turner's, English St. (☎3752 2028), across from the Shambles. The newest hot spot; comfortable drinking in a mixed crowd. 20-sumthins clique off and gossip to the strains of a live band on F and a DJ on Sa.

The Shambles Lounge, 9 Lower English St. (☎3752 4107). An older crowd shuffles over to Shambles for after-work pints and weekend dinners. Cover £5. Open 6-9:30pm.

Platform 1, Railway St. (☎3752 2103). Cluttered bar attracts the youngest of Armagh's nocturnal creatures. F disco, Sa live band.

The Northern Bar, Railway St. (☎3752 7315), across from Platform 1. Live entertainment and dancing 3 nights a wk. at 9:30pm; Tu trad.

SIGHTS

THE CATHOLIC CATHEDRAL OF ST. PATRICK. Armagh's cathedrals watch over the city from opposing hills. To the north on Cathedral Rd. sits the 1873 Roman Catholic **Cathedral of St. Patrick.** The imposing exterior and exquisite mosaic interior contrast mightily with the ultra-modern granite sanctuary, which seems to have been designed by a federation of pagans and Martians. *(☎3752 2802. Open daily until dusk. Free.)*

THE PROTESTANT CATHEDRAL OF ST. PATRICK. To the south of the city is the **Cathedral of St. Patrick,** or rather, the Protestant incarnation thereof. Authorities claim that this 13th-century church rests upon the site where St. Paddy founded his main house o' worship in AD 445. The cathedral is also the final resting place of the great Irish King Brian Ború. *(☎3752 3142. Open Apr.-Oct. daily 10am-5pm; Nov.-Mar. 10am-4pm. Tours June-Aug. M-Sa 11:30am and 2:30pm. Free.)*

ST. PATRICK'S TRIAN. In the center of town, **St. Patrick's Trian** shares a building with the tourist office. Most exhibits emphasize St. Pat's role in Armagh, although his link to the town is historically dubious. The **Armagh Story** is a walk-through display and audio-visual presentation in which plaster Vikings, priests, and pagan warriors relate the lengthy history of the town. A smaller, fanciful display, geared toward the little people, recreates **Swift's Land of Lilliput.** *(☎3752 1801. Open M-Sa 10am-5pm, Su 2-5pm. £3.75, students and seniors £2.75, children £2, families £9.50.)*

OBSERVATORY AND PLANETARIUM. Up College Hill, north of the Mall, is the **Armagh Observatory,** founded in 1790 by Archbishop Robinson. The star-stricken can observe a modern weather station and an 1885 refractory telescope. *(☎3752 2928. By appt. only, though the grounds are open 9:30am-4:30pm.)* More celestial wonders await in the nearby **Planetarium,** where a few centimeters of Mars are on display. *(☎3752 3689. 45min. shows July-Aug. 3-5 times per day; Apr.-June M-F 1 per day. Open M-F 10am-4:45pm, Sa-Su 1:15-4:45pm. Seating limited; book ahead. £3.75, students £2.75.)*

NORTHERN IRELAND

PALACE DEMESNE. Palace Demesne (dah-MAIN) sprawls south of the town center. The palace, chapel, and stables were another of the Archbishop of Armagh's efforts to rebuild the city. The County Council now occupies the main building, relegating the public to the **Palace Stables Heritage Centre,** where a slick multimedia show presents "A Day in the Life" of the closed palace. A **Franciscan Friary** occupies a peaceful corner of the grounds. *(☎3752 9629. Open May-Aug. M-Sa 10am-5:30pm, Su 1-5pm; Sept.-Apr. M-Sa 10am-5pm, Su 2-5pm. £3.75, children £2.)*

OTHER SIGHTS. You can take a peek at a first edition of **Gulliver's Travels**—covered with Swift's own scrawled comments—at the **Armagh Public Library,** Abbey St. *(☎3752 3142. Open M-F 10am-1pm and 2-4pm. Access to rare books by appointment.)* Bargain-hunters should tour the walled **Shambles marketplace,** at the foot of the hill where Cathedral Rd., Dawson St., and English St. meet. Regular "car boot" sales dredge up old records, Jackie Collins best sellers, and other "antiques"; a farmers market makes an irregular appearance. *(☎3752 8192. Open Tu, F, and alternate Sa 9am-noon.)* At the **Armagh County Museum,** on the east side of the Mall, historians have a panoply of 18th-century objects—old wedding dresses, pictures, stuffed birds, jewelry, and militia uniforms. *(☎3752 3070. Open M-Sa 10am-1pm and 2-5pm. Free.)*

ENTERTAINMENT

Armaghnian aesthetes enjoy a varied program of theater, music, dance, and visual arts within the white-tiled confines of the **Marketplace Theatre and Arts Centre,** on Market Sq. The theater also organizes the **Music in Armagh Festival.** (☎3752 1921. Open M-Sa 9am-5pm, performance nights 9am-7pm.) Around the first week of June, Armagh holds an annual **Comhaltas Ceoltori Traditional Music Festival** (for info call Liz Watson ☎3752 5353), and in mid-August, the Ulster **Road Bowls Finals** (see **Sports,** p. 77) are held on highways and byways throughout the county (for info call Sammy Gilespie ☎3752 5622). **The Apple Blossom Festival,** in the second week of May, brings a number of events to the city, culminating in a lavish **May Ball** (contact the tourist office for info and schedules). On March 17, the **St. Patrick's Day** revels bring people together from far away to celebrate Big Paddy.

If you've had enough of other peoples' history, look into your own at the **Armagh Ancestry,** 40 English St. (☎3752 1802). Who knows? Maybe you'll find a long-lost relative willing to take you in and show you Irish hospitality firsthand. You don't need relations to take in the ***céilí*** dancing at St. Patrick's Parochial Hall on Cathedral Rd. (Th 9-10pm. Contact Brendan Kirk or Seamus McDonagh ☎3752 6088.) **Set dancing** also welcomes visitors on Monday nights at the **Pearse Og Social Club** on Dalton Rd. (contact Pat Prunty ☎3752 6929).

 SPORTS AND ACTIVITIES

The area surrounding Armagh offers a multitude of outdoors activities. **Angling** is a popular pastime; you can obtain daily permits from GI Stores, including the one on Dobbin St. (☎3752 2335). **Loughall County Park** promises a 37-acre fishery with daily permits at £3; yearly permits are only £25. Break out your 9-iron at the 18-hole **County Armagh Golf Club.** (☎3752 2501. BYO-clubs. Non-members £12-18. Open daily 8am-dark.) If you need more horsepower than the golf carts provide, head to the **Moy Riding School,** where your equine escort awaits. (☎8778 4440. £8 per hr.) The school also presents **show jumping** on Friday nights. Finally, if it's the need for speed you need to feed, **Gosford Karting** will let you make like Tom Cruise, in the days when he was cool. (☎3755 1248. £5 per 7-10min.; £10 per 10-15min.)

DAYTRIPS FROM ARMAGH

NAVAN FORT

Navan Fort is on Killylea Rd. (A28), 2 mi. west of Armagh. ☎01861 525 550. Open M-Sa 10am-5pm, Su noon-5pm. £3.95, students £3.

On the outskirts of Armagh, the mysterious Navan Fort, also called *Emain Macha* (AHM-win maka), played host to the capital of the Kings of Ulster for 800 years. This may look like a grassy mound of dirt, but with a lot of imagination you might see extensive fortifications and elaborate religious paraphernalia strewn across the site. In 94 BC, a huge wooden structure 40 yd. in diameter was constructed where the mound now stands; it was filled with stones, burnt to the ground in a religious rite, and covered with soil. Queen Macha (see **Legends and Folktales,** p. 71) is said to have founded the fort, although it is also associated with St. Patrick, who probably chose *Ard Macha* (Armagh, for those of you who weren't paying attention earlier) as a Christian center because of its proximity to this pagan stronghold. Following a series of tragic circumstances beginning with fire and ending with bankruptcy, the once-famous Navan Centre is now closed.

LOUGH NEAGH AND OXFORD ISLAND

Route A3 runs northeast from Armagh to loughside towns Craigavon and Lurgan. Discovery Centre ☎3832 2205. Open Apr.-Sept. M-Sa 10am-6pm, Su 10am-7pm; Oct.-Mar. W-Su 10am-5pm. Last admission 1hr. before closing. Audio-visual displays £1.50.

Birdwatching and various aquatic activities are the primary amusements in the towns around Lough Neagh; its shores are best seen by car during daytrips from Belfast or Armagh. Sources tell us that a giant once scooped a heap of prime Ulster real estate out of the ground and hurled it into the Irish sea, creating not only the Isle of Man but also Lough Neagh, the UK's largest lake. The **Lough Neagh Discovery Centre,** on the **Oxford Island National Nature Reserve** in **Craigavon,** contains acres of wooded parkland for exploration. Audio-visual displays inside the center detail the lake's ecosystem and wildlife. **Boat rides** to the island run June to August. The **Kinnego Caravan Park,** on the Kinnego Marina in Lurgan, is home to hundreds of species of wild campers. (☎3832 7573. £6 per 2-person tent.)

GOSFORD FOREST PARK

To get to the Forest Park, take the A28 for about 7 mi. or hop the #40 bus to Markethill. ☎3755 1277; ranger ☎3755 2143. Open daily 10am-sunset.

The Gosford Forest Park, 7 mi. southeast of Armagh, cordially invites you to spend a nice day with its castle, old walled garden, and miles of nature trails. Please direct your attention to the sheds full of unusual roosters—and do take note of the Transylvanian Naked Neck. **Horse-riding** and **golf** are also in the area. Visitors are welcome to **camp** in the Gosford Forest. (£5.50-10 per 2-person tent.)

UNTANGLING THE TROUBLES

Protestant vs Catholic? Republican vs Loyalist?

For more than three decades, the bloody conflict in the North has mystified visitors. People have explained the Troubles as Catholic versus Protestant, as Republican versus Unionist, as Irish versus British, but each of these dimensions tells only part of the story.

To vastly oversimplify, the Troubles started as a Civil Rights movement gone bad. In the late 1960s, the minority Catholic population of Northern Ireland, dissatisfied with the continuing system of discrimination in housing and employment, began to hold marches and protests. This angered Protestant Unionists, who feared that concessions to the Catholics would eventually break their union with Great Britain. Unionist paramilitary groups, like the Ulster Defense Association (UDA), began a campaign of killings and arson to intimidate the Catholics. The Irish Republican Army (IRA) which had been languishing up to that point, found new life as the "defender of the Catholics." They began a wave of murder against Protestant civilians and the Royal Ulster Constabulary police force (RUC) to "encourage" the British to leave. Westminster responded by sending in the British army, which further inflamed the Catholic population. By 1999, 3,636 people were dead and more than 36,000 injured.

The roots of this conflict were laid long ago. In the 17th century, King James I of England (and all of Ireland at the time) saw Ulster as particularly savage. To change this, he encouraged English and Scottish Protestants to settle there. This "Ulster Plantation" brought a culturally-separated Protestant population to Northern Ireland. In the 19th century, while agrarian southerners were embracing nationalist revolutionary principles, this Protestant Ulster population was embracing the Industrial Revolution. By the time of Irish Independence Ulster was far more economically advanced than its agricultural cousin down south, in large part due to the British state. Consequently, the Northerners viewed the revolutionary farmers in the South as ungrateful to the empire—the Southern Republicans never quite understood this. Southerners fought the Anglo-Irish War and the Irish Civil War to keep the northern counties as part of the new republic, not realizing that the Protestant northerners had no intention of leaving the Empire. The result of these conflicts was a polarization of the Catholic community as Nationalist and the Protestants as Loyalist, divisions that have continued to this day.

There are a number of reasons why the Troubles were so difficult to end. One was the stubborn extremism of both sides; the IRA would accept nothing less than Britain's complete withdrawal, while the UDA saw any British concession as a mortal betrayal. Another problem was basic misunderstandings. The IRA stubbornly insisted that the main obstacle to Irish reunification was British Imperial policy. In truth, British governments throughout the century have been more than happy to compromise on Northern Ireland, but they have been held back by the staunch opposition of Ulster's 700,000 fiercely loyal subjects. The British, in turn, misunderstood the conflict as essentially a problem with the IRA; by ignoring the atrocities committed by Unionist groups, they further inflamed Catholic anger. These misunderstandings fueled the conflict, but the greatest difficulty was the culture of brutality it engendered.

The Good Friday Agreement of 1998 brought new hope. As a result of these agreements, and based upon the IRA's commitment to decommission their weapons, Catholics and Protestants now share power and the RUC has been reorganized. While these developments are positive, relics of the old hatred linger. Though the IRA and the UDA have held their cease-fire, as of August 2002, they both continue to retain large arsenals. The cease-fire gets tested each summer during the Protestant Marching season, when "Orange-man" Protestants march antagonistically through Catholic neighborhoods. More chillingly, extremist splinter groups on both sides have threatened and even murdered civilians in attempts to destabilize the peace process. Despite these difficulties, the peace has held, thanks to the efforts of Gerry Adams, David Trimble, John Hume, and Tony Blair. We can only hope that these voices of reason will continue to prevail.

Ryan Hackney was the Editor of Let's Go: Ireland 1996 and a Researcher-Writer for Ireland 1995 and Ecuador 1997. He is now pursuing a career as a novelist.

ANTRIM AND DERRY

The A2 coastal road skitters along the edge of Antrim and Derry, connecting the scenic attractions of both counties. West of Belfast, stodgy and industrial Larne gives way to lovely seaside villages. The nine Glens of Antrim offer scenery fiends plenty to get excited about. Near the midpoint of the island's northern coast, the Giant's Causeway spills its geological honeycomb into the ocean; this middle section of the coast road is a cyclist's paradise. Urban sprawl reappears just past the Causeway, with the carnival lights of Portrush and Portstewart. The road terminates at the turbulent, walled city of Derry, the North's second largest city.

LARNE (LATHARNA)

Though it claims aristocratic roots—Prince Lathar lent his name to the original settlement of *Latharna*—today's Larne is a working man's town whose major attraction is the ferry it runs to and from Scotland. The town also serves the surrounding rural communities with a **livestock fair,** held on Fridays in the Market Yard. **P&O Ferries** (☎087 0242 4777; www.poirishsea.com) operates boats from Larne to Cairnryan, Scotland and Fleetwood, England. The **train station** lies adjacent to a roundabout, down the street from the tourist office on Narrow Gauge Rd. (☎2826 0604. Open daily 7:30am-5:30pm.) Trains chug from Central Station in Belfast to Larne Town and Larne Harbour, a 15min. walk from the town (50min.; M-Sa 17-20 per day, Su 6 per day; £3.60). The **bus station** is just south of town, on the other side of the A8 overpass. (☎2827 2345. Open M-F 9am-5:15pm.) Buses leave from Station Rd. for Laganside Station in Belfast (1½hr., express 50min.; M-Sa 12 per day, Su 2 per day in summer; £3.20) and points north along the Antrim coast.

To reach the town center from the harbor, take the first right outside of the ferryport. As the road curves left, it becomes **Curran Rd.,** and then **Main St.** It's a good idea to take a cab in the evening, as this route passes through a fairly rough Unionist neighborhood. The **tourist office,** Narrow Gauge Rd., offers accommodations booking and a free town map. (☎2826 0088. Open July-Sept. M-F 9am-6pm, Sa 9am-5pm; Oct.-Easter M-F 9am-5pm; Easter-June M-Sa 9am-5pm.) **Northern Bank,** 19 Main St. (☎2827 6311) has a 24hr. **ATMs.** Larne's **post office** is at 98 Main St. (☎2826 0489. Open M-F 9am-5:30pm, Sa 9am-12:30pm.) **Postal code:** BT40.

Larne's not the sort of town where people tend to linger. Rather than crashing at the harbor near the ferry, you'll be better off heading to **Glenarm Rd.,** a more affluent area closer to town that is lined with B&Bs. **Inverbann ❷,** at 7 Glenarm Rd., is one such establishment, with spacious TV- and bath-endowed rooms. (☎2827 2524. £15 per person.) **The Aardvark ❷,** 21 Curran Rd., has beautifully decorated, luxurious rooms complete with TV and tea/coffeemakers. (☎2827 0898. £16-17 per person.) **Curran Caravan Park ❶,** 131 Curran Rd., between the harbor and town, is a congested campground. (☎2827 5505. £1.50 per person; £5 per tent.) The giant **Co-op Superstore** is on Station Rd., next to the bus station. (☎2826 0737. Open M-W 9am-9pm, Th-F 9am-10pm, Sa 9am-8pm, Su 1-6pm.) Larne's main street is littered with cheap sandwich shops. **Caffe Spice ❶,** 7 Dunluce St., is especially popular with the younger crowd. (☎2826 9633. Open M-W 10am-5pm, Th-Sa 10am-10pm.) Those who appreciate substance over style will enjoy **The Big Sandwich Company ❶,** 27 Point St., where an assembly line manufactures sizable lunches. (☎2826 0410. Open M-Sa 9am-5pm. Sandwiches around £2.) **Chekker's Wine Bar ❷,** 33 Lower Cross St., serves a broad selection of bistro food in a take-your-time atmosphere. (☎2827 5305. Most meals £5; food served daily noon-9pm.) The smoky, lamp-lit **Bailie,** 111-113 Main St., distributes congratulatory pints to brave ocean voyagers. (☎2827 3947. Entrees £4-5; food served daily 11:30am-2:30pm and 5-8pm.)

GLENS OF ANTRIM

During the last Ice Age, glaciers ripped through the mountainous coastline northeast of Antrim, leaving in their wake nine deep scars. Over the years, water collected in these "valleys," spurring the growth of trees, ferns, and other lush flora not usually found in Ireland. The A2 coastal road connects the mouths of these glens and provides entry to roads leading inland, allowing weekenders easy access to the area. The glens and their mountains and waterfalls can best be seen on daytrips inland from the coastal villages of Glenarm, Waterfoot, and Cushendall.

Most visitors travel the glens by car, but two **Ulsterbus** routes serve the area year-round (Belfast ☎9032 0011; Larne ☎2827 2345). Bus #156 from Belfast stops in Larne, Ballygally, Glenarm, and Carnlough (summer M-Sa 6-7 per day, Su 3 per day; off-season M-Sa 5-7 per day, Su 1 per day; £2.80-5.20) and sometimes continues to Waterfoot, Cushendall, and Cushendun (summer M-F 4 per day, Sa-Su 2 per day; off-season M-F 2 per day). Bus #150 runs between Ballymena and Glenariff (M-Sa 5 per day, £2.60) then to Waterfoot, Cushendall, and Cushendun (M-F 5 per day, Sa 3 per day; £4.30). The **Antrim Coaster** (#252) runs year-round, following the road from Belfast to Coleraine and stopping at every town along the way (2 per day, £7.50). **Cycling** the glens is fabulous—the coastal road from Ballygally to Cushendun is both scenic and flat. Once the road leaves Cushendun, though, it becomes hilly enough to make even motorists groan; the **Ardclinis Activity Centre** in Cushendall **rents bikes** (see p. 515). The winding, narrow road between here make drivers feel less guilty about not stopping for hitchhikers. Crossroads are the best places to find a lift, but *Let's Go* does not recommend hitchhiking.

GLENARM (GLEANN ARMA)

Six flat, winding, coastal miles lead through increasingly pristine and isolated vistas to lovely Glenarm ("Glen of the Army"), which was once the chief dwelling place of the **MacDonnell clan.** The village comprises several centuries-old houses, a couple of pubs, and a collection of short walks. Just before you enter town, look for **madman's window** on your right; four boulders have fallen down to look like a window at this famous outcropping. The huge arch at the top of Altmore St. marks the entrance to **Glenarm Forest,** where trails trace the river's path. (Open daily 9am to dusk.) **Glenarm Castle,** set just off the main street behind the trees north of the river, is the current residence of the 13th Earl of Antrim. The castle's 17th-century gate is visible from Castle St.—plan ahead if you want to enter the castle, as it's only open two days each year: the Monday and Tuesday following July 12. The **gardens** are open year-round by appointment (inquire via the tourist office); to enter them take the Ballymena road toward Cushendall and fork left. The town also boasts a **heritage trail** and a **waterduck walk;** brochures on both are available at the tourist office or from your B&B. If you're up for a real hike, the local section of the now-defunct **Ulster Way** trail passes through town.

The **tourist office,** in the town council building by the bridge, provides friendly advice on the attractions of the area. (☎2884 1087. **Internet access** £4 per hr. Open M 10am-4pm, Tu-F noon-7pm, Su 2-6pm.) Glenarm's **post office** is on Toberwine St. (☎2884 1218. Open M-Tu and Th-F 9am-1pm and 2-5:30pm, W and Sa 9am-12:30pm.) The **postal code** is BT44. **Margaret's B&B ❶,** 10 Altmore St., provides comfortable rooms with 1950s decor. (☎2884 1307. Tea and toast breakfast included. Full Irish breakfast £4. £10 per person.) **Costcutters,** 22 Toberwine St., has all you need to create your own feast. (☎7084 1629. Open M-Sa 8am-8pm, Su 8am-6pm.) The **Poacher's Pocket ❷,** 1 New Row, will provide you with beefed up meals. (☎2884 1221. Entrees £6-7, burgers £3.50; food served daily noon-9pm.) **The Coast Road Inn,** 3-5 Toberwine St., draws young and old alike for its great *craic.*

(☎2884 1207. Food in summer daily noon-7pm.) You'll find nothing fancier than pints and good company at the **Bridge End Tavern,** 1-3 Toberwine St. (☎2884 1252).

GLENARIFF

Mirror, mirror, on the wall, who's the fairest Glen of all? The answer, my dear, is the beautiful, broad, Glenariff. Guarded from any would-be wicked stepmothers by the village of **Waterfoot,** the glen is 9 mi. up the coast from Glenarm. Thackeray dubbed this area "Switzerland in miniature" because of the steep and rugged landscape. The glen lies inside the large **Glenariff Forest Park,** 4 mi. south of Waterfoot along the Glenariff road (A43 toward Ballymena). The **bus** between Cushendun and Ballymena (#150) stops at the official park entrance (M-Sa 3-5 per day). If you're walking from Waterfoot, however, you can enter 1½ mi. downhill by taking the road that branches left toward the Manor Lodge Restaurant. (☎2175 8769 or 2177 1796. Open daily 10am-dusk. £3 per car; £1.50 per pedestrian.) Once inside the park, you'll be confronted with trails ranging in length from half a mile to 5 mi. round-trip. All paths pass the Glenariff and Inver rivers and the three waterfalls that feed them. The awesome 3 mi. **Waterfall Trail,** marked by blue triangles, follows the cascading, fern-lined Glenariff River from the park entrance to the Manor Lodge. The entrance to the **Moyle Way,** a 17 mi. hike from Glenariff to Ballycastle, is directly across from the park entrance. All of the walks begin and end at the carpark, where you will also find the **Glenariff Tea House ❷.** This bay-windowed restaurant offers fresh snacks (sandwiches £2), exotically seasoned meals (£5-8), and free **maps** of the park's trails. (☎2565 8769. Open Easter-Sept. daily 11am-6pm.)

Those wishing to commune with beautiful Glenariff for longer than an afternoon should seek lodging in Waterfoot. **Lurig View B&B ❷,** at 4 Lurig View on Glen Rd., off Garron Rd. about half a mile past town on the waterfront, provides big, comfy beds and big, tasty breakfasts. (☎2177 1618. £17 per person.) **Glenariff Forest Park Camping ❶,** 98 Glenariff Rd., is self-explanatory. (☎2175 8232. Tents £7-10.) Stock up at **Kearney's Costcutter,** 21 Main St., before your trek into the waterfall wilderness. (☎2177 1213. Open daily 7am-10pm.) Run out of a family home, **Angela's Restaurant and Bakery ❷,** 32 Main St., serves home-cooked meals (£4-7) with names like Knickerbocker Glory. The back patio has grand views of Lurigethan Hill to the left and Garron Point to the right. (☎2177 1700. Takeaway available all day. Open M-W 10am-8pm, Th-Su 10am-11pm.) **The Saffron Bar,** 4-6 Main St. (☎2177 2906), is just wild about hurling. The owners seek to inject this mellow pub with new life by offering an indoor bar and outdoor beer garden. The **Cellar Bar,** downstairs, has live music ranging from country to trad on weekends. **The Mariners' Bar,** 7 Main St. (☎2177 1330), has live music of various sorts on Friday and Saturday nights.

CUSHENDALL (BUN ABHANN DALLA)

Cushendall is nicknamed the capital of the Glens, most likely because its village center consists of four streets instead of just one. The storefronts on all those extra streets house a variety of goods, services, and pubs unavailable anywhere else in the region. In addition to its importance as a commercial center, Cushendall is also well-situated less than 5 mi. from Glenaan, Glenariff, Glenballyeamon, Glencorp, and Glendun. Unfortunately, the closing of its hostel may mean that Cushendall's days as a budget travel mecca are over.

TRANSPORTATION

Buses: Ulsterbus (☎9033 3000). Bus #162 has limited service from **Belfast** (£6.20) via **Larne** (£5.20) and **Cushendall,** then north to **Cushendun** (July-Aug. M-F 4 per day, Sa-Su 2 per day; Sept.-June M-F 2 per day). #252 (a.k.a. the **Antrim Coaster**) goes

NORTHERN IRELAND

coastal from **Belfast** to **Coleraine,** stopping in **Cushendall** and most everywhere else (July-Aug. 2 per day; Sept.-June M-Sa only and with fewer stops). #150, from **Belfast** via **Ballymena,** stops in nearby **Glenariff** (a.k.a. **Waterfoot;** M-Sa 5 per day, £2.60).

Bike Rental: Ardclinis Activity Centre, 11 High St. (☎2177 1340). Mountain bikes £10 per day; deposit £50. **Wetsuits** £5 per day. They also provide advice on hill-walking, canoeing, and gorge-walking.

ORIENTATION AND PRACTICAL INFORMATION

The busiest section of Cushendall is its crossroads. From the center of town, **Mill St.** turns into **Chapel Rd.** and heads northwest toward Ballycastle; **Shore Rd.** extends south toward Glenarm and Larne. On the north side of town, **Hill St.** leads uphill from **Bridge Rd.,** a section of the **Coast road** (an extension of the A2) that continues toward the sea at Waterfoot.

Tourist Office: 25 Mill St. (☎2177 1180), near the bus stop at the northern (Cushendun) end of town. Has a wealth of info and may be able to wrangle you a ride to Glenariff. Open July-Sept. M-F 10am-1pm and 2-5:30pm, Sa 10am-1pm and 2-4:30pm; Oct. to mid-Dec. and Feb.-June Tu-Sa 10am-1pm.

Banks: Northern Bank, 5 Shore Rd. (☎2177 1243). Open M 9:30am-12:30pm and 1:30-5pm, Tu-F 10am-12:30pm and 1:30-3:30pm. 24hr. **ATM.**

Pharmacy: Numark Pharmacist, 8 Mill St. (☎2177 1523). Open M-Sa 9am-6pm.

Internet Access: Cushendall Development Office (☎2177 1378), behind the tourist office. £1.50 per 30min.; students, seniors, and other jobless types £1. Open M-F 9am-1pm and 2-5pm. When that's closed, access at the tourist office (£1 per 15min.).

Post Office: Inside the Spar Market on Coast Rd. (☎2177 1201). Open M and W-F 9am-1pm and 2-5:30pm, Tu and Sa 9am-12:30pm. **Postal code:** BT44.

ACCOMMODATIONS AND CAMPING

B&Bs occupy every other house on Kilnadore Rd. From the Coast road, turn inland at the RUC station. The town's caravan parks aren't particularly suited to tents, but campers in need should be able to find a bit of earth.

Glendale, Mrs. Mary O'Neill's, 46 Coast Rd. (☎2177 1495), south of town overlooking the sea. It's hard to imagine a warmer welcome. Rooms are huge and as soothing to the weary traveler as the proprietress's colorful company. Tea, coffee, biscuits, and bath in each room. £17 per person. ❷

Ballyeamon Camping Barn (☎2175 8451 or 077 0344 0558), 6 mi. south of Cushendall on the B14. Far from town, but overlooking the Glenariff Forest Park and only a few hundred yards from the Moyle Way. Owner is a renowned storyteller. Book ahead and call for pickup. Blankets £2. Dorms £7. ❶

Cushendall Caravan Park, 62 Coast Rd. (☎2177 1699), adjacent to Red Bay Boat yard. Strong winds can make camping "rugged." No kitchen. 2-person tent £5.70; family tent £9.50. Free showers. Wash £1, dry £1.50 per 15min. ❶

FOOD AND PUBS

Spar Market, 2 Coast Rd., just past Bridge Rd., has plenty of fruits and veggies. (☎2177 1763. Open daily 7am-10pm.)

Arthur's, Shore St. (☎2177 1627). The bold new crusader in town, seeking to bring princely sandwiches and freshness to the masses. Panini £3. Open daily 10am-5pm. ❶

Harry's, 10-12 Mill St. (☎2177 2022). Pub grub that transcends the usual fare; alongside the traditional fish and chips you'll find inventive dishes such as orange chicken. Bar food served daily noon-9:30pm; a la carte dinner 6-9:30pm. ❸

The Half Door, 6 Bridge St. (☎2177 1300). A takeaway pizza and chipper joint. Try some of the funkier pizzas with inexplicable names and ingredients (chicken+pineapple+banana+bacon = "The Maryland"). Medium pie £4. Open daily 5-10:45pm. ❷

Gillan's Home Bakery and Coffee Shop, 6 Mill St. (☎2177 1404). Vinyl booths lend this excellent bakery a diner atmosphere. A meal for a fiver. Open summer M-Sa 9am-6pm; winter M and W-Sa 9am-6pm, Tu 9am-3pm. ❷

Joe McCollam's (Johnny Joe's), 23 Mill St. (☎2177 1876). One of the best pubs on the island. Features impromptu ballads, fiddling, and slurred limericks. Exciting most nights of the wk., but musicians are guaranteed to gather F-Su.

An Camán, 5 Bridge St. (☎2177 1293), in an inconspicuous off-white building across from the Half Door. Come for the pints, stay for the *craic.* Sa-Su live bands.

SIGHTS

The sandstone **Curfew Tower** in the center of town, on the corner of Mill St. and High St., was built in 1817 by the eccentric and slightly paranoid Francis Turley. This Cushendall landlord made a fortune in China, and when he returned he eagerly wanted to protect his riches. He built the tower with features that include openings for pouring boiling oil onto non-existent attackers, and a bell that was rung every night at the town's "quiet time"—hence the tower's name. Today, the structure is privately owned and closed to the public. The extensive remnants of **Layde Church,** a medieval friary, lie along Layde Rd. When it was established in 1306, the church was valued at 20 shillings. Its ruins are noteworthy for their surrounding graveyard and spectacular seaviews, and for the pretty **seaside walks** that begin at its carpark. (Always open. Free.) The graveyard includes **Cross Na Nagan,** a pagan holestone used for marriage ceremonies and Christianized into a Celtic cross with four clever strokes. **Tieveragh Hill,** half a mile up High St., is known locally as Faery Hill for the otherworldly "little people" who supposedly reside in the area. Quaint locals still refuse to cut the hedgerows in which the wee folk are reputed to dwell. **Lurigethan Hill** (1153 ft.) would soar above town, if only its summit weren't flattened on the way up. A climb to the top rewards with up-close access to a virtually intact Iron Age promontory fort. Locals race up the hill for a "Lurigethan Run" during the **Heart of the Glens** festival, a ten-day affair starting the second week of August and leading up to a giant block party. (Contact the development office ☎2177 1378.) **Ossian's Grave** rests a few miles away on the lower slopes of **Tievebulliagh Mountain.** Actually a neolithic burial cairn dating from around 4000 BC, it is linked by tradition with the Ulster warrior-bard Ossian, who was supposedly buried here 'round about AD 300. The A2 leads north from Cushendall toward Ballymoney and the lower slopes of Tievebulliagh, where a sign points the way to the grave. The steep walk up the southern slope of **Glenaan** rewards with views of the lush valley. The Glens of Antrim **Rambling Club** plans a series of short and long walks throughout the year. Contact the chairman (Liam Murphy ☎2565 6079) or the Cushendall tourist office for details.

CUSHENDUN (BUN ABHANN DUINNE)

In 1954, the National Trust bought the tiny, picturesque seaside village of Cushendun, 5 mi. north of Cushendall on the A2; since then, the Trust has protected the town's "olde," squeaky-clean image. Its white-washed, black-shuttered buildings lie next to a vast beach perforated by wonderful, murky **caves** that are carved into red seacliffs. The largest cave, located just south of town off the Coast road, serves as the only entrance to **Cave House,** built in 1820 but now occupied by the Mercy religious order and closed to the public. From behind what used to be the hotel, an excruciatingly steep path leads to the clifftop. Other less painful walks meander around the **historical monuments** in town and in nearby **Glendun,** a preserved village that is a fine example of Cornish architecture. The **"Maud Cottages"** that line the main street were built by Lord Cushendun for his wife in 1925; tourist information signs in town remind visitors not to mistake them for almshouses.

Buses pause on the Coast road at Cushendun's grocery shop on their way to Waterfoot via Cushendall (#162; July-Aug. 2-4 per day; Sept.-June M-F 2 per day). Just west of town on the A2 is **Drumkeerin,** 201a Torr Rd., where visitors can choose between their immaculate **B&B ❸** and **camping barn ❶** (hostel) facilities, each with a gorgeous view of Cushendun and the rest of the coast. Owners Mary and Joe also offer **painting courses** for those looking to improve their talents, or develop talents yet undiscovered. Mary was just named Landlady of the Year for the whole of the UK in 2002; it's no wonder—she makes her own bread and jams, and offers eggs from her hens. Simply put, you're in good hands. (☎2176 1554. Blankets, sheets, and towels £2. Camping barn £8. B&B with-bath singles £20; doubles £35.) Camping at **Cushendun Caravan Site ❶,** 14 Glendun Rd. (50 yd. from the end of the beach), is cheap and presents the exciting possibility of lounging in a TV- and game-room. (☎2176 1254. No kitchen. Open Mar.-Sept. £6 per small tent. Laundry £2.) The town's most popular attraction is also its only real pub: **Mary McBride's,** 2 Main St., used to be in the *Guinness Book of World Records* as the smallest bar in Europe. The original bar is still there, but has been vigorously expanded to create a lounge that seems to have been designed for the viewing of GAA matches (see **Sports,** p. 77). Cushendun's characters leave the bar only when musicians start a session in the lounge. (☎2176 1511. Steak and Guinness pie £5. Food served daily noon-9pm. Music summer Sa-Su; usually trad or country.) **Cushendun Tea Room ❷,** across the street, serves typical chipper fare. (☎2176 1506. Burgers and sandwiches £1.70-2.50; entrees around £4.50-8. Open July-Aug. daily 11am-7pm; Sept.-June weekends only, noon-6:30pm.)

CAUSEWAY COAST

Past Cushendun, the northern coast shifts from lyrical to dramatic mode. Sea-battered cliffs tower 600 ft. above white, wave-lapped beaches before giving way to the spectacular Giant's Causeway. Lying between stretches of colossally beautiful scenery, the Causeway is a hopscotch of 40,000 black and red hexagonal stone columns, formed by volcanic eruptions some 65 million years ago. Thousands of visitors swarm the site today, but few venture beyond the visitors center to the miles of stunning and easily-accessible coastline that stretch beyond.

The A2, which is suitable for **cycling,** is the major thoroughfare between the main towns along the Causeway. **Ulsterbus** (☎7043 3334 or 7032 5400) #172 runs between Ballycastle and Portrush along the coast (1hr.; M-F 6 per day, Sa 4 per day, Su 5 per day; £3.70) and makes frequent connections to Portstewart. The "Triangle" service (#140) connects Portrush, Portstewart, and Coleraine (9am-5pm every 10min., less frequent service 6:55am-9am and 5-10:30pm). The #252 "Antrim Coaster" bus runs up the coast from Belfast to Portstewart via just about every town *Let's Go* can think of. Ulsterbus also runs package **tours** in the area that leave from Belfast, Portrush, and Portstewart (£3-9). The orange open-topped **Bushmills Bus** outlines the coast between Coleraine, 5 mi. south of Portrush, and the Causeway. (Coleraine bus station ☎7043 3334. July-Aug. 7 per day.) Those hitching along the A2 or the inland roads find that the lack of cars and high ratio of tourists slows them down. All together now: *Let's Go* does not recommend hitchhiking.

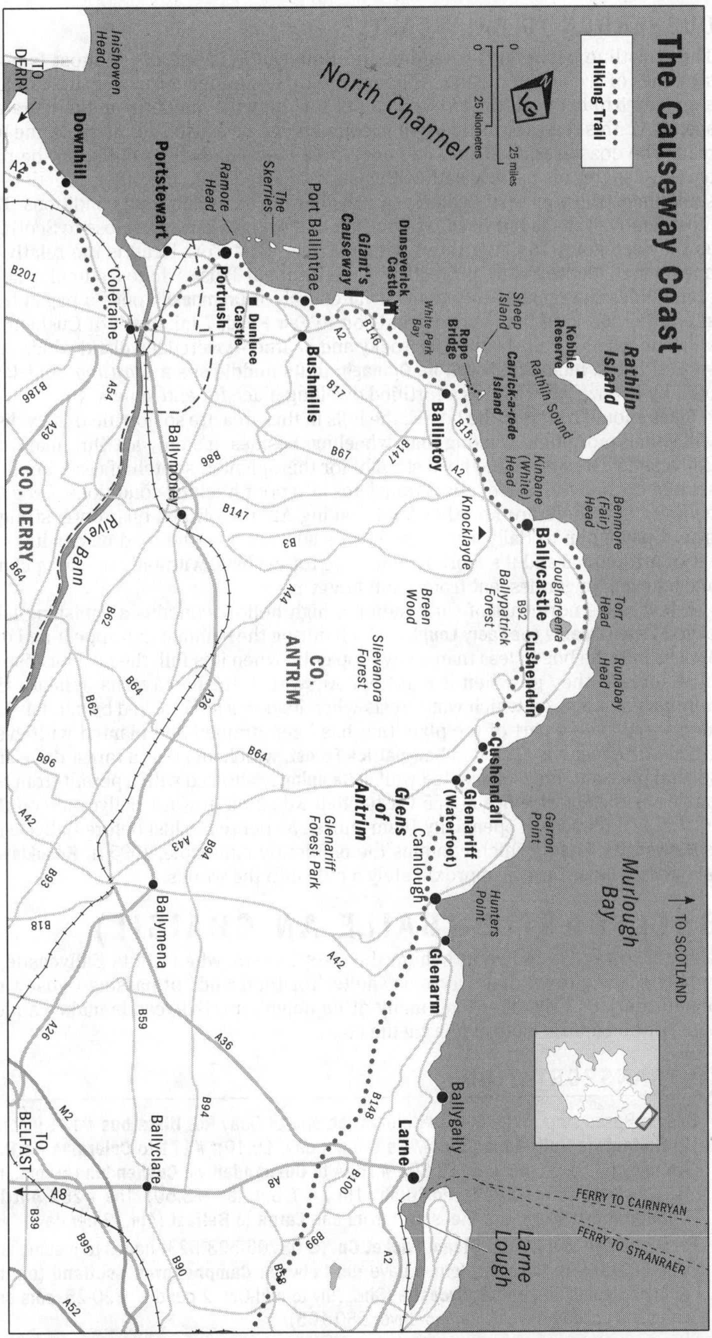

NORTHERN IRELAND

The Causeway Coast

Hiking Trail

0 25 kilometers
0 25 miles

North Channel
Murlough Bay
TO SCOTLAND
Rathlin Island
Kebble Reserve
Rathlin Sound
Sheep Island
Carrick-a-rede Island
Rope Bridge
White Park Bay
Dunseverick Castle
Giant's Causeway
Port Ballintrae
The Skerries
Ramore Head
Portrush
Dunluce Castle
Portstewart
Coleraine
Downhill
Inishowen Head
TO DERRY
Bushmills
Ballintoy
Kinbane (White) Head
Benmore (Fair) Head
Ballycastle
Lougharema
Torr Head
Runabay Head
Knocklayde
Ballypatrick Forest
Breen Wood
Slievanora Forest
Cushendun
Cushendall
Garron Point
Glenariff (Waterfoot)
Glens of Antrim
Glenariff Forest Park
Carnlough
Hunters Point
Glenarm
Ballygally
Larne
Larne Lough
FERRY TO CAIRNRYAN
FERRY TO STRANRAER
Ballymoney
Ballymena
Ballyclare
TO BELFAST
CO. ANTRIM
CO. DERRY
River Bann
A2 A26 A29 A36 A42 A43 A44 A52 A54 A8 M2 B15 B17 B3 B39 B58 B59 B62 B64 B67 B86 B90 B92 B93 B94 B95 B96 B100 B146 B147 B148 B186 B18 B201

CUSHENDUN TO BALLYCASTLE

The coastline between Cushendun and Ballycastle is one of the most famous stretches of scenery in Ireland. Although motorists and other travelers in search of a speedy trip between the two towns opt for the wide, modern, and moderately scenic A2, this road seems tame when compared to its coastal counterpart, the **Torr road.** The coastal road affords incomparable views and sheer cliffs, but be prepared to share this narrow path with visitors coming from the other direction—a sometimes tricky prospect when you consider the turns and road conditions. The most famous vista is **Torr Head,** a peninsula that brings visitors as close to Scotland as they are going to get without wings or fins. Past Torr Head is the relatively unexpected **Murlough Bay,** protected by the National Trust, where a stunning landscape hides the remains of the medieval church of **Drumnakill,** once a pagan holy site. The road then bumps and grinds on to **Fair Head,** 7 mi. north of Cushendun and 3 mi. east of Ballycastle. This rocky and heather-covered headland winds past several lakes, including **Lough na Cranagh;** in its middle sits a *crannog*, an island built by Bronze Age Celts as a fortified dwelling-place for elite chiefs.

Bikes should be left at the hostel: the hills in this area are so horrific that cyclists will spend more time walking than wheeling; besides, it's only a 1½hr. hike from Ballycastle. Drivers should head straight for this splendid stretch of road, but they seldom do, and the lack of autos translates into poor hitching conditions; *Let's Go* believes that there are no other kind. Taking A2, the official bus route, straight from Cushendun to Ballycastle also has its advantages—the road passes its own set of attractions and it's more manageable for cyclists, with only one long climb and an even longer descent from a soft boggy plain.

A few miles northeast of Cushendun, a high hollow contains a vanishing lake called **Loughareema** (or **Faery Lough**), which during the summer can appear and disappear into the bog in less than a day. Pop quiz: When it is full, the lake has fish in it. Where do they go when it empties? Answer: Into the caverns beneath the porous limestone, on which water rests when its pores are blocked by silt. Farther along you'll see a part of the plain that has been drained and planted with evergreens. The result is secluded **Ballypatrick Forest,** which includes a forest drive and several pleasant, Pinesol-scented walks. **Camping** is allowed with a permit from the ranger or the **Forest Office** at 155 Cushendall Rd., 2 mi. toward Ballycastle on the A2. (☎2076 2301. Park open daily 10am-sunset. £5 per tent.) Just before Ballycastle is **Ballycastle Forest,** which contains the eminently climbable, 1695 ft. **Knocklayde Mountain,** whose base is approximately a mile into the woods.

BALLYCASTLE (BAILE AN CHAISIL)

The Causeway Coast leaves behind the sleepy Glens when it hits Ballycastle, a bubbly seaside town that serves as shelter for thousands of passing Causeway-bound tourists. Friendlier than many of its neighbors, Ballycastle makes a nice base for budget travelers exploring the coast.

TRANSPORTATION

Buses: Buses stop at the Marine Hotel at the end of Quay Rd. **Ulsterbus** #131 vrooms to **Belfast** via **Ballymena** (3hr., M-Sa 5-6 per day, £6.10); #171 to **Coleraine** via **Ballymoney** (M-Sa 5-6 per day, £3.80); #162A to **Cushendall** via **Cushendun** (50min., M-F 1 per day, £3); #172 to **Portrush** (1hr., 4-7 per day, £3.50). The #252 **Antrim Coaster** runs through the **Glens of Antrim** and **Larne** to **Belfast** (4hr., 2 per day).

Ferries: Argyll and Antrim Steam Packet Co. (☎08705 523 523) hopes to resume service in 2003. In the past, ferries have run between **Campbeltown, Scotland** (on the Kintryre Peninsula), and **Ballycastle** (3hr.; July to mid-Oct. 2 per day; £20-25, cars and caravans accepted, vehicles and driver £80-105).

Bike Rental: Cushleake B&B, Quay Rd. (☎2076 3798). £6 per day.

Taxis: Castle (☎2076 8884); **Grab-a-Cab** (☎2076 3451 or 077 1495 9245).

ORIENTATION AND PRACTICAL INFORMATION

Ballycastle's main street runs perpendicular to the waterfront, starting at the ocean as **Quay Rd.,** becoming **Ann St.,** and then turning into **Castle St.** as it passes **the Diamond.** Most restaurants and shops are found along Ann St. and Castle St. As Quay Rd. meets the water, the road takes a sharp left onto **North St.,** where more stores and food await. Directly east of Quay Rd. is a park and the town strand; beyond them is **Mary Rd.,** where lies the tourist office. B&Bs nest on Quay Rd.

Tourist Office: Sheskburn House, 7 Mary St. (☎2076 2024). Info on the entire Antrim coast. Also books accommodations. 24hr. computerized info kiosk outside. Open July-Aug. M-F 9:30am-7pm, Sa 10am-6pm, Su 2-6pm; Sept.-June M-F 9:30am-5pm.

Banks: First Trust Bank, Ann St. (☎2076 3326). Open M-F 9:30am-4:30pm, W open 10am. **Northern Bank,** 24 Ann St. (☎2076 2238). Open M-F 9:30am-12:30pm and 1:30-3pm, F until 5pm. Both have 24hr. **ATMs.**

Pharmacy: McMullan's NuMark, 63 Castle St. (☎2076 3135). Open M-Sa 9am-6pm, alternating Su noon-1pm.

Emergency: ☎999. **Police:** Ramoan Rd. (☎2076 2312 or 2076 3125).

Internet Access: Ballycastle Library (☎2076 2566), on the corner of Castle St. and Leyland St. £2.50 per hr., members free (sign up for a card). Open M and Th-Sa 10am-1pm and 2-5:30pm, Tu 6-8pm. **Herald's** restaurant, 22 Ann St. (☎2076 9064), has a single terminal for public use. £1 per hr. (See **Food,** below.)

Post Office: 3 Ann St. (☎2076 2519). Open M-Tu and Th-F 9am-1pm and 2-5:30pm, W 9am-1pm, Sa 9am-12:30pm. **Postal code:** BT54.

ACCOMMODATIONS

Most of Ballycastle's housing clusters around the harbor at the northern end of town. Look out for the Ould Lammas Fair, held the last Monday and Tuesday in August—B&Bs fill almost a year in advance, and hostels fill weeks before the fair.

Castle Hostel (IHH), 62 Quay Rd. (☎2076 2337), just out of town, next to the Marine Hotel. 40-bed hostel with a relaxed and welcoming atmosphere. Laundry wash £2, dry £2. Dorms £7; private rooms £8.50 per person. ❶

Ballycastle Backpackers (IHO), North St. (☎2076 3612 or 077 7323 7890), also next to the Marine Hotel. The view of the strand's sunrises makes up for somewhat absentee management. Dorms £7.50; singles £10, with bath £12.50-15. ❶

Fragrens, 34 Quay Rd. (☎2076 2168). Although the house is one of Ballycastle's oldest, recent renovations have brought a modern sheen to all the bedrooms. Fresh fruit at breakfast is a welcome change from greasy meat. £17-18 per person. ❷

Marine Hotel, 1-3 North St. (☎2076 2222). Beautiful views, spacious rooms, and on-site dining makes your stay especially enjoyable. Singles £65-80; doubles £70-90. ❺

FOOD

Your friendly local **SuperValu,** 54 Castle St., is a 10min. walk from the hostels. (☎2076 2268. Open M-Sa 8am-10pm, Su 9am-10pm.)

Flash-in-the-Pan, 74 Castle St. (☎2076 2251). Pretends to be a humble chipper, but the specialty would more properly be called a £3 tour-de-force fried-fish-fiesta. Open Su-Th 11am-midnight, F-Sa 11am-1am. ❶

Herald's, 22 Ann St. (☎2076 9064). Serves huge, fleshy portions at cheap prices. The wonderful staff is just the icing on the cake. **Internet access** available. Entrees £4-8. Open daily 8am-9pm. ❷

The Cellar, the Diamond (☎2076 3037). Eat-in or takeaway yummy homemade pizza or calzones (£3-7). Evening meals £7-12.50. Open daily noon-10pm. ❸

Wysner's, 16 Ann St. (☎2076 2372), caters to seafood lovers, and prides itself on using local ingredients. Lunch around £5, dinner special £6-15. Open June-Aug. daily 8am-11pm; Sept.-May 8am-8pm. ❹

PUBS

Trad can be hard to come by in the North, even in tourist-subservient areas. Not so in Ballycastle, where pubs satiate the masses with frequent summertime sessions.

House of McDonnell, 71 Castle St. (☎2076 2975). Tourists come for Trad F, Folk Sa, and the more elusive Spontaneous Trad, which pops up sporadically during the wk.

McCarroll's Bar, 7 Ann St. (☎2076 2123). The place to be for reels and jigs (Th). Nicely lit, and a bonus beer garden sits out back for the more relaxed guzzler.

Central Bar, 12 Ann St. (☎2076 3877). Musical fun ranging from piano sing-alongs (Th) to karaoke (Sa) to the ever-popular trad (W). Always lots of *craic* on tap.

Boyd Arms, 4 the Diamond (☎2076 2364). Once a weekly trad-type bar; now a constant consumption of alcohol-type bar. Not that that's necessarily a bad thing.

SIGHTS AND FESTIVALS

The Holy Trinity Church of Ireland—a.k.a. **Boyd Church**—is responsible for that octagonal spire you've been wondering about. Built by 18th-century landlord Hugh Boyd, the same guy who brought you Quay Rd., Ann St. (named for his wife), and local industrialization, the improvements fell into ruin when industrial profiteering lost its groove. Half a mile out of town on the Cushendall road, the 15th-century **Bonamargy Friary** sits in the middle of a golf course. Pretty impressive, this: nice graveyard, climbable priory, and a par-3 hole.

For those who'd rather *do* than *see*, **Moyle Sightseeing Tours** produces fishing and sightseeing tours, and sells local fishing licenses. (Contact Dan McCauley ☎2076 9521. One-day license £11, 8-day £23.50.) The **Ould Lammas Fair,** Northern Ireland's oldest and most famous fair, has taken place in Ballycastle for 413 years. Originally a week-long fiesta, the festival is now crammed into two frenzied days, the last Monday and Tuesday in August. Following the traditions of the ancient Celtic harvest festival, the fair jams Ballycastle's streets with vendors selling cows, sheep, crafts, and baked goods, as trad musicians pack the pubs.

NEAR BALLYCASTLE: RATHLIN ISLAND (REACHLAINN)

Just off the coast at Ballycastle, bumpy, boomerang-shaped Rathlin Island ("Fort of the Sea") offers the ultimate in escapism for 20,000 puffins, the odd golden eagle, 100 human beings, and four daily ferries of tourists. Its windy surface supports few trees, but does harbor an eco-paradise of orchids, purple heather, and seabirds. The contrast between the white chalk and black basalt cliffs that encircle the island led the novelist Charles Kingsley to compare Rathlin to a "drowned magpie." During 20 years of Famine-ravage, the island's population dwindled from 1000 to half that; most of Rathlin's emigrants set sail for America and created a community in Maine. Even though electricity only arrived in Rathlin in 1992, the island holds a unique place in the history of technology: in 1898, the Italian scientist Marconi sent the first wireless telegraph message from here to Ballycastle.

A leaflet available at the Ballycastle tourist office contains a decent map and description of the island's walks and sights. For a more complete presentation of its intricately intertwined history and myths, visit the island's **Boat House Heritage Centre** (a.k.a. the Rathlin Island Visitors Centre), at the southeastern end of the harbor opposite the ferry. (☎2076 3951. Open May-Aug. daily 10am-4pm, other months by arrangement. Free.) **Irene's minibus** service (☎2076 3949) will drive you from the ferry docks to the **Kebble Bird Sanctuary,** at the western tip of the island, 4½ mi. from the harbor (20min., every 45min., £2.50 each way). Peak bird-watching season lasts from May to mid-July. The **lighthouse** is the best place to view the enormous colony of puffins, guillemots, and gulls nesting in the cliffs, but it's accessible only with the warden's supervision. (Call in advance ☎2076 3948.) A walk to **Rue Point,** 2½ mi. from the harbor, allows visitors to marvel at the crumbled remains of **Smuggler's House,** which has wall cavities that once hid contraband during the days when pirates and smugglers fueled Rathlin's economy. **Fair Head** and its frolicking **seals** loom a few miles away from Rue Point.

Caledonian MacBrayne runs a **ferry** service to the island from Ballycastle. In the summer, the ferry runs four times daily from the pier at Ballycastle, on Bayview Rd., up the hill from Quay Rd. and by the harbor. The small MacBrayne office at the Ballycastle pier, open before each departure, sells tickets, but buying at the central office ensures a timely return. (☎2076 9299. 45min. June-Sept. 4 per day, Oct.-May 2 per day. £8.40 return, children £4.20.)

If you need a break from it all, spend the night at the **Kinramer Camping Barn (ACB)** ❶, a 4½ mi. hike from the harbor, where clusters of bunks are isolated by plywood partitions. (☎2073 3948. Dorms or camping beds £5.) The **Soerneog View Hostel** ❶ provides an option closer to the hustle and bustle of the ferry landing. To get there, take a right from the dock and turn left at the side road before the pub. At the top of the road, turn right; the hostel is a ¼ mi. down on the left. Call ahead for pickup. This place's six beds fill up quickly, so be sure to secure your spot by calling ahead. (☎2076 3954. **Bike rental** £7 per day. Wash £3, dry 50p. 2-bunk private dorms £8.) Either way, remember to stock up on groceries on the mainland. **McCuaig's Bar** ❷ sometimes allows free **camping** on its grounds. The bar is the single entertainment center for the entire island, as well as its only food source. (☎2076 3974. Sandwiches, toasties, and burgers £1-2, limited selection of entrees £4-6. Food served 9am-9pm.)

BALLINTOY AND THE ISLANDS

Five miles west of Ballycastle on the B15, the modest village of **Ballintoy** *(Baile an Tuaighe)* consists of a church, a harbor, a hostel, and a fisherman's bridge that is one of the most frequented tourist destinations in all of Northern Ireland. Two diminutive but remarkable islands, Sheep and Carrick-a-rede, put Ballintoy's name on the map. Visible from Ballintoy village, **Sheep Island** is home to puffins, razor bills, kittiwakes, and the largest cormorant colony in Ireland. Even smaller but better-known **Carrick-a-rede Island** lies offshore to the east of Ballintoy. Meaning "rock in the road," Carrick-a-rede presents a barrier to migrating salmon returning to their home rivers. For over 250 years, fishermen have set up their nets at the point off the island that the migrating salmon have to pass. To reach the nets, the fishermen string a **rope bridge** between the mainland and the island, where it hangs from April to September. Crossing the shaky, 48 in. wide, 67 ft. long bridge over the dizzying 100 ft. drop to rocks and sea below is now the business of thousands of tourists every year. Wardens are on site during opening hours, and the bridge is certainly a lot safer than the days when it had only one handrail to cling to, but you should still be **extremely careful** in windy weather. A sign about ½ mile east of Ballintoy on the Coast road marks the turnoff for the bridge; the carpark is a ¼ mile farther, and the bridge is less than 1 mi. beyond that.

I AM A CERTIFIED HERO

I, ______________________________, devotee of *Let's Go: Ireland 2003* and all it stands for, am hereby to be referred to as "hero" because I have crossed the treacherous rope-bridge to Carrick-a-Rede Island. Possession of this certificate entitles me to hero-worship and all the privileges contained therein.

Witness: ______________________________

Date: ______________________________

The walk out to the bridge leads courageous crossers along the heights of the **Larrybane sea cliffs,** where you're likely to see at least one of the many native species of birds, including the unusual black-and-white razor bill, the quirky brown- and white-bellied guillemot, and the mundane gull. Ask the wardens for the National Trust's leaflet on the site, which provides a map of the area's geological notables. On the eastern side of the island, a fishing hut totters and salmon nets stretch out into the sea. The **tearoom** by the parking lot sells snacks, posts information, and offers a bit of local advice. For 50p, they'll also give you a certificate stating that you successfully crossed the bridge, but *Let's Go* recommends that you save your money for bubble gum and use our certificate instead (see **I Am a Certified Hero,** above). Free **camping** can be arranged with the wardens. Access to the parking lot is zealously protected by officious National Trust employees. (☎2076 2178. Carpark closes 8pm. Tea room open July-Sept. daily 10am-8pm. £3 per car.)

Quiet Ballintoy provides beds and grub for Carrick-a-rede's daredevils. A local grocer (open daily 9am-5pm) spawned the aptly-named **Sheep Island View Hostel (IHH)** ❶, 42A Main St., which has one of the biggest kitchens you'll ever see. Call the hostel for pickup from anywhere between Ballycastle and Portrush. (☎2076 9391; www.sheepislandview.com. Wheelchair-accessible. Continental breakfast £3, Ulster fry £4.50. Laundry £2. Dorms with bath £10. **Camping** £5 per person.) In town, **Fullerton Arms** ❸ serves non-transgressive pub food and other treats behind frosted-glass windows. They also have three-star **B&B** accommodations if you ask nicely at the bar. (☎2076 9613. Pub food £5-7; served 12:30-9pm. Restaurant open M-F 6-9pm, Sa-Su all day. B&B £25 per person.) Across the street, **Carrick-a-rede Pub** is cheaper and less ostentatious, food-wise and music-wise. *Let's Go* prefers ostentation. (☎2076 2241. Food £3.50-5.50; served noon-9pm. Tu, F and Su trad.)

Three miles west along the coast road from Ballintoy is the **Whitepark Bay Youth Hostel (HANI)** ❶. Its out-of-the-way setting, overlooking one of the most famous—and least swimmable—beaches on the Antrim Coast, is either a blessing or a bane, depending on whether or not you have a car. The Portrush-Ballycastle bus (#172) or the Antrim Coaster (#252) will drop you off 200 yd. from the hostel, but there are no shops or pubs for miles. A **restaurant** sells the most basic food stuffs. (☎2073 1745. Breakfast £2.50. 4-bed dorms £11; doubles £13. Under 18 £1 less.)

PORTRUSH (PORT RUIS)

Portrush's name should be taken quite literally: in the fall, when the universities reopen, students flood the city center; in July, when their summer holidays begin, they race back out again in order to make room for an even more vicious influx, that of holiday-making tourists. The streets boil over on summer days with families flocking to amusements and carnival rides; in the evenings, teenly elements swamp the town's discos. Despite its flaws—or charms, depending on your taste—Portrush remains the town most convenient to the region's major attractions.

TRANSPORTATION. Trains run from Eglinton St. (☎7082 2395) in the center of town (open July-Aug. M-F 11am-8pm; Sept.-June 7:45am-3:30pm) to Belfast (2hr.; M-F 9 per day, Sa 7 per day, Su 4 per day; £5.30) and Derry (1hr.; M-F 9 per day, Sa 7 per day, Su 3 per day; £5.90). Most causeway-bound **buses** stop in town at Dunluce Ave. Ulsterbus #140 ("Triangle Service") runs to Coleraine via Portstewart (30min.; every 10min. 6:55am-10:30pm). #172 runs along the coast to Bushmills (20min.; 5-6 per day), Giant's Causeway (25min.), Ballintoy (40min.), and Ballycastle (1hr.). The open-topped **Bushmills Bus** (#177) goes to Portstewart, Bushmills, and the Giant's Causeway (summer only, 5 per day). **Rent** your **bike** at **Thompson Cycles,** 77b Lower Main St. (☎7082 9606. £7 per day; ID deposit. Open daily 10am-5pm; after closing return bikes at the hostel.)

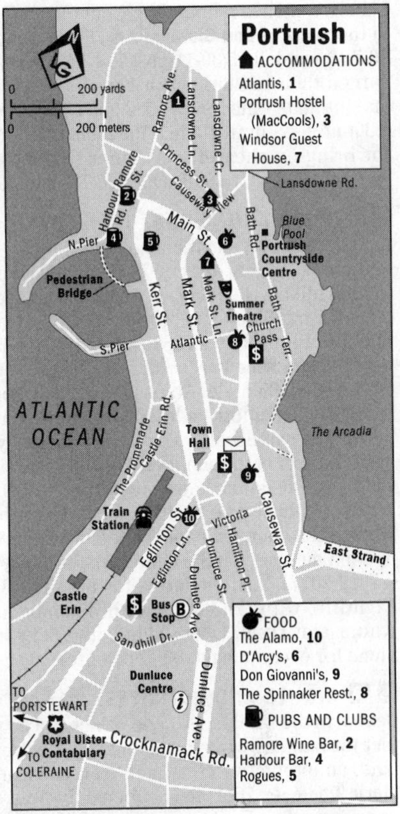

PRACTICAL INFORMATION. The **tourist office,** in the Dunluce Centre off Sandhill Dr. and just south of the town center, will book accommodations and **bureau** your **de change,** for a fee. (☎7082 3333. Open mid-June to Aug. daily 9am-7pm; Apr.-June and Sept. M-F 9am-5pm, Sa-Su noon-5pm; Mar. and Oct. Sa-Su noon-5pm.) For more money stuff, including getting some, hit up **First Trust,** 25 Eglinton St. (☎7082 2726. Open M-F 9:30am-4:30pm, W open 10am.) Outfit your **surfing** excursion at **Trogg's,** 88 Main St. (☎7082 5476. Open July-Aug. daily 10am-9pm; Sept.-June 11am-6pm). The **post office** is on Eglinton St. (☎7082 3700. Open M-Tu and Th-Sa 9am-12:30pm and 1:30-5:30pm, W 9am-1pm.) The **postal code** is BT56.

ACCOMMODATIONS AND FOOD. The owners of the **Portrush Hostel (MacCool's) ❶**, 5 Causeway View Terr., are as of press time attempting to sell the property. Until they do, though, travelers are warmly encouraged to relax in their homey common room and partake of the owner's informative hiking advice. (**Internet access** £2 per 15min. Laundry £3. Dorms £7.) One place that seems sure not to go out of business is the very large **Windsor Guest House ❷**, 67-71 Main St., which provides professional service and sunny rooms. (☎7082 3793; www.windsorguesthouse.com. Lunches £3; dinner £8; full board £10. £18 per person.) **Atlantis ❷**, 10 Ramore Ave., has what passes in Portrush for an ocean view. (☎7082 4583. Dinner £5. Singles £18; doubles £32, with bath £37.)

Portrush's coterie of chippers and too-expensive-for-budget-travel options is spurred by a tiny **Spar,** 106 Lower Main St. (☎7082 5447. Open daily 7am-11pm.)

Lonely wenches rebounding from plate after plate of greasy chips will find solace in the arms of **Don Giovanni's ❷**, 9-13 Causeway St. (☎7082 5516. Pizza £4-7, pasta £6-7. Open daily 5:30-11pm.) The new management at **D'Arcy's ❹**, Main St., have earned their reputation for ambitious cuisine (mint almond pesto; ostrich filets) and intimate dinners. (☎7082 2063. Lunches £4-6, dinners £8-14. Open daily noon-9:30pm; F-Sa until 10pm.) **The Alamo ❷**, Eglinton St., will always be remembered for bringing cheap food, rather than non-indigenous disease, to supplicants. (☎7082 2000. Pizza £3-5. Open M-Th 5pm-2am, F-Sa 5pm-3am, Su 5pm-1am.)

PUBS AND CLUBS. The nightlife scene in this once-and-future metropolis has increasingly been consolidated into a collection of multi-venue complexes, with pubs feeding directly into live music clubs and discos. Although bar crowds remain mixed, the (very) young set does seem to prevail on disco nights. The newest such multiplex sits at the top of the North Pier, off Harbour Rd. The **Harbour Bar,** 5 Harbour Rd. (☎7082 2430), tries its darndest to remain a sailor pub, but the new **Ramore Wine Bar** (☎7082 4313), at the top of the hill, aspires to a more lofty, well-heeled clientele. Across the harbor, **Rogues,** 54 Kerr St., (☎7082 2946) tries to teach the behemoths a lesson by offering nightly live bands and almighty alcohol within the same walls. The crowd varies by season: students in the winter, more aged tourists in the summer. The crowd at the **Trak's Complex** remains more consistently inconsistent; the **Station Bar** feeds relative innocents to the hard-techno **Trak's Nightclub** and relative oldsters to the live-music **Shunter's.** (☎7082 2112; www.traks-complex.com. Nightclub cover £7; open M and Th-Sa. Music cover £3-5; open summer Tu-Sa, winter Th-Sa.) **Kelly's** (officially "Beetle's Bar and Disco"; ☎7082 2027), just outside of town on the Bushmill's road, is the Original King of Nightlife, with ten bars and three clubs, including the main disco and jailbait wholesaler **Lushi.** Overwhelmingly tacky, this juggernaut-cum-behemoth has a niche for every imaginable type of teenager.

SIGHTS AND ACTIVITES. Portrush's best-advertised attraction is **Dunluce Centre,** in the Dunluce Arcade, which is a sort of kiddie ride of a heritage sight. Perfect for families with young 'uns, the Centre hosts the largest soft-play area in Ireland, an interactive computer Treasure Hunt, as well as the **Turbo Tours Hydraulic Movie Room.** (☎7082 4444. Open July-Aug. daily 10am-7pm; May-June and Sept. noon-5pm; Apr. Sa-Su noon-5pm. Turbo tours £2.50, whole enchilada £5.) The yin to the Dunluce Centre's yang is the **Portrush Countryside Centre,** 8 Bath Rd., next to the East Strand. The displays here, which cater to the same kiddies but with less exclusivity, include wildlife exhibits and a tidal pool with sea urchins and starfish. (☎7082 3600. Open July-Aug. daily 10am-6pm; June by pre-booking only. Free.)

To escape all this amusement-park silliness, head over to the **East Strand Beach,** which stretches 1½ mi. from town toward the Giant's Causeway (see below). At the far end of the beach is a carpark; from here, it's another 1½ mi. along the main road to **Dunluce Castle,** a surprisingly intact 16th-century fort. The castle was built close to the cliff's edge—so close, in fact, that one day the kitchen fell into the sea. (Open Apr.-Sept. M-Sa 10am-6pm, Su 2-6pm; June-Aug. M-Sa 10am-6am, Su noon-6pm; Oct.-Mar. Tu-Sa 10am-4pm, Su 2-4pm. Last admission 30min. before closing. £1.50, students 75p.) Near the edge of the castle, the mouth of a **sea cave** stretches down to the water. Getting down can be quite slippery, but the adventurous are rewarded with outstanding sea views.

The best **surfing** on the North Antrim coast is at **Portballintree Beach,** where the waves soar almost as high as the nearby castle. If the sea proves intimidating, contact **Gareth Becket,** who can teach you how to conquer the **surf** and **hang ten** like a pro (☎028 7032 9468 or 078 8430 6795). After a hard day of surfing, retire to **Waterworld's Pirate's Cove,** where two water slides, a water playground, and a swimming area await. When you've had enough liquid, try your hand at one of the center's

Pirate Bowl bowling lanes while you wait to dry. (Pirate's Cove ☎7082 2001; open July-Aug. M-Sa 10am-8pm, Su noon-8pm; Sept. Sa 10am-7pm, Su noon-7pm. Last tickets sold 1hr. before closing. Pirate Bowl ☎7082 2334; open July-Aug. M-Sa 10am-10pm, Su noon-10pm; Sept. F 6-10pm, Sa 10am-10pm, Su 12-10pm.)

For those with a yarnin' fer culture, mosey on over to Portrush's **Summer Theatre** stage, St. Patrick's Hall, Causeway St., which provides a venue for several Northern Irish theater companies but has nothing to do with cowboys. (☎7082 2500. Performances W-Sa 8pm. Tickets £4. Box office open W-Sa 11am-noon and 6-8pm.)

DAYTRIPS FROM PORTRUSH

THE GIANT'S CAUSEWAY

The Causeway is always open and free to pedestrians. Ulsterbuses #172 to Portrush, the #252 Antrim Coaster, the "Causeway Rambler," and the Bushmills Bus all dump visitors at the Giant's Causeway Visitors Centre (in the shop next to the carpark). Every 15min., the Causeway Coaster minibus runs to the columns (£1.20, 2min.). Centre info ☎2073 1855; open June daily 10am-5pm; July-Aug. 10am-6pm; Sept.-May 10am-4:30pm. Parking £5.

Geologists believe that the unique rock formations found at the **Giant's Causeway** were formed some 60 million years ago, when molten lava broke through the surface, cooled, and shrank at an unusually steady rate. Though locals have very different ideas (see **The Real MacCool,** below), everyone agrees that the causeway is an awesome sight to behold. Comprised of over 40,000 perfectly symmetrical hexagonal basalt columns, the sight resembles a large descending staircase that leads out from the cliffs to the ocean's floor below. While most simply enjoy the causeway proper, the site offers more than just stone-hopping. In addition to the Grand Causeway itself, several other formations, such as **The Giant's Organ, The Wishing Chair, The Granny, The Camel,** and **The Giant's Boot,** can also be viewed. Advertised as the eighth natural wonder of the world, the Giant's Causeway is Northern Ireland's most famous sight, so don't be surprised to find that 2000 other travelers picked the same exact day as you to visit.

Once travelers reach the visitors center, they have two options: the more popular low road, which directly swoops down to the causeway from the center (20min.); and the more rewarding high road, which takes visitors the 4½ mi. to the overwhelmingly romantic Iron Age ruins of **Dunseverick Castle,** which sit high above on a sea cliff. Bus #172 and the #252 Antrim Coaster stop in front of the castle, from which it's 4½ mi. farther to Ballintoy. The trail is well-marked and easy to follow, but those looking for additional help should consult the free map available from the visitors center. Two miles west of the Causeway, **Bushmills** (of distillery fame) is the next place you'll probably want to check out (see below).

THE REAL MACCOOL Legend has it that the Giant's Causeway was formed when the warrior giant Finn MacCool fell in love with Una, a lady giant who lived off the Scottish coast on Staffa Island. Finn, devoted that he was, built the Giant's Causeway in order to bring Una to Ulster, which explains why there are similar honeycomb-esque rock formations on Staffa. Benandonner, a vexed and Scottish giant, followed the lovebirds to Ireland, intending óto defeat Finn and take Una home with him. When Big Mac realized just how large his Scottish rival was, he recognized the folly of his physical confidence and turned instead to his massive wit for guidance. With the help of darling Una, the wily Finn disguised himself as an Irish-giant infant. When the Scot got a load of the size of that baby, he imagined how big the father must have been and quickly fled back to Scotland, destroying the Causeway in his wake to ensure that Papp Finn wouldn't be able to pursue.

NORTHERN IRELAND

BUSHMILLS DISTILLERY

The distillery and its Bushmills are 3 mi. east of Portrush and 2 mi. west of the Causeway, at the intersection of A2 and B17; they are served by The Causeway Rambler bus and the Bushmills bus. ☎2073 1521. Open M-Sa 9:30am-5:30pm; last tour 4pm. Closed around Christmas. Tours Apr.-Oct. when enough people accumulate; Nov.-Mar. daily at 10:30 and 11:30am and 1:30, 2:30, and 3:30pm. £3.95, students and seniors £3.50.

Ardently Protestant Bushmills has been home to the **Old Bushmills Distillery,** creator of Bushmills Irish Whiskey, since 1608, which makes it the oldest licensed whiskey producer in the world. Travelers have been stopping here since ancient days, when it was on the route to Tara from castles Dunluce and Dunseverick. The tour allows you to see whiskey being thrice-distilled when the plant is operating; during the three weeks in July when production stops for maintenance, the far-less-interesting experience is redeemed only by the free sample at its end. Serious whiskey fans (and who isn't these days?) should shoulder their way to the front as the tour winds down and volunteer when the guide makes his cryptic request for "help."

PORTSTEWART (PORT STÍOBHAIRD)

The twin ports of Portstewart and Portrush have enough in common to have developed a friendly rivalry. Although it's as crowded as Portrush, Portstewart feels far less claustrophobic. 'Stewart's crowds remain more affluent, lending the town a more refined, ice-cream-parlor-rather-than-fast-food aesthetic, but recent overcrowding in 'Rush has pushed some of its famous nightlife over the border, allowing 'Stewart's visitors to couple their beachy fun with lusty clubbing.

TRANSPORTATION AND PRACTICAL INFORMATION. Buses stop in the middle of **the Promenade.** Ulsterbus #140 ("The Triangle") connects Portstewart, Portrush, and Coleraine (M-Sa 21-28 per day, Su 9 per day). Portstewart's **tourist office,** in the red-brick library/town hall complex, sits on the crescent at the southern end of the Promenade. The library also provides **Internet access** for £1.50 per 30min. (☎7083 2286. Open July-Aug. M-Sa 10am-1pm and 2-4:30pm.) **First Trust,** 13 the Promenade, offers financial services inside and out with a 24hr. **ATM.** (☎7083 3273. Open M-F 9:30am-4:30pm, W open 10am.) The **post office,** 90 the Promenade, waits inside the Spick and Span cleaners. (☎7083 2001. Open M-Tu and Th-F 9am-1pm and 2-5:30pm, W 9am-1pm, Sa 9am-12:30pm.) The **postal code** is BT55.

ACCOMMODATIONS, FOOD, AND PUBS. The Victoria Terr. area, on the left as you head out of town on the Portrush road, has beds galore. From the bus stop, face the sea, turn right, and follow Main St. around the corner; Victoria Terr. juts out to the left. **Rick's Causeway Coast Independent Hostel (IHH/IHO) ❶,** 4 Victoria Terr., is friendly and comfortable. (☎7083 3789. Barbecue available. Laundry £2, free if you stay for more than one night. £2 key deposit. Dorms £7; doubles £17.) **Wanderin' Heights ❷,** 12 High Rd., near Victoria Terr., provides B&B and yellow-print wallpaper. (☎7083 3250. All rooms with bath. Singles £20-25; shared rooms £20-25 per person.) **The Anchorage Inn ❹,** of Skipper's Wine Bar fame, provides luxury rooms, all with bath. (☎7083 4401. Singles £35; doubles £60.)

Portstewart cultivates both good cooks and a tradition of superb ice cream. **Centra** supermarket, 70 the Promenade, has an impressive selection of cheeses. (☎7083 3203. Open daily 7am-midnight.) **Morelli's Sundae Garden ❶,** 55-58 the Promenade, provides Portstewart's indispensable gustatory experience—the unnaturally good waffle cone sundae. (☎7083 2150. Open July-Aug. daily 9am-11pm; Sept.-June variable weekend hours only.) **Good Food and Company ❷,** 44 the Promenade, serves sandwiches (£1.50-1.70) and baked goods. (☎7083 6386. Open M-Sa 8:30am-10pm; Sept.-June M-Sa 8:30am-6pm.) **Ecosse Restaurant ❹,** Atlantic

Circle, serves sit-down dinners and ocean views for those with time to dine. (☎7083 5822. A la carte dinner F-Sa 6-10pm, Su 6-8:30pm £8-15. Su brunch £6-8.)

Portstewart's two major entertainment monoliths are at the southern end of the promenade: **O'Hara's** and **The Anchor.** Each are comprised of a couple of bars and a music club/venue. Anchor Pub, 87 the Promenade, provides less self-conscious pints. Upstairs houses a live music venue, as does the nearby **Skipper's Wine Bar.** Both The Anchor and Skipper alike serve food, though the food at Skipper's is a bit more expensive. (☎7083 2003. M and Th-Su live music.) Across the street, O'Hara's public bar has as mixed a crowd as the multiplexes get, with a pool table and a cool lounge for the kids; **Shenanigan's** serves up sophisticated and adventurous fare to a thumpin' dance beat; **Bar 7** courts a mature crowd with upscale and upprice whiskeys; **Chaines** is the weekend disco for youngsters. (☎7083 6000. Restaurant open noon-2:30pm and 5-9:30pm. Disco F-Sa.)

SIGHTS AND ACTIVITIES. Beachcombers have a full day ahead of them on the 6½ mi. coastal path that leads east from Portstewart Strand, on the west side of town, toward Portrush. The path takes you past sea cliffs, blow holes, an ancient hermit's house, and plenty of other odd sights that a free map from the tourist office will help you recognize. **Portstewart Strand,** less than a mile west of town, is owned and preserved by the National Trust. (Visitors facilities open daily May-Aug. 10am-6pm. £3 per car, free after 6pm.) The **Port-na-happle rock pool,** located between town and the beach, is ideal for bathing. A small but dedicated group of surfers call these waters home; the town's two surf shops serve those who dare to take on the Irish waves. **Troggs,** 20 the Diamond, rents wetsuits, surfboards, bodyboards, and wild things. (☎7083 3361. Equipment £3-10 per day. Open July-Aug. daily 10am-6pm; Apr.-June Sa-Su 10am-6pm.) **Ocean Warriors,** at 80 the Promenade and on the Strand, rents similar equipment. (☎7083 6500. Open daily 10am-6pm.) According to locals, the best waves hit the shore from September to March and reach 5-6 ft. The **Flowerfield Arts Centre,** 185 Coleraine Rd., shelters traveling art exhibits and holds lectures on subjects ranging from local history and folklore to the royal family. (☎7083 3959. Open M-F 9am-1pm and 2-5pm.)

DOWNHILL

The land between Castlerock and Downhill once belonged to the Earl Bishop Frederick Hervey, Earl of Bristol and Derry, who will long be remembered as one of the wackiest members of British aristocracy ever to tamper with the Irish landscape. His construction of **Downhill Castle** in the late 18th century challenged the coast's stoic sea cliffs with the heavy hand of human decadence. His house was once one of Europe's greatest treasure troves, but it suffered a disastrous fire and was abandoned after WWII. The residence was later bought by a Yankee Doodle Dandy, who gutted it and sold the windows, chandeliers, furnishings, and even the roof, leaving behind only the stone shell of a former palace.

On the cliffs in front of the castle, **Musendun Temple** all but teeters over a precipitous drop to the sea. This circular library was based on the Temples of Vesta in Italy and was named after the niece with whom locals speculated Earl Bishop Fred had an affair. Behind the castle sit the remains of another of Hervey's architectural frivolities—the **mausoleum** he built for his brother, which sings a cautionary song. Ignoring warnings that the windy clifftop would not long support the structure he had planned, Herv erected a monument twice the height of the one that now stands. Needless to say, a second tier and the statue atop it both toppled in a windstorm. (Temple open July-Aug. daily noon-6pm; Apr.-June and Sept. Sa-Su noon-6pm.) **Downhill Beach,** one of the most gorgeous on the Northern coast, lies below.

Getting to Downhill is surprisingly easy; **bus** #134 from Coleraine to Limavady swings right by (7-8 per day)—ask the driver to drop you at the hostel, which will be a 2min. walk straight ahead. The **train** stops at Castlerock on its way from Belfast to Derry, and from there the hostel will pick you up for free if you call ahead. Leaving may be more difficult—the **Downhill Hostel's** ❶ gentle embrace can prove mighty addictive. This dreamhouse has a beach out front, is backed by cliffs, and is bordered by a rocky stream. High bunks, hand-sewn quilts, and a luxurious shower provide more reasons to stick around. (☎7084 9077. Wetsuit and boogie board rental £6 per day. Laundry £3.50. Dorms £7.50; private rooms £9 per person.) The closest food source other than Downhill's pub is the grocery store 2 mi. away in **Castlerock,** so do your shopping before you arrive. In the nearby library, you'll find books galore, and **Internet access.** (☎7084 8463.)

DERRY (DOIRE CHOLM CILLE)

Derry became a major commercial port under the Ulster Plantation of the 17th century (see p. 58). Under the English feudal system, the city became the outpost of London's authority, who renamed it Londonderry. (Phone books and other such bureaucratic traps use this official title, but many Northerners refer to the city as Derry.) The past three centuries of Derry's history have given rise to the iconography used by both sides of the sectarian conflict. The city's troubled history spans from the siege of Derry in 1689, when the now-legendary Apprentice Boys closed the city gates on the advancing armies of the Catholic King James II (see p. 58), to the civil rights turmoil of the 1960s, when protests against religious discrimination against Catholics exploded into violence publicized worldwide. In 1972, the Troubles reached their pinnacle on Bloody Sunday, a tragic public massacre in which British soldiers shot into a crowd of peaceful protesters. None of the soldiers were ever convicted, and Nationalists are still seeking redress from the British government (see **The Troubles,** p. 455). Hearings into the Bloody Sunday Massacre were recently reopened, and will be held in Derry's Guildhall over the next few years.

INTERCITY TRANSPORTATION

Airport: Eglinton/Derry Airport, Eglinton (☎7181 0784). 7 mi. from Derry. Flights to **Dublin, Glasgow, London-Stanstead,** and **Manchester.**

Trains: Duke St., Waterside (☎7134 2228), on the east bank. A free **Rail-Link bus** connects the bus station to the train station. Trains from Derry go east to **Belfast** via **Castlerock, Coleraine, Ballymoney, Ballymena,** and **Lisburn** (2½hr.; M-F 7 per day, Sa 6 per day, Su 4 per day; £7.80). Connections may be made from Coleraine to **Portrush.**

Buses: Most stop at the Ulsterbus depot on Foyle St. between the walled city and the river. **Ulsterbus** (☎7126 2261) serves all destinations in the North and a few in the Republic. #212 to **Belfast** (1½-3hr.; M-Sa 14-16 per day, Su 6 per day; £8); #234 to **Coleraine** (M-F 4 per day, Su 1 per day; £5.40); #275 to Donegal (90min., M-Sa 1 per day at noon); #274 to **Dublin** via **Omagh** (4-6 per day, £10.31); #296 to **Galway** via Longford and **Athlone** (7hr., M-Sa at 9am); #273-4 to **Omagh** (M-Sa 13 per day, Su 8 per day; £5.40). **Lough Swilly** bus service (☎7126 2017) heads to the **Fanad Peninsula,** the **Inishowen Peninsula,** and **Letterkenny,** and other parts of northwest Donegal. Buses to: **Buncrana** (35min.; M-Sa 10-12 per day, Su 4 per day; £3); **Letterkenny** (1hr.; M-F 10 per day, Sa 13 per day; £4); **Malin Head** (1½hr.; M, W, and F 1 per day, Sa 3 per day; £5). **Northwest Busways** (Republic ☎077 82619) heads to **Inishowen** from Patrick St. opposite the Multiplex Cinema and to **Buncrana** (M-Sa 9 per day, £2.50), **Carndonagh** (M-Sa 7 per day, £3.20), and **Malin Head** (2 per day, £4.20).

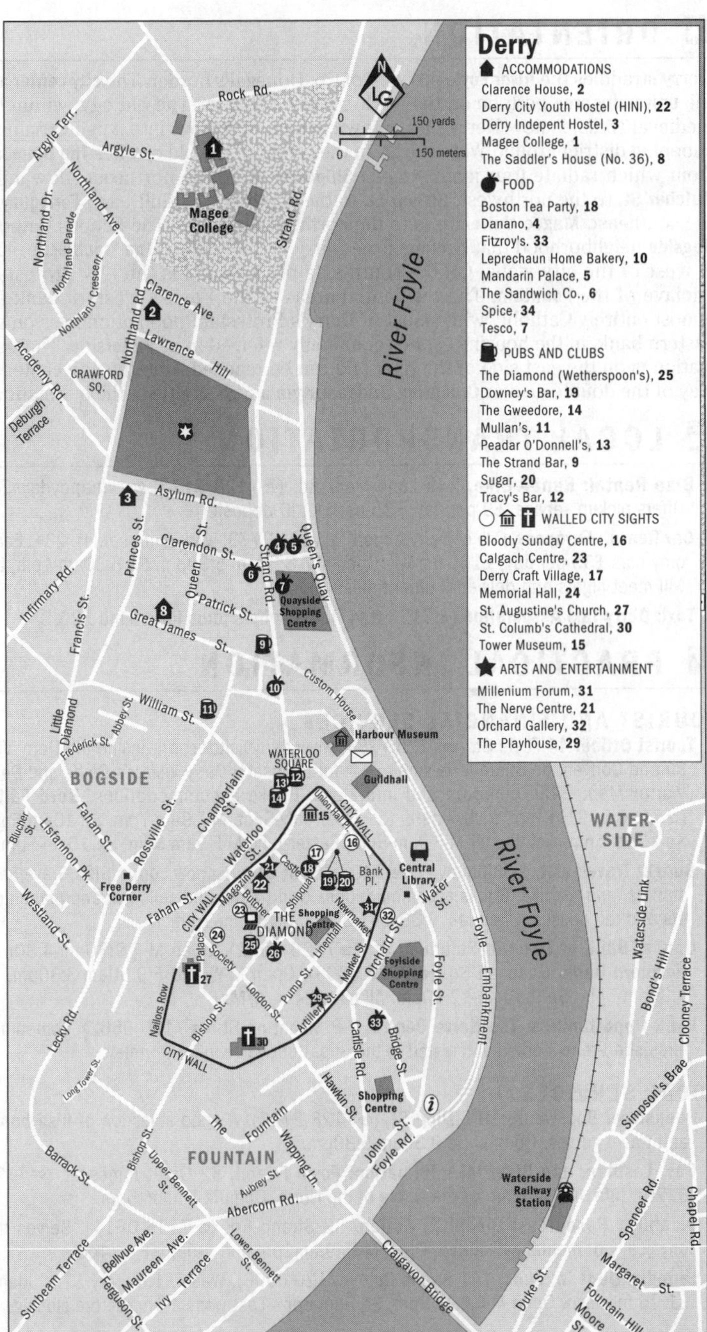
Derry
ACCOMMODATIONS
Clarence House, 2
Derry City Youth Hostel (HINI), 22
Derry Indepent Hostel, 3
Magee College, 1
The Saddler's House (No. 36), 8
FOOD
Boston Tea Party, 18
Danano, 4
Fitzroy's, 33
Leprechaun Home Bakery, 10
Mandarin Palace, 5
The Sandwich Co., 6
Spice, 34
Tesco, 7
PUBS AND CLUBS
The Diamond (Wetherspoon's), 25
Downey's Bar, 19
The Gweedore, 14
Mullan's, 11
Peadar O'Donnell's, 13
The Strand Bar, 9
Sugar, 20
Tracy's Bar, 12
WALLED CITY SIGHTS
Bloody Sunday Centre, 16
Calgach Centre, 23
Derry Craft Village, 17
Memorial Hall, 24
St. Augustine's Church, 27
St. Columb's Cathedral, 30
Tower Museum, 15
ARTS AND ENTERTAINMENT
Millenium Forum, 31
The Nerve Centre, 21
Orchard Gallery, 32
The Playhouse, 29
150 yards
150 meters
River Foyle
Magee College
Quayside Shopping Centre
Harbour Museum
Guildhall
WATERLOO SQUARE
BOGSIDE
Free Derry Corner
THE DIAMOND
Shopping Centre
Foyleside Shopping Centre
Central Library
WATER-SIDE
FOUNTAIN
Waterside Railway Station
CITY WALL
Craigavon Bridge
Foyle Embankment

NORTHERN IRELAND

ORIENTATION

Derry straddles the **River Foyle** just east of Co. Donegal's border. The **city center** and the **university area** both lie on the Foyle's western banks. The old city, within the medieval walls, is now Derry's downtown, which overflows into a pedestrianized shopping district around Waterloo St. In the center of the old city lies **The Diamond,** from which radiate four main streets: **Shipquay St.** to the northeast (downhill), **Butcher St.** to the northwest, **Bishop St.** to the southwest (uphill), and **Ferryquay** to the southeast. **Magee University** is to the north off **Strand Rd.** The famous Catholic **Bogside** neighborhood that became Free Derry in the 70s (see **The Troubles,** p. 455) is west of the city walls. On the south side of the walls is the tiny Protestant enclave of the **Fountain.** The residential areas of the Foyle's western bank are almost entirely Catholic, while most of Derry's Protestant population lives on the eastern bank, in the housing estates commonly referred to as **Waterside.** The train station is on the east side of the river and can be reached from the city center by way of the double-decker **Craigavon Bridge,** or via a free shuttle at the bus station.

LOCAL TRANSPORTATION

Bike Rental: Rent-A-Bike, 245 Lone Moor Rd. (☎7128 7128; www.happydays.ie). Offers pickup service. £9 per day, £35 per wk.; ID deposit.

Car Rental: Europcar, City of Derry Airport (☎7181 2773; www.europcar.ie). 23+. Economy cars £35 per day, £165 per wk. Open M-F 8:30am-5:30pm, Sa 8:30am-1pm, but will meet flights and deliver at other times.

Taxi: Derry Taxi Association (☎7126 0247). Also offers tours for around £20.

PRACTICAL INFORMATION

TOURIST AND FINANCIAL SERVICES

Tourist Office: 44 Foyle St. (☎7126 7284; www.derryvisitor.com), inside the Derry Visitor and Convention Bureau. Be sure to ask for the useful *Derry Visitor's Guide* and *Derry Visitor Map*. 24hr. computerized info kiosk. Books accommodations. **Bord Fáilte** (☎7136 9501) keeps a desk here, too. Open July-Sept. M-F 9am-7pm, Sa 10am-6pm, Su 10am-5pm; Oct.-Easter M-F 9am-5pm; Easter-June M-F 9am-5pm, Sa 10am-5pm.

Budget Travel: usit, 4 Shipquay Pl. (☎7137 1888; www.usitnow.com). ISICs, TravelSave stamps, and the like. Books accommodations world-wide, and sells bus and plane tickets and rail passes. Open M-F 9:30am-5:30pm, Sa 10am-1pm.

Banks: Bank of Ireland, Shipquay St. (☎7126 4992). Open M-F 9:30am-4:30pm. **Northern Bank,** Guildhall Sq. (☎7126 5333). Open M-W and F 9:30am-3:30pm, Th 9:30am-5pm, Sa 9:30am-12:30pm. All have 24hr. **ATMs.**

Work Opportunities: The Nerve Centre, 7-8 Magazine St. (☎7126 0562), sometimes hires short-term workers interested in the arts. Contact Jennifer Gormley.

LOCAL SERVICES

Bookstore: Bookworm, 18 Bishop St. (☎7128 2727). A good selection of Irish books and travel guides. Open M-Sa 9:30am-5:30pm.

Gay, Lesbian, and Bisexual Information: Foyle Friend, 32 Great James St. (☎7126 3120). Info and support for the whole of the North. Open M-F noon-5pm.

Disability Resources: Disability Action, 52 Strand Rd. (☎7136 0811). Serves the physically or mentally disabled. Open M-Th 9am-1pm and 2-5pm, F 'til 4pm.

Laundry: Duds 'n' Suds, 141 Strand Rd. (☎7126 6006). Wash £1.80, dry £2; students £1.25 for each. Open M-F 8am-9pm, Sa 8am-6pm. Last wash 1½hr. before closing.

EMERGENCY AND COMMUNICATIONS

Emergency: ☎999; no coins required. **Police:** Strand Rd. (☎7136 7337).

Pharmacy: Gordon's Chemist, 3a-b Strand Rd. (☎7126 4502). Open M-Th and Sa 9am-5:30pm, F 9am-8pm.

Hospital: Altnagelvin Hospital, Glenshane Rd. (☎7134 5171).

Internet Access: Central Library, 35 Foyle St. (☎7127 2300). £3 per hr. Open M and Th 9:15am-8pm, Tu-W and F-Sa 9:15am-5pm. **bean-there.com,** 20 The Diamond (☎7128 1303). £2.50 per 30min. Open M-F 9am-7pm, Sa 10am-6pm, Su 2-6pm.

Post Office: 3 Custom House St. (☎7136 2563). Open M-F 8:30am-5:30pm, Sa 9am-12:30pm. **Postal code:** BT48. Unless addressed to 3 Custom House St., *Poste Restante* letters will go to the **Postal Sorting Office** (☎7136 2577) on the corner of Great James and Little James St.

ACCOMMODATIONS

Derry provides a number of excellent accommodation options for travelers, from a friendly hostel and a self-catering townhouse, to the city's many B&Bs.

Derry Independent Hostel (Steve's Backpackers), 4 Asylum Rd. (☎7137 7989 or 7137 0011). Down Strand Rd. 7min. from the city center; Asylum Rd. is on the left just before the RUC station. Welcome to the Derry Vortex; once you stay, you'll have a hard time leaving (the 5th night is free). The owner has filled this hostel with various items from his own travels, as well as an eclectic assortment of music, books, and movies. Free breakfast, free **Internet,** and frequent all-you-can-eat barbeques for £1.50. Organizes trips to Giant's Causeway in the summer (£16). Dorms £9; doubles £24; triples £36. ❶

The Saddler's House (No. 36), 36 Great James St. (☎7126 9691; www.thesaddlershouse.com). Friendly, historically knowledgeable owners welcome you into their lovely Victorian home. French coffee, fresh fruit, and homemade jam make for excellent breakfasts. The same family also runs **The Merchant's House,** an award-winning, restored Georgian townhouse with fluffy beds. Both houses £20 per person, with bath £25. ❸

Derry City Youth Hostel (HINI), Magazine St. (☎7128 0280), off Butcher St. A large and institutional hostel located within the city walls. 24hr. access with night watchman. The 1st floor lounge has a TV and pool table. Lockers in rooms; BYO lock. Wheelchair-accessible. Continental breakfasts £1.50, full Irish £2.99. **Internet** £3 per hr. Towels 50p. 10-bed dorms £9, with bath £10; 6-bed £10.50; 4-bed £12.50. B&B singles without bath £15; doubles with bath £35. ❶

Magee College (☎7137 5255), on the corner of Rock and Northland Rd. Walk ½ mi. up Strand Rd. and turn left onto Rock Rd.; Magee College is at the top of the hill on the left. The Housing Office is on the ground floor of Woodburn House, a red brick building just past the main building. Rooms with desk, drawers, and sink. Available mid-June to Sept. Wash and dry £1 each. Wheelchair-accessible. Mandatory reservations M-Th 9am-5pm, F 9am-4pm. Singles in 5-bedroom flats £14.10, students £11.75. ❷

Clarence House, 15 Northland Rd. (☎7126 5342; www.clarenceguesthouse.co.uk). Accommodating owner pleases all with a range of breakfast offerings and quality rooms stocked with phones, hair dryers, TVs, irons, and bottled water. £19 per person, with bath £25. Reduced prices for longer stays. ❷

FOOD

Tesco supermarket, in the Quayside Shopping Centre, is a few minutes' walk from the walled city along Strand Rd. (Open M-Th 9am-9pm, F 8:30am-9pm, Sa 8:30am-8pm, Su 1-6pm.)

Fitzroy's, 2-4 Bridge St. (☎7126 6211), next to Bishops' Gate. Modern cafe culture and filling meals, from simple chicken breast to mango lamb. During the day most meals £4-6; dinners £7-12. Open M-Tu 9:30am-8pm, W-Sa 9:30am-10pm, Su noon-8pm. ❸

The Sandwich Co., The Diamond (☎7137 2500), and 61 Strand Rd. (☎7126 6771). Your choice of breads stuffed with a wide range of tasty fillings. Journey to the Strand location at lunch to avoid queues. Sandwiches £2-3. Both open M-F 8:30am-5pm. ❶

Spice, 162 Spencer Rd. (☎7134 4875), on East bank. Cross Craigavon Bridge and continue as it turns into Spencer. Rumored to be the best food in Derry. Appetizers £3-4. Daily veggie specials £7.95; sesame seed pork with ginger dressing £8.50; seabass with tomato and coriander salsa £11.50. Open 12:30-2:30pm and 5:30-10pm. ❸

Danano, 2-4 Lower Clarendon St. (☎7126 9034). A tasty Italian restaurant where you can watch your pizzas (£4-6) form or see your lobsters pushed into the only wood-burning oven in Northern Ireland. Anticipation is half the pleasure. Adjoining takeaway offers pizzas, pastas, and salads for slightly less, but call ahead if you're in a hurry. Ask about promotions on M-Tu. Open daily 5pm-midnight. ❸

Mandarin Palace, Queen's Ct., Lower Clarendon (☎7137 3656). A stylish Chinese restaurant that looks onto the River Foyle. Adjacent takeaway is cheaper, with most meals £5-6, and always open until midnight. Restaurant open Su-Th 4:30-11pm, F-Sa 4:30pm-midnight. ❸

Leprechaun Home Bakery, 21-23 Strand Rd. (☎7136 3606). Eclairs, buns, cakes, and whatnot; sandwiches (£3), salads (£3), and meals (£4). Open M-Sa 9am-5:30pm. ❷

Boston Tea Party, 13-15 Craft Village (☎7126 9667), off Shipquay St. Delicious cakes and surprisingly inexpensive food for a touristy area. Outside seating is a rare pleasure in Derry. Meals £2-3. Open daily 9:30am-5:30pm. ❶

PUBS AND CLUBS

Most pubs line Waterloo and the Strand, though a growing number are popping up within the walls. Trad and rock can be found almost any night of the week, and all age groups keep the pubs lively until the 1am closing time. Many bars have cheap drink promotions on weeknights; just read the chalkboards out front.

Mullan's, 13 Little James St. (☎7126 5300), on the corner of William and Rossville St. An incredible pub with idiosyncratically lavish decor, from stained-glass ceilings and bronze lion statues, to huge flat-screen TVs. More eye-candy than should be consumed in 1 night; hopefully your drinking buddies won't notice your wandering eye. Hosts excellent jazz W nights and Su afternoon. Open M-Sa 10am-2am, Su noon-12:30am.

Peadar O'Donnell's, 53 Waterloo St. (☎7137 2318). Named for the famous Donegal Socialist who organized the Irish Transport and General Workers Union and took an active role in the 1921 Irish Civil War. On nights with trad, the floor is littered ankle-deep with *craic.* Open M-Sa 11am-1am, Su 7pm-midnight.

The Gweedore, 59-61 Waterloo St. (☎7126 3513). The back door has connected to Peadar's since Famine times. An intimate venue where crowds listen attentively to rock, bluegrass, and funk bands nightly. Open M-Sa 4:30pm-1am, Su 7pm-midnight.

The Diamond (Wetherspoon's), The Diamond (☎7127 2880). Cheap meals (£2-4) and even cheaper drinks make this a good place to start the night before moving onto pubs with more character. Frequent promotions make your few quid go a long way. Food until 10pm. Open M-W 11:30am-11pm, Th and Su 11:30am-midnight, F-Sa 11:30am-1am.

The Strand Bar, 31-35 Strand Rd. (☎7126 0494). 3 floors of decadently decorated space pull in young partiers, especially on F when DJs occupy every floor. The downstairs has live music Tu-Th and the top floor is a nightclub (cover £3-6). Open M-Sa 11:30am-1am, Su noon-midnight.

Tracy's Bar, 51 Waterloo St. (☎7126 9770). Locals circle the straw-ringed central bar nightly; bands play frequently. Open M-Sa 11:30am-12:45am, Su 12:30-11:45pm.

Downey's Bar, 33 Shipquay St. (☎7126 0820). 20-somethings people this bar to play pool on purple tables and pretend that they can hear each other over the pulsing music. In nice weather, the ceiling over the bar opens up. Tu karaoke, W-Sa DJs.

Sugar, 33 Shipquay St. (behind Downey's). Downey's sweaty cousin and the newest nightclub in Derry. Big-name DJs drop in on weekends. Th 18+, F-Sa 21+. Cover £3-5.

TOURS

THE DERRY VISITOR AND CONVENTION BUREAU GUIDED TOURS. Walking tours are an excellent way to see many of the city's sights while getting an introduction to its history-laden geography. Most walks circle on top of the city walls, stepping down to visit various sights. The Derry Visitor and Convention Bureau Guided Walking Tours leave from the tourist office and take visitors around the city, including a brief tour of St. Columb's Cathedral. *(☎7126 7284. 1½hr. tours. July-Aug. M-F 11:15am and 3:15pm, Sept.-June M-F 2:30pm. £4; students, seniors, and children £3.)*

MARTIN MCCROSSAN TOURS. Martin, of Derry City Youth Hostel fame, runs highly-acclaimed City Tours from 11 Carlisle Rd. Put on your shoes and be prepared to pound the pavement for close to 2hr. *(☎7127 1996 or 7127 1997; www.irishtourguides.com. Depart daily at 10am, noon, and 2pm. Book ahead. £4.)*

NORTHERN IRELAND

SIGHTS

Derry was once the main emigration point in Ireland—massive numbers of Ulster Catholics as well as Presbyterians fled the area's religious discrimination from the city. Around the time of the Famine, many Catholics gave up on emigration and formed the **Bogside** neighborhood outside the city walls. The creation of the Republic made Derry a border city, and a Catholic majority made it a headache for Unionist leaders; it became the site of blatant civil rights violations, including gerrymandering and religious discrimination. The civil rights marches that sparked the Troubles originated here in 1968. The following became powerful touchstones for Catholics in Derry and Nationalists everywhere: **Free Derry,** the western, Catholic part of the city, controlled by the IRA and a "no-go area" for the army from 1969 to 1972; **Bloody Sunday,** January 30, 1972, when British troops fired on demonstrators and killed 14 (see p. 456); and **Operation Motorman,** the July 1972 army effort to penetrate Free Derry and arrest IRA leaders. Although the cityscape was once razed by years of bombings, Derry has since been rebuilt and looks sparklingly new. Violence still occasionally erupts during Marching Season and other contentious sectarian events, but, on the whole, recent years have seen the relatively peaceful coexistence of Derry's Catholic and Protestant populations.

THE CITY WALLS. Derry's city walls, 18 ft. high and 20 ft. thick, were erected between 1614 and 1619. They have never been breached, hence Derry's nickname "the Maiden City." Such resilience did not save the city from danger though; during the **Siege of 1689,** 600 mortar bombs sent from the nearby hills were able to go over what they could not go through, devastating the 30,000 Protestants crowded inside. This sad irony of intent has caused some to quip, "The first planned city, the first planned mistake." A walk along the top of its mile-long perimeter affords a far-reaching view of Derry from its self-contained early days to its present urban sprawl. Seven **cannons**—donated by Queen Elizabeth I and the London Guilds who "acquired" the city during the Ulster Plantation—are perched along the northeast wall between Magazine and Shipquay Gates. A plaque on the outside of this section of wall marks the water level in the days when the Foyle ran right along the walls (now 300 ft. away). The raised portion of the stone wall past New Gate was built to protect **St. Columb's Cathedral,** the symbolic focus of the city's Protestant defenders. Stuck in the center of the southwest wall, **Bishop's Gate** received an ornate face-lift in 1789, commemorating the victory of Protestant William of Orange 100 years earlier. The northwest wall supports **Roaring Meg,** a massive cannon donated by London fishmongers in 1642 and used in the 1689 siege. The sound of the cannon alone was rumored to strike fear into the hearts of enemies.

ST. COLUMB'S CATHEDRAL. Built between 1628 and 1633, St. Columb's Cathedral was the first Protestant cathedral in Britain or Ireland (all the older ones were confiscated Catholic cathedrals). The spire of the cathedral, in the southwest corner of the walled city, is visible from almost anywhere in Derry. Today's steeple is the church's third. The original wooden spire burnt down after being struck by lightning, while the second (a leaden and rounded replacement) was smelted into bullets and cannonballs during the siege. The interior is fashioned of roughly hewn stone and holds an exquisite Killybegs altar carpet, an extravagant bishop's chair dating from 1630, and 214 hand-carved Derry-oak pews, of which no two are the same. A tiny, museum-like **chapterhouse** at the back of the church displays the original locks and keys of the four main city gates, relics from the 1689 siege. Cecil Francis Alexander, author of the children's hymn "All Things Bright and Beautiful," is in a picture that is half photo, half drawing, as early subjects of photography still sought the beautifying treatment of traditional portraiture. More fun, however, is the comparison of the photograph and portrait of her husband, Rev. William Alexander. The official portrait shows an abundant and pompous figure while the photograph of the posing man shows the diminutive reality. In the **graveyard** outside, the tombstones flat on the ground were leveled during the siege to protect the graves from Jacobite cannonballs. *(Off Bishop St. in the southwest corner of the city. ☎ 7126 7313. Open Easter.-Oct. M-Sa 9am-5pm, Nov.-Mar. M-Sa 9am-1pm and 2-4pm.)*

MEMORIAL HALL. The Apprentice Boys have had their headquarters here for centuries. Inside the clubhouse there is (supposedly) a museum's worth of historical items dating back to the Apprentices who shut the 1689 closure of the gates. Admission is strictly regulated and highly unlikely, except during the Walled City Cultural Trail in July and August. Membership is open only to Protestant men, though they generously allow women to cook and clean. *(Between Royal Bastion and Butcher's Gate. Contact ☎ 7126 7284 for current information about the Walled City Cultural Trail.)*

GUILDHALL. This neo-Gothic building was formerly home to the City Council. First built in 1887, wrecked by fire in 1908, and destroyed by bombs in 1972, today's structure contains replicas of the original stained-glass windows. Among the bountiful rarities is the mayor's chain of office, which was officially presented to the city by William of Orange. Upstairs, the hall houses an enormous organ with over 3000 pipes. The hall also sponsors various concerts, plays, and exhibitions throughout the year. The ghost of Sam Mackay, a former superintendent, is rumored to haunt the place. *(Shipquay Place at Shipquay Gate. ☎ 7137 7335. No tours due to the ongoing Bloody Sunday inquiry, but the council chamber is open Sept.-May M-F 9am-5pm.)*

TOWER MUSEUM. Derry's top attraction utilizes engaging walk-through dioramas and audio-visual displays to relay Derry's intriguing history, from its days as a mere oak grove, through the siege of 1689, 20th-century wars, and the troublesome Troubles. A series of short videos illustrate Derry's economic, political, and cultural past. The whole museum deserves at least 1½hr. *(Union Hall Place, just inside Magazine Gate. ☎ 7137 2411. Open July-Aug. M-Sa 10am-5pm, Su 2-5pm; Sept.-June Tu-Sa 10am-5pm. Last entrance 4:30pm. £4.20, students and seniors £1.60, families £8.50.)*

HERE, KITTY-KITTY... In the last century, Derry's statesmen and merchants bought opulent homes within the city walls, and their wealthy wives would order their fashionable dresses from London. When the frilly frocks arrived, the ladies would don them and meet to stroll about on the city walls. The residents of the Bogside, looking up at the wall-wenches from their own poverty-stricken neighborhood, were enraged at the decadent lifestyle on display. On one occasion, several Bogsiders took it upon themselves to write a letter of complaint to the London papers about the parading "cats." The press in London were so amused by the nickname for Derry's finest ladies that it stuck, and the phrase "cat walk" fell into common usage.

WORKHOUSE MUSEUM. Located in a recently restored Victorian building on the east side of the River Foyle, this workhouse-turned-showplace now dons displays dealing with poverty, health care, and more importantly, the history of the Famine in Northern Ireland. The museum also houses the Atlantic Memorial exhibition that examines the role of the city in World War II. *(23 Glendermot Rd. ☎7131 8328. Open July-Aug. M-Sa 10am-4:30pm; Sept.-June M-Th and Sa 10am-4:30pm.)*

MAGEE COLLEGE. This neo-Gothic building, found outside the city walls, shines among its clumsier neighbors. The university has changed its affiliation several times: originally a member of the Royal University of Ireland in 1879, by 1909 it had become part of Trinity College Dublin. It has been part of the University of Ulster since 1984. *(12min. walk east of the city center. ☎7137 1371.)*

OTHER SIGHTS. Maritime buffs might head to the **Harbour Museum,** which features paintings and artifacts related to Derry's harbor history. *(Guildhall St., on the banks of the Foyle. ☎7137 7331. Open M-F 10am-1pm and 2-4:30pm. Free.)* The **Bloody Sunday Centre,** though primarily for families and friends of those directly affected by the tragedy, also has a small exhibition space with moving black-and-white photographs and news footage of the marches. *(Bank Place. ☎7136 0880. Open M-F 9:30am-4:30pm. Free.)* The **Calgach Center** has two locations. On 14 Bishop St. is the Genealogy Centre, which conducts research on ancestry in Counties Derry and Donegal. *(☎7126 9792. Open M-F 9am-5pm.)* The larger location at 4-22 Butcher St. houses **The Fifth Province,** a flashy multimedia display on the history of Celtic Ulster. Children might enjoy the simulated space and time travel, though some older viewers might find the show, which focuses on the origins of Irish names and Ireland's many successful emigrants, less stimulating. *(Shows M-F 11:30am and 2:30pm. £3, students and seniors £1.)* The **Derry Craft Village,** Shipquay St., was built from cast-away building materials by entrepreneurial youth in an abandoned lot in the Bogside. The village encompasses a pleasant courtyard surrounded by cafes, kitschy craft shops, and **Bridie's Cottage,** the summertime host to Derry's award-winning **Teach Ceoil (Music House).** In July and August, the Cottage offers lunchtime performances of Irish music, reading, and dance, as well as "Irish suppers" (tea), with *céilí* dancing and trad sessions. *(Lunchtime performances Tu-Th 1-2pm; free. Irish supper Th 8:30pm; £6.)*

RESIDENTIAL NEIGHBORHOODS AND MURALS

Near the city walls, Derry's residential neighborhoods, both Catholic and Protestant, display brilliant murals. Most pay tribute to past historical events, such as the civil rights movements of the 1970s; though many show scenes of violence and terror, most shine with a spirit of strength and hope. Several murals can be seen from the viewpoints on the city wall. For a key to their iconography, see **The Mural Symbols,** p. 484. A sculpture at the west-side end of Craigavon Bridge looks forward optimistically, with two men reaching out to each other across a divide.

WATERSIDE AND THE FOUNTAIN ESTATE. These two neighborhoods are home to Derry's Protestant population. The Waterside is nearly split in its percentage of Catholics and Protestants, but the Fountain is almost entirely Protestant. The Fountain is reached from the walled city by exiting through the left side of Bishop's Gate; it is contained by Bishop, Upper Bennett, Abercorn, and Hawkin St. This small area of only 600 residents holds the more interesting of the Protestant murals. The few Loyalist murals in the Waterside lie along Bond and Irish St.

THE BOGSIDE. The Bogside is hard to miss—a huge facade just west of the city walls at the junction of Fahan St. and Rossville Sq. declares "You Are Now Entering Free Derry." Surrounded by other, equally striking, nationalist artistic creations, this area is referred to as **Free Derry Corner.** Of all the murals perhaps most arresting is **The Death of Innocence.** From this mural the image of young Annette McGavigan leaps from the dark and disheveled backdrop to flaunt her life-spirit; the blue butterfly in the painting suggests peace and hope. **Bernadette** depicts Bernadette Devlin, who, at the age of 22, became the youngest woman ever to win a seat in the House of Commons. Here she is shown leading the '69 Bogside fighters with her megaphone. The black-and-white **Petrol Bomber** shows a young boy in a gas mask armed with a bottle of petrol, fighting in the Battle of Bogside.

ARTS AND ENTERTAINMENT

The Millenium Forum, Newmarket St., has a 1000-seat theater that shows big name performances. (Box office ☎7126 4455; www.milleniumforum.co.uk. Performances from £16, concessions often available.) **The Nerve Centre,** 7-8 Magazine St., is Derry's newest venue for local and international performances; it most recently played host to rising star David Gray. Various types of lessons in music and the arts are also available. (☎7126 0562; www.nerve-centre.org. Bar and music venue £8-15. Open Th-Su 9pm-1:30am. Films play at 8pm, and sometimes 2pm; £1. Group guitar lessons £5 per class.) **Orchard Gallery,** Orchard St., is one of the best spots on the island for viewing well-conceived exhibitions of contemporary Irish and international art. (☎7126 9675. Open Tu-Sa 10am-6pm. Free.) **The Playhouse,** 5-7 Artillery St., specializes in the work of young playwrights and performers. (☎7126 8027. Tickets £7, students £5.) **St. Columb's Hall,** Orchard St., houses the **Orchard Cinema.** Renovations are due to be completed November 2002. (For info call ☎7126 2045.)

Derry's most boisterous and festive time of the year is Halloween, when the whole city, including thousands of visitors, dresses up and revels at the **Banks of the Boyle Halloween Carnival** (☎7126 7284). The event culminates in a fireworks show over the river. In early June, the **Walled City Festival** turns Derry into "Carnival City," with a weekend that includes a free outdoor concert and various events around the city's walls (☎7126 7284). August brings the **Maiden City Festival;** organized by the Apprentice Boys, this week-long event features pageantry, drama, and music commemorating the siege of Derry (☎7134 6677).

SPORTS AND ACTIVITIES

Sporting events in Derry are as prevalent and exciting as in any good city. **Gaelic football** and **soccer** are both played at **Brandywell** on Lone Moor Rd. (Gaelic info ☎7126 7142. Games June-Sept. Su afternoon. Tickets £6. Football info ☎7128 1337. Games Aug.-May. Tickets £7.) Brandywell also hosts **greyhound racing** (about £5). **Rugby** can be caught at **Judges Rd. pitch.** (☎7186 1101. Sept.-Mar. Sa 2:30pm. Tickets £2-5.) If you'd prefer to take part in the fun, **Brooke Park Leisure Centre,** Rosemount Ave., offers plenty of activity options; it houses tennis and squash courts, a fitness room, and lends exercise and sporting equipment. (☎7126 2637. Prices generally range from £2-7.) Or, have a swimmingly good time at the **City Baths,** on William St., for only £2. (☎7126 4459. Open M and W 10am-2pm and 6-8pm; Tu and Th 10am-2pm and 6-7pm; F 10am-2pm; Sa noon-4pm.)

THE SPERRIN MOUNTAINS

The Sperrin Mountains span a 40 mi. arc northeast from **Strabane** to **Milltown** to **Downhill.** The new **Sperrin Way,** an ambitious collection of way-marked trails, aims to make a portion of this land more accessible to outdoors enthusiasts. **Hikers** and **bikers** who embark on the trail can expect rambles through the best-preserved high elevation blanket bogs and moorlands in Ireland, as well as some fantastic inland stretches of lush countryside. A number of maps and guided walks to the area are available; for travelers expecting an extended stay in the Sperrins, *Ordnance Survey Discoverer Series #13* is an invaluable guide to the southern part of the range. *Walking in the Western Sperrins* (£3) has concise instructions and miniature maps for five short walks (5-10 mi.) focused on the area around **Gortin,** north of Omagh, while *Walk the Sperrins* (£4.95) provides a broader selection of ten hikes (5-13 mi.) with more detailed narrative descriptions of the routes and focused geological information about the area. Maps and guides are available at the Omagh tourist office (see p. 540) and the Sperrins Heritage Centre (see below).

Hikers can also take advantage of the **Central Sperrins Way,** newly signposted in August 2001. A product of the fragmentation of the former Ulster Way into several more manageable pieces, the Central Way runs 30 mi. through the mountains between the **Glenelly** and **Owenkillew Rivers** in Co. Tyrone. The route can be picked up at any point, but the carpark at **Barnes** (where there is also free **camping**) is a logical starting location. The longest segment of the trail extends northeast from Barnes, following the **Glenelly River** to **Corratary Hill.** The Way then crosses the mountains and circles back to **Scotch Town,** which is connected to Barnes by a well-trod path. To the west of Barnes and Scotch Town is the Way's shorter loop, which traverses higher elevations and the expansive bogs of **Craignamaddy Hill.** The *Central Sperrins Way* (50p) brochure details the route's segments and sights.

The bounty of the Sperrins is not restricted to pedestrians. **Cyclists** can enjoy the **National Cycle Network,** which connects Derry, Strabane, and Omagh via smooth, low-traffic roads. The route is labeled on *Ordnance Survey* maps and is signposted in most areas. Further options for Sperrin-edification abound. For starters, the **Sperrins Heritage Centre,** 1 mi. east of **Cranagh** on the Plumbridge-Draperstown road, presents some state-of-the-art multimedia ballyhoo, featuring storytelling ghost bartenders, glaciation, and the discovery of gold. (☎8164 8142. Open May-Oct. M-F 11am-5:30pm, Sa 11:30am-6pm, Su 2-6pm. £2.20, seniors and children £1.30, families £6.90.) You might consider hiring a private guide; **Sperrin Guides** (☎8164 8157 or 7126 1148), an organization of specialists in local geology, ecology, and archaeology, offers individually tailored local hikes. Visitors to the Sperrins often base themselves in **Gortin** (see p. 543) or **Omagh** (see p. 540), the towns closest to the most traveled part of the range. Distant **Dungiven,** on the A6 in Co. Derry, provides access to the less-traveled northeastern region.

DUNGIVEN (DUN GEIMHIN)

Dungiven is located on the main road between Derry and Belfast. Perfectly situated at the foot of the Sperrins, the town also sports sights of its own; the ornate 14th-century tomb of Cooey na Gal, a Chieftan of the O'Cahans, is one of the best preserved tombs in Northern Ireland. The town is also home to two of the North's most interesting accommodations.

Before checking out the local abodes, you may want to stock up on some food at **Mace** (Main St.; open M-Su 7:30am-11pm) or **Spar** (Main St.; open M-Sa 9am-10:30pm, Su 1-10:30pm). **Northern Banks** (☎7774 1215) has a 24hr. **ATM** on Main St. And don't forget to send home some postcards from the **post office,** Main St. (Open M-W and F 9am-12:30pm and 1:30-5:30pm, Th and Sa 9am-12:30pm.)

Whether you're heading to the peaks or simply passing between major cities, the **Flax Mill Hostel (IHH) ❶,** just outside of town, is an anachronistic treasure. The owners charm visitors with their pastoral utopia; they mill flour for delicious homemade bread, grow organic vegetables, and make jam, cheese, and muesli. Though without electricity much of the time, the hostel facilities remain top-notch thanks to the ingenuity of the owners: gas lamps glow throughout the building, and gas heating warms water for showers or dips in the incredible bath. The hostel also hosts a variety of cultural programs, including weaving demonstrations and trad sessions, the biggest of which is the **Yard Session Festival,** a weekend of great trad and tasty food in mid-September. (☎7774 2655. Festival suggested donation £10. Dorms £5.50. **Camping** £3.50.) For travelers with a taste for modern amenities, the **Dungiven Castle ❶** has a wide range of "budget accommodation" facilities that bear a striking resemblance to those of a hostel, though it prefers to avoid the name. The castle grounds are surrounded by 22 acres of be-trailed land that hovers somewhere between wilderness and domestication, and all of the rooms afford great inland views. (☎7774 2428. 1 wheelchair-accessible room. Laundry wash £2, dry £1. Dorms £12; doubles £32; family rooms £16 per person, children £7.)

COUNTY TYRONE

As lakes are to Fermanagh, forests are to Co. Tyrone. Indeed, the only thing the county is more proud of than its forests is its history of emigration; the Ulster American Folk Park is a paean to Ulstermen who made it in America. Omagh is a large town that provides bus access from the rest of Ireland; it's also your last chance to pick up supplies before heading to grandmother's house in the Gortin Glen Forest Park, a scant 8 mi. from town.

OMAGH (AN OMAIGH)

On August 15, 1998, a bomb ripped through Omagh's busy downtown area, killing 29 people and injuring hundreds more. Later, "The Real IRA," a splinter group of the Provisional IRA, took responsibility for the act. Despite persistent memory of this tragedy, the town's sloping main street is once again a center for frenzied commercial activity. Tourists rarely stay in Omagh for long, and most often simply see the bus station and river in the rear view mirror as they head to the Ulster American Folk Park, the nearby forests, and the mountains to the North.

TRANSPORTATION. Ulsterbus runs from the station on Mountjoy Rd. (☎8224 2711. Open M-F 8:30am-5:45pm.) Buses go to: Belfast (2hr.; M-Sa 11 per day, Su 5 per day; £7.10); Derry (1hr.; M-Sa 11 per day, Su 5 per day; £5.20); Dublin (3hr.; M-Sa 6 per day, Su 5 per day; £11); Enniskillen (1hr., 6 per day, £4.80). **Taxis** await at the bus depot, or can be contacted at ☎8229 1010. Cabs have fixed fares to all destinations in the town center (£3), the hostel (£4), and the Folk Park (£6).

ORIENTATION AND PRACTICAL INFORMATION. Omagh's buildings cluster to the south of the **River Strule.** The town center, across the bridge from the bus depot, is bounded by three streets: **Campisie, Market,** and **High St.** At the top of

the hill, High St. splits into pub-lined **John St.** and **George St.** Town maps and warm welcomes are free at the **tourist office** on Market St., but that lovingly detailed *Ordnance Survey* (#13) of the Sperrin Mountains will cost you £6. (☎8224 7831. Open Apr.-Sept. M-Sa 9am-5pm; Oct.-Mar. M-F 9am-5pm.) Nab cash from the 24hr. **ATM** at **First Trust.** (☎8224 7133. Open M-F 9:30am-4:30pm, W open 10am.) **Boots** pharms out potions at 47 High St. (☎8224 5455. Open M-Sa 9am-5:30pm.) To **get 'netted,** walk down Market St. and turn onto the Dublin Rd; the **library** is at 1 Spillars Pl. (☎8224 4821. £2 per hr., free M-F 9:15am-1pm. Open M, W, and F 9:15am-5:30pm; Tu and Th 9:15am-8pm, Sa 9:15am-1pm and 2-5pm.) The **post office** is at 7 High St. (☎8224 2970. Open M-F 9am-5:30pm, Sa 10am-12:30pm.) **Postal code:** BT78 1AB.

ACCOMMODATIONS, FOOD, AND PUBS. The **Omagh Hostel ❶**, 9a Waterworks Rd., perches atop a hill overlooking the town, sharing its space with several cattle and sheep. The building itself has been expanded to include a small conservatory in which you can have a cuppa and watch the sun set. Call the owners for pickup or head north from town on the B48; turn right and follow the signs that start about a mile out of town. (☎8224 1973; www.omaghhostel.co.uk. Laundry £3. £7 per person.) At the **4 Winds ❷,** 10min. from town at 63 Dromore Rd., the owner (a former chef) provides a filling Irish breakfast and packs lunches on request. Call for pickup or directions. (☎8224 3554. £18 per person, £20 with bath.)

THE LOCAL STORY

An interview with Paddy Fitzgerald of the Ulster American Folk Museum.

LG: Being from the North, how do you define your "Irish identity?"

PF: Ah, right. It's a very important question. I think it's an issue that everyone in Northern Ireland, and probably in all of Ireland, are obsessed with. I think we spend most of our time belly-button gazing trying to define ourselves. My own identity fluctuates. I used to tell myself that I was "Bri-rish" to negotiate my dual identities. And that's not just a cute way of saying something or nothing at all. The word "Bri-rish" addressed the fact that I was an Ulster Protestant, that I have areas culturally and so on where I feel attached to the British heritage, but that I also have areas where I would see myself relating to an Irish Catholic culture, or an Irish Gaelic culture if you want to use those terms. The word is a way to negotiate the two. I tend to see myself as Irish, even though I am also an Ulster Protestant. Let me give you an example: Gaelic rugby is something I've played since I was a kid. I often find meself screaming in joy at the TV in Belfast when the Irish score a goal against England. So I see meself as Irish, even though I'm also a 'Proddie.' I mean, there have been people who played on the Irish team and had UVF tattoos. That should give you a good sense of the multi-faceted cultures and identities in the North. I mean, I'm a Northern Irish Protestant named Paddy Fitzgerald. If that doesn't explain the torn identities in Northern Ireland, I don't know what will.

Pitch a tent 8 mi. north of Omagh at **Glen Caravan and Camping Park ❶**, on the Gortin road. (☎8164 8108. **Bike hire** £7 per day. £4-9 per tent.)

Grant's ❸, 29 George St., lets visitors raze their way through a hearty range of pasta, steak, and seafood. Dinner is pricey (£8.95-15.95), but lunch (about £5) and the evening special (£5-7.50) fits most budgets. (☎8225 0900. Open M-Th noon-10pm, F-Sa noon-10:30pm, Su 5-10pm.) The **Riverfront Coffeehouse ❶**, Market St., lures in the lunch swarms with the glow of swank blue lights and an industrial-strength sandwich bar. (☎8225 0011. Sandwiches £2, daily special £4. Open M-Sa 9am-6pm.) **McElroy's ❷**, on Castle St., serves up sandwiches, chicken nuggets, and seafood at reasonable prices. (☎8224 4441. Club sandwich £3.50.) **Dragon Castle ❷**, High St., captures its maidens with affordable, yummy takeaway and lunch specials (Th-F £5-6). (☎8224 5208. Open M-Th 5-11:45pm, F-Sa 5pm-12:45am, Su 5-11:45pm.) **Sally O'Brien's,** cowering down the street from the Dragon, began as a tea merchant in the 1880s but has since moved on to stronger brews. On weekend nights, clubbers shake it upstairs. (☎8224 2521. Cover £5-6.) Other gotta-dance youngsters join the suits of armor and a wooden tiger at **McElroy's.** (☎8224 4441. Cover £4-6. Open Sa.)

SIGHTS. The **Ulster American Folk Park,** 5 mi. north of Omagh on the Strabane road (A5), proudly chronicles the experiences of the two million folk who left Ulster in the 18th and 19th centuries, including exhibits on Andrew Jackson, Davy Crockett, and Ulysses S. Grant. The indoor museum has full-scale tableaux of a Famine cottage and a New York City tenement. Frequent special events include July 4th celebrations, farming demonstrations, and craft workshops. The Omagh-Strabane bus (M-Sa 5-7 per day, Su 2 per day; £1.20) brings you directly to the Folk Park. (☎8224 3292. Open Apr.-Sept. M-Sa 10:30am-6pm, Su 11am-6:30pm; Oct.-Mar. M-F 10:30am-5pm. Last admission 1½hr. before closing. £4, students £2.50.)

Next door is the **Emigration Database,** which includes an extensive collection of books on Irish-Americana and emigration, and provides free **Internet access.** (Open M-F 9:30am-4:30pm.) The **Ulster History Park,** 7 mi. out of town on the Gortin road, is a theme park whose theme is historical Irish structures. The many replicas include a dolmen, an early monastery, a crannog, and a Plantation settlement. The park hosts periodic special events, such as St. Patrick's Day festivities and a craft fair in August. The Omagh-Gortin bus also stops here. (☎8164 8188. Open July-Aug. daily 10am-6:30pm; Apr.-June and Sept. 10am-

5:30pm; Oct.-Mar. M-F 10am-5pm. Last admission 1hr. before closing. £3.75, students £2.50; joint ticket with Folk Park £6.50/£4.)

The **Gortin Glen Forest Park,** brimming with deer, nature trails, and breathtaking views, is a 3min. walk to your left as you leave the History Park. (Open daily 10am-sunset. Cars £3.) Archaeology enthusiasts—you know who you are—should check out Ireland's answer to Stonehenge: situated on the A505 between Omagh and Cookstown, **An Creagán** has 44 well-preserved Neolithic monuments. (☎8076 1112. Open Apr.-Sept. daily 11am-6:30pm; Oct.-Mar. M-F 11am-4:30pm. £2, students £1.50.) During the first weekend in May, born-again Celts descend on the village of **Creggan** for the **Bealtaine Festival,** an ancient rite of fertility and fun.

NEAR OMAGH: GORTIN

Ten miles north of Omagh on the B48, one-street, two-hostel Gortin provides access to the walking trails of the **Central Sperrins Way** and the **Gortin Forest Park** (see above). Despite its ideal location—right on the edge of the **Sperrin Mountains**—Gortin feels largely undiscovered. Short walks surround the town—the **Gortin Burn Walk,** for instance, offers a gentle 2 mi. meander along a riverbank toward the forest park. (The trailhead is up a gravel road just before the post office.) For **guided walks** of the Sperrins, contact Una McKenna (☎8164 8157).

Gortin is easily reached by **bus** from Omagh (30min., 4 per day, £2). The **Ulster Bank** has a 24hr. **ATM.** (Open M-F 9:30am-12:30pm and 1:30-4:30pm.) An anonymous **pharmacy** at the end of Main St. dispenses relief for all manner of malady. (☎8164 8020. Open M-F 9:30am-1pm and 2-6pm, Th-Sa 9:30am-1pm.)

The **Gortin Tourist Accommodation ❶,** down Main St., is modern and child-friendly, with a family room and a playground out back. (☎8164 8346. £7.50 per person.) That renovated schoolhouse on the Omagh road is actually the **Gortin Hostel ❶,** where the comfitude of the beds in the lofty rooms is matched by the hearthside chairs. (☎8164 8083. **Bike rental** £6-9 per day for hostelers. Dorms £6.) Pitch a tent in a forest plot at the **Gortin Glen Caravan Park ❶,** 2 mi. south of town on the Omagh road. (☎8164 8108. Laundry £1.60. 2-person tent £4.50 per night, £25 per wk.) **McSwiggen's Costcutters** sells groceries. (☎8164 8810. Open M-F 8am-9pm, Sa 8am-10:30pm, Su 9am-8pm.) **Glenview ❶,** down the street, fries up takeaway goodies. (☎8164 8705. Open Su-Th 5-11:30pm, F-Sa 5pm-1:30am.) **Badoney Tavern** complements its pints with cheap tasty meals. (☎8164 8157. Food served noon-10pm.)

FERMANAGH LAKE DISTRICT

Driving across the border into Co. Fermanagh from Sligo is a jarring experience. Heading inland, the landscape changes dramatically, and hills begin to be peppered with trees and herds of placid cattle. In Fermanagh, fields are tidy and walled, with firm rectangular boundaries; everything here seems just slightly more ordered than in the neighboring counties to the south. Eventually, hills descend into small valleys filled with wide, clear lakes. Along with Upper and Lower Lough Erne, a number of these smaller lakes intertwine into a matrix of waterways, whose placid waters creep from Sligo in the west, across Enniskillen, and south into County Cavan. Vacationers, mostly from Northern Ireland, crowd into the lake district in July for their summer vacations.

CHARTER A CRUISE

A week of boating on the Shannon-Erne Waterway is an interesting and surprisingly inexpensive way for the aquatically inclined to explore the Fermanagh Lake District. The original Shannon-Erne link was built in 1846, abandoned in 1869 in favor of the steam engine, and restored for tourism in 1994 as the longest navigable inland waterway in Europe. Many companies now offer travelers the option to rent out boats—complete with bedrooms and kitchenette—to groups for week-long trips along the waterway. Many cabins also come with TV, radio, and full kitchen cutlery. When divided among a group, what seems like a splurge quickly becomes a rather unique travel/lodging deal. Two- to eight-person boats only cost £13-40 per person per night and come fully equipped with all linens. Most marinas on the lakes are free, mechanical services along the way are plentiful, and no boating experience is necessary.

Belleek Charter Cruising *in Belleek, located next to ExlorErne, is extremely accessible and offers decent rates. (☎028 6566 8027; www25.brinkster.com/belleekcruising. July-Aug. 4-6 person boat £995 per wk., 6-8 person £1200 per wk.; May-June £850/£1050; Sept.-Apr. £730/£800.) An alternate company,* ***Carrybridge,*** *is based in Enniskillen. (☎028 6638 7034. July-Aug. 2-4 person boat £550 per wk., 5-person £740 per wk.; May-June £450/£610; Apr. and Sept. £350/£530.)*

ENNISKILLEN (INIS CEITHLEANN)

Busy. Clean. Industrious. The flavor of Enniskillen seems best captured in single words, so fast is the pace of life in this tidy market town compared to its country neighbors. The major transportation hub between Northern Ireland and the Republic, Enniskillen is nonetheless relatively manicured and neighborly, and its abundant shops and services make it a thoroughly pleasant base for explorations of the Lake District. The town center's shops and pubs rest on an island between Upper and Lower Lough Erne, connected to the mainland by five traffic-choked bridges. Though undetectable on its neat streets or in the faces of its people, Enniskillen still bears the emotional, though not the physical, scars of an IRA bombing on Remembrance Day, 1987, which killed 11 and injured 61.

TRANSPORTATION

Buses: Wellington Rd. (☎6632 2633), across from the tourist office. Open M-F 8:45am-5:15pm, Sa 8:45am-2:45pm. Service to: **Belfast** (2½hr., 5-9 per day, £7.80); **Derry** (3hr.; M-Sa 4-8 per day, Su 1 per day; £7.40); **Dublin** (3hr., 4-5 per day, €13.90); **Galway** (5hr.; M-Sa 3 per day, Su 1 per day; €17.10); **Sligo** (1hr., M-Sa 3 per day, €9.30).

Taxis: Speedy Cabs (☎6632 7327; toll-free ☎0800 666 666).

Bike Rental: Lakeland Canoe Centre. Bikes £10 per day.

PRACTICAL INFORMATION

Enniskillen's primary streets run laterally across the island: **Queen Elizabeth Rd.** to the north, the five segments that compose the island's main street in the middle area, and **Wellington Rd.** to the south.

Tourist Office: Fermanagh Tourist Information Centre, Wellington Rd. (☎6632 3110), across from the bus station. Open July-Aug. M-F 9am-7pm, Sa 10am-6pm, Su 11am-5pm; May-June and Sept. M-F 9am-5:30pm, Sa 10am-6pm, Su 11am-5pm; Oct.-Mar. M-F 9am-5pm; Apr. M-F 9am-5pm, Sa 10am-6pm, Su 11am-5pm.

Banks: Bank of Ireland, Townhall St. (☎6632 2136). Open M-F 9:30am-4:30pm, W open 10am. **Ulster Bank,** Darling St. (☎6632 4034). Open M-F 9:30am-4:30pm.

Luggage Storage: Ulsterbus Parcel-link (☎6632 2633), at the bus station. 50p per bag. Open M-F 9am-5:30pm; no overnight storage. Closed on bank holidays.

Pharmacy: P.F. McGovern, High St. (☎6632 2393). Open M-Sa 9am-5:30pm. Rotating Su hours.

Emergency: ☎999; no coins required. **Police:** Queen St. (☎6632 2823).

Internet Access: Intech Centre, the orange building on E. Bridge St. (☎6632 2556). £2 per hr. Open M-F 9am-5pm.

Post Office: E. Bridge St. (☎6632 4525), at the back of the Spar. Open M-F 8am-5:30pm, Sa 9am-5:30pm. **Postal code:** BT747BW.

ACCOMMODATIONS AND CAMPING

Backpackers have a couple of hostel options in Enniskillen, while quality B&Bs are surprisingly scarce and are much farther from the town center. Those blessed with wheels may want to check out the **HINI** hostel 10 mi. north of town in **Castle Archdale Country Park** (☎6862 8118).

The Bridges (HINI), Belmore St. (☎6634 0110; www.hini.org.uk). A 5min. walk from the bus depot. Turn right on Wellington Rd., take the 1st left after the Erneside Shopping Centre, and turn right onto E. Bridge St., at the end of which you'll spot the futuristic building. This shiny new hostel is clean, spacious, and environmentally friendly (it's the first building in Ireland to use both photo voltaic cells *and* solar panels for energy). The kitchen closes at 10:30pm, but the TV, dining, and quiet rooms are open all night. **Internet access** coming soon. Laundry £3. 2- to 6-bed dorms £12, under 18 £10. ❷

Lakeland Canoe Centre, Castle Island (☎6632 4250). Walk down from the tourist office to the river, ring the bell for a ferry, and prepare to wait. Last ferry-crossing at midnight. The hostel is in 3 interlocking pagodas on the island. Often filled with youth groups. Showers in the "boys" bath are communal. Continental breakfast £2. Kitchen closes at 10pm. Bike rentals £10 per day; **canoe rentals** £18 per day. 4- to 16-bed dorms £10. **Camping** £4.50 per person, including ferry and use of hostel facilities. ❶

Sharredda, Dublin Rd. (☎6632 2659), a 12min. walk from town. Guests are lodged in the privacy of converted stables behind the main house. Pillowy bedspreads are comfort itself. Singles £25; doubles with bath £40. ❸

FOOD AND PUBS

The most budgelicious option for gustation in Enniskillen is to scavenge through the grocery stores lining the main streets; **Dunnes,** Belmore St., is the largest (☎6632 5132; open M-Tu and Sa 9am-6pm, W-F 9am-9pm, Su 1-6pm).

Kamal Mahal, Water St. (☎6632 5045). Portions of Indian food large enough to satiate an army of carnivores or a cadre of vegetarians. Lunch buffet £4.95, served noon-3pm. Takeaway or sit-down. Dinner served 5pm-midnight. ❷

Franco's, Queen Elizabeth Rd. (☎6632 4424). Cozy nooks, wooden tables, and red napkins fill the front rooms of this popular bistro, while the newly refurbished back rooms suffer from faceless modernity. Pizza from £6.75, mix and match pasta from £6.95. Takeaway available. Open M-Sa noon-11pm, Su noon-10:30pm. ❸

Oscar's, Bemore St. (☎6632 7037). Serves a Mediterranean-influenced menu in a unique atmosphere that is 1 part pub, 2 parts library. In homage to Oscar Wilde (who went to secondary school in Enniskillen's Portora Royal School), books—both real and painted—line the walls. Upstairs, the candlelit **Writer's Room** seduces book lovers. Most meals £8-12. Veggie menu. Open daily 6-10pm. ❹

Blake's of the Hollow, 6 Church St. (☎6632 5388). Reads "William Blake" on the facade, which is so old and red they put it on a postcard. The front pub is dark and traditional, with gated snugs behind, while large, modern pubs are up the stairs with a Greco-Roman themed wine bar in the cellar. F trad.

The Linen Hall, Townhall St. (☎6632 4055). Weatherspoons recently bought and refurbished this large bar, formerly called The Vintage. As is its custom, the chain offers frequent promos, the cheapest drinks in town, and inexpensive pub grub until 11pm most nights, luring students and other young customers. The medieval back room and lights produce a festive atmosphere for the bump 'n grind crowd. Disco W and F-Sa. 18+.

Bush Bar, 26 Townhall St. (☎6632 5210). The place for trad and folk F and Su, while W and Sa welcome a free (top-40) nightclub out back in **'Havana,'** with lots of promos on its tropical drink concoctions.

Pat's Bar, Townhall St. (☎6632 7462). Live music all weekend long, from trad to rock. Sa is a big night, with one band downstairs and one of the most popular clubs with the younger set pulsing above. Open late.

The Crowe's Nest, High St. (☎6632 5252). Gas masks, swords, and other digestive aids are hung around this central pub-and-grill. Live music nightly at 10pm ranges from country to trad. Upstairs, the **Thatch Niteclub** offers free admission W and Su, and charges £3 for its F-Sa discos out back.

SIGHTS AND ACTIVITIES

The jumbled buildings of **Enniskillen Castle** were home to the fearsome Gaelic Maguire chieftains in the 15th century before becoming Elizabethan barracks; these days they house two separate museums. The castle's **heritage center** presents a comprehensive look at rural Fermanagh, beginning with a pottery display and culminating in a large-scale tableau of an 1830s kitchen. The **Museum of the Royal Inniskilling Fusiliers and Dragoons,** in the castle keep, is a militarophile's playground, with guns, uniforms, and row upon row of medals. (☎6632 5000. Open M 2-5pm, Tu-F 10am-5pm; May-Aug. also Sa 2-5pm; July-Aug. also Su 2-5pm. £2.)

One and a half miles south of Enniskillen on A4, **Castle Coole** rears up in Neoclassical pride, with a hauteur that was justified when the National Trust spent £7 million restoring it. James Wyatt completed this impressive mansion in 1798; while Bartoli designed its numerous scagioli columns. A less celebrated feature delights the gadget-lover: the face of the **French clock** in the dining room turns while the hands remain immobile. The castle grounds are 10min. along on the Dublin road; the castle itself appears at the end of a 20min. hike up the driveway. (☎6632 2690. Open July-Aug. daily noon-6pm; June W-M noon-6pm; mid-Mar. to May and Sept. Sa and Su noon-6pm. Last tour 5:15pm. Admission to house by guided tour only. £3.50.) Diagonally across the street from the castle, the **Ardhowen Theatre** poses by the shore, satisfying enthusiasts of dance, drama, music, and comedy. (☎6632 5440. Performances generally Th-Sa. Box office open M-Sa 10am-4:30pm, until 7:30pm performance nights. Tickets £7-15.)

The **Fermanagh Lakeland Forum,** behind the tourist office, offers a swimming pool, tennis courts, squash, badminton, and pitches. (☎6632 4121. Open M-F 8am-10:30pm, Sa 8am-6pm, Su 2-6pm. Tennis £3 per hr. Racket rental 50p. Pool £2.) The 18-hole **Enniskillen Golf Club,** Castle Coole Rd., is within walking distance from town. (☎6632 5250. M-F £15, Sa and Su £18.) If watersports are your thing, make waves at the **Drumrush Watersports Center,** Boa Island. (☎9693 1578. Open June-Sept. daily 10am-6pm. Sailing £20 per hr.; £100 per day. Waterskiing £30 per 30min. Jet skiing £35 per 30min. Canoes £7.50 per hr. Paddleboats £10 per hr. Powerboats £30 per 30min.) Slightly cheaper **waterskiing** can be found at **Tudor Farm,** also on Boa Island. (☎6863 1943. Open daily 11am-7pm. £15 per 25min. lesson. Experienced skiers £10 per run.) Rent your own boats at the **Castle Archdale Marina,** where an extra £25 will get you the boat overnight and free **camping** on one of the lough's islands. The marina also **rents bikes** (£6 per half day, £10 per day), sells **fishing rods** and bait (£30), and runs **pony trekking** expeditions. (☎6862 1892. Boats £50 per day; £25 per 2hr. Fishing rod and bait £5.) There's a **GAA Field** on Factory Rd.

DAYTRIPS FROM ENNISKILLEN

FLORENCE COURT AND FOREST PARK. Florence Court, which once housed the Earls of Enniskillen, is a mid-18th-century Georgian mansion built by John Cole. The third Earl left behind his fossil collection for visitors' delectation; the rocks have been supplemented by the return of much of the original artwork and furniture in recent years. To reach the castle and its artwork, take the Sligo road out of Enniskillen, then turn left onto the A32 (Swanlinbar Rd.) and follow the signs. *(☎6634 8249. Open June-Aug. daily noon-6pm; Apr.-May and Sept. Sa-Su noon-6pm. £3.50.)*

MARBLE ARCH CAVES. Four miles farther down the road from Florence Court to Belcoo, and easily combined with Florence Court as a comfortable daytrip from Enniskillen, are the Marble Arch Caves, a subterranean labyrinth of hidden rivers, waterfalls, and strangely sculpted limestone. An underground boat trip begins the 1¼hr. tour, which leads to impressive creations carved by nature's weird hand over thousands of years. The reflections of stalactites in the river are a sight to behold. To get to the caves, take the Sligo bus to Belcoo and follow the signposts for 3 mi. *(☎6634 8855. Open Mar.-Oct. daily 10am-4:30pm. Tours every 15min. £6, students and seniors £4. Book ahead. Tours may be canceled due to heavy rain.)*

BELLEEK. Belleek lies 25 mi. from Enniskillen on the A46. Buses run there six times per day (1hr.) from Enniskillen. At the northern tip of Lower Lough Erne, tiny Belleek would go unnoticed were it not for its famously delicate china. Tours of the **Belleek Pottery Factory** tell the story of young John C. Bloomfield's quest to turn a humble toilet manufacturer into the powerhouse of kitsch it is today. *(☎6865 8501. Open Mar.-Oct. Sa 10am-6pm, Su 2-6pm; Nov.-Feb. M-F 9am-5:30pm. 2 tours per hr. Last tour 4:15pm. £3, seniors £2.)* The exhibits at **ExplorErne,** also in Belleek, provide a concise introduction to the geology, anthropology, and history of the Lough Erne region, all accompanied by spooky Celtic elevator music. *(☎6865 8866. Open June-Sept. daily 11am-5pm. £1, children and seniors 50p; free coffee or tea with admission.)*

DEVENISH ISLAND. Today the ruins on Devenish island mostly function as a playpen for young children, but can also provide insight into the culture of the early Irish monking life; St. Molaise founded a monastic center here in the 6th century. Today all that remain are **St. Molaise's House,** an oratory; an 81 ft. **round tower** dating from the 12th century; and St. Mary's 15th-century Augustinian **priory.** To get to the island, contact the friendly people at **Devenish Ferries,** which push off ferries from Trory Point, 4 mi. from Enniskillen on Irvinestown Rd., or a 1 mi. walk to the left from the Trory ferry bus stop on the Pettigoe route. *(☎07702 052873. 4 boats run Apr.-Sept. daily 10am-5pm. £2.25.)*

LONDON

Given its close proximity to Ireland, and the plethora of cheap flights that connect the two, tourists often travel to or from London on their way to Dublin or Belfast. What follows is enough information to find a good place to sleep and plan a short stay. This is the bare-bones highlights of the majestic city and its history, culture, and bloody good times; for more detailed information on sights, museums, shopping, restaurants, nightlife, and more, be sure to pick up a copy of *Let's Go: London 2003*.

TRANSPORTATION

Airports: Heathrow Airport (www.baa.co.uk/main/airports/heathrow). The slowest but cheapest way to get to central London is the **Tube:** Heathrow is in Zone 6, on the Piccadilly Line (40-60min. to Zone 1; every 4-5min. M-Sa 5am-11:34pm, Su 6am-10:43pm; £3.60, under-16 £1.50). The costly **Heathrow Express** (www.heathrowexpress.co.uk) travels to **Paddington Station** in 15min. every 15min. (5:10am-11:40pm, £11). Travel to and from **Gatwick Airport** (www.baa.co.uk/main/airports/gatwick) is superior. Trains to London leave from the **South Terminal. Gatwick Express** (☎08705 301 530; www.gatwickexpress.co.uk) and the cheaper **Connex** (☎0870 603 0405; www.connex.co.uk) both run to **Victoria Station;** Connex takes 7min. longer. (Gatwick Express: 35min., every 15min. 6am-8pm and every 30min. through the night. £11. Connex: 42min., every 15-20min. 5am-midnight and hourly through the night. £8.20.)

Public Transportation: The **24hr. help line** (☎7222 1234) helps plan travel. London's subway system is divided into 6 concentric transport zones; fares depend on the distance of the journey and the number of zones crossed (central London £1.60). The **Underground** (or **Tube**) is fast, efficient, and crowded. (Open 6am-approx. midnight.) Buying a **Travelcard** allows unlimited trips—on the Underground, regular buses, British Rail, and the Docklands Light Railway—within certain zones. Available from any station in 1-day, 1-week, and 1-month increments. The **bus** network is divided into 4 zones. 1-way fares range 70p-£1; a 1-day bus pass is £2. **Night buses** (the "N" routes) run throughout London 11:30pm-6am. All pass through Trafalgar Sq. Pick up free maps and guides at **London Transport's Information Centres** (look for the lower-case "i" logo on signs) at the following Tube stations: Euston, Victoria, King's Cross, Liverpool St., Oxford Circus, Piccadilly, and Heathrow Terminals 1, 2, and 4.

Taxis: A light signifies an available taxi. Fares are steep, and 10% tip is standard.

PRACTICAL INFORMATION

TOURIST AND LOCAL SERVICES

London Visitor Centres (www.londontouristboard.com): **Heathrow Terminals 1,2,3:** In the Tube station. Open Oct.- Aug. daily 8am-6pm; Sept. M-Sa 9am-7pm and Su 8am-6pm. **Liverpool St.:** In the Tube station. Open June-Sept. M-Sa 8am-7pm, Su 8am-6pm; Oct.-May daily 8am-6pm. **Victoria Station:** Open Easter-Sept. M-Sa 8am-8pm, Su 8am-6pm; Oct.-Easter daily 8am-6pm. **Waterloo Int'l.:** Open daily 8:30am-10:30pm.

Embassies and Consulates: For a full list of those in London, see p. 7.

Gay, Lesbian, and Bisexual: London Lesbian and Gay Switchboard (☎7837 7324; www.queery.org.uk). 24hr. helpline and info resource. **Boyz** (www. boyz.co.uk) and **Gingerbeer** (www.gingerbeer.co.uk) are gay and lesbian web portals respectively with listings of clubs, bars, and restaurants. **GAY to Z** (www.gaytoz.co.uk). Directory of gay resources and gay-friendly businesses in Britain.

Disability Resources: RADAR, 12 City Forum, 250 City Rd., EC1V 8AF (☎7250 3222; www.radar.org.uk), is a network of 500 charities that offer info and support.

Pharmacies: Most "chemists" keep regular store hours; late at night, try: **Bliss,** 5-6 Marble Arch (☎7723 6116). Tube: Marble Arch. Open daily 9am-midnight. **Zafash Pharmacy,** 233 Old Brompton Rd. (☎7373 2798). Tube: Earl's Court. Open 24hr.

EMERGENCY AND COMMUNICATIONS

Emergency: ☎999; no coins required. ☎112 from a mobile (cell) phone.

Hospitals: The following have 24hr. walk-in A&E departments: **Charing Cross Hospital,** Fulham Palace Rd. (entrance St. Dunstan's Rd.), W6 (☎8846 1234; Tube: Baron's Ct. or Hammersmith); **St. Thomas's Hospital,** Lambeth Palace Rd., SE1 (☎7928 9292; Tube: Westminster); **University College Hospital,** Gower St. (entrance on Grafton Way), WC1 (☎7387 9300; Tube: Euston or Warren St.).

Internet Access: easyEverything (☎7241 9000; www.easyeverything.com). Constantly expanding empire: 9-16 Tottenham Court Rd. (Tube: Tottenham Court Rd.); 358 Oxford St. (Tube: Bond St.); 9-13 Wilson Rd. (Tube: Victoria); 160-166 Kensington High St. (Tube: High St. Kensington). From £1 per hr.; min. charge £2. Open 24hr.

Royal Mail (www.royalmail.co.uk). Delivers twice a day M-F, once Sa. Rates within the UK: 1st class letter (next business day) 27p, 2nd class letter (3 business days), 19p. Airmail letters 37p within Europe, 47p intercontinental. Offices all over London.

ACCOMMODATIONS

Accommodations in London average 2-3 times what you would normally find in the Republic of Ireland or Northern Ireland. Family rooms are often your best deal. The area near Victoria station (Westminster) is convenient for major sights and transportation. Bloomsbury, near the British Museum, has affordable accommodations. While in West London, posh Kensington and less-so Bayswater offer a few reasonably priced B&Bs. Call ahead to book, especially in summer.

WESTMINSTER

Westminster House Hotel, 96 Ebury St. (☎7730 7850; www.westminsterhousehotel.co.uk). Tube: Victoria. The extremely welcoming Joneses run this small B&B as if it were their home, which it is. The 10 spotless rooms each have TV, hospitality trays with hot drinks, and almost all have private baths. Full English breakfast included. 48hr. cancellation policy. Singles £50, with bath £55; doubles £70/£80; triples with bath £90; quad with bath £100. ❺

Luna Simone Hotel, 47/49 Belgrave Rd. (☎7834 5897; www.lunasimonehotel.com). Tube: Victoria or Pimlico. Victorian facade conceals ultra-modern yellow rooms with TV, phone, kettle, safety deposit box, and hair dryer. On the downside, some singles are cramped. English breakfast included. Reserve 2 weeks ahead; 48hr. cancellation policy. **Internet access.** Singles £40, with bath £60; doubles £60/£80; triples £80/£110. 10% discount for stays over 7 nights in low season. ❹

Surtees Hotel, 94 Warwick Way, SW1 (☎7834 7163/7394; www.surtees-hotel.co.uk). Tube: Victoria. A flurry of flowers welcome guests to this hospitable B&B. Larger rooms range from a bunk-bed quad to the giant 6-bed, 2-room basement suite. Doubles and triples are on the small side but are bright and pleasingly decorated. English breakfast included. Singles £30, with bath £50; doubles £55/£70; triples £70/£80; quad £80/£90; family suite with bath £100. ❹

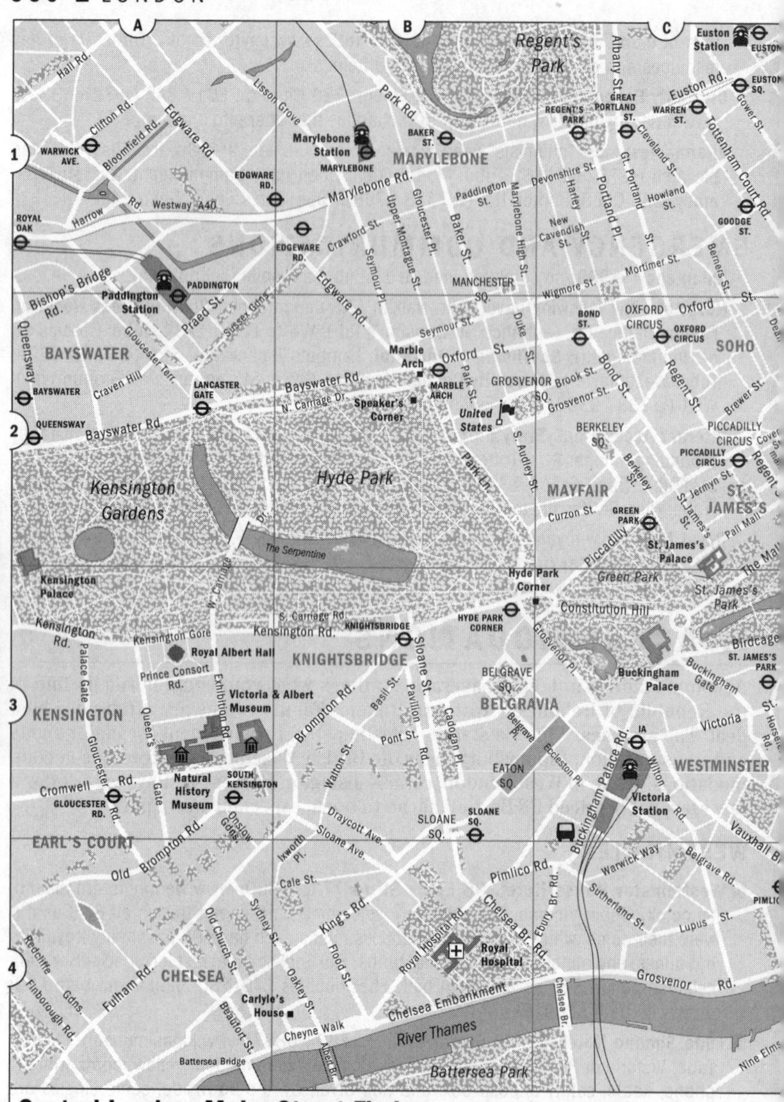

LONDON

Central London: Major Street Finder

Albert Embankment **D4**
Aldersgate **E1**
Aldwych **D2**
Audley(N&S) **B2**
Baker St. **B1**
Bayswater Rd. **A2**
Beech St./Chiswell St. **E1**
Belgrave Pl. **B3**
Beaufort **A4**
Belgrave Rd. **C4**
Berkeley St. **C2**
Birdcage Walk **C3**
Bishops Br. Rd. **A1**
Bishopsgate **F1**
Blackfriars Rd. **E2**
Bloomsbury Way **D1**
Bond St. (New&Old) **C2**
Bow St./Lancaster Pl. **D2**
Brompton Rd. **B3**
Buckingham Gate **C3**
Buckingham Palace Rd. **C3**
Cannon St. **F2**
Chancery Ln. **D1**
Charing Cross Rd. **D2**
Charterhouse St. **E1**
Cheapside **E2**
Chelsea Br. Rd. **B4**
Chelsea Embankment **B4**
Cheyne Walk **B4**
City Rd. **F1**
Clerkenwell Rd. **E1**
Constitution Hill **C3**
Cornhill/Leadenhall St. **F2**
Coventry/Cranbourne **D2**
Craven Hill Rd./Praed St. **A2**
Cromwell Rd. **A3**
Curzon St. **C2**
Drury Ln. **D2**
Eastcheap/Great Tower **F2**
Eccleston Pl. **C3**

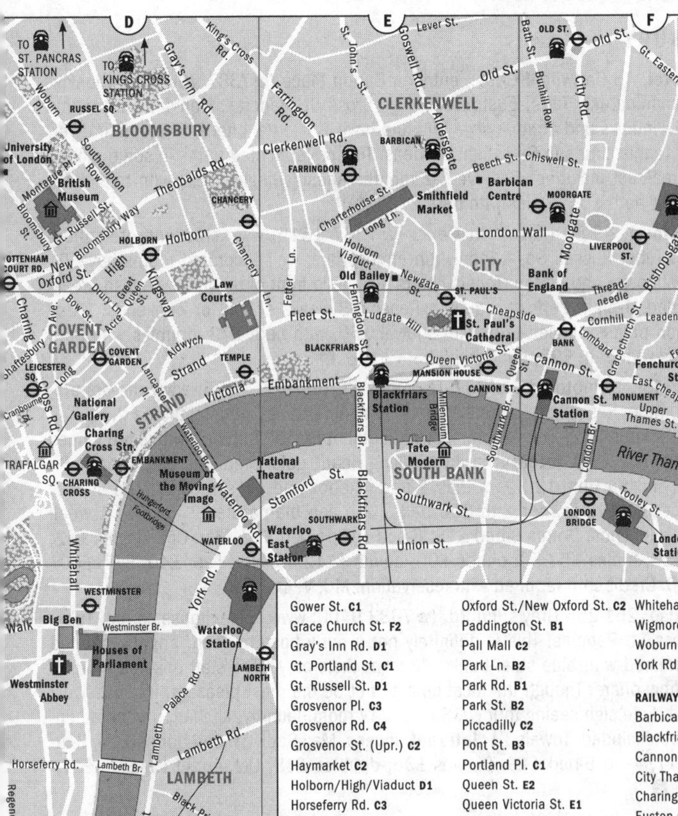

Edgware Rd. **A1**
Euston Rd. **C1**
Exhibition Rd. **A3**
Farringdon Rd. **E1**
Fenchurch/Aldgate **F2**
Fleet St. **E2**
Fulham Rd. **A4**
Gloucester Pl. **B1**
Gloucester Rd. **A3**
Goswell Rd. **E1**
Gower St. **C1**
Grace Church St. **F2**
Gray's Inn Rd. **D1**
Gt. Portland St. **C1**
Gt. Russell St. **D1**
Grosvenor Pl. **C3**
Grosvenor Rd. **C4**
Grosvenor St. (Upr.) **C2**
Haymarket **C2**
Holborn/High/Viaduct **D1**
Horseferry Rd. **C3**
Jermyn St. **C2**
Kensington High St./Rd. **A3**
King's Cross Rd. **D1**
King's Rd. **B4**
Kingsway **D2**
Knightsbridge **B3**
Lambeth Palace Rd. **D3**
Lisson Grove **A1**
Lombard St. **F2**
London Wall **E1**
Long Acre/Gt. Queen St. **D2**
Long Ln. **E1**
Ludgate Hill **E2**
Marylebone High St. **B1**
Marylebone Rd. **B1**
Millbank **D4**
Montague Pl. **D1**
Moorgate **F1**
New Bridge St. **E2**
New Cavendish **C1**
Newgate St. **E1**
Nine Elms Ln. **C4**
Oakley St. **B4**
Old St. **F1**
Old Brompton Rd. **A4**
Onslow Sq./St. **A3**
Oxford St./New Oxford St. **C2**
Paddington St. **B1**
Pall Mall **C2**
Park Ln. **B2**
Park Rd. **B1**
Park St. **B2**
Piccadilly **C2**
Pont St. **B3**
Portland Pl. **C1**
Queen St. **E2**
Queen Victoria St. **E1**
Queen's Gate **A3**
Queensway **A2**
Redcliffe Gdns. **A4**
Regent St. **C2**
Royal Hospital Rd. **B4**
St. James's St. **C2**
Seymour Pl. **A1**
Seymour St. **A2**
Shaftesbury Ave. **C2**
Sloane/Lwr. Sloane **B3**
Southampton Row **D1**
Southwark Bridge Rd. **E2**
Southwark Rd. **E2**
Stamford St. **E2**
Strand **D2**
Sydney St. **A4**
Thames St.(Upr. & Lwr.) **F2**
The Mall **C2**
Theobald's Rd. **D1**
Threadneedle St. **F2**
Tottenham Ct. Rd. **C1**
Vauxhall Br. Rd. **C4**
Victoria Embankment **D2**
Victoria St. **C3**
Warwick Way **C4**
Waterloo Rd. **E1**
Whitehall **D2**
Wigmore/Mortimer **C1**
Woburn Pl. **D1**
York Rd. **D3**

RAILWAY STATIONS

Barbican **E1**
Blackfriars **E2**
Cannon St. **F2**
City Thameslink **E2**
Charing Cross **D2**
Euston **C1**
Farringdon **E1**
King's Cross **D1**
Liverpool St. **F1**
London Bridge **F2**
Marylebone **B1**
Moorgate **F1**
Old St. **F1**
Paddington **A2**
St Pancras **D1**
Victoria **C3**
Waterloo East **E2**
Waterloo **D3**

BRIDGES

Albert **B4**
Battersea **A4**
Blackfriars **E2**
Chelsea **C4**
Hungerford Footbridge **D2**
Lambeth **D3**
London Bridge **F2**
Millennium **E2**
Southwark **E2**
Tower Bridge **F2**
Waterloo **D2**
Westminster **D3**

BLOOMSBURY

Jenkins Hotel, 45 Cartwright Gdns., entry on Barton Place (☎7387 2067; www.jenkinshotel.demon.co.uk). Tube: Euston or King's Cross St. Pancras. Non-smoking rooms with large windows and antique-style furniture have TV, kettle, phone, fridge, hair dryer, and safe. Tennis courts in Cartwright Gardens. Tiny prefabricated baths in some rooms. English breakfast included. Reserve 1-2 months ahead. Singles £52, with bath £72; doubles with bath £85; triples with bath £105. ❺

Crescent Hotel, 49-50 Cartwright Gdns. (☎7387 1515; www.crescenthotelsoflondon.com). Tube: Russell Sq. A family-run atmosphere; well-decorated rooms have TV, kettle, washbasin, and phone. Tennis courts also lie in front of the hotel. English breakfast included. 1-night deposit required. Reserve 3 weeks ahead for weekends. 7-day cancellation policy. Singles £45, with shower £50, with bath £72; doubles with bath £87; triples with bath £97; quads with bath £106. ❺

The Generator, Compton Pl. off 37 Tavistock Pl. (☎7388 7655; www.the-generator.co.uk). Tube: Russell Sq. or King's Cross St. Pancras. Less a hostel than a dystopian vision of the future: cell-like sleep units with metal bunks; a "Turbine" with video games and pool tables; 24hr. **Internet** in the "Talking Head" quiet area. The bar, open M-Sa 6pm-2am and Su 6pm-12:30am, has a free jukebox and big-screen TV. The staff is quite strict about rules, but with 800 beds, who can blame them? Reserve 1 week ahead for weekends. Dorms 8-bed £15; 6-bed £16; 4-bed £17. Mar.-Oct. singles £42; doubles £53; triples £67.50; quads £90; quints £112.50. Nov.-Feb. £40/£47/£60/£80/£100. Credit card required with reservation. MC, V. ❹

Ashlee House, 261-265 Gray's Inn Rd. (☎7833 9400; www.ashleehouse.co.uk). Tube: King's Cross St. Pancras. This is definitely not a party hostel. Clean, brightly painted rooms crammed with blue steel bunks. "Backpackers only." The staff ensures a quiet, friendly atmosphere. Though the location may not be the most pleasant, it's massively convenient. Free sightseeing tour (Th-Sa). Lift, TV room, laundry, kitchen, and continental breakfast included. Towels £1. **Internet access.** May-Sept. 16-bed dorms £15; 8- to 10-bed £17; 4- to 6-bed £19. Singles £36; doubles £48. Oct.-Apr. £13/£15/£17/£34/£44. ❷

KENSINGTON

Five Sumner Place Hotel, 5 Sumner Pl. (☎7584 7586; www.sumnerplace.com). Tube: South Kensington. Boasts all the amenities of a luxury hotel without losing the charm of the small, independent converted Victorians in the area. Surprisingly spacious rooms with large windows have private bath, TV, fridge, phone, and hair dryer, and are each accessible by lift. Unbeatable location and warm staff—it's no surprise it won the award for the best small hotel in London. Full English breakfast. 14-day cancellation policy, book 1 month ahead in summer. Singles £85; doubles £130. ❺

Vicarage Private Hotel, 10 Vicarage Gate, (☎7229 4030; www.londonvicaragehotel.com). Tube: High St. Kensington. Beautifully kept Victorian house with ornate hallways, TV lounge, and superbly appointed rooms, all with kettle and hair dryer (rooms with private bath also have TV). English breakfast included. Reserve months ahead with 1 night's deposit. No credit cards accepted. Singles £46; doubles £76, with bath £100; triples £93; quads £100. ❺

YHA Holland House, Holland Walk, (☎7937 0748). Tube: High St. Kensington or Holland Park. On the edge of Holland Park, this accommodation is split between a 17th-century mansion and a less attractive 1970s unit; dorms in both are similar, with 12-20 interlocking bunks. TV room, luggage storage, lockers, laundry, and kitchen. Breakfast included. Book 2-3 weeks ahead in summer. £21 per person, under-18 £18.75. ❸

BAYSWATER

Hyde Park Rooms Hotel, 137 Sussex Gdns. (☎7723 0225). Tube: Paddington. The jovial London natives who run the hotel take great pride in every detail of the airy, spotless rooms they provide, as well as the helpful assistance they offer. Expansive elbow room compensates for the quad's dim lighting. English breakfast included, served in the beautiful, homely dining room. Call ahead in summer. 24hr. cancellation policy. Singles £30, with bath £40; doubles £40-45/£50-55; triples £60/£72; quads £80/£96. ❹

Hyde Park Hostel, 2-6 Inverness Terr. (☎7229 5101; www.astorhostels.com). Tube: Queensway or Bayswater. Backpacker spirit pervades—flimsy foam-pad mattresses; quarters a bit cramped—but what it lacks in comfort it makes up in fun. Basement bar and dance space with frequent DJs, and theme parties, both restricted to residents only (open W-Sa 8pm-3am; food also served). Kitchen, laundry, TV lounge, and secure luggage room. Continental breakfast and linen included. Ages 16-35 only. Reserve 2 weeks ahead; 24hr. cancellation policy. **Internet access.** Online booking with 10% non-refundable deposit. 10- to 18-bed dorms £11-13.50; 8-beds £14.50-15.50; 6-beds £15.50-16.50; 4-beds £16.50-17.50. Doubles £42-45. 10% ISIC discount. ❷

OTHER NEIGHBORHOODS

Travel Inn County Hall, Belvedere Rd., the South Bank (☎0870 238 3300; www.travelinn.co.uk). Tube: Westminster or Waterloo. Seconds from the South Bank and Westminster. No river views but rooms are clean and modern, with bath, kettle, and color TV in each. Facilities include elevator, restaurant, and bar. Reserve at least 1 month ahead; cancel by 4pm on day of arrival. Continental breakfast £5, English £6, children £3.50. Only rents by the room (which sleeps four individuals); perfect for families. F-Su £75 per room, M-Th £80. ❷

International Student House, 229 Great Portland St., Marylebone (☎7631 8300; www.ish.org.uk). Tube: Great Portland Street. Great location near Regent's Park and just minutes from Oxford Circus. Most rooms are of similar size, varying only in the number of beds—singles seem huge, bunk-bedded quads less so. Spartan 8- to 10-bed dorms have sink and lockers. 3 bars, cheap cafeteria, fitness center (£3 per day), cinema (Su only), and laundry; guests get 15min. free **Internet,** then £2 per hr. Continental breakfast included except for dorms (£2); English breakfast £3. £10 key deposit. Reserve 1 month ahead during the summer. All dorms £10. Singles £31, with bath £33; doubles £50/£52; triples £60; quads £72. ❶

High Holborn Residence, 178 High Holborn, the West End (☎7379 5589; www.lse.ac.uk/vacations). Tube: Holborn or Tottenham Court Rd. One of the nicest university dorms to rent hostel-style rooms in the summer, with a great location for Covent Garden exploits. Accommodation is in "flats" of 4-5 rooms, each with a phone, sharing well-equipped kitchen and bath; rooms with private bath are much larger. Some rooms wheelchair-accessible. Bar, elevator, laundry, TV room, and games room. Continental breakfast included. Open June to late Sept. Singles £29-36; doubles £48-58, with bath £58-68; triples with bath £68-78. Rates lower after mid-Aug. ❹

NEIGHBORHOOD HIGHLIGHTS

THE WEST END

Whether it's shopping, eating, theater-going, or clubbing, the West End is London's popular (and populist) heartland. **Soho** is the nightlife nexus—and, around Old Compton St., its gay vanguard. The fashion-conscious head to the boutiques of **Covent Garden,** southwest of Soho. South of Covent Garden, **the Strand** offers glimpses of London's past—along with a smattering of theaters and touristy restaurants—

on its way to majestic, pigeon-infested **Trafalgar Square.** Tube: Piccadilly Circus, Leicester Sq., and Covent Garden.

Sights: Soak in the atmosphere—prestigious **Mayfair;** smug **St. James's;** overwhelming **Oxford St.;** classy **Covent Garden;** slinky **Soho.**

Museums: A plethora of artistic greats at the **Royal Academy,** Burlington House (☎7300 8000); Tubes and trams at **London's Transport Museum,** Covent Garden Piazza (☎7565 7299).

Food: Monorail-delivered fusion sushi at **Itsu,** 103 Wardour St. (☎7479 4794); high tea with a postmodern twist at Ian Schrager's **St. Martin's Lane Hotel,** 45 St. Martin's Ln. (☎7300 5588); a truly bazaar experience at **Mô's Moroccan Tea-room,** 23 Heddon St. (☎7434 3999); the **cafes** of St. Christopher's Place, near Oxford St.

Shopping: The hottest **fashions on Floral St.,** Covent Garden; top DJs' favorite **record stores in Soho;** window-shopping at the *couture* **boutiques on Bond St.; Selfridges,** 400 Oxford St. (☎0870 8377 377), London's favorite department store.

Entertainment: Blockbusters, classic films, and *Sing-a-long-a-Sound-of-Music* in and around **Leicester Sq.;** jazz legends at **Ronnie Scott's,** 47 Frith St. (☎7439 0747); big people, big voices at the **Royal Opera,** Bow St. (☎7304 4000), and the **Coliseum,** St. Martin's Lane (☎7632 8300); the funniest of funny-men at the **Comedy Store,** 1a Oxendon St. (☎7344 0234).

Nightlife: Plumbing the depths of 60s and 70s at **Madame Jojo's,** 8-10 Brewer St. (☎7734 3040); Brazilian dance at the **Velvet Room's** *Swerve,* 143 Charing Cross Rd. (☎7734 4687); chilling on the couches at **Freud,** 198 Shaftesbury Ave. (☎7240 9933).

Gay and Lesbian: Old Compton St., the heart of gay London including pubs **Comptons of Soho,** 53 Old Compton St. (☎7479 7461), and **Admiral Duncan,** 54 Old Compton St. (☎7437 5300); the labrynthine **Heaven,** Britain's most famous gay nightclub, is at The Arches, Craven Terrace (☎7930 2020).

LONDON

WESTMINSTER

Home to Parliament, the Prime Minister, and the Queen herself, Westminster exudes power and privilege. But away from the bureaucracy of Whitehall and the Gothic grandeur of the abbey, this area is surprisingly down-to-earth. **Pimlico,** south of Victoria, is a quiet residential district with some of London's best B&Bs. Don't come here for food, shopping, or—unless you count late-running debates in the House of Lords—nightlife; but with some of London's top sights, and the West End, Knightsbridge, and Chelsea within easy reach, whatever you don't find in Westminster can't be far away. Tube: Westminster, St. James's Park, Victoria, Charing Cross, and Pimlico.

Sights: The **Houses of Parliament** seen from Westminster Bridge at dusk; the resting places of England's great and good (and Cromwell) in **Westminster Abbey** (☎7222 7110); a proud Nelson in triumphant **Trafalgar Sq.;** the neo-Byzantine splendor of **Westminster Cathedral** (☎7798 9055), Inigo Jones's masterpiece.

Museums & Galleries: Leonardo, Michelangelo, et al. at the **National Gallery,** Trafalgar Sq. (☎7747 2885); the heart of a nation at war in the **Cabinet War Rooms,** King Charles St. (☎7930 6961); the art of a nation through the ages in **Tate Britain,** Millbank (☎7887 8008).

THE SOUTH BANK

Close to the City but long exempt from its party-pooping laws, the South Bank has been for centuries London's entertainment center, renowned of yore for its theaters, cock-fighting, bull-baiting, and other (less reputable) gentlemanly diversions. Now, the **Millennium Mile** stretches from the twirling London Eye past the cultural powerhouses of the Festival Hall, Hayward Gallery, National Theatre, Tate Modern, and Shakespeare's Globe Theatre, as well as the quirky riverside shops and eateries of Gabriel's Wharf and the OXO Tower. Tube: Southwark, Blackfriars, or Waterloo.

Sights: London–all of it, as seen from the **London Eye** (☎0870 5000 0600); **HMS Belfast** (☎7940 6300), one mother of a WWII warship; the graceful (recently stabilized) span of the **Millennium Bridge.**

Museums & Galleries: Tate Modern, the world's largest, most unusual modern art museum, Bankside (☎7887 8006); the meaning of modernity at the **Design Museum,** 28 Shad Thames, Butler's Wharf (☎7403 6933).

Food: A trio of affordable lunches with brilliant food and great riverside views: the **People's Palace,** Royal Festival Hall (☎7928 9999), **Tate Modern** (☎7887 8888), and **Cantina del Ponte,** 36c Shad Thames, Butler's Wharf (☎7403 5403); top Turkish treats at **Tas,** 72 Borough High St. (☎7403 7200).

Entertainment: World-beating drama at the **National Theatre,** just downriver of Waterloo Bridge (☎7452 3400), the **Old Vic,** Waterloo Rd. (☎7928 2651), and **the Globe,** 21 New Globe Walk (☎7401 9919); classics, world music, and jazz at the **South Bank Centre** (☎7960 4201); celluloid variety at the **National Film Theater** and mind-boggling cinematic experiences at the **BFI IMAX,** Charlie Chaplin Walk (☎7902 1234).

THE CITY OF LONDON

The City is where London began—indeed, for most of its history, the City *was* London. Today, not much happens here outside office hours; the only restaurants and pubs that don't close entirely are those aimed at the millions of tourists who outnumber the pigeons at **St. Paul's Cathedral** and daily storm the **Tower of London.** The City's gems are the 24 surviving churches built by Christopher Wren following the Great Fire of 1666. Tube: St. Paul's, Tower Hill, and Monument.

Sights: London at your feet from the top of **St. Paul's Cathedral** (☎7264 8348) and **Monument** (☎7626 2717); Elizabeth II's baubles at the **Tower of London** (☎7709 0765); the gigantic Gothic **Guildhall** (☎7606 3030), seat of the Lord Mayor's Great Council, off Gresham St. (☎7606 3030).

Museums & Galleries: 1970 years of history at the **Museum of London,** London Wall (☎7600 3699). Enter through the Barbican Centre.

Food: The best of a new breed of Indian restaurants, **Cafe Spice Namaste,** 16 Prescot St. (☎7488 9242).

Entertainment: Top plays and musical acts in the **Barbican Centre** (☎7638 8891).

BLOOMSBURY

Home to dozens of universities, colleges, and specialist hospitals—not to mention the British Museum and the British Library—Bloomsbury is London's undisputed intellectual powerhouse. Tube: King's Cross, Euston, Goodge St. and Russell Sq.

Sights: The **British Library** (☎7412 7332) and **St. Pancras Station,** forming an odd but intriguing architectural contrast; both make for rewarding visits.

Museums: The **British Museum,** Great Russell St. (☎7323 8000), in which whole vacations can be swallowed; a past world of playthings in **Pollock's Toy Museum,** 1 Scala St. (☎7636 3452), with not a Playstation in sight .

Food: Da Beppe, 116 Tottenham Court Rd. (☎7387 6324), serving huge portions of London's best Italian food; **Diwana Bhel Poori House,** 121-123 Drummond St., (☎7387 5556), a vegetarian's paradise of South Indian food at unbeatable prices.

KENSINGTON

Until recently the stomping ground of Princess Diana, Kensington divides between the consumer mecca of **Kensington High St.** (in the west) and the incredible array of museums and colleges of **South Kensington's** "Albertopolis" (in the east). Tube: High St. Kensington or South Kensington.

Sights: The Royal Dress Collection in **Kensington Palace** (☎7937 9561), Diana's former home.

Museums: The **Victoria & Albert Museum,** Cromwell Rd. (☎7942 2000), tops most people's lists, but those with kids run to the **Natural History Museum,** Cromwell Rd. (☎7942 5000) and **Science Museum,** Exhibition Rd. (☎0870 870 4868).

Food: Tea at the Palace in the **Orangery** (☎7938 1406); a taste of France at **Raison d'Être** in South Kensington's Little Paris, 18 Bute St. (☎7584 5008).

Shopping: Oxford St. variety without Oxford St. crowds on **Kensington High St.**

NOTTING HILL

For decades it was one of London's most vibrant, ethnically mixed neighborhoods, but over the past few years (helped on by a certain movie) Notting Hill has become a victim of its own trendiness. Only at the edges can you catch glimpses of the old magic: to the south, where the ugly 1950s facades of **Notting Hill Gate** do their best to keep yuppieville at bay, and in the north around **Portobello Road** and **the Westway.** Tube: Notting Hill Gate and Ladbroke Grove.

Shopping: Portobello Market on a Saturday; vintage Westwood, Gaultier, and other outrageous *couture* at **One of a Kind,** 259 Portobello Rd. (☎7792 5853).

Food: Top fish'n'chips at **George's,** 329 Portobello Rd. (☎8969 7895); fresh Portuguese pastries at **Lisboa,** 57 Golborne Rd. (☎8968 5242); taste the latest recipes at **Books for Cooks'** in-store demo kitchen, 4 Blenheim Crescent (☎7221 1992).

HOLBORN

London's second-oldest area, a center of medieval monasticism, today Holborn is associated with two unholy professions: lawyers and journalists. If you thought lawyers had it good at home, wait until you see the **Inns of Court,** colleges-cum-clubs for barristers that have been growing in wealth and power for centuries. Though **Fleet Street** remains synonymous with the British press, the newspapers have since moved on, sapping Holborn of much of its vitality. Home to some sterling sights, after hours there's little to do but sit in one of the many historic pubs once frequented by local lads Samuel Johnson and Samuel Pepys. Tube: Temple, Blackfriars and Chancery Lane.

Sights: Lawyers in wigs at the **Royal Courts of Justice,** where Strand becomes Fleet St. (☎7936 6000); lawyers in digs in the **Temple,** south down a Middle Temple Ln. from Fleet St. (☎7353 3470); gothic splendor of **St. Etheldreda's,** Ely Place (☎7405 1061).

Museums & Galleries: Monet and Manet at the **Courtauld Institute,** Somerset House, Strand (☎7848 2526); the incredible maze-museum of architectural innovator **Sir John Soane,** 13 Lincoln's Inn Fields.

Food: Brilliant British food at the **Bleeding Heart Tavern,** corner of Greville St. and Bleeding Heart Yard (☎7404 0333); 300 years of drinking at **Ye Olde Cheshire Cheese,** Wine Office Ct. by 145 Fleet St. (☎7353 6170).

CLERKENWELL

Behind the grim industrial facade, Clerkenwell is one of London's most fascinating and historic districts. Good food, great bars, *and* historic sights? Get outta town. Tube: Farringdon or Barbican.

Sights: The ancient church of **St. Bartholomew the Great,** off West Smithfield (☎7606 5171); **Smithfield,** London's largest meat market; a tour of the **Charterhouse** (W 2pm), a fascinating, living Elizabethan institution (☎7251 5000).

Food: Affordable bar food at **St. John,** 26 St. John St. (☎7251 0848), British Restaurant of the Year; artery-hardening breakfasts with beer at the **Fox & Anchor,** 115 Charterhouse St. (☎7253 5075), one of London's earliest-opening pubs.

Nightlife: Louder than you thought possible, top dance nights at megaclub **Fabric,** 77a Charterhouse St. (☎7336 8898); go crazy at **Cafe Kick's** multiple foosball tables, 43 Exmouth Market (☎7837 8077).

CHELSEA

Chelsea has the cachet of Knightsbridge and Kensington without their stuffiness. In the 19th century, **Cheyne Walk** hummed to the discussions of Edgar Allen Poe, Dante Gabriel Rossetti, and Oscar Wilde among others. While, in the 1960s and 70s, **King's Rd.** was the launching point for miniskirts and punk rock. Today's Chelsea now includes a string of B-list celebrities and trust-fund kids known collectively as "Sloane Rangers." Nonetheless, Chelsea retains a little of that old-time glamour, helped along by the presence of numerous modeling agencies around **Sloane Square.** Tube: Sloane Sq. although take the #11 bus down the King's Rd.

Sights: The envy of all retirement homes, Christopher Wren's **Royal Hospital** home of the Chelsea Pensioners (Royal Hospital Rd.).

Shopping: A last stand against global brands, the **unique boutiques** of the King's Rd.

Entertainment: New plays and iconoclastic classics at the **Royal Court Theatre,** Sloane Sq. (☎7565 5000); underground jazz in the hard-to-find **606 club,** 90 Lot's Rd. (☎7352 5953).

KNIGHTSBRIDGE & BELGRAVIA

London's most desired addresses for the last two centuries—Apsley House, the Duke of Wellington's former abode, revels in the address "No. 1, London." But now only foreign embassies and consulates can afford the land anymore. High prices mean that finding anything affordable is not easy, and the primary draw is the windowshopping. **Knightsbridge** provides the foil to the West End's shopping stranglehold: like the locals, famed department stores Harrods and Harvey Nichols are secure in their sense of superiority. **Belgravia,** east of Sloane St., is a cultural desert of grand 19th-century mansions occupied by aforementioned billionaires and embassies. Tube: Knightsbridge and Hyde Park Corner.

Sights: Apsley House, Hyde Park Corner (☎7499 5676), proving that real men can have interests beyond football; the **Wellington Arch,** Hyde Park Corner (☎7930 2726), providing a rare glimpse into Buckingham Palace gardens.

Shopping: Harrods, 87-135 Old Brompton Rd. (☎7730 1234), to be seen to be believed, especially the prices; **Harvey Nichols,** 109-125 Knightsbridge (☎7235 5000), Diana's favorite department store and still the most fashionable; **designer collections** on Sloane St.

APPENDIX

TIME DIFFERENCES

Ireland and the UK are on **Greenwich Mean Time (GMT),** which means they are: 1hr. earlier than (most of) continental Europe; 5hr. later than New York (EST); 6hr. later than Hibbing, Minnesota (CST); 7hr. later than Phoenix, Arizona (MST); 8hr. later than Los Angeles, California (PST); 8, 9½, and 10hr. earlier than Australia; and 12hr. earlier than Auckland, New Zealand.

MEASUREMENTS

MEASUREMENT CONVERSIONS	
1 foot (ft.) = 0.30 m	1 meter (m) = 3.28 ft.
1 yard (yd.) = 0.914m	1 meter (m) = 1.09 yd.
1 mile = 1.61km	1 kilometer (km) = 0.62 mi.
1 acre (ac.) = 0.405ha	1 hectare (ha) = 2.47 ac.
1 square mile (sq. mi.) = 2.59km²	1 square kilometer (km²) = 0.386 sq. mi.

2003 BANK HOLIDAYS

Government agencies, post offices, and banks are closed on the following days (hence the term "Bank Holiday"), and businesses—if not closed—may have shorter hours. Sights, on the other hand, are more likely to remain open.

DATE	HOLIDAY	AREAS
January 1	New Year's Day	Republic of Ireland and Northern Ireland
March 17	St. Patrick's Day	Republic of Ireland and Northern Ireland
April 18	Good Friday	Republic of Ireland and Northern Ireland
April 21	Easter Monday	Republic of Ireland and Northern Ireland
May 5	May Day Bank Holiday	Republic of Ireland and Northern Ireland
June 2	First Monday in June	Republic of Ireland
July 12	Battle of the Boyne (Orangeman's Day)	Northern Ireland
October 27	Halloween Weekend (last Monday in October)	Republic of Ireland
December 25	Christmas Day	Republic of Ireland and Northern Ireland
December 26	Boxing Day/St. Stephen's Day	Republic of Ireland and Northern Ireland

AVERAGE TEMPERATURE AND RAINFALL

Avg. Temp. (lo/hi), Precipitation	January			April			July			October		
	°C	°F	mm	°C	°F	mm	°C	°F	mm	°C	°F	mm
Dublin	2/7	37/46	63	5/11	41/52	48	12/18	54/66	66	7/12	46/55	73
Cork	3/7	38/46	124	4/11	40/52	66	11/18	53/65	68	7/12	46/65	106
Belfast	4/7	40/45	83	6/10	44/51	51	13/17	56/63	79	8/11	47/52	85
London	2/7	36/45	60	5/12	41/55	43	13/22	56/72	45	7/14	46/58	78

GLOSSARY

For a brief history of the Irish language, see our brief history of **The Irish Language,** p. 70. On the left-hand side of this table you will find a list of Gaelic/Irish words (or English words marked by a distinct Irish dialect) that you are likely to encounter during your time in Ireland. The glossary on the right-hand side of the table should help you sort things out. Spelling conventions do not always match English pronunciations: for example, "mh" sounds like "v," "dh" like "g", and "ai" like "ie."

IRISH	PRONUNCIATION	(AMERICAN) ENGLISH
	Getting to know the locals	
Ba mháich liom point.	ba WHY-lum pee-yunt	**I would like a pint.**
Cann eille led' thoil.	cahn EYE-leh led-TOIL	**Another one, please.**
Conas tá tú?	CUNN-us taw too	**How are you?**
dia dhuit	JEE-a dich	**Good day, hello**
dia's muire dhuit	Jee-as MWUR-a dich	**The reply to "good day"**
fáilte	FAHL-tshuh	**Welcome**
go raibh maith agat	guh roh moh UG-ut	**Thank you**
mór	more	**Big, great**
ní hea	nee hah	**No (sort of; it's tricky)**
oíche mhaith dhuit	EE-ha woh dich	**Good night**
sea	shah	**Yes (sort of; it's tricky)**
sláinte	SLAWN-che	**Cheers, to your health**
slán agat	slawn UG-ut	**Goodbye**
Tá mé i mo idirgalachtach bhithiúnach.	ta-MAY imah va-HOO-nock idder gah-lachtach	**I am an inter-galactic space criminal.**
Tá sé fluic.	tah SHAY fluck	**It's raining.**
Tá sé trim!	tah SHAY trim!	**It's not raining!**
tóg é go bog é	TOG-ah BUG-ay	**Take it easy**
tuigim	tiggum	**I understand**
	Sleeping and Living	
bedsit		**One-room apartment, sometimes with kitchen**
biro		**Ball point pen**
caravan		**RV, trailer**
dust bin		**Trash can**
fir	fear	**Men**
first floor		**First floor up from the ground floor (second floor)**
flat		**Apartment**
ground floor		**First floor (are you confused yet?)**
half-ten, half-nine, etc.		**Ten-thirty, nine-thirty, etc.**
hoover		**Vacuum cleaner**
lavatory, lav		**Bathroom**
leithras	LEH-hrass	**Toilets**
loo		**Bathroom**
mná	min-AW	**Women**
Oifig an Phoist	UFF-ig un fwisht	**Post office**
to queue up, "the Q"	CUE	**Waiting line**
teach	chock	**House**
torch		**Flashlight**
siopa	SHUP-ah	**Shop**

APPENDIX

IRISH	PRONUNCIATION	(AMERICAN) ENGLISH
		Locations and Landmarks
An Lár	on lahr	**City center**
Baile Átha Cliath	BALL-yah AW-hah CLEE-ah	**Dublin**
drumlin		**Small hill**
Éire	AIR-uh	**Ireland; official name of the Republic of Ireland**
gaeltacht	GAYL-tokt	**A district where Irish is the everyday language**
inch, innis		**Island**
quay	key	**A waterside street**
slieve *or* sliabh	shleev	**Mountain**
sraid	shrawd	**Street**
strand		**Beach**
trá	thraw	**Beach**
		Getting Around
coach		**Bus (long distance)**
hire		**Rental**
left luggage		**Luggage storage**
a lift		**A ride**
lorry		**Truck**
motorway		**Highway**
petrol		**Gasoline**
roundabout		**Rotary road interchange**
self-drive		**Car rental**
single ticket		**One-way ticket**
		Sightseeing
Bord Fáilte	Bored FAHL-tshuh	**Irish Tourist Board**
concession		**Discount on admission for seniors and students**
dolmen		**Chamber formed by huge stones**
dún	doon	**Fort**
gaol	jail	**Jail**
kil	kill	**Church; monk's cell**
ogham	Oh-um	**Early Irish, written on stones**
rath	rath *or* rah	**Earthen fort**
tumulus		**Stone burial mound**
		Money Please
cheap		**Inexpensive (not shoddy)**
dear		**Expensive**
fiver		**€5 note (used to mean £5 punts)**
sterling		**British pound**
tenner		**€10 note (used to mean £10 punts)**
		Civic and Cultural
chemist		**Pharmacist**
garda, Garda Siochána	GAR-da SHE-och-ANA	**Police**
OAP		**Old age pensioner, "senior citizen"**
RTÉ		**Radio Telefis Éireann, the Republic's broadcasting authority**
RUC		**Royal Ulster Constabulary, the police force of Northern Ireland**

IRISH	PRONUNCIATION	(AMERICAN) ENGLISH
	Please Sir, May I Have Another	
bangers and mash		**Sausage and mashed potatoes**
bap		**A soft round bun**
bill		**Check (in restaurants)**
biscuit		**Cookie**
candy-floss		**Cotton candy**
carvey		**Meal of meat, potatoes, and carrots/vegetables**
chips		**French fries**
chipper		**Fish and chips vendor**
crisps		**Potato chips**
rashers		**Irish bacon**
takeaway		**Take-out, "to go"**
	Pubs & Music	
bodhrán	BOUR-ohn	**Traditional drum**
brilliant		**Great, "awesome"**
busker		**Street musician**
céilí	KAY-lee	**Irish dance**
to chat up		**To hit on**
concertina		**Small, round-button accordian**
craic	krak	**Good cheer, good pub conversation, a good time**
faders	FOD-ers	**Party poopers who go to bed early**
fag		**A cigarette**
feis	fesh	**An assembly or Irish festival**
fleadh	flah	**A musical festival**
knakered		**Exhausted and very tired**
off-license		**Retail liquor store**
pissed		**Drunk**
poitín	pa-CHEEN	**Moonshine; sometimes toxic homemade liquor**
pub grub		**Quality bar food**
publican		**Barkeep**
to slag		**To tease and ridicule**
to snog		**To kiss**
to take the piss out		**To make fun of in a joking way**
trad		**Traditional Irish music**
uilleann pipes	ILL-in	**"Elbow pipes," a form of bagpipes**
táim	thaw im	**I am...**
súgach	SOO-gakh	**Tipsy**
ar meisce	uhr MEH-shka	**Drunk**
caoch ólta	KWEE-ukh OLE-ta	**"Blind drunk"**
	Sports	
football		**Gaelic football in the Republic, soccer in the North**
GAA		**Gaelic Athletic Association; organizes Gaelic sports**
iománaíocht	umauneeakht	**Hurling**
peil	pell	**Football**
snooker		**A game similar to pool**

APPENDIX

IRISH	PRONUNCIATION	(AMERICAN) ENGLISH
		Politics and the North
Bobby Sands		**The first IRA member to die during the 1980s hunger strikes; also a member of British parliament**
Catholic		**Someone of the Roman Catholic faith: usually implies loyalty to the Republic of Ireland**
Dáil	DOY-il	**House of Representatives in the Republic**
dole, on the dole		**Welfare or unemployment benefits**
DUP		**Democratic Unionist Party; right-wing N.I. party led by extremist Ian Paisley**
Fianna Fáil	FEE-in-ah foil	**"Soldiers of Destiny," political party in Éire**
Fine Gael	FINN-eh gayl	**"Family of Ireland," political party in Éire**
INLA		**Irish National Liberation Army, an IRA splinter group**
IRA (Provisional IRA)		**Irish Republican Army; a Nationalist paramilitary group**
Loyalist		**Pro-British Northern Irish (see Unionists)**
Nationalists		**Those who want Northern Ireland and the Republic united (see Republicans)**
Oireachtas	OR-uch-tus	**Both houses of the Irish Parliament**
Orangemen		**A widespread Protestant Unionist secret order**
Protestant		**Someone of the Anglican Protestant faith: usually implies allegiance with the British Crown.**
Provos		**Slang for the Provisional IRA**
Real IRA		**Small splinter group of radicals who claimed responsblity for the 1998 Omagh bombing**
Republicans		**Northern Irish who identify with the Republic (see Nationalists)**
SDLP		**Social Democratic and Labor Party; moderate Nationalist Party in the North**
Seanad	SHAN-ud	**The Irish Senate**
Sinn Féin	shin fayn	**"Ourselves Alone," Northern political party; affiliated with the IRA**
Sunday, Bloody Sunday		**Refers to 30 January 1970, when 13 Catholic civilians were gunned down by the British army**
Taoiseach	TEE-shukh	**Irish Prime Minister**
the Troubles		**The period of violence in the North that started in 1969 and continues today**
UDA		**Ulster Defence Association; Unionist paramilitary group**
UFF		**Ulster Freedom Fighters (synonymous with UDA)**
Unionists		**Those who want Northern Ireland to remain part of the UK (see loyalists)**
UUP		**Ulster Unionist Party; the ruling party in the North**
UVF		**Ulster Volunteer Force; Unionist paramilitary group**

INDEX

INDEX

Book your air, hotel, and transportation all in one place.

Hotel or hostel? Cruise or canoe? Car? Plane? Camel? Wherever you're going, visit Yahoo! Travel and get total control over your arrangements. Even choose your seat assignment. So. One hump or two? travel.yahoo.com

powered by hp

YAHOO!
Travel

MAP INDEX

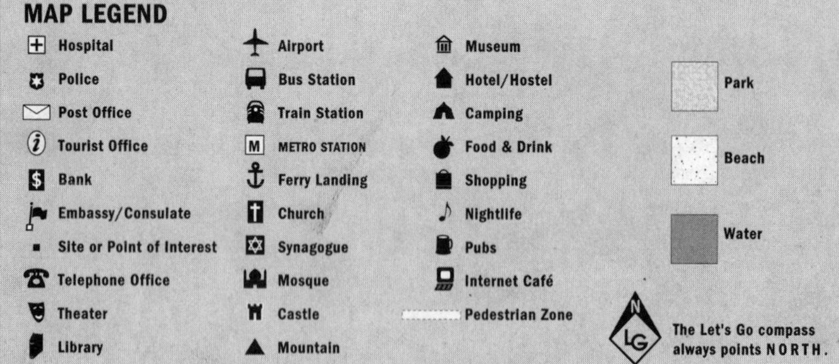

MAP LEGEND
Hospital
Police
Post Office
Tourist Office
Bank
Embassy/Consulate
Site or Point of Interest
Telephone Office
Theater
Library
Airport
Bus Station
Train Station
M
METRO STATION
Ferry Landing
Church
Synagogue
Mosque
Castle
Mountain
Museum
Hotel/Hostel
Camping
Food & Drink
Shopping
Nightlife
Pubs
Internet Café
Pedestrian Zone
Park
Beach
Water
N
LG
The Let's Go compass always points NORTH.